ILLINOIS
WISCONSIN
INDIANA
PURDUE
IOWA

THE BIG TEN

1895

OHIO STATE
MICHIGAN
NORTHWESTERN
MICH. STATE
MINNESOTA

THE

PRENTICE-HALL, INC.

BIG TEN

by Kenneth L. (Tug) Wilson
and Jerry Brondfield

ENGLEWOOD CLIFFS, NEW JERSEY

The Big Ten

by Kenneth L. (Tug) Wilson and Jerry Brondfield

Library of Congress
Catalog Card Number: 67-20746

SECOND PRINTING ..... NOVEMBER, 1967

PRINTED IN THE UNITED STATES OF AMERICA
B & P

DEDICATION

This book is dedicated to the memory of Amos Alonzo Stagg, athletic director and coach at the University of Chicago, whose 40 years of service to his university and to The Big Ten provided an example, without parallel, of what is right and fitting in college sports.

THE BIG TEN TRADITION IS BORN

It was officially organized as The Intercollegiate Conference of Faculty Representatives.

To the public it is commonly referred to as the Western Conference or, more popularly, The Big Ten.

By any definition it is the oldest, continually operated collegiate athletic conference in America and, even more importantly, one of the most prestigious groups in the field of higher education.*

Stated statistically, and with no attempt to claim more than is universally acknowledged to be true, the Big Ten, as a group of mutually-motivated universities, offers more areas of professional and technical education, as well as Liberal Arts education, than any other educationally or athletically-aligned group in the nation. From agriculture and architecture through visual perception and zoology, the catalogues of the Big Ten schools offer just about every educational pursuit known to man. And while size is not meant to be translated as superiority these schools as a group have granted more degrees—undergraduate and graduate—than any other American collegiate federation. And, in fact, in just a little more than an average of a century of existence as separate universities (as distinguished from their history as an athletic conference) they have conferred more degrees than all the universities of Europe throughout history. On a graduate level the Big Ten grants almost a third of the doctorates conferred in the U.S. each year.

The pursuit and attainment of academic excellence has long been the cherished goal of the Big Ten universities, and their record in producing national leaders and in preparing young people for responsible leadership has been a proud one.

All but one—Northwestern—are state-supported, public institutions and all have played magnificent roles in providing the broadest opportunities for their students; yet, at the same time, maintaining the vibrancy and challenge of modern education.

In athletics the Big Ten has been absolutely pre-eminent. Again, statistically, these midwestern schools have produced more All-America football and basketball stars; more national championship teams; more national and world record holders; more Olympic team members; more pro ball players; more Heisman Trophy winners; more coach-of-the-year winners; more top-ten teams in the annual football and basketball polls; and more NCAA team and individual titlists than any other collegiate conference in the country.

If the scope of spectator interest is still another measure of greatness it should also be noted that The Big Ten paces all collegiate conferences in yearly spectator attendance. (One Big Ten school, Ohio State, has, in fact, been the perennial football attendance leader for more than a decade.)

Here, then, is a history of The Big Ten from the time a few worried college presidents met in Chicago's Palmer House in 1895 until the present . . . A Chronicle of events and decisions which gave the Conference its firm fabric of regulatory practices . . . And a Chronicle of great athletes and coaches whose accomplishments will forever be listed among the finest chapters of American intercollegiate athletics.

In describing this year-to-year history the authors found it impossible, because of space limitations, to deal elaborately with every Big Ten athlete or coach who attracted headlines, and, inevitably, there will be raised the cry of dismay: "What about so-and-so!"

Five volumes this size would not do credit to the missing. Let the few, then, represent the many, with nobody tarnished by omission.

—Kenneth L. (Tug) Wilson
Jerry Brondfield

* The representatives of some colleges which subsequently would become the Southeast Conference met informally to discuss athletic problems a few months before the organization of The Western Conference, but the Big Ten was the first to proceed on a formally organized basis.

ACKNOWLEDGEMENTS

In assembling the hundreds of photographs and source material used in this book we acknowledge a large debt of gratitude to the following for their contributions:

The Columbus, O. *Dispatch*
Cover photo of Rainy Day at Ohio State Stadium
   by Wilbur Downing, courtesy of The Columbus
   Dispatch Sunday Magazine
The Columbus, O. *Citizen-Journal*
The Detroit *News*
The Decatur, Ill., *Herald Review*
NEA Service, Inc.
The Office of the Big Ten Commissioner
Carl Voltmer, Big Ten historian

And the university archives and public relation departments of The University of Chicago; The University of Illinois; Indiana University; The University of Iowa; The University of Michigan; Michigan State University; The University of Minnesota; Northwestern University; The Ohio State University; Purdue University; and The University of Wisconsin.

And particularly to the Directors of Sports Information at The Big Ten schools, without whose wholehearted cooperation the task would have been impossible.
—*Tug Wilson*
Jerry Brondfield

Ever since the turn of the century, among the best friends The Big Ten ever had were Midwestern sports writers. The early ones quickly grasped the significance of the national leadership displayed by the young league, and writers who followed them covered the Conference in such a thorough and entertaining way that they made thousands—hundreds of thousands—of friends for The Big Ten. The Conference owes a tremendous debt of gratitude to these columnists and writers. Those whom I met and worked with include the following. To them—to their papers—and to all others who have been involved with Big Ten sports coverage—I want to add my deep, personal note of thanks. We would have been a lesser league without them. Instead, they helped us become the greatest.

(K. L. W.)

Harvey Woodruff, Chicago Tribune
Arch Ward, Chicago Tribune
Wilfred Smith, Chicago Tribune
Dave Condon, Chicago Tribune
George Strickler, Chicago Tribune
Warren Brown, Chicago American
Leo Fischer, Chicago American
Jim Enright, Chicago American
John Carmichael, Chicago Daily News
Jim Kearns, Chicago Daily News
Francis Powers, Chicago Daily News
Bill Jauss, Chicago Daily News

Bill Fox, Indianapolis News
Gordon Graham, Lafayette Journal-Courier
Jack Clarke, Chicago Sun-Times
Irv Kupcinet, Chicago Sun-Times
H.G. Salsinger, Detroit News
Sam Greene, Detroit News
Watson Spoelstra, Detroit News
Sec Taylor, Des Moines Register-Tribune
Bert McGrane, Des Moines Register-Tribune
Maury White, Des Moines Register-Tribune
John O'Donnell, Davenort Times-Democrat
Gus Schrader, Cedar Rapids Gazette
George Alderton, Lansing State Journal
Mil Marsh, Ann Arbor News
Bert Bertine, Urbana Courier
George Barton, Minneapolis Tribune
Sid Hartman, Minneapolis Tribune
Charley Johnson, Minneapolis Star Tribune
Dick Cullum, Minneapolis Star Tribune
Ed Hayes, Detroit Times
Lew Byrer, Columbus Citizen
Paul Hornung, Columbus Dispatch
Kaye Kessler, Columbus Citizen Journal
John Dietrich, Cleveland Plain Dealer
Jack Clowser, Cleveland Press
Si Burick, Dayton Daily News
Jim Schlemmer, Akron Beacon-Journal
Oliver Kuechle, Milwaukee Journal
Lloyd Larson, Milwaukee Sentinel
Henry J. McCormick, Wisconsin State Journal
Henry Casserly, Madison Capital Times
Charles W. Dunkley, Associated Press
Jerry Liska, Associated Press
Harry Grayson, NEA Service
Ed Sainsbury, United Press International

CONTENTS

The Big Ten Tradition Is Born

Presenting the Schools

Historical Campus Scenes 13
Modern Campus Scenes 13

The "Official" Families

The Men Who Make the Programs Go 37

Presidents, Faculty Advisors, Athletic Directors, Sports Information Directors, Head Coaches

The Birth and Growth of a Conference

A History of Accomplishment, and a Long Championship Trail 50

Alan Ameche, Howard (Hopalong) Cassady, Jim Counsilman, Chuck Davey, Duffy Daugherty, Randy Duncan, Terry Dischinger, Paddy Driscoll, Chuck Fenske, Ed Gordon, Don Gehrmann, Johnny Green, Willie Heston, Bill Haarlow, Billy Hillenbrand, Pat Harder, George Huff, Ford Konno, Don Lash, Tim Lowry, Pug Lund, Matt Mann, Biggie Munn, Stretch Murphy, Mike Peppe, Pete Pihos, John Pingel, Pug Rentner, Walter Ris, Joe Reiff, Tom Robinson, Cazzie Russell, Karl Schlademan, "Germany" Schulz, Don Schlundt, John Walsh, Pest Welch, Bud Wilkinson, The Wisterts of Michigan, and many, many others.

The Tug Wilson Story

The Personal Account of a Lifetime in Sports 100

The Great Athletes and Coaches

Profiles and Sketches of Some of the Most Glittering Stars in Collegiate Sports History 54

Jay Berwanger, Bernie Bierman, Lou Boudreau, Herbert Orrin, (Fritz) Crisler, Aubrey Devine, Walter Eckersall, Dwight (Dyke) Eddleman, Ray Ewry, Wesley Fesler, Benny Friedman, Harry Gill, Otto Graham, Harold (Red) Grange, Charles W. (Chic) Harley, Tom Harmon, Woody Hayes, Nile Kinnick, Noble Kizer, Ward (Piggy) Lambert, Jerry Lucas, Branch McCracken, Alvin Nugent, (Bo) McMillin,

Walter Meanwell, Michigans Point-A-Minute Machine, Bronko Nagurski, Nels Norgren, Pat O'Dea, Elmer Oliphant, Bennie Oosterbaan, Jesse Owens, Harlan (Pat) Page, Bob Richards, Duke Slater, Amos Alonzo Stagg, Chris Steinmetz, The Whiz Kids—Art Mathisen, Ken Menke, Andy Philip, Art Smiley and Gene Vance, Dr. Henry Williams, Fielding (Hurry-Up) Yost, Bob Zuppke.

Official All-Time Big Ten Records, Statistics and Awards

Football, Basketball, Baseball, Track, Swimming, Wrestling, Gymnastics, Hockey, Fencing, Tennis, Golf, Cross-Country 415

Traditional Trophies

The Colorful Symbols of Intense Rivalry 463

Where Are They Now?

Big Ten Athletes Who Went On To Eminence In Every Walk of Life 465

HISTORICAL

AND

MODERN

CAMPUS SCENES

ILLINOIS

HISTORICAL CAMPUS

Engineering Classroom

Members of Class of 1901 as Sophomores (posing for Hoboes Union party)

University Hall

Science Class

Illinois R.O.T.C. Regiment of 1906

Steam Roller Used to Drag Infield of Baseball Diamond

Illinois Campus in Early 1900's

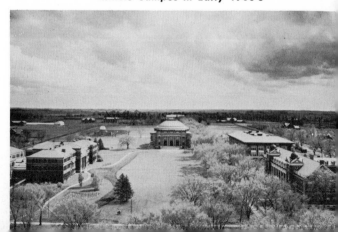

MODERN CAMPUS

Krannert Art Museum

Alma Mater Group (by Lorado Taft)

Illini Union

Memorial Stadium

Mechanical Engineering Building

Assembly Hall

INDIANA

HISTORICAL CAMPUS

Owen Hall (for Medical Studies)

Owen Hall (for Home Economics)

Lindley Hall (Erected 1902)

Wooden Walkway & Horse and Buggy Path

Indiana Campus in 1880

MODERN CAMPUS

Fine Arts Building & Showalter Fountain

Memorial Union Building

Ballantine Hall

Indiana University Stadium & Fieldhouse

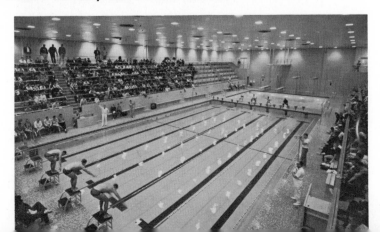

Kirkwood Hall

Robert Royer Pool

R.O.T.C. Artillery Battery in 1899

Medical College Class in 1897

Commencement Procession in 1905

Dental Laboratory in 1900

MODERN CAMPUS

Iowa Campus

General Hospital

School of Fine Arts

Dramatic Arts Building

Iowa Football Stadium

Iowa Field House

MICHIGAN

HISTORICAL CAMPUS

Main Classroom Buildings in 1900

Haven Hall

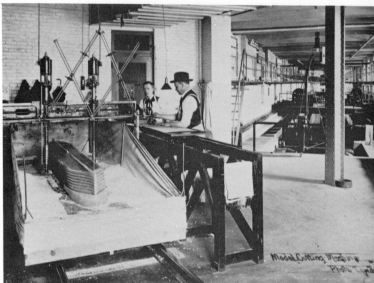

Engineering Laboratory

Physics Lecture in 1900

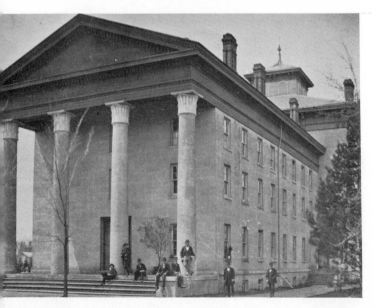

Medical Building

South Hall Biology Class

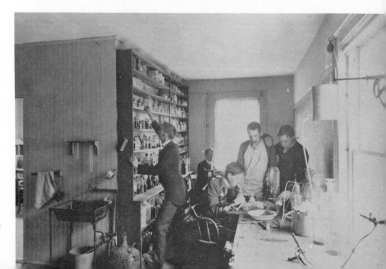

MODERN CAMPUS

Law Quadrangle

Burton Memorial Tower

Athletic Office Building

Mason-Hauen Hall

Michigan Football Stadium

Michigan Swimming Pool

Michigan Agricultural College in 1904

MICHIGAN STATE

HISTORICAL CAMPUS

Old College Hall—Original Building at Michigan State. Erected in 1862, it was the first college structure in the United States devoted to the teaching of scientific agriculture.

Michigan State Library in 1890

Chemistry Laboratory in 1896

Physics Class in 1892

MODERN CAMPUS

Library

College of Education

Men's Intramural Building

Kellogg Center for Continuing Education

Spartan Stadium

College of Engineering

Company Q, Women's R.O.T.C. Drill Team in 1890

Northrop Field

Football in 1900

MINNESOTA

HISTORICAL CAMPUS

Classrooms in the 1980's

Burton Hall & Old Main

Coffman Memorial Union

Ford Hall

MODERN CAMPUS

Mayo Memorial Hospital

Veterinary Medicine

Memorial Stadium

Sheppard Field

NORTHWESTERN

HISTORICAL CAMPUS

Northwestern's First Gymnasium in the 1890's

Interior of First Gymnasium

Northwestern's Mandolin Club in 1890's

Campus Scene in early 1900's

MODERN CAMPUS

Deering Library

Kresge Centennial Hall

Patten Gymnasium

Dyche Stadium

McGaw Memorial Hall (Basketball)

OHIO STATE HISTORICAL CAMPUS

Faculty-Senior Baseball Game in 1892

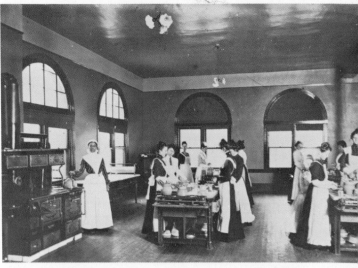

Home Economics Class in Hayer Hall (1896)

Tally-Ho's seat spectators at 1901 Ohio State-Michigan Game

Early Veterinary Medicine Ambulance

North Dormitory Students in 1889

Freshman Women's Physical Education Class in 1903

MODERN CAMPUS

University Hall

Library

University Hospital

Ohio Union

St. John Arena & French Field House

Stadium

PURDUE

HISTORICAL CAMPUS

Purdue Commencement in 1903

Original Women's Dormitory at Purdue

Fences kept College cattle from straying onto campus.

Memorial Union

Field House

MODERN CAMPUS

Hall of Music & Executive Building

Life Science Building

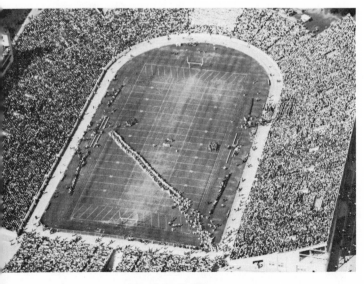

Ross-Ade Stadium

Golf Starter House

State Street in 1896

WISCONSIN

HISTORICAL CAMPUS

Intramural Field in 1900

Camp Randall Stadium Entrance (Originally, Camp Randall was a Civil War Training Camp on Wisconsin Campus.)

Women's Field Hockey Team in 1912

Freshman-Sophomore "Bag Rush" in 1919

MODERN CAMPUS

Wisconsin Campus

Lincoln Statue Before Bascom Hall

Memorial Library

Observatory Hill

Camp Randall Stadium

Cobb Hall

CHICAGO

Walter Museum & Women's Residence Hall

University of Chicago Campus

HISTORICAL CAMPUS

Chicago vs. Wisconsin in 1904

THE
OFFICIAL
FAMILIES

David Dodds Henry
President

Leslie A. Bryan
Big Ten Faculty Representative

Gene Vance
Athletic Director

ILLINOIS

Charles P. Pond
Gymnastics Coach

B. R. Patterson
Wrestling Coach

A. L. Klingel
Swimming Coach

Robert C. Wright
Track Coach

Maxwell R. Garret
Fencing Coach

Lee Eilbracht
Baseball Coach

Harvey Schmidt
Basketball Coach

Charles Bellatti
Athletic Publicity

Jim Valek
Football Coach

Ralph E. Fletcher
Golf Coach

Dan Olson
Tennis Coach

Edwin H. Cady
Big Ten Faculty Representative

Bill Orwig
Athletic Director

Dr. Elvis J. Stahr, Jr.
President

INDIANA

Otto Ryser
Gymnastics Coach

Charley McDaniel
Wrestling Coach

Ernie Andres
Baseball Coach

Jim Lavery
Track & Cross-Country Coach

Lou Watson
Basketball Coach

Jim Counsilman
Swimming Coach

John Pont
Football Coach

Bill Landin
Tennis Coach

Tom Miller
Athletic Publicity Director

Robert E. Fitch
Golf Coach

Howard R. Bowen
President

Dr. Robert Ray
Big Ten Faculty Representative

Forest Evashevski
Director of Athletics & Football Coach

IOWA

Charles Zwiener
Golf Coach

Bob Allen
Swimming Coach

Francis X. Cretzmeyer
Track Coach

David McCuskey
Wrestling Coach

Sam Bailie
Gymnastics Coach

Ralph Miller
Basketball Coach

Richard Schultz
Baseball Coach

Eric Wilson
Athletic Publicity Director

Dick Marks
Fencing Coach

Ray Nagel
Football Coach

Donald D. Klotz
Tennis Coach

Marcus Plant
Big Ten Faculty Representative

H. O. (Fritz) Crisler
Athletic Director

Robben W. Fleming
President

Al Renfrew
Hockey Coach

Gus Stager
Swimming Coach

Don Canham
Track Coach

MICHIGAN

Chalmers "Bump" Elliott
Football Coach

Milbry E. (Moby) Benedict
Baseball Coach

David Strack
Basketball Coach

Bill Murphy
Tennis Coach

Cliff Keen
Wrestling Coach

Newt Loken
Gymnastics Coach

Bert Katzenmeyer
Golf Coach

Les Etter
Sports Information Director

Dr. John A. Hannah
President

Dr. John A. Fuzak
Big Ten Faculty Representative

Clarence Munn
Athletic Director

MICHIGAN STATE

Charles McCaffree
Swimming Coach

Danny Litwhiler
Baseball Coach

Fran Dittrich
Track Coach

Karl Schlademan
Cross-Country Coach

Fred Stabley
Sports Information Director

George Szypula
Gymnastics Coach

Amo Bessone
Hockey Coach

Hugh (Duffy) Daugherty
Football Coach

Stan Drobac
Tennis Coach

Bruce Fossum
Golf Coach

Grady Peninger
Wrestling Coach

Charles R. Schmitter
Fencing Coach

John Benington
Basketball Coach

Max O. Schultze
Big Ten Faculty Representative

Marshall Ryman
Athletic Director

O. Meredith Wilson
President

Murray Warmath
Football Coach

John Kundla
Basketball Coach

Glen Sonmor
Hockey Coach

MINNESOTA

Joe Walsh
Tennis Coach

Roy Griak
Track Coach

Les Bolstad
Golf Coach

Ralph Piper
Gymnastics Coach

Otis J. Dypwick
Sports Information Director

Wally Johnson
Wrestling Coach

Dick Siebert
Baseball Coach

Robert Mowerson
Swimming Coach

Dr. J. Roscoe Miller
President

Prof. T. Leroy Martin
Chairman, Faculty Athletic Committee

William H. H. (Tippy) Dye
Director of Athletics

NORTHWESTERN

Alex Agase
Football Coach

Walter Paulison
Athletic Publicity Director

George McKinnon
Baseball Coach

Bob Ehrhart
Track Coach

Clare Riessen
Tennis Coach

Ken Kraft
Wrestling Coach

Sid Richardson
Golf Coach

Larry Glass
Basketball Coach

Bill Peterson
Swimming Coach

James R. McCoy
Big Ten Faculty Representative

Richard C. Larkins
Athletic Director

Novice G. Fawcett
President

W. W. (Woody) Hayes
Football Coach

Wilbur E. Snypp
Athletic Publicity Director

Joe Hewlett
Gymnastics Coach

OHIO STATE

Robert Epskamp
Track Coach

Fred Taylor
Basketball Coach

Roderick W. Myers
Golf Coach

Casey Fredericks
Wrestling Coach

Charles Simonian
Fencing Coach

Marty Karrow
Baseball Coach

Robert Bartels
Swimming Coach

John Hendrix
Tennis Coach

Frederick L. Hovde
President

Dean V. C. Freeman
Big Ten Faculty Representative

Guy J. "Red" Mackey
Athletic Director

PURDUE

Sam Voinoff
Golf Coach

David Rankin
Track Coach

Joe Sexson
Baseball Coach

Claude Reeck
Wrestling Coach

Richard Papenguth
Swimming Coach

Jack Mollenkopf
Football Coach

George King
Basketball Coach

Ed Eicholtz
Tennis Coach

Karl Klages
Sports Information Director

Frank Remington
Big Ten Faculty Representative

Ivan Williamson
Athletic Director

Fred M. Harrington
President

George Martin
Wrestling Coach

Archie Simonson
Fencing Coach

Norman Sonju
Crew Coach

WISCONSIN

Robert N. Johnson
Ice Hockey Coach

Arthur "Dynie" Mansfield
Baseball Coach

John Coatta
Football Coach

John C. Hickman
Swimming Coach

Charles Walter
Track Coach

John Erickson
Basketball Coach

John Jamieson
Golf Coach

George Bauer
Gymnastics Coach

Jim Mott
Sports Information
Director

ILLINOIS
WISCONSIN
INDIANA
PURDUE
IOWA
OHIO STATE
MICHIGAN
NORTHWESTERN
MICH. STATE
MINNESOTA

THE
BIG
TEN

1895

Grover Cleveland was President of The United States, and the nation was just beginning to pick itself up out of the Great Panic and Depression . . . Immigration from Europe was at flood-tide, and people with foreign-looking faces and alien tongues were setting down roots all over the land.

There were still Indian uprisings in the West, and in Chicago a young woman named Jane Addams had an idea called "Hull House" to help bring a social consciousness to the poor and disadvantaged . . . John Drew and Julia Marlowe were giants of the American theater, and down in the hills of West Virginia two families named Hatfield and McCoy were destroying each other from ambush . . . An angular mechanic in Detroit was working on a two-cylinder gasoline engine which he would install in a horseless carriage called a "Quadrangle," but which in a couple of years would be given his own name: Ford.

The people were discovering leisure time and finding entertainment in sports. They were attending sports events in great numbers . . . by the thousands, because it was something robust and rollicking and competitive, and so typically American. There was already a National Professional Baseball League; a Rowing Association of America; an American Hockey Association; and the United States Golfing Association. There had already been the first Intercollegiate Track and Field Meet, and the sports "hero" was beginning to be a new personality on the American scene.

The year was 1895 . . .

1895

The year was 1895 and President James H. Smart of Purdue University was troubled, and had issued invitations to the presidents of six other universities besides his own, to attend a meeting in Chicago. It was a meeting, he felt, that was long overdue . . . it was high time responsible people should discuss the problem of, and possible means of control of, intercollegiate athletics . . .

High time, indeed! The problems were awesome. . . !

And so they came—the presidents of Purdue, Minnesota, Wisconsin, Illinois, Northwestern, Michigan, and Chicago.

With the growth of the state universities had come a burgeoning interest in intercollegiate athletics. The new interest meant new loyalties—and loyalties, fanned by the hot breath of competition, fed best on success.

Now there were *games* to be played, and people to watch the players, and the best way to play

'em was to *win*. Who cared if the methods were less than altruistic and sporting!

In the 10 or 15 years prior to 1895, when sports began taking hold with a hoot and a holler, football, baseball and track were the three so-called "varsity" sports—with football just beginning to catch up with (and soon to *replace*) baseball as the leading attraction. By 1890 the game was pretty much on an intercollegiate basis in the midwest, and the desire to clobber the team from a neighboring state was just about the reigning emotion on any midwest college campus. After all, the rumble seat, hip-flasks and the swallowing of live goldfish was a couple of generations away—and what else *was* there?

Trouble was, all university sports were operated on an unofficial, informal basis. College administrators and faculty (at first) seemingly couldn't have cared less about "agitating a pig's bladder full of wind!" (as an Eastern college president once put it) and allowed the undergraduates to proceed their

PRESIDENT JAMES H. SMART, of Purdue, whose invitation to six other university presidents to meet with him January 11, 1895, in Chicago, led to formation of The Big Ten.

NING...

merry and freebooting ways. If there was an ounce of standardized control and a glimmer of ethics no one was aware of it.

But there was a Press, even then, which enjoyed nothing better than to make news of skullduggery, chicanery and frequent blood-letting, all in the good name of student sporting instincts.

There is no better environment for rampant irregularity and evil than where there is no control. And in those days there were no codes of eligibility rules, and no organization to draw up or enforce any. The one purpose was to win and games frequently broke up because of a savage—and often free-swinging—quarrel over team personnel or playing methods.

Some colleges bolstered their squads with strong-armed high school boys playing under assumed names. Some athletes actually played football for one school and baseball for another, in the same year. A baseball team thought nothing of pressing a professional pitcher into service if it could get up his asking price—which wasn't too astronimical in those days. Coaches who were young and vigorous (and they were the only kind around) often inserted themselves in their line-ups. Tramp athletes played for as many as three and four different schools; often, by some strange oversight, without undergoing the amenities of enrolling.

Perhaps nowhere was the spirit of the times better expressed than by young writers for campus newspapers who were no less sophisticated than the events they described. The writer for the *Purdue Exponent* explained a loss to Wabash: "The story is quickly told by stating that Wabash used a professional pitcher of eight years standing!"

In the Iowa *Vidette-Reporter*, a football game with Missouri took on the following tinge: "Many of our team say that during the trouble which arose, several persons in the crowd drew knives on our team . . . Later, there was a slight altercation between Missouri's center and our quarterback . . . But it is impossible to give a detailed account of the game from this point on because your humble servant was a very busy man for the next seven minutes . . . The faculty and students of M.S.U. . . . should never again ask college men to play football in Columbia, Mo., without a strong guard of armed men without which no team seems to be safe . . ."

At Illinois, the *Daily Illini* described part of a game with Chicago as follows: "At this point Stagg stopped the game and in trotted Chicago's professional star . . . It being evident that the referee had determined Illinois should not score." A few lines later the paper claimed that the "star" most certainly "has been in athletics there since the institution opened."

One football manager of the period stated that on the Michigan team in his charge in the early 1890's, seven players were not on the university's enrollment books during the football season.

So, this in essence epitomized the rambunctious and colorful chaos which, after several years, convinced university heads that sports were getting to be a sorry reflection of their growing citadels of learning. Sports, which had been regarded by the uneasy savants as nothing more than a tolerable nuisance, were rapidly becoming an intollerable noose around their reddening intellectual necks. In short, when they finally got around to asking: 'What's going on around here?" they almost choked on the answers they got.

Luckily there were some who agreed there were a few salvageable ideas in sports which might even have some educational value if viewed under proper perspective. It meant saying "Whoa!" to several thousand young undergraduates who had gone too long unbridled, but at least this was the horse-and-buggy age and they might still know what "whoa" meant. And maybe if the educators could come up with a semblance of standardization there'd be a fighting chance to get the whole runaway thing on a new road.

It was that friendly but firm attitude that prevailed on Jan. 11, 1895, when into a darkly-paneled conference room in Chicago's Palmer House came the dignified seven: President Angell of Michigan; President Rogers of Northwestern; President North-

WILLIAM RAINEY HARPER, one of the most distinguished educators in American history, was the first president of the University of Chicago and attended the historic Conference "launching" meeting of January 11, 1895 in Chicago's Palmer House.

rop of Minnesota; President Draper of Illinois; President Adams of Wisconsin; President Harper of Chicago, and President Smart of Purdue. The University of Chicago and Northwestern were the only private schools, the others being state universities, but they were all together because of geography and natural interests and somebody had to start this thing. If other sections of the country would see fit to follow suit, so much the better.

They sat down . . . and at the end of the day there emerged the first attempts at concrete management of intercollegiate athletics by any collegiate group in the country. They started with a basic set of rules. In succeeding years these would be amplified, reconsidered, made stronger, made weaker, praised with religious fervor, jeered and winked at, followed to the letter. But always there would be one general direction they would take: upward and firmer, toward more and sensible control.

Before these and succeeding presidents and school representatives were through, they would have established a conference of 10 of the largest and greatest universities in the nation, and although these first seven gave it its still formal designation of the "Intercollegiate Conference of Faculty Representatives," it would come to be known as the Big Ten.

They had made a start . . . There would be so much that would follow.

Here were their first set of rules:

RULES

1. Each college and university which has not already done so shall appoint a committee on college athletics which shall take general supervision of all athletic matters in the respective college or university, and which shall have all responsibility of enforcing the college or university rules regarding athletics and all intercollegiate sports.

2. No one shall participate in any game or athletic sport unless he be a bona fide student doing full work in a regular or special course as defined in the curriculum of his college; and no person who has participated in any match game as a member of any college team shall be permitted to participate in any game as a member of another college team, until he has been a matriculate in said college under the above conditions for a period of six months. This rule shall not apply to students who, having graduated at one college, shall enter another college for professional or graduate study.

3. No person shall be admitted to any intercollegiate contest who receives any gift, remuneration or pay for his services on the college team.

4. Any student of any institution who shall be pursuing a regularly prescribed resident graduate course within such institution, whether for an advanced degree or in one of its professional schools, may be permitted to play for the period of the minimum number of years required for securing the graduate or professional degree for which he is a candidate.

5. No person who has been employed in training a college team for intercollegiate contests shall be allowed to participate in any intercollegiate contest as a member of any team which he has trained, and no professional athlete or person who has ever been a member of a professional team shall play at any intercollegiate contest.

6. No student shall play in any game under an assumed name.

7. No student shall be permitted to participate in any intercollegiate contest who is found by the faculty to be delinquent in his studies.

8. All games shall be played on grounds either owned by or under the immediate control of one or both of the colleges participating in the contest, and all games shall be played under student management and not under the patronage or control of any other corporation, association or private individual.

9. The election of managers and captains of teams in each college shall be subject to the approval of its committee on athletics.

10. College teams shall not engage in games with professional teams nor with those representing so-called athletic clubs.

11. Before every intercollegiate contest a list of men proposing to play shall be presented by each team or teams to the other or others, certifying that all the members are entitled to play under conditions of the rules adopted, such certificate to be signed by the registrar or the secretary of the college or university. It shall be the duty of the captain to enforce this rule.

12, We call upon the expert managers of football teams to so revise the rules as to reduce the liability to injury to a minimum.

It was decided to give everyone concerned some time to digest the startling impact of what they'd laid out for their universities. They were to go home, sound out their faculty and administration and see if they wanted to support an athletic program built on some orderly process of good behavior. It would, of course, be a rather radical departure from the prevailing norm, but if they were serious about this thing they could prove it by selecting and sending their first faculty representative back to Chicago a year later, and start *moving forward*.

For this was to be the new concept of control of intercollegiate athletics—by the *faculty*, not athletic personnel.

Seemingly, there was one exception to the rule that all representatives were to be faculty members at their schools. The University of Chicago a few years previously, had taken a startling step. It had decided to dignify its coach and athletic director by giving him faculty status—a move which fluttered a lot of pedagogical eyebrows in shock and dismay on Chicago's Midway—and elsewhere, as well. Therefore, the Chicago Director would attend the meeting as a faculty man and not as an itinerant muscle-maker.

His name was Professor Amos Alonzo Stagg.

The influence he would eventually have on this new conference and on American athletics in general, would be monumental.

The group now had decided it would be a permanent body to meet twice a year, and to expand as it saw fit by taking in other neighboring schools who wanted to see the ball bounce this new way. It spelled out the system by which its member programs of intercollegiate athletics would be controlled —by Faculty Committee, or so-called Board in Control.

In the next three years, an elaboration upon those original rules made something quite clear. There was to be no hanky-panky. Each lodge member not only was to police its own backyard but any member could bring charges against another if circumstances seemed to point toward a violation of the code. It was a little bit vague as to how these charges were to be investigated and what punitive action would be administered—if any. That was still several years away. The Founding Fathers evidently placed a lot of faith in individual soul-searching, a system which usually leaves something to be desired when the searchers lose their way among the boondocks and brambles of too many clobberings on the playing fields.

It was, however, a start. At least the members' representatives were classical faculty men who were not supposed to care quite as much about victory and winning streaks.

It is a tribute to the wisdom of the seven original presidents that the system they hit upon was, perhaps, the solid foundation upon which the future of *all* collegiate conferences, and college sports in general, was built. Every league that followed in years to come borrowed its founding philosophy from this Midwestern group.

Even the public was becoming aware of the significance of the action taken in Chicago. Caspar Whitney, of New York, probably the best-known sports writer of the time, in an article in Harper's Weekly, stated:

"The most notable clearing of the atmosphere is to be seen in the West. Football—indeed all Midwestern college sports—was very near total extinction because of a rampant professional spirit that had ranged throughout nearly all the universities, leaving corruption in its wake . . . The meeting last winter in Chicago marked the beginning of a new and clarified era in Western collegiate sport!"

Soon Mr. Whitney was to publicly recommend this Conference system of control to Eastern schools.

Meanwhile, in the East, Harvard had set up some standards for administration of its own athletic policies, and the Midwestern group decided to make the Cantabs' certificate of eligibility the standard requirement for the entire Conference. Among other things it stipulated that a student who had failed his courses or who had been dropped temporarily from school, would be ineligible for athletics for a

More than anyone else, a brace of Northwestern halfbacks, JESSE VAN DOOZER, left, and AL POTTER, brought national attention to the newly-formed Western Conference in its inaugural year of 1896. Casper Whitney, foremost football writer of the period, in summing up the season in Harper's Weekly, acknowledged: ". . . Van Doozer is undoubtedly the best halfback in the West and . . . close to the most brilliant players in the East. I consider him as good a natural halfback as is playing football today."

There was no explanation by Whitney as to why Van Doozer was left off his All-America, which, for a few more years was to be the almost exclusive Pantheon of the Big Three of Harvard, Yale and Princeton. Both Van Doozer and Potter did make All-Western, but the frosting which Big Van wanted for his cake—the Conference title—was denied to him. Northwestern which had lost only one game that season, met undefeated Wisconsin for the first league championship. It came up rain and mud but, late in the game, Van finally slithered through for a touchdown. With only three minutes remaining Wisconsin lost the ball on downs on the Northwestern 20-yard line and it appeared to be all over, but Northwestern had to punt. The slippery ball, snapped from center, sailed high over the kicker's head and was downed behind the goal line for a Badger touchdown, a tie game, and a Wisconsin championship in the first year of league play.

1896

year, or until he had returned to school and made up his deficiencies. It also limited athletes to four years of competition, and ruled out athletes who were taking post-graduate work. (Walter Camp had played football for six years at Yale, and the Crimson, perhaps, thought four years should be enough for *anybody*.)

By 1897 the Conference Faculty Representatives had decided that henceforth no team in the league would be allowed to play against professionals or a club team using professional players. There was a sort of momentum at work, now. Sports would be

1897

tolerated on an amateur basis, played by bona fide students who would have to do creditable work in the classroom.

The idea was catching. In 1899 Indiana University and University of Iowa decided they wanted in. The Conference admitted them and, for the first time, the popular name of the new Conference broke into print and public use: it was called The Big Nine.

Meanwhile, within the framework of the New Idea, only three sports enjoyed the status of varsity competition: football, baseball and track. (James Naismith had already devised his peach basket game as a gymnastic exercise out East at Springfield College, and for the past few years college boys in the midwest were indulging in a crude form of Roundball charades in gym classes. The Big Nine, however, disdainfully claimed it wasn't a sport. It would not be until 1906 that basketball would climb out from under its humiliating cloud and be legalized for Big Nine Collegiate competition.)

Football in the 1890's displayed some startling differences from today's game. The field was 330 feet long without end zones of any kind. There were two fifty-yard lines, 10 yards apart. The halves were 45 minutes long, and, considering that nobody wore helmets, that was a lot of head-knocking. Touchdowns and field goals were worth five points each (the field goal would be cut to four points in 1904 and three in 1909; the touchdown would go up to six).

With no forward pass, it was strictly a ground offense and the defense played it accordingly to stop the running game. Therefore only five yards were needed for a first down, but you had only three downs instead of four to make it. There was no rule requiring seven men on the offensive line and bulky linemen frequently were called back to lead a formation on momentum plays. This was a rough game the boys played, with little padded equipment. (Spaulding Bros., advertised a knitted cap guaranteed to be "an absolute protection for sore ears.")

Michigan, Wisconsin, Minnesota and Chicago were the strong teams in the 1890's, and in 1895 Michigan and Chicago, balked by bad weather, were the first collegiate football teams to play a game indoors, using the Chicago Coliseum and playing before a paid gate of $10,812, a record for Western football. Chicago won, 7-6.

Soon, back East, Caspar Whitney and Walter Camp, the two selectors of the All-American teams, found themselves forced to acknowledge the presence of some pretty good country football players west of the Alleghenies. In 1898 Whitney named William Cunningham as Michigan's All-America center, and Camp spotted Clarence Herschberger, of Chicago, at fullback. They were first in a long line of midwesterners which ultimately would dominate the All-America selections.

Even as the 20th century beckoned, and with it a whole new era of intercollegiate sports, there were

1898

It was a bitter cold night—a good night to be on the inside looking out at the deep-drifted snow and glazed, frosted trees. Given a choice, no sensible person would have poked his nose beyond the door, but 400 people exercised a choice and crunched across the snow toward the armory on the University of Iowa campus because they were curious about a new game called basketball.

It was the night of January 18, 1896 and the 400 witnessed the first game of intercollegiate basketball ever played under conditions similar to what we now know— five players to a side, and rules and regulations arbitrated by a referee on the floor.

That afternoon a train had bought into Iowa City nine youths from the University of Chicago. Four of them made up the Chicago debating team which was to engage in forensic combat that afternoon with a Hawkeye foursome. The other five made up the Maroon basketball team that would meet five Iowa students who were representing the local Y.M.C.A. as well as the University.

The game had been scheduled as a result of a friendship between H. F. Kallenberg, a member of the Iowa physical education department, and Amos Alonzo Stagg, the University of Chicago's Director of Athletics. They had been graduate students together at Springfield College where basketball had been invented just a few years before by Dr. James Naismith.

Up until now the new sport had been played with seven, then nine, and finally eight on a side. It made for a lot of congested traffic and not a very popular team game. Now Kallenberg and Horace Butterworth, the Chicago basketball instructor, thought there could be a vast improvement with only five to a side and wanted to try out the new idea.

Before the game started Kallenberg got up and ex-

In 1898 Chicago's great fullback, CLARENCE HERSCHBERGER, along with Michigan's William Cunningham, a center, made history for the Western Conference by cracking through the Eastern monopoly on All-America. They were the first of many to come from the Big Ten.

plained the rules to the spectators who previously had had their competitive corpuscles stirred into a frenzy of excitement by the Iowa band, and weren't quite sure they wanted the match to be too encumbered by rules.

It turned out to be a close game. All scoring, whether from the floor or foul line, counted only one point per shot. Chicago, smaller but faster than Iowa, led 7-5 at the half and took it at the end, 13-12. The Maroon cashed in on 10 free-throws and three field goals. Iowa had three field goals and nine foul shots. There was a lot of uncertain and strange skirmishing between scores, and every shot was either an upward, underhand toss or a two-handed push shot from the chest. Lay-ups, one-handers, hooks and jumpers weren't even in the game's vocabulary or, for that matter, within the skill range of any of the players. No matter which man on a team was fouled, his free-throw could be taken by someone on his side who was a better foul shooter. Scoring was enough of a novelty so that each successful shot was accompanied by the kind of roar reserved for a game-winning, fullback smash into the line on fourth-and-one and 10 seconds to play.

Even though it may have been the first college game under a semblance of modern rules, one newspaper account of the contest indicated that some things still haven't changed much, today. Said the reporter: " . . . Strict officiating was a source of intense dissatisfaction to the audience . . ."

Iowa, incidentally, was able to salvage an even split for the day. In the afternoon its debaters won the match with Chicago, upholding the affirmative on the question that "Further Territorial Expansion of the United States is Undesirable."

The forensic victory perhaps could have been a source of some concern to people in Oklahoma, New Mexico and Arizona which, although territories, had not yet been admitted to the Union as states.

---

those who still would remember, for example, that in 1894, when Wisconsin beat Minnesota in football for the first time, the Wisconsin *Daily Cardinal* rushed out with an "Extra" after the game, printed on red paper. Badger fans would remember it, too, as the same year Dick Arms, Wisconsin's baseball captain, a tiny 5-foot, 7-inch second baseman, pulled off the first unassisted triple play in collegiate baseball history. In the Michigan game, with runners on first and second, the Wolverine batter drilled a high liner directly over second base. Arms leaped up unbelievably for his height, snared the ball with his bare right hand, came down on the bag to double the runner off second, then ran down the Michigan runner trying to get back to first.

In 1896, other sports fans were discussing the fact that, just before the Oberlin game, Ohio State football captain, Ed French, became the Midwest's first academic casualty, and was barred from further play because of his scholastic standing. After the Buckeyes lost, the student paper, *The Lantern*, ran a headline which read: "Who Defeated the Ohio State team—Oberlin or the Ohio State University Faculty?"

That same year Michigan State's baseball team was allowed $10.00 for a dozen balls, which had to last all season—and was allowed another $1.20 for chewing gum. The Spartans were more fortunate than the 1898 Ohio State team; the Buckeye faculty would not approve a diamond schedule at all, because the Student Athletic Association had debts of $14.00 and cash on hand of two cents.

At Northwestern, a benign administration started something in 1898 when it raised a $100 fund for the first Northwestern band.

The same Northwestern faculty was embarrassed no end a year later when Charley Ward, a big football lineman, pulled off a hoax that became a national sensation. En route to a game with Wisconsin, Ward stepped onto the rear platform of the train when it stopped at a small town and made a ringing political speech. The trouble was, Ward was giving a perfect imitation of still-youthful Presidential Candidate William Jennings Bryan, and his remarks were duly noted in the press.

Although the Founding Fathers had decreed that no official champion would be crowned in any Conference sport, they were bucking a burgeoning public interest in competitive collegiate sports, as well as an alert press which cannily decided it would give that public what it wanted. It wanted champions, and Wisconsin was popularly tabbed as such in the first football season under Conference regulations, in 1896.

The faculty delegates wisely refrained from protesting the trend but simply refused to award any team trophies. As various sports were added to Conference activity, the press and public continued to crown the champs. Eventually, there would come a day when involvement with National Collegiate Athletic Association tournaments and Rose Bowl games would call for official recognition.

It was shortly before the turn of the century, too, that the germ of an idea was spawned along the shores of Lake Mendota in Madison, Wisconsin. Rowing had long been a colorful and popular college sport in the East, but midwest collegians, lacking either the sophistication or the facilities, had done little with it beyond paddling their girl friends around in a canoe or pushing a flat-bottom rowboat in pursuit of catfish. Neither, it seemed, was competitive enough for Wisconsin students who thought the beautiful Mendota was made to order for more strenuous things; club rowing had, for some years, been big stuff on Campus. By 1892, two eight-oared gigs had been purchased for class races and it took just two years for Wisconsin officials to hire the school's first coach. He was Amos Marston, a former Cornel rower. Marston was followed a year later by Andrew O'Dea who had rowed for a club in Melbourne, Australia. (O'Dea brought with him from Australia his famous so-called Yarra Yarra stroke, but many Badger sports fans thought it was equally important that he subsequently brought with him his younger brother, Pat, who became Wisconsin's legendary football star.)

Wisconsin took rowing to its heart almost as enthusiastically as football. In fact, it became the only

1899

It was the Minnesota-Wisconsin game of 1899, and it looked as though it would be one of those fiercely bitter, scoreless deadlocks. Then, midway through the second half, the Minnesota punter booted the ball from deep within his own territory. The Badger safetyman waited for it, his arms and hands cupped to receive it . . .

Gil Dobie, the Minnesota end (later a great coach at Cornell) dived for the safety man at a spot somewhere five yards beyond the center stripe at midfield. Take an instant, now, to recall that there were two fifty-yard lines on the field in those days, 10 yards apart. Thus, with the full field 110 yards long, when Pat O'Dea, the Badger safety man, caught the ball five yards beyond the center stripe, he was 60 yards from the Gopher goal.

What happened next was described by newspapers of the day as "unbelievable."

Dobie was closing in fast as O'Dea waited for the ball, and three other Gophers weren't far behind. Somehow O'Dea fielded the punt cleanly without being decapitated by Dobie who was merely waiting for the instant of contact between the ball and O'Dea's hands.

Dobie dived but O'Dea wasn't there. Eluding Dobie, O'Dea headed for the sidelines on his left, shucking other Gophers as he went. Then, without so much as coming to a full stop, and despite the fact that he was a right-footed kicker going to his left, O'Dea got off a drop-kick.

He was an even 60 yards away from the goal posts as far as the field stripes were concerned; the angle of his kick would make it closer to 65.

The ball sailed squarely over the Minnesota cross-bar. It was the longest successful drop-kick in the history of American football. Dobie, who subsequently saw a lot of spectaculars in his brilliant coaching career at Washington and Cornell, later said that O'Dea's kick that day was the greatest individual play he'd ever seen in footbll.

O'Dea's fantastic footwork wasn't exactly a new act. It had been demonstrated time and again, ever since the afternoon he'd arrived on the Madison campus, a lithe, fresh-faced immigrant from Melbourne, Australia.

Australian football was a modified form of English Rugby, with all scoring accomplished only by field goals —either drop- or place-kicked. The youngster, who had come to Wisconsin, where his older brother, Andy, was crew coach, had been one of the outstanding kickers in Australia. When he went out for American-style football, Phil King, the ex-Princeton All-America who was coaching the Badgers, immediately tabbed the 6-1, 173-pounder as a once-in-a-lifetime secret weapon. Here was somebody who could score for him anywhere within the 50-yard line—unerringly—and whose punting, when necessary, could keep the opposition disconsolately bottled up near its own goal line.

For four years Pat O'Dea was the greatest kicker in American football. He had more than a dozen goals from midfield; anything (and they were numerous) from within the 40-yard line drew notice only on the scoreboard. All his drop-kicking was done from scrimmage but his place-kicking was a story in itself.

In those days the rules permitted a field goal attempt on a free kick. In order to get this free kick, all you had to do was signal for a fair catch on a punt. You gave

up a run-back but if you had a kicker you got a crack at a five-pointer, unopposed, from wherever you fielded your fair catch. With O'Dea's magic toe Wisconsin rarely returned a punt short of midfield.

O'Dea's greatest place-kick for a goal does not appear in the official records, although it is well-authenticated. It was made against Illinois at Milwaukee, November 11, 1899. Pat was handicapped that afternoon by an injured leg and hadn't even been in uniform for twelve days before the game.

The game was played in the old Milwaukee baseball park. After one of O'Dea's long punts had gone over the goal line for a touchback, Illinois punted out from the 25 yard line, as the rules then required. The ball was dropping just in bounds near the sidelines when O'Dea shouted to Bill Juneau, playing right end: "Fair catch, Bill, fair catch!" Juneau heeled the catch, just a few feet inside the sideline and 60 yards from the goal line.

A moment later, O'Dea calmly kicked a perfect goal— the longest unofficial place-kicked goal in American football history. Actually, O'Dea's kick against Illinois that day would have been good had the distance been 80 yards, because it cleared the baseball bleachers behind the Illinois goal, the high fence behind them and landed in the street, outside the ball park.

As a punter, O'Dea used the Australian system of kicking the ball end-over-end instead of booting the spiral. O'Dea's punts soared fifty, sixty, and more than seventy yards, with tremendous height, enabling his ends to get down and be waiting for the receiver. It was almost impossible to hurt Wisconsin with punt returns. O'Dea also kicked with such quickness and explosive force that never in four years did he have one blocked. Often, when opposing linemen broke through on him, O'Dea would electrify the crowd by dashing four or five steps to the right and nonchalantly booting the ball on the run—still getting his sixty yards.

Statistics weren't kept in those days. Nobody knew Pat O'Dea's average, but everybody was aware that his drop-kicking, place-kicking and punting had made him the most publicized football player of the day.

Because O'Dea was such a valuable offensive weapon, the Wisconsin coach rarely used him as a line plunger, the usual role for the fullback of that era. In the mass and momentum ground game, too many defenders had an opportunity to take a shot at that gifted leg—and they often did.

It made O'Dea furious to be used so sparingly as a ball carrier because he had tremendous speed, power and competitive fire, and he took a lot of needling from the enemy who claimed he was something less than an honest fullback. (Consequently, when he did carry the ball from scrimmage it usually took two to stop him!) O'Dea, however, made believers out of them on defense where his deadly tackling as a safety man time and again kept opposing backs from going all the way.

Yet, somehow, the charges, unfair as they were, sifted back East where Caspar Whitney and Walter Camp picked the All-America. Somehow, they passed over the greatest kicker the game had ever developed.

Certainly, nobody ever kicked a goal for a more rollicking reason than the one that inspired O'Dea as he booted the first play after Wisconsin got the ball against Northwestern, November 15, 1898.

Phil King, the Badger coach, feared his players were overconfident and in a pre-game pep-talk hammered out the importance of scoring first. In fact, he dangled a special incentive. "It's your last game of the season," he said shrewdly. "You can break training tonight, so, if you score in the first two minutes I'll buy you a case of champagne!"

When Northwestern won the toss, however, and elected to receive, the Badgers naturally took a dim view of their chances for the quick score and the case of Bubbly. Wisconsin, in a fine frenzy, forced Northwestern to punt on the second series of downs. O'Dea signalled for a fair catch and gathered in the ball well past midfield, almost 65 yards from the Wildcat goal.

With only seconds to go before the two-minute deadline, O'Dea screamed for a field goal attempt. The field was muddy but O'Dea calmly toed into the heavy ball and split the uprights 65 yards away for the five points and the champagne chaser.

The last field goal of O'Dea's career, however, was not the end of the story. For the full story of Pat O'Dea there would be a strange and haunting climax.

O'Dea had gone to San Francisco after leaving college and began to practice law. A dozen years later he dropped completely out of sight. It was as though he'd never existed. Sports fans remembered his exploits but nowhere was there a clue to a living—or even a dead—Pat O'Dea. During World War One, word circulated that he'd enlisted in the Australian army and had died a hero's death in France. Yet, there was no clear record of that, either.

Then, in the summer of 1934, almost twenty years later, a man named Charles Mitchell came forward with an electrifying announcement. Mitchell was in the lumber business in Westwood, California, a small mountain town not far from San Francisco. Mitchell also was Pat O'Dea.

A business acquaintance named Walker who'd played football for Minnesota many years before, had become intrigued by Mitchell's looks, his movements, his apparent knowledge of football—but his reticence to talk about the sport. Finally, Walker got Mitchell to confess—and the story made headlines from coast-to-coast.

After college, O'Dea's law practice began to fade with World War One. He started to brood. He became obsessed with the fact that he was a big-time football star who had failed in life. Pat O'Dea considered himself a classic has-been. The only thing to do was assume a new identity and escape from his past.

Asked in 1934 why he had decided to assume his true identity again. O'Dea said: "It took me more than fifteen years to realize there was more shame in hiding than there could ever be in the reason I'd disappeared. I suddenly wanted to become myself again . . . and see a football game once more."

Pat O'Dea kicks off while Red Grange holds.

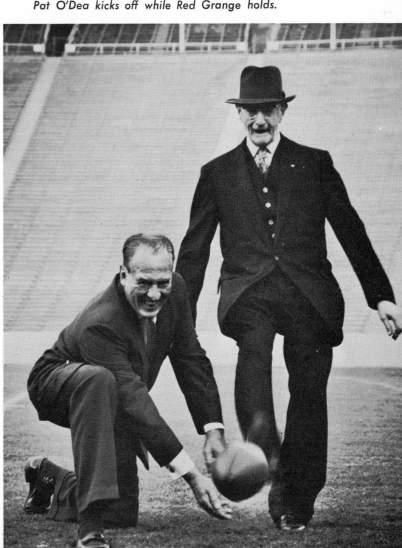

school in the Conference to ever float a varsity boat. So quickly did it catch on that by 1898 Wisconsin entered its crew in the famed Poughkeepsie Regatta, for years a strictly Eastern blue-ribbon event. The Badgers astounded everyone by finishing third, and the following year were the heroes of the famous "berry crate affair." Pennsylvania, Cornell and Columbia were heavily favored and, despite the warning which the raw Midwesterners had served up the previous spring, nobody gave them a chance. A poor start left Wisconsin astern of everybody but by the first mile the powerful Badgers had taken the lead. They easily maintained their position until there was only a quarter of mile to go in the four-mile pull, with Penn more than a boat-length behind.

Suddenly, a large berry crate drifted dead into the Wisconsin boat's course. The coxswain had to swerve his craft to avoid fouling it, because the thin, slim racing shells aren't built for ramming. This took the Badgers on a long diagonal, and, because of the mechanics and rhythm of rowing, the cox figured if he tried to straighten his course he'd lose more ground than he could by staying on the diagonal. He kept the shell on a diagonal all the way to the finish line, adding considerably to the distance Wisconsin had to row. It didn't quite work, and Pennsylvania crossed the line a scant five feet in front.

The following year when Wisconsin returned to the Regatta, the Penn crew saluted them by lining up on the Quaker boat dock with each Quaker oarsman wearing a quart-sized strawberry box on his head.

From then on the Badgers were to be recognized as a national rowing power, and would be a frequent threat at Poughkeepsie.

1900 In 1900, Michigan and Iowa, both undefeated in league play, and losers only once outside of it, were declared Conference football champions, and although the Wolverines would soon make it a habit, Iowa would have to wait more than 20 long years to do it again.

The athletic board at Michigan State (then known as Michigan Agricultural and Mechanical College), noting that the baseball team was hampered each spring by the flooding of the Red Cedar River, hired 100 students at 15 cents an hour to build a protective dike—which still stands. Ohio State got a new grandstand for its athletic field through some expert maneuvering by Prexy William Oxley Thompson, who presented the athletic board with a contract which stipulated that Dean George B. Kauffman of the College of Pharmacy would personally advance the money to build it. Kauffman was also president of a big drug firm. A rider to the agreement was that the faculty, and not the students, would be given control of contributions collected to pay off the loan.

In 1900 Ray Ewry of Purdue became the first

GEORGE HUFF arrived at Illinois in 1895 and took over the dual job of Athletic Director and varsity baseball coach a year later. In very short order his Illini ball clubs became the scourge of the Western Conference and, before he gave up his coaching duties at the end of the 1919 season the Orange and Blue had won 12 league championships and were second 11 times for the most impressive record in the history of Big Ten baseball coaching . . . Not only for the number of titles captured but for the 23 firsts or seconds in his 25 seasons at the helm.

Although he gave up his diamond duties in 1919, Huff continued as Illinois athletic director until 1935. His 41 years give him the longest tenure of any Big Ten athletic director and it is generally acknowledge that "Mister Huff," as he was commonly referred to, was one of the men whose wisdom and energy was responsible for the successful creation of the Western Conference.

Coach George Huff pegs one down during Illinois infield drill.

Conference athlete to win an Olympic championship when he took the first pair of his astounding total of eight titles in the standing broad jump and standing high jump in four Olympiads.

The same year marked the start of one of the most phenomenal sports dynasties in Conference history. George Huff, who had come to Illinois in in 1895 to serve a single year as football coach, had given up the gridiron to take over the following year as athletic director and baseball coach. In 1900 Huff led the Illini to its first championship in any sport, winning the Conference diamond title and launching an incredible 20-year span in which the Orange and Blue won 11 championships and finished second the other nine times!

Up at Minnesota, a husky young medical doctor named Henry Williams took over as Gopher football coach; within a very few years he would not only make the Vikings the scourge of the West but would come up with one of football's most re-volutionary inventions. More about him, later.

In 1900, too, Joe Hunter of Northwestern, finally made it. Elected football captain in 1898, he'd never served because he'd left school to fight in the Spanish-American War. Returning in 1899 he was chosen captain again but was so weak from malaria and typhoid he never played. Elected captain a third time, in 1900, he failed to return in time from a tour of Europe and got back to play only in the

final game—under somebody else's leadership. Later, he was on time for his wedding, when he married the daughter of Georges Clemenceau, Premier of France.

In 1901 football raised some significant portents in the Big Nine. Michigan and Wisconsin both had perfect seasons (11-0 for the Wolverines and 9-0 for the Badgers with neither team being scored upon). It also marked the cranking up of Michigan's awe-some Point-a-Minute machines under Fielding H. (Hurry-Up) Yost, with their first year being climaxed by a 49-0 victory over Stanford in the first Rose Bowl game.

Northwestern scored its first sports victory of any kind over Notre Dame with a 2-0 gridiron triumph, when Harry Allen tackled an Irish halfback behind the goal line as he was trying to punt the soggy ball. Against Chicago, the Purple's Alton Johnson inadvertently inaugurated the huddle (later formal-

The 1901 Michigan team which launched the Wolve-rines' "point-a-minute" era and which crushed Stanford in the first Rose Bowl game. Front row: Everett Sweeley; Harrison Weeks; Curtis Redden; Arthur Redner; Albert Herrnstein. Middle Row: Ebin Wilson; Neil Snow; Captain Hugh White; Bruce Shorts; Willie Heston. Back Row: H. K. Crafts, manager; Dan McGugin; George Gregory; Coach Fielding Yost; Herb Graver; Athletic Director Charles Baird; Keene Fitzpatrick, trainer.

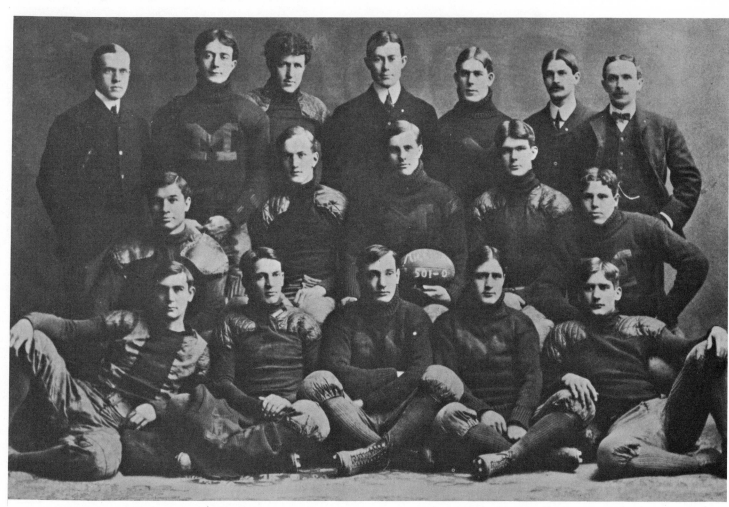

ALTON JOHNSON, a slashing halfback, was Northwestern's first All-America in 1901 and, with Michigan's Neil Snow, shared the distinction of being only the third in Big Ten history.

ized by Bob Zuppke). Unable to remember the signals after a bump on the head, Johnson called his mates around him to get him straightened out for the next play. Johnson made Casper Whitney's All-America but Johnson never found out about it until years later. Then after almost 40 more years had passed he wrote to Collier's Magazine requesting official confirmation of his honor because his daughter had refused to believe it.

It was a year of sadness for Ohio State, which marked the only grid fatality in its history, when John L. Sigrist, the Buckeye center, was fatally injured in a game against Western Reserve.

In the same year, the Big Nine faculty representatives were warming up to their work. They voted to limit preliminary football practice to the two weeks immediately preceding the start of the opening of college, and they declared Mueller of Minnesota ineligible for future athletics because he'd accepted a $5 prize for winning a Fat Man's Race.

In 1901 the Big Nine had begun to flex its organizational muscles in new directions. Up until then, there had been an annual midwest intercollegiate

The first Indiana basketball team (1901) led by Captain Ernie Strange, with hand on ball, had only limited success, but the Hoosiers would later become a perennial power in the Big Ten.

track and field meet promoted by a loosely-knit organization known as the Western Intercollegiate Amateur Athletic Association. It's handling of the affair left something to be desired, and, realizing it, they invited the Big Nine to take it over. The Conference agreed, and decided it would continue it as an open championship with any school eligible to enter. From 1901 until 1926, when the Conference meet became strictly one for the lodge members, colleges such as Notre Dame, Stanford, California, Kansas, Nebraska, Drake, Beloit, Marquette, and others, competed in the annual festival.

Michigan won that first meet in 1901 with 38 points to runner-up Wisconsin's 28, and it's interesting to take a look at the kind of performances typical of the period. Marks held by Conference athletes as of 1901 indicate that the record-holders of their day wouldn't even win their events in a state high school meet today; but, they were establishing standards for others to shoot at, and it wouldn't be long before the Conference, with some of the fiercest competition in the nation, would set a whole swarm of world records.

Conference Track & Field Records As of 1901

100 Yard Run		
John V. Crum, Iowa	0:10.0	
100 Yard Run		
Chas. L. Burroughs, Chicago	0:10.0	
220 Yard Run		
John V. Crum, Iowa	0:22.0	
220 Yard Run		
Chas. L. Burroughs, Chicago	0:22.0	
440 Yard Run		
W. E. Hodgeman, Michigan	0:50.6	
880 Yard Run		
W. A. Moloney, Chicago	2:02.0	
One Mile Run		
Byron B. Smith, Chicago	4:33.0	
120 Yard Hurdle		
J. R. Richards, Wisconsin	0:14.8	
200 Yard Hurdle		
Alvan Kraenzlein, Wisconsin	0:25.6	
200 Yard Hurdle		
John F. McLean, Michigan	0:25.6	
Discus Throw		
C. G. Stangel, Wisconsin	117 ft.	4 in.
Running High Jump		
J. J. Louis, Iowa	5 ft.	11 in.
Putting 16 lb. Shot		
H. E. Lehr, Michigan	38 ft.	11 in.
Running Broad Jump		
James A. Leroy, Michigan	22 ft.	7.5 in.
16 lb. Hammer Throw		
T. W. Mortimer, Chicago	121 ft.	2 in.
Pole Vault		
Chas. Dvorak, Michigan	11 ft.	6 in.

Michigan continued its domination of the Big Nine in 1902 but Michigan State (a half century away from admittance to the Conference, and still called Michigan Agricultural & Mechanical College) made history of sorts by installing electric lights on its practice field . . . And Capt. Charley Ward, of Northwestern—who had imitated William Jennings Bryan so successfully three years earlier—completed a remarkable performance record. With the exception of the last half of the Chicago game in his senior year, Ward played every minute of every game for four years—and played every position but quarterback. (His iron-manship did not, however, come up to that of one of Stagg's early gridders at Chicago before the Conference was formed. Andrew R. E. Wyant had played four years at Bucknell, then three more for Chicago and never missed a minute of play in seven years and 98 games. He became a Baptist minister and lived to the age of 97.)

Meanwhile, the Conference added a third sport to its roster of official athletic activities, with Wisconsin taking the first team title in gymnastics.

When President Charles Van Hise, of Wisconsin, rode his horse out each night to watch football practice in 1903, it was an indication of the hold football (and sports in general) was beginning to take on midwest college administrators. The public demonstrated the same thing by turning out more than 20,000 fans, a new Midwest record, to see mighty Michigan and equally potent Minnesota clash at old Northrop Field in Minneapolis. It was a game ballyhooed as the most titanic clash in the annals of a still young intercollegiate football history.

Michigan's point-a-minute express was rudely held up somewhat in its unobstructed rush. The game ended not only in an epic 6-6 tie (with both teams sharing seasonal honors with 11-0-1 marks) but it was the beginning of the Little Brown Jug tradition, college football's first nationally-known trophy. Willie Heston, Michigan's thunderbolt halfback, was not only All-America but considered by most critics as the greatest back in the nation.

There was tragedy that year, too. The train carrying Purdue's team to Indiana was in a wreck and more than 20 players were killed or injured.

In gymnastics, the Conference recognized the first all-around performance winner, J. W. Dye, of Minnesota . . . and Michigan won its third straight Conference track championship.

1902

1903

WILLIE HESTON

There was no such thing as a monopoly on collegiate football success early in the twentieth century. Nobody was beating everybody and everybody was getting their lumps once in a while. Not even Harvard and Yale, the almost legendary titans of the East, were immune to a clobbering frequently enough to prove them less than immortal.

This was all changed with dynamic and dramatic suddenness by Fielding H. Yost, the rough-hewn West Virginian who had taken over as coach at the University of Michigan.

From 1901, his first season at Ann Arbor, through 1905, Yost and his Wolverines established the greatest gridiron dynasty of all time. There can be no more effective description of their accomplishments than a recital of the record.

In those five years Michigan won 55 games, lost one and tied one.

It piled up 2821 points to its opponents' 42. (This, in the days before the forward pass and with a touchdown counting only five points.)

In 1901 the Wolverines tallied 550 points to 0.

In 1902 it was 644 to 12.

In 1903 a 6-6 tie with Minnesota made it 565 to 6.

In 1904 the count was 567 to 22.

In 1905 it was 495 to 2.

The two points in 1905 were scored on a game-winning safety by Chicago in the next-to-last game of the season, breaking the Wolverines' winning streak.

The 1901 team, Yost's first at Michigan, steam-rolled for 8000 yards (4½ miles). The longest single gain by an opponent was 12 yards. No foe got beyond Michigan's 35-yard line. Some representative scores that year: Michigan 107, Iowa 0; Michigan 86, Ohio State 0; Michigan 128, Buffalo 0.

At the end of the season, Stanford, which was undefeated invited Michigan to a New Year's Day game which would be the climax of the Pasadena Rose Festival. It was hoped that this New Year's Day game would become an annual event between the leading teams from East and West. It became just that, although Stanford on that particular day, January 1, 1902, was sorry it started the whole thing.

The game was 30 minutes late because the Michigan boys insisted on riding one of the floats in the Rose Parade, but didn't start quite late enough for Stanford.

Yost played eleven men without substituting. They ran 142 plays from scrimmage and gained 1,463 yards in a 49-0 victory. Fullback Neil Snow scored five touchdowns (still an all-time Rose Bowl record) and the Wolverines pulled off something Stanford (or anybody else, for that matter) had never seen on their way to their first touchdown. Ten men lined up to the right of the center. The quarterback handed off to Willie Heston who swept all alone to the left, 40 yards. It was the first bootleg play in football history.

This was only the first of five great Michigan teams in an incredible era. It featured Heston, Boss Weeks, Neil Snow, Dan McGugin, Dad Gregory, John Herrnstein, and others. A couple of years later they would be joined by Adolph Schulz, nicknamed "Germany," who would have no peer as a center.

Finally, fifty-six games after it started, the remarkable Point-A-Minute machine hit its only roadblock. Amos Alonzo Stagg of Chicago had put together his finest team

Neil Snow

thus far in his career when it met Michigan on the Midway in the second last game of the 1905 season. More than 20,000 people were in the stands, a Midwest record crowd.

Ferocious defensive play blunted both teams' offenses. Then, with only four minutes to go, a pint-sized Chicago quarterback named Walter Ekersall, got off a 60-yard punt which went into the Michigan end zone. Denny Clark, the Wolverine safety-man, tried to run it out. He almost made it, but just behind the goal line he was hit by Maurice Catlin, the Maroon captain. The referee signaled a safety, and Chicago won, 2-0.

Ring Lardner, the great sports writer who covered the game, later wrote it was the first time anyone had ever seen him cry.

It was the end of an era.

The almost legendary Heston, unquestionably the greatest halfback of early collegiate football, had his own formula for success: "Use your searchlights and jump the dead ones."

Translated by the star of the Wolverines' Point-A-Minute scourge, it meant that Willie used his eyes to spot the slimmest sliver of daylight in the stacked defensive lines of the day, and hurdled anybody who wasn't in an upright position.

Actually, there were other skills that went into the more than 100 touchdowns Willie scored in his four years of play. The 5-10, 190 pounder had the reflexes

The 1901 Michigan team on Tournament of Roses sightseeing tour.

and balance of a cat. He was a master at changing speed and direction. His natural aggressiveness and competitive fire gave him an explosive force at ramming a line or bowling over tacklers. Only once in his career did a single man stop him in the open field. Willie was swift enough to beat Archie Hahn, Michigan's Olympic sprint champion, in impromptu races at 40 and 50 yards. With his brown hair flowing like a great, curling chrysanthemum around his helmetless head, Willie was the most electrifying sight of his day.

Heston's abilities, in fact, led to two innovations in football. Fielding Yost, in order to take advantage of his star's unstoppable power and dazzling running, devised football's first tailback formation in 1901. It allowed Heston to be put in position to run either right or left on a direct snap from center or on a hand-off.

Then, because of the devastating success of the Wolverine attack, Dr. Henry Williams, Minnesota's famed early coach, pioneered the seven-man line and diamond secondary. Football did not yet have the forward pass, pitch-outs and reverses of a later-day open game. Everything was mass momentum or direct sweeps. A run of 10 yards was considered by spectators to be a big thrill. Consequently, the defense played a nine-man line with two men back.

With Heston having the stunning power to tear nine-man lines to bits and constantly elude the two secondary defenders, Williams, at the suggestion of Pudge Hefflefinger, the Yale immortal and a Minneapolis resident, experimented with the seven-diamond defense. Williams reasoned that as long as Willie was going to crack his forward wall anyway, he might as well have four men in the secondary to converge on him when he came through.

The stratagem not only modified all football defenses thereafter but led to a classic stalemate between the irresistible force and immovable object. In the stretch of 55 Michigan games without defeat there came a 6-6 tie with Doc Williams' Gophers in 1903. Williams' new defense held Michigan to two first downs. Heston got away just once to put the Wolverines ahead. But Minnesota came back with a touchdown and the point-after by its great Indian end, Ed Rogers, to tie it up. Aside from interrupting Michigan's victory string and temporarily derailing Heston, the really conclusive result of the game was the success of Williams' seven-man line. It became football's standard defense for a quarter of a century until the ball was redesigned in a more slender shape for forward passing.

MICHIGAN'S POINT-A-MINUTE HISTORY, 1901-1905

1901

Michigan	50;	Albion	0
Michigan	57;	Case	0
Michigan	33;	Indiana	0
Michigan	29;	Northwestern	0
Michigan	128;	Buffalo	0
Michigan	22;	Carlisle	0
Michigan	21;	O. S. U.	0
Michigan	22;	Chicago	0
Michigan	89;	Beloit	0
Michigan	50;	Iowa	0
Michigan	49;	Leland Stanford, Jr.	0

Season Summary

Games won, 11; Lost, 0; Tied, 0.
Points for Michigan, 550; For Opponents, 0.

1902

Michigan	88;	Albion	0
Michigan	48;	Case	6
Michigan	119;	M. A. C.	0
Michigan	60;	Indiana	0
Michigan	23;	Notre Dame	0
Michigan	86;	O. S. U.	0
Michigan	6;	Wisconsin	0
Michigan	107;	Iowa	0
Michigan	21;	Chicago	0
Michigan	63;	Oberlin	0
Michigan	23;	Minnesota	6

Season Summary

Games won, 11; Lost, 0; Tied, 0.
Points for Michigan, 644; For Opponents, 12.

1903

Michigan	31;	Case	0
Michigan	79;	Beloit	0
Michigan	65;	Ohio Northern	0
Michigan	51;	Indiana	0
Michigan	88;	Ferris Institute	0
Michigan	47;	Drake	0
Michigan	76;	Albion	0
Michigan	6;	Minnesota	6
Michigan	36;	O. S. U.	0
Michigan	16;	Wisconsin	0
Michigan	42;	Oberlin	0
Michigan	28;	Chicago	0

Season Summary

Games won, 11; Lost, 0; Tied, 1.
Points for Michigan, 565; For Opponents, 6.

1904

Michigan	33;	Case	0
Michigan	48;	Ohio Northern	0
Michigan	95;	Kalamazoo	0
Michigan	72;	P. & S.	0
Michigan	31;	O. S. U.	6
Michigan	72;	Am. Col. M. & S.	0
Michigan	130;	West Virginia	0
Michigan	28;	Wisconsin	0
Michigan	36;	Drake	4
Michigan	22;	Chicago	12

Season Summary

Games won, 10; Lost, 0; Tied, 0.
Points for Michigan, 567; For Opponents, 22.

1905

Michigan	65;	Ohio Wesleyan	0
Michigan	44;	Kalamazoo	0
Michigan	36;	Case	0
Michigan	23;	Ohio Northern	0
Michigan	18;	Vanderbilt	0
Michigan	31;	Nebraska	0
Michigan	70;	Albion	0
Michigan	48;	Drake	0
Michigan	33;	Illinois	0
Michigan	40;	O. S. U.	0
Michigan	12;	Wisconsin	0
Michigan	75;	Oberlin	0
Michigan	0;	Chicago	2

Season Summary

Games won, 12; Lost 1; Tied, 0.
Points for Michigan, 495; For Opponents, 2.

The Ohio State basketball team in 1904 had as its "big man," lanky George Bellows, third from left, who later would be hailed as one of America's greatest painters, particularly famed for his "Stag at Sharkey's."

1904

Two familiar names—Michigan and Minnesota—dominated Big Nine and midwest football in 1904, and it was disappointing that they didn't meet. Michigan scored 567 points to its foes' 22 in its 10-0 season; the Gophers piled up 618 to 12 in their perfect 12-game campaign. In addition, it was Dr. Henry Williams, the Minnesota coach, who, as a member of the football rules committee, in 1904, first advocated legalization of the forward pass. It would not get into the rules for two more years but Williams deserves the main credit for arguing for its adoption.

For the first time, a Conference team placed two men on the All-America when Chicago's Walter Eckersall was named as quarterback, and Maroon end, Fred Speik, joined him. With Willie Heston of Michigan again named as a halfback, the Conference had a terrific all-star trio on the honor squad—the first collegiate conference, aside from the entrenched Eastern group to do so.

In track, a lanky Canadian named Harry Gill showed up at Illinois to begin a fabulous 30-year coaching regime in which the Illini took the Conference team title 11 times and finished second seven others. The big news in track in 1904 was the remarkable representation of Big Nine athletes on the U.S. Olympic team. More track and field athletes from the Conference competed for the United States in the Olympics in St. Louis than any collegiate contingent. Archie Hahn, of Michigan, took the 100- and 200-meters; the Wolverines' Ralph Rose and C. E. Dvorak added the shot-put and pole vault. James Lightbody, of Chicago, took the 800-meter and 1500-meter events. Ray Ewry of Purdue captured the standing high jump and standing broad jumps. Indiana's Thad Shideler was second in the high hurdles and the Hoosiers' LeRoy Samse was second in the pole vault. Wisconsin's Frank Waller was second at 400-meters. Walter Eckersall, Chicago's legendary quarterback, was a sprinter on the team but didn't take a medal, and another non-winning team member was Michigan State's Harry Moon. Altogether, 10 Western Conference track and field athletes competed for Uncle Sam.

Meanwhile, the Big Nine faculty representatives pioneered a new rule that was hailed throughout the country as a radical departure in college athletics. It required that a student, to be eligible for intercollegiate athletics, must first complete a full semester's work in residence. It not only meant freshmen couldn't play on varsity teams but discouraged easy transfer from college to college by "tramp" athletes.

A trio of Big Ten stars who shone for the United States Olympic team in 1904. ARCHIE HAHN, of Michigan, scored a brilliant sprint double with firsts in the 100- and 200-meters; teammate RALPH ROSE, took the shot-put; and Indiana's LEROY SAMSE was second in the pole vault and later, in 1906, set a world record of 12 feet 4 and 3/7 inches—although it is a bit hazy as to how the fraction was established.

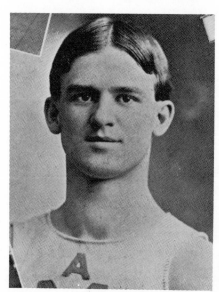

ARCHIE HAHN

RALPH ROSE

LEROY SAMSE

CHRIS STEINMETZ

The word is, perhaps, "unbelievable."

In this day of run-and-shoot, fling-em-up basketball where more than 200 points are often scored in a single Big Ten game, it will come as quite a seismic shock to Wisconsin fans—and others—to learn that most Badger scoring records are held by a Wisconsin player of almost 60 years ago—when two teams usually staggered in with a total of 20 points or so for an evening's effort . . . Except when Chris Steinmetz played, and then the official scorer became more of a bona fide working stiff and less of a spectator.

Getting right to the heart of the matter, here are Steinmetz' records, still all-time Wisconsin marks, established in the 1904-5 season:

Most points in a single game—50
Most field goals in one game—20
Most free throws in one game—26
Most free throws, one season—233
Most points in a single season—462

No screens, picks, pivot-plays or pin-point passing marked Wisconsin's play (or anybody else's!) in those days. The whole idea was to let Steinmetz, a rangy six-footer, get the ball as often as he could. One player could still shoot all the foul shots for his team and since free throws were also awarded for such violations as double-dribble and traveling, Steinmetz wore a steady path to the foul line. His 20 field goals against Beloit on January 7, 1905, established an inter-collegiate record.

Although there was yet no Big Ten basketball championship (but there would be the following year, for the first time) Steinmetz put Wisconsin on the cage map, and within a few years Wisconsin would hire, as coach a lean young physician named Walter Meanwell, who would become one of the all-time great teachers of the game.

Heady with success, the Badgers late in 1905 embarked on a nine-game Eastern trip. Unaccountably, Wisconsin won only two games on that tour but Steinmetz later remembered ". . . at least we got a great send-off from Madison. They sent up an elaborate fireworks display for us, and subsequently the old State Capitol Building burned down."

Steinmetz also recalled that in a game with Columbia the baskets were perched atop iron poles, without backboards. Every time Wisconsin shot, a Columbia player would grab the pole and shake the ball off the hoop.

Two men played every minute of every game for Wisconsin on that trip. One was Steinmetz. The other was an obscure, stumpy youngster named Bob Zuppke—who, not too many years later, would not be so obscure.

There came, in 1905, the end of an era. Michigan's juggernaut, undefeated in 55 games over a five-year span, met Chicago in the final game of the season—and it was a Chicago team judged to be the greatest in Amos Alonzo Stagg's career. Mighty Mite Walter Eckersall was an All-America

"The Greatest Team that Ever Wore The 'C' " is the way Amos Alonzo Stagg referred to his 1905 undefeated club which ended Michigan's "Point-a-Minute" undefeated streak at 55 games, in an epic 2-0 victory. Walter Eckersall, the incredible 145-pound All-America quarterback, is second from right in the bottom row.

quarterback who had magnificent support from such as Mark Catlin, All-America center; Babe Meigs, Hugo Bezdek (later a coaching genius at Penn State) and Jesse Harper, who would subsequently put Notre Dame on the map. It was a safety that gave the Maroon a 2-0 win in the struggle of two superteams, with Willie Heston of the Wolverines being stopped cold for the first time in his career, before a crowd of 25,791 that set a new Conference and western attendance record. Chicago, of course, with a 10-0 mark for the season, was the new Big Nine champion.

1905

BABE MEIGS, a tough, brilliant lineman, was a big factor in the success of the 1905 Chicago football team, said to be the greatest of Stagg's early clubs. Meigs also starred on undefeated Maroon basketball teams.

WILLIAM OXLEY THOMPSON, president of Ohio State University in 1905 stated in his annual report that athletics were "an inescapable part of the college scene." One of the first college leaders to make such a public statement, he added: ". . . faculties must recognize not only their right but their duty to lead in all forms of college athletics."

There was celebrating up at Wisconsin, too. The first Badger victory in the Conference in three years was scored in a 16-12 upset of Minnesota, with major heroics provided by A. R. Findlay, Badger halfback, who had two 85-yard runs for touchdowns.

Lean, wiry Zora G. Clevenger began a career of sports service at Indiana that would make him one of the most venerable administrators in the Western Conference. (Clevenger would coach the Hoosier baseball and basketball teams briefly and later spend 23 years as athletic director.)

ZORA G. CLEVENGER, an all-time great football, basketball and baseball player at Indiana where he starred in the early 1900s, coached the Hoosier baseball team in 1905 and basketball in 1905 and 1906, then subsequently moved on to Tennessee where, as varsity football coach he led the Volunteers in 1914 to their first undefeated grid season. After stints as Athletic Director at Missouri and Kansas State he returned to his Alma Mater in 1923 to become Indiana's most venerated Athletic Director. During his 23 years at the helm of Hoosier athletics (he retired in 1946) he became one of the nation's most respected leaders of intercollegiate sports.

In 1905, also, midwest athletics got a big boost when William Oxley Thompson, president of Ohio State, in his annual report to the university called athletics "an inescapable part of the college scene." He was of the opinion, however, that college faculties " . . . must recognize not only their right but their duty to lead in all forms of college athletics."

He continued: "An absorbing interest of the public, alumni and students has created an atmosphere not always the purest. For 10 years or more, commendable efforts have been made to regulate excesses and irregularities of athletics. There has been evident improvement in the rules; what is needed at present is to improve the ethical standards of all persons interested in athletics. Conformity to rules . . . is too much a technicality and not enough of a principle . . . Athletics like every other form of amusement or business must eventually rest on sound ethics. . . .

"It is unfortunate that the public . . . is so eager for amusement that it becomes indifferent to ethical conditions surrounding the game. It is a waste of energy denouncing athletics; what is needed is efficient leadership by men to whom principle is dearer than anything else. If university faculties are set for education of youth, it is little more than a corollary to add that they cannot ignore the ethical conditions surrounding college sports . . . So long as there are institutions there will be students, and so long as there are games there will be problems. We will never reform athletics simply by rules; we shall reform it only when we have inspired young men to high ideals and to be governed by sound ethics. . . ."

Thompson's encouragement and good sense not only helped strengthen the Conference faculty representatives' administrative position but paved the way for the eventual admission of Ohio State as the 10th and final member of the league a few years later.

WALTER ECKERSALL

He was a little squirt who, in 1897, began his football days by fetching the water bucket to University of Chicago players in a game with the Carlisle Indians, and he decided he'd be a football player, himself. Two years later Walter Eckersall entered Hyde Park High School and began his career as football's Mightiest Mite.

Eckersall, who later became one of Walter Camp's most enthusiastic All-America choices, was a 118-pound end and quarterback for the Chicago prepsters in an era when high schools thought nothing of rostering returning Spanish-American war veterans, or 20-year-olds who showed up to take a single course in woodshop while they played football. With tiny Walter Eckersall cracking the whip over his bigger mates, Hyde Park not only mopped up every high school in sight by 40 or more points but took on the University of Chicago and Wisconsin teams, beating the Maroon and losing to the Badgers. Hyde Park played the first intersectional high school game in history, inviting Brooklyn Tech, the best in the East, to a post-season game, and utterly crushed the visitors, 105-0.

Eckersall was the running, kicking and defensive star of the club, and although he had ballooned up to 140 pounds when he was ready to enter the University of Chicago, Amos Alonzo Stagg welcomed him with the mental reservation that the youngster would probably get killed in the first inter-squad scrimmage.

Eckie, as he was known, not only survived the first scrimmage; he awed Stagg with his ferocity and his skills. Stagg installed him first at end and then at quarterback, where he led the Maroon to 32 victories against four losses and two ties in four years. An All-America in 1904-05-06, Eckie was a brilliant strategist, phenomenal kicker and an unbelievably tigerish safetyman on defense. His heroics would have been sensational for a full-sized performer; for a 140-pounder they were nothing short of fantastic.

In the days when a field goal was forth five points he kicked three against Wisconsin for a 15-6 win. He booted five field goals against Illinois and five against Nebraska, all drop-kicks. Against Wisconsin another year he had returned a kick-off 106 yards to a touchdown.

Eckersall, a wildly-daring young man who was also a legitimate 9.8 sprinter, probably displayed his brightest pyrotechnics in the famous 1905 clash with Michigan's Point-A-Minute wonders. Chicago put up a tremendous goal line stand in a game that would decide the Big Ten championship, and took over the ball on its own two-yard line. Going back to punt Eckersall noticed the Michigan ends playing tight in order to knife in to block the kick. Without even signalling to his team-mates Eckersall sized things up in a flash. Instead of kicking he took the snap from center and streaked around the charging Wolverine end and up the field where a Michigan safety man just barely succeeded in pushing him out of bounds at the fifty.

Halted by the Michigan line Eckersall dropped back to punt again. This time he actually laid into it and sent the ball on a booming kick over the goal line where Denny Clark, Michigan halfback, caught it and decided to run it out. He was tackled behind his goal for a safety which won the game 2-0 for Chicago, halting Michigan's Point-A-Minute victory string at 55, and capturing Chicago's first Big Ten title since 1899.

The two-point lead, however, might not have held up if the 140-pound Eckersall, whom Walter Camp called the "greatest quarterback of all time" had not pulled off a defensive maneuver which never before had been successful.

The incomparable Willie Heston, breaking through the line, bore down on Eckersall, the lone defender in his path. Eckersall dove low for the Wolverine star but missed. Heston hurdled the diving Chicagoan and continued on his way. Eckersall after missing, had made a complete revolution with his body, and wound up on his feet, still in motion, in pursuit of the fleeing Heston. He dragged Willie down from behind on the Chicago 20. It was the first and only time in his four-year career that the fleet Willie Heston had ever been nailed from behind.

There was no end to the Mighty Mite's virtuosity. By Eckie's final year, 1906, the forward pass had been legalized. "Think you can throw this thing with any accuracy?" Amos Alonzo Stagg asked him. "I'll throw it," Eckersall grinned. "Just make sure you have someone who can catch it."

Chicago waited until its fourth game, with Illinois as its opponent, before taking to the air. Eckersall, who had never thrown a pass in a game, gave a perfect exhibition of pigskin pitching, completing every pass he threw in a 63-0 rout of the Illini. His very first toss wound up in a 75-yard touchdown play to Wally Steffen, later a famed coach of Carnegie Tech and a distinguished judge on the Federal Bench.

Natuarlly, it was the longest touchdown pass play of the year.

Meanwhile, 1905 provided some new accents in other sports. The Michigan Aggies' track team defeated Notre Dame for the first Spartan victory over the Irish in any sport. The Northwestern baseball team accomplished the same thing for the Purple over Chicago, but the 6-5 Northwestern victory so stunned Chicago that the Maroon couldn't accept it and challenged Northwestern to another game, this time for a team dinner. The Purple repeated, 1-0, in an 11-inning game and dined sumptuously at the old Edelwiess Cafe.

Chicago, meanwhile, having ended Michigan's era of football domination in the Big Nine, proceeded to do the same thing to the Wolverines in track. After four straight championships, Michigan bowed to Alonzo Stagg's Maroon in the annual outdoor meet.

Suddenly, with dramatic impact, the announcement came from Northwestern that it was withdrawing from football competition. A lot of people were not at all shocked. The 1905 season in college football had been something of a carnage, and it was only the intervention of President Teddy Roosevelt that saved the sport, at all. He literally forced the national rules markers to make drastic changes to open up the game and reduce the possibility of injuries. The most notable improvement, of course, was the legalizing of the forward pass as an offensive weapon; but high on the list of improvements were the cutting down of playing time for each half to 30 minutes, and the provision that at least six men must be on the line of scrimmage.

The excesses of a burgeoning big-time sport, aside from the physical aspect of the game, continued to resist change and the Western Conference decided to go a bit further.

President J. B. Angell, of Michigan, taking the lead, suggested other needed reforms (which were soon to have violent repercussions on the Wolverines' own campus). In a letter to the Conference officials he suggested that...

"... The general complaint in the public press is of the roughness and dangerous character of the game. Now while it is desirable and I hope practicable to remove some of the objections to the present style of playing, I think that we who administer universities will agree that there are other objections to the present mode of carrying on the game quite as serious as the roughness of the play. Let us notice some of them.

"1. The absorbing interest and excitement of the students — not to speak of the public — in the preparation for the intercollegiate games make a damaging invasion into the proper work of the university for the first ten or twelve weeks of the academic year. This is not true of the players alone, but of the main body of students, who think and talk of little else but the game. The season given up to this excitement is too long. The games are too many. The number should be reduced. It is a fair question whether, without resorting to intercollegiate games, the competition of classes and departments in any university would not furnish games enough for healthy rivalry. It would probably spare us the presence of thousands of spectators from outside.

"2. The present conditions constantly hold before the students and before the world false ideals of college life. Not only in the college journals, but in the newspaper press of the whole country, the students who by daily descriptions and by portraits are held up as the great men of the university are the men of brawn rather than the men of brains. Their slight ailments are chronicled with as much promptness as are those of a King in his Court Gazette. Their names are daily carried by the Associated Press from ocean to ocean. Not only undergraduates but schoolboys are filled with aspirations to follow in the footsteps not of the best scholars, but of the best players.

"3. The university is necessarily viewed in a wrong perspective. It is looked on as training men for a public spectacle, to which people come by thousands, instead of quietly training men for useful intellectual and moral service while securing ample opportunity for reasonable athletic sports. Indeed the intellectual trainers are made to appear as of small consequence compared with the football coach and trainer.

"4. The expenditure of money in the preparation for the game is out of all proportion to what a rational provision for exercise and games for students ought to call for. I need not go into detail. I will only add that where so much money is handled for such purpose, the temptations to misuse are not wanting."

PRESIDENT J. B. ANGELL, of Michigan, not only was one of the founders of the Big Ten but was one of the most courageous college leaders in the nation when he offered his platform of badly needed reforms.

AMOS ALONZO STAGG

James J. Corbett had just won the heavyweight title of the world from John L. Sullivan.

Knute Rockne was a four-year-old growing up in Norway.

The American Baseball League would not be born for another eight years.

It was September, 1892 and a ram-rod-straight young man with bushy hair had just arrived on the raw new campus of freshly-minted University of Chicago. He had been hired by famed William Rainey Harper, Chicago's president, to become the school's first athletic director and coach—and as an Associate Professor. Harper, who had been the young man's professor of Hebrew at Yale, thus conferred upon Amos Alonzo Stagg the distinction of being the first athletic coach in America to receive academic status.

What happened in the next 70 years (yes, 70) is the story of the most remarkable man in the history of American collegiate sports.

The figures, alone, found in his record would have established Stagg as a monumental success; but Knute Rockne, among others, said: "All modern football comes from Amos Alonzo Stagg."

Stagg pioneered the T-formation, the quick kick, the man-in-motion, the fake hand-off, the flanker, cross-blocking, the double-delayed pass, and was the first to put numbers on his players' jerseys for the spectators' benefit.

It is Stagg, himself—the man and his background—which is infinitely more astounding than the record.

Amos Alonzo Stagg had hoped to be a minister of the gospel. He could have been a big league pitcher. It was inevitable that he chose the life he did.

It is almost symbolic that Amos Stagg, the fifth of eight children, who was born August 16, 1862, to a humble shoemaker in West Orange, N.J., should have been a descendant, on both sides of his family, of colonial stock who fought in the Revolutionary War. Stagg finished district school in West Orange but the community had no high school. Three years later, after deciding he would get more education at any cost, he entered Orange High School at 18, rising at five in the morning to tend furnaces to earn out-of-district tuition money. He graduated from high school at 21, with his eye on the ministry via Yale University. Lacking credits to enroll as a Boola Boola, he talked his way into admittance to Phillips Exeter Academy—the oldest boy in the school—and again had to work to pay his way. While doing so he lived in a drafty garret without heat, and mostly on a diet of soda crackers and beans.

Tuition at Yale in those days was $50 a term. This astronomical sum was beyond him but President Noah Porter told the young Stagg he'd see to it that he had enough campus work to swing it. Stagg had entered Exeter with $21. Things were looking up; he entered Yale with $32. Several major colleges had wooed him because, despite his almost starvation diet at Exeter, he was the best pitcher ever to perform in the posh Eastern prep school league. He picked Yale because of its Divinity School.

Stagg's athletic record at Yale from 1884 through 1889 was phenomenal even in that day of comparatively low-pressure collegiate competition. He pitched Yale to five straight league titles. In 1888 he set a record of 20 strikeouts in one game against Princeton. He later said he'd put a little bit extra on the ball against the Tigers

because Mrs. Grover Cleveland, wife of the President of the United States, had attended the game and stayed on the Princeton side for the entire contest. Young Stagg thought she was violating the spirit of neutrality.

In the four years Stagg played football for Yale (he didn't take up the game until he was in graduate school) the Elis lost only one game—the last one of his career, against Princeton. Stagg, a stocky, 5-foot, 10-inch end, made the first All-America team ever picked by Caspar Whitney, in 1888, and during the time he was a demon flanker Yale scored 1820 points to its opponents' 45. By the time he'd graduated in 1889 Stagg had invented the tackling dummy, and his pitching feats had attracted tempting offers from virtually every professional team in baseball; but, he was set on becoming a minister and enrolled in Yale's Divinity School.

He lasted one year because he found he had a complete inability to speak in front of groups of people.

Emotionally bruised, he did what he thought was the next best thing: he launched a coaching career at the YMCA training school at Springfield, Mass. Two years later he received the fateful call from William Rainey Harper at Chicago.

When Stagg called his first football practice October 1, 1892 the very day the University opened its still unfinished doors, only 13 boys responded. After a week of practice the team played its first game, defeating Hyde Park High School. Stagg, himself, captained the team and played end.

Suddenly the young man who couldn't talk effectively to groups of people, began to find his way—through sports. As the University grew, so did its football team until it became one of the mightiest in the Midwest and the nation. Stagg's reputation grew right along with it. (The

Amos Alonzo Stagg in 1888 when he played right end on Yale's championship team.

A. A. Stagg with Mrs. Stella Robertson Stagg who was a coed at Chicago when he began his work on the Midway.

headline "Stagg Fears Purdue" became a bit of national gridiron folklore.)

In 1894 Stagg made the longest trip ever taken by a college team when he took Chicago to California for two games. Soon he was visiting the East, where he'd first gained fame, to play Cornell and Pennsylvania. His teams were veteran travelers long before a latter-day traveling team from South Bend, Indiana had barely got itself a football.

It was a rousing, almost chaotic world of football in which young Stagg found himself. He often inserted himself into the lineup, but not because he was being devious; with limited manpower this was an acceptable and standard coaching gambit of the period. Once, in the early 1890's, the crowd at a Chicago game became so excited that mounted policemen were called in to keep the fans from surging onto the field at old Washington Park where the Maroon played. At a crucial moment one of the cops actually took a position on the playing field. At that instant Stagg was carrying the ball on a wide sweep. As a local historian reported it at the time, Stagg whacked the cop's steed on the flank and, with the horse galloping down the sideline, Stagg fled behind this improvised interference 60 yards for a winning touchdown.

In the 40 years Stagg coached at Chicago, from 1892 to 1932 his teams won 229, lost 108, and tied 27. He won Conference championships in 1896, 1899, 1905, 1907, 1908, 1913, and 1924, more than any other coach in the

Big Ten up until that time. It should be noted, too, that most of his defeats came in his last 10 years after a new Chicago president, Robert Maynard Hutchins, almost fanatically anti-football, so successfully de-emphasized sports that Stagg had virtually no material. Before he was hobbled by Hutchins' New Concept, however, Stagg was the man to beat if you wanted to win the Big Ten title. (Even with a final decade deep in frustration, Stagg, over his entire Chicago career, outscored his opponents 5827 to 2724.) In 1905, in one of the historic games in early football, his Maroon ended Michigan's and Fielding H. (Hurry-Up) Yost's fabulous five-year winning streak by scoring a 2-0 victory over Willie Heston and his Point-A-Minute mates.

The stars who played for him were among the brightest in football's constellation: Clarence Herschberger, the Maroon's first All-America; Walter Eckersall, Wally Steffen, Tiny Maxwell, Hugo Bezdek, Ralph Hammil, John Schommer, Andy Wynant, Babe Meigs, Nels Norgren, Paul Des Jardiens, Pat Page, John Thomas, Charles McGuire, Fritz Crisler, Austin (Five-Yards) McCarty, Ken Rouse and Joe Pondelik.

Aside from his inspired inventiveness and his mastery of all phases of the game, Stagg's success was due mostly to two things: his way of growing close to his players and thereby inspiring them with a sense of personal loyalty, and an ability to demonstrate techniques in an era when candidates reported without the prior benefit of the expert high school coaching so prevalent in later days. Many a raw, unknowing recruit, who reported to Stagg with a limited prep background, was handtooled by the Grand Old Man into an All-Big Ten star.

It was not just as a coach that Amos Stagg left his mark. He was one of the first to recognize the evils of unregulated collegiate athletics, and when President Smart of Purdue called his historic conference in 1895, it was Stagg's eloquence and common sense which did much to shape the new-born league. In 1904 he became a member of the national Football Rules Committee and helped save the game from almost universal condemnation and impending banishment because of its savagery and numerous injuries. Stagg was one of the committee's most vociferous members in favor of introducing rules which would open up the game and make it less injury-prone. Thus, when Teddy Roosevelt summoned college representatives to the White House in 1905 and threatened to abolish the sport virually by presidential decree unless something was done, his visitors had something to offer.

A. A. Stagg and Hugo Bezdek, one of his football pupils, on a vacation in Hot Springs, Arkansas in 1905. Bezdek was later coach at Penn State.

WILL BE Home Soon.

For openers they suggested elimination of the flying wedge, mass-momentum plays from behind the line of scrimmage, and introduction of the forward pass. Teddy Roosevelt accepted and the game was saved.

Too many people forget—or are not aware—that Amos Stagg was virtually as successful a coach in baseball and track as he was in football. His baseball teams won five Big Ten titles before he gave up diamond duties in 1909; and he won four Conference track championships before devoting his attention exclusively to football and athletic administration in the twenties. He served on the American Olympic Committee for several years and in the 1924 games in Paris he coached the middle distance runners and relay team.

No man in football was more honored than Stagg. In 1931 to help observe his 40th anniversary as coach and molder of men, his Alma Mater, Yale University, consented to make its first trip west of the Alleghenies to play Stagg's Chicago team. The night before the game, 1500 Yale alumni gathered at a dinner at the Hotel Stevens to pay their respects to one who was now popularly known as *The Grand Old Man.* The next day Albie Booth, Yale's famed Little Boy Blue, led the Elis to a decisive victory over Chicago but Stagg was still the hero of the weekend festivities.

In 1933 at age 70 Amos Alonzo Stagg grudgingly bowed to University regulations and accepted mandatory retirement; but, he had no intention of retiring from football. He was promptly hired by College of the Pacific. Two years later he brought his COP team to Chicago and walloped the Maroon 32-0 on Stagg Field.

In 1943, after spectacular COP successes over major opposition, Amos Stagg, at age 81, was elected Coach-of-the-Year.

Forcibly retired again in 1947, Stagg age 85, promptly moved to Susquehanna College in Pennsylvania where he assisted his son, Alonzo, Jr., who was head coach. Be-

A. A. Stagg became Athletic Director and football coach of the University of Chicago when it opened in 1892. He is shown above at the start of his forty-first season.

cause of his wife's ill health he had to go back West again in 1953, and took an assistant coaching job at Stockton Junior College. ("I am fit and able," he noted firmly, "and I refuse to become an idle nuisance.") Two years later he gave up coaching and at age 93 was named the greatest living American by the U.S. Chamber of Commerce.

In 1958 he became the only man to be named to the Football Hall of Fame for both playing and coaching.

On August 16th, 1962 at Stockton, California, Amos Alonzo Stagg celebrated his 100th birthday—and was still mowing his own lawn.

What made the Man? It can be summed up in one word—Integrity—and, perhaps, his integrity can best be illustrated by an incident in one of the greatest football games ever witnessed in the East.

"The Grand Old Man of Football" is piloted around the field by his wife in his electric carriage as he recovers from an injury sustained while showing his boys proper blocking techniques.

A. A. Stagg (left) chats with Purdue coach Jimmy Phelan.

Members of a Minnesota Indian tribe attempt to put a hex on Stagg and his players prior to their game in Minneapolis.

One of his finest Chicago teams was locked in titanic battle with one of Bill Roper's great Princeton elevens at Palmer Stadium. The teams had traded scores until, in the fourth quarter with Chicago trailing 21-18, the Maroon had the ball in Tiger territory with a touchdown situation clearly set up. It was obvious on the Chicago bench, if not so clear to the Chicago players on the field. The Tiger defense was so tightly deployed that a wide sweep would undoubtedly bring the winning touchdown.

Stagg's assistant was a young man named Fritz Crisler who immediately spotted the possibilities and grabbed Stagg's arm impulsively. Substitutes at that time were forbidden to talk to teammates until a play had been run off; but, there was nothing in the rules against sending in a fresh quarterback who could immediately call the right play. Chicago's second-string quarterback was Alonzo Stagg, Jr.

"Let's put Lonnie in there to call the end run," Crisler said eagerly.

Stagg shook his head. "The rules committee deprecates the use of a substitute to convey information—even though, in this case it would be legal."

Lonnie Stagg didn't go in and Chicago didn't score. A few minutes later the game ended with Chicago on Princeton's one-yard line. It could have been Chicago's greatest win of many a year but Amos Alonzo Stagg didn't want it that way.

The Grand Old Man Speaks

"I invite a man out for football only once. Never a second time. Football is here for those who will participate. If you have to urge a man he'll lack confidence and aggressiveness."

*　　*　　*

"There is too much intemperance in eating. Too many people dig their graves with their teeth." (Stagg ate only simple foods, never ate a hot dog in his life.)

*　　*　　*

"Whenever I get mentally sluggish during the day I get up from my desk, promptly, and run around the block."

*　　*　　*

"Learn to understand your own bodily machinery and then take care of it like a master mechanic."

*　　*　　*

"I will never consent to select an All-America team or candidate for one. The individual is only part of the whole. It's the combined labors of players and coaches that produce results."

Amos Alonzo Stagg was still interested in football at 81 years of age after 54 years of coaching. Here he advises his quarterback, Irwin Barnickle, during College of Pacific—Coast Guard Game.

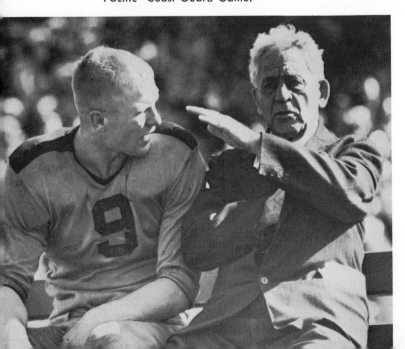

"Well, my gosh! Tell those coaches thanks. I certainly didn't expect any honors at my time of life. You see, I don't move around in that world anymore." (On being notified he'd been elected Coach-of-the-Year at age 81, at College of Pacific.)

* * *

"Golly!" (On learning in 1914 that the new football stadium at Chicago would be dedicated to him and named Stagg Field, the only coach in the history of football so honored in his lifetime. Chicago had played its early games at Washington Park, but in 1893 the school received a gift of land from a local merchant named Marshall Field, which later was the site of Stagg Field.)

* * *

"You jackass!" (A player who made an error.) "You double jackass!" (A player who committed a grievous error.) "You triple jackass!" (A player who pulled a colossal boner.) Stagg never swore, smoked or drank. One day Bob Zuppke, the Illinois coach, attended a Chicago practice. Nobody was doing much that was right and Stagg, in good voice, was handing out the jackass label liberally. "By the time practice was over," observed Zup drily, "there wasn't a human being on the field. The whole squad was grazing."

* * *

"Yes, I am a little disappointed about the way things turned out today. I've misplaced my topcoat and Mrs. Stagg will be furious." (His only comment after one of his better Chicago teams lost a heartbreaker to Ohio State on an obviously bonehead decision by an official. Stagg had uncorked a surprise flanker play which resulted in a 57-yard winning touchdown, but the official, unfamiliar with the play, nullified the score.)

* * *

"This is despicable; I will not avail myself of it." (In the old days, signals were called at the line of scrimmage, and on many occasions spies sent him full sets of signals used by opposing teams.)

A. A. Stagg and eight of his former University of Chicago football captains at a luncheon held in his honor in 1944. Left to right, Back Row: Lawrence Whiting, 1910; Charles Higgins, 1919; Dr. A. R. E. Wyant, 1893; Hal Lewis, 1922; Charles H. McGuire, 1920; Don Birney, 1932; Front Row: Pete Russell, 1915; Coach Stagg, and Pat Page, 1909.

Even though they were in their 90's, the Staggs still enjoyed a good football game, and Mrs. Stagg was as knowledgeable as her husband about the game's finer points.

1906

At Angell's urging, representatives of the Conference met in Chicago, in January, 1906, and again in March, to discuss the ideas he had offered in his letter. The result was a set of stringent restrictions which was officially adopted as Conference policy:

1. One year of residence was necessary for eligibility. This rule also declared that an athlete meet all entrance requirements of his university and that he complete a full year's work before playing.
2. Competition would be limited to three years, and no graduate student would be eligible.
3. The season would be limited to five games (as compared to as many as 12, previously).
4. Training tables and training quarters were prohibited.
5. Student and faculty tickets were not to cost more than fifty cents.
6. Coaches were to be appointed only by the university itself, and at moderate salary.
7. Steps would be taken to reduce receipts and expenses of athletic contests.

This was reform with a vengeance. Ironically, Michigan, whose President Angell had started the thing in motion, was the first to recant. Because of its geographical location, Michigan had planned on playing many eastern colleges, and a five-game schedule would, obviously, prevent it. The Wolverines also resented certain other restrictions in the new regulations and there were mutterings from Ann Arbor that Michigan intended to go its own way unless there was a relaxation of the rules.

The Wisconsin faculty, meanwhile, was in a mood to go beyond the provisions of the "Angell Conference." Fed up with proselytizing and the bad name the Big Nine was receiving in the press, the faculty first voted to abolish football; then, after a furious uproar by students and alumni, reconsidered and merely banned "big games," instead. This meant the Badgers could not play their traditional rivals, Chicago, Minnesota and Michigan. Since these were the only games producing any revenue it became apparent that Wisconsin's role on the midwestern sports stage would be reduced to a walk-on. Before that could happen, however, there was a walkout as the Badger football, baseball, track and crew coaches immediately resigned. President Van Hise promptly decided that all coaches henceforth would be full faculty members. Under the new system things weren't too bad on the field. The Badgers, with a perfect 5-0 season, shared Conference honors with Minnesota; but, it was disastrous at the box office. From $35,000 the previous year, Wisconsin dropped to a take of $3400 without its "big games."

1907

Minnesota's successful season, incidentally, was saved by Bobby Marshall, its great Negro end, and the first of his race to play in the Big Nine. Marshall booted a soggy ball 60 yards for a field goal that beat Chicago, 4-2, a field goal at the time still counting four points.

This early photo of the 1907 Iowa football team may surprise fans by revealing that even way back then there was a T-formation, with a split end. Modern refinements and complexities came later, of course.

The Big Nine, in 1906, also saw its first outstanding passer in Pomeroy Sinnock of Illinois, who completed more than a dozen the first season the pass was legalized. Amos Alonzo Stagg in 1906 claimed to have had 64 different forward pass formations off a six-man and seven-man line.... "Of course, I only selected the best ones to be used," he recalled later, "but since we were winning without them in our early games that year I kept them under cover for the Minnesota game on November 10, knowing it would probably decide the league championship. But it rained all day Friday and Saturday and the field was a mess of mud, and Eckersall didn't use a single pass—and we lost."

Basketball in 1906 finally achieved championship recognition by the Conference fathers, and to Minnesota fell the honor of taking the first league title with a 6-1 record in Conference play and 13-2 overall. In Olympic track and field, Hahn of Michigan, Lightbody of Chicago, and Ewry of Purdue repeated their 1904 victories.

In 1907 Michigan made good its threat to leave the Conference and played no Conference teams. Chicago took the league's first five-game football championship and much of the Maroon's success was due to a young man named Harlan O. (Pat) Page, an end who was destined to become the Conference's first nine-letterman in football, basketball, and baseball, and one of the greatest athletes Stagg ever coached.

Up at Minnesota Dr. Henry Williams became the first college coach to use a flanker in connection with the forward pass, and George Capron, the Gophers' great drop-kicker, scored all his team's points in the first three games, and three quarters of its points for the entire season... And at Michigan, Adolph (Germany) Schulz, the Wolverines' mastodonic center, became the first glamorized football lineman, whose All-America feats were mentioned in the same breath as the most scintillating backs.

The year also marked the first of four straight Conference basketball championships which Chicago would win—a feat not to be duplicated until more

HARLAN (PAT) PAGE

Here is a statement of fact: no roster of early 20th century super-athletes can be complete without Harlan O. (Pat) Page, of Chicago. The first man to star on Conference championship teams in three different sports, Page was a magnificent end on the Maroon's Big Ten title teams of 1907 and 1908; in 1909 he played quarterback on the team that lost only to Minnesota. He played guard on the Conference basketball championship teams of 1908-09-10 and was one of the nation's outstanding collegiate baseball pitchers. His pitching was a big factor in winning the 1909 title for the Maroon and brought him a dozen Big League offers. Page declined them all to remain at Chicago as a coach.

In his senior year he was the star of the Chicago team which was the first American collegiate squad to be invited on a tour of Japan. Chicago won 10 straight, and the Japanese were so impressed with Page and his teammates (and the whole idea, generally) that it led to a series of similar invitations to other American college nines.

In 1913, just three years after graduation, and now the youngest coach in the Western Conference, Page's Maroon baseball team won the league title.

Meanwhile, Chicago hadn't won a basketball title in 10 years, or, since Page's playing days. As coach, Page got the Maroon robust again. In 1919 the club dropped its first two games, then won 10 straight, almost overhauling Minnesota for the title. The next season Page brought them home in first place.

Page's big love, however, was football and the following fall he left Chicago to become head coach at Butler, and subsequently at Indiana. There he became involved in one of the weirdest and hottest hassles in Big Ten history.

Asked to resign after five straight losing seasons (1926-30) Page raised eyebrows all over the Midwest when he threatened to sue Indiana University for breach of verbal contract and for several thousand dollars he said the school still owed him. It would have been the only such suit in league history but the altercation never got to court. The most startling thing that came out of it was the revelation that part of Page's salary was being paid by zealous Hoosier alumni. This led to subsequent Conference regulations against such practices.

HARLAN "PAT" PAGE

ADOLPH "GERMANY" SCHULZ, a 6 foot 2, 240-pound young giant from Fort Wayne, Indiana, reported to Fielding Yost on the first day of Michigan's 1904 football season and was immediately installed as varsity center. Four years and more than 45 games later Schulz was still varsity center and All-America—and was eventually to be named by Walter Camp as the greatest pivotman in the history of collegiate football.

Schulz, who had the brawn of a blacksmith and the reflexes of a panther, early in his career revolutionized center play for all time to come.

He was the first center to drop behind the line on defense.

The first time Yost saw this he was horrified and as soon as he could call a time out frantically beckoned Schulz to the sidelines.

"Hey, Dutchman, what're you trying to do?" the Michigan coach barked. "You're supposed to play in the line!"

"I think it'd be better to play behind the line," said Schulz calmly.

"They'll run over us!" Yost screamed.

"Listen, Yost, I can see things better back there. If anybody gets by me I'll move back into the line and stay there!"

Yost, who was never able to fault Schulz' judgment or performance, went along with him.

From that day on, Schulz played behind the line on defense, stopping everything aimed at the slightest semblance of a hole.

Not too many years later, the center used as a linebacker became a permanent part of the game.

than a half century later by Ohio State. Pat Page, Babe Meigs, and John Schommer sparked those Maroon quintets, and all three men would subsequently become famous in other fields—Page as a coach; Schommer (who was chosen player of the year in his senior season) as one of the Conference's leading football and basketball referees; and Meigs as a distinguished Chicago newspaper publisher.

The Michigan Aggies saw cross-country get off to a humble start with an intramural race. (A half-century later, the Spartans would have a virtual national monopoly in the sport.)

1908

Chicago, in 1908, repeated as Conference football champion and once again, Amos Stagg's inventiveness stood the league on its ear and signalled something new for coaches all over the country. At quarterback for the Maroon was Wally Steffen, a swift, stocky, versatile performer whom Stagg trained to become the first man to use the pass as a feint. With strong hands and adept ball control, Steffen would fake to a receiver then streak wide when the defense backed off. Steffen chosen All-America that year, ran wild against Minnesota in a 29-0 romp that was the key to the Chicago season.

His faking was made all the more potent by the fact that, in John Schommer and Pat Page, he had the league's first brace of star pass-catching ends.

One of the great quarterbacks of the early 20th century, WALTER (WALLY) STEFFEN, a 5-10, 170-pounder, was the first man to use the forward pass as a fake, resulting in a sprint through a hole in the line. After Steffen had played his last game in 1908, Amos Alonzo Stagg, his Chicago coach, described him thusly:

"I have never seen anyone who was Steffen's equal as a dodger, in cleverness and instinctive resourcefulness, supported by such splendid speed. In running from the quarterback position there has been nobody who could come close to him in ability . . . (ED. NOTE: Until 1910, the quarterback when carrying the ball had to run at least five yards to either side of the point where the ball was centered, before starting up field.)

"He had more art and finesse in his ball-carrying than Eckersall because Eckie ran chiefly to his right. Steffen ran right or left equally well . . . He was a clever passer, a deadly tackler . . . adept at catching and returning punts . . . a good kicker . . . and an inspiring leader and field general."

(Although Stagg thought Steffen a better runner than Eckersall, he never claimed Steffen was a better all-around player than Eckersall, who was sensational for three years.)

Later, Steffen became a brilliant and highly-respected Federal Judge who took time off from the bench each fall to coach Carnegie Tech.

1909

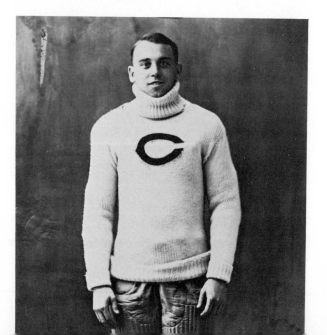

Meanwhile, a great clamor had gone up on the Northwestern campus to restore football, and, after a petition had been presented with signatures of 90% of the student body, the Board of Trustees found itself pressured into action. A committee of the trustees, meeting with student and alumni groups decided that the reforms instituted by the national rules committee resulting in a safer, more open game, and the eligibility and conduct regulations passed by the Conference two years previously, were effective enough to make the game worthwhile. The Board agreed to re-instate football at Northwestern "if the alumni would establish a guarantee fund of $1000 to cover any possible deficit."

That autumn, the Conference held its first cross-country meet and, much to its embarrassment, promptly saw its first team championship carried off by an outsider—Nebraska.

Chicago, in winning its second straight basketball title in 1908, had defeated Wisconsin in a play-off, the only one in Conference history. The two teams were tied with 7-1 records at the end of the season (having lost to each other) and the Maroon edged the Badgers 18-16 for the crown before 1500 spectators at Madison, the largest crowd yet to see a Conference game. John Schommer, the Maroon's star center, was considered the finest player in the nation, and in an era of strictly man-to-man defense, scored 39 field goals that season against a total of four for his opponents..

Illinois became the first conference team to win the baseball championship three years in a row, and four Conference athletes represented the United States in the Olympics at London. Ray Ewry won the last brace of standing high jump and standing broad jump events that would ever be held (the event was abolished after that); Michigan's Ralph Rose took his second shot-put championship; Johnny Garrels, Michigan's great halfback, took second in the high hurdles and third in the shot-put; and Chicago's Ned Merriam ran for Uncle Sam but did not win a medal.

With Michigan out of the Conference, Minnesota was dominant in Big Nine football competition for several seasons, although it is not to be assumed the Gophers would not have done as well even with the Wolverines in the lodge. The 1909 Gophers featured their first All-America in John McGovern, a quarterback who stood only 5 feet 5 inches and weighed 155 pounds—the smallest All-America quarterback since Eckersall. Yet McGovern was an offensive and defensive terror. He had great speed in the open and often hit for big yardage between the tackles. He was a brilliant tactician and a fine drop-kicker and punter.

In the final game of the 1909 season, against Michigan, McGovern, who had broken his collar bone the week before against Wisconsin, took the field protected by heavy padding and yards of tape, and played the full 60 minutes in a 15-6 loss that was the Gophers' lone defeat in 1909.

RAY EWRY

He was barely in his teens when the doctors, mystified by his weakness and muscular instability, were afraid he'd be an invalid all his life, and that ultimately he'd even be unable to walk. One doctor, however, urged him to go into his backyard, near the Wabash Canal in northwest Indiana, and try jumping over things. Anything. A barrel, a bush, the back fence . . .

Before he stopped jumping, Ray Ewry of Purdue had won more Olympic titles than any man in history and had starred in the Games of 1900, 1904, 1906 and 1908. Incidentally, he didn't win his first title until he was 28 years old.

When Ray Ewry entered Purdue in 1890, track athletics featured two events no longer held: the standing high jump and standing broad jump. By 1900 he'd added the standing-hop-step-and-jump to his repertoire and that year in Paris he won all three Olympic crowns.

Conditions in Paris were far from ideal for jumping. No hard take-off ground had been provided. The contestants had to jump from wet, soggy grass. Ewry took off from this spongy surface and leaped five feet five inches for a new world's standing high jump record. Next, he took the standing broad jump with 10 feet 6 and 2/5 inches. Then Ewry reported for one of the most difficult field events of the day: the standing hop-step-and-jump and captured it with a mark of 32 feet, 7 inches.

In the 1904 games at St. Louis, Ewry again won his three specialties, setting world records in two of them. In the standing broad jump he leaped 11 feet 6 and 5/8 inches. Then he reported for the triple-jump. His hop took him over 10 feet; his step carried him 11 feet; then, with the momentum generated by his first two movements he catapulted an astounding 14 feet 8½ inches for a world record total of 35 feet 9 and 5/8 inches. Without a running start!

The Games were held two years later at Athens (before an official four-year cycle was established) and although the standing triple-jump had been abolished by then, Ewry added the standing broad and standing high jump crowns to his collection. Two years later in London, by then known as The Human Frog, he repeated his victories for a total of 10 Olympic gold medals. He was then 36 years old.

He won his events at the National AAU meet the next two years and then in March, 1912, at age 40, started training for the Olympic Games in Stockholm. Everything was going smoothly until he was slowed down by a crick in his shoulder from an old football injury. (He'd played end one year for Purdue.) When Matt Sheridan, a good friend and former Olympic teammate, heard of it he approached Ewry and said with a smile: "Ray, you're getting to be an old man. Maybe you ought to quit."

Ewry looked at Sheridan and said three words. "Matt, you're right."

Ewry walked off the field and never competed again.

JOHN McGOVERN, Minnesota's first All-America, back in 1909, was a 5-foot, 5-inch quarterback, the shortest All-America ever selected. At 155 pounds the stocky Gopher was a great runner and kicker as well as a defensive demon.

Football, which had been re-installed at Northwestern after a lapse of two seasons, was further fortified when President Harris wrote a personal letter to every man on the team after a 21-11 loss to powerful Wisconsin, complimenting the players on their magnificent effort.

Chicago made it three straight in basketball and Schommer was the league's leading scorer for the third successive season. In all the history of the Conference there would be only two others who would do this.

Big Nine sports enjoyed a banner year in 1910, with the most dramatic item being Dr. Henry Williams' invention of the Minnesota Shift, which revolutionized football by having all backs and both ends spring into different positions just before the ball was snapped, thus confusing the defense. Despite the Gophers' tactical brilliance, however, it was Illinois which won the Conference title with a perfect 4-0 record and 7-0 overall, for the first undefeated season in Illini history.

Minnesota had played only two Conference games

1910

that year, winning both, but Illinois, generally, was acclaimed champion. The Gophers, however, might have been awarded greater national honors had they not been involved in a weirdly disputed game with Michigan, which they lost 6-0. There were observers, though, who declared the game should have been a 6-6 tie, a scoreless tie, or even a 6-0 Minnesota victory, all three possibilities being valid because of apparent officiating lapses.

The Wolverines got their winning touchdown on a march featuring two plays which Dr. Williams insisted were illegal forward passes. In that era, passes were limited to 20 yards. One of the Wolverine passes clearly appeared to travel 30 yards through the air, and the other went 24 yards. Meanwhile, Jim Walker of Minnesota had blocked a Michigan punt which was scooped up by the Gophers' Leonard Frank who ran it over for a touchdown. One of the officials, however, nullified the score, saying the ball had touched him after it was blocked, and thereby was a dead ball. Despite protests by the entire Minnesota team he refused to change his decision. Walker became Minnesota's third all-America; and, although temporarily out of the Conference, Michigan celebrated the selection of two men on the All-America; Stanfield Wells at end, and Al Benbrook, for the second year in a row, at guard.

Amos Alonzo Stagg, ever alert to what new rules could mean, took advantage of the ruling in 1910 which, for the first time, allowed the quarterback

AL BENBROOK, a rugged guard from Michigan, was the first lineman from a Western Conference school to be All-America two years in a row, gaining the honor in 1909-10.

DR. HENRY WILLIAMS

The well-muscled young man in the shawl-collared sweater and checkered cap who was barking out instructions to some Minnesota linemen early in the fall of 1900, had arrived in Minneapolis on the crest of his own conditions—and a wave of fame that had preceded him. His conditions, first of all, were that he would consent to become the first full-time coach in Minnesota grid history only if he be allowed to continue his medical practice at the same time—and that he be the judge of which would take priority over which.

The fame was based on several things. As an undergraduate at Yale a few years previously, he was a halfback teammate of Amos Alonzo Stagg and the immortal Pudge Hefflefinger. He had also set a world hurdles record in track. After graduation he became a teacher at Newburgh, N. Y. High School, just down the road a bit from West Point, and one autumn, in 1891, he took a horse and buggy over to The Plains to instruct the Army football squad. He kept on doing it, and did it well enough to give the Cadets their first victory over Navy.

So, Dr. Henry Williams was welcomed somewhat as a Deliverer when he stepped onto the raw campus of the Minnesota Northland. He was hired at the suggestion of Amos Alonzo Stagg of Chicago, after a succession of part-time graduate tutors, some of whom were only too content to sidle away from their minor and sporadic rag-tag successes. A few, such as Frederick S. Jones, Dean of the Law School, and the gigantic Pudge Hefflefinger, performed comparative miracles with the time and material they had. Often, when no coaches were available, the instruction fell to the players, themselves. On of them, Alfred F. Pillsbury, subsequently helped establish the Pillsbury flour-milling dynasty.

Things could only take a Minnesota bounce under Williams, and, as Hefflefinger growled, ". . . these dumb Swedes will finally get some mind to go with their muscles!"

What they also got was the first Golden Era of Minnesota Football, and giving off the brightest glow of all was a Williams invention which completely revolutionized the game. It was called "The Minnesota Shift" and all future offenses could trace their genes to the Good Doctor's bold blood lines. It would take 10 years before he would come up with it, however, and a lot would happen previously to help dramatize the day it would finally burst upon the football scene. In sum, however, Minnesota under Williams during his first 16 years would win eight Conference titles, four of them outright and four ties, and in those days of fervent, governmental anti-trust action this was referred to by some as the "Minnesota Monopoly."

to run anywhere with the ball. Formerly, the signal-caller had to run at least five yards left or right of the center. Now Stagg artfully directed Chicago quarterback Norman Paine in a brand new maneuver. He taught Paine to fake to the fullback or halfback, then whirl around and into the line over center or guard. It was the first quarterback spinner, and would lead to all sorts of offensive mischief to devil the defense. (Meanwhile, at Oak Park High School in Chicago, a bantam-sized coach named Robert

Williams, in his first season of 1900, took the Gophers through an 11-game schedule undefeated, but with two ties—one of them, incredibly, with a high school team. Minnesota swept over such as Wisconsin, Illinois, Nebraska, Northwestern, and others, but a game also had been arranged with Minneapolis Central High School to open the season. (There was no way of knowing that the young preppers would field a team that would include a bevy of future college stars, including Sig Harris and Bob Marshall, who later helped Williams make more history at Minnesota.) The game ended in a scoreless tie.

Hefflefinger's prediction that Minnesota would develop smarter muscles under Williams proved true. After a rousing 24-1-3 record for 1900-01-02, Minnesota's next club had a full head of student and civic steam behind it. On the way to a 12-game undefeated season the Gophers played an historic 6-6 tie with one of Fielding Yost's mightiest Point-A-Minute teams featuring Willie Heston. It was a game described by the press as bringing together the two strongest clubs in Western football history, and a remarkable crowd—for the period—of 20,000 people had filled the stands by 10:00 a.m. The outcome made Williams a national figure. (It was also a game which launched the Little Brown Jug series between the two schools.)

By the middle of the 1905 season, Minnesota under Williams was 52-3-3 and had rolled up a staggering 2131 points to its opponents' 93. Then came a 16-12 defeat by Wisconsin, the first loss since 1901, and it would be several years before Minnesota would make big news again.

The Big News came in 1910 when Dr. Henry Williams came up with his famed shift . . .

Until the physician-grid master popped up with his startling prescription, all backfields took a static position and remained frozen until the ball was snapped to one man who either ran with it or, if he were the quarterback, handed off to somebody else. (The advent of the forward pass in 1906 had given football more offensive opportunities, of course, but the backs were still arrayed in set posts behind the line.) Defenses, if they were smart enough and quick enough, had a fair idea of how to meet the offense head-on.

Williams changed all this. From the backs' first set position, on a pre-arranged signal, they would quickly spring into different positions and formations behind the line just an instant before the ball was snapped, giving the defense little chance to gauge the type of play or the direction it would go.

This opened up all sorts of attacking maneuvers and for many years the offense was considered to have an edge over the defense. The new idea swept the country and within two seasons every college coach put its advantages to use, including eventual refinements by Pop Warner and Knute Rockne among others. The national rules committee in later years would get around to declaring that all four backs would have to come to a complete stop for at least one second before the ball was snapped; but, football, with the advent of the forward pass and the introduction of Williams' shift, could now enter the beginning of its modern era.

Dr. Henry Williams remained at Minnesota until 1921, when he became the first of famous Big Ten coaches to fall victim to the twin disasters of dwindling material and mounting alumni displeasure over defeats. Yet he left a remarkable record behind him—one that was all the more impressive when it is realized he managed to carry on a large and successful medical practice throughout his career, and that he never had more than one varsity assistant. The first was Gil Dobie, his quarterback of 1902, later the "Gloomy Gil" Dobie of the University of Washington and Cornell coaching fame. The second assistant was Sig Harris, who succeeded Dobie as Gopher quarterback and also replaced him as Williams' assistant in 1907 . . . The same Sig Harris who, as signal caller for a Minneapolis high school team, had played Williams' first varsity team to a tie.

Zuppke, who a couple of years hence would make the jump to college ranks at Illinois, also sparked a new concept. He dropped his guards back to protect his forward passer—and opened still another path for offensive shenannigans.)

Ohio State, which had been playing Michigan regularly since 1897, finally scored against the Wolverines, and a 3-3 tie further convinced the Buckeyes that maybe they should pursue the dream of seeking admittance to the Western Conference—a dream which had been dancing like so many pigskin-coated sugarplums in Buckeye heads.

Chicago won its fourth straight Conference basketball title in 1910 and E. B. Styles, of Illinois, took the first of the three straight all-around gymnastics titles he would win in his varsity career.

Meanwhile, Northwestern provided a big boost for track in the midwest when alumnus James Patten, a Chicago grain broker and member of the Northwestern Board of Trustees, gave the money to build

It was a bright, fall afternoon in Champaign, Illinois. The date, October 5, 1910—and tradition was being born as Illinois alumni returned to the campus for the first "Homecoming" game in collegiate football history. The idea was spawned and planned during the preceding year and came to fruition with a full panoply of color and campus activities. Today, on virtually every campus in the country, it is the big event of the year.

Chicago, whom the Illini hadn't beaten in nine years, was their foe—and again living up to the label of "Monsters of the Midway." In the previous four seasons the Maroon had a record of 23-2-1 while winning three Big Ten titles.

1911

Otto Seiler, the Illinois quarterback pictured above, became history's first homecoming hero. One of the greatest kickers in Big Ten annals, Seiler, who had been ill, was discharged from the hospital on the day of the game, and it was his talented toe which gave Illinois a 3-0 win on a 38-yard drop-kick field goal.

Three times that year Seiler's drop-kicking brought 3-0 victories for Illinois' Big Ten champions. It was the only undefeated, untied, unscored-upon team in Illini history.

Patten Gymnasium. It was the first indoor facility in the midwest, (with a big infield and a 10-lap track). There was such an immediate upsurge in the sport that the Conference scheduled its first indoor championships for Patten Gym the following year.

The Big Nine also arranged its first Conference tennis tournament for the spring of 1910, with Paul Gardner, of Chicago, crowned as the league's first singles champion.

Although Illinois had won the Big Nine baseball championship, Chicago received an invitation to send its team on a tour of Japan, a nation that had been running up a rather high fever for the sport. The Maroon was the first American college to be so invited, and promptly whacked their hosts for 10 straight victories.

The Conference, having allowed outsiders such as Stanford, Missouri, Kansas, Notre Dame, and others, to participate in annual outdoor track championships, got some unkind treatment from the visitors, and Notre Dame went home with the league's own championship.

Minnesota rolled to its third straight undefeated football season in 1911 (although tied by Wisconsin) but, for the first time since the Conference became a national power the league failed to place a man on the All-America. It would never happen again—and no other collegiate conference in America would be able to make the same claim.

In basketball, Purdue ended Chicago's domination of the past few seasons and took its first league title. The Boilermakers would have to wait a long time for another, but later would become the hardwood scourge of the Conference.

In other highlights of the year, Illinois won the

In 1910 Northwestern opened Patten Gymnasium, (a later photo, here) a gift of University Trustee, James Patten, which was the first indoor track facility in the *Midwest. It gave a tremendous boost to the sport and set the pattern for similar structures at other Conference schools.*

ELMER OLIPHANT

Elmer Oliphant once kicked a field goal against Illinois with a broken ankle, and friends who heard of it remarked that it wasn't at all an unusual feat for someone who'd worked in the coal mines at the age of 14. An almost legendary figure at Purdue, Oliphant, who spent every summer of his high school years in southern Indiana mines, was considered by many people to be the toughest, most versatile athlete of his day—Jim Thorpe notwithstanding. He certainly won more varsity letters than any man in the history of intercollegiate sports, dividing his glory days between Purdue and West Point, where he became All-America. His fantastic total: 24 letters in seven different sports. He won nine at Purdue, 15 at Army.

A blond, stocky youngster who packed 178 steel-hard pounds on a squat, 5 foot 8-inch frame, Oliphant was a brilliant halfback at Purdue in 1911-12-13, winning All-Western honors. Only a poor team record kept him off the All-America teams which featured the stars of winning casts. He sparkled in basketball in 1913-14 and, in those same years, was a great catcher, outfielder and prodigious hitter in baseball, and a sprinter and hurdler in track. (He set a world record for the low hurdles on turf.)

In those days athletes frequently received appointments to the service academies after graduating from college, and Oliphant went on to even greater renown at West Point where he played four more years. His hard-running, drop-kicking and punting talents brought him All-America honors in 1916. Knute Rockne, then a young coach, declared that Oliphant belonged on any all-time All-America and insisted he was the peer of Thorpe and Charley Brickley of Harvard as a drop-kicker. (The Rock had never seen Wisconsin's Pat O'Dea so he declined a comparison there.)

"Nobody has ever seen a more devastating stiff-arm in all the history of football!" rhapsodized one critic of the era in describing Oliphant's ball-carrying technique.

"The thing we fear the most," said an Army lineman, "is Ollie, with those churning legs of his, running up our backs if we don't charge fast enough."

The stiff-arm was part of a natural sequence of events. Oliphant was also the Corps heavyweight boxing champion. During the winter, whenever the Cadet basketball schedule permitted, he was also a star freestyle swimmer and a crack hockey player. His locker at any given time, it was said, held the most chaotic collection of varied sports gear short of a Spaulding Bros. warehouse.

Modern linemen who are star field goal kickers are common, but in 1911 WILLIS (FAT) O'BRIEN, an outstanding Iowa center, was a rarity. He was not only one of the nation's top pivotmen but was a deadly dropkicker. His 52-yarder against Minnesota that season was the longest in the nation.

first Conference swimming meet, held in Northwestern's magnificent new Patten Gym, and, at the same site, Amos Stagg's Chicago Maroon won the first Conference indoor track meet. In outdoor track, Missouri succeeded Notre Dame as the second straight outsider to romp off with the league's title.

That same year, the Michigan Aggies appointed John F. Macklin athletic director and made sure he'd be the busiest man in midwest sports by also naming him head coach in all sports—football, basketball, baseball and track—the first man since Stagg to attempt such a load—and the last in major college history. It was the beginning of one of the most honored careers in college athletic ledaership, and subsequently he would be honored as the second man in Conference annals to have school's stadium named after him. Stagg, of course, was the first, with Stagg Field.

At Ohio State, the athletic board marked the year as the first time the expenses of a cheerleader were paid to attend a football game on the road. The cheerleader (chosen, incidentally, in a student election) was Hub Atkinson, who years later would become a member of the University Board of Trustees.

JOHN F. MACKLIN, who was named athletic director at Michigan A. & M., (later Michigan State) in 1911, also coached the football, basketball, baseball and track teams—the only man aside from A.A. Stagg, who handled such a load.

The Conference representatives, meanwhile, took a slap at Michigan by passing a "non-intercourse" rule. Michigan, while out of the Conference, had played Minnesota twice, in football, but now the league decided no school could schedule any kind of competition with a university that had ceased to be a loop member.

In 1912 Wisconsin, for the first time, was rated a national football power, when its championship team, coached by Bill Juneau, an ex-Badger kicking star, had an undefeated season, scoring 246 points to 29, and Robert (Butts) Butler, the Badgers' powerful tackle, became Wisconsin's first All-America. In the matter of honor selections, Walter Eckersall, by then a leading sports authority for the *Chicago Tribune*, absolutely went overboard for the great Wisconsin eleven. He named no less than nine Badgers to the All-Conference first team. In addition to Butler he selected Ed Samp, the other tackle; Ed Hoeffel and Hod Ofstie at ends; Max Gelein and Ray Keeler, guards; Eddie Gillette, at quarterback; John Van Riper at halfback, and Al Tanberg, fullback. No other Conference team in history ever placed as many men on a recognized honor team.

Badger football, perhaps, had merely taken its cue from basketball. Youthful, spare, Dr. Walter Meanwell, one of many MD's who, strangely, were to become associated with athletics in the Western Conference, took over as Wisconsin cage coach for the 1912 season—and launched a career which made him the first nationally-known college basketball coach in America. In his first season at Madison, his Badgers mounted a perfect season, 12-0 in the Conference and 15-0 overall, sharing the league title with Purdue, also undefeated with 10-0 and 12-0 overall. It would be the only time in history that the Conference would have two unblemished records in the same year.

1912

The undefeated Wisconsin team of 1912 must be considered one of the greatest clubs in Big Ten history and probably deserves all-time national ranking, as well. Efforts were made to bring the Badgers together with unbeaten Harvard in a post-season "national championship" game, but the Wisconsin faculty squelched the idea. The Chicago Tribune was so impressed by the Badgers it named nine of them to its All-Conference team. Included were tackles "Butts" Butler, second from right in fourth row; and Ed Samp, second from right, third row; ends Ed Hoeffel, Captain (with ball), and Hod Ofstie, second from right, front row; guards Max Gelein, extreme right, front row; and Ray Keeler, third from left, third row; quarterback Eddie Gillette, third from left, second row; halfback John Van Riper, third from right, third row; and fullback Al Tanberg, fourth from right, third row. Head coach was W.G. "Bill" Juneau, seated, extreme left.

WALTER MEANWELL

The young graduate of the University of Maryland Medical School was practicing medicine in a Baltimore slum area in 1909 when he decided he'd like to spend some time working in a local recreation program for boys. He found out pretty quickly that the kids didn't enjoy the mass gymnasium drills so widely used in that day, so, to enliven the boys' interest, he started teaching them to play the comparatively new game called basketball.

The young doctor had never played the game, either in high school or college; but, in Rochester, N. Y., where his family had settled after emigrating from England, young Walter Meanwell had been active in sports at the Rochester Athletic Club. There he had won boxing and wrestling championships and played on the club's baseball and basketball teams.

When he became interested in community recreation work in Baltimore, Dr. Walter Meanwell drew upon a limited basketball background, buttressed it with an analytical mind, and developed some theories of his own. He passed them on to the kids who loved the new game and who provided the young medico with a proving ground for ideas that would ultimately make him the first famous college basketball coach in the nation.

In 1911, "The Little Doctor," as he came to be known (he was barely 5 feet 7 inches), was offered a post at the University of Wisconsin on the basis of his recreational background. It was vaguely referred to as "Director of the Gymnasium," and young Dr. Meanwell took it and looked forward to practicing some medicine on the side. He found, on his arrival at Madison, that he was also expected to coach the fencing team. He knew little about fencing but allowed the word to get around that he did know something about basketball, and the following year Wisconsin asked him to forget his foils and sabres and take over as cage coach.

"Basketball was a rough sport in those days," Meanwell later recalled. "In fact, it was so rough that many schools and colleges dropped the game between 1905 and 1915, so I decided to go against the trend and emphasize finesse. I'd done some experimenting with the slum kids back in Baltimore, but because they were kids nobody paid much attention to the stuff I'd devised, even though we'd been remarkably successful. So, I figured I'd put my ideas to work at Wisconsin and see what happened."

The Little Doctor merely prescribed a pattern of play that became the bedrock of college basketball. It was subsequently described, aptly, as "The Wisconsin System." Most basketball offenses of the day were static and unimaginative, with lots of long passes down court and across court; with waist-high dribbling and virtually all shooting done by the forwards and center. Meanwell put his Badgers into five-man motion, using short passes and a revolutionary criss-cross and weave involving all his players, which never gave the defense a chance to get set. He also taught his players to pivot in motion, which added still another dimension to the short pass and the return pass to a man cutting. Finally, with so much fluidity going for him, it was inevitable that he pioneer the slickest offensive maneuver of all: the screen for the shooter.

The net effect of The Little Doctor's regimen was the first great dynasty of college basketball. His style of play so demoralized the opposition that his first three teams at Wisconsin won the Conference title and, overall, were 44-1, with the Badger offense piling up 1426 points to 685. Only an upset by Chicago in the 1913 season marred the Badgers' total domination of the Big Ten. Although offense-minded, Meanwell proved he could teach defense, too, and his 1914 team scored the only whitewash in league cage history with a 50-0 shellacking of Parsons College. Three times that year Wisconsin held Conference foes to nine points or under.

Altogether, Meanwell in his first 10 years at Wisconsin won seven league titles, four outright and three shared. His overall record for the period was 142 wins and only 25 losses for the highest winning percentage (.850) of any major college coach in the business.

Meanwell's 1916 team was the greatest scoring machine college basketball had ever seen, racking up 634 points to its foes' 337, with the highest average per game (31.7) the collegiate sport had yet produced. George Levis, considered the best center in the nation; Bill Chandler, at center; and Harold Olsen (later a great coach in his own right at Ohio State) at guard, formed three fifths of the Conference all-star team. One night Levis popped in 11 field goals in less than 30 minutes against Iowa, and, remember, it was an era still using the center jump after each basket. So slick was Meanwell's offense that it allowed Lyn Smith, a "stationary" guard to slip through for four goals against Northwestern, convincing coaches throughout the league—and nation—that the day of the static, offensive zone play was coming to an end.

Meanwhile, it was an amazing tribute to Wisconsin team play that only one of Meanwell's nine championship Badger teams (his first) produced the league's leading scorer!

The Little Doctor took time out in 1918 to serve in the Army Medical Corps during World War One, and didn't return immediately to Wisconsin after the war. Missouri talked him into building up its basketball fortunes in the then-constituted Missouri Valley League, and Meanwell proved he had the right touch no matter where he operated. He coached the Tigers to the first title they'd ever won, but pined too much for Badgerland, and since there was a strong reciprocal feeling, he came back to the shores of Lake Mendota for the 1921 season. Naturally, he picked up right where he'd left off by winning another Big Ten title although he had to share it with Purdue and Michigan. It was not until 1922, incidentally, that the Badgers lost their first non-Conference game under Meanwell, bowing to Butler, 26-20. Wisconsin was destined to win three more titles with Meanwell, in 1923, 1924 and 1929. By 1934 the Little Doctor, who coached Wisconsin basketball 20 years and who did more to launch modern basketball than anyone else, gave up his whistle to become Badger athletic director—and, ultimately, to return to the practice of medicine he'd interrupted somewhat in 1909 to teach slum neighborhood boys how to play a new game.

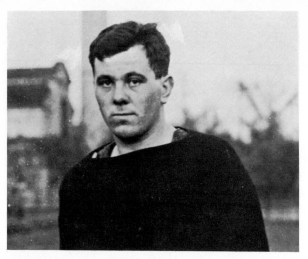

ROBERT (BUTTS) BUTLER, *a tremendous tackle, who in 1912 was Wisconsin's first All-America.*

When the Badgers placed Wallie Scoville at guard, and Otto Stangel at forward, it was the first time any school landed two men on the All-Conference team. Stangel also led the loop in scoring with 177 points, the first time anyone had reached the then magic plateau of 150. Basketball games, at the time, were still being decided by scores such as 18-15 or 21-17, and it was an event when a team went over 30 points, so Stangel's accuracy made him the dead-eye of his day. The Badgers as a team, meanwhile, went over 30 points a game seven times as they averaged 33.3 a game and more than doubled their opposition for the season 489 to 233.

The Wisconsin baseball team, having taken the Conference championship in the spring of 1912, set a record by winning four league titles in a single year. In the fall, the Badger cross-country squad won the Conference crown, led by Irving White, who captured the individual title. Four team crowns in a single year was a new Conference record, (no school had won more than two) and although other schools have done it since, 1912 stands as Wisconsin's peak effort—and a mighty one.

In track, California was the third straight outsider

Michigan's RALPH CRAIG, Olympic sprint champion at 100-and 200-meters in 1912, was the only athlete in Big Ten history who was both an Olympic tytlist and All-America footballer. He made the honor eleven as a halfback in 1913.

to waltz off with the league's outdoor track crown, but again Conference schools had a sizable contingent on the 1912 Olympic team. The Wolverines' Ralph Craig, an outstanding halfback, scored a gold medal sprint double in the 100- and 200-meters, and Carol Haff ran in the 400 but did not place. Ira Davenport of Chicago and Garnett Wikoff, of Ohio State, were middle-distance runners, and the Buckeyes' Clement Cooke was a sprinter on the team. Ken Huszagh, Northwestern freestyler, was a sprinter on the swimming team.

Meanwhile, 1912 had been a year of great activity on the administrative front. For Ohio State it was possibly the most important year in its athletic history. The Buckeyes, it seemed, were in a dilemma. For years they had enjoyed a varied athletic association with neighboring Michigan. Certain Ohio State officials had claimed that the competition with the Wolverines was the most helpful factor in a growing Ohio State athletic program. The two teams had been meeting in football since 1897 and, since 1900, had started an annual rivalry that was destined to become the most intense on the two school's schedules. Gradually, there had been a momentum in

AVERY BRUNDAGE, *a great all-around track star for Illinois before World War One, shown here competing for the Chicago Athletic Club, went on to international eminence as President of the U.S. Olympic Association and later President of the International Olympic Committee.*

Columbus leading toward a quest for membership in the Western Conference. Geographically and emotionally the Buckeyes felt they belonged. They thought they were ready. On the other hand, if they applied for membership and were accepted, they could no longer meet Michigan in any sport because of the "non-intercourse" rule adopted by the league as sanctions against a one-time Brother who had left the Lodge. It was decided after much soul-searching that the best interests of the university

would lie in membership in the Conference, and application was made.

On April 6, 1912, Ohio State was voted in, making possible (with the return of Michigan a few years later) the ultimate popular label for the nation's mightiest collegiate athletic conference—The Big Ten.

Ohio State, however, need not have been too concerned over its relationships with Michigan. On the Wolverine campus, the student body was violently disenchanted with its non-conference status. A long and chronic protest had been under way for some time, and a strong overture was made to the university to re-apply for admission to the Conference. It would take a few years before it would be accomplished but it was a start.

The Conference athletic representatives in 1912 were busy on other matters, too. They voted that "faculty representatives of each university in the Conference must hereafter be a person who receives no pay for any services connected with athletics or the Department of Physical Culture." The league was simply determined that its administrative officials be simon-pure academicians who had no sportive axes to grind. They also voted that Conference basketball teams henceforth would play a 12-game league schedule and could add a maximum of five non-league games if desired.

At Ohio State it was decided, with great regret, that Steve Farrell who had served since 1910 as

It was on a winter day in 1912 that John R. Richards resigned as athletic director at Ohio State, and, according to legend, his successor never knew he was being appointed.

The Athletic Board held a meeting and decided to promote the young man who had been brought to the campus the year before as varsity baseball and basketball coach, and line coach in football (as well as athletic business manager). Then the Board notified LYNN W. ST. JOHN that he was the new Athletic Director at the Big Ten's newest member school.

Up until then, the young man still nursed hopes of becoming a doctor. The dream was ended, now, but he was launched on one of the most eminent careers ever attained in the Big Ten and intercollegiate athletic circles. "Saint," as he was known to players and administrative colleagues, was to remain as Buckeye boss until his retirement in 1947—the second longest tenure in the Conference—and would be responsible for much of the leadership not only in the Big Ten but in NCAA affairs.

A freshman halfback at Ohio State in 1900, St. John had to drop out of school when his father died. Subsequently he coached high school ball in Fostoria, and then at Wooster College, where he coached the Compton brothers—Arthur and Karl—who later became world-famed scientists and college presidents.

"Saint" then moved to Ohio Wesleyan as coach and athletic director and while there commuted daily for two years to Starling-Ohio Medical College in Columbus, studying medicine in the morning and returning 17 miles to the Wesleyan campus in Delaware, Ohio, for afternoon athletic duties. Eventually he had to interrupt his medical studies as he became more involved in sports. When he accepted the Ohio State athletic directorship he knew he would have to make a choice.

Medicine's loss was a gain for collegiate sports.

In 1912 Ohio State regretfully announced it "could not afford to employ more than two men to handle all coaching chores," so STEVE FARRELL, who enjoyed the luxury of just coaching track and serving as chief trainer, was reluctantly let go and given a $200 bonus "in appreciation of his excellent services." Farrell immediately was signed by Michigan and became one of the greatest coaches in the history of collegiate track and field. The Wolverines were temporarily out of the Conference, then, but after they returned in 1918, and under Farrell's leadership, they took four titles and four second places, indoors, and five titles and three second places, outdoors, in his 11 seasons.

varsity trainer and track coach, would have to be released because . . . "financial conditions made it impossible to employ more than two high class men for the entire management and coaching of all athletic teams, thereby rendering it necessary for each man to coach two athletic teams in addition to performing numerous other duties." The athletic board hailed Farrell for his "earnestness and ability . . . his success in winning the confidence and loyalty of the athletes." The board also voted him a bonus of $200 for his services and said it would do all in its power to assist Mr. Farrell in becoming located at some other institution. The students gave Farrell a silver cup and a purse of $126 and Farrell, without breaking stride, went off to Michigan where he became one of the greatest track coaches in collegiate history.

1913

Another great Chicago production highlighted the football stage for 1913, as Stagg's undefeated Maroon dominated the Conference and laid claim to national honors. This remarkable team was led by Captain Nels Norgren, a four-sport athletic virtuoso at halfback, and Paul Des Jardiens at center. Walter Camp named Des Jardiens as his All-America pivotman but placed Norgren on his second team. Keeping Des Jardiens company were Michigan's wondrous halfback, the Olympic sprint champion, Ralph Craig, and tackle Miller Pontius; along with Ray Keeler, of Wisconsin, at guard.

Iowa, coached by Jesse Hawley, just missed grabbing the brass ring, as the Hawkeyes, with their most explosive offense to date, tallied 310 points in seven games, the most any Conference team had posted since the sport was redesigned in 1906. A 6-0 loss to ultimate champion, Chicago, kept the Hawks from their first league crown; and, down at Champaign, Illinois, a sandy-haired bantam named Robert Zuppke had come from Oak Park High School outside of Chicago, to take over the Illini coaching job. Many Illinois alumni sniffed it was a sorry day for Illinois when the best that could be found was a high school coach who had never even played college ball, himself.

CLARK SHAUGHNESSY was one of the most versatile athletes in Minnesota's pre-World War One history. In 1912-13 he played end, tackle and fullback and won All-Big Ten football honors; starred as a guard on the Viking basketball team; and ran the 440, 880 and competed in field events, in track. Later, after coaching at Tulane and Chicago he would go to Stanford to become the father of the modern T-formation.

The 1913 season was the first for Ohio State in the Conference and the Buckeyes were sure they were ready for it under John W. Wilce. Wilce, a young medical student, had starred in football and track at Wisconsin and had stroked with the Badger crew. He was only 25 when he took over as Buckeye grid coach but his eagerness and technical grasp of the game would soon pay off for Ohio, but not that first season. A 7-6 loss to Indiana marred the Buck's Conference debut and their next league start was another good—but losing—effort in their first road trip, a 12-0 loss to Wisconsin.

Helping to make history at that Wisconsin game however, were 76 loyal rooters who made that first trip—including four who shipped themselves as "blind baggage" at a cost of eighty cents each.

It was during the 1913 season, too, that a Big Ten game produced one of the weirdest incidents in football history. Indiana had held Iowa on downs within the shadow of the Hoosiers' goal posts, and now, in possession of the ball, Indiana sent its punter back to kick. A 50-mile-per-hour gale was blowing as the Hoosier punter got his kick away, high into the air. Leo Dick, the Hawkeye safety man, was back about 25 yards awaiting the ball when suddenly he realized that after the pigskin had advanced almost to him the wind stopped it, then started blowing it back toward the punter. Dick nimbly advanced with and under the ball until it had blown back over the goal line—where he simply caught it for a touchdown!

In basketball, Wisconsin, except for a shocking setback by Chicago in the final game of the season, was the class of the Conference again and would have been ranked as the best in the nation, along with Navy, the only major college team to go through undefeated that season. Except for a one-point victory over Illinois, the Badgers had mauled the Conference with ease. They were led by Gene Van Gent, called the best center in the nation; Allan Johnson, a forward, who in two years had scored 86 field goals to four by his opposition; and Captain John Van Riper and Carl Harper, two great defensive guards. All four made the Conference honor team, the only time a league school would ever so dominate the selections. Following the Badgers' stunning 23-10 setback by Chicago in the season finale, Walter Meanwell said it was the only time he'd ever seen one of his great teams go into a game so grossly overconfident, and the scrappy Maroon, sensing it, rose to the heights for the upset of the year.

Although Illinois in 1913 won its third straight Conference swimming title it took an ineligibility ruling at Northwestern to give the Illini the winning edge. Ken Huszagh, the Purple's Olympic sprinter, was ruled scholastically ineligible just before the meet. There was, for Northwestern, however, the first indication of the big splash in the making at Evanston. where tall, husky Tom Robinson had taken over as the Purple's first swimming

NELS NORGREN

If he had never done anything else, Nels Norgren, Chicago 1914, would have been remembered for having been awarded a silver-handled shaving brush as the winner of the Class Mustache Contest. Handsome, husky Nels Norgren didn't have to rely on that event for fame. He was, in addition, the first man in Western Conference history to win 12 varsity letters in four different sports. In football Norgren never missed a game in three years as he starred as a hard-running halfback and magnificent punter. (The best punter in the nation, he made Walter Camp's second team All-America.) In basketball he was an All-Conference forward. He played on the Conference championship baseball team and threw the discus and shot-put in track.

Graduating with a degree in Philosophy, Norgren, at 22, became Director of Athletics at the University of Utah and was the youngest and busiest coach in the Rockies when he found himself also handling the Utah football, basketball, baseball and track squads. Two years later Norgren's Utes astounded the sports world by coming out of Salt Lake City unheralded to win the National A.A.U. basketball championship. It was on the trip to Chicago for the tournament that Norgren started demonstrating the sense of humor that was to endear him to players, coaches and officials wherever he went. Bringing his mountain boys to Chicago for the A.A.U. tourney he quickly found they were borrowing their etiquette cues from him. Nels couldn't resist the temptation one night while they were dining in an elegant Chicago restaurant. Every eye was constantly on him to see what fork or spoon to use, and how to use the napkin. When finger bowls were finally brought around with after-dinner mints, the boys stalled just long enough for their coach to proceed. Casually, Norgren dipped a mint into the finger bowl and began polishing his nails with it. When he had 10 basketball players following suit he broke up.

Later, after returning to the University of Chicago in 1921 as head baseball and basketball coach, Norgren took the Maroon diamond team on tours of Japan. Players who made the first trip with him in 1925 recall when, sailing westward over the Pacific Ocean, one prairie state farmboy approached Norgren and said: "Coach, that's certainly a lot of water out there." Norgren nodded. "Yes," he replied, "and you're only seeing the top of it."

On a subsequent trip, Roy Henshaw, one of his stars, noticed that a nautical chart aboard the ship indicated they were in an area where the water was more than two miles deep. Henshaw nervously asked Norgren: "Coach, do ships sink here very often?"

Norgren shook his head negatively. "Only once, son! Only once!"

A brilliant tactician and handler of personnel, Norgren was prevented from becoming a nationally-acclaimed coach only by the fact that, by the mid-twenties, athletics were beginning to be de-emphasized at Chicago and after 1925 the Maroon would never again be able to compete on even terms with other Conference teams.

coach after the building of Patten Gym and its magnificent pool, the first in the midwest if not the nation, at the time. The National Collegiate Athletic Association had not yet sponsored its annual tournament but, after winning all its dual meets, including one with Yale, champion of the East, Northwestern laid claim to the 1913 national championship. Huszagh, the Purple's sensational freestyle sprinter had set world marks of 19.4 for 40-yards, and 23.8 for 50-yards, and had posted a new Conference record of 58.4 for the 100 (before the Australian crawl was refined, of course). He was considered an absolute cinch for his events in the Conference meet until his ineligibility was announced. Northwestern finished third behind the Illini and Wisconsin. What would follow after that, for Northwestern however, would become an epic era of the aquatic sport.

In track, Illinois was the first to win both the indoor and outdoor championships in the same season, and in doing so ended the string of outdoor titles which had been dragooned off by rude outsiders. Never again, in fact, would an outside school go home with the title. The year had also marked the arrival of Tom Jones as Wisconsin track coach, and for the next 35 years the Badgers would be a power on the cinder track.

Speaking of arrivals, 1913 saw a young sophomore pitcher reporting to Coach Branch Rickey at Michigan. The youngster's name was George Sisler, and after starring as a Wolverine hurler for three years he would jump right to the majors and score a victory over the legendary Walter Johnson in the ex-collegian's first start. Subsequently, Sisler would be switched to first base and become one of the all-time great hitters in baseball, and post the highest seasonal average (.420) in American League history.

GEORGE SISLER was a Michigan pitcher under Coach Branch Rickey, and both went on to major league fame —Rickey in managerial ranks and Sisler, converted to a first baseman, as one of baseball's all-time great hitters.

GEORGE SISLER, who was a Michigan pitcher in 1913-14-15, switched to first base when he leaped from the campus to the major leagues. As first baseman for the St. Louis Browns he set an all-time American league batting mark of .420. (He is shown here years later as Commissioner of the American Softball Association.)

JOHN W. BRICKER was the star catcher for the Ohio State baseball team in 1915-1916. He was later governor of Ohio, U.S. Senator and GOP vice-presidential nominee in 1944.

BOB ZUPPKE called his undefeated 1914 team the greatest he'd ever coached—better, even, than any of the clubs which starred Red Grange.

CONFERENCE   FOOTBALL TEAM 1914   CHAMPIONS

Lindgren · R. Petty · Madsen · Glimstedt, Tr. · Squier · Derby · Rayburn, Mgr
Graves · Clark · Pogue · Zuppke, Coach · Nelson · Stewart · Macomber
Rue · Wagner · Watson · Chapman, Capt. · Schobinger · Armstrong

For the first time wrestling appeared as a championship sport in the Conference, although it was not an official and exclusive Conference activity but was part of the overall Western Intercollegiate Wrestling Association. All the Conference schools entered, however, and the first title was shared by Illinois and Minnesota. Later, the sport would become an official, closed-competition tournament for the Conference only. All in all, it was a big year for Illinois.

Little Bob Zuppke wasted little time making his presence felt in the Western Conference, and in 1914, his second year in the league, he turned out what he later described as the greatest Illinois team of his career. ". . . Better, even, than the Red Grange teams of 1923-24-25," Zup declared. In posting a 7-0 undefeated season and taking the Conference title the Illini not only had brilliant individuals but, according to Zuppke, was the only team he ever had that had the versatility to deploy from several offenses.

The basic Illinois attack was a balanced alignment now recognized as the "I" formation. To support this, Zuppke added liberal doses of a spread and a deep T, and a punt formation which was adapted to quick openings, wide running plays, passes, and the surprise kick used as an offensive weapon. Zuppke later said his 1914 team played the most modern football yet attempted.

Sparking the attack was, perhaps, the slickest all-around backfield yet put together in this Conference. At quarterback was George (Potsy) Clark, who became an early pro star and coach. Harold Pogue, a swift, slashing runner, and tough Bart Macomber, were the halfbacks; and Gene Schobinger was a power fullback in the modern mold. Up front, a fast, hard-charging line was led by Captain Ralph (Slooie) Chapman, a guard, and Illinois' first All-

RALPH (SLOOIE) CHAPMAN, slashing Illinois guard, was first All-America for Illinois. Teamed with speedy halfback BART MACOMBER, they were the brightest stars of the 1914 team described by Coach Bob Zuppke as the greatest he ever had at Illinois. Macomber was All-America the following season.

1914

America. Scoring 224 points to only 22 for its opponents, this Illinois team was clearly the class of the country. Also selected for All-America that season were Arlie Mucks, Wisconsin guard, and John Maulbetsch, Michigan fullback, who at 172 pounds, was the lightest man yet chosen at the position.

It was a big year all around for the Illini, who also won the Conference baseball, tennis, and indoor and outdoor track titles for a total of five team titles in one year—a new league record.

In basketball, it was three straight (35-1 for three years) for Wisconsin under Walter Meanwell, as all five Badger starters were among the top eight Conference leaders in field goals. Captain Gene Van Gent, the most versatile player in the league, led with 40, but Glenn Whittle, of Northwestern, was the loop's top scorer because of the free throw rule. In those days, and until 1925, the best foul shooter on the team went to the line for the entire team's free throws, and Whittle did the chores for Northwestern, while Carl Harper, Wisconsin guard, performed for the Badgers. The other Wisconsin starters on this, possibly Meanwell's greatest team, were Ernie Lange, Al Sands and Mell Hass. It was a team that scored the only shut out in Big Ten history, whomping Parsons College 50-0.

This was the year, too, when Indiana became a champion for the first time in its Conference history—and swung it twice in the same season. The Hoosiers won the swimming title outright and took the unoffical crown in wrestling, at it led all Conference entries in the annual Western Intercollegiate Wrestling Association.

JOHN MAULBETSCH, Michigan's 172-pound All-America fullback in 1914, was the lightest man yet picked at his position.

The little man with a lank cowlick hanging over his forehead allowed his face to relax in a twisted, whimsical smile. "I am Louis XVI," he said in a flavorful Germanic accent, "and you are my court. After us, the deluge."

His audience stared as though he were some kind of a nut, but he went right on. "Let them eat their cake today. We'll live on bread. All I ask is that every man on this team have a lot of fun out on that field. No matter what the score, I want you fellows to have a good time. If you miss a tackle don't worry; I'll get off the bench and tackle the man myself."

The speaker was Robert C. Zuppke, making a pre-game speech to his Illinois football team in the locker room at Minnesota, and suddenly everybody began to laugh. "Come on," said a halfback named Joe Sternaman who weighed 139 pounds. "Here's to the deluge!"

Bob Zuppke had broken the tension and they surged past him to take the field for a game that is often called the greatest collegiate football upset of all time. Bob Zuppke, master psychologist, eventually became famous for his upsets.

It was October, 1916 and as Zuppke was talking to his men, Mighty Minnesota had already loped onto the field almost diffidently. No team had a right to be more confident. The big, veteran Gophers were the Wonder Team of the year. In its first four games it had rolled up 236 points to its foe's 14. Illinois had a lone victory in four games and against Minnesota was considered at least a 40-point underdog. A special section had been built in the Press Box for Walter Camp, the premier poobah of football, who had honored the Big Ten by attending this game because he was considering at least five of the Gophers as All-American candidates. Among them were Pudge Wyman, a halfback, and Bert Baston, an end, the best passing combination in the country; and George Hauser, a talented tackle. It was to be a frollicking Viking feast for the Norsemen, and hapless Illinois was to be the sacrifice.

Just before his relaxed players left the dressing room Zuppke had given only one set of instructions. The first three times Minnesota put the ball in play, Illinois was to concentrate on tackling three different Gopher backs, in order, with no deviation. "But what if they don't have the ball when we tackle them?" a lineman said timorously. Zuppke nodded. "They'll have it," he said, "in exactly the order I gave you."

Minnesota got the ball first. On three straight plays the Illinois line paid no attention to possible fakes or hand-offs and converged on the backs Zuppke had named. Three straight plays cost the Gophers 18 yards in losses. They never recovered from that onslaught—and the subsequent first Illinois play from scrimmage.

Getting the ball as Minnesota punted, Illinois, on its first play, lined up strung completely across the field. When the ball was snapped there was an eternity of hocus-pocus behind the line that didn't resolve itself until suddenly Bart Macomber was tossing a 25-yard pass to Sternaman, completely alone behind the thoroughly bolixed Gophers. The biggest mis-match since David and Goliath resulted in the same stunning reversal of form. While Illinois scampered gleefully off the field with a 14-9 victory Walter Camp turned to a colleague in the press box. "Will somebody please tell me," he said tartly, "how something like this could happen?" Camp was not exactly being complimentary to Illinois. He had already made public utterances about Minnesota's thunder-

ing power and here, in the Norsemen's own wind-nipped lair, he was suffering some of their loss.

It was not, however, the first nor would it be the last time Bob Zuppke would prove to be the master psychologist without peer among football coaches—and why he would ultimately rank with Stagg and Fielding Yost in the Big Three of Big Ten grid masters.

His 29 campaigns at Illinois from 1913 to 1941 established him second to Stagg in length of service, but second to nobody in overall success and matchless color. The only coach in the history of the Big Ten who never played varsity football in college, Zup was born in Berlin, Germany, in 1879, and two years later was brought by his parents to Milwaukee. When he enrolled at the University of Wisconsin to major in philosophy he was a sturdy 5 feet 7, and 140 pounds. He wanted to play football but never succeeded beyond taking a lot of lumps with the scrubs who were used as varsity practice fodder. He did play varsity basketball, though, (height was no particular disadvantage in those days) and played an important part in the Big Ten's first cage championship.

When he graduated Zup had no idea at all, so he thought, of ever coaching football. He was an accomplished artist and painter and set out for New York to study, visit galleries and take his first steps at setting the art world on fire.

He was there a year and spent most of it as a sign-painter, sometimes working on a scaffold swinging high over Times Square. (Later he would be acknowledged as one of the finest amateur artists in America.)

He also saw many of the big Eastern college football games and suddenly decided that art would only be a hobby and football his business. He packed up his brushes and easel and returned to the Midwest where he took a job teaching and coaching at Muskegon, Michigan. It was soon apparent he was an artist in both his chief interests. In four years at Muskegon he won two state championships before being lured to Oak Park High School in Chicago and making it a nationally known power. He lost his first game at Oak Park but didn't lose another in three years. So impressive were his

Coach Zuppke works with Carney, one of his All-Americas in the early 1920's.

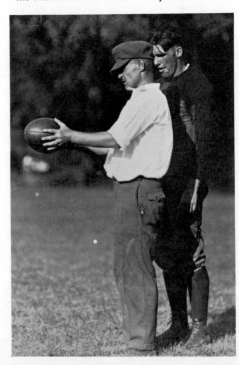

Bob Zuppke just prior to the Grange era.

successes and his scores that Oak Park was challenged by high school teams all over the United States, and Zup took his preppers to Oregon, Washington and Massachusetts, among other places, and clobbered them all.

In 1913, George Huff, athletic director of Illinois, summoned him for a chat. Illinois had only a tie for the 1910 championship to show for 17 years of Big Ten competition, and Huff coaxed the little Dutchman into taking over. It took Zup just one year to make Illinois a national power, and before he retired he would hold victory margins over 8 of the 10 teams in the Big Ten, trailing only Michigan and Ohio State.

He won the title in 1914, shared it in 1915, took it outright in 1918-19, shared it again in 1923 and won it undisputed in 1927-28, for seven titles in 16 years. Three of his clubs were designated national champions, in 1914, 1923, and 1927. Zup's teams won a total of 132 games, lost 79 and tied 12. From 1913 until 1930 his record was an astounding 90-24. Then high-pressure recruiting entered the college grid picture and Zup flatly refused to go along with it. "I'm at a disadvantage," Zup once growled in his thick German accent. "I'm a poor handshaker. I'm blunt and direct. And I can't go into the home of some poor Italian or Polish mother, present her with a bouquet of gardenias and tell her that if she sends her boy to Illinois he'll surely make All-America and marry the bank president's daughter."

What Zup didn't attract in the way of pre-guaranteed grid talent he made up for in creativity—the kind that gave football many of its most effective weapons. In 1906 as a high school coach, he invented the spiral snap from center. Previously the ball came back floating end-over-end, or with just a dead push. Often a defensive lineman arrived right with it. You couldn't "lead" a back with the dead snap. Zup fiddled around with placing the hands in varying positions around the ball and suddenly came up with the technique which produced a smooth, fast spiral to a waiting punter or a running back.

In 1912, still a high school mentor, he invented the screen pass. In fact his Oak Park team featured a whole pattern of beautifully executed forwards, laterals, for-ward-laterals, screen passes and shovel passes years before they were taken up seriously in the college game.

"I dislike the obvious," was the way Zup once put it. He preferred deceptive ball-handling and intricate stuff behind the line, as well as in the air, to power, no matter how successfully that power could be harnessed. (Zup created the most quixotically-named and one of the most effective multiple-pass plays in modern football. It was called The Flying Trapeze and involved a man-in-motion, a direct snap from center, a shovel pass, a lateral and then a long forward pass downfield—often for a touchdown. He perfected it in 1934 with slick Jack Beynon usually on the final throwing end.)

In 1922 Zuppke devised the first huddle. Until then signals were called at the line of scrimmage, with attendant mistakes and confusion, failure to hear over roaring crowds and inability of a quarterback to get anything more across to his team than a bare play-call. In a huddle Zup found he could offer variations of a play; could learn valuable information about a defensive man; and could send a line off on a rhythmic charge on a specified count. It led to the intricate football play of today.

In 1924, on the day of Red Grange's famous afternoon against Michigan, Zuppke sent his whole team out in short socks instead of the long, heavy wool stockings which became heavy with perspiration and were worn by every team in football. Not only was it a hot day but the typical Zuppke sense of psychology made the Illini appear snappier and zippier to the heavy-garbed Wolverines. The next year virtually every team in the land threw away its long wool stockings and wore either half socks or long cottons.

Zuppke had even applied psychology to Grange, himself. "I was the one who gave him that number 77," he later admitted. "I saw Red was a natural when he first reported as a freshman and I wanted him to start out with a proper set of symbols. Seven is a natural in dice. So I decided to give him two of them. It didn't make Red run any faster or shiftier, maybe, but once the opposition saw those two sevens—from the rear—as they

Bob Zuppke in his studio in Urbana, Illinois. The famous Illini coach often passed time with palette and brush creating masterpieces in oil.

were bound to, they'd do a lot of thinking that would do 'em no good."

It was Zup, himself, incidentally, who had the perfect squelch for a disgruntled student sportswriter from Michigan after Grange had wrecked the Wolverines. "All Grange can do is run," sour-graped the young critic. Zup cocked his head and, alluding to the greatest opera star of the era, remarked: "Yes, and all Galli-Curci can do is sing!"

No coach in the Big Ten pulled off as many legitimate upsets as Zup. Ohio State, led by the magical Chic Harley, had man-handled the Conference in 1916-17, and in 1919 again came into its season finale undefeated, and heavily favored over Illinois. Going into the closing minutes the Buckeyes led, 7-6, and the Ohio State student paper, The Lantern, showing unusual verve for a campus publication, decided to let its presses roll with an "extra," which was rushed to Ohio Field just 300 yards from the Journalism building. The edition carried a blaring headline proclaiming an Ohio victory, but stunned fans, who still couldn't believe what they saw, bought no papers as they came off the field. In the last 10-seconds, Illinois' Bobby Fletcher calmly wiped the mud and dirt from his cleats and booted a perfect field goal for a 9-7 win and the Big Ten title.

In 1921 these same Buckeyes with one of their great teams, again were favored for the title—and again were undefeated going into the finale with Illinois, which hadn't won a single Conference game. This time Zup concentrated on defense. Score: Illinois 7, Ohio 0 as Ohio could do nothing against the fired up Orange and Blue.

It was this totally unexpected win over a superior foe which prompted Harvey Woodruff, the eminent sports editor of the Chicago Tribune, to pin on Zuppke's team a label which was to become the school's official athletic nickname: The Fighting Illini.

Despite the presence of Red Grange, the Illini's 24-2 win over Penn in 1925 was a definite upset. Illinois, beset by injuries and a weak bench, had dropped two games that season. Penn hadn't been beaten in two years, and had great defensive ends and linebackers. Zup figured they might contain the Redhead unless something special could be set up. Zuppke wisely guessed that Penn would over-shift to stop Grange's sweeps to the strong side of Illinois' unbalanced line. All afternoon he had Red fake toward the strong side and then, with his amazing ability to change direction, had him wheel to the weak side. All Red needed was one block to spring him into maneuvering position. Penn didn't dare disregard the fake completely because the merest hesitation was a signature on a defense's death warrant. That was the day Grange rambled through the mud for three TD's.

One of the upsets that gave Zup his biggest glow came late in his career, in 1939, when he pitted his non-recruited, sub-par material against a Michigan team led by the superlative Tom Harmon. Harmon had run wild as the Wolverines, racking up 165 points, won their first four games. The Illini were still looking for their first win. They got it when Zup installed six different defenses, described later as "on loan from Barnum & Bailey." Michigan blockers never knew whom to block and couldn't find their man when they did. Harmon was stopped cold. Meanwhile, Zup had fashioned a sleeper-pass play on which Jimmy Smith, a rookie fullback, passed all the way across the field to George Rettinger

for a touchdown in a 16-7 hatchet job on the bigger, faster but thoroughly frustrated Wolverines.

After the game Zup revealed his personal prescription for springing a major upset. Said Zup: "When you're faced with one of those years when your material is only fair and you're not going to win many games, put your eggs in one basket. Pick out a tough team and lay for it. Knock it off and you've got yourself a season."

At the end of the 1914 season Robert C. Zuppke retired. After 29 years, at the time of his resignation, he had served longer as head coach than any major college mentor in the country. Zup felt that his attitude toward recruiting was causing too much bickering between university officials and alumni and he loved Illinois too deeply to allow such friction to continue. Virtually every summer, Zup had packed off to Alaska, the Rocky Mountains or Canada to paint the vistas of nature he loved so much. Zup had a lot of things to say when he finally put aside his whistle. One of his first comments was: "Where are my brushes . . ? Now I can paint without interruption."

And he did. His pictures hang in some of the finest collections in the Midwest.

His artistry in football exists prominently in the record books.

"Football is a brutal game," Bob Zuppke once said, "but brutes can't play it. It's more than a grunt, a lunge and a surge of muscle. It's a truly intricate thing that needs cohesion and integrity and rhythm—especially rhythm. There's beautiful rhythm in the shift of a back-field, in the co-ordinated charge of a lineman. It's the same in a painting. There can't be awkward expression in an effective painting. It must have cohesion and a rhythm of its own. Football and art are so much alike . . . And neither is for brutes."

Up on the shores of Lake Mendota where rowing had become a fixture on the Wisconsin athletic scene, dramatic but disappointing news burst upon the campus, where Harry (Dad) Vail, who had become coach in 1911, was just beginning to make the Badgers a national power. His 1912 crew, in fact, had finished second to Cornell in the famed four-mile Poughkeepsie Regatta by barely three seconds (after Wisconsin had lost its number two oarsman with an infected hand), and Vail was determined that the Badgers would be the first Western crew to break the Eastern monopoly in the historic event. In 1914, however, members of the medical faculty at Wisconsin convinced the Athletic Board that four-mile crew races were injurious to health, and the Board voted to send no more crews to Poughkeepsie. For the next six years rowing would languish afoul of this arbitrary edict, with only intramural racing on the program.

It was an action taken on December 5, 1941, by the Conference, however, that was acclaimed throughout the nation—and in particular by the National Collegiate Athletic Association—as one of the most significant gestures yet made in college sports. To support the avowed position of educational emphasis on athletics, it was decided that recognition should be given to scholarship. As a consequence, the Conference authorized $2000 to be set aside (a sum greatly increased over the years) to provide revenue for what became known as the Conference Medal of Honor, to be awarded one senior for each school who has "attained greatest proficiency in athletics and scholastic work." The medal, designed by R. Tait McKenzie, was to be awarded annually, with each university making its own selection. (It is an award still unique among college athletic conferences today.) It was announced that the first awards would be made in 1915.

Much has been said about the early Notre Dame passing combination of Gus Dorais and Knute Rockne, but there are critics who have declared that the finest aerial combo in college football prior to World War One was the Minnesota duo of Arnold (Pudge) Wyman and Bert Baston. With Wyman, a halfback, throwing to Baston, at end, the Gophers in 1915 were seemingly headed for Conference and national honors until Illinois, also unbeaten, loomed ahead in a battle that undoubtedly would decide the title. In practice that week, the Minnesota attack was blunted when Bernie Bierman, the Gophers' brilliant running back sprained an ankle. Without the running attack to complement the Wyman-Baston aerial game, the Gophers muffed one of their last chances to give Dr. Henry Williams another undefeated season as the Illini fought them to a 6-6 tie and a deadlocked Conference title.

With ARNOLD (PUDGE) WYMAN, throwing, and BERT BASTON, an All-America end, catching, Minnesota's great 1915 team boasted the best aerial duo college football had yet seen.

At Northwestern, the season saw the debut of John Leo (Paddy) Driscoll, a local boy from Evanston, who was hailed as another Walter Eckersall. The same size as Eckie at 145 pounds, Paddy Driscoll exhibited a similar brand of running, kicking and field generalship and in another year he would succeed in making the Purple a nationally recognized power. Meanwhile, the Michigan Aggies offered a halfback hero on a "here-and-now" basis, as the Spartans scored their first win in history over Michigan, 24-0, and Aggie star, Jerry De Prato become his school's first All-America. Stopped only

"DAD" VAIL, who took over as Wisconsin crew coach in 1911, led the Badgers to second place at the famed Poughkeepsie Regatta the following year, and for 17 years was one of the nation's most distinguished rowing coaches.

Two great Michigan Aggie stars of pre-World War One era who helped put the Spartans on the football map. GIDEON E. SMITH, brilliant back who was a leader of the 1913 team, the first undefeated club in Michigan State history. They posted a 7-0 record, including three shut-outs, and a stingy, single touchdown apiece for the other four foes. It was also the first Spartan club to beat Michigan. NENO (JERRY) DePRATO, Michigan State's first All-America (1915), led the nation that year in scoring with 188 points in six games. Gideon and De-Prato played together in 1915 when the Spartans missed another undefeated season by a lone loss to Oregon State.

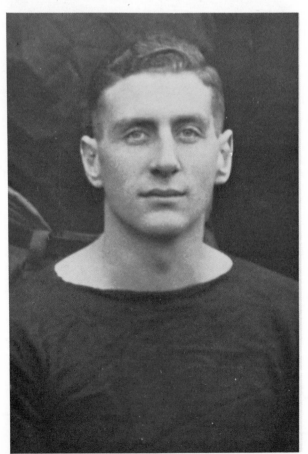

in the Spartan's sole loss that year to Orgeon State, De Prato was the nation's leading scorer with 188 points in six games. Baston and Bart Macomber, Illinois halfback, were also All-America.

In basketball there was a slight interruption in what appeared to be the natural order of events, and Wisconsin, for a change, was jarred loose from its Conference supremacy by Illinois, which posted its first undefeated season. It took an unusual play to do it when Ernie Wilford, second in Conference scoring that year, pulled out a one-point victory for the Illini over second-place Chicago when he batted the ball through the net on a tossup.

CHARLES CARRAN had the honor of taking Ohio State's first Big Ten title when he won the Conference tennis singles crown in 1915.

In other Conference highlights, Illinois became the first school to take three straight league swimming championships; Wisconsin, making its presence felt under Tom Jones, won its first Conference outdoor track title by scoring 38 points to runner-up Chicago's 37 in the closest finish yet witnessed; and the 1915 baseball season at Ohio State featured a battery destined for greatness in later life. Pitching was George (Red) Trautman, who was to become Commissioner of Baseball Minor Leagues; and catching him was stocky, hard-hitting John W. Bricker, subsequently a famed U.S. Senator, a Vice-Presidential running mate with Thomas E. Dewey, and a long-time member of the Ohio State University Board of Trustees. F. O. Watson, the wiry Minnesota cross-country star, won his third straight individual title, the only man in Conference history, ever to do so.

Administratively, the Conference Representatives made two pronouncements. They declared (for reasons not too clear) that henceforth Conference football teams would be limited to two secret practices a week; and they released the names of the inaugural year winners of the Conference Medal of honor for scholastic achievement by athletes. First

In 1915 Wisconsin won its first track title and when the Badgers, coached by TOM JONES, repeated the following spring it was obvious that young Tom Jones knew what it was all about. So well did he know it that he remained for 35 years, the longest track tutorship ever held by a Big Ten coach. Further testimony to his ability is offered by the record book: in 23 of those 35 years, indoors, he was never out of the top three positions in the Conference tourney. Outdoors he was in the top three spots 15 out of the 35 years. He had two indoor team titles and three outdoors, and his cross-country teams won team honors twelve times, a record for a single coach in Conference cross-country annals.

For many years Jones also was a professor in the Physical Education Department and stoutly insisted he got his biggest thrills at Wisconsin by taking unheralded boys out of gym classes, talking them into trying out for track and then turning them into varsity letter-winners. Meanwhile, he subsequently developed champions galore, including distance stars Don Gehrmann, Chuck Fenske and Walter Mehl; pole vaulter Milt Padway; hurdler Ed Smith; sprinter and broad-jumper Lloyd LaBeach; and middle-distance man Ed Buxton.

recipients of what would become the most prestigious scholar-athlete awards of any college conference were:

F. T. Ward, Chicago
Edward A. Williford, Illinois
Edward Winters, Indiana
Herman L. Von Lackum, Iowa
Boles A. Rosenthal, Minnesota
Harold G. Osborn, Northwestern
Arthur S. Kiefer, Ohio State
Harold B. Routh, Purdue
Martin T. Kennedy, Wisconsin

In 1916 the baby of the Conference came of age quickly, suddenly and with stunning impact upon the sports scene. Ohio State, a lodge member for just three years of actual league play, fielded a football team that listed at halfback a slight, black-haired boy named Charles (Chic) Harley who weighed 162 pounds. At the end of the season Harley was an All-America and the Buckeyes were undefeated Conference champions. Harley was the loop's first soph to make All-America since Eckersall in 1904. Only five others would do the same in the next half century.

Northwestern, which had finished a solid last the year before with 0-5 in league play made a remarkable turnabout in 1916, led by the little virtuoso, Paddy Driscoll, and everything came up climactic in the final game of the season: Northwestern vs. Ohio State for all the marbles. It was easily the best Purple team since the turn of the century and, in fact, had scored the first Northwestern victory over Chicago since 1901 when Driscoll added a 43-yard drop-kick field goal to his touchdown to upset the Maroon.

In Harley (and a tough line led by tackle Bob Karch) the Buckeyes simply had the answer to everything and this was a year that not too many questions were proving embarrassing to the speedy Buckeyes. It was a close game for the first three quarters but in the final period Harley slashed the Purple to pieces with some of the most dazzling running pigskin critics had ever witnessed, and the Buckeyes had a 23-3 victory and their first title.

JOHN LEO (PADDY) DRISCOLL, a 145-pound triple-threat quarterback, was hailed as another Walter Eckersall for his brilliant all-around play from 1915 to 1917. He led the Purple to the best season they'd ever had, in 1916, when only a season finale loss to champion Ohio State ruined what would have been Northwestern's first undefeated season. Driscoll was a particularly deadly drop-kicker and frequently split the cross-bar from 40 yards out.

1916

CHARLES W. (CHIC) HARLEY

If it can ever be said that one man is responsible for a school's entire football success, then the claim can justly be offered that Charles W. (Chic) Harley made Ohio State a leading and lasting football power, and applied the first brush to the creation of the image that is said to make Columbus the football capital of the world. (Who is to argue against the fact that the Buckeyes today lead the nation year after year in attendance, and for almost a decade have averaged 82,000 people per home game!)

Let's go back, however, to an earlier year. Back to a day before World War One when Ohio State was the newly-admitted baby of the Western Conference—a handy door mat for mighty Michigan, Minnesota and Chicago who would, of course, fatten up on the upstart Buckeyes with their delusions of grandeur—upstarts who had been humbled in recent times by Oberlin, Case and Western Reserve among others, and by lopsided scores.

Still, the Buckeyes had made a good, neighborly case in seeking admission to the midwestern lodge, and had been accepted. During their first three years as a member, Ohio had made a few threatening gestures but nobody was about to predict the Buckeyes would soon— if ever—become the bully on the block. In 1916, much sooner than anyone expected, something happened. It happened in the person of 5-9, 165-pound Chic Harley a local boy who had been the hottest thing ever seen in Columbus prep grid annals. When Dr. John W. Wilce, the young Buckeye varsity coach, first saw him perform

Running, passing or kicking, Harley was superb.

with the freshmen, he made a big speech about Harley. He said, "Hmmm-mmm!" The way he said it spoke volumes.

The quiet, black-shocked boy with the high cheekbones and innocent black eyes looked like a third-string book-keeper in a losing business; but, the books kept on Chic Harley told of one of the greatest success stories in the history of football. Before the books were closed on him, the speedy, slippery Buckeye, would be the first three-time All-America in modern football. In his three years of varsity play Ohio State would win 21 games, tie one and lose one; and would win two Conference titles and come within 10 seconds of a third. The Buckeyes would also score 726 points in his three seasons, still a Big Ten team record, and forever after Chic Harley would be a legend.

When he first pulled on a varsity uniform, somebody, according to legend, asked Coach Wilce what Harley could do best. As the story goes, Wilce pondered a bit and said: "Probably run—" Then, after a pause: "No, he's possibly a better punter." Another pause. "Could be as a passer." A final hesitation: "Of course, you ought to see him drop-kick!"

During the next three years, Chic Harley displayed all those talents in a manner that had critics claiming the slim Ohioan was the greatest all-around back yet turned up, Jim Thorpe notwithstanding. (The big Indian rarely was used as a passer or pass receiver.)

It became quickly apparent that it was not only his natural gifts which would stamp Harley with greatness. He was cut out for the kind of heroics that made for sheer drama. As in the first Conference game he played . . .

The Buckeyes had launched Harley's sophomore season with a 12-0 win over Ohio Wesleyan and followed it with a 128-0 clobbering of Oberlin for the highest score ever run up by an Ohio team. Now the first real hurdle lay ahead for the Bucks and their heralded but yet untested sophomore. Thousands of hopeful fans made the trip to Illinois to see Harley's Conference debut against wily Bob Zuppke's favored Illini. It was a muddy day, the field almost ankle deep in ooze. Illinois had pushed over a touchdown but failed to make the extra point, and going into the final quarter Ohio's hopes looked dim. Because of the slippery footing and some bad breaks Harley had been unable to break away. Time was slipping by. There was a minute to play, and Ohio had the ball inside the Illinois 20-yard line. Suddenly there was a slender, muddied scarlet jersey streaking toward right end. Faking an inside thrust, Harley sped outside, got around, cut back slightly, sliced between two defenders and out-raced them to the goal. It was a 6-6 tie, and the try for the extra point was coming up. Ohio took a time-out as their student manager ran onto the field. Harley had asked for a dry right shoe. Harley knelt, took off his heavy, mud-caked cleats and pulled on the dry shoe. He tied the laces carefully, gave the a shoe a pat and stood up. The teams lined up. The ball was snapped directly to Harley who took one step and split the goal posts with a perfect drop-kick for a 7-6 victory.

It was the type of theatrical performance that would be repeated time and again. In fact, the Wisconsin game just a week later was almost an encore for Harley. The Badgers were leading 7-0 in the third quarter when Harley, from mid-field, fired a perfect pass to Peabody, an Ohio end, who was pulled down on the Wisconsin 27. On the next play Harley cut back over tackle and slipped wraith-like through the Wisconsin secondary and went

Chic Harley executes a perfect play in 1916 Northwestern Ohio State game.

all the way without being touched. His drop-kick tied it up. Then, mid-way through the final period Harley broke loose from his own twenty and picked his way 80 yards with virtually every Badger having a shot at him somewhere along his route. Again, calmly, he drop-kicked the extra point which proved the difference because Wisconsin put on a late scoring drive that clicked for a TD but failed to convert the extra point that would have tied it up. (Wisconsin, incidentally, missed its chance to tie because of the existing rule governing extra points. A touchdown that crossed the goal line in a corner of the field necessitated a strange gambit to qualify for the point-after. The scoring team was given an unimpeded kick-out from the corner, leading to a fair catch by a teammate on the playing field at as good a spot in front of the goal as the kicker could accomplish; but, the ball had to be caught to protect the attempt for goal. A Badger blew the easy catch and there was no extra point attempt.)

The following week Harley ran for 107 yards in the first eight minutes of play against Indiana and was promptly taken out by Wilce to save him for the season finale against Northwestern.

Ohio needed him for that one. It would be, up until then, the most important football game the Buckeyes had ever played. A victory would give them their first Conference championship, and it was something Ohio fans could virtually taste in their agonized expectancy. It would not be easy going against a good Northwestern team, led by the dynamic Paddy Driscoll. The date, because so much was riding on the game, became a memorable one: November 25, 1916. A bright but bitterly cold day, with 12,000 well-bundled fans jamming old Ohio Field.

In the first quarter Harley drop-kicked a 34-yard field goal and the ecstatic Ohio fans would have settled right then and there for a 3-0 game. In fact, as the third quarter ended it was still 3-0, and anything could happen. Paddy Driscoll removed some of the uncertainties shortly after the final period started by squaring things, 3-3, with a beautiful 40-yard dropkick field goal. If he got into range again . . .

The Ohio anxiety was short-lived. The first time Northwestern punted in that fourth quarter, Harley fielded the ball on the Ohio 33, took a couple of tentative steps while sizing up the onrushing Purple and then shifted gears. No one touched him on his skittering 67-yard jaunt to the goal.

Three minutes later Ohio was on Northwestern's 20 again. Harley was the tailback in a pass formation, the ends split. The Purple put on a rush that was fatal. It was a fake all the way, but the 20-yard sprint through the Northwestern defense was real for Harley. He booted the second of two drop-kick extra points but his fourth quarter pyrotechnics were not yet over. A few minutes later, on the Northwestern 40, he dropped back to pass and this time it was no fake as he hit McDonald on the two-yard line. Sorenson slammed over for the final touchdown, Harley booted the extra point, the Buckeyes had their first championship, and Walter Camp in naming Chic Harley All-America (the Buckeye's first) said: "It doesn't seen possible he could have done everything credited to him but the fact is he did, and proved he is as great as any claim made for him."

The claims held up for two more years. In 1917 the Buckeyes were among the favorites for the title and Harley was a marked man, with every foe keying on him. These were not the days of complex offenses and intricate pass patterns; the defense figured their opponents' star would be involved in the majority of plays and simply built their strategy to stop him. It mattered little as far as Harley was concerned. In 1917 Ohio opened against Indiana and Coach Wilce allowed a substitute to start in Chic's place while he sized up the opposition. The Hoosiers promptly out-played the Bucks, and Wilce rushed Harley into action near the end of the first quarter with the game a scoreless deadlock. Harley ran 40 yards, 8 yards, 11 yards and 33 yards for all of Ohio's four touchdowns.

Against Wisconsin the following week he demonstrated his versatility when he tossed a 25-yard scoring pass to Bolen and one of 32 yards to Courtney for another TD. He also kicked a field goal and once again had a hand in all his team's points. Against Illinois he again promoted all the Buckeye scoring by kicking two field goals from the 14 and 29 and passing 17 yards to Courtney.

No point he ever scored, however, got a greater ovation than the touchdown Harley tallied in the Buckeyes' first Big Ten game in 1919. The slender All-America had been in the army in 1918, along with many other Conference

Halftime at Ohio Field—That's L. W. St. John on the extreme left in the senatorial hat, and just behind him is coach Jack Wilce. The player pulling up his socks is Captain Hap Courtney. Others, left to right, are Kelly Van Dyne, Howard Courtney, Bob Karch, Chic Harley, Bill Styker, Howard Yerges and Truck Myers.

stars, and had returned in 1919 for his final season of eligibility. By this time Chic Harley was perhaps the first super-star whose exploits and private life were blown up into public-property status. The new era of sports hero imagery was beginning to emerge. The press was looking for campus heroes, and the big midwestern schools were going to provide them, as opposed to the sedate, cloistered institutions of the East which had produced the Poes, Mahans, Coys, Brickleys and others, but who had never been adopted by Joe Fan as his Very Own.

In Chic Harley the press had its first post-war, all-purpose football hero. The headlines and pictures could have tripped a more sophisticated, more out-going boy, but fame never once threw the quiet, humble Harley for a loss. When Ohio went up to Ann Arbor to meet Michigan in its 1919 Big Ten opener all the elements were present for a slightly hysterical drama. Ohio had been playing Michigan since 1897 and had yet to beat its northern neighbor. The closest the Bucks had come was a 3-3 tie. In fact, over the years Ohio had only three touchdowns to show for its head-knocking with the Wolverines. Buckeye fandom had dreamed of a victory over Michigan with the fervor of religious fanatics. Heaven could wait but a clobbering of the Wolverines could only be savored in a man's lifetime. When Ohio and Harley turned up with victories of 38-0 over Ohio Wesleyan, 46-0 over Cincinnati, and 49-0 over Kentucky, there was a general feeling that the Conference opener against Michigan might be as historic as the toppling of George the Third.

It was October 25, 1919, a late Conference opener for the Buckeyes, as they opposed Michigan on old Ferry Field in Ann Arbor. Ohio scored first, early in the game, when Iolas Huffman and Cyril Meyers blocked a Michigan punt and Buckeye end Jim Flowers smothered the ball over the goal line. Harley converted for the 7-0 lead, but when Cliff Sparks,, the Wolverine quarterback, drop-kicked a 40-yard field goal in the second quarter, the 7-3 score at half-time was still an iffy thing for Ohio fans.

Late in the third quarter, Ohio got the ball on its own 32. The Buckeyes carved out two first downs and then Harley took off again. He sped toward right end, got a block, cut inside and, as the Associated Press described it, "ran around and through the entire Michigan team a dazzling 40-yard touchdown run."

The extra point was missed but the scoring was ended

for the day, with a 13-3 Ohio victory—the first, ever, over Michigan, and there were Ohio fans who wept unashamedly in the stands.

For the essence of tragic drama, however, nothing in football could ever match the final game of Chic Harley's fabled career. Driving for an unprecedented third straight undefeated season and third straight Big Ten title, Harley led his mates into the season finale against a good but not great Illinois eleven at Ohio Field, on a sullen, gray day in late November, 1919.

An Ohio victory would be the logical glittering climax to the Harley epic. An Illinois win was unthinkable except in the unremitting desire of Bob Zuppke to be the spoiler of the century—even more so than on that day a few years previously at Minnesota when he made his famed "I am Louis the XVI" speech.

The Ohio State Lantern, the student daily, was well aware of the Olympian aura surrounding Harley and his farewell appearance. The editors had planned a special "extra," covering the game, which would be rushed from the journalism building nearby and distributed to fans leaving the field, within 10 minutes after the game's end.

Who could have blamed the enthusiasm of the student editor who, with three minutes to play, and Ohio leading 7-6 and in possession of the ball, shouted to the pressman: "Let 'er go!" A headline had been set to scream an Ohio victory and a Big Ten title.

Zuppke's defense had done a magnificent job of blunting the Buckeye attack on the slippery field—but not entirely, of course. Harley's running had put the ball in scoring position and then he flipped a nine-yard pass to McDonald to place the ball on the two. On the next play Harley squirted through the Illini for a touchdown. Then he kicked the extra point. Illinois roared back to score but missed the extra point attempt, and, with three minutes to go the score was 7-6 and the ball in Ohio hands.

Illinois, however, took over on downs, put on one more offensive drive and got down to the Ohio 12 with less than 10 seconds to go. There was time for one more play and it had to be a field goal. An agonized hush settled over the stands as chunky Bobby Fletcher, arms outstretched, awaited the snap of the ball. Back it came, Fletcher swung his leg and the most fateful drop-kick in Big Ten history fluttered toward the cross-bar—and went over for a 9-7 Illinois victory. In the stands grown men stood mute and numb as student newsboys came along clutching newspapers whose headline unwittingly bore false witness to the end of Chic Harley's career.

Discounting what was considered an unofficial wartime season in 1918, Ohio State had come within 10 seconds of pulling off an unprecedented third straight championship. No one could have asked more of Harley, of course, even in the Buckeyes' failure. In the three years of his brilliant play, the Buckeyes had lost one ball game. In those three years Harley had failed to score in just three games, and in one of those three he played only eight minutes. In those three years he had scored more than half of his team's points, had done virtually all of its extra-point and field goal kicking, all its punting and most of its passing.

Never had one man so dominated the Conference for three years with his display of virtuosity. As one commentator remarked at the time: "Harley simply HAD to lose his final game. It was fate. Nobody could be that perfect."

Walter Camp trumpeted Harley, on his first team All-America, as the most sensational back of the year for his running and kicking feats. Other Conference All-Americans that season were Karch, the Buckeye tackle; Fred Becker, Iowa's first All-America, at tackle; and Bert Baston, of Minnesota, repeating at end. Still another Gopher star was husky George Hauser, a second-team All-America, who would go on to join the long line of physicians who became great coaches.

Minnesota, incidentally, was only one game away from challenging Ohio for the Conference crown and establishing a claim to national honors—but what a game! It was a game the Gophers lost to Illinois in what was described at the time as the King of Upsets, not only because of the shocking reversal of form, itself, but because of a remark made by the winning coach. Early in the season the Gophers, with possibly the best club Dr. Henry Williams ever turned out, had posted such romps at 67-0 over Iowa, and 81-0 over South Dakota. Later they would clobber a fine Wisconsin team 54-0 and a great Chicago team 49-0. For the fifth game of their season, however, the Gophers were to take on a very mediocre Illinois team that was to win only three of seven for the year.

It was considered a three touchdown mismatch for the Gophers; but little Bob Zuppke, on arriving in Minneapolis, was among those who'd heard rumors that Dr. Williams had worked his Vikings unusually hard all week and had even kept them on the drill field until almost nine o'clock the night before the game. All this prompted Zuppke to come up with two startling statements in the locker room before the Illini took the field. One was psychological; the other was tactical. He felt his players were physically ready and well-drilled but they were edgy. They knew everyone considered them doomed but felt they should do something about it.

To break their mood Zup stood up and postured: "I am Louis the Fifteenth—and, after me, the Deluge!" The Illinois players stared at him for an instant then roared their delight and defiance. Then Zup assured them the mighty Vikings could be had, and outlined two special maneuvers. If Minnesota won the toss and received, he predicted (on the basis of scouting reports and a Minnesota superstition) that the Gophers' first three running plays would be successive carries by three different backs. He named each in order, (Sprafka, Wyman, and Long), and told his Illini to forget everything else and key on these men. Zup said he would bear the responsibility if any Gopher carried out of turn and ran for a touchdown. Then Zup outlined a special play the Illini were to use the first time they got their hands on the ball. Bart Macomber was to pass on first down (unheard of) to Eddie Sternaman, to an exact spot.

Sure enough, the Gophers seemed listless as they took the field. Sternaman turned to Zuppke. "Hey, Coach, they don't look so big and tough!" Zup nodded. "Not only that," Zup shot back, making sure the Vikings could hear, "but the whole crowd of 'em, together couldn't add two and two!"

Minnesota took the kick-off and failed to gain on the first series of downs because three straight ball carriers were smacked down in their tracks before they got to the line of scrimmage, in the very order Zuppke had predicted. The Gophers then got off a poor punt which Illinois put into play on the Minnesota 45. Then, just as Zup had directed, Macomber stunned the Gophers with a perfect 20-yard pass to Sternaman. From there Illinois drove for a touchdown on a half dozen running plays as the Gophers came completely unstuck. Following the kickoff, Minnesota was faced by tigers. Pudge Wyman dropped back to pass. The entire Illinois line poured in on him and he threw wildy—and directly into the hands of Ken Kraft, who raced 50 yards untouched for the second Orange and Blue touchdown. Minnesota never recovered as Illinois won 14-9 for the second greatest upset victory in Illinois history. The *Chicago Tribune's* headline for the story was: WAIT TILL YOU READ THIS! (Illinois' *greatest* upset victory would come just three years later . . .)

It was undoubtedly the most ignominous defeat in all Minnesota football history. Word of this team's greatness had swept the country and Walter Camp, himself, decided to make his first visit to Minneapolis to see the Gophers in action. A special vantage point in the press box had been built for The Great Man, from which he could properly observe this Marvel of all Gridiron Marvels. Never were hosts more embarrassed. Yet, after this loss, Minnesota closed its

FRED BECKER gave Iowa its first breakthrough in the All-America ranks when the Hawkeye tackle was selected in 1916.

season by beating a strong Chicago team, at Chicago, 49-0, for the worst defeat in Amos Alonzo Stagg's tenure as coach.

(And, making his first appearance on the scene in the fall of 1916, as a freshman at the University of Illinois, was a big, raw-boned farm boy from Atwood, Illinois, (Pop. 680). His name: Kenneth Leon Wilson, and future events in his lifetime would lead to authorship of this book.—THE EDITORS.)

The year marked, too, the coaching debut at Iowa of Howard Harding Jones, a former Yale end, and older brother of Tad Jones, an Eli immortal. In just a few years Jones would give the Hawkeyes their first taste of national football fame.

In basketball, Doctor Meanwell's Badgers made it five titles in six years for Wisconsin, with 11-1 in the league and a gaudy 18-1 overall. For the second time, Wisconsin placed three men on the Conference honor team: forward George Levis, center Bill Chandler, and guard Harold Olsen. Wisconsin was generally considered the number one team in the nation.

The Badgers repeated as outdoor track champions, the only time in their history they ever did so, and the Conference fathers set a record for rapid reversal of themselves on the administrative front; in December of 1915 it was decided that baseball would be discontinued as an intercollegiate sport because it had become too difficult to police the summer professional baseball shennanigans of so many Conference players. Just six months later, somewhat ashamed to admit they couldn't keep their house in order, they repealed the ban in the fastest administrative double-play in Conference history. Not a single year's schedule was lost in the procedure, it having been decided, when the ban was laid, that the 1916 program would be the last.

1917 Mercurial Chic Harley led Ohio State to its second straight grid championship in 1917, as the Buckeyes went undefeated in nine games, with a

Ohio State's second straight Big Ten title team in 1917 featured a brilliant backfield of CHIC HARLEY, left, and PETE STINCHCOMB, right, as halfbacks; DICK BOESEL, center, fullback; and, kneeling, HOWARD YERGES, quarterback. (Yerges' son later starred for Michigan teams which twice defeated the Buckeyes.)

scoreless tie with Auburn providing the only blemish. Not a single touchdown was tallied by the opposition as the Bucks rolled up 292 points to six—on field goals by Indiana and Wisconsin. Along with Harley, Ohio placed guard Charles Bolen on the All-America. Charley Higgins of Chicago was an All-America guard, along with Ernie Allmendinger of Michigan, whose teammate, Cedric Smith, was named All-America fullback.

Minnesota made its presence felt in basketball for the first time since it had won the title in the league's debuting year of cage competition in 1906. The Gophers, however, had to share the championship with Illinois when the two teams divided their home-and-home games. Fred Stadsvold at forward and Harold Gillen, a great center, paced the Go-

THE TUG WILSON

Often, you never know where or when a career is starting. I certainly didn't realize it in my case, back in the autumn of 1912, when a man named Tom Samuels took over as high school principal in Atwood, Illinois, a farm community of 600 people, in the central part of the state.

Tom Samuels had just returned from a tour of Europe, including Stockholm, Sweden, in order to see the 1912 Olympic Games. He'd been hired as principal in Atwood because one of his qualifications was the ability to teach track and field.

There were 33 students in Atwood High School—nine of them boys. One of Samuels' first acts was to gather those nine boys around him and tell them of the glories

phers, while Illinois was led by the first great brother combination in Conference basketball—Ray and Ralph Woods who had played together for three years at guard and forward along with Chuck Alwood at center. Gillen and Ralph Woods tied for the Conference scoring lead, and Stadsvold and Alwood were All-America. Wisconsin again came up with three all-league players in Bill Chandler and Harold Olsen, who repeated as center and guard, and Paul Meyers, who also received prominent mention as a guard.

Meanwhile, at Lafayette, Indiana, Ward (Piggy) Lambert, a wiry towheaded newcomer to the Conference sports scene, took over as Purdue basketball coach. He would soon take a year off for mili-

RALPH WOODS, and his brother, Ray, of Illinois, formed the first great brother combination in Conference basketball, starring for three years and pacing Illini to the 1917 title. Ralph Woods tied for the league scoring crown with Harold Gillen, of Minnesota.

HAROLD GILLEN, front row, right, the league's leading scorer in 1917 and a two-time All-Big Ten choice, led Minnesota to a share of the Conference championship with Illinois, and tied for the scoring title with the Illini's Ralph Woods.

tary service, but would subsequently establish the second great cage dynasty in the Big Ten, following Meanwell's Wisconsin teams.

At Michigan, where the game had been abandoned as a collegiate sport a few years previously, basketball had been restored on an intramural basis. An all-out campus drive was under way to regain membership in the Conference, and the Wolverines didn't want to be too far behind their brother lodge members if their application was made—and accepted.

In other sports, Binga Desmond, Chicago's great Negro quarter-miler, was the first of his race to win a league championship as Amos Alonzo Stagg's Maroon trackman took both the indoor and outdoor team titles. They were the last that Chicago would ever win.

STORY...

of the Olympic games—and of Jim Thorpe, the incredibly talented and versatile Indian who had made a personal extravaganza of the Games and who, on being presented to His Royal Highness, Gustave of Sweden, had said: "Hello, King."

Samuels told us that if we started training now, someone in the group might qualify for an Olympic team in the future. He turned to me and asked how far my farm

was from the school. I told him it was just a mile. Despite the fact that I weighed 190 pounds, he assured me that if I would run back and forth each day and continue my training I would make an Olympic team some day. It sounded all too simple to a 16-year-old, but years later when I was picked for the 1920 Olympic track and field team I had the immense satisfaction of writing him from Antwerp, Belgium, where the Games were being staged, and thanking him for starting me on my athletic career.

When I was five years old, our family had moved from Atwood to the family farm about a mile from town. The privilege of a small boy growing up on a farm is an experience I wish more boys could have. Everyone works and makes a contribution to the family welfare, shares in its fortunes—and misfortunes, and there are plenty of both on a farm. My father would

101

WARD (PIGGY) LAMBERT

Chemical science lost a promising professor and—who knows?—maybe an ultimate genius, when young Ward (Piggy) Lambert hung up his laboratory smock and put aside his test tubes and formulae one day back in 1917.

The decision which science lost was to a peculiarly local disease known as Indiana Fever, a lingering malady picked up at instant contact with a basketball and hardwood floor.

Ward Lambert, head cage coach at Purdue University from 1917 to 1946, was able to concoct a potent mixture, using a championship formula with its chief ingredient being Lambert's uncanny ability to take an average boy and transform him into a poised, polished perfectionist on the basketball floor.

In the three quarters of a century the sport has been played, no major college coach anywhere, has been able to do this more successfully in undiluted big-time competition than Lambert, who had 371 wins and 152 losses for a .710 average. No Big Ten coach has come close to his 28-year tenure. No Conference coach has been able to match his 11 league championships; his 19 All-Conference players; his nine All-Americas, his nine league-leading scorers.

Piggy—that's a name, incidentally, which was given to him as a kid in Crawfordsville, Indiana, when he wore a stocking cap with pigtails—wasn't able to get too worked up over his accomplishments the last time he was interviewed shortly before his retirement in 1946. He muttered something about getting a few breaks, but you know quite well that Lady Luck was never that constant in her affections.

Rather, success was due to Lambert's ability to repeat time and again what he did with a frail, left-handed kid named Bob Kessler, who was cut from his high school squad because his coach didn't think he could make it in such a rugged game. Kessler's case was just one of many where Lambert was able to spot latent talent and bring it out when no one else dreamed it existed. "There," Lambert beamed later about Kessler, "was a real contortionist. He wasn't a natural player but he had mental aggressiveness and great speed—and we were able to get him to harness them together."

Kessler went on to lead the Big Ten in scoring in 1937 and make All-America in his senior year.

Jewell Young was just a 120-pound kid at Lafayette, Indiana, High School when he graduated a couple of years after Kessler, and there wasn't a single college who made overtures toward him because of his basketball ability. Jewell went to a Civilian Conservation Corps camp for a year, put on a few pounds and decided to go to college in his own home town.

He was just one of 125 freshman who turned out for basketball every year at Purdue. He didn't set the place on fire right away but Piggy taught him a little trick—to get his defensive opponent in motion and then use a foot or head fake to get by him, or get his shot off. Young set a Big Ten scoring record and also made All-America.

Lambert's biggest reconstruction job was his biggest prize of all: a 6-foot 6-inch boy named Charles (Stretch) Murphy. Murphy enrolled at Purdue a victim of a common practice among high school coaches in the late 1920's. Usually, when they got hold of the rare big kid like that, they went to no great lengths to develop him. The coach merely planted his giant under the basket and had the other kids feed him. (He could stay there all night under the rules existing then.) Even with two or three men desperately draped over his torso, the big kid could turn around with the ball, shake one of his foes off his shooting arm and claw his way up to the basket for two points. It was a good way to draw fouls, too.

That was Stretch Murphy's background when Lambert got hold of him. He had to change every basketball habit the boy had. According to Piggy, the young giant had two left feet, both always on the floor. He didn't have balance. He swayed like a reed in the wind. He couldn't move, had no sense of timing. He didn't have much besides altitude.

Stretch Murphy didn't have much to start with but in a very short time he acquired poise, balance and a scoring eye from anywhere on the court, and didn't have to depend solely on his wrestling ability under the bucket. He fit in beautifully two years later with a 5-9 guard named Johnny Wooden, a master dribbler and play-maker who, the old-timers tell you, was the greatest small man in the history of the game. Both made All-America, and Murphy led the Big Ten in scoring.

---

rouse me out of bed at 4:30 a.m. and by the time I'd finished the early chores I was ready to eat an enormous breakfast which, in those days, usually consisted of three or four eggs, bacon, several slices of bread, and milk, which would barely keep me going until noon.

There was fun, too. With the other boys from our neighborhood I'd go fishing in the creek, learned to swim, and even performed some awkward if not foolhardy high dives from the top of a boxcar when a freight train stopped to take on water from a tank-tower by the side of the creek. I can well remember once, just after I'd jumped off a car, seeing a large water moccasin swimming down the middle of the creek towards the spot where I would surely land. If any small boy ever tried to fly, I did right then, and consequently my dive turned into a panicked belly-flop, landing me right on the moccasin who was even more frightened than I was. Anyway, he retreated in a hurry,

with me going in the opposite direction much faster, I am sure, than any future Olympic swimmer ever managed.

On Wednesdays during the summer, Dad would always let me go to the town baseball game where I sometimes got to shag flies in the outfield before the older fellows got down to business. There really wasn't much time for athletic competition except at the many little country fairs held in the surrounding towns. My first such experience was a 50-yard dash for boys under 10 years. I got off to a good start but suddenly my suspenders parted from my pants and my pants started south. I finished with one hand clutching them, but luckily I had enough of a lead to win. The fifty-cent prize, I suppose, made me a pro, but because I was only 10 years old my conscience didn't bother me later on.

The nickname of Tug had been given to me at an

Lambert had a solid background in overcoming obstacles. When he entered Crawfordsville, Indiana, High School shortly after the turn of the century he reported for basketball weighing a not impressive 112 pounds. He immediately was tabbed by the coach as good managerial or waterboy material. That is, with a little more size and experience.

Piggy couldn't see it that way so he became the team's leading scorer, instead.

After starring in football, basketball and baseball at Wabash College, Piggy took post-graduate work in chemistry at the University of Minnesota and went back to Crawfordsville to teach and coach basketball on the side. He moved on to Lebanon, Indiana, where his results in both chemistry AND basketball were such that he received an offer from Purdue University in 1917. Purdue, however, wanted him on a one-field basis, and Lambert made his choice.

Lambert was an early advocate of fire-wagon basketball, the blistering, perpetual-motion game which was to become the pattern for the sport a few years later. Lambert was obsessed with speed and the idea of moving the ball around. In a player he looked for qualities in this order: mental aggressiveness; stability of temperament, or belief in himself; speed, and then size. Thus, size, the factor so paramount today, was last on Lambert's list.

On his 1934 championship team there wasn't a man over six feet, probably the only instance of its kind in Big Ten history.

Regardless of material at hand at the beginning of the year, Purdue never was counted out of the title picture. It is not so much lese majeste as it was common sense.

There were no better spoilers than the Boilermakers. In the 1936 Purdue-Wisconsin game the title was at stake. Half the state of Wisconsin, it seemed, tried to get tickets and journey to Lafayette for the kill.

It was in the bag for the Badgers . . . Purdue had been lucky all season . . . the Boilermakers had fattened up on second division clubs . . . getting the breaks.

Now, after 12 years, Wisconsin was knocking at the throne room door again. The state of Wisconsin clamored for a radio broadcast of the game. Purdue allowed no such broadcasts but pressure was brought to bear from the Wisconsin governor on down, and the request was finally granted.

Thousands of Wisconsin fans who had to remain at home were told in a play-by-play broadcast how Purdue went out to take a 19-2 lead at the half and win as it pleased.

Lambert's last-minute change of plans did it. Instead of using a zone defense to combat the Badger's slick blocking plays, Lambert took a gamble and had his boys "overplay" the offense of their foe, dangerously working out in front of the offensive men instead of remaining between them and the basket. Purdue intercepted the first nine passes Wisconsin tried. The demoralized Badgers never had a chance for the rest of the game.

On the other hand, no team ever had the idea that it had Purdue beaten if it found itself on the long end of the score with only a few minutes to play. A 10-point lead with two minutes to go usually was safe enough 99 times out of 100 in those days of low-scoring basketball, but the odds weren't good enough when you were contending with a Lambert-coached club.

"Mental attitude is the most important thing in the game," Piggy always insisted. "The doctrine I preach is to never get panicky when you're behind in the stretch."

In the final game of 1940, Purdue had to beat Illinois to win an undisputed title. With three minutes to play,

early age. My father was also called "Tug," a name he'd sort of inherited from a famous English fighter named Tug Wilson who had come to America to take on John L. Sullivan in a special challenge match. There was a purse of $5000 for any professional challenger who could stay in the ring three rounds with Sullivan. The Englishman was content with just keeping out of Big John's way and went back to Britain $5000 richer, and subsequently launched a successful business career with the money. The fight had received a lot of publicity, even for those late 19th Century days, and as my father had acquired some sort of notice as a strongman and athlete around Illinois he began to be called "Tug." The name was passed on to me and I was known by it through all my competitive days and in my administrative career. I guess I wouldn't even turn around, now, if someone shouted "Hey, Ken!" (And now I have a grandson called Little Tug.)

Tug Wilson with older sister Winifred and younger brother Henry on April 14, 1907.

Stretch Murphy

Jewell Young

John Wooden

Bob Kessler

Anyway, it was a thrilling time to grow up in the Midwest. I remember how exciting it was to use the telephone in the early 1900's and how I tried vainly to understand how a voice could be transmitted across a wire. Kids today are raised on such miracles from the cradle onward and take them as a matter of course, with no wonderment attached to such things as telephones, television and the like. I'll never forget the delight of my first ride in an automobile at a 1909 Country Fair, when a promoter charged twenty-five cents for a ride around the trotting-horse track.

There was also the thrill my brother and I received a couple of years later when our father brought home a second-hand Buick from a winter farm sale and simply stored it in the machine shed because he didn't know how to run it. My brother and I decided to take things into our own hands, and one day when my father was away we hitched a team of horses to the car, towed it out into the middle of a 40-acre pasture and learned to drive the car ourselves, purely by trial and error—with mostly the latter. How we managed not to strip the gears or batter a cow or two I'll never know. Of course we hauled it back to the shed, covered up the tracks and, when Spring came, astonished our parents by showing them how to handle the car.

While I didn't wreck any family property that time, I certainly did soon after. My parents, overlooking the hands I was developing, decided I should start taking music lessons and picked on the violin, and I, in turn, was picked on by my pals who teased me unmercifully. One day returning from a lesson I smashed the violin over the head of one of my tormentors. My music career ended abruptly and left me time to take up sports more seriously.

Donald White

the Illini led, 29-19. In three minutes Purdue rained a 12-point barrage on the basket to win, 31-29.

The Michigan game of 1936 was another title-teller and Michigan went into the final minutes with a 25-12 edge. Throughout the game Michigan worked with a terrific size advantage, converging Johnny Gee, 6 feet 8, and John Townsend, 6 feet 4, near the basket on defense. They snatched just about every rebound as luckless Purdue peppered the backboard.

The situation was acute. Lambert switched his tactics and ordered long shots. Three clicked. The Michigan defense got nervous, moved out to mid-floor to check the long-range thrust. Quickly, before the Wolverine defense could readjust itself, the crazy Purdue race horse attack moved in again and, before Michigan could recover, hit for three more buckets which won the game and the title.

Piggy Lambert himself was as much a show as the game his boys played. Nowhere in the sport was there a bundle of nervous intensity quite like Lambert on the bench during a game.

All 5 feet 6 inches of him was as much on the floor in spirit as his players. He squirmed, he fidgeted, he clapped his hands over his eyes and muttered to himself. He shouted, screamed at, cajoled, even cussed out his players as they raced by.

Legend is (and some say it is absolute fact) that the Purdue athletic department ordered two student managers to sit right alongside Lambert to be ready to grab him whenever he showed signs of racing onto the floor. The restraint didn't always work. One veteran referee always claimed it was a mental hazard working a Purdue game. "I never felt Piggy trying to intimidate me," he said, "but it's an uncomfortable feeling to be calling them as you see 'em, knowing the little guy over there has never been wrong on a basketball floor in his life."

The record would seem to bear him out. After winning the Big Ten titles in 1921 and 1922, there was a truly amazing and unique pattern: starting in 1926 Lambert's Boilermakers won the league championship every other year from 1926 through 1940.

It made people wonder about those odd years. Piggy Lambert, a Hardwood Houdini if ever there was one, used to say he was just getting ready.

As I had mentioned earlier, we had only nine boys in Atwood High School, but young Tom Samuels, the principal and an avid sports fan, kept us all busy from September to June. Football, however, was taboo in our town because several years previously two boys in a neighboring community had been killed in a football game. (As a matter of fact, the first football game I ever saw was when an alumnus of Illinois took me to Champaign when I was a senior in high school and saw Potsy Clark, one of Illinois' greats, win the game by a long, twisting run through a fine Chicago team.)

We started playing basketball, still in its embryonic stage, in the fall. We had no gymnasium and played on an outdoor court. When cold weather came we played our games in the town Opera House, enabling us to pull off some of the most bizarre plays anyone ever saw, such as disappearing through one door under the

stage and coming out the other door, completely unguarded.

Atwood had no running track, either, but Samuels was determined to have a track team even though we had to run everything down the middle of a wide, dusty, dirt road. The only time we competed under any sort of normal foot-racing conditions was in the County Meet, held at the old county trotting track at the fairgrounds. We had a very good team in my senior year and the meet came to the final event, the half-mile relay. We had no batons to exchange so the rules allowed us to simply touch the next runner as we came up to him. I was running the second leg and in my excitement at the end of my 220-yards I belted my teammate so hard on the back I knocked him sprawling on his face. Instantly realizing by the time he got up the other runners would have passed him and left him com-

1918

LYMAN FRIMODIG, only man in Michigan State history to win 10 varsity letters—two in football, two in basketball and four in baseball. After graduation in 1917 and service in World War One he returned to campus for almost 30 years of teaching and athletic administrative service.

Ohio State, riding the impetus that had given the baby of the Conference two straight grid titles, won its first baseball championship, and the Michigan Aggies said farewell to Lyman Frimodig, the only Spartan athlete to win 10 varsity letters—two in football, two in basketball and four in baseball. (Frimodig played varsity baseball as a frosh, since the Aggies, as a non-Conference team, were not bound by league rules.)

Perhaps the biggest news of the year was made on November 17, when Michigan finally did re-

apply for membership in the Conference and was accepted. For the first time, now, the league could be called The Big Ten.

The year also marked the appearance of two men who would be around for a long time, and highly respected for every minute of their stay. Dave Armbruster, appointed swimming coach at Iowa, would compile the longest service record of any coach or athletic official in Conference history, not stepping down until 1958—forty-one years later. In addition, Michigan named as its Conference faculty representative a young instructor named Ralph W. Aigler, who until he gave up the post in 1955, would be regarded as one of the most influential men ever to serve the Big Ten.

World War One put a serious crimp in Big Ten sports activity in 1918, as it did throughout the nation, and before the football season started the Conference suspended its activities "as a controlling body" and tendered to the War Department "its services in carrying on athletic activities, both intramural and intercollegiate, in and among its members."

Many Big Ten stars were in active military service, and all teams were understandably sub-par. Illinois was generally recognized as Conference unofficial football champion with a perfect 5-0 record, but lost to two service teams: Great Lakes Naval Training and Municipal Pier, both by 7-0 for the only points scored against the Illini that year. Chicago gave Amos Stagg his only season without a win, dropping all five games.

Frank Steketee, Michian fullback, was the league's lone All-America selection—but it would be the last time the Big Ten would be limited to a single All-America.

Norman Elliott, a young doctor, coached Northwestern's basketball team in 1918 but, perhaps more important, became the father of two boys, Bump and Pete Elliott, who later would become the first

pletely out of it, I just kept on running another 220 and we won the race. The meet officials had never seen this happen before and tried to disqualify our team but they couldn't find anything in their rule book that precluded one man from running two sections of the relay, so we were declared winners. Today, of course, the rule is clearly understood, and one man may not run two legs.

I had also become interested in the hammer throw but because our high school didn't own a hammer I took the event literally and threw a 12-pound sledge hammer, instead, in training. We finally got the real equipment and because I was the only hammer thrower on the squad I was allowed to take it home and practice in the cow pasture. One day my father, who was watching me, told me he thought I could throw the thing farther if the wire were longer. I lengthened the wire and he was right; I set a new county record that stood

for years. Nobody knew that the rules listed a required length and so I had what might be called an "innocent" advantage.

It was baseball, however, that I loved the most. I not only played for the high school but for the town team, too, and many were the times I drove 10 miles or more with a horse and buggy to play a Sunday evening game.

Meanwhile, Tom Samuels, our principal and coach, decided to go back into law practice (he later became one of the most distinguished lawyers in the state of Illinois) and a friend of his from the University of Illinois, Warren Madden, took over at Atwood. He stepped up our training considerably, brought Illinois athletes down to Atwood for exhibitions, and often went hunting quail and rabbit with me. Both Samuels and Madden had given me encouragement to go on to college but the

brace of brothers to coach Big Ten football teams (at Michigan and Illinois). The Conference managed to play a full cage schedule, with Wisconsin taking the title, but gymnastics and cross-country became wartime casualties with no championship meets being held. Northwestern took its fifth straight swimming championship, and Michigan, restored to Conference membership, wasted little time in getting back on the title trail, taking an abbreviated-schedule baseball championship and both the indoor and outdoor track crowns. It was Floyd Smart of Northwestern, however, who was the most versatile trackman the Conference had yet seen—and he proved it by taking six first places in a dual meet with Indiana and five against Ohio State .

Among Conference athletes who graduated in June of that year was a slender three-sport man at Illinois (football, basketball, and baseball) named

George Halas, who told friends he was thinking of putting in a few licks with a rag-tag operation known as professional football. There were ex-collegians getting as much as $25 a game and, who knows, the thing might grow to a point where maybe there'd be regular teams in a regular league and good players might get as much as $500 for a season. It might even be fun some day, said Halas, to coach or even sponsor such a team. Some of his friends implied he was some kind of a nut and had better look for a steady job.

The war was over. Young athletes, now older and more mature, took off their service uniforms and came back to the campuses. It was a return to normalcy on the Big Ten sports front, and Illinois posted the most dramatic last-second upset in its history to win the 1919 Conference football crown

1919

GEORGE HALAS was a smart, wiry but tough end for Illinois in 1918, one of the best in the Midwest, but he would achieve even more fame a few years later when he put together one of the great teams in professional football—the Chicago Bears.

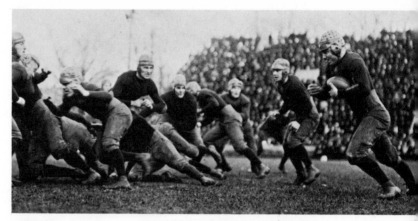

GAYLORD (PETE) STINCHCOMB, brilliant Ohio State halfback, takes off for a substantial gain against Illinois in 1919 but just a few minutes later Bobby Fletcher booted the last-gasp field goal which gave the Illini a 9-7 upset victory to thwart the Bucks' bid for a third straight championship. The following year Stinchcomb, no longer playing in Chic Harley's shadow, was an All-America in his own right.

matter of finances was a difficult one. Farming had been a rugged, marginal business and my parents certainly couldn't afford to send me. Yet I knew they had secret hopes for me. Both my father and mother had been school teachers. My father had started teaching country school when he was 17 years old, although he, himself, had just finished high school. My mother taught country school after only one year at Valparaiso College in Indiana. My older sister who had graduated from Atwood High School two years ahead of me, also taught country school to earn some money to go on to college.

The president of the school board of a nearby town knew of our family and came around to my parents and said he'd like to hire me as a teacher. It was the last thing I'd ever considered at the time but the salary offer of $75 a month was just too tempting to turn down—

even though "country school" meant teaching every grade from first through the 8th grade, and often with everybody in the same classroom.

I agreed to try it, and the next thing on the program was for me to get a teaching certificate. So, at the age of 17, I took the certification exam given that very next week. I didn't have much time to prepare for it and the results were less than impressive. The County Superintendent of Schools, a good friend of my parents, said he'd pass me with a special provision if I'd go to the University of Illinois summer school for one session and complete six hours of satisfactory work. He specified that two hours must be in English. I thought about it and figured I had nothing to lose but a summer in Champaign-Urbana, and a few dollars.

When I arrived on the Illinois campus I found it was the first summer of the Illinois Coaching School given

from an Ohio State team that had welcomed back the imcomparable Chic Harley for his final season. The Buckeyes, undefeated, among other big moments had beaten Michigan for the first time in their history, 13-3. The Illini had been rudely dumped, 14-10, by Wisconsin for their only loss but, nevertheless, were a two or three touchdown underdog to the Mighty Buckeyes in the season finale. Ohio led 7-6 going into the final minutes. Chic Harley had tallied Ohio's lone touchdown and kicked the extra point, but a tigerish Illinois effort was keeping things close.

The Ohio State *Lantern,* the student daily, had previously decided to bring out a Football Extra to be sold to fans leaving the field at game's end. Just minutes before the final gun, the editors decided to gamble on a headline proclaiming a 7-6 Ohio win. The extra was brought off as a shining example of student enterprise; but, just seconds before the game ended, Bobby Fletcher, of Illinois, who had never tried a field goal before, stood poised in the darkening gloom on an oozy, muddy field and booted an 18-yarder that provided a 9-7 Illinois victory, an erroneous headline in the *Lantern,* and the lone defeat in Chic Harley's fabulous career.

On the All-America scene, Harley became football's first three-time nominee since the game went modern with the forward pass. Joining him from the Conference were Charles Carpenter, Wisconsin center, and Lester Belding, Iowa end.

It had been a season, too, which produced a note of tragedy stemming, perhaps, in part from the final Northwestern game of the year. A Notre Dame halfback—the greatest back yet to perform for the Irish—had been sub-par because of injuries and illness but he was determined to play anyway. His accurate passing and inspired running led Notre Dame to a 33-7 victory over the Purple, but two weeks later the great George Gipp was dead of

BOBBY FLETCHER, whose dramatic last second field goal on a drop-kick deprived Ohio State of a championship in 1919 and gave the legendary Chic Harley his only defeat in the three years he starred for the Buckeyes.

ARNIE OSS, a crack Minnesota halfback, also was a star of the 1919 undefeated Gopher basketball team, described by many critics as the outstanding college team in the country.

by the Athletic Department. I registered for the two hours in English and then became intrigued by the idea of learning something formally about sports and coaching them. George Huff, already a leader in Western Conference athletics, had promoted the coaching school idea. He felt there was a tremendous need for high school and college coaches who could be chosen for their knowledge of sports and an ability to teach them. One of Mr. Huff's cardinal beliefs was that before you could teach an athlete anything you should be able to demonstrate it yourself. I was hooked. I signed up for the rest of my four hours in this Coaching School.

There were more than 200 coaches enrolled, and I was the youngest student of the lot. Baseball and basketball teams were organized within the entire group and each candidate had to demonstrate his ability. Our basketball group was one of the best, mainly because

one of its members was a young man named Piggy Lambert, who later would become one of the greatest coaches in the history of the game at Purdue. My real enjoyment came in baseball. The teams from the coaching school played various town teams on Sunday. In our final game of the season I had a great day, getting a homer, a double and three singles in five times at bat. Yet I was absolutely deflated when Mr. Huff came over to me after the game and said: "Son, you didn't hit a good ball the whole afternoon!" He was undoubtedly right. In my anxiety I'd done some rather free swinging and luckily I was connecting against bad pitches. Needless to say, I got an "A" in all the coaching courses and a respectable "B" in English, and I ended up qualifying for my teaching certificate.

Early that September I reported to my first job, teaching school at the age of 17. I found to my astonishment

pneumonia—and the basis of a legend called "Win one for the Gipper," was born.

Minnesota, with 10-0 in the Conference and 13-0 overall, was the Conference cage king, and it would be the last time that the Gophers would be undisputed champs until the present date. Led by Captain Erling Platou, Arnie Oss, the Vikings great football halfback, and N. W. Kingsley, Minnesota was judged by many critics to be the best team in the country that year.

Michigan repeated as league baseball and indoor and outdoor track champions, going undefeated in Conference diamond competition and dropping a 3-2 decision to Notre Dame for 13-1 on the season.

Michigan's Walter K. Westbrook won the first of two straight tennis singles titles, and George Huff served his last year as Illinois baseball coach to commit himself to full-time duties as Athlete Director, where he would be hailed as one of the Conference's great leaders. As baseball coach he had compiled the astounding record of 11 championships and 11 second place finishes in 24 years!

As the year drew to a close there was something in the air—a feeling around the league that a curtain had been lowered on the past, and that something new and vital was coming up. Those who shared the feeling were right.

The year 1920 heralded a whole new era in American sports, and there are those who claim there had never been one like it nor would there ever be one again to compare with it. Perhaps they are right. Perhaps the 1920's epitomized the emergence of sports as a truly national concept of life. With the end of World War One there came new freedoms, new drives, new searchings for emotional and physical outlets; and sports seemed to provide the one big national denominator.

The public wanted new heroes. It got them. It got them in a decade that produced Jack Dempsey, Red Grange, Babe Ruth, Bobby Jones, Bill Tilden, Gene Tunney, Charley Paddock, Johnny Weismuller, Helen Wills and Earle Sande.

Suffice to say, The Big Ten did more than its share in producing public heroes. It did something else. As a group, the 10 schools led the nation into the era of huge concrete stadiums. Sprawling wooden bleachers and grandstands could no longer hold the crowds seeking the excitement and color of collegiate football which, by now, was beginning to be really big business.

In the East, Harvard (1903) had been first with its historic horseshoe-shaped Soldier Field stadium, followed by Yale (1913) with its Bowl. But that was about it as far as collegiate concrete structures were concerned. Now the Big Ten with its large, state-supported universities and leading football powers began blueprinting the construction program that would be emulated on college campuses all over the country.

In 1920 Gaylord (Pete) Stinchcomb, who as a sophomore and junior had been eclipsed by the meteoric Chic Harley, streaked across the football firmament in his own right and the Buckeyes again had the championship which had been denied them in the final seconds of the previous year. The brilliant running and pass-receiving of the 165-pound halfback led Ohio to an undefeated season but there was a rude roadblock ahead for the Buckeyes. They were invited to the Rose Bowl for the first appearance by a Big Ten team since Michigan and Stanford inaugurated the affair in 1902. However, Stinchcomb and his mates could never get untracked and on New Year's Day, 1921, one of Andy Smith's best "Wonder Bear" teams clobbered Ohio 28-0, as Brick Mueller, a California end, used as a passer instead of a receiver, got off the longest scoring aerial in Rose Bowl history. It has since been ticketed variously as 55 yards, 65 yards and 70 yards, but regardless of the lack of consistent and accurate

1920

At 19 Tug Wilson was an experienced teacher, having been on the job for two years.

reporting, it completely demoralized the Buckeyes.

Stinchcomb was a unanimous All-America that year, and joining him as honor selections were Chuck Carney, possibly the best end in Illinois history and Frank Weston and Ralph Scott, end and tackle from an outstanding Wisconsin team that lost only to Ohio, 13-7.

Chicago took the Conference basketball title in 1920, and Carney set the stage for his becoming the first Big Ten athlete to be named All-America in two sports by first gaining national cage honors in the winter of 1920 when he led the league in scoring with 188 points, the highest total yet in Conference play.

If there was any doubt about what Piggy Lambert was up to at Purdue, his Boilermakers, although finishing second to the Maroon, hit for a 712-point season and a 35.6 average per game—a new Big Ten record. A sports writer noted that offense was getting too much ahead of defense and predicted gloomily that basketball would soon be spoiled by 40-point games.

Illinois took both the indoor and outdoor track titles. Michigan was baseball champ again, and the second year in a row Iowa State, an outsider, took the Big Ten cross-country championship. After that, non-members were barred from the meet. The Big Ten's first golf tournament was held in 1920 on a match-play basis, and here, too, the lodge brothers were humiliated by strangers as Robert McKee of Drake won the individual championship and led his club to the team trophy.

Among personalities of note in 1920, Joe Steinauer took over as Wisconsin swimming coach and launched the fourth longest tenure of any Conference tank tutor. He was to stay on until 1951. The Badgers also appointed their first Athletic Director that year, with track coach Tom Jones assuming the title of "acting director," for the next five years until the school decided the position warranted a full time man. It left Minnesota as the only league school operating without an Athletic Director.

The Conference delegation to the 1920 Olympics in Antwerp was the smallest in the history of the games, with only two schools supplying athletes for the United States' squad. Michigan's Carl Johnson took second place in the broad jump and Illinois contributed four men who competed but did not place: Kenneth L. Wilson and Milt Angier in the javelin; Basil Bennett, hammer throw; and Bob Emery, 400-meter dash. For youthful Tug Wilson it was merely the beginning of an association with the Games that would one day find him President of the U. S. Olympic Committee.

In Iowa today there are still legions of fans who remember the Golden Era of Iowa football that

GORDON LOCKE, a thundering Iowa fullback and the Big Ten's leading scorer, was selected as an All-American in 1922.

that there were 48 students in eight grades, and the average length of the class period was 15 minutes. Many of the students were as big as I was, and had problems to match. They stayed out of school in the fall to shuck corn and left early in the Spring to help with the planting and other farm work, and in between I was supposed to educate them. It didn't take me long to realize, in all probability, that I'd been hired because I was big enough, physically, to control this group.

The best way to do it, I figured, was to immediately form some athletic teams. We made a crude outdoor basketball court on the bare ground and put up some flimsy baskets. The problem of competition was solved when I discovered there were four country schools within a radius of six miles and I promptly organized a small league. We kept everyone busy, and found an event for just about every kid in school. We had races

for both boys and girls in each grade from first to eighth. For those who didn't like to run we had a mile bicycle race. The more rugged kids played basketball. All the kids loved it and a lot of farm chores went unattended, but if this was the only way I could keep kids interested in school I was willing to face up to the ire of a lot of farmer-fathers. The only trouble I had was that I had to be on hand, at school, at 7:00 o'clock in the morning because that's when the kids wanted to practice and work out.

There was little supervision of country teachers then in Illinois but occasionally we might expect a visit from the County Superintendent. One brisk fall morning I had ridden a horse from the farm to the schoolhouse but just before I arrived the horse decided to get obstreperous and bucked me off. I wound up with a big rip in my pants. I didn't have time to go back home for another

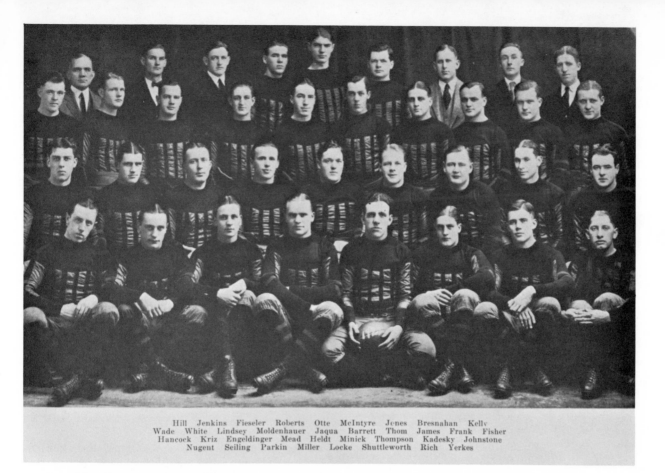

Hill   Jenkins   Fieseler   Roberts   Otte   McIntyre   Jones   Bresnahan   Kelly
Wade   White   Lindsey   Moldenhauer   Jaqua   Barrett   Thom   James   Frank   Fisher
Hancock   Kriz   Engeldinger   Mead   Heldt   Minick   Thompson   Kadesky   Johnstone
Nugent   Seiling   Parkin   Miller   Locke   Shuttleworth   Rich   Yerkes

The Iowa squad of 1922, the second straight undefeated Iowa team, captained by Locke.

began in 1921. The bedrock of success perhaps had been laid in the last half of the 1920 season when all the pieces started falling in place for Howard Jones, with three straight wins. Returning with pretty much the same material in 1921 Jones and Iowa were ready for bigger things — but no one really dreamed of the gigantic success lying ahead.

In the Hawkeye backfield there was the brother combination of quarterback Aubrey Devine and blocking back Glenn Devine. Craven Shuttleworth,

a talented sophomore was the other halfback, and at fullback was bushy-browed Gordon Locke who had few equals anywhere, anytime, as a line-smasher.

Up front was a fierce line headed by Duke Slater, a magnificent tackle; Les Belding, the great pass-receiving end who had received prominent All-America mention in 1919; Paul Minick, a rugged guard, and John Heldt, a pudgy but tough center who was never outplayed.

Superimposed over a collection of remarkable tal-

1921

Dramatic action shot of the 1921 Iowa team on offense. Note bareheaded Duke Slater (he never wore a helmet) blocking in ferocious line action as Gordon Locke blasts through his hole for touchdown which

proved decisive in 10-7 victory over Notre Dame. The Notre Dame defensive end coming around, right rear, is Eddie Anderson, who later would become the coach of another great Iowa team.

GORDON LOCKE   **DUKE SLATER**   **EDDIE ANDERSON**

AUBREY DEVINE

Minnesota's homecoming game in 1921 was a big bust for the Gophers—and a big burst for Iowa captain and quarterback, Aubrey Devine, who raced for four touchdowns and kicked five of six extra points for a 29-point individual total, the highest ever posted in a modern Big Ten game, as the Hawkeyes smashed Minnesota 41-7. Where did the other Iowa points come from? Devine passed to Les Belding, the Hawkeyes' star end, for the other two touchdowns, one covering 43 yards, the other 25. In the less than 50 minutes he played, Devine accounted for 162 yards on 34 plays from scrimmage and returned seven punts and kickoffs for 180 yards.

For Minnesota fans it was a revelation. For Iowa partisans it was "I told you so!" all the way.

Aubrey Devine was the first truly nationally-acclaimed hero in Iowa grid history. He had already starred for two years with the Hawks but 1921 was Devine's and Iowa's year of legendary greatness, and the tip-off came early when Iowa defeated a dazzling Notre Dame team that was to go through an 11-game season with just this lone, 10-7 defeat. The three-point difference? A drop-kicked field goal by Devine after calling a perfect game. The Hawkeyes went on, of course, to a perfect season themselves, their first Big Ten title and a vigorous claim to top national honors. Aubrey Devine was a unanimous All-America.

The 5-10, 175-pound triple threat was one of the early wizards at the running forward pass and had all-around skills which he put to work not only in football; but in basketball and track as well. He was one of only four men in Iowa history who won nine major letters.

ent was the genius of Howard Jones, the ex-Yale Blue. Devising a shift which featured ends dropped off into the backfield, Jones fashioned an offense which ripped the Big Ten apart, and the Hawkeyes in 1921 had their first undefeated season, their first Conference title, their first claim to national honors and their first unanimous All-America in multiple threat Aubrey Devine.

Joining Devine on the All-America team were his teammates Duke Slater and Gordon Locke; Charles McGuire of Chicago, repeating at tackle; Ernie Vick of Michigan at center; and Iolas Huffman of Ohio State, repeating at tackle.

Football news was simmering in other ways as refinements of the game were being cooked up by Big Ten people. At Illinois, Bob Zuppke was first to experiment with the modern huddle. (Two years later he would make it a permanent part of his tactics as he turned loose a mercurial halfback who in 1921 was just winding up a fabulous high school career.) At Wisconsin, Coach John Richards developed the screen pass and, coaching at Montana, a young Big Ten graduate of Minnesota named Bernie Bierman installed something known as the buck-lateral which would become a standard weapon in every single wing offense.

Meanwhile, in June of that year, the Conference fathers had passed an official ban on post-season football games. Somehow, there were suddenly a lot of people with short memories, and when Iowa found itself invited to the Rose Bowl at the end of the 1921 season there was state-wide anguish when it was realized the Hawkeyes would have to decline.

Also among the crestfallen—but for another reason —was Northwestern to whom had fallen the dubious distinction of being the first Big Ten team, since the game went "modern" with the advent of the forward pass in 1906, to go through a five-game league schedule without scoring a point.

In basketball, Michigan had its first taste of a Conference title but had to share the full flavor

---

pair so I stopped at a neighboring farm and borrowed some. The pants were very much on the short side and came almost up to my knees. The man looked at me with a grin and said we could fix things up by adding a pair of his gumboots. I explained all this to my pupils when I got to school but just then I looked out the schoolhouse window and saw an old Stanley Steamer car pull up, and printed on the side were the words: "STATE SUPERINTENDENT OF SCHOOLS."

He came in and told me he was on his way from Champaign to Springfield, the state capital, and since he was so close by he thought he'd stop in and observe some classes. I was very jittery but managed to get through the morning without any kind of pedagogical disaster, and the Superintendent left at noon. Years later, a friend of mine in the Department of Education at Springfield told me he'd been reviewing some of the

State Superintendent's reports and came across this item: "Harsburger School: taught by K. L. Wilson. Doing an acceptable job of teaching but extremely eccentric in his dress."

Looking back, I like to believe that because of this "acceptable job of teaching," I later received my finest compliments in the form of letters from former pupils who told me that the happiest times of their lives had been spent while attending my little country school.

At the time, however, it was a lot of work and I wasn't too sure of myself when it came to grading papers and planning programs. Since I figured I'd never get to go to college, I looked for relief in baseball, my favorite sport, during the Spring and Summer when I could be spared from chores on the family farm.

I thought I was quite a pitcher. In fact, I had learned to throw a spitball—still legal in those days—by sub-

with Purdue and Wisconsin with 8-4 records all around. Arnie Oss, Minnesota's great center, was given All-American honors, but Don White of Purdue led the league in scoring. At Indiana, an outstanding center named Everett Dean made his first impression on Hoosier fans, but would later make an even stronger one as Indiana coach, and one of the greatest the game has produced. Although no

ERNIE VICK, Michigan's rock-like center, and IOLAS HUFFMAN, a mobile tackle from Ohio State, were 1921 All-America choices in a year which produced five from the Big Ten, including Iowa's fabulous twosome of Aubrey Devine, at quarterback, and Duke Slater, at tackle; and Chicago's Charley McGuire, at tackle.

EVERETT DEAN, as basketball captain at Indiana, in 1921, wasn't fortunate enough to lead the Hoosiers to a title but four years later he was head coach at his Alma Mater—the youngest coach in the Conference—and soon established himself as one of the most astute in the business. His Hoosiers finished second in his first campaign but he led them to Indiana's first crown a year later. After another second place finish in 1927 he came back for a second title in 1928, and until he turned over coaching chores in 1938 to Branch McCracken, one of his former stars, Dean's Hoosiers were always a factor in the race.

scribing to a correspondence course taught by Big Ed Walsh, the famed White Sox star. I had just about worn out one side of the barn and a half dozen or more old baseballs experimenting with the pitch because I couldn't get anyone to catch me. It was hard to control but when it worked it was a tough pitch to hit.

Every town had a baseball team, then. Some, of course, were better than others but all played before good crowds as part of community life. Wednesdays and Sundays were the usual game days, and players were ex-high school players or young men around town who stayed in shape. There was also the occasional "ringer," imported from elsewhere. I did rather well in these games and I must confess I was one of the "ringers" who got calls from neighboring towns to come over and pitch a game or two for them.

One day I got a call from a neighboring town that

had arranged a fall exhibition game with a team made up of several members of the Chicago Cubs, plus a few others. The manager of the town team had hired a pitcher from Chicago but he hadn't looked too good in practice and the manager said I might have to pitch a few innings. I drove over with my horse and wagon and he was right about his Chicago import. In the first two innings the visitors scored 15 runs. At the start of the third inning the manager motioned for me to go in and relieve.

I took the mound, warmed up and got set to throw my best pitch, the spit ball. Joe Tinker, the Cubs' manager and one-third of the famed double-play combination of Tinker-to-Evans-to-Chance, was at bat. My first pitch nearly took his cap off as the ball took a wild hop. I was surprised to see him back away from the plate. Then he tapped my next pitch for an easy

one ever thought anything would come of it, somebody at Michigan A. & M., in what was called a "radio station," thought it would be interesting to describe a basketball game on the air. The station, WKAR, promptly made a little bit of history by being the first to do so, although not many people knew it at the time.

Illinois repeated as indoor and outdoor track champions, but the big track news of the year was the inauguration of the National Collegiate Athletic Association track meet—and the honor of winning this first NCAA spectacle made Illinois' cinder season complete. Three Conference performers won individual titles. Pete Stinchcomb, Ohio State's All-America halfback, became the first All-America gridder to win one when he took the broad jump; Lloyd Wilder of Wisconsin captured the pole vault, and Eric Wilson of Iowa, who later would become the Hawkeyes' able sports publicity director, won the 220-yard dash.

Illinois added to its big year by taking the baseball title and B. E. Ford of Chicago became the first man from a Conference school to win the league's individual golf crown.

1922

The Big Ten wondered, in 1922, how Howard Jones and Iowa would do without the services of fabulous Aubrey Devine; his path-clearing brother, Glenn; the versatile Les Belding and the awesome Duke Slater. The uncertainty didn't last long. Gordon Locke, now the marked man in the Hawkeye backfield, and a supporting cast of Craven Shuttleworth and Lee Parkin furnished the offensive spark, ably abetted up front by Johnny Heldt, Paul Minick, Chet Mean and Max Kadesky. It was another Hawkeye hurricane that blew across the land as the Black and Gold posted its second straight undefeated season. Even the skeptical East was convinced as Howard Jones took his cornfeds to New Haven to post a 6-0 win over a great Yale team headed by Century Millstead and Bill Mallory—both destined

HARRY GILL

Canadian-born Harry L. Gill who had the longest tenure as varsity track coach of anyone in The Big Ten, also had the winningest teams in the Conference during his 30 years from 1904 to 1933.

He produced 11 outdoor and eight indoor Conference championship squads and had an astounding dual meet mark of 111 wins against only 24 defeats. He also had the satisfaction of outscoring his perennial rival, Michigan, 1025-736, the only coach to hold an edge over the Wolverines.

Gill helped organize the first National Collegiate Athletic meet in 1921—and promptly won it. He took another NCAA title in 1927.

Probably the height of his coaching career came in 1924 when his Illinois athletes scored more points in the Olympic Games than were scored by any other single nation. The Illini 35-point-production in Paris was paced by Harold Osborn who captured the high jump and decathlon; Dan Kinsey who won the 110-meter high hurdles; and Horatio M. Fitch, second in the 400-meter run.

Gill also turned out Avery Brundage, three times winner of the all-around track and field championship of the U. S., and who later became President of the International Olympic Committee; Kenneth L. (Tug) Wilson, former Big

grounder right back to me. I threw him out at first. The next batter struck out and I got the third on a little pop fly. That was the pattern of the game for seven innings. Not a Cub player got on base as I held them hitless and gave no walks.

After the game I waited for somebody to come rushing over to sign me to a contract but, instead, the Cubs hastily gathered their equipment and ran to the railroad station a couple of blocks away to catch a train that was waiting there.

Years later I met Carl Lundgren, the baseball coach at Illinois, who had seen that game and I asked him why the Cubs hadn't made me an offer after holding them hitless for virtually the whole game. Lundgren burst out laughing. "Do you remember," he said, grinning, "how Joe Tinker called all his players together when you came in to relieve? Well, he told the Cubs

that anyone who got a hit, got on base or slowed up the ball game in any way would be fined $100 for making the team miss their train and causing everyone to stay all night in a hick town!"

I was finally convinced I'd never be a big league ball player and would stick to teaching country school and farming.

Of course it wasn't a completely orderly existence, if my memory serves me well. I particularly remember one county fair which featured a wrestler on its Carnival Midway. A large sign was posted, offering $25 to anyone who could go five minutes with the wrestler, a quiet, muscular man who seemed bored with it all. I watched him throw three husky young farmers in a hurry and decided to try it myself, recalling the story of the Englishman who'd taken on John L. Sullivan and left me the legacy of his name.

Ten Commissioner, later President of the United States Olympic Committee and who was, himself, an Olympic performer; and hurdler Lee Sentman; half miler John Sittig; two-miler, Dave Abbott; discus thrower Frank Purma, and pole vaulter Verne McDermott, all of whom were national champions.

Gill, who was born in 1876 in Coldwater, Ont., got his early indoctrination at the Harvard School of Physical Training. By 1900, Gill, who was six feet and 165 pounds, had become Canadian all-around champion, and challenged Ellery Clark, the U. S. Champ for three straight years. The all-around was similar to the modern decathlon except that the 56-pound weight throw and the hammer throw were programmed instead of the javelin and discus. The two-man contest took place in New York before several thousand partisan Yankee spectators. Gill, comparatively unknown in the U. S., won with ease.

In those days there was money to be made in professional track and for three years Gill barnstormed profitably until he decided to take a crack at college coaching. He was one of the first track coaches who understood the physiology and mechanics of the human body, and out of this he devised training programs for the different track and field events which went far beyond mere muscle and stamina-developing exercising. His immediate success at Illinois was a recognized bellwether in promoting track and field in the midwest.

DUKE SLATER

DUKE SLATER

Cutting Mississippi River ice in sub-zero weather for a commercial ice company wasn't for him, and 15-year-old Fred Slater knew it. He'd quit high school to take a job, but his father, a Clinton, Iowa, minister, who wanted him to finish school, actually got the job for him. The selection worked. Young Fred Slater returned to school, acquired the nickname of "Duke," and, as Duke Slater, went on to the University of Iowa where he became an All-America and one of the greatest tackles the Big Ten had ever seen.

Not big by modern standards, Duke Slater was 6-2 and 210 pounds but he had phenomenal brawn, with such strength in his hands that he tossed blockers aside like toys, and when his hands fastened on a ball carrier there was no way out and nowhere to go. The opposition often played two men against him and even then couldn't keep him out of the play. To add to his opponents' misery, Slater was so fast he was usually the first man downfield under an Iowa punt.

On offense it was his bruising blocking which opened up huge holes for Aubrey Devine and Gordon Locke, the Hawkeyes' great backs, and there was unanimous agreement that, despite the all-around brilliance of the undefeated Hawkeyes of 1921, there would have been a blemish or two on their record were it not for Duke Slater.

Slater played four years at Iowa, making the varsity as an 18-year-old freshman in 1918 under wartime rules, and never once did he have to take a time out for injury. Howard Jones, the canny coach of the Hawks who later turned out some of the nation's greatest linemen and national championship teams at Southern California, said he'd never coached a lineman who made so few errors either on offense or defense. "And in Slater's case," he once remarked wryly, "you might translate 'so few' as 'none.' He was simply never out of position, never fooled by a fake, never mistaken on where the opposing ball carrier was going, never late on his offensive charge."

After graduating from Iowa, Slater played pro ball with the old Chicago Cardinals, then returned to Iowa to get his law degree. Later, for many years he was a judge of the Superior Court of Cook County (Chicago), until his death in August, 1966.

When I climbed into the ring the wrestler looked me over, noted my size and said softly: "Son, let's make this easy on both of us. Don't try too hard and I'll go easy on you."

I knew nothing about wrestling but we put on a great show. He'd toss me around for a bit and then pretend to have a bit of trouble with me. Finally I threw him to the mat, but just as I was feeling heady with success and about to pin him—I thought—he whirled over, picked me up, waved me around his head a couple of times, slammed me to the mat and ended my wrestling career. Later I discovered he was Doc Roller, one of the claimants to the world heavyweight title in a day when legitimate wrestling meant something.

Among my chores on the farm was shucking corn, for which my father paid me three cents a bushel for all I could shuck. We also had a couple of Kentuckians who

had drifted north to help us finish the crop, and because of them I almost succeeded in ending any sort of athletic career to which I might have aspired. We made a fifty cent bet one day on who would be first to fill their wagon and get back to the corn crib with it. I got my wagon filled and was getting ready to start for the barn when my team of mules balked. It was as if for no reason at all they'd had it for the day and weren't going anywhere for anyone. That's why they're mules, I guess. Nothing I could do, including beating them over the head with a corn stalk, could budge them.

Suddenly I recalled an old farmer's advice that if ever a mule balked you should pour some water in his ear and he'd get going again. I took an old jug, filled it with water from a creek just a few feet away, but then I found I couldn't quite reach my mules' ears with the jug. It was a pretty big team of mules. So I climbed up onto

There is little doubt that HARRY KIPKE, Michigan's great All-America halfback of 1922, was the greatest spot kicker in Big Ten, if not collegiate, history. A nine-letterman who starred for three years in football, basketball and baseball, Kipke's amazing coffin-corner punting was not only a defensive but offensive weapon for the Wolverines. Virtually any time he punted from anywhere around midfield or slightly into an opponent's territory, he was a threat to put the ball out-of-bounds within the 10-yard line. For three years he was the leading punter in the Conference and was also a deadly place-kicker on field goals with more than a half dozen to his credit of 40 yards or more. A Michigan immortal, he later coached the Wolverines from 1929 through 1937, giving the Maize and Blue four straight titles in 1930-31-32-33 and then suffering lean years when his material thinned out.

to be All-America—and a Yale team coached by the other Jones Brother, the Boola Boola immortal, Tad.

Locke was a unanimous All-America quarterback, and was joined on the honor team by Conference colleagues John Thomas, Chicago fullback; Harry Kipke, Michigan's hard-running halfback and fabulous punter, and Paul Goebel, Michigan end.

Although considered the finest team in the Conference, if not the nation, Iowa was forced to share the league title with undefeated Michigan and once-tied (in the Conference) Chicago. Michigan's lone blemish in 1922 came when Fielding Yost tangled with Brother-in-Law Dan McGugin's Vanderbilt team in a scoreless tie, while Alonzo Stagg's mighty Maroon dropped an epic 21-18 battle to Princeton. It was the first triple tie for the championship in Conference history, and it would happen only once more.

There were football highlights elsewhere than at Iowa, of course, and Northwestern claimed two of them—and both in the same game. With the Purple locked in bitter battle with Minnesota, President Walter Dill Scott of Northwestern climbed out of the stands to lead a series of cheers—the only time in Big Ten history that such an eminent campus leader would become that intensely involved. For Walter Dill Scott, however, it was only natural. As a 170-pounder, Scott had been a tough, scrappy guard on the 1892 Northwestern team—always out-weighed but seldom outfought. One year he had broken a hand in an early game but came back two weeks later, wearing a boxing glove on the injured hand, to finish the season. When Walter Dill Scott led the cheers against Minnesota the Northwestern fans went wild. They went sky-high a few minutes later when Chuck Palmer, a Northwestern halfback, set a Big Ten record that still stands. Minnesota had driven to the Purple goal line. Then, a Gopher back, starting to plunge for the touchdown, fumbled, with the ball popping into the air. Palmer, plucking it off well behind the goal line, streaked 105 yards for a

the wagon tongue between them and started pouring the water into their ears.

Nobody had been more right than that old farmer. My mules not only started but left the mark like record-holding sprinters. I was knocked sprawling onto the wagon tongue, holding on for dear life while they were on the dead run. I started praying I wouldn't fall off because if I did I could fall right under the plunging wagon wheels. Meanwhile, the Kentuckians saw my wagon racing toward the barn and immediately leaped aboard their wagon behind a pair of mules who didn't need water in their ears. They caught me after about 100-yards and then it was neck-and-neck, with my driver-less mules, for some strange reason, heading straight for the corn crib where my father was standing, smoking his pipe and watching the race curiously.

My mules got there first, by about a wagon-length,

and, for reasons of their own, came to a dead stop right by my father. He took his pipe out of his mouth and said quietly: "Just who do you think you are—Ben Hur?" Years later while speaking at an AAU convention in Miami I sat next to Charlton Heston, who had starred in the motion picture, "Ben Hur." When I told him about my particular version of the chariot race he cracked up so hard that people started staring at us.

Somehow I got through two years of country school teaching and then, at 19, I made up my mind. I had saved up nearly $800 and I thought I could swing it. I was going to college. I would go to the University of Illinois and somehow work my way through. The day I left home in September, 1916, my father had planned to drive me to Champaign in the old family car but there'd been a pouring rain the day before and since there were no paved roads in our area he knew it would

JOHN THOMAS, one of the great plunging fullbacks of the early 1920's, was Chicago All-America of 1922.

PRESIDENT WALTER DILL SCOTT, of Northwestern, who had been a tough, 170-pound guard on the Purple team in 1892, made news in 1922 when he leaped out of the stands to lead student cheers during a bitter battle with Minnesota. It was the only such presidential gambit in Big Ten annals—and it worked, as the undermanned Wildcats pulled off a 7-7 tie.

touchdown that tied the game. It was the longest scoring run with a fumble in league play.

Ward (Piggy) Lambert, who had coached Purdue to a share of the league title the year before, led the Boilermakers to their first undisputed crown in 1922 and, from then on, the Conference would regard Lambert as its biggest hurdle until his retirement 24 years later. His string of titles would be unmatched and only once in his long career would he have a losing season. In 1922, also, Chuck Carney, the Illinois All-America, came back after a slight junior year slump to win the Conference scoring crown he had first taken as a sophomore.

Illinois won the indoor and outdoor track titles for the third straight year—the first school to do so —and again the Big Ten was a major part of the

When CHUCK CARNEY, of Illinois, was named All-America in basketball in 1922 he became the first man in Big Ten history to gain All-America honors in two sports, having previously been selected as an end in football in 1920. He led the league in scoring in 1920 as a sophomore and again in 1922 as a senior.

be impossible to get through. So he hitched up the mule team and we plodded through the mud to Tuscola, on the Illinois Central rail line. It was a 10-mile trip and in the couple of hours it took to get there he had plenty of time to give me all the advice he felt in his heart. There was one thing I'll never forget as the train pulled in. He handed me a checkbook and said: "Son, even though money is hard to come by on the farm, if you ever need any just go ahead and write a check on my account." The confidence he had in me was enough for me to make a silent promise never to let him down.

At Champaign I took lodgings in a rooming house and then went over to register in the College of Agriculture. Naturally, I figured that when I'd acquired some modern ideas about farming I'd go back to take over the family acreage and turn it into a profitable venture; but, often things happen very quickly to change

the whole course of our lives. The next day was the start of freshman football practice and since it was just about the only sport I'd never tried I figured I'd give it a fling and see what happened. I was 6-1 and weighed about 195 pounds so I thought I'd at least survive, physically. In a very short while, after some calisthenics, the frosh coach, Ralph Jones looked me over and told me to take the right tackle position in a run-through of some plays. Well, I'd only seen one football game in my life and had never even touched a football so, with some embarrassment, I had to ask what and where right tackle was.

I caught on quickly, however, and enjoyed the contact. With quite some pride two months later I was able to write my Dad that I'd won my freshman numerals. I did not write him that I was beginning to think more about athletics than a career as a modern farmer. When football was over, I immediately went out for freshman

show in the NCAA meet. Iowa's Charles Brookins won the 120-yard high hurdles; Harold Osborne, of Illinois, won the high jump crown; Michigan's John Landowski was co-champ in the pole vault; and the Wolverines' Howard Hoffman won the javelin throw with 203 feet 3 inches, the first time anyone exceeded 200 feet.

Michigan and Minnesota won team titles for the first time in cross-country and swimming respectively. Michigan would never do it again strangely enough, but Chicago, however, was making it a habit in gymnastics, with its fourth straight team title.

From the graduating classes of 1922 there came some headline names who proved that scholarship and athletics can be mutually attractive. Among the winners of the Conference Medal were Aubrey Devine, Iowa's All-America quarterback; Iolas Huffman, Ohio State's All-America tackle; Arnie Oss, Minnesota's All-America cager; and a fine end from Chicago named Herbert Orrin (Fritz) Crisler, who would be heard from in other ways later on.

Perhaps the biggest news coming out of the Big Ten in 1922 was the announcement on June 2 that the Conference had established the office of "Commissioner of Athletics," with the Commissioner to serve as "general secretary, promote educational campaigns on amateurism and carry on investigations regarding intercollegiate athletics problems." It was a significant event in the history of American collegiate sports, and, with the Big Ten showing the way, most of the major conferences in the nation would eventually follow suit. The first man elected to the post by the Big Ten directors was Major John L. Griffith, an ex-Army officer and athletic director.

1923

In some respects it is impossible to think of a more portentous year for the Big Ten than 1923. It was then, in the brilliant light and lengthening shadows of a midwestern autumn, that a ghost was born. Embodied, he was the most famous football player in the history of football.

Before his career would be ended, children, housewives, and any manner of people who never saw a football game would recognize as household words more nicknames for him than had ever been bestowed upon a football star. The Wheaton Iceman . . . The Wheaton Redhead . . . Number 77 . . . The Illinois Flash . . . And the one that would become a part of gridiron immortality: *The Galloping Ghost.*

Red Grange was, simply, the most electrifying ball-carrier the sport had ever seen and his speed, shiftiness, change-of-pace and swivel hips left a trail of frustrated tacklers in his wake for three years. It mattered little to Illinois that, with a perfect season, it had to share the Conference title in 1923 with also undefeated Michigan; Illinois still had Grange. Nobody else could come close to that.

Major John L. Griffith became the first Commissioner of the Big Ten in 1922.

basketball where I did pretty well against the varsity as a center. My frosh coach, who was Bob Zuppke, the famed varsity football coach, told me the varsity was counting on me for the following year. Then, toward the end of the season, I had my first bit of tough luck (more would follow). I got knocked off my feet going for a rebound and fractured my left wrist. They put my arm in a cast and when I took it off eight weeks later my wrist was stiff as a board. In fact, my whole hand resembled a claw. Athletic Director George Huff, after consulting the team doctor, decided to send me, with a couple of varsity athletes, to a famous healer named Bone-Setter Reese in Youngstown, Ohio. Reese wasn't a doctor but had achieved great fame in curing professional baseball players of all kinds of injuries.

The other two athletes who went with me were Swede Rundquist, captain of the football team, and George Halas, one of the greatest athletes Illinois had ever produced, and who was having trouble with his arm and shoulder. Bone-Setter Reese had little difficulty in fixing them up and they both came out of his office jubilant over the way he had apparently cured them. Now it was my turn. I was quite a little apprehensive when I went in. On his wall dangled a skeleton and there were also pictures of the human anatomy. Reese examined me once very carefully, then went over and studied his charts. "Son," he said, "this is going to hurt. I have to break all the adhesions that have formed on your wrist." With that, he placed my wrist on the table and with his strong hands proceeded to break them. It was a very painful process but it did the trick and I eventually healed in good shape.

HAROLD (RED) GRANGE

The husky deputy sheriff of Wheaton, Illinois, clapped a hand heartily on his son's shoulder. "Football?" he said to the 125-pound boy. "You want to go out for the high school football team? Okay—and I'll tell you what I'll do. I'll give you two bits for every touchdown you score!"

So the boy went out and played high school football, then he played college football, and then played pro ball, and when they totaled it all up they found Harold (Red) Grange had carried the ball 4013 times for 33,820 yards (19¼ miles) for an average of 8.4 yards per carry and had scored 2366 points in 247 games.

He'd never really needed the incentive of twenty-five cents for every touchdown. Once past his freshman year in high school it was apparent to anyone who saw him that Red Grange was born to play football. He became the most famous player in the history of the game. He made a national byword out of a mere number. Seventy-seven. There was only one seventy-seven. There was only one Red Grange.

Before leaving the University of Illinois he received more than 5000 letters and telegrams in the autumn of his senior year from fans and business entrepreneurs seeking to tie-in with him. More than a half-million dollars was flung rapturously at him before he could vote. Sports writers and columnists bestowed superlatives on him such as never before had been torn out of their sizzling typewriters, and Grantland Rice, in one poetic passage, composed something that began as follows:

> A streak of fire, a breath of flame
> Eluding all who reach and clutch;
> A gray ghost thrown into the game
> That rival hands may never touch.

Grange hadn't even intended to go out for football when he entered Illinois in September, 1922. He preferred basketball and track, but he'd joined a fraternity and the upperclassmen at his house ordered him out for the freshman football team. Red went, hoping by that time that all the suits had been issued. There were a couple left. One of them fit him. Then he took a look at the awesome competition on that Illini frosh squad. (Among them Moon Baker, later to transfer to Northwestern; Earl Britton and a whole bevy of all-state stars.) Grange decided he didn't have a chance and went right back to the fraternity house. He was honest enough to tell the upperclassmen the truth—that he was scared stiff—and was promptly ordered to report back to the frosh squad the next day or take a fraternity paddling.

Within a week the lithe redhead was in the first-string backfield, and in the first varsity-frosh scrimmage he fielded a punt and snaked 65 yards through the entire varsity for a touchdown. Bob Zuppke, the Illini coach, pursed his lips in a silent whistle and thought cozily of the three promising years ahead.

Actually, it was out-of-character for Grange to have been faint-hearted about his chances to make it. At Wheaton he'd built himself up from 125 to 170 pounds, and for three years was the team's best running back. He won the Du Page County scoring title and kicked 30 consecutive points-after-touchdown. In one game against Downers Grove he tallied six touchdowns and booted nine field goals.

Despite all this, Grange's reputation had been submerged under that of a fine Wheaton team which was selected in 1921 to play Scott High School of Toledo for a mythical midwest prep school championship. The young redhead might have attracted some real attention in that post-season game but got little chance; he was knocked out on the first play and didn't regain his speech for almost two weeks.

He was better known as a trackman. In his senior year at Wheaton he entered 19 events in the hurdles, high jump and broad jump. He won all 19.

The early stamina and strength so evident in the boy was no accident—and yet, perhaps, could be called just that. As a promotional stunt, the owner of a local icehouse announced he'd offer a prize of a dollar to any boy who could hoist a 100-pound block of ice to his shoulder. Red, just 14 years old, was one of three kids who did it. He soon got a job helping out on a wagon for $5 a day, and by the time he was a high school junior he was a wagon boss at $50 a week. Later, he would be known as the Wheaton Ice Man, and there wasn't a daily newspaper in the country that wouldn't eventually carry a picture of the Illinois star grinning widely, lugging a cake of ice on his shoulder. His horse was more photographed than Man O' War.

Actually, Red had carried much of his ice from a truck and it was a truck which almost ended his football career in high school. As a helper one week before he got his own wagon Red was hopping on and off the running board at each house. One day the truck started to roll before the boy was solidly aboard. Red fell off and rolled under the truck loaded with several tons of ice. A back wheel crunched over his left leg just above the knee. The leg was crushed so badly that the doctors feared amputation was necessary, but a closer examination showed that the knee joint had been missed by just an inch and they decided to give the leg a chance to heal—although he was never expected to play football again. All he did in three years as a high school halfback was score 255 points on 36 touchdowns and 39 conversions.

Grange's varsity debut at Illinois was strictly in keeping with his promise as a freshman. In his sophomore season, opening against a tough Nebraska team, Grange took a punt in the first quarter and before the startled Cornhuskers steaming down could converge on him he slipped among them like a wraith and was gone 66 yards for a touchdown. He scored twice more on end runs, racked up a total of 208 yards gained and sat out the entire fourth quarter with the game safely on ice.

In seven games that year Grange tallied 12 touchdowns and led the nation in yards gained with 1260. Walter Camp hadn't seen him play and the East was skeptical, but Camp acknowledged that the record was too convincing to leave Red off his All-America.

Grange's ability, in addition to tremendous speed, was his knack of switching directions, an exquisite sense of timing in controlling his speed in different situations; a gymnast's sense of body co-ordination and balance, and a triphammer stiff arm that stretched many a tackler prone on the turf if his hip fake already hadn't. In his 31 collegiate touchdowns, Grange scored in almost every possible way except on the receiving end of a pass. He skirted the ends, exploded through the line with fullback fury, and frequently brought the ball all the way back on kick-offs and punts. There simply was no way he couldn't beat you. He returned an intercepted pass 95 yards against Northwestern and once, with his

Red Grange tears off yardage against Chicago in 1924.

cat-like reflexes, dashed in from his defensive position to scoop up a blocked punt and ramble 35 yards for the score. Although he was a marked man in every game he played and extravagant heroics were expected of him each time, Grange seldom let the fans down.

When Zuppke switched his brilliant star to quarterback in his senior year to take advantage of his experience and gridiron savvy, Grange proved not only his tremendous versatility but his sportsmanship and unselfishness. In his junior year, with defenses over-committing themselves because of his virtually unstoppable running threat, Grange became even more of a menace because Zup had developed him into a passer. Red tossed 27 completions that year. As a senior he frequently took to the air but, as quarterback and mindful of possible criticism as a ball-hog, Grange cut down both his passing and running (although he still had 15 completions for the year).

He often allowed other backs to score when he himself could and should have carried the ball on short sweeps that were tailor-made for him against tight defenses. With a hard-charging line in front of him (to which Red, incidentally, constantly gave credit game after game) Grange's particular backfield favorite was Earl Britton, who often blocked for him. Several times he sent the big fullback into the line on short scoring plunges, even though Grange had set up the situation with long, brilliant runs and might have deserved the opportunity to complete the job, himself, over the last two or three yards. His selflessness at quarterback also accounted for the fact that of the five games in his college career in which he was held scoreless, four of them came while he was calling signals.

Except for two games when he was hobbled by injuries Grange was the star of every game he played. Three in particular will always be recalled as examples of his genius. On a crisp, sun-drenched afternoon in October, 1924 at Champaign, 60,000 fans at the dedication of Illinois Memorial Stadium not only witnessed Grange's finest hour but what indisputably was the most glittering one-man performance in the history of college football. Illinois' guest was a typically tough Michigan team, and Fielding Yost had an idea that he'd spoil the Illinois dedication weekend.

What happened to Michigan in the first twelve minutes

of play had never happened to a major team before, or since.

Illinois won the toss and chose to receive. Michigan booted the ball high, end-over-end, down to the 5-yard line. Fate, not a Wolverine foot, perhaps, had directed the ball straight to No. 77. Red Grange gathered in the pigskin, took three or four steps to the right and then seemingly headed straight toward a horde of blue shirts bearing down on him. Grange burst between the first two, skittered to the left and back to the right again between two more, then broke into the clear and streaked 95 yards for a touchdown.

Illinois kicked off to Michigan. They stopped the Wolverines cold and immediately forced them to punt, with Illinois taking over on its own 33. A direct snap to Grange on the first play and he started toward end, cut back off tackle, stiff-armed the linebacker and spurted through the Michigan secondary. Two defenders took shots at him but he slipped past them and dashed 67 yards for the touchdown.

A few minutes later, again unable to move, Michigan gave up the ball on the Illinois 44. Again a snap to Grange, who cut toward tackle, suddenly veered sharply out and around the end and raced, untouched, 56 yards to the goal line.

Two minutes more and again Illinois had the ball, on the Wolverine 44. Yost and the entire Michigan team knew what to expect, but it really didn't matter much. Another direct snap to Grange—only the fourth time he'd had his hands on the ball—and again, with the defense spread wide to keep him from getting out and around, Grange suckered the end and defensive halfback out of their shoes and left them grasping as he ran at them and then away from them, 44 yards to another touchdown.

Literally panting from all that sprinting in such a short time, Red leaned one hand against the goal post for support while he waited for the two teams to arrive at the goal line to take position for the try for extra point. Only then did the idea occur to Zuppke that his star might be legitimately pooped, and took him out. The din which reverberated from the densely-packed fans was described by one witness as: "Something not heard since Ceasar's return to Rome in triumph from the Wars." If this were true then, obviously, the Redhead's deeds were as mighty as Ceasar's. Anyway, Zup kept Grange on the bench during the second quarter but sent him back to the wars to start the second half. Red promptly galloped 15 yards for his fifth touchdown and a couple of minutes later he fired a touchdown pass to Marion Leonard for Illinois' sixth and final touchdown. By game's end he had carried the ball 21 times for 402 yards and had six pass completions for 64 more in a 39-14 rout.

Two weeks later the Galloping Ghost, as he was now known, had to make some last-minute wraith-like moves to get the Illini past one of Amos Alonzo Stagg's last great teams which featured Austin (Five Yards) McCarty. Chicago was leading 21-7 when Grange went to work. Somehow, his end runs hadn't been too effective against the Maroon, but Red's passing was brilliant that day as he completed seven for 177 yards. He had scored Illinois' first touchdown on a four-yard punch into the line. In the third quarter his aerials put the Illini into scoring range again. Suddenly there was No. 77 ramming through a slight hole five yards to a touchdown that brought Illinois up to 21-14.

Time was running out. Then, in the fourth quarter,

Chicago punted and Illinois took over an its own 20. There was a long, long way to go and not much time left to get there. Illinois did it the easy way. In the translation of the day it meant a direct snap to Grange who followed his interference toward end. The end committed himself to Grange's feint inside. Grange swept past his interference, past the defensive end and turned the corner. Nobody laid a finger on him as he streaked 80 yards down the sideline. The score was tied at 21-21. In the final minute Red burst through tackle and sped 55 yards for another touchdown—but Illinois was called for holding and the score was nullified. That was it. Injuries and the clock were the only things that stopped Grange.

Only once did Red Grange have to rise to an occasion because his personal pride was stung. Illinois had never appeared in the East. Smug fans and critics along the Atlantic seaboard in those days before TV and radio, still weren't convinced that the balance of football power had swung from the game's birthplace to the hinterlands. Grange could not be that good. Nobody could be as good as the Corn Belt sportswriters claimed.

So, in Grange's senior year when Illinois came to Franklin Field to play Pennsylvania, long one of the titans of Eastern football, the general attitude was still one of unkind skepticism.

It came up rain that Saturday late in November, 1925 and the Eastern fans were disappointed. Now the Redhead would be hampered and excuses would be made for him. They preferred to see him stopped on a dry field.

It had started to rain long before game time and at the kick-off the field was ankle-deep in ooze. Two and a half hours later Eastern sportswriters stared silently at each other and wondered how it could have happened.

With mud squirting from his cleats at every step, with his face twisted gleefully in a gooey-streaked grimace, Red Grange had run for 363 yards and three touchdowns. On his first scoring play he rocketed through tackle, pivoted away from a linebacker and invited the secondary to race him to the goal line 56 yards away. The pleasure of their company was soon parted.

Red's second score was a duplicate of the first at 13 yards. His third and last in the 24-2 Illinois victory was a 20-yard scamper around end. The number 77 on his jersey had long since been obliterated but nobody in the huge throng needed any further indentification. They were now Believers and Witnesses. Laurence Stallings, the great playwright who had authored "What Price Glory," had been hired by a New York newspaper to cover the game and do a special color story. At the game's end Stallings shrugged and put the lid on his typewriter. "I can't write it," he sighed. "The story's too big for me."

There were only two games left in Grange's college career—Chicago and Ohio State—both of which Illinois were to win handily. Now, however, with the season drawing to a close, a strange phenomenon of American sports was being born. For the first time, a national sports figure would be merchandized as an outright commercial product. Letters and telegrams had been pouring into Grange's fraternity house at the rate of a hundred a day, offering the footballer every possible financial opportunity. Marriage proposals were as numerous as the financial gambits. Bewildered, Red took his problem to a local businessman named C. C. Pyle who operated two movie theatres. Pyle, a red-hot football fan, had seen Red in

every game he'd played, including road trips, and they had become good friends. Pyle convinced Grange to take him on as his manager. Then the fun began.

First, it was announced that Red would sign a lucrative contract to finish the rest of the professional season with the Chicago Bears. Pro football was scrabbling for a foothold as a spectator sport, and the announcement that Grange would appear in the line-up sold thousands of extra tickets wherever he would play, The claim is made that pro football as it is known today, was rescued from collapse and oblivion the day Grange signed with the Bears. At any rate, Grange and Pyle split $2,000,000 for Red's appearance with the Bears after the Illinois season ended.

Grange was also immediately offered his first movie contract for $300,000; the first of many. He provided his name for testimonials at the rate of $12,000 for a particular sweater; $10,000 for a football doll with red hair; $5,000 for shoes; $5,000 for a brand of ginger ale; $2,000 for a cap, and, even though he didn't smoke, $1,000 for a tobacco company. It was just the start for what would follow.

It was, of course, The Era of Wonderful Nonsense, as social historians later termed it. It was also Sport's Golden Era. It was not a day like all days because football has produced only one player who was cloaked in an aura of drama, color, hero worship and legend, and who was able to match it all with commensurate ability. There was, indeed, only one Red Grange.

A Fabulous Career In Capsule Form

OPPONENT	TOUCH-DOWNS	MINUTES PLAYED	YARDS GAINED	PASSES AND YARDS
SEASON OF 1923				
Nebraska	3	39	208	
Iowa	1	60	175	
Butler	2	28	142	
Northwestern	3	19	251	
Chicago	1	59	160	
Wisconsin	1	30	140	
Ohio State	1	60	184	
	12	295	1260	

Number 77 made its last appearance on an Illinois football jersey at the Ohio State game in 1925. Illinois retired Grange's number and placed his jersey on display as an inspiration to all its athletes.

OPPONENT	TOUCH-DOWNS	MINUTES PLAYED	YARDS GAINED	PASSES AND YARDS
SEASON OF 1924				
Nebraska	0	60	116	6 for 116
Butler	2	16	104	2 for 30
Michigan	5	41	402	6 for 64
Iowa	2	45	186	3 for 98
Chicago	3	60	300	7 for 177
Minnesota	1	44	56	3 for 39
	13	266	1164	27 for 524
SEASON OF 1925				
Nebraska	0	51	49	1 for 18
Butler	2	41	185	2 for 22
Iowa	1	60	208	2 for 24
Michigan	0	60	122	....
Pennsylvania	3	57	363	1 for 13
Chicago	0	60	51	....
Ohio State	0	48	235	9 for 42
	6	377	1213	15 for 119

Grand Totals: Touchdowns—31; Yards Gained—3,637; Passes Completed—42 for 643 yards.

Single Game Feats: Most touchdowns—5 against Michigan, 1924; most yards gained—402 against Michigan, 1924; most passes completed—7 for 177 yards against Chicago, 1924; least yards gained—49 against Nebraska, 1925; longest run—95 yards with opening kick-off against Michigan, 1924.

(Note: Yards gained includes runs from scrimmage, and return of punts and kick-offs.)

Summary of Grange's Touchdowns:

SEASON	YARDS	TYPE PLAY	OPPONENT
1923	66	Returned punt	Nebraska
"	5	End run	Nebraska
"	11	End run	Nebraska
"	3	Line plunge	Iowa
"	22	End run	Butler
"	7	Line plunge	Butler
"	90	Intercepted pass	Northwestern
"	35	Recovered blocked punt	Northwestern
"	15	End run	Northwestern
"	3	Line plunge	Chicago
"	26	End run	Wisconsin
"	34	Through center	Ohio State
1924	13	End run	Butler
"	48	End run	Butler
"	95	Returned opening kick off	Michigan
"	67	End run	Michigan
"	56	End run	Michigan
"	44	End run	Michigan
"	15	Through line	Michigan
"	11	Through line	Iowa
"	2	Through line	Iowa
"	4	Line plunge	Chicago
"	5	Line plunge	Chicago
"	88	End run	Chicago
"	10	End run	Minnesota
1925	60	Returned punt	Butler
"	10	End run	Butler
"	83	Returned opening kick off	Iowa
"	56	Through tackle	Pennsylvania
"	13	Through tackle	Pennsylvania
"	20	End run	Pennsylvania

JIM McMILLEN was the first guard to gain national fame as a leader of interference. Speedy, agile and tough, McMillen made All-America in 1923 with his superlative blocking for Red Grange at Illinois.

(It also had, in Jim McMillen, the first great guard to attain national prominence for the kind of interference he and fullback Earl Britton a year later ran for Grange.)

Grange, of course, was a unanimous All-American, and the selectors also honored McMillen. Other Conference stars on the honor team were Michigan's marvelous center, Jack Blott; Earl Martineau, Minnesota's swift halfback; and Martin Below, versatile Wisconsin end.

Meanwhile, it was not a Big Ten season without controversy, as the closest thing to an absolute riot erupted over the Michigan-Wisconsin game at Madison. The Badgers, consigned to mediocrity that year, were trying to pull off the impossible and salvage their season by topping high-flying Michigan —and could have done so, 3-0, on a field goal, but fate and "the biggest robbery ever pulled off in Madison, Wisconsin," prevented it.

The highly-respected Walter Eckersall was referee that day, but the violently disputed decision made on a play that snatched victory from defeat for Michigan, was handed down by Colonel Mumma, the field judge, who had been in position to see it. Wisconsin had punted, and Tod Rockwell, Michigan's clever quarterback and safety man, tucked in the ball and ran it back about 20 yards

EARL MARTINEAU, Minnesota's brilliant halfback, was an outstanding choice for the 1923 All-America.

We came back through Chicago in the late evening and when the two "elder statesmen" athletes, Halas and Rundquist, who were both from Chicago, found out that this was my first trip to the great city, they insisted on showing me a little night life. They took me to a famous old tavern, the "Marx Beer Tunnel." The highlight of the evening was to see and meet Jim Jefferies the ex-heavyweight champion. For a country boy, I was really getting around.

The small measure of success I'd had as a freshman in winning two freshman numerals had caused me to get a tremendous rush by several fraternities on campus. I finally decided on Delta Upsilon. Many unkind things had been said through the years about fraternities but from my own experience I know that I owe a great deal more to my fraternity than I can ever pay back. They knocked a lot of the rough, rural edges off me, kept me at my studies and gave me a lot of encouragement when the going was tough.

Illinois was a very friendly university. The enrollment was around 6,000 students at that time but everyone spoke to you and I made many friends. I was doing fairly well in my studies except for chemistry, and this was a must if I was to stay eligible for next year. World War One had broken out and while the United States had not entered the war, all the agricultural schools in the United States were asked to let their students go up to Canada to help with the spring wheat. I was elated to find out they would give us our grades as of March 1st, if we had passing grades in the various subjects. That got me through chemistry! I was elected to go with the group and they sent us by train up to Regina, Saskatchewan. They were in the midst of a live stock show there and I entered and won a live stock judging contest for college

before being dumped by two Wisconsin tacklers near the sidelines at midfield. Rockwell was on the ground for several seconds before he got up casually with the ball, walked nonchalantly out of a group of players who had come up, then suddenly turned and madly dashed 50 yards to the Wisconsin goal while everyone watched him with stupefication.

The official judgment was that Eckersall had not blown his whistle, and Mumma declared the forward progress of the ball had not been stopped while the Wisconsin tacklers had Rockwell in their grasp. Technically, if true, it was a touchdown. Coach Jack Ryan, the Badger bench, and more than 20,000 rooters at Camp Randall Field went into a mass seizure. Eckie stood rock-like, arms folded and steadfastly refused to reverse the decision. The ruling held and Michigan went off the field with a 6-3 win which preserved its tie for the Conference crown. Eckersall went off the field surrounded by a protective ring of Wisconsin football players who in a display of fine sportsmanship, were the only thing that saved Eckie from immediate and complete dismemberment.

Eckersall also had the last word on the subject. He was not only the referee but as the eminent Chicago *Tribune* football writer he defended his decision in print over and over again.

The 1923 season saw the introduction of a new nickname for Northwestern sports teams. Up until then they were referred to as the "Fighting Methodists" or The Purple, but Wallace Abbey, a Northwestern graduate who was writing for the Chicago *Tribune*, covered the Chicago-Northwestern game in which the Maroon was a least a three touchdown favorite. It took a field goal in the last three minutes to give Chicago a 3-0 win as a ferocious Northwestern defense evoked from Abbey the observation that ". . . Wildcats would be a name better suited to Coach Thistlethwaite's boys . . . The (Chicago) eleven that had tied Illinois a week before was unable to score for 57 minutes . . . stopped dead by a

ERIC WILSON

Big Ten stars who shone in the 1923 NCAA track tourney included ERIC WILSON, and CHARLES BROOKINS of Iowa. Wilson who had won the 220 as a sophomore, came back as a repeater in his senior year. Brookins was a two-time champ in the 220-low hurdles in 1922-23. Both were on the U.S. Olympic team in 1924 and Wilson later became sports publicity director at his Alma Mater.

CHARLES BROOKINS

students, and then found myself a little later helping a young farmer put in his wheat. After the wheat was put in, it was a custom for all the ranchers and farmers to come down for a baseball game. At the first game I attended, the local pitcher was knocked all over the field and I told my boss I knew I could do better than that, so he talked to the manager. I was put in the box and won the game. Next thing I knew, I was playing all over Canada, including such romantic-sounding places as Saskatoon, Medicine Hat, and others I had read about.

When I returned to Illinois for my sophomore year I went out for football, of course, but I didn't do too well although I got into a few games. When football was over I immediately reported for basketball and made the varsity as a center; but, in the middle of the season I suffered another injury—a torn semi-lunar cartilage in my knee. It was serious enough to look as though it

would ruin my athletic career and I'd be back to farming, yet. The team doctor didn't think the knee could be mended.

I'd heard of a doctor in Chicago named Porter who had had unusual success in knee operations even though they were rarely tried in those days, and I asked Mr. Huff if the school would send me to see him. Huff said he didn't think they could because it might might make me a permanant cripple—and besides, it was too expensive. (What a far cry from today when no expense is too much to repair an athletic injury at any Big Ten school even if the boy never competes again.)

I went home and talked it over with my Dad and he urged me to see the doctor, anyway. I was pretty well crippled up as it was and I thought I may as well take the chance. Dr. Porter looked my knee over and said he was sure an operation would be successful. This type

Purple wall of Wildcats." Beginning with the following season all Northwestern teams were referred to as "Wildcats."

Iowa gained the basketball heights for the first time in 1923, but shared the Big Ten title with Wisconsin with 11-1 marks. The Hawkeyes' Funk led the league scorers and Gus Tebell and Rollie Williams of Wisconsin provided the best brace of guards in the midwest.

It was another big year in track for the Big Ten with Michigan dethroning Illinois in both the indoor and outdoor meets—the latter being decided by the closest margin ever posted: 57½ to 57. In the NCAA meet, Conference athletes dominated the festival with Michigan taking the team title and five individual titles going to Big Ten performers. Jim Brooks, the Wolverines' pole vaulter was joined by a versatile sophomore teammate who was destined to become one of the great names in Michigan track history: William DeHart Hubbard, who won the broad jump crown. Iowa's Charles Brookins repeated as low hurdle champ and Eric Wilson, who had won the 220 as a sophomore two years pre-

HARRY FRIEDA, Chicago javelin thrower, was one of the Big Ten's early national champions, winning the 1923 NCAA title, and later representing the U.S. in the 1924 Olympics.

viously, came back as a senior to do it again, and Harry Frieda of Chicago took the javelin throw.

Noteworthy on the administrative front was Conference legislation which raised the limit on football games from seven to eight a season, giving the lodge members more of a chance to spread the gospel of Big Ten greatness among non-believers in other areas.

No one quite realized it at the time, but 1924 marked the beginning of the final chapter of one of the great American sports stories—the story of Amos Alonzo Stagg and the magnificent Maroon teams in all sports. In fact, the 1924 football season produced the last major team title Chicago would win when Stagg led Chicago to an undefeated Conference season that included three ties. One of the deadlocks was an epic 21-21 affair with Illinois which subsequently enabled the Maroon to take the title when the Illini inexplicably dropped a late season game to Minnesota. The Maroon-Illini game was a classic bludgeon vs. rapier affair, with Austin (Five-Yards) McCarty, the colossal Chicago line-buster running over the Illini and the elusive Red Grange running through and around the Maroon. (The Redhead scored all three of his team's TD's.)

It was an epic event three weeks earlier, however, that immortalized Red Grange forever in the lore of collegiate football. It was the dedication game for Illinois' magnificent new stadium and elaborate ceremonies had been scheduled. Nothing was more elaborate than the performance by Grange which since then has been called the most fantastic one-game effort in the history of the college sport. In the first 10 minutes—the first four times he touched the ball—The Redhead streaked for touchdown runs of 95, 66, 55, and 40 yards. He went to the bench before the quarter was over. Zuppke put him back in shortly before the half ended, and then in the third period Grange zipped 15 yards for his fifth touchdown. In the final quarter he threw a pass for

1924

of operation was so revolutionary then that he performed it before an intrigued audience of 200 doctors and surgeons, and it was one of the first knee operations of a kind which is so commonplace today.

Following the operation he put on a heavy cast from my hip to my ankle and told me I'd have to wear it for two months.

This ended my athletic competition for the time being, but not entirely. Just before the cast was to come off, there was a track meet between Illinois and Notre Dame —and something happened at that meet which came close to affecting an important area of American sports. The javelin throw was being introduced that day for the first time. Since it was a new event none of the tosses by either the Notre Dame or Illinois entries was very impressive. Nobody was quite sure how the long, steel-tipped spear should be thrown.

Watching them I turned to a couple of fraternity brothers with me and snorted, "I think I could toss that thing farther than those guys even with this cast on my leg!"

I took an awful needling from them in the next two minutes and one word led to another. All the words led us over to where an unused javelin was lying on the ground. I picked it up, balancing it awkwardly in my hand and put it down again. They asked me why I didn't throw it and I nodded toward a group of coaches standing downfield and said I was afraid of hitting them. My pals groaned in derision. The men were standing far beyond the farthest effort of any of the contestants. Finally, I had no choice but to try to match my muscle with my arrogance. I hefted the javelin again, hobbled a couple of steps on my gimpy, cast-enclosed leg and let fly. The javelin soared high in the air and started to

FRANKLIN GOWDY

JOE PONDELIK

Stagg's 1924 Chicago team was truly the last of the great Maroon clubs before de-emphasis set in, and, leading the Big Ten champs were two All-America linemen, FRANKLIN GOWDY, tackle; and JOE PONDELIK, guard. AUSTIN (FIVE-YARDS) McCARTY, a rampaging fullback, was barely nipped for All-America by Elmer Layden, of Notre Dame "Four Horsemen," fame.

AUSTIN (FIVE-YARDS) McCARTY

Illinois' sixth score. He had played 41 minutes, carried the ball 21 times for 402 yards and five touchdowns and completed six passes for 64 yards.

Illinois' rude setback by the Gophers came the week after the tie with Chicago. Early in the first quarter Grange swept right end for an Illinois score but thereafter it was all Minnesota as the Gopher line prevented the Illinois interference from springing Grange loose again. Led by Carl Lidberg and Clarence Schutte, the Gophers went on to score three touchdowns.

Grange, of course, with a career high of 13 touchdowns for the season, was again a unanimous All-America, with the Conference also contributing three great linemen to the honor team: Frank Gowdy and Joe Pondelik, Chicago tackle and guard; and Ed Slaughter, a guard from Michigan. This was the year too, that the Chicago *Tribune* established its annual Big Ten most-valuable player award. It was no contest—Red Grange all the way—for the inaugural trophy.

Chicago had also shared in the Big Ten basketball title that year—the last it would claim—deadlocked with Wisconsin and Illinois. George Spradling, Purdue's great three-sport star, who took the league scoring title, and Harry Kipke, Michigan's All-America gridder, received national prominence along with Marshall Diebold of Wisconsin. For Chicago, Harrison Barnes, was the Maroon leader, while Illinois was paced by Leland Stilwell, a star for three years, who much later became physician and surgeon to his Alma Mater's athletic teams.

Among other highlights of the Conference year were the feats of two great wrestlers—Ed (Killer) Temlin, of Wisconsin, and Perry Marter, of Ohio State. Temlin, at 145 pounds, was the first man to win three straight Conference mat crowns. Marter, an amazingly strong and fast welterweight, won Conference titles twice but the incredible part of his performance was the fact that, in winning 19 of 20 bouts over three years, he frequently wrestled out

come down from a perfect trajectory. Suddenly everyone realized, in horror, that it would carry right to where two of the coaches were standing with their backs turned to us. We all screamed in unison, and one of the coaches turned, startled, just as the steel-tipped javelin whistled within inches of his throat and buried itself in the ground.

Six inches to the right and my errant throw would have killed Knute Rockne of Notre Dame.

I was petrified when Rockne, the Irish track coach as well as football coach, yelled for me to come over. I hobbled over as quickly as I could, and I'll never forget his reaction. Instead of chewing me out for nearly skewering him, his first words were: "Son, how did you throw that stick?"

I started mumbling something about doing it naturally, the way I used to hurl cornstalks as spears on the farm

for fun, and maybe the motion I used on the javelin was just instinctive. Anyway, I demonstrated my grip and arm motion for Rockne, and our own coach said: "We've got a meet coming up next Saturday with Wisconsin and I want you to throw the javelin for us."

Well, even with the cast on my leg I came out for track the following Monday and won every dual meet javelin throw for the rest of the season. That year, 1918, the Conference meet was held at Chicago and, because World War One was still on, there was still another added event, never held before or since: the hand-grenade throw. The contestants threw an unfused grenade at a bull's-eye target and I was lucky enough to hit the bull's-eye five out of five times. A French general who was instructing doughboys in grenade-throwing at nearby Camp Grant astonished me greatly by proceeding to kiss me on both cheeks as he presented me with a

Basketball in the early 1920's was hazardous for player and spectator alike. Wisconsin's great teams under Dr. Walter Meanwell played in this "Old Red Gym," as the natives called it, where players frequently landed in the fans' laps a foot from the sidelines, and the ball frequently bounced into the hanging pressbox.

Leaders of 1922 tri-championship basketball teams: GEORGE SPRADLING, of Purdue, led the league in scoring as a sophomore; LELAND STILLWELL starred for Illinois for three years (later he became team physician to all Illini teams); and HARRISON BARNES, of Chicago, paced the Maroon to the last Big Ten cage title it would ever claim. Two years later, as a senior, Spradling would be named an All-America.

gold medal, no doubt wondering how soon he could get me to the trenches in France.

My training with Harry Gill, the track coach, was a tremendous experience. The tall, lanky Canadian talked very little but liked to ask a lot of questions. In my junior year he decided the javelins we were using could be greatly improved if they were made of hickory instead of spruce which all the javelins of that day were fashioned from. He wanted to know if we had any rail fences on our farm. What he needed was a stick of well-seasoned hickory. We had the fences, all right, and we drove down and picked out several rails. Out of these rails, which had been weathering and drying for years, Gill made a javelin, turning it out on a hand lathe and sandpapering it down to specified measurements. It was Harry Gill's ingenuity which proved to be my round-trip ticket to the Olympic Games at Antwerp a couple of

years later. It was also the start of the Gill Manufacturing Co., which went on to become a leading athletic equipment organization.

The United States was now in World War One and I tried to get into Officers Training School but was turned down because of my knee. The Air Force then rejected me for poor eyesight so it was back to college for me.

The Army medics must have known what they were doing, though, because my knee prevented me from playing much varsity football after that, but I continued with basketball where my luck held up a bit better, and I led the team in scoring and was elected captain for my senior year. In track we won the Conference championship and I won points in the shot-put, discus, hammer, and javelin. If it was hardware, I could manage it.

I was beginning to branch out in other directions, too, in a way that was to have as much benefit for me as

ED (KILLER) TEMLIN

Two of the finest wrestlers yet to appear in the Conference: Ohio State's PERRY MARTER, shown here in a training match with a teammate, although a natural welterweight he frequently went out of his class to take on light-heavies and heavyweights. He won 19 of 20 bouts in three years (1922-23-24), and captured two league crowns as a welter. ED (KILLER) TEMLIN, of Wisconsin, a 145-pounder, was the first man to win three straight mat crowns (1922-23-24).

of his class, taking on light heavyweights and heavyweights. The only time he lost was to a 175-pounder and wound up in a hospital, afterwards.

Dick Howell and Ralph Breyer, two of the greatest swimmers in early Big Ten tank history, between them broke every Big Ten and NCAA record from 40- to 440-yards with Breyer also taking the 100- and 200-meter NCAA titles and Howell the 400- and 1500-meter events. Northwestern had missed out on the Big Ten team title only three times since 1914, and Tom Robinson, coach of the almost perennial Purple champions, tried in vain to arrange a dual meet with Yale, the customary Eastern ruler, but

the Boola Boolas somehow never seemed to have an opening on their schedule.

Michigan and Ohio State shared the 1924 baseball title and the Buckeyes for the first and only time in their history also took the cross-country championship, with H. R. Phelps, of Iowa, winning the individual crown for the second straight year. At Michigan State College, young John Kobs signed on as baseball coach to start a 35-year tenure that would be the longest in league annuals.

In the spring of 1924, what was possibly the finest crew in Wisconsin rowing history, stroked by Howie Johnson, was only half a boat-length from

had been gained from athletics. During my junior year a group of campus politicians came to me and asked me to run for the biggest student job on campus—President of the Student Union. I finally agreed to run but things didn't look too rosy. The fraternity political alignment seemed pretty well balanced away from the slate which my house was backing and it appeared that I'd take a sound drubbing. I talked it over with some of my professors. One, in particular, Lou Sarret, was a well-known poet and was in the department of public speaking. He'd taken an interest in me and had previously gotten me to take several public speaking courses. (At the time, I didn't see how this would help me communicate with livestock and chickens but his reply was you'd never know what kind of work you might get into after graduation. It might NOT be farming.)

He helped me analyze the campus political situation and come up with a startling suggestion, "Tug," he said, "why don't you spend all your efforts working on the BIG vote. Not the fraternities and sororities but the numerous rooming houses and the dormitories where the independent students live. No campus politician has ever paid any attention to them."

It was revolutionary, but it made good sense. For too many years campus elections had been managed and won by the Greek-letter houses. So I hit every rooming house on the campus, whether they had two students or twelve. I went to every dormitory. They always wanted to talk about sports, and I was more than willing, but I always managed to get across the idea I was running for office and would appreciate their support.

I was an easy winner, and I don't know who was more

HAROLD PHELPS, *distance star for Iowa track teams in the early twenties, won the individual cross-country crown two years in a row, 1923-24.*

Two of the brightest stars in early Big Ten swimming annals: RALPH BREYER, and DICK HOWELL, North-western freestylers. Between them they broke every Con-ference and NCAA mark from 40- to 440-yards. Breyer won the 100- and 200-meter NCAA titles and Howell took the 400- and 1500-meter crowns, in the 1924 tourney.

JOHN KOBS *took over as Michigan State baseball coach in 1924 and began a 35-year career that would be the longest in Big Ten history.*

surprised: the University administration; the fraternity-sorority aligned parties; the independent students; or Kenneth L. (Tug) Wilson.

My first experience as President of the Student Union was quite exciting. The freshmen who had patiently worn the green caps had a big celebration and burned them which symbolized that they were getting ready for upperclass work. To celebrate this momentous occasion they decided to raid the Orpheum Theatre and demand free tickets. The Orpheum manager at first refused them admission but after they had battered down a couple of doors, he opened all entrances for them.

Word in the meantime filtered out to the members of the sophomore class who decided that now they had the freshmen penned in and it would be a good time to haze them. Soon the entire theatre was surrounded by several

hundred vigorous upperclassmen clamoring to get in. I received a frantic call from Dean Clark asking me if I could help quiet the groups down, as he was fearful there might be a lot of damage and many people might get hurt. I got down there in a hurry and came in the back door where the manager escorted me to the stage. I told the freshmen class to sit quietly and they would not be disturbed until the show was through. I then went outside where they perched me on a big swinging door and pleaded with the upperclassmen to go back to the campus and if they wanted to do any hazing, they could catch the freshmen as they came through the park through which meandered a little stream called The Boneyard. This I told them would be a fitting place to meet the freshman.

Thank goodness it worked out perfectly. The scene of

129

victory at Poughkeepsie. A dead last at the half-way mark in the four-mile race, the Badgers put on a blazing sprint that all but caught the winning Washington shell at the wire.

Illinois, which for years was vying with Michigan for track supremacy, took both indoor and outdoor crowns, but Conference stars were denied national glory when the NCAA decided not to hold a meet during an Olympic year.

It was, however, a highly respectable year for the Big Ten in Olympic competition as more than a dozen Conference stars represented Uncle Sam at Antwerp. Michigan's DeHart Hubbard won the broad jump. Harold Osborn, of Illinois, made Olympic history when he became the first man to win both an individual event (in this case the high jump) and the grueling decathlon. Ohio State's Harry Steel won the heavyweight wrestling crown; the Buckeyes' George (Phin) Guthrie, took third in the high hurdles; and Michigan's Jim Brooker took third in the pole vault. Other Conference stars who participated but who weren't medal winners, were: Chan Coulter and Charles Brookins, 400-meter hurdles, from Iowa, along with Hawkeye teammates Eric Wilson and Harold Phelps in the 400- and 5000-meter events; Ralph Breyer and Dick Howell, 400-meter and 1500-meter swimmers from Northwestern; Bryan Himes, Northwestern wrestler at 125 pounds; Minnesota's first Olympian, Karl Anderson, in the hurdles; Ohio State's Perry Marter, who wrestled as a welterweight, and Buckeye Russ Payne, who ran the 3000-meter steeplechase.

1925

Although Michigan took the Big Ten football title in 1925 with a single loss for the season, the lone setback will go down in Conference history as one of the most dramatic games ever played. More than 75,000 fans had bought tickets for the Wolverines' games with Northwestern at Soldier's Field in Chicago, but it had rained so hard all morning there was consideration given to cancelling or postponing. With 40,000 sodden spectators actually

DeHART HUBBARD

Three Big Ten stars won gold medals for the U.S. in the 1924 Olympics. DeHART HUBBARD, Michigan's great broad-jumper, won with 24-5 and 1/4. (The following year he would set a world record of 25-10 and 7/8.) HAROLD OSBORNE, of Illinois, became the first man in Olympic history to win both an individual event (the high jump with 6-6) and the grueling decathlon. HARRY STEEL, of Ohio State, captured the heavyweight wrestling crown.

HAROLD OSBORNE   HARRY STEEL

combat was changed from a crowded theatre to the park, and outside of a lot of freshmen getting ducked into the stream, there was little damage. Many, many times I would run into Illinois Alumni all over the world, and they would tell me that this was the first time they ever met me and we would have a good laugh about the whole affair. Dean Clark appreciated my help in this adventure very much as did Dr. David Kinley, President of the University.

Life suddenly took on an added dimension for me, apart from sports and farming. As president of the Student Union I was now part of various faculty meetings and made some fine friendships with men who impressed me very much, including Thomas Arkle Clark, the Dean of Men, a legendary figure on the Illinois campus. One of my responsibilities was to run the student dances, a delightful duty but time-consuming. On weekends we'd

have two large dances, one at College Hall and the other at the Men's Gym if there were no athletic events taking place. I had to make all arrangements, including the dance bands, the program and the chaperones among other things. Previously, two couples had been hired for the entire year as chaperones for all dances but I changed this. I began hiring my own professors and their wives. I was also able to get a lovely orchid corsage from the horticulture department for $1.50 each, and some of the faculty wives, whose husbands were earning small salaries, thanked me with tears in their eyes because it was the first orchid they'd ever received. It was surprising how this raised their feminine morale—along with some of my college grades!

Much to everyone's surprise, for the first time in history, the Student Union instead of losing money on its dances, wound up $4000 in the black at the end of the year.

RALPH (MOON) BAKER

LELAND (TINY) LEWIS

The first Northwestern team to go through a Big Ten campaign undefeated hit the headlines in 1926, with only a last-minute 6-0 defeat by Notre Dame marring what could have been a national championship season. There were stars galore, including All-America back RALPH (MOON) BAKER; All-America tackle, BOB JOHNSON; fullback TINY LEWIS, and end WALDO FISHER. Fisher was one of a comparative handful who won All-Big Ten honors in both football and basketball.

WALDO FISHER

BOB JOHNSON

showing up, however, it was decided to go on with the game, even though the field was an absolute sea of mud, and the rain showed no sign of stopping.

Early in the first quarter, Michigan quarterback, Benny Friedman, misjudged a punt in the slanting sheets of water and fumbled the ball. Northwestern fell on it on the Michigan five-yard line. Three plays later, after Leland (Tiny) Lewis had been stopped for no gain, the big Northwestern fullback booted a field goal.

Thereafter, the game was strictly a kicking duel as neither team found it possible in the gooey mire to put more than two first downs back-to-back. In

the fourth quarter Michigan finally drove to the Wildcat 10-yard line but failed to keep the drive going. Northwestern took over, but a roaring gale was blowing torrents of water directly into the Wildcats' faces. Fate, as well as the wind, would have decreed it a perfect spot for a blocked punt. Captain Tim Lowry and quarterback Bill Christmann made a hasty decision which they communicated to Tiny Lewis who stood on the goal line in punt formation. Lewis took the snap, stepped back over the goal line and downed the ball for an intentional safety. With more margin for error, now, Northwestern got off its free kick and held the Wolverines for the final few minutes. It was the

There were no ground rules and I wondered what to do with the money. Eventually, I was asked by the administration if I had any ideas. I did, indeed. I reported that the Union Building, an old brick building purchased from the YMCA, badly needed repairing, and that additions were needed for the permanent staff. Lloyd Morey, the university business manager and later president of the university, agreed with me and okayed the expenditures, complimenting me upon my success and for my ideas. When the repairs had been made, Mr. Morey said we should have a dedication ceremony. I represented the men and a lovely coed by the name of Dorothy Shade, who was junior class vice-president, represented the girls. She later was to become Mrs. Tug Wilson.

Later that Spring I was deflated a bit, however, when I was notified that because I'd taken so many courses

in public speaking I'd neglected my requirements in the agricultural college, and I'd have to go to summer school if I was going to graduate on time. This would have been a financial fiasco because I needed whatever money I could make from summer jobs, but, luckily, wheat and corn prices soared that year because of the War and my father was able to bail me out. I promised him I'd pay back every penny, and I did.

My preoccupation with public speaking soon paid off, as far as Illinois football fortunes were concerned. We were expected to have a good if not a championship team that fall (1919) but the dramatic word came through that Jack Crangle, our star fullback, was going to be declared ineligible. I learned a few facts and then went to George Huff, the athletic director. Crangle's faculty advisor, it seems, had given him a course for which he hadn't yet taken a pre-requisite, and

It had been a long time between All-Americans for Northwestern, from Alton Johnson, the first Purple pick in 1901, until 1925 when TIM LOWRY made up for the honor drought with a tremendous year as center and most-valuable-player in the Western Conference, to become a virtually unanimous pick as All-America pivot-man.

EARL BRITTON, Illinois' hard-hitting fullback and a great blocker for Red Grange in 1924-25, was one of the unsung Big Ten heroes.

only 3-2 score in the history of Big Ten football, and, for the losers, it wrecked a perfect season.

Yet, subsequently, Fielding Yost called this the greatest team he ever coached. "The majority of teams we played made fewer first downs against us than they scored touchdowns against other teams," said Yost wryly. "If you were even to count first downs against us as touchdowns we'd still have been winners!"

There was also less than a perfect season, elsewhere, where one had been expected. Illinois, with Grange and Britton still on hand, was hoping to regain the heights of the Redhead's sophomore year. A stubborn Nebraska team had other ideas and stopped Grange in the season opener for a 14-0 win, and Michigan, with the two fabulous Benny's together for the first time—Friedman and Oosterbaan—stopped him again and won on a field goal, 3-0. In fact, Grange, who had been injured earlier, was held in check for a third time that year when he failed to score in his career finale. Ohio Stadium was jammed for the occasion. Much was being made of the fact that Grange would duel with the Buckeyes' tremendous football-basketball-baseball star, Cookie Cunningham. Their first names were Harold; they wore the same number, 77; they were the respective captains closing out great careers; and Grange might have to turn Cunningham's end. Not only did Grange fail to out-slick Cunningham but he failed to score in his farewell appearance. He did, however, spark the Illini offense for a 13-7 victory.

Grange no longer had to prove himself, of course. The last doubts had been erased three weeks earlier on a gridiron ankle deep in mud, at Franklin Field, Philadelphia. Dubious Eastern critics, getting a first and only look at the Galloping Ghost from the Midlands, saw him slither through, around and past an entire Penn team time and again, and, expressly, for four touchdowns, in a dazzling exhibition of running that no one expected to see on a perfectly dry field, let alone the quagmire Grange had underfoot.

Crangle flunked. Mr. Huff studied the case and said that in all his years as athletic director he'd never asked a professor to change a grade. So I asked Mr. Huff if I could take the protest before the Senate Group of the University, comprised of all the department heads. It was the last court of appeal.

Huff was startled but said he'd arrange for my appearance at their monthly meeting if I thought I could go through with it. I was more nervous about this appearance than at any time during all my athletic competition, but I went in there and spoke heatedly but eloquently on the poor advisory system the students had to rely on. I further stated that too many advisors took the easy way out and assigned students to a class that was open, regardless of whether the subject was proper for the student's course or whether the student had the right preparation for it.

It raised several faculty eyebrows and set off quite a debate right in front of me. Quickly I managed to review Crangle's academic record which, while it would never qualify him for Phi Beta Kappa, was really quite creditable. I argued passionately for justice and understanding and heaven knows what else and after a while the "court" went into a huddle and voted to remove Jack's failing grade and make him eligible as he had enough credits without this course. I guess in my three years of football I never helped the team as much as I did that night. It might even be said that my action got us the Big Ten championship, which we did win in 1919 with Crangle's efforts playing a big part in the proceedings.

Certainly I didn't do too much for the team on the field and, in fact, wasn't even included in the traveling squad for the final game against Ohio State in Colum-

FIELDING "HURRY-UP" YOST

It was the summer of 1901 . . .

The train from the West had chugged into the depot at Ann Arbor, Michigan, and a tall, powerfully built man of about 26, stepped down and looked around. Nobody was there to greet him. Down the steps behind him came three youths who later admitted they wished they were back in Grants Pass, Oregon; San Francisco, and a sleepy village in Iowa.

The man was Fielding Harris Yost and he was the new football coach at the University of Michigan. The boy from Iowa was Dan McGugin. Later he would become the coach's brother-in-law. The boy from San Francisco was named Gregory, and implausibly called "Dad." The third boy, from Oregon, was a solidly-built six footer named Willie Heston. It is not important how Fielding Yost managed to talk them into accompanying him to a town they'd literally never heard of. The important thing was that they ultimately were to provide a robust part of the most successful football dynasty of all time—Fielding (Hurry-Up) Yost's fantastic Point-A-Minute teams of 1901-1905. The boy named Heston would score more than 100 touchdowns . . .

The arrival of Fielding Yost at Michigan put an end to the wandering of a restless pioneer who was looking

Fielding Yost when he arrived on the Michigan campus in 1901.

for a spot to sink a taproot. Football coaches at the turn of the century were hardly considered men of stature. Nobody enticed them away from other schools with sweeter contracts; and Cadillacs presented to a coach at half-time appreciation ceremonies were a long time coming. In 1900 the alumni weren't even thinking about oats for his horse.

Michigan had started playing football in the 1880's and wasn't doing exceptionally well at it. A winning season was a rarity, but President Angell got around to thinking that if the game was worth playing at all it was worth playing well. He'd heard about this young chap who was coaching successfully and simultaneously at four schools out West and figured a man like that could really do a job if he settled down in one spot and stayed a while.

Nobody was more willing to settle down than Fielding Yost. Born in Fairview, West Virginia, Yost first played football as a student at the University of West Virginia in 1894-95. He was a tackle, and such a hamhanded terror that Lafayette College decided to lure him away to help in its crusade against the University of Pennsylvania. Penn, with its crunching guards-back formation, was whomping everything in sight, including Lafayette, an Eastern power at the time. There was no transfer rule then, and Yost, the following season, immediately pulled on a Lafayette uniform. Almost single-handedly he demolished the Quakers' attack and Lafayette scored the biggest upset of the Eastern season.

Yost stayed on at Lafayette to take a law degree but couldn't develop enough desire to make a living that way. He decided his happiness lay in football and, when he graduated in 1897, he set out looking for a coaching job. A friend invited him to meet a professor at Ohio State who was influential in hiring Buckeye football coaches. Yost met with the professor and, using chairs, a sofa, and the horrified faculty member as movable props, proceeded to demonstrate how he smashed Penn's guards-back formation.

"Get this madman out of here!" the professor gasped to the man who'd invited Yost.

Yost clamped his hat on his head, shrugged, and journeyed 17 miles further up the road where he had better luck convincing Ohio Wesleyan of his talents. Yost coached Wesleyan in 1897 then moved on to the University of Nebraska. A year later he went to Kansas, and after one season leaped all the way out to Stanford.

When he got to California for the season of 1900 he found himself coaching not one team but four. At 10:00 a.m. he tutored the local high school squad; at 2:00 the Stanford freshman; at 4:00 the Stanford varsity; and after supper he coached the nearby San Jose State Teachers College eleven. Significantly, every year from 1897 through 1900 his teams were league champions. "San Jose didn't pay me," Yost later reflected good-naturedly, "but I got something out of it anyway. That's where I met a kid named Heston, and when I went to Michigan he decided to come along with me."

At his first practice at Ann Arbor, Yost appeared in his black Lafayette sweater and battered felt hat perched precariously on the back of his head. That very first day provided a clue to how he'd managed to coach four football teams in one season. Yost was in perpetual motion around the practice field, constantly clapping his hands and shouting: "Hurry-up . . . Speed it up . . . Let's hurry, now . . . Hurry-up, there! If you can't hurry, make way for someone who can . . . !"

The famous nickname, "Hurry-Up" Yost was born. It was part and parcel of the man's philosophy and the legendary results he obtained during the next 27 years.

Although football was still in its Neanderthal stage when Fielding Yost arrived at Michigan, the big West Virginian had some ideas which are very much in evidence today. The forward pass was yet to come into the game, and raw, straight-ahead power was nine-tenths of football. Yost, however, insisted that speed, agility and surprise were more valuable than slow-moving beef, and designed his Michigan attack accordingly.

On Yost's practice field in those early years, anyone who was stationary for three seconds was positively loitering. His drill sessions were models of organization and efficiency, and he was still young enough—and tough enough—to show his boys how to block and tackle . . . And he never wore the rudimentary pads of the period in demonstrating his techniques.

In 25 years as Michigan's head coach, Yost won 164 games, lost only 29 and tied 10. His Wolverines ran up 6305 points to 894. He produced 21 All-Americans, more than thirty All-Conference players, eight undefeated teams, seven Big Ten champions, and his 1901 team played in the first Rose Bowl game, smashing Stanford, 49-0. (A few years later Yost admitted he allowed the game to be shortened by almost 10 minutes because Stanford was utterly exhausted.) His Big Ten title record undoubtedly would have been more impressive, but in 1907 Michigan dropped out of the Conference because of a schedule squabble, and didn't return until 1917.

As soon as the forward pass was legalized in 1906, Yost was the first to devise a method of spiraling the ball. Until Yost discovered you could get more speed, distance and accuracy with the spiral, the forward pass was nothing more than a clumsy, end-over-end basket push. Soon there were two theories on the use of the pass. (1) It was sheer folly and shouldn't be used at all. (2) It should be used as often as possible without regard to strategy. Yost was the first proponent of the pass as a weapon of surprise to keep the defense off-balance.

One forward pass always rankled Fielding Yost in those early days. Using it against Penn, at Philadelphia in 1911, when he needed a long-gainer, Yost startled 15,000 people by spreading his linemen all across the field. Penn's defenders went into a crazy-legged dither when the ball was snapped, trying to cover. There were two Wolverine passes behind the line and then, suddenly, the Michigan quarterback flipped the ball downfield to a halfback who scampered for the touchdown. Penn screamed frantically, claiming the whole nightmare was illegal, but didn't seem to know exactly why. The bemused officials finally upheld the Quakers by claiming the ball hadn't been passed five yards outside center of the scrimmage line, as the rules required. Yost knew it was at least 10 yards outside of center but allowed the official to skin him of his touchdown because it was a matter of official judgment—albeit hastily reconstructed.

From that decision came the present custom of informing officials before a game of any unusual plays to be used.

The vision of Yost, himself, racing up and down the sidelines, arms flailing, a huge, black unlighted cigar clamped between his teeth, was a sight fans began to find colorfully familiar. Coaches accused him of calling every play from the sideline, certain that his gymnastics were camouflaged signals; but, his game soon influenced

Fielding Yost in the mid 20's when he produced what he termed his greatest team featuring Benny Friedman and Bennie Oosterbaan.

every coach in the Mid West and the East as well, where defense was the keynote of football philosophy. Yost's aggressively scornful assertion that "A good offense is the best durned defense there is!" changed the entire Eastern style of play. He was the first to use a man-in-motion as a decoy, and immediately a whole new concept of pigskin pyrotechnics was sparked by the Wolverine formation.

Many of his teams, and the talented players who performed for him, were among the greatest in collegiate football. The achievements of the Point-A-Minute crowd provided a rocketing impetus for future Wolverine glory. Under Yost, Michigan soon became the most intersectional-minded football club in America, playing several Eastern or Southern colleges year after year. (A situation that led to severance of Michigan's Big Ten membership for several years.)

Albert Benbrook, guard, 1909-10; Stanfield Wells, end, 1910; James Craig, an Olympic sprinter and halfback, 1913; and John Maulbetsch, an incredible 170-pound fullback, 1914, won approval of Walter Camp, the only man who dared pick All-American teams by himself, prior to World War One.

After the war, Yost, who had fallen on (what was for him) a few lean years, welcomed a stocky, thick-legged youngster named Harry Kipke who was soon hailed as nothing more than the greatest college punter (to date) of all time, and very likely deserved the honor. Kipke, Harry Vick, a center; Paul Gobel, an end; and Jack Blott, another center, were the chief aiders and abetters who gave Michigan three years (1921-22-23) in which Yost lost a total of one game. Then, in 1925, Yost turned out what he claimed was his greatest team—greater, even, than any of his Point-A-Minute clubs.

Losing only to Northwestern by a 3-2 baseball score, the 1925 Wolverines rolled up 227 points to their opponents' 3, sparked by Harry Hawkins, a speedy, thumping guard, and the famed combination of Benny Friedman and Bennie Oosterbaan. Friedman throwing and Oosterbaan receiving was undoubtedly the most effective aerial duo collegiate football, to that day, had ever witnessed.

Among other notable victories, Michigan swamped Navy that year, 54-0 and turned back Illinois in one of Red Grange's finest years.

All the while Yost was fashioning champions at Michigan during the early part of the 20th century, he invariably spent the off-season in Nashville, Tennessee, where he practiced law and became a bellwether in some of the South's biggest businesses. He promoted and developed a huge hydroelectric plant for the Tennessee Power Co., and became a director of many other corporations. In 1921, however, Michigan appointed him its first full-time Director of Athletics, in addition to his football coaching duties.

In that capacity, Fielding Yost became one of the first college athletic administrators to pioneer sports for all students in the university, instead of just for varsity squads. He demanded that the University and its Board of Regents erect a Field House that would take care of the individual physical education needs of the entire student body as well as indoor facilities for an intercollegiate program of 19 different sports. Yost said it might cost somewhere around $3,000,000 and state officials immediately branded him the nineteen-twenty-ish version of "some kind of a nut!" They said he'd get no such sum and no such building.

In 1928 Fielding Yost chomped sagely on his unlighted cigar in self-satisfaction as proud officials spouted flowery words of wisdom as they opened the Michigan Field House. It was just as Yost had envisioned it, except that it cost a million more than he'd requested. Nowhere in America at the time was there such a college sports building and it became the prototype for many which followed.

Yost retired as football coach in 1929 and from the Athletic Directorship in 1941. Both he and Michigan had come a long way since that garrulous voice had barked out over wind-swept Ferry Field: "Hurry-up! Hurry-up . . . If you can't hurry-up make way for somebody who will!"

Representing a combined total of almost 50 years of coaching brilliance, Fielding Yost and Amos Alonzo Stagg met at Michigan when their schools clashed in a dual athletic meet.

bus. I simply had to get over there, though, and talked to Dean Clark about it. With a twinkle in his eye he came up with the wildest gimmick that any administrator ever created. He suggested that it'd be a good idea if the head of the Illinois Student Union would go over to Columbus and inspect the Ohio State Student Union on an official basis. "I think you've earned it for the work you've done here," the Dean said, and then staggered me by adding: "And I think you ought to take along that coed who helped you dedicate our building—what's her name—Dorothy Shade . . .?"

I knew her name, all right. She was thrilled to go, and was properly chaperoned by Mrs. Bob Zuppke, the wife of our coach, and other ladies in the official party.

It was on this trip that one of the most amazing incidents I'd ever witnessed unfolded itself the night before the game, but to understand it better you'd have to know

the background. The setting for the game was just short of fantastic. Ohio State had won two straight Big Ten titles in 1916-17 before the somewhat unofficial wartime season of 1918, and now were favored to make it three under their brilliant young coach, Dr. Jack Wilce, and led by their super-star, Chic Harley. Harley was quite probably the greatest running back the Conference had yet seen and was a unanimous All-American from his sophomore year on. Now, in this third year, Ohio State had yet to lose a game in his three seasons of play, and were favored over the Illini even though such stars as Bert Ingwerson, Dutch Sternaman, Ralph and Bob Fletcher, and Chuck Carney, made it one of Zuppke's finest clubs.

It was Harley's last game of his fabulous career, and with the Buckeyes trying to make it three big undefeated seasons, there was tremendous interest in the game. On

In regard to playing under adverse conditions, however, the prize for the year would have to go to Iowa and Wisconsin who, early in November, met in a snowstorm that obliterated the sidelines and every yard-line stripe. The score of the game may not have gone down in history (a 6-0 win for Wisconsin) but another item did. Thirty four fumbles were listed, with eighteen coming in the first quarter alone.

It was an Iowa team, incidentally, that rostered Nicholas (Cowboy) Kutsch, a transfer from Trinity College in Sioux City. Kutsch, a demoniac, slashing runner, scored 50 points and ripped off 427 yards in Iowa's first three games, then was injured against Ohio State and was never in top form the rest of the season. He was to come back for his final year in 1926 and set two-year running records that no Big Ten performer has ever equalled.

Grange led a contingent of six Big Ten stars on the All-America at season's end. Others were Bennie Oosterbaan, Michigan's great end, the first Wolverine sophomore to make it; Dick Romney, Iowa end; Harry Hawkins, Michigan guard; Ed Hess,

In an era when nicknames for sports stars were not only commonplace but somewhat corny and forced, an Iowa halfback was an exception. He was well-named. NICHOLAS KUTCH was called "Cowboy," and as Cowboy Kutsch he made the headlines come to life.

A transfer from little Trinity College in Sioux City, Kutsch was a 5-10, 178-pounder who, installed as a triple-threat in his first varsity game in 1925, ran with a wild, free-wheeling motion and hit with monstrous power for a man his size. In general, his reckless abandon and sheer love of contact had rarely been seen on a Conference football field.

In his first three games for Iowa he scored 50 points, smashed for 427 yards rushing and averaged 8 yards per carry. It was his third game which brought him he's-for-real prominence. The Hawkeyes were supposed to be a set-up for Illinois and Red Grange, with the Illini inclined to discount the rambunctious deeds of the Cowboy. When Grange returned the opening kickoff 89 yards for a touchdown the expected rout seemed to be on.

The Cowboy stampeded right down the Illini's throats, gained 144 yards rushing, kicked two 25-yard field goals and bulldozed across the goal in the final minute to score the winning touchdown in a 12-10 upset of the touted Orange and Blue, who, along with the rest of the league, suddenly became Believers.

Badly hurt in the first quarter against Ohio State the following week, Kutsch played only part time the rest of the season. The next year he came back as good as ever. In his two seasons he rushed for more than 1200 yards in 15 games, in three of which he saw only limited action because of injuries, and averaged 6 yards per carry. In 1926 he tore off 781 yards rushing. Five times in his two campaigns he smashed for 140 yards or more. No two-year performer had ever matched his marks. Although he made All-Big Ten, Iowa's mediocre record caused the selectors to pass him over for All-America. Those who had tried to lasso the Cowboy figured the selectors would have made poor range bosses.

---

the Monday preceding the game, a fraternity brother from the Ohio State chapter of Delta Upsilon arrived in Champaign-Urbana and visited our chapter house and asked to talk to us at our weekly Monday night meeting. He really amazed us. He informed us that the Ohio State DU's thought the Buckeyes were the greatest team ever to come down the Pike and solemnly proceeded to take out a roll of bills and count out $500 which he laid on table. This was what the Brothers from Columbus really thought of their team and did we have the same affection for Illinois . . .?

Well, we didn't have $500 but a quick trip up and down fraternity row netted us the money in a hurry. This experience, plus what I was to see when I arrived in Columbus, was to acquaint me with one of the great national dangers of college football in that era.

In Columbus, after depositing Miss Shade at a sorority

Kenneth L. (Tug) Wilson as Illinois basketball captain in 1920.

Ohio State guard, and Tim Lowry, the marvelous Northwestern center who also was named the most valuable player in the Conference.

The basketball season of 1925 had seen a breakthrough for Ohio State as the Buckeyes, led by Cookie Cunningham at center, and Captain Johnny Miner, at forward, took their first Conference crown. Miner, who was only 5 feet 8, was probably the shortest man ever to capture the league scoring title, and was given All-America honors along with Wisconsin guard, Marshall Diebold.

Michigan took both the indoor and outdoor track titles, and Wolverine performers were particularly outstanding in the revival of the NCAA meet which never again would be given a hiatus during an Olympic season. DeHart Hubbard closed out his remarkable three-year career by becoming the first Big Ten athlete to be an NCAA double winner when he took the 100-yard dash and broad jump, setting a record in the latter of 25 feet, 10-⅞ inches. Another Wolverine, Philip Northrop, was practically

JOHNNY MINER, a speedy, 5-8 sharp-shooting All-America and big HAROLD (COOKIE) CUNNINGHAM sparked Ohio State to its first Big Ten basketball title in 1925. Cunningham, one of the greatest three-sport stars in Conference history, also starred in football and baseball. He was All-Big Ten on the gridiron as an end, on the hardwood, as a center, and on the diamond as a hard-hitting first sacker.

ED HESS, a rugged 190-pound guard, was a two-time All-America guard for Ohio State in 1925-26.

house, I took a cab back to the Deshler-Wallick Hotel. I saw things there that I'd never even dreamed about. Right in the lobby of that famous hotel was a big table where bets of thousands of dollars were being made. There were several policemen hovering around and I asked one of them, half jokingly, what they were doing there and one of them told me, quite seriously, that they were on duty to protect the wagered money against hijacking.

Although just a student I felt tremendously troubled by what I'd witnessed, and I thought it significant when a vigorous campaign was initiated the following year to end this kind of blatant betting on college games. The campaign was led by four famous directors of athletics—George Huff, of Illinois; Amos Alonzo Stagg, of Chicago; Fielding Yost, of Michigan, and L.W. St. John, of Ohio State.

Meanwhile, Fraternity Row at Illinois became $500 richer because in the last seconds of play, Bobby Fletcher of Illinois, booted a field goal that gave the underdog Illini a tremendous upset victory over the Buckeyes, spoiling their bid for a third straight Big Ten Championship and inflicting the only defeat that Ohio's immortal Chic Harley ever knew in his three-year varsity career. I might add that Bob Fletcher had never kicked a field goal before in a varsity game.

That winter I got a good insight, personally, into the disappointment that can crop up in a collegiate athlete's life. I was captain and center of the Illinois basketball team but Chuck Carney, a sophomore who had been named All-America end in football, proved he was just as good on the basketball floor and took my position away from me. The only thing that gave me any solace was the fact that Carney immediately was recog-

137

JOHN FARICY was Minnesota's first great swimmer, and was the Gophers' first NCAA champion, taking the 200-yard breaststroke in 1925 after winning three straight Big Ten breaststroke crowns. He was undefeated in three years of college competition, set a world mark for the 100-yard event in 1922; broke it again the following year, and was a member of the U.S. Olympic team in 1924.

Dick Howell repeated in the NCAA meet, with Breyer winning the 100 freestyle and Howell the 220. Minnesota's John Faricy became the first Gopher athlete to win an NCCA crown in any sport when he took the 200-yard breaststroke.

Another historic development in 1925 was Indiana's first Conference championship in any sport when the Hoosiers took the Big Ten baseball flag. Butler University made off with the league tennis title and became the only outsider ever to do so. Among the scholar-athletes who won the Conference Medal that year were Harry Frieda, Chicago's Olympic javelin thrower; Larry Breyer, Northwestern's Olympic swimmer, and Lawrence M. Snyder, Ohio State track star, who, later, as Buckeye coach, would send a multitude of men to wear the United States Olympic uniform, and who would, himself, be a head Olympic coach.

Meanwhile, on the administrative front, the Big Ten directors rounded out the full slate of league championships by adding Conference tournaments in wrestling, fencing and gymnastics to replace the individual championships previously held.

At East Lansing in 1925, two changes were instituted that made people happy at Michigan Agricultural College. The name of the school was changed to Michigan State College, and team nicknames were switched from Aggies (and sometimes "Farmers") to Spartans. There was a resultant lifting of spirit which soon would directly lead to greater athletic glory. (Perhaps the spirit took its first wings the following year when a madcap cheerleader named Skinny Skellenger set off a wild celebration when the Spartan baseball team beat Michigan for the first victory over the Wolverines in 11 years. At game's end, with Skellenger serving as pace-setter, Michigan State students started a round of festivities by burning down the ancient center field bleachers. With this as a starter, Skinny led his buddies downtown where they torched up a few more fences and corner-lot bon-

in the same dual win category when he won the javelin throw and wound up in a five-way tie for the pole vault title. Other Conference winners were Ray Bunker, Ohio State hammer thrower; Justin Russell, of Chicago, who was in a three-way tie for the high jump crown; and Northwestern's Royal Bouschor who tied for the pole vault title.

Tom Robinson's Northwestern swimmers added another league championship to the Purple skein, which made it nine in 12 years. It would be the last one for some time, though, as a new aquatic power was being fashioned by a crusty Englishman named Matt Mann, at Michigan. For Northwestern, meanwhile, the fabulous duo of Ralph Breyer and

nized as the finest basketball player Illinois had ever had, and eventually he was to become the first Conference athlete to make All-America in both football and basketball. I was happy to get in enough games to make my letter.

Even while I was riding the bench, I was looking forward to the track season because the 1920 Olympic Games were coming up after having been cancelled in 1916 by World War One. There was a lot of excitement generated in the renewal scheduled for Antwerp, Belgium; and, somehow, I was nursing the thought that maybe I could make the U.S. team as a javelin thrower.

I did well enough that Spring to keep my crazy dreams alive but the problem was to get to the Olympic tryouts at Harvard Stadium, in Boston. Few universities in those days sent their athletes to Olympic tryouts, and if a boy

couldn't afford it he either stayed home or convinced a local A.A.U. organization or Athletic Club that he was good enough for them to pick up his traveling tab and maybe they would receive the glory of rostering an Olympian in return. Much to my relief I got such an invite from Martin Delaney, Athletic Director of the Chicago A.C., who said they'd see to it that I and a few others would represent the Chicago A.C. in the trials and would send us East.

When the Spring semester was over I went to Chicago, lived at the Club and trained under Delaney in both the discus and javelin. I was so confident I could make the Olympic team that I got my passport ahead of time and, embroidered with $20.00 for expenses, I made the trip to Boston. Then came near disaster. The day before the javelin trials I was stunned to learn that the international

fires before the cops decided to put the damper on the leader. When they finally cornered Skellenger he was perched atop a telephone pole with a basket of overage eggs, the kind of amunition which enabled him to remain king of the perch for quite a while.)

In 1926 the big story in the Big Ten could well be the emergence, finally, of Northwestern as a national football power. For the first time in their history, the Wildcats had an undefeated league season, with a lone loss outside the lodge handed to them, 6-0, by Notre Dame. It was a perfect combination of seasoned veterans and fired up sophomores which Coach Glen Thistlethwaite put together. The irrepressible Moon Baker and jarring Tiny Lewis headed the attack, while up front there was a great tackle in Bob Johnson; a versatile end in Waldo Fisher, and a couple of sophomores who fought their way into starting positions: tough, agile,

GLEN THISTLETHWAITE, Northwestern's football coach in the mid-Twenties, was distinguished on two counts: he brought the Wildcats to their finest football hour with two great teams in a row (1925-26) and he possessed the most misspelled name of any Conference coach, ever. With him is the great Ralph (Moon) Baker, All-America halfback in 1926. Another All-America from that club was Bob Johnson, a stonewall defensive star, at tackle.

rules had changed the throwing style for the event. For more than two years I'd been holding it at the end, or close to it, but now I found out the stick had to be grasped at the middle. Later I discovered that the AAU had been given this information but had neglected to pass it along to everyone. I had just two days to get ready for this change.

Then, as if things weren't tough enough, I got into a battle with the meet officials who had never seen a homemade, handmade javelin whose ancestor had been a hickory fence rail on an Illinois farm. They simply wanted to throw it out, and if Martin Delaney hadn't proved it met all specifications I'd have had to compete with something which really would have felt strange in my hand. By the time the event was called I felt I'd already been through a wringer. When my turn came

Tug Wilson throwing javelin for Illinois just before Olympic trials.

Justin Dart, at tackle, and big, strong Luke Johnsos, at end. (Both would be heard from later: Dart as president of the Rexall Drug chain, and Johnsos as a pro star and coach.) Another soph who couldn't be kept out of the backfield was a great runner named Walt Holmer.

It was an aggregation that all but blew its opposition off the field. Only three touchdowns were scored against the Purple that year, but it was the one put over by Notre Dame that was the costliest. The year before, the Irish with a national championship team featuring the immortal Four Horsemen, almost had their perfect season spoiled by the Wildcats. Moon Baker had booted two drop-kick field goals in the first half—from the 34 and 36—to give Northwestern a 6-0 lead at halftime, and it took a big second half comeback for the Irish to pull it out—the winning score coming on a pass interception by Elmer Layden who ran it back for the TD that gave Notre Dame the 13-6 win. Thus, the 1926 contest held a lot of previous memories and inspiration for both clubs.

The sturdy Purple line headed by Bob Johnson, time and again stopped Christy Flannagan, the Irish All-America fullback, and it looked like a scoreless tie would go into the books. Finally, late in the fourth quarter, Art Parisien, the Irish quarterback, caught the Purple secondary off-guard when he tossed a left-handed pass to John Niemic for the game's lone touchdown.

Meanwhile, in an unusual situation never again repeated in the Big Ten, Minnesota and Michigan wound up playing each other twice in 1926. In those days there were no precise league rulings on the number of games a team had to play, and Minnesota had been having difficulty lining up as many as four Big Ten contests. Under Dr. Clarence Spears, Viking football was rough and rugged and, although clean, the Gophers couldn't convince too many of the lodge brethren that a game wouldn't be less than a Saturday afternoon social.

As a final solution, Fielding Yost, of Michigan, agreed to take on the Gophers twice in a home-and-home arrangement. The first was played at Ann Arbor, and so high was the feeling at Minneapolis that two scrub teams re-acted each play at Ann Arbor as it was telegraphed to the Gopher stadium. Proceeds from the fans were donated to the Walter Camp Memorial being erected at Yale.

In the second game, at Minneapolis, the Gophers took a 6-0 lead into the fourth quarter only to see Bennie Oosterbaan the brilliant Wolverine All-America end, scoop up a Gopher fumble and run 55 yards for a touchdown. It was only natural for the other Bennie (Friedman) in the famed Wolverine combination, to boot the extra point for a Michigan victory.

Although Northwestern shared the league title with Michigan in 1926, it took an epic 17-16 victory over Ohio State to bring it off for the Wolverines. Ohio Stadium, at the time, seated only 65,000 but, unofficially, more than 90,000 were inside the huge horseshoe with thousands of fans having literally stormed and climbed over the huge iron gates to pack the aisles for what everyone figured would be a bloodletting. Nobody was disappointed. Both teams scored two touchdowns and a field goal. Benny Friedman place-kicked the Wolverine three-pointer from the 47-yard line just a minute before the half ended to tie it up at 10-10, after Meyers Clark had previously booted a goal for Ohio. Michigan scored its second touchdown in the third quarter after Elmer Marek, brilliant Ohio halfback, had fumbled a punt deep in Buckeye territory with Michigan recovering and going in for the TD.

In the final quarter, with just a few minutes to play, Ohio scored again to make it 17-16. The agonized expectancy of the 90,000 fans was truly a physical thing as Clark, a magnificent quarterback all afternoon, stepped into the snap-back from center for the boot that would have added the game-tying extra point—and missed.

---

to throw I was so anxious I stepped over the toe board and fouled. My second throw was woefully short, and finally I heard my name called for the third and last time.

This was it. A lot of things went through my head. I thought of my family back home, and the hopes they'd had for me. I thought of the time and effort put into me by Coach Harry Gill at Illinois and Martin Delaney at the Chicago A.C. I even thought of the hickory fence rail we'd liberated from the farm.

My third throw turned out to be the best I'd ever made in competition, and when I saw it sail out past the flag marking the best previous throw of the day I knew I'd made the Olympic team. It was one of the greatest thrills in my career in sports.

The next day we were taken to Travers Island in New York where we were to train until it was time to sail for Antwerp. Everything was in a terrible state of confusion. The AAU had had difficulty in raising funds and securing transportation. There was still a lack of space on ocean-going vessels because the war was only 18 months finished and there was still a lot of military and other official transport needed. Finally, in desperation, the Olympic Committee obtained a troop ship, the "Princess Matoika." It had just returned from Europe with more than 2000 bodies of U.S. dead, killed in France. The ship reeked of disinfectant. Team members slept in hammocks deep in the hold of the ship and this huge compartment was infested with the largest rats I'd ever seen. The eating facilities were so poor that the team had to be fed in three shifts. Since my name started with "W", I was always on the last shift and there wasn't always an abundance of food.

These were the conditions we had to put up with for

In sports there is always the temptation to debate the undebatable. Like, who was football's most famous collegiate forward passing combination? Was it Gus Dorais—Knute Rockne of Notre Dame? No; they came on big because of the publicity surrounding a single, dramatic Irish win over Army. Neither ever made All-America, as good as they were. Dixie Howell—Don Hutson of Alabama? Great, but again a one-year stint.

The vote here, and from most of the balloteers who saw them, has to go to Michigan's Benny Friedman and Bennie Oosterbaan, the only aerial combo in the history of college football who were named All-America two years in a row (1925-1926) and this criterion in itself is not all-important.

They were the super-stars and the super-charge of the team which the immortal Fielding H. ("Hurry-Up!") Yost called the greatest team he ever turned out. Enough evidence to stand on, right there.

The two Bennies almost never got together. The first Benny to arrived at Ann Arbor was Friedman. As a Cleveland prepper he'd first gone to East Tech High School, open to any boy in town, and which had a very successful coach named Sam Willaman. Friedman wanted to play for him. Willaman took a look and gently told the boy he didn't have it and suggested he go back to his regular neighborhood school, Glenville.

A week later Willaman saw the Glenville coach who told him he was trying the boy at quarterback. Willaman snorted, "He'll never get you past the line of scrimmage!"

Young Benny Friedman in 1922 got Glenville to the city championship and a date with Oak Park High School in Chicago, in a game billed as a national schoolboy title contest. Glenville won in a romp.

At Michigan the 5-10, 175-pounder with the raven hair and black eyes was a quiet kid who had a so-so freshman season and who, at the end of the semester, felt so lonely and socially out of things that he packed his trunk and was about to leave school and transfer to

In 1925 Bennie Oosterbaan joined Benny Friedman on the Wolverine varsity and collegiate football's most famous passing combo was born.

Dartmouth to join some Cleveland friends. An assistant Michigan coach heard about it just in time, unpacked the trunk, talked him into staying and steered him to some new social contacts.

Even so, things didn't seem to improve much for Friedman as a sophomore. The first two games in 1924 he rode the bench. Then Michigan visited Illinois to help dedicate the Illini's new stadium, and Red Grange had his Day of Days in running for four touchdowns the first four times he touched the ball. When Fielding Yost surveyed the ashes of his 39-14 defeat he knew he might as well start rebuilding, this time with a passing attack. He inserted the soph, Friedman, at quarterback, against Wisconsin. Friedman tossed two touchdown passes and the Wolverines were off on a five-game winning streak and Benny Friedman was launched on a fabulous career.

Meanwhile, Michigan coaches had begun to worry about a big frosh end who'd shown flashes of brilliance between bouts with a bad back. There was, indeed, cause for alarm . . .

In the early 1920's it was a rare thing for a high school boy to be so famous that newspapers headlined his choice of college, but the 6-2, 198-pound Dutch boy from Muskegon had simply been too much. When Bennie Oosterbaan announced he would attend Michigan, papers all over the midwest trumpeted his decision. He'd been a super-end in football; a basketball center who had led Muskegon to the finals of a national prep tournament in Chicago; a baseball pitcher, and a weightman in track. Yet, a tragedy almost took away the whole thing. An older brother, while starring at Muskegon, developed a blister on his foot. The blister became infected and the boy died of blood poisoning.

Bennie Oosterbaan's parents in their grief vowed their second son would give up athletics. Only a visit by a delegation of leading citizens and high school students subsequently got the Oosterbaans to change their minds and Bennie became the greatest schoolboy star in Michigan history.

At Ann Arbor, the back trouble which hit him as a frosh gridder worried him so much he passed up fresh-

Benny Friedman came off the bench in 1924 to launch a five-game winning streak for Michigan and another fabulous football era for Coach Fielding Yost.

Bennie Oosterbaan made All-America for 3 straight years and earned a total of 9 letters in football, basketball and baseball at Michigan.

man basketball. Wolverine coaches were sure they'd had it. Friedman, the rising young aerial wizard, would be returning as a junior and the thought of having the big, talented sophomore to throw to even had Old Man Yost drooling a bit.

Oosterbaan's back ailment disappeared almost as mysteriously as it had come and Michigan in 1925 featured the junior passer and the sophomore end who led the team Yost called his greatest ever. (It scored 227 points to three; actually tallied more touchdowns than the opposition got in first downs; and among its victories, beat Iowa 63-0; Michigan State 39-0; Navy 54-0; and Minnesota 35-0).

Most national observers called the Wolverines the best team in the land despite a 3-2 loss to Northwestern in the famous game at Soldiers Field, Chicago, played in a driving rainstorm of such intensity that it was almost postponed. The Wildcats kicked a wobbly field goal from up close and later took an automatic safety rather than chance a blocked punt within its own 5-yard line.

One high spot of the season was a 3-0 win over Red Grange's last Illinois team, on a field goal by Friedman, the best place-kicker in the country. "Grange carried more than 20 times that day and I swear it was for minus-yardage," Friedman recalls with a grin. "I think Bob Brown, our center, stopped him behind the line six times, and I even came up from my safety position three times to nail him at the line of scrimmage. He never went near Bennie Oosterbaan at end after the first quarter. And that was virtually the same Illinois team that devastated us 39-14 the year before!"

In remarking on the collaboration between the Passing Benny and the Catching Bennie, Friedman said: "It was the confidence we had in each other that made us so successful. Bennie would tell me exactly where he'd go and I knew he'd be there, and he knew I'd deliver the ball to that point. When we beat Ohio State, 17-16, for the title in 1926 Oosterbaan told me he'd go to the extreme corner of the end zone and I should put the ball to the outside of him and there'd be no way it could be stopped. It was a touchdown, of course. That Oosterbaan! What fluidity of motion he had! What sneaky speed and great hands! In another game where he was being closely guarded from behind he told me to throw the ball almost into the ground in front of him and he'd dive for it. He did—and got it." Incidentally, in that 17-16 affair with the Buckeyes it was a 45-yard field goal from near the sideline (the ball wasn't brought in 15 yards in those days) which tied it up 10-10 at the half and gave the Wolverines the locker-room lift they needed to go on and win.

Friedman, who could chuck the bulbous ball of the period either short or long, with a feathery touch, recalls that Yost borrowed P. T. Barnum's philosophy and applied it to football. "There's a sucker born every minute, Benny," he told me, "so don't be afraid to pass on first down."

"As a result," Friedman continued, "We were probably the first major college team to do this. It was not only revolutionary but downright heresy. Yost trusted Bennie and me. 'Get there fast,' Yost always said. 'Get touchdowns. First downs don't go up on the scoreboard.'"

(To fully appreciate the effectiveness of the Friedman-Oosterbaan passing combination you have to realize how new their impact on the game really was. The forward pass, legalized in 1906, had been part of football for only 19 years when they first got together!)

As a rule, Michigan got their TD's fast and in quantity;

the 13 days it took to sail to Belgium. I can only contemplate how differently a U.S. Olympic team travels these days, with the finest food and fastest jets. Meanwhile, virtually everyone on the team that summer of 1920 was seasick and digusted with the whole idea of competing if we had to approach it that way. When some of the competitors ventured into the first class accomodations and saw Olympic officials installed in lovely staterooms, and all that went with it, it nearly led to mutiny among the American athletes.

Many years later Mrs. Wilson and I were entertained at the Outrigger Canoe Club on Waikiki Beach in Honolulu. They showed me a copy of a letter of protest that the athletes of the 1920 Olympic Team had registered gainst the A.A.U. and Olympic Committee for the poor facilities we had been given on the trip and in

Antwerp. Along with all the other athletes was the signature of one K. L. Wilson. Apparently it did some good as we were sent back first class.

Things didn't improve much when we got to Antwerp and found we were to be quartered in a schoolhouse with about 30 athletes to a room, sleeping on cots. By this time, however, we were so thrilled by the impending Games that we overlooked everything that had happened and concentrated on putting out our best efforts. As I look back, it is interesting to note that the average age of our 1920 Olympians was much in excess of today's. There were few if any teenagers. Many athletes were in their mid-twenties and some were in their thirties and older, including two giant weightmen from the New York police force, Pat McDonald and Pat Ryan, who had competed in two earlier Olympiads before the war. I'll

Benny Friedman, Coach Fielding Yost and Bennie Oosterbaan leave the White House after visiting President Coolidge before traveling to Baltimore to challenge the Naval Academy.

but, Bennie Oosterbaan said his greatest thrill in football came on the lone touchdown the Wolves got in the last game of the 1926 season. Because of a scheduling controversy, Minnesota had been unable to fill a full Conference slate. Finally Yost got the Gophers off the hook by agreeing to play them twice that year. At Ann Arbor the Wolverines won handily, 20-0. The return was in Minneapolis a week after the emotion-packed 17-16 game with Ohio State and Michigan was still somewhat drained. Minnesota held a 6-0 lead at half-time and had piled up 12 first downs to Michigan's none. It looked hopeless.

The Gophers were on another drive in the fourth quarter and were deep in Michigan territory when a Minnesota back bobbled the snap from center. Oosterbaan, crashing in, scooped up the ball and raced almost 60 yards for a touchdown. Friedman calmly booted the point-after and the Wolverines had sewed up another title.

In 1925 both Bennies had been All-America. They repeated in 1926. Oosterbaan was judged the finest all-around end collegiate football had yet seen and Friedman was easily the smartest field general and most brilliant passer the sport had yet produced.

Friedman graduated, leaving Oosterbaan to finish out a third year as All-America and a nine-letter career in football, basketball and baseball. He also earned All-America honors in basketball. Friedman went on to become the first truly great professional quarterback, starring with the New York Giants, then went into coaching and later a business career. Oosterbaan, after graduation, remained at Michigan as an assistant coach, became head basketball coach, then head football coach and subsequently assistant athletic director. Bennie Oosterbaan never left the campus. From the time he appeared in the fall of 1924 as a freshman he stayed 42 consecutive years as player, coach and administrator, a record second only to that of George Huff, of Illinois, who put in two or three years more than that.

never forget Ryan. The athletes of all nations were to parade before King Albert of Belgium at the opening ceremonies. The American team was ranked in marching order with the tallest in the lead and naturally these two big Irishmen were in the front row. We'd been carefully briefed that as we passed the royal box there'd be a signal for eyes right and the removal of all hats.

We swung proudly past the royal box, all right, but everyone was horrified to see Pat Ryan striding by with his hat firmly anchored to his head. Later, when Pat was receiving his Gold Medal for the hammer throw, the King, who was a great sportsman, chided Pat about the "oversight" on the hat incident. Pat looked the King squarely in the eye and said, "I'll take off my hat to no man, not even a king!" Albert laughed heartily and shook Pat's hand enthusiastically.

Although interest in Olympic competition in those days centered mostly around track and field, and swimming, there was an unusual interest in boxing in 1920, and, along with Brutus Hamilton, later to become the famed track coach at University of California, I found myself cheering loudly for Eddie Egan, our heavyweight fighter from Yale. Unfortunately, Brutus and I weren't aware that cheering was considered bad taste at Olympic bouts and when we looked around we found we were the only ones in the audience making such a racket. A moment later we also found a gendarme at our arms, escorting us out of the building.

Meanwhile, it hadn't taken me long to find that I was completely outclassed in the javelin by the Finns and Swedes, but even though I won no medal it was a thrilling experience to compete. I was also making a lot of

Both Michigan and Northwestern had 5-0 league marks and 7-1 overall. The Wolverines' lone loss was an inexplicable 10-0 affair with Navy, although a 54-0 clobbering of the Middies by Michigan the year before might have had something to do with it.

The Conference had its finest year yet in placing men on the All-America, with nine on the honor rolls. Northwestern supplied the brilliant Moon Baker at halfback, and the crushing Bob Johnson at tackle. Michigan provided the most famous aerial battery in Big Ten history: Benny Friedman at quarterback and Bennie Oosterbaan at end. Other linemen were Bernie Shively, Illinois guard (now athletic director at Kentucky); Emerson Nelson, Iowa tackle, and Ed Hess, Ohio State guard. Two robust fullbacks were honored: Minnesota's bull-dozing Herb Joesting and Marty Karow, Ohio State's deluxe line-smasher.

Meanwhile, at Chicago—and, in fact, throughout the league—there was sadness for the plight in which Amos Alonzo Stagg had found himself. The flow of athletic talent which had brought such honor to the Maroon had begun to dry up on the Midway, and for the first time in his long and envied career, the Grand Old Man fielded a team which failed to win a Conference game.

The only quadruple tie in the history of Big Ten basketball was the highlight of the 1926 cage season, with Indiana, Michigan, Purdue and Iowa sharing the title. Captain Julius Kreuger and Art Beckner led Indiana, with Beckner taking the league scoring title, while Dick Doyle, George Spradling and Charley McConnell paced the Wolverines, Boilermakers and Hawkeyes, respectively with Spradling honored as an All-America.

Iowa won its first track title when it took the indoor crown, but couldn't handle Michigan outdoors. Four Conference stars took NCAA titles. Michigan's Phil Northrop repeated in the javelin; the Wolves' Harry Hawkins won the hammer throw; George (Phin) Guthrie of Ohio State skipped off

Michigan's HARRY HAWKINS in 1926 became the second man in Conference history to win both All-America honors in football, as a guard, and an NCAA track crown for the hammer throw.

with the 120-yard high hurdles and Alvo Martin of Northwestern won the 880.

Minnesota ended Northwestern's domination of Big Ten swimming by winning the Conference team crown. The Wildcats, who had won it in 1914-15-

When JIM HILL, Minnesota backstroker, took the 150-yard event in the 1926 NCAA meet it was the last time in the history of the national tourney that the Big Ten was limited to a single individual crown.

mental notes about sports and competition in general, although at the moment I wasn't sure why I was doing so, because I knew I was headed right back to the farm in Illinois. I did note that athletes of the day didn't seem to take their competition as seriously as I'd expected them to. I had finished my event when one of the American coaches asked me to run to the dressing room and tell our hammer-throwers they were late for reporting. The event was about to start and our entries hadn't even been around to warm up!

Dashing to the dressing room I found our three giants sitting around polishing off a bottle of ale apiece. Stunned, I told them to hurry up and get out onto the field. Pat Ryan waved his bottle majestically. "Keep your pants on, m'boy. They can wait for us!"

I finally got them out just as Pat's name was being called for his first throw. I'll never forget how he saunt-

ered to the ring, a mountain of a man, 6-4 and close to 300 pounds, to make his first Olympic throw without a single practice throw or even some warm-up calisthenics.

Pat merely won the event on his first throw!

Following the Games I was lucky enough to be included with a touring team of Americans for meets in Paris and London, and I began to dream of continuing my Olympic activities in one form or another.

Arriving back in the U.S., and having received my diploma from Illinois, I was all set to take a job as a county farm advisor. First, I thought I'd pay a courtesy call on George Huff, the Illinois athletic director who had been such a good friend while I was in school. He'd certainly like to hear about my Olympic adventures first-hand.

After we were through chatting about what had hap-

16-(co)-17-18-20-23-24-25 would take the title only once more in their history, but Tom Robinson had already established himself as one of the great coaches in aquatic history. Jim Hill, of Minnesota, won the NCAA 150-yard backstroke championship but from that year on the Big Ten would never again be limited to just one title in the NCAA festival.

Tom O'Connell, of Illinois, won the first of an eventual three straight tennis singles titles (the first man to do so) and K. E. Hisert, of Chicago, successfully defended his Conference golf championship in the first medal play tournament. Previously, the title had been decided on match play.

CAPTAIN RUSS CRAIN, an inspiring guard, who led Illinois to a Conference championship, and HERB JOESTING, rampaging Minnesota fullback, were All-America selections in 1927, with Joesting repeating his previous year's selection.

T. F. O'CONNELL, of Illinois, first man ever to win three straight Conference tennis singles titles, 1926-27-28. In 1926 he also paired with Ed Shoaff for the doubles crown, and repeated with Gordon Brandt in 1929.

1927

One of Bob Zuppke's greatest Illinois football teams ruled the Conference along with Minnesota in 1927. Led by Captain Russ Crain, fiercely competitive and versatile guard; Al Nowack, a tough tackle; and Jud Timm, a fine halfback, the Illini had a spotless league record but, to the shock and surprise of everyone, had a 12-12 tie early in the year with an Iowa State team that would win only four games that season. The Gophers still had the rampaging Herb Joesting at fullback, and clearing the way for him was a vintage Viking line headed by guard George Gibson, end Ken Haycraft and a raw, rousing, rambunctious sophomore tackle named Bronko Nagurski who, said the critics

---

pened in Europe he tilted back in his chair and asked if I had a job. To this day I've never know what possessed me to say there was nothing in sight.

He gave me a long look. "How'd you like to come in here and help us in the athletic department?" he said bluntly. "I think we could put you to very good use."

With all my public speaking courses, I was at a complete loss for words. Mr. Huff smiled and went on. He said he was convinced there was tremendous good in athletic competition and there was too little publicity about it in the small, Midwestern country papers. He wanted someone to send them weekly articles about Illinois teams. He thought I was just the one to do that and that I could also earn my keep by helping Ralph Jones with the freshman football team and assist Huff, himself, with other duties.

At that moment, any career I might have had in

agriculture vanished out the window. I was so excited I didn't even ask him about salary arrangements. I didn't know about it, didn't care about it, and therefore found myself utterly delighted when I got my first monthly check of $200.00.

One day, Mr. Huff called me into his office to meet a man who'd just joined his staff as head of the Illinois coaching school which was rapidly gaining in stature. The man's name was Major John L. Griffith and, although I didn't know it at the time, he was to have a tremendous influence over my career. Major Griffith had just returned from military service where he had headed up the army's physical training program. Huff said my first assignment with Griffith was to acquaint the Major with student groups on the campus. I arranged a series of dinners for him at fraternity houses and restaurants where he could talk to boys about the growing import-

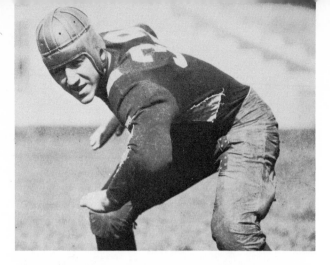

LEO RASKOWSKI, Ohio State's All-America defensive standout in 1927.

seat 15,000 and later would be expanded to accommodate 20,000, the largest collegiate cage arena in the land. Iowa's Field House had room for 15,000 and Indiana was scheduled to open its Field House the following season with room for 10,000. (Post-World War Two basketball arenas in the Big Ten would become architectural all-purpose show places that would seat 15,000.)

In swimming, Matt Mann launched Michigan on a wave of supremacy that, with exceptions in only three years, would last until World War Two. In

In 1927 WALLY COLBATH, of Northwestern, first of what would become a long line of Big Ten diving stars, took the first of his three straight NCAA low-board diving titles. The following year he was an Olympian.

might turn out to be quite a football player in a couple of years. A 14-14 tie with Indiana and a 7-7 stalemate with Notre Dame spoiled what might have been the first perfect Gopher season since 1904.

Joesting repeated as All-America fullback, as did Michigan's brilliant Bennie Oosterbaan at end, while guard and tackle spots were won respectively by the Illini's Crain and Ohio State's Leo Raskowski. Chicago, coming back a bit with a 3-3 Conference mark that would be its final high-water mark, still managed to produce the league's most valuable player in brilliant, inspiring Ken Rouse, the Maroon captain and center.

Michigan, led by Bennie Oosterbaan, won its first undisputed basketball championship in 1927, with the Wolverines' star center gaining All-America mention. Cummins, of Purdue, was the league scoring champion, and big news was being made on the construction front as basketball entered an era of burgeoning spectator interest. Huge arenas were now being built throughout the land, and, as with football stadiums, the Big Ten was showing the way. Williams Arena at Minnesota was built to

ance of coaching and physical education, hoping he could interest them in careers in those fields. It was the start of an important association with the man who subsequently would become the first Commissioner of the Big Ten.

I was also getting some firsthand coaching experience, myself, assisting Ralph Jones with the freshman football squad. He had decided to cut the 200 candidates to a manageable 60 and, after viewing all our prospects, it was my job to notify the boys who were being dropped, and suggest they go out for some other sport. On some of our decisions we missed by plenty. One candidate, upset by being cut from the squad, quit Illinois and the following September entered another University where he became an All-Western fullback, a Phi Beta Kappa student and a Rhodes Scholar. It impressed upon me,

at an early age, that coaches aren't infallible, no matter how long a winning streak they can put together.

Late in the Spring of my first year at Illinois, Major Griffith called me into his office and dropped the bombshell that was to be a turning point in my future. He told me that Drake University, where he had once coached, was looking for a Director of Athletics, a job that included the staging of the famed Drake Relays. He said he was sure I could handle the position. I was dumfounded. Here I was, just 24 years old, and someone whose judgment I respected was suggesting I was ready to head up the entire sports program at one of the finest colleges in the Midwest. I didn't tell the Major he was shellshocked but I implied that he was making a big mistake, and that I was much too inexperienced.

He wasn't an easy man to brush off once he took a

the NCAA meet the Wolverines' star freestyler, Paul Samson, won the 220- and 440-yard events; Winston Kratz, in taking the 200-yard breaststroke became Wisconsin's first and only NCAA champion in history; Wally Colbath, of Northwestern, first of the great diving champions the Big Ten would produce, took the first of three straight one-meter crowns he would wear; Carl Darnall, of Michigan, captured the 100-yard freestyle; the Wolverine foursome of Allan Seager, Tom Watson, Samson and Darnall won the 200-yard freestyle relay, and the Minnesota trio of Jim Hill, Charles Purdy and Sam Hill won the 300-yard medley relay.

The track wars found Wisconsin winning its first Conference indoor title but couldn't stave off Illinois outdoors. Two Conference stars and one from

Michigan State won NCAA crowns as John Sittig, of Illinois took the 880, Bill Droegemueller, of Northwestern won the pole vault, and Fred Alderman became the first Spartan athlete to win a national collegiate title when he took the 100- and 220-yard dashes. Meanwhile, Tiny Lewis, the big Northwestern fullback, made Big Ten track history of sorts when he scored in six events in a dual meet with Indiana, winning the shot-put, tying for first in the broad jump; taking second in the discus; tying for second in the pole vault; placing second in high hurdles and taking a third in the javelin.

In other highlights of the year, Wisconsin won its fourth straight cross-country team title, as the Badgers' John Zola romped home in 24:57, fastest time yet in the league meet. Les Bolstad became Minnesota's first Conference individual golf champion, and Chicago launched an unusual domination of gymnastics. In seven of the next eight years the

From 1926 to 1934 inclusive, one of the major dominations of Big Ten sports saw Chicago winning the league gymnastics crown eight times in nine years. Leading the Maroon surge were three athletes who won the all-around title two years in a row: FLOYD DAVIDSON in 1927-28; JOHN MENZIES, 1929-30; and George Wrighte, 1933-34.

FRED ALDERMAN *was Michigan State's first NCAA champion. He took the 100- and 220-yard dashes in the 1927 track tourney, and ran a leg on the winning 1600-meter relay team for the U.S. in the 1928 Olympics.*

fix on an idea and insisted I go to Des Moines, anyway, for an interview he would set up. Just to please him, I said I'd go. The Drake Athletic Board met me, treated me with politeness, asked me some personal questions and then corroborated my own judgment by telling me that, yes, indeed, I was too inexperienced. They asked me, however, if I'd stay that evening and be a speaker at an alumni dinner and perhaps offer some ideas on Drake's athletic program.

Well, since I knew I wasn't getting the job anyway, and with the heat off me, I just relaxed at the dinner, got up when they called upon me and chatted quite informally, but at some length, about what I felt Drake could or should do in athletics.

When I was finished there was a burst of applause and an almost instant huddle between some influential

alumni and members of the Athletic Board. Next thing I knew, the Board took me back into another meeting and I left Des Moines the next day as the brand new Drake Athletic Director. I knew, now, that athletic administration was the thing that would always hold my most intense interest. Nevertheless, I was to wear two hats for awhile, because I was also to coach the Drake track team. As Director of the Drake Relays, I would have a chance to make friends all over the country.

Prior to my taking over at Drake in 1921, the Drake Relays had always been held a week before the Penn Relays. After discussing the matter with Amos Alonzo Stagg of Chicago, Tom Jones of Wisconsin, and Notre Dame's Knute Rockne, we were convinced that we should butt head-on with the Penn Relays and compete for attention with the big Eastern spectacle and hold our

Maroon would win the team title and Floyd Davidson began a long string of Maroon all-around individual champions. Davidson would win in 1927-28; John Menzies in 1929-30, Everett Olson in 1931-32, and George Wrighte in 1933-34.

In baseball, Iowa broke the title barrier for the first time, although the Hawkeyes tied with Illinois in a situation unique in Conference history when the two teams not only posted 7-3 records but played a tie game to help preserve the deadlock.

On the administrative front, the Conference directors decreed that athletes may not engage in athletic writing or use their names for commercial advertising. It was also decided that no Big Ten school could employ a coach from another Conference school without obtaining permission from that school to negotiate with the candidate.

Among 1928 All-America designees were AL NO-WACK, a tackle and prime mover in Illinois' surge to its second straight Big Ten title, and KEN HAYCRAFT, Minnesota's slashing end.

1928

Illinois made it two grid titles in a row in 1928, and, although nobody would have predicted it at the time, it was the last championship Bob Zuppke would win. A lone field goal was all the scoring as Michigan handed the Illini their only loss of the season in a battle of strong lines.

Perhaps the key touchdown of the championship season for Illinois came in the Northwestern game when Jud Timm swept end for 26 yards and the only score of the game in the most doubt-filled Illinois victory of the year.

The Illini's Al Nowack and the Wolverines' Otto Pommerening were All-America tackles. Other honor selections were Ken Haycraft, a versatile end from Minnesota; Chuck Bennett, a triple-threat halfback from Indiana (the Hoosiers' first All-America) and a handsome, blond sophomore end from Ohio State named Wesley Fesler—the first sophomore to be a unanimous honor choice since the Buckeyes' own Chic Harley. Midwest critics were convinced from the start—and Eastern observers got on the bandwagon when the Buckeyes played a superior Prince-

ton eleven to bone-bruising 6-6 tie. Sportswriters said the defensive play of the slashing Ohio end was the finest witnessed on historic Palmer Stadium turf in a decade.

Although Chuck Bennett performed for an Indiana team that won only two league games, the Hoosier iron-man was judged the most valuable player in the Conference.

An Iowa team that could have been one of the best in Hawkeye history brushed aside six straight victories before, strangely, running out of steam in its last two games, and lost, 13-0 to Wisconsin, and 10-7 to Michigan. Nevertheless, the Hawks put on exhibit three of the best backs yet seen in the same offensive unit: Bill Glasgow, and Oran Pape, two speedy halfbacks, and burly Mayes McClain, a tranfer from Haskell Indian Institute. As a fullback, the mighty Indian at Haskell in 1926 had set a modern collegiate scoring record that still stands. Against highly respectable opposition that included Tulsa, Bucknell and Michigan State, McClain rambled for 253 points. The following year Pape and Glasgow would become the central figures in a

meet the same day. I obtained the wholehearted co-operation of the Big Ten coaches who said they'd send their athletes to our affair and, for an added event, I persuaded my old Olympic teammate, Charlie Paddock, to come out for a spring exhibition. We jammed Drake Stadium for the event, with the biggest crowd in Drake Relays history. From then on it shared the spotlight with the Penn Relays as the nation's most prestigious track and field carnival.

I had realized quickly that our main problem at Drake would lie in the fact Drake was one of the smaller schools with ambitious athletic aims. First I tried to develop a new attitude based on optimism, determination and quality performance. We began to attract good boys and we had a fine staff to train them. Young Ossie Solem, later head coach at Iowa and Syracuse, did a terrific job for us. In our first seson, 1921, we posted a

5-2 mark, the best Drake record in 10 years, and the next season we had the first undefeated club in Drake history. While our material was limited in quantity it was long on quality—indicated by the fact that three of our athletes became Big Ten Athletic Directors in subsequent years.

Ike Armstrong, our great fullback, we recommended to the coaching staff at the University of Utah where, subsequently, as head coach, he dominated the Rocky Mountain Conference for 20 years before moving on to become Athletic Director at the University of Minnesota. Another Drake star, Paul Brechler, later became Athletic Director of the University of Iowa and then became Commissioner of the Mountain States Conference. Ted Payseur, one of Drake's greatest basketball players, later accompanied me as a member of my staff at Northwestern when I became Athletic Director there, and

racking controversy that would result in the suspension of Iowa from the Big Ten.

For sheer virtuosity, however, the finest performance of the season might have been that of Joe Steinauer, the veteran and colorful Wisconsin swimming coach and physical education instructor, who broadcast Badger football games. In describing the Badger-Minnesota game that year Steinauer used five different languages in describing the play-by-play. Examples included the following.

Indiana celebrated a long-awaited "first" in 1928 when chunky, hard-running CHUCK BENNETT became the Hoosiers first All-America. Although Indiana had a mediocre 4-4 record for the season, Bennett's brilliant running and fierce, all-around play drew raves from every coach who had to stop him, and from critics who observed him.

WESLEY FESLER

It's a shame the Big Ten didn't keep permanent records prior to 1939. They certainly would have shown that Wesley Fesler, of Ohio State, set one that would stand forever when, in a 11-6 Buckeye baseball victory over Illinois in his junior year, he hit for 16 total bases and drove in all 11 Ohio runs on a double, a homer, another double, a grand slam homer and another grand slam homer, in that order. Seemingly this was the type of heroics expected of the handsome, blond first sacker who was probably the greatest all-around athlete in Buckeye history and who has few contenders for the honor on a league-wide basis.

Fesler, who came to Ohio State as a football center, was shifted to end as a sophomore in 1928 by Dr. John W. Wilce and immediately became an All-America end on the basis of his brilliant offensive and defensive play. He repeated as a junior and a senior but not before the versatile Buckeye had seen service as quarterback and fullback as well, as the occasion demanded.

An All-Big Ten basketball star for three years and a baseball first sacker good enough to attract numerous Big League offers, Fesler elected, however, to go into coaching. He eventually returned to lead his Alma Mater into the Rose Bowl with his 1949 team and then, after resigning inexplicably because of a temporary distaste for coaching pressure, moved up to Minnesota for three more years before turning to a business career for good.

then succeeded me as Director when I became Big Ten Commissioner.

Although I had concentrated on building Drake's athletic fortunes from an administrative level some of my fondest memories from Des Moines came from my coaching activities. Oddly enough, it was in golf that Drake first gained national prominence. In those days the Big Ten allowed outside teams to enter their track and golf tournaments and Drake won three Big Ten golf crowns in a row, coached by that confirmed hacker (lucky to break 90), K.L. Wilson.

Track had been a long, hard struggle on a limited budget with limited material and my hope was that I'd be able to develop a relay team that could take a championship at our own prestigious Drake Relays. In 1924 I thought I could bring it off with my two-mile team. On the day of the Relays it was cold, raw and

MINNEAPOLIS NORWEGIAN: *Foiste stop, tee yard til et go.*

ST. PAUL SWEDISH: *Foist standstil te mere till et go.*

MILWAUKEE GERMAN: *Erste anhaltung, stein za gehen.*

CHICAGO YIDDISH: *Ahsawraw meedohs lawvoh.*

WISCONSIN CHINESE: *De e ting su mah wong chan.*

All this simply meant: "First down, 10 yards to go."

Two heartbreaking one-point decisions kept Minnesota from a perfect season that year, with two startling long runs figuring in the dramatics. Against

FRED HOVDE's brilliant Minnesota quarterbacking in 1927-28 was merely a portent of things to come. He was later a Rhodes Scholar and president of Purdue University.

Iowa on a muddy field, the Gophers were in a scoreless deadlock until Fred Hovde, brilliant Gopher safety man, picked up a Hawkeye punt that had sailed over his head and streaked and slithered back 91 yards for a touchdown. Unfortunately for the Gophers they missed the extra point and, after Oran Pape, had ripped off a 62-yard TD of his own, Hawk Coach Burt Ingwersen called upon Irv Nelson to try for the extra point because Glasgow had been injured in the preceding play. Nelson, a drop-kicker, made it—and it was the first time he had ever appeared in an Iowa football game.

The following week Minnesota dropped its other one-point heartbreaker to Northwestern, 10-9. The Gophers, leading 9-0 late in the game on a touchdown and safety, appeared to be home free when Bill Calderwood of Northwestern picked up a Gopher fumble and raced it back 70 yards for a touchdown. Walt Holmer then booted the extra point and shortly afterward kicked a field goal to win, 10-9.

Indiana and Purdue, who had tied for second the year before, moved up together and shared the 1928 basketball title with 10-2 marks, dividing their home-and-home series in the process. Benny Oosterbaan, Michigan's All-America forward, and the second man in league history to become All-America in two sports, led the loop in scoring. Elmo Wells and Bob Correll had led the Hoosiers to their league honors while the Boilermakers featured a senior, Lloyd Kennen, and an amazing sophomore: Charles (Stretch) Murphy.

Michigan was off and splashing in earnest, in the Big Ten swimming wars, as the Wolverines took their second team title in a row. In the NCAA meet Carl Darnall retained his 100-yard freestyle; Wally Colbath, of Northwestern made it two straight in the one-meter dive; the Wildcats' Dick Hinch won the 150-yard backstroke; and Michigan relay teams won the 200-yard freestyle event and 300-yard medley. The freestyle quartet included Bob Walker,

blustery, and I told my foursome to keep their sweat clothes on until the very last minute before each ran their leg. Coming into the third leg we were in good running position and my third man was beginning to remove his sweat pants. To my astonishment I heard him let out an agonized yell. "Coach, I forgot to put on my track pants!"

I think I then made the quickest decision I ever made in sports. "You're going to run, anyway!" No track crowd was ever more amazed than this overflow crowd at the Drake Relays when they saw our third man racing around the track wearing only a shirt and his athletic supporter! Rather than giving him an advantage in weight I think it cost him something in poise and embarassment because we blew a race we could have won.

Despite the success I was having as Drake's Athletic

Director I wasn't entirely happy in Des Moines. I was too far way from Dorothy Shade, my campus sweetheart at Illinois, to whom I was now engaged. She was living in Bloomington, Illinois, and I wangled many a trip eastward out of Des Moines so I could stop off and see her.

Once, knowing her love for pets, I bought the cutest little pedigreed Persian I could find and carried it from Des Moines to Chicago in a Pullman berth, without the conductor or porter knowing it, and the only way I could keep it from crying was to cradle it in my arms all night. When I got to Bloomington where Dorothy lived I knocked on the door and when she answered I merely held the little kitten out to her. I think it speeded up our marriage plans somewhat.

That summer I scraped up all my available assets and

RALPH LUPTON, of Northwestern, was one of the Big Ten's finest wrestlers during the 1920s. Twice he was Conference and NCAA champion at 125 pounds (1928-1929) and missed a chance to make the 1928 Olympic team when he sustained a broken rib in the final round of the Olympic tryouts.

RALPH LUPTON   **DAVE ABBOTT**

DAVE ABBOTT, an Illinois distance star of the late twenties, was the first of only two men in Conference history to win the NCAA two-mile crown for two straight years. His victories came in 1928 and 1929. He was also 1928 individual cross-country champ.

Frank Walaitis, Allan Seager and Darnall, the medley trio featured George Hubbell, Jay Thompson and Bob Walker.

The NCAA sponsored its first wrestling tournament in 1928 and the Big Ten lost no time in making its presence felt as Ralph Lupton, Northwestern's great 125-pounder took the title in his division and Les Beers, an Iowa stand-out, triumphed at 158.

In other highlights of the year, Dave Abbott of Illinois was the cross-country individual champion and Indiana romped off with the first of a string of team titles that would hit six straight years—the longest string until Michigan State entered the Conference and turned the event into a perennial, personal carnival for more than a decade.

Illinois captured both the indoor and outdoor track championships and, in the NCAA tournament which was re-established as a team championship after several years of individual recognition only, five Conference teams finished in the top 10, with Ohio State second to Stanford, and Illinois third, Iowa fifth, Northwestern seventh and Michigan eighth. Frank Cuhel of Iowa took the 220-yard low hurdles crown in a record time of 23.2; Dave Abbott of Illinois set a new record of 9:28 in the two-mile, and Wilford Ketz of Michigan won the hammer throw.

The 1928 Conference Scholarship Medal went to some particularly outstanding athletes: Ken Rouse, Chicago's inspiring football leader; Art Beckner, Indiana's league-leading basketball scorer; Mal Nydahl, Minnesota's great halfback, and Bill Droegemueller, Northwestern's Olympic pole vaulter.

Once again the Olympic Games found a strong contingent of Conference athletes bolstering Uncle Sam's team.

Iowa's George Baird and Michigan State's Fred Alderman ran legs on the winning United States' 1600-meter relay; Iowan Frank Cuhel took second in the 400-meter hurdles, and another Hawkeye, Ed Gordon, competed in the broad jump. Northwestern's Bill Droegemueller captured second place in the pole vault, in which Wisconsin's Chuck McGinnis also competed; and Michigan's George Hester was a sprinter on the Canadian team. The Wolverines also contributed heavily to the wrestling squad. Ed Don George won the heavyweight title and Bobby Hewitt wrestled as a bantamweight, with Russ Saver and Al Watson making the trip as alternates. Michigan's Paul Samson swam a leg

bought an engagement ring. I had also accumulated a racy old Buick Roadster and was driving from Des Moines to Bloomington carrying the ring in my pocket, when somewhere around Grinnell, Iowa I foolishly picked up a tired and dirty hitchhiker who said he was going to Chicago. He was a disreputable looking character, and I soon realized I had made a mistake. Along the roadside was a small tree with a crow sitting on the top branch. Suddenly my passenger pulled out a rusty old "forty-five" and proceeded to kill the crow with one shot even though we were moving at a pretty fast clip. Now the question was how to get rid of him. When we got into Iowa City he decided he was hungry and said he would get some sandwiches. The minute he was out of sight I went rolling out of town as fast as I could go. The ring and I reached our destination safely.

I had hoped we could be married that summer, but Dorothy had taken a job teaching in Bloomington High School, and her family thought she should finish out her contract. When I came back to see her at Christmas, however, we decided to get married and I returned to Des Moines after the Christmas holidays with my bride. Her folks had given her a beautiful grey squirrel coat for a wedding present and I'll never forget the sensation she created on the campus, when I took her to her first chapel service.

Des Moines was a wonderful city to live in, and we both enjoyed the many friends we made there. To augment my salary I frequently went out officiating in football and basketball, and Dorothy always went with me.

I always enjoyed having her with me as she took such a keen interest in my work and helped me tremendously

GEORGE BAIRD

PAUL SAMSON

Among the Big Ten contingent on the 1928 Olympic team were GEORGE BAIRD, of Iowa, who ran a leg on the winning 1600-meter relay; PAUL SAMSON, Michigan freestyle swimmer who swam a leg on the winning 800-meter relay; Iowa's FRANK CUHEL who took second in the 400-meter hurdles; Iowan LES BEERS who wrestled at 158 pounds; and Northwestern's star pole-vaulter, BILL DROEGEMUELLER.

FRANK CUHEL

LESLIE BEERS

BILL DROEGEMUELLER

1929

on the winning 800-meter relay; Northwestern's Wally Colbath was a U.S. diver, and the Wildcat's Harry Daniels was a member of the water polo team. Iowa's Leslie Beers wrestled at 158 pounds; Illinois' Dave Abbott ran the 5000-meters, and the Illini also contributed wrestling star, Albie Morrison.

It was a long time in coming and everyone in the midwest agreed that no one deserved it more than Purdue as the Boilermakers highlighted the 1929 Conference football season with their first title in 30 seasons and the first undefeated team in Black and Gold history. True, Jimmy Phelan, the brilliant

especially during our twenty years at Northwestern in our faculty contacts. After I became Commissioner, the many Rose Bowl trips were a delight to the whole family as we always took our daughters Nancy and Suzanne along. We took them to many athletic contests in the Big Ten and when it became time for them to go to college we were delighted to have Nancy choose Illinois and then finish getting her Masters degree in the School of Journalism at Northwestern. Suzanne chose Michigan for the first two years and then transferred to Northwestern where she received her degree in the School of Education. We were truly a Big Ten family. Later on Dorothy and I were to take many Olympic trips together, attending the summer games at Amsterdam, London, Helsinki, Melbourne, Rome and Tokyo, and the winter games at Cortina, Innsbruck and Squaw Valley.

At Drake, it was my handling of the famed Drake Relays which brought me more national attention than the overall job of improving the sports program at the University, and in the summer of 1925 I got a phone call from Major Griffith again. Now I'll have to backtrack a bit.

The Big Ten universities had wisely recognized the problems being faced by intercollegiate athletics as World War One came to an end. The presidents and athletic directors of the league had correctly anticipated an increased college enrollment and a mushrooming interest in collegiate sports in the nation's "Return to Normalcy," as the politicians put it in those early post-war days. The Directors were also concerned with the "tramp athlete" who transferred from school to school and often played out several years of so-called eligibility

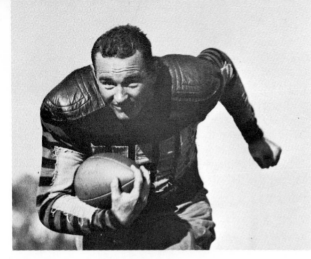

Nobody was more appropriately nicknamed during the 1929 Big Ten football season than RALPH (PEST) WELCH, of Purdue, a 6-1, 190-pound triple-threat halfback from Whitesboro, Texas, who could beat you five ways on his running, kicking, passing, defending and inspirational leadership. The opening game of the season found favored Michigan leading the Boilermakers 16-6 at the end of the third quarter. Welch ran wild and lifted his teammates to a four-touchdown effort in the final period to smash the Wolverines 30-16. The game provided the springboard for an undefeated season for Purdue, the Boilermakers' first undisputed Big Ten crown and their first claim to national honors—with Pest Welch a unanimous All-America, the Boilermaker's first man to make the honor squad. Purdue was the last Big Ten school to produce an All-America but would shortly make up for any time lost in the honors department.

young Purdue coach, had the horses but he also knew how to handle them. Ralph (Pest) Welch, one of the league's all-time great triple-threat halfbacks; slick quarterback Glen Harmeson, a three-sport star; and Elmer (Red) Sleight, a brilliant and mobile tackle, led the Boilermakers to their 8-0 season. Against five Big Ten foes the Boilermakers racked up 108 points, with Michigan the lone team able to score against them in a 30-16 affair. (It was the first Purdue win over the Wolverines since 1892.) Only once was Purdue in jeopardy that year—in a decisive

title showdown against stubborn Iowa, led by the talented Bill Glassgow and Oran Pape. Purdue tallied on a 17-yard pass from Harmeson to Woerner, and made the score hold up to nail the flag.

It was Glassgow, however, who was awarded the league's most-valuable-player award for his running, kicking, and passing virtuosity with a team that was not able to give him as much support as Purdue gave Pest Welch, for instance.

GLENN HARMESON, Purdue three-sport man in football (1927-28-29), basketball (1928-29-30), and baseball (1928-29-30) was the Boilermakers' second nine-letterman. First was Mel Taube in the same sports four years earlier. Harmeson's older brother, Harold, was a four-sport man the same years as Taube with seven letters (three in football, two for baseball and one each in basketball and track).

at more than one college. Each individual college, whether it was the Big Ten or elsewhere, was the sole judge, then, of whether to accept a transfer student and grant him additional athletic eligibility on the basis of the first school's academic standing and accreditation. A lot of athletes obtained additional years of competition because of this loosely applied philosophy. There were also the first glimmerings (and not so faint, at that) of intensified and alarming recruiting practices.

Overall, the Big Ten took the lead, nationally, to head off trouble before it could get started. The first step the Conference took was to appoint its first "Commissioner of Athletics." June 2, 1922 became an historic date in Big Ten history with the announcement that Major John L. Griffith, the former coach and U.S. Army physical training director, was to be the man who would "...

serve as a general secretary, promote educational campaigns on amateurism and carry on investigations regarding intercollegiate athletic problems."

It caused quite a stir in the Midwest, particularly, and it caused a lot of coaches, not only in the Conference, but all over America, to do a lot of thinking about how they would handle their programs. Fortunately, with coaches such as Stagg of Chicago; Yost of Michigan; Zuppke of Illinois, Wilce of Ohio State, and others of high integrity, there was the basis for leadership in a common cause for the good of American collegiate athletics. In Major Griffith the Big Ten had the right man to get things in motion.

Griffith had been in office three years when he put through that phone call to me in the summer of 1925. He told me Northwestern University was in the market

WILLIS GLASSGOW

Central figures in the suspension of Iowa from the Big Ten in 1929—the only time in league history a member was ousted from the lodge, albeit temporarily—were WILLIS GLASSGOW, All-America halfback and Conference MVP, and ORAN PAPE, his running-mate. Conference punitive action focused on irregular financial aid to the two Hawkeye backs.

ORAN PAPE

Yet, there was no greater or more colorful player in the Big Ten—or the nation, for that matter—than football's Paul Bunyan of the Northland—Minnesota's unique Bronko Nagurski who, for two years had played fullback on offense and tackle on defense. Nobody ever blocked him out on defense and never did anyone succeed in completely hobbling him when he had the ball tucked into his belly and

blasted a line. Virtually unanimous All-Americas that year included Welch and Sleight of Purdue; the fabulous Nagurski; Wes Fesler, of Ohio State, making it two in a row at end; Glassgow, the stocky, versatile Iowan; Henry Anderson, a quick, tough Northwestern guard, and Lou Gordon, Illinois tackle, who was one of the best blockers in the land.

In basketball, Michigan and Wisconsin shared the title with 10-2 marks, with Harold (Bud) Foster and Ed Chinielewski leading the Badgers, and Ernie McCoy sparking the Wolverines. Stretch Murphy of Purdue, who led the Conference scorers; Michigain's McCoy, and the lanky, sharp-shooting Foster were All-Ameica.

Never in collegiate football had one Conference contributed as many All-America tackles to the honor squad as did the Big Ten in 1929; ELMER SLEIGHT, the Purdue terror who ripped big holes for All-America teammate Pest Welch; LOU GORDON, one of the best blockers in Illinois history; and the immovable, irrepressible Bronko Nagurski of Minnesota. Other Big Ten All-America designees that year were Ohio State's legendary Wes Fesler, showcased elsewhere in this book; Henry Anderson, Northwestern's tough, smart guard; and Willis Glassgow, the mercurial Iowa halfback.

ELMER (RED) SLEIGHT   **LOU GORDON**

Gathering at the 1924 meeting of the Conference Athletic Directors were some of the most famous administrators in collegiate sports history. Bottom row, left to right: Zora G. Clevenger, Indiana; Fielding Yost, Michigan; Amos Alonzo Stagg, Chicago; George Huff, Illinois; Dana Evans, Northwestern. Top row, left to right: Tom Jones, Wisconsin; Major John L. Griffith, Commissioner of the Big Ten; Ned Kellogg, Purdue; Fred Leuhring, Minnesota; L. W. St. John, Ohio State; Howard Jones, Iowa.

Minnesota had the ball on the Northwestern 12-yard line, fourth down and goal to go. The Gopher quarterback handed off to Bronko Nagurski who hurtled his 225 pounds straight ahead into the massed Wildcat forward wall. Absolutely everything gave way as the ball carrier smashed through, his momentum carrying him 12 yards to and over the goal line, through the 10-yard end zone and beyond to a stack of 100-pound bags of cement piled up for a construction project. The wall of cement bags went over, too, before Nagurski could flag down his runaway power.

The story goes that when Bronko Nagurski was born on November 3, 1908 in Rainy River, Ontario, the legendary Paul Bunyan sensed it and said to Babe, his famed blue ox: "We have a challenger!"

Bunyan needn't have been concerned. Bronko Nagurski never became a woodsman, although there were those who wished he had.

He did, however, become the Bunyan of college football. Even the name helped. Say it. Bronko Nagurski. Say it again. Notice how it measures and menaces in tone and feeling. Bronko Nagurski. A perfectly proper Ukrainian name, but most people believed it was a nickname derived from the wild, strong, fierce bucking bronco of the Western plains. Unlike that bronco, however, the gridiron version rarely, if ever, was bridled and tamed. In 1929, the New York Sun in picking its All-America football team paid the Minnesota superman an accolade never before or since tendered a college gridder. Whereas various honor teams named Nagurski at fullback and others had him at tackle, The Sun, in effect, said to hell with it, we'll do the only sensible thing and just name ten men instead of eleven, and promptly awarded Nagurski two positions: fullback and tackle.

There was never a more characteristic player in a sport founded on the basic principals of atavistic physical contact. It is said the real football player must merely meet one, overriding requirement: he must have an appetite for the nature of the game. In essence, Bronko Nagurski simply had to be himself—the most guileless, unfanciest man on the field. He was about as subtle as a hangman's noose. Nobody ever completely cured him of occasionally glancing toward the hole he'd be hitting. Big deal. So they knew he was coming. That was their misfortune. He simply tucked the ball into his rock-like belly, lowered a pair of shoulders a water buffalo could envy, and ran into, through, and over people. Never around them. That was being subtle, and maybe cowardly. When he was blocking or tackling, there was simply an upright object ahead that had to be converted to the horizontal. All at once.

It should have been a source of great satisfaction for Nagurski to trumpet his collegiate career on a lofty note after a high school record which never found him playing in a winning game. Dr. Clarence Spears, who coached Nagurski at Minnesota, once was asked how he happened to land his biggest prize. The story, later trotted out at a hundred banquets, told how Spears was lost while driving along a lonely road up in the north woods and encountered a farmboy plowing a field. "Which way to the nearest town?" Spears asked.

"Thataway," the youth pointed.

"Right then and there I signed him up for Minnesota," said Spears. "Anybody who could point with a plow would have to be a prospect."

Actually, Bronko Nagurski had shown up at Minnesota in the autumn of 1926 in a prosaic, unheralded manner, and carrying a mere 190 pounds on his 6-foot, 2-inch frame. No scholarship, no plushy alumni "patronage," no purple promises had lured him. Arnie Oss, an ex-Minnesota grid and basketball star, had met the quiet boy from International Falls (pop. 4000), suggested he might be able to make the grade in Minneapolis and said he'd try to get the lad a job to help meet expenses.

No press clippings had preceded Bronko. There had been only two high schools in Nagurski's county, and, until Bronko joined the team as a sophomore, International Falls had never even scored on the tough teams from the neighboring iron-mining region. The high school coach took a look at the youthful Nagurski, noted how quick he was and thought how marvelous it would be if the boy could run interference for himself. The closest the coach could come to that Utopian gridiron gambit was to install Bronko at fullback on offense and tackle on defense. Nagurski, however, was all the coach had, and while International Falls managed to get an occasional touchdown during the next two years the team never did win a game.

Nagurski also played center and guard on the basketball team, and it was a rhubarb in this sport which cost him his final year of high school football. His principal, in disciplining two other basketball players, cancelled the team's trip to the district tournament. Nagurski resented this treatment and when some friends suggested he transfer to Bemiji High School for his senior year, Bronko got a job in Bemiji and began to work his way through his final year. International Falls promptly protested that he was a non-resident of Bemiji and therefore ineligible until he had put in a semester of residence as a transfer student. The state high school athletic commission upheld the beef and Bronko lost his senior year of football but he did play basketball and, in the spring, turned out for the track team to put the shot, throw the discus, high jump, and run a leg on the sprint relay team.

It was football, however, that Bronko Nagurski's psyche thirsted for. This was a game where a formal set of rules had given mayhem a semblance of respectability. In the fall of 1926 he reported for freshman football at Minnesota and, as the story goes, Clarence Spears, the Gopher coach, wandered over to meet the newcomers, offering a friendly hand to each, and a hearty, "My name's Spears—what's yours?"

"Mine's Nagurski—Bronko Nagurski," the big kid from International Falls said hesitantly.

Spears squinted humorously. "Bronko, hey? That's a strange name!"

The hulking frosh glowered. "Well, Clarence ain't so hot, either!"

It was obvious to the Gopher coaching staff that Nagurski would have to be tried at both fullback and tackle until they decided where he would fit best. So, during the first scrimmage, when the varsity was told to move the ball against the frosh, Bronko was installed at tackle. The only thing the varsity moved were several pair of startled eyebrows as Nagurski devoured ball carrier after carrier. Next, the varsity went on defense and Bronko was told to carry the ball from fullback. Varsity linemen banged through the green freshman blockers and converged hungrily on the big frosh fullback with the ball. There was a loud meeting of muscle as Nagurski came through, shedding tacklers with every step. The

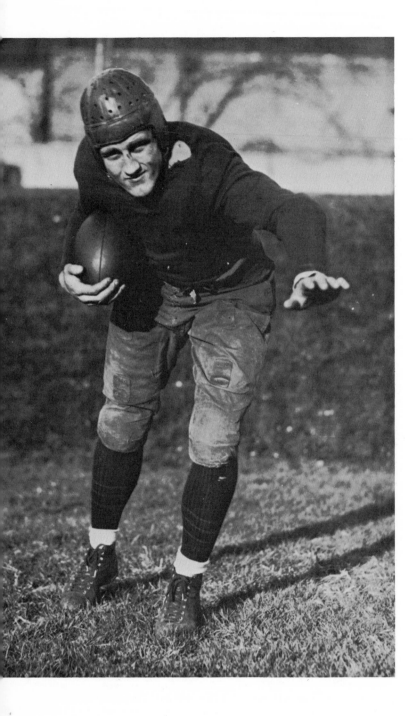

performance was repeated many nights thereafter, and around Minneapolis there commenced a murmuring in half a dozen Swedish and Norwegian dialects, all of which, translated, meant: "Wait'll next year!"

Spears, however, had no intention of using Nagurski at fullback in his sophomore year. With All-America Herb Joesting stationed there it would have been superfluous. "Bronk," he said to the young giant (now up to 220), "we're using you in the line this season." So, in his first game against North Dakota State, Spears had Nagurski make his debut at end. Bronko crashed interference, smeared ball carriers, blasted big holes on offense and drew raves as the best end prospect in years. Again, it was pointless. In Bob Tanner and Ken Haycraft, the Gophers had the best two wingmen in the league. Spears bowed to the inevitable (for the time being) and switched Nagurski to tackle for a big part of his first year and it was as such that Nagurski gained his biggest thrill in college ball.

"We were playing Notre Dame at old Cartier Field in South Bend," he recalled later. "Notre Dame hadn't been defeated or tied there in 22 years. Here I was, only a soph, playing against one of Rockne's good clubs. They'd gotten a quick touchdown when Fred Hovde fumbled for us on our own 17. (I don't think I ever forgave Fred until he became a Rhodes Scholar, and later president of Purdue, and I figured I should be proud just to know him.) Anyway, Notre Dame had this 7-0 lead and time was running out. Then it happened. I was at tackle and they had the ball inside their own 20. There was the snap from center and somehow I knocked a couple of guys down and got to the ball carrier before he could do much of anything besides fumble. There we were, both of us after the bouncing ball. I shucked him aside and beat him to it on their 15-yard line. Herb Joesting crossed up everybody by passing to Walsh for the touchdown. Barnhardt kicked the point and we'd tied Notre Dame. Nothing I did afterwards in college could compare with causing and recovering that fumble."

That was just one man's opinion, of course, albeit the view of the management. Other witnesses would claim that was three-penny stuff from the inventory of Nagurski heroics.

Before he was through at Minnesota, Nagurski had played every position but quarterback, halfback and center. Although the Gophers were destined never to win a Conference title with him in the line-up he was, nevertheless, the most talked-about and most feared and respected football player in the loop.

After playing most of 1927 at tackle, Nagurski inherited Joesting's fullback post in 1928. The Bronk had spent most of the summer working on a cement crew in northern Minnesota and was ready. On occasion, when the defense needed shoring up, Nagurski slipped into a defensive tackle spot but mostly it was his incredible bull-like rushes that posed a problem for the enemy. If a couple of tacklers got to him before he had taken more than two steps they had a fifty-fifty chance of stopping him. If they hit him after he'd gotten to the hole unimpeded, or into the secondary at full speed, they stood a fifty-fifty chance of hanging up their suits for the season. He ripped opposing lines to shreds the first three games as though they were schoolboys. Then Minnesota took on tough Iowa, and, for the only time in his college career, Bronko Nagurski was injured. (It was later discovered three ribs were torn at the juncture of the spine.) Bronko couldn't bend over to receive a snap from center and couldn't generate his normal speed so he stayed at tackle and played all but five minutes of the remainder of the game which Iowa won, 7-6.

He played only a few minutes against Northwestern the following week, again at tackle, and just sporadically against Indiana and Haskell Indian School. This brought the Gophers to their traditional finale against Wisconsin —and a display of heroics such as never had been witnessed in the Northland. The Badgers had been in a title drought since 1912 and now, with only a tie marring their record, were shooting for the crown. Nothing could be sweeter, too, than for Wisconsin to use their neighboring rival as a stepping stone to the throne.

Nagurski was determined to play despite his painwracked condition. The Gopher trainers, bowing to his insistent and virtually threatening demands, fashioned a special brace for his ribs and back, and Bronko went in at fullback.

It was a sullen, bruising battle, with neither team penetrating the other's 20-yard line in the first quarter. Nagurski was being used mainly as a decoy or to run interference for Hovde and Win Brockmeyer, a gritty 155-pound halfback. Then, on the first play of the second period there was a Wisconsin fumble by Russ Rebholz, the Badgers' great fullback, and Minnesota recovered on the Wisconsin 18. Canny quarterback Hovde looked over the Badger defense and said to Nagurski, who had been injured again in the opening period: "Can you do it?" The Bronk just snorted.

On the first lunge Nagurski got nine yards. Another blast by the Bronk and it was first down on the seven. Nagurski again—this time to the four. Then he smashed to the one and a half. Hovde and Nagurski exchanged looks. Not a word passed between them, and then the future Rhodes Scholar and Purdue president barked his signals. The ball was snapped. Captain George Gibson, Minnesota's All-America guard, hit straight ahead, budged his man just enough and the Bronk roared up both their backs for the touchdown. Five straight times the injured Nagurski had carried the ball for the most grueling and longest 18 yards ever measured. It was enough for a 6-0 victory for Minnesota, and the upset knocked the Badgers out of the title.

In 1929, the critics claimed Nagurski was the finest tackle of the year—yet he played less than 120 minutes, or a total of less than two games, in the line. Only a man of Nagurski's strength, speed and zest for contact could have shuttled back and forth between the line and backfield game after game. He put in 50 minutes at tackle against Vanderbilt; less than 30 against Coe; only two minutes against Northwestern. He started the Iowa game at tackle, ruined the Hawkeye forwards and ball toters for 28 minutes, then switched to fullback and soon bolted through the entire Hawkeye team 45 yards for a touchdown. Most of the time that season he had been a fullback; 58 minutes against Northwestern; 58 against Indiana; 32 against Iowa and 60 each in the Michigan and Wisconsin games.

Two chancy, slim points-after-touchdown (a 7-6 loss to Iowa and a 10-9 decision to Northwestern) cost the Gophers Big Ten and national honors in 1929, but Nagurski, himself, missed nothing in the way of honors. He made every All-America team picked, either at tackle or fullback. It remained for the New York Sun, of course, to point up the Bronk's true worth when they named him to both positions on its 10-man team.

A modest, almost shy student, Nagurski took his football ability for granted, but only within himself. He still had to work to get through college and at various times he was night watchman at a lumber yard; messenger boy for a firm of lawyers; and put in more than 30 hours a week in a restaurant (where his duties included that of "bouncer").

He permitted himself very little in the way of personal high jinks and the closest he came to tooting his own horn was when he insisted, despite his 225 pounds, that he was faster than Shorty Almquist, a speedy, 180-pound Gopher halfback. The Bronk challenged Almquist to enter the fraternity intramural track meet in the spring. Almquist laughingly accepted. Bronk beat him by two yards in the 50-yard dash. Mortified, Almquist entered the shot-put against the mighty Nagurski who had flung the iron ball in high school. Almquist beat Bronko by six inches.

The pro league was just beginning to prove its stability and attraction at the gate as Bronko Nagurski finished college. Several teams panted after the Gopher star, knowing he would not only be a great fullback but a sure-fire box-office draw. They all wanted him, but in those days most collegiate stars signed for a straight salary or a per-game fee. At least four clubs, realizing what Nagurski was worth, offered him hard cash to sign. Eventually the Bronk bowed to the blandishments of the Chicago Bears' George Halas. The owner-coach of the Midway Monsters was willing to part with a fortune to get the mighty Bronko.

He signed Nagurski for $5000.

The Bronk went on to become the greatest running back the pro game had ever known. He gained 3946 yards in eight seasons for an average of almost five yards a carry. Later, when the pro game would open up, his yardage marks would be wiped out by such as Steve Van Buren and Jimmy Brown, but in the era of tight-knit, power football this was considered the greatest bit of ground-grabbing since the Oklahoma land-rush.

In 1934 when Beattie Feathers joined the Bears, the Tennessee flash set a new league mark of 1004 yards rushing for one season. Every foot of it was accomplished behind Nagurski's blocking.

When the pros started fiddling around with the jump pass in the middle thirties, Halas figured he had the proper technician to execute it—a fullback blasting toward the line and suddenly leaping up to flip the short one. "Think you can throw?" Halas inquired.

"Let's try it, Coach," Bronko growled, wrapping a huge paw around the ball, almost obscuring it.

Nagurski attempted the jump pass 73 times in pro competition, completing 36, with nine going for touchdowns.

Bronko Nagurski retired after the 1937 season but when World War Two posed a manpower problem for most of the teams, Halas in 1943 talked him into coming back at the age of 35. "I'll try it at tackle, Coach," said Bronko, "where I won't need as much speed."

Subsequently, after playing a full 60 minutes in a 21-21 donnybrook, Nagurski turned to a teammate, lineman George Musso, and said: "This is the first time I've never been tired after a pro game. You know, linemen should be able to play until they're 45."

Musso looked over at him suspiciously. "You sure you weren't kicked in the head out there?"

Of course Bronko had, and many times before, but what damage could be done by a flea booting a horse on the noggin?

GEORGE SIMPSON, *with a smashing sprint double in the 100 (a 9.4 world record) and 220, led Ohio State to its only NCAA track championship in 1929.*

One of the outstanding athletes in Northwestern history, RUSSELL (RUT) WALTER was a three-time winner of the Big Ten quarter-mile championship, took the NCAA title in 1929 and captained the 1930 Purple basketball team, winning All-league honors.

In track, Iowa took the indoor crown, and Illinois the outdoor title, but it was Ohio State which grabbed off the major honors of the year when it won the NCAA team title behind the brilliant performances of sprinter George Simpson who won both the 100 and 220 and set a world mark of 9.4 in the century. Dick Rockaway, the Buckeyes' swift, graceful hurdler, took the high hurdles and teammate Pete Rasmus set a new NCAA discus mark with 159-1⅞. (The four Buckeye individual titles also constituted a new NCAA high.) Tom Warne, Northwestern pole vaulter, took the first of what was to be three straight NCAA crowns by tying Bill Graber of Southern California with a new NCAA mark of 13 feet 10-5⁄16 inches; teammate Rut Walter won the 440; Dave Abbott, of Illinois repeated in the two-mile, and Ed Gordon, of Iowa, won the first of what would be three straight broad jump crowns. It was a big year for the Big Ten with eight individual titles. No collegiate conference would ever again win more in a single NCAA track tournament. (The Big Ten would equal it in 1936.) Six Conference teams placed in the top ten finishers. Behind Ohio were Illinois, third; Iowa, sixth; Michigan, seventh; Northwestern ninth; and Chicago, tenth.

In swimming, Michigan took its third straight team crown, and the Conference won three titles in the NCAA, all by Northwestern. Al Schwartz, first of the league's truly great freestylers, set a new NCAA mark of 53.2 in the 100; Wally Colbath, captured his third straight one-meter diving title (the first three-timer in any NCAA sport in Big Ten history), and the Northwestern trio of Dick Hinch, Don Peterson and Schwartz posted a new 300-yard medley relay mark of 3:09.4.

On other league fronts, Michigan won the first Conference team championship in wrestling, with a tournament replacing the previous system of team titles determined by dual meet standings. The Wolverines were then runners-up to Oklahoma A. & M., as NCAA team champs, in the second year of NCAA

for an Athletic Director and he'd taken the liberty of recommending me highly to President Walter Dill Scott. Without waiting to gauge my reaction he suggested that I come to Chicago immediately. I did. I met with President Scott and the Athletic Board and they offered me the job. I said I was still under contract for another year at Drake and would like to talk it over with the Drake people. The Drake president urged me to accept because it was obviously a big step up on the career ladder. Even after he said he'd release me from our contract if I desired, I still had some reservations. I went to see George Huff, my old Athletic Director at Illinois. Quite bluntly I asked him what kind of future Northwestern might have.

Huff spelled out what I already knew but he wanted me to be sure of the facts. Northwestern was the small-

est school in the Big Ten, and the only private institution in the league aside from Chicago. The other eight were state supported schools, with certain financial advantages. Northwestern had higher tuition fees than its sister schools and, for the most part, higher entrance requirements. It all added up to a tougher row to hoe in athletic competition. As a farm boy I knew about tough rows to hoe and I didn't scare too easily. "I can't be too optimistic about Northwestern's athletic future in the toughest Conference in the land," said Huff, "but I'll say this . . . ," and he paused. "They can't go any lower in the league standings and directed by the right person they might very well improve."

I knew, then, what his advice was, without him having to tell me precisely what to do. There was only one more person whose counsel I knew I had to seek—my wife. I

mat tournaments. Among individual titlists, Illinois' Joe Sapora was the 115-pound champion, and teammate George Minot ruled the 135-pounders.

The year before, Chicago had won the first Conference team title in fencing, but in 1929 Illinois swordsmen launched a domination of the sport that has continued to this day with few interruptions. In the next 37 years, the Illini would wear the crown 21 times. Two great coaches won all the crowns between them: Herb Craig, who started Illinois on its winning ways in 1929, continued to 1938; and Max Garret, who took over in 1941, has been there since.

In tennis, George Lott, of Chicago won the Conference singles championship, and would go on to even greater glory as a member of the U.S. Davis Cup team and, with Lester Stoefer, would win the world doubles championship.

Among the winners of the Conference Medal for scholarship in 1929 was Ernie McCoy, the Michigan cage and baseball star, who later would become the highly-respected athletic director at Penn State.

Despite a highly successful year in the athletic arena, the Big Ten in 1929 gave itself a self-dosage of the bitter along with the sweet, when, on May 25, it handed down the first and only suspension of a member in the league's long and honored history. Iowa, accused of "infractions of an athletic nature," involving financial aid to football stars Willis Glasgow and Oran Pape among others, was dropped from the Conference amid the most heated controversy ever witnessed in the Big Ten. The fact that Iowa was readmitted nine months later was anticlimactic to the high personal drama involving Hawkeye athletes and administrative personnel. Meanwhile, Iowa schedules were flipped completely awry. The Hawkeyes managed to get in only one football game against a league foe—Purdue—and took advantage of hastily made dates with outsiders to fill their slate. No Conference basketball and baseball teams were met.

Little JOE SAPORA, Illinois' 115-pound Big Ten wrestling champ, was the first Conference mat man to take two NCAA crowns in a row, winning in 1929-30.

GEORGE LOTT, Chicago's Big Ten singles champion in 1929, went on to become one of the world's greatest stars in international tennis, winning the U.S. doubles championship with Lester Stoeffen twice.

Tug Wilson in 1925 when, at age 29, he became Athletic Director at Northwestern—the youngest director the Conference ever had.

told her I was very happy at Drake, that the new job would be a tough one, and asked what she thought of making a change when Drake represented all the security we'd ever need.

"When do we leave?" was all Dorothy said.

Five minutes later I made a telephone call to O.F. Long, Chairman of the Northwestern Athletic Committee, and found myself the youngest Athletic Director in the Big Ten. I was just 29 years old, bringing a pair of shaky knees to the arena of big-time collegiate sports.

We moved immediately, finding a nice apartment near the University. My first day on the job I went over to old Patten Gym to meet my coaches and take stock of the situation. It wasn't rosy. I was the most disillusioned man in American sports. To begin with, 22 members of the football squad were in summer school and if they didn't

159

Just as the Twenties had ushered in a decade in which Americans became avidly involved with sports as a way of life, so did the Thirties leave its mark upon the sports scene—not only in the Western Conference but throughout the land.

Colleges began to get athletes who had more and better coaching in high school, and with the nation entering the Great Depression sports would become the only means by which many a deserving boy could go on to college, either through an athletic scholarship or jobs provided by athletic departments or alumni. On the other side of the coin, as compared to the Twenties when many athletes found their own way to the college of their choice without too much pressure on them, the Thirties saw the real beginning of all-out recruiting procedures on the part of coaches and alumni. Before too many years would pass, recruiting would become The Name of the Game, and survival on the athletic fields would depend on the horses you could lure into your corral.

The Thirties also were a decade of change in the sports, themselves. The football, for instance, was redesigned to give it more pointed dimensions. It became a passer's ball and opened up aerial tactics almost undreamed of before. (It also spelled doom for the drop-kick because the slimmer ball would not rebound as predictably when dropped.)

During the Thirties the size of the basketball, too, would be slightly reduced, with a consequent improvement in ball-handling, and the center jump would be eliminated after each goal, opening the way for the race horse, fast break game. Even swimming gear would come in for alteration, and full-length tank suits would give way to trunks as performers gave up some of their modesty for more speed. (Men only, of course. Topless attire for women would be a conversation piece and a designer's gambit for a still later decade.)

In track, sprinters in the Thirties would make use of starting blocks instead of digging holes in the cinders.

REB RUSSELL, a line-smashing fullback; WADE WOODWORTH, an explosive guard; and talented end, Frank Baker, led Northwestern to an unbeaten Big Ten season and a title tie with Michigan. All three were rewarded with All-America honors along with Wisconsin's tough Milo Lubratovich, at tackle, and Ohio State's incomparable Wes Fesler, at end.

As far as the single year, 1930, is concerned, the question may be asked: Is there such a thing as an absolute jinx, and can it make or break a team's season? The answer is affirmative on both counts if you're talking about Hank Bruder and the 1930 Northwestern campaign. It might well be that Dick Hanley, who replaced Glenn Thistlethwaite in 1927

pass their courses we'd be lucky to field a team of any sort. Then I learned that an alumni group had been helping some of our athletes get jobs and tuition money. The alumni had become disgusted with the procedure and suddenly turned things over to the new, young Athletic Director. They felt that the University was heavily enough endowed so that the athletic department could handle all such financial matters.

I realized, after a quick survey, that things were going on outside the scope of Big Ten rules. I didn't want to start my career at Northwestern with that hanging over me.

So, quite bluntly, I went to Commissioner John L. Griffith. I admitted a lot of things had been done improperly in the past but, although I was determined to run the department under Conference rules, it looked like a hopeless job.

Griffith was more than understanding. He suggested I call a meeting with President Scott, Dean Heilman of the School of Commerce and William A. Dyche, the University business manager. A week later we all spent a full day behind closed doors, and, with Griffith's blessing, worked out a plan whereby the University would help with needy athletes' tuition fees if they would sign notes for the money advanced to them. The gesture helped Northwestern start afresh with a clean slate. It also meant that I, as Director, was starting off the same way, and I never forgot the Major's contribution to our solution.

I spent a lot of time that first summer riding herd on the athletes in summer school and got a lot of help from some of the younger faculty members who tutored them. They were going to have to make it legitimately

had come up with one of the finest clubs in Big Ten history. Up front was a remarkable brace of tackles in Dallas Marvil and Jack Riley; Wade (Red) Woodworth the best guard in the Conference, and a talented sophomore end in Dick Fencl, among others.

Then there was the backfield—and what a backfield! Felix (Lefty) Leach, was a heady, blocking quarterback. Captain Hank Bruder was one halfback, and two big, rough newcomers—Ernest (Pug) Rentner and Fayette (Reb) Russell—were the other halfback and fullback respectively. It is the almost unbelievable story of Bruder that marks the saga of a Northwestern team which, with Michigan shared the Big Ten title with unblemished Conference slates—and which found the Purple deprived of the national championship in the final game of the season against Notre Dame.

A six-foot, 180-pound swifty who could do everything (run, pass and kick), Bruder had clinched the left halfback position in pre-season drills two years previously as a sophomore. He injured his hip a week before the season opened, missed the first five games and was sub-par in the last three. Obviously, as a junior, he figured to be an all-time Purple great. In the Conference opener against Wisconsin, however, he broke his leg, and his junior year was wiped out. The Wildcats, nevertheless, elected Bruder captain for his senior year and everyone hoped he could cast aside the nickname "Hard-Luck Hank." In fact, the 1930 season loomed a gigantic success for both Bruder and the Wildcats. In the opener against Tulane, Bruder romped 50 yards for the first Purple touchdown and Pug Rentner put the frosting on his collegiate debut by ripping 30 yards for the second Northwestern score.

A few days later Hank Bruder was stricken with smallpox!

No jinx had ever been so consistent for player or school in the history of the Conference. Yet, Northwestern almost beat it, on the strength of heroics by Rentner, Russell and Woodworth. In his first

Conference game, against Ohio State, Rentner scored one touchdown himself and passed for two others to Frank Baker and Lee Hanley. Against Illinois, Rentner was on target for two more TD aerials to Baker and scored, himself, on a dazzling 98-yard kickoff return. Meanwhile, Russell was shredding defenses every week, with his pulverizing fullbacking preventing Purple foes from keying on Rentner. Even Woodworth, a lineman, got into the act by scoring on an old-fashioned guard-around play against Minnesota. (A costly touchdown for the Wildcats as Rentner sustained a shoulder injury while blocking, and was lost for the rest of the season.)

Captain Hank Bruder, beating the smallpox siege; came back for the last three games, and Northwestern eyed the conclusion of its greatest season ever. Bruder, his weight down drastically from his bout with smallpox, caught a pass for one score and passed for two others against Indiana. Reb Russell

"HARD-LUCK" HANK BRUDER, Northwestern halfback, was one of the Conference greats in 1928-29-30 but never enjoyed a complete season because of physical set-backs that ranged from broken legs to smallpox.

or not at all. It was part of my determination that I was going to launch my career in the Big Ten as clean as possible. Only two boys failed to regain their eligibility. I was proud of the big group that did.

Then, before the fall term began I decided I'd visit the Athletic Directors at some of the other Conference schools having great success in their varsity programs. First, I saw L.W. St. John at Ohio State who gave me a lot of suggestions and solid encouragement. Very pointedly he stated it was important to the Conference that Northwestern have good athletic teams. It was one of two private schools in the league and the smallest, and, he implied it would be unhealthy for the Conference to have a perennial weak sister.

Next, I talked to Fielding Yost at Michigan, who convinced me there was nothing I faced that couldn't be whipped into shape. He, too, had some solid ideas, and

I wound up my tour with Amos Alonzo Stagg, at the University of Chicago, our cross-town neighbors. Frankly, Stagg was a bit pessimistic about Northwestern's chances of competing with the large state universities in the Conference. I told him I thought we could handle things as well as Chicago, the other private college in the Big Ten, but he declared that things were going well at Chicago with lots of tradition and the impetus of success behind the school. Northwestern was rebuilding and I might have a tough time keeping our alumni on the straight and narrow. As grand a person as he was, and as astute, Amos Alonzo Stagg didn't realize that within two or three years athletic catastrophy would strike Chicago, and Northwestern was destined to go on to some great days.

The tour, however, was one of the smartest things I could do. Huff, Stagg, Yost and St. John really ran the

and Lee Hanley sparked a rout of Wisconsin the following week and suddenly Northwestern had come up to the season finale with unbeaten Notre Dame in what simply had to be for national honors.

Notre Dame in 1930 was just a team-wide collection of current and future All-Americas. Up front, Bert Metzger, the famous watch-charm All-America guard; Joe Kurth, tackle; Frank Hoffman, guard; and Tommy Yarr, center, who would be All-America the following season. In the backfield, a trio of All-Americas in quarterback Frank Carideo and halfbacks Marchy Schwartz and Marty Brill.

It was this bunch which Northwestern rocked back on its heels in a scoreless deadlock for 53 of the 60 minutes in jam-packed Dyche Stadium. In fact, it looked as if the Wildcats would have little trouble with the Irish. Russell made a sieve of the Notre Dame line and battered his way to the Irish four, but there he fumbled and Notre Dame recovered. Then Bob Clark picked off a Carideo pass and the Wildcats were knocking on the Irish door again. With the ball on the one-yard line the Purple switched strategy, faked to Russell and gave it to Hard-Luck Hank Bruder, who hit the goal line—and fumbled. Notre Dame recovered again and Northwestern seemed to lose some of its spark. Notre Dame had been completely dominated by the Wildcats but, suddenly, with seven minutes to play, Marchy Schwartz cracked over tackle and went 27 yards for a TD. Two minutes later Carideo intercepted a Purple pass and took it to the Northwestern 10. The Northwestern defense, magnificent all day, had suffered too much letdown from its offense, and Dan Hanley, Irish fullback, eventually crashed over to end the scoring for the day. The Wildcats who had averaged 26 points a game, had suffered their lone loss and their only whitewash.

Michigan, meanwhile, had only a scoreless tie with arch-rival, Michigan State, as the only blotch on an otherwise spotless record. Harry Kipke, former Wolverine star who had coached the Spartans the

Conference in those days and the frequent counsel I had from them over the next few years meant a great deal to me.

Meanwhile, as I started my first year at Northwestern I had to reflect that my new school had had the poorest record of any in the Big Ten. Although a founding member in 1896 they had never won a football title, never won a baseball or track title. Our old football stands were a wooden affair into which you might cram 25,000 people. Dressing quarters were in an old building that contained just enough hot shower water for half the squad. On the plus side, however, Northwestern had one of the nation's finest field houses where the Conference indoor track meet was held each year. They had the best swimming record in the Conference and Tom Robinson was certainly an outstanding coach—if not the best in the country.

After several dismal football seasons we were beginning to show some strength. In fact, the year before I arrived, in the last two games, we'd battled champion Chicago scoreless for 27 minutes before the Maroon got a field goal and the only score of the game. The following week Northwestern gave Notre Dame's Four Horsemen club fits before losing in the last few minutes, 13-6. Incidentally, before the Chicago game Northwestern teams had been known as the Fighting Methodists or simply The Purple, but their ferocious play against mighty Chicago moved a sports writer to refer to the club as "Wildcats," and the name was immediately adopted.

It was in my first year as Director that Northwestern came up with possibly the most dramatic football game to date. Michigan was coming in to play us at huge Soldier's Field in Chicago, utilized to accomodate the

year before, had returned to his Alma Mater to take over the Wolverine reins, and had been replaced at East Lansing by Sleepy Jim Crowley, the young Notre Damer of Four Horsemen fame. It took Crowley just two weeks to endear himself to Spartan fans who had seen Michigan State defeated by the Wolverines every year since 1915. The scoreless tie in the Spartans second game of the 1930 season, seemed proof enough that better days were coming.

The All-America teams listed three Northwestern stars in 1930, the first time a Conference school had placed three men since Michigan's trio of Culver, Smith and Allmendinger in 1917. The pass-catching wizardry and all-around play of Frank Baker earned him an end spot; Reb Russell was a popular fullback pick; and Wade Woodworth was honored at guard. Milo Lubratovich, a tough, nimble Wisconsin tackle was the first Badger All-America in seven years, and Ohio State's versatile Wesley Fesler who was used at quarterback as well as end, was honored for the third straight year and was selected as the Conference's most valuable player, as well.

The 1930 basketball season was the year Piggy Lambert got Purdue rolling in a manner that would find the Boilermakers winning six championships in the next 10 years. It was Purdue's first under-feated team and it was the first time the league flag had been nailed without a loss since Minnesota did it in 1919. Leading the Boilermaker surge were Stretch Murphy and Johnny Wooden, the peerless center and guard, both of whom made All-America, along with Wisconsin's Bud Foster. The Big Ten scoring crown was worn by Indiana's Branch McCracken, however—the Hoosier three-sport star who just missed All-America honors in both football and basketball. Subsequently he would become one of the most successful basketball coaches in America and lead Indiana to national prominence. Never had the Conference seen three such great centers in the

DR. JOHN W. WILCE, center, came to Ohio State in 1913 after a brilliant athletic career in Wisconson, got his medical degree while coaching the Buckeyes and led them to their first years of glory with Big Ten titles in 1916-17-20. With him are two of his "finest, ever," as he termed them. Left, WES FESLER, the three-time All-America end, and his inseparable campus buddy, DICK LARKINS, also a football and basketball star, and who is now Ohio State's nationally-prominent athletic director.

same year as Murphy, Foster and McCracken and it was the only time three pivotmen were ever placed on the first All-Big Ten team because it was impossible to leave off any of the three.

In swimming, Michigan had its championship skein temporarily snapped by Northwestern—and it was the 10th and last time the Wildcats took the title. The first of the Big Ten aquatic powers had run its course. The Purple were also the only Conference team to make a noteworthy splash in the NCAA meet as freestyler Al Schwartz became the first man in NCAA history to take three titles in one year when he swept the 50-, 100- and 220-yard events, and the Wildcat trio of Dick Hinch, Bob Howlett, and Volney Wilson won the 300-yard medley relay.

In NCAA wrestling, Illinois' scrappy little Joe Sapora successfully defended his 115-pound title,

huge alumni groups which both schools had in the area. Fielding (Hurry-Up) Yost's Wolverines were undefeated, and his team, which included Benny Friedman and Bennie Oosterbaan, was subsequently called by the Michigan coach "my best team ever." We weren't exactly novices at Northwestern, with Tiny Lewis at fullback, Waldo Fisher, at end, and Captain Tim Lowry at center, but we just didn't have Michigan's depth and experience.

Saturday brought the worst weather I'd ever seen for a football game—driving rain and snow coming off Lake Michigan, and the field was covered with water. (It was the days before big, expensive tarpaulins.) Conditions were so bad Yost appealed to me to postpone the game. Here I was, just 29 years old, the youngest athletic director in the Western Conference, and more than 75,000 tickets had been sold—and almost 50,000 people had shown up at game time. I had to make a decision,

and as home-school director it was solely mine to make. I told Yost the 50,000 fans had a right to see a game and I thought we should play. I finally got his grudging consent, although there really wasn't much he could do about it as long as I'd made the decision.

It was an incredible game. I would see hundreds more in my lifetime but this one I'd never forget. Shortly after the kickoff Northwestern recovered a Michigan fumble on the Michigan five-yard line. Three times in that muck and rain Tiny Lewis blasted into the Wolverine line and somehow they kept him from slithering over. So, on fourth down Lewis kicked a field goal that just got there, and we led 3-0. From that point on, normal football was impossible. Running and ball-handling were impossible. (It would be exactly 25 years before this eerie situation would be repeated in an incredible Blizzard Bowl in Columbus.) Both teams resorted to a punting duel just to

HAROLD (BUD) FOSTER   DOUG MILLS

Possibly the most famous All-Big Ten basketball team of any given year was that of 1930. It included HAROLD (BUD) FOSTER, of Wisconsin; DOUG MILLS, of Illinois; Branch McCracken, of Indiana, and George (Stretch) Murphy and John Wooden of Purdue. Mills, who was twice All-Big Ten and among the top five scorers for three years, went on to become a great coach at Illinois and subsequently athletic director. Wooden later led UCLA to national cage heights. McCracken became Indiana's coach and turned out some of the Hoosiers' finest teams during a distinguished 24-year career at Bloomington. Murphy, of course, was recognized as one of the greatest "Big Men" in the early years of basketball history.

1931

and Otto Kelley, of Michigan, won the 155-pound crown.

There were loud noises raised at Wisconsin as the Badgers captured their first baseball championship since 1912, led by Captain Moe Winer, a short-stop, and pitchers Nello Pacetti and Art Sommerfield. Wisconsin also took the indoor track crown, but Michigan came through outdoors, and six Conference stars won NCAA titles. George Simpson, Ohio State's great sprinter, made it two in a row in the 220, setting a new record of 20.7 as he did so. Lee Sentman of Illinois tied the 220-yard low

hurdles mark of 23.2 set by Iowa's Frank Cuhel two years earlier. Orval Martin of Purdue took the 880; Tom Warne of Northwestern won his second straight pole vault title; Ed Gordon of Iowa took his second broad jump crown; and Michigan's Holley Campbell took the javelin throw.

When EDWARD L. GORDON, JR., was only 14 years old, in Gary, Indiana, he was six feet tall but weighed a mere 115 pounds. To improve his gawky, weak-limbed physique his father urged him to get active in sports. Six years and 50 pounds later Ed Gordon was well along toward becoming the nation's greatest broad-jumper. He had tried the event only once in high school (where he'd been just a fair sprinter and high-jumper) but when he came to the University of Iowa, veteran track coach George Bresnahan took one look at his wiry physique and sinewy strength and thought he had enough speed to make a good broad-jumper—despite the fact that Gordon appeared almost awkward as he raced down the runway with tremendous stride, feet turned outward and arms flailing without grace. Something told Bresnahan not to try to change the boy's style.

So the "good" broad-jumper won more major titles than any trackman in Iowa history and became the first Big Ten athlete to win three straight NCAA championships when he won the broad jump title in 1929-30-31. Meanwhile he was also taking three straight Big Ten crowns in the event. He captured 17 major broad jump championships in all and climaxed his career with the Olympic crown in 1932. In an era when a single 24-foot leap was a superlative jump in an athlete's career, Gordon had 16 of them in championship meets, alone, not counting the dozens of times he did it in his trial jumps. Bresnahan estimated that he reached 24 feet or better in at least four of every six trial jumps. Only once, in the rain at the Drake Relays, was Gordon under 24 feet. As a freshman, Gordon made the 1928 Olympic team but a strained muscle kept him at least a foot under his usual efforts. In 1932, however, a healthy Ed Gordon climaxed his career by winning the Olympic title with 25 feet 3/4 inches.

It was a wild football season in 1931, and even the Great Depression had a hand in determining the championship. Northwestern (putting together

get rid of the ball and hope the other guy would fumble. Then, late in the fourth period Michigan sloshed its way to our 10-yard line but Northwestern held for downs. Then came a brilliant bit of strategy. Bill Christmann, our quarterback, and Captain Lowry, decided to go back into punt formation with Tiny Lewis standing on the goal line—and then take a deliberate safety. It made the score 3-2, gave us a chance for a free kick, and there was Michigan putting the ball in play again in its own territory with miles to go in the mud, it seemed. There were just two or three minutes left, and they didn't get there. It was the upset of the year.

Then, in our final game it looked as though we'd pull off another big upset, this time against Knute Rockne's Four Horsemen team. We led 10-0 at half-time and the Irish fans were stunned. As the two teams left the field to go to their dressing rooms I suddenly found myself

walking right next to Rockne. I wanted to get to our own dressing room but Rock grabbed my arm. "Stay with me!" he said, and first thing I knew I was with him in the Notre Dame locker room. Everything was quiet. Rockne stood there a moment, his lips tight, his eyes cold. Then he said, scornfully: "I thought I was coaching the Fighting Irish but you're getting beat by some Fighting Wildcats!" I don't know what he said after that; I tore out of there to get to our own dressing rooms. It must have been a typically effective Rockne speech. The Irish came back to score two touchdowns to beat us, 13-10.

It had been the greatest football season in 10 years for Northwestern and at the annual dinner for the squad, Robert Campbell, President of the Board of Trustees, announced that the 1926 team would play in a new stadium. It would be called Dyche Stadium in honor

EDWARD GORDON

circumstances. The Wolverines, who were to go through the season shutting out eight opponents and holding a ninth to a single touchdown, had a poised, versatile ball club featuring brainy Harry Newman at quarterback; hard-running halfback, Herman Everhardus, and a line anchored by Maynard Morrison, a great pivotman, and Ted Petosskey, a brilliant end—plus a big, strong sophomore tackle named Francis Wistert who was destined to be the first of three brothers who would be All-America tackles for the Wolverines—a record no other school or family would ever match. Somehow, all the talent got slightly unstuck at the same time, and Michigan dropped a 20-0 shocker to an undermanned Ohio State team that got a lot of offensive mileage out of versatile Stu Holcomb, Lew Hinchman, a hard-nosed halfback, Mickey Vuchinich, a plugging fullback, and a line bolstered by Joe Gailus, a great guard and Sid Gilman, a fine, all-around end. Nobody believed the score of that game except the Buckeye players who suddenly considered themselves championship contenders.

Purdue, which had been upset early in the year, 21-14, by Wisconsin, romped through the rest of its season undefeated. Roy Horstman, a fast, jarring fullback; and Jim Purvis, a big, triple-threat halfback, provided the offensive fireworks behind a line that featured Chuck Miller, a mighty center, and Paul Moss, a dazzling, pass-catching end. The Boilermakers, however, were not through yet. There was still a big depression-spawned surprise to come.

Northwestern, meanwhile, looked as if it had come up with a team fully as brilliant as its almost-national champion of the previous season. After opening with a clean clobbering of Nebraska, the Purple played a fierce scoreless tie with Knute Rockne's last Notre Dame team—a great one—then went on to turn back UCLA and five straight Conference foes for an undefeated season. Leading the Wildcat surge were Pug Rentner, probably the best all-around halfback in the country; and a mighty line

two straight titles for the only time in its history), Michigan and Purdue wound up locked in a triple tie with each team losing one game under unusual

---

of William A. Dyche, for many years the Business Manager of the University and a great football fan.

It was to be a hectic year and, in fact, just short of chaotic in some aspects. There were endless hours with the stadium architects on last minute details, and in getting ready for the season, itself. At least summer jobs for our athletes were no problem because the contractors put many of them on construction work.

Of paramount concern to us was the dedication game which was to be played late in the season. We wanted the University of Chicago to be our opponent. Northwestern had few victories over the Maroon down through the years and a dedication win over Chicago would be a big boost for us. Both schools, of course, had large alumni right there in the area and that made it a natural, too.

It wasn't easy to get Chicago. I think Amos Alonzo

Stagg was suspicious of our motives because he knew we had a fine club coming up, but we finally got Mr. Stagg to agree to be our dedication opponent. (Actually, Stagg had reason to be wary of us. Led by our great quarterback, Moon Baker, and some terrific sophomores such as Justin Dart, Luke Johnsos, Yatz Levinson, and others, it was due to become the best team Northwestern had to date.)

That dedication game was a nightmare from an administrative viewpoint. We had fine, new dressings rooms in the stadium, but Stagg refused to use them. He insisted his team be allowed to dress in Patten Gym, several blocks away and this presented a sudden and acute transportation problem the day of the game. We just got his team to Dyche Stadium in time, or so we thought. Both teams were now in their stadium dressing rooms waiting until the dedication ceremonies were over.

CHUCK MILLER, *All-America center, was a line stalwart in Purdue's championship grid team of 1931.*

bulwarked by tackles Jack Riley and Dallas Marvil, and a fine, place-kicking guard, Paul Engegretsen, whose extra point beat Iowa, 7-6 in the closest victory margin of the year for Northwestern. The Wildcats, like Purdue, Michigan, and Ohio State, weren't in the clear yet. Even though the schedule was completed and, seemingly, Northwestern was the undisputed champion, one more hurdle suddenly arose where none had been anticipated. The nation was in the depths of the depression. Millions were unemployed. As participants in a varied, nation-wide charity program, the Big Ten decided to play five post-season games with proceeds to go to the poor. Results of the games were to count in the final championship standing which Northwestern previously had dominated.

In the extra-game draw, Northwestern was paired with Purdue; Michigan with Wisconsin, and Ohio State with Minnesota. Only the Wildcats were undefeated. The Wolverines, Boilermakers and Buckeyes had lost only once. Never were there so many grab bag possibilities at the close of a season. The grab bag burst in some surprised faces as the favorites overreached themselves. If the Buckeyes defeated the Gophers they would have shared the title, but Minnesota, which had lost three games, upset the Bucks, 19-7. Michigan, fighting to salvage a share of the title, did manage to turn back Wisconsin, 16-0. It was Northwestern that had the most to gain by a win over tough Purdue, but there had been an ill omen at the Chicago hotel where the Wildcats were staying the night before the game at Soldier's Field. An elevator with several players aboard fell out of control, and although nobody was badly hurt, many players were shaken up. The next afternoon the Purple appeared sluggish. For 50 minutes the teams battled without a score. Then Fred Hecker of Purdue intercepted a Wildcat pass and returned it 40 yards to the Wildcat 30-yard line. Three plays got 11 yards, and then Jim Purvis broke loose for 19 yards and the only touchdown of the game, and the only blemish on a great Northwestern season. As one Wildcat supporter mournfully described the charity game. "We gave more than our share—we gave up an undisputed title!"

It was a season of stars for the Big Ten. Not only did Northwestern provide the brilliant, triple-threat Pug Rentner for the All-America, but it became the first Conference team in history to turn up two linemen at the same position for the honor squad, in Jack Riley and Dallas Marvil. Michigan supplied Maynard Morrison as an All-America center, as did Purdue with Chuck Miller. It was a big year for the Boilermakers as the versatile Paul Moss also made it at end.

Playing with a mediocre team that had dropped three games, chunky, quiet but immensely dedicated

Now this was in the early days of loud-speaking mechanisms, but we'd obtained the best available and tested it thoroughly that morning. I got the University President, the Chairman of the Board of Trustees, and other dignitaries in front of the mike at mid-field and they made speeches that fell on an absolutely dead loud-speaking system. I was almost ill. The crowd started chanting for the teams to come out, but neither one appeared although it was well past starting time. I ran to the Chicago dressing room and told Stagg it was time to get cracking and would he please take the field. He quietly asked if Northwestern was out there yet.

"No, not yet," I began, and he interrupted me.

"Then we'll wait until they get out there," Mr. Stagg snapped.

I rushed to our own dressing room and was horrified to listen to Coach Glen Thistlethwaite say he wouldn't budge out there until Stagg was on the field.

The crowd began clamoring for a ball game, and I couldn't seem to give them one. The only thing I could do was tell a lie. I ran back to Stagg's quarters and said Northwestern was on the field. I then broke all records for the 100-yard dash when I fled back to Thistlethwaite and said Stagg was on the field.

Both teams came out together and I didn't wait around for the looks which Stagg and Thistlethwaite aimed at me. I guess it was fated that on a day like this the game should start the way it did when Captain Vic Gustafson took the Chicago kickoff and ran it back 88 yards for a touchdown. It was the best dedication game anyone could have dreamed up but I must confess I didn't have a hand in it. It also launched a 38-7 rout of Chicago

PUG RENTNER

DAL MARVIL

Three stars from Northwestern's title-sharing team were featured in the All-America selections for 1931, along with the Big Ten's most-valuable-player. PUG RENTNER, the wildcats' triple-threat, was a do-everything who slashed opponent's ground defense with his running and riddled their secondary with pin-point passing. Meanwhile, the Purple's JACK RILEY and DAL MARVIL became the league's first and only brace of tackles from one school to gain All-America honors. Minnesota boasted a converted fullback, CLARENCE

(BIGGIE) MUNN, who sacrificed his more glamorous ball-toting duties of the previous season to turn himself into an All-America guard who became the loop's MVP. Later, Munn would have a brilliant career as coach and then athletic director at Michigan State. Other Conference All-Americas for the year were Maynard Morrison, also a converted fullback and a tower of strength in the Wolverine line, and Chuck Miller, of Purdue, who attracted similar raves for his all-around play as Boilermaker pivotman.

JACK
RILEY

CLARENCE
(BIGGIE) MUNN

for the first Northwestern win over the Maroon in 10 years and I mentally complimented myself for working so hard to get Chicago into the picture. I might add that the stunning victory helped me forget the fury of a prominent Northwestern alumnus I'd startled underneath the stands when I'd been running from one dressing room to the other to get the game started. I'd come upon him as he was taking a long pull at a bottle to bolster his spirit. He was, in fact, so startled he dropped his precious bottle. "Wilson," he roared, "haven't you got anything else to do but go around snooping under the stands?"

Little did he know what his neophyte Athletic Director had to do.

The season itself ended in a rapturous blaze for all of us when we beat Iowa, 13-6, in the finale, to complete

Northwestern's first undefeated Conference season and earn a tie with Michigan for the league championship—the Wildcats' first.

The football banquet planned that year was to be the greatest in Northwestern's history. A great surprise however was in store for Northwestern. Coach Glen Thistlethwaite who had completed a five-year contract, decided to accept an offer to be head coach at Wisconsin. The fact that he had been recruited secretly by another Conference school to a similar position was not only a shock to Northwestern but to the Conference as well. In the May meeting of the Big Ten in 1927, the Directors voted that Conference schools should not employ a coach from other Big Ten members without first obtaining permission to negotiate from his employers.

There were many applications for the Northwestern

Clarence (Biggie) Munn—also a star shot-putter—was named the league's most valuable player.

In basketball, the 1931 season had been marked by the success of the one team which had not yet won a Conference title—and for Northwestern it had been a long, long wait. Arthur (Dutch) Lonborg, a quiet young man from Kansas, had taken over

ARTHUR (DUTCH) LONBORG who had taken over as Northwestern basketball coach in 1927 to begin one of the longest and most respected careers in Big Ten cage history, molded one of the Wildcats' finest teams, ever, in 1931, a championship outfit that was the first in Wildcat history, with 13-1 in the league and 16-1 overall.

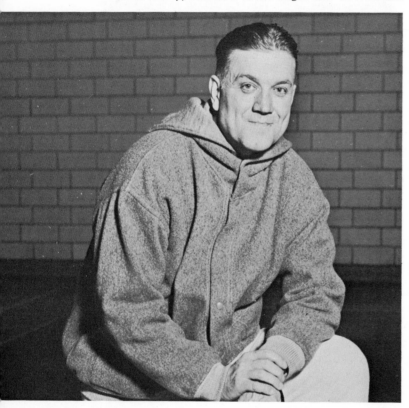

as Purple coach in 1927 to begin one of the longest and most respected coaching tenures in Northwestern history, and in 1931 he put together an outstanding team that was 16-1 for the season overall, with the lone loss handed to the Wildcats by Illinois, 34-28, in an upset. Leading the Purple surge were Captain Bert Riel at forward, Bob McCarnes, center, and Frank Marshall, guard, plus a red-hot sophomore whiz, Joe Reiff, the league's leading scorer.

Purdue, which had bid an almost tearful farewell to Stretch Murphy, still had Johnny Wooden, the best play-maker in the Big Ten, and the dazzling junior guard again was All-America, along with Rieff, the brilliant Northwestern center.

Michigan took the indoor track title, and Wisconsin which hadn't won the outdoor crown since 1916, finally did it again. In the NCAA meet, although Southern California won the team title handily, the Big Ten followed the Trojans in remarkable fashion, with Ohio State second, Illinois third, Iowa fourth, Indiana fifth, Wisconsin sixth, and Michigan seventh. There were individual heroes galore from the Big Ten. Ohio State's swift, lanky Jack Keller scored an impressive double by winning the 120-high hurdles and 220-lows. Ed Gordon, Iowa's brilliant broad jumper won his third straight crown; Tom Warne, Northwestern's dextrous pole vaulter, accomplished the same trick by sharing a three-way tie with Illinois' Verne McDermott and Southern California's Bill Graber, at the record height of 13 feet 10 and $^{15}/_{16}$ inches. Eddie Tolan, Michigan's blazing sprinter, took the 220-yard dash and barely missed out in the century. Chicago's Dale Letts set a new NCAA mark of 1:53.5 in the 880, and Michigan State's Clark Chamberlain became the second Spartan titlist by winning the two-mile.

In other NCAA action, John Schmieler, one of the stars of Michigan's Big Ten swimming champions, took the NCAA 220-yard breaststroke and Lowell March, of Minnesota, captured the 150-yard backstroke event. (Never again would the Confer-

vacancy but we finally decided on Dick Hanley who had had a tremendous coaching record at Haskell Indian Institute.

Despite our flurry of success, there was still a lot of spade work to be done if we were to continue to win. I had gotten off to a good start with the "N" Men's Club and each month we would have meetings at which I would present my problems. Sometimes their enthusiasm almost got us in trouble, but I will always have the utmost admiration for alumni of Northwestern. They were a loyal and enthusiastic group and I could see that if I could harness all this interest and enthusiasm they would be an invaluable aid to us in promoting strong athletic teams.

I worked with our venerable alumni secretary, Charlie Ward, and he arranged many meetings in and around the Chicago area. One thing I noticed right at the start was that Northwestern had few graduates in the high

school coaching field. Neighboring state institutions with large coaching schools had literally hundreds of high school coaches throughout the middle west. I remembered my days at the University of Illinois coaching school and thought it might serve as a model. The trouble was that a six-week school was rather expensive for high school coaches. I conceived the idea of a short two-week summer coaching school which would give class work in football, basketball, track and administration. The tuition for the course would be $25.00, which was very nominal.

We had an ideal situation. We could house the visiting coaches at Northwestern's fine dormitories and fraternity houses right on the lake front at reasonable cost and could offer many diversions such as big league baseball games; both the Chicago Cubs and the White Sox were very happy to give us complimentary tickets for one game at each park.

While I had a very fine coaching staff at Northwestern,

CLARK CHAMBERLAIN became Michigan State's second NCAA champion when he took the two-mile crown in the 1931 nationals.

CLARK CHAMBERLAIN   JOE RIEFF

JOE RIEFF, of Northwestern was the first man in history to win the Conference scoring crown three years in a row. (There have been only three to do so.) As a sophomore center (6-3) in 1931 Rieff led the Wildcats to their long-sought first league championship and was named All-America, along with Purdue's Johnny Wooden.

ence be limited to only two titles.) In wrestling, Jack Riley, Northwestern's All-America tackle became the second Big Ten all-star to win an NCAA crown in another sport when he won the heavyweight title.

In other highlights of the year, Richard Martin, of Illinois won the Big Ten individual golf crown for the second year in a row, and Chicago's Scott Rexinger did the same in tennis. Henry Brocksmith of Indiana took the individual cross-country title to lead the Hoosiers to their fourth-straight team championship.

In the awarding of the Conference Medal for scholarship, stardom didn't get in the way of the books for Chicago's NCAA track champion Dale Letts; Purdue's great football guard, George Van-Bibber; Illinois' NCAA hurdle champ, Lee Sentman, and a talented football and basketball star from Ohio State who later would become the Buckeyes' brilliant and respected athletic director—Richard C. Larkins.

1932

Under Harry Kipke, Michigan was becoming the dominant force in Conference football in the early thirties, and for the third year in a row the Wolverines in 1932 had a title, although the Wolves had to share it with Purdue which was undefeated but tied once. Under the custom which existed then, tie games didn't count in the standings.

For Michigan, the story was one of a beautifully balanced club playing sound football. Captain Ivan Williamson was a brilliant end and leader. As juniors, Ted Petoskey at end, and Francis Wistert at tackle, had matured into great linemen. In Chuck Bernard, Coach Harry Kipke again had a fine center whom he'd converted from fullback, just as he had done with Morrison in 1931. Herman Everhardus was now the tough, dependable, bread-and-butter halfback, and running the whole show was Harry Newman, the most dazzling quarterback the Big Ten had seen since the Wolverines' own Benny

---

I realized it would help if I could get clinic coaches of national reputation from other parts of the United States. The star-studded list I came up with through the years was outstanding: Bob Zuppke of Illinois; Pop Warner of Stanford; Knute Rockne of Notre Dame; Fritz Crisler of Michigan; Bernie Bierman of Minnesota; Bo McMillin of Indiana; Frank Leahy, then of Fordham; Howard Jones of Southern California; Harry Stuhldreher of Wisconsin; Ward Lambert of Purdue; and Sam Berry of Southern California. They were just a few of my illustrious faculty.

The response was almost unbelievable. High school coaches came from all over the United States and, to my surprise, many college and university coaches. From a modest 160 coaches the first year, the attendance grew to 480 in one year. I asked many of the big name coaches to give us a few of their plays and some of their defensive and offensive patterns. We mimeographed

Good friends get together on the steps of Patten Gym at Northwestern during 1927 summer coaching school. Left to right: Knute Rockne, Notre Dame; Kenneth L. Wilson, Northwestern Athletic Director; and Dick Hanley, Northwestern football coach.

Friedman. A squat, 5 foot 8 inch, 170-pounder, Newman was not only the finest passer in the nation that year but a tricky runner and canny safety man. An iron-man who took fearful punishment because of his size, Newman played 437 minutes out of a possible 480 for the season. He had demonstrated his varied heroics ever since he was a sophomore when he either passed for touchdowns or completed passes inside the 3-yard line against half the teams he played against, and, as a senior, did the same thing against six of Michigan's eight foes. He failed to turn the trick only against Chicago and Minnesota —but against the Maroon he ripped off dazzling touchdown runs of 78 and 26 yards, and against the Gophers he booted a field goal that provided the only points in the game.

Michigan that year was the epitome of the Punt-Pass-and-a-Prayer legacy handed down from Fielding Yost to Kipke. As Kipke, himself, declared: "In 1932 we gained about 1100 yards punting in seven of our eight games. . .Of course, a team can't score with punts but we try to work ourselves into scoring territory by kicking, and then we go to work with the passes—and an occasional prayer for deception. Our 1932 game with Princeton was a perfect example. . .We'd expected to handle Princeton all right but as it turned out they had us with our backs to the wall most of the afternoon. Jack James, their fullback, probably gained more yardage than our whole backfield but we kept protecting our kicker and punted out of danger a dozen times. Then our prayers came through when Ivy Williamson blocked a Princeton kick and Chuck Bernard fell on it for a touchdown. Later, Harry Newman got our passing game going and he completed a short one for the final score and that was the ball game."

Meanwhile, Purdue was also going through somewhat of a Golden Age of Football which had been launched by Jimmy Phelan in 1929 and was now being directed by the brilliant Noble Kizer. It took a vengeance-minded Northwestern team to put the

PAUL MOSS, Purdue's versatile end, made All-America for the second year in a row, in 1932, and JOE GAILUS, Ohio State's quick, slashing guard, was another Big Ten star honored, along with Michigan's quarterbacking genius, Harry Newman; a fine Wolverine end, Ted Petoskey, and Purdue's jolting Roy Horstman, a fullback who was responsible for much of the Boilermaker's unbeaten but once-tied season.

only blemish on a perfect Boilermaker season. The year before it was Purdue which had shattered the Purple dream of a perfect, national championship season by upsetting Northwestern in the post-season charity finale—and now the Wildcats were taking dead aim at the glory-bound Boilermakers. Purdue almost thwarted them, at that, and were leading 7-0 with 55 seconds to play when Pug Rentner passed to George Potter in the end zone for a touchdown, and Oliver Olson calmly booted the extra point for the tie that took the blush off Purdue's peach of perfection.

When All-America time came it was Michigan's Newman who was the glamor boy of the year—a unanimous pick for quarterback. Teammate Ted Petoskey was honored for his all-around, slashing end play, as was the versatile Paul Moss, repeating a second year for Purdue. Roy Horstmann, the Boilermakers' rough-riding fullback, was another Conference selection, along with Ohio State's talented Joe Gailus, an offensive and defensive demon at guard. For the Conference's most-valuable-player award it was Newman virtually unanimously.

these so the coaches could take them home. Some of the sessions were truly outstanding. One year I had Knute Rockne and Pop Warner of Stanford arguing the merits of the Notre Dame shift against the Warner double wing attack, nor can anyone ever forget the tremendous talks Coach Amos Alonzo Stagg gave at our coaching sessions.

Over the years many fine athletes came to Northwestern as a result of contacts we'd made with high school coaches at our annual coaching school. (I estimate that during these years we had over 1500 high school coaches in attendance.) I kept up a continual correspondence with those in neighboring states, sending them an occasional play or some defensive maneuvers helpful to them. I was also able to place some of the more successful coaches in college jobs, and as I look back over

a long athletic career, these memories bring some of my happiest moments.

Not all of the high school coaches needed assistance from me. You could tell some were heading for the top. Paul Brown, who was later to coach at Ohio State and the Cleveland Browns, was a student, as was Weeb Eubank, now coaching the New York Jets. Blanton Collier was coaching a small Kentucky high school when he first came to our school. He later coached at Kentucky and now heads the Cleveland Browns. Another of my students, Dr. W.S. Davis who, after coaching a few years, took his PhD. and is now the very successful President of Tennessee State.

In 1933, with the World's Fair in Chicago as a big attraction, I decided to go for the jackpot. I imported Howard Jones and Sam Berry from Southern California

NOBLE KIZER

The farm boy from Plymouth, Indiana, was a star basketball player and track man at tiny Plymouth High School, and a lot of colleges who were beginning to consider themselves big-time cage powers shortly after World War One, wanted young Noble Kizer to cast his lot with them.

It was quite a surprise, therefore, when young Nobe said he'd go to Notre Dame, just 20 miles from home, where football under Knute Rockne completely overshadowed what passed for basketball under the Golden Dome. Furthermore, young Kizer decided to put in two years as an instructor at the South Bend Y.M.C.A. before entering Notre Dame. His decision would later have immense benefits for Purdue, but, meanwhile fate would flutter a somewhat weird flick of her hand.

Noble Kizer not only had never played football (Plymouth didn't have a team) but he had seen exactly one game in his life. Nevertheless he decided to go out for his dormitory team at Notre Dame. Two weeks later Knute Rockne happened to pass by and saw a dormitory scrimmage. He also saw a 160-pound lineman tearing people apart. Rock took the boy aside. "Tomorrow," he ordered briskly, "you report to the freshman team!"

"Who, me?" the astonished boy said, implying furthermore that he'd probably get killed.

"I think you'll survive," Rock snapped. "Three-thirty tomorrow!"

Rock was right. Noble Kizer survived and, ballooning up to 165 pounds as a sophomore, promptly became a varsity guard in the fall of 1922. By his senior season he had achieved fame as the first of Notre Dame's great "watch-charm" guards, with his explosive blocking accounting for a lot of the success of Notre Dame's legendary "Four Horsemen" backfield of Stuhldreher, Miller, Crowley, and Layden.

Rockne was subsequently quoted as saying that Kizer and Rip Miller, the other guard, were the best brace of guards he'd ever had at Notre Dame up to that time. Coincidentally, Kizer and Miller became brothers-in-law when they married two sisters.

Meanwhile, he had fulfilled his original promise and intent as a basketball player and became the star and captain of the first Notre Dame team to attract any attention. He was All-Western in both football and basketball.

Joining the Purdue coaching staff the following fall, Noble Kizer brought with him a dynamism that was to revitalize the Boilermakers and, in the process, gain for Purdue its first recognition as a modern football power. Starting as an assistant coach under Jimmy Phelan, Kizer developed the kind of lines that led, in 1929, to Purdue's first undefeated season and first Big Ten title, and kept every Conference foe, except Michigan, from scoring. In 1930 Phelan left for Washington and Kizer succeeded him as head coach—the youngest in the Big Ten, and the only major college coach in the country under the age of 30.

In the next seven years Purdue became synonymous with gridiron greatness. Kizer's teams in that period lost only nine games with an overall record of 58-13-3. This occurred despite the fact that Purdue was renowned primarily as a basketball school, and prep football in the state of Indiana was not exactly brimming with pigskin talent. Kizer, however, every once in a while, by sheer force of personality, was able to lure an occasional recruit from

Noble Kizer, one of Notre Dame's great "watch-charm" guards, gets ready to meet Army.

out-of-state to Lafayette, such as Pest Welch, Jim and Duane Purvis, Cecil Isbell and others whom he developed into All-America and All-Big Ten performers.

Kizer's first team finished second, and the following year, 1931, he tied for the title with Michigan and Northwestern. In 1932 Kizer brought the Boilermakers home undefeated to share the title with Michigan. No Kizer-coach team ever finished out of the first division in the Conference, and in 1934 the brilliant young tactician was chosen in a nation-wide poll to be the first coach of the College All-Stars in the inaugural charity game with the pros in Chicago. In a titanic struggle with the Chicago Bears, Kizer's collegians battled the Monsters of the Midway to a scoreless tie.

Kizer, meanwhile, in 1933 had become Purdue's athletic director, the youngest with that portfolio in the Big Ten. In 1937 he relinquished his coaching duties following an illness, and three years later died at age 40, from a kidney ailment.

Noble Kizer, Purdue's head football coach, with Captain Ed Skoronski (left) and John Drake.

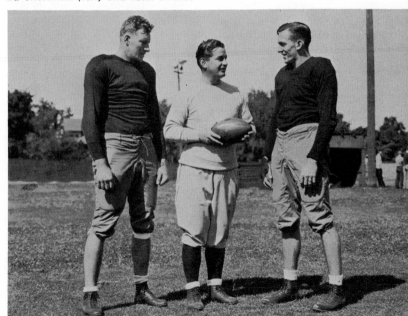

From Chicago came the word so long expected but not so easily accepted. Amos Alonzo Stagg was nearing the retirement age of 70, and despite his desire to stay on, University officials were adamant. The Grand Old Man of the Midway was through. Officially, he would not leave the University until July, 1933, but the 1932 football season was his last. It was not only a loss for Chicago, but for the entire Big Ten.

In basketball, Purdue took what was to become a patented, biennial championship with a gaudy 17-1 overall and 11-1 in the Conference, as most critics regarded the Boilermakers as the best in the land—and Captain Johnny Wooden as the best player in the nation as he led the Boilermakers with his play-making, defensive ball-hawking and his shooting eye. Leading the Big Ten in scoring (the first backcourt man to do so), he was a unanimous All-America. Not far behind in ability were Joe Rieff and Virgil Licht, of Northwestern and Minnesota, respectively, who tied for second place in the league.

In swimming, Michigan not only won the Conference title but dominated the NCAA festival with four titles. Taylor Drysdale, one of the greats in a glittering Wolverine aquatic history, won the first of three straight 150-yard backstroke titles and swam a leg on Michigan's winning 300-yard medley relay, along with Lou Lemak and Bob Lad as the trio set a new mark of 3:08.6. John Schmieler, retained his 200-yard breaststroke crown with a new mark of 2:33.4 and added the 220-freestyle, also with a new record of 2:15.4. Northwestern added to Conference glory when a Purple foursome of Paul Troup, Volney Wilson, Art Highland, and Mert Wilcox won the 400-yard freestyle relay.

Indiana took the indoor track title from Michigan by the margin of a spike—27-⅚ to 27—but the Wolves took the title outdoors. The Hoosiers, however, rebounded again to win the NCAA team crown, and for the first and only time in history the first three places went to one collegiate conference:

behind the Hoosiers were Ohio State and Minnesota. Leading the Hoosiers were Charles Hornbostel with the first of what would be three straight 880-yard crowns; and Bryce Beecher. who won the pole vault. Ohio State's great Jack Keller repeated his low hurdle triumph of the year before, but was upset in the highs by a 14.2 record-breaking performance by Iowa's George Saling.

Among other highlights of the year, Michigan's Johnny Fischer not only led the Wolves to the Con-

JOHN FISCHER, *Michigan's Big Ten individual golf titlist for two straight years in 1932-33 was the first Conference entry to take the NCAA individual title when he cracked through the usual Harvard-Yale-Princeton monopoly in 1932.*

and along with our own Coach Hanley, they generated a tremendous interest in our school program for that year. I, however, had even bigger things in mind.

During the early spring, the World's Fair directors announced they wanted some athletic events. They had tried track, but it had been a dismal failure at the gate. Now they wanted to try a football game.

I talked this over with Hanley, and together with Howard Jones we decided to put on an all-star game involving seniors who had finished their college competition. We divided the country at the Mississippi River. Everything to the west would belong to Jones, everything to the east to Hanley. We limited each squad to 25 players, and some of the greatest names in college football—including many All-Americans—were more than glad to come for a modest fee and expenses.

These players were utilized for demonstrations before the coaching school, and the visting high school coaches simply ate it up. The railroads gave us the transportation on credit. We had optimistically printed 50,000 tickets at $1 each, and hoped to have all our expense money in the bag long before game time.

About two weeks before the game at Soldier Field, Hanley and I realized we were $28,000 in the hole. I was learning a lesson in promotion of athletic events, namely that people will not buy unreserved tickets ahead of time.

The sports writers had been very generous with their publicity and there was a great deal of interest, but the day before the game we still were $25,000 in the red. Luckily for us, the weather was good. It was Iowa Day at the fair, and more than a half million persons were in

ference team title in golf but cracked what had been a virtual Ivy League monopoly on the NCAA individual crown since the turn of the century. (Fischer subsequently would become a U.S. Amateur champion in 1936, the only Big Ten star to do so.)

Another monopoly was broken by a Big Ten team when Indiana ended a four-year domination of NCAA wrestling by dethroning Oklahoma A. & M. as team champion. Among Conference mat stars who took individual titles were Ed Belshaw, the Hoosiers' 135-pound star who was voted the outstanding wrestler in the tourney; Joe Puerta, of Illinois, at 123 pounds; Carl Dougovito, Michigan's 158-pounder and Jack Riley, of Northwestern, repeating as heavyweight champ.

Indiana, meanwhile, had kept a good thing going for itself in cross-country, winning the Big Ten team title the sixth straight year, although Illinois' Dean Woolsey won the individual crown.

In the 1932 Olympic Games, the Big Ten again played an impressive role.

It was a glittering record for the Big Ten in the 1932 Olympics at Los Angeles. Michigan's Eddie Tolan scored a brilliant double with firsts in the

EDDIE TOLAN

Big Ten point scorers in the 1932 Olympics: Michigan's EDDIE TOLAN, former Big Ten champ, posted a brilliant sprint double winning gold medals at 100- and 200-meters. GEORGE SALING, of Iowa, the 1932 NCAA champ, set a new Olympic record in taking the high hurdles—and was tragically killed the following year in an auto accident. Ed Gordon, his Iowa teammate, captured the broad jump; and scholarly JACK KELLER, Ohio State's sparkling NCAA high and low hurdles titlist in 1931, and Big Ten champion, took a fourth place in the 110-meter hurdles, with teammate George Simpson, the Bucks' double sprint king of the 1929 NCAA tourney, coming back for a silver medal in the 200-meters.

GEORGE SALING

JACK KELLER

attendance. I had traded a handful of tickets to the men who ran the loudspeakers, and in return got announcements that could be heard all over the fair grounds. I also hired a man to shoot fireworks salutes starting a couple of hours before game time.

People simply jammed the gates. We ran out of printed tickets, so I told the ticket sellers to accept dollar bills and let the people through. Even the ushers and policemen were out at the gates selling tickets. Not all of the money was turned in, but we collected on nearly 60,000 people. It was a good game, too, and the crowd's interest was intense as the East finally won.

I shudder every time I think that had it rained that day the game couldn't have been postponed, because the Ringling Brothers circus had reserved the whole week at the stadium.

Before the game, Hanley and I had desperately tried to get financial backing. We offered it to the Northwestern Alumni Association, but they turned it down. As it turned out, it was a very profitable deal for the two promoters, Hanley and Wilson. It was a thrilling—and lucky—promotion of the first college all-star game.

At the meeting of Big Ten faculty representatives and athletic directors the following December, however, legislation was passed forbidding any director or football coach to foster any promotion of this kind. Shortly after that, Arch Ward, sports editor of the Chicago Tribune, approached me and said I'd had a wonderful idea, and that he'd like to continue the all-star game, matching the best college players who had just graduated against the defending National Football League champion.

I was only too glad to turn whatever vested rights I

100- and 200-meters. Iowa's Ed Gordon won the broad jump and teammate George Saling captured the high hurdles. Ivan Fuqua of Iowa ran a leg on the triumphant 1600-meter relay team, and Ohio State's George Simpson and Jack Keller took second in the 200-meters and fourth in the high hurdles respectively. Other Conference competitors were Indiana's Charley Hornbostel at 800-meters; Northwestern's Jack Riley; heavyweight wrestler; Michigan State's Tom Ottey and Ernie Crosbie in the 10,000-meter run and the 50,000-meter walk. (Crosbie also represented the U.S. in that event in the 1936 and 1948 games, one of the few athletes who was a three-timer for America.) Michigan's Jim Cristy was a 1500-meter freestyler on the swimming team; the Wolverines' Dick Degener was a diver; Carl Dougovito was a wrestling alternate, and the Wolves' Ned Turner represented Canada at 800-meters.

1933

Michigan in 1933 no longer had the mercurial Harry Newman and dependable Ivy Williamson, but there was enough left from the Wolverines' 1932 champions to take dead aim at what might be a fourth straight title. It turned out just that way as Harry Kipke forged the greatest line of his career, linked to veterans such as Ted Petoskey at end; Francis Wistert at tackle and Chuck Bernard at center. With Newman gone, Herm Everhardus carried most of the offensive load, and it was good enough to get the Wolves past every obstacle except one. Up until the 1933 Michigan-Minnesota game the Gophers had dropped 19 straight contests to Michigan, and Gopher fans were hurting. Perhaps Bernie Bierman could finally end the galling string.

It was a head-butting such as fans hadn't seen in years and neither side ever allowed more than three first downs back-to-back. It wound up a scoreless tie. For Minnesota it was their fourth Conference deadlock of the season—a Big Ten record—and although both clubs finished undefeated Minnesota

gallantly conceded it deserved no title consideration, even unofficially. The Gophers, of course, were merely biding their time. Only one senior was in the starting line-up at season's end. Pug Lund, the magnificent triple-threat, had already come into his own as a junior, along with Butch Larson, a big, rough end, and behind them was a whole clutch of old-style Vikings with new-style mobility. There were Gopher fans willing to give up a year of their lives if it could be October, 1934, right then.

Meanwhile, Michigan's success was causing repercussions in Columbus, where Ohio State, under Sam Willaman, had lost only two games in two years. The cardinal sin had been commited, however; both losses had been to Michigan. There would have to be some changes . . . on the bench as well as the scoreboard. Even before the season was over, Buckeye fans, who had not hailed a champion in 13 years, were literally mailing outward-bound train schedules to the man known as "Sad Sam," who was, in fact, a sound, successful football coach whom fate had denied the privilege of giving his constituents what they wanted most: victory over Michigan.

It was a good year for the Conference on the All-America lists, with seven Big Ten stars named. The fabulous Michigan trio of Petoskey, Wistert and Bernard made it at end, tackle and center. Minnesota contributed the irrepressible Pug Lund and versatile Butch Larson. Edgar (Eggs) Manske, Northwestern's holy terror on defense and a fine pass receiver, made it at end. Duane Purvis, younger brother of Purdue's Jim, and a triple-threat in his own right, was honored at halfback, and Iowa's rugged Francis Schammel was named as a guard. Despite the stars that had sparked and wheeled across the Big Ten firmament, it was an unbelievably rugged and dependable iron-man halfback from Iowa—Joe Laws—who received the league's most-valuable-player award.

Not only did Laws lead the league in scoring, with only moderate blocking assistance, but he was

In 1933 when the Directors met with Commissioner Griffith there were some new faces on the administrative front. Bottom row, left to right: Fielding Yost, Michigan; L. W. St. John, Ohio State; George Huff, Illinois; Dr. Walter Meanwell, Wisconsin; Major John L. Griffith. Top row, left to right: Noble Kizer, Purdue; Kenneth L. Wilson, Northwestern; Frank McCormick, Minnesota; Nelson Metcalfe, Chicago; Edward Lauer, Iowa; Zora G. Clevenger, Indiana.

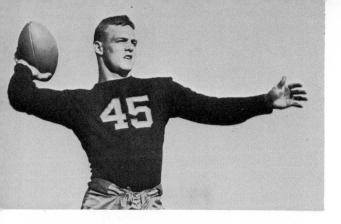

DUANE PURVIS, *Purdue's exciting triple-threat halfback, in an era when a real triple-threat was a tailback who ran, passed, and kicked equally well, was one of the Big Ten stars on the 1933 All-America, along with Francis Wistert, Michigan tackle, and the first of an unprecedented three-brother act for the Wolves—the only such in the history of All-America selections.*

JOE LAWS, *an inexhaustible, hard-running, slick-passing Iowa halfback, was the Big Ten's most-valuable-player in 1933. They beat his team twice in the league that year but they never fully stopped Laws.*

capable of the kind of heroics that saw him, virtually single-handed, end Purdue's unbeaten streak at 20 games when he scored the Hawkeyes' winning touchdowns—one on a 27-yard romp from scrimmage and the other on a dazzling 55-yard punt return. He had previously scored one of the most dramatic touchdowns in Iowa history when, in the season opener against Northwestern, he raced 31 yards late in the game to give the Hawkeyes a 7-0 victory. . . the first Big Ten triumph the Hawks had tasted since November, 1929. The taint of suspension that season had left Iowa in the doldrums and the victory gained by Laws' run in 1933 was packed with emotion.

It was a year, too, that saw one of the finest crops of sophomores ever to arrive on the Conference campuses at one time, and headlines in subsequent years would be filled by such names as Jay Berwanger, Bud Wilkinson, Bill Bevan, Gomer Jones, Ozzie Simmons and others.

BILL HOSKET, *Ohio State's All-Big Ten center and one of the nation's best pivotmen and early hook-shot artists, led the Buckeyes to a 1933 title-tie with Northwestern. (A generation later, Ohio teams would be led by Bill Hosket, Jr.)*

had in the promotion over to him, and the next year was the beginning of the Tribune All-Star Game that has run ever since, earning hundreds of thousands of dollars for charity.

With football going along very satisfactorily, my attention was next directed at building up the Northwestern coaching staff in other sports. Frank Hill, our veteran track coach, was doing an excellent job. Tom Robinson was the dean of the athletic staff, having had charge of swimming since Patten Gym was completed in 1910. One of the first rules he succeeded in getting passed through the faculty was that every Northwestern student, man and woman, must learn to swim before he could graduate. He estimated that he taught more than 50,000 persons how to swim during his career, and he brought championships galore to Northwestern: 10 Big Ten titles and five NCAA championships, along with numerous Olympic performers.

After a long search for a new basketball coach, A.C. (Dutch) Lonborg was added to the staff. A star at the University of Kansas, he got results in a hurry at Northwestern, giving the Wildcats their first undisputed championship in basketball in 1931. This was followed in 1933 by a championship tie with Ohio State.

He was ably assisted by Ted Payseur, who had been one of my outstanding athletes at Drake in basketball, golf and track. He became freshman basketball coach, varsity golf coach and several years later athletic ticket manager. He was to play a tremendous role in the NCAA golf tournaments as chairman for many years.

Paul Bennett, a former Canadian Davis Cup player, took charge of tennis, giving us championship teams in 1936, 1940 and 1942.

These were just a few of the fine men who came to work for me.

The 1933 basketball season saw Northwestern and Ohio State go down to the wire with the championship riding on the final game of the season. The Buckeyes, playing Indiana, were 10-1 and in first place, and could snatch the flag from the clutches of Northwestern, who was already finished with 10-2. A so-so Indiana team stunned the Buckeyes 40-28, and dropped them back into a tie with the Wildcats. The Bucks, who had not tasted title nectar since 1925, were led by Big Bill Hosket, the finest pivot man in the league if not the country, with captain Howie Mattison, footballer Lew Hinchman, star sophomore Bill Beitner and chubby Bobby Colburn rounding out the first five.

The Big Man in those days could still station himself under the bucket and it was a fascinating thing to watch the Buckeyes work the ball into Hosket for his sweeping right- and left-handed hooks underneath, just as Stretch Murphy had done a few years previously.

Joe Reiff led the Wildcats to their title share, with the slender, tireless forward leading the league in scoring for the second time, and teammate Elmer Johnson right behind him in second place. They got valuable aid from Don Brewer, Nelson Culver and sophomores Al Kawal and Eggs Manske. Reiff gained All-America honors that year.

The swimming season produced another team title for Michigan and, in the NCAA meet, helped launch the beginning of the domination of a single event such as had never been witnessed in any sport in collegiate history. Donald Horn of Northwestern had won the 200-yard breaststroke and a Wildcat trio of Bernard Hahn, Horn, and Art Highland had taken the 300-yard medley, but nobody at the time could ever dream what would follow in years to come when Dick Degener, Michigan's great diver, captured the 3-meter crown. What would follow, is this: from that year to the present there would be 65 individual titles in both the one-meter and 3-meter events. Big Ten divers would win 57 of them. Even

JOHN BROOKS, *Chicago's NCAA broad jump champ in 1933, was the last Maroon athlete to take a national collegiate track crown.*

more amazingly one school—Ohio State—would win 42 of this number.

In track, Indiana repeated as indoor champion but Michigan came back to successfully defend its outdoor crown. In the NCAA meet, Rod Cox, of Michigan, took the hammer throw; Duane Purvis, Purdue's All-America halfback, set a new mark in the javelin with 216 feet, 6¼ inches; Charles Hornbostel, Indiana's superb middle-distance runner, repeated in the 880, and John Brooks, of Chicago won the broad jump. He would be the last Maroon athlete to win an NCAA track title.

Pat Devine, Indiana's tough little 135-pounder, won the NCAA wrestling title in his division, and Johnny Fischer, the Michigan ace, successfully defended his Conference golf crown. Among the winners of the Conference Scholarship Medal were Ivan Williamson, Michigan's great end; Roy Horstmann, Purdue's All America fullback, and Jack Keller, Ohio State's Olympic hurdler. The Depression spelled out one discomforting note in 1933 when, for reasons of economy, it was decided to cancel out the Conference cross-country meet, and uneasy athletic directors, coaches and athletes wondered how far such measures might spread.

I also had desperately needed an assistant and was fortunate enough to get Ade Schumacher to help me. He developed a tremendous intramural program, directed and channeled all of our recruiting activities and kept close watch on our athletes' grades. I needed an athletic publicity man badly and was fortunate to secure the services of a student from the Northwestern Journalism School by the name of Walter Paulison. In terms of length of service, he is today one of four ranking men in that position in the nation.

When Dick Hanley resigned in 1935, I faced the problem of hiring a new football coach. We had literally dozens of applications from some of the greatest coaches in the country and hundreds of recommendations. Then one day President Walter Dill Scott asked me to represent him at a banquet being given by the Woman's Christian Temperance Union in Chicago for Amos Alonzo

Stagg, honoring him for the wonderful Christian life he had lived. I found myself sitting next to Bishop Waldorf of the Methodist Church. In talking about my problems to the Bishop, he looked at me and smilingly said he had a son by the name of Lyn, who was going to be a great football coach and urged me to look into his records. I had never met Lynn Waldorf but I sure looked up his record after I got to the office. He had been an outstanding player at Syracuse and had won football championships every place he had coached, which included Oklahoma City College and Kansas State. I went out to see his final game with Nebraska where he licked one of Dana Bible's great teams for the Missouri Valley championship. Having started with a recommendation from a Bishop, I couldn't go wrong, I figured, and we hired the Bishop's son. He subsequently gave us our first victory over Notre Dame since 1901 and our

It might well be that the 1934 football season in the Big Ten could be summed up by just a few of the quotes of the following nature:

(Grantland Rice, writing from Minneapolis): "Football fans here are no longer discussing whether Minnesota's team is the best in the country. They are taking it for granted. What they want to know is: Shouldn't it be rated the greatest of all time? In this debate they speak in terms of a squad—not eleven men—as they point to at least thirty men, most of whom are big, fast, and replete with skill. . ."

Allizon Danzig, the New York Times: "One of the great football machines of all time has had its

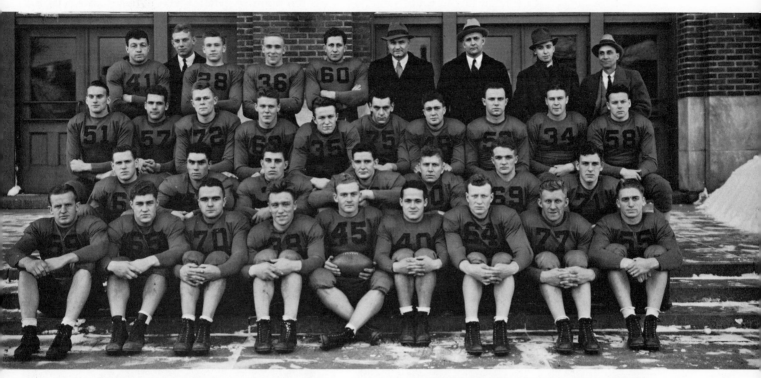

The finest collegiate team, ever. . . ? That was the label, at any rate, pinned on Minnesota's 1934 marvelously cohesive and talent-rich undefeated National Champions by every gridiron critic who saw the Gophers in action. FRONT ROW: *Maurice Johnson, Bob Tenner, Phil Bengston, Bill Bevan, Francis (Pug) Lund, Dale Rennebohm, Vern Oech, Ed Widseth, John Roning.* SECOND ROW: *Whit Rork, Art Clarkson, Milt Bruhn, Dick Smith, Stan Kostka, Bill Proffitt, Selmer Anderson.* THIRD ROW: *Glenn Seidel, George Roscoe, Les Knudsen, Charles Wilkinson, Jay Bevan, Bill Freimuth, Willis Smith, Frank Dallera, Ray Antil, Dick Potvin.* BACK ROW: *Julie Alphonse, George Svendsen, George Rennix, Vern LaVoir, Sheldon Beise, Head Coach Bernie Bierman; Frank McCormick, athletic director; Paul Berggren, student manager; Oscar Munson, equipment custodian.* MISSING: *Frank (Butch) Larson.*

first undisputed Big Ten football title in 1936. A big, genial, energetic individual with a tremendous capacity for work, he soon became one of the most respected coaches in the Conference. He was so popular with his players that he quickly acquired the name of "Pappy." What a thrill it was later on to see him elected to the Football Hall of Fame as a coach.

This was a staff that gave Northwestern its Gold Era with four football championships; two in basketball, one in baseball, two in swimming and three in tennis. I really felt, now, that I belonged in the Big Ten.

Meanwhile, the depression of the 1930's was beginning to run its course and it was obvious that the Western Conference would soon be launched on a whole new era of sports and expansion. In fact, the Big Ten record books term 1939 the start of The Modern Era. Even as it began I couldn't help but look back and take stock of

what had happened in the league's first few decades; and I can't help but marvel at the wisdom of the seven college presidents whom President James H. Smart of Purdue called together in Chicago that January day in 1895. Athletics were in such a sorry state that it was a wonder these educators didn't take a stand against them instead of what they actually did in founding the Western Conference.

When you consider that at that time football contests had served to engender great bitterness among rival schools, that many of these were followed by fist fights and often the winning team (if visiting) would be run out of town, the situation as it existed can be better understood. The problem of tramp athletes was a critical one, and there were several instances where an athlete played on one team one year and at a neighboring school the next. In the early days of baseball, before

last roundup. With its smashing 34-0 victory over Wisconsin, the Minnesota varsity of 1934 passed into history leaving the Midwest dazed in its trail of destruction, but proud of. . .a team that has caught the national imagination as have few others. . ."

Harry Kipke, Michigan coach: "It is the greatest team I ever saw as a player or coach. Their reserves would beat almost every team in the country. . ."

They (and others) were talking, of course, about Bernie Bierman's magnificent creation—the 1934 Minnesota team which won the Conference title, and was, indeed, the finest club in Gopher history and, who knows, year-for-year, the finest team in the history of collegiate football.

If, as Bo McMillin, Indiana coach, declared, it was "a team without a weakness," it was because it not only had the advantage of Beirman's brilliantly-sound coaching but was made up of personnel that was astoundingly talented on an individual basis and unbelievably dedicated in its team effort.

Essentially, it was the same team which had gone through undefeated in 1933 but with four ties. At ends there were All-America Butch Larson, Bob Tenner and John Romig; tackles were Dick Smith, Phil Bengston, and a sensational sophomore, Ed Widseth. Bill Bevan, the last man in the Big Ten to play without headgear, was a devastating blocker who led a guard corps including smart, aggressive Milt Bruhn, who later would be the highly successful head coach at Wisconsin; swift, heady Charles (Bud) Wilkinson, who would later achieve almost Olympian fame as head coach at Oklahoma, and steady Vern Oech. Dale Rennebohm and Earl Svendsen were centers of the sort that had people debating which was the better. At quarterback was a straight "A" engineering student named Glenn Seidel, who never called a bad play. Captain Pug Lund, the triple-threat All-America; Babe LeVoir, who could play quarterback or halfback and was

magnificent defensively; and Julie Alfonse, a star of 1933, were the halfbacks—and Alfonse had a devil of a time beating off the challenge of Art Clarkson, another great sophomore. At fullback it was merely a battle between Sheldon Beise, the powerful regular of 1933 and Stan Kostka, a transfer from Oregon, who at 230 swift-moving, bone rattling pounds was aptly referred to as the "Hammer of the North." There were others, such as Bill Freimuth, George Roscoe, George Rennix, and still others unmentioned, who could have been stars elsewhere, and one critic claimed his Aunt Clara could have coached this team merely by closing her eyes and pointing blindly eleven times down the bench.

GLENN SEIDEL, a straight-A engineering student, was the quarterback who "engineered" Minnesota's all-winning drive in 1934.

---

the Conference was formed, two professionals per team were permitted, and the school that found the best professionals usually won.

Not only was the practice of tramp athletes prevalent, but also tramp coaches. Sometimes their coaching record listed a single Saturday, and it was the accepted custom for them to play if they could strengthen the team. In my research, I read with great interest an account of one of the very first Northwestern-Chicago football games; how the Northwestern team drove to the South side on a tallyho; how Northwestern led at halftime, and how at the start of the second half, the Chicago coach, Amos Alonzo Stagg, went in at quarterback and quickly changed the situation. The loose regulation of collegiate athletics at this stage proved to be of great concern to many college presidents, some of whom considered discontinuing football.

Yet, here were seven great educators who recognized the intrinsic value of a controlled, well-managed program of athletics for their students. In 1898 the record showed the number of men available for athletics as follows: Northwestern, 317; Purdue, 569; Illinois, 746; Wisconsin, 1,229; Chicago, 1,345; Minnesota, 1,813; Michigan, 2,081; a total of 8,100. Now the total men at each Conference school, with the exception of two, exceeds that Conference total of 1898.

The seven original members and their faculty representatives were: Minnesota, Conway MacMillan (Chairman); Wisconsin, C.R. Barnes; Illinois, H.H. Everett; Northwestern, J. Scott Clark; Purdue, W.E. Stone; Michigan, Dr. Joseph Nancrede; and Chicago, A.A. Stagg.

It was fortunate that Amos Alonzo Stagg was a faculty representative in the early days. A more qualified individual could not have existed. He was a tremendous

BERNIE BIERMAN

An underdog Tulane football team had worked itself into a slightly hysterical froth just before it took the field against Vanderbilt in 1931. Suddenly, somebody ripped open the dressing room door and the Tulane team started to thunder toward it to race emotionally upon the field, intent upon tearing the enemy limb from limb.

"Hold it!" a flat, metallic voice called out. "I want you to trot out there calmly. Keep your brains quiet and your legs will take care of themselves."

The subsequent 19-0 win turned Tulane into a well-knit club that racked up an undefeated season.

The restraining voice had been that of Bernie Bierman who just a few years later as coach at Minnesota would terrorize the Big Ten. The advice he had just given was one-half of the credo responsible for his success, namely, that he preferred a calm, deliberate team rather than one keyed up emotionally. It was a reflection of the man, himself. ("I never made a fiery or emotional speech to a team in my life," he once said. "I'd have broken down laughing at myself if I'd tried it.")

The other half of his successful formula once made a sideline spectator stare in complete puzzlement. Bierman had just halted a Minnesota scrimmage session and was walking in a deeply stooped over position behind the line, as though examining the ground very closely. "What's the matter?" the spectator queried. "He got a crick in his back, or did he lose something?"

The answer was "neither." Bierman was a compulsive stickler for blocking and timing. His pulling linemen and blocking backs were taught to travel such a precise path in getting out in front of the ball carrier that mere inches counted. Bierman, stooped over, was checking footprints to prove to a guard that he'd strayed wrong by the width of a few blades of grass.

When Minnesota tapped Bernie Bierman for its head coaching job in 1932 it had had only indifferent results in the years following the retirement of the brilliant Dr. Henry L. Williams. In three seasons at Tulane, from 1929 through 1931, Bierman's Green Wave lost a grand total of one game. An early season loss to Northwestern in 1930 came after 10 straight wins, and was followed by a string of 18 more victories when the call came from the North.

In the 10 years that followed at Minnesota, Bernie Bierman eclipsed, by far, the accomplishments until then of any coach in the history of football, in a similar length of time. Laced through his 10-year record of 63 wins, 12 losses and five ties were five undefeated seasons (1933-34-35-40-41), five national Championships (1934-35-36-40-41); seven Big Ten titles (five outright and two ties) and 12 All-America selections. It took World War Two and resulting changes afterwards to stop Bierman.

Meanwhile, he'd become the first college coach ever to have two different victory strings of 20 games or more each. His first streak began at the tail end of '33, went through '34-'35 and was stopped at 21 straight by Northwestern in mid-1936 in a sea of mud at Evanston. The score was 6-0. The Wildcats won it with a 15-yard Gopher penalty stepping off the ball, in Northwestern's possession, to a first down on the Minnesota one-yard line.

Bierman's second string—again 21 straight—began at the end of 1939 and took the Gophers through 1940-41 for 17 in a row. Then Bierman, a Marine in World War One, was called back to service in World War Two as a Lieutenant Colonel. When he returned in the fall of 1945 he

Bernie Bierman with Minnesota's 1913 basketball squad.

continued for five more wins before being stopped by Ohio State.

Only one other coach would come along to surpass his records. Fittingly and symbolically, the man would be a former pupil of his at Minnesota—Charles (Bud) Wilkinson, of Oklahoma.

Bernard W. Bierman was the full name, and it was only natural that Minnesota should have summoned him from his successes in the Southland. A great halfback at Minnesota, Bierman had captained the Gophers' 1915 Big Ten champions and also starred in track and basketball.

At Minnesota he also won the Western Conference Medal for all-around academic and athletic ability.

Born of pioneer German parents on a farm near Springfield, Minnesota, on March 11, 1894, Bierman as a child was frequently confined to bed and forced to use crutches because of a chronic bone infection in his leg. A series of operations restored moderate use of the limb and he was advised to go into sports to build it up. As though sports were a new found toy, of which he'd been unfairly deprived, young Bernie soon became a star at Litchfield High School.

After graduating from Minnesota he took a job teaching and coaching at Billings, Montana, High School. His first team scored 300 points to six for the opposition and was considered state champion. He went into the Marines during World War One, and afterwards took a series of coaching jobs at Montana, Tulane (where he was an assistant to Clark Shaughnessy) and Mississippi A. & M.

Bernie Bierman as captain of Minnesota's 1916 football team.

When Shaughnessy left Tulane, Bierman was called back as head coach. Bierman could have stayed the rest of his life in New Orleans. The Yankee from Vikingland who turned Tulane into a national power, was the Toast of the Town, but Bierman frankly admitted he was homesick. His wife also was a Minnesota graduate. When he was approached by his Alma Mater, Bierman and his wife looked at each other and both nodded silently at the same split second. "We were going home," Bernie said simply.

"Home" was soon the most thunderous heartbeat of college football. Here he installed his famous, virtually unstoppable single wing from an unbalanced line, with the backs to the right and the wingback set almost even with the fullback. The Gophers liked to shift, but they often struck from a set position.

Bierman's material was mostly home-grown talent from the state of Minnesota. He insisted that football success was 85% material and 15% coaching. Astute gridologists claimed that with Bierman it was at least 50-50. Whatever the scientifically unprovable ratio, Bierman was a superb handler of material. Jock Sutherland, the great Pitt coach who dropped two titanic struggles in a row to Minnesota in 1933-34 said: "Don't ever hurt a Minnesota player so that he has to leave the game. Bierman will only put in a better guy."

Often his "better guy" was someone who'd been switched from another position. In 1935 Bierman had a great 198-pound junior guard who was an All-America. Bierman, noting the young man's intelligence, knowledge of the game, his speed and co-ordination (the kid was also a superb varsity hockey player) decided to recast him in another and much-needed mould. So, the following year Charles (Bud) Wilkinson became a magnificent quarterback for the Gophers. A couple of years later Bob Sweiger, a hard-hitting fullback, was switched to left half. Centers became guards; tackles became centers.

Bierman always thought his 1934 team, which scored 270 points against 38, was his greatest. It may have been—but his team a year later furnished no less than a then record of four men to the various All-America selectors: Sheldon Beise, halfback; Bud Wilkinson, guard; Dick Smith and Ed Widseth, tackles.

One of Bierman's major accomplishments was stopping Michigan's famed Tom Harmon, three years in a row, 1938-39-40. The brilliant Wolverine tailback never enjoyed a Michigan win over the Gophers and was held scoreless all three times. The Michigan shutouts were the only ones of his junior and senior season.

In reviewing the reasons behind his Viking Victories, Bierman always liked to recall two plays in particular which epitomized his teams' machine-like blocking.

"My nomination for the most perfect running play I've ever seen," he says, "is the one which sent Julie Alphonse on a long touchdown gallop in the Iowa game of 1933. Everybody on our team carried out their assignments flawlessly. It was a short-side end run. Alfonse was the back man in the formation. He took a direct snap from Rennebohm, our center, and cut to the left. Fullback Sheldon Beise, left half Pug Lung, quarterback Glen Seidel and guard Bill Bevan swung out for interference.

"Lund smacked the end.

"Bob Tenner from his left end position hit into the Iowa tackle. Our other linemen held fast against the Iowa charge, blocking beautifully, while Butch Larson our right

Bernie Bierman as U.S. Marine in 1917.

end, and Dick Smith, our right tackle, cut through and started downfield. Now, keep an eye on Larson . . .

"As Alfonse turned the corner and tore up field, Seidel cut down the Iowa right half who'd come up quickly. Bevan and Beise took the fullback and roving center. Smith mowed down the defensive left half who was cutting across toward Alfonse. Larson was continuing on a long, diagonal course. Don't lose sight of Larson . . .

"It was a perfect path which Alfonse sped through toward the goal, and now there was only the deep safety man to consider. Larson had already done the 'considering' . . . He entered the safety man's territory just a second before Alfonse. You could hear the impact from the bench. The Iowa man seemed to be going straight up for the clouds. Alfonse just cut slightly to the right and completed a 65-yard touchdown run without a finger being laid on him. It's blocking execution like that which made me feel like a football coach."

Often it would be a combination of blocking and quick thinking which paid off for the Gophers. "Our kids were frequently referred to as 'Big dumb Swedes.' I never saw one on my football teams," said Bierman. A 7-0 win over a great Pitt team proved it. "We had the ball on their 20. Bob Tenner, wheeling off behind the line from left end, took a shovel pass from Lund and drove between Pitt's left tackle and end. Meanwhile, Sheldon Beise had swung to the right and up field; the play called for Tenner to flip a lateral to him. (We could be tricky, too.) But Tenner saw a clear field ahead and kept driving. Larson cut down one man in the secondary but three others converged on Tenner just before the goal line. Beise, still in motion, re-entered the picture in a flash. Putting on speed he cut diagonally in front of Tenner and blotted out the three Panthers with one crunch. It was the only touchdown of the game."

When Bierman returned to Minnesota after World War Two things had changed. Material was of an inconsistent

Coach Bernie Bierman at University of Minnesota in 1936 with his co-captains Julius Alfonse (left) and Ed Widseth. His 1936 team added to victories of previous years and set a new win record.

stripe. Freshman were allowed to play, and boys 18 were being deployed with returning servicemen of 24 and 25—who weren't sure they still wanted to play a boy's game any more. For two or three years college football would have a rough transition period.

At that time, the T-formation was coming in strong, but Bierman stuck with the single wing, much to the displeasure of Downtown Quarterbacks. Two or three

Head Coach Bernard W. (Bernie) Bierman of the University of Minnesota.

losing seasons provided bait enough for the Wolves to howl over. The Wolves, it seemed, had short memories of previous feasts. At the end of the 1950 season Bernie Bierman, who had been known as the Hammer of the North, lowered his arm. He resigned and retired from football.

It would be a long time before anyone would strike like that again.

BIERMAN GUIDE LINES FOR VIKING VICTORIES

"Only one thing is worse than going into a game convinced you can't win. That's going into a game convinced you can't lose. The best psychology is to feel you can win but will have to put out everything you have to do it." (Bierman's severest critics grudgingly admitted that only twice in more than 100 games at Minnesota did his team lose when it was expected to win. Both were against Nebraska, in 1937 and 1939, when, admittedly, the Gopher players got chesty before the game.)

*　　*　　*

"You cannot design a play that will fool all of the opposition at the same time—or one that will fool them for very long. It is our aim to fool just a few defensive players for a limited time and depend upon our perfect execution to take the split-second advantage of this which is all we need."

*　　*　　*

"It was always good to realize my boys believed in my philosophy that perfect blocking would win football games. Yet I was always pleasantly surprised to see them go off on their own time, or before practice started, and work on the blocking machines by themselves or with a buddy, without having to be told to do so by a coach."

*　　*　　*

"I hear people saying the pressure on the fans is tougher than on my players while we're on a long winning streak. Fine. Let's keep it that way."

Bierman, himself, admitted his team was two deep and, at some spots, three deep, with little if any drop-off talent, and that his line speed was almost equal to that of his backs. "We didn't have a really outstanding passer or receiver," he testified, "but our passing game was nevertheless effective because of the running pressure we could put on."

How well the single wing Gophers put these elements together (plus a defense that never allowed a touchdown to be scored against the first team) is indicated by the 267 points scored in eight games. The one close game of the year was an epic 13-7 win over Pitt which some experts called the "perfect football game." Bierman, himself, termed Jock Sutherland's 1934 Panthers "the strongest opponent I've ever played against in college coaching. . ."

An example of the kind of game it would be came in the first quarter when the Panthers recovered a Minnesota fumble on the Gopher six-yard line and four plays later were back on the 12. The eventual scoring on both sides came on beautifully executed plays. In the second quarter the Pitt fullback, Weinstock, blasted through the line at midfield and then immediately lateraled to Nicksick, a halfback, who raced 50 yards for the score.

So rock-like were both teams' defenses that sustained drives were impossible. Spectators were treated to the rapier when the bludgeon failed. In the third quarter, Julie Alfonse, after Seidel had sent a fake into the line at midfield, whipped around end and got back Nicksick's 50 yards for a Gopher touchdown. When Bill Bevan converted, it was a 7-7 game and only a certified Swami would have dared predict the outcome. The turning point came on the heels of the only sustained drive of the day, starting on the Minnesota 22-yard line. Pug Lund and Stan Kostka took turns at blasting to the Panther 45-yard line, and then Kostka exploded in an exhibition of raw power that had not been witnessed since Nagurski's day. At least five men had a shot at Kostka as he barreled through the line and

into the secondary, and at least three Panthers rode his back and shoulders at various times until he collapsed on the Pitt 23. Pitt stiffened here and three plays netted Minnesota six yards. On fourth down quarterback Glenn Seidel called for a play the Vikings had perfected in practice but had never used in a game.

With Pitt fully expecting Kostka to blast again, Seidel let the Panthers confirm their suspicion by handing off to the 230-pound fullback straight ahead; but, just as the "Hammer of the North" got to the line, and with the Pitt secondary converging toward the spot, he flipped a little lateral out to Pug Lund who sprinted wide, then suddenly stopped dead and pegged a perfect pass to end Bob Tenner who took the ball near to the goal line and raced over for the winning touchdown. The flawlessly executed buck-lateral, ending in a forward pass, was subsequently described as "The Picture Play of 1934."

The following Saturday, to give Minnesota fans a surfeit of dramatic satisfaction, the Gophers swamped Michigan, 39-0, in the first Gopher home-field victory over the Wolverines since 1900.

Meanwhile, one game, one point, one missed conversion attempt, kept Ohio State from filing counter-claim to Minnesota's lofty position. Francis Schmidt who had come up from Texas Christian to replace Sam Willaman as Buckeye coach, had installed, by everyone's concession, the wildest offensive patterns the Big Ten had ever seen. The big Texan was a former army bayonet instructor whose bluff, salty language was as colorful as the imaginative pyrotechnics which would earn him the title of "Close-the-Gates-of-Mercy Schmidt," and he was an immediate success where success was not immediately expected. Schmidt used a tandem formation which 30 years later would be called an "I" formation; any of three men who lined up in a straight front-to-back formation behind the quarterback could and did carry the ball. He used forward passes after

performer in any sport he undertook, and an outstanding coach guided by the finest practices and integrity. He gave life blood to the young Conference, which expanded by two more in 1899, when Indiana and Iowa received membership.

In the meeting of November, 1900, Professor H.S. White of Northwestern presented legislation providing that any university may object to new legislation if the objection is made within 30 days after legislation is passed. Otherwise, the Conference action would be binding on all members. (The following year, this time limit was raised to 60 days and final action on the subject specified that these days must be during school session.)

The thinking behind this legislation, unique in the history of the Big Ten, was to prevent any hasty change of rules. Sometimes it really slowed up progress, but the

faculty representatives have stuck with it through the years.

During this early era, the 51 faculty representatives and 39 athletics directors who guided the destiny of the Conference were men of integrity and dedication, and they cast long shadows through the years. Some of the Big Ten institutions made frequent changes in both positions. An interesting observation, as one scans the list, is that the schools which had the most successful athletic programs are those that had few changes, with many men serving for 30 years or more. This gave them the vast experience necessary to see through many problems. The Conference today owes a tremendous debt of gratitude to these outstanding individuals. Of the faculty representatives, I must certainly mention George A. Goodenough, Illinois; O. F. Long, Northwestern;

BEVAN

LARSON

LUND

Stars from the 1934 Minnesota team that was described by many critics as the "greatest in the history of collegiate football," were prominent on the 1934 All-America selections, with three Gophers being honored. BILL BEVAN, a guard who weighed under 200, was devastating on both offense and defense, and was the last Big Ten player to perform without a helmet. (Shortly thereafter helmets became mandatory.) FRANK (BUTCH) LARSON, a repeater from 1933, was a great blocker and pass receiver—the target for one of the nation's finest backs of the decade, and certainly the greatest yet to play for Minnesota—FRANCIS (PUG) LUND, a triple-threat in every sense of the label, Lund was a slashing runner, a booming punter and a deadly passer.

laterals; laterals after forwards; laterals after laterals, and reverses flowed from all points of the backfield compass. Buckeye point production was prodigious. Stan Pincura, Dick Heekin, Buzz Wetzel and Jack Smith were backs who could move the ball, operating behind a great blocking line featuring Merle Wendt, Charlie Hamrick, Inwood Smith, Captain Regis Monahan and Gomer Jones.

When the last cleat mark had been planted for the season, the similarity between Minnesota's and Ohio's record was remarkable. The Gophers tallied 267 points to their opponents' 38. The Buckeyes went 271 to 34. Against four common foes—Michigan, Chicago, Indiana, and Iowa—the victory margins were virtually the same even when the scores mounted into the 30's and 40's!

It was against one of Bob Zuppke's last good teams featuring Jack Beynon, Les Lindberg, Frank Froschauer, and Chuck Galbreath, that the Bucks stumbled in their lone loss of the year. It was the second game of the season, before Schmidt got his Scarlet Scourge in full sweep, and Zup demonstrated he could come up with something pretty exotic himself. He dusted off an oldie called "The Flea Flicker," two laterals followed by a forward, and for the Illini it proved to be the winning touchdown. The Buckeyes subsequently had a chance to tie the game 14-14, but their two-touchdown comeback fell short when Regis Monahan, a great guard and unerring place-kicker, missed the extra point. It was one of only two he was to miss all season.

Pug Lund, at halfback; Bill Bevan, at guard; and Frank Larson, at end, were Minnesota's contributions to the All America that year. Ohio State was represented by Regis Monahan, while Duane Purvis, Purdue halfback, and Ellmore Patterson, Chicago guard, were the other Conference representatives. For Conference M-V-P it was a clear-cut case of Francis (Pug) Lund, the Gophers' do-all, be-everywhere halfback. Speaking of most valuable players, there was a Michigan center named Gerald Ford,

---

Thomas F. Moran, Purdue; James Paige, Minnesota; I. F. Pyre, Wisconsin; Ralph Aigler, Michigan; and Thomas E. French, Ohio State.

The combined years of service of that dedicated group was 210 years, and their wisdom brought the Conference through many critical times. At the beginning, it was Goodenough, Long, Paige and Moran who were the outstanding leaders. A decade or so later, it was French, Aigler and Pyre who were to leave their indelible imprint on the Big Ten. These men, you might say, wrote the rule book of the Conference, and they were instrumental in the organization of the NCAA and the shaping of the entire intercollegiate program.

Of the early athletic directors, you could start with George A. Huff of Illinois and Amos Alonzo Stagg of Chicago. They were in from the beginning, and their

guidance was simply tremendous, as was that of L. W. St. John of Ohio State and Fielding H. Yost of Michigan, whose influence was soon to be felt. When they spoke, others listened.

The thing that has impressed me through endless hours of reading the minutes of old meetings was the determination of the faculty representatives to maintain control and to see that athletics were promoted on the highest possible plane. The Conference pioneered the resident rule requiring that a student, to be eligible for intercollegiate sports, must first complete a full semester's work in residence. No such rule had been enacted before. It was termed a radical departure in college athletics.

Other conferences, after first scorning this rule, reluctantly adopted it.

ELLMORE PATTERSON

GEORGE H. WRIGHTE

The 1930's saw the beginning of Chicago's decline as a Big Ten athletic power but the Maroon still came up with some of the most brilliant individual performers of the decade. ELLMORE PATTERSON was a tremendous All-America guard in 1934 although he only weighed 185 pounds, and GEORGE H. WRIGHTE, in 1933 and 1934 was Conference all-around gymnastics champ.

whose fierce, competitive drive and wide-ranging talents in a dismally losing cause became the talk of the Big Ten. Today he is Representative Gerald Ford (R.-Mich) and House minority leader.

A great Purdue team that placed two men on the All-Conference club and a third man on the second team, took the league basketball crown in 1934. Paced by Conference scoring leader Norm Cottom, and Ray Eddy, co-captains, and three-sport star Emmett Lowery, who was the league's fifth leading scorer, the Boilermakers were the highest-scoring team to date in Big Ten history as they hit for a then astronomical 831 points for their 17-3 season.

Although Michigan finished last in the 1934 Conference football race for the first time in its history, all its foes had nothing but praise for the Wolverines' most-valuable-player that season, a fiery, shock-haired center named JERRY FORD, who went on to become a U.S. Congressman and minority leader of The House of Representatives.

Purdue's Big Ten champs in 1934, one of the great teams in Conference history (10-2, league and 17-3 seasonal), were led by All-Americas NORM COTTOM, and EMMETT LOWERY, and Captain Ray Eddy, later the Boilermaker coach.

NORM COTTOM   EMMETT LOWERY

The Conference next turned its attention to other sports such as track and swimming, which were having a struggle to keep alive. On May 13, 1905, the Intercollegiate Conference Athletic Association (ICAA) was incorporated under the laws of Illinois "to promote public interest in track and field and other forms of amateur sports, to maintain a high standard of amateurism in athletics and to conduct and manage athletic contests, exhibitions and meets in furtherance of the purpose above named."

Members of the corporation were the institutions making up the Conference. Operating the corporation were graduate directors representing each member institution, and their work was important because it helped promote Conference meets in other sports on the same amateur basis being insisted on for football.

In 1906, a particularly important meeting was called by President A. A. Angell of Michigan, bringing together presidents and faculty representatives of the member institutions. This farsighted group took only one day to adopt five most significant rules: (1) One year of residence necessary for eligibility, with this rule also requiring the meeting of all entrance requirements and completion of a full year's work; (2) Only three years of competition allowed, and no graduate student to be eligible; (3) Football season limited to five games; (4) No training table or training quarters permitted; (5) Student and faculty tickets not to cost more than 50 cents. These rules again met with much skepticism from the rest of the country; but, after seeing they could operate a good athletic program under them, every other conference adopted them.

The ban against training tables subsequently caused Michigan to withdraw from the Conference in protest

The only Purdue losses in the Conference were to Illinois by one point and to Iowa by two points, along with a loss to Notre Dame outside the league. Other Conference stars of the year were Frank Froschauer, of Illinois, Lyle Fisher, of Northwestern, and a slim sophomore from Chicago, who, although his team would finish a dead last for three years, would, amazingly, be virtually unstoppable. His name: Bill Haarlow, and, a generation later, he would become Chief of Referees for the Big Ten, and would see three of his own sons go on to star at Princeton.

Michigan took the indoor track crown, Illinois won it outdoors, and, generally, it was a slim year for the Conference in the NCAA, with only one individual title taken. Charley Hornbostel closed out his glittering collegiate career at Indiana by winning the 880 for the third straight year.

In 1934, for the first time, the Big Ten team championship in wrestling was decided on a point system

AL SCHWARTZ

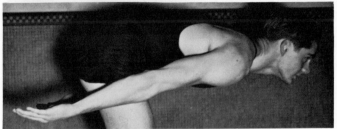

CHARLEY FLACHMAN

TAYLOR DRYSDALE

DICK VOLIVA, 175-pounder, was the star of the 1934 Indiana wrestling team that was the first to win the Conference championship based on a team tourney, rather than dual-meet standings. Voliva went on to win the NCAA title at his weight and represent the U.S. in the 1936 Olympics, where he won the silver medal.

The 1930's ushered in a Big Ten domination of the national swimming championships such as never before, or since, had been matched by any collegiate conference. Two-time and even three-time winners became commonplace. Northwestern's AL SCHWARTZ, started things off in 1929 with a 100-yard sprint victory, and scored the first triple in NCAA history in the 50, 100 and 220 in 1930. Illinois' CHARLEY FLACHMAN posted a 50 and 100 in 1935 after taking the 50 the year before. TAYLOR DRYSDALE, Michigan's great backstroker, won the 150-yard event in 1932, missed a year of competition, then came back for wins in 1934-35. The Wolverines' brilliant Ed Kirar scored twin doubles in the 50 and 100 in 1937-38; and Michigan's Tom Haynie won the 220 in 1937 and again in 1939. Meanwhile, the most incredible aquatic supremacy of all was in the making by Big Ten divers.

against retroactive provisions of certain Conference enactments. This was truly a serious blow to the young and struggling Conference, because Michigan, which had been one of the strongest members from the start, remained outside the league until 1917.

On January 2, 1909, Conference institutions took an active part in the creation of the National Collegiate Athletic Association.

March 25, 1911, marked the first Conference indoor track and swimming meets at Northwestern.

In 1912 another new member—Ohio State University—was admitted to the Conference. The Conference was really beginning to grow in size and strength. In 1917 when Michigan decided it wanted to return, and was accepted, the Conference achieved its first final makeup of 10 schools.

In exploring the historical data of the Conference, I

have been amazed to see so many of its problems centered on baseball. Few people of this generation fully realize what an important part baseball played in the development of sports throughout the country. College games frequently outdrew the attendance of the big league games. Every small town had a baseball team, and it soon became apparent that many Big Ten players were playing for pay in the summer or even on Sundays during the school year.

The faculty representatives and directors felt it was almost impossible to control the situation, which had its parallels in other sports as well, and after many meetings decided that the best way to cope with the problem would be to hire a Commissioner. It took one of the wildest episodes in Conference history to really convince them—an event without parallel.

November 27, 1921, convinced the faculty representa-

in a Conference tournament, instead of on dual meet records, and Indiana was the first tourney champion. Dick Voliva, the Hoosier's star 175-pounder, went on to take the NCAA crown in his division.

In swimming, after Michigan had won its seventh league crown in eight years, Taylor Drysdale, the Wolverines' great backstroker, won the NCAA 150-

AL PATNIK

DICK DEGENER

Starting in 1933 and continuing for the next 30 years there were 58 high and low board national collegiate titles at stake in the NCAA meet. (There was no low board event in 1933-34.) Of this total, 49 of the 54 crowns were won by Ohio State and Michigan—with the Buckeyes taking an amazing 42 of the 49. DICK DEGENER, Michigan, started things off with high board victories in 1933-34, followed by the Wolverines' Frank Fehsenfeld in 1935-36. The gaudiest multiple winner, however, was Ohio State's slim AL PATNIK, the greatest diver the world had yet seen. Patnik captured five NCAA crowns: the low board in 1938-39-40, and the high board in 38-39. (He was barely nipped by teammate Earl Clark, in '40).

Championships on a team basis were not instituted until 1937 and in the next 30 years 24 of them would go to Big Ten schools: 11 to Ohio State, 10 to Michigan, and three to Indiana. (Four others would go to Yale and two to Southern California.)

1935

yard championship again; Charles Flachman of Illinois took the 50-yard freestyle; Michigan's Dick Degener repeated as 3-meter diving champ, and a Wolverine quartet of Julian Robertson, Ogden Dalrymple, Henry Kamenski and Bob Renner, splashed home first in the 400-freestyle relay.

John Kocsis, a brilliant sophomore with all the shots, came along to lead Michigan not only to the Big Ten golf title (in which Kocsis won the individual crown) but also the NCAA team title. It was the first time the team crown had left the Ivy League. (In fact, the Ivies, who had taken it every year since 1897 would win it only four more times after 1935.)

At Wisconsin, which had sponsored varsity boxing since 1933, Irish John Walsh, became the Badger coach—and started down the road which would make him the most successful collegiate ring coach in America. As a student at St. Thomas College in 1933, Walsh not only was a member of, but coached the school's boxing team which met Wisconsin in the latter's first collegiate match. A few years later when the Badgers were looking for a coach, George Downer, known as the "Father of Boxing" at Wisconsin, remembered the young man who had impressed him so much. Downer, the director of sports publicity, urged the university to hire Walsh, a young attorney in Madison. The young Irishman signed on and subsequently turned out squads that won more matches and more NCAA titles than any other school in America.

In 1935 the Minnesota football juggernaut rolled on.

Ohio State matched it, fury for fury—almost.

A Notre Dame-Buckeye game went down in history as perhaps the most dramatic game ever played on a college gridiron.

The exploits of a halfback from the University of Chicago, of all places, defied belief, and the trough of mediocrity into which mighty Michigan had

---

tives and directors that a Commissioner of the Conference was not only desirable, but essential. The National Football League had not yet been born, but there was a sturdy semi-pro team in Decatur, Illinois, led by player-manager George Halas. There were other strong semi-pro teams around the country: the Rock Island Independents, the Minneapolis Marines and the famed Canton, Ohio Bulldogs. Every good-sized city in the Midwest boasted a semi-pro team. It was not unusual for some of the Big Ten players to play a college game on Saturday and then on Sunday appear in a semi-pro lineup, where satisfactory performance might earn them $15 to $25 a game. Often they played for nothing, just for love of the game.

During that period, a tremendous rivalry developed between two Southern Illinois towns, Taylorville and Carlinville, county seats of adjoining counties. Taylor-

ville had long been a leader in downstate semi-pro football, with its team—founded in 1914—building a record of 58-5 over the years. Carlinville, on the other hand, was organized in 1920. It had been undefeated that year, and had won a treasured victory over perennial champion Taylorville. The rivalry between these two towns was unbelievable. A great deal of money changed hands whenever they met. Carlinville's 1920 triumph was a bitter blow to Taylorville, and the small town buzzed all winter with plans to field a stronger team the next fall.

Carlinville decided 1921 was the time to make the killing. To make sure of winning, it proceeded to get the strongest group of players possible. Notre Dame, under Knute Rockne, had just finished an undefeated season, and Carlinville quietly planned to bring 11 of the best Irish players to represent it in the big game

fallen was for real and not just a bad dream of the previous season.

It was, in brief, a year the Big Ten would not soon forget.

Gone from that great 1934 Minnesota team were such as Pug Lund, Butch Larson, Bill Bevan, and others. The Gophers had also received a severe jolt when Kostka, George Svendson and Art Clarkson were ruled ineligible by the Big Ten. They had played one year of freshman football and one year of sophomore football at Oregon under Clarence Spears before transferring to Minnesota. When Spears resigned at Oregon to take over at Wisconsin, the trio came back to Minnesota but, as it turned out, were allowed to play only one year. There was a strong nucleus of stars remaining and some precocious sophomores for Bernie Bierman to work with. Glenn Seidel was still around at quarterback. George Roscoe, Babe LeVoir and two sparky sophomores, Tuffy Thompson and Andy Uram, ran from halfback, and Sheldon Beise blasted from fullback. Two brilliant sophomores, Ray King and Dwight Reed, started at end; Ed Widseth and Dick Smith were still rampant at tackle; Bud Wilkinson and Vern Oech headed the guard corps and Dale Rennebohn held down the center post. The Gophers were not quite as deep as the previous year but behind the regulars were still half a horde of reserves who could have started on most college teams. The only thing lacking as the season began was some tangible proof that all the ingredients would fit nicely into place.

The second game of the campaign, after a reasonable drubbing of North Dakota in the opener, would provide the test—and the test was a powerful Nebraska team considered the best Cornhusker eleven in a decade or more. In fact, the Huskers were installed as slight favorites over the Norsemen on this steamy, hot day at Lincoln, Nebraska, and among the experts there were strong doubts that Minnesota could bring it off.

The experts had a clue to the future on the opening kick-off. George Roscoe tucked in the ball on the Minnesota goal line and, with hard-nose interference ahead of him, sped to the Nebraska 26-yard line before being tossed out of bounds. Beise and Roscoe took turns ripping chunks to the Husker three and a first down, but three plunges got nowhere and then Seidel called for mind over muscle. Beise plunged directly into the line but handed the ball behind him to Seidel just before he hit. Seidel then pivoted and flipped a lateral out to George Roscoe cutting wide to the right. Touchdown! Then, after Bud Wilkinson missed the extra point, Nebraska went ahead on a 33-yard scoring sprint by Jerry La Noue and the extra point by Sam Francis. The Gophers scored again after a poor Nebraska punt, and again Wilkinson's boot failed. If this was to be another Minnesota team of destiny, their 12-7 lead would take a lot of protecting. It was never so apparent as when the Nebraska punter booted one from his own 25 and bounced it around on the Minnesota two, where Roscoe chased it and decided to pick it up and run. He was hit just as his fingers touched the ball, which squirted away to be smothered by a Nebraskan on the Gopher one-yard line. The final quarter was rapidly running out and with an inevitable Nebraska touchdown coming up, Minnesota's victory hopes seemed to be melting away in the hot sun—a sun which had the Viking line sagging and spent.

On first down, Nebraska sent Lloyd Cardwell, their fastest back, on an end sweep. Ray King cut him down for no gain. In fact, he hit him so hard that King himself, was knocked out and carried from the field. On second down, La Noue hit tackle and the whole Minnesota line smashed him back again for no gain. On the third try, Cardwell slightly juggled a direct snap from center just long enough for Babe LeVoir to streak through and toss him back to the eight. On fourth down, center Dale Rennebohm batted a pass away from a Nebraska receiver

---

against Taylorville. This was done in the utmost secrecy, so that bets could be placed on a sure thing.

The disturbing information reached Taylorville fans through an unsigned letter. The writer said he was well acquainted with both Taylorville and Carlinville, but refused to sit idly by and let Carlinville slip anything over on Taylorville, where he had many friends. The bitter blow came in the last sentence; he revealed they would have to play most of the Notre Dame team Sunday. The fact that Carlinville fans had chartered a special train of 15 cars for the trip to Taylorville lent validity to the letter. The Taylorville coach, remembering that one of the University of Illinois players had once told him that any time he needed help he could have the services of anyone from the Illini squad, called Champaign and the following phone conversation ensued:

"We've got some bad news," said the Taylorville man.

"What's the matter, did they cancel the game?"

"No, but they're bringing the whole Notre Dame team."

"To hell with them! We'll bring the Illinois team and kick the pants off 'em!"

The result of this conversation was that most of Illinois backfield and several linemen came to play for Taylorville. So the semi-pro championship between two small coal-mining towns actually was developing into a game between stars from two great institutions that had never met on the modern gridiron—Notre Dame and Illinois.

Most of the players were seniors but a few, unfortunately, had competition left.

All negotiations had been made very quietly, so the fans in Carlinville thought the game was in the bag for them. Taylorville even sent a man to Chicago, and when he saw 12 husky football players get on the train heading downstate, he was able to give the Taylorville coach

on the goal line, and the Gophers took over to preserve their 12-7 victory. Later Bernie Bierman described the goal line stand as the moment that made
the Gopher season. It was what the Gophers needed
to jell them as a team and enabled them to survive
what, to other teams, could have been a disastrous
personnel loss in a 20-0 victory over Tulane the following week. On its lone major scoring threat, Tulane sprung Bernie Mintz loose behind perfect interference for what should have been a 20-yard touchdown payoff. Streaking across field, Gopher quarterback Glenn Seidel knocked Mintz out of bounds a
foot from the goal line. It was a magnificent defensive play but a costly one for Minnesota as Seidel
was taken from the field with a broken collar bone
that kept him out for the remainder of the season—
and probably cost him All-America consideration.

Handy Babe LeVoir moved to quarterback and
the Gophers swept their eight-game slate, scoring
194 points to 56 and preserving their No. 1 status
for the second year in a row. Also, for the second
straight year it was a talent-rich Ohio State team
under imaginative Francis Schmidt which kept pace
with the Golden Gophers and shared the Big Ten
title with them with a clean Conference record.

It was a big, fast and daring Buckeye crew which
featured slashing runners when the ball wasn't being whipped around in the air—forward and later-
ally. Trevor Rees and Merle Wendt, a great pass
receiver and defensive star, were at the ends;
Charley Hamrick and Gil Harre were tough tackles;
smart, mobile Inwood Smith and Jim Karcher
headed a strong guard corps, and Captain Gomer
Jones, an amazing 5-foot, 9-in, 220-pounder who
could range all over the field, was at center. Stan
Pincura and Tippy Dye, both brilliant passers, were
at quarterback; the halfbacks were manned by big,
slashing Dick Heekin, swift, hard-running Franklin
Boucher, Dick Beltz, and Jumping Joe Williams, a
fireplug squat sophomore who was one of the year's
most exciting runners. John Kabealo, the best punter

*The Big Ten had never seen anything like it when
FRANCIS SCHMIDT came up from Texas Christian in
1934 to take over at Ohio State. His intricate, wild-and-
woolly offense took the Buckeyes to national ranking,
and the tremendous scores run up by the Scarlet brought
the World War One bayonet drillmaster the label, "Close-
The-Gates-of-Mercy-Schmidt."*

in the Big Ten, Frank Antenucci, and another great
sophomore, Jim McDonald, were the fullbacks.
These and a dozen brilliant reserves enabled the
Scarlet Scourge to make the pre-season experts look
good by running up an awesome 150 points to 26
in their first four games against Kentucky, Drake,
Northwestern and Indiana.

This brought the Buckeyes to the point in their
schedule that loomed not only as the game-of-the-
year but an almost hysterical rallying point for
Scarlet and Gray fandom such as hadn't been witnessed since Ohio Stadium was opened in 1922.

Notre Dame, heralded as a great team, undefeated
in its first five games, and coached by Elmer Layden, one of the immortal Four Horsemen, was
meeting Ohio State for the first time. The drama was
laid on as though by a trowel. Three-dollar tickets,
even in these depression days, were being scalped
for fifty dollars a pair, and more. The elite of the
sportswriting world, as well as special columnists,

verification that Carlinville was using most of the Irish
team. When the special pulled in early Sunday morning
from Carlinville, its passengers could hardly wait to get
off the train to place their bets. Much to their amazement, they found Taylorville fans willing to cover everything.

A tremendous crowd banked the field on all sides,
and excitement ran high. Taylorville decided to start its
regular lineup, but Carlinville started three Irish All-
Americans—Chet Wynne, Eddie Anderson (later a great
Iowa coach) and Roger Kiley—and a line also made up
mainly of Notre Damers. Frank Thomas, the regular
Notre Dame quarterback, had missed the train, a blow
to Carlinville in that it was unable to use the Notre
Dame shift with any success. Despite this, Carlinville had
all the best of it in the first half. Winning the toss, Carlinville chose to receive. Wynne returned the kickoff past
midfield before he was pulled down. He then advanced

the ball to the Taylorville 15, but failed to score.

After an exchange of kicks, a punt was blocked and
Taylorville gained possession on Carlinville's one-yard
line. Two line plays lost three yards. Then Taylorville's
Charlie Dressen (later to manage in the Big Leagues)
called his prize play, the quarterback sneak, actually a
spinner. Despite the fact he had to go around All-
American end Roger Kiley, he made it. The score at
halftime was Taylorville 7, Carlinville 0.

Between halves, Coach Hoover of Taylorville was in
a quandary. He had not yet used his imports from
Illinois, and hated to do so, holding a temporary lead.
He knew he couldn't hold back the opposition with all
its Notre Dame strength. (His own players had a poor
opinion of Illinois, as the Illini had won but one game
that season, though it was over Ohio State, Big Ten
champion.) Hoover's decision, finally, was to put in the
Illinois stars, including Captain Laurie Walquist, half-

jammed the press box. From the East came Damon Runyon, Grantland Rice, Paul Gallico, Allison Danzig of the *New York Times,* and the sports editors of all the wire services. From the midwest came top sportswiters of all the leading papers in the Big Ten area. It was stated in many quarters that, regardless of what Minnesota might do from there on in, the winner of the Ohio-Notre Dame game would have to be considered national champion. (It was inconceivable that the victor could be defeated after this day.)

Thus was the stage set under gloomy, overcast skies at 2:00 p.m. when Kabealo of Ohio State kicked off to Notre Dame.

The Notre Dame backfield included Bill Shakespeare, a fine passer-runner; Joe Carrideo, younger brother of All-America Fred; Mike Layden, younger brother of the Notre Dame coach; Jim Miller, a hard runner, and Andy Pilney another runner-passer. They operated behind a big, rugged line but, in the first quarter against Ohio, couldn't move the ball. The second time the Irish went on offense, Buckeye lightening struck. Mike Layden shot a pass over the line. The Bucks' Antenucci leaped high to intercept, took three or four steps and obeyed Francis Schmidt's littany of "look for a guy to lateral to!" Antenucci fiicked it off to Franklin Boucher and the big halfback, behind one gorgeous block by Trevor Rees, raced 70 yards for a touchdown. Dick Beltz' conversion made it 7-0.

The Irish again got nowhere against the ferocious Ohio line and early in the second quarter the Buckeye offense tore great gaps in the Notre Dame forward wall and sifted through its secondary until, finally, Joe Williams jammed over from the three. The point was missed but it didn't seem to matter. The Buckeyes were going to roll it up.

Between the halves a young sports writer for the Columbus *Dispatch* was assigned to extract statements (flattering, it was presumed) from the famous experts in the press box on their opinion of the Ohio team thus far. The comments were like this:

Runyon: "I'm glad I was here to see 'em. I wouldn't have believed it, otherwise."

Rice: "This Ohio State team in the first half has shown me the greatest display of football I've ever witnessed!"

Gallico: "It'll take Congressional action to stop these guys."

The second half, of course, was supposed to be a continuation of the first, but somebody forgot to inform Notre Dame. Especially the Irish line which suddenly started commiting mass mayhem on every Scarlet sortie. Meanwhile, Miller, Shakespeare, Pilney and Layden, behind revitalized blocking, were beginning to dent the Buckeye forward wall. Then, on the last play of the period, Pilney took an Ohio punt on the Buck 35 and slashed down to the 12.

The fourth quarter opened, it seemed, with Notre Dame still having about fifty miles to go and no time to do it in. After one line thrust and an incomplete pass, Pilney pegged one to Frank Gaul on the two. Miller slammed into the line for the TD but the Irish missed the conversion and Ohio breathed more comfortably. The sense of security didn't last long. The Notre Dame line stifled Ohio, and Pilney went to work again, by land and by air. He ran, he bucked, he took laterals and eventually he passed to Layden on the Ohio one-yard line. Then Miller hit center and fumbled—and Ohio recovered behind the goal line for a life-saving touchback. From the 20, Joe Williams streaked around the end for 24 yards and would have gone the distance had he not been pulled down by (it was almost ordained, by now) Andy Pilney. The Bucks got no further and had to punt. A Layden plunge and then Pilney, again, passing to the Ohio 33. Two more Pilney passes and the Irish were on the 15. Everybody in the Stadium was calling the play now, as time began to run out on the Irish. So, nobody was surprised— just delighted or stunned, as the case may be— when Pilney threw a touchdown pass to Layden.

---

back; Jack Crangle, Big Ten all-star fullback; and Joe Sternaman, quarterback.

The second half was a different story when Sternaman started to bark out his signals. The Illinois backfield quickly made its presence felt. Walquist's passes got the ball near the Carlinville goal line three times, each time close enough for little Sternaman to kick a field goal. The game ended: Taylorville 16, Carlinville 0.

No lineups were printed and few in the crowd realized they were seeing some of the finest college players in the country in action. The bets were all paid off and finally, as the players were about to leave, a Notre Dame player who had starred in the game, said: "Well, we know that *you* know who we are, and we know who you had. But we aren't going to say anything about being here and we hope you won't either!"

For two months nothing more was heard of the game. Then, as Illinois went into a basketball game against Wisconsin, Walquist's eligibility was challenged. The investigation that followed was sensational. Both Illinois and Notre Dame promptly declared non-seniors who had been involved in the game ineligible for further college competition.

The faculty representatives after carefully studying the problem with the Directors in a joint meeting now decided a Commissioner simply had to be selected, and a committee consisting of George Huff of Illinois, A. A. Stagg of Chicago and Tom Jones of Wisconsin was appointed to survey the field. After reviewing many fine candidates they came up with a unanimous choice: Major John L. Griffith, a man who was destined to leave his mark on the pages of history of intercollegiate sports as the first Conference Commissioner of Athletics in the United States.

His qualifications were excellent. He was a fine athlete in several sports at Beloit College in Wisconsin, where

There were less than two minutes to play. The conversion must tie it up for the Irish or it was all over. Ohio would receive and eat up the clock.

Wally Fromhart's kick was low and a roar of relief rolled up from the Ohio fans.

As expected, Notre Dame tried an on-side kick in a desperate attempt to regain possession. It didn't work and Ohio had the ball on its 47, with 1:30 to go. The 70,000 hysterical fans figured the clock was as good as eaten; salted for the Irish, sweetened for the Bucks. On the first play from scrimmage, Dick Beltz slanted into the Notre Dame line, picked up good yardage—and fumbled. The ball squirted toward the sideline. When the officials restored order, it was Notre Dame's Pojman who owned the ball on the Irish 40.

Less than a minute to play? Impossible. Ohio would back up its entire secondary against long passes and concede the short ones.

The prevailing rules, however, forbade a player from returning in any quarter in which he had already played. Francis Schmidt had given a badly-needed rest to Dick Heekin, Frank Boucher and Jim McDonald, all of them six-foot backs. In the line-up were Vic Dorris, Dick Beltz and Jack Bettridge. Nobody over 5-9. Wayne Millner, the Irish end, was 6-3.

So Notre Dame had the ball for one final effort. Andy Pilney, in deep formation, circled and skittered to pass, found himself hemmed in and decided to run. With the Ohio secondary pulled back he slashed to the 19 before being spilled. He didn't get up. They carried him off on a stretcher, and Bill Shakespeare replaced him.

The stretcher bearers were carrying Pilney along the sidelines toward the dressing room. He signaled them to stop, then raised up painfully to take a look. In the pressbox somebody shouted: "Look at Pilney . . . What's that old chestnut about the Spartan warrior coming home victorious or being borne home on his shield . . .?"

Somebody snarled it was no time for a reference to classics. There was a classic down on the field, and the play had started.

As Pilney raised up on one elbow to look, Shakespeare threw toward a receiver in the medium flat. Beltz rushing up, almost intercepted, but batted the ball down. Pilney sagged back to the stretcher. Time left: 20 seconds. Shakespeare took the direct snap from center, ducked under and between charging Ohio linemen, got the ball away, arching it toward a spot in the end zone where big Wayne Milner had gotten behind a defender.

The spot was exactly five yards deep in the end zone, exactly 12 yards from the west sideline.

The time was 4:24 p.m. as Millner pulled in the ball for a touchdown just as Pilney raised up on the stretcher for another look.

For the third time in the final quarter the Irish missed the extra point. Who cared? It was still an 18-13 victory on three touchdowns in the last quarter—two of them in the last two minutes.

Nobody believed it. The silence, except from a small Notre Dame rooting section, was a testimonial to stunned incredulity.

A half hour later fans were still on the field, drawn irresistibly to a spot in the south end zone, five yards deep, 12 yards from the west sideline. They stared down at the turf as though there was a marker, or a plaque already on the spot. Twenty-five years later the young sports writer from the *Dispatch*, on a visit from the East, wandered into the empty stadium, then over to the unlined end zone. He stopped and stared down. A veteran groundskeeper, working nearby, looked up and grinned. "That's the spot," he said simply.

For Notre Dame, the afternoon produced victory for the day—and disaster for the season. Physically and emotionally exhausted the Irish couldn't get up for a Northwestern team that had dropped three out of five games, and lost to the Wildcats, 14-7. The week after that they were tied, 6-6, by Army,

---

he graduated in 1902. He became a successful coach in all sports at Yankton College, South Dakota, then at Morningside College, Sioux City, Iowa, and finally at Drake University, Des Moines, in 1908, where he coached all sports. In 1909 he founded the Drake Relays, which were to become one of the outstanding relay meets of the country.

He entered the military service in 1916 and was assigned to Camp Dodge to handle the athletic activities and coach the football team, and later to Camp Pike. His success at these two large army camps and the enthusiasm he generated in their athletic program brought him to the attention of the War Department, and he ended up heading physical training for the entire U. S. Army.

There was much speculation as to what Griffith's exact duties would be as Commissioner. The Conference minutes

of June 2, 1922, are as follows: "Established the office of Commissioner of Athletics with the Commissioner to serve as general secretary, promote educational campaigns on amateurism and carry on investigations regarding intercollegiate athletic problems."

I doubt very much that even Major Griffith, with his background, fully realized the tremendous job he faced and the importance of the work he was to do. He was now at the helm of the most powerful Conference in the United States.

The Big Ten Conference served as a model for many of the conferences organized in later years. The prestige of Big Ten teams was tremendous. Their football teams were coached by some of the greatest names in coaching history, including Fielding Yost of Michigan, Bob Zuppke of Illinois, Jack Wilce of Ohio State, Amos Alonzo Stagg of Chicago, Dr. Harry Williams of Minnesota and others

which had lost two in a row prior to their annual game with the Irish. The Buckeyes also showed signs of what they'd been through when they traveled to Chicago for a meeting with the Maroon and just squeaked through to a 20-13 win after the scintillating Jay Berwanger led an assault that produced a 13-0 Maroon lead.

On one epic run, Berwanger got credit for a 60-yard touchdown play but everybody in the park saw him, on a soggy field, slip off tackle, cut toward the sideline, cut back toward the middle, give way backwards for a few yards, slither through two defenders at midfield, cut back to the original sideline and then to the goal line—a total distance of well over 100 yards. It was merely typical of the

triple-threat heroics displayed for two seasons by the big blond—the last All-America Chicago would ever produce.

And Michigan? Evidently what the single victory of the 1934 season had implied, apparently was true. The Wolves got back to a 4-4 year in 1935 (including three shut-outs pinned on them in their last three games) and a pigskin depression obviously was on at Ann Arbor.

All-American from the Big Ten that year included Chicago's Jay Berwanger; Bud Wilkinson and Dick Smith, Minnesota's great guard and tackle; Ohio State's brilliant line trio of end Merle Wendt, guard Inwood Smith, and captain Gomer Jones, center; Paul Tangora, Northwestern guard; Ozzie

It took Michigan State 20 years to produce its second All-America but SID WAGNER, the Spartans' tremendous guard in 1935, left no doubts that he deserved all-star rating. Other Big Ten stars on the All-America included GOMER JONES, Ohio State's rotund but remarkable

center, and BUD WILKINSON, the brilliant Minnesota guard under whom Jones served as line coach at Oklahoma where Wilkinson's teams were the class of the nation for many years.

BUD WILKINSON	GOMER JONES	SID WAGNER

who were then ranked with them as tops in football coaching. Basketball was but a step behind, with such famous names as Dr. Walter Meanwell of Wisconsin, Ward Lambert of Purdue, Dr. L. J. Cooke of Minnesota and Ralph Jones of Illinois.

In track the outstanding coaches included Tom Jones of Wisconsin, Harry Gill of Illinois, Steve Farrell of Michigan, Frank Hill of Northwestern and Riley Castleman of Ohio State. These were truly legendary names; men who had produced many Olympic stars, and were the best of the lot.

In swimming, Tom Robinson of Northwestern, Dave Armbruster of Iowa, Ed Manley of Illinois and Neils Thorp of Minnesota were the men whose teams were usually to be found at the top. In a few years they were to be joined by Matt Mann of Michigan and Mike Peppe of Ohio State.

In baseball two of the most famous coaches in the Conference were Carl Lundgren of Illinois, a former great Cub pitcher, and Ray Fisher of Michigan, former Yankee star. This is just a sampling of the many distinguished coaches with whom Major Griffith was to work.

The Conference had grown tremendously in student enrollment from the days when the football games were witnessed by scattered crowds, to a time when they were filling inadequate stadiums to overflowing at every game. The Big Ten was just on the threshold of the roaring 20's, the era of athletic expansion and growth that will probably never be equalled in intercollegiate athletics. There was little professional football played in the United States at that time, and football enthusiasts gloried in college football alone.

One of the amazing things was the development of the

Iowa, who had the first Negro lineman to make All-America from the Big Ten (Duke Slater, 1921), also provided the first Negro back in fleet OZZIE SIMMONS in 1935, one of the most exciting runners the Conference had seen in years.

JAY BERWANGER

During the 1935 football season the Downtown A.C. in New York had announced it would make an annual award to the most valuable collegiate football player in the United States. It would be known as the Heisman Trophy, in honor of John Heisman, one of the nation's great, early grid coaches at Georgia Tech.

That same season, the University of Chicago, already deep in the throes of de-emphasis decreed by President Robert Hutchins, had managed to beat Indiana, Wisconsin and Illinois but had lost to Ohio State, Nebraska and Purdue. With two other victories over little Cornell College of Iowa and Western State, it was nevertheless a decidedly unimpressive year for the once Mighty Men of the Midway.

Yet it was from this team which came the first recipient of the Heisman Trophy—John Jacob Berwanger, more familiarly known as Jay.

There was absolutely no surprise or criticism when the award was announced. There simply couldn't be any. Jay Berwanger just happened to be the greatest all-around back since Jim Thorpe, and one of the coziest questions of the past three years had been: "I wonder what Berwanger could have done behind one of those Minnesota lines . . . ?"

A good question, and it almost could have been answered. After making All-State at Dubuque, Iowa High School, Berwanger considered Minnesota, Purdue and Iowa before deciding on Chicago—a decision, incidentally, he never regretted.

Chicago's day as a football power had long since waned, but the young Berwanger had come to know Ira Davenport, a Chicago Olympian of 1912, who headed the Dubuque Boat and Boiler Co., where Jay worked as a prepper. Davenport sold the boy on Chicago's great academic heritage and assured Berwanger he could participate in sports without a lot of win-win-win pressure being exerted on him. So Berwanger enrolled at Chicago where there were very few Big Ten-type football players, and Chicago proceeded to do some serious winning, anyway. The victories were due, mainly, to the 6-foot, 200-pound, tough-muscled halfback who not only had great speed and power but who was described by Red Grange as having "that faraway look."

Simmons, Iowa's fleet, tricky halfback; and Sid Wagner, a slashing guard from fast-rising Michigan State which, by now, was beginning to play one of the toughest independent schedules in the midwest.

Jay Berwanger, who was a predictable choice for the league's most-valuable-player, was further honored by being the first recipient of what would become the most prestigious individual award in collegiate football—the Heisman Trophy for the outstanding football player in the nation.

tremendous Big Ten football marching bands with their intricate field formations, the first of their kind in the nation. Oddly enough, many of these bands had been originated and supported for the purpose of taking part in the ROTC military program. Austin Harding, Illinois band director, gave football marching bands an entirely new dimension by instituting elaborate field formations that quickly spread to other Big Ten bands and eventually were copied by bands throughout the country. It was carried to the West Coast by the University of Michigan in 1948 in the Rose Bowl game against Southern California. Despite the fact that the football team won 49 to 0, the team was forced to share the headlines with the accounts of Michigan's tremendous marching band.

Meanwhile, radio was in its infancy and TV still a dream. Consequently, the only way to enjoy a football

game was to go and see it, and there were just not enough seats in any Conference stadium to accomodate the thousands of alumni and visitors. This led to what we could call "The Age of Stadium Building." It's true that each Big Ten university had a stadium, but most of them were wooden and few could seat in excess of 25,000, and would not begin to hold half the crowds that wanted to go to the game. Adding to the size of the crowds was a growing appreciation by the Universities of the attraction that football held for alumni. The administration recognized that the games could serve as a rallying point to bring alumni back to campus, or contribute to development funds, and this gave rise to the institution of football homecoming games, a tradition created at the University of Illinois before World War One.

The pressure created by the need for vastly larger

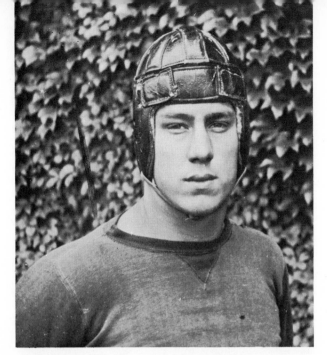

Jay Berwanger as All-America captain of Chicago's 1935 football team.

By that, Grange meant an ability to swiftly photograph downfield situations while cutting back, changing speed and dealing with immediate tacklers. "He had a rare gait," Grange said. "A change of pace is not, as some people believe, running slow or medium speed one second and fast the next. It is running hard at top speed and then reaching down within the body and getting an extra burst of momentum to flash past or between defensive men. Berwanger also had an uncanny ability at hitting a hole that was closing on him. His feet would drum the ground lightly, in momentary hesitation when blockers or tacklers were locked in front of him, then he would be away in a flash when a slit of opening showed."

Riding with this ability was tremendous desire and pride, and nothing illustrated it more than the Purdue game of 1934 when the Maroon was trailing by two touchdowns late in the game. Storming back, Chicago still lost it, 26-20, but on the Maroon's third touchdown drive which carried 85 yards, there were three occasions when it was third and 10. All three times Jay Berwanger

ripped off 10 yards for the vital first down to keep the drive alive.

Perhaps the greatest run of Berwanger's career came in 1935 against powerful Ohio State, which had just come off its stunning upset by Notre Dame and was driving toward an unbeaten Big Ten season and a co-championship with Minnesota. The Maroon had the Bucks on the verge of still another upset and were leading 13-0 at the half, with Chicago's second touchdown coming on what was described as a 140-yard scoring gallop which found Berwanger slithering through the mud off tackle, then down a sideline, then crossing back to midfield between tacklers, then back to the sideline again where he burst through two converging Buckeyes who had their hands on him.

One wonders, too, how Berwanger developed his "faraway look," because for three years he was known as "The Man in the Iron Mask." He had broken his nose as a frosh and when it refused to heal properly and left him vulnerable, the doctors said he couldn't play without protection. A sort of half baseball catcher's mask was devised, made of spring steel bars covered with leather. At first he had difficulty adjusting his sight but for three years he never set foot on the field without that mask.

For those three years he compiled some remarkable statistics while playing for a team that never enjoyed a winning season—on the record, that is, because Berwanger and his mates were winners in more ways than one. As a sophomore he played 60 minutes of all five of Chicago's league games; carried the ball 184 times from scrimmage for just under a four-yard average; scored eight touchdowns and did all the punting. Against Illinois he lugged the ball 37 times, the same number as the entire Illinois backfield. At season's end he was named Chicago's most-valuable player, the only sophomore in the league ever to gain that honor.

As a junior Berwanger carried 119 times for just under five yards per carry, picked up some passing chores and completed 14 for 196 yards, and punted 77 times for 3,026 yards (which exceeded modern records which were not kept by the Big Ten Service Bureau until 1939). More astonishing he placed 30 punts out of bounds and only five of the 77 went over the goal line. Meanwhile, as a safetyman he returned 18 punts for 186 yards. He had eight touchdowns, and to give you an idea of his defensive

---

stadia resulted in the construction during the 1920's of seven new facilities: Ohio State, 1922 (81,109); Illinois, 1923, (71,227); Minnesota, 1924 (63,430); Purdue, 1924 (62,000); Northwestern, 1926 (55,000); Michigan, 1927 (101,001); and Iowa, 1929 (60,150). Since then, many of these have been enlarged.

These magnificent stadia were to play a very important part in the athletic history of the Big Ten. The increased capacity brought in tremendous revenue, and this revenue was plowed right back into the athletic departments and into sports that had little crowd appeal. Along with these benefits, however, it was only natural that it brought problems. You can't fill a gigantic stadium with a losing team. Consequently, the pressure on recruiting began to increase.

It didn't take long for Commissioner Griffith to get into action. His first evidence was against a number of

baseball players who had been playing in violation of the Conference rules. The directors promptly disqualified these men, a number of them having received varying amounts of money from semi-pro teams. Major Griffith asked the Conference for permission to hire an investigator to help run down the many rumors going around concerning the offers being made to outstanding athletes. As he proceeded with this work, he found the great majority of illegal offers came from alumni. So he began an extensive educational campaign with the alumni groups concerning Big Ten rules.

Despite all these precautions, in May, 1929, action was taken that shocked the Conference to its very roots. As I was host to the Big Ten track meet at Northwestern, I also served as chairman of the Conference Directors, an honor which rotated each year. I received a call from Major Griffith a week prior to the meeting, asking me to

Jay Berwanger carries against Michigan in 1934. Chicago won 27-0 and Berwanger scored two touchdowns.

In 1934, Captain Ellmore Patterson, an inspiring leader and great blocker, was Chicago's MVP (and an All-America) but in 1935 Berwanger's teammates again chose him for the honor. Berwanger was also acclaimed the league's MVP and for the second straight year he was a unanimous choice for All-America.

Meanwhile, Berwanger had also demonstrated his versatility in track where he was a natural. So much so that he took fourth place in the Decathlon at the Kansas Relays in his sophomore year—his very first attempt at the event. He could do everything, but his best events were the hurdles and broad jump. There was simply not enough time for Berwanger to concentrate on track, and he competed only two years. There were no athletic scholarships or grants-in-aid of any kind at Chicago and he supported himself by working three hours a day in

ability, in the Minnesota game which wasn't too far from typical, he made 14 tackles in the first half alone from his left corner post, and even the mighty Vikings ran mostly to the other side in the second half.

By the end of his senior year Berwanger had compiled the following career marks, and although he always gave full and grateful credit to his mates who put out for him with 100 percent of their ability, it was all too true that there weren't too many big holes opened for him, and his pass and punt protection broke down not infrequently. All of which makes these career figures more remarkable.

> Figures covering Berwanger's performances in the 23 games he played during his three years' competition. (He missed the Chicago-Ohio State contest in 1934 because of injury):
> GAINS FROM SCRIMMAGE—Carried the ball 439 times for net gains of 1,839 yards and an average gain of 4.19 yards per try.
> PASSES—Threw 146 forward passes, of which 50 were complete, for total gains of 921 yards, or an average of 6.3 yards per attempted pass; 22 of Berwanger's passes were intercepted. He received 12 passes for total gains of 189 yards; intercepted eight opponents' passes and returned them a total of 79 yards.
> PUNTS—Punted 223 times for total yardage from the scrimmage line of 8,325 [excluding one punt blocked because of bad pass from center], or an average of 37.3 yards per punt; 80 of his punts were placed out of bounds and only nine crossed the opponent's goal line; returned 20 punts a total of 207 yards, or an average of 10.3 yards per return.
> KICK-OFFS—Kicked-off 31 times for total yardage of 1,435, or an average of 46.3 yards per kick-off; returned 34 opponents' kick-offs a total of 873 yards, or an average of 25.7 yards per return.
> SCORING—Scored 22 touchdowns and 20 points after touchdown for 152 points.

Jay Berwanger, Chicago's last All-America and America's first Heisman Trophy winner, gains ground for Chicago Rugby Team on way to victory over New York.

the office of the University Engineer and waiting on tables at his Psi Upsilon fraternity house.

Clark Shaughnessy, the Maroon coach who had succeeded Amos Alonzo Stagg, and who did wondrous things with the material at hand, summed it up for everybody when he said of his super-star: "I've never met a finer boy nor seen a finer football player—and I don't expect to. You can say anything superlative about him you like . . . and I'll double it!"

FRANK FROSCHAUER   ROLF POSER

ED SHAVER

FRANK FROSCHAUER, Illinois forward (and star half-back in football), led the Illini to a triple tie for the 1935 Big Ten cage crown with Wisconsin, paced by star guard ROLF POSER, and Purdue, paced by Co-Captains ED SHAVER and Norm Cottom.

In basketball, the Conference turned up another dogfight for the 1935 season, with Wisconsin, Purdue, and Illinois finally battling to a three-way tie. For the Badgers it was history repeating. Harold (Bud) Foster, the former Wisconsin great, had taken over for Dr. Walter Meanwell, who had stepped down at the end of the 1934 season. Just as the tutor had done in 1912, so had the student in 1934 by debuting with a league title. The Badgers were led by two fine guards, Rolf Poser and Gil McDonald. For Purdue, a new star had risen in Bob Kessler, second-leading scorer in the league, to assist North Cottom and Ed Shaver. Big Bob Riegel, a great sophomore center, and the tireless Frank Froschauer who was also a fine halfback, paced Illinois. The leading scorer in the Conference, however, was the man who had the least assistance from a 10th place club: All-America, Bill Haarlow of Chicago.

In track, the big news was not that Michigan took both the indoor and outdoor crowns, but rather it was the bursting upon the scene of the most famed track star in the history of the sport—Jesse Owens of Ohio State. The fluid, lithe Owens who had been a national schoolboy sensation in Cleveland, used a series of dual meets as a tune-up in this, his sophomore season, and then electrified the entire sports world one day in May when, at the Big Ten outdoor meet at Michigan, he turned in the performance that has since been declared the greatest display of track virtuosity ever witnessed in one day of effort.

In less than 45 minutes, the slim Buckeye Bullet tied a world record and broke three others as he equalled the 100-yard standard of 9.4; and set new world marks of 20.3 in the 220; 26-8¼ inches in the broad jump; and 20.6 for the 220-yard low hurdles. He repeated his four triumphs in the NCAA meet, and became the first athlete ever to

come to his home in the evening. When I got there, I was amazed to see Fielding Yost of Michigan and L. W. St. John of Ohio State, two of the veteran directors. The Major informed us that the University of Iowa had been in direct violation of the Conference rules. A number of Iowa football players had been receiving an illegal monthly stipend. These facts had been verified by the Iowa athletic director, Paul Belding, who had been unable to control the situation and had resigned. Enraged students, in fact, came close to storming Belding's house.

It was a very emotional meeting. The directors and faculty felt that severe action had to be taken if irregularities of this type were to be stopped. After three days of careful study, the University of Iowa was suspended from Conference membership, and its Conference football schedule cancelled. The feeling against the Con-

ference and Commissioner Griffith was intense in the state of Iowa. Many prominent Iowa alumni felt they should withdraw from the league; thinking they would never be able to recover from this drastic action. The faculty, athletic authorities and regents of the University, however, valuing their Big Ten membership, did a magnificent job of cleaning up the situation. Consequently, on February 1, 1930, the University of Iowa resumed membership in the Conference.

It was the first time in athletic history any institution had ever received such a severe penalty and its effect was studied and felt all over the nation.

Through all these troublesome years, the strength of faculty control in Big Ten athletics was firmly maintained. Early in 1936, the regents of the University of Wisconsin, following several disastrous football seasons and internal strife in their athletic department, decided to take

The circumstances surrounding the epic performances of *BILL HAARLOW* were, in a word, unique. You start with the statistics. Chicago, deep in its mid-thirties athletic doldrums, wound up dead last in the Big Ten basketball races of 1934, 1935, and 1936, with league seasonal records of 2-10, 1-11 and 0-12, respectively. Against this dismal collective record of 3-33 the situation quickly becomes unbelievable; because, with the kind of supporting cast which the record suggests, the Maroon ace was still unstoppable.

It quickly became apparent to Chicago's foes that the 6-1, 170-pounder was the only Maroon threat on the floor, so they mostly double-teamed Haarlow and let the other chips fall where they may. (Mostly at some distance from the hoop.) Yet, in his sophomore year Haarlow was third in Conference scoring, edged only by All-America Norm Cottom of Purdue's championship club, and Lyle Fisher, of second-place Northwestern. In his junior year,

Purdue was still a first place club and Chicago still a 10th place team, but it was Haarlow who led all scorers, this time edging Bob Kessler, the new Boilermaker phenomenon. In his senior year Purdue was again at the top—Chicago at the bottom, but Haarlow was still able to give Kessler a battle for top scoring honors, but had to settle for second as they exchanged places by just a few points.

An All-America if ever there was one, Haarlow had a deadly shot from outside and was a whirling-dervish of a dribbler. He had moves that were a decade or two before his time. Piggy Lambert, the veteran Purdue coach, paid him the supreme compliment. "You spend years telling your kids that basketball is a five-man game, and then that Haarlow goes ahead and destroys the evidence every time he sets foot on the floor."

Later, Haarlow became chief of basketball officials in the Western Conference.

Big Ten meeting in Chicago in December 1929. Left to right, back, are George Little (Wisconsin), Tug Wilson (Northwestern), George Huff (Illinois), N.A. Kellogg (Purdue), Z. E. Clevenger (Indiana), and Fred W. Luehring (Minnesota). In front are Commissioner John L. Griffith, E. H. Lauer (Iowa), Fielding H. Yost (Michigan), Amos Alonzo Stagg (Chicago), and L. W. St. John (Ohio State).

take four individual NCAA titles—and they were the only four the Big Ten accounted for that year.

Michigan, coming off its eighth Big Ten team title in nine years, dominated the NCAA swimming meet as no team ever had before, taking four titles. (It would not be until 1937 that an NCAA team title would be recognized.)

In a new event on the program, Jack Kasley won the first of what would be three straight 220-yard butterfly titles. Teammate Taylor Drydale successfully defended his 150-yard backstroke crown, his third straight, and two Wolverine relay teams triumphed. A Michigan quartet of Drysdale, Bob Renner, Julian Robertson and Ogden Dalrymple won the 400-yard freestyle event, and a trio of

CHARLEY McDANIEL, Indiana's sophomore football lineman, won the Big Ten heavyweight wrestling title in 1935 and went on to take the NCAA crown, too. He competed in the 1936 Olympics and then, after missing competition for a year, he picked off the NCAA title again in 1938.

Kasley, Drysdale and Dalrymple smashed the 300-yard medley mark by more than four seconds. Meanwhile, Illinois star, Charley Flachman scored a sprint double when he set a new mark of 23-flat in the 50-yard freestyle and then added the 100-yard crown to give the Big Ten six championships, a high for any collegiate conference—but a figure that would be exceeded over and over by the Big Ten.

Illinois cracked through Chicago's five-year domination of the Big Ten gymnastic tournament but Gene Wettstein, of Iowa, was the individual titlist. The Illini also took the Conference wrestling crown, and Ralph (Ruffy) Silverstine was the NCAA winner at 175 pounds, with Charley McDaniel, of Indiana, taking the heavyweight crown. Johnny Fischer, who had dropped out of school for a year, returned to Michigan for his final year and, along with Charley Kocsis, led the Wolverines to a successful defense of their Big Ten and NCAA golf championship.

Bill Schommer, winning the singles, and Schommer and Roy Huber, taking the doubles, came close to giving Minnesota its first and only Conference team tennis crown, but Chicago, on the basis of number of winning matches, carried off the team trophy.

Among winners of the Conference Medal were Bob Tenner, Minnesota's outstanding end; Ellmore Patterson, Chicago's All-America guard; Don Veller, Indiana's M-V-P halfback; and Rolf Poser, Wisconsin's crack basketballer.

The football was on Minnesota's 16-yard line in Northwestern possession and what happened on the subsequent play was to lead to the big story of the 1936 season. The Wildcats drove into the line, an official tossed a flag, and the Gophers were penalized 15 yards for unnecessary roughness, putting the ball on the Minnesota one-yard stripe, first down and goal.

Now, let's back up a bit . . .

1936

things into their own hands and hire coaches of their own choosing. The Conference immediately informed the administration at Wisconsin that if this happened the University would be suspended from the Big Ten. On May 22, 1936, the Conference, having received assurance from the Wisconsin faculty that they were in complete charge of athletic affairs, withdrew the threat of suspension.

Officiating at football games was another growing problem. In the early years of the Conference this had been handled, oddly enough, by a committee of the faculty. The officiating chores in the early years had been delegated to former football players who were interested enough to devote their time for a small fee.

When the office of Commissioner was created, one of his duties was to help assign officials and develop and train these important people. The Major was outstanding

in this capacity, as he had been a coach and a very competent official himself.

He finally developed a great group: Jim Masker, John Schommer, Frank Birch, Fred Young, Col. Hackett, Meyer Morton, Cap Hedges, Ernie Vick, Dutch Clarno, Joe Lipp, Col. Mumma, Don Laurie, Bill Knight and Meyer Morton, Ted Curtiss, Russel H. Rupp, and Dave Noble, just to mention a few whose abilities put them in constant demand. These men, all prominent in business and professional life, gave up endless hours attending official meetings and studying the rules. Their services through the years were invaluable to the development of football in the Western Conference. If there was a football hall of fame for officials, the list would be studded with names of many from the Big Ten; they were truly among the finest.

A previous source of irritation had been football

Twenty-eight games in a row without defeat was the record Bernie Bierman's Golden Gophers had brought into Dyche Stadium in Evanston that rainy, muddy October 31. With such as Tuffy Thompson, Andy Uram and Julie Alphonse in the backfield, and Ray King, Ed Widseth and Horace Bell in the line, there was enough left over from the

A tremendously adjustable athlete, Minnesota's BUD WILKINSON was not only an amazingly versatile football player but was the star goalie on Minnesota's hockey team. On the gridiron it was Wilkinson's dramatic conversion from All-America guard in 1935 to brilliant quarterback in 1936 that gave the Vikings a leg up on their national championship that season.

great 1935 team to predict similar success in 1936. Besides, Bierman had brought off perhaps the most remarkable personnel switch of his career. He took big, hard-charging Bud Wilkinson, a bona fide All-America guard, and installed him at quarterback. With Wilkinson's brains, football savvy, dexterity for ball-handling, and speed that would make him a bone-rattling blocker, it was a brilliant move. Wilkinson didn't have to pass. Uram was available for that in the Vikings' power-packed single wing.

So, the Gophers performed pretty much as expected in their first four games although it took some rather explosive heroics to get by their first two games. Opening against eventual Rose Bowl entry Washington, at Seattle, the Gophers had to survive a long, tiresome train ride, a dust storm, a hotel fire, a climate change and limited practice time. Deadlocked 7-7 in the fourth quarter, the Gophers pulled it out, 14-7, on a pass from Uram to King.

The following week they shaved it even closer against tough Nebraska. With less than two minutes to play in a scoreless dual, Wilkinson fielded a Nebraska punt and lateraled to Uram who, after getting a key block from Svendson, raced 78 yards through and around the entire Cornhusker team for a 7-0 win.

Thus, after picking up steam with smashing defeats of Michigan and Purdue, the Gophers came to grips with a Northwestern team that, somehow, had exceeded Pappy Waldorf's expectations. As weeks had gone by, it was evident this was going to be one of the better Purple grid machines although a "starless" one.

Fred Vanzo was a big, blocking quarterback; Don Heap, Ollie Edelman, and Bernie Jefferson were hard-running halfbacks, and Steve Toth and Don Geyer provided straight-ahead punch at fullback. Up front, Johnny Kovatch, Hi Bender, John Zitko and Cleo Diehl made up a strong end corps; and the tackle spots were deep with Park Wray, Dewit Gibson, Vange Burnett and Bob Voigts. Captain

schedules. At the beginning, it was simple enough. A Big Ten school, with a large stadium had no trouble getting a good team scheduled. The institutions with a smaller capacity found themselves playing the majority of their games away from home. As these schools developed larger stadia, they required better home schedules, and consequently there was a lot of ill feeling developing between directors and among football coaches from unsatisfactory meetings. (Truth of the matter was that Fielding Yost and one or two others would stride to the blackboard in a meeting, write out the games they wanted and stalk away, leaving other schools to scratch out a schedule as best they could.)

Following a very difficult football scheduling meeting, Major Griffith called me to his office and said he had

an idea that might be helpful. He suggested getting the Conference directors and football coaches together at a golf outing where they could just have a good time playing golf without discussing business. The outdoor track meet that year was at Northwestern, so he suggested I find a golf course where we might have this spring party.

The party, at Old Elm Country Club, was a tremendous success. Everyone forgot his private grudges and thoroughly enjoyed the outing. The idea was continued from that time on. Wherever the outdoor track meet was held, they arrived a day early for golf, and it was always called the Old Elm Party. Coaches from all the outside teams that competed in Conference events were invited, and many non-Conference schedules were dis-

In 1936, after a few lean years, Northwestern summoned LYNN (PAPPY) WALDORF from Kansas State, and suddenly there was a new air on the Wildcat campus. Taking a team that was expected to go nowhere, Waldorf had the Purple in a world-beating attitude by season's end. They whipped Illinois, Notre Dame and Wisconsin and played a scoreless tie with Iowa to round out a campaign that saw Waldorf chosen Coach-of-the Year in the first season the award was made.

Steve Reid, Carl De Vry, Mike Galvano and Les Shreiber shaped up at guard; and Lee Fuller and Erwin Wegner held down center. Voigts, Jefferson and Diehl were brilliant sophomores.

Waldorf brought his crew through their first three games in good style, turning back Iowa, Ohio State and Illinois, but against Ohio it took a last-ditch, long TD pass from Heap to Jefferson and a dramatic conversation by Geyer to snatch a victory from the Bucks.

With a Conference crown a distinct possibility, the Wildcats went into their rainy day meeting with Minnesota with the distinct impression they had a chance against the mighty Norsemen who hadn't tasted defeat since 1932. With Steve Reid and linebacker Fred Vanzo leading the defensive charge, Minnesota's attack was completely blunted. In the muck and mire, the Purple couldn't dent the Gopher defense, either, and the game went into the third quarter a scoreless tie.

Then came the break. A recovery of a Minnesota fumble deep in Gopher territory gave the Wildcats their big chance. It might be their last, and they lined up determined to take advantage of it.

On the first Northwestern slant into the line an official considered Ed Widseth, the Gopher tackle, to be overly aggressive and blew his whistle for a 15-yard unnecessary roughness penalty, giving Northwestern a first down on the Vikings' one-yard line.

On the next play, the two lines hit, locked and went down into the mud while fullback Steve Toth cracked between guard and tackle. Gopher hands grabbed wildly for him as the secondary closed on the small hole, but Toth was over. The conversion attempt was missed and that was the scoring for the day. The Minnesota string was broken, and the Wildcats win provided enough impetus for victory over Wisconsin and Michigan for the first undisputed league championship in Northwestern history.

Now, only one foe—Notre Dame—remained be-

cussed at that time. The word of this party spread to other Conferences and soon they, too, adopted the idea.

My proximity to the Conference office in Chicago and a desire to be of real service to the man who had helped me get into the Big Ten as a director led me to invitations of many kinds. The Big Ten had been having trouble again with baseball in the 1930's because the Big League scouts were continually raiding the college teams of their best talent.

Griffith was an old-time friend of Judge Kenesaw M. Landis, the Baseball Commissioner. He arranged a meeting with the Judge and invited me to attend. We quickly stated our case and asked Landis if he could help us get an arrangement with the Major Leagues so this practice could be discontinued. Landis was very

sympathetic, but said he doubted if anything could be done. Still, he would put it on the agenda of the next annual baseball meeting.

We thought we had a good case, because few college men signed out of school made the grade, most of them being shipped to minor leagues where they were poorly paid, and few ever came back to complete their college education. The judge was certainly right. The owners listened politely, but outside of Branch Rickey and Connie Mack, we received little encouragement.

In later years as secretary and treasurer of the NCAA, I attended many meetings trying to get some sensible rules that would prohibit the signing of a boy until his college class had graduated. It is interesting to note that an agreement was finally consummated late in 1966.

tween the Purple and its first undefeated season, ever.

The Irish were out to demonstrate how much motivation there would be in revenge. The year before the Wildcats had knocked them off, 14-7 right after Notre Dame's epic victory over Ohio State. This season the Irish already had lost to Pitt and Navy and were out of the national recognition picture, but Northwestern was very much in it.

In football you never know. Final score: Notre Dame 26—Northwestern 6.

At "honors" time, it turned out that Northwestern wasn't as starless as the critics had figured earlier. Captain Steve Reid (now a brilliant surgeon) was named All-America guard, and Ed Widseth, the great Minnesota lineman, was picked at tackle.

ED WIDSETH and STEVE REID were the Big Ten's All-America designees in 1936, with the slashing Widseth performing prodigious heroics on Minnesota's national championship team which lost only one game—an upset by Northwestern. It was Reid of Northwestern, who was greatly responsible for the Viking setback in an epic battle in the mud, and who had every attribute needed by a great guard: speed, toughness and alertness.

Vern Huffman, Indiana's versatile halfback, was the league's most valuable player, and there were several others, including fullbacks John Drake of Purdue; Ed Jankowski of Wisconsin, and Cliff Kuhn, Illinois guard, who were do-everything guys on teams with lesser records.

Once again Michigan failed to win a Conference game and, as in 1934, the first year of their gridiron doldrums, the Wolverines were able to handle only one outsider, Columbia, 13-0. Michigan alumni were beginning to wonder whether Harry Kipke, virtually a Michigan immortal as a player, might not be all too human as a coach. In the early 30's Kipke, of course, had proved he could coach with the best of them; but, the alumni habit of inquiring: "What have you done for us lately?" was becoming the yardstick by which too many good coaches were being unfairly measured—even when material was sub-par as was the case at Michigan.

Of significant note, too, during the 1936 season was the appearance of the collegiate football poll conducted by the Associated Press. Despite the loss to Northwestern, it was Minnesota's Golden Gophers whom the experts honored as the first "elected" national champions.

Leaping Bob Kessler, a tireless whirling-dervish, had come of age in the 1936 basketball season, and the Purdue captain not only led his team to a share of the Conference title, with Indiana, but wrested the scoring crown from Chicago's Bill Haarlow, reversing their one-two positions of the previous year. The figures show what a torrid duel these two fought. In 1935 it was Haarlow, 156 points to 150 for Kessler. In 1936 it was Kessler, 160 points to Haarlow's 151. Again, Purdue had a senior-sophomore combination going for them as newcomer Jewell Young backed up Kessler, with valuable help from Glen Downey and Jim Seward. For the title-sharing Hoosiers, slick Ken Gunning was the league's third hottest scorer, and Vern Huffman, the football star, exhibited such brilliant all-around play he received All-America listing along with Haarlow and Kessler.

Eppie Barnes, president of the NCAA, who had fought this battle down through the years, headed the committee that found a successful conclusion. Serving with him was Bill Reed, later my successor as Commissioner of the Big Ten.

Reed's long association with the Conference began in 1939, when Major Griffith hired him to establish the Conference Service Bureau in response to the growing demand for statistical and publicity material on the Big Ten.

Reed, following his graduation from Michigan in 1936, had been active in newspaper and athletic publicity work. A young man with tremendous ability and dedication to his work, he proved an invaluable assistant to Griffith and the Conference.

(In 1942, Bill entered naval service as an ensign. After a year at the Iowa pre-flight school, he was assigned to armed guard duty with service in both the Atlantic and South Pacific. He returned to the Conference office in the fall of 1945.)

In 1939, I agreed to hold the first NCAA basketball finals at Northwestern. The two finalists were Ohio State and Oregon. There was little local interest and the only way we could fill Patten Gym was to give tickets away to the sororities and fraternities in order to muster up a decent crowd. The date was March 27, which happened to be my birthday, but there was little for the Big Ten to celebrate as Oregon defeated Ohio State, 46 to 32. The idea would soon catch on and from this inauspicious beginning, the NCAA basketball tournament became

One of the greatest athletes in Big Ten history, VERN HUFFMAN, of Indiana, was not only an All-America basketball player in 1936 but the following year on the gridiron he was an All-Big Ten halfback and the league's most-valuable player.

IVAN FUQUA

CHARLES HORNBOSTEL

HENRY BROCKSMITH

TOM DECKARD

DON LASH

BILLY HAYES, great Indiana track coach from 1925 to 1943, never saw his Hoosiers fail to make the first division in the 1930's. Much of Indiana's success was due to the brilliant success of its middle distance and distance men. IVAN FUQUA, Big Ten 440 champ, also ran a leg on the winning 1600-meter relay team for the U.S. in 1932. HENRY BROCKSMITH, two-mile star, was also Big Ten cross-country individual champ in 1931 and was a big factor in Hoosier team titles as they won five straight from 1929 through 1932 for the most complete domination, yet, of the annual cross-country meet. CHARLES HORNBOSTEL, the Hoosiers' great half-miler, was the first Big Ten athlete to take three straight NCAA titles, 1932-33-34. DON LASH and TOM DECKARD were the Hoosiers' distance twins of the 1935-36-37 team: Deckard, a two-miler, was also AAU steeplechase champ and ran the event for the U.S. in the Olympics in 1936.

Lash, the first of the Big Ten's great modern milers, broke the Conference record as a sophomore in 1935 and set a world record for the two-mile in 1936, the year he ran the 1500-meters for the U.S. in the Olympics.

BILLY HAYES

The 1936 track season again featured Jesse Owens, although the Buckeyes still could not take a Conference crown. Indiana, led by Don Lash, the first of the great modern milers in the Big Ten, and Tom Deckard, took the outdoor title, and Michigan, paced by sprinter Sam Stoller and hurdler Bob Osgood, captured the indoor championship. In the NCAA meet, Ohio State won six individual events—a new high for one school, and still unmatched—with Owens repeating his triumphs of 1935 in the 100, 220, broad jump and 220 low hurdles; Charlie Beetham, a magnificent half-miler, taking the 800-meters, and Dave Albritton and teammate Mel Walker tieing for the high jump crown. For Albritton (later a member of the State Legislature) it was the first of three straight crowns he would win. Michigan's Bob Osgood, in the 400-meter hurdles, and Indiana's Don Lash in the two-mile, were the other Conference first-place winners.

Despite the six Ohio State individual titles, the Buckeyes had to settle for second place in the team standings as Southern California, with victories only in the pole vault and discus, nevertheless had such all-around strength that the Trojans scored heavily in nearly every event.

For Beetham, the Buckeye star, the year was one of triumph and tragedy. The 1:50 half-miler who scored a Grand Slam in winning the Big Ten, NCAA, and AAU titles, expected to cap the season with an Olympic championship, but in the finals of the Olympic tryouts, just as he was about to make his move going into the final turn, he was spiked, inadvertently, by Duke Hobbs, of Indiana, and knocked to the cinders and out of contention.

In swimming, Iowa stunned the Big Ten by breaking Michigan's strangle hold on the team title. It was the Hawkeyes' first and only Conference championship, as all-around balance, led by Ray Walters, a great freestyler, was enough to stave off Michigan's brilliance in fewer events. Subsequently,

in the NCAA meet, Walters also won the 50-yard freestyle and swam a leg on the Hawkeyes' winning 400-yard freestyle relay, with a quartet that also included Adolph Jacobsmeyer, Bob Christians and Jack Sieg. Dan Zehr, of Northwestern, set a new 150-yard backstroke mark of 1:36.8 and Jack Kasley of Michigan ably defended his 200-yard butterfly, and then swam a leg on the Wolverines' 3:35.3 record-breaking 300-yard medley relay. Teamed up with him were backstroker Harry Rieke and freestyler Bob Mowerson.

Michigan's individual brilliance was on display again when Frank Fehsenfeld retained his 3-meter diving crown, but he was dethroned by teammate Derland Johnson in the one-meter event.

In other highlights of the year, Charley Kocsis, Michigan's wizard of the fairways, led the

CHARLEY BEETHAM, Ohio State half-miler, scored a spectacular triple in 1936, winning the Big Ten, NCAA and national AAAU titles only to tragically miss the Olympic team when he was spiked and tripped just as he was making his stretch run in the final Olympic trials.

tremendously successful and now sells out within a few days after the tickets are placed on sale.

World War Two brought tremendous problems. The great facilities of the Big Ten were turned over to the military for officer training programs, which greatly enlarged the existing ROTC and NROTC programs. A large pre-flight school was placed at Iowa City, and many of the great athletes of the Conference and other conferences received training there. Meanwhile, in 1940, the Big Ten had voted to permit nine football games a season, six Conference games to be required, with at least two home games for everyone. This was for the season beginning in 1943. With the war, certain other rules were waived, permitting a 10-game football schedule and inter-freshman team competition. Games with teams that did not observe Conference rules, primarily service teams, were also permitted.

It became a struggle to field good athletic teams, and in 1943 the eligibility rules were waived to permit use of freshmen on varsity teams. Summer practice also was permitted. Finally, in order to maintain athletic programs, the Conference waived its eligibility rules with two exceptions: (a) regular enrollment as a student; (b) non-receipt of compensation for athletic participation. The war years were proud years, and also sad ones, as many of the great athletes of the Big Ten lost their lives.

The scheduled December meeting in 1944, held in Chicago, was a dramatically sad one. Major Griffith had not been in the best of health, but insisted on conducting the meeting, and at the end of the day the directors were going to join the faculty representatives at the University Club for dinner. L. W. St. John and I were waiting in the lobby of the Sherman Hotel (where the Conference office was located at that time) for the Major

BOB FADNER, *125-pound NCAA boxing champion in 1936, was the first of a long line of Wisconsin ring rulers who would establish the Badgers as the premier collegiate boxing school in the nation.*

NORM BICKELL, *Chicago tennis ace, won the league singles crown in 1936 and teamed with Norb Burgess for the doubles title.*

WALTER JACOBS, *Michigan State 158-pounder, was first Spartan matman to take a national crown when he won the National Collegiate title in 1936.*

Wolverine golfers to the Big Ten team title and also took the individual crown in the NCAA, although Yale stripped Michigan of the team crown it had held for two years. Bob Fadner of Wisconsin won the NCAA 125-pound boxing title, and Walt Jacobs became Michigan State's first wrestling champion when he won the 158-pound title.

Norm Bickell of Chicago won the league singles tennis title and then teamed up with Norbert Burgess to win the doubles and lead the Maroon to a team title that had almost become habit. In winning the U.S. National Amateur golf tournament that year, John Kocsis, of Michigan, became the first Conference golfer to attain such eminence.

The Conference continued to contribute important elements to the U.S. Olympic team in 1936 with a gaudy collection of medals falling to Big Ten stars. Jesse Owens, of course, not only led the team but the world in sparkling performances as he took the 100- and 200-meter dashes, the broad jump, and ran a leg on the 400-meter relay. The Buckeyes' Dave Albritton, Big Ten and NCAA champ, took second in the high jump. In other track events Charley Hornbostel of Indiana ran the 800, and the Hoosiers' Don Lash competed in the 5000-meters along with teammate Tom Deckard.

to come downstairs. After a long wait, Saint asked me to go up and see what was keeping him. The Major's door was open. I walked in and found the Major dead on the floor. It was a terrific shock. He had been my best friend through many years. The meetings were cancelled, and the following Monday, the 10 directors carried Major Griffith to his grave.

In the 22 years he served as Commissioner, Griffith was a man with strong convictions who dedicated his life to youth and sports. His successful years of work inspired every other athletic conference in the country to appoint a commissioner. The value of this man can scarcely be measured.

The imprint he left on intercollegiate athletics was not confined to the Big Ten alone. He gave the same wise leadership to the NCAA, which he had served for many years as secretary-treasurer, helping to develop that

Amos Alonzo Stagg and Tug Wilson in the early 40's.

JESSE OWENS

The simple fact of the matter is that Jesse Owens was the most famous track and field athlete of all time, and that goes back as far as the first Greek in the first competitive foot-race ever held. You could look it up.

Think of the great names of today and the near past —Paavo Nurmi, Charley Paddock, Bob Hayes, Dallas Long, Valerie Brumel, Peter Snell. All are great names, but a generation from now, most likely, they will be merely names in a record book. They will not have had Jesse Owens' charisma. Charisma . . . The word has something to do with a magical image, and let it go at that. In this case it is an image that translates into "legend," and that is what the lithe, graceful Ohio Stater became.

In 1950 when the Associated Press conducted a poll to determine the greatest track and field athlete of the first half of the Twentieth Century, the result wasn't even close—Owens by plenty.

It all started when a Cleveland, Ohio, junior high school physical education teacher looked at the frail 8th grader who had moved up from the South a couple of years previously. The boy obviously needed building up and the teacher suggested he come out for track. The boy's name was really James Cleveland Owens but when he first went to school he told his teacher his name was J. C. Owens, using the initials only. The teacher misunderstood his drawl and the name was instantly Jesse.

So the physical education teacher took Jesse out on the city street which the junior high school used as a running track and lined up a few boys for a 100-yard dash. The untrained Jesse beat them all by 15 yards. The teacher looked at his stop-watch and later that day took it to a jeweler to repair. Obviously it was off because the youngster had run the 100 yards in floppy rubber sneakers in near world record time. The jeweler assured the teacher there was absolutely nothing wrong with the watch.

A couple of years later, in high school, Jesse Owens was running the century in 9.5 and broad-jumping 25 feet. He went to Ohio State where Coach Larry Snyder

Jesse Owens demonstrates his famous flying start.

Jesse Owens, the Buckeye Bullet, made collegiate and Olympic history in the 1930's.

worked on his start and put him on a development program to make fullest use of his versatility.

It was this versatility which on May 25, 1935 electrified the sports world as it hadn't been in decades. The setting: the Western Conference Outdoor Track and Field meet at Ann Arbor, Mich., and the expectation that the Ohio State sophomore sensation would give them something to remember had brought out the largest crowd yet to see a Big Ten meet—more than 10,000 people, packed into Michigan's ancient Ferry Field wooden stands.

For three weeks Jesse had had an aching back which hadn't responded too well to treatment. Therefore, it must have been pure adrenalin which, in the space of 45 minutes, took his mind off his ache and enabled him to put on the greatest one-man, one-day performance the sport had ever known. Jesse broke three world records and tied a fourth.

The time-table went like this:

At 3:15 he flashed down the track to win the 100-yard dash in 9.4 seconds, tying the world mark.

At 3:25 Jesse removed his sweat suit, bent over at the top of the broad jump runway and hurtled forward toward the take-off board. In his first and what was to be his only jump of the day he rocketed out 26 feet 8¼ inches, breaking the world record by more than half a foot.

At 3:34, just nine minutes later, Owens again slipped out of his sweats, this time for the 220-yard dash. He took his mark, went to the set position, was off with the gun and streaked home almost 15 yards ahead of the second man in 20.3 seconds, slashing three-tenths of a second from the world mark.

At exactly 4:00 p.m., 16 minutes later, he again took off his sweats and eyed the long row of barriers placed in position for the 220-yard low hurdles. Again the gun, and again there was Owens ripping away from the field, flying over the timbers to the tape. The time: 22.6 seconds, four-tenths of a second shaved from the world record.

The 5-10, 165-pound paragon of poetry in motion was to add verse upon verse to his accomplishments. A few weeks after the Conference meet, he scored an unprecedented sweep of the same four events in the National Collegiates. He swept the same four at the Conference meet the following May, 1936. Then he repeated his NCAA triumphs in June, 1936. Eight Big Ten outdoor crowns; eight NCAA crowns. The figures stand alone in track history. He never got the chance to add the senior year championships which surely would have made his figures as permanent as those at Mt. Rushmore. The 1936 Olympic Games altered his whole life.

From the moment the American contingent arrived in Berlin the so-called Buckeye Bullet was the man most marked for distinction. The 110,000 who jammed Adolf Hitler's new stadium, and fans at home throughout the world, wondered whether Owens would be vulnerable to the pressure of international competition and show a crack in his invincibility.

At no Olympiad, past or future, would an athlete be subjected to such searching scrutiny. Correspondents converged in platoons around Owens in the Olympic Village where the athletes were quartered, prying into every facet of his past, of his personality, into his minute-by-minute activities in Berlin. Some European papers and magazines even sent female writers in an attempt to whip up a special perspective. Finally, the American coaching staff had to blow the whistle on the intensive coverage. There was just too much danger that Jesse would be badgered into a state of nerves. They needn't have bothered. Larry Snyder, Owen's coach and assistant coach of the Olympic team, could have pointed to Jesse's amazing ability to hang loose. Relaxation, in fact, was the key to his performing style. He didn't know what it was to be tense either before or during competition and his flawless style reflected it.

Jesse Owens made a one-man show of the 1936 Olympics. He was entered in the 100- and 200-meter dashes; the broad jump; and scheduled for a leg of the 400-meter relay.

First he streaked to victory in the 100 meters in 10.3 but was denied a new Olympic record because of a slight breeze. Then came the broad jump and a display of sportsmanship rarely if ever seen in an Olympic setting. In the preliminaries Owens was ahead of Lutz Long, Germany's great leaper, by a few inches with one more prelim to go. Long had strained a leg muscle and now there was the sight of Jesse Owens down on the grass reassuring the blond Nazi entry, and rubbing his leg. Long got up, took his final jump which was a few inches under 26 feet—but enough to take the Gold Medal unless his non-Aryan rival could really get out there on his last attempt.

Owens poised at the end of the runway, raised up and took off down the strip, gathered momentum, hit the take-off board solidly and soared up and out into the sand as the crowd roared, knowing it was a tremendous effort. The measurement confirmed it: a new Olympic mark of ·26 feet 5 and 5/16 inches, the first time anyone had ever gone over 26 feet in Olympic history.

Jesse Owens sets new NCAA broad jump mark in 1935 with a leap of 26' 1½". He also won both dash events and the low hurdles.

Came the 200-meter dash, on a raw, damp day, the worst of the Olympic festival. The finalists waited until the last second before removing their sweat clothes. A fine rain started to fall as the runners went to their set position. Owens exploded off his mark at the gun, swept around the turn two yards in front, then went into his rhythmic over-glide to pull away and win by five yards in 20.7, a new Olympic mark—the first time anyone had bettered 21 seconds for 200-meters around a curve.

In his huge, private box Adolf Hitler glowered and bit at his mustached upper lip. It was the third time Der Fuehrer had to rise to his feet to acknowledge the ceremonious draping of a Gold Medal around the neck of the American Negro on the victor's stand.

There would be a fourth Gold Medal for Jesse. He ran the lead-off leg for the American team in the 400-meter sprint relay. He rocketed off to give the Yankee quartet such a tremendous lead there was no chance of overtaking them as they sped to a new Olympic record of 40.0.

Der Fuehrer didn't see Jesse Owens receive his fourth Gold Medal. He couldn't take it. Tight-faced, his fists clenched at his side, he got up from his seat just before the award ceremonies began and sulked from the stadium.

It had been a busy three days for Jesse Owens. In winning his four Gold Medals he had to run the 100-meters four times, including preliminary heats; the 200-meters four times; the 400-meter relay twice, and had to make two broad-jump appearances with several trials, each. In these 12 performances he bettered or equalled nine Olympic and four world records. There had been no such hero in the annals of international sport. Even

Jesse Owens ties the world record for the 100-yard dash in 1935 with a time of 9.4.

before Jesse returned home he announced he would turn professional to take advantage of some of the hundreds of commercial offers he had been bombarded with before he left Berlin.

He came home to a Broadway ticker-tape welcome, passed up his senior season at Ohio State and embarked on a world-wide professional tour which included running against horses and dogs. Later he went into business and youth activities work in Chicago.

Then, 15 years later, in August, 1951, Jesse once again appeared on the running track of the giant stadium in Berlin, which was unharmed by bombing in World War Two. This time he was there at the invitation of the U. S. High Commission to Germany. The war was over but the Cold War with Russia was eroding the spirit of the vanquished German people who had been sustained by the Berlin Airlift when the Reds cut off food and fuel from the West.

Jesse Owens, in his Olympic track suit, addressed 75,000 Germans in the stadium, asking them to ". . . Stand fast with us in the fight for freedom and democracy under the protection of Almighty God."

Then Owens jogged around the same track that had been his glory path 15 years before. The entire crowd stood in thunderous salute as he jogged and waved. He was still the winner they'd never forgotten.

Jesse Owens and Lutz Long, Germany's broad jump star, at the 1936 Olympics in Berlin. Owens helped Long limber up a strained leg muscle just before the German's final jump. Long got up and jumped almost 26 feet—the best mark of the day. Owens had one try left—and it turned out to be a new Olympic record of 26' 5-5/16".

The Hoosiers also supplied two wrestlers, with Dick Voliva winning a silver medal at 174 pounds and Charley McDaniel a reserve entry at 191. In swimming, three Michigan stars were on hand with Dick Degener soaring to a gold medal in the three-meter dive and Taylor Drysdale and Jack Kasley competing in the backstroke and breatstroke. John Higgins, Ohio State breaststroker, and Ralph Gilman, Buckeye freestyler, were other U.S. Olympians, and Minnesota contributed Phil LaBatte to the hockey squad.

Under CHARLEY BACHMAN, Michigan State continued its quest for national honors and in 1937 the Spartans scored their fourth straight win over Michigan, dropped a 3-0 thriller to Manhattan, then went on to win six straight and gain the Orange Bowl invitation, its first Bowl game in history, but dropped a 6-0 decision to Auburn.

The Conference medal was won by some outstanding athletes in 1936, including Glenn Seidel, Minnesota's great quarterback; Bob Kessler, Purdue's All-America basketball player; Francis Cretzmeyer, Iowa track star and current coach; and Bruce Laybourne, Ohio State basketball and tennis star, and senior class president.

It didn't take too long for Bernie Bierman to get his Gophers cranked up again for the Conference football race, and 1937 found them making their usual run for it after being temporarily sidetracked by Northwestern in 1936.

It was not the usual strength-at-every-position kind of team the Gophers usually fielded, but there were no pushovers any place in the line-up. Up front were two fine ends in Ray King and Bob Johnson, and a couple of hard-nosed guards in Francis Twedell and Horace Bell made things easier for the Gopher backfield. Offensively it was a Viking attack built around Rudy Gmitro, a smallish but tough halfback who was a slashing runner and fine pass receiver, and Harold Van Every, a versatile sophomore, who did most of the throwing. Billy Mathena, Wilbur Moore and Marty Christiansen piled up a lot of yardage at halfback and the bulk of the fullbacking chores were handled by powerful Vic Spadaccini.

It turned into still another perfect league season, 5-0, for the Vikings, although they dropped two of their three outside affairs, losing 14-9 to Nebraska, and 7-6 to Notre Dame in games that could have gone the Gopher way. The Cornhuskers, twice trailing Minnesota, completed fourth-down passes for touchdowns after running attacks had stalled. A single defensive lapse against Notre Dame also proved fatal when Andy Puplis, the Irish safetyman, took a punt and raced it back 33 yards before Gopher tacklers could get into position to nip him off. Puplis' subsequent plunge for the extra point was the difference. Minnesota tallied on a triple-

---

organization from its inception. Along with Tom Jones of Wisconsin and Amos Alonzo Stagg of Chicago he helped inaugurate the first NCAA track and field championships at Chicago in 1921, and this meet rapidly grew to be the outstanding college and university track meet in the country. He fought strenuously to see that the colleges and universities had adequate representation on the Olympic Committee. He spearheaded a drive that in 1929 finally earned equal representation for the NCAA with the AAU on sports committees. This resulted in a period of harmony for nearly 20 years, and was the biggest boost to Olympic activities the United States ever had.

The problem now was to select the new Commissioner. The directors were asked by the faculty representatives to survey the field and recommend a man qualified to

hold the job. I can well remember that my choice was Fritz Crisler of Michigan. He was a man who had proven himself to be a great administrator and director at Minnesota and at Michigan. I felt he would be the perfect man to run the Conference. Fritz, however, was happily situated at Michigan and felt his future was wrapped up in that great institution.

I had not considered myself at all for the job. After 20 years at Northwestern, I, too, felt I had a very happy situation. I was stunned when St. John of Ohio State, Guy Mackey of Purdue and Doug Mills of Illinois proposed my name, and was, of course, greatly honored to think I was even being considered. When I was formally offered the position, I really had a tough decision to make, and I wanted to talk it over with Mrs. Wilson before I gave them the go-ahead signal. There was no

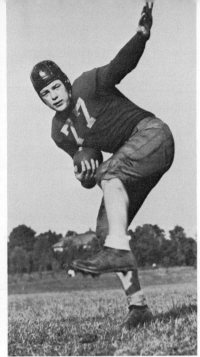

GUS ZARNAS

RAY KING

CORBY DAVIS

pass behind the line which ended with Van Every throwing to Ray King for the TD, but George Faust's placekick for the extra point was blocked.

King, the Gophers versatile end, was chosen on the All-America along with Gust Zarnas, Ohio State guard, and Corby Davis, Indiana's bulldozing fullback, who for the second year in a row gave the Hoosiers the honor of supplying the league's most-valuable-player, echoing Vern Huffman's choice the year before. A great kicker, blocker and defensive player, it was Davis who almost single-handedly knocked Ohio State out of a title share in a 10-0 Indiana victory—the first for the Hoosiers over the Bucks since 1924.

Among others who pressed closely upon Davis for MVP honors were two triple-threat halfbacks; Northwestern's Don Heap, and Purdue's Cecil Isbell. At

Three Conference stars were honored on the All-America lists for 1937, headed by Indiana's versatile and inspirational halfback, CORBY DAVIS, who was also the league's MVP; the second in a row for the Hoosiers. A 6-foot, 195-pound fullback, Davis did it all, on offense, and backed up the line on defense. RAY KING, Minnesota's great blocking and pass-snatching end, and GUS ZARNAS, Ohio State's rugged guard, were the others honored.

Ann Arbor, Harry Kipke, definitely on the griddle after four straight lackluster if not disastrous years, was frequently seen glancing longingly toward the freshman practice field and thinking he'd still like to be around the following fall to inherit some frosh named Tom Harmon, Forest Evashevski, Paul Kromer, Ed Frutig and others who had been giving the varsity fits in practice.

Kenneth L. "Tug" Wilson in 1945 when he took over as Commissioner of the Big Ten.

hesitancy in her advice to me. She told me she thought it was a wonderful opportunity and a great honor, and hoped I would accept the appointment.

The next day I accepted the directors' vote and, at the March meeting in 1945, the faculty representatives approved the directors' recommendation and gave me until May 1 to wind up my affairs at Northwestern and move into the Conference office.

I left Northwestern with many regrets, but with the feeling of satisfaction over what I had accomplished there.

During the past years it had been my good fortune to work closely with Major Griffith. We didn't live too far apart on the North Shore and often he had me drop in to talk over things, not only relating to Northwestern but to the Conference as well. I'll never forget one of

Critics also were beginning to work up an anvil chorus at Illinois where Bob Zuppke's teams had finished in the second division six times in the last seven years—critics with short memories who had hailed the same Bob Zuppke—just as the whole nation had hailed him—as one of the game's greatest coaches during the previous two decades.

Minnesota, solidly entrenched as the nation's dominant football power, for years had languished in the basketball doldrums, a perennial second division team, and nobody paid much attention to the Gophers as the 1937 season got under way. After all, they hadn't won a title since 1919, so why should anything happen now? This, however, was the year Dave MacMillan, the Original Celtic, got his hands on some material, most notably Marty Rolek; and two hot sophomore prospects, John Kundla and Gordon Addington, and the Gophers surprised everyone as they battled Illinois to a title deadlock with 10-2 records. Some famous names were to emerge from this 1937 season. In addition to Jewell Young, then a bonafide All-America at Purdue, and the league's leading scorer, there were three Conference stars who would later coach at their Alma Maters: Kundla at Minnesota; Harry Combes at Illinois, and Tippy Dye the Mighty Mite, at Ohio State. Who would have thought that a slick backcourt operative for the Illini would not too many years later become manager of the Cleveland Indians at age 24, and one of the greatest shortstops in major league baseball history? This, of course, is exactly what Lou Boudreau did.

To Michigan in 1937 fell the honor (richly deserved, as it turned out) of winning the first team championship in NCAA swimming history. Prior to 1937, there had been titles awarded only in individual events. Under the new setup, the Wolverines, who had resumed their winning ways in the Big Ten meet after a one-year reign by Iowa, made a shambles of the NCAA opposition, as they took the first of what would be five straight team crowns.

One of the smallest athletes (and the best of the Mighty Mites) to appear on modern Big Ten teams was 138-pound WILLIAM HENRY HARRISON (TIPPY) DYE, who starred for Ohio State in 1935-36-37 as a tricky, fine-passing quarterback, a slick back-courtman in basketball, and a fine shortstop in baseball. Later he would coach the Buckeyes into the NCAA basketball tourney.

these meetings. He said the presidents of all the Southeastern Conference institutions were coming into Chicago to meet with him and to discuss their plan of giving athletic scholarships to their athletes consisting of board, room and tuition. There was to be no high scholastic attainment; simple admission to the university was the only academic requirement. They maintained that they wanted to be honest and above-board and preferred this to alumni help and a pay-off under the table. I could see there would be a lot of trouble ahead not only for the Big Ten but for other neighboring conferences if the southeastern group could give a full ride to all their athletes while the Big Ten and other groups were trying to work on tuition scholarships and job programs.

We talked about this for a full day. I didn't realize it at the time but I was receiving terrific training in the administration of athletics. We lost the argument; we couldn't convince them their plan was wrong. I did, however, have to admire the candor and honesty with which these Southern schools were announcing their programs.

The Major asked them an interesting question. How did they expect to finance their program which would cost each institution a lot of money? Their answer was they hoped to obtain this money from their appearances in bowl games. It was an argument I was able to use with great effect in later years in urging the Big Ten hookup with the Rose Bowl. It would curb a lot of other teams from getting lucrative bowl money which they could use for recruiting athletes in our own territory.

The 20 years I spent at Northwestern had been tough ones, but also very enjoyable. I had had the finest cooperation from a great athletic staff and from my

When Lou Boudreau entered Illinois in 1936, a sub-sequent event which took place just five years later was almost predictable. That event coming after the 1941 American League baseball season, saw Lou Boudreau, age 24, appointed manager of the Cleveland Indians, the youngest major league manager in history.

Leadership was the basic talent of the boy from Thornton High School in Harvey, Ill. The 5-foot 11-inch, 180-pounder was the first player in Illinois scholastic basketball history to make all-state three years in a row, and the first boy to make it as a sophomore as he led his team to a state title and two runner-up trophies.

In his first varsity season at Illinois he scored 157 points in an era before the game had turned into the run-and-shoot net-burner it is now. His play-making, calmness and inspired leadership impelled his teammates to elect him captain of the 1938 team although he would only be a junior.

His brilliant fielding and hard hitting as a sophomore third baseman on Illinois' Conference baseball team drew a similar response from his diamond-mates: captaincy in his junior year.

Lou Boudreau, one of the finest athletes in Big Ten history, was destined to miss half his junior year and all his senior season completely. Nobody would ever know how great a collegiate basketball and baseball player he would have been.

Midway through his junior year Boudreau was declared ineligible by the Big Ten because he had innocently made a verbal agreement with the Cleveland Indians, permitting the Indians to make financial contributions to his mother for family support.

After only a few weeks in the minor leagues Boudreau was brought up to the Tribe varsity in 1939 and immediately set about establishing himself as one of the game's greatest shortstops. Two years later he was named manager. For nine straight years he led American League shortstops in fielding and once won the league batting title with .327. In 1948 the Tribe won the American League title in a tie-breaking playoff with the Red Sox, with Boudreau hitting two homers and two singles for a perfect day at bat. No one even remotely approached him in the balloting for MVP that year. He subsequently played for and managed the Red Sox, Kansas City Athletics and Chicago Cubs before going into sportscasting in Chicago.

Six individual titles and two relays went to Matt Mann's swimmers. Ed Kirar took the 50- and 100-yard freestyle; Tom Haynie the 220- and 440-yard freestyle; Jack Kasley the 200-yard butterfly, for the third straight year; and Ben Grady the one-meter dive and two relays. In the 300-yard medley, a trio of Fred Cody, Kasley, and Bob Mowerson set a new record of 2:57.8, and in the 400-yard freestyle affair, a quartet of Waldemar Tomski, Ed Hutchens, Haynie and Kirar turned in a new mark of 3:32.2. Other Conference winners were Bill Neunzig of Ohio State in the 150 backstroke and Jim Patterson in the three-meter dive, as they paced the Buckeyes to second place behind Michigan.

The Wolverines were having a good year in 1937. They also took both the indoor and outdoor track titles, and Sam Stoller, their star sprinter, took the NCAA 100-yard dash crown. Dave Albritton of Ohio State tied for his second NCAA high jump crown, this time with Gil Cruter, of Colorado; and Chuck Fenske, the first of a string of great Wisconsin distance men, took the mile run.

Illinois won the Big Ten wrestling crown, but Minnesota's John Whitaker, at 175 pounds, was the league's only NCAA winner.

Sid Richardson, the finest golfer in Northwestern history, and, in fact, one of the all-time collegiate greats, won the Big Ten individual crown and led the Wildcats to the team title.

Gene Wettstone, who had won the all-around title in gymnastics as a sophomore but relinquished it as a junior, came back in his senior season to regain the honor and lead Iowa to its only NCAA team title in its history. Later, Wettstone would become one of the nation's finest coaches at Penn State, building the Lions into a national power.

---

faculty athletic committee. The greatest help, of course, had come from a lot of wonderful athletes who had been at Northwestern during those 20 years.

There had been many serious moments, and also some that were very humorous. I can remember one occasion in particular. The directors of the Conference had begun to wage a campaign against drinking at the games, which had gotten slightly out of hand, especially in the late fall. At first, a request was printed in the football program, but this seemed to get little results. Then each director was asked to make a dignified announcement before the game started, asking for full cooperation from everyone. I had just finished making my announcement before one of our biggest games. The crowd had been listening in respectful silence, but all of a sudden broke into a roar of laughter. As I looked around in a confused state, someone pointed into the sky. There was a plane trailing a banner that read: "Drink Wilson's Whiskey; It's the Best." It was a well-known commercial brand and a legitimate advertising gimmick, but the coincidence broke everybody up.

There was another time in the early Thirties when I was on the sidelines before a game and saw one of our Northwestern stars, Reb Russell, our fullback, talking to a stranger in a light, belted camel's hair coat and a white felt hat. We didn't allow strangers near our bench and I noted, too, that several photographers had started to drift over to take pictures. I hurried up and curtly told the cameramen to disperse and snapped to Russell that he should join his teammates. I barely glanced at the man he'd been chatting with, but I was pretty sure I knew who it was.

DAVE ALBRITTON, Ohio State high-jumper, not only was a Big Ten titlist, but was the only man in history to win the NCAA championship three years in a row (1936-37-38), although he had to share the honor each time. In '36 it was with Buckeye teammate Mel Walker; in '37 and '38 with Gil Cruder, of Colorado. Albritton later became a member of the State Legislature.

Never had one Big Ten school produced two successive distance stars of such magnitude as did Wisconsin in CHUCK FENSKE and WALTER MEHL. In 1936 Fenske won the league indoor mile crown; in 1937 he took the indoor title again and added the NCAA championship. In 1938 he captured both the indoor and outdoor honors in the Big Ten tourneys, and in 1940 he picked off the AAU title. Mehl scored victories in the two-mile, in the 1938 Conference indoor and outdoor meets and won the NCAA crown the same year for a spectacular sweep. In 1939 he came down to the mile and won the Conference indoor and outdoor crowns; in 1940 he added the AAU mile to his collection, and in 1941 the AAU indoor crown for a total of seven major championships.

SID RICHARDSON was the third of the Conference's great golfers in the 30's. The Northwestern ace won the Big Ten title in 1937 and 1938 and took medalist honors in the 1939 NCAA tourney.

Iowa won only one team title in the history of Big Ten gymnastic tourneys (1937) and it was GENE WETT-STONE, champion in all-around, who led the Hawks. He had gained the all-around title two years previously as a sophomore, missed out in his junior year, but came back strong as a senior.

1938

Some of the Big Ten's greatest athletes were equally brilliant in the classroom in 1937 as the Conference Medal was won by Bud Wilkinson, Minnesota's All-America football guard and quarterback; Inwood Smith of Ohio State, also an All-America guard; Bob Kessler, Purdue's All-America basketballer; Vern Huffman, Indiana's All-America cager; and John Gee, Michigan's 6-8 basketball center and pitcher who subsequently hurled in the big leagues.

The way things were going in the Big Ten during the 1930's, an African explorer might return after many years in the Congo, say to a football fan: "What's new?" and be told, in reply: "Nothing's new; it's still Minnesota."

As indeed it was, in 1938, as the Gophers continued to find new personnel and new ways to hoist the Conference flag. Larry Buhler had come into his own as a senior fullback; Harold Van Every, a junior tailback, was blossoming as a real star; people were predicting a rosy future for a sophomore halfback named George (Sonny) Franck; and Francis Twedell, a smart, fierce guard, anchored the line with running-mate Horace Bell.

After victories over Washington, Nebraska and Purdue, the Gophers came up against Michigan, a team rejuvenated by a new coach, Fritz Crisler, and a bevy of star sophomores led by Tom Harmon and Forest Evashevski. The Wolves also had three straight wins in the young season, and this was to be a big hurdle for both clubs. It was a bruising defensive battle until the final quarter when Michigan banged across but failed to convert. A few minutes later Harmon fumbled. Van Every not only re-covered for the Gophers but immediately completed two passes, one to Bill Johnson and the second to Wilbur Moore for the touchdown. When George Faust kicked the extra point the Gophers were on their way to the Big Ten title. Strangely enough, Harmon, the greatest all-around back in Michigan history, was destined never to play in a winning game against the Gophers, was never to score against them, and, despite his individual brilliance, never in these three years would Michigan win a Conference title.

Although Minnesota's 4-1 record was good enough for the championship (Michigan also played a 0-0 tie with Northwestern), the Gophers tripped twice during the year. Against Northwestern a field goal by Horace Bell was standing up until the Wildcats recovered a Minnesota fumble on the Viking 19, and after a first down, Bernie Jefferson scored the winning touchdown on an 8-yard sprint. Two weeks later Minnesota took on Notre Dame, still looking for its first win over the Irish. The Gophers limited Notre Dame to two first downs for the day but three perfectly executed plays produced three touchdowns and a 19-0 win for the Irish.

The Gophers' Francis Twedell was honored as an All-America guard, as was Michigan's 187-pound wonder Ralph Heikkenen. Bob Voigts, Northwestern's great tackle, was another line choice; Howie Weiss, Wisconsin's line-blaster made it at fullback, and was also named the league's most valuable player; and at East Lansing, Michigan State fans hailed the selection of brilliant triple-threat John Pingel, the Spartan halfback who became his school's third All-America.

Prominent on the All-America lists for 1938 were five Big Ten stars, including Michigan State's JOHN PINGEL; Northwestern's BOB VOIGTS; and HOWIE WEISS, of Wisconsin. Pingel, a legitimate triple-threat star led the Spartans to a fine 6-2 season as they continued their football renaissance under Coach Charley Bachman. Despite Northwestern's lacklustre 4-3-1 season, Voigts was such a tremendous blocker and defensive stand-out he simply couldn't be overlooked when it came to individual brilliance. Weiss, also playing for an average club, was one of the hardest-hitting fullbacks the league had seen since Bronko Nagurski, and contributed so much in so many ways he was chosen the Conference MVP. Other Big Ten stars selected for All-America in 1938 were Minnesota's Francis Twedell and Michigan's Ralph Heikkinen, both guards. Voigts later returned to coach the Wildcats.

JOHN PINGEL   BOB VOIGTS   HOWIE WEISS

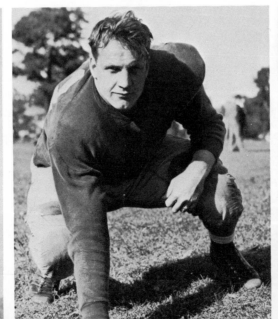

A few days before football practice began in 1933 at Horace Mann High School in Gary, Indiana, a 14-year-old freshman had won a bubble gum contest at a local theater. He could blow 'em bigger and faster than any kid in the neighborhood and won a pair of roller skates for a prize.

Blowing bubbles almost ruined a great football career before it started for Thomas Dudley Harmon. He was still working on his specialty when he reported for football practice. The coach became irritated while talking to his assembled squad because Harmon was blowing big plastic poppers instead of listening to the coach's words of wisdom. He ordered the kid to get off the field and turn in his uniform.

The young frosh slunk off to the sidelines, but no further, and made no move to start stripping off his suit. A few minutes later, the coach spotted him and crooked a finger ominously. The varsity was just about to practice kick-offs and the coach figured this was a chance to discourage the kid once and for all. "Get down there with that receiving unit," he barked, "and return one of these kicks!"

The kid silently and obediently trotted toward the goal line. Seconds later the ball came sailing straight toward him. He tucked it under an arm and proceeded to thread his way through the entire varsity, 90 yards to the opposite goal.

Doug Kerr, the coach, a graduate of Michigan, stared slack-jawed, then recovered to call the boy over. "Harmon," he began haltingly, "If you're willing to give up bubble gum—"

The youngster was willing and the rest became football history. Before he graduated, Tom Harmon would be described by many critics as better than Heston, better than Thorpe, better than Grange . . . Comparison of players from different eras isn't exactly an exact science but in this instance the evidence wasn't without startling substance.

Long before young Tom Harmon ran back that kick-off as a high school freshman, all the signs and portents were there for eventual greatness. First, he was a member of an athletic family. His father, a Gary policeman, had been a crack high school sprinter. Three older brothers had been college stars; Lou and Harold in basketball and track at Purdue; Gene as basketball captain at Tulane. Two uncles, Leo and Doyle, played football for Wisconsin, and Doyle had been the Badger captain.

At age 10 young Tom, wearing cut-down, castoff equipment from his uncles, was playing on the sixth grade team at Holy Angels grammar school. The field was cinder-encrusted but this kid, like many of his playmates, was hard-nosed long before his time. His older brothers for years had instilled in him the idea that nobody gets anywhere in sports without taking some lumps. They'd even run him through an ordeal in which they put him in a room, or garage, and forced him through a yelling and hollering drill so he'd develop a firm, commanding voice. "I could have sung bass by the time I was 12," Harmon drily recalled later.

Meanwhile, he was developing the speed of a sprinter and the natural co-ordination of a Nijinsky. In the eighth grade, as player coach, he led his school team to 10 straight victories, the last one a win over the high school freshman team.

In high school Tom Harmon was virtually a living

Tom Harmon of Michigan.

prep legend in his time. As a 145-pound frosh he played mostly with the reserves, but the following summer he operated a compression drill and dug ditches on a road gang, and reported as a 165-pound sophomore to nail down a starting halfback berth on the varsity. The next summer he worked in a Gary steel mill and, as a 185-pounder, made all-league in the tough Northern Indiana League. As a 195-pound senior he was one of the highest-scoring backs in midwest prep football.

He was a 14-letterman at Gary, starring in four sports: football, basketball, baseball and track. He won the state high school championship in the 100-yard dash and 220-yard low hurdles. A good student, he was sought by the Ivies, Big Ten, The South and Far West. You can box the compass and find a dozen campuses at each of the 32 points who were wooing him.

Doug Kerr, his Gary coach, who had become a close friend and adviser, had taken his backfield every year to the high school football clinic held on the University of Michigan campus during spring training. Harmon, after three trips, grew to like the atmosphere. Michigan had suffered through three straight disastrous grid seasons and was 6-18 for the three years, and Coach Harry Kipke, with a run of sub-par material, was rumored to be in trouble. Despite the low estate of Michigan football fortunes Harmon decided this was the place for him. (Kipke, unfortunately, was never to reap the benefits of this decision. Had Harmon shown up in Maize and Blue a year earlier, Kipke probably would have stayed and become a Coaching Great.)

It was Fritz Crisler, brought in from a highly successful coaching stint at Princeton, who inherited Tom Harmon—and a delicate situation involving player relationships. There was no doubt that Harmon's arrival in Ann Arbor was accompanied by the Sound of Trumpets, but, as it turned out, there'd been some other pretty fair country football players rounded up by Wolverine recruiters. There was a young husky from Hamtramck named Forest Evashevski; Paul Kromer, a swifty from Lorain, O., Big Ed Frutig, from Dearborn, and others. In order to slow down the publicity on his tinseled, cocky, hot-shot, Crisler thought of converting Harmon to a blocking back during spring drills prior to Tom's sophomore year. Using the Kohinoor Diamond as a paperweight would have been equally wasteful. Crisler needed just one look to realize the folly of the move, and Harmon became the triple-threat tailback in Michigan's tricky single wing.

Even before he pulled on a varsity shirt, Harmon became the storm center of a national controversy. In the winter of his freshman year, an assistant coach at Tulane, which had tried desperately to recruit the Gary flash originally, sent Harmon a telegram. In essence the message contained the suggestion that Harmon pack his bags, pack in Michigan and transfer to Tulane, which dangled some rather tempting inducements. The Big Ten, in those days, had no such thing as athletic scholarships and Conference athletes had to make it on their own finances or through campus jobs. Harmon, among other chores, washed dishes three hours a day in the Michigan Union. Tulane thought this was sheer nonsense and offered Harmon a full, free, and gaudy ride, and also thought it could provide Harmon with a better football showcase for his talents than was then thought possible at low-tide Michigan.

Somehow the telegram got printed in the Michigan Daily, the campus newspaper, and for several days the headlines had Harmon teetering on the plank of a pigskin piracy scandal. When he announced he was remaining at Michigan it was a bigger local relief than anything coming out of alphabetized Washington in those depression days. (After all, Harmon and his freshman mates had twice defeated the varsity in regulation scrimmages, 7-6 and 14-0, and there was strong evidence that Harmon had been the difference.)

As a Michigan varsity tailback, Harmon became everything that was predicted of him. As the headlines grew bigger and more frequent there grew along with them a general air of discontent on the part of his teammates. It was Evashevski, a born leader, who wisely found the pressure vent that kept things from exploding. The gimmick was a sort of straight-faced ridicule along with a smidgeon of mock servility in Harmon's presence. "We really laid it on," Evashevski recounted later. "We'd be getting dressed for practice and Tom would come in and somebody would say, 'Here comes the team, men. We can practice, now!'

"Every once in a while we'd pass Tom on the campus and sort of give him a silent, respectful, Hindu-type salaam and move right on," said Evashevski. Once, Evy, himself, went around the locker room with a sheaf of dollar bills in his hand, passing them out with the following spiel: "Here it is, men; your chance to join

Tom Harmon, Michigan's All-America halfback in 1940, made six touchdowns in two games with the season only beginning.

the world's most exclusive organization. It's called the I-Block-For-Tom-Harmon Club, and acceptance of a dollar makes you a bona fide member." The gag was elaborately carried out with certain players pulling off a straight-faced refusal to join and others hesitating. Some would make a show of grabbing the dollar bills avidly.

The tactics seemed to be working but the headlines were getting more obtrusive and insinuating. "Harmon a One-Man Team . . ." "Harmon Greater Than Grange . . ." Then some sports wag suggested calling the school at Ann Arbor, "Tom Harmon University."

By Harmon's junior year, although he was running wild, it was still touch and go whether Michigan would fulfill the promise inherent in its fine material, or fragmentize on the rocks of discord. That's when Evashevski took it upon himself to call a squad meeting. Evashevski was not only Harmon's chief blocker from his quarterback post but he had been drawing closer to Tom as a personal friend. Although Harmon knew what the meeting was to be about he insisted upon attending. "This was one time I didn't want anybody blocking for me," Harmon said to friends. "I wanted a chance to tell the other guys that nobody knew better than myself that I'd be just another back if they didn't do the job up front."

It was Evy who took right over at the meeting. Harmon, he said in his opening gambit, was indeed a great halfback, and as long as everybody blocked for him it was only natural for him to score a lot of touchdowns and get big headlines. Of course, there was a simple way to choke off those headlines. Simply do a lousy job of blocking and there'd be no touchdowns. There'd be no Michigan victories, either, but maybe that didn't matter to the rest of the team . . .

It was a frank, completely objective analysis and the squad realized Harmon was only doing what they'd hoped he'd do, based on all-out team effort.

The headlines for three years were merely post-game reflections of the actual heroics on the field. As Michigan's tailback, Harmon broke Red Grange's Big Ten scoring record by slamming across the goal 33 times to the famed Redhead's 31. Nobody has ever come close to that, since; but, it was his remarkable versatility that led to a glory road that, in some people's estimation, not even the Galloping Ghost traveled. The gifts which made it all possible for Harmon were a combination of physical skills and intense personal drive. The 6-foot, 195-pound frame that filled out the uniform that became known as Old No. 98, was his basic asset. In addition he had jack rabbit pick-up and tremendous speed once under way. He had an uncanny sense of anticipation, much like Grange, and a tricky change of pace. His powerful stiff arm, which he used often, was undoubtedly better than Grange's because of his physical strength. He had high, driving leg action and in addition to his running skills he was an excellent blocker, defender, passer, punter, place-kicker, kick-off specialist and quick-kicker in the Wolverine single wing.

Harmon's first varsity touchdown came in the second game of his sophomore year when he swept 59 yards against Chicago—only the first of many long-gainers to come. The following week it was a Harmon pass that brought the lone Wolverine score in a 7-6 loss to Minnesota. His passes paralyzed Yale the next time out and then, against Illinois in a colorful Homecoming game at Ann Arbor, the big sophomore put all his talents together in an exhibition of virtuosity that was to become commonplace, and which told Crisler and Michigan fans that their promised prize package was finally delivered. In the first quarter he darted 17 yards through the Illinois line, shaking off three defenders who had clear shots at him. In the third quarter he dropped back, eluding a furious Illini rush, and drilled a 40-yard scoring toss to Evashevski. The 1938 season was not only Harmon's inaugural, but that of many of his mates, and it served as a good pump-priming for the more glittering successes that would follow.

His junior year found Harmon ready for the first of two back-to-back All-America seasons that made him probably the most heralded back of the decade. In eight games he handled the ball 224 times, carrying 130 trips for 956 yards, and, although not the caliber of a modern-day T-quarterback, he completed 37 of 94 passes for 543 yards. He scored 14 touchdowns, himself, and tossed for six others for a total of 102 points, including 15 points-after and one field goal.

Against Iowa he scored all of Michigan's 27 points, and one of his touchdowns, coming early in the third quarter, broke open the game when he made a spectacular interception of a Hawkeye pass on the Michigan 10 and streaked 90 yards down the sidelines.

He scored four touchdowns against Iowa, three against

Yale and two against Pennsylvania in three of his major triumphs, the latter two making believers out of Eastern critics. A kick-off return against Penn just might have been the longest run, unofficially, in the history of collegiate football. Taking the ball on the Michigan 17 he ripped down the right side of the field where he was hemmed in by three Penn tacklers. He spun out of their clutches, reversed his field all the way to the opposite side and raced down to the Penn 20 only to be pinched in by two more desperate Quaker defenders. Again he reversed his field to the original sideline, tore loose from another clutching Quaker and crossed the goal standing up. It was estimated later that he had gone close to 175 yards, around, through, between and over Red and Blue jerseys.

In the season finale against Ohio State he again demonstrated the amazing versatility that made him The Complete Football Player. He had scored once against the Bucks, passed for another TD to Evashevski and kicked both points-after to bring the Wolverines into a 14-14 tie after trailing 14-0. Then with three minutes to go, and Michigan in possession, fourth down on the Ohio 24, the Wolves lined up for a field goal. Fred Trosko knelt to hold the ball for Harmon's boot. But it was a beautifully conceived fake, in just the right spot, because Ohio had a huge, hard-charging line, making the attempt problematical. When the ball was snapped, Trosko, whose knee was not in contact with the ground, got up with the ball and started to skirt right end. Harmon, who was behind him, roared on past Trosko and blotted out two Buckeye tacklers as Trosko crossed the goal with the winning touchdown.

Two blemishes marred Harmon's junior year, however. Minnesota, led by George Franck and Bruce Smith, turned back Michigan 20-7 for the second time in Harmon's career. The year before, the Gophers had capitalized on a Harmon fumble to win, 7-6. (Tom's sister later knitted him a woolen football for his birthday and the football had handles on it.) The other Michigan setback was an amazing 16-6 upset by a mediocre but fired-up Illinois team that was going all-out for Coach Bob Zuppke who was on the Alumni griddle.

Harmon was, in fact, the center of two jinxes, one operating for him, the other against him, in Michigan's two major rivalries. Despite his individual brilliance and the caliber of three great Michigan teams, Harmon was destined never to play on a Big Ten championship squad —deprived of it three straight years by losses to Minnesota. Again, in his senior year, Michigan would drop its only game to the Gophers, 7-6, with Bruce Smith doing the main damage.

It always rankled Harmon that he never scored a touchdown against the Gophers and this game was a particular disappointment. Both teams were undefeated as they met on a muddy field in Minneapolis, with the first quarter a punting duel between Harmon and Franck. Once, the Wolves powered 86 yards to the Gopher one-yard line but on fourth down Harmon slipped in the ooze. Minnesota punted out, Harmon kicked back and then there was a Gopher fumble. Promptly, Harmon passed to Evashevski for a touchdown, but Harmon's kick failed. Then, when a Harmon pass was intercepted in the Minnesota end zone and put in play on the 20, Smith sprinted 80 yards for a TD and then kicked the extra point for the 7-6 victory.

On the other hand, against its chief traditional rival,

Tom Harmon piles up yardage for Michigan in 1939 clash with Ohio. That's Forest Evashevski, Harmon's favorite blocker, on his back on the right.

Ohio State, Michigan scored three straight victories with Harmon, including the final game of his career which was, in itself, a valedictory beyond any player's fondest dreams.

Harmon had always claimed his personal destruction of Iowa had been his best game, but nobody among the 60,000 in Berkeley, California, who saw Michigan open its 1940 season against California's Golden Bears, would ever agree with him. The date was September 28, and it was Harmon's 21st birthday. Just before the kick-off Evashevski sidled up to him and said, "Let's celebrate it in a big way. If you get the kick-off, run like a thief and we'll knock a lot of guys down for you!"

It happened just that way, with Harmon streaking 94 yards to one of the easiest touchdowns of his life. It was particularly memorable for him because he knew,

then, that he'd come a long way in his teammates' estimation—a long way from the brash, cocky freshman days when he was more than willing to be his own cheerleader. It was the first of four thrilling touchdowns he scored against the Bears, in a 41-0 Michigan victory. The second came on a 72-yard punt return. The third was an 86-yard jaunt through the entire California team, plus an irate Golden Bear fan who jumped out of the stands and tried to haul down Harmon just before he crossed the goal line. The Wolverine flash scored once more on an 8-yard off-tackle slant and passed to Dave Nelson, for still another.

The pattern was set for the rest of the season. Harmon tallied all 21 points in a 21-14 win over Michigan State; he got three TD's, passed for another and did all the passing and kicking to wallop a great Harvard team featuring All-America Chub Peabody; he ran for one touchdown, passed for another and kicked a field goal to smash Illinois; and, he got all of Michigan's 14 points to whitewash Pennsylvania.

By now, the hottest topic of conversation in the Big Ten was whether Harmon would break Red Grange's record of 31 TD's. Grange, himself, was in the stands at Evanston as Harmon got his 30th to beat Northwestern, 20-13.

There was one game left. The annual donnybrook with Ohio State, Michigan's bitterest foe. More than 75,000 were on hand in Ohio Stadium. It was a chance for a potentially great Buckeye team to salvage something out of a dismal season. The veteran club had started with hopes for a national championship, but had been upset by Northwestern, Minnesota and Cornell. A win over Harmon and his mates might even save Francis Schmidt's job. This, plus Harmon's quest for Grange's record, made it a Roman Holiday for fans on both sides.

Nobody could have demanded more for a farewell appearance. In the first quarter Harmon cracked over from the 8-yard line to tie Grange's mark. In the second period he flipped to Evashevski for Michigan's second touchdown, but the magic moment had not yet arrived. He returned Ohio State's second half kick-off 70 yards to the Buckeye 22, and almost went the distance. It was enough to put him in position to toss another touchdown pass, this time to Ed Frutig, the Wolverines' great end. As great as his performance had been up to now, there was still something missing . . . The thing everyone had come to see. Then, in the closing moments of the third quarter, following an interception of an Ohio pass, there came the moment everyone had waited for. From the Ohio 18 Harmon raced wide, cut back over tackle, stiff-armed one defender, out-raced the rest and sprinted over the goal line to break Grange's scoring record. The sound was deafening, with most of it contributed by partisan Ohio fans, many of whom had seen Grange wind up his career in this same stadium in 1925.

Harmon was not yet through. In the final quarter he faked a pass and kept going around end from the six to complete a 40-0 rout of the Buckeyes and to score the 33d and final touchdown of his fabulous career. He had, meanwhile, punted three times for a 50-yard average and made an even dozen tackles on defense.

In 24 games in three years he had carried the ball 398 times for 2338 yards and 33 touchdowns. He had completed 101 of 233 passes for 1359 yards and 16 touchdowns, and had, himself, scored 237 points on his 33 TD's, 33 points-after, and two field goals. He was a fraction short of six yards per carry on his ball-lugging.

With 30 seconds to go in that final game, Crisler took out his super-star who trotted to the bench to a standing ovation and a weird ordeal that would await him in the locker room.

"It was a mad-house," Harmon recalled later. "People were stampeding past the guards, climbing over the high, iron, protective fences leading to the backdoor of the locker room, and even pushing past the cops at the dressing room door itself. The trouble was, most of them were after my signature, but not as an autograph trophy. They wanted my name on contracts for all kinds of merchandise, testimonials, jobs and promotion schemes. Even though there was big money involved for me, it was almost terrifying."

It was something that had been building up all season long. Contracts for cigarettes, beer and clothing endorsements could have made him wealthy. He turned them all down. Shrewdly, Harmon wanted only one thing. He had majored in speech and radio communications at Michigan and wanted to become a sportscaster and produce sports programs. Pro football, not then the big-time business it was destined to become, was still a possibility. Before he made up his mind on anything definite, Harmon got involved in a frantic banquet circuit that earned him big fees—and almost got him flunked out of school. In one month he logged 25 hours of flying time getting to and from his appearances. After winning the Heisman Trophy and being named Athlete of the Year by the AP, he needed a secretary to handle his various dates and fill requests for hundreds of photos. (Once, in a reverse procedure, he got a crate of razzberries from Minneapolis city councilmen, along with a note implying he was a bum sport for telling the press that Michigan should have scored three times against Minnesota in his senior year. Actually, Tom had been somewhat misquoted by a sportswriter.)

After graduation Harmon made a movie called "Harmon of Michigan," and bought a new home for his parents with some of his loot. Then, suddenly, there was a priority on his services. He was drafted into the army as America prepared for entry into World War Two, and became an air cadet.

Typically, he was the hero of two headlined stories that had sports fans throughout the nation holding their breath. In April, 1943, word flashed over the United States that Lieut. Tom Harmon, on submarine patrol over the South American coast, was missing in his bomber.

For six days there was only ominous silence. Then, on the seventh day, there was the electrifying news that Lieut. Harmon, covered with cuts, bruises and sores, had walked into a U. S. base, led by some jungle natives he had come across the day before, after wandering, helplessly lost, through some of the most savage country in the world. He had parachuted out of his crippled bomber, along with his mates, but never made contact with any of them.

Several months later, after having switched to pursuit planes, Harmon volunteered to join a group of 25 fighter pilots being assigned to Gen. Chenault in China. Then, on November 30, 1943, another telegram from the War Department was delivered to his parents in Ann Arbor. Lieut. Harmon's P-38 had been shot down by the Japs over China. This time 32 days were to pass before the word came that Harmon had been smuggled back to an Allied base by Chinese guerilla fighters. Meanwhile, he had destroyed his share of Jap Zeros. It was typical that he should receive a telegram after shooting down his first two, which said: "Congratulations on your victory but how did you ever do it without me?" It was signed by Forest Evashevski.

Shortly after the war was over Tom Harmon came home to marry beautiful Elyse Knox, a movie star he had met in Hollywood.

After the war Harmon tried pro football briefly with the Los Angeles Rams, but his legs had been burned and injured in his two unlucky aircrafts and, although he showed flashes of his former wizardry, the legs couldn't take it and he retired to go into sports broadcasting. Today he is West Coast sports director for ABC and his voice is as familiar to the nation's sports fans as the number 98 was to a generation of football fans.

JOHN TOWNSEND

MARTY ROLEK

In addition to Jewell Young, who led Purdue to the Big Ten basketball title in 1938, the Conference supplied three other All-Americans. LEW (PICK) DEHNER, Illinois' slick center was the first Illini honored in 16 years. MARTY ROLEK, whose scoring and play-making almost gave Minnesota a second straight league crown, was a forward; and JOHN TOWNSEND, of Michigan, a shining light for three years with average Wolverine clubs, and a track star as well, was also selected as a center.

LEW (PICK) DEHNER

A weird start in the 1938 basketball season kept Minnesota from a share of the title again, and Purdue slipped in with a 10-2 mark to the Gophers 9-3. It was puzzling, indeed, to Minnesota fans, after a bright early season spurt which found the Vikings knocking off such Eastern powers as Long Island University and N.Y.U., to see their team come up with the jitters for three straight losses to Wisconsin, Indiana, and Michigan—all of whom were destined to be second-division clubs. Suddenly Minnesota did a complete turnabout and tore off nine straight Conference victories, but the damage had been done as Purdue dropped only two games.

Jewell Young, the demon scorer who led the loop for the second straight year, and Gene Anderson, paced the Boilermakers, while once again Marty Rolek sparked Minnesota. Both Young and Rolek received All-America honors, along with John Townsend, a smooth shooter and accomplished pivotman from Michigan, who had been a star since his sophomore year.

There was a significant arrival among the swimming elite in the 1938 season, when Mike Peppe brought Ohio State into the Big Ten title picture for the first time, upsetting Michigan. Yet, so closely matched were these two squads that the Wolverines were able to reverse things in the NCAA, 46-45. It was the second straight Wolverine-Buckeye finish

Later, Russell grinned as he described out the scene. The man had jerked a thumb in my direction after I'd walked away and said: "Who's that jerk? You want me to have him taken care of?"

"No, I don't think you'd better," Russell said he told the man. "That's Tug Wilson, our athletic director and a good friend of mine."

"Okay, okay," said Al Capone, "I just thought I'd ask!"

From the very beginning of my career at Northwestern, I had become very active in the NCAA, attending all the meetings and serving on several important committees. This, too, had been valuable training because I was to assume the job of secretary-treasurer in that organization in future years. I had also been extremely active in Olympic affairs, serving on the Olympic track and field committee, and working with the NCAA Olympic Committee right from the start. I had attended the Olympic

Games in Paris in 1924, Amsterdam in 1928, and Los Angeles in 1932.

At the time of my selection as Commissioner, the directors and faculty representatives of the Big Ten had increased the powers and duties that were to go with the position. I was hardly prepared to read the headlines in the papers the day after my selection: "Tug Wilson Appointed Czar of the Big Ten." This was not the case at all. Although Michigan's Ralph Aigler, chairman of the faculty representatives, had put out a carefully prepared statement about the scope of my duties, some of my good friends among the sports writers tacked on the title "Czar", which embarrassed me no end.

I knew, of course, that my duties put me in the category of an enforcement officer, which was in contrast to Major Griffith's limited power, in which he merely dug up infractions and placed evidence before the faculty rep-

in the nationals, and for the next two decades the rest of the country would have to get used to these two teams battling it out for the team title.

Ed Kirar, Michigan's swift freestyler, took the NCAA 50- and 100-yard events. Michigan's foursome of Waldemar Tomski, Ed Hutchens, Tom Haynie and Kirar repeated the Wolverine triumph of 1937 in the 400-meter relay; and a slim sandy-haired youngster from Ohio State named Al Patnik began his mastery of the diving events that would bring him acclaim as the greatest springboard artist yet seen. He took both the one-meter and three-meter events, and before he would finish he would collect five NCAA crowns. Only one other diver in history would ever exceed that.

Michigan swept both the indoor and outdoor Conference track titles. In the NCAA Dave Albritton of Ohio State again tied with Colorado's Gil Cruter in the high jump, in which they also shared a new record of 6 feet 8¼ inches; and Wisconsin's Walter Mehl established a new two-mile mark of 9:11.1.

In other sports, Northwestern's gifted golfer, Sid Richardson, won his second straight Conference individual crown, but Minnesota dethroned the Wildcats as team champion.

Meanwhile, cross-country had been resumed on a Conference championship meet basis after a five-year depression layoff, and Billy Hayes' Indiana team, led by Mel Trutt, not only won the Big Ten team crown but romped off with the NCAA crown, the first time a national meet was held in the sport.

In wrestling, things were a bit topsy-turvy. Illinois was runner-up to Michigan as Big Ten team champion, but the Illini finished the year strong by taking a runner-up spot to Oklahoma A. & M., in the NCAA meet. Individual titles were won by Allen Sapora, Illinois' 126-pounder, and younger brother of former Illini great, Joe Sapora; John Ginay, Illinois 165-pounder; and Charlie McDaniel, Indiana heavyweight.

Chicago and Illinois pulled off the same kind of

MEL TRUTT, Indiana distance ace in track, turned to cross-country and led the Hoosiers to the Big Ten title and the NCAA championship in 1938, the first time it was held as a national collegiate team tourney.

turnabout in gymnastics when, after placing second and third to Minnesota in the Conference team championship, the Maroon and Illini came back to place one-two in the first NCAA team tournament, with Minnesota third. Two Conference stars immediately made gymnastic history by taking three individual event. Illinois' Joe Giallombardo won the tumbling, flying rings, and all-around crowns; and Erwin Beyer of Chicago took the side horse, long horse, and parallel bar titles.

In tennis, Chicago not only won the Conference

resentatives, who were to determine and inflict the penalty.

In this transition period of the office of Commissioner, I found immediate tasks confronting me, the first of which was to assign the basketball officials for a season that was just around the corner. Griffith had not yet done this before he died. I shall never forget the help that Dutch Lonborg, my basketball coach at Northwestern, gave me in this most difficult assignment that was accomplished on a crash basis. It could have been disastrous.

My next piece of luck was to find that Bill Reed was finishing his military stint and would soon be available. I wasted no time in negotiating with him and he joined me in the fall of 1945. In the meantime, the council of the NCAA had asked if I would assume the duties of Secretary-Treasurer of the National Collegiate Athletic Association, a position Major Griffith had held. I knew I would also need help in appointing and directing football and basketball officials; this is almost a fulltime job in itself. Again, I was fortunate in being able to secure the services of Jim Masker who had retired from officiating at 65 but still wanted to keep his hand in the game. Jim was one of the best and most respected officials the Big Ten has ever had and he helped me tremendously.

This was my first staff and no one was ever blessed with two more loyal, dedicated individuals than Reed and Masker, each of whom devoted himself to the Conference and possessed outstanding ability.

Later I was to hire Bill Haarlow, one of the all-time basketball greats at Chicago and an outstanding basketball referee who assisted me in the selection and training of basketball officials. When Bill Reed left to join the staff of Senator Ferguson of Michigan in Washington in

JOE GIALLOMBARDO, *Illinois' muscular but lithe gymnastics star, was one of the greatest gymnasts in the history of the sport. In the first NCAA tourney ever held, in 1938, he took three titles: tumbling, all-around and flying rings; and repeated in tumbling and all-around in 1939-40 for a total of seven individual championships, the most ever taken by one collegian.*

1939

team title but produced a Conference "first" when the Maroon brother combination of Chet and Bill Murphy took the doubles championship.

On the administrative front, the Conference voted to re-establish a training table for football players, and also reaffirmed the ruling that the football season would end the last Thursday before Thanksgiving Day. The Conference Medals went to John Townsend, Michigan's All-America basketball player;

The Maroon's remarkable twin brother combination of CHET and BILL MURPHY were the league's doubles champs in 1938 and 1939, with Chet also winning the singles crown in 1939.

Chuck Fenske, Wisconsin's great miler; Ralph Wolf, Ohio State's outstanding football center; Danny Zehr, Northwestern's 1936 NCAA swimming champ; and Allen Sapora and Charley McDanield, Illinios and Indiana NCAA wrestling kings, respectively.

The year 1938 also brought another honor to the Big Ten and Indiana in particular, when Don Lash, the Hoosiers' great distance runner, won the Sullivan Award as the most outstanding amateur athlete in America.

Francis Schmidt came up with a combination of plentiful talent and a versatile attack in the 1939 football season and Ohio State wrote much of the drama in a campaign which found the Scarlet playing roles ranging from heroic to tragic (as far as Buckeye fandom was concerned).

This was a big, fast Scarlet team that had all the ingredients for a varied attack. Quarterback Don Scott (later to be killed in World War Two) was the most versatile Buckeye back in a decade. A 6'-1",

1947, I was fortunate in hiring a young newspaper man who had graduated from the University of Iowa, Walter Byers, who was to serve as my assistant and director of public relations for the Conference, and assist me with my NCAA duties. Later he was to be selected as the Executive Director of the NCAA and would become one of the most important figures in intercollegiate athletics. When Byers left to join the NCAA on a full-time basis I talked Reed into leaving Washington and coming back on my staff. There were others who were to help me during the next 16 years: Bill Blake, as supervisor of officials, who contributed greatly to the development of young football officials; and Cap Hedges who assisted me in this same role. Most of all I remember Irish Krieger, who brought his vast technical knowledge to the Conference concerning the problems of football officiating. Krieger dedicated practically his whole life to football

officiating and not only gave valuable aid to the Big Ten but the national football rules committee as well.

Following Krieger's untimely death, Carlisle Dollings at Columbus, a retired Conference official, gave valuable service as a technical advisor for football officials. There was also Jack Ryan, former Big Ten athlete who gave me tremendous service as my chief investigator, and last but not least, there was John Dewey, who came to us in a new capacity as Conference Examiner.

In the December meeting of 1945, the waivers which were so necessary during the wartime years, were ended and the Conference went back on its regular schedule of rules. At this same meeting a nine-game football schedule was adopted as permanent legislation. This had been discussed and argued over at length many times but the experience during wartime rules had proved to the satisfaction of the directors and faculty representa-

205-pounder he was a smart signal-caller, a fine passer, superb punter (Conference leader), a strong runner, an unerring place-kicker for points-after and capped it all with bearish defensive ability. Jim Strausbaugh was a swift, picture-runner at left half; Frank Zadworney a devastating blocker and a power runner on reverses; and Jimmy Langhurst a fast, smashing fullback. The line was bulwarked by Captain Steve Andrako, a tigerish center; Thornton Dixon and Charley Maag at tackle, and Esco Sarkkinen, a versatile, all-around end.

As a heady quarterback and superb blocker, FOREST EVASHEVSKI was responsible for much of the success of teammate Tom Harmon in 1938-39-40. Evy went on to coaching greatness at Iowa.

Opening with solid wins over Missouri and Northwestern, the Buckeyes set the stage for burgeoning national honors when they turned in an offensive masterpiece against tough Minnesota for a come-from-behind 23-20 victory paced by Scott, Strausbaugh, Langhurst and a field goal by Maag.

The next week the Buckeyes were to take on Cornell, the best of the Ivies that year, but the football differential of the two areas—Big Ten and the East—made the Scarlet an overwhelming choice. In fact, the Bucks jumped off to a 14-0 first quarter lead on two long, sustained drives and it looked like a rout until suddenly, in the second quarter, Cornell deep in its own territory, sprang Walt Scholl loose around end and the little halfback sprinted 79 yards without a hand laid on him. Three minutes later, Scholl twisted away from onrushing Ohio linemen and fired a long pass to Swifty Bohrman who had slipped beyond the Buck secondary, and the game was tied up at 14-14.

The Buckeyes, stunned by this unexpected lightning, never quite got over it. Cornell got a third touchdown in the third quarter and field goal in the fourth to nail the Scarlet with a 23-14 defeat that was perhaps even more galling than the one pinned on them by Notre Dame a few season earlier. After all, Cornell was still an Eastern team—although it was realized subsequently that the Easterners that year were loaded with personnel that could have played anywhere, and were one of the best teams in the nation.

Schmidt was able to pick up his Buckeyes for three straight shut-out wins over Big Ten foes, and then came the season finale for everyone—with only two teams left in contention for the title: Ohio and Iowa. Michigan was out of it following two mid-season upset losses to Illinois and Minnesota—and both are worth examining. With the great Harmon-Evashevski combination clicking beautifully the Wolves had won four straight when it met mediocre Illinois. An active movement was under way to get

tives that a nine-game schedule was not too much. The only qualifications were that the first game of the season should not be played before the last Saturday in September and the last game not be played after the last Saturday before the last Thursday in November. There was a plea from the football coaches at this time to have limited freshmen competition in football and basketball. This had apparently worked out very satisfactorily during the wartime years but after considerable debate, it was turned down. My personal opinion then, and now, is that a limited amount of competition for freshmen could be very beneficial. In the first place, it is drudgery for freshmen to merely scrimmage against the varsity and there would also be an incentive to keep up their grades so they could compete. Other conferences throughout the country, including the Ivy League had adopted this practice; in fact the Big Ten was the only major conference in the country that prohibited freshmen competition.

The March meeting in 1946 was another sad one. T. N. Metcalf, the Director at the University of Chicago, came in with a formal notice that Chicago wished to withdraw from the Conference due to its inability to provide reasonable equality of competition. The faculty representatives and directors in a joint session regretfully accepted. This brought to a close a great and glorious record of competition in the Big Ten by the Maroon. Only the old timers and avid sports fans would probably remember that Chicago had won 58 championships and 13 co-championships in Conference sports, a record that ranks them high in the Conference for all-time championship competition. As I sat there listening to the discussion, my mind went back to one of the first Illinois football games I ever played against Chicago before packed stands. Neither team was able to make

rid of Bob Zuppke, and alumni were taking red-hot positions for and against Zup. The football team knew that a petition had actually been tendered, asking Zuppke's removal. As far as the ball club was concerned, there was only one way to answer it. Led by Jimmy Smith, Chuck Bernhardt, and George Rettinger, backs with a mission that day, and Bill Lenich, a terror at center, the embattled Illini stunned Michigan—and the football world—by clobbering the Wolverines, Harmon and all 16-7.

The following week, determined to get back into the race, the Wolves entertained a Minnesota team that was nowhere-bound (3-4-1 for the season), with Harmon determined to atone for the fumble that had led to a Gopher win the year before. The Gopher line, however, with everything to gain and nothing to lose, put on a display of rousing, clean mayhem, stopped Harmon cold and sprung loose Sonny Franck, Harold Van Every and Bruce Smith for touchdowns in a 20-7 rout of the Wolverines.

While this had eliminated Michigan from title contention, the Wolverines had previously managed to do some spoiling of their own. Against an Iowa club that had appeared to have a label of "team-of-destiny" tied to it, the Wolverines—and Tom Harmon—played perfect football to pin a 27-7 loss on the Hawkeyes. This was an Iowa team, however, that had come from nowhere, with no expectations, to make a title bid out of solid and imaginative coaching by Dr. Eddie Anderson in his first year, brilliant leadership by the talented Nile Kinnick, and so many 60-minute performances that the Hawks gained and deserved an "Iron-Man" designation.

Bill Osmanski, a star at Holy Cross under Anderson, had come to Iowa City to help Anderson with spring training, and when he went back East a month later he was quoted as saying: "There are 5000 male students at Iowa, and only five of them are real football players." He was wrong, by plenty. Captain Edwin Prasse, Ken Pettit and Dick Evans turned out to be a crack trio of ends; Jim Walker,

EDDIE ANDERSON was a native Iowa boy who had gone off to star for Notre Dame, but everyone remembered him. When Hawkeye football fortunes dwindled in the thirties he was lured away from Holy Cross in Worcester, Massachusetts, where he had nothing but smashing success. By now it was Edward Anderson, M.D., and the "doctoring" he did to the Hawkeyes gave the patient one of the quickest recoveries in Big Ten history. One year of organization and Anderson had the Hawks off and winging in 1939 with his famed "Iron Men." His rebuilding job and his well-decorated 6-1-1 season brought him Coach-of-the-Year honors.

Mike Enich, and Wally Bergstrom a terrific set of tackles; Max Hawkins and Charley Tollefson functioned fiercely as guards; and Bill Diehl and Bruno Andruska split the job at center. At quarterback was Al Coupee, a fine blocker. Buzz Dean was a slashing runner on the reverse and an excellent receiver. At fullback was work-horse Bill Green; and at tailback was the almost indescribable Nile Kinnick, one of the most inspiring and talented players in the history of collegiate football.

much yardage and it ended in a scoreless tie. There was the usual fight and scramble for the ball as the gun ended the game, and to my surprise it bounced crazily into my hands and I meant to keep it for the team. Just then Amos Alonzo Stagg walked out onto the field and I gave the ball to him. He asked who the captain of the Illinois team was and when he appeared, Stagg presented him with the ball, saying: "you boys deserve to win; you played better than we did." It was the first time I had ever seen Mr. Stagg.

The directors and faculty representatives of the Conference expressed extreme regret and told Metcalf that if Chicago ever wished to resume membership, the door would be open for them. (Today, despite the fact that Chicago does not play a Conference schedule, under the leadership of Walter Hass, the present director of athletics, it maintains a fine intramural program for the

undergraduates and a modest varsity program with small colleges.)

Despite the pressures of just the routine matters in my first years as Commissioner, there was one new item I wanted to get to as soon as I could. I thought the time was ripe for me to try to steer the Western Conference into a permanent involvment with The Rose Bowl—the grand-daddy of all the Bowl games with the most interesting background. Some of it is worth mentioning here before we get into that word "involvement."

The Big Ten played a very important part in Rose Bowl history. Michigan and Stanford were the first teams to be invited in 1902. Prior to that time, the Tournament of Roses, the heart of a winter flower festival, had put on a Parade of Floats patterned after the Carnival of Flowers in Nice, France. They also had a program of foot races, tug-of-war and other athletic events, but

NILE KINNICK

The waters of the Gulf of Paria in the Caribbean Sea churned and spouted as the U. S. Navy fighter plane, its motor conked out, plunged into the swell. After a few moments the plane settled beneath the waves. A crash boat from a U. S. aircraft carrier, hurrying to the spot, found nothing but an oil slick on the surface.

The date was June 2, 1943, and at the University of Iowa the news was received with stunned disbelief that this could have happened to a young man who was almost a legend in his time. Iowa was not alone in its grief. Throughout the Big Ten, throughout the nation, in fact, Ensign Nile Kinnick—athlete, scholar, gentleman, inspiring leader—was considered something quite special and not likely to be duplicated too often.

Kinnick, a stocky, 5-9, 170-pounder, came to Iowa from Benson High School in Omaha. A quietly confident athlete, he immediately displayed the abilities and characteristics which prompted one sports writer to decare Iowa was breaking the rules because "They have a coach on the field."

Kinnick played football at Iowa in 1937-38-39, and despite the fact that the Hawkeyes failed to win a game his first year he was an All-Big Ten quarterback. The following season he was handicapped by a bad ankle and Iowa was lucky to win exactly one game.

In 1939, however, Kinnick led Iowa to what was possibly the most amazing—and certainly the quickest—reversal of football form ever seen in the Western Conference. From 1930 until 1938 Iowa had won just 22 of 72 games, with 16 of those 22 wins coming at the expense of such non-Conference opposition as Carlton, Bradley, South Dakota, George Washington, Temple and others. Only five league victories in all that time was the dismal record in Big Ten play. In 1938, with things going from bad to unbelievably worse, a loss to Colgate had been followed by some rather plaintive talk in the press. One Iowa paper remarked: "Iowa's football hopes, such as they were, painfully passed away yesterday afternoon . . . Interment services will be held on any Iowa City street corner . . . The sooner the better."

A few weeks later the Chicago Tribune, feeling that Iowa was going the way of de-emphasized Chicago, stated: "Nearly every Saturday afternoon the gridiron has enhanced scholarship and endowed it with new luster at Chicago and Iowa . . . It is proposed that Robert M. Hutchins, of Chicago, be named the first All-America prexy and E. A. Gilmore, of Iowa, the second All-America prexy."

Irl Tubbs, who had coached the Hawkeyes in 1937-38, had managed a single victory each year, and finally the Iowa administration reached Eastward to Holy Cross and lured Dr. Eddie Anderson back to his native state where he'd been a schoolboy star before entering Notre Dame to shine for Knute Rockne.

Anderson, in 1939, knew what he was inheriting in Nile Kinnick, of course. In his sophomore year Kinnick had gained national prominence as the nation's leading punter who had boomed out 70 kicks for a gaudy 43-yard average. Anderson also knew the stocky, tow-head had been hobbled by injuries as a junior, but one look at Kinnick and some of his teammates in spring drills prior to the 1939 season and The Good Doctor sensed just how far Kinnick might take the Hawkeyes.

So it was Nile Kinnick's senior year that went down in history as a monument to individual virtuosity when,

Nile Kinnick, Iowa's ironman, played 402 minutes out of a possible 420 in the last seven games of his senior season.

as a tailback out of Anderson's single wing, he led Iowa to a glorious season that was built mostly on an ironman stunt never before seen, or since equalled, in The Big Ten. After playing only half the game in Iowa's opener with South Dakota, Kinnick proceeded to play 402 minutes out of a possible 420 in the final seven major games, including successive 60-minute stints against Indiana, Michigan, Wisconsin, Purdue, Notre Dame and Minnesota. Only Michigan, with Tom Harmon having one of his greatest days, was able to halt the Hawkeyes.

In that South Dakota opener, Kinnick ran for three touchdowns and drop-kicked five extra points in less than 35 minutes. The following week against a strong Indiana team led by the sensational Hal Hursch, a passing wizard, came the evidence that Kinnick not only was a mechanical marvel but a lodestone of inspiration. Trailing 29-26 midway in the final quarter, the Hawks had a fourth down and three. They were well within field goal range and Kinnick was a deadly drop-kicker. "Forget the tie," he barked in the huddle, "we're going all the way!" On the snap from center he dropped back, evaded two charging Hoosiers, then a third, calmly searched downfield and fired a perfect pass to Erwin Prasse who raced into the end zone for a 32-29 victory. In that instant when Nile Kinnick gambled for victory instead of a certain tie, a new Iowa football philosophy was born.

Next, against Wisconsin, Kinnick tossed three touchdown passes in a 19-13 win as Max Hawkins, Mike Enich, Wally Bergstrom, and Charley Tollefson joined Kinnick in 60-minute stints. Purdue, a week later, was a violent defensive battle with Iowa's 4-0 victory coming on two safeties, both on blocked punts by the mighty Mike Enich. This time there were no fewer than seven other Hawkeyes who emulated Kinnick's 60-minute heroics.

Then came Notre Dame and another display of Kinnick's brilliance. The undefeated Irish, with a tremendous size and depth advantage, hammered fiercely at the

Nile Kinnick and University of Iowa football coach, Dr. Eddie Anderson.

courageous Hawks, but 16 punts by Kinnick, averaging 46 yards, kept the frustrated Irish from mounting a real drive. Then, finally, Iowa recovered a Notre Dame fumble on the Irish four, and Kinnick went strategic. Quickly he switched positions with Buzz Dean who had been at right half. Then Kinnick called for an improvised play in which he took a direct snap from center, got just enough blocking to give him a chance, and crashed through for a touchdown. Calmly he drop-kicked the extra point which proved the difference when Notre Dame came back to score but missed the PAT. To cap it all, Kinnick saved the day in the last two minutes when he put up the last of his 16 punts, an awesome clutch effort of more than 60 yards which went out of bounds on the Irish five.

Kinnick's next performance, against Minnesota, was described thusly by one Chicago sports writer: "Nile Kinnick 13, Minnesota 9. Tersely, that tells the story of the most spectacular football game in modern Big Ten history."

The Gophers, ferociously determined to retain their Big Ten title, or at least a share of it, had gone into the fourth quarter with a 9-0 lead over Iowa, which now had the ball on its own 20. It took Kinnick just four plays to engineer a touchdown. He passed to Dean for 18 yards; lofted another to Dean for 15 yards; loosened up the Gopher defense by rushing for 2; then dropped

back again, pumping, looking for receivers, twisting and pulling away from clutching Minnesota linemen. He spotted Erwin Prasse and laid the ball perfectly into his hands far downfield, and Prasse took it in. Kinnick drop-kicked the point and it was 13-7 with 11 minutes to go; but, with each team having the ball twice more, time began to run out. There was about a minute and a half left when Minnesota punted to Kinnick who took the ball on the 10 and returned to the 21.

The minute and a half seemed translatable into a mile and a half.

On first down Kinnick threw incomplete. Then he hit Buzz Dean for 17 yards. A pass to Erwin Prasse was incomplete but there was interference and the Hawkeyes had the ball on the Minnesota 45. Bill Green blasted for 7 yards and then Kinnick slashed off tackle for 10 more. There were only seconds remaining. Kinnick took a direct snap, faded back while Gopher linemen smashed at his protection trying to get to him. Downfield, Green was racing into the end zone. Two huge Gophers lunged for Kinnick who waited until the last split second and fired as they closed in on him. On the seat of his pants Kinnick never saw Green take the ball for the touchdown as the gun went off on an Iowa victory. Again, for Kinnick and six of the Hawkeye linemen, it had been the full 60, savage minutes of play.

Then, in the final game of the season against Northwestern the ironman was found to be human after all. After 402 minutes without relief—virtually seven full games—Nile Kinnick was taken out of the game with a ripped shoulder muscle, his arm hanging limp and useless. It was, perhaps, the most tragic injury in Iowa grid history because without his usual last-minute heroics the Hawks were lucky to settle for a 7-7 tie. A win would have given them the Big Ten title because, at Ann Arbor, Michigan was upsetting Ohio State, and the once-defeated Buckeyes backed into the title that had slipped away from the Black and Gold Ironmen who had one loss and a tie.

When they toted up his accomplishments at season's end there was plenty of statistical evidence to proclaim Nile Kinnick's multi-skilled brilliance. He had tossed 11 touchdown passes, drop-kicked 11 extra points and was personally involved in 107 of Iowa's 130 points. He led the nation in runback of kick-offs with 377 yards and in pass interceptions with eight. He had been the prime mover in 197 plays for Iowa—104 rushing and 93 passing—a modern season record for an eight-game schedule, as was his 998 yards gained.

Although not particularly fast, Kinnick was a hard, slashing runner, and Dr. Eddie Anderson often said Kinnick was the hardest worker on the squad—the first on the practice field every day. "He was a perfectionist," said Anderson. "Never satisfied unless he could come as close as he could to absolute perfection in any move he made. He could never feel convinced there was no room for further improvement, and his spirit was transmitted to his teammates.

"More often than not," Anderson continued, "as a result of his inspiration we had as many as seven or eight players who'd go the full 60 minutes with him in a particular game. And they knew Nile was never wasting himself; when Kinnick wasn't running the ball, or passing it, he was blocking for somebody else. There was no such thing as using Nile Kinnick on a fake."

It was that kind of leadership which five times in 1939 brought victory in the fourth quarter for Iowa.

Small wonder the honors piled up at the end of the season: the Heisman Trophy, Maxwell and Camp Trophies as No. 1 player of the year; unanimous All-America selection, topping the balloting on every team selected, and honorary captain of the team picked by the All-America Football Board—the only honor team that designated a leader. Kinnick was also chosen the No. 1 Athlete in America in the annual wire service poll, beating out Joe DiMaggio for the honor. The following summer Kinnick was ranked first in the national poll to name the college all-stars for their annual game against the pro champions.

Although remembered chiefly as a football player, Kinnick played basketball in his sophomore year and was second highest scorer on the Iowa team. He gave up basketball after that to concentrate on his studies—the kind of concentration which got him elected to Phi Beta Kappa.

Kinnick rejected a glittering offer to play pro football because it would have conflicted with law school, which he entered in 1940. There's no telling where or how high that career might have taken him, but shortly before Pearl Harbor he was called up for training as a naval aviation cadet.

On that fatal day in the Caribbean, it was not the perfectionism of Nile Kinnick that failed. It was the machine which faltered and brought an end, all too soon and tragically, to a remarkable career.

Nile Kinnick crosses goal line for Iowa in 1939 clash with Notre Dame. Seconds later he drop-kicked the extra point to provide the 7-6 victory margin for the Hawkeyes.

nothing very exciting. Then someone got an idea for a football game.

The first game had many unique features. The players took part in the Rose Bowl Parade. Each team was decked out in turtle-necked sweaters, proudly wearing the emblem of their university as they were transported in tallyhos down the parade line.

The stadium in contrast to the magnificent one of today, could only accommodate 2,500. However, thousands more crashed the gate and lined the field, protesting the exorbitant prices of 50¢ and $1.00 for seats. There was so much confusion the game didn't start until 3:30 P.M. and the first half wasn't over until 4:30 P.M. The game eventually had to be shortened because of darkness. That day Michigan gained a total of 1,463 yards in 142 plays for an unbelievable average of over 10 yards per try as the Wolverines won, 49-0.

During the next few years the Tournament of Roses Committee was unable to schedule another football game. They had chariot races which proved very spectacular but also extremely dangerous, and, following an incident where several people in the crowd were injured by a runaway chariot, they returned to football in 1916 and have continued with it ever since. That year Washington State and Brown University were the featured teams.

From 1916 on, no Big Ten team appeared at the Rose Bowl Game until 1921, when a game was scheduled which had a terrific impact on the Rose Bowl. The year before, Tournament officials had approved a plan to build a stadium to hold 60,000. The proposals to sell stadium membership at $50 and $100, each carrying exclusive seat privileges for five- and ten-year periods, had met with very poor response. That year, however,

Virtually every regular played the full 60 minutes in at least one game; most of them went the distance in two or three. Kinnick, the truest iron-man of them all, at one stretch played 402 minutes out of a possible 420 in seven straight games. In one contest, against Wisconsin, he was joined in a 60-minute stint by Hawkins, Enick, Tollefson, and Bergstrom. The story of Bergstrom is perhaps typical of this Hawkeye team. Bergstrom was a senior who'd never played high school football, and had seen no service in his first two years at Iowa. When Walker was injured in the third game of the season Bergstrom was thrown into the Wisconsin game where, in a 19-13 victory over the Badgers, Bergstrom, according to Kinnick, ". . . finished a college football course in one afternoon."

It had been that third game of the season, however, against Michigan, which had been the big stumbling block for the Hawkeyes. Traveling to Ann Arbor, where Iowa had never won a football game, the Hawks got off to the kind of start which, hopefully, for Iowa, was history-in-the-making. Kinnick completed a 50-yard pass play to Dean for a touchdown but the 7-0 lead didn't last long. Moments later, Tom Harmon intercepted a Kinnick pass and raced it back 90 yards for a score. Harmon went on to tally all 27 points for Michigan that afternoon as his mates put on a dazzling offensive and defensive display. (Later, Harmon described it as his greatest day in football.)

Thus, the last day of the season came down to a title decision that would go either to undefeated Ohio State or once-defeated Iowa. The Bucks were going against Michigan who were out of it; the Hawkeyes against Northwestern, also a non-contender with two defeats. Both Ohio and the Hawkeyes were clear favorites, but only experts predict. The football never indicates how it will bounce. It exercised its persnickety prerogative in both contests.

The Ohio-Michigan game in Columbus was one which the two opposing coaches, Francis Schmidt and Fritz Crisler, would never forget. The Scarlet led, 14-0 at the half, but Harmon, Evashevski and mates roared back to tie it up. Then, late in the fourth quarter the Wolves had possession, fourth and long yardage on the buckeye 25, shortly after Harmon had caught Frank Zadworney from behind when the Buck halfback seemed on his way to a TD that would have iced the game. (The Buckeyes fumbled on the next play. Michigan recovered and put on a drive that stalled deep in Ohio territory.) Michigan now lined up in field goal formation, with Fred Trosko holding for Harmon. The kick never came. The resultant play had been planned and was now beautifully executed as Trosko leaped up with the ball and raced around the Ohio end, past a stunned secondary, for the winning touchdown.

Starting their game an hour later in the Central time zone, Iowa had only to beat Northwestern for a fitting climax to a fabulous season.

Fearfully battered in its previous game with Minnesota and in the first half against the Wildcats, Iowa now saw its star, Nile Kinnick, his shoulder badly bruised, leave the game with the Hawks trailing 7-0. With a stupendous effort, the Hawkeyes roared back with a touchdown by fullback Ray Murphy and an extra point by Buzz Dean and it was 7-7. That's the way it ended. A victory would have given Iowa the Big Ten title over the vanquished Buckeyes, but with the Iowa-Northwestern tie, Ohio State backed into the championship.

The valorous Hawkeyes, however, were recognized nationally for their magnificent season-long effort, and their 9th ranking spot in the year-end poll was the highest recognition an Iowa team had received since the glory days of 1921-22. With the pride felt for the Hawks, went a note of sadness which the Conference felt for Chicago. It was the Maroon's last football season within the league. All that had gone before—the Staggs, the Eckersalls, the Steffens, the Pages, Kelloggs, McCarthys, the Berwangers—was now only a memory of a glorious past, and there would be no new names added to an illustrious list. At honors time it was Nile Kinnick, of Iowa, who

---

Ohio State and the University of California were tentatively announced as opponents. The Buckeyes were Conference champs and the Big Ten alumni clubs on the coast put up a terrific clamor to see a Western Conference team in the Bowl again. Howard Lucas, President of the Ohio State Alumni Association of Los Angeles, sent the following wire to L. W. St. John, Buckeye athletic director:

> "Informal invitation goes to you tonight from Tournament committee. Desire reply at once whether or not you will accept. Invitation absolute certainty. Formal invitation will follow your acceptance."

St. John, a man of quick but incisive decision, obtained consent from President William Oxley Thompson, and the Ohio State faculty. However, when Saint placed the matter before the Big Ten it took considerable urging on the part of Professor Thomas E. French, Ohio's faculty representative, to get an official okay. After all, the first appearance by Michigan in 1902 had been just a casual thing. There had been no Rose Bowl build-up; no publicity; and no problems. Now it was an annual event and maybe caution was the word. Ohio was given permission and the Buckeyes, the Conference champs, led by a great All-American, Pete Stinchcomb, were undefeated and nationally-known. Coach Andy Smith's "Wonder Bears" of California were no strangers to the limelight either. No Bowl game or intersectional game to date had received so much publicity. The Buckeyes lost,

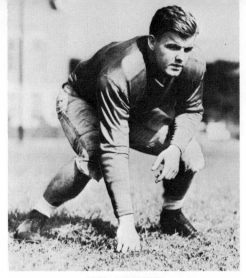

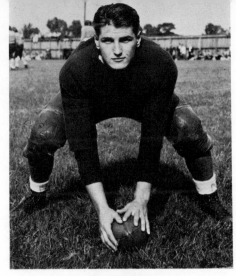

DON SCOTT   ESCO SARKKINEN   JOHN HAMAN

In 1939 the biggest of the All-America headlines went to the remarkable Nile Kinnick, Iowa's all-everything, including league MVP; and Tom Harmon, the Michigan whirlwind; but, the Big Ten had others who were honored by the selectors for their brilliant play. Among them was JOHN HAMAN, a magnificent center for Northwestern.

Ohio State's Big Ten champions supplied ESCO SARK-KINEN, a slashing defensive star and pass-catcher; and DON SCOTT, a 200-pound halfback who called signals, was a punishing runner, accurate passer, punter, extra-point kicker and defensive star—and, like Kinnick, he was a flyer who died in World War Two.

led the Big Ten's delegation. Heisman Trophy Winner, Big Ten MVP, and unanious All-America, he headed a Big Ten All-America contingent that included Tom Harmon of Michigan, the league's top scorer and total offense leader; Don Scott, Ohio State's triple-threat halfback; Esco Sarkkinen, the Buckeye's talented end; John Haman, Northwestern's great center; and Jim Reeder, Illinois' outstanding tackle.

Ohio State, like Minnesota, a ranking national football power, had suffered through a long basketball drought, not having tasted championship nectar since 1925. In 1939 Harold Olsen, the calm, genial Buckeye coach had speed and balance led by Captain Jimmy Hull. Ohio's great shooter and inspirational leader and his forward running-mate, Dick Baker.

The Bucks dropped only two Conference games, an early season loss to Illinois and one of the home-and-home bouts with second place Indiana, who was led by Ernie Andres, a hot shooting guard, and Bill Menke, a net-bombing forward. Andres, Hull, and Lew Dehner of Illinois, who had been a top Conference scorer for two years, were All America.

The NCAA, meanwhile, recognizing the growing popularity of basketball, got around to its first national championship tournament and when the district and regional warfare was over the finalists were Oregon, of the Pacific Coast Conference, meeting Ohio State of the Big Ten. The Buckeyes had to be content with the honor of making the first tourney finals without taking home the championship because the tall and talented westerners, led by Laddie Gale and Slim Wintermute, two All-Americas, over-

28-0, which was, to say the least, regretted in the Midwest, but the game had other implications as far as the Conference was concerned.

On June 2, 1921, official action against post-season football games was taken by the Conference, and consequently, during the next twenty-six years, although informal invitations were issued by the Rose Bowl, no Big Ten team was permitted to go.

The representatives of the Pacific Coast Conference came back almost annually with splendid arguments why a Big Ten team should appear each year. These arguments were augmented by pressure from our fine Big Ten Alumni Clubs on the coast, numbering thousands of members, who demanded that the rule be changed. The majority of the directors were for one post-season game

but many of our faculty representatives who had repeatedly taken this before their entire faculty groups were convinced the football season was long enough and should end with the regular schedule. It was argued by the various faculties that this was far too much emphasis on football. No item ever appeared with more regularity at the Big Ten meetings than that of the Rose Bowl.

Major Griffith was a strong advocate for a rule change and his untimely death just prior to the December meeting found the item still on the agenda when I became Commissioner in 1945.

At that time, I sincerely felt this question of Rose Bowl participation should be settled once and for all. The directors of the Conference at that time were Doug Mills

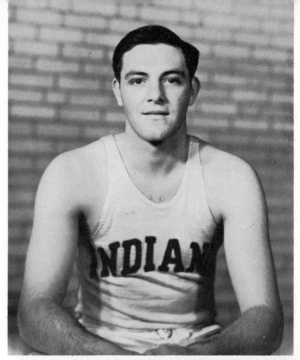

All-America JIMMY HULL, Ohio State forward, was the Big Ten scoring leader in 1939 and led the Buckeyes to the league championship and finals of the first NCAA basketball tourney, dropped by the Bucks to Oregon. Hull, however, was the tourney's leading scorer.

ERNIE ANDRES, Indiana's great play-making guard, joined Ohio State's Jimmy Hull and Illinois' Lou (Pick) Dehner, who was repeating, on the All-America basketball lists in 1939. Andres, also an outstanding infielder, later became the Hoosiers' baseball coach.

powered the Bucks, 46-33. Jimmy Hull, the Buckeye star, was high man for the tournament with 58 points in three games.

Michigan, with good team balance, took both the indoor and outdoor track crowns in 1939, but for the first time since the inception of the NCAA meet in 1921 a Conference team failed to win an individual national title.

Such was far from the case in the NCAA swimming meet, however, after the Wolverines had swum back into their accustomed title spot in the Big Ten meet, leaving Ohio State, the previous year's champ, slightly awash. Michigan stars accounted for five individual titles in the NCAA meet as the Wolverines

won the team championship for the third straight year with Ohio State right behind them. Michigan's Charley Barker succeeded Wolverine Ed Kirar as 50- and 100-yard freestyle champ, tying with Southern California's Paul Wolf in the latter. Tom Haynie scored a double in the 220 and 440 freestyle, and a Michigan foursome of Barker, Ed Hutchens, Haynie and Waldemar Tomski captured the 400-yard freestyle relay. Meanwhile, Ohio State's Harold Stanhope took the 1500-yard freestyle, and the Buckeyes' Al Patnik repeated his double diving triumphs in the one- and three-meter events.

In winning the 1939 NCAA team boxing title, Wisconsin served notice it had arrived as a peren-

of Illinois, Zora Clevenger of Indiana, E. G. Schroeder of Iowa, Fritz Crisler of Michigan, Frank G. McCormick of Minnesota, Ted Payseur of Northwestern, L. W. St. John of Ohio State, Guy J. Mackey of Purdue and Harry Stuhldreher of Wisconsin.

No Commissioner ever started with a better group of Directors and faculty representatives than I did in 1945. The big job would be selling the game to the faculties. A careful study was made showing how we could insure there'd be practically no absences from classes by the participants, and that football as a sport had fewer class absenses than any other sport. This meant that both the Pacific Coast and the Big Ten would have to agree on a definite starting time for Rose Bowl practice, that a Big Ten team should not depart for the West Coast until classes had adjourned for the holidays.

A second major point for us, was that no member of

the Big Ten could go out two years in a row. This was to meet the arguments that one school might monopolize the Rose Bowl game by a long winning streak. It was also agreed that Conference proceeds of the game would be divided into twelve equal shares, each member of the Conference to receive one share; the participating team to receive two shares plus its traveling budget; and the Conference office to receive one share.

This was the first time that bowl receipts had ever been distributed evenly among the members of any conference and in later years the plan was to be adopted by many others. Thus, no team could get wealthy by getting the assignment. These in brief were the main arguments the Directors and Faculty Representatives carried back to their various faculty meetings.

I would be remiss in my role as a historian if I did not mention the wonderful support given by members of the

nial contender, and, in fact, in the 21 tournaments held before the NCAA dropped the sport as a team tournament event, the Badgers were to top the all-time tourney record with eight team titles and 38 individual crowns. To indicate how completely the Badgers dominated this event until its final year, 1960, it took 12 schools to capture the remaining 18 team titles, and 33 schools to collect the 161 individual crowns the Badgers missed—or an average

DALE HANSON, Minnesota's Big Ten and NCAA wrestling champ in 1939 at 128 pounds, also received the Outstanding Wrestler Award in the national collegiate tourney, the first Conference matman to gain the honor.

Although official team championships in NCAA boxing were not established until 1948, unofficial designations were made from the tourney's inception in 1932, and Wisconsin got into the act for the first time in 1938 when the Badgers took four of the eight individual titles in the national tourney. RAY CROCKER, 145-pound king, was probably the most successful fighter in Wisconsin history. In 21 dual-meet bouts from 1938 to 1940 he won 20 and had one draw, with 14 of his wins coming on knockouts. He was defeated once in five NCAA bouts in two years, losing in the semi-final of the 1940 tourney when a judge admitted he got his cards mixed and turned in his decision on the wrong fighter.

of less than three per college as compared to Wisconsin's 38.

In their title-debuting year of 1939, the four Badgers belters came out of it with individual crowns: Gene Rankin, winning the first of three 135-pound titles; Omar Crocker at 145; Woody Swancutt at 155, and Truman Torgerson at 175 pounds.

Following a team victory by Indiana in the Conference wrestling tournament, four Big Ten stars won NCAA individual titles. Dale Hanson of Minnesota not only took the 128-pound crown but was voted the outstanding wrestler of the tourney. Archie Deutschmann of Illinois took the 136-pound title; Harold Nichols of Michigan the 145-pound championship, and Chris Traicoff of Indiana the 175-pound crown.

faculty representatives: Ralph W. Aigler of Michigan, whose skill and enthusiasm in helping to sell his colleagues was tremendous; Frank E. Richart of Ilinois, William R. Breneman of Indiana, Karl E. Leib of Iowa, Henry Rottschaefer of Minnesota, Dr. G. R. Lindquist of Northwestern, James E. Pollard and Wendell Postle of Ohio State, Vern C. Freeman of Purdue and Dr. William F. Lorenz of Wisconsin.

At a special meeting of the Faculty Representatives and Directors on September 1, 1946, the deadlock which had existed for twenty-six years was ended by a favorable vote for a five-year agreement with the Pacific Coast Intercollegiate Conference permitting a Big Ten team to play a Pacific Coast team in the January 1, 1947 Rose Bowl Game. At the first meeting of the Rose Bowl Committees from the two conferences it looked like the agreement might never be signed. The Pacific

Coast Conference didn't like our no-repeat provision. They wanted our champion each year. There was a lot of controversy about the number of tickets to be allocated to the Big Ten which was finally settled at 12,500 tickets. Other provisions were hammered out, item by item until agreement was met, and the contract approved by both Conferences.

The uniting of these two great Conferences was not met with much enthusiasm on the Coast by the sports writers. They wanted the agreement to be postponed a year so that Army, which had one of their greatest teams, could appear in the Rose Bowl and many caustic things were said about both Conferences. Following the end of the football season, Illinois was selected as our representative and the Pacific Coast named UCLA.

In the first place, Illinois, although Conference champions, had lost two games to Notre Dame and Indiana

Illinois, coached by Hartley Price, succeeded Minnesota as Big Ten and Chicago as NCAA gym titlists, and it would be the first of a glittering four-year domination by the Illini. Joe Giallombardo successfully defended his tumbling and all-around titles; Erwin Beyer of Chicago held onto his side horse crown, and teammate Marv Forman picked off the long horse title.

In 1939 the NCAA began its sponsorship of the national collegiate golf championships, previously administered by the United States Golf Association. Sid Richardson of Northwestern, who had given way to teammate Chase Fannon as Big Ten Champ, was NCAA medalist, but was upset in his quest for the individual title by Vince D'Antoni of Tulane.

Iowa, which had shared the baseball title with Indiana the previous season, made history when its 1939 club won the first undisputed championship the Hawkeyes ever owned, behind Harold Haub, the league's leading pitcher with a 4-0 mark, and outfielder Jim George, the leading hitter in the Conference with .452.

In tennis, Chet Murphy, of Chicago, took the Big Ten singles title and the brother combination of Chet and Bill Murphy repeated as doubles champs, as the Maroon took their third straight team championship.

Among the winners of the Conference Scholarship Medal in 1939 were Johnny Kundla, Minnesota's great basketball player; and NCAA wrestling kings Archie Deutschman of Illinois and Chris Traicoff, of Indiana.

1940

Hitler had marched into Poland the year before. The world was at war again as the 1940's got under way. For the Western Conference it was to be a decade of doubt, uncertainty, restricted programs and a scrambled eligibility pattern. Special wartime personnel rules would create unique situations, as 17-year-old freshmen enacted varsity starring roles on campus after campus, and as the army, navy and air force shuttled service trainees from college to college for special programs, turning Badger into Wolverine, Gopher into Wildcat, Hoosier into Hawkeye. In some cases, friend became foe, and vice versa on the playing field, and in other cases trainee-athletes were denied varsity competition by military regulation.

When it was all over, great players would return from three or four years of military duty and, even though they had eligibility remaining, would find they had lost some zip on the field and some zest for the whole idea of sports as they failed to mesh, philosophically, with youngsters of 19, and became more interested in the pressing problems of getting on with their life's work.

The depression was definitely ended, by now, as colleges entered a new era of affluence and of burgeoning enrollment lists at war's end, and there was a noticeable pickup in recruiting drives and pressures. Football would reach out for new highs in attendance, and basketball would begin a quest to attain nation-wide attention virtually on a level with football. The Conference Commissioner and the member schools would, indeed, have their work cut out for them on the administrative front.

Looking, then, to the fields of competition . . . Just as anyone is entitled to an occasional off-day, so had Minnesota been entitled to its off-season in 1939, but the Gophers lost no time in reasserting themselves in 1940. There were some close escapes, however, and it took some glittering heroics to turn a few doubtful situations into a perfect season.

George (Sonny) Franck, the chief architect of the Viking assault; Bruce Smith, Bob Sweiger, Bob Paffrath and a brilliant sophomore, Bill Daley, operated behind a line featuring Urban Odson at tackle; Helge Pukema a great guard; and Bob Fitch and Bill Johnson, two superlative ends. If reaction to pressure is a mark of a good team, the 1940 Gophers were well-stamped. Six times that year

and there was some West Coast suspicion that the Illini weren't exactly a glamour club. In fact, critical sports writers on the Coast bluntly referred to them as second-rate. (The taste of that phrase would come back, soon, to haunt them.) UCLA was immediately installed as a heavy favorite, but the damage had already been done to the West Coast cause.

Illinois read all the papers calling them a second class team, and the Illini were really ready to go. As Commissioner, I had an opportunity to sense the feeing that had been created against the start of the Bowl Pact, when I spoke briefly at the Los Angeles Times Sports Awards Dinner. It was my bad luck to follow a young football player named Glen Davis. A California boy, he was the star of the great team from West Point that year, and he was receiving an award as the best college football player in the country. When he spoke, he said it had always been his hope to play in the Rose Bowl but, evidently, this could never happen.

I was the next speaker, and was actually booed when I was introduced. At first, I was tempted to sit down, but finally waited until they quieted down. I told them Illinois was not a second class team and that the Conference had worked hard on this pact with the Pacific Coast for many years. I even stuck my neck out by saying I thought Illinois could take care of the situation.

A crowd of 93,000—the largest yet to see a Rose Bowl game—saw the Illini do just that. They virtually scored at will on UCLA, winning 45-14. There was no more talk about a second-rate team from the Big Ten. From then on, the Coast fans would be quite willing to take our Conference selection.

HELGE PUKEMA　　　　　**BOB FITCH**

Much of Minnesota's championship success in 1940 was attributed to two exceptional linemen: HELGE PUKEMA, a tremendous guard, and BOB FITCH, a talented end.

they had to come from behind. In the opener against Washington, for instance, Minnesota trailed at half-time, 14-10, but on the second half kick-off Sonny Franck shook himself loose on a dazzling 98-yard touchdown run to put the Norsemen ahead to stay. (Franck also saved a 19-14 victory in the fourth quarter when he knocked a Washington runner out of bounds on a Statue-of-Liberty play that almost went the distance.)

It took a 42-yard scoring pass from Bruce Smith to Co-Captain Bill Johnson to break a tie with Nebraska. Against Ohio State, on a murky, muddy field in Columbus, Smith turned in a magnificent two-touchdown, 134-yards-gained performance to defeat a Buckeye team that had held a 7-6 lead. Once again Franck saved a 13-7 victory by putting a tremendous block, instead of a tackle, on goalbound Don Scott, knocking the Buckeye quarterback out

of bounds on the one-yard line as time ran out after the inspired Gopher line had held the Bucks on downs inside the five. (Amazingly enough, the Gophers brought off their victory without attempting a single pass!)

Iowa took a 6-0 lead over the Gophers but Franck quickly went on a four-touchdown rampage in a 34-6 victory. Northwestern led Minnesota, 6-0, and it took Joe Mernik's chips-down place-kick for the extra point for the 13-12 win, after Bob Sweiger took the starring role with two slam-over touchdowns.

Tom Harmon tossed a touchdown pass to Forest Evashevski to give Michigan a 6-0 lead in a game billed as a battle for the national championship. Soon afterwards, Michigan's Ed Frutig blocked one of Franck's punts and when the Wolverines recovered on the Minnesota two it looked like it was all over, but the Gopher line stacked up Harmon and West-fall, and then Bob Paffrath intercepted Harmon's pass in the end zone.

Taking over on their twenty, Minnesota switched halfbacks on second down, with Bruce Smith going to right half to execute Bierman's machine-like single wing reverse. With the Michigan line not quite knowing whether to key on Franck or Smith, the latter took the hand-off, smashed over his own left tackle on the reverse and went 80 yards for the score. Again, Joe Mernik's toe brought the extra-point victory. For the third straight year Tom Harmon had failed to score against Minnesota, failed to beat Minnesota, and failed to play on a title team.

In the finale with Wisconsin, a whole season's work seemed headed for the drain when the Badgers took a 13-0 lead before Bill Daley and Bruce Smith got touchdowns which tied things up. Joe Mernik's talented toe produced a field goal for the go-ahead points and Franck took an intercepted pass 20 yards for the final score as the comeback Gophers nailed the title and another national championship.

The season was notable, too, for other developments. Ohio State, with a wealth of material, and

---

In the 1947 Spring meeting, the Conference took official notice of the retirement of four veterans who had a combined total of nearly 80 years of service to the Big Ten, and had played a tremendous part in its affairs. They were L. W. St. John, Ohio State's athletic director for 34 years; Z. G. Clevenger, who had served Indiana for 23 years as coach and director; Dr. William F. Lorenz, faculty representative at Wisconsin for 11 years; and E. G. Schroeder, University of Iowa, director for 11 years. The Conference membership had been changing rapidly. Fritz Crisler had succeeded Yost at Michigan; Doug Mills was now the athletic director at Illinois. Dick Larkins had taken up the reins at Ohio State from L. W. St. John; Paul Brechler took over the directorship at Iowa; Bo McMillin had succeeded Clevenger at Indiana. (He was to remain there only one

year and then the lure of professional football took him from the Conference and he was succeeded by Paul J. Harrell.) At Minnesota, Frank McCormick was in charge. Northwestern had selected Ted Payseur when I had resigned to become Commissioner. At Purdue, Guy J. Mackey had been made director, and at Wisconsin, Harry Stuhldreher was director.

These were men who would have charge of the athletic destinies of the Conference in the post-war era now under way. They were all capable and dedicated men but I doubt if any could foresee the tremendous problems ahead. All had tremendous athletic facilities, which their schools were outgrowing and had to be replaced with better and larger ones. Many of them had athletic budgets that had grown to over $1 million a year, and their budgetary troubles were just getting started. These

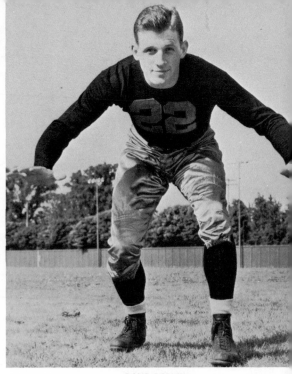

GEORGE (SONNY) FRANCK   MIKE ENICH   DAVE RANKIN

picked as potential national champion, unexplanably collapsed. First, the Buckeyes blew a 6-3 decision to underdog Northwestern, with Bill De Correvont grinning widely as he cracked over from the five with the winning touchdown.

Next, it was the Gophers who stopped Ohio on downs inside Minnesota's five-yard line in pinning a 13-7 defeat on the Scarlet. Cornell then repeated its Ivy-tinged humiliation of the year before with a 21-7 smacking, and Tom Harmon and his mates ran wild in a 40-0 affair destined to be the last game for the Bucks under Francis Schmidt.

At Illinois, disenchanted fans were chipping away at Bob Zuppke who for only the second time in his 38-year career had failed to win a Conference game.

There was a generous contribution of Big Ten stars in the galaxy of honor listings in 1940. Tom Harmon and Sonny Franck were unanimous All-

Conference All-America designees in 1940 included Minnesota's brilliant triple-threat halfback, SONNY FRANCK; Iowa's ironman tackle, MIKE ENICH; and Purdue's swift versatile end DAVE RANKIN.

America halfbacks; Mike Enich, of Iowa, and Minnesota's Urban Odson were All-America tackles, and Ed Frutig of Michigan and Purdue's Dave Rankin were named as ends. The league's MVP: Harmon of Michigan, who closed out his fabulous three-year career in all games with 33 touchdowns, 237 points, and 3438 net total yards gained—the most glittering collection of offensive records in Conference history.

The 1940 basketball season again proved out the biennial pattern for Purdue. The Boilermakers took the league title but suffered the unusual humiliation of dropping its two Conference losses to second place Indiana. The Hoosiers, however, had trouble

---

were the men I had literally grown up with and I knew I would have their wholehearted cooperation in Conference matters.

One of the important things in a well-run Conference is to have a similarity of academic rules. I saw some immediate difficulty in a regulation two institutions had regarding eligibility. These two members had a faculty ruling that a failing grade could be removed by a special examination. Several of their top athletes availed themselves of this opportunity. It was like getting a second turn at bat after you had struck out. This we prohibited in the meeting in May, 1947.

There were other things I found that also needed immediate attention. First was football officiating. With the advent of a 9-game schedule and the pressure of a 5-man officiating crew, I found it necessary to enlarge my

officiating staff. We had also begun to lose some of our capable men to the professional league. I had inherited a great group from Major Griffith: men such as Cap Hedges, Irish Krieger, Frank Birch, Don Lourie, John Schomer, Ernie Vick, and many others, but they were beginning to age and were not as active on the field as they had been in the past. Now I was in the recruiting business. I quickly found that the best method was to hire young officials who had made their reputation in smaller conferences and, of course, desired to work in the Big Ten. This took a lot of screening and careful observation of their capabilities because with our tremendous crowds and pressure, good officiating was extremely important. Some of the first men that I added were Jay Berwanger, Mike Delaney, Ross Dean, Elliott Hansan, Charles Leadbetter, Dewitt Gibson, Dal Marvil,

handling some lower-rung lodge members—Minnesota, Northwestern, and Ohio State—and thus blew their big opportunity.

Strangely enough, Purdue took the title without a single player in the top five Conference scorers, the first time this had ever happened. The Boilermakers had fine balance, and were led by Captain Fred Beretta, a superb all-around star, and sizzling sophomore Don Blanken, their leading scorer.

The outstanding player in the Conference, however, was Bill Hapac, Illinois forward, the loop's number one scorer and one of its top rebounders. Hapac was a virtually unanimous All-America. At Michigan State, Chet Aubuchon, a star backcourt

man for three years, was being hailed as the greatest player thus far in Spartan history.

The NCAA tournament of 1940 provided the Big Ten with a chance to come up with high drama. In the early years of the tourney, eight teams were selected by vote to represent eight districts of the nation. (In 1951 the rules would be changed to give certain league champions automatic nomination.) In the midwest district embracing the Big Ten, the judges noted the fact that Indiana, after a shaky start in the Conference race, came back with nine straight league victories, including two conquests of Purdue, the Conference champion. Indiana was selected as the district representative to the NCAA

Captain FRED BERETTA, Purdue guard, led the Boilermakers to the 1940 basketball championship and won All-America honors along with Illinois' BILL HAPAC,

the league's outstanding performer, and CHET AUBUCHON, of Michigan State, a three-year backcourt star for the Spartans and their first All-America cager.

CHET AUBUCHON   FRED BERETTA   BILL HAPAC

Remy Meyer, George Rennix, Bill Orwig, Mike Layden and Don Elser. I put in a suggested retirement age of 55. This didn't meet with a lot of enthusiasm with some of the older officials, but the changing style of football required speed and agility. I made it a rule to never hire an official until I had first carefully investigated his business or professional work. These men met several times during the season, took rule examinations and, at each game, I had an observer give me a report on their work.

The advent of football movies had presented quite a problem. A football coach might write me a letter on Monday saying what a fine job our officials had done but two or three days later, after he had carefully reviewed his films he might tell me that there were glaring mistakes made in the game. I wanted the coaches to

know the officials better so each Spring we would have a two-day outing, inviting the football coaches to play golf with the officials and we soon established a better *rapport*.

Training and hiring basketball officials was equally important. With the advent of great field houses and tremendous crowds, we needed the best basketball officials we could obtain. As I started as Commissioner there was a fine nucleus headed by: Jim Enright, Bill Haarlow, Nick Kearns, John Schomer, Stanley Feezel and Lyle Clarno. Some of these men also officiated in football. As these men grew older I tried to obtain good officials from all over the Conference territory and found that the states of Ohio and Indiana furnished the most because they had many small colleges where these men were being developed. When it came time for Bill Haar-

Captain MARV HUFFMAN led the 1940 Indiana basketball team to the first 1000-point season in league history, and then paced the Hoosiers to a resounding victory over Kansas for the NCAA title. Huffman also won the first MVP award given in the tourney.

The key to Branch McCracken's success as one of the nation's outstanding basketball coaches might be a competitive spirit best exemplified by a unique record. Any time a dubious foul was called against one of his Indiana University cagers, Branch McCracken emitted a sound like a steam calliope gone amok, and then exploded off the bench, straight up, to a consistent height of 9 feet 4½ inches. (Verified by no less than three official observers as required by Irate Basketball Coach-Watchers rules.)

It was not always like that. Once upon a time, just after World War One, Branch McCracken was a farm boy in Monrovia, Indiana. He was one of the most placid kids in Morgan County until one day, as the story goes, a friend came by with a pig bladder and a bicycle pump. They pumped the pig bladder full of air until it reached a lop-sided but somewhat roundish proportion. The next step was to nail a bottomless peach basket to the barn door. That was it. Instant basketball, barnyard style. Branch McCracken was hooked, and the genesis of a unique record was spawned for posterity in addition to a lot of other things that would go into the make-up of the man who became, and still is, an institution at Indiana University.

For instance, in McCracken's area of Indiana, as a youth, no high school played football. Indeed, young Branch had never even seen a game of football before he entered college—but that didn't prevent him from becoming one of the great ends in the Big Ten of his day.

First, however, back to Monrovia. Young Branch, sprouting like a Hoosier corn stalk, got his hands on a real basketball when he entered high school, and starred for four years as a husky, 195-pound, 6-3 center. On entering Indiana he was called "Doc," because he'd always loved domestic animals and fully intended to be a veterinary doctor and go back to Monrovia to hang out his shingle. Shortly after McCracken arrived on the Bloomington campus, veterinary medicine lost out to Indiana Fever, the endemic malady that made the Hoosier state the number one basketball area in the nation. It was apparent from the start that McCracken was going to be high on the list of all-time Hoosier hot-shots.

He starred immediately as a sophomore, leading Indiana to a Big Ten title. He made All-Conference his junior

tournament. Youthful Branch McCracken, in his second year at the helm, led his Cinderalla team to early round triumphs over Springfield and Duquesne and then turned them loose in the finals against a Kansas team that had been the first club in the Big Eight to score over 1000. Indiana was, itself, the first Big Ten team to go over 1000 points in a season. The Hoosiers, led by Captain Marv Huffman, Bill Menke and Bob Dro, blew the bigger Jayhawkers off the floor, 60-42, to become the first Big Ten team to take the NCAA title. Huffman won the first most-valuable-player award to be given in the tournament.

low to retire, he took a tremendous load off my back by proving to be a genius in selecting and training officials who were to become known all over the United States.

The directors gave me fine backing in this respect. The Big Ten paid the highest fees for football and basketball officials of any Conference in the country with the exception of a few individual games worked in the Ivy League. Basketball officiating had especially come under close scrutiny because of scandals rising out of point-fixing arrangements with gamblers.

Naturally, this caused a close scrutiny of the basketball officials who, if they were so inclined, could call fouls at the right time to make the score come out as the gamblers wanted. After a close study, the Conference put in many precautionary measures, starting with the players. They were given firm instructions to report any individual who

approached them with point-fixing suggestions. Secondly, all coaches were told to restrict any calls to the hotel rooms where the team was housed, and each coach was to ask his players not to discuss team injuries. I instructed officials not to discuss the teams, or players in any games to which they had been assigned. Working with Bill Reed, we arranged to get information from one of the major odds-making centers where the line odds for all games were established. If the odds suddenly shifted drastically in a situation where any of our officials were working, we observed this man with great care, especially if he had called an unusual number of fouls. We had some stiff interrogations at times to determine whether a couple of our officials might be under suspicion. While the reports on these men were not conclusive, there was enough evidence so that I could ask

Indiana's Branch McCracken demonstrates the one-hand push shot. Although considered a showboat shot, McCracken used it as a deadly scoring weapon.

and senior years and climaxed his career as All-America after he'd broken the existing Big Ten scoring mark with 147 points in his final season. His 366 points for three years was more than a third of his team's total point production for the three seasons. This was still the day of the center jump after each goal, and scoring, of course, was slowed down. It also took a lot out of the center who had to get up there for forty or fifty tip-offs each game. Control of the tip meant control of the ball and, although he wasn't always the biggest man around at 6-3, McCracken seldom lost it.

He was particularly adept in the standard pivot play of the day, stationing himself just underneath or out front of the bucket (the rules, then, permitting an unlimited time in the scoring area). He had great fakes with head and hands, and had marvelous agility in whipping around his defensive man for a lay-up. Meanwhile, he was one of the first collegians to use the one-hand push shot. Later, it would be permanently popular-

ized by Hank Luisetti of Stanford, but in the late 1920's it was considered showboating to shoot with one hand, except for the lay-up, and coaches quickly yanked a player who tried it. Hoosier coach, Everett Dean, knew McCracken was far from a showboat; it was a quick, natural move for Branch and he used it anywhere up to 20 feet, considered long-range bombing for that kind of shot. "I was a bit self-conscious at first," McCracken recalled later, "because I was often the only man on

Branch McCracken also played end on the Hoosier football team. He made the varsity in his sophomore year and was named All-Big Ten.

for their immediate resignation. All this was quite distasteful to me but I can happily say that Big Ten players and officials came through the era without any scandal.

Another problem in the late 1940's and early 1950's was television. I remember back in the days of radio when our schools thought that radio might hurt attendance at the games, but instead it increased football interest. Television was a different matter. Here a sports fan could often have a better view of the game than he could from the stands. After a great deal of study, the Conference voted to prohibit from the 1950 football season telecasting of games played on the home grounds of Conference institutions. At this same meeting, however, we did okay the use of football films to be made available for post-game telecasts.

Naturally, the NCAA was right in the middle of all

this. It was important that there be similar rules throughout the country. Asa Bushnell of the Ivy League was placed in the important position of director of the NCAA TV Committee. Experimentation was made and surveys carried out to study the damage television might present to attendance.

Probably the most alarmed of all the NCAA members were the small colleges who feared that football fans instead of attending their local games would sit at home and watch the big games on television. Rules were put in that no game could be televised if there were other small college games in that vicinity at the same time.

All this was working up to a large network televising of the NCAA program and the Conference in 1951 voted to go along with it.

There were many tempting offers to the Big Ten for

the floor who used the shot. But I didn't overdo it and after a while it felt natural."

McCracken was too much a natural athlete to confine himself to one sport. He had never touched a football in his life, and the game was as foreign to him as noodles to a Nigerian, but McCracken was fascinated by the sport's dynamic demands and physical contact, and decided to give it a try. With the rangy 195-pounds, a try was translatable into instant success. In his sophomore year he promptly nailed down a starting end position and, against a great Minnesota team that went through an undefeated season that year, he twice scooped up Gopher fumbles and raced for two touchdowns to gain a 14-14 tie with the mighty Vikings.

A tough blocker and tackler and a glue-fingered pass receiver because of his basketball ability, McCracken was All-Big Ten and, according to many experts, would have merited All-America with a more successful team.

Basketball, however, was McCracken's big love and when he graduated he was offered the head coaching job at Ball State Teachers College of Muncie, Indiana, where at age 22 he became the youngest college varsity coach in the country.

Eight years later, after Everett Dean decided to leave Indiana to go west to Stanford, the Indiana Athletic Board didn't even bother to set up machinery to screen applicants for the job. At Ball State McCracken had compiled one of the best small college records in the country (knocking over a lot of big-timers in the process) and the Board immediately and unanimously tendered the post to Favorite Son McCracken.

McCracken, like the Board, was no time-waster. "To play for me," he told his first Hoosier squad at the beginning of the 1938-39 season, "you've got to be ball-handlers and be able to run all night." What it meant was Indiana would play what McCracken called "common-sense" basketball which left plenty of leeway for individual initiative and frowned on too many set plays. He kept his drills under two hours daily, with the final hour devoted to race horse scrimmage with no time-outs.

Soon McCracken was the New Influence in the Midlands. His very first Hoosier club, in 1939, was mostly sophomore, held together by Captain Ernie Andres, a great guard. They were expected to be a deep second division team but they stunned the Big Ten by finishing second.

Branch McCracken was one of the few coaches in the nation to achieve a 500-victory mark. His coaching tenure covered almost a quarter of a century.

Winning 17 of 20, Indiana's three losses were all in league play, and only an upset by a lowly Michigan team in the final game of the season prevented the Hoosiers from tying Ohio State for the title—and kept McCracken from becoming the first Conference coach to win a flag his first year.

The following season McCracken took his team as far as anybody could go—winning the N.C.A.A. crown, knocking off Kansas in the finals.

Indiana finished second in the Big Ten six years in a row, but in 1953 the Hoosiers were the class of the country again, winning the Conference title and defeating Kansas again for the N.C.A.A. crown. Indiana repeated in the league the following season but faltered in defense of their N.C.A.A. title. In those two seasons Indiana won 29 of 32 games in league play.

One of the few coaches in the nation with a 500-victory mark, McCracken was the dean of Big Ten mentors, when he retired just before the 1965-66 season that would have been his 25th anniversary year as Hoosier coach.

their exclusive television rights, which would be shown regardless of the NCAA program but this would have meant loss of our NCAA membership, and was wisely turned down.

As the NCAA TV program developed, their TV Committee tried to spread the financial benefits to different areas. They limited the number of games on which an institution might appear and, consequently, many of the best games were left out. The network and sponsors naturally wanted the finest contests they could get and the Big Ten games were very much in demand. However, football fans of the Midwest wanted still more TV and, consequently, a program of regional games, which would allow more Big Ten appearances in District 4, was suggested. There was tremendous opposition at first but in the December meeting in 1953, the Conference ap-

proved an operating principle for regional televising of football games, but also released a critical statement on NCAA television plans. In Bill Reed, incidentally I had an individual who was, in my opinion, one of the best TV authorities in the NCAA. In fact, I was so immersed in my own duties as an enforcement officer that I turned much of the TV responsibility over to him.

Walter Byers, whom I had brought into athletic administration as an assistant to me, had also grown in stature in guiding the NCAA in these problems. While the Big Ten did not always agree with some of his decisions, Byers did a remarkable job in attempting to protect the interest of all NCAA members. As these progressed, we began to find out that TV created many new fans and the attendance at football games instead of suffering, showed an increase each year. Small col-

On other fronts, action was highlighted by an event a long time in coming—the first baseball championship ever won by Northwestern. Although the Wildcats had to share the flag with Illinois, with 9-3 records, there was a lot to celebrate including the fact that Stan Klores, at age 23 was the youngest coach ever to lead a Conference team to a title. (A year later Flores enlisted in the Navy and was killed in action aboard the destroyer U.S.S. Cooper in the battle of Leyte Gulf.) It was a well-knit combination of good hitting and solid defensive strength which Klores put together. Captain Fred Shinkevich, Alex Lustig, Henry Clason and sophomore footballer Bill De Correvont patrolled the outfield; Nick Conteas was at first; Dick Erdlitz, at second; George McKinnon at shortstop, and Erwin Madsen was the third-sacker. Ash Arnold was the catcher, with Fred Rosch and John Goldak providing the pitching strength.

In track, Michigan took its seventh straight indoor track title and followed it up with a fourth straight outdoor title. Four in a row, indoors and outdoors, was a new Conference record and remains so to this day. Title defenses were almost routine with the Wolverines that year as the Maize and Blue added another swimming trophy to its growing collection. Illinois did the same in gymnastics, and Delver Daly of Minnesota launched a long line of all-around championships that would be won by Gopher stars. Northwestern's tennis team took a cue from their baseball colleagues and the Wildcats netmen nailed their first tennis title in Purple history, paced by brilliant sophomore, Seymour Greenberg, who took the singles title and paired with Captain Jerry Clifford to win the doubles. In the matter of "firsts," Bill Gilbert of Ohio State became the first Buckeye to win the individual Conference golf crown, as Illinois won the team title.

It was a glittering year for Big Ten athletes in NCAA competition. In leading Illinois to the national gymnastics championship, the talented Joe Giallom-bardo became the only three-time double winner in NCAA competition when he took his third straight tumbling and all-around titles. It gave the Illini star an unprecedented career including seven individual titles. (He had also won the flying rings in 1938.) Teammate Lou Fina tied Giallombardo in the all-around, as Bob Hanning, of Minnesota, captured the parallel bars and Chicago's Earl Shanken took the long horse.

In NCAA wrestling, Michigan's brilliant Don Nichols not only took the 175-pound crown but won the Outstanding Wrestling Award in the tourney. Other national triumphs went to Bob Antonucci, the great little Indiana 121-pounder who had led the

ARCHIE HARRIS, a great halfback for Indiana in 1938-39-40, also achieved fame as Big Ten and NCAA discus champion, and was national collegiate titlist in 1940-41.

leges were not damaged as much as they thought they would be, as they readjusted their schedules, playing many of their games on Friday night.

The money going into several of the Conference schools was getting to be a sizable amount but, nevertheless, some of the members had not been chosen very often for the national NCAA program. In order to equalize the benefits of TV, I called a special meeting in March of 1955, when the Conference approved pending NCAA TV plans and voted to pool all football television rights of members and to share television proceeds equally. This meant that each director would have a substantial amount of money coming to him each year for his athletic budget.

It also helped soften the blow when the gate receipts fell off if a great Big Ten game was on the air in this territory, as all Big Ten schools share in the television rights.

The Conference was located right in the middle of a great professional football area: The Green Bay Packers, Detroit Lions, Cleveland Rams (before they moved to Los Angeles), Chicago Bears and Cardinals, who were then operating in Chicago, and later there was to be another entry, the Minnesota Vikings.

The popuarity of these teams hurt the attendance very badly at first. It is a tribute to the brand of football that is played in the Conference that the attendance has held up remarkably well.

The high schools and colleges must be protected on their Friday and Saturday schedules from professional games, or irreparable damage will result.

Meanwhile, ever since Chicago had dropped out of

Hoosiers to the Big Ten team title, and George Downes, Ohio State heavyweight.

In NCAA track, Campbell Kane, Indiana's picture-runner, won the 880 in 1:51.5; Roy Fehr, Michigan State's finest distance man to date, captured the two-mile in 9:18.9; Don Canham of Michigan tied John Wilson of Southern California in the high jump at 6'-6-⅜" and Archie Harris, Indiana's versatile football and field event star, won the discuss throw with 162'-4½".

It was in swimming, however, that it became increasingly apparent that the Big Ten—and Michigan and Ohio State in particular—was making the NCAA tournament pretty much of a private plunge, and would continue to do so for years to come. For Michigan it was the fourth straight team championship. Gus Sharement, one of two Wolverine brother stars, took the 100 freestyle in 51.8. The Maize and Blue foursome of Ed Gutchens, John Gillis, Charles Barker and John Sharemet won the 400-yard freestyle relay in 3.31; and a Michigan trio of Francis Heydt, and John and Gus Sharement sped to a 2:54.9 triumph in the 300-yard medley. Ohio State's John Higgins scored a smashing 2:23.7 victory in the 200-yard butterfly; the Buckeye's Harold Stanhope retained his 1500-meter crown in 20:15.8; and Ohio State divers were now embarked on a winning habit that would, in time, be hailed as the most astounding in acquatic history. Earl Clark displaced teammate Al Patnik as three-meter champion, but the slim, graceful Patnik took the low board championship for the third year in a row.

Among the winners of the Conference Scholarship Medal in May, 1940, were All-America Esco Sarkkinen of Ohio State, and Minnesota's fine halfback, Harold Van Every.

1941   The historian might not quite know how to highlight the 1941 Conference football season. Does he point to another in a long line of Minnesota successes (six titles in eight years) or does he recall

that for the second year in a row, Illinois—proud, honored Illinois—failed to win a Big Ten game? A saddening thing for the veteran, revered Bob Zuppke.

As far as the Gophers were concerned, it was a typical Bernie Bierman construction job, led by the brilliant Bruce Smith and Bob Sweiger at halfback and fullback, and little Herman Frickey, a scatback. They deployed behind still another typical Viking forward wall anchored by Urban Odson, Dick Wildung, and Len Levy, superlative tackles; Helge Pukema, a fine guard; and Bob Fitch, a crack end. So, the Gophers stormed to their second straight 8-0 season, Big Ten title, and National Championship. Only once, as opposed to six times the year before was there truly an anxious moment.

DAVE NELSON, Michigan's brilliant quarterback of 1941, went on to become one of football's great innovators and offensive tacticians as coach at Delaware where many of his ideas became widely copied.

---

the Conference in 1946, the league had operated as a nine-member group but there was no doubt it would eventually return to its traditional "Big Ten" status. There had been much speculation—particularly in the newspapers—over who would fill the vacancy. The University of Pittsburgh, an Eastern Independent, had made overtures to the Conference through its president, who happened to be an Iowa alumnus. The University of Nebraska, of the Big Eight, on the Western side of the Conference, had also quietly indicated it would like membership. The school that was beginning to get the most consideration however, was Michigan State College in East Lansing. Michigan's athletic director, Ralph Young, was expanding the athletic program each year, and members of the Big Ten already were scheduling the Spartans in many sports. Through President John Hannah, they made a formal request for consideration.

Prior to this, faculty representatives and directors had been invited on several occasions to different athletic events on the campus, and all were impressed with the fine athletic and academic program fostered at Michigan State College.

It was pointed out by several of our directors, however, that the Michigan State athletes were receiving Jennison scholarships, which entitled them to board, room and tuition. This was all legal under NCAA rules, but, at the time, was prohibited by the Big Ten. There was a feeling that Michigan State might have a tough time accomodating Big Ten rules, and that their athletic program would suffer.

At our December meeting in 1948, the Conference voted that Michigan State College be admitted to membership, the admission to take effect at such time as a committee of faculty representatives shall have certified

OTTO GRAHAM

Otto Graham, Northwestern's brilliant halfback, as a sophomore.

It was the 1943 football finale between Northwestern and Illinois, and a somewhat bemused charade was being presented on the field just seconds after the gun had ended the game. The scoreboard proclaimed a 53-6 Northwestern victory but the Illinois team was engaged in a rousing post-game battle for the football. It was the only thing Illinois could salvage for the day, if they could get it. In fact, the battle for the game ball was considerably closer than the contest that just ended, and the 50,000 spectators cheered wildly.

Suddenly the pigskin slithered away from a group of players just as a husky young man in civilian clothes darted onto the field from the sidelines, scooped up the ball, dashed nimbly through a knot of Illinois gridders closing in on him and escaped to the Northwestern dressing room.

It figured. The young man in civies was Otto Graham. In or out of uniform he was a tough man to bring down, and only Otto Graham would have had the irrepressible nature to do what he'd just done. It was with the same enthusiasm that Otto Graham performed on the football field, and had, in fact, that very afternoon, run for two touchdowns and completed four of six passes to lead the rout before Coach Lynn Waldorf removed his star from the game shortly after half-time and sent him in to get dressed. The week before Graham had scored three touchdowns on slashing runs and kicked three extra points in the first 12 minutes against Wisconsin, left the game, then re-entered to run back a punt 55 yards for another TD and passed to Bob Motl for a fifth score before retiring to the sidelines.

With the final game of his career, Otto Graham, a 6-1, 190-pound halfback, had closed out one of the most glittering grid careers the Big Ten—and the nation—had ever known. Nobody ever completely stopped him in 1941-42-43. In an era that preceded the T-formation and the emphasis on passing, Graham was the triple-threat in Waldorf's single wing attack. Nile Kinnick, Tom Harmon and Jay Berwanger notwithstanding, there were critics who said Graham may well have been the best pure running-passing combo the Conference had ever seen.

While the superlatives are being wheeled out, there is evidence that the black-haired, dark-eyed youth from Waukegan, Ill., rated favorable comparison with Michigan's Bennie Oosterbaan, Ohio State's Wes Fesler, and Indiana's Branch McCracken as a nominee for the most versatile Conference athlete on a genuine star basis. A three-sport performer, Graham was All-America in both football and basketball and was a fine baseball player even though he'd never played the sport in high school and had only played softball before pulling on the spikes for Northwestern.

Graham's biggest headlines—in football—were almost never printed. A knee injury as a freshman required an operation and he withdrew from school so that he might have three years of varsity basketball left if he chose to return to sports. Football was assumed to be a lost cause because, even when the injury healed, he still couldn't pivot or cut, or put much strain on the leg.

As great a prospect as he was, sports were not a one-way street for Graham. He was a music major at Northwestern. His father for 22 years had directed the Waukegan High School band; his mother was a grammar school music teacher; his older brother, Gene, had been an oboe player and soloist with the United States Marine Band. With the marine band, Gene was frequently a soloist at the White House and a favorite of President Roosevelt. Otto, himself, played the piano, violin, cornet and French horn, and was headed for a musical career.

The Big Ten, because of his injury, had granted him an extra year of eligibility if he wanted it, and in the spring of his freshman year his leg felt pretty good and he allowed his friends to talk him into trying football again and he reported for spring drills. The rest is history.

Waldorf installed Graham as his single-wing tailback and later remarked that ". . . with Otto's sense of timing, his peripheral vision and his natural physical gifts of size, strength and toughness, he was the ideal running-passing threat." So Otto began threatening the league from his sophomore season on. He scored two touchdowns in his Big Ten debut against Wisconsin, followed it with a TD and a 6-yard per carry average against Michigan in a losing cause, then tossed two touchdown passes to hand Paul Brown's first Ohio State team its only defeat of the 1941 season. Before Otto was finished he set a career mark of 157 completions for 2163 yards on 334 attempts—very fancy flinging for those days before the aerial blizzards we have today. He led the league in passing in his junior and senior seasons and was total offense leader as a junior. His 104 aerials as a sophomore marked the first time a Big Ten passer had come anywhere near attempting 100 tosses in one year and his 714 yards gained would stand up until the real aerial barrages of the 1950's came into play.

Graham's 1942 season record of 89 completions out of 182 attempts, including a brilliant 20 for 29 against Michigan, merely set the stage for his senior year when his all-around virtuosity brought him All-America honors and the Conference MVP award. Yet, strangely enough, Otto later insisted that his greatest thrill in football came on a single play in the College All-Star game against the Washington Redskins in August, 1943.

Graham had yet to play his final collegiate season but was one of several undergraduates selected to play against the Pros—whom they beat in an incredible 27-7 upset. Otto Graham's scythe-like block which took out two Redskins to pave the way for Bob Stuber's 50-yard touchdown on a punt return was, as Otto said, his biggest moment in football—even though he went 55 yards for a TD, himself, on an intercepted pass in the same game!

Meanwhile, Arthur (Dutch) Lonborg, Northwestern's astute basketball coach, always felt Graham was as good a cager as he was a gridder, and Lonborg had plenty of corroborative testimony from other critics. "He was a tremendous rebounder at 6-1," Lonborg said later. "Remember, there weren't the 6-5 and bigger guys around that came along after him. His fighting off the boards was ferocious, and when we had to get the ball Otto got it for us. And his passing . . . the boy was phenomenal! That football peripheral vision of his found our open man in a flash."

Graham was also one of the hottest shooters around. He was the Big Ten's second leading scorer as a sophomore (runner-up to Wisconsin's All-America John Kotz) and was second again as a junior (this time to Illinois' All-America Whiz Kid, Andy Phillip). Otto was All-America that year, himself, and would have had an even greater season as a senior but, as a Naval Air Corps officer trainee on campus, he was called into active service mid-way through the campaign.

The Otto Graham story, of course, had its most brilliant chapter written after the war when Paul Brown decided not to return to Ohio State and cast his lot with the Cleveland entry in the new All-American Conference pro league. The canny Brown of the Browns (with the club named after him) had known from the start that his building keystone for a new team would have to be a T-quarterback. There was no doubt in his mind that the best T-quarterback in the business was a man who'd never played the position: Otto Graham, the ex-single-wing tailback.

Paul Brown's perception paid off. With Otto at the throttle the Browns for 10 years were unqualifiedly the greatest organization the game had yet known. In the four years the All-America Conference existed, the Browns won 47 of 50 games and four titles. When the club moved into the NFL in 1950, Otto Graham played six more seasons, with the Browns winning three NFL championships and losing in the other three title games. Thus, Graham was the only back in the history of pro football to go to a championship game 10 times in 10 years. Along the way, his passing exploits (and quite a bit of running) brought him All-Pro selection for 10 straight years before he retired at the close of the 1955 campaign.

It is worth noting, too, that Graham, with his genius for timing and his whip-like arm, developed one of pro football's great clutch plays—the down-and-out sideline pass. Until Otto came along, the maneuver was a rare and chancy thing, particularly vulnerable to wasted efforts out-of-bounds and interceptions. Graham, however, proved it could be done, and evolved the sideline pattern into a strategic play not only effective as a ground-gainer but as a clock-stopper. Nothing illustrated this point better than the 1950 championship play-off against the Los Angeles Rams, the Browns' first such effort in the NFL. With only two minutes to go, the Browns trailed, 28-27, in possession of the ball but deep in their own territory. The Rams were in a deep-prevent and a long bomb wasn't the answer. A series of short completions might work but would kill the clock. So, with ineffable skill and aplomb Otto ate up yardage with four completed side-line passes, three of which carried out of bounds to stop the clock. It was just enough time to take the Browns to the Ram 16-yard line from which point Lou Groza kicked a field goal to win it, 30-28.

To a generation of Northwestern and Big Ten fans it was no surprise at all.

Otto Graham picks up yardage for the Wildcats against Iowa. His dazzling play earned All-America honors and the Conference MVP award.

"This club was possibly just as good as our 1934 team," Bernie Bierman later declared, "and a lot of folks have described that '34 club as the best thing college football ever put out. Well, I won't downgrade my '41 team. Our line was probably even better and if our backs had been in better physical shape I could say the same thing about them."

The one time the Gophers were in jeopardy came against Northwestern when the Vikings had to resort to an amazing bit of flim-flammery to pull off an 8-7 win. A safety on a poor Northwestern pass from center had given the Gophers a 2-0 edge, but then Otto Graham went to work for the Wildcats. First, however, there was a big hunk of frustration for the Purple when Graham fired a pass good for 78 yards and a touchdown to Bob Motl, only to have an official detect an ineligible receiver downfield, nullifying the score. A few minutes later, after an exchange of punts, the Wildcats clawed back and this time Graham flipped one to Budd Hasse that stayed on the scoreboard.

The 7-2 count loomed grim for the Gophers in the second half, with both Bruce Smith and Herm Frickey out with injuries. It was time for the hanky-panky. Bierman had conceived it as a last-ditch measure in a scoring emergency. Minnesota got the ball on a blocked punt on the Purple 41, and, as previously planned, the first play in the next series was to be a set-up with Bob Sweiger deliberately being stopped for no-gain on a play near the left sidelines that would necessitate bringing the ball in 15 yards.

Alf Bauman, the Wildcats' great tackle, was the lone defender who smelled something. "Watch out!" he yelled, but it was too late. The Gophers had lined up in a hurry without huddling, with every lineman to the right of the center, Gene Flick, who stood facing the Minnesota goal. Flick snapped a quick shovel pass to scatback Bud Higgins and Higgins set sail for the opposite sideline. Then he turned the corner and headed toward the North-

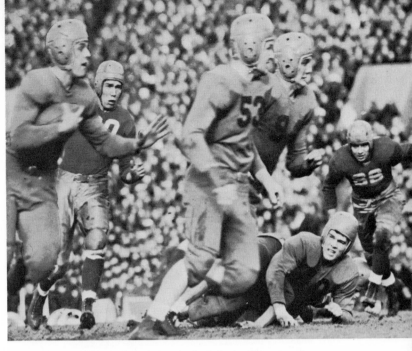

It was blocking like this which led to Minnesota's triumphant season in 1941. Captain BRUCE SMITH sweeps to a touchdown against Wisconsin behind blocking by JOHN BILLMAN, No. 53, and tackle DICK WILDUNG, No. 94. Halfback BILL GARNAAS, No. 40, has already leveled a Badger.

western goal 41 yards away. Urban Odson wiped out two Purple defenders with a single block near the goal line and Higgins was across for an 8-7 Minnesota victory. Northwestern raised a storm of protest, claiming an illegal play. Referee John Getchell— coincidentally the official who had called the crucial slugging penalty against Ed Widseth in 1936, enabling the Wildcats to snap Minnesota's great winning streak— affirmed, however, that the ball was in play and that all Minnesota players were on-side and upheld the legality of the maneuver.

Successive triumps over Nebraska, Iowa and Wisconsin firmly established the Golden Gophers as the nation's number one team for the second year in

---

to the Conference that the rules and regulations and other requirements of the Conference were completely enforced at that institution.

I accompanied the committee of faculty representatives to East Lansing early in April and, after going through all of Michigan State's various phases of administration of athletics, concluded they were in compliance with the Conference rules. We reported this to the faculty representatives and directors at the May meeting in 1949, and they were admitted to membership. It was also voted that Conference competition by Michigan State College would begin with the academic year of 1950-51, and in the case of football at the expiration of schedules previously drawn (at the December, 1948, meeting Conference football schedules had been drawn through the 1952 season). By the time tne Spartans were included for football in 1953, the Conference learned that the

infant member was a very lusty one on the field of play.

There was no question by now, after each directors and faculty meeting, that the trend definitely was toward tightening our rules. Probably the best example of this was in the meeting of March 11, 1950, when the Conference adopted an eligibility rule requiring that a student, to be eligible for intercollegiate athletic competition, must maintain normal progress each year toward his degree. The significance of this was that it stopped the isolated practice of an athlete gaining eligibility in his sophomore year, playing through the football schedule and completing that semester, then withdrawing from school and not re-entering until the next fall, when he would play again. The new eligibility rule required that a boy who, for example, was in his third football season also had to be a junior in academic standing.

Then, in May of 1951 the faculty representatives and

For two years, 190-pound JACK GRAF had been an obscure third-string quarterback at Ohio State, and did not even win a letter. As a senior in 1941, in Paul Brown's first year as coach, Graf moved into the number-one spot and his running, passing and punting won him the league's MVP trophy.

a row, but there were other events of a football nature worth noting. Michigan and Ohio State played their first tie game in Big Ten competition, and it was a 20-20 bash which saw the teams incredibly alternate six touchdowns and two of three extra points en route to the stand-off for second place in the standings. Each had only one loss for the season: The Wolves losing to Minnesota, and Ohio falling before Northwestern, 14-7.

Jack Graf, the Buckeyes' versatile quarterback, was the comeback story of the year as he went from two seasons of third-string substituting to the kind of stardom that brought the Conference MVP award. Illinois, with an unprecedented two straight season's without a league victory, accepted with mixed emo-

tions the news at season's end that the brilliant and honored Bob Zuppke had resigned. For Illinois, the Big Ten, and for college football, it was the end of an era.

On the All-America rolls for the season, the Big Ten took pride in Heisman Trophy winner Bruce Smith, Minnesota's superlative halfback; Bob Westfall, Michigan's battering fullback; Alf Bauman, Northwestern's brilliant tackle, and Wisconsin's Dave Schreiner, a gifted, all-around end.

In basketball, Wisconsin dropped its first Conference game of the season to Minnesota, checked its errors, and went on to knock over 11 straight league foes and nip Indiana for the title in a head-to-head meeting. It was a great comeback for a team that had finshed ninth the year before. In fact, it was the first and only time in loop history that such a reversal had been made from one year to the next. Largely responsible for the Badger surge were Captain Gene Englund, an All-America center; sparkling sophomore John Kotz, and steady Teddy Strain. Meanwhile, Joe Stampf, of Chicago, had taken a leaf from Bill Haarlow's book and the Maroon sharpshooter, with a 10th place team, won the league scoring title.

Selected as district representative to the NCAA tournament, Wisconsin disposed of Dartmouth and Pitt in elimination rounds and then, in a thrill-packed final in which the score was tied five times, the Badgers defeated Washington State for the national championship, 39-34. Englund and Kotz got 25 points between them and Kotz received the tourney MVP award.

Michigan, in 1941, had another go-go year in other sports. The Wolverines pinned up the baseball flag and won their first tennis title in Big Ten history, dethroning Northwestern despite the fact that the Wildcats' great Seymour Greenberg repeated as singles champ and won the doubles crown with Gene Richards. Michigan also took an unprecedented fifth straight swimming championship and added the NCAA crown as well.

directors voted approval of a reorganization of the Conference rules and regulations which more clearly defined the jurisdiction of the faculty representatives and the directors in matters of Conference legislation, and which established the Commissioner as the primary enforcement agency of all legislation. This more clearly defined my duties and laid absolute responsibility of enforcement in my hands.

After long discussion, it was provided that all penalties imposed by the Commissioner and the Conference would be announced publicly. It was felt that when these penalties were carried by the press it would serve as a deterrent to similar offenses. The ironic part was that the more I dug up with my investigations, the worse it made the Big Ten appear to the public. I shuddered many times when the reports of the big investigations took

place. During all of them I worked hand in hand with the NCAA and frequently they would place their own investigators at my disposal. Our faculty, directors and presidents backed me completely, and I believe, distasteful as it was, we were serving to clean up intercollegiate athletics, not only in the Big Ten, but in other areas as well.

I think I should point out that, inevitably, one of the critical areas of a Commissioner's job in the Big Ten or any Conference, is the constant headache brought on by the intensive recruiting of high school athletic stars. Though a Commissioner's job is one of the most interesting in athletic administration he must be constantly on the alert for the excesses which creep into college sports. It is because of these excesses that the Big Ten has such stringent rules and regulations, and it

DAVE SCHREINER

ALF BAUMAN

BOB WESTFALL

BRUCE SMITH

Four Big Ten stars were high on the lists of All-America selectors in 1941: Minnesota's BRUCE SMITH, the superlative triple-threat halfback; BOB WESTFALL, Michigan's great spin-buck fullback; ALF BAUMAN, Northwestern's tackle terror; and DAVE SCHREINER, Wisconsin's gifted end, who later was killed in World War Two.

Captain GENE ENGLUND and soph JOHN KOTZ led Wisconsin to the league cage title in 1941 and then on to the NCAA championship. Englund capped his career with All-America honors and Kotz was awarded the NCAA MVP trophy.

Wisconsin's Big Ten and National Collegiate champions of 1941. First row, left to right: Bob Alwin, Bob Sullivan, Fred Rehm, John Kotz, Gene Englund, Charles Epperson, Ted Strain, Harlow Scott, Ed Scheiwe. Back row: Manager Morris Bradley, Trainer Walter Bakke, Ed Downs, Bob Roth, George Affeldt, Warren Schrage, Don Timmerman, Ted Deppe, John Lynch, Ed Jones, Coach Bud Foster, Assistant Coach Fred Wegner.

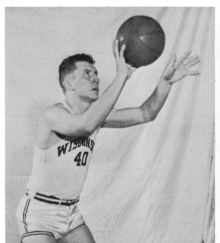

JOHN KOTZ

GENE ENGLUND

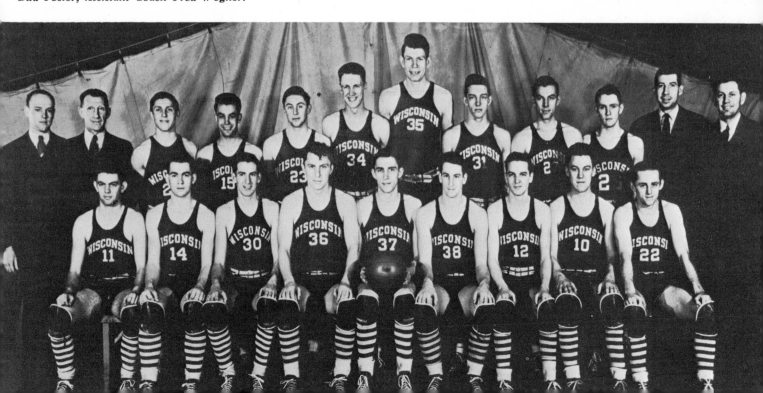

CATON COBB

COURTNEY SHANKEN

EARL SHANKEN

Big Ten gymnasts had a sparkling year in 1941. Illinois' CATON COBB, and Chicago's brother combination of COURTNEY and EARL SHANKEN, all won Big Ten and NCAA championships. (The following year Earl Shanken's third straight side horse victory would make him the only Chicago athlete ever to win three NCAA crowns.)

SEYMOUR GREENBERG was the first in a long line of great Northwestern tennis stars. He was two-time Big Ten singles champ in 1940-41 and three times paired with a teammate to take the doubles crown.

FRED WILT

CAMPBELL KANE

FRED WILT, Indiana distance ace, was NCAA two-mile champ and Big Ten and NCAA cross-country champ in 1941. Teammate CAMPBELL KANE repeated as national half-mile king; Archie Harris, Indiana football and track star, repeated as national discus champ; and Ohio State's league champ, Bob Wright, scored a double in NCAA low and high hurdles.

BOB WRIGHT was one of the all-time collegiate hurdling greats at Ohio State. He was Big Ten champ and scored brilliant doubles in the NCAA high and low hurdle crowns in 1941 and 1942.

Michigan State had the distinction of providing twin wrestling champions for the only time in NCAA history *when BURL, left, and MERLE JENNINGS took the 128 and 121-pound crowns respectively in 1941.*

Minnesota had gone a long time between wrestling championships but under Coach Dave Bartelma the Gopher matmen took their first crown since 1913. Illinois for the fourth year in a row captured the Conference gymnastics title, but the all-around individual crown went to Minnesota's marvelously co-ordinated Newt Loken, later coach at Michigan. Alex Welsh, Illinois' golfing great, taking individual honors, led the Illini to a repeat team championship, and Indiana swept both the indoor and outdoor track championships. Fred Wilt, the Hoosiers' great distance star, won the individual cross-country crown but Purdue nosed out the Hoosiers for the team title. Wilts' clocking of 21:01.5 was a new Conference record for the standard four-mile course.

In was a good year, too, for Conference schools in NCAA competition. In gymnastics the league won more titles than any other conference in the history of the sport as Illinois ran off with the team crown for the third straight year. Caton Cobb took the side horse and parallel bars for the Illini, and teammates John Adkins and Lou Fina won the tumbling and free exercise respectively. Courtney Shanken, of Chicago, captured the rope climb and the all-around upsetting Big Ten title-holder, Newt Loken, in the latter event. Loken, however won the horizontal bars with Gopher teammate Del Daly winning on the flying rings. Earl Shanken's win on the long horse made it quite a family affair for Chicago.

In NCAA track, Indiana's long-striding Cambell Kane retained his 880-yard crown in a sizzling 1:51.2 as teammate Fred Wilt took the two-mile in 9:144.4. Still another Hoosier, Archie Harris, repeated as discus champ with a record toss of 174 feet, 8 and three quarter inches. (Wilt, incidentally, made it a big year by also taking the NCAA individual cross-country title.) The Big Ten added two more track crowns when Bob Wright, a speedy perfectionist from Ohio State, captured the 120-yard high hurdles in a scorching 14-flat and the 220-lows in an equally brilliant 23.4.

Two Conference swordsmen took individual championship with Ed McNamara of Northwestern and G.H. Borland of Illinois winning in foil and epee respectively.

Three league stars won wrestling crowns, with Michigan State's twin combination of Merle and Burl Jennings taking the 121-and 128-pound titles, and Len Levy, Minnesota footballer, capturing heavyweight honors. Wisconsin's tough, speedy Gene Rankin won the 135-pound NCAA boxing championship and in swimming Michigan poured it on again as Matt Mann's splashers took their fifth straight team title. Charley Barker regained the 50-yard freestyle crown he had won as a sophomore but lost as a junior, when he sped home in 23.5; Jim Welsh took the 440-yard freestyle in 4:51.4; Francis Heydt won the 150-yard backstroke in 1:37.7, and Jim Skinner won the 200-yard butterfly in 2:25.9 for the fourth Wolverine individual title. Then a Michigan trio of Heydt, Skinner and Clair Moore added the 300-yard medley in 2:58. Meanwhile, Earl Clark, Ohio State's graceful diver, retained his three-meter championship and added the one-meter title which his graduated teammate Al Patnik, had held for three years.

Again headliners were among the Conference Medal winners, the honor going to Sonny Franck, Minnesota's All-America halfback, and Forest Evashevski, Michigan's great quarterback.

The 1942 football season was the last normal campaign of the wartime years before emergency regulations and quixotic personnel switches came along to make a guessing game of the sport. The lodge members made the most of what turned out to be a brilliantly wild season.

Paul Brown, having taken one year to familiarize himself with big-time head-butting after his amazing career at Massillon, Ohio High School, came up to his second season at Ohio State ready to hand-wrestle a grizzly bear. His Bucks had the muscles

1942

---

is the enforcement of these rules that any Commissioner must contend with at all times. It is truly a complex situation.

Let's take a look at the Big Ten with thousands of alumni concentrated in the Midwest. The alumni are the real strength of an institution in many different facets. They work unceasingly, give generously to the university foundations and take great pride in their Alma Mater's accomplishments; academic, scientific and athletic. Usually the place to blow off steam and to become vocal with their feelings is while watching their teams on the athletic field. The transformation of the dignified business tycoon who can handle his affairs with quiet demeanor, to the uninhibited cheerleader is truly a social study.

The impact of the college athletic programs has made

its imprint on the social life of America. It's a tremendous thing to have thousands of alumni and friends come to games. Football and the other sports have been the means of keeping alumni interest centered around their university and I have admired the skill with which Presidents of the Big Ten, alumni secretaries and faculty make the most of these alumni visits.

Now, the Big Ten is a conference so evenly matched that on any given Saturday any team could conceivably defeat any other. Sometimes this is where your troubles start as a Commissioner. Alumni of one institution see their team hopelessly outmatched. They realize they have a good, sound coaching staff, so the next thing is for them to get better material for the team. They insist on the recruiting program being stepped up.

This, of course, is met with great approval by the

PAUL BROWN, after a sensational career at Massillon, Ohio, High School, replaced Francis Schmidt at Ohio State in 1941, and in 1942 led the Buckeyes to the national championship. Later, he would achieve lasting fame in professional coaching ranks with the Cleveland Browns.

nomenal; Les Horvath and Tom James at wingback, and Gene Fekete, a sensational sophomore fullback who was to lead the league in scoring. The Ohio line was not overly large but was tough and agile, and the Buckeyes, in all their history, had never presented a better end-tackle-guard trio than Bob Shaw, Chuck Csuri and Lindell Houston.

Brown, the precision-minded drill-master, provided the Scarlet with a mixture of single wing, short punt and the new-fangled T, and his pupils made it go. The Conference went to 10 games that season to accomodate service teams on the schedule, and the high-geared Buckeyes rolled to a Big Ten and National Championship with a season total of 337 points, the second highest output in modern Big Ten history, just under the Minnesota record of 348 in 1916.

The Buckeye effort, however, suffered a single flaw. Romping along with five straight wins and basking in a barrage of superlative adjectives, they invaded Wisconsin to meet a Badger team whose record showed five straight victories and a 7-7 tie with Notre Dame. The Bucks were a solid 10-point favorite but this was a Wisconsin club which felt it should rate some flattering adjectives themselves. Slick quarterback, Jack Wing, called the shots for a backfield that included rampaging Pat Harder at fullback, and a wild-running halfback named Elroy (Crazy Legs) Hirsch. Up front Coach Harry Stuhldreher had such superlative operatives as the brilliant Dave Schreiner at end; Paul Hirsbrunner at tackle; Fred Negus at center, and a brace of great guards, Ken Currier and Evan Vogds.

It turned out to be a ball game long to be remembered by Badger fandom. There was evidence that several Buckeyes had taken ill before the game with faulty food or water, but there was also evidence on the field that the Badgers were up for some magnificent football, and they got off to a 10-point lead in the first half. Ohio came back with a third period touchdown but Wisconsin matched it

and the mind for it, too. A big, strong backfield was headed by George Lynn, a smart, blocking quarterback; Paul Sarringhaus, a swift, 190-pound running-passing tailback who, although nearsighted, operated on an amazing, private radar system that was phe-

coaches but here is where guidance must come from the Commissioner, down through the directors and to the coaches. There is nothing wrong with good, sound recruiting kept within the rules. Our Big Ten universities recruit the top scholars and, the best graduate students as much as they would an athlete, and many times these scholars receive far greater rewards than are permitted athletes. The difficulty comes when someone,—an individual or a group, and quite often not alumni, but avid boosters of a school—decide that the legal method is too slow; that they have to have faster action. Despite the warnings of a Commissioner, or a coaching staff trying to live within the rules, they want to get the job done. What they do is nobody's business but their own, they think. The folly of such thinking is they haven't realized what it is doing to a boy's career. He is suddenly subjected to the most lavish entertainment he has ever

known. Boosters of that kind have just one idea and that is to get a boy enrolled in school. The harm comes in when an athlete finally enters the university after receiving illegal help and must falsify his eligibility statement. This fact alone could undermine the boy's character so that his whole life may be affected. He is the youngster who gets the exaggerated idea of his importance and finally adopts a policy that the world is pretty much his oyster because he can play football or basketball. Secondly, he forgets what he is really attending college for, and that is to get an education. Recruiting of this nature cannot be tolerated and in these cases, any Commissioner worth his salt must deal with a iron hand.

In contrast you find the legitimate recruiting methods which operate under the rules, where the alumnus and friends make the main selling point to the athlete on

BOB SHAW

CHUCK CSURI

LIN HOUSTON

BOB SHAW, a superlative end; CHUCK CSURI, a tremendous tackle; and LIN HOUSTON, a quick, rugged guard, helped pave the way for Ohio State's national championship season in 1942 and were the first end-tackle-guard trio to be named All-America from one school in modern history.

with another score of its own and pulled off a 17-7 victory that was one of the big upsets of the year.

Ohio State went on to roll up 165 points in its last four games, smashing Pitt, Illinois, Michigan and the Iowa Seahawks, one of the better service teams, but the Bucks needed two bizarre results from other quarters before nailing the Big Ten and National Championships. Wisconsin surely would have been recognized as the top team in the nation coming off its victory over Ohio but the triumph over the Buckeyes drained the Badgers so much they were smacked down the following week, 6-0, by an Iowa club that was a four-time loser on the season. The Hawkeyes stopped the Badgers on the one-foot line on the last play of the first half and went on to a

third period score themselves, on a Tom Farmer to Bill Burkett pass that meant the ball game.

The other assist the Buckeyes got came from still another four-time loser—Auburn—who took on all-winning Georgia, the heir-apparent to national honors after Ohio and Wisconsin had been tripped, and stunned the Bulldogs, 27-13. The Buckeyes' driving finish in their last four games was enough to impress the pollsters and the honor team pickers. Shaw, Csuri and Houston made All-America at end, tackle and guard, and were joined by no fewer than seven other Big Ten stars for the largest total yet contributed by any collegiate conference. Also named were the Badgers' Harder and Schreiner at fullback and end; Michigan's tough Albert Wistert, at tackle,

the advantages of the education he can obtain. He takes the athlete to his school and shows him every facet of college life. In his recruiting, he also attempts to acquaint the father and mother with the careful guidance their son will receive at the university, and parents certainly lend a tremendous influence when the time comes to make the decision. (After watching years of recruiting in the Big Ten, I've observed that the mother is the one to sell. The father may become enraptured over the possibility of his boy becoming an All-American but the mother wants to know what kind of a place her son is going to live in, what kind of food he will eat, what kind of coaching and guidance he is going to get, how much attention will be focused on her son's studies, and so on. She often has the last word.)

The high school athlete who is outstanding and who, in addition, is a good student has terrific pressure put on

him. Let us say he begins to show outstanding potential as a sophomore or junior. He quickly becomes a marked man for recruiters from many universities. The fact that several high schools play their football and basketball games on Friday means he will have an invitation from dozens of universities to attend the big college game on Saturday. The race is on.

The average person or fan who has no idea of what goes on in college recruiting today, can hardly believe the typical example of the red-hot halfback or the 6-8 basketball center who is being wooed by half a hundred colleges across the land. If a prospective college on his list is any distance from his home he is provided with jet plane transportation. He is met at the airport by an assistant coach; and, if he's really a tremendous candidate, the head coach, himself, will meet him. If he isn't put up at a dormitory ("to see how our boys live") he is

PAT HARDER

Wisconsin's rampaging fullback, PAT HARDER; and Minnesota's terrific tackle, DICK WILDUNG, were among the seven Conference stars on the All-America in 1942.

and aggressive Julius Franks, at guard; Illinois' Alex Agase, at guard (the first sophomore lineman honored since Bennie Oosterbaan in 1925); Minnesota's wide-ranging Dick Wildung, at tackle; and Billy Hillenbrand, probably the greatest triple-threat in Indiana history, at halfback.

Schreiner, the Badgers' brilliant wingman who could do it all on both offense and defense, was the

DICK WILDUNG

Many followers of Indiana football claim that BILLY HILLENBRAND was probably the greatest triple-threat back in Hoosier history. A 1942 All-America the 6-foot, 190-pound Indiana halfback was a swift, slashing runner who was a threat to go all the way any time he had the ball; a hard hitter inside; a fine passer and punter and a tough defensive player.

installed in a plush hotel or motel during his stay. He dines at the best restaurants, not only with the head coach but a prominent alumnus who may be an important lawyer, corporate president, or local congressman, and maybe a clutch of local All-Americans. He is taken to a fraternity and given the royal tour around campus. Someone arranges a Saturday night date with a cute freshman co-ed. With a big flourish he is taken to the Business School (to meet the Dean), or the Engineering School (to meet the Dean), or the Law School (to meet the Dean), depending on where his interest lies. Finally, the head coach, himself, takes the boy into his office, closes the door and makes the final pitch about this wonderful place "to get a good education and play good ball." Sometimes the pitch is reversed. Some coaches (I'm not talking about The Big Ten) don't pay too much attention to the educational end.

All along, this 17-year-old boy knows he's regarded as visiting Royalty. In fact, he's KING, and it's going to be HIS choice where he'll go to college. He'll let THEM know where it'll be, not vice-versa. In any event, he usually goes home after a two day stay (that's all that's allowed under current NCAA rules) feeling THIS was the place for him. He'll repeat this visit, however, five or six more times to other schools and, as often as not, he'll have much the same feeling. If he isn't level-headed and getting proper guidance from his family or high school coach, he's going to have a tough time making a final choice. (Incidentally, today he is only allowed one free trip to each school on his list. Some schools get around this by having a wealthy alumnus transport the boy for a second trip and pay all his expenses, but the alumnus must actually accompany the boy.)

As far as the Big Ten is concerned, the boy may not

Conference choice for MVP, the first lineman to be honored since Biggie Munn, of Minnesota, in 1931.

For uniqueness, a gridiron gambit pulled off by the Illini's Alex Agase, must be recorded as the item of the season. Against Minnesota, the ubiquitous Agase (subsequently to become the most-travelled All-America in Big Ten history) turned up as the only guard in league annals to score two touchdowns in one game. He stole the ball from the Gophers' Bill Daley and ran 35 yards for his first score, and late in the game picked up an errant Gopher snap from center, in the end zone, to score the touchdown that won the game, 20-13.

Tommy James, the swift Ohio State halfback, set a league rushing record when he averaged an eye-popping 11.8 yards per carry on 20 attempts.

For the 1942 basketball season, a group of sophomores had reported to Doug Mills, Illinois cage coach, and before the whistles would toot an end to their careers they would have written one of the most glittering pages in the sport's history. They also acquired the most famous nickname of any Big Ten court team—The Whiz Kids. Andy Phillip, Gene Vance, Ed Smiley, and Ken Menke were the sophs who combined with junior Art Mathisen to take the Conference title with a mark of 13-2 and 18-3 overall for the regular season. Eliminated by Kentucky in the NCAA tourney, the youthful Illini were, nevertheless, the team of the future and fans were wondering just how great they might turn out to be.

Meanwhile, John Kotz, a great Wisconsin shotmaker, led the loop in scoring and set a new league record of 16.1 points per game as he gained All-America honors. Forrest Sprowl of Purdue, Andy Zimmer of Indiana, and the great Iowa duo of Kuhl and Chapman were other Conference stars of the year, along with a Northwestern sophomore who had already made his presence known on the football field; the Purple's Otto Graham was the second leading scorer in the league.

There were some noteworthy firsts—and a last—

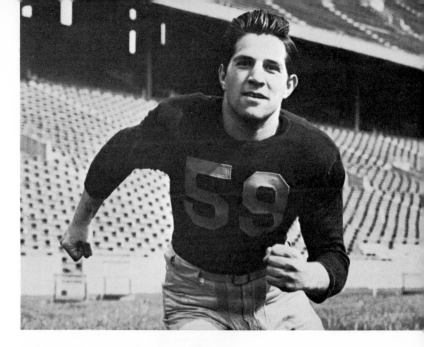

ALEX AGASE, the "wandering guard," was unique in Big Ten history. He was the only man ever to make All-America at two schools. A designee at Illinois in 1942, he was shifted to Purdue the following year for naval officer training and made the honor team again as a Boilermaker. At war's end he returned for his final year at Illinois in 1946 and was honored a third time.

among highlights of other sports of 1942. Purdue, an original member of the Conference, won its first wrestling title and Ohio State, in the lodge since 1912, captured its first track title, with the Buckeyes winning both the indoor and outdoor crowns. It was hard to believe it was the first ever for the Scarlet, but even in the glory days of Jesse Owens the Bucks had never been better than second. As for the "last," there was the Big Ten singles tennis crown won by Chicago's Cal Sawyier—the last Conference title ever to be taken by a school which, as a founder of the Western Conference, had compiled one of the most honored and successful athletic histories in American collegiate sports.

---

make his choice before April 1 (a later date for basketball and spring sports) when a letter of intent is mailed to him in which he declares his intention of going to the particular school in the Conference which has sent the tender. He has 10 days in which to sign the agreement and return it. If he doesn't return a particular tender within 10 days he automatically declares himself out of the picture for that school. (The tender, incidentally, guarantees the boy free tuition, books, room and board. Nothing more. No transportation between school and home, or spending money. It is in these areas that complexities arise and make for possible violations.)

The intelligent recruiters who spend more of their time selling the athlete on the advantages their university holds in the way of a sound education are the ones, I think, who get the best results in the long run. It is true they don't exactly talk down the athletic possibilities but they impress the boy that athletics is just one phase of their university; but the important thing is to get an education. This makes a great impression on the individual's parents.

There are certain types of recruiters with whom every Commissioner has to cope. He may be a sporting goods salesman or he may be employed by some large corporation headed by an enthusiastic alumnus and he becomes a bird dog for a particular school. He might have played football or basketball for the coach at his Alma Mater and probably merely started out as an enthusiastic booster. When it becomes apparent that he is spending at least half his time during the football or basketball season transporting athletes back and forth to the games, you have ample grounds for suspecting there might be more involved than just Alma Mater. It is hard to prove this recruiter received any compensation

CASEY FREDERICKS was the star of Purdue's first Conference wrestling champions in 1942. A Big Ten titlist at 128 pounds, he had been the 121-pound king the previous year.

It was in the late 1930's that an astounding Stanford basketball team, led by the wondrous Hank Luisetti, established itself as the first of the great modern teams featuring the then-unheard-of one-hand shot and the fast-break offense.

"How're they ever going to match 'em!" was the awe-struck cry of the nation's fans. Luisetti . . . Calderwood . . . Stoeffen . . . Lee, and the others. How do you get that many great ones to mesh as one unit?

Illinois had the answer in "The Whiz Kids," a label borrowed from the immensely popular radio program of the late '30's which purveyed the precocity of some of the nation's most brilliant children. The same label, applied to the Illinois varsity of 1941-42 and 1942-43 was the first time it was used in sports, and the hardwood precocity of five remarkably talented athletes made it appropriate. Their names: Andy Phillip, Ken Menke, Art Smiley, Gene Vance and Art Mathisen. Mathisen was a junior when the group came together; the other four were sophomores.

Dutch Lonborg, veteran coach of Northwestern, in 1943 probable epitomized the feelings of most coaches who battled Illinois those years. For thirty minutes he twisted in coachly torment on the bench one night as his nifty Wildcat team dropped deeper and deeper into defeat. After the Illinois lead got up to 22 points he sort of sighed, collapsed into a slouched position on his seat, stopped agonizing and began to enjoy it.

When the Whiz Kids had ceased their bombardment at 86 points (astonishing for that era) Lonborg leaped to his feet at Chicago Stadium and voiced the sentiments of the 19,000 fans who made up the largest college basketball crowd in history. "We've just seen," Lonborg shouted to anyone who'd listen, "we've just seen the greatest basketball team ever put together!" (Almost 20 years would pass before the names of Lucas-Havlicek-Nowell would grace one line-up, but in those earlier days of modern basketball, the Whiz Kids would reign supreme.)

Playing together as a starting unit for two straight years beginning with their sophomore season, the Whiz Kids, coached by Doug Mills, racked up records unmatched by any previous modern college team in percentage of games won and the caliber of the competition they faced.

As a sophomore-dominated team in 1942, the Illini

from the athletic department of a university but it was always amazing to me to note the tremendous activity of some of these individuals.

As Commissioner, I simply had to take their word. These statements could not be taken under oath and I had no power of subpoena if they refused to answer questions. Many recruiters of this type, I am convinced, did the job just for the privilege of being allowed to sit on the coaches' bench, receiving free tickets, and even attending the coaches' meetings and secret practices.

During my first few years as Commissioner, I uncovered something that would have led to commercialized recruiting on an inconceivable basis. A bright young avid sports fan started to send out letters to coaches, not only in the Big Ten but all over the country, in which he would list the most promising athletes in the Chicago area, giving height, weight, academic records, and other data

that many an athletic department would take weeks to accumulate. His description of some of these athletes would make any coaches' mouth water and, for a reasonable fee, he would attempt to deliver the athlete to that university. It was fortunate that one of the coaches sent me a copy of this sales sheet and I immediately contacted the young man and told him this must be discontinued. It took several hours with him, but he finally agreed to stop the publication. About that time, too, there was an all-star high school game being conducted down in Memphis, Tennessee. The promoters, in order to attract college coaches, would put out the same sort of records on the athletes. The NCAA was unable to cope with this, nor did I have any great success in convincing the sponsors this was the wrong thing to do. (The NCAA has forbade any institution to allow their coaches to participate in this type of thing but the

The Whiz Kids in 1942. From left to right—Jack Smiley, Art Mathisen, Ken Menke, Gene Vance and Andy Phillip.

won 13 of 15 to take the Big Ten crown, and were 18-3 overall. As juniors, they were undefeated, 12-0 in Conference play, and 17-1 overall, with only an upset by a talent-packed service team from Camp Grant as their lone blemish. Along the way that year, Illinois set Big Ten records of 755 points for a season; a high of 92 for a single game; the widest victory margin (62) in a game; and were the first team to win two consecutive titles since Wisconsin swung it in 1913-14.

No one could deny that the five individuals did not mesh beautifully—knowing and taking advantage of their strength and weaknesses. By the same token, there could be no denial that the one who had chief responsibility for their greatness as a unit was Andy Phillip.

Phillip arrived at Illlinois via Granite City High School, where he had led his team to the state prep title. Lithe and quick at 6-2, Phillip had been a center in high school but Mills switched him to forward. The speedy soph immediately led his yearling teammates to the Big Ten title and was named the Illini MVP. The virtually all-sophomore team lost to Kentucky in the N.C.A.A. tournament, but things looked brighter for the future.

The following season the stage was set and Phillip filled the leading role with star billing. He set Big Ten records for most points in one Conference season (255); most field goals in one season (111); most goals in a single game (16); and most points in a single game (40). Phillip's value extended far beyond his scoring. His play-making, dribbling, deft passing and rebounding made the Illini fast-break really go. He constantly set up his mates when he didn't have the shot, himself, and his defensive ball-hawking brought him the nickname

"The Thief." He was unanimous All-America and most-valuable player in the Big Ten, but disappointment was to strike Phillip, his teammates, Coach Doug Mills and Illini fans. Normally, Illinois with its 17-1 record and unblemished league mark, would have been an overwhelming favorite for the N.C.A.A. crown, but America had gone to war, and the tournament was cancelled.

Phillip was called to active duty with the Marine Corps and served three years in the Pacific. Mathisen, Vance Menke and Smiley went into the army. What would have been (for four of them) their third year together as a unit —unparalleled in major collegiate cage history—was sacrificed to a more important line-up, but not before a poll of 15 outstanding college coaches called them the top collegiate team of all time. "Most of them had not even reached their peak," Doug Mills said ruefully. "There's no telling how great they would have been as seniors."

Only Mathisen, captain of the 1943 team, had run out of varsity eligibility, but Phillip, Vance, Menke and Smiley survived the war and returned to the campus. Joining them was Fred Green who took over at center for Mathisen, but three years of military service had taken their toll just enough to dull the reflexes a smidgeon, cut the speed by a step, and put a tiny crick in the marvelous team co-ordination. The post-war Whiz Kids finished second in the Big Ten.

One year later, however, Phillip whipped himself into his old-time condition and signed with the Boston Celtics in the pro league, where he starred in the back-court for the next 10 years as one of the finest play-makers in the league.

Illinois was triumphant in gymnastics and fencing; Iowa and Michigan shared the baseball crown with 10-2 marks; Earl Mitchell, with the individual title, led Indiana to the cross-country championship; Michigan remained on its remarkable swim-crown course, and Northwestern, once again led by Seymour Greenberg in singles, and Greenberg and Bob Jake in doubles, dominated the tennis picture.

Big Ten athletes again led all collegiate conferences in snatching up NCAA championship medals. Wisconsin won the first of many team boxing crowns that would come, with four Badger belters

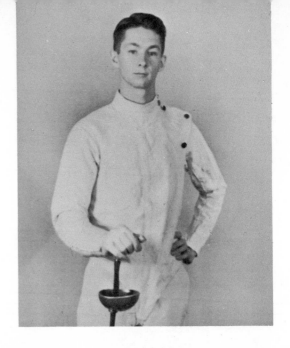

BEN BURTT became Ohio State's first national fencing titlist when he took the epee event in the 1942 NCAA tourney.

GENE RANKIN, repeating as NCAA 135-pound champ in 1942 (his third crown), was one of four Wisconsin boxers who led the Badgers to the national collegiate team title.

taking individual honors: Gene Rankin repeating at 135 pounds; Warren Jollymore winning at 145; Cliff Lutz at 155; and George Makris at 175. Jollymore also took the Outstanding Boxer Award in the national tourney.

In wrestling, Michigan State's twin duo of Merl and Burl Jennings retained their 121- and 128-pound crowns for the independent Spartans, and Illinois won its fourth straight gymnastics crown under the astute Hartley Price. Caton Cobb, leading the Illini all year, retained his side horse laurels. Newt Loken, the Minnesota whiz, repeated his all-round triumph of the year before; and Earl Shanken, of Chicago, in winning his third straight long horse title became the only Chicago athlete to win three NCAA crowns.

Indiana tied Rhode Island State for the cross-country team title and Ben Burtt became Ohio State's

sponsors got around this by hiring professional coaches to handle the teams.) Fortunately, this game did not prove a success and it was finally cancelled.

Last but not least in the recruiting picture were the high school coaches who felt they could enhance their reputations by the number of athletes they sent to big-time colleges. On the face of it, it seemed a laudable thing to have their athletes continue school but when it got to the point where they were virtually making a beaten path to any one university, you had to start looking into the whole maneuver. Many high school coaches did this, I am sure, simply to become better acquainted with some of the prominent football coaches who, in turn, would look over their offense and defense and give them suggestions that might be helpful.

High school all-star games presented many problems. Some of the stars would play in two or three games in

the summer. Some of these games were well-regulated, every precaution observed to protect the athletes from injuries and a portion of the gate receipts went to local charities. Others were not so well run, with only a couple of days practice, and many promising athletes ruined their careers in such games. These contests, of course, attracted coaches from everywhere, including the Bib Ten. It was a chance to observe some of the boys in which they were interested and see how they measured up in tough competition. It was almost impossible to police these contests and they created many recruiting problems. Probably the greatest headache of regulating the recruiting was controlling the coaches in visiting prospective athletes.

Early in my career as Commissioner, I began to get letters and calls from superintendents of high schools telling me of numerous alumni and coaches visiting the

first national fencing titlist when he took the epee event. In swimming Yale nosed out Michigan and Ohio State for the team championship and would be one of only three schools in the long history of NCAA swimming to interfere with the Wolverine-Buckeye domination of the tourney. The Big Ten was still well-represented among individual winners, however. Northwestern's Bob Amundsen took the 50-yard sprint in 23.4; Michigan's John Patten won the 220-freestyle in 2:10; John Skinner, the Wolves' star breaststroker, repeated as 200-yard butterfly champ in 2:23.7; Ohio State's Frank Dempsey, continuing the long line of crack Buckeye divers, captured both the low and high board events; and a Michigan foursome of Bill Burton, Lou Kivi, Patten and John Sharemet set a new 400-yard freestyle relay mark of 3:27.8.

Among the Conference Medal winners were Dave Nelson, Michigan's brilliant halfback and later a remarkably successful coach at Delaware; Cal Sawyier, Chicago's Big Ten tennis champ; and Ben Burtt, Ohio State's national fencing titlist.

In 1943 it was the year of the 17- and 18-year-olds as Big Ten football players went into the armed forces by the hundreds. Freshmen were made eligible for varsity play, and youngsters not yet of draft age, or 18-year-olds not yet called up, filled out squads that rostered 4-F's (physically unfit for military service) plus veteran players assigned to a college which had special naval training programs. (The army refused to allow its special trainees on college campuses to participate in varsity sports.)

Michigan and Purdue pulled some good ones out of the service grab bag as stars from other schools were assigned willy-nilly to schools which formerly were their toughest rivals. Thus did Michigan get Bill Daley, Minnesota's mighty fullback, and Elroy (Crazy Legs) Hirsch, the Wisconsin great, along with his teammate Jack Wink, among others. Purdue suddenly found itself suiting up Alex Agase, Illinois'

ELROY (CRAZY-LEGS) HIRSCH was a rampaging running star at Wisconsin in 1942 and then at Michigan in 1943 when transferred to the Wolverine campus in the wartime naval training program. He went on to become one of the greats in the National Football League as a tremendous pass-receiving end.

In 1943, BOB (HUNCHY) HOERNSCHEMEYER, an 18-year-old Indiana freshman halfback, playing under wartime eligibility rules, astounded the Conference—as well as the nation—by leading the league in total yardage gained with 277 rushing and 596 passing for an aggregate of 873, breaking marks previously set by Tom Harmon and Otto Graham.

1943

Lord Phillip Mountebatten and Tug Wilson at the British Empire Games in 1948.

star guard. Three other Minnesota luminaries, Herm Frickey, Herm Hein and Jerry Carle, got tickets to Northwestern. And so it went, with Big Ten coaches not knowing what kind of assistance they might get from Washington until the personnel popped up unannounced. Meanwhile, certain schools, such as Ohio State, Iowa, Illinois and Wisconsin had no naval trainees on campus, but at college after college the peach-fuzzed 17- and 18-year-olds performed staggering deeds alongside their older teammates. Indiana had a triple-threat phenomenon in Bob (Hunchy) Hoernschmeyer, who was gobbled up by

Annapolis the following year. Ohio State offered speedster Dean Sensanbaugher, picked off by West Point a year later. Wisconsin had a precocious triple-threat in Earl (Jug) Girard.

Almost predictably, the war of the Haves vs. Have-Nots resulted in Michigan and Purdue tying for the title with 6-0 seasons. The Boilermakers also came up with a spotless 9-0 for the year, their first undefeated campaign since 1929, and only the second in their Conference history. Much of their success was due to rampaging fullback Tony Butkovich who in only four games against Ohio State, Illinois, Wis-

TONY BUTKOVICH, Purdue fullback, who set an all-time Big Ten scoring record of 13 touchdowns (in just four games, before being assigned to active naval duty) led the Boilermakers to a share of the 1943 Conference

title and an undefeated season which was only the second in Boilermaker history. BORIS DIMANCHEFF, a nifty halfback, and DICK BARWEGAN, a great guard, were other Purdue leaders.

TONY BUTKOVICH

DICK BARWEGAN

BORIS DIMANCHEFF

high schools to find out the academic records of the better prospects. They would also use their visit to check the high school's game film and it was not unusual for the prospect himself to casually drop in and meet the coach. High school administrators felt these visits were a serious distraction to the athlete's school work because he was frequently called out of class. Corrective legislation had to be passed. I couldn't blame the coaches for doing every possible thing to attract desirable athletes; but, it was in the best interests of their schools—and of the Conference—that they stay within the rules. It was my task as Commissioner to see that they did.

The enforcement duties of a Commissioner represent his toughest and most exacting work. Granted that the responsibilities of selecting and training officials can always be demanding, and that the myriad of other duties required can be time consuming and important;

but, a Commissioner's true worth to his conference is measured by his ability to see that there is uniform adherence to the rules, not only by the athletic departments but by the thousands of alumni and friends from each school.

At this time, I think it is important to give you the rules that were published by the Conference in 1949—particularly Rule 6 dealing with Compensation, and Rule 7 on Unearned Financial Aid. These two rules will give you a background of what was permitted and what was illegal at the time. They represented years of study and covered practically every situation that could come up in the way of unearned or illegal aid. Lack of compliance with these two rules were the basis of many of my investigations. It is true that there were many other restrictions and ways in which an athlete might become ineligible but I will discuss those facts later on.

consin and Iowa set an all-time Big Ten scoring mark of 13 touchdowns, breaking the record of 12 set by Iowa's Gordon Locke in 1921. Butkovich, who was summoned to active duty before the season ended, and who subsequently was killed in action, had real help from Boris Dimancheff, a nifty halfback, and a line led by Alex Agase, the former Illinois star, and Dick Barwegan, probably the best brace of guards in the nation.

The Michigan backfield, featuring Daley and Hirsch, deployed behind a tough line led by big Merv Pregulman, an explosive tackle, and the Wolverines racked up every foe but one—Notre Dame—as the national championship Irish, led by the great Angelo Bertelli, did a 35-12 hatchet job on the Maize and Blue.

With Otto Graham having the best year of his collegiate career, Northwestern failed by one game to nail a share of the Conference title. The one loss, 27-7 to Michigan, was enough to drop the Wildcats to second and allow Purple fans to commiserate over a crazy season in which a former Minnesota back named Bill Daley showed up in a Michigan uniform and tore off two blazing touchdown runs of 37 and 64 yards to pull out the victory over the Cats. It was that kind of year and one result of it was some crazy-quilt All-America selection. Herb Hein, the ex-Minnesota star, made it at end for Northwestern, and Daley, the other former Gopher, at Michigan, was the popular pick at halfback. Alex Agase, already an honor choice at guard for Illinois, now was an All-America for Purdue. There were some loyal home-bodies being honored, too. Otto Graham, Northwestern's magnificent halfback, was installed virtually unanimously. Tony Butkovich, Purdue's high scorer was a fullback. Michigan's Merv Pregulman was a tackle designee, and Pete Pihos, at end, meant that Indiana for the first time in its history had All-American players two years in a row. For the league's MVP there was no disputing the selection of Northwestern's versatile and inspirational Graham.

Indiana's tough, smart end, PETE PIHOS; and Northwestern's HERB HEIN were among the Big Ten's All-America selections in 1943.

Rule 6. Compensation.

Section 1. No student shall be eligible who:

a) has ever used his knowledge of, or skill in, athletics for financial gain; (The acceptance of employment as a playground director, life guard or similar work, which does not require technical preparation in, or coaching of, athletic sports shall not be a violation of this rule. The publication of technical articles upon athletic subjects shall be a violation if compensation is received.)

b) has taken part in an athletic contest in which a money prize was offered, regardless of the disposition made of the money prize. Participation in contests involving sports other than those recognized as intercollegiate sports by any member of this Conference shall not be a violation of this rule;

c) lends his name to any form of commercial advertising;

d) receives compensation from any employer unless, (1) he is performing useful work; (2) he is being paid at the going rate in his locality for the work performed; and (3) he is working on the job all the time for which he is being paid.

Rule 7. Unearned Financial Aid

Section 2. *Scholarship Requirements.* No student shall be eligible who receives any type of unearned financial aid, other than from persons upon whom he is naturally or legally dependent unless he qualifies either by superior scholarship, or by a level of scholastic achievement plus demonstrated need as outlined below.

b) *Aids Which May not Exceed Tuition and Incidental Fees.* A student may receive unearned financial aid not exceeding the tuition and incidental fees of his institution, without loss of eligibility, if he presents clear evidence of need for financial aid, and he has demon-

For the weirdest finish of any football game played in the nation that year, the nod must surely go to the wind-up of the Illinois-Ohio State game at Columbus where, at the end of 60 minutes it was all tied up, 26-26, and the Bucks had just thrown an incomplete pass from the Illini 35 when the gun went off. The teams left the field, went into the locker rooms and started undressing when an official appeared and announced that Illinois had been off-side on the final play. The game could not end on a penalty; the infraction had been noted while there were still a couple of seconds of playing time left. The crowd, filing from the Stadium, was startled to see both clubs straggling back on the field, uncertainly, lining up on the Illinois 30, with a few of the lineman actually in their sweat sox. Then, with 60,000 pair of eyes staring unbelievingly, John Stungis, an 18-year-old freshman quarterback who had never tried a field goal in a game in his life, swung his toe into the ball and got it away wobbling toward the cross-bar. Two seconds later a network radio announcer, completely overwhelmed by excitement and this quixotic turn of events, screamed into the mike: "The son of a bitch made it!" Ohio State had a 29-26 "fifth quarter" victory.

The 1943 All-Big Ten basketball team listed four members of Illinois' "Whiz Kids,"—Andy Phillip, Gene Vance, Ed Smiley, and Art Mathisen—and the fifth man, Ken Menke, made the second team. It was the only time in Conference history this had happened, and the circumstance was pretty much the story of the season. Their 12-0 Conference mark was the first all winning performance in 12 years; the Illini's 755 points in league play wiped out their own mark of 694 set the previous year; and Andy Phillip, leading the league in scoring, was the first man in loop history to average more than 20 points a game, with 21.9. Illinois' lone loss was an outside affair with Camp Grant, a service team featuring an ex-collegiate all-star cast.

Phillip was All-America, and once again, North-western's Otto Graham took second in the league scoring race, having the misfortune for two years to be eased out of the top spot by super-shooters such as Wisconsin's great John Kotz and Phillip.

Strangely enough, Illinois was by-passed as a district representative to the NCAA tourney in favor of De Paul (18-4). Later, in 1951 under a revised set-up, Big Ten champs automatically went to the tourney.

The year provided the low spot in Conference sports history as the war wiped out half of the NCAA

TOM ROBINSON, who took over as Northwestern swimming coach in 1910, retired at the end of the 1943 season, his 34 years giving him the longest tenure of any Big Ten tank coach in history. Nine league titles went to the Wildcats under his tutelage and he was the nation's first famous collegiate swimming coach after the Purple took five straight crowns from 1914 through 1918. He was back on top again in 1920 and then put three more titles back-to-back in 1923-24-25.

strated the level of scholastic achievement outlined below.

(1) If an entering freshman, he must rank in the upper one-half of his high school graduating class; or above the 50th percentile of entering college freshmen on either a standard college aptitude examination or standard college entrance examination.

(2) If an entering transfer student, he must have achieved a cumulative scholastic record in college which places him no lower than one-fourth of the way between the "C" and "B" grades in an ABCD-Fail grading system or its equivalent in other grading systems.

(3) If a continuing student, he must have achieved a cumulative scholastic record in college which places him no lower than the "C" level in an ABCD-Fail grading system, or its equivalent in other grading systems.

(4) Eligibility for continuance of unearned financial aids shall be based upon the student's cumulative scholastic record at the end of the academic year.

Section 4. Loans. A student may receive, without loss of eligibility, loans which are made or approved by the regular agency established by his institution for granting loans to all students.

My first couple of years as Commissioner were filled with problems resulting from World War Two. There had been many waivers of rules during the war years. These were gradually cancelled, and the full rule structure brought back into effect. I had appeared before the athletic staff of each Big Ten member, carefully going over the entire rule book but dealing in more detail those points covered in Rules 6 and 7. I had met with many alumni groups giving them a full explanation of what they could, and could not, do.

As a further precaution, these rules were printed in

tourney program and weakened virtually all the action within the Big Ten. Ohio State, for the first time, took three team titles in one year, with two of them coming as big "firsts." The Buckeyes won their first undisputed baseball flag, and their first tennis championship, led by the Conference championship doubles duo of Wasserman and Samson. Ohio also interrupted Michigan's domination of the swimming picture. Soon, the Buckeye-Wolverine battle for aquatic supremacy would become a unique chapter in Big Ten sports history as they totally dominated things for two decades.

Michigan took both the indoor and outdoor track titles; Indiana won the wrestling crown; and Illinois retained its fencing championship and clearly established the fact that by now it was apparent that the Illini—first under Herb Craig, and now under Max Garret—were going to set up a swordsmen's dynasty that would be unparalleled in the nation.

In NCAA competition, gymnastics, fencing, wrestling and cross-country were wiped off the books, not to return until the end of the war. In boxing Wisconsin set a record that still stands—and combined with a later-to-be lodge brother, Michigan State, in setting still another. Between them the two schools took every individual title but one as the Badgers won the team crown. Bill Zurakowski won at 120 pounds and Chuck Davey triumphed at 127 for the Spartans. (After the war Davey would return to become the most famous collegiate battler of all time.) For Wisconsin, Badger belters captured every division crown from 145 through heavyweight. Cliff Lutz won at 145; Don Miller at 155; Myron Miller at 165; George Makris (repeating) at 175; and Verdayne John, the tourney's Outstanding Boxer, heavyweight. (That left one division—135 pounds—for Dave Knight, an outsider from Washington State.)

In track the Conference was limited to a single champion as Minnesota's Jack DeField, the league's first 14-foot pole vaulter, retained his title with a 14-1 effort, matching his mark of the previous year.

GEORGE MAKRIS, *Wisconsin 175-pounder, won his second straight NCAA boxing crown as the Badgers repeated as team champs in 1943.*

Swimming was another story as Ohio State broke Michigan's title string at five. Leading the Buckeyes were Bill Smith was a 2:09.8 record-breaking 200-yard freestyle; Keo Nakama, who took the 1500-meters in 19:18.6 and the 440 in 4:43.2; and Earl Clark, who retained his high and low board championships. Smith and Nakama were first of a school of Hawaiian fish who would help keep the Bucks aquatically supreme for years to come. For second-place Michigan there was glory enough, however. Harry Holiday set a new NCAA mark of 1:35.5 for the 150-yard backstroke; John Patten won the 100-yard freestyle in 52 flat; the trio of Holiday, Irv Einbender and Patten set a new mark of 2:53.4 for the medley relay; and Holiday, Patten, Mert Church and Ace Cory took the 400-yard freestyle relay in 3:31.1. Seldom had a Wolverine swimmer been as happily busy as Holiday. Meanwhile, Northwestern

alumni magazines and many of the athletic directors put a simple condensation of the rules in locker rooms where the athletes could see them. The trouble was, they were similar to the fine print on an insurance policy; not everyone would take the trouble to read the information.

When I started my investigation work, I found a number of athletes scattered through the Big Ten who were in direct violation of Rule No. 7—Unearned Aid. Money that had been given to them was practically all from alumni or sports fans of their home town. It was not excessive but, nevertheless, I ruled them ineligible for a period of one year. Penalties of this kind were very painful to me. Here was a youngster who seemed unaware he was jeopardizing his eligibility by accepting unauthorized help. In fact, many alumni donors had told them it was okay. I kept track of a dozen or more of these boys I'd penalized for one year and found that

few of them remained in college. It pointed out to me that here was a field of education with the alumni and friends of a university that had to be watched very closely.

Although I had had staff meetings and had carefully instructed coaches what they could and could not do, I was soon to find there were several little violations of conduct with athletes off-campus and gave this phase a careful study. Sometimes this would happen at All-Star high school games; sometimes at banquets and it seemed hard for a coach to resist taking a chance. After receiving direct evidence of a violation of off-campus recruiting by one of the most popular basketball coaches in the Conference, I dug up an unusual penalty. For a period of one year I grounded this coach from all recruiting activities. He was not to be allowed to talk to athletes, even those who came to the campus for a visit. He

KEO NAKAMA

EARL CLARK

HARRY HOLIDAY

KEO NAKAMA, one of the first of many Hawaiian stars who would sparkle for Ohio State, won the 1500-meter freestyle and EARL CLARK, who scored a high and low board double for the second straight year, led the Buckeyes to the 1943 NCAA team title in swimming. HARRY HOLIDAY, one of the great all-time collegiate swimmers, set a new backstroke mark in the tourney and Hank Kozlowski, of Northwestern, became the first collegian to break the 23-second barrier for the 50-yard freestyle.

also got into the championship act when Henry Kozlowski, the Purple sprinter, became the first collegian to break 23 seconds in the title meet with a 22.1 for the 50-yard freestyle.

Two star footballers won the Conference Medal as the academic honor went to crack Michigan halfback, George Ceithaml, and Ohio State's fiery center of its 1942 national championship team, Bill Vickroy.

Temporary wartime regulations worked their strangest ways of all in 1944 football. Carroll Widdoes, who took over at Ohio State when Paul Brown entered the Navy, looked at his leading quarterback candidate and pinched himself unbelievingly. The

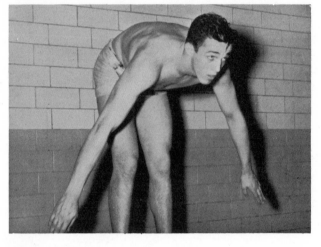

1944

HENRY KOZLOWSKI, Northwestern's Conference sprint champ, was the first swimmer to crack the 23-second barrier in the NCAA championships when he took the 50-yard crown in 22.1 in 1943.

could not make speeches at high school banquets. He could handle his team but that was all. The coach complied 100% with the rule but I will be the first to admit it didn't have the desired effect. Alumni and friends of that institution treated him as a martyr and proceeded to do all the leg work recruiting for him.

There were numerous cases where, upon investigation, the alleged violations proved to be nothing more than suspicion and gossip and no actual infraction of the rule had been made. There were other cases, however, when I found it necessary to reprimand a coach where I felt he was violating the rules consistently. While a reprimand sounds like a mere slap on the wrist, a copy of the reprimand was also sent to the faculty representative and president of the university. This frequently caused the coach to be called on the carpet for an explanation

and in the great majority of these cases, it straightened him out.

I think at this time it might be well to examine what was happening to intercollegiate athletics following World War Two. Thousands of students were returning from service, many of whom had gone into service from high school. The GI Bill was in vogue and these youngsters could now go to college and the enrollments swelled in all the colleges and universities in the country. These young men had been through a vigorous training program in the service. Many had been in combat. They had learned what tough competition meant and had their first experience in athletic competition in their training programs. They wanted and demanded an opportunity for the chance to compete. They were a rather unusual lot. Whereas the athlete of the early years following

candidate had been a fine halfback for the Bucks in 1940-41-42 and now was in Dental College on an Army deferment. When the Conference allowed freshmen to play varsity ball it also added a fourth year of eligibility to any player still working toward a higher degree on campus. A handful of medical, dental and science majors benefitted by the rule and among them was the 5-10, 170-pound Leslie Horvath of the Buckeyes. Horvath provided the maturity to go with three sensational 17-year-olds in the Scarlet backfield: swift halfbacks Bob Brugge and Dick Flannagan, and a crushing fullback, Ollie Cline. Up front there were Jack Dugger, a 220-pound end militarily deferred for bad eyesight; Bill Willis, a great tackle later to star with the Cleveland Browns, deferred for a chronic illness; and Bill Hackett, a fierce smart guard who was a veterinary medicine student.

When Paul Brown went into the Navy in World War Two, CARROLL WIDDOES, his number one assistant at Ohio State, took over the Buckeyes, molded them into an undefeated team and was chosen Coach-of-the-Year for his great job with 18-year-olds, 4-F's and a sprinkling of veterans.

For the second time in three years, Ohio State came up with an end-tackle-guard All-America trio when the undefeated Buckeye champions of 1944 presented JACK DUGGER, a big, tough flanker; BILL WILLIS, a crushing tackle who went on to pro fame with the Cleveland Browns; and BILL HACKETT, an aggressive, slashing guard.

World War One had usually gone to college in his home state, these youngsters had been trained in camps all over the United States and their selection of colleges covered just about the whole country.

Colleges were keeping pace with the athletic facilities. The period following World War One was the "Age of Stadia," and the era following World War Two could aptly be known as the "Era of Field Houses and Indoor Facilities." The expansion of the intramural programs in the Big Ten had been tremendous. Here, a student, regardless of his size or athletic ability had a chance to learn the values of athletic competition and the playing fields were crowded with thousands of competitors.

Now let's take a look at the Big Ten Conference comprising a seven-state area in which 3318 high schools fielded football teams. Students received fine high school

coaching. They were tough, able athletes, coming from mill towns, farms and industrial centers. I doubt if there was any conference territory in the United States that contained so many fine prospects or where there were more skilled high school coaches. They had fine athletic facilities and developed hundreds of outstanding athletes each year.

With this great potential source of athletic material, why couldn't any Big Ten school easily obtain all the talent it needed? The trouble was that the Big Ten was surrounded by conferences and universities offering the so-called straight athletic scholarships with no academic requirements other than admittance to the university. The Big Ten area became the happy hunting ground and many of the best athletes went to other than Conference schools. It was truly rugged competition.

Others included in the line were Captain Gordon Appleby, a light, scrappy center; Russ Thomas, tackle; Tom Snyder, a guard, and Cecil Souders, the other end.

Widdoes cranked them up, installed Horvath as the spark, sold 'em all on a mission and turned them loose for possibly the most astounding cohesive effort ever put forth for an Ohio State football team. They creamed the bigger opposition loaded with veterans and service trainees, and led the league in scoring with a 25.5 average per game. Their virtuosity was tinged with cool-nerved precision as they also led the loop in fewest fumbles, making only six bobbles all year.

Widdoes used the forward pass just enough to keep the defense honest for a devasting running attack that saw Horvath leading the league in rushing with 669 yards and a 5.3 average per carry—a new loop yardage mark. With his 284 yards passing, on 12 of 24 attempts, he was the Conference ground-gaining champ with 953 yards. He was also a virtual 60-minute player in most of the key contests, and a hawk on defense. Not until the final game of the season against Michigan were the Bucks seriously threatened. It was a good, solid Wolverine club which had dropped only one game, 20-0, to a high-scoring, fired-up Indiana team in the league opener, and thereafter the Wolves had scored five straight one-sided wins over Conference foes as well as a 41-19 walloping of a strong, trainee-loaded Penn team. With talented Don Lund at halfback and a remarkable spin-buck fullback in Bob Wiese the Wolverines mounted an offense which racked up 204 points of their own, and came into Ohio Stadium determined to gain a tie for the title and keep the Bucks from their first perfect season in 24 years.

It was a bruising, drama-packed affair under sullen, gray skies. Ohio scored first but missed the point-after. Michigan came back with a TD and converted for the 7-6 lead. Once again the Bucks pulled out in front with a TD but again missed the extra

When Ohio State dental student LESLIE HORVATH was given a fourth year of football eligibility in 1944 through the relaxed World War Two regulations it came as a complete surprise to him. He hadn't expected it but the 5-11, 172-pounder took the opportunity and went to work.

Leading a young Buckeye team to undefeated championship status, he called signals from his halfback position; rushed for 669 yards for a record-breaking 5.3 average, passed, punted, plied his 18-year-old teammates with unlimited inspiration and was a 60-minute performer in every key game—and practically every game was a key game for the Bucks that seasons.

Net result of all this was his virtually automatic selection for the Conference MVP tropy and the Heisman Award—along with All-America honors, of course.

The Big Ten also had some rigid rules about coaches visiting athletes in their homes and transporting prospective athletes for visits. There were occasions where plane loads of fine prospects who had been carefully hand-picked, would be flown from the Big Ten area to other parts of the country and given most unusual entertainment. On frequent occasions, these athletes were given tryouts to make sure they possessed the necessary skills and ability. It was not uncommon to pick up a roster of a Southern team and see a high percentage of the starting line-up was made up of athletes from the Big Ten territory. Naturally the result of these raids was a step-up in our recruiting by alumni and coaches to keep our boys home.

Realizing the Western Conference would not stand as an island, giving vigorous enforcement, while the majority of our surrounding conferences were running

wide-open, I, along with members of the Big Ten, became a leader in bringing this important matter squarely before the NCAA membership at their annual meeting. In fact, I found myself at one of the conventions as chairman of a round-table discussion on recruiting and proselyting. I presented a statement on the necessity for all of us to work together to curb the evils that had crept in. Having done that, I asked for a discussion to start. Not a soul offered to speak. I called on representatives of various conferences around the country and got very little response. It was a topic everyone shied away from.

At the next convention a year later, legislation had been carefully worked out which we thought would lead to a sane and direct approach to the problem. I am happy to say that all the Big Ten directors and faculty representatives backed it to the limit. For want of a

point. When the Wolverines tallied again with less than five minutes to play, and led 14-12, it looked like the ball game and the end of the Buckeye dream for a perfect season after 24 frustrating years.

There was an air of destiny, however, that seemed to hover over this talented but patchwork Ohio club as Horvath marshalled his youthful troops for what certainly had to be their last drive following the Michigan kickoff.

It was Flannagan wide. Cline blasting, and blasting again. Brugge reversing. Horvath flipping a short pass. Horvath running, running, running, and coolly calling plays, carrying the club on his back when he wasn't directing traffic. With time slipping by the Bucks had put together a half dozen first downs until there it was—all the chips stacked on the two-yard point.

line, and Les Horvath hurling himself over for the winning touchdown.

No wonder the slender dentist-to-be not only won the Big Ten's MVP trophy but the Heisman Award as well. Only Army, studded with veterans not affected by the draft, plus a liberal sprinkling of stars appointed to the Academy from other colleges, was listed above the young Buckeyes in the polls, and many critics referred to Ohio as the best "civilian team" in the land. With Carroll Widdoes named Coach of the Year in his first season as head coach, it was a big year for the Buckeyes.

Horvath, of course, was a unanimous All-America, and when Jack Dugger, Bill Willis and Bill Hackett joined him for a total of four Ohioans it represented the biggest contingent yet turned up from one Big

The 1944 All-America selections included eight Big Ten stars, the most yet chosen from any single Conference, and included EARL (JUG) GIRARD, the talented, do-everything Wisconsin halfback; JOHN TAVENER, the *great Indiana center; and CLAUDE (BUDDY) YOUNG, the chunky little trackman-halfback from Illinois who was the most electrifying breakaway back in the Conference.*

EARL (JUG) GIRARD   JOHN TAVENER   CLAUDE (BUDDY) YOUNG

better name, it was termed the Sanity Code. It was not a complicated set of rules but simply stated that all aid must be administered by a university's Scholarship Committee, and that this aid could not exceed the normal expenses of an athlete coming to college. This was adopted and the membership of the NCAA was informed that any violation of these rules would be handled in a drastic manner.

When the 1950 NCAA convention rolled around, its Infractions Committee had accumulated a number of serious violations; in fact, the Committee recommended the termination of NCAA membership for seven prominent institutions because of violations of the Code. It brought a furious battle to the floor of the meeting, including speeches by the presidents of these institutions, and in the end the motion was lost. There seemed to be a feeling among the membership that the NCAA should

not enter into regulatory matters of this type. However, there was enough strong leadership in the NCAA group to realize there must be a uniform set of rules and that they must be enforced.

The setback was only temporary and in the years that followed, strong leadership prevailed and rigid resolutions were passed regarding the conduct of recruiting. Boiled down they were as follows.

1) No coach could offer financial aid or inducements not permitted by his institution or conference.

2) No member institution could pay the expenses of more than one trip for a prospective athlete to visit the university.

3) No member institution could conduct tryouts on the campus of prospective athletes.

From this simple beginning, rules were added from year to year and to the credit of the NCAA leadership,

Ten school. Honored along with the Buck foursome were Claude (Buddy) Young, the sensational, squat, speedy halfback from Illinois; his teammate, Ralph Serpico, a guard; John Tavener, a great center and inspirational leader from Indiana; Boris Dimancheff, the crushing Purdue fullback who led the league in scoring (second year in a row for a Purdue player); and Earl (Jug) Girard, the running-passing-kicking whirlwind from Wisconsin, at halfback.

Meanwhile, no story of the 1944 season would be complete without noting that Indiana, long the step-brother of Big Ten football, was beginning to flex its muscles. Although the Hoosiers dropped three games, to Illinois, Minnesota and Ohio State—all close ones—the Hoosiers were one of the top teams in the land and tallied 292 points, the most ever run up by an Indiana football team. There were Hoosier fans who, for the first time, could mutter "Wait till next year!" and mean it.

By the 1944 basketball season, wartime manpower regulations had limited Conference schools to 18-year olds; upperclassmen excused on phsyical grounds, and on-campus naval trainees. Surprisingly, it still produced possibly a better brand of basketball than was being shown by wartime football. Led by Don (The Great) Grate, and 6'-8" Arnie Risen, the first of the outstanding big, big men in modern basketball, Ohio State took the championship with a 10-2 mark. Nor was there a lack of glittering performers throughout the Conference. Runner-up Iowa displayed a slick trio in Dick Ives, who was the league's leading scorer, Herb Wilkinson and Dave Danner. Headlines also went to Paul Hoffman, a great Purdue sophomore and, of course, the ubiquitous Otto Graham of Northwestern, who was an All-America selection. Ohio State represented the District in the NCAA tourney but after disposing of Temple, was eliminated by a strong Dartmouth team led by the brilliant Audley Brindley.

On other sports fronts, if Michigan could have taken the 1944 cross-country title, the Wolverines

DON GRATE

Forward DON GRATE, and ARNIE RISEN, 6-8 center, led Ohio State to the 1944 Big Ten basketball championship.

ARNIE RISEN

a remarkable job of restoring a semblance of order was accomplished among the hundreds of institutions who held membership. It was a fine beginning but really only the start. In a noteworthy convention held in Dallas, the NCAA published in its yearbook a statement that the following rule had become legislation:

Section 4. Principle Governing Financial Aid—Any college athlete who receives financial assistance other than that administered by his institution shall not be eligible for intercollegiate competition; provided, however, that this principle shall have no application to assistance received from anyone upon whom the athlete is naturally or legally dependent.

This rule, of course, had been in vogue in the Big Ten for some time.

Now let us take a look at aid that was available in the 1950's in the Big Ten for athletes. An incoming athlete

who was a superior student might receive a scholarship through the regular scholarship committee in excess of his tuition and incidental expenses, but the requirements were tough. He had to be in the upper third of his graduating class and must also maintain a "B" average if he was to retain this scholarship. These were truly the "blue chip" students but they were being recruited by practically every large university in the country, and many left the Conference territory. Now let's examine the category into which most of the athletes fell. If they were in the upper half of their high school graduating class, tuition help was available. They had to maintain grades above a "C" level. The rest of their school expenses would have to come from their parents or from jobs that might be found for them while they were attending college.

The third classification comprised student athletes who were admissible to the university but because they were

might have been brought to court on monopoly charges. The hill-and-dale crown was the only one that failed to rest on Wolverine heads as they swept indoor and outdoor track, wrestling, swimming, golf, tennis and baseball. In baseball the Maize and Blue posted the first perfect season in Conference play since a previous Michigan team had done it 21 years earlier. The Wolves' netmen won the team crown without winning either the singles or doubles honors which were taken respectively by Wisconsin's Ted Park and Ohio State's duo of Franklin and Mitchell. John Jenswold, capturing the individual title, led Michigan golfers. Wisconsin's Bill Lawson, in winning the individual championship, paced the Badgers to the league cross-country crown for the lone minor sports title not taken by the Wolverines.

LOU LICK, in 1944 became Minnesota's first and only national collegiate golf champion when he took the 1944 NCAA national crown.

ROSS, left, and ROBERT HUME, Michigan's Canadian twin brothers, fittingly enough scored the only tie victory in NCAA mile history in the 1944 meet.

Illinois sparkled in the war-shortened NCAA program, as the Illini became the first Conference team to win the track championship since Indiana's great year in 1932. Leading the Illini triumph were Buddy Young, the All-America halfback, who scored a sprint double in the 100 and 220 with 9.7 and 21.6; Bob Kelley, who took the 880 in 1:55.1; Dave Nichols, a high hurdles victor in 15.3; and Bob Phelps, who tied for first in the pole vault at 13-6 with Ohio State's John Schmidt, and two others from outside the Conference. Ralph Tyler, Buckeye broad jumper, took home a crown with 23-4½; and Michigan's Canadian twin brothers, Bob and Ross Hume, managed a dead heat to share mile honors in 4:18.5.

In swimming, Yale, led by the great Alan Ford, temporarily sidetracked Michigan and Ohio State. Meanwhile, a Wolverine foursome of Mert Church, Charley Fries, Bill Kogen and Gurdon Pulford won the 400-yard relay in 3:35; and Ohio's Keo Nakama

---

not in the upper half of their graduating class, no unearned aid was available. This type of athlete was a poor risk at best but the coaches could not resist passing up a tremendous prospect in the hopes he would turn over a new leaf and become a good student. This youngster had to earn the full shot if he was poor and it placed an awful burden on him in regard to a work program. You must remember that in any job, the work must be of a bona fide nature; the athlete must put in full time and the rate of pay must be the same as received by any person performing a similar task. A few made it but the attrition of this third group was tremendous.

You might question why a Big Ten institution would accept any students of this type. You must remember that the majority of our Conference members were state institutions and some were required to admit any high school graduate of their state. The faculties of these institutions

simply weeded out the poor prospects, usually during the first semester.

I think it is readily apparent that, as Commissioner, first of all I had to seek complete compliance and cooperation from the athletic directors and coaches. I was justly proud of this group. I do not think any conference in the country had a finer group of coaches than the Big Ten in the 1940's and 1950's. In football, for example, there were Bernie Biernam, Fritz Crisler, Woody Hayes, Murray Warmath, Ray Elliott, Bo McMillin, Clarence (Biggy) Munn, Lyn Waldorf, Ivy Williamson and Forest Evashevski, to name just a few in this period. All Big Ten institutions had capable staffs of assistants. They believed in the value of competition and had developed many fine teams that attained national recognition. Their athletes not only excelled in football but later many made distinguished records in business or professional life.

1945

retained his 1500-meter and 440 titles in 20:02.2 and 4:47. Ohio's domination in diving was interrupted—but perhaps not really—as Charley Batterman, a superb, former Buckeye star, shipped off to Columbia by the Navy for officer training, won both the low and high board titles.

In golf, Minnesota hailed a first time individual champ in Lou Lick, as Notre Dame took the team crown.

Gigantic TED KLUSEWSKI, a talented end; quarter-back BEN RAIMONDI, the league's leading passer; and HOWARD BROWN, a smart rugged guard who was Indiana's MVP for two years, as sophomore and senior,

On a Saturday afternoon in late September, 1945, when all the football results were in, grid fans were not quite prepared to believe that Indiana was really making a run for it that year. One of those opening day scores was Indiana 13—Michigan 7, and it was the first indication that the Hoosiers were serious about shooting for the Big Ten title after decades of almost automatically finishing in the second division.

paced the Hoosiers to their first undefeated season and first Big Ten championship in 1945. Big "Klu" later went on to become a slugging first baseman for the Cincinnati Reds.

HOWARD BROWN   BEN RAIMONDI   TED KLUSEWSKI

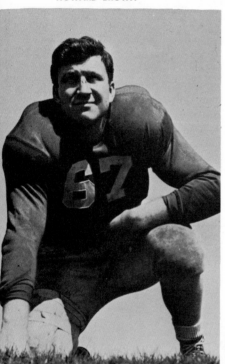

Here was a different type of coach than had been prevalent in the early years. These men had faculty tenure and were given support and backing by their presidents in good years and in bad. Nevertheless, they all wanted to win and knew full well that without good material this was an impossible task. The whole attitude of the blue chip athlete seemed to have changed. I received many reports from coaches that were very discouraging. After an attempt to sell a prospect on the academic advantages of his university and what a fine place it was to get an education, the prospect would often interrupt and say, "Coach, you don't need to go into all that. What's the deal?" This was indeed a deplorable situation. What had caused it? I felt then, and still feel, that many of these boys had visited too many schools, and had been subjected to a lot of high pressure. They began to feel they were a privileged class, the world owed them a living and if they could help attract great crowds to the games, they

should be amply rewarded. Too many of them were thinking only of football or basketball competition and not about the splendid education available to them.

The fact that the situation was serious was shown rather dramatically by prominent educators throughout the country. A special committee on athletic policy had emerged from the American Council on Education. This committee included some of our Big Ten presidents. I had the honor to be asked to appear before them and give my views. Following the publication of their conclusions, a meeting was called by the Big Ten presidents with faculty representatives and athletic directors present, and the group noted that our Conference rules were stricter than even those proposed by the American Council on Education. At that same meeting, it was decided that the Commissioner should hereafter be employed by the Big Ten presidents (on recommendation, of course, by the faculty representatives) and that he should report to them at their

It was, by far, the happiest, headiest day in Indiana sports history—that last Saturday in November, 1945.

The gun went off, signalling a 26-0 victory over Purdue in the annal battle for The Old Oaken Bucket, and for a change nobody really cared about the venerated prize. The big thing was that the Hoosiers had completed their first undefeated season in almost 60 years of football and had won their first Big Ten title.

Ol' Bo had done it, just as he promised he would, just as they knew he would.

Even so, the actual beginning of this day had gone back more than two decades, back to October 20, 1921 which was without doubt one of the most implausible days in the annals of football. On this day Centre College ("Who . . . ?") had come from Danville, Kentucky, ("Where . . . ?") to tradition-soaked Soldier Field across the river from Cambridge, Massachusetts, to play a football game with Harvard, mighty Harvard, hallowed Harvard, the paragon of Eastern football.

It was preposterous on the face of it. Nobody was quite sure how the match had been made in the first place. The only common ties between the two schools was that they spoke a common language, and even that was debatable if you compared Beacon Street English with Bottom Hollow twang.

The match had been made, however, and the only thing little Centre College wanted to compare was the quality of the rocking and socking on the Crimson's aristocratic turf.

Harvard had been undefeated in 25 straight games over three seasons, with one of the string being a Rose Bowl win over Oregon. So, this was the mismatch of the century.

On this day, Red Roberts, a bruising end, made a key block that laid low two Crimson defenders, and a tough, nimble Centre quarterback was suddenly scampering between and around everybody else, 35 yards for the touchdown that shocked the football world. That was it. Final score, 6-0. Nobody was on hand from Danville, Kentucky, so the sporting Harvard followers did the proper sporting thing. They hoisted Alvin Nugent McMillin, the Centre quarterback, to their shoulders and carried him to the Kentuckians' dressing room.

It should be pointed out, however, that a big part of that Centre College team were not Kentuckians but transplanted Texans. Transplanted in a sort of package affair. Bob Meyers, a Fort Worth high school coach, with fiery Indian blood in him, told a half dozen of his prep stars that he was moving up to his Alma Mater, Centre College, in the Blue Grass region, and would take them all with him.

"We'll beat Kentucky and be famous," he said heatedly. "Then we'll challenge Harvard or Yale and beat them, too, and be even more famous, and some of you guys will make All-America!"

None of the kids bothered to find out that Centre College had only 375 students. This was exotic dream stuff, and the number one dreamer was scrawny Alvin McMillin from the wrong side of the tracks in Fort Worth, one of 12 children, and whose mother adopted three more "to have a nice crowd around."

All five went off to Danville in 1917 with Chief Meyers, who promptly made himself Athletic Director and hired Charley Moran, the hard-nosed big league baseball umpire, as football coach. The year before Centre had lost to Kentucky 68-0. Now, with the five Texas frosh sparking

them, Centre took on virtually the same Kentucky personnel and beat them, 3-0, on a McMillin field goal. Centre also gained a nickname that swept the nation, "The Prayin' Colonels." As McMillin later told it, "We never prayed to win but we had such a small squad we couldn't afford to lose anyone, so one of the boys suggested, just as we were taking the field to play Kentucky, that we get down on our knees and pray we wouldn't have any injuries. After we upset Kentucky, we just naturally got on our knees before every game for real sincere prayers. We also prayed that if we were beaten we'd be big enough to take it."

It wasn't often they had to take it. There was time out for a year of military service and then in 1919 Walter Camp recognized Centre's undefeated season by naming Bo McMillin and Red Weaver, a center, to his All-America team. "Now get us Harvard like you promised," said Bo and his buddies, and Chief Meyers did just that. He conned the Crimson into believing it would be a nice, democratic gesture, or something, to give his "pore little boys" the thrill of coming East and providing a "breather" for Harvard.

In the first game, in 1920, it was a breather for sure as Harvard demolished Centre, 31-14, but as The Prayin' Colonels left the field Bo McMillin said, softly, to one of the Crimsons, "Don't go too far away, buddy—we'll be back next year."

As McMillin related it later, "We were lower than a snail's basement but the thought that we WOULD be back gave us something to chew on."

When they came back on October 20, 1921 it was to post the stunning 6-0 victory over the Harvard team that hadn't been whipped in 25 straight games. Even so, the five Texans almost hadn't come back as a group. One of them had received a pro baseball offer—a five-year contract at $10,000 a year, a ton of money then. Fortunately they'd been granted another year of eligibility because of the war, and the baseball star said he'd pass up the diamond if they all agreed to play another football season and take aim at Harvard. They agreed. The boy who gave up the baseball riches was Bo McMillin.

Alvin (Bo) McMillin, Centre College quarterback in 1921, led his team to victory over mighty Harvard who was riding a 25-game winning streak at the time.

He gained his fame soon enough in football, becoming head coach at little Geneva College in Pennsylvania, and with stars such as mountainous Cal Hubbard, later a great pro and chief umpire for the American League, McMillin produced an instant winner. One of his early victims was a team that just didn't learn to stay away from Bo McMillin: Harvard.

Bo was a natural for the coaching profession. A canny field general, a great passer, kicker and runner at Centre, he could teach all the skills—and inspire those who were learning them. Boys took to the "Prayin' Colonel" as he came to be known. He was firm, fair and colorful, and they put out 100 percent.

From Geneva, McMillin went to Kansas State in 1928, made the Wildcats a power in the old Big Six and then was summoned to Indiana in 1934. His mission was to end the Hoosiers' historical position as patsy for her Big Ten lodge brothers. Not enough high schools in the state played football to produce a fair work force for the ambitious McMillin but, as he told a friend when he took the job: "They're used to losin' and I'm used to winnin', but I'm the boss so these pore li'l boys are gonna have to get used to my way of doin' things!"

"Pore li'l boys," soon became a standard label for Hoosier football teams but not in a qualitative sense. Bo referred to them thusly more out of affection, and the affection was mutual because for the first time in the modern era the rest of the league could no longer look on Indiana as an automatic pushover.

It had been 14 years since Indiana had a winning team when Bo took over in 1934. He installed his imaginative wide-open offense of single wing, double wing and "McMillin Maverick" and his first year was break-even. The next was a winning one, and in 1937 only an early season 6-0 loss to eventual champ Minnesota cost the Hoosiers their first title.

Bo McMillin was winning confidence as well as games and was beginning to attract some bona-fide star talent. In 1942 he developed Billy Hillenbrand into one of the nation's truly great triple-threats. The following year Bob (Hunchy) Hoernschmeyer, a 17-year-old wartime freshman, led the nation in total offense.

Alvin (Bo) McMillin with members of his 1945 Big Ten championship team. From left to right—C. A. Timerario, Line Coach; McMillin; Pete Pihos, end; and George Taliaferro, halfback.

The trouble was, Indiana simply never had enough depth to make a real run for the flag. Then came 1945. In June the Hoosiers had signed Alvin Nugent McMillin to a 10-year, $95,000 contract, then the longest pact ever offered in the league. By September, Indiana fans were ready to collect their first big dividend on the investment, and Bo was ready to prove he could compete in anybody's race if he had some horses.

Ben Raimondi, the Brooklyn Bomber, was the Big Ten's most effective passer. Freshman George Taliaferro and George Groomes were a pair of big, fast halfbacks; and Pete Pihos, who had been an All-America end in 1943, had returned from two years service as a paratrooper and, with only one week of practice, took over a new position—fullback—and in Bo's own words was "the finest all-around football player in America." A tough, fast line featured two great ends in Bob Ravensburg and Ted Kluzewski, later the Cincinnati Reds' home run star; Howard Brown, a magnificent guard; and a great frosh tackle, John Goldsberry.

Raimondi fired two touchdown passes to beat Michigan in the opener and the Hoosiers were on their way, despite a 7-7 tie with Northwestern in the second game. From then on a devastating Hoosier attack rolled up such scores as 54-14 over Nebraska, 52-20 vs. Iowa and a 49-0 shellacking of mighty Minnesota which was the worst defeat in the Gophers' history. When the gun went off to mark Indiana's 26-0 whitewash of Purdue in the finale the Hoosiers had their first unbeaten team; and their first Big Ten title. Once again Bo McMillin was carried off the field on the fans' shoulders but in this dramatic instance it was on the shoulders of friends and not strangers as at Cambridge in 1921. The man they carried off was chosen Coach-of-the-Year in a virtual sweep of the election as the Hoosiers earned a fourth place ranking in the polls, the highest in their history.

The following year Bo was made Athletic Director, and a year later he announced his retirement from coaching. It was a blow to Indiana's fast-rising football fortunes that the disease that was to kill him very shortly ended one of the most colorful careers of any man in Big Ten history.

Alvin (Bo) McMillin accepts Coach-of-the-Year award for his championship Illini team of 1945.

Alvin (Bo) McMillin was finally about to prove that given a few horses he could plow under a lot of opposition. After that big opening win, however, fans weren't so sure. The next week Northwestern held the Hoosiers to a 7-7 tie. Maybe it wasn't to be, after all. Then, whammo! The Hoosiers knocked off Nebraska, 54-14, followed it with a 52-20 clobbering of Iowa, and suddenly there were believers all over the Midlands. This was a talented, power-packed outfit with a mission. At the ends were the gigantic Ten Kluzewski, later a slugging first-sacker for the Cincinnati Reds, and Bob Ravensberg, a nifty pass receiver. The tackles were John Goldsberry, fastest lineman in the Big Ten, and Russ Dean. At guard were tough Joe Sowenski and the brilliant, versatile Howard Brown who could block,

lead interference and defend. The center was smart, rugged John Cannady. Chunky Ben Raimondi, the Brooklyn Bomber, was at quarterback; George Taliaferro at one half; hard-running Dick Deranek at the other and, rounding things out, possibly the best all-around football player in the nation: ex-All America end Pete Pihos, back from service and performing block-busting chores at fullback.

After a close 7-2 bout with a great Tulsa team, the Hoosiers went on to lopsided victories over Cornell College, Minnesota, Pitt and Purdue, among others, and posted the first undefeated season in Indiana football history. Along the way the Hoosiers were the league scoring leaders with a 25.5 average per game.

Although Indiana was not too aerial-minded, Raimondi, the all-purpose quarterback, was the

Big Ten contributions to the All-America lists were all linemen in 1945. Featured were BOB RAVENSBERG, Indiana's swift, adept pass-snatcher; MAX MORRIS, Northwestern's prize flanker; TOM HUGHES, Purdue's

great tackle, and WARREN AMLING, Ohio State's quick, aggressive guard, who would repeat in 1946 while attending Veterinary Medicine school.

| BOB RAVENSBERG | MAX MORRIS | WARREN AMLING | TOM HUGHES |

frequent meetings on the enforcement of Conference rules and regulations. It would be far better, of course, to be responsible to the presidents in the ultimate sense, than to the directors.

I felt very encouraged by their action. I have always maintained that a college president could have any type of athletic program he wanted. After all, he is responsible to his Board of Trustees or regents for the conduct of all the educational programs. The difficulty is that the position of president at any large university is one of the most complicated imaginable. His biggest worries are, of course, to meet the demands of soaring enrollment; housing and classroom space; to seek larger endowments; to search for the finest teaching staff available and to present the finest possible image of the university to the alumni and public. Consequently, too many educators have turned over the athletic problems to their faculty

representatives and directors. The fact that our Big Ten presidents regarded these problems seriously and required frequent reports was extremely encouraging. Now I would have the opportunity to present Conference problems right at the top. In my reports, I tried to show what must be done to correct various situations. I now felt I had the entire support of the Big Ten Conference in back of me, top to bottom.

I found in my subsequent meetings with the President's Council that they asked very intelligent questions and, as a group, surprised me with their knowledge of intercollegiate athletics. I was particularly glad that one of the Council had been a great football player at Minnesota, Dr. Fred Hovde, President of Purdue. Few men I've dealt with in my administrative work had a better working knowledge of the problems that faced the Conference. If I could sell him on the merits of some suggested change,

passing leader with 31 completions in 62 attempts, and was second to Ohio's Ollie Cline in total offense. As a team, Indiana led in punting with a 37.1 average, further pointing up the all-around excellence of Bo McMillin's "pore li'l boys," as he was so fond of calling his clubs.

Ravensberg, the swift, 185-pound versatile wingman was an All-America and was joined on the honor lists by Max Morris, Northwestern's big, pass-snatching flanker, Warren Amling, a great guard at Ohio State while attending veterinary medicine school; and Tom Hughes, Purdue's dynamic tackle. A sophomore was selected as the Conference MVP, with Ollie Cline, Ohio State's blasting fullback getting the honor.

To cap things properly for the Hoosiers, the nation's coaches showed no hesitancy in recognizing Indiana's magnificent season by hailing Bo McMillin as Coach of the Year.

DICK IVES, Iowa's slick, hot-shooting forward in 1945 led the Hawkeyes in their first Big Ten basketball title in 22 years, and capped his performance with All-America selection.

In 1945 Iowa won its first basketball title in 22 years as the sparkling duo of Dick Ives and Herb Wilkinson, plus a shining soph star, Murray Weir, led the Hawkeyes to a 11-1 Conference mark and 17-1 overall. Only a 43-42 loss to Illinois spoiled what could have been the only perfect season in Hawk history. Northwestern star, Max Morris, led the league in scoring and Ives, and Walton Kirk, the versatile Illinois ace, were listed as All-America.

Unfortunately for Iowa, the Hawkeyes' with service trainees on their team, were unable to participate in the NCAA tourney, and second place Ohio State was picked to represent the District. The Bucks got by Kentucky but were rudely dumped by New York University, 70-65 in overtime, after leading by 10 points with two minutes to play in regulation time.

Aside from football and basketball, in which they hadn't won titles in a dozen years or so, Michigan's Wolverines continued to cut a winning swath through other sports and, in 1945, took four more team titles in indoor track, swimming, baseball and tennis. The baseball season found the Wolves becoming the first Conference team ever to turn up two straight perfect seasons, and Bliss Bowman, their star pitcher, was also the only league hurler to lead the loop in winning percentage two years in a row.

In tennis, although Ohio State's Aris Franklin took the singles crown and combined with his twin brother, Alex, to capture the doubles, Michigan managed to come through for team honors. Ohio's Howard Baker and John Lorms tied for the individual golf championship in leading the Bucks to team laurels. Purdue won its second straight wrestling title and Wisconsin took its second straight cross-country crown, with Illinois' Vic Twomey winning individual honors.

NCAA competition found Ohio State splashing back into national swimming honors again, ahead of Michigan, the Big Ten champ, as Seymore Schlanger and Hobie Billingsley scored doubles for the Buckeyes. Schlanger took the 440-freestyle in 4:55.4

he was invaluable in helping to get the proposition across. Each member of the Council of Ten contributed much to these meetings. They were men of quick decision, extremely articulate and their advice proved extremely helpful. Their introduction into the picture was not in any way a take-over policy; they all believed strongly in faculty control. I think the meetings that followed had an extremely salutary effect on the whole Conference. I felt also that the fact that I was hired by the ten presidents on the recommendation of the faculty representatives gave me added protection in my work. There was no question in anyone's mind in the Big Ten that they wanted and expected a job to be done, regardless of whose toes were stepped on.

Now, the question I am probably asked most is, how did you hear about infractions? Many came from coaches who were outraged at losing a valuable prospect at the

last minute. They would scream to anyone who would listen to them. Some of their listeners were often friendly sports writers and these complaints meant juicy items for their columns. Many complaints upon investigation proved so erroneous that the Conference soon passed regulations that these charges must be reported to the faculty representative and athletic director and not to the press. They were supposed to first sift the details and determine in their minds whether there were actual grounds for charges.

Of course, the majority of the complaints really came from alumni who seemed to feel that, while they were obeying the Conference rules, everyone else was not. Their stories would grow with every telling. Many times I found they were grossly misinformed.

I soon found I needed help in investigation work. Remember, each member of the Big Ten had, in round

GEORGE WALKER, Illinois' Big Ten champ, took an NCAA double in 1945 with victories in low and high hurdles.

Ohio State's JOHN LORMS, who had tied with teammate Howard Baker for the Big Ten individual golf crown in 1945, went on to take the NCAA individual title and lead the Bucks to their first national team championship.

A twin brother combination of ALEX and ARIS FRANKLIN led Ohio State to its third straight league title in tennis in 1945 when they won the doubles crown and Aris took the singles championship.

and the 1500-meter freestyle in 20:11.4. Billingsley, continuing Buckeye domination on the springboards, took both low and high diving events. Meanwhile, Michigan's Mert Church was scoring a double of his own. He won the 50-freestyle with 23.2 and the 100-freestyle with 52.3. Wolverine relay teams continued their annual successes as a foursome of Charley Frues, Bill Breen, Gurdon Pulford and Church won the 400 in 3:39.8, and a trio of Pulford, Heini Kessler and Frues ripped off a 3:05.2 for the 150-yard medley.

In NCAA golf Ohio State's John Lorms took individual honors as the Bucks won their first national team title. In track, Michigan and Illinois placed second and third to champion Navy (the Middies first and only title). The Wolves' durable Ross Hume pulled off a double with a 1:55.8 half-mile

numbers, between 200 and 300 athletes on the eligibility list. That called for policing a group of more than 2,000 individuals. Granted, that most of the hard recruiting was done on football and basketball prospects, there was still a great deal of pressure on the top track and field athletes; on great swimmers and exceptional base-ball material. I was to learn that the toughest, roughest recruiting came in regard to basketball talent. As the game had developed, it called for at least two tall men who must be from 6'6" on up. (What a contrast this was from the days when I had competed and was ranked as one of the big men in basketball at 6'2½"!) Now it was a must to get a big boy who could move and when they located one, the race was on.

The directors and faculty representatives encouraged me to add to my staff. At first I experimented with a couple of ex-high school coaches who knew the high

school field pretty well. I found in a short time that they had too much sympathy for the athlete and hated to dig up information that might cost him his eligibility.

I then hired Jack Ryan, a former Conference athlete who had lettered in football at Northwestern, had had a fine record of seven years of service in the FBI and, having resigned from that service, was doing private investigation work.

He knew the problems confronting us and his help through the years was invaluable. I quickly found it was impossible for one investigator to do the job completely and with Ryan's assistance, obtained the services of other former FBI men now in private practice and living in key spots in the Conference. These men were employed on a day-to-day basis and helped us get the work done in a hurry. I don't believe in the entire history of intercollegiate athletics that any conference has ever taken a more

and a 4:18.5 mile. George Walker, Illinois hurdler, did the same with victories in the low and high sticks with 24.0 and 14.9 Other Illini victories included Bob Phelps' pole vault crown with 11-6 and Henry Aihara's broad jump crown with 23-1 and ⅝.

On the Academic side, two more grid stars were honored with the Conference Medal: Michigan fullback Bob Wiese and Ohio State's All-America end, Jack Dugger.

1946

The Conference was back to a nine game football schedule in 1946—the veterans were back from military service—the freshmen were back where they belonged—and Big Ten football was back to a semblance of normalcy—except that two things were unexpected. Nobody thought the older players would have such difficulty picking up where they left off as underclassmen three and four years previously. Many had simply lost their spark and zest for the game, if not their physical edge. Nobody expected Illinois to be the league representative in the first Rose Bowl game in a new, closed contract with the Pacific Coast Conference. The Illini pulled it off with a smallish, scrappy gang which Ray Elliot led through some early season erratum and honed them to a sharp, late-season surge that put the Orange and Blue among the nation's elite.

A big item in the first Illinois title since 1928 was quarterback Perry Moss who was granted an extra year of eligibility by the Conference after returning from military service—and who was one who DID retain his competitive edge. A smart signal caller, strong runner and pinpoint passer, Moss engineered an offense that made big use of the mercurial Buddy Young and hard-nosed, hard-running Julie Rykovich at halfbacks. They deployed behind a line that featured (here he comes again!) Alex Agase at guard, and a couple of fine ends in Ike Owens and sophmore star Jim Valek.

Agase is unique in collegiate grid annals. He is the only man ever to hopscotch back and forth

PERRY MOSS

PERRY MOSS, a canny, slick-passing quarterback, and JULIE RYKOVICH, a hard-running halfback, were important factors in Illinois' championship drive in 1946 and a subsequent victory over UCLA in the first Rose Bowl game between the Coast Conference and Big Ten in their closed pact arrangement.

JULIE RYKOVICH

determined stand to find out what was actually being done and to stamp out undesirable practices of recruiting and subsidizing.

The Big Ten, however, was not alone in its attempt to curb undesirable practices. The Pacific Coast Conference which had worked so closely with us during our years of Rose Bowl competition and in inter-conference track meets, was having its troubles. Their very able Commissioner, Victor O. Schmidt, had also undertaken one of the most exhaustive investigations of their conference, interviewing each incoming athlete in each institution as well as examining the work programs that existed in each university. (The results of these investigations were to have very serious implications, finally leading to a dissolution of that fine conference that had contributed so much to intercollegiate athletics during the years. In passing, I am happy to relate that the new conference,

known as the Athletic Association of Western Universities, subsequently reconstituted itself and, headed by their very able Commissioner, Tom Hamilton, has resumed the prominence in the athletic world it justly deserves.)

In the Southeast Conference, Bernie Moore had led a relentless struggle against improper recruiting and subsidizing. Bernie, in my book, was a commissioner's commissioner and we frequently traded opinions and aid on our various problems. Dick Romney, Commissioner of the Mountain States Conference, was a legendary figure in that region and did much to keep things in order. Reeves Peters, Commissioner of the Big Eight Conference was one of the first to bring the presidents of his institutions into the picture. Jim Weaver in the Atlantic Coast Conference was a tower of strength to that league. Lloyd Jordan in the Southern Conference

three times between two schools and make All-America all three years. Since the Navy shuttled him around, the brilliant blocker and defensive stand-out was able to receive national honors at Illinois in 1942; at Purdue in 1943; and then, after active Navy duty for two years, returned to Illinois and all-star status in 1946.

In compiling its 6-1 Conference mark and 7-2 overall, the Illini first dropped a 26-6 decision to eventual National Champion Notre Dame in the second game of the season and, half way through the year were rudely upset, 14-7, by Indiana, After that, however, came five straight decisive victories over Wisconsin, Michigan, Iowa, Ohio State and Northwestern. It was the Michigan game which made the season for Illinois and kept the Orange and Blue in the national spotlight. To protect a 13-9 lead in the fourth quarter the Fighting Illini rose up four times in the last 12 minutes to throw back Wolverine marches that ended inside the Illinois 10-yard line.

Strangely enough, this was an Illinois team that got the job done in an orderly, workmanlike manner without posting a host of statistical records. In fact, Illinois won the title without leading in a single set of statistics—neither by an individual or as a team, in any of the more than a dozen categories in which records are kept.

It was a marvelous team effort for the Illini and it was to pay off handsomely in the Rose Bowl where, by the West Coast critics' own admission, UCLA had the strongest, most experienced team in its history. In fact, there had been extreme displeasure among Coast fans and sportswriters at the selection of Illinois as the Bruins' opponent instead of Army or Notre Dame—neither of which could accept a post-season invite. Besides, the Coast Conference-Big Ten pact had been signed, and UCLA was stuck with the uninspiring Illini.

All that happened was that Perry Moss pitched perfectly, Julie Rykovich ran wild, Alex Agase and his teammates up front littered the turf with Bruin

bodies, and Illinois had inaugurated the new Rose Bowl era with a smashing 45-14 rout of the embarassed Westerners and their fans.

Honors at year's end found Agase named Conference MVP as well as All-America, and he was joined by Elmer Madar, Michigan's great end, and Warren Amling, of Ohio State, who switched from his 1945 guard spot to tackle for his second straight all-star designation.

Among other accomplishments worth noting for the season, Michigan's fine center, Jim Brieske, set a new league mark for points after touchdown with 22. He missed only one place-kick. Norm Maloney, Purdue's versatile end, set a new record when he picked off an Indiana bobble and went 90 yards for a score; and Red Williams, Minnesota halfback, tied the Conference mark of four touchdowns in one

HERB WILKINSON, brilliant Iowa guard, and Max Morris, Northwestern's great shot-making forward, were Big Ten All-America selections in 1946.

---

had demonstrated great ability. The largest group of colleges and universities, the ECAC, which comprised not only the Ivy League schools but many fine small colleges on the easten seaboard, was under the extremely capable direction of Asa Bushnell. Bushnell was not vested with enforcement powers, yet he exerted tremendous influence in regulating and keeping things in order in that large group.

Paul Brechler who succeeded Dick Romney as commissioner of the Mountain States Athletic Conference, has helped reorganize and enlarge this conference which is now known as the Western Athletic Conference. He faced many problems in the reorganizational work and has shown tremendous administrative ability in solving them.

Along with these men, I was a member of the National Association of Collegiate Commissioners. This group held

long sessions in which they discussed mutual problems and developed many guidelines toward the best way of officiating football and basketball. At each meeting the chairman of the football rules committee would be invited to relate, in detail, problems facing the rules committee. Walter Byers, Executive Director of the NCAA would give a report on the inforcement procedures and rule changes that were being contemplated in the NCAA.

In looking back, I will not attempt to give a detailed account of the many investigations I held in the Big Ten but will try to pinpoint a few of the major ones I think were extremely important, not only for the impact they had on the Western Conference but on intercollegiate athletics all over the country. Every Big Ten university was involved at one time or other.

Now let us take a quick look at an era that furnished considerable difficulties and involved many alumni and

game when he cracked across for a quartet against Iowa.

Ohio State drove to the 1946 basketball championship with a 10-2 mark, just nosing out Indiana with whom the Buckeyes divided the home-and-home series. Whereas the Bucks lost only one other game, to Michigan, the Hoosiers dropped two, to Minnesota and arch-rival Purdue. Indiana had a chance to snatch the title in its second game with Ohio but the 53-52 decision and the crown went to the Scarlet.

For the second season in a row it was Max Morris, of Northwestern, who led the league scorers —only the second man in modern Conference history to stay on top for two years running—and the Purple star paced such headliners as Tony Jaros, of Minnesota; Ohio State's Jack Underman and Paul Huston; Purdue's Paul Hoffman, and Iowa's Herb Wilkinson, all of who dominated most of the Conference all-star listings. Wilkinson and Morris were All-America. Morris, having made it in football a few months earlier, was the first in modern Conference history to be a two-sport All-America. Ohio State went to the NCAA tourney but, after knocking off Harvard, was eliminated in a 60-57 squeaker with North Carolina.

Illinois, under the canny leadership of Leo Johnson, started reaching out for another period of track supremacy such as had been enjoyed earlier under Harry Gill, and the Illini in 1946 were one of the most powerful teams ever seen in the Conference as they swept both the indoor and outdoor tourneys. Illinois also took its first and only team title in tennis, but Northwestern's Bob Jake won the Conference singles crown and Jake and Larry Daly hooked up for doubles honors. Michigan won the golf flag as the individual honors went to John Jacobs, of Iowa, the first Hawkeye to win the championship. In baseball it was Wisconsin for the first time in more than 15 years, with Gene Jaroch, the Badger pitching star, becoming the first Conference hurler to win six games in a season.

GENE JAROCH, Wisconsin pitching ace in 1946, was the first hurler in league history to win six games in a season.

The Badgers also made it three straight in cross-country, although they had to share the title with Indiana, whose Earl Mitchell romped off with the individual crown.

It was Ohio State's turn to splash home ahead of Michigan in the turnabout swimming war between the two schools. The Buckeye tank squad also repeated in the NCAA tourney, with six individual events captured by the Scarlet. Halo Hirose, lastest Hawaiian to find his way to Columbus, won the 100-yard freestyle in 52.1; and Jack Hill scored a double in the 220 and 440 with 2:11.3 and 4:47.2. The Buckeye diving dynasty was firmly established, now, as Miller Anderson, a returning war hero, took both the low and high board events, and a Buckeye trio of Dick Fetterman, Jim Counsilman, and Ted Hobert captured the 300-yard medley in 2:57. (The swimming world would hear much more of Counsilman a dozen years later when, as Dr. James Counsilman, he would establish a swimming dynasty of his own, as coach at Indiana.) Michigan for the first time in years, was limited to a single triumph, but

friends of Big Ten universities. As I've said before, the alumni are the life blood of any institution. They have a tremendous pride in their university.

The difficulty begins in the fact that a typical alumnus always wants and expects his team to win. Sooner or later they want to get into the act. Usually they don't do it individually but some enterprising person calls an alumni meeting and starts making plans to recruit outstanding material, regardless of method. A more serious alumnus in the crowd might say, "What about the rules?" Too often the reply might come back, "the rules were made to be broken," or "we are going to do this on our own and what the university doesn't know, won't hurt it," or "the other schools' alumni are doing the same thing."

The first step is usually to collect money to use for transporting the athletes, entertainment and so forth. This became known as a "slush fund" and the fund was available for whatever it took to get the blue chip athlete. This was in direct violation of the rules that stated, "no athlete would be eligible if he received unearned aid from individuals other than his family or relatives." If they wanted to keep within the rules, all they had to do was to see that the money collected went to the university for scholarships or loans. I hasten to add that sometimes these groups did keep within the rules, helping to get good jobs for the athletes during the summer and selling the educational values of their university. Many college presidents felt hopeless about such groups and would frequently ask how the president could be responsible for the actions of thousands of friends of the university.

a solid one, when the foursome of Ziggie Indyke, John DeMond, Jim Quigley, and Bob Allwardt zipped through the 400-freestyle relay in 3:37.2.

In other NCAA action three Conference stars scored individual triumphs in the wrestling tourney, with Bill Courtwright winning the 155-pound crown for Michigan; Dave Shapiro taking the 165-pound title for Illinois; and Ohio State's George Bollas being crowned heavyweight king.

The most impressive NCAA triumph of the year went to Illinois' national championship track team, with four titles collected en route to the flag. Bill Mathis took the 100-yard dash in 9.6; the incomparable Herb McKenley roared to a smashing double with 21:3 in the 220 and 47.5 in the 440; and Bob Rehberg was the mile king in 4:15.2. Meanwhile, Northwestern's Bill Moore was taking the pole vault with 13-8, and a Minnesota soph named Fortune Gordien won the first of three straight discus titles he would collect before he was through, with a toss of 153-10 and ¾. Later he would reach world record achievements.

Bob Phelps, Illinois' two-time pole vault champ and Bliss Bowman, Michigan's pitching star, were among the prominent recipients of the Conference Medal.

Historically, two events had been big news in the Conference in 1946. In March, Chicago had formally withdrawn due to inability ". . . to provide reasonable equality of opposition." Secondly, the Big Ten had voted to enter into a five-year agreement with the Pacific Coast Conference permitting a league representative to play a Coast team in the annual Rose Bowl game. It was an epoch in Conference history as it rescinded the Big Ten's long opposition to post-season games, and set up a contractual agreement that would truly make the Rose Bowl the most exciting of all post-season football spectacles.

Make no mistake about it. Anyone who attempts a list of the five greatest football teams in Western Conference annals can be sure that the 1947 Michigan club *Belongs*.

Fritz Crisler, the brilliant, imaginative coach who tutored this early post-war outfit, drew from a rich mine of basic talent that had started to surface the previous year. Crisler was the kind of coach who never needed more than one season to refine good ore. His refinements for '47 found Michigan restored to the glory days of the Twenties and early Thirties as he brought the Maize and Blue their first championship in 15 years—cutting off the longest title drought in Michigan history as the Wolverines made a runaway of the Conference race.

Crisler, who has been credited with pioneering the two-platoon system, later described his '47 club as the epitome of platooning perfection. "We had great speed, mobility and precision on offense, and strength, toughness and quick reactions on defense."

Individually, he was talking about Bob Mann and Dick Rifenburg, fine blockers and receivers at end; Captain Bruce Hilkene and Bill Pritula, machine-like operators at tackle; Don Tomasi and Stu Wilkins, two tough, cat-like guards, and Jim Brieske, the all-purpose center and ace place-kicker.

Howard Yerges, a master strategist and slick ballhandler was at quarterback. (Yerges broke Ohio State hearts because he was the son of an old-time, great Buckeye quarterback; as a boy the Michigan star lived near the Ohio campus and came down every afternoon to watch the Bucks work out.) The Michigan halfbacks were the sensational triple-threat Bob Chappuis and the brilliant, pass-snatching Bump Elliott. The fullback, Jack Weisenburger, was a typical, quick, power runner in the successful Michigan spin-buck mold, but adaptable to the T. This group of offensive specialists posted a 6-0 Conference mark and a perfect 10-0 overall record, including a 49-0 bashing of Southern California in the Rose Bowl, and ran up an awesome total of 394 points that is still a season scoring record for all major college teams.

Policing these groups was really a tremendous job. Each Big Ten school had thousands of alumni and friends. I realized, however, that if their actions could not be controlled, we were in a hopeless situation. Some way or other, all this enthusiasm had to be channeled into legal activities. I had spent a great deal of time at meetings attempting to acquaint alumni with what they could and could not do legally, and had fine cooperation from all Big Ten members. The "friends" of a university were another unique problem. These men usually lived in the cities where the university was located. They were usually highly successful businessmen, often graduates of other colleges, but they, too, had become ardent rooters for their adopted school and wanted to help. This was the group that was the backbone of the many Quarterback Clubs, that listened with great interest to the coach after big games, and watched the football movies. These were the men who usually dug up the jobs or contributed quite liberally to the various funds.

The investigations I made were long and tedious and many times I grew disgusted at my inability to get the job done. Remember, in my investigations I didn't possess the power of subpoena. I had to accept that which was told to me as factual. I was not dealing with immature youth but sharp businessmen who seemed to regard this as just a game, and who took care to cover up their tracks.

The question is often brought to me, why investigate one institution rather than another. You simply had to wait until there was a substantial number of complaints and charges that slowly began to fit into a pattern and

HERBERT ORRIN "FRITZ" CRISLER

It was October, 1945, a couple of weeks before a youthful Michigan football team was to play unbeaten Army in Yankee Stadium. Mighty Army, with Glenn Davis, Doc Blanchard, and several tons of supportive All-America linemen up front, who, for two years had been as Huns and Tartars to wartime college football's fuzzy-cheeks.

Michigan, with a couple of 4-F holdovers and a gaggle of 18-year-old frosh who were eligible under wartime rules, headed for the slaughter. "All we wanted to do was survive—with honor," was the fervent hope of Herbert Orrin (Fritz) Crisler, the Wolverine coach.

So, to implement the hope, Crisler came up with the invention which revolutionized football as it hadn't been reshuffled since the forward pass appeared in 1906.

Crisler simply devised two-platoon football.

"Coaches had long known that some boys were better offensive players than defensive, and vice versa," Crisler said at the time. "But the custom leaned toward fielding a team mostly of offensive experts who could do a creditable job of tackling on defense."

Everybody also knew it was a severe physical drain on a boy to play 50 or more minutes of football, going both ways, but coaches had to put up with it because the rules on substitution just didn't permit much else. Once a boy was taken out in a particular quarter he couldn't return in that same period. So, except in one-sided affairs, or in case of numerous injuries, not more than 17 or 18 boys got to play.

"I knew we couldn't stay on the same field with Army, playing nose-to-nose," said Crisler, "but the rules had been liberalized during the war so coaches could substitute freely with small squads and sub-par material. Suddenly it occurred to me. . . . If we could use any kid whenever we wanted, why not look for the best ball carriers, passers and receivers, put the best blockers up front ahead of them, then take 'em out when the ball changed hands and throw in the best tacklers and pass defenders. We worked on it for two weeks and sprung it on Army, who figured to beat us by 40 or more, if they desired."

By the end of the third quarter it was a 7-7 ball game. Amazement was spread an inch thick on the faces of Eastern sportswriters witnessing the event. The fact that Army finally got rolling and beat the young Wolverines, 28-7, failed to dim the luster of Crisler's innovation. Immediately the thought was: "What could he have done with normal material. . . ?"

The idea of offensive and defensive units was a radical concept of football and in the week after the Army game Crisler began to get a lot of publicity. He got calls from coaches all over the country—some of them in the middle of the night, with next-game desperation apparent in the caller's tone. The free substitution rule had been invoked in 1941 as a wartime manpower measure but nobody had examined its possibilities beyond getting a couple of kids in and out of the game for frequent rests. Two years after Crisler's eye opener, platoon football was thoroughly launched on a high tide of acceptance —both college and pro.

Football people have a smug way of describing the sport in various ways. Like: "The name of the game is defense." Or, "Football is a game of third downs." Or, "Nothing builds character like football."

Then there are the people who took their cue from Fritz Crisler, and they say, "Football is a game of sales-

Herbert Orrin "Fritz" Crisler, Director of Athletics and Head Football Coach at the University of Michigan in 1931.

manship." Salesmanship as demonstrated by the man who brought Minnesota back, and then brought Princeton back, and then brought Michigan back, all because he knew what to do before he stepped onto a practice field.

Chronologically, the process demonstrated by the Wolverines' eminent Director of Athletics went like this: in 1930, after serving as a top aide to Amos Alonzo Stagg, at Chicago, Crisler was summoned to his first head coaching job at Minnesota, which, for several years under coaches who'd followed Dr. Williams, had enjoyed only desultory success. At the age of 30, Herbert Orrin Crisler was expected to plow a rather fallow field, without the horses. Minnesota, in the mid and late twenties, had produced great football players, but usually only one at a time, and they rarely had enough supporting cast to make any Gopher production a huge success.

"What's first on your program?" Minneapolis and St. Paul sportswriters demanded critically of the tall, handsome newcomer with the black hair parted severely down the middle like something out of the gay nineties.

"I'm going to make a few speeches," he told them.

What Fritz Crisler did in the next five months was to stump the state, and surrounding areas, addressing by actual count 103 Gopher Alumni Clubs. It was hailed as the first world record ever set by a Minnesota athletic figure. He developed an allergy to chicken and peas but succeeded in arousing enough Gopher alumni to forge a pact of Mutual Assistance. In effect, he told them, "You send me enough talent and I'll give you enough victories to keep you reasonably happy."

How well Crisler sold the alumni was reflected in the fact that the freshmen recruited in 1931 later were to give Minnesota undefeated seasons in 1933-34, but Fritz Crisler wasn't to share the glory with them. Two short years after he'd taken over in the Northland he was lured East to, of all places, Princeton, which in 65 years of football had never had a non-alumnus as football coach. It was a challenge such as never before had been flung at a Midwesterner. Glorified Princeton . . . Home of the Poes, the Bakers, the Leas and other such legendary heroes. Mighty Princeton . . . which, in the five seasons before hiring Fritz Crisler, had won a grand total of nine games! What they had at Tigertown were Tabby-cats, and what they'd been playing hadn't been football. Furthermore, when Old Orange and Blacks heard the news in their Eastern Clubs and speak-easies they almost popped their aristocratic seams. An unwashed, non-alumnus, midwestern bumpkin holding the Chair of Gridology at Nassau. . . ? The Depression was bad enough, but this was carrying things too far; but, they wound up buying him all the way. Salesman Crisler spoke at all 86 Princeton Alumni Clubs all over the country and, instead of the uncivilized rustic, they met one of the most polished and urbane men who ever hung a whistle around his neck, and Fritz blew it on them. First, however, he revealed he had nothing against gentlemen playing football. . . . As long as they had a smart head, a hard nose, and some latent meaness in them. He further suggested that some of these types could be found in the steel centers and coal towns of Ohio and Pennsylvania.

That whistle around the Bumpkin's neck, meanwhile, had also been blown in a most startling fashion. Old Princeton grid heroes had been in the habit of returning uninvited each fall, donning uniforms and imparting their wisdom to members of the team while the coaching staff helplessly cursed The System that gave alumni these weird privileges. This was the area in which Crisler brought the first change to Tigertown—but the manner in which he did it was typically Crisler. He sent letters to all alumni which, in essence, stated the following: the new coaching staff was eager to retain alumni interest and invited them to be part of the new Princeton Football Plan. Practice would be held in secret but the staff would never think of barring football-minded alumni, and if they wanted to attend practice they should simply use the enclosed card of admittance. Under the plan, how-

Herbert Orrin "Fritz" Crisler and Captain Bruce Hilkene plan the 1947 Wolverine campaign.

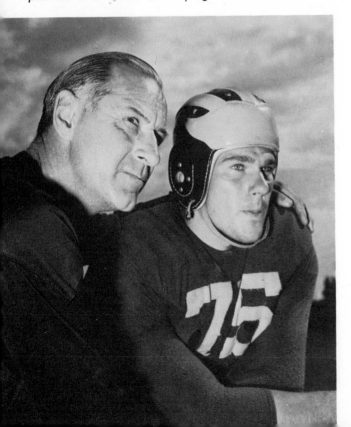

ever, all visitors would confine themselves to the stands alongside the field and keep in confidence whatever they saw on the practice field.

The Old Grads were so delighted to get such a special pass that they never realized they were being snowed out of their former coaching privileges. From then on, all Crisler had to do was coach football. He did it with a single wing virtuosity that gave Princeton its greatest victory orgy in 40 years. Starting out with some diffident, warmed-over material, his first club in 1932 broke even, but the following year Princeton was undefeated, scoring 217 points to its opponents' eight. His 1935 team like-wise was unblemished, with 256 points scored against 32, and was hailed by many critics as the top team in the nation. In between these two, the 1934 Tigers just missed setting up Old Nassau with three perfect seasons in a row, when a fired-up Yale team, a three-touchdown underdog, took its cue from an irrepressible Larry Kelley and dumped the Tigers in a horrendous 7-0 upset. The Tigers that year hung 280 points on the board against 32, and their three-year total of 753 points was the highest in modern major college history.

After six years, Princeton under Crisler had a 35-9-5 record and it was duly noted back in the Midwest where there had been the greatest debacle in the history of Michigan football fortunes. Harry Kipke, the one-time heir to Fielding Yost's dynasty, had fallen upon anti-royalist times. Successful football at Michigan, traditionally, had been built upon a Punt, a Pass, and a Prayer. Kipke in the mid-thirties had no one who ever punted as he had done in his own All-America days; nobody who could pass like Benny Friedman or Harry Newman; and what-ever prayers had been answered must have been on the other side of the field, because in four seasons, 1934 through 1937, the Wolves won a not-so-rousing total of 10 games out of 32. President Alexander Ruthven called a big Revival Meeting and the assemblage offered up one final prayer, asking Fritz Crisler of Princeton to come home to the Midwest and Michigan in particular. The prayer was answered. Crisler accepted the head coaching job after demanding and getting certain spiritual benefits that guaranteed him the athletic directorship when Yost was due to step down a few years hence.

The miracle needed at Michigan might have had to be performed by somebody else if young Herbert Orrin Crisler, a freshman at the University of Chicago in 1917, had taken another route to the library one day on the Maroon campus. Instead, he wandered too close to the football practice field where he failed to get out of the way when a play was run in his direction. Four players tripped over him, and the pile-up also claimed Amos Alonzo Stagg.

Brushing himself off Stagg sputtered, "Obviously you're a freshman! Well, make yourself more useful than this; get a suit and come out for practice!"

Although the frightened frosh considered it an order it was strange that he accepted it. Earlsville, Illinois, where he came from, had only 15 boys in its high school. All but two played football; one of the two was a crippled lad; the other was lanky Herbie Crisler who had won a scholarship to the University of Chicago with his brilliant academic record.

From that humiliating beginning, sprawled in the dust of the Maroon practice field, Crisler went on to become one of Chicago's greatest all-around athletes, and one of only two in Maroon history to win nine letters in three sports. He was, first of all, a brilliant end, gaining All-

Western recognition by his senior year. He was captain of the basketball team and an All-Conference guard. As a baseball pitcher he led the Maroon on a tour of Japan and was good enough to be offered a major league contract from the White Sox, which he turned down in favor of a coaching career. One of Crisler's best days on the gridiron, incidentally, was on the turf of Palmer Stadium where he would later direct Princeton's great revival. His magnificent blocking against big Stan Keck, Princeton's All-America tackle, led the way for the victorious rampaging of Jud Timme and John Thomas, Chicago's star backs. Later, Keck moaned: "I couldn't get past him and I couldn't get out of his way!"

Meanwhile, the handsome, studious Crisler had already gained the nickname that would stick with him through life. He had been having a bad day in practice, during his sophomore year, with his mistakes lousing up four straight plays. Stagg, exasperated, said to the disgusted youth: "Crisler, from now on your name is 'Fritz,' after the famous violinist. Not because you resemble him in any way but because you're so different!" Years later Crisler met Fritz Kreisler and the great musician roared hilariously when he heard the story. After that, whenever Kreisler gave a concert at Michigan he played the Wolverine coach's favorite number, "Londonderry Air."

Crisler's arrival at Ann Arbor in the Spring of 1938 was the beginning of a new era of Michigan pigskin pros-perity. It helped, of course, that he fell heir to a couple of sophomore backs named Tom Harmon and Forest Evashevski, and some beefy, hard noses up front, but once again it was his superb sense of organization and his mastery of both offensive and defensive football which gave him a winning insight to the complex tactics of modern football.

Under Crisler, Michigan brought to the acme of perfection the modern single wing offense featuring the buck-lateral and spinner sequences for which the Wolves became famous. With backs such as Tom Harmon, Bob Westfall, Tom Kuzma, Bob Chappius, and Pete and Chalmers Elliott, the ground-gaining talent was available and Crisler supplied the wizardry that made them go.

Over the 11 years he was head coach, Michigan clearly was the class of the Conference, the team that had to be beat before a championship was settled. The Wolverines shared the title with Purdue in 1943, won it outright in 1947 and were second six times.

Nine years in a row, during Crisler's regime, the Wolverines were voted among the nation's Top Ten in the annual polls—a record no other coach has approached. His magnificent, undefeated 1947 team undoubtedly was one of the great gridiron machines of all time, featuring Bob Chappius, the Elliott brothers, Bump and Pete, Al Wistert, a great tackle, and Len Ford and Dick Rifenburg, two magnificent ends. It was inevitable that Crisler would

Herbert Orrin "Fritz" Crisler (left) retired as Wolverine coach in 1948. His former backfield coach and three-time All-America, Bennie Oosterbaan, (right), took over the coaching reins. Crisler then devoted full time to his Athletic Director's post at Michigan.

be selected Coach-of-the-Year, and just as inevitable that Michigan would crush Southern California in the Rose Bowl, 49-0, the exact same score by which a much earlier Michigan team had opened the Rose Bowl series almost half a century earlier. Then, at the very pinnacle of success —after an era in which his Maize and Blue had won 71 games, lost only 16 and tied three—Herbert Orrin Crisler surprised the football world by announcing his retirement from coaching to concentrate on his duties as athletic director which he had taken over in 1941 from Fielding Yost.

As Athletic Director, Crisler, a natural leader, has been one of football's most eminent statesmen. Suave, polished, articulate and forceful he has had tremendous success as chairman of the College Football Rules Committee. It was under his guidance that the first change in football's scoring system since 1912 came about: the two-point option following a touchdown. It took imagination, daring, courage and diplomacy to steer this one to adoption. Herbert Orrin Crisler was equal to it.

More than anything else, perhaps the following anecdote reveals the true stature of Fritz Crisler. It concerns a boy who entered Michigan heralded as a can't-miss star. His freshman and sophomore years were disappointing. His junior season was Crisler's first as Michigan coach. As Crisler recalls it, "We were playing Minnesota and leading 6-0 late in the fourth quarter. It looked like we were on the title road. We fumbled a punt and Minnesota recovered. I sent this boy into the game to stop a long pass I expected Van Every to toss. On the first down Van Every flipped it, all right. My boy started to cover. He slipped. The pass was completed and Minnesota won, 7 to 6.

"The boy blamed himself bitterly for the loss.

"We played Northwestern for a possible share in the Big Ten title. The play seesawed. Neither team could score. We pushed down to the 4-yard line and I sent this boy in to kick a field goal. The day before he had booted 10 straight beauties under pressure. But he missed. He probably tried too hard. It was one of those things nobody could help.

"But the boy blamed himself bitterly.

"He became depressed and flunked a course that semester. He flunked another course the next semester. In June he came to me and said he was quitting school.

He was no good to the team, no good to himself. I talked him out of it and he made up his work that summer and came back the following fall.

"We played Illinois. The first time the boy touched the ball he fumbled. Illinois picked it up and went for a touchdown.

"He fumbled a punt. Illinois recovered and kicked a field goal.

"He fumbled again. Illinois recovered for another touchdown.

"We rolled through the schedule to the Ohio State game. We didn't have a chance for the title, but we needed that game—badly. I went to the boy's room that morning, found him sitting morosely on the bed. I told him to cut out the moping. I told him I had complete confidence in him and that he was starting against Ohio.

"The first time he touched the ball, he fumbled. Ohio recovered . . . a touchdown.

"He threw a pass. Ohio intercepted . . . a touchdown.

"At the half I found him in a room by himself, tears pouring down his cheeks. I told him to cut it out because I had complete confidence in him. I told him he was starting the second half.

"In the waning minutes of the game the score was tied. We shoved the ball down to Ohio's 14 but got pushed back to the 21.

"It was too far to kick, but I had a fake kick we'd practiced for the Minnesota game but never used. The boy's position was the key spot. I motioned another halfback from the bench to replace the boy who couldn't deliver in the clutch.

"Then I stopped. I said to mself, 'Crisler, you're a rat. You've told this boy all along you had confidence in him. This is his last game for Michigan. You'll destroy all you've tried to build up in him. You can't do it.'

"I motioned the substitute to sit down. I felt sick. I sat on the bench, eyes closed, fists clenched, afraid to watch the play. The crowd's roar brought me to my feet just in time to see the boy racing over the goal line from the fake field goal formation. We'd won—he'd won. And I think he was glad he played football. I was."

The boy was Freddy Trosko, whose famous 21 yard dash for the winning touchdown brought a standing ovation from the 85,000 spectators who saw his last game for Michigan.

---

to use the old adage, "where you have smoke, you usually find fire."

The first real sweeping investigation I was to make in the early 1950's, concerned the baby member of the Conference, Michigan State, which had been admitted to the Big Ten in 1949. A lusty, growing institution, it was destined to become one of the largest in the country. They had a fine athletic program and before entering the Big Ten had given their athletes athletic scholarships, permissible under NCAA rules but not (at the time) under the Big Ten setup. When they were accepted as a member in 1949 they agreed to comply with all Conference rules and regulations. I knew, of course, that this transition period might be a difficult one.

I began to get many complaints and charges that unearned aid was being made through an organization called the Spartan Foundation. The complaints stated

that these funds were being used for the benefit of the athletes and were not administered by the university. In undertaking the investigation I had three objectives in mind: to find out the size and scope of the Spartan Foundation, identify the athletes receiving the illegal aid and also to find out if there was any connection between members of the athletic staff and the Spartan Fund group.

I first contacted Ralph Young, the Athletic Director and Biggy Munn, the football coach, but they could give me no information on the membership of the Spartan Foundation, except that they'd heard of it. To the best of their knowledge, no money had been dispersed to the athletes. Through their help, I found out who was president of this group and he turned out to be a city engineer, highly respected in the community but extremely difficult to interrogate. He refused to divulge any in-

CHALMERS (BUMP) ELLIOTT, Michigan halfback and Conference MVP; and BOB CHAPPUIS, talented triple-threat halfback, were outstanding All-America choices for the 1947 Wolverine Conference champions. (Teammates

HOWARD YERGES and JACK WEISENBURGER, left and right center, were the quarterback and fullback in one of the great all-time versatile backfields for Michigan.)

Throttling the opposition's attack was the job of a fast, tough, ball-hawking defensive unit featuring a line consisting of Len Ford and Ed McNeil at ends; Alvin Wistert and Ralph Kohl at tackle; Joe Soboleski and Quent Sickels at guard, and Dan Dworsky at center. There wasn't much that sifted through that forward wall but when it did there was a quick-reacting secondary group including Pete Elliott (Bump's brother), Dick Kempthorn, Gene Derricotte, Bump Elliott and Weisenburger. Bump Elliott and Weisenburger were the only two Wolverines to consistently go both ways.

Never has a league champion dominated seasonal statistics as did this Michigan team. They led in team scoring with 28.7 per game; first downs with 17.5; rushing with 242.5; passing with 136.8; total

net yardage gained with 379.3; and, to prove how meticulous they could be, the Wolverines tied with Minnesota with lowest penalty yardage per game, with only 25.8 per game assessed against them.

Nor was that all. Impeccable triple-threat Bob Chappuis led the league in passing and total yardage gained, with 655 yards overhead and 364 on the ground for a 1019 total. Fullback Jack Weisenburger paced all rushers with 503 yards on 82 carries for a 6.1 average. Proving the fine balance of the Wolves' attack, Bump Elliott led Big Ten scorers on only six touchdowns as Chappuis, Weisenberger, Yerges and the ends, Mann and Rifenburger, repeatedly got into the act in the end zone.

Opposing end zones, incidentally, were violated by the Wolverines as follows: 55-0 over Michigan State;

formation concerning the size of the fund or how it operated, stating it had no connection whatsoever with Michigan State and it would be illegal for him to furnish me with any information concerning the money they held or the membership.

Following this unproductive visit and after repeated requests to him, on February 25, 1952, I wrote him a letter pointing out that the Spartan Foundation activities were a serious matter and that unless he would divulge the information I needed, it would be necessary to make a formal request to President John Hannah for help in clearing up the Foundation's alleged activities. Getting no response, I requested assistance from Dr. Hannah in obtaining access to the records and informed him that if nothing were resolved it would be necessary to bring formal charges against Michigan State.

This brought a prompt reply from Dr. Hannah. He told

me the Spartan Foundation had agreed to turn over $2,000 to the Michigan State scholarship fund and that after May 1, 1952, all scholarship funds would be processed through the college channels. While this was helpful, it did not give me the full information that I desired. Therefore, I suggested a meeting in East Lansing with the president, staff members and the faculty representative, Lloyd Emmons. The meeting did not produce much information except to strengthen my opinion that this fund was being operated entirely without the knowledge of the members of the athletic department. Through the help of a lawyer, I was later able to get a look at the corporate records which were filed in the State House as of July 12, 1951. The records stated that the assets of the foundation were $38,209.92, and also that approximately $17,500 had been dispersed during the year of 1951. Not all of this sum had gone to athletes,

49-13 over Stanford; 69-0 over Pitt; 49-21 over Northwestern; 13-6 over Minnesota; 14-7 over Illinois; 35-0 over Indiana; 40-6 over Wisconsin, and 21-0 over Ohio State. Despite the seeming mid-season letdown against the Gophers and Illini, Michigan never was in jeopardy and quickly resumed its swashbuckling ways the last half of the campaign.

When honors were being handed out at season's end, Michigan was not exactly by-passed. In the final AP poll, Notre Dame barely edged the Wolves for first place, but in an unprecedented supplementary poll taken by the wire service after the Bowl games were out of the way, the Wolverines took over the top spot. Crisler was named Coach-of-the-Year; Bump Elliott was the Conference MVP, and Chappuis and Elliott were named All-America. They were the only Big Ten nominees—and it was the last time the league was represented by only one school.

The only thing left for Michigan to do was take care of the Rose Bowl business on January 1, 1948. The 49-0 creaming of Southern California barely found the Wolverines working up a sweat. "It was almost a perfect game for a winning team," Crisler reported, "and it was called without a single mistake by quarterback Yerges." Later, in describing his backfield as a unit, Crisler termed it "the greatest group of ball-handlers I ever saw. All played baseball or basketball and spent hours of early season football drills in perfecting their technique to the point where they could even fool the coaches closely observing the action."

After all, it was that kind of a team . . .

Illinois' "Whiz Kids" had come back from the wars for the 1947 basketball season, but something was missing; some of the magic had disappeared while they were on military service and they were nipped for the title by Wisconsin which had a 9-3 mark to Illinois' 8-4. The Badgers, led by Bob Cook and Don Rehfeldt, split the home-and-home series with the Illini, but a 48-41 Illinois loss to Indiana

in the last game of the season provided the final upending of the glittering gang from Champaign-Urbana. It might have been otherwise because Wisconsin also dropped it finale, 58-55 to Minnesota. However, the Minnesota game turned out NOT to be the league windup for the Badgers who were involved in the weirdest situation in Big Ten cage history and were not actually crowned champions until a week after the official season was ended because of an unfinished ball game.

Two weeks previously a bleacher crash at Lafayette, Indiana had halted the Wisconsin-Purdue game at half-time. The contest was ordered to be completed on a neutral floor and the result could still

<table>
<tr><td style="text-align:center">BOB COOK</td><td style="text-align:center">RALPH HAMILTON</td></tr>
</table>

Among Big Ten headliners for 1947 were BOB COOK, Wisconsin's ace forward who led the league in scoring, and RALPH HAMILTON, Indiana slickster, whose shooting and all-around play-making at forward brought him All-America honors.

some went to members of the band and some to non-athletic upperclassmen who were in financial difficulty. I had also located and investigated certain individuals who were members of the Spartan group. I found they were at great odds with the university's athletic policies on aid and they felt they could do a better job than the university. Apparently their policy had been to assist senior athletes, who had completed their eligibility, but were without enough funds to graduate. There were many vague references that these were loans but when I questioned the athletes involved, they said they weren't expected to pay back the money.

Under the rules of the Conference, an institution being investigated is entitled to a hearing to answer the charges. Dr. Hannah said he felt there should be no grounds for suspicion of violations of any Conference regulations of the Spartan Foundation and further stated

"you have about all the information obtainable on the Foundation activities." In my letter to Dr. Hannah of May 27, 1952, I agreed with him and informed him of my conclusion to assess the penalty of one year probation against Michigan State.

This brought an immediate answer from him and a request for a formal hearing which took place on June 4, at which time Bill Reed, my assistant who had aided in the investigation, and myself were in attendance. Michigan State was represented by President Hannah, Kim Sigler, former Goveror of Michigan and now Chief Counsel for Michigan State; Dean Lloyd C. Emmons, Faculty Representative; and Dean Thomas King, Dean of Students. Clearly, we were outnumbered and the meeting was a most interesting one from the outset. I found we were in honest disagreement apparently on two major points. Number one, the liability of Michigan State

determine the league championship. Playing the second half on the Northwestern court, the Badgers took a 72-60 victory and the title.

Wisconsin's sparkling Bob Cook led the Conference scorers and shared headlines with Jim McIntyre, of Minnesota, and Ralph Hamilton, of Indiana, who also received prominent All-America listing. The Badgers went to the NCAA tourney but didn't get past the opening round. In the first half of their game with City College of New York, Wis-

MARV ROTBLATT, Illinois pitcher, won top league mound honors in 1947 with a 6-0 season as he led the Illini to the Big Ten title. A Michigan State hurler by the name of ROBIN ROBERTS, not quite as successful, went on to all-time greatness with the Philadelphia Phils.

HERB McKENLEY, Illinois' superb 220- and 440-yard dashman not only led the Illini to indoor and outdoor league championships two years in a row (1946-47) but led the Orange and Blue to two straight NCAA team championships with a two-year sweep of his favorite events.

for the operation of the Spartan Foundation. Number two, the Commissioner's authority to impose a penalty, specifically one in the nature of a probationary status, not expressly referred to in the Conference Handbook. On both these question I felt that I was on sound ground; if a university could not be held responsible for the operations of an outside slush fund, I could conceive that this would repeatedly become the pattern for illegal aid. On the second point, I agreed the probationary status was not spelled out in the penalty structure of the Conference, but I was sure the Conference faculty representatives would back me up in this respect. To my knowledge, it was the first time this serious penalty was ever invoked, although it has been used continually by the other conferences and the NCAA would use it in subsequent years.

Following the meeting, there was an exchange of letters between President Hannah and myself. In a letter dated February 14, 1963, I wrote to President Hannah as follows:

"Dear Dr. Hannah:

"I have your letter of February 10, in reply to mine of the 3rd with its enclosure.

"In response to the request in the last sentence of your letter, accepting fully the spirit in which the letter was written, I have earnestly sought means whereby I could 'reframe my position.' In the light of the conclusions I have conscientiously formed and sought to state in the undated letter you have, I find it impossible to alter my position.

"We are in honest dispute, apparently, on two major points:

1) The liability of Michigan State College for the operations of the Spartan Foundation.

consin could do no wrong and virtually toyed with the Easterners; but in an amazing turnabout the Badgers couldn't locate the basket in the second half and allowed a 15-point lead to slide into a 70-56 loss.

In track, Illinois, led by the incomparable Herb McKenley, retained both its indoor and outdoor championships, and also captured the Conference baseball title as Marv Rotblatt led the league pitchers with a perfect 6-0 campaign. There was a Michigan State pitcher, however, who, not quite as successfull, was destined to become the greatest hurler ever to come out of the Big Ten. A tremendous right-hander with the Phils, he would set a major league mark by winning 20 or more games for six straight years. His name: Robin Roberts.

Two other sports long dominated by the Illini came up with new champions. Northwestern, with its first fencing title in league history, turned back the Illini, 10 to 9½, the narrowest margin ever recorded in the Conference tourney. Led by Gordon Groh, the league foil champ, the Wildcat swordsmen came out of nowhere with an inspired performance in the grueling day-long competition following a dual-meet season which found them winning only one of nine matches. It was also a triumph for Tully Friedman, Purple captain in 1939, who brought off the title in his first year of coaching.

Minnesota interrupted Illinois' long-time hold on gymnastic honors as Ralph Piper, the Gopher coach (and a nationally known square dance caller), got the Gophers off to the first of a three-year reign, with Jim Petersen, Minnesota sophomore, capturing the first of three all-around crowns.

Illinois added the cross-country title to its trophy case but a newly-rising distance star, Don Gehrmann, of Wisconsin, won the individual crown.

Northwestern, strengthening its position as a collegiate tennis power, also took the team net title led by Ted Petersen's triumph in singles, with Illinois' Downs and Migdow winning the doubles.

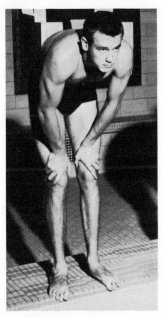 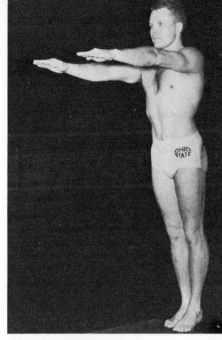

GEORGE HOOGERHYDE   **MILLER ANDERSON**

MILLER ANDERSON, Ohio State diving virtuoso who had swept Big Ten boards for two straight years, completed his mastery of collegiate high and low boards in the 1947 NCAA with a double for the second straight year as the Buckeyes splashed to their third straight team title. GEORGE HOOGERHYDE gave Michigan State its first NCAA championship when the Spartan ace took the 1500-meter event.

Ohio State repeated as Conference swim titlist and also made it three straight in NCAA competition nosing out (naturally) Michigan. In the nationals the Buckeyes were led by Hawaiian star, Bill Smith, and their magnificent diver, Miller Anderson, both of whom scored double triumphs. Smith, returning from four years of wartime service, and destined to become one of the greatest collegiate swimmers of his era over the next three years, took the 220-freestyle in 2:10.4 and the 440 in 4:45.2. Anderson, wounded in the knee when his fighter plane was hit over Germany, and who had to restyle his take off technique from one leg to the other when he re-

2) The Commissioner's authority to impose a penalty, specifically one in the nature of a probationary status, not expressly referred to in the Conference Handbook.

"I regret that my conclusions regarding each of these points are not such that I believe we can resolve them between us. The very nature of our respective contentions, in fact, suggests that if the issues are to be resolved it can be done only by orderly reference to the specified channels of appeal. I can conceive of no 'other action for the best interest of the Conference and all the members thereof' that could be appropriate, and I believe that in the present instance an appeal to the Faculty Representatives would be both appropriate and desirable.

"I am, accordingly, enclosing formal notice of action being instituted with respect to Michigan State and the Spartan Foundation of Lansing, in the form of the undated letter previously submitted to you. In accordance with Conference procedures a copy of the enclosed will be distributed to the Council of Ten and members of the Conference Joint Group. This communication will be covered by a memorandum imposing an injunction of secrecy until appellate procedures have been observed, and, for information purposes, a copy of this letter."

The enclosed letter, as referred to above, was a long review of the entire case containing the facts that had been disclosed by my investigations, and the letter ended with my conclusions as follows:

"My conclusions concerning the Spartan Foundation of Lansing, based on known facts, are summarized as follows:

1) Violations of Rule 7 governing the award of un-

BOB RICHARDS

The kid from a tough neighborhood may have been headed for delinquency, but at age 16 he developed an interest in the church, went to live with the family of a minister and turned to sports. (Five members of his old gang went on to jail.)

Subsequently, he became a minister, himself, but that was after young Robert Richards had gone off to college and became, at the time, the best-known pole-vaulter in the history of track and field. In the days before anyone ever dreamed of making a vaulting pole out of glass, Bob Richards dominated the nation's and the world's high-flyers with standard metal poles. The second man ever to vault 15 feet (Cornelius Warmerdam was the first) Richards soared 15 feet or better, more than 100 times, and more than any man in history. What he would have done with the fiber glass pole can only be sky-scraping speculation.

Only 5 feet 11, Richards was considered by coaches to be too short for the ideal vaulter but, as the star of Illinois track teams of 1945-46-47, the 180-pound Richards won Big Ten and N.C.A.A. titles twice and won two Olympic gold medals, in 1952 and 1956. A remarkably versatile performer who could run, jump and throw assorted hardware, he also won the A.A.U. decathlon title three times and took the bronze medal in the event in the 1948 Olympics—the only decathlon athlete in the games who also won an individual event.

An "A" student at Illinois, he became an ordained minister of the Church of Brethren while still in college. In 1951 he won the Sullivan Award for sportsmanship, the highest accolade an amateur can win in the United States, the second Big Ten athlete to receive it. There was subsequent agreement among the Russians that he surely must have earned it. At the Olympic Games of 1952 it was the Rev. Bob Richards who, for the first time, spent much of his own time explaining to the Russians the best training methods, techniques, and equipment to use. He then proceeded to garner the gold medal in the Decathalon and repeated his performance for a second gold medal four years later at the Melbourne games.

In 1948, Illinois' BOB RICHARDS, shown getting some last-minute words of advice from U.S. Olympic Coach Dean Cromwell, had to settle for a Bronze Medal in London, but in 1952 and 1956 at Helsinki and Melbourne the Illini star won the Olympic Gold Medal both times.

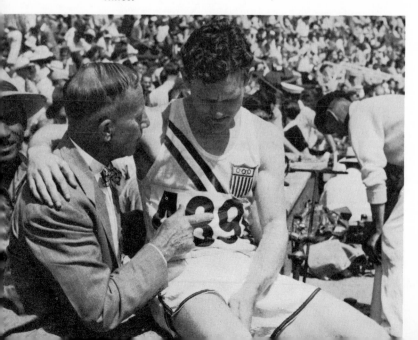

turned to college, repeated his low and high board triumphs of the previous year. A Buck foursome of Bill Zemer, Ted Hobert, Halo Hirose, and Smith, captured the 400-yard relay in 3:30.2, and a Michigan trio of Harry Holiday, Bob Sohl and Dick Weinberg took the 300-yard medley in 2:54.9. Holiday also took the 150-yard backstroke in 1:33.6, and Weinberg, one of the best Wolverine sprinters in years, scored a double with a 23.3 in the fifty and a 52.2 in the hundred. Meanwhile, Michigan State was also getting into the individual title picture with a 19:44.2 triumph by George Hoogerhyde in the 1500-meters.

Illinois scored an impressive repeat performance by taking its second straight NCAA track title, with Herb McKenley, the Illini's Jamaican import, winning the 220 in 20.7 and setting a new mark for the 440 with 46.2. Bob Richards, subsequently to become the world's greatest pole vaulter of his era, helped the Illini cause by placing in an uprecedented six-way tie for first, at 14 feet, with Bill Moore, of Northwestern, also sharing the honor he'd won undisputed the year before. Bill Clifford, Ohio State's crack half-miler, took the 880 in a scorching 1:50.8; Charles Fonville, Michigan's great field-eventer, took the first of his two shot-put titles with 54-7/8; and Fortune Gordien, of Minnesota, repeated as discus champ with 173-3.

In wrestling, Gail Mikles, Michigan State's tough, aggressive 155-pounder, took his division crown, and Joe Scarpello, of Iowa, won at 175. Boxing returned to the NCAA lists after a wartime layoff, and Wisconsin lost no time in nailing the team title again, led by Cliff Lutz, who took his third 145-pound championship, and John Lenski, who won at 165. Michigan State's Chuck Davey not only captured the 135-pound crown but was given the Outstanding Boxer Award for the tournament. (Davey would be hailed as the best collegiate boxer of all time before he finished his career.)

One other NCAA title went to the Big Ten as

earned aid to athletes appear to have existed in the operations of the Spartan Foundation of Lansing.

2) The existence of an organization of the Spartan Foundation's apparent character and the extent to which its activities have been established reflects directly on Michigan State's lack of diligence and attention to compliance with Rule 7.

3) The nature of the operations of the Spartan Foundation cannot be fully evaluated nor the full extent of possible violations determined because there has been no complete disclosure of the past activities of the Spartan Foundation.

4) A full disclosure of the Spartan Foundation's disbursements is essential to the establishment of adherence, on the part of Michigan State College and its athletes, to the provision of Rule 7.

CLIFF LUTZ, Wisconsin 145-pounder, won three straight national collegiate boxing championships in 1945-46-47.

Dave Barclay, Michigan football and basketball star, proved his versatility by winning the individual golf crown.

Among winners of the coveted Conference Medal for scholarship were Warren Amling, Ohio State's All-America lineman; Paul White, Michigan's star grid center; and Bob Richards, Illinois' great pole vaulter.

If there were any Michigan football fans who wondered what their 1948 team would do for an encore following that fabulous '47 season, you couldn't blame them. After all, those '47 Wolves had been undefeated and National champions; had provided two All-Americas and the Coach-of-the-Year.

Now Fritz Crisler had stepped out of the coaching ranks to devote all his time as athletic director, and had turned over the team to long-time assistant, Bennie Oosterbaan.

The encore went like this: Michigan was undefeated Big Ten and National champion; provided three All-Americas; and Bennie Oosterbaan succeeded Crisler as Coach-of-the-Year. The latter event was unprecedented; it was the first time any college had ever turned up two successive Coach-of-the-Year designees, but Oosterbaan had lost little time in demonstrating that the Pupil could quickly become the Master.

Much of the '47 talent had graduated but there was enough left to form a nucleus around which Oosterbaan could build with reserves and bright sophomores. Dick Rifenburg, Ed McNeil and Harry Allis were back at end; Joe Soboleski and Ralph Kohl still manned the offensive tackles; Captain Don Tomasi and Stu Wilkins were still at guard, and Bob Erben took over at offensive center. Alvin Wistert, probably the best defensive tackle in the nation,

DAN DWORSKY   **ALVIN WISTERT**

Two of the stars who helped Michigan to its second straight undefeated football team in 1948 were DAN DWORSKY, a tremendous linebacker, and ALVIN WISTERT, a tremendous tackle and last of the three Wistert brothers to make All-America for Michigan. (And he made it at age 32 after entering college much later than most youths.)

1948

"Based on known facts pertaining to the Spartan Foundation of Lansing I hereby institute the following action, subject to the process of review available to you as a member institution:

"Michigan State College shall be placed on probation as a member of the Intercollegiate Conference for a period of one year. The following conditions for the faithful discharge of probation shall be:

1) During this period there shall be full compliance with Rule 7 of the Intercollegiate Conference to the satisfaction of the Commissioner and the Conference.

2) It shall be incumbent on Michigan State College to secure, or exhaust every possible remedy in an effort to secure, detailed and complete information concerning all financial disbursements of the Spartan Foundation to the time of its dissolution.

3) When called upon by the Commissioner, Michigan State College and its officials shall render every possible assistance in the examination and inspection of the operations of other Michigan State alumni clubs or clubs operating on behalf of Michigan State College.

"For your information, I expect to review the status of Michigan State College periodically during the probationary period in the hope that the Conference and I will be satisfied that, the purposes and conditions of the probation having been fulfilled, the probation can be terminated prior to the expiration of the year."

Michigan State College (later, University) then requested an appeal be made to the Conference which was within their rights and on February 22, 1953, the

Begining his career in 1945 under World War Two regulations that made freshmen eligible for varsity, PETE ELLIOTT became the only 12-letterman in Michigan history and modern Big Ten annals. Here he recounts his four years each of football, basketball and golf exploits with grid coach BENNIE OOSTERBAAN, who, in his playing days at Michigan, was the Wolverines' most famous nine-letterman in the mid-Twenties, in football, basketball, and baseball.

bulwarked the defensive line whenever the Wolverines gave up the ball, and was ably assisted by veterans Dan Dworsky and Dick Kempthorn whom Oosterban called "the best pair of linebackers I've ever seen at Michigan." He was equally high on Gene Derricotte as a safteyman.

Although the talented foursome of Howard Yerges,

Bob Chappuis, Bump Elliott and Jack Weisenburger had graduated, Oosterbaan invested his newcomers with the same brand of magic. First, he shifted Pete Elliott to quarterback. Two precocious sophomores were installed at halfback: Leo Koceski and Chuck Ortmann, and the latter immediately provided the triple-threat virtuosity that Chappuis had given the Wolverines the year before. Another smacking fullback in Don Peterson, and additional help from Wally Teninga, filled out the Michigan attacking forces.

Posting 252 points for the year the Wolverines were pressed only in a 13-7 opener with Michigan State. After that it was Rompsville all the way as Michigan led the league with a 31.7 scoring average. Ortmann, the sophomore whiz, who did most of the passing, led the league in total yardage gained, ground and air, with 712. Dick Rifenburg, the towering end, was the Big Ten's outstanding receiver, and Harry Allis, still another Michigan end, not only equalled Jim Brieske's PAT mark of 22 for the season but, with three touchdown passes added to his point production, became the only lineman ever to lead the Conference in scoring.

It was not, however, Michigan's good fortune to go to the Rose Bowl again. The post-season pact didn't prevent the Coast league from naming a repeater but the Big Ten had insisted it would not allow one of its representatives to go two years in a row; therefore, second place Northwestern was tendered the invitation. Young Bob Voigts in his second year as Wildcat coach had done the kind of job that put the Purple in readiness. With Captain Alex Sarkisian as a rallying point at center, the Wildcats presented a line which for the most part played both ways, although with frequent relief. Chuck Hagmann and Joe Zuravlef were a pair of sharp ends; Steve Sawle and crack sophomore Rudy Cernoch, were tackles who knew their business; and Eddie Nemeth and Larry Day manned the guards. Behind them the Wildcats featured smart, pass-

faculty representatives of the Big Ten met in special session to hear their appeal. Their action was as follows, as stated in the minutes of that meeting:

"After detailed consideration of the grounds for the appeal and of the Commissioner's explanation of the basis for his action it is the decision of the Faculty Representatives, sitting as an appellate board, that the appeal of Michigan State College from the action taken by the Commissioner as set forth in his letter of February 2, 1953, be denied, and the Commissioner's action sustained."

This case not only received great publicity throughout the Big Ten area but throughout the nation in collegiate circles. Many college presidents throughout the country had concurred with President Hannah that it was impossible to police the thousands of alumni and friends in their recruiting and subsidizing activities, and

they had watched with great interest the outcome of the case. It meant if this decision stood up, then they, too, would be responsible for their own alumni and friends.

It was the first time in athletic history an important institution had been put on probation. Although this was not a listed penalty in the rule book, I felt it was a fair and just penalty. In other words, it gave Michigan State a year to put its house in order or face the loss of membership in the Conference. It is noteworthy that that this quickly became standard practice in all Conferences and in the NCAA as well. Frankly, it was one of the most significant actions taken by the Big Ten since the Conference had been formed. The wisdom and firm resolution of the faculty representatives in taking the stand they did was a real milestone in Big Ten history. The NCAA which had been intensely interested in these investigations and, in fact, had done considerable in-

throwing Don Burson at quarterback; two brilliant ball-carriers in Frank Aschenbrenner, left halfback, and Art Murakowski, a stupendous fullback. Ed Tunnicliff and Tom Worthington shared the other halfback spot.

There was every indication this Wildcat team was going to be a factor in the Conference and even national picture when it not only smashed highly favored Purdue in an early game but pulled off the incredible defensive feat of not allowing the aerial-minded Boilermakers to complete a single pass. The following week the evidence was complete—this time on an offensive basis—when Minnesota jumped off to a 16-0 first quarter lead over the Purple with two touchdowns and a safety coming after Wildcat fumbles. Northwestern came back with one of the great rallies in Purple history. Spearheaded by Burson's passing, some wild running by Aschenbrenner and Murakowski, and deft pass-receiving by Hagmann and Worthington, the Wildcats scored 19 points before the half ended, then protected the lead through a scoreless second half.

Michigan was too much for Northwestern in a 28-0 setback and, a few weeks later, Notre Dame took a 12-7 squeaker, but Northwestern went into the season finale against Illinois with its Rose Bowl hopes dangling before them. The Purple wasn't about to blow it. Aschenbrenner scampered 22 yards for a score; Burson flipped 23 to Zuravlef for another; and Loran (Pee Wee) Day, twin brother of Wildcats guard, Eddie, picked off a fumble and lateralled to Hagmann who sped 65 yards for the final touchdown in a 20-7 performance that was Rose-scented all the way.

It was a unique situation as the post-season spectacle loomed. Lynn (Pappy) Waldorf had left Evanston two years before, and now, as head coach at University of California, was taking on his former club that was tutored by his former pupil.

Any petulance the Coast fans may have had over getting the Big Ten's second best team in the Bowl

Slick quarterback DON BURSON and hard-running halfback ED TUNNICLIFF were big reasons why Northwestern finished a strong second in the Conference and went to the Rose Bowl when Michigan stayed home on the no-repeat ruling. It was Tunnicliff's 50-yard TD sprint with a minute to play which gave the Wildcats the Bowl victory over California.

vestigation on their own, promptly placed a similar probation on Michigan State.

To Michigan State's great credit it cleared up the situation in a hurry and, our subsequent investigation showed that all Spartan Foundation funds had been turned over to the Scholarship Committee. It also gave me an opportunity to state, when alumni asked what they could do, that they could raise all the money they liked but it must be turned over to the university and be administered by the regulating agencies in conformity to the rules.

A Commissioner's life is never dull. One of the next problems I faced were rumors and allegations that some of the coaches of the Big Ten had held tryouts of prospective athletes on the campus. This was against Big Ten rules and also against NCAA rules and, looking back over the years, it is not hard to see how a coach

would be tempted. The customary plan to entertain prospective athletes was to invite them to the university over the weekend where they would be entertained and meet the coaches. In order to break the monotony, their hosts would frequently take them over to the gymnasium where they could shoot some baskets or take a swim. I could see nothing wrong with this but when a coach had some of his varsity players suit up and engage in a minor scrimmage, with the coach present, this, in my opinion, constituted a tryout. Looking at it from the coach's viewpoint, here was a 6'6" basketball player who looked like the answer to his prayers but he wondered how this big fellow could move. Nothing would be more natural than to put a varsity man on him and see how he reacted. There were further charges that some of the football prospects in the fall were given wind sprints.

I had reprimanded the basketball coach at Michigan

was dissipated midway in the first quarter when Aschenbrenner cracked over tackle and went 73 yards for a score. Jackie Jensen evened things up for the Golden Bears on the first play after the subsequent kickoff and it was 7-7 until early in the second period when Murakowski repeatedly tore the Bear line apart, finally going over from the two. He fumbled going over but the officilas ruled he had possession long enough to score.

After repelling several California drives in the last half, Northwestern, leading 13-7 and in jeopardy if the Bears were to score again, got the ball on their own twelve with three minutes to go. After a first down on the ground, Aschenbrenner, seldom a passer, crossed up everybody and completed the Wildcats' only pass of the game, to Don Stonesifer on the Purple 30. With only seconds left, North-

western lined up with Tunnicliff taking a direct snap from center—the only time in the game when the quarterback didn't handle the ball—and behind scythe-like blocking, Tunnicliff raced 45 yards for the touchdown that iced the Roses.

Murakowski, who had been the take-charge guy for the Purple all season, wound up not only as the Conference MVP but All-American, as well, along with Alex Sarkisian, the great Wildcat center. All-conquering Michigan placed the brilliant Dick Rifenburg at offensive end, and the redoubtable Alvin Wistert at tackle—the third Wistert brother to make

Among Big Ten stars who wound up as Al-America designees in 1948 were DICK RIFENBURG, Michigan's towering, pass-grabbing end; ART MURAKOWSKI, Northwestern's line-battering fullback; and ALEX SARKISIAN, the Wildcats' terrific center.

ALEX SARKISIAN   ART MURAKOWSKI   DICK RIFENBURG

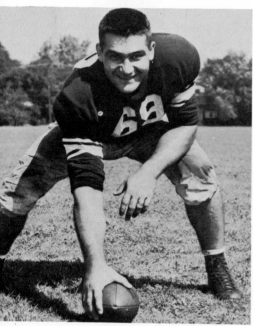

State for a couple of these tryouts and finally issued a rule that no competition of this type could be held with the coach or any of his assistants present, and that no equipment could be issued. This led to several problems. In many cities where our Big Ten institutions are located, the high school athletes of that area, having no indoor facilities, would frequently go over to the university field house for a work out. The track coach of that institution might be working his own men out at the same time so the rule had to be modified. As long as the high school coach was present, the situation was acceptable. Many of the college coaches were particularly unhappy about this, stating they believed it was their duty to help any high school athlete they could, if he asked for help. I can well remember long discussions with one of the finest baseball coaches the Big Ten ever had, Ray Fisher, a former Yankee baseball pitcher, who was reported to

have helped a young high school pitcher develop his curve ball and had several sessions with the youngster in the field house at the University of Michigan. Ray argued vehemently that the rule was unjust but I had to tell him that while I believed he was not giving the boy a tryout, it might be construed as one. The ironic thing in this case was that Ray's coaching evidently helped the boy a lot because he became one of the great pitchers of the Big Ten and later in the major leagues, but he didn't go to Michigan.

There were also problems in other sports, especially in swimming. Many Conference swimming coaches ran summer camps and it was only natural that a good high school swimmer would think of nothing better than attending a camp and learning the techniques from the great coach who was running it. I ruled at the time that this was not a violation, if the high school athlete payed

Soph flash MACK SUPRUNOWICZ led Michigan in 1948 to its first league basketball title in 19 years.

MACK SUPRUNOWICZ   MURRAY WEIR

Iowa's sensational MURRAY WEIR set a new league scoring record of 279 points and an average of 22.7 on his way to All-America honors in 1948.

All-America—and do-everything Pete Elliott at defensive halfback. Leo Nomellini, Minnesota's magnificant tackle, was the other Conference designee.

Nineteen years without a Conference championship was the resident shame of Michigan basketball fans but in 1948 the Wolverines finally had something to posture about. Mack Supronowicz, leading Wolverine scorer; Pete Elliott, of football fame, and Bob Harrison led Michigan to a 10-2 title mark. However, it was Iowa's sensational Murray Weir, an All-America pick, who led Conference scorers with a new league high of 279 points and the highest average yet tacked up, of 22.7 points per game. Other stars of the season were Minnesota's Jim McIntyre;

Wisconsin's Bob Cook; and Dwight Eddleman, the versatile, three-sport star from Illinois.

The Wolverines went to the NCAA but were tripped by Holy Cross, 63-45, in the first round.

Track fans in Ohio look back with a sigh when the 1948 season is recalled. It was a double win for the Buckeyes—indoor and outdoor team titles—and it was also the last time the Scarlet took a Conference team crown. The Buckeye's indoor record included Harry Cogswell's victory in the 440; a mile relay triumph by a foursome of Russ Owen, Mark Whitaker, Bill Clifford and Cogswell; and a brillant double by Lloyd Duff, who took the broad jump and set a new Conference record of 8.4 in the 70-

LLOYD DUFF, hurdler and broad jumper, was one of the stars of the 1948 Ohio State track team, the only squad in the school's history to win the indoor and outdoor titles the same year.

his full camp fee. In addition, any varsity swimmers attending the camp must have regular duties as counselors and actually perform them.

Baseball continued to present problems in summer competition. With the great promotion of American Legion baseball throughout the country, many teams had been organized and were playing in small towns throughout the Midwest. Nothing is more natural than to have a baseball player play all he can during the summer months. The Big Ten had operated for years under a rule that Conference baseball players could not play in a game where admission was charged. The rule had been passed because of the fear that if money was taken in at the gate, eventually the players would share in the receipts.

This proved so totally unrealistic that in order to avoid any complications, some of the athletes were simply play-

ing under assumed names. The rule was then modified to state that where admission was charged, a Conference athlete must secure a statement from the manager of the team, stating he would not participate in the gate receipts. There was also legislation enacted to fill a particular situation where a Conference athlete played on a team competing in a tournament for a cash prize. It was the custom of many of these baseball teams to wind up the season in several tournaments, where as much as $1000 might be offered the team that won. To remove several of their best players at tournament time destroyed the strength of the team. Consequently, the Conference, along with the NCAA, passed legislation banning participation in baseball tournaments unless the management could furnish a sworn statement that the athletes were not receiving money.

The NCAA took a prominent part in these regulatory

287

FORTUNE GORDIEN, *of Minnesota, the greatest discus thrower in Conference history, completed a three-year sweep of Conference and NCAA titles in 1948 en route to world records and Olympic fame.*

yard low hurdles. In the record department, Charley Fonville, Michigan's star weightman, set a new shot-put mark of 56-3 and 5/8.

Outdoors, the Bucks were led by Mal Whitfield's victory in the 440; Bill Clifford's win in the 880; and a mile relay triumph by Whitaker, Ed Porter, Cogswell and Whitfield. A new Conference mark went into the books with the 178-11½ discuss thrown by Minnesota's Fortune Gordien.

In swimming, Michigan returned to the throne room, led by Harry Holiday, one of the greatest swimmers of his day, with a victory in the 150-yard backstroke; a 1500-meter win by Matt Mann III, the son of the famed Wolverine coach; and by a winning medley relay team made up of Holiday, Bob Sohl and Bill Kogen. Other stars of the meet were Keith Carter, the greatest swimmer in Purdue history, who took the 50-yard freestyle and 200-yard

breaststroke; and Miller Anderson, the Ohio State diving whiz who scored a double in the high and low board events.

Michigan also shared the baseball crown with Illinois, whose second-baseman, Herb Plews, led the Conference in hitting with a gaudy .404. Purdue dethroned Illinois as wrestling champion with individual titles taken by Arnold Plaza, at 121; Joe Patascil, 128, and Wald Van Cott, 175. Northwestern repeated as fencing king, with the Wildcats' Humphrey Sullivan and Ralph Tykodi taking the foil and saber crowns, and Tom Spellerberg, of Ohio State, the epee. Northwestern also continued its supremacy in tennis but Michigan, ironically a frequent team winner without taking the singles or doubles championships, found itself reversed for the first time as the Wolves failed in team honors but turned up the singles champ in Andy Paton and followed with Paton and Mikulich in the doubles.

The Wildcats, embarked on a successful year, added the team golf championship to their bag, but

KEITH CARTER, *possibly the best swimmer in Purdue history, was a highlighter of the 1948 Conference meet with freestyle and breaststroke victories.*

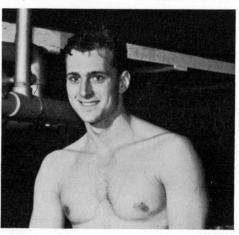

problems and along with my Conference investigators made a thorough check of the many summer baseball leagues that were in vogue. It did an outstanding job in passing legislation preventing a college athlete from participating in summer baseball unless the league was registered with the NCAA, and its amateur status carefully checked.

Throughout the years, I can remember many amusing things in regard to baseball. Driving through the countryside one Sunday afternoon, I saw a game being played and stopped to take a look. When the team at bat finally took the field again, their shortstop was missing. The reason: he had recognized me and had decided to hide under the bench until I left.

Another famous case that came to my attention was that of Moose Skowron who later became the star first baseman of the New York Yankees. He was a sophomore

at Purdue and not only was a great baseball player but one of the finest football prospects the Conference ever had. The investigation started as a result of rather elaborate gifts he had received for playing softball, and then turned into an investigation because he was burning up an industrial baseball league in Minnesota. I was just on the verge of questioning his eligibility at Purdue (he was then a sophomore) when he beat me to the punch by signing up with the N.Y. Yankees.

The next months were extremely busy in the maze of details that the new aid program brought in. There was hardly a day when there were not half dozen calls or letters regarding technical aspects.

My investigations soon became directed toward the work programs at the Big Ten schools. These were the basis on which many athletes earned the extra money they needed to continue in college. On the face of it the

Minnesota's national collegiate track champions of 1948. Left to right, front row: Clark Rice, Lloyd LaMois, Fortune Gordien, Charles Lindekugel, Jim Niel-sen. Second row: Roy Good, Fred Brass, Bill Ewing, Lee Hofacre, Bob Comer. Back row: Scott Nelson, manager; Tom Mason, Paul Neff, Dick Kilty, Coach Jim Kelly.

a Purdue sophomore, Fred Wampler, served notice that he would be a dominant links figure in the league by taking the first of three individual titles. Minnesota and its brilliant all-around titlist, Jim Peterson, took its second team and individual gymnastic laurels, respectively, and Don Gehrmann, repeating his individual honors of the year before, led Wisconsin to the cross-country flag.

In NCAA competition, Minnesota scored its first and only national championship in track, with Fortune Gordien taking his third straight discus title with 164-6½. Michigan's Charley Fonville repeated in the shot-put with 54-7; Dike Eddleman, Illinois' football and basketball star, tied for first in the high jump at 6-7; Ohio State's Mal Whitfield took the 800-meters (an Olympic year distance) in 1:51.1,

work program idea was a sound one. There is no question that a student working part of his way through college is better off for it. The question I had to determine (and I had begun to receive considerable complaints against some of my Big Ten members) was to find out the validity of the job. Was the athlete being paid the going rate and did he put in full time? Like all commissioners, I decided to investigate where most of the complaints were being directed and this led me to Ohio State University. Columbus, Ohio has often been called the football capital of the United States. Win or lose, they usually played to capacity crowds of over 80,000. The businessmen of Columbus and, as far as that goes, the whole state of Ohio, were rabid football fans.

I decided to do a full scale investigation of all jobs held by the athletes there. Dick Larkins, Athletic Director, gave me full cooperation and told me their records were

all available. There were two types of jobs held by the Buckeye athletes. Ohio State University is located in the capital of Ohio and, I found there were numerous state house jobs. This type of work had been investigated by my predecessor, Major Griffith, on several occasions. Apparently, they were well regulated and supervised by the different department heads. They were not highly paid jobs but were extremely valuable to an athlete because the hours could be filled during the evening, or weekends. The average number of hours put in by the athletes was a 16-hour week, for which the pay could be anywhere from $50 to $75 a month. The state not only employed athletes but hundreds of other Ohio State students (non-athletes) as well. One of my investigators, after spending a whole week at the state house, during the fall, reported that a few of the players had an agreement with the departments where they worked

DON GEHRMANN was another of Wisconsin's nationally acclaimed track stars, appearing just a few years after Gene Fenske and Walter Mehl had flashed across the Conference firmament for the Badgers. Gehrmann was Conference indoor and outdoor mile champ in 1947, was a repeater in 1948, and was NCAA king for three years in a row, becoming only the second man in Big Ten history to be a three-ply national winner. In 1948 he won the Olympic trials finals at 1500-meters and represented the United States in London. The Conference individual cross-country crowns in 1947-48 were other honors the Badger star collected in his brilliant career.

and Don Gehrmann of Wisconsin scored the first of three brilliant triumphs he would have in the 1500-meters.

Matt Mann's Wolverines out-splashed Ohio State for the swim title on the basis of all-around strength as they took only one first place, the 300-yard medley relay, won by the ubiquitous Harry Holiday, Bob Sohl and Dave Tittle, in 2:51.9. Michigan State's foursome of Abel Gilbert, George Hoogerhyde, Bob Allwardt, and Jim Duke, ripped off a record-tying 3:31.0 in the 400-yard freestyle relay. Among individuals, Ohio State's Bill Smith scored a brilliant repeat double, setting a new mark of 2:09.5 for

the freestyle, and won the 440 in 4:43.8. Wally Riis, of Iowa, one of the finest freestylers the Big Ten has ever turned out, took the 100 in 51:5, and Bill Heusner, Northwestern's great distance ace, won the 1500-meter in 19:28.2. A new star ascended on the diving scene, as Ohio State's Bruce Harlan, destined to be hailed as the greatest diver in the history of the sport, scored his first double on the high and low boards. Before he would be finished, he would own an unprecedented set of three double victories.

Wisconsin repeated as NCAA boxing champ, with the Badger cause led by individual titlists, Steve Gremban at 119 pounds; Don Dickenson, 147; Cal Vernon, 176; and Vito Parisi, heavyweight. Two Michigan State battlers also captured individual crowns—Ernie Charboneau at 112 and the incomparable Chuck Davey at 136. Davey, for the second straight year won the John S. LaRowe trophy for sportsmanship and skill.

In wrestling, Arnold Plaza, Purdue's mighty mite, took the NCAA 114½-pound title; Dick Dickenson,

WALLY GACEK, leading the tourney scorers, led Michigan to victory in the first national collegiate hockey tournament in 1948.

---

that if they couldn't complete the 16 hours, the time could be made up after football season was over but that they would still receive the full amount of their pay. Obviously, this was not according to the rule and I made a hurried trip to the Ohio State campus.

After going through the records at the state house, I convinced myself these could be accurately checked. I could determine absolutely when the athlete checked in for work and when he checked out. There was another point here that, while these were bona fide jobs, they might be called patronage jobs dispersed by the political party in power. However, the minority group was always looking for irregularities. If there was any discrepancy in time put in, they would let everybody know.

The job program I was really concerned over was the one provided by hotels and various business places. On many of these, I found the statement, "no work during

football season; make it up later." It was an out-and-out violation and, frankly, I didn't see how a student athlete could find the time in the second semester to comply fully with this demand. The situation began to look serious.

I also ran into an unusual situation with the head football coach, Woody Hayes. Woody was an intelligent, energetic type who insisted on complete control of all football activities. He was an unusual character. No football fan who has watched him during a game will ever forget him. It might be almost zero weather but Woody was out on the side lines in his shirt sleeves. (I thought possibly that his observation of the football officials was what kept him so steamed up.) He not only was the coach but the close advisor and counselor of every one of his football players and it was this unusual care for his boys' welfare that got him into trouble. There had been an article published in the October, 1955 edi-

In the rainy mist at London's Wembley Stadium, Ohio State's MAL WHITFIELD (number 136) breaks the tape in a new record of 1:49.2 for a Gold Medal in the 800-meters. At Helsinki, Finland, four years later, he won the Gold Medal again in the same time.

of Michigan State, won at 136½; and Vern Gagne, Minnesota footballer, triumphed at 191. In addition, a new event was added to the NCAA tourney program and Michigan had the honor of winning the first national collegiate hockey title, defeating Boston College in the finals, 8-4, with Wolverine Wally Gacek leading the tourney scorers with eight goals for two games.

Gold Medals galore were draped around the necks of Conference stars on the Olympic victor's stand in 1948. Bill Porter, Northwestern's hurdling great, won the 110-meter high hurdles in a record-smashing 13.9. Ohio State's picture-runner, Mal Whitfield, posted a new mark of 1:49.2 for the 800-meters and ran a leg for the Yanks' victorious 1600-meter relay team, along with Indiana's Roy Cochrane, who also set a new mark of 51.1 to win the 400-meter hurdles.

In swimming, Walter Ris, Iowa's brilliant free-styler, splashed to a new record of 57.3 for the 100-meter sprint and swam a leg on the record-

smashing U.S. 800-meter relay. Ohio State's almost legendary Hawaiian flash, Bill Smith, posted a new mark of 4:41 for the 400-meter freestyle and teammate Bruce Harlan captured the high dive. Michigan's John Davies, on lend-lease, academically, from Australia, swam for his homeland and won the 200-meter breaststroke in a record-breaking 2:34.4. The Wolverines' Bob Sohl took a Silver Medal in the 200-meter backstroke. The swimming squad also rostered Michigan State's Howard Patterson and George Hoogerhyde, and Buckeye diver Miller Anderson.

ROY COCHRANE, Indiana's Big Ten champ, was an Olympic hero for the U.S. in 1948 setting a new Olympic mark of 51.1 in winning the 400-meter hurdles.

tion of Sports Illustrated that stated he had used his personal income, derived not from his salary for coaching but from making speeches and appearing on local TV shows, to help football players in need.

I questioned Woody about the article and while he said it had been somewhat blown up, he did admit to helping his players when they came to him in dire distress. It might have been money to keep an athlete from being evicted from a rooming house; or money for bus fare home when one of his parents was seriously ill. He also told me he had saved several of his players from dropping out of school and felt it was his right to do this. I told him that as laudable as his help was, unfortunately it was absolutely against the Conference Rule which dealt with unearned aid. His contention was these advances were in the nature of loans but that he had not required the athletes to sign notes for the money be-

cause often they were very small amounts. He also stated he had never kept a record but would endeavor to give me an accounting.

Finally, after a long talk, I told him I would have to take action against Ohio State. When President Howard Bevis heard about this, he requested that I meet with him and Woody to discuss the matter.

After several hours of discussion, I pointed out to the President of Ohio State that it would be necessary to get a full accounting of the football coach's loans or gifts to members of the football squad. This, Coach Hayes insisted he would do. In regard to the work program, the Athletic Department was to make a more rigid inspection, and no advance payments could be made where the actual work had not been performed.

As I studied all the investigating reports, I realized the almost impossible task faced by the Athletic Directors,

Other Big Ten track entries were Michigan's Herb Barten and Erkki Koutenen in the 800-meters and hop-step-jump; Indiana's Fred Wilt, 10,000-meters; Wisconsin's Don Gehrmann, 1500-meters; Michigan State's Ernie Crosbie and Adolph Weinacker in the 50,000-meter walk and Illinois' Bob Richards and Dwight Eddleman in the pole vault and high-jump.

The wrestling squad listed Minnesota's Verne Gagne; Michigan State's Bob Maldegan and Leland Merrill; and Iowa's Joe Scarpella.

Minnesota placed Allan Opsahl and Rube Bjorkman on the hockey team; and Michigan State's Chuck Davey and Chuck Speiser were on the boxing team.

The administrative scene was an active one for 1948. First, the directors reaffirmed a rule requiring Junior College transfers to spend a year in residence before becoming eligible for varsity competition. Next, the Conference administrators ruled 11 athletes from various schools ineligible for one year because of violations of league regulations dealing with aid to athletes. Most importantly of all, perhaps, was the decision to admit Michigan State to membership replacing departed Chicago, with the admission to take effect after Spartan athletic representatives had certified that Conference rules and other requirements were completly in force on the Michigan State campus. (The certification subsequently was made in May of 1949, and the Spartans were voted into formal membership for the academic year of 1950-51, but with football representation not to begin until the Spartans had played out their previously-drawn schedules and were free to embark on a full Conference card beginning in 1953.)

1949

It was late in the last quarter of the annual Ohio State-Michigan finale, at Ann Arbor. The Buckeyes had just tallied a touchdown that made it 7-6 in favor of Michigan, and now Jimmy Hague, Ohio's place-kicking end, was poised for the point that would decide the 1949 title and a Rose Bowl

CLAYTON TONNEMAKER

LEO NOMELLINI, Minnesota's mastodonic tackle, repeating the honor he'd won the year before, was an outstanding All-America choice in 1949, along with teammate CLAYTON TONNEMAKER, the Gophers' great center.

LEO NOMELLINI

or individuals they assigned to supervise the work program. Here, for instance, were jobs concentrated all over Columbus, Ohio, some of them offered by people who would tell the athlete that during the football season just forget it, and make up the time later. On April 26, 1956, I recommended that Ohio State be placed on probation for one year, with the following provisions:

1) During this period Ohio State shall under no circumstances be considered a representative team eligible to represent the Conference in the Rose Bowl football game.

2) That there will be diligent supervision by the University of the work program of athletes to assure full compliance with the rules. This would include a complete job record accounting which would permit a check on that compliance to my satisfaction.

3) That the university shall cooperate in obtaining a can-

did and full disclosure from Coach Hayes of any assistance to Ohio State University athletes to which he has been a party outside the limits and channels of aid permissible under the Conference rules, and also will provide an assurance of Mr. Hayes' literal compliance during the term of his future employment by the University with all rules of the Conference governing financial assistance to athletes.

4) That none of the athletes who were beneficiaries of the irregularities in the work program which permitted them to draw pay in advance of performing work therefore shall be presented for eligibility until I have approved satisfactory evidence that they have actually repaid fully in services the wages received.

The faculty representatives concurred with my decision and Ohio State was placed on probation and I was instructed to make periodic investigations to see that all

nomination. Pandel Savic knelt, took the snap from center and Hague swung his leg.

The kick was wide.

But a Michigan lineman had been offside and the Bucks got another boot out of it. Hague split the uprights this time and the Scarlet, with a 7-7 tie, went Bowling. In case of a title tie, the rule keeps home the team that last went to the Coast—in this case, Michigan.

Before all this happened, however, there had been a lot of surprises in this Conference race that went right down to the wire.

Minnesota, with a great line, and Michigan, coming off of two straight titles, were favored for the top spot. The Gophers had a torrid threesome in Dick Gregory, Billy Bye, and Frank Kuzma advancing the ball; and great linemen in Leo Nomellini and Clayt Tonnemaker to bolster a forward wall that also featured crack ends in Bud Grant and Gordy Soltau. The Gophers looked like the Norsemen of old, and manhandled their first four foes, including a 27-0 shellacking of Ohio. It was, apparently, a shoo-in for the Gophers; but, somebody forgot to tell Michigan and Purdue in the Gophers' next two games. The Minnesota offense sputtered badly, and all of a sudden there were 14-7 and 13-7 splotches on the Gopher record and their season was in ashes.

Michigan seemed loaded, too. Up front there were two marvelous tackles in Alvin Wistert and Allen Wahl; a great guard in Lloyd Heneveld, and Harry Allis was still a welcome sight at end. In Chuck Ortmann, the Wolverines had the top running-passing threat in the Conference. Don Dufek and Don Peterson were the best brace of bruising, alternating fullbacks in the league; and Wally Teninga, Dick Kempthorn and Chuck Lentz were the kind of Handy-Andy's that give a club real depth. Ortmann again wound up leading the league in total offense, and Lentz, alert and cat-like, picked off more enemy passes than anybody in the loop.

It wasn't as strong a club as the '47-'48 teams (who was?) and there was some errant staggering earlier in the year when Army smacked down the Wolves 21-7 and Northwestern pulled one out 21-20 in successive games. Ironically enough, it was a missed PAT by Harry Allis, one of the great booters in Michigan history, which cost the Wolverines a tie when Steady Eddie Nemeth made good on all three of his attempts for the Wildcats. A late season drive by the Maize and Blue found them sniffing roses as they squared off in the big finale against Ohio State.

The Buckeyes the year before had had their worst season since they were in the Big Ten, winning only two games out of nine; but old-hero Wes Fesler, in his second year, was beginning to put the pieces together neatly. At quarterback was Pandel Savic, who came to the United States from Yugoslavia as a boy of 12. A smart signal-caller and fine passer, Savic presided over a bevy of swift halfbacks that included hard-running Jerry Krall; Walt Klevay, Jimmy Clark, and a squat, versatile sophomore named Vic Janowicz who, the following year would be Mr. Unbelievable. At fullback was Fred Morrison, a rampaging line-smasher and terrific punter. Fesler put this group behind a line that featured Ralph Armstrong and Jim Hague at ends; Dick O'Hanlon and Bill Trautwein at tackles; a great guard in George Toneff and his fine running-mate, Bob Momsen; and a nifty center in Jack Lininger.

After a heart-stopping 35-34 win over Missouri, Fesler figured he might make some waves. A big victory over Indiana, and a 13-13 tie with Southern California, followed, but then the Bucks were taken apart by what appeared to be the Minnesota juggernaut. After that, they settled down to a pattern which Fesler later described somewhat whimsically. "We never really felt comfortable until we fell behind and had to rally."

After a 21-0 win over Wisconsin the Buckeyes fell into their strange ways: they trailed Northwestern

stipulations concerning the probation were carried out.

The NCAA concurred with this action and they, too, placed Ohio State on probation and requested that I make a periodic report to their committee on infractions, concerning Ohio State's compliance with the requirements. I am happy to say that Ohio State's Athletic Department did a very fine job in meeting all my requests. Several of their athletes had to work their entire spring vacation and even part of their summer vacation until they had made up all the deficiencies. Hayes later furnished me with a report which showed that a relatively small amount of money had not been repaid and this amount was really inconsequential.

President Eisenhower and Tug Wilson confer on upcoming Olympics in 1954.

7-0 before winning 24-7; trailed Pitt 10-7 before pulling it out 14-10; trailed Illinois 17-14 and then ran wild for a 30-17 count; trailed Michigan 7-0 before evening it up for the Bowl assignment. Then, against California in the Rose Bowl, the Golden Bears had the Bucks 14-7 before Fred Morrison cracked over for the tying TD and Jimmy Hague

FRANCIS, ALBERT and ALVIN WISTERT, collegiate football's most-famed brother trio, and the only such threesome in grid history to win All-America honors: Michigan's tackle triumverate (top to bottom) Francis (1933); Albert (1942); and Alvin (1948-49).

again came through with the PAT and a subsequent field goal for the win.

For the first time in 30 years—going back to 1919 —a big Ten champion, or co-champ in Ohio's case— failed to place a man on the All-America, but Michigan, the other flag-sharer, placed their great tackle, Alvin Wistert, third and last of the all-star brothers. Leo Nomellini, the mastodonic Gopher tackle, and teammate Clayt Tonnemaker, at center, were other Conference contributions. Bob Wilson, Wisconsin's versatile center, was chosen Conference MVP. Meanwhile, Michigan State, with an eye on the Big Ten vacancy created by Chicago's withdrawal, had turned up with its second straight high scoring team in a row. The year before, the Spartans had posted 359 points in winning six, tying two and losing two—dropping early season games to Michigan, 13-7 and mighty Notre Dame, 26-7. The Wolverines and Irish pinned losses on the Spartans again in 1949, as did Oregon, but again Michigan State rolled up the points for 309, and in Lynn Chandnois had one of the best backs in the land, along with a great pair of guards in Ed Bagdon and Don Mason. Bagdon, Mason, and Chandnois were named All-America (with Bagdon winning the Outland Award as the nation's best interior lineman) and soon there would be a veritable wave of Green and White all-stars rolling from the East Lansing campus.

Meanwhile, there had been a record set by Michigan which brought envious sighs from college ticket sellers all over the land. The Wolverines had set an all-time attendance mark of 772,482 for nine games. A neat average of 85,831 per game.

Although defending champion Michigan returned to the 1949 cage season with a veteran nucleus headed by Mack Supronowicz and Bob Harrison, the Wolverines lost their impetus, and a well-disciplined, hot-shooting Illinois team regained the heights once known by the "Whiz Kids." Scoring 1530 points for the season, overall, a new high for

The result of this sweeping investigation, and others that had been made at different Big Ten schools, showed how impractical and unrealistic a work program had become. There simply were not enough hours in the day to permit an athlete to meet all his college expenses by a work program. There were questions continually being raised as to when an athlete should receive portal pay if his job required some distances of travel. I had also become aware of the fact that there were injustices being done to some athletes because of the difference of the pay structure in various states, which was hard to equalize.

In a special Joint Group meeting on August 4, 1956, the Conference received a report from a Special Committee appointed months before to give a critical self-appraisal of Conference policies and practices. There were now two ways the Big Ten could go. One was to

adopt a practice of athletic grants-in-aid for athletes which was in vogue in many conferences in the United States. These were commonly known as athletic scholarships and in most conferences there were no academic restrictions governing their award. The other was to give up the work program and, perhaps, award aid on a proven need basis.

This might be a good time to review the whole unearned aid situation, the existing legislation which had been passed in 1952 and which was a determined effort to tighten the rules on aid rather than to lighten them.

Under this legislation, no scholarship aid could be given to an athlete unless the applicant possessed superior academic standing, defined as being in the upper third of his high school graduating class. To continue this aid in college it was mandatory that he maintain a cumulative scholastic average between B and C.

Michigan State, just a few seasons away from admittance to the Big Ten grid wars, was tuning up in 1949 with three All-Americas: LYNN CHANDNOIS, a slashing halfback, and ED BAGDON, who with his All-America running mate, Don Mason, gave the Spartans the finest guard duo in the nation.

a Big Ten team, the Illini were led by Dwight Eddleman and Bill Erickson, and finished with a 10-2 league mark just ahead of Minnesota. Once again, as so often happens in the Big Ten, last game pressure with the title at stake tripped the Gophers. With a chance to tie, the Vikings, paced by Jim McIntyre and Meyer (Whitey) Skoog, a brilliant sophomore, blew a 45-43 windup to Wisconsin.

Big Don Rehfeldt of Wisconsin led the league scorers, and shared all-around honors with Eddleman, Erickson, Ohio State's Dick Schnittker, and McIntyre. Erickson was an All-America choice, and

A further stipulation was that he must make quantitative progress toward a degree. If he satisfied all these requirements, he could receive a scholarship on a yearly basis not to exceed the normal expenses of attending the university, and this aid would come under review each year. This was fine for the excellent scholar-athlete. He had it made. He would be sought after by every Big Ten school, as well as many other colleges throughout the country. The unfortunate part of the legislation was that the majority of the athletic prospects did not graduate in the upper third of their class and, therefore, couldn't qualify for full aid. Many came from families of moderate means, usually from large families and could expect very little, if any, help from their parents.

It is true that the athlete could qualify for a tuition grant if he were in the upper half of his high school

DWIGHT (DYKE) EDDLEMAN

In 1942 when a 6-2 forward led Centralia, Ill., High School to a state basketball championship, the game had not yet reached its high-scoring, firehorse style of play. Dwight (Dyke) Eddleman, however, was a portent of the future. In four seasons he had scored 2702 points and, in one year, his junior season, he had gone over 40 points a game on three occasions. Since there were considerably fewer team shots per game in those days the youngster was doing it on uncanny accuracy—almost a .600 shooting percentage for four years.

The black-haired youth had gone out for football in his freshman year in high school and was injured, so he passed up the gridiron for his sophomore and junior years. He decided to pull on his cleats again for his senior season and promptly ran and passed for 1000 yards, and added All-State grid honors to the similar honors he'd won in basketball for three straight years.

The track coach had a crack at him, too, and Dyke Eddleman obligingly won state championships in the hurdles and high jump. He was invited to make a guest appearance at the annual Big Ten-Pacific Coast Conference track meet and the high school boy outjumped the collegians with a 6-foot, 6-inch effort, pretty amazing stuff for 1942.

There was ample reason to believe Dyke Eddleman would cut a similar swath through collegiate circles. Illinois won the Eddleman sweepstakes and, after three years of World War Two military service, Eddleman showed up at Champaign-Urbana.

At Illinois he won 11 varsity letters—more than any man in modern Illini history. He played four years of basketball, capping his career with a 329-point senior year as he led the 1949 Illini to a Big Ten title. A magnificent all-around halfback, he was undoubtedly the greatest punter in recorded Big Ten annals. In his senior year his 52 high, booming kicks for 2252 yards averaged 43.3 yards for the season.

In track he took five out of six Big Ten outdoor and indoor high jump titles and gilded his performance with a 6-8 leap for second place in the 1948 Olympics in London.

All this—and the Western Conference Honor Medal for Scholarship, as well!

Dwight (Dyke) Eddleman, Illinois' 11-letter star and Conference Medal winner.

BILL ERICKSON, a sparkling backcourtman who could shoot and hawk the ball, led Illinois to the league title in 1949 and was named All-America.

JACK BRUNER, Iowa ace who was the league's leading pitcher; and DON RITTER, Indiana's Conference batting champ, both were named to the collegiate All-America in 1949.

Illinois went to the NCAA where it got by Yale but was dumped, 76-47, by Kentucky, the eventual champion.

Indiana, which hadn't won a track title since 1930, came through with the indoor crown, but Minnesota claimed the honors outdoors. The Hoosiers also shared the baseball championship, with Michigan and Iowa making it a three-way split. Indiana's first-sacker, Don Ritter, led the league in hitting with a robust .439, and Iowa's Jack Bruner paced the pitchers with a 5-1 mark, and was selected for the All-America team.

Mike Peppe's Ohio State swimmers launched the longest reign in Conference annals when the Bucks, paced by Bill Smith, Bob deGroot and Bruce Harlan,

DON RITTER

graduating class, but that was all. If he could not earn enough on his summer job, the athlete had to work his way through the university. In past years, this had been possible but now university food and housing costs in the dormitories were at record heights. A large percentage of the athletes belonged to fraternities and the cost there had almost doubled in a 20-year period. A portion of the cost was often defrayed by the athlete who waited on tables at his fraternity in addition to working at other odd jobs.

My hat is off to those who made it and many did, and in doing so received the valuable training of learning to budget their time. Frankly, many could not meet this survival program and either flunked out or quietly withdrew to re-enter neighboring conferences where they could get an athletic scholarship. The attrition of Big Ten freshmen athletes became quite alarming.

Through the mid-1950's the Conference had stubbornly stuck to its program but finally concluded that the job program was unsatisfactory in that it placed an almost impossible burden on an athlete who had to work all the way through. A Special Committee had been appointed and spent a year studying the situation. On August 4, 1956, they made their final report to the faculty representatives and athletic directors at a special meeting. They endorsed and suggested a practice of administering financial aids to athletes on a basis of proven need.

The Conference okayed this principle and directed the Special Committee to submit the necessary legislation for this principle. It was a tough decision for the Conference leaders to make. There were those who felt the best way would simply be to give athletic grants-in-aid across the board. There were others who stubbornly wanted

JIM PETERSON of Minnesota was the only man in Big Ten gymnastics history to win the undisputed league all-around title three straight years (1947-48-49).

took the first of what would become eight straight league titles.

Purdue, with 121-pound Arnold Plaza winning his third straight crown, took the league wrestling championship, and Jim Peterson, with his third straight all-around title, led Minnesota to its third consecutive gymnastic championship.

Northwestern, with Ted Peterson's singles title leading the way, won the Conference tennis crown, and Michigan took team golf honors as Ed Schalon tied Purdue's Fred Wampler for the individual crown.

Wisconsin picked off the cross-country crown but Michigan's Don McEwan, one of the greatest dis-

tance men in Wolverine track history, nipped the Badgers' fabulous Don Gehrmann for the individual title and the only defeat of Gehrmann's Conference career. In a stupendous upset, however, Michigan State, under Karl Schlademan, the most successful cross-country coach in Big Ten annals, came on to take the NCAA team crown. Schlademan, before retiring, would win more national championships than any coach in history.

In other NCAA action, Ohio State captured another swimming team title for the Big Ten in what was now a common turnabout with Michigan, the defending titlist. The Buckeyes were led by Bill Smith's double: a 2:08.5 record in the 220-freestyle which lowered the standard he'd set a year. before; and another typically Smith victory in the 440 freestyle, in 4:43.8. Lanky Bob deGroot captured the 150-yard backstroke for the Bucks in 1:34, and Bruce Harlan, the superlative diver, again won both the low and high board titles. Other Conference members took their usual share of championships: Dick Weinberg, the Michigan ace, won the 50-yard sprint; Wally Ris, the Iowa sensation, repeated in the 100 with a time of 50.4; Bill Heusner, of Northwestern, retained his 1500-meter championship in 19:04.8; and Keith Carter, the great Purdue butterfly artist, won the 200-yard event in 2:14.8. In the relay section, a crack Iowa trio of Duane Draves, Bowen Stassforth, and Erv Straug took the 300-yard medley in 2:54.1.

Louisiana State interrupted Wisconsin's domination of the NCAA boxing tourney, as the Badgers, for the first time, failed to win a single division crown. There were laurels aplenty, however, for Chuck Davey of Michigan State, the most-decorated boxer in NCAA history, who became the only man ever to win four crowns as he triumphed at 135 pounds and again was awarded the trophy for the outstanding performer in the tourney. Colin Connell, Minnesota's aggressive 165-pound belter, was the league's only other titlist.

to continue with the job program and doubted that an aid-based-on-need plan would be workable. The Special Committee had investigated how this had been handled in the Ivy League. Bill Reed, my assistant, had made several trips to the Ivy League schools, studying how they had worked out their problems. We had invited two of the administering officers of these institutions to talk to our faculty representatives and directors. It was touch-and-go as to whether a common agreement could be arrived at but in the Conference meeting on December 8, 1956, a new rule was passed governing financial assistance on a basis of demonstrated need. After a 60-day period under the so-called White Resolution, the Conference confirmed the enactment of the new financial assistance rule and created a financial aid service to make determination of financial need.

Briefly stated, this financial aid service had to deter-

mine, in the case of each entering athlete, how much his parents should be expected to contribute. This meant that when athletes applied for aid, parents must submit a confidential statement of their net income. Some parents refused to do this, stating it was their own business, but after finding out that no aid would be available unless they complied, the plan began to work.

Reed, who had done such a tremendous job securing information about the plan, was given the task of evaluating the parent's confidential statements. It took hours and hours of careful work and the statements were often checked through the home town banker or someone who knew the family circumstances. Many times the parent's financial fortunes would vary from year to year and this meant the amounts they could be expected to pay had to be adjusted.

In theory this was a just plan. There was no reason

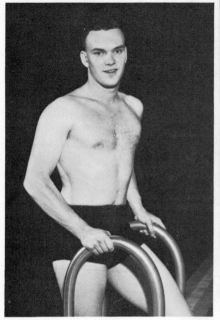

BILL SMITH **BILL HEUSNER** **WALTER RIS**

Ohio State's Big Ten and NCAA championship swimming team in 1949 owed much of its success to Hawaiian star BILL SMITH. Other stars from the Conference who won national crowns were WALLY RIS, Iowa sprint ace, and Northwestern's great distance swimmer, BILL HEUSNER, at 1500-meters. Heusner was a repeater from 1948, as was Ris, Olympic champion in 1948 and the greatest tankman in Iowa history. The Buckeyes' Smith was merely a legend in his time. The Big Ten champ at 220-and 440-yards, he was a three-timer in the NCAA 440 freestyle (1947-48-49) and the only man in history to splash to four victories in the 220 freestyle (1943-47-48-49, with time out for wartime military service). Altogether, Smith won three Conference crowns, seven NCAA titles, seven AAU championships, and an Olympic victory in 1948.

Arnold Plaza, the little whiz from Purdue, repeated as NCAA 121-pound wrestling champ, and Minnesota's Vern Gagne, a winner at 191 pounds the previous year, moved up to heavyweight and triumphed impressively.

CHUCK DAVEY of Michigan State was the most decorated boxer in collegiate history. He won four NCAA crowns at varying weights from 127 to 145 pounds (1943-47-48-49, with time out for military service), and was three-time winner of the LaRowe Trophy as the outstanding boxer in the national tournament.

why parents in the higher brackets, who frequently allowed their son to have a car at school, should not have to pay the whole shot. Very often they didn't agree and even more often an athlete from a wealthy family thought he should get full help just like the rest of his teammates. Many staff members, especially the football and basketball coaches, heartily disapproved of the plan; they said it made recruiting a tougher task, but there were also many parents of moderate means who complied with the regulations. They took pride in the fact they were helping their boy through school.

The financial aid program added so much work to the Conference office that we employed an examiner, John Dewey, a very capable young graduate of Northwestern. He had spent several years working at Purdue as an auditor in the business department and was thor-

oughly conversant with Big Ten problems and rules. His duties were to make regular inspections of intercollegiate athletic practices at the member schools and particularly of the administration of financial aid to athletes. His investigations brought to light many technical irregularities, most of them inconsequential but others were more serious.

When a new coach came into the Conference, I tried to use unusual diligence in seeing that he fully understood our rules of recruiting; what was permissible and what was not. These rules, of course, were all a matter of record and could be referred to at any time.

Indiana University had had its ups and downs through the years in football. In the 58 years they had been a member of the Big Ten they had only been successful in winning one clear-cut Conference championship in 1945

In hockey, Michigan's Gil Burford was the leading scorer with seven points in the tourney won by Boston College, and in track, three Conference stars took individual crowns. Don Gehrmann, of Wisconsin repeated as mile king in 4:09.6; Ohio State's brilliant Olympian, Mal Whitfield, repeated in the 880 and equalled the NCAA record of 1:50.3; and Fred Johnson, Michigan State's fine broad jumper, leaped 25-2½ for the crown.

Among the winners of the Conference Medal for scholarship were Dike Eddleman, Illinois' great three-sport star in football, basketball and track; Michigan grid and basketball star, Pete Elliott; Northwestern's crack swimmer, Bill Heusner; Purdue's aquatic star, Keith Carter; and Ohio State's great diver, Bruce Harlan.

VERN GAGNE, Minnesota grid lineman and Big Ten champ, won the NCAA heavyweight wrestling championship in 1949 after competing for the United States in the 1948 Olympics.

Coming off a decade in which World War Two brought more problems than the Conference had ever experienced in one period, the Big Ten was hoping to welcome The Fifties as an era of progress. The dream was quickly shattered as the Korean War put a crimp in personnel and physical expansion plans. Once again freshmen were declared eligible for varsity competition and some of them immediately made national headlines, most notably Indiana's Don Schlundt in basketball and Ohio State's Hopalong Cassady in football.

It was also a decade which found the Conference restored to its traditional ten members as Michigan State was admitted, and a period which saw the start of the second great athletic building boom as basketball arenas, field houses and golf courses blossomed all over the Big Ten, or went onto the drawing boards. Talent-wise, the decade was to provide more All-America football and basketball players and more national swimming champions than any other 10-year period in history. Perhaps more significantly, the decade was to see the advent of the grant-in-aid for student athletes.

The 1950 football season followed a rather predictable pattern for seven weeks, took a strong detour on the eighth weekend and wound up with the most bizzare finish in the history of Western Conference football. National magazines were still doing feature stories more than 10 years later about the title-deciding game between Michigan and Ohio State which, for sheer, zany unbelivability might go unequalled in football annals.

The campaign leading up to that day is worth reviewing. Wes Fesler's Buckeyes, with a sizeable group of veterans left over from his '49 co-champions, plus some prize sophomores, were favored to lead the Big Ten pack and even make a run for national honors. Why not, said the critics? Vic Janowicz, the stocky do-everything halfback was now a mature junior, and if he needed help there was fleet Walt Klevay at wingback; stampeding

under Bo McMillin. Part of this difficulty came from the fact that high schools in Indiana were mostly rabid basketball schools. As a matter of fact, at one time only 59 high schools in the State of Indiana fielded football teams. This, of course, confronted them with a distinct disadvantage because there wasn't a big pool of athletes to draw from in the state.

In the past few years the enrollments at Indiana University had grown tremendously. They now possessed fine dormitories, a wonderful student union building and under the dynamic leadership of President Herman Welles, Indiana made amazing progress. They had on the drawing boards plans for a fine new stadium, a new field house and also a wonderful practice area blocked out for all their athletic teams. Then, following a disastrous season in 1956 when they finished at the bottom of the

Big Ten they hired a new coach, Phil Dickens, who had a remarkable coaching record at the University of Wyoming. In his last year there he was 10-0. His arrival on the Hoosier campus was heralded as the beginning of a new era in Indiana football.

A tremendous worker and fine speaker, he talked to Indiana alumni groups throughout the state. He implanted confidence in his listeners that the job could be done providing he obtained good material. Since he'd come in at a time when many changes had been made, I took extra precautions in going into detailed instructions concerning the rules. I felt sure there would be mistakes made but was hardly prepared for the reports that began to come in. Most of them were minor in detail and only called for a clarification, but it was not long before word began to filter in that the new coach at

VIC JANOWICZ, Ohio State's 5-9, 185-pound Mr. Versatility not only was a unanimous All-America in 1950 but was a natural for the Heisman and UPI Player-of-the-Year Award. The chunky Buckeye who ran, passed, punted, and place-kicked with equal brilliance, led the league in scoring, rushing and, naturally, was Conference MVP.

Chuck Gandee at fullback, and Tony Curcillo, a sophomore quarterback whiz who was a fine passer and strong runner. Fesler, who believed in platooning as much as possible, also had a bevy of hawk-like defensive backs in Karl Sturtz, Bob Demmel, Dick Widdoes and Bob Bruney. Up front, there were featured performers in Tom Watson, a great pass-catcher at end; a trio of terrific tackles in Bill Trautwein, Joe Campanella and Dick Logan; a brace of bruising guards in Bob Momsen and John Biltz, and a talented center in Bob McCullough.

The total picture became somewhat fuzzy, however, when a tossup opener with Southern Methodist found the Mustangs, led by shotgun passer Fred Benners and Kyle Rote, scoring twice in the final few

minutes to pull out a 32-27 victory over the Bucks. From then on, the Scarlet went on an awesome, five-week, 230-point scoring rampage featured by an 83-0 devastation of Iowa. By this time sports writers were referring to Ohio as ". . . Vic Janowicz and his 40 All-America playmates."

The Iowa game resulted in a rash of records as the Buckeyes ran and passed in an orgy of point-making that found second and third stringers sharing prominently in the proceedings. Tony Curcillo tossed four touchdown passes for a new Conference mark (to be broken by Iowa's Fred Riddle a decade later) and also set a record, which still stands, for 308 total yards gained on 10 of 14 completions for 292 yards and 16 more by rushing. The Buckeyes' 12 touchdowns tied the league mark and Janowicz swung his leg for 11 PAT attempts and made 10 of them for two more records. (An Ohio sub made good on the 12th.)

After two more Ohio wins over Northwestern and Wisconsin the football world was rocked by the news that an underdog Illinois team had upset the Buckeyes 14-7. It was a sound Illinois team, with a fine backfield of Fred Major at quarterback; Johnny Karras and Don Stevens at halfback; and a pile-driving Dick Raklovits at fullback. Raklovits was also the league's leading rusher. The line had particularly brilliant performers in Tony Klimek at end; Al Tate at tackle; Chuck Brown, a guard, and Bill Vahaska at center. The Illini kept the Bucks off balance all afternoon and their stunning victory threw the Conference into a three-way battle for the title and Rose Bowl assignment going into the final day of the season—a day never to be forgotten by fans, players, and the weatherman.

As it turned out, the Illini, with only a 7-6 loss to Wisconsin, could have been Bowl-bound by beating Northwestern, who was going nowhere but home after the game.

Meanwhile, at Columbus, the Buckeyes needed only a win over a lacklustre Michigan team which

Indiana was making fantastic offers of financial assistance to prospective athletes in excess of aid permissible under Conference regulations.

At first I thought these assertions could not possibly be true. The rule clearly stated that the unearned aid was to be determined by the Conference financial aid service. The next rule was, of course, that this aid could not be larger than the normal expenses of any student going to that university. These charges were immediately called to the attention of the athletic director at Indiana University and to the coaching staff. They continued to come in, however, so I put my investigators to work. There were cases where athletes had been brought to the Indiana campus and then on their way home had visited other schools and asked why they could not get as good deal there as that which had been offered

to them at Indiana. I got calls from high school coaches who had talked to the boys after they got home. I told them the alleged offer was absolutely illegal.

I knew that high school athletes would sometimes brag about the offers they had received and enlarge on them, but in these cases the whole pattern seemed to be exactly the same. The boys were brought to the campus, which was legal. They were entertained over a weekend, which was within the rules. They met the coaching staff who enlarged on their chances of making the team there, which is a customary selling talk of all coaches. Their last port of call, however, was to talk alone with the head coach in his private office. All of them had the same story to relate—there they were offered aid in the amount of board, room, books, tuition and meals but would also receive $50.00 a month for

had lost to Illinois, had been tied by Minnesota and had been dumped outside the lodge by Army and Michigan State (not yet a league member). It was a spotty Wolverine record and a spotty club whose most redeeming features were Chuck Ortmann and Don Dufek, two exceptionally fine backs, a terrific tackle in Allen Wahl; a fine end in Lowell Perry; a whale of a center in Tony Momsen—whose brother, Bob, would be playing opposite him, at guard, for Ohio State.

All week the Buckeyes, who had scored 283 points in eight games, had been sizzling over their defeat by Illinois, and Fesler had the Scarlet in a savage mood for a comeback victory over archrival Michigan that would insure the Rose Bowl bid. Early Friday morning it started to snow all over the state. Nobody paid much attention at first, but by evening the white stuff, blown by gale-force winds, was piling up in alarming fashion. It kept snowing all through the night. By Saturday morning the temperature had dropped to three degrees above zero and the snow in some portions of Ohio was 25 inches deep and still rising. In other places it was in four- and five-foot drifts. Ohio Stadium was a muffled, arctic fantasmagoria. Somewhere, beneath thousands of tons of snow was the tarpaulin covering the field, and it was frozen stiff. Stranded on highways throughout central Ohio were thousands of cars headed for Columbus and the game. All public transportation—plane, train, bus and taxi—had been shut down tight. Columbus was a sealed city. As one witness put it: "Only Peary, Cook and Amundsen could get through to this game!"

He was wrong. More than 50,000 of the 80,000 ticket-holders somehow showed up at the big horseshoe where many tried to build small bonfires under the Stadium while others swept monstrous piles of snow off the seats to find their numbers.

The question was, would there be a game; Fritz Crisler of Michigan and Dick Larkins of Ohio State, the two athletics directors, went into a huddle after discussions with Bennie Oosterbaan and Wes Fesler, the coaches. (Fesler later decided he didn't think anybody should be forced to play under such conditions.) Even if they were able to pry the frozen tarp loose with bulldozers and push off most of the snow it was still a blizzard out there and the field would be covered again in a short while, and maybe knee-deep by game's end. Nobody could find a yard stripe. No official would ever see what was going on; but it was up to the home director, and Larkins, feeling that Crisler preferred to play, agreed to let the game go on. It started 20 minutes late, and what happened between opening whistle and final gun was not exactly football—a sport which both teams immediately discovered could not be played.

ALLEN WAHL, All-America tackle, and CHUCK ORT-MANN, triple-threat halfback who punted 24 times for 723 yards in a single game—the famed "Blizzard Bowl" against Ohio State—were big factors in Michigan's 1950 championship season.

their incidental expenses, which was clearly a violation of the rule.

In a letter to President Wells of Indiana University dated July 18, 1957, I enumerated in full the violations I had found and gave my conclusions as follows:

"On the basis of the facts and testimony which have been brought forth, I have concluded that, for reasons which must be known only to him, Coach Dickens did offer or promise to various individuals financial aid which is not permissible under Conference rules. The compelling basis for this conclusion is that, whatever mental reservations Coach Dickens may have had, there was established in a consistant pattern a firm and unmistakable impression the expectancy of such excessive aid on the part of several prospects he had interviewed, and that there was totally absent in their minds, on the basis of anything he had said or communicated to them, an understanding or appreciation of the needs basis for the award of aid which is inherent in Rule 7.

"A question has been raised as to whether such a conclusion as to fact constitutes a violation of Rule 7, or is subject only to the provisions of the Conference regulation governing recruiting as an improper inducement to enrollment. While it may be contended that Rule 7 is not explicit in this respect (and I would cite Section 3(f) of the Rule as well as the Summary of Prohibitions and Penalties in the Financial Aid Manual as being sufficiently explicit), it would not be contended that a staff member's complicity in the acceptance or receipt of unauthorized aid was not a violation. That being true, I cannot escape a conclusion that any invitation

Deception, ball-handling and trap-blocking were out. A lineman was lucky to make contact on a block. A ball-carrier had to go it alone and his feet betrayed him on every start. It became a record-shattering kicking duel as both clubs got off (nobody knew how) a total of 45 punts. Mostly on third down, often on second down, and sometimes on first down—hoping the congealed receiver would never see the ball or bobble it if he tried for it.

Chuck Ortmann, the Michigan tailback, booted the ball 24 times, the most ever in a Big Ten game, for a 723-yard total. Vic Janowicz got off 21 for 672 yards in the nightmarish exchange.

From whistle to gun, Michigan gained 27 yards and never made a first down. Ohio got three first downs.

Janowicz carried 19 times for a net loss of nine yards—despite the game's longest gain of 11 yards.

Ortmann's six-yard skid around end was the Wolverines' longest gain.

Eighteen passes were thrown by both teams when they found it impossible to run.

Michigan didn't complete a single one and Ohio completed three, as Ortmann, Janowicz and Curcillo could only guess where shadowy receivers were (nobody ever came close to running a prescribed pattern) and whether a receiver was wearing Scarlet or Blue.

It was a miracle anybody scored. Late in the first quarter Ohio was surprised to find itself on the Michigan 27. "I can see the goal posts," Janowicz chattered through chilled teeth to Curcillo. "Let's try a field goal." Somehow he converted this mad gambit into a 3-0 Ohio lead.

Early in the second quarter the Bucks were backed up to their goal and had to punt out. The kick was blocked and the ball rolled out of the end zone for an automatic safety and a 3-2 score.

Thus it continued—along with the snow and a lot of guessing by the officials as to where the yard-

stripes were at times. Then, with 40 seconds in the half to play, Ohio again had a third down on their own four-yard line and Michigan called time so the Bucks couldn't run out the clock. Maybe, the Wolves figured, they could force the Scarlet to kick. Maybe there'd be a bad pass from center or Janowicz would fumble the ball. Maybe there'd be time for one lucky Wolverine offensive play if this happened . . .

The 50,000 fans became quarterbacks and coaches. Eat the clock . . . Punt it out, now . . .

Fesler figured Michigan was smart enough to call time again if Ohio ran the ball on third down. That meant there'd be a gamble in running out the clock on fourth down, too. There might still be time for Michigan to run one lucky play from the four-yard line. The Bucks decided to punt on third down.

The ball was snapped, and blurred, blue figures sifted through the blizzarding snow, arms upraised, ghost-like. Janowicz swung his leg and the ball bounded off some random Wolverine anatomy, and suddenly everybody was diving into snowbanks all over the end zone looking for the ball. Tony Momsen, the Michigan center, found it first and Michigan had a touchdown.

There was no scoring in the second half. Ortmann and Janowicz kept up their kicking marathon, the backs kept falling on their faces, the blizzard grew worse, and, finally, Michigan had won it, 9-3.

That night the state of Ohio lay under its worst snowstorm in history. Buckeye fans lay under the stupor of bizarre defeat, and Ralph Guarasci, the Stadium groundkeeping boss had a gnawing worry as he and his crew searched every piece of rolled up canvas tarpaulin that had had to be cut into sections to be removed before the game. Hundreds of boy scouts on ushering duty at the stadium had helped the ground crew during the blinding storm and with kids slipping and falling all around there'd been a genuine fear that somebody might

or solicitation to accept improper aid, which in essence is the offense of which I consider Coach Dickens guilty, is also culpable and accordingly itself a violation of the rule.

"It is the privilege of Indiana University to appeal my decisions, both as to fact and as to the nature of the violation, to the Conference Faculty Representatives within five days of your receipt of this notice of my conclusions.

"In the absence of an appeal, or in the event of the Faculty Representatives sustaining my conclusions upon appeal, it will be necessary for Indiana University, in the terms of Section 9(b) of Rule 7 to "show cause why its membership in the Conference should not be suspended or terminated" if Coach Dickens remains in the employ or on the athletic staff of the University as one "who has violated or been a party to the violation of

the provisions of this rule." Such a proceeding would be before the Faculty Representatives as a group, whom I would call together at a date as early as may be possible."

At the special meeting on July 28, 1957, the Conference faculty representatives weighed carefully the assurance that from here on no member of the Indiana coaching staff could enter into any discussion of financial aid opportunities with prospective athletes, and that this responsibility would be delegated solely to an administrator under the athletic director, and that the athletes in quesion would be informed by letter what the limits of their unearned aid would be. Coach Dickens gave the Conference representatives his firm assurance that he and his staff would comply 100% with all the rules of the Conference. The faculty representatives then took the following action:

still be rolled up, helpless, in canvas, and freezing to death. Until midnight Guarasci's crew searched the canvas piles and every rest room and passageway in the huge horseshoe looking for fans who'd passed out from too much frostbite serum and who might freeze to death if not found.

"It was bad enough losing the title and the Rose Bowl trip," Guarasci moaned. "All we needed was to find some kid or fan stiff on us."

It wasn't until Monday that Columbus Airport was reopened . . . Not until Wednesday that classes met again . . . Not until a week later that the last of 20,000 stranded cars was removed from drifted highways. Eventually, the effects of the weird game and the deep disappointment of Buckeye fans began to wear off. Then, suddenly, there was another delayed reaction when Wes Fesler resigned as Ohio coach for personal reasons. "He just couldn't live with that blocked punt," one fan muttered morosely, and everybody immediately replayed the craziest football game in Big Ten history.

Meanwhile, getting back to that fateful Saturday . . . Illinois, which, coupled by an unseeming Ohio defeat could have taken the Big Ten title and the Rose Bowl trip by defeating underdog Northwestern, went down in a shocking 14-7 upset and the Wolverines, of course, went to Pasadena. There, the team with limping credentials, the team that had won the title game without making a first down and which had failed to lead the league in a single set of statistics, was still strong enough to knock off California, the pride of the West, 14-6.

For Vic Janowicz, there were honors galore at season's end. The running, passing, punting, placekicking virtuoso had led the league in scoring, total offense and handy-andy tactics. To such an extent, in fact, that he gained All-America, the Heisman

Among the nine stars from Conference schools who received All-America honors in 1950 were BOB MOMSEN, Ohio State's great guard; DON STONESIFER, Northwestern's slick pass receiver at end; and AL TATE, Illinois' wide-ranging tackle.

BOB MOMSEN   DON STONESIFER   AL TATE

WHEREAS, it is the responsibility of the Faculty Representatives to determine and impose a penalty or penalties for violations of Rule 7 and General Regulation VIII;

NOW THEREFORE BE IT RESOLVED, that Indiana University is deemed to have shown sufficient cause why its membership in the Conference should not be suspended or terminated, provided that Coach Phil Dickens be suspended as a coach of the football team for one year, during which period he shall not perform any of the professional duties or functions of a member of the intercollegiate football staff; and

BE IT FURTHER RESOLVED, that Indiana University shall have no right prior to the December, 1957 meeting of the Faculty Representatives to petition for permission to reinstate Coach Dickens; and

BE IT FURTHER RESOLVED, that as a penalty for vio-

lation of General Regulation VIII, during the period of suspension Coach Dickens shall have no contact with any prospective students.

It was probably the first time in the history of athletics at any institution where a football coach had been forced to sit out the whole season before he had fielded a team. The NCAA concurred with this penalty and placed a similar one through their committee on infractions, and requested that I keep them informed on my investigations that would follow. During the following year a careful check by many investigations demonstrated that Indiana had complied with all the stipulations of the probation. Coach Hicks, an assistant to Coach Dickens, did the coaching while the head coach was forced to sweat it out from a press box seat.

In a December meeting of the Faculty Representatives, the faculty representative from Indiana, John Mee, pre-

Michigan State, admitted to the Big Ten in all sports but football (set for 1953), launched an incredible decade of All-America football selections in 1950, with the naming of hard-running halfback EVERETT (SONNY) GRANDELIUS and end Dorne Dibble. Between 1950 and 1960 the Spartans would have 20 players honored as All-America, the most ever from any college in the land in a single decade.

Trophy and, of course, the Conference MVP award. Joining him as All-America designees were teammates Bob Momsen at guard and Bob McCullough, at center. From other Conference schools came Don Stonesifer, the great Northwestern end who led the league in pass receptions and who set a mark of 13 in a single game, against Minnesota; Dorne Dibble, the versatile Michigan State wingman; Everett (Sonny) Grandelius, Michigan State's great halfback; Al Wahl, the mighty Michigan tackle; Al Tate and Bob Vohaska, Illinois, stand-out tackle and guard; and Ed Withers, Wisconsin's defensive halfback demon.

Another Conference mark set that year, which still holds, was the sensational .642 percentage for pass completions set by Wisconsin's brilliant John Coatta. The busiest kicker in Big Ten history also cropped up that year when Don Roedel, a Minnesota guard, who was called upon for 56 kicks in six league games, established an all-time record.

Tippy Dye, the pint-sized three-sport star of yesteryear who had returned to Ohio State as basketball coach in 1946, laid a deft title touch on his 1950 group and molded the Buckeyes into a brilliantly-meshed cage machine. Dick Schnittker, the lanky shotmaker who was second only to Wisconsin's deadeye Don Rehfeldt in the Conference

JOHN COATTA, Wisconsin quarterback who led Big Ten passers two years in a row (1950 and 1951), set an all-time Conference record completion average in 1950 with 52 tosses out of 81 attempts for .642.

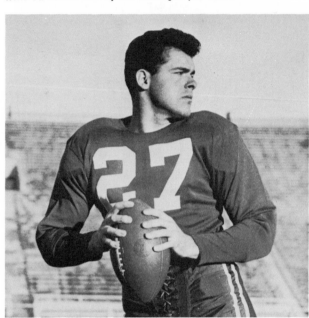

Kenneth L. "Tug" Wilson surrounded by George Halas, Red Grange, Bob Richards, Lou Boudreau & Dike Eddleman.

BOB DONHAM

Leading Ohio State to the Conference basketball championship in 1950 were smooth, dead-eye DICK SCHNITTKER at forward and his running mate, BOB DONHAM. Schnittker's all-around talents making him an All-America along with Wisconsin's Don Rehfeldt, the big center who led the league in scoring for the second year in a row.

DICK SCHNITTKER

scoring race, paced the Buckeyes to an 11-1 league mark and 22-4 overall, and a new team scoring mark of 1697 points for the season. Schnittker was the only super-star on the club but had valuable aid from four other cool, poised players who were a perfect complement to his brilliance: Bob Donham at the other forward spot, Bob Brown and Bob Burkholder in the backcourt, and a smallish but rugged center named Fred Taylor who, less than a decade later, would himself return to coach Ohio State to national basketball heights never before reached by a Big Ten school.

Schnittker, and Wisconsin's Rehfeldt, whose 265 points gave him the loop scoring title for the second

Wisconsin's DON REHFELDT took triple honors in 1950 as the Badger center, winning All-Big Ten, All-America and Conference MVP laurels.

---

sented a petition on behalf of Indiana University for permission to remove the suspension of Coach Dickens and on December 14, 1957, this received a unanimous vote of the institutions present with Indiana abstaining. Dickens was now permitted to field his first football team in the fall of 1958, where he made a very creditable record of 4 wins, 4 losses and one tie.

John Dewey proved to be a great aid in the examination of all the records at each university. He was also invaluable in being a kind of sounding board regarding the charges of one school against another, and when he found those that seemed to be of substance, he referred them to me and I checked them out.

One of the pieces of Conference legislation which had been passed, along with NCAA legislation in 1952, was the limitation of spring football practice. The allowable

time was 20 practice sessions in a period of 30 days. The 30-day period the Big Ten schools wanted had to be registered in my office and the 20 practices must come within that period. Our faculty representatives wanted to protect the athlete from any coach who might conceivably insist on a couple of months practice. The Big Ten had taken an early stand in this regard, not only limiting practice during the football season to a daily 2-hour period but also curtailed spring practice to make it possible for football players interested in track or baseball to go out for a spring sport. One day, a friendly sporting goods dealer, who was making the rounds, came in the office and reported to having seen a spirited practice in the field house during the winter months at the University of Minnesota. I checked the date he'd been there and found it didn't coincide with the 30-day period

straight year; Lou Watson, of Indiana; and Minnesota's scorching Whitey Skoog, were easily the brightest stars in the league. Schnittker was the first unanimous All-America from the Big Ten since Andy Phillip of Illinois pulled it off in 1943. Schnittker led Ohio into the NCAA where they were eliminated in a wild, 56-55 first round battle with CCNY, the eventual champion.

Not in years had the track championships been so hotly contested, as Ohio State nipped Michigan, 35 to 32-¾ indoors, and Indiana edged Minnesota, 37-36 outdoors. Indoors, the Buckeyes took only one first, with a mile relay triumph by Harry Cogswell, Gene Cole, Howie Kunz, and Herman Turner, but the Bucks built up supporting points in eight of the 12 events. The star of the meet, however, was Wisconsin's super-gaited Don Gehrman, who set new Conference marks of 1:53.1 and 4:10.4 in scoring a smashing double in the 880 and mile. Don Laz, Illinois' high-flying pole vaulter, hung up another new mark with his 14-3 and ⅞.

Outdoor, the team title achievement was much the same pattern. Indiana took only three individual crowns on Charley Peters' sprint double in the 100 and 220, and Cliff Anderson's shot-put triumph, but the Hoosiers scored heavily in eight of the 14 events. Again Gehrman was a stand-out, with victories in the half-mile, mile, and a great anchor lap in the mile relay.

In baseball, it was Michigan and Wisconsin sharing the crown with 9-3 marks, with the Badgers featuring a great battery in league-leading pitcher, Thornton Kipper, and Bob Wilson, probably the finest backstop in Badger history; along with two slugging outfielders, Paul Furseth and Bruce Elliott, both hitting .333. Michigan was led by a hard-hitting third-sacker, Gerry Dorr (.341); Pete Palmer, a smart catcher (.340) and outfielder Leo Koceski (.333). The league's top hitter, with a new league mark of .500 was a burly Purdue shortstop named Bill Skowron. Skowron was also a great Boilermaker

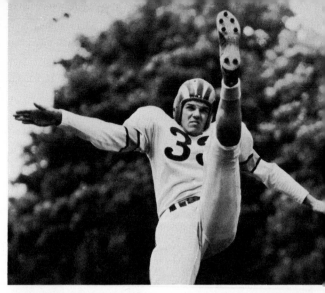

In 1950, Purdue three-sport star, BILL SKOWRON (football, basketball, baseball) led the league baseball campaign in hitting with the then highest average ever (.500). Later, Skowron starred for the New York Yankees. Skowron, a shortstop in college, had his batting mark broken in 1961 by Michigan's star catcher, Bill Freehan (.585) who went on to big league greatness with the Tigers.

halfback, and would later star with the New York Yankees. The Big Ten's first All-America, as selected by the newly-formed American Association of College Baseball Coaches, was Fred Taylor, a lanky Ohio State first baseman (.326) who starred in basketball and who would later coach the Buckeye basketeers to their greatest successes.

Purdue reached an all-time high in individual wins to take the league wrestling title for its third straight crown under Coach C. C. Reeck, and it was little Arnold Plaza at 121 pounds who set an unique mark that may never be matched, as he became the only man ever to win four titles. It was all made possible when he entered college in the fall of 1946 under the wartime freshman-eligible rule, and won his first championship in March, 1947. Other Boilermaker winners in 1950 were Joe Patascil, 128;

Coach Murray Warmath had selected. I decided to go up and take a look for myself and found out that there was considerable football activity going on.

It proved to be a class in an athletic coaching course—called theory and methods in football—and I found that all the athletes who were participating were enrolled in the course. The classes consisted of two parts: lecture and demonstration work. In discussing it with the athletic director and coach, they asked me what could be wrong with the situation. "Certainly there is no better way to teach a sport than by actually participating in it." I had to agree with the theory. The thing that bothered me was that nearly all the freshmen football players were enrolled in the class and were quite active in the demonstration work. Many of these youngsters were not taking physical education as a major but were enrolled in commerce, liberal arts or agriculture. There were only certain elective classes they could enroll in. Further, in questioning some of the boys, I found that members of the football staff had urged them to enroll in this class.

I informed the athletic department that I thought this was a violation of the rules and the practice must be discontinued. This was immediately appealed to the President of the University of Minnesota who, after listening to the facts, to my surprise, agreed with the coach; there was, he thought, no better way to teach a sport than to have a student actually participate, and he felt that my decision was wrong. I pointed out that to permit this would cause every member of the Big Ten which had athletic coaching courses to do the same thing. In other words, they would have the whole spring semester devoted to coaching their freshmen prospects. If the football candidates wanted to enroll in this course it was their privilege but they could not receive any

Charles Farina, 136; Charles Moreno, 145; and Wald Van Cott, 165.

Ohio State was off on the longest title streak in Big Ten swimming history, and the Bucks took seven events in their 1950 victory splash. Jack Taylor was the individual star of the meet, as the Buckeye flash took the 150-yard backstroke; 440-freestyle; and set a new Conference mark of 18:58.1 in the 1500-meters. An Ohio trio of Bill Sonner, Jose Balmores, and Frank Dooley won the 300-yard medley relay; Sonner added the 100-yard backstroke in a record 59.1, and Bruce Harlan, the Buckeyes' magnificent diver, scored a double for the second

Ohio State's Big Ten and NCAA swimming champs were led in 1950 by JACK TAYLOR and BRUCE HARLAN. A versatile swimmer, Taylor took three crowns in the Conference meet in backstroke and freestyle events, and added two more in the nationals. Harlan wound up his three-year varsity career as undoubtedly the greatest diver of all time. His three-year sweep of the high and low boards in the NCAA meet (1948-49-50) had never been done before or since. In all, the graceful blond won five Big Ten titles, six NCAA crowns, and eight AAU titles in addition to his 1948 Olympic championship. Not too many years later he died tragically and ironically in a fall from a high diving platform to the cement poolside below while making adjustments on the board.

ARNOLD PLAZA, Purdue wrestler, proved that a small man can win a big honor when he won the Gimlet Award in 1950 as Purdue's outstanding athlete of the year after a career which saw him win four straight Big Ten titles and two National Collegiate crowns. He was undefeated in dual meets for four years (freshman were eligible under Korean War regulations) and won Conference titles in 1947-48-49-50 at 121 pounds. He was NCAA champ in 1948 at 114½ pounds and NCAA ruler at 121 pounds in 1949, the year he won the Big Ten's "Outstanding Wrestler" award.

special instruction and, as a further precaution, they should not suit up. As a penalty, I cut down the number of regular practice sessions they were entitled to for the year.

Other Big Ten schools had violated the rule unknowingly by permitting a freshmen game the week after the football season had closed. This was promptly discontinued. Occasionally, the limited period of practice sessions worked a hardship. I remember one late Spring where the weather had been almost impossible and it cut the allowable outdoor practice almost in half. There was weeping and wailing from the coaches but we stuck to the rule. It is interesting to note that the rule was observed in all the conferences with the exception of one, the Ivy League, and there, by agreement of their presidents, they allowed no Spring practice at all.

My own thought on the rule was that it was not a

hardship to the football coaches in the Big Ten. The 20 allowable practices gave a coach a good opportunity to evaluate his new material coming up, which was important. On the other hand, I told our football coaches that if they had a two-sport man in the program he should be allowed to compete in his spring sport. To my satisfaction, the majortiy followed this practice but a few did not.

The whole athletic picture seems to be changing through the years. In the old days there were many outstanding athletes who won letters in many sports but now the pressure of extensive training seems to force an athlete to confine his activities to one sport.

Basketball at one time also came under the restricted out-of-season practice, with 20 sessions in 24 days. It was even a more difficult job to control this than football. Coaches normally would encourage their players

year in a row on the high and low boards. Meanwhile, other highlights were being posted by Iowa's Ed Garst with a sprint double in the 50- and 100-yard freestyle; and by Michigan's Charley Moss who turned in a 1:00 record 100-yard breaststroke.

In gymnastics, Illinois ended Minnesota's three-year reign and resumed its accustomed spot in the championship tourney, led by versatile Frank Dolan, who took the side horse, horizontal bar and all-around titles; Dick Palmer, on flying rings; and Irvo Bedard, who won in tumbling. The Illini also returned to fencing supremacy and did it by winning 24 tourney bouts to Northwestern's 22, but without a single Illinois victory in individual events. Bill Barton, of Ohio State, won the individual foil crown, and Don Olander and Bill Witsiepe, of Northwestern, took the epee and saber, respectively.

In golf, Purdue's Fred Wampler became the first

Purdue's FRED WAMPLER became the only golfer in Big Ten history to take the league individual crown three straight years when he won the title in 1950—and followed it up with the national collegiate championship.

Conference golfer to win three straight individual championships as he led the Boilermakers to the team honors. In tennis Northwestern made it four straight, led by Grant Goldin's singles play and a double win by Goldin and Bill Landin.

In NCAA competition, Ohio State repeated as collegiate swimming champion as the Bucks took five events. Jack Taylor won the 150-yard backstroke in 1:32.1, and set a new NCAA mark of 18:38.3 for the 1500-meters. Bruce Harlan completed an unmatched feat of taking the high and low board diving crowns for the third straight year; and Bill Sonner won the 100-yard backstroke in 59.1. Other Conference stars were Clark Scholes of Michigan State, who took the first of his eventual three straight 100-yard freestyle victories in 50.9; and Ed Garst, of Iowa, who sped the 50-freestyle in 23.4.

For the first time in history, the Big Ten failed to place a team in the top ten finishers of the NCAA track meet, but two Conference stars shone brightly. Don Gehrmann, the Wisconsin ace, in winning the mile in 4.12.4, became the first man ever to take the event three years in a row, and Don McEwan, Michigan's great distance star, won the first of two two-mile crowns in 9:01.9.

Hartley Price had left Illinois to become gymnastic coach at Florida State, but, under Charley Pond, the Illini lost little time in regaining the team title they had dropped for two years to Penn State and Temple. Although Irv Bedard, in tumbling, was the only individual winner, the Illini showed strength in all events. Edsel Buchanan, of Michigan, was the league's only other individual winner, repeating in the trampoline.

Fred Wampler, Purdue's smooth-swinging triple golf champ in Big Ten play, capped his career by taking NCAA individual honors, and in wrestling, Purdue's Joe Patascil and Iowa's Joe Scarpello triumphed at 128 and 175 pounds.

Among Conference Medal winners were such top-

to keep in shape and urged them to go out and shoot baskets. Other coaches would have the players run cross-country to develop their wind and legs. I felt this was okay but attempted to enforce a ban on organized coaching except for the allowable time. Many of the coaches, both football and basketball, were vehement against these restrictions, claiming that track and field candidates competed in the fall with cross-country, then competed indoors all winter and finally competed outdoors again in the spring. They had a point, but in track and field it was possible for an athlete to take his practice training practically to suit his own convenience and he could arrange these sessions without harm to his school program.

Frankly, these were more or less routine matters, time consuming and disagreeable, it is true, but necessary steps had to be taken and enforcement handed down from time to time to keep things in hand.

The big concern of the Conference was to seek rigid enforcement on aid to athletes; to see that all aid came through legal channels and did not exceed the amount as had been determined by the need principle. Again the danger signals seemed to point directly to Indiana. During the year that Dickens had been on probation and in the year that followed, my office was involved in many quiet investigations of reported irregularities. At first these seemed to be centered around the action of irresponsible alumni and then seemed to revolve around individuals who could only be construed as having come from representatives of the athletic interests of the university. Some were alumni but others were not, one being a former player under Dickens at Wofford College. These men had close contact with football coaches, drove high school athletes to games and consequently could only be labeled as representing the interests of the football staff.

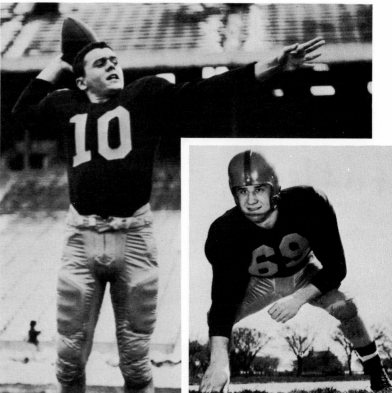

Repeating as Big Ten champ in 1950 and winning the National Collegiate title the same year at 128 pounds, Purdue's JOE PATACSIL was named the Big Ten's outstanding wrestler for the 1950 season.

notchers as Wisconsin's football and baseball star, Bob Wilson; Ohio State's diving ace, Bruce Harlan, and football stars, Norb Adams, of Purdue; Don Burson, of Northwestern; and Tom Peterson, of Michigan.

It was another example, in 1951, of a football team that could do a crisp, workmanlike job on every phase of the game without drawing raves in any one department—and with this kind of thorough effort Illinois was back in the title business. Only a scoreless tie with Ohio State sullied the Orange and Blue record which was capped by a rousing 40-7 clobbering of Stanford in the Rose Bowl.

Offensively, the Illini had a perfect blend of go-go. Tommy O'Connell, an ideal, pass-throwing quarterback who would set all kinds of records before he was through the following year, had a prime target in Rex Smith, a nifty, sticky-fingered

end. When O'Connell wasn't throwing, the Illini displayed a ground game which featured Johnny Karras, a swift, elusive halfback who tore off real estate in huge chunks, and Dick Racklovits.

Providing the flash of daylight (which was all Karras and Racklovits needed) was a hard-charging

1951

TOMMY O'CONNELL

CHUCK STUDLEY

Important cogs in Illinois' 1951 championship team were quarterback TOMMY O'CONNELL and Captain CHUCK STUDLEY, a terrific guard. O'Connell, the finest passer in Illinois history, would make a shambles of Conference aerial records the following year when he hit 108 completions on 191 attempts for 1308 yards—more than twice the previous record.

The investigating was stepped up to a high degree. Every complaint or charge we received from different parts of the country was carefully checked. The NCAA had also received numerous complaints about some of the offers that had been made and it instructed their top investigator to run these down. I doubt if any university had ever gone through such a sweeping and thorough investigation and it was to bring out many weird cases of illegal help. In the case of a few freshmen who had entered in the fall of 1957 and 1959, the detailed report showed they had admitted receiving illegal assistance amounting in three instances to $50.00 a month and in one case, $60.00 a month over and above the allowable normal expenses of attending the university. Three freshmen who had entered in the fall of 1958 and 1959 admitted to having received monthly payments of between $15.00 and $60.00. Five prospective athletes, who never did enter the university, furnished sworn affidavits

that in the spring of 1958 and 1959 they had received offers of illegal payments varying from free transportation home at vacation time; the promise of a bonus; plus $50.00 a month over school expenses for one boy while in residence if he would enroll at Indiana. I was always a little skeptical about some of these fantastic offers submitted by athletes who did not enter the university but the details seemed to fall in the same pattern that had caused Indiana to be placed on probation in 1957.

The freshmen who had been the beneficiaries of illegal aid in 1957 had flunked out of school. My investigators asked them who had paid them the money and how they had received it. They said it was in a plain envelope and that they had picked it up in their mail at the gymnasium. They could furnish no information as to where it had come from or who had supplied it. In another isolated case there were others who had

Page 309

line led by two of the best blocking guards Illinois ever had: Captain Chuck Studley, a great inspirational leader, and Don Gnidovic.

Defensively, the Illini were fortunate to have, among other assets, the best defensive halfback and linebacker in the Big Ten. Al Brosky, a sure tackler and ball-hawk, picked off enemy passes as though he'd been in the opposition's huddle, while Charley Boerio, backing up the line, was in on a third of his team's tackles on anything that didn't go outside the ends.

Meanwhile, Michigan State, admitted to the Big Ten but sitting out its waiting period before embarking on a full Conference schedule, was launched on a Golden Era of Spartan football. Under Clarence (Biggie) Munn, the Green and White had posted an 8-1 record the year before, but now they soared to the heights. Once past a 6-0 opener with Oregon, the issue was never in doubt as the Spartans smashed nine straight opponents for their first perfect season in 38 years. Along the way, the Spartans flattened Michigan, 25-0; Ohio State 24-20, and Notre Dame 35-0, among others.

It was an intricate but beautifully executed attack which Munn designed for the Spartans, who operated out of a multiple style offense presided over by Al Dorrow, a deft quarterback who could do it all. Working with him were a trio of halfbacks who were always threats to go all the way: Don McAuliffe; Vince Pisano; and Leroy Bolden, while Dick Panin was a smallish but hard-hitting fullback. Captain Bob Carey, and twin brother, Bill, were outstanding offensive ends; Don Coleman was the finest tackle in the league; and Frank Kush and Dick Kuh were great defensive guards. Jim Ellis was probably the finest safety man in the nation, and Dick Tamburo was a magnificent linebacker.

Although the Spartans looked like the greatest thing that ever came down the pike in creaming Notre Dame 35-0, it was an earlier game that really typified the daring and brilliance of Biggie Munn's legions. Trailing Ohio State, 20-10 with less than 10 minutes to play, Michigan State stormed back

for two touchdowns, the last of which clearly registered as the picture play of the season. With two minutes to go, the Spartans were still 30 yards away, third down and long yardage. Into the game rushed Tom Yewcic, a sophomore tailback, with a play from the bench. The Spartans lined up in a modified double wing. The ball came back to Dorrow and the quarterback flipped behind the line to Yewcic starting wide to the right. Then Dorrow scooted through the left side of the line and down the sideline. With the Ohio secondary drawn over toward the flow of the play. Yewcic suddenly stopped and tossed a pass diagonally across the field to Dorrow, who took the ball on the 11 and beat three defenders across the goal.

The all-winning Spartans, although not yet officially a Conference member, equalled Ohio State's record of four All-America choices, as the selectors named Dorrow, Bob Carey, at end; the punt-return star Jim Ellis, at defensive halfback; and Don Coleman, at tackle—who promptly had his number 78 retired after being called "the finest lineman in Michigan State history."

Illinois' Johnny Karras was named at halfback, and the ball-hawking Al Brosky was given a post as a defensive star. In addition to Carey, Lowell Perry of Michigan, Leo Sugar of Purdue, and Pat O'Donahue and Hal Faverty of Wisconsin, all great ends, were also named on various offensive and defensive units for the largest contingent ever selected from one athletic conference at the same position. Although his team was not much of a factor in the Big Ten race, Bill Reichardt, Iowa's amazingly versatile and hard-hitting fullback, was named Conference MVP.

There were other names and other moments worth recalling in 1951. A bull-like Wisconsin freshman named Alan Ameche was the first and only frosh ever to lead the Conference in rushing, with 774 yards and a 5.3 average, and in years ahead he would be rated the most-talked-about fullback the league had known since Bronko Nagurski.

John Coatta, Ameche's quarterbacking teammate,

---

received a plain envelope containing the money at the dormitories where they lived.

A young football coach had been added to the staff in 1958 and immediately his progress in recruiting became apparent. On two recruiting trips he registered under an assumed name at a hotel. I grilled him as to why he had done this and he told me that the territory he was covering had been in West Virginia, and that the hotel clerks there would very likely have informed other colleges nearby that a recruiter from another institution was in that area. The young coach usually worked with an alumnus of Indiana. They would interview the parents and the athlete and then the coach would excuse himself and, while he was gone, the alumnus would make the illegal offer. When the coach returned to the group he would always say, "You can depend on what my

friend has told you and the offer will be carried out."

There was another mysterious incident about this time, which seemed to tie in with recruiting at Indiana. In Ohio and West Virginia, where there were many fine high school prospects, several boys reported to their coaches that they had received a telephone call from an individual who introduced himself as "Dr. Palmer," stating he was an Indiana alumnus and lived in Louisville, Kentucky. The conversation with the prospective athlete was always the same. After chatting about the glories of Indiana, "Palmer" would end by saying that if the boy went to Indiana he would receive $50.00 a month above expenses, plus a round-trip plane fare at Christmas and Thanksgiving.

I immediately started to track down and locate the mysterious "Dr. Palmer." There was no such man in Louis-

LEO SUGAR

JOHN KARRAS

DON COLEMAN

Despite nine All-Americas in Conference ranks, Iowa's fullback, BILL REICHARDT, won the league's MVP award in 1951 for his one-man gang tactics and inspirational qualities.

The Big Ten rostered a rousing nine players on the All-America selections of 1951, including Illinois' sensational halfback, JOHNNY KARRAS, whose speed, power and deception was unexcelled by any back that year; LEO SUGAR, Purdue end, one of the most versatile wingmen the league had seen in years; and DON COLEMAN, an amazing 190-pound tackle from Michigan State—the lightest regular tackle in the league—whose jersey number was retired at the end of the season as Spartan officials called him the finest lineman Michigan State had yet produced.

led the passers for the second straight year. In 1950 he had posted the highest completion percentage (.642) in Conference history, and in '51 came back with .521. George Rice, of Iowa, equalled the league mark for a kick-off return when he raced one back an even 100 yards against Purdue, and Tony Curcillo, Ohio State quarterback, set a new league mark for yards gained in one game when he passed for 292 on 10 completions in 14 attempts, and rushed for 16, for a total of 308 against Iowa.

The Big Ten went to a 14-game league basket-

ville or the vicinity. I checked all the doctors in Bloomington, Indiana and the surrounding area but to no avail. Indiana University gave me full access to their alumni records but I could not uncover the individual. The thing that bothered me was that every time the mysterious Dr. Palmer contacted a prospect, there would be a follow-up call from an interested Indiana alumnus in that area who would tell the athlete, "Don't worry, you can always depend on what Dr. Palmer tells you." Then one day, the young Indiana coach who was doing a great deal of recruiting in that area, was introduced by an Indiana alumnus as "Dr. Palmer" in the presence of the parents of the athlete and the athlete himself. That was enough for me. I promptly reported these facts to the University and the coach was allowed to resign at once. Indiana stated that the coach

had acted solely on his own but I could not be convinced that someone had not given him guidance. Furthermore, the university was responsible for the actions of a staff member.

My investigation led me to demand a complete audit of the alumni foundation funds collected and turned over to the university for administration in assisting athletes under Conference rules. Their records were very complete and I could find no case of where sums had been taken from the fund to make payments to athletes. Nevertheless, there was such a preponderance of evidence against the way the recruiting was taking place that it could not be overlooked.

One of the most unusual cases I ran into started with a letter from an athlete who had transferred from West Point to Indiana and which stated categorically he had

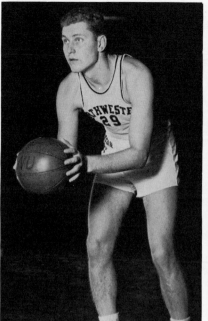

The Big Ten furnished four All-America cagers in 1951, including DON SUNDERLAGE, the hot-shooting backcourtman who led Illinois to the Conference championship; BILL GARRETT, Indiana's tremendous center;

Northwestern's deadly RAY RAGELIS, a forward who had starred for three years and who led the league in scoring; and MYER (WHITEY) SKOOG, the three-year Minnesota sharpshooting star.

ball schedule in 1951, and it was Illinois who took the first crown in an extended campaign. Posting a 13-1 mark (19-3 overall) the Illini also set a new season scoring mark with 1921 points. Led by Dandy Don Sunderlage, Irv Bemoras and Rod Fletcher, the Illini's lone league loss was to second-place Indiana with the two teams splitting their home-and-home. Ray Ragelis, Northwestern forward, set a new high of 277 points in taking the league scoring crown, and the Conference all-star selections were dominated by Sunderlage, Ragelis, Minnesota's Whitey Skoog, Paul McNulty of Purdue, Ab Nicholas of Wisconsin, and Indiana's sharpshooting Bill Garrett whose all-around play made him an All-America designee. Also named to the

All-America were Sunderlage, Northwestern's Ragelis, and Minnesota shooting star, Skoog.

The Illini went to the NCCA and, in fact, almost went all the way to the throne room. After disposing of Columbia and North Carolina State without much difficulty, the Orange and Blue dropped a 76-74 heartbreaker to Kentucky in the finals.

Illinois and Ohio State captured practically all of the remaining team titles between them. The Illini swept both the indoor and outdoor track crowns; and fencing and gymnastic championships, while the Buckeyes triumphed in swimming, wrestling, baseball and golf. Victories by Joe Gonzales in the 60-yard dash; Cirilo McSween, in the 440; Tom Floyd with a tie in the high jump, and a

received an illegal offer and had received illegal help. John Dewey, the Conference examiner, was in Bloomington at the time. I called him up and the boy reported the same information to Dewey. He added that his reason for writing was he was disgusted with the whole set-up and wanted to help clear up the situation. Dewey suggested the matter was important enough for me to fly down to Indiana, and after talking to the boy, I, too, felt he was telling the truth. I placed these facts before President Wells and the Board of Directors. They asked that I bring the boy before them so they could hear his story personally. I did. He repeated the statement and nothing their cross-examination could do would change his story. The youngster had had trouble with the coaches and was no longer a candidate for the team and they felt he was nothing more than a malicious malcontent trying to harm the reputation of the univer-

sity. There were other facts in his statement, however, that bothered me tremendously. When he came to the university he had been housed at the leading hotel in Bloomington for several days until he could find a house for his wife and himself. The bill had been mysteriously taken care of. In order to establish the veracity of his statement, I asked the athlete if he would consent to taking a lie-detector test in Chicago. He agreed and a couple of days later, a lie-detector expert assured me that the boy's statement was absolutely true.

As a result of nearly two years investigation of dozens of individuals; parents of the boys; the athletes themselves; and many of their high school coaches, I was thoroughly convinced there was need for drastic action. I had never been able to pinpoint that any illicit aid had come from the university but I had proof that the athletes had received it. All my investigations had revealed no

swift mile relay foursome of Nast, Gilbertson, Swank, and McSween, paced the Illini indoors. Outdoors it was Gonzales in the 220; McSween with a new Conference mark of 47.7 in the 440; Don Laz with a brilliant double in the broad jump and a 14-foot, 10-inch record in the pole vault; and another mile relay triumph by Swank, Stacey Siders, Gilbertson and McSween. Don McEwan, the crack Michigan distance runner, completed the league's first two-year distance double by taking the mile and two-mile for the second year in a row, with a new mark of 4:09 in the mile.

Fencing found the Illini not only taking the team title with 43 bouts, but Orange and Blue swordsmen grabbed off all three individual crowns: Allen Mills, in foil; Leonard Atkin, in epee; and Jorge Quiros in saber. In gymnastics, Frank Dolan took the side horse title and Bob Sullivan scored a double in long horse and tumbling to lead the Illini

MEL STOUT was the first Michigan State gymnast to win the Conference all-around crown in 1951.

to the championship, as Michigan State supplied the all-around winner in versatile Mel Stout, the first Spartan to win a Big Ten gym crown.

Ohio State's swim champs, taking the title for the fifth time in six years, were led by one of the Scarlet's all-time greats, Jack Taylor. The lanky Buckeye scored a brilliant triple as he won the 100-yard backstroke and set Conference records of 2:08 in the 220-yard backstroke and 18:43.3 for the 1500-meters. Jose Balmores captured the 150-yard medley, and Bob Clotworthy (now a successful coach at Princeton) came along as the latest wearer of the crown in Coach Mike Peppe's diving dynasty, with a low and high board double; and a Buckeye foursome of Dooley, Kobayashi, Stephanos and Whiteleather splashed to victory in the 400-yard relay. Meanwhile, Michigan State's great Clark Scholes was continuing his own string of starring performances with a 50- and 100-yard sprint double, the latter in a new record of 50.7.

Ohio State wrestlers took the first and only team title in Buckeye history, as Bryce Keough, at 147 pounds, and football tackle, Bill Miller, heavyweight, led the way for individual titles.

Buckeye baseballers were effective 10-2 championship winners, with good pitching by Ed Bohnslay, and solid hitting. The Bucks, who led the league in team batting, were paced by third-sacker Bob Montebello, the Big Ten batting leader with .467, and the hardest-hitting outfield the Conference had seen in years, with Dave Leonhart, at .333, Stew Hein, .327, and Elbert Gutzweiler, .308. Hein, also a fleet fly-chaser, and Illinois' grid star and third baseman, Dick Raklovits, were named All-America.

The Buckeyes were also busy on the golf course, winning the league team title for their fourth Conference flag, although it was Purdue's Gene Coulter who won the individual crown.

Tennis provided another first for Michigan State, as the Spartans took their first net crown, with

cases of athletes then in the university or any who had ever taken part in varsity athletics at Indiana, as being recipients of illegal aid. My investigations had paralleled those of the NCAA and in order to bring the matter to a close, I wrote a letter to Dr. Wells, President of Indiana University, on July 29, 1960, in which I summarized my findings by saying:

"I find in these cases a widespread practice of offers of illegal financial assistance to prospective students and of the receipt of illegal financial assistance by students, once they have enrolled at Indiana University." . . . "It is submitted by Indiana University that to the extent these practices existed, they were the workings of unknown uninstructed or irresponsible friends or alumni of the University." . . . "To the extent that I have been unable to identify unnamed persons who in certain cases made promises of financial assistance which are acknowl-

edged by the recipients, I will concede that I cannot beyond all reasonable doubt contradict this contention . . ."

"I must say, however, that I have grave doubts that any such practices on the scale suggested by the cases at hand could possibly have been carried on without the knowledge of and, indeed, the approval of the football coaching staff. It is only because I cannot bring myself to employ circumstantial evidence in so serious a matter as one involving a person's livelihood that I do not, in the present circumstances, cite Indiana University under the provisions of Rule 7, Section 15."

The rule referred to requires any member institution to show cause why its membership in the Conference should not be terminated if it retains in its employ a staff member who has been found in violation of the financial rules.

BOB MONTEBELLO

STEW HEIN, Ohio State outfielder whose clutch hitting and nifty glove brought him All-America honors, and third sacker BOB MONTEBELLO, who won the league batting crown with .467, led Ohio State to the 1951 baseball championship.

STEWART HEIN

Leonard Brose capturing the singles title and Brose and John Sahratian taking the doubles crown. It was a year, also, that saw Michigan State launch one of the most complete dominations of a sport ever seen in the Big Ten, as the Spartans, under the astute Karl Schlademan took their first cross-country championship in a string that would come to nine titles in 11 years.

In NCAA competition, the Michigan-Ohio State entry had one of its rare lapses as Yale slipped by them for the team title in swimming. There was plenty of individual glory, however, for Conference stars. Michigan State's Clark Scholes won the 50-yard freestyle and repeated in the 100, for a double. The backstroke went from 150-yards to 200-yards, but Ohio State's Jack Taylor, a winner the previous year, didn't let the additional 50-yards

JOHN SAHRATIAN and LEONARD BROSE

Michigan State celebrated its entry to the Big Ten in 1951 by immediately winning the Conference tennis championship, sparked by LEONARD BROSE, singles titlist, who combined with teammate JOHN SAHRATIAN for the doubles crown.

I then concluded the letter by stating the following:

"I consider it incumbent upon the University to make redress for the illegal practices which have occurred for the benefit of its football program. I hold it imperative that the University shall provide positive assurances to the Conference that there is and can be no continuation or reoccurrece of those practices.

"I therefore hold that Indiana University's Conference membership shall be placed in probationary status for a period of one year. As a condition of restoration to good standing the University shall demonstrate to the satisfaction of the Conference Commissioner and Faculty Representatives, by its existing practices with regard to financial aid, by diligent further investigation of the responsibility for improper financial aid practices in the past three years, and by such corrective action as any investigative findings may demand, full assurance of

adherence to the financial aid regulations of the Conference on the part of the University's staff and representatives. Such a showing, prior to the expiration of one year, may be considered as a basis for restoration to good standing.

"Further, I hold that ... the University be denied the right to participate in the Conference sharing of football television receipts in 1960.

"Further, in recognition of the fact that illegal financial aid practices have occurred for the benefit of the Indiana University football program, I hold that Indiana University's football games with Conference members in 1960 shall not be counted in any tabulation of relative Conference standings for the 1960 season."

It was a most drastic penalty and came at a most unfortunate time for Indiana. Its fine new stadium had just been completed and yet the results of their games

DON LAZ scored a double in the broad jump and pole vault to lead Illinois to the outdoor track crown in 1951, and added the NCAA crown in the pole vault. DON McEWAN, of Michigan, pulled off the league's only two-

year distance double in history with victories in the mile and two-mile in 1950-51, and made it two in a row in the NCAA two-mile. It was Michigan State's sparkling WARREN DREUTZLER who took the NCAA mile.

stop him. A Michigan State foursome of Dave Hoffman, Jim Quigley, Scholes, and George Hoogerhyde ripped off a record 3:26.7 in the 400-yard relay, and an Ohio State trio of Taylor, Gerry Holan and Herb Kobayashi, won the 300-yard medley in 2:52.2. For the first time in 17 years, the diving titles went to other than Ohio State or Michigan as Skippy Browning, of Texas, triumphed on both boards.

In track, Michigan State's Warren Dreutzler won a great mile victory in 4:08.8; Don McEwan, of Michigan, scored his second straight two-mile triumph in 9:03.2; and Illinois' Don Laz set a new NCAA pole vault record of 14-9 and ¾ inches.

Michigan State made it its biggest year, ever, in the NCAA lists, with successes in boxing, wrestling, and gymnastics. Spartan belters took their first team title in the ring wars and Wisconsin, as runner-up, made it a one-two punch for the first

CHUCK SPEISER, Michigan State 175-pounder, took an NCAA crown in 1951 as the Spartans won their first national collegiate team title.

would have no bearing on the Conference championship. The fact that they were not allowed to participate in the TV receipts of the Conference meant a direct loss to the athletic department of nearly $100,000. More than that, however, it would seriously interfere in Indiana's recruiting because of the bad image it had created of their fine university. To get down to facts, it simply meant that if Indiana could not bring this situation under control in a year, its Conference membership was in real jeopardy.

The penalty was an extremely unpopular one and I received numerous letters of protest from Indiana alumni. The student's reaction was as expected—bitter. I was hung in effigy from a tree on the campus. There was a torrent of bitter comment. The majority of these included: "Why did you pick on us, we're the doormat of Big Ten football. Why don't you go after the people at

the top?" Among my most drastic penalties, they could have noted that Ohio State and Michigan State who were consistently in the upper half in the win and lose columns had already been put on probation and given a year to put their house in order.

As a result of this case the NCAA infractions committee placed Indiana on probation for a period of four years from April 27, 1960 to April 27, 1964 for these violations. They, too, denied them any participation in TV programs but one other stipulation was the toughest; it declared that for this four-year period, Indiana University would be ineligible to enter its teams or athletes in NCAA championship competition. I felt myself that the last probationary measure was an extremely rough one. In all the sweeping investigations of all athletes at Indiana University, I had never found irregularities in the recruiting or subsidizing of any group except foot-

time by any collegiate conference. Coached by George Makris, an ex-Badger 175-pound king, the Spartans also had individual winners in Gerald Black, 145 pounds; and Chuck Speiser, at 175. Minnesota's Neil Oftshun won at 125, and Wisconsin's Dick Murphy and Bob Ranck, were crowned as 155-pound and heavyweight kings.

1952

Michigan State's Gene Gibson took the 167-pound wrestling championship and Ohio State's Gene Nieport, was the NCAA individual golf titlist.

In gymnastics, Michigan State boasted still another champion in Mel Stout on the flying rings, as Illinois' Bob Sullivan won in tumbling, and Michigan's Edsel Buchanan won his third straight trampoline title to become the Wolverines' only three-time gymnastics winner. Michigan also took home a team title in hockey that year, as the Wolves, led by Gil Burford, clawed Brown, 7-1, in the tourney final.

The Conference Medal for scholarship went to such headliners as Don Laz, Illinois' great pole vaulter; Everett (Sonny) Grandelius, Michigan State's All-America halfback; and Myer (Whitey) Skoog, Minnesota's All-America basketballer.

The Conference fathers also had a busy year on the administrative front. Because of a probable manpower shortage brought on by the Korean War, they voted to suspend the one-year residence rule for the 1951-52 academic year for students who had entered Conference schools during 1950-51 but who hadn't completed a year of residence by the time the 1951 fall term started, and for junior college transfers. They also agreed to allow freshman football candidates to report for 1951 fall practice on September 1, instead of waiting until the usual start of school. The Rose Bowl agreement with the Coast Conference was renewed for three more years, and Athletic Directors, instead of Faculty Representatives, were to vote for the Big Ten's representative. Indicating a desire to tighten standards for assistance to athletes, the Conference re-

jected a proposed work-aid program for athletes described as "an equality of offer" basis for aids. William R. Reed, a Michigan graduate, became Assistant Commissioner.

It was Ray George, the Texas A. & M. coach, who furnished the best clue to the 1952 football season when, after losing to Michigan State 48-6, he declared: "It isn't so much what their first and second teams do to you—but the third, fourth and fifth teams simply murder you!"

This was after Biggie Munn surveyed his material in pre-season drills and discovered he had to replace his entire offensive line, and a good part of his defensive corps. No matter. Biggie had his single wing, double wing, straight-T, winged-T, split-T, short punt, plus some random variations of his own devising, and he was determined that the new boys would carry on a winning streak that had reached 15.

The Spartans proceeded to tack on nine more for a gaudy 24.

They did it with a pony backfield behind a light, green line. Reserve tailback Tommy Yewcic at 178 pounds became a cool-headed, sharp-passing quarterback. Billy Wells at 168 was one halfback, teamed up with Captain Don McAuliffe, the big man at 190; and a 170-pound fullback in quick, squat Evan Slonak who hit like a 200-pounder. To clear the way for them, Munn and a tough, fast-talking assistant named Hugh (Duffy) Daugherty, installed Doug Bobo and Paul Dekker at ends; Gordon Serr and Larry Fowler at tackles; Ferris Hallmark and Bob Brenniff at guards, and Jim Neal at center. Neal was the biggest man in the line at 215, but this was a line that came off the mark with mayhem in mind, and the holes opened big and frequently.

When the Spartans gave up the ball they inserted Ed Luke and Don Doheny at ends; Jack Morgan and double-duty Larry Fowler at tackle;

ball players. It meant that Indiana, which had had the best swimming team in the country, would be denied a crack at the NCCA championship, always the top goal. It also banned any chance for their basketball team to compete in the NCAA championship. I felt so keenly about this that along with President Wells, I appeared before the NCAA Infraction Committee in Atlanta, Georgia, to see if the penalty might be modified for the other sports.

I told the Council members I had definitely pinpointed the area in which recruiting and subsidizing violations had been made and that it was only in the area of football, and since no other sports were involved, the penalty should be on football alone.

The NCAA council was adamant in their decision and felt that inasmuch as some of these rule violations had occurred while Indiana had been on probation, that the

penalty should be very drastic across the board in all sports.

To the everlasting credit of the Hoosier Athletic Department, now headed by Bill Orwig, and the capable faculty representative, John Mee, they really did a clean-up job. They demonstrated thoroughly to the Conference that future action would not only be within the rule structure but also within the spirit of the rules as well. It was with a great deal of pleasure that one of my last official actions as Commissioner was to recommend to the Conference that they be restored in good standing in May, 1961, and this received approval by the faculty representatives.

As I look back over the last 10 years of my stewardship of the Conference, I cannot help but remark that while these were troublesome years, full of many unpleasant investigations; they were, at the same time,

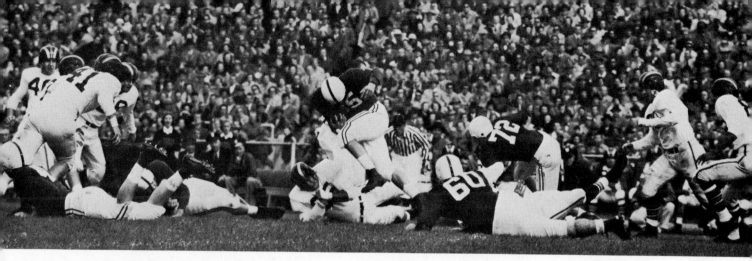

Hank Bullough and the amazing 180-pound Frank Kush at guard, with Ed Timmerman and the bruising Dick Tamburo at linebacker. John Wilson and Rex Corless were alert, hard-hitting defensive halfbacks and the incomparable Jim Ellis put in his second year at safety.

With this group in control, the Spartans were rarely in trouble. "This was undoubtedly the strongest, deepest club we'd yet had at Michigan State," Munn recalled later. "Only twice were we in what might be called trouble. In our second game against Oregon State we needed another chance on a penalty when we missed a field goal attempt with seven seconds left, but Gene Lekenta made good on his second effort with two seconds on the clock. Against Purdue we needed an interception to protect our 14-7 lead in the fourth quarter. Otherwise we rolled along under pretty good steam."

The pretty good steam accounted for 312 points for the season, including such routs as 48-7 over Syracuse; 34-7 over Penn State; 21-3 over Notre Dame; 48-6 over Texas A. & M.; 41-14 over Indiana; 62-13 over Marquette; and decisive wins over Michigan, Oregon State and Purdue. It was small wonder the Spartans gained the national championship.

One of the most familiar and awesome sights in Big Ten football in the early 1950's was that of ALAN (THE HORSE) AMECHE, Wisconsin's incomparable fullback, blasting through opponents' lines, as he does here against Purdue.

Although a member of the Big Ten, Michigan State had not yet played a full Conference schedule and therefore was not eligible for the Rose Bowl—an assignment that went to Wisconsin, which tied Purdue for the league title but was selected for the New Year's Day frolic because of a better record. It ended the longest title drought in the Conference; the Badgers hadn't flown the flag since 1912 and Ivan Williamson had made good on the promise shown the previous season when his youthful club ranked first in both total offensive and total defense in the Conference. Now, in 1952, they were ready to turn statistics into a pay-off.

The hub of the Badger attack was the maturing sophomore fullback, Alan Ameche, soon to be dubbed "The Horse." The jarring 19-year old had led league rushers as a frosh, and repeated as a sophomore with 721 yards for a 4.9 average. There was strong half-backing help from Gerry Witt, Harland Carl, Bill Hutchinson, and Archie Burks,

---

probably the most important years the Conference has ever gone through. First of all, it had given the job program a good try but found it unreasonable and actually unenforceable because coaches and directors didn't believe it workable. It had been found impossible for a boy to play ball, study and work 16 hours a week at a job. The program governed by the financial need principle had been given a thorough trial but it, too, was unsatisfactory, as it had placed the Big Ten in an island surrounded by vigorous other leagues who recruited in this area, and it wasn't hard for the others to convince a boy that ". . . we are not concerned with how much your father makes and, in fact, we will guarantee your college expenses without going through all this red tape about financial reports." As a consequence, hundreds of the best athletes in a seven-state area were leaving for other conference institutions.

It is significant that, as each step was taken through 10 troubled years, the academic requirements for unearned aid were tightened up, always keeping in mind that the student's primary function in college was to enjoy a sound academic program and make progress toward graduating with his class.

The principle had been firmly set in 1958 when a rule was adopted limiting eligibility, except in hardship cases, to a four-year period following initial enrollment. This securely curbed the practice that had grown in some conferences throughout the nation, called "red shirting;" a deplorable idea where a coach would keep an athlete out of competition as a sophomore, knowing the boy would be a better player if he were a year older and had more practice sessions under his belt. He would then extend his college career by a year. This was legal under NCAA rules which provided that an

Two of the many stars who led Michigan State to the national championship in 1952 were Captain DON McAULIFFE, a big, slashing All-America halfback; and

FRANK KUSH, a fierce guard, who at 180 pounds was the lightest All-America lineman in almost 20 years. McAuliffe was also UPI Back of the Year.

while a brilliant sophomore quarterback Jim Haluska, turned in a .587 pass completion mark on 74 for 126 and six touchdowns.

Up front, the rock-ribbed Badgers featured a great sophomore end in Don Voss; a stupendous tackle in Dave Suminsky; and hard-hitting guards, Bob Kennedy, George O'Brien, Clarence Stensby and George Steinmetz.

Upset by a weak Ohio State team early in the year, the Badgers went into their finale with Minnesota needing at least a tie for the title—and got it in a wild 21-21 affair which found the ball changing hands five times in the last two minutes on fumbles and interceptions.

It was a well-deserved share of the championship the Badgers owned as the final statistics showed they led in scoring, first downs, rushing, pass completion percentage and total yards gained. Purdue, the title co-holder, had been a factor in the race

throughout. The Boilermakers under personable Stu Holcomb, were led by little Dale Samuels, a strong-armed quarterback who completed 71 of 116 for eight touchdowns and the league's top completion mark of .612. Max Schmaling, a jarring fullback, was the loop's third leading rusher, and a lot of the reasons for Samuels' and Schmaling's success were up front in a line bulwarked by Bernie Flowers, a marvelously talented end; two fine guards in Jack Houston, one of three great linemen brothers from Massilon, Ohio, (the other two, Lin and Jim, played for Ohio State) and Tom Bettis, a brilliant freshman who would go on to even greater days; Ken Panfil, a hard-nosed tackle, and Walt Cudzik, a fine center.

Michigan State furnished a trio of All-Americas in Don McAuliffe at halfback; Frank Kush at defensive guard; and Dick Tamburo at linebacker. Six other Conference stars joined them: Paul Giel,

athlete was allowed a 5-year period to complete his competition. Colleges which participated in this practice argued that many of the university courses were five-year courses but few of the athletes were enrolled in them.

The current athletic scholarship system devised by the Conference in 1960, however, made coaches and athletic directors happier than they'd been in a long time. It was the most sensible and enforceable system the Big Ten had yet devised. Financial aid was tendered based on acamedic achievement but without regard to a financial need factor. Now, as long as a boy met a prescribed standard of scholarship it didn't matter how much money his family had. The boy would receive aid amounting to tuition, books, room and board, but with no transportation expenses or spending money.

The tenders were to be an official invitation by each

school to prospects of their selection but which could not be offered until a certain, common date which all Conference members had to observe (currently April 1 for football prospects, with a later date for spring sports candidates).

A boy could receive tenders from several Conference schools but after studying them for 10 days he could only select one. This was then to be filed in the Commissioner's office and the boy could not, then, at a later date, change his mind and select another Big Ten school. If he did he would be ineligible for financial aid on his second choice. (To my knowledge this has never happened.)

Incidentally, the academic achievement standards today require the applicant to be in the upper half of his high school graduating class. If below that, his performance must be compensated for on a scale of

Minnesota's superb triple-threat halfback, who was also the Conference MVP; Mike Takacs, a brilliant guard from Ohio State; Bernie Flowers, one of the best ends in Purdue history; Joe Collier, Northwestern's deft, pass-snatching end; and two stars from Wisconsin's line, Dave Suminsky, tackle, and Don Voss, Wisconsin's sensational sophomore end.

Although Michigan State was not yet a head-butting brother in football, the Conference was proud of the fact that Clarence (Biggie) Munn was elected Coach-of-the-Year.

Also, at season's end, fans talked about George O'Brien's longest Conference punt in history, when the Wisconsin kicker got off a 96-yard effort, with roll, against Iowa. Tommy O'Connell, Illinois' passing star, set an aerial mark of 306 yards on 22 completions out of 34, also against Iowa, but chalked up another record in reverse when the Hawks in the same game picked off six interceptions. The Illini's Rex Smith used the Iowa game for 11 completions for 190 yards and wound up the season with a league high of 36 for 515 yards.

Among the Big Ten's All-America performers in 1952 were DAVE SUMINSKI, star tackle for Wisconsin's co-champions; DON VOSS, Wisconsin's swift sophomore end; and DICK TAMBURO, the tremendous linebacker for Michigan State's national champions.

As a portent of things to come, Ohio State displayed an 18-year-old freshman halfback, eligible under Korean War regulations identical with those of World War Two. He was a slight, 175-pounder of no particular high school reputation, but Woody Hayes liked what he saw and started him in the opener against Indiana. The redheaded halfback tore up the turf at Ohio Stadium, racing for three touchdowns in a debut even more remarkable than that of the immortal Chic Harley, and sent fans away at game's end talking not of the Buckeyes slim chances for the season but about Howard (Hopalong) Cassady.

In basketball for 1952 the word was "wunderkind," as far as the Conference was concerned. Never in league history had so many sensational first-year men made their debut. In fact, because the Korean War had resulted in freshmen being made eligible for varsity play, there were even some glittering frosh who made their league bow an auspicious one, along with the sophomores. It was a year, too, that Illinois successfully defended its title with a 12-2 mark, with Iowa runner-up at 11-3.

The biggest stars, sizewise, yet to play in the Conference showed up at Illinois and Indiana

DON VOSS   DICK TAMBURO

adjusted College Board Scores or scores on the American College Testing Program. There can be no conniving on this. Official scores from the College Board or ACT people must be filed in the Commissioner's office. This was a tremendous step forward as it did away with the frantic rushing and pressure recruiting at the last minute just before the colleges started the fall term. A great share of illegal offers had occurred in the past during the final summer month. If an athlete had performed unusually well at a state high school all-star game, he would literally be swamped with offers, many times by irresponsible people.

It is true that our tender did not prevent him from going to another conference but as various leagues adopted the system, some of them suggested a national letter of intent. This was truly a step forward and in the years to come would serve a most laudable function.

In recent years the Council of 10, made up of the presidents of our institutions, began to be apprehensive over the rising costs of athletic administration. Some of the athletic budgets in the Big Ten were well in excess of $1,000,000 a year. The cost of maintenance for the athletic facilities had increased tremendously each year; transportation costs had advanced; and while the presidents believed in a strong athletic program they advocated arriving at some reasonable basis.

The problem was not unique to the Big Ten. The NCAA had called for a frank and candid revelation of how much was being spent in the athletic activities of athletic departments of their member insitutions. The names of the schools were withheld but the amounts revealed were astounding and rather awesome. Some member institutions reported their recruiting costs alone had exceeded $200,000 a year. There were many others

honors and, of course, league laurels along with Ohio's Ebert, Purdue's Carl McNulty, and Ab Nicholas of Wisconsin.

In the NCAA, Illinois got past Duquesne in the first round but fell before St. Johns, 61-59, in the Eastern finals.

Illinois scored impressive repeat championships in both indoor and outdoor track, dominating the meets with a rash of individual victories. Indoors, Hank Cryder set a new Conference mark of 1:52.9 for the 880. Joel McNulty won the 70-yard high

WILLIE WILLIAMS, Illinois sprinter and hurdler, was a big winner as the Illini took both indoor and outdoor league championship, in 1952. In 1953-54 he scored 100-yard dash victories in the NCAA.

Leading Illinois to the Big Ten cage crown in 1952 was ROD FLETCHER, sparkling backcourtman who gained All-America honors along with Iowa's brilliant center, CHUCK DARLING, who set a new Conference scoring mark.

where Bob Kerr, a soph, and Don Schlundt, a frosh, both at 6-10, were instant, authentic greats. Paul Ebert, at Ohio State; Bob Leonard, at Indiana, and Chuck Mencel, of Minnesota were the sophomore luminaries, and all five newcomers were destined to dominate individual play in the Conference for the next few seasons. Not until the Lucas-Dischinger-Havlicek crop of eight years later would the loop see such brilliant talent enter in one class.

Meanwhile in 1952, Chuck Darling of Iowa smashed all existing scoring marks with a 364-point total and a 26.0 average per game, as he and Illinois' brilliant Rod Fletcher gained All-America

who operated on a more reasonable basis but it was quite easy to see that unless some curbs were put on these practices, the situation might get entirely out of hand. Positive steps have been taken to limit the number of visits an athlete could make to a school, and rigid enforcements of these practices was instituted.

The Big Ten had exerted a great deal of leadership in all these matters, as their rules had been more restrictive than those of the NCAA. I was particularly glad to see the joint committee of faculty and athletic directors, after a long and careful study of the duties and responsibilities of the Commissioner in the matter of enforcement procedures, realign the rules giving the athletic directors new responsibilities with the Commissioner for the determination of violations and imposition of penalties. The Commissioner under these revised rules would place his findings before the athletic directors and they would

determine whether or not violations had been committed. It was no longer a case of sitting back and feeling that if there were any infractions taking place, let the Commissioner find them. It placed the important responsibility right where it belonged—with the director who knew what was going on, not only in his own department but now, also, in the rest of the Conference.

The Conference now has rules it believes in and can support 100%. This had not been true in the past. There had been much division of opinion from time to time and a stubborn resistance to new legislation until it had been given a thorough trial.

Certainly, the new ruling covering aid, which was advanced in 1960 and thoroughly worked out and enacted in 1961, was one I approved of whole-heartedly. The device for administering aid to athletes on the "need"

HARVEY KUENN, Wisconsin's All-America shortstop in 1952, went on to major league all-star fame.

hurdles in 8.7; Willie Williams skimmed the lows in 8.1; Dick Coleman took the pole vault with 14-3, and Ron Mitchell set a new league standard in the high jump with 6-7¼. Other Conference marks were set by a swift Iowa foursome of Boylan, Wheeler, Ebert and Scott, with 3:18.3 in the mile relay, and Michigan's John Ross posted a 4:09.4 record in the mile.

Outdoors, still another Illinois half-miler set a record when Stacey Siders came home in 1:52.2. Cirilo McSween captured the 440 in 48.7 for the Illini, and McNulty and Williams scored hurdle victories again with 14.4 in the 120-yard highs, and 21.7 in the 220-lows, respectively. Dick Coleman tied for first in the pole vault with Ohio State's Jerry Welbourn, at 14-1¼, and Ron Mitchell shared the high jump honors with Michigan's Milt Mead, at 6-15 and ¹⁵⁄₁₆.

It was an Illinois-Michigan deadlock in baseball, with 10-5 and 8-4 records respectively, and the same .667 percentage. Gerry Smith, Illinois' top

pitcher, shared the league lead of 5-0 with two illustrious rivals, Paul Giel, Minnesota All-America footballer, and Paul Ebert, Ohio State's star basketballer. Also aiding the Illini cause were Bruce Frazier, hard-hitting catcher (.345); John Davis, shortstop (.333) and Bob Moore, first baseman (.326). For Michigan, success came with dependable, all-around team effort rather than individual brilliance as the Wolverines failed to place a hitter in the top 20, nor a pitcher among the top five. Third baseman Don Eaddy was the Wolverines' top hitter with .311, and hurlers Jack Corbett and Dick Yirkoski were 7th and 8th in pitching percentages.

Purdue's Harold Hanes, a swift outfielder, led the league in hitting with .450 and in second spot, with .444, was Harvey Kuenn, Wisconsin shortstop and All-America, who, many claim, was the finest ball player ever to come out of the Big Ten, and who went on to become an American League all-star.

It was Ohio State repeating in swimming, led by a Hawaiian freshman who, before he would be through, would be hailed as one of the greatest swimmers the world has ever known: Ford Konno. The slim stylist set three Conference records—never before accomplished at one meet—when he posted a time of 2:06.7 for the 220 freestyle; splashed home in 4:35.9 in the 440 and devastated the 1500-meters in 18:11.5. Meanwhile, teammates Dick Cleveland and Jack Taylor were setting new marks of 22.7 in the 50-yard sprint, and 2:07.2 for the 200-yard backstroke, respectively. Taylor, an all-time Buckeye great, also took the 100-yard backstroke in 58.2, and a trio of Taylor, Gerry Holan and Herb Kobayashi set still another mark of 2:50.7 in the medley relay. Kobayashi, Nick Silverio, Frank Dooley and Cleveland combined for a record 3:25.4 in the 400-yard freestyle relay, and Morley Shapiro and Bob Clotworthy, continuing Ohio State's springboard mastery, took the low and high board diving events as the Buckeyes, with a

principle had been opposed by the majority of Big Ten coaches. It had caused the loss of many fine athletes to schools with more liberal inducements. To prevent losing these boys some Big Ten alumni atttepted to corrupt the rules in an effort to recruit them—and, in turn, to corrupt the boys.

I was also particularly happy to see the special Conference committee work out sound and definite standards on academic achievement for scholarship eligibility, which had to be maintained by the boy thereafter if he was to hold his aid.

No longer would the coach waste his time or the university's money in attempting to recruit an athlete who didn't have a reasonable chance of being eligible. These standards, it is true, were higher than any of the other conferences but the whole theory was technically sound and it was laying the basis for a program

of aid to athletes that Big Ten schools would not be ashamed of.

These grants of aid programs recognized the place of a vigorous athletic agenda in our growing institutions, and was one of the great milestones in solving the tremendous problems we'd struggled with for years. I was delighted that this program came about; I felt that here was a standard that coaches and athletic directors alike, could support. The rigid academic requirements pleased the Big Ten faculties and subsequent years have shown the wisdom of the action.

As I approached the May meeting in 1961, I realized it would be my last one. The Conference had adopted a rule along with the Council of 10 that executive officers should retire at age 65. They had worked out a generous retirement program for me, and I would close my office as Commissioner as of July 1, 1961.

rash of seconds and thirds, piled up 125 points to Michigan's 66 for the most complete domination of the annual festival in Conference history. In diving, for instance, of the 12 point-producing places in the low and high boards combined, Buckeye divers took eight of them, with the other four distributed between Purdue and Iowa.

Illinois continued its hot streak in both gymnastics and fencing. In fencing, Vince D'Orazio, with an individual title in foil; Allen Mills with second in foil; and Phil Urso and Bruce Sublette, second in epee and saber respectively, led the Illini to a sweeping team victory. In gymnastics the Illini were led by Bob Sullivan who took the tumbling and all-around crowns; Frank Bare won on the side horse, and Harry Luchs scored on the parallel bars.

The Illini also went home with the team wrestling trophy, although it was a rare enough triumph

NORM BARNES, 1952 tennis singles champ, was the first Hawkeye to take a title in Iowa net history.

with only one individual crown gracing an Illinois' matman: tough, little Nort Compton, at 137 pounds. The Illini did, however, score points in six of the 10 weight divisions to pile up their team triumph.

Indiana, which had never made a threatening gesture in tennis, came through for its first team title in 1952 with 70 tourney matches to Michigan State's 56, although the Hoosiers failed to win either the singles or doubles crown which were taken respectively by Iowa's Norman Barnes (an historic first for the Hawkeyes) and Michigan State's Stan Drobac and Tom Belton. Iowa's little Rich Ferguson also gave the Hawks the individual cross-country crown, although Michigan State's tremendous all-around strength kept the team trophy in its perennial East Lansing resting place.

Wisconsin's Doug Koepcke brought the Badgers their first individual golf crown in history, but Michigan won the team title as Russ Johnson, Dean Lind, Lowell Le Clair and John Frazer all wound up among the top eight finishers in an unusual show of team strength.

NCAA competition found the Big Ten at its usual productive level, with four Conference schools taking team titles. Ohio State recaptured swimming laurels from Yale, with two wartime eligible frosh playing big roles in the proceedings. Ford Konno, who had made a shambles of Big Ten records, now won the 440 in 4:30.3 and set a new national mark of 18:15.5 for the 1500-meters. Yoshi Oyakawa, the other first-year sensation, took the 200-yard backstroke in 2:07.3. Meanwhile, star sprinter, Dick Cleveland had sped to a 22.3 victory in the 50-yard freestyle and the perennially brilliant Jack Taylor won the 100-yard backstroke in 57.3 as the Buckeyes piled up points in most of the events on the card. Michigan wasn't exactly idle, either. John Davies, the Wolverine's butterfly star, took the 100 in 58.8 for a new NCAA record and came back for still another new mark of 2:12.9 for the 200.

The search for a new Commissioner presented no problem at all. When I was approached by the committee for a suggestion, I felt there was only one candidate to be considered: my capable assistant, Bill Reed. He'd had wonderful training for the position. His connection with the Conference had begun in 1939 when he'd assisted my predecessor, Major Griffith, during which time he had organized the Big Ten Service Bureau. He took a leave of absence from the Conference in 1942 through 1945 to enter naval service as an Ensign. After a year at the Iowa Pre-Flight School, he was assigned to Armed Guard duty in both the Atlantic and South Pacific, where he reached the rank of Lieutenant and returned to the Conference in the fall of 1945.

He helped organize the central office of the National Collegiate Athletic Association at the time I was serving as Secretary-Treasurer. In 1947 Bill resigned to take

a position as Administrative Assistant to United States Senator Homer Ferguson of Michigan until the fall of 1951, when I brought him back to the Conference as Assistant Commissioner. He was a close friend and most loyal helper. No job was too tough for him to tackle regardless of the time and energy needed to complete it. He was extremely skillful in his relations with the press, having been a charter member of the American Football Writers' Association and had helped draft their constitution. The field in which he was most interested seemed to be television problems and there were many. He helped promote the sale of our basketball games to television and gave our TV committee much valuable assistance.

I was happy to see that the faculty representatives and the Council of 10 concurred with my belief that Bill was the man and at a special meeting on April 24,

Teammate Burwell Jones did some record-smashing, too, with a glittering 1:29.8 for the individual medley, and a Michigan foursome of Tom Benner, Jones, Don Hill and Wally Jeffries posted a new record of 3:25.7 for the 400-yard freestyle relay. It was a high mark for the number of records by one Conference team.

In boxing it was Wisconsin for the NCAA team title by reversing the order of the year before, when Michigan State had been first and the Badgers second. Bob Morgan, champion at 147 pounds, and Bob Ranck, heavyweight king, led Wisconsin, as Michigan State's Chuck Spieser took the 175-pound title again and Minnesota's speedy Neil Oftshun repeated as 125-pound champ.

Michigan State took the cross-country title, and Michigan, under new coach, Vic Heyliger, won the NCAA hockey crown, defeating Colorado College in the final, 4-1, as Wolverines Doug Philpott and George Chin shared tournament scoring honors with four points each.

In gymnastics, Illinois provided two individual champs in Frank Bare, on side horse, and Bob Sullivan repeating as tumbling titlist.

It was a comparatively slim year for the Conference in NCAA track, with Jim Golliday, Northwestern's crack sprinter, taking the 100-meters (Olympic year distance) in 10.4; Illinois' Dick Coleman sharing a 4-way tie in the pole vault at 13-9; and Wisconsin's Walt Dieke capturing the 10,000-meter run.

The contingent sent to the 1952 Olympics in Finland by Conference schools (37 athletes) was the largest, by far, ever contributed by a collegiate conference. The 13 swimmers and divers from Ohio State alone constituted still another mark.

The most dramatic performance, probably, was that of Ohio State's Mal Whitfield. Then an Air Force sergeant who had flown more than 30 missions as a tail gunner in Korea, the ex-Buckeye star came back from the Wars, got into shape again

FRANK HILL *of Northwestern was one of the great producers of track champions in the Big Ten's middle years. In his 31 years as Wildcat coach from 1921 to 1952, he was one of the nation's most distinguished track and field mentors.*

and repeated his triumph of the 1948 Games by retaining his 800-meter championship in his own record-equalling time of 1:49.2. Then Whitfield and Buckeye teammate Gene Cole ran legs on the Yanks' 1600-meter relay which finished second.

Bob Richards, Illinois' great pole vaulter, took a Gold Medal with a record-setting mark of 14-11¼, beating out teammate Don Laz, who took second. The Illini's incomparable Herb McKenley, running for his native Jamaica, took second in the 100- and 200-meters and ran a leg for the Jamaicans' winning 400-meter relay. Milt Campbell, Indiana's

1961, he became the third Commissioner of the Big Ten Conference. He promoted John Dewey, the capable examiner, to the position of Assistant to the Commissioner and brought in Kay Schultz to act as Service Bureau Director.

The May meeting was the last I presided over as Commissioner. The faculty representatives and directors held a dinner at the University Club in Chicago, the same place at which I was elected to the job some 16 years previously. I received a lovely silver bowl with the names of the faculty representatives and athletic directors engraved on it. I thoroughly appreciated the many laudatory comments that went with it and sometimes wondered if I deserved it all. In my response, I thanked them for their patience and assistance and predicted that the Big Ten was on the threshold of even greater years. They were beginning a new era and I

was confident that under Bill Reed's leadership things would be in good hands.

There were other farewell parties but those tendered to me by the basketball officials and, at a later date, the one given by the football officials, really hit me the hardest. These dedicated men in the striped shirts were my gang. Practically every man on these two lists had been my selection. Saturday after Saturday, I had watched them officiate the tough games of basketball and football before tremendous crowds in pressure-packed situations. They were, in my opinion, the best officiating corps in the whole country. In my book, they are the unsung heroes of the athletic picture. It is true they are paid for their services but this is small compensation for the hours of study and preparation. Few people realize the importance of sound officiating. A good official must command the respect of the players.

football star and do-everything trackman, won the Silver Medal in the decathlon; and Minnesota's Fortune Gordien took fourth place in the discus. Indiana's Fred Wilt competed at 10,000-meters and Michigan State's Warren Drestzler at 5,000. Three

CLARK SCHOLES of Michigan State was one of the greatest sprinters in Big Ten swim history. He was Conference champ at 50- and 100-yards in 1951; repeated as century champ in 1952; scored a brilliant three-year sweep of the 50 in the national collegiates in 1950-51-52, the only man ever to do so; then climaxed his career by winning the Gold Medal for the 100-meters in the 1952 Olympic Games. (Incidentally, Scholes scored no victories in the 1950 Conference meet because the Spartans were not league members until 1951.)

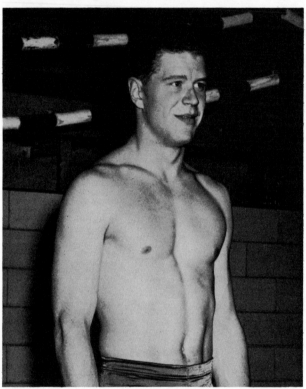

Michigan track stars, meanwhile, competed for foreign nations: Roland Nilson in the shot-put and discus for Sweden; John Ross at 800- and 1500-meters for Canada; and Jack Carroll in the 400- and 1600-meter relay for Canada.

In swimming, the Ohio State contingent piled up a ton of points for the United States, headed by Ford Konno's record-breaking 18:30 for the 1500-meters; his second place in the 400 and his great leg for America's winning 800-meter relay, which also got a leg from Indiana's Bill Woolsey. Still another Buckeye, Yoshi Oyakawa, set a new mark of 1:05.4 for the Gold Medal in the 100-meter backstroke, and Buckeye teammate Jack Taylor was third. Two Ohio divers, Miller Anderson and Bob Clotworthy, won Silver and Bronze Medals in the 3-meter event; Iowa's Bowen Stassforth won the Silver Medal in the 200-meter breaststroke which was won by Michigan's John Davies, swimming for Australia, in a new record of 2:34.4. Still another Gold Medal went to the great Clark Scholes of Michigan State, who posted a new mark of 57.1 for 100-meters.

Other swimmers who competed in the Games were Dick Cleveland, Frank Dooley, and Gerry Holan, and diver Jack Calhoun, in addition to four Buckeyes who competed for their native lands: Leo Portelance, Gerry McNamee and Lucien Beaumont for Canada, and Nick Silverio for Cuba. Michigan contributed Burwell Jones and Ron Gora, and also sent the Wardrop brothers, Jack and Bob, to the British team.

Michigan State's Chuck Speiser was on the boxing team and the Spartans' Dale Thomas and Allan Kwartler were on the wrestling and fencing squads. The Spartans also contributed pretty Virgina Baxter to the women's figure skating squad. Minnesota's Jim Sedin, Allan Van, Rube Bjorkman and Ken Yackel skated with the U.S. hockey team.

Meanwhile, the Conference Medal for academic proficiency in 1952 had gone to stars such as Don McEwan, Michigan's great track champion; Chuck

He must always be in a position to call infractions and must call them as he sees them.

The advent of the football movies and television with the "instant replay" furnished many opportunities of second guessing the men in the striped shirts. Coaches would review for hours the game films and often would arrive at the conclusion that the correct call had not been made. (The whistle blower had only seconds to determine the same call and once the call was made that was it!)

However, I don't think any problem has the importance and complexities of rule enforcement in regard to athletic personnel within the Conference, and I would be remiss if I did not review here the most significant crisis in recent league history.

On December 16, 1966, the Big Ten was rocked to its foundations when Dr. David D. Henry, president of the

University of Illinois, asked Commissioner Bill Reed to investigate some alleged irregularities in aid to athletes at Illinois. The university, itself, was asking for the investigation of a $21,000 slush fund which, apparently, had been in operation since 1962. The revelation had been made to Dr. Henry by Mel Brewer, an assistant director of athletics who asked to be relieved of his duties.

Doug Mills, Athletic Director at Illinois since 1941, had resigned on November 23 for personal reasons. Leslie A. Bryan, the Faculty Representative to the Conference, was serving as acting Director until the post was filled permanently.

On December 23, the university, complying with established Conference rules, suspended seven football players, four varsity basketball players and one freshman basketball player. On the same day, it was announced by Dr. Henry that varsity grid coach, Pete Elliott, varsity basket-

Darling, Iowa's basketball whiz; and Stew Hein, Ohio State All-America baseballer. In significant adminstrative action, the Conference adopted an 18-game round robin basketball schedule; announced that the Conference Commissioner henceforth would be employed by the 10 Conference presidents and would report to them semi-annually on enforcement of league regulations. They also ruled that all penalties imposed by the Commissioner would be announced publicly; and established new regulations for aid to athletes, as follows: institutional aid on the basis of superior scholarship would be limited to renewable one-year terms in an amount not exceeding normal expenses for attending that institution; it defined "superior scholarship" as the upper third of the high school class or, in college, a cumulative average no lower than mid-way between B and C. An athlete receiving unearned aid from a school would be notified in writing of the terms and basis of the award. A "qualitative progress" rule of eligibility paralleling the rule of normal underclass qualitative progress toward a degree was established as was a limit of athletic eligibility to a residence period of ten semesters or 15 quarters.

Nobody could possibly have predicted it—and it was incredible when it happened on that Saturday in November in 1953. Michigan State, with the nation's longest winning streak, 28 straight, was shooting for its 29th against a Purdue team that had lost four in a row and was destined that season to win only two of nine. The Boilermakers, fired up and capitalizing on Spartan mistakes, made a lone touchdown stand up for the 6-0 win that rocked the football world. It was the Spartans' first official Big Ten grid season and Biggie Munn's last at the coaching helm; but the inexplainable loss to Purdue deprived the Spartans of only a smidgin of luster as they recovered to sweep decisively through the rest of the season to a title tie with Illinois and a dramatic victory over UCLA in the Rose Bowl.

The rules-makers had done away with platoon football in 1953 and suddenly collegians who had been specialists found themselves playing both ways. "In fact," said Munn, "the key to our success in 1953 was the remarkable adjustment many of our players made to the sudden demands upon them. Stars such as Captain Don Dohoney, LeRoy Bolden, Billy Wells, Larry Fowler, Tommy Yewcic, Jim Neal, Evan Slonac Ellis Duckett, and others, had played only one way and had to start all over again to learn aspects of the game they'd never been called upon to use. Dohoney is a prime example of how well we made the switch. He'd been a great defensive player as a sophomore and junior, but when he was suddenly forced to go both ways he mastered the skills along with the strategic fine points, and despite the fact he hadn't played a single minute of offensive football he became an All-America for us."

In Yewcic, Bolden, Wells and Slonac the Spartans had the smallest backfield ever to play for a Big Ten champion, but they were tough, instinctively smart and whippet-fast. In front of them was a line that made up in mobility and aggressiveness what it lacked in size. Heading up this forward wall were Dohoney and Ellis Duckett at ends; two all-purpose tackles in Randy Schrecengost and Hank Bullough; a great guard in Ferris Hallmark, and rock-hard center, Jim Neal.

"Another factor in our success," recalled Biggie Munn, "was our great desire to win. Several times we had to come back from what was shaping up as an obvious defeat. Against Texas Christian we trailed 19-7 late in the third quarter and we exploded for 19 points in the next 13 minutes. Against UCLA in the Rose Bowl they had us 14-0 before we got up from the floor, took a good look at what was happening and then went out and got 28 points."

The Spartans got to go to the Bowl in their first year in the Conference because Illinois, the co-sharers of the title had been out to Pasadena two years previously and the last-to-go rule gave the invitation

1953

ball coach, Harry Combes, and his assistant, Howard Braun, had been placed on two years probation and were forbidden to participate in any recruiting activities for one year. These sanctions, however, were purely "local," so to speak. There would yet be official word from Commissioner Reed's office.

On January 20, 1967, there was word, indeed, when Reed announced he had concluded his investigation of the irregularities, and had called a meeting of Conference Athletic Directors for February 22, at which time he'd place his evidence before them. Because of the gravity of the charges—the most serious in modern Big Ten history—it is fitting that we print, here, Reed's statement following that meeting.

"The athletic directors of the conference [Illinois not voting] have concluded that football Coach Pete Elliott, basketball Coach Harry Combes, and assistant basketball

Coach Howard Braun of the University of Illinois have been in violation of certain Conference rules and regulations relating to financial assistance to athletes and to the source and uses of funds in the recruiting of athletes.

"The athletic directors have further voted to invoke the penalty described in these rules and regulations, which reads as follows:

" 'Any member university which employs or retains on its athletic staff anyone who has violated or who has been a party to a violation of the provisions of this rule, or who encourages others to violate this rule, shall be required to show cause why its membership in the Conference should not be suspended or terminated.'

"These actions represent the unanimous position of the directors voting.

"These actions are subject to appeal to the Conference

J. C. CAROLINE

BOB LENZINI, a terrific tackle, and J. C. CAROLINE, a swift halfback, led Illinois to the co-championship in 1953 and a Rose Bowl triumph over UCLA. Caroline, an

BOB LENZINI

All-America, was Conference rushing leader with 919 yards (a record) and tore off at least one run of 40 yards or more in every game he played.

to Michigan State. It was a solid creation that Ray Elliot had forged again at Champaign-Urbana, however—a team that led the league in scoring, first downs, rushing, and total yards gained. Two great sophomore halfbacks paced the Illini and it was doubtful if a better brace of newcomers had shown up in the league in the last decade. J. C. Caroline, a swift, long-striding 186-pounder, was a wraith-like, go-the-distance threat who ripped off at least one run of 40 yards or more in every game he

played, and wound up as Conference rushing leader with 919 yards for a record that still stands, and a phenomenal 6.9 average per carry. His running-mate, Mickey Bates, was a 195-pounder who, though not quite as swift, was a powerhouse who led the Big Ten in scoring. Backing them up were fullback Stan Wallace, quarterback Ken Miller and halfback Elry Falkenstein, who added offensive depth and defensive ability to the cause. Ahead of these backs was a line led by two great tackles, Bob Lenzini and

faculty representatives by the University of Illinois or the affected staff members.

"In the absence of any appeal, the recommended penalty will necessarily be referred to the faculty representatives for implementation since only that group can act upon membership status.

"The athletic directors have also referred to the faculty representatives final determination of the eligibility status of students who were the recipients of financial assistance not authorized by the rule.

"To protect rights of appeal, the athletic directors have agreed they will make no further comment at this time and have directed me to make no further comment at this time.

"The athletic directors have recorded their appreciation of the initiative and responsibility of the University of Illinois in making initial and voluntary disclosure of facts in this matter."

In essence, it meant that Illinois had to fire the coaches involved or get out of the Conference. President Henry immediately issued a statement protesting the decision pertaining to the coaches as, "too harsh," and added: "we intend to appeal to the faculty representatives for release from that decision."

With respect to the eligibility status of the students, Henry said: "We shall ask the faculty representatives for the greatest possible ameliorative action under the rules."

On March 2, the Faculty Representatives met in Chicago and listened to stirring pleas from Dr. Henry, University Legal Counsel, James Costello, and Prof. Leslie Bryan, the Illini faculty representative. It was a day-long session, and certainly not a comfortable one for all involved. These were all good friends sitting there. Dr. Henry spoke of Illinois' "historic position in the Conference and the way in which we have fully participated in all its activities through the years." Prof. Bryan spoke

Don Ernst; two terrific guards, Jan Smid and John Bauer; a quick, tough center, Herb Borman; and an exceptionally fine two-way end, Cliff Waldbesser.

There was a gaudy selection of Big Ten stars on the various All-America's in 1953, and again Michigan State led the pack with three: Don Doheny at end; LeRoy Bolden, at halfback, and the tough, mobile Larry Fowler at tackle. (The Spartans were well on their way to setting a Conference record for number of All-Americas produced in one decade.) Paul Giel, considered by some critics as the finest halfback in Minnesota history and one of the greatest ever produced in the Big Ten, was a unanimous choice at his position. He also was named Conference MVP for the second year in a row, and barely

lost out to John Lattner of Notre Dame for the Heisman Award. J. C. Caroline, Illinois' hip-swinger, was another all-star designee at halfback; Joe Collier, Northwestern's versatile end, made it two years in a row; and Jerry Hilgenberg, the first Iowa center ever to make the honor squad, ended a Hawkeye All-America drought that went back to 1940.

The Conference experimented with an 18-game basketball schedule in 1953, with full home-and-home series all around, but the idea was abandoned the following year. It was just too much basketball. Meanwhile, it was Indiana's honor to win the longest league warfare ever waged, with a runaway 17-1 mark and 23-3 overall. A 65-63 loss to Minnesota was the Hoosiers' lone league blemish. There were

LEROY BOLDEN, Michigan State's swift 165-pound halfback; and Captain DON DOHENY, a fine end, were two of the Spartans' All-Americas in 1953, along with teammate Larry Fowler, a tremendous tackle. JOE COL-

LIER, Northwestern's superb pass-catcher, was another Big Ten All-America, as was JERRY HILGENBERG, Iowa's great center, and the first Hawkeye to be All-America at that position.

| DON DOHENY | JERRY HILGENBERG | JOE COLLIER | LEROY BOLDEN |

on behalf of 14 affected athletes—two more than originally involved. And Costello, as legal counsel, pleaded for Elliott, Combes and Braun, the coaches.

The following day the Faculty Representatives upheld the Athletic Directors' decision by unanimous vote. Chairman Verne C. Freeman, of Purdue, sent Dr. Henry the following wire:

Dear Dr. Henry:

The faculty representatives of the Intercollegiate Conference, after full consideration of the University of Illinois' appeal from decisions recorded by the directors of athletics of the Conference on Feb. 22, have voted to concur in those decisions as follows:

1. That Coaches Elliott, Combes and Braun have been in violation of certain of the Conference rules and regulations;

2. That in consequence there be invoked the penalties stated in rule 7, section 12 [a] and regulation VIII,

section 11a of the Conference handbook, to wit: "Any member university which employs or retains on its athletic staff anyone who has violated or who has been a party to a violation of the provisions of this rule [regulation], or who upon inquiry by the Commissioner withholds knowledge of the violation of this rule [regulation] by others, shall be required to show cause why its membership in the Conference should not be suspended or terminated."

In accordance with the latter action, the University of Illinois is invited to respond to the Commissioner on or before March 17, 1967 concerning the following:

a. Will the university retain on its athletic staff Coaches Elliott, Combes and Braun? If the answer is "no" the case is closed.

b. If the answer to the above question is "yes" as to any of these coaches, will you discuss with the Commissioner dates convenient for a hearing at which the uni-

Indiana's 1953 Big Ten and National Collegiate championship starting five: Charley Kraak, Bob Leonard, Don Schlundt, Dick Farley, Burke Scott, and Coach Branch McCracken.

also early season setbacks by Notre Dame (71-70) and Kansas (82-80), and keep an eye on those barn-burners because there would be some sweet revenge for Indiana on a more significant basis than usually accrues to ordinary games.

Don Schlundt, the Hoosiers' big center, became the first sophomore in modern Big Ten cage history to lead the league in scoring, with 459 points and a 25.5 average. He paced such brilliant Conference stars as Illinois' Irv Bemoras; Ohio State's Paul Ebert; Minnesota's Chuck Mencel; John Kerr of Illinois, and Indiana's sparkling Bob Leonard.

There were two Conference contributions to the All-America listings, Indiana's Schlundt and Leonard who did so much to make the Hoosiers the first league team to wear the NCAA crown. Along the tournament route they disposed of DePaul, 82-80; avenged their earlier loss to Notre Dame, 79-76; smashed Louisiana State, 80-67, and then got even with Kansas by toppling the defending tourney titlists, 69-68 for all the marbles.

Led by Willie Williams, Stacey Siders and Joel McNulty, Illinois swept both indoor and outdoor track championships for the third year in a row. On the boards, Williams took the 60-yard dash and 70-yard low hurdles, while Siders set a new Conference record of 1:52.7 for the 880, and McNulty captured the 70-yard high hurdles. Outdoors, the

versity is invited to show cause why its membership in the Conference should not be suspended or terminated? We are grateful for your cooperation.

Sincerely yours,
Verne C. Freeman, Chairman

Marcus Plant, of Michigan, secretary of the Faculty Group, in a press interview said: "There was no new evidence (in the appeal) but we didn't approach it with the feeling we had to go back to the Directors. The question before us was, 'is the action too harsh?' Our conclusion was that the action by the Athletic Directors was *not* too harsh."

Then the faculty representatives met again the following day to decide on the eligibility of the athletes who had been suspended by Illinois. Five were declared permanently ineligible for Big Ten competition; two others had their eligibility limited; six were cleared and one was barred from competition until his sophomore year.

Faced with these decrees, President Henry, the next day, March 6, made public a nine-page statement outlining an offer of compromise he had made before the Faculty Representatives, and said the University intended to show cause why its membership in the Conference should not be terminated if Illinois should refuse to fire the three coaches.

It was a forthright statement which admitted that the three coaches had erred grievously in knowing about the slush fund but Dr. Henry felt the penalties should be exacted on an institutional basis—that Illinois, itself, should handle it—and the coaches should be given a second chance. He also added that the illegal funds structure had been organized and authorized by the former athletic director and that Elliott, Combes and Braun had merely acted in compliance with the Director's plan.

Henry's statement also contained a plea that the

streaking Williams scored a double in the 100- and 220-yard dashes; Siders repeated as half-mile champ; McNulty replaced Williams in the low hurdles and took the 220-yard event; Tom Floyd won the broad jump; Willard Thomson the high hurdles; Jim Wright tied for first in the pole vault and Dick Wham did likewise in the high jump.

Illinois also shared the baseball title with Michigan, although it must have been done with mirrors. Both clubs had 10-3 marks but arrived at them in considerably different fashion. Michigan led the league in both team hitting (.288) and team fielding (.971). For the Wolverines, outfielder Paul Lepley hit .396; outfielder-pitcher Jack Corbett swung for .375; All-America shortstop Bruce Haynam posted

PAUL GIEL, Minnesota's two-time All-America halfback in 1952-53, was one of the finest offensive threats, running and passing, in Conference history. Winner of the Walter Camp Memorial Trophy for back-of-the-year, and of the UPI player-of-the-year award, Giel was the only halfback even to win the Conference MVP award two years in a row.

.360; second baseman Gil Sabuco hit .327 and third-sacker Don Eaddy, although only hitting .250 was so valuable he made All-Conference along with Haynam and Lepley. Meanwhile, the Wolverines were getting crack pitching performances from John Ritter, Jack Corbett and Dick Yirkoski.

The Illinois story was statistically different. The Illini got there on hustle and headiness. First baseman Bob Moore was their top hitter at .292, and four pitchers divided their 10 victories: Carl Ahrens, 3-0; Clive Follmer, 3-1; Gerry Smith, 3-1, and Jim Schuldt, 1-1.

Gene Steiger, Minnesota catcher, was the league's top hitter with .462, and Merle Jensen, Iowa pitcher, led the hurlers with 4-0.

In swimming, Ohio State won its fifth straight team title, and their seventh in eight years, with seven first places falling to the Buckeye splashers. Ford Konno took the 1500-meters but suffered a rare defeat as Michigan's Burwell Jones nipped him by a touch in the 220 freestyle. Yoshi Oyakawa triumphed in the 100- and 200-yard backstroke; Gerry Holan took the 200-yard breaststroke; Bobby Clotworthy scored a typical Ohio State double on the low and high diving boards; and a Scarlet trio of Oyakawa, Holan and Nick Silverio picked off the 300-yard medley relay. Strangely enough, it was the last Conference meet in which the athletes failed to set a single record.

Michigan took the wrestling championship, led by Snip Nalon's victory at 130 pounds, and Dick O'Shaughnessy's 177-pound laurels, with football center O'Shaughnessy coming down from his gridiron heft of 190 pounds to make his mat weight. Illinois won its fourth straight fencing crown, with John Cameron's sabre title leading the Illini's 40-bout victory list. It was also the fourth straight championship for the Illinois gymnastics team as Bob Sullivan paced things with a free exercise title. Minnesota's Kent Bartlett took the prestigious all-around crown.

Little Rich Ferguson of Iowa repeated as individ-

athletes who'd received illicit financial aid should have their eligibility suspension limited to one year in all cases. Dr. Henry published the case history of each athlete and the amount he'd received from the slush fund. The sums involved for the five who'd been declared permanently ineligble ran from $83.00 to $1645.00 beyond their grant-in-aid of room, board, books and tuition.

The final meeting was on March 18 in Chicago. Dr. Henry, the only Illinois official present, spoke for three hours. The Faculty Representatives deliberated that afternoon and made the following announcement at a press conference:

"Having weighed carefully the seriousness of the infractions involved and all of the information of record, including that furnished by the representatives of the University of Illinois, the faculty representatives have decided that the University of Illinois did not sufficiently

show cause under the provisions of rule 7, section 12[a], and regulation VIII, section 11a.

"Therefore, if after March 21, 1967, Coaches Peter Elliott, Harry Combes, and Howard Braun, or any one of them, be retained in positions in the coaching of any sport in the intercollegiate athletic program or in the direction or administration of intercollegiate athletics at the University of Illinois, the membership of the University of Illinois in the Intercollegiate Conference of Faculty Representatives shall be suspended indefinitely as of that date.

"In taking this action the faculty representatives are mindful of the honored position of the University of Illinois in the long history of the Conference and are unanimously hopeful that this association will continue."

The vote of the Faculty Representatives was announced as eight to one, with Illinois abstaining.

Illinois now had two options. They could dismiss the

ual cross-country champ, but as usual, there was no stopping Michigan State for the team title as three Spartans—John Cook, Ron Barr and Lyle Garbe—placed among the first ten finishers. Michigan State's Stan Drobac also brought home the tennis singles cup for the Spartans and Drobac and teammate Tom Felton repeated as doubles champs but couldn't overcome the overall strength of Indiana which repeated as team champ. Don Albert, the latest in a long line of Purdue golf stars, won the individual title and, with teammate Bob Benning, led the Boilermakers to the team title.

Two team titles went to the Big Ten in NCAA activity and both went to Michigan. The Wolverines became the first Conference club to take the national baseball crown when they defeated Texas, 7-5, in the tourney final, and the Wolves and Minnesota faced off in the first all-Conference hockey final, with Michigan downing the Gophers 7-3. Once again Michigan's Doug Philpott and George Chin shared tournament scoring honors with six points each.

In track, Willie Williams, winning a 9.7 century, led Illinois to second place behind U.S.C for team honors, while Iowa's Rich Ferguson set a new two-mile mark of 9:02.7 and Michigan's Milt Mead tied for first in the high jump with 6-8½.

In swimming, it was Yale, the only foreign intruder in the waters usually controlled by Ohio State and Michigan, which took the team crown, but there were a flock of first-place medals that went to Big Ten tankmen. The Buckeyes' Yoshi Oyakawa, posted a brilliant double with the first of what would be three straight titles in the 100-yard backstroke in record time of 56.9, and his second victory at 200-yards, also in record-shattering time of 2:05.1. Ohio's Gerry Holan won the 200-yard butterfly in 2:14; the Buckeye trio of Oyakawa, Holan and Dick Cleveland captured the 300-yard medley in a 2:47.2 record effort; and Buckeye divers took home both titles, with Gerry Harrison scoring

Iowa's **RICHARD FERGUSON** *won the Conference individual cross-country crown for the second year in a row in 1953.*

BOB CLOTWORTHY, *Ohio State diving star, captured both the high and low board events as the Buckeyes won their fifth straight team title in 1953, and then went on to take the high board crown in the NCAA tourney.*

three coaches and the case would be closed; or, if they retained them Illinois would be suspended from the Big Ten. Marcus Plant defined suspension in this manner: "Suspension places an institution in the same position as any non-Conference university. As against *termination* of membership, suspension carries the possibility of further re-instatement."

The next day, Elliott, Combes and Braun tendered their resignations to Dr. Henry who accepted them but revealed that their termination of their coaching duties didn't affect their faculty status in the College of Physical Education if they chose to remain.

Although Elliott, Combes and Braun candidly said they'd resigned because they didn't want to put Illinois in an impossible situation, a furor of indignation broke out among Illinois alumni, fans and sympathizers in the press, particularly the press in Chicago. The three coaches

had been immensely popular. The Illinois State Legislature, incensed, voted for an investigation that would include the Commissioner's office in Chicago. Much of the bitterness poured forth by Illini sympathizers had been predicated on their allegations that the Illinois coaches had merely been victimized by practices universal in intercollegiate athletics as well as the Big Ten; but their charges were not backed up by proof of this. It was, indeed, the most trying hour in Conference history, not forgetting a similar uproar when Iowa's membership was suspended in 1929.

Through all the furor, the Conference position emerged strong and clear. The Athletic Directors and Faculty Representatives, necessarily mindful of implications regarding the programs for which they were individually responsible, had faced up to the harshest of their obligations—protection of the integrity of Conference rules. In

on the low and Bobby Clotworthy on the high board. As usual, Michigan was very much in the picture. Don Hill took the 50-yard sprint in 22.4; Burwell Jones won the 150-yard medley in 1:30 and a crack Wolverine foursome of Ron Gora, Jones, Tom Benner and Hill set a new mark of 3:24 for the 400-yard freestyle relay. The Conference took home one other title when Bob Clemons, of Illinois, captured the 100-yard butterfly in 1:00.9.

In boxing, Ray Zale, Wisconsin's 178-pound champ, was chosen for the John S. LaRowe Award as outstanding performer in the NCAA tourney; teammate Pat Screen, triumphed at 147 pounds; and Michigan State's Tom Hickey won at 165.

Dick Mueller, of Minnesota, at 123 pounds, and Norvard (Snip) Nalon, of Michigan, at 130, were wrestling titlists. In gymnastics the Conference came up with titles for Carlton Rintz of Michigan State

RAY ZALE, Wisconsin 178-pound NCAA champion of 1953, won the LaRowe Award as the tourney's oustanding boxer.

on side horse; Bob Sullivan of Illinois in free exercise; Minnesota's Ken Bartlett on flying rings; and Iowa's Bob Hazlett on the trampoline.

The big news of the year, administratively, was the disciplinary action which the Commissioner took against Michigan State for delinquencies in permitting the existence of a private organization known as the Spartan Foundation which solicited funds to assist Michigan State athletes. The Spartans were put on probation as of February 22 and ordered to clean up the situation.

The Conference also limited football traveling squads to 38 and got rid of the 18-game Conference basketball schedule which was found to be just too much, and restored the 14-game program.

The faculty representatives also voted to renew the Rose Bowl Pact with the Coast Conference for three more years, and, just before the year was out, the Conference Representatives, on the Commissioner's recommendation, removed Michigan State from probation after it was established that the school had forced the dissolution of the Spartan Foundation. On December 10, 1953, Prof. Ralph W. Aigler, of Michigan, retired as Chairman of the Big Ten Eligibility Committee after serving more than 25 years with that body. It marked the end of one of the most illustrious careers in athletic administration the Conference had ever seen.

By 1954, Wayne Woodrow Hayes who had weathered three mediocre years at Ohio State, had started to put a few things together, and his philosophy of football was beginning to emerge. A few years later, after Woody Hayes was hailed as one of football's coaching greats, his philosophy would be described as "three yards and a cloud of dust." The description, however, was an unfair catchall that didn't tell the story. What Woody Hayes was working on was a ball-control game that featured a sound, precise running attack with just enough passing to keep a limited aerial franchise. To make

1954

doing so they had committed themselves in the future to such a confrontation wherever and whenever it might occur.

A look into the future is always hazardous but I can only predict success for the Big Ten in the coming years. The problems ahead will be simply tremendous. Some of the Big Ten schools have over 30,000 students enrolled on campus. While the Conference now possesses the finest athletic facilities of any in the country, future years will find them inadequate. Television will continue to present problems, along with the financial awards of the sponsoring programs.

The relationship between professional football and professional basketball will cause great problems from time to time especially if the pro teams start encroaching on what has come to be known through the years as high school and college time, namely Friday night and

Saturday afternoon. If, in their greed for bigger television money, the pros start to schedule games on these dates, it will cause unbelievable damage to the amateur program. I have bemoaned the sight of the professional scouts signing up a college athlete under the goal posts as he completed his eligibility. If this continues, it will undoubtedly cause athletes to go to college not for an education but simply as a training ground for professional football. When you realize the limited span of competition for most professional athletes, you realize the great need for them to acquire a sound education that will enable them to take an important part in business or professional life when they are through playing.

I have no quarrel with professional athletics. They have become an important part of our way of life. To thousands of sports fans who did not attend college, the pros become their teams and they take pleasure in

Woody Hayes, Ohio State football coach, is truly a man on his toes.

WOODY HAYES

One way to discuss Wayne Woodrow Hayes of Ohio State is to wind up, take a deep breath and describe him as one of the nation's most successful and colorful football coaches . . . Who wears nothing but a short-sleeved shirt even during games in 20-degree weather . . . Who once tried to order the Buckeye band off the muddy field during half-time at the Rose Bowl because he was afraid it would chew up the field too much . . . Who once was accused of slugging a sportswriter at the dressing room door (but really didn't) . . . Who drew a probationary period from the Commissioner's office for helping financially distressed football players out of his own pocket . . . Who once in a heated argument told a faculty colleague that he (Woody) could do the colleagues' job but the prof couldn't do his . . . Who once chased an official all the way down the sideline to protest a call (for one of the great all-time sports page pics) . . . Who is an authentic history scholar and who can quote Herodotus by the yard . . . Who once said "there are three things that can happen on a forward pass and two of them are bad" . . . Whose offense has been described as "three yards and a cloud of dust," (Although actually he's been near the top of Big Ten passing statistics for many years) . . . Who has been Coach-of-the-Year and President of the American Football Coaches Association. . . .

No, there is no doubt that the Buckeyes' Woody Hayes, Dean of the Big Ten football coaches, is the most colorful coach in the Conference. Just as there is no doubt he is one of the most successful in Conference history.

Since he came to Ohio State in 1951, via Miami of Ohio, he has won four Conference crowns and two national championships, set a league mark of 17 straight Conference wins (1954-55-56); has been to the Rose Bowl twice (victoriously) and was denied a third trip by an anti-Bowl faculty at the time; has the best winning record and has produced more All-America players than any Conference coach; has sent more players into the pro ranks and has seen to it that a remarkably high percentage of his players get their degrees. (More than 90%; considerably higher than the average for the student body as a whole.)

rooting for them. I have watched with some alarm the inroads they have made on college attendance in various parts of the country. It is true they play great football but they still lack much of the excitement and glamor of a college game with its colorful rooting sections, the tremendous marching bands, things that professional football games have never quite attained.

I have spent considerable time lauding the Big Ten for what it has done for intercollegiate athletics but there are some phases that I think are open for criticism. If the football and basketball teams are truly representative of the student body, why is it that practically the only athletes who go out for the team are those who have been carefully recruited and who are beneficiaries of financial aid? It is inconceivable to me that with a student body of 20,000 to 30,000 there are not more students who would like to enjoy an opportunity to try out for the various teams. The coaches' response

Under Woody Hayes the Buckeyes have won two national championships and four Conference titles.

One significant measure of his sound coaching: Hayes' teams in his 16 seasons have had less penalty yardage assessed against them and have fumbled the ball fewer times than any other club in the Conference.

Handsome, rotund, and urbane and colloquial by turns, Woody Hayes, as an accompanying picture illustrates, has truly been a man on his toes and seldom caught off balance.

his game go, however, Hayes put a premium on superb line blocking; on backs who would rarely fumble; and on the kind of all-around execution that would result in a minimum of mistakes and penalties. As a result, the Buckeyes under Hayes for many years would have the lowest fumble average and penalty rate in the league. They would hold onto the ball, point their way up the middle and defy the defense to stop them.

By 1954 Hayes not only had established his pattern of play but he had the personnel to make it go —and the Woody Hayes Era had come to Big Ten football. The personnel was deep, dedicated and disciplined—and the name of the game was blocking. Up front was a machine of many parts. Ken Vargo and Bob Thornton, two brilliant centers, had three great guards spotted at various times alongside them: Jim Reichenbach, a four-year regular, and Dave Weaver and Jim Parker, who was to go on to all-time pro stardom. Dick Hilinski, Frank Machinski, Jerry Krisher, another four-year regular who had been a Korea-ruling frosh, and Don Swartz gave Hayes four hard-hitting tackles. Co-Captain Dick Brubaker and big, tough Dean Dugger, younger brother of former All-America Jack Dugger, were the ends.

The backfield started out with a bad break and ended with all-around superlatives. Co-Captain John Borton as a sophomore had been one of the greatest prospects in league history—an impeccable signal-caller, a brilliant passer and fine runner. Hurt halfway through his junior season he was expected to regain his form as a senior. He came back from a Naval R.O.T.C. cruise overweight, then broke a thumb the second week of practice and had to sit by as Hayes was forced to turn to Dave Leggett as first-string quarterback. Borton became a brilliant defensive star, as he had been as a freshman. Leggett, a good if not great passer, and a strong runner on the keeper-play, presided over possibly the best rushing backfield yet put together in the

to this is invariably the same. They simply do not have the time, equipment, space or coaching staff to waste on an untried prospect. I violently disagree with this premise. If the university is being represented only by athletes who have been recruited, it places this group apart from the rest of the student body. I think of my own experience. Coming from a small high school where there were only nine boys enrolled, there was no football team. I wanted to try out. I was welcomed to the squad but when they told me to line up at right tackle, I had to ask another squad member where to go. It is true I never burned up the Conference as a football player but I had a wonderful experience in being a squad member for a four-year period and received a training that was invaluable to me in later years. I think of Fritz Crisler. As a tall, skinny freshman he had not gone out for freshmen football at the start of the season at Chicago. He was seen by Amos Alonzo Stagg

one day who noticed his casual ability on the sidelines and told him to draw a suit. This was the first step of his illustrious career as he became a great player and later one of the outstanding coaches of all time. I think of George Gipp standing on the sidelines at Notre Dame watching practice, picking up a loose ball that came bouncing toward him and kicking it some 60 yards back on the field. When Knute Rockne saw this he was put on the squad the next day. These things simply do not happen today.

As Commissioner, I frequently visited Big Ten campuses the day before a game and loved to go out and watch the hundreds of students playing touch football. Their enthusiasm and skill was sometimes astonishing. At one of these intramural contests I spotted a big 6'4" end. I watched him go up high in the air and snare a pass with one hand, then fake a defender out of position and score a touchdown. I couldn't resist

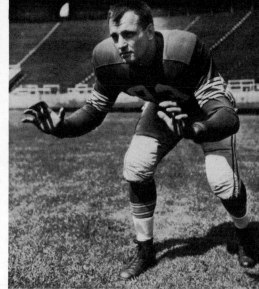

HOWARD (HOPALONG) CASSADY

DAVE LEGGETT

DEAN DUGGER

Three of the talent-studded 1954 Ohio State team who led the Buckeyes to the national championship were cool quarterback DAVE LEGGETT; DEAN DUGGER, a versatile end; and HOWARD (HOPALONG) CASSADY, the brilliant redhead who, with Dugger, was named All-America, and who the following season would gain even greater honors.

First, there were the irrepressible heroics of Howard (Hopalong) Cassady at left half. Bobby Watkins, a quick-hitting 190-pounder, was at right half; and hard-nosed, rampaging Hubert Bobo, a sophomore was at full back, where he was also a devastating blocker and a fine punter. For the first time in history, three backs from the same team wound up in the top 10 rushers for the season as Cassady raced 472 yards on 87 carries for a 5.4 average; Watkins 464 yards on 73 efforts for a bumptious 6.3 average; and Bobo 332 yards on 53 attempts for a 6.3 average. Incredibly, Watkins lost only two yards all season and Bobo never lost an inch. Leggett, meanwhile, completed 32 of 72 attempts as a passer as the Buckeyes enjoyed one of their greatest seasons ever.

Two games stood out as the Buckeyes smashed to a perfect 9-0 season, the Big Ten and National

The Chair of Applied Gridiron Science at Michigan State was turned over to HUGH (DUFFY) DAUGHERTY in 1954 by CLARENCE (BIGGIE) MUNN, standing, as the latter retired from coaching to take over as Athletic Director. Two years before, Munn, the Master, had been Coach-of-the-Year; a year later, Duffy, the pupil, achieved the same honor.

hunting him out and asking why he was not out for the varsity. His reply almost bowled me over. He said he would not have had a chance as they had recruited all the other candidates. I told him this was all poppycock and he agreed to give it a try. He reported to me later that after standing on the sidelines for a couple of weeks and receiving no coaching or encouragement, he was back playing touch football for his fraternity team.

It is true the Big Ten has done a remarkable job in furnishing tremendous intramural programs but they could not take the place of actual varsity play. I think there is no question in anyone's mind of the value of sport competition. A youngster learns what it means to be a team player, to block for someone else. He learns the joy of picking himself up out of the dirt and going back after his opponent. He is getting a terrific lesson

in discipline, a quality he will need the rest of his life.

As I was preparing for my final meeting as Commissioner in the Spring of 1961 I was glancing over the records of games played against teams outside the league since 1945 when I had taken over. I cannot claim much of a role in the success of our Conference on the field of play but the results were indeed impressive. In football our average was .670. In basketball, baseball, track, swimming and other sports the record was just as good. In 16 years of Rose Bowl competition there were 13 victories and only three losses. The Conference had supplied dozens of Olympic performers, and, in total number, more than any other league.

All these things I remembered with deep satisfaction as I prepared to leave the Commissioner's office and concentrate on my newer duties as President of the

Championships and a 20-7 conquest of Southern California in the Rose Bowl. Along the way there were two dramatic mileposts in the Scarlet surge. At midpoint in the season they were trailing Wisconsin 14-10 and the Badgers were getting stronger by halftime. Then Cassady, who for four straight years turned in game-breaking long runs against the Badgers for come-from-behind Ohio victories, led the Bucks on a three-touchdown rampage that tore the game apart.

In the season finale with Michigan, all the chips were shoved to the center of the table as the Wolverines battled the Buckeyes for the Bouquet of Roses. Michigan had been upset 13-9 by Indiana, but a victory over Ohio would send them to Pasadena. It was a high-potential Wolverine club, spearheaded by three great backs in Lou Baldacci, Terry Barr and Tony Branoff, behind a line featuring the magnificent Ron Kramer and Tom Maentz at ends; a terrific tackle in Art Walker, and Jim Bates, a fine center.

The game was still up for grabs at 7-7 late in the third quarter when a Michigan drive reached a climactic spot with a first down on the Buckeye four. Three plays later the Wolverines were on the 1-foot line and Ohio Stadium was a huge sea of sound. The two lines smashed together, the Michigan ball carrier hurtled into them, and then the officials started digging into the bodies for the ball.

It was still on the one-foot line.

The Buckeyes took over and put on a 12-play drive that measured 2600 miles, 99 and two-thirds yards, or the distance from the shadow of the Ohio goal-line to the turf in Pasadena. It was an epic march. Lining up for the first play virtually in his end zone, Dave Leggett decided to sneak to get at least a yard onto the field. He got two. He sneaked again and got four. Incredibly he sneaked a third time and got a first down. The Bucks could at least take a deep breath. On the next play Cassady got them a big chunk of air by streaking 52 yards into

Wolverine territory. Seven more running plays took the Bucks to the 8-yard line, and then Leggett pegged a pass to Dick Brubaker for the go-ahead touchdown. The Scarlet, out of immediate danger, capped the day with another drive of 62 yards (again in 12 plays) with Cassady blasting over from the two, with 14 seconds left, and their 21-7 victory was one of their most dramatic victories in history.

In the entire history of collegiate football there were few fullbacks who could match the feats of Wisconsin's fabulous ALAN (THE HORSE) AMECHE. A two-year All-America (1953-54), Ameche was a four-year star with the Badgers, courtesy of Korean War regulations, and was the first freshman in Conference history to lead the league in rushing. As an 18-year-old he blasted 147 times for 774 yards and an awesome 5.3 average. As a sophomore he led the loop again with almost identical figures, 146 for 721 and 4.9. Coach Ivan Williamson took some of the pressure off the big kid in his junior and senior years by passing more, but the 220-pound bulldozer was still so devastating he was his team's MVP for both years and the Conference MVP as a senior in 1954. Small wonder he was a virtually automatic Heisman Award winner that season. After that came his fabulous years as all-pro fullback with the Baltimore Colts.

United States Olympic Association, a post I had assumed prior to the 1956 games in Australia.

All the pleasant memories of my Big Ten association I remembered with deep satisfaction; but, the deepest of all came from the knowledge that the Big Ten now had rules the league could believe in and live with. Yet, I suppose, there will always be infractions or there would never be a need for a Commissioner. The people in sports are no more immune from human error than those in business, or law, or government, or cement-mixing. At least, as I look at it, the sins committed in the Conference stem more from emotional reasons than economic. The desire to WIN, when carried to an excess, is certainly evil; but, I reject any charge that this excessive desire to WIN can be laid primarily to economics. Too often I've heard the trite claim: ". . . They've

got to have a winning team to pay off the bonds on the stadium!" Coaches may want to win to hold onto their jobs but the original costs on Big Ten stadiums have long since been paid off.

I firmly believe the athletic program of any university will be only as honest as the integrity of the athletic director and his staff. The type of aid now given to athletes in the Big Ten (tuition, books, room and board) is sufficient. There is no need—nor place—for slush funds, and in any real emergency each school has loan funds at a very low rate of interest which a boy doesn't have to pay back until after graduation.

Now, as an observer, I can watch from the sidelines, figuratively as well as literally, as the Conference continues its growth, and I heartily applaud many of the things accomplished after I stepped down. Of particular

Cassady was a unanimous All-America, as was Alan (The Horse) Ameche, Wisconsin's battering fullback, whose feats on both offense and defense also brought him Conference MVP honors. Joining them on the All-America lists were Calvin Jones, the great Iowa guard; Art Walker, Michigan's mighty tackle; Tom Bettis, one of the best guards in Purdue grid annals; and Bob McNamara, Minnesota's outstanding halfback. Two new scoring records went

Among the seven Conference stars who made All-America in 1954 were TOM BETTIS, a tremendous all-around guard from Purdue; BOB McNAMARA, Minnesota's brilliant halfback; and Iowa's CALVIN JONES, one of the mightiest in Hawkeye grid history, who would repeat his honor the following season, and who a few years later would be tragically killed in a plane crash.

into the books that year as Iowa's Eddie Vincent went 96 yards for the longest touchdown from scrimmage in modern Conference history, and Billy Lowe, of Wisconsin, set a new standard on a pass interception when he picked off an Iowa aerial to go 98 yards and tie a mark previously set by Illinois' Julie Rykovich.

The state of Indiana has long been noted as the nation's hottest basketball area but it wasn't until 1954 that Indiana University was able to put two Big Ten cage titles back to back. Branch McCracken's Hoosiers, repeating their triumph of '53, again got their leadership from their remarkable Big Man, Don Schlundt and slick, deft Bob Leonard in backcourt. With Dick Farley and Charley Kraack operating at forward and Burke Scott pairing off with

note was the 10-game football schedule, putting the Conference on a par with virtually every other major group. (The Ivies still play only nine.) Originally, the added game was to make way for an eventual round-robin schedule with each Conference school playing every other, but that would have meant only one outside game a year. The provision eventually was tabled; I think it a good idea for Conference teams to play three teams from other sections of the country each year. It's a good-neighbor policy in which the Big Ten has always been a leader.

In the last couple of years claims have been made that the Big Ten is no longer King of the Collegiate Conferences. The Big Ten has been taking a few more lumps than usual in interconference football and basketball but, I'm sure, this is only a transient situation. One reason, of course, is the high academic requirements for

athletic scholarships in the Big Ten and many great prospects from our seven Midwest states have gone to schools with lower standards.

Equally restrictive are the rigid recruiting regulations imposed on member schools today. Big Ten institutions may not grant more than 100 athletic scholarships for all sports combined (football, basketball, track, baseball, swimming, etc.) to an incoming freshman class. Not more than 33 of this total may be in football, nor more than six in basketball, lowest numbers of any conference. A coach may not go to a boy's hgih school to interview him and not more than one visit may be made to the boy's home. These and other regulations are considerably more strict than those observed by other institutions.

Also, high school coaching in other geographical sections of the country has been improving rapidly, al-

Leonard, the Hoosiers hustled to a 12-2 Conference mark as the league abandoned the 18-game slate that had lasted only the previous season.

Second-place Iowa, led by center Bill Logan and forward Carl Cain, had cut the Hoosiers down to size, 82-64, in a late season game, but failure to handle Minnesota, Ohio State and Illinois in earlier games cost the Hawkeyes a possible title.

The 6-10 Schlundt was probably the most difficult big man for defense's to halt so far in modern league history. His 27.1 average per game on an amazing variety of hooks with either hand; tap-ins and soft sets was a new Big Ten record, erasing the 26-point mark set by Iowa's Chuck Darling in 1952. The op-

DON SCHLUNDT   BOB LEONARD

The rare feat of putting two Big Ten basketball championships back-to-back was brought off by Indiana in 1953 and 1954, with 6-10 DON SCHLUNDT and slick backcourt man BOB LEONARD leading the way. Both were named All-America for the two seasons. Schlundt was also the first man in modern history to lead the league in scoring as a sophomore, and before his four-year career would be finished he played as a wartime frosh) he would have more records in the book than any player in Conference history.

PAUL EBERT, Ohio State senior All-America forward in 1954, was the first man in league history to be chosen his team's MVP for three straight years. Also a great pitcher for the Buckeye baseball team, he led the league with an ERA of 1.50 and was named All-America. He passed up a pro contract to go to medical school.

position was so desperate in their defensive zeal in trying to choke him off that they provided Schlundt with a new league high of 10.9 free throw attempts per game.

The All-Big Ten team of '54 was undoubtedly the strongest yet picked. In addition to Schlundt and Leonard (16.9 per game) of Indiana, there was Bob Kerr, Illinois' great center, who set a school career scoring mark of 880 points for his 1952-53-54 seasons; Paul Ebert, the stylish Ohio State forward who, during the same period set a Buckeye all-time mark of 1027 points, and Dick Garmaker, the Minnesota backcourt whiz whose 24.6 gave him third place in

though the best programs, I feel, are still in the Midwest; but, as I say, these other areas are catching up.

If the Western Conference has to rise to a challenge it will be neither news nor a hardship. The Big Ten has been challenged before. Without challenge there is no progress. If anything, the great universities that make up the Big Ten stand for progress whether it is in science, technology, the arts—or football and fencing. May it ever be thus.

THE OLYMPIC CHAPTER: A PROLOGUE

For an added chapter, I wish to put on another hat, my Olympic one. It might seem strange that this should be included in a history of the Big Ten, but the Conference had so many men active in Olympic affairs for so many years, contributing so much to the success of the games,

President Lyndon B. Johnson and Tug Wilson in 1964.

the Big Ten scoring race behind Schlundt and Kerr (25.9).

Schlundt, Leonard and Ebert were All-America, but to Kerr, the do-it-all guy for Illinois, went the league's MVP trophy.

Indiana went to the NCAA tournament but failed to get past its first opponent, Notre Dame, which avenged an early, regular season loss to the Hoosiers by dumping them, 65-64 in overtime.

By now, Leo Johnson was working up a pretty good domination of Big Ten track, and the Illini again won both the indoor and outdoor titles, with speedster Willie Williams, middle-distance star Gene Maynard, and hurdler Willard Thomson leading the way. Indoors, it was Williams taking the 60-yard dash and Maynard the 1000-yard run. (He also had a first in the 880 but was disqualified for a foul on a turn.) Ralph Fessenden won the 440; Willard Thomson took the 70-yard high hurdles; football halfback Abe Woodson won the 70-yard lows and Ron Mitchell, with a new record of 6-7½ in the high jump, all played leading roles in the Illini cause.

Among the noteworthy performances at the indoor meet was a record-shattering mile relay in 3:17.6 by an Indiana foursome of Mike Cusick, John Howe, Mel Edwards and Len Robinson. Outdoors, Williams sped to a triumph in the 100 and 220; Maynard whipped through in the 880; Fessenden took the 440; Thomson captured both the low and high hurdles; Dale Foster and Jim Wright tied for first in the pole vault with Northwestern's Bob Errhart; and an Illini foursome of Ralph Peterson, Joe Corley, Maynard and Fessenden won the mile relay.

Ohio State set a new Conference record by winning its sixth straight team crown in swimming, with its Hawaiian contingent again leading the way. The remarkable Ford Konno posted a blazing triple with victories in the 1500-meters, 220 freestyle and 440 freestyle, with new records of 2:06.3 and 4:28.8 in the two shorter events. Yoshi Oyakawa the wind-milling backstroker, captured the 100- and 200-yard events in his specialty; and a third islander, Ed Kawachika, swam the freestyle leg of the winning medley relay along with Oyakawa and Bob Van Heyde. Meanwhile, speedster Dick Cleveland was setting a new mark of 49.5 for the 100-yard sprint; and Morley Shapiro, the new Buckeye King of the Boards, won the low and high dives.

Other Conference stars who shone brightly in the meet were Michigan's Don Hill, who smashed the

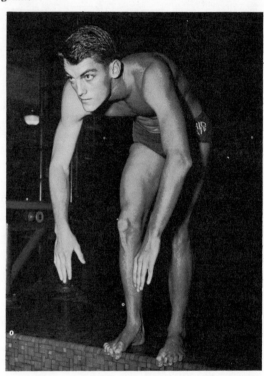

DICK CLEVELAND, Ohio State's league sprint champion, scored a double win in the NCAA 50-and 100-yard free-style in 1954 as the Buckeyes made aquatic history by taking nine individual titles out of 14 on the national program.

that I would feel remiss in my duties as an athletic historian if I did not mention some of the early history. It is not my purpose to go through the worrisome and aggravating accounts of administrative warfare in track and field the last few years, but to attempt to show the importance of this great international contest.

Many sports fans are under the impression that the battle between the AAU and the NCAA has only occurred during the recent few years, and are not aware of the fact that the real struggle began back in the early 1920's. The question often has been posed to me as to why the United States seems always to be embroiled in difficulties over amateur athletics, while other countries contribute every bit of their money, energy and skill to turning out Olympic champions. This is not a hard question to answer. The United States is the only nation in the Olympic picture where the great majority of the athletes that make the Olympic team get their real training in the high schools and universities of our country. It is true that many of the other Olympic nations have great universities, but very few of their institutions have any athletic programs at all. In many of these countries, the sole control is vested in their Olympic committee or in their international sports foundations.

As a competitor in the Olympic Games at Antwerp and even as a brash young collegian, I saw many things that needed correction in the management of Olympic affairs. I was to be a part of a long 15-year struggle before there would emerge any strong working agreement between our two major sports bodies. During these years, it was my privilege to work with many strong individuals on various committees. Gen. Palmer Pierce, president of the NCAA, was one of the first of these

The varied faces of a great figure in American collegiate sports—Michigan State's RALPH YOUNG. He was a pre-World War One football star at Washington and Jefferson College, and football coach and athletic director *at Michigan State (then known as Michigan A. & M.) in 1925. He retired as Michigan State Athletic Director in 1954 after serving the Spartans in that capacity for 21 years.*

50-yard mark with 22.1; Burwell Jones, the Wolverines' medley marvel, with a new record of 1:29.5 for the 150-yard three-ply event; John Dudeck, Michigan State's sparkling breaststroker, who cracked the 100-yard standard with 59.7; and a Michigan foursome of Ron Gora, Jones, Tom Benner and Hill, with a new record of 3:23.8 for the 400-yard relay.

Purdue captured the wrestling championship, led by three individual winners: Al Vega, at 123 pounds; Bob Weick, 147 pounds, and Ahmet Senol, 177 pounds. Illinois took its fifth straight gymnastics title with Frank Bare winning on side horse; Tom Garden taking the parallel bars and Jeff Austin the free exercise. Michigan State's brilliant Carlton Rintz captured the all-around title. Illinois also took its fifth straight fencing crown, as Herman Velasco and Bill Shewchuk led the Illini with titles in foil and sabre.

In baseball Michigan State, with an 11-2 mark,

won its first Conference diamond championship as the Spartans fielded a club that posted one of the highest team batting averages in league history, at .317. Jack Risch, .433 (second to Indiana's Bob Robertson with .438); Ray Collard, 341 and Bob Powell, .326, gave Coach John Kobs a slugging outfield, with additional attacking power from football quarterback Tom Yewcic, a .370-hitting catcher; Charley Matthews, .362 at first base, and George Smith, second baseman, with .300. Jack Zeitler, .290, at third base and shortstop John Matsock, at .283, were the only regulars below .300, and both were brilliant fielders. Bud Erickson, who led the league in victories with a 5-0 mark, and Ed Holbaugh, with 4-0, were the Spartan pitching mainstays, and Risch, Yewcic and Matthews made All-Conference. Yewcic also was named All-America, along with Ohio State's pitching ace, Paul Ebert, who had the league's lowest earned run average with 1.50. The 6-5 Ebert, who

men who recognized and insisted that the colleges and universities of the United States should have a strong say in the management of the U.S. Olympic team.

Maj. John L. Griffith, who served not only as Commissioner of the Big Ten but also was Secretary of the NCAA, was a leader in insisting on more representation and authority for the colleges during his long career. I was privileged to be on many of these committees along with L. W. St. John, director of athletics at Ohio State University; Frank McCormick, director of athletics at the University of Minnesota, and Willis O. Hunter, athletic director at the University of Southern California. Times were hectic, as they are today. One of the controversies that threatened a wide open break was the refusal of the AAU to sanction a swimming meet between Northwestern University and the Chicago Athletic Association because Northwestern had competed in meets not sanc-

tioned by the AAU during the previous summer. At the time, I was athletic director at Northwestern and I issued the following statement upon cancellation of the swimming meet:

"The men who have been disqualified by the AAU competed in amateur swimming last summer with our permission. These were annual meets. No admission was charged, and all who competed were certified amateur by some reputable and responsible organization. The AAU has not charged that the men violated any amateur laws. Their only offense in the eyes of the AAU is that they competed in meets not controlled by the AAU. Northwestern University does not acknowledge that the AAU has supreme control over swimming and other sports, and in the future we will schedule our meets with colleges, universities and such clubs as are not subject to AAU control."

BURWELL JONES

FORD KONNO

YOSHI OYAKAWA

Among the dozen or more truly magnificent swimmers turned out in the Big Ten during the 1950's there is no doubt that the three pictured here deserve all-time accolades. In his day, in fact, Ohio State's slender Hawaiian, FORD KONNO, was simply the greatest freestyle swimmer the world had yet seen. He won more major collegiate titles than any man in the history of the sport: three NCAA crowns in the 440, in 1952-54-55 (he did not compete in 1953); three 1500-meter titles in the same years; and nine Big Ten championships, more than any swimmer in league annals. His high mark, of course, was the 1500-meter Olympic championship in 1952.

Buckeye teammate and fellow Hawaiian, YOSHI OYA-KAWA, was the world's greatest backstroker of his day.

His title bag: the NCAA 200-yard backstroke in 1952-53-54-55 (only man in the history of the nationals to take four straight championships); three NCAA 100-yard crowns in 1953-54-55; six Big Ten championships; and, like Konno, the Olympic crown in 1952 in the 100-meters.

Michigan's powerful BURWELL JONES, meanwhile, was certainly the most versatile swimmer the nation had yet seen. His specialty was the 150-yard individual medley: three 50-yard legs of backstroke, breaststroke and freestyle. For three years in a row (1952-53-54) the great Wolverine star took the NCAA crown. He also won five Big Ten titles, three in the medley and one each in the 220-freestyle and 200-breaststroke.

This agreement led to the Big Ten's decision on January 18, 1929, to break off relations with the AAU. AAU president, Avery Brundage, appointed a special committee to meet with the NCAA committee, and out of this meeting came an agreement in regard to certification of college athletes, which was the first ray of sunshine in a long, bitter battle. The final resolution adopted between the NCAA and the AAU reads as follows:

"Resolved, That it is the sense of the meeting that it is unnecessary and unwise for international intercollegiate competition that it should require any so-called sanction or permit from the Amateur Athletic Union of the United States, the Amateur Athletic Association of England, the International Amateur Athletic Federation or any international federation."

This was the first sign of any peaceful settlement. It was followed by a compromise which resulted in giving to the NCAA, for the first time, representation on the Sports Games committees equal in numbers to that of the AAU, six for each organization, and one appointed by the president of the American Olympic Committee. That was something Commissioner Griffith had battled for over many years. As a further concession, following World War Two it was mutually agreed by the AAU and the NCAA that the four officers of the American Olympic Committee would be divided, two from each group, and this led to the election of Asa Bushnell as secretary and myself as vice-president in 1945. At that time an alliance was agreed upon, the two most important paragraphs being:

"The Amateur Athletic Union recognizes the right of member colleges of the National Collegiate Athletic Association to govern themselves and to compete among themselves or with non-member colleges, under eligibility rules considered satisfactory to the National Collegiate Athletic Association.

was also named All-America in basketball in 1954, thus became the first Big Ten athlete to gain the honor in those two sports.

Indiana won a third straight tennis team title, led by its crack doubles duo of John Hironimus and Bob Martin, with Northwestern's Al Kuhn taking the singles crown. Michigan won the cross-country title for the first time in history, although the Wolverines had been a perennial track power for years. Indiana's Jim Lambert, however, romped home as the individual winner by almost a half minute. Only John Moule, among the Wolverine runners, finished in the first five. Team-wise, Michigan had five men in the first 20, to take the title.

Ohio State won the golf title with George Smith, Francis Cardi, Larry Harper and Fred Jones finishing among the top ten, but Purdue's Bob Benning won the individual crown.

Although only two team titles went to the Big Ten in NCAA wars, Conference athletes harvested a bumper crop of individual crowns. Mike Peppe's Ohio State swimmers regained the aquatic supremacy after allowing Yale to hold it for a year, and set an all-time NCAA record in the process when the Buckeyes took nine individual titles. With Michigan taking three others it meant that only three events were captured by the rest of the nation. Leading the Buckeye surge were the Hawaiian super-stars, Ford Konno and Yoshi Oyakawa, and the brilliant Dick Cleveland, all of whom scored impressive doubles. Cleveland took the 50-yard sprint in 22.3 and the 100 in 50.0. Oyakawa won the 100- and 200-yard backstroke in 57.0 and 2:09.8, and Konno merely broke two records when he swam the 440 in 4:28.6 and the 1500-meters in 18:14.4. Konno posted a 18:11 time in 1952, although it wasn't in an NCAA meet. A Buckeye trio of Oyakawa, Bob Van Heyde and Tom White-leather took the 300-yard medley relay in 2:49.3, and Morley Shapiro repeated as high board diving

champ. He was turned back in his defense of his low board crown, but it took another in the growing line of Buckeye springboard stars to do it—Fletcher Gilders.

For Michigan, the great Burwell Jones won his third straight individual medley in 1:30; Jack Wardrop set a new record of 2:05.0 for the 220-free-style, and a foursome of Tom Benner, Ron Gora, Don Hill and Jones picked off the 400-yard relay in 3:26.1.

In track, Illinois took three individual crowns when Willie Williams repeated as 100-yard dash champ in 9.5; Willard Thomson captured the 120-yard high hurdles in 14.2, and Joe Corley took the lows in 22.6. The Illini also had an individual winner in gymnastics as Dick Browning triumphed in tumbling, with Iowa's Jim Norman scoring on the trampoline.

Wisconsin won its 7th title in boxing for the second Big Ten team championship for the year, although the Badgers had only one individual champ in Bob Meath, who not only won the 156-pound crown but was chosen the tournament's outstanding boxer. Herb Odom, Michigan State 147-pounder, was the league's only other division ruler.

Minnesota came close to giving the Conference a third crown when it lost, 5-4 in overtime, to Rensselaer Polytech in the finals of the NCAA hockey tournament. However, two Gopher stars, John Mayasich and Dick Dougherty, along with Michigan's Bill McFarland, led the tournament scorers with nine goals each. Mayasich, incidentally, set an all-time NCAA tourney mark for goals in one game when he canned seven against Boston College in an early round victory.

Michigan State was another that almost got to the throne room as the Spartan baseball team went all the way to the fifth round of the NCAA baseball tourney before losing, 4-3, to Missouri, the eventual champion. The Spartans, however, had the satisfac-

Tug Wilson heading up the U.S. Olympic delegation in Tokyo in 1964.

JOHN MAYASICH starred for the Minnesota hockey team which went to the finals of the 1954 NCAA hockey tournament, losing to Rennselaer Poly for the title in overtime. Mayasich, however, had set an all-time tourney scoring mark with seven goals in one game, against Boston College.

1955

TOM YEWCIC, Michigan State's star quarterback, also distinguished himself on the baseball diamond where his superb catching and hitting was a big factor in the Spartans' drive to the 1954 league title. Although Michigan State was eliminated in the NCAA tourney, Yewcic was named All-America and won the tournament MVP trophy.

tion of seeing Tom Yewcic, their catcher, being named MVP for the tourney.

Three Conference stars also won individual crowns in wrestling as Iowa's Dick Govig won at 123 pounds; Michigan's Norvard Nalon repeated at 130 and Michigan State's Bob Hoke, took the 157-pound title.

The Conference Medal for scholarship went to headliners such as Paul Giel, Minnesota's All-America halfback; Paul Ebert, Ohio State's All-America basketball and baseball star; Bob Lenzini, Illinois' great linebacker, and Michigan State's NCAA wrestling champ, Bob Hoke.

"Unpack! Unpack!" It was the weirdest battle cry ever chanted by a football team. To Ohio State who was singing it out it was a keynote to fun, but to Michigan, listening with rabbit ears, it was a note of fury in a bizarre 1955 finale between these two teams—but more about it, later. Before the season reached that point there'd been a few surprises and a few moments that had gone as expected during the Big Ten football campaign.

Ohio State had lost a ton of talent. Gone were Brubaker and Dugger, the ends; Hilinski, Reichenbach, Thornton and other interior linemen. Gone, too, were Borton, Leggett, Watkins and Bobo, the latter an academic casualty.

There was still Hopalong Cassady . . . But would it be enough?

Tom Spears, Fred Kriss and Bill Michael moved up from reserve status at end and were joined by an amazing little 5-10, 165-pound sophomore, Leo Brown. Bill Whetstone and Dick Guy were new tackles, and Bill Jobko joined Jim Parker and Dave Weaver at guards, alongside Ken Vargo, the holdover center.

On paper it wasn't as strong a line as the previous year's, but it became one of the finest blocking lines the Scarlet ever turned out. The backfield ap-

Kenneth L. "Tug" Wilson & Douglas Roby (New President of United States Olympic Association).

Only seven times in this century has a Big Ten football team won two titles back-to-back, and when Ohio State did it in 1954-55 it was the brilliantly-versatile HOWARD (HOPALONG) CASSADY, a two-time All-America half-back, who was the spark in the Buckeyes' two straight undefeated Conference seasons. In 1955 Cassady not only was Conference MVP and All-America but was the league's fourth recipient of the Heisman Award, and also won the Walter Camp Trophy, the Maxwell Award, and the UPI Award as Player-of-the-Year. Among other heroics, *the 5-11, 175-pounder led the league rushers with 711 yards and an incredible 6.0 average per carry; was top scorer with 11 TD's; led in kick-off returns with a fraction under 30 yards per runback, and was a ferocious defensive star and alert pass-interceptor. It was his impetus which put Ohio State on the path to 17 straight Big Ten victories over three seasons, then the longest winning streak in league history. The above shot is typical of Hopalong's range-riding as he leaves Indiana tacklers sprawling en route to a touchdown.*

parently wasn't as strong as '54, either, but football games aren't played on paper. Frank Elwood, a reserve end, was a straight-A student with fine leadership qualities and Hayes installed him at quarterback (where he'd had some high school experience) and said: "Let's run." The Buckeyes had to run. Nobody ever said Ellwood couldn't hit a barn, passing, but don't narrow the target to the barn door—

and at the end of the season the Buckeyes were to go down in Conference history with the lowest passing average per game—a miserly 12.8 yards per contest!

If the cue was "run," the Buckeyes followed direction (and their interference!) and rambled for 309.7 yards per game, second highest in league history.

"In competition conducted by members of the National Collegiate Athletic Association where both college and open events are included the rules of the National Collegiate Athletic Association shall apply to college events and the rules of the Amateur Athletic Union shall apply to the open events."

Big Ten representatives played a tremendous role in working out this alliance, which was to give peace and harmony for several Oylmpiads. Avery Brundage, Commissioner Griffith, L. W. St. John, Frank McCormick and I —at that time at Northwestern—were those involved.

In the years that followed, there were many Big Ten coaches and managers and imporant Olympic chairmen who helped make Olympic history.

In track and field, Jim Kelly of the University of Minnesota coached the Olympic track team in the games at Melbourne. Larry Snyder from Ohio State was the

track coach at Rome. Frank Jones of Wisconsin was assistant track coach at Helsinki.

Matt Mann of the University of Michigan was the swimming coach at Helsinki, while Mike Peppe of Ohio State was in charge of the divers. At Tokyo, Dr. James Counsilman of Indiana, along with Richard J. Kimball, of Michigan, took charge of the swimming and diving, respectively.

In wrestling, Buel Patterson of Illinois and Cliff Keene of Michigan were the coaches at Helsinki and London, respectively.

John Walsh of Wisconsin was the boxing coach at Helsinki with Norm Sonju of Wisconsin serving as crew manager at Tokyo. Walter Brake of Wisconsin was a trainer for the team at Rome.

This fine array of Big Ten coaches did a magnificent job and helped bring many Olympic medals back to

Cassady led the loop rushers with 711 yards for a 6.0 average carry, and was top scorer with 11 touchdowns and 66 points. He also led in kick-off returns with a fraction under 30 yards per effort as the opposition desperately tried to keep the ball away from him. The all-purpose redhead, a brilliant defensive player as well, had excellent ball-toting help from Jerry Harkrader and Jim Roseboro, halfbacks who could have starred for any team that didn't have a Cassady; and two ram-jamming fullbacks in Don Vicic and Galen Cisco, a baseball star who later would pitch for the Mets.

Not only was this backfield a fearsome unit on the ground but it exercised the kind of precise ballhandling that resulted in an incredibly low average of only 0.8 fumbles per game, and anytime you're dropping that pumpkin less than once per contest you've got an edge.

In spite of all this Ohio was upended twice. In their second game, Stanford made a lone first-half touchdown stand up as the game's only score as the Indians succeeded in completely stopping Cassady for the only time in Hopalong's four years of unmatched range-riding. Two weeks later Duke tripped the Bucks 20-14 on a disputed touchdown pass in the last second of the first half. A Blue Devil receiver appeared to take the aerial while on his knees on the one-foot line and topple backward into the end zone, but the officials legalized it and it eventually meant the ball game.

The Bucks roared back for six straight decisive Conference victories and thereby put together two undefeated league seasons. It was the finale against Michigan, however, that provided a weird climax at Ann Arbor. With the Bucks ineligible to succeed themselves in the Rose Bowl, the invite was up for grabs between the Wolverines and Michigan State which had already wound up its league campaign with a 5-1 mark and had a no-count finish with Marquette. Michigan, if it could beat Ohio, could post a similar mark but would go to Pasadena because they had upset the Spartans in their head-to-head meeting.

With no Bowl tension to mar their performance, the Buckeyes took command early as the Wolverines made mistake after mistake and never succeeded in putting together two consecutive first downs.

By the third period, the Buckeyes, with a 9-0 lead and mindful of Michigan's westward hopes, were grinning across the line at the Wolves and

When Michigan's PROF. RALPH AIGLER retired in 1955 as the Wolverine's Big Ten Faculty Representative, his 38 consecutive years of service marked the longest career of its kind in Conference history. One of the league's truly great leaders, Aigler started in 1917.

the United States, with many Big Ten athletes among those earning the medals.

From the administrative side, you start with Avery Brundage, a track star at the University of Illinois, who competed in the 1912 Games at Stockholm. He served seven terms as president of the AAU, became president of the U. S. Olympic Association, as it was then known, and served for six consecutive Olympiads. In 1936, he became a member of the International Olympic Committee, and in 1952, was elected president of that powerful group. He is known and respected throughout the world for his years of service and dedication to the Olympic ideals of amateurism.

I had the honor to represent the United States as vice-president of the U. S. Olympic Committee for two Olympiads, and served as president for the games at Melbourne, Rome and Tokyo. When I retired in 1965, I was succeeded by Douglas F. Roby, a graduate of the University of Michigan who had been my vice-president for the three terms I was in office.

As President Emeritus, I was retained on the Board of Directors.

At this quadrennial meeting, Arthur Lentz, graduate of the University of Iowa who had served for many years as assistant to the executive director, Lyman Bingham, was elected to that important post himself.

I was pleased to see William Reed, Commissioner of the Big Ten, and Charles M. Neinas, a graduate of the University of Wisconsin, elected to the board of directors.

The Big Ten has played a vital part in Olympic history from every viewpoint. There still is much to be done if the athletic prestige of the United States is to be maintained in the years to come. I am confident that this will be done and that the uneasy truce that prevails now will be replaced by an all-out effort of the combined sports governing bodies of the U. S. working as a team.

singing out: "Unpack! Unpack! You guys aren't going anywhere!"

Somebody chanted "unpack" on virtually every play, and the Wolverines went to pieces. It got so bad Michigan completed a forward pass in their own end zone for an Ohio State safety as Terry Barr was dumped by Aurelius Thomas before he could advance. By then, the unnecessary roughness and unsportsmanlike conduct penalties were being flagged down in bunches, with three and four whistles tooting on every other play. The game was almost not completed at all. It was one of those days when everybody concerned was having a bit

EARL MORRALL

An opening game tie with Michigan slightly tarnished Michigan State's early hopes in 1955 but when the Spartans roared back for an undefeated season and Rose Bowl victory, Hugh (Duffy) Daugherty, in his second year as head coach, was a rousing choice for Coach-of-the-Year. He gave much credit for his team's success to EARL MORRALL, quarterback passing star; and Captain CARL NYSTROM, the complete, all-purpose guard. Both Morrall and Nystrom were All-America, along with two other Spartans stars, Gerry Planutis, fullback, and Norm Masters, tackle.

CARL NYSTROM

LEN DAWSON, *Purdue's outstanding quarterback in 1954-55-56, was the only man in the history of the Big Ten to lead the league in total offense for three straight years. He was the Conference leading passer all three seasons and could rush when he had to.*

of illicit fun, including spectators who had begun to line the field. The Bucks wound up with a 17-0 victory, scoring in every possible way except point-after-touchdown: two TD's, a field goal and a safety. Michigan crossed the fifty-yard line for the first and only time late in the fourth quarter—on a penalty—and saw the Rose Bowl assignment go to Michigan State.

Duffy Daugherty, who had succeeded his boss, Biggie Munn, the year before, had come up with another great Spartan eleven, despite a 14-7 loss to the Wolverines in their first Conference game of the season, when fumbles and miscues all but drove Duffy from the bench to the dressing room in frustration.

It was a fine Spartan team that took a second-place status into Pasadena. It featured an astute, pinpoint passing quarterback in Earl Morrall; a hard-hitting halfback in Clarence Peakes; and Gerry Planutis, a swift, knifing fullback in the 175-pound Spartan mold so common during the Fifties. Up front, Norm Masters, a terrific tackle, and Captain Carl Nystrom, a do-everything guard, held things together and headed the go-direction on attack. All but Peakes were All-America selections. They were joined by Ohio's Cassady, who was not only the Conference MVP but was also winner of the Heisman Trophy, the Walter Camp Award as Back-of-the-Year, and the United Press award as Player-of-the-Year. Jim Parker, Ohio's magnificent two-way guard; Ron Kramer, Michigan's tremendous end; and Cal Jones, of Iowa, repeating at guard, and winning the Outland Award as the country's best interior lineman, were other All-America selections.

345

Hugh (Duffy) Daugherty, in his second year at the Michigan State helm, had his fine season further rewarded by his selection as Coach-of-the-Year.

Two eye-popping individual performances went into the books for '55, as Len Dawson, Purdue's nifty quarterback, set a new Big Ten record with a scoring pass to Erich Barnes that covered 95 yards against Northwestern. Kevin Kleberg, Minnesota fullback, put on a tremendous punting display to set a new punting average of 44.2 yards on 25 kicks.

If anything, the 1955 basketball season proved that even a super-star can't do it by himself, as Indiana found out. There's a lot to be said for team balance and consistency of performance, as Iowa demonstrated in dethroning the Hoosiers. Big Don Schlundt, who wound up his career with more listings in the Conference record book than any man in history, was still the unparalleled shooting threat and, in fact, led the league in scoring for an unprecedented third straight year; but when your second man is only 25th in the league point-producing column, you're not likely to win a championship. The Hoosiers dropped to a 5-9 record and a deep second-division finish.

The Hawkeyes, meanwhile, although they didn't place a man in the top 10 point-makers, got steady production from all five starters. Led by center Bill Logan's 16.6, Iowa's starting five averaged virtually in double figures, with Logan followed by guard Bill Seaburg (14.6), forward Carl Cain (14.5), forward McKinley Davis (11.8), and guard Milt Scheuerman (9.5), with Seaburg and Scheuerman starring as play-makers. It wasn't so much that

BILL LOGAN, Iowa's slick center; and CARL CAIN, a speedy forward, led Iowa to the 1955 basketball championship.

BILL LOGAN   **CARL CAIN**

they were high scorers in Iowa's 11-3 finish for the flag, but the Hawkeyes led the league in field goal percentage with .413, the first time in Conference history a champion hit over .400. That kind of accuracy for an entire team, including subs, never hurt anybody.

Seven men dominated the All-Conference selections with Schlundt, of course, pre-eminent. Dick Garmaker, the Minnesota flash who was second in league scoring with 24.8; Fred Ehmann, Northwestern's hottest scorer, ever, with 24.5 per game, and Bill Logan, Iowa's slick center, were designated as forwards. Chuck Mencel, of Minnesota; Paul Judson of Illinois; and Ohio State's Robin Freeman were backcourt selections. Freeman, giving promise of things to come, hit for a fabulous 27.8 average for six Conference contests as injuries robbed him of a full year's play.

Mencel, the Gophers' superlative play-maker, was Conference MVP, and he and hot-shooting team-mate, Dick Garmaker, were All-America, along with Schlundt, Ehmann, and Freeman.

Iowa went to the NCAA tourney where the Hawkeyes disposed of Penn State and Marquette before losing to LaSalle, led by the great Tom Gola, 76-73, for the Eastern play-offs, with LaSalle subsequently bowing to San Francisco and Bill Russell, for the national title.

Michigan's trophy case was bulging before the year was over as Wolverines carried off four team titles: indoor and outdoor track (putting an end to Illinois' four-year domination), wrestling and tennis. Michigan runners and field men were led by Pete Gray, John Moule, Dave Owen and Mark Booth who posted wins both on the boards and outdoors. In the winter carnival Gray took the 880 in 1:54.7; Moule won the mile in 4.21.3; Owen captured the shot-put with 53-¼; Booth tied Jim Boyd of Indiana in the high jump at 6-5 and ⅞; Ron Wallingford won the two-mile in 9:26.4 and Jim Love took the 70-yard low hurdles in 8.0. Meanwhile, two Michigan State stars were brilliant double winners, with Ed Brabham winning the 60-yard dash in 06.2 and the broad jump with 23-8; and Kevan Gosper streaking the 440 in 48.2 and setting a new Conference mark of 1:11.3 for 1000-yards.

Outdoors, Gray came back for another half-mile win in 1:51.4; Moule again took the mile, in 4:14.8; Owen won the shot with 54-4 and ¾; Booth took the high jump with 6-6; Bob Apoleman picked off the pole vault with 13-8 and ¾; Clarence Stielstra won the broad jump with 23-5 and ¾; and a Wolverine foursome of Laird Sloan, Gray, Dick Flodin and Grant Scruggs ripped off the mile relay in 3:14.4. Northwestern's Jim Golliday, who that year was to set a new world record of 9.3 for the hundred, scored a sprint double with a 9.5 century and a 21.3 effort in the 220; and Illinois' great Willard Thomson posted a hurdles double with a

CHUCK MENCEL   DICK GARMAKER   FRANK EHMANN

CHUCK MENCEL, Conference MVP, and Minnesota teammate DICK GARMAKER, were All-America back- *court men in 1955; along with Northwestern's center and all-time hottest scorer, FRANK EHMANN.*

Northwestern's Big Ten sprint champ, JIM GOLLI-DAY, added to his star-lustre in 1955 when he set a new world record of 9.3 for the 100-yard dash, and also took the century in the NCAA meet.

record-equalling 14.0 in the 120-yard highs and captured the 220 lows in 23.0.

The Wolverines also pretty well dominated the wrestling tournament as Cliff Keen's grapplers took four individual titles: Max Pearson, 130 pounds; Andy Kaul, 137; Don Haney, 147, and Mike Rodriguez at 157. The Michigan tennis triumph was led by Barry MacKay, a sophomore, who was destined to become one of the all-time greats in Big Ten net play, as well as a future national and international star. MacKay and Dick Potter took the doubles crown, but the singles title went to Warren Mueller, of Wisconsin, who thereby became the Badgers' first and only net champion in Conference history. Wisconsin also chalked up a big first in fencing as Badger swordsmen won the Conference crown for the first time, dethroning perennial champ, Illinois, 40 bouts to 34. Jack Heiden, in foils, was the Badgers' only individual champ, but valuable victories were also posted by Eric Kindwall in epee; Charley Kortier in sabre, and Bruce Bachmann in foil.

Ohio State came through for an astonishing seventh straight swimming title, breaking their own record set the year before when the streak hit six. Again, it was the scintillating Hawaiians who led the way. Ford Konno set a new mark of 4:28.4 in the 440, and won the 1500-meters in 18:21.8. Yoshi Oyakawa posted a new mark of 56.5 for the 100-yard backstroke and set a new Conference and national record for the 200-yard event, with 2:06.1.

347

WARREN MUELLER was Wisconsin's only Big Ten tennis singles champion. He won the crown in 1955.

There is no doubt that the two most successful swimming coaches in the history of the Big Ten—if not the nation—were Michigan's MATT MANN and Ohio State's MIKE PEPPE. In any pantheon of aquatic greats they must be paired as equals, not only because of their accomplishments but because of their impact on collegiate swimming during virtually the same era.

Mann's family had emigrated to America from Leeds, England, where as a boy he'd been a professional club swimmer. In the U.S. he coached club teams and various schools before coming to Michigan in 1926. During his 29 years at Ann Arbor (he retired after the 1954 season), his Wolverines won 96 Big Ten individual titles, 68 national collegiate crowns, and 23 of his boys were Olympians. His teams won 16 Conference championships (more than any coach in league history) and six NCAA crowns. (Team titles in NCAA competition were not awarded until 1937; prior to that there were only individual titles to be won in the nationals.)

Al Wiggins gave the Buckeyes another record-breaking performance in taking the individual medley in 1:24.3; and Gerry Harrison, the new Buckeye ace on the springboards, took the high dive but made possibly even bigger news when he lost the low board crown to Michigan's Jim Walters, for the first Buckeye diving setback over a 17-year, 34-event skein.

Walters had some teammates who grabbed off headlines of their own—all with record-breaking performances. Jack Wardrop set a new world mark of 2:03.4 in the 220-freestyle nipping Konno for a rare defeat; Burwell Jones splashed to a brilliant

Peppe was a young physical education instructor at Ohio State when he was asked in 1930 to form the first varsity swimming team for the Buckeyes—the last Conference school to launch swimming on a varsity basis. The Bucks, until Peppe's retirement in 1963, won 64 individual Conference crowns; a record crop of 104 national collegiate titles; and sent a record number of 28 stars to the Olympics where they won eight Gold Medals. His teams took 12 Big Ten titles and a record-high 11 NCAA crowns. At one stretch his Buckeyes won a record-setting eight straight (1949-56) league championships. Of more monumental significance was Peppe's success with his divers. From the time Peppe won his first national diving crown in 1937 until his retirement there were 50 national collegiate diving titles up for grabs. Peppe-trained divers won 42 of them against the rest of the nation!

Between them, Mann and Peppe so completely dominated the national collegiate swimming picture that the figures are startling. To begin with, hundreds of NCAA-affiliated schools have competed for the 528 titles won through the 1966 season. Michigan and Ohio State between them have won 210 of them. During the Mann-Peppe years there were 327 titles available, and the Mann-Peppe performers won 183 of them—more than half!

Both Mann and Peppe were Olympic coaches, Mann as swimming coach in 1952 and Peppe as diving coach in 1948 and 1952.

MATT MANN | **DICK CLEVELAND** | **MIKE PEPPE**

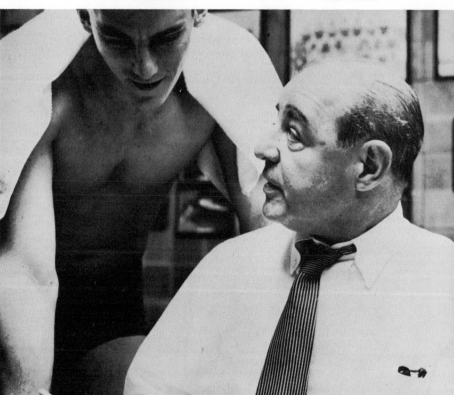

Michigan third-sacker, DON EADDY, slick fielder and .353 hitter, was named to the All-America baseball team in 1955.

double with records of 2:27.3 and 2:15.1 for the 200-yard breaststroke and 200-yard butterfly, respectively; and a Wolverine trio of Wardrop, John Delaney, and Ron Gora flashed home in 2:49.3 for the medley relay.

The Buckeyes also picked off the Conference baseball flag on a combination of timely hitting and tight pitching. First-sacker Don Kelley led the Bucks in batting, with .422, with All-Conference second baseman Chuck Ellis not far behind at .395. Howard (Hopalong) Cassady, who had scorched many a football field, was a .324-hitting outfielder. All-Conference Hal Northrup, with 4-1; Dick Finn, with 3-0, and Bill Rutenschroer, 2-0, were the Buckeye pitching mainstays. George Smith, of Indiana led league hitters with a rousing .485, and Michigan provided the league's lone All-America in Don Eaddy, a slick-fielding third baseman who hit .353.

Illinois took its sixth straight gymnastics championship, winning three individual titles: Tom Gardner on parallel bars; Jeff Austin in free exercise, and Austin tying with Iowa's Walt Patterson in tumbling. Indiana's Dick Albershardt was trampoline champ and the all-around crown went to Michigan State's magnificent Carlton Rintz, undoubtedly the finest gymnast in Spartan history. Another Spartan all-time great, Henry Kennedy, led Michigan State to another cross-country title as he took the individual crown, and Bob Rubendall, of Wisconsin, won the individual golf championship, although the team title went to Purdue.

In NCAA competition there was no letup in the virtual monopoly held by Conference swimmers as

Ohio State won another—it's 9th—team title. Ford Konno added two more national crowns in the 440 freestyle (4:31.1) and the 1500-meters (18:16.1). Yoshi Oyakawa took his third straight 100-yard backstroke, in 58.0, and made history when he became the only man in the annals of NCAA swimming to win four straight titles in one event when he captured the 200-yard backstroke in 2:07.7. (An earlier Buckeye, Bill Smith, had won four championships in the 220-freestyle but World War II had prevented him from doing it in consecutive years.) Al Wiggins set a new mark of 1:26.5 in winning the individual medley for the Bucks; Gerry Harrison and Fletcher Gilders took the high and low dives, respectively; and a Buckeye team of Oyakawa, Higgins and Ed Kawachika added the medley relay in a record-shattering 2:42.2. Still another record went to a Conference star as Michigan's brilliant Jack Wardrop repeated as 200 freestyle champ in 2:04.2.

Michigan won the NCAA team hockey crown, defeating Colorado College, 5-3, and the Wolverines' Bill McFarland tied Harvard's Bill Cleary for tourney scoring honors with five goals each. Illinois won the national gymnastics championship without taking an individual title but the Illini piled up points in most of the events for an 82-69

CARLTON RINTZ, of Michigan State, a multiple champ in Big Ten gymnastics, proved in 1955 that he was one of the all-time Conference greats when he became only the second man in league history to win three NCAA crowns in one year: side horse, horizontal bar and parallel bar.

349

JOE CAMPBELL, another in a string of fine Purdue golfers, took the NCAA individual crown in 1955 and in 1956-57 was Conference king.

victory over second-place Penn State. Carlton Rintz, of Michigan State, and Indiana's Dick Albershardt kept alive the Big Ten's proud boast of being the only Conference never to be shut out of an individual crown. Rintz merely took three of them: side horse, parallel bars and horizontal bar; and Albershardt won on the trampoline.

Michigan State gave the Conference a fourth NCAA crown by taking the team boxing title, with hard-punching Herb Odom repeating as 147-pound titlist. In wrestling, Terry McCann, of Iowa, captured 115-pound honors; Herman Velasco, of Illinois, was an NCAA fencing winner, in epee; and Purdue's Joe Campbell became the second Boilermaker to take the individual golf crown.

1956

In a state like Iowa, thirty-four years between blue ribbons—whether it's on the farm or in football—is a mighty long time, neighbor! So, in 1956 the Hawkeyes down at the University finally beat the biggest drought since the Dust Bowl when they harvested their first Big Ten title since the glory days of the Devines, the Lockes, and the Slaters of 1921-22. They did it with a 5-1 Conference mark and 9-1 overall, including a 48-0 rout of Notre Dame and a 39-14 hoisting of Oregon State in the Rose Bowl. It was the beginning of a new era of grid greatness for the Gold and Black and from then on Iowa would be a considerable factor in every Conference campaign.

The prime movers in this rousing resurgence started first of all with Forest Evashevski, the brilliant, offensive-minded ex-Michigan star who arrived in 1952 and brought new verve and purpose to the Hawkeye scene. The first thing Evy did was to install the wing-T and balanced line from which he could get real faking preceding the actual exchange of the ball, and with the faker plugging the hole left by a pulling lineman. He then fielded a team that was not so deep and strong as it was fiercely determined to put out 105 percent of what it had in talent—and don't anybody sell that talent short.

There was a brace of brilliant ends in Jim Gibbons and Frank Gilliam; three fine tackles in Alex Karras (a great one), Dick Klein and Frank Rigney; three booming guards in Frank Bloomquist, Bob Commings, and Gary Grouwinkel; and a topnotch center in Don Suchy. The Hawks had the ideal quarterback to make the wing-T go. Kenny Ploen, a fine passer, was a master at keeping or pitching out, and in operating the bootleg. The halfbacks weren't big, but Mike Hagler, Fred Harris, Bill Happel and Don Dovrino were fast and heady, and John Nocera was a strong fullback and a defensive standout.

The first indication that things were looking up came in the opener against Indiana when the Hawks put on crisp scoring drives of 82 and 69 yards in the first quarter, and the critics who had relegated Iowa to a deep, second division berth suddenly had to revise their thinking. Their thinking jelled the following week when, after trailing a powerful Oregon State team 13-0 in the last quarter the Hawks picked themselves up for a smashing 14-13 comeback win on a Nocera to Gilliam 10-yard pass and a Randy Duncan to Gibbons aerial good for 33. (Duncan, a sophomore, was filling in for the injured Ploen, and more of him would be heard in future years.) Two perfect PAT's by Bob Prescott spelled the point difference against the Westerners.

Victories over Wisconsin, Hawaii and Purdue followed, and suddenly the Hawkeyes were a contender—and meeting Michigan in a game that could be crucial to their hopes. It was Homecoming at Iowa, and Forest Evashevski had never known defeat in a Homecoming game, either as player or coach. At half-time, two Hawkeye touchdowns gave them a 14-3 lead over the Wolverines who'd started the scoring with a field goal by Ron Kramer, and it looked as though Evy's victory pattern was still in style. Michigan got a third quarter TD but with time running out in the last quarter the Hawks appeared home free. It wasn't to be. The Wolves, led by fullback John Herrnstein who six times in a row smashed for vital first downs with only inches to spare, got a final touchdown with only 66 seconds to play.

Yet, as far as the title was concerned, Iowa was not yet out of it. Minnesota subsequently walloped Michigan by two touchdowns and suddenly the Gophers were favored for the flag and the Rose

Bowl—if they could get by the Hawks over whom they were heavily favored.

On the fourth play of the game, the Gophers fumbled. The Hawks recovered on the Minnesota 38 and launched a drive to the one-yard line, with a Ploen to Gibbons pass keying the assault. From the one, Fred Harris cracked over and that was it. There was no more scoring for the next 55 minutes and the Hawks now had only one obstacle left: a dangerous Ohio State team that was riding a Big Ten record of 17 straight Conference victories.

Before the game Evashevski told his squad: "You have only 60 minutes to play football, and the rest of your life to remember it!"

The Hawks played it and had something to remember. After a scoreless first half they went 63 yards in 10 plays in the third period, climaxed by a 17-yard touchdown toss from Ploen to Gilliam for the game's only score. It ended the Bucks' record string of victories and put the Hawkeyes in the Rose Bowl. There, in an historic meeting which for the first time found regular season rivals meeting again at season's end in Pasadena, Iowa rolled up 408 yards rushing and passing to swamp Oregon State 35-19. In between Ohio and the Bowl, however, the Hawks had ended their regular season by handing Notre Dame a stunning 48-8 defeat to become the first Iowa team to beat the Irish in 16 years and the first Hawkeye team in 51 years to win more than eight games. Forest Evashevski later admitted that the one game that got away—the upset by Michigan—was the biggest disappointment of his football career, as he recalled that he and his boys were only 66 seconds away from a perfect season.

There was glory enough for Evy and his Hawkeyes, however. Evy, himself, was high on the Coach-of-the-Year lists; big aggressive Alex Karras was an All-America tackle; Kenny Ploen was Conference MVP, and the Hawkeyes were the third-ranked team, nationally. Joining Karras on the All-America squads were Minnesota's Bob Hobert, another great

JIM PARKER, Ohio State guard, made All-America for the second straight year in 1956. He also won the Outland Trophy as the best interior lineman of the season.

KENNY PLOEN, a brilliant passer and master of the keeper play, earned All-America quarterback honors and the Conference MVP trophy as he and teammate FRANK GILLIAM, a swift, adept pass receiving end, led Iowa to the Big Ten title in 1956.

Big RON KRAMER, Michigan's tremendous end, earned All-America honors for the second straight year in 1956. (A great basketball center, he also pulled off the rare trick of being his team's MVP cager for three straight years, a feat accomplished only three times in Big Ten history.) Also an All-America grid choice in 1956 was Minnesota's BOB HOBERT, another in a long line of mighty Gopher tackles.

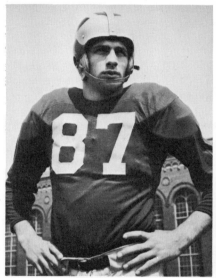

tackle; Jim Parker, Ohio State's thundering guard, who won the Outland Award as the nation's best interior lineman; and Ron Kramer, Michigan's stupendous end who, like Parker, was repeating from '55.

Frank O'Connor, who had replaced Rollie Williams as Iowa basketball coach in 1952, brought the Hawkeyes to their pinnacle of cage success in 1956 by completing the first back-to-back title surge in Iowa history. In making it two in a row, the Hawkeyes presented the best club Iowa had ever fielded as Carl Cain and Bill Logan at forward and center had remarkable senior seasons, with deft backing up at guard from Bill Seaburg and Milt (Sharm) Scheuerman.

The Hawkeyes were 13-1 in Conference play and 20-6 overall with a 65-64 defeat by Michigan in the league opener coming as the lone loss within the lodge. After that the Hawks ran off a brilliant string of 13 straight league victories to take the title, and went all the way to the finals of the NCAA tournament before falling before two-time winner San Francisco. En route to their defeat, the Hawks eliminated Morehead State, Kentucky and Temple, but Bill Russell and his mates were a bit too much.

On an individual basis, the Big Ten produced an unprecedented display of scoring pyrotechnics. Ten men averaged 20 or more points a game—a feat never again matched by any major college conference in the country.

Robin Freeman, the whirling dervish jump-shooter from Ohio State, completely obliterated all previous standards with his 32.5 average on 455 points in 14 games. Following him came Julius McCoy, the hottest shooter in Michigan State annals, with 27.3; George Bon Salle, of Illinois, with 22.9; Joe Sexson, of Purdue, with 21.8; Wally Choice, of Indiana, with 21.5; Dick Miller, Wisconsin with 20.7; Jed Dommeyer, Minnesota, with 20.7; Ron Kramer, the Michigan grid star, with 20.4; and Dick Mast, of Northwestern, with 20.2.

Brightest star of the 1956 Conference basketball season was ROBIN FREEMAN, Ohio State's fantastic guard. As league MVP he set an all-time loop scoring mark of 32.5 per game and was the Big Ten's lone All-America, repeating his selection of the previous year. JULIUS McCOY, Michigan State's amazing leaper and shotmaker at forward, was another league luminary. His 27.3 per game was the best average in Spartan history, and his 918 points for three years (1954-55-56) was a Michigan State career record.

Carl Cain, of Iowa, at forward; Julius McCoy, Michigan State forward; Paul Judson, Illinois guard; and Robin Freeman, Ohio State guard, (who was also Conference MVP) were unanimous All-Big Ten selections. Bill Logan, the Iowa star, and center George Bon Salle, of Illinois, alternated for the center post on most of the all-star teams picked, and Bill Ridley, of Illinois, received first team designation at guard. The league's national limelighter: Robin Freeman, of Ohio State, repeated as All-America.

It was a heady eight championships in a row for Mike Peppe's Ohio swimmers as they turned back Michigan—who, thusly, had its eighth straight second place finish—which was also something of a record.

Leading the Buckeyes to the team title were Don Harper, the newest star in Ohio's diving line, who scored a double on the high and low boards; powerful Al Wiggins with a new league record of 2:08.3 for the 200-yard individual medley; and Van Hoffman, with a new mark of 2:25.4 for the 200-yard breaststroke. Wiggins, a nautical ironman, also played a major role in the Buckeyes' two victorious relays. He swam the backstroke leg with Canfield and Kawachika in a 2:46.2 medley and with Kawachika, Kimmel and Ledger in a 3:26.9 400-yard freestyle win.

The brightest star of the meet, however, was Indiana's Bill Woolsey who scored a smashing triple with 19:06.8 for 1500-meters; 2:05.9 for the 220-yard freestyle, and 4:40.1 for the 440 freestyle. Double winners were Lincoln Hurring, of Iowa, who took the 100-yard backstroke in 59.1 and the 200-yard event in 2:08.4; and Northwestern's Al Kuhn, who captured the 50- and 100-yard sprints in 22.6 and 50.4.

If Michigan had to settle for second place in the water there were honors galore in other arenas for the Wolverines, who took team titles in indoor track, wrestling and tennis. On the indoor boards the Wolverines were led by Pete Gray's 1000-yard victory in 2:14.4; Ron Wallingford's victory in the two-mile in 9:19.3; Eeles Landstrom's winning pole vault effort of 14-2; Dave Owen's shot-put victory with 54 feet 7 and 1/8; and a tie for first in the high jump by Mark Booth, at 6-6 and 3/8. Greg Bell, of Indiana, set a new broad jump mark of 24-11 and 5/8 and impressive doubles were scored by Michigan State's Ed Brabham in the 60-yard dash and 300-yard run with 6.3 and 31.3; and by Iowa's Ted Wheeler who took the 880 in 1:55.1 and the mile in 4:12.5.

Outdoors, Michigan had repeat triumphs by Landstrom with 14-6 in the pole vault; by Owen, with 53-6¼ in the shot-put; and two shares of a three-way tie in the high jump by Booth and Brendon O'Reilly, at 6-5 and 5/8. Brabham picked up another brilliant sprint double with 9.7 for the 100 and a record-equalling 21.2 for a 220 around a turn. Indiana's Don Ward tied the mark of 47.7 for a 440

Brightest swim star of the 1956 season was Indiana's Hawaiian freestyler, BILL WOOLSEY, Big Ten triple champ at 220- and 440-yards, and 1500-meters; and NCAA champ at 220 and 440. LINCOLN HURRING, Iowa's great backstroker, one of the nation's best ever, scored brilliant doubles in both the Big Ten and NCAA championships and 100- and 200-yards. AL WIGGINS, of Ohio State, one of the most versatile swimmers of his day, was Big Ten and National Collegiate 200-yard individual medley champ (he had won at 150 the year before) and the following season he took Conference titles in the backstroke and butterfly events. Woolsey also repeated his NCAA double in 1957.

around two turns; and Iowa's Wheeler made it another double with a 1:51.7 time in the 880 and a 4:12.7 mile.

In wrestling Mike Rodriguez at 157 pounds and Jack Marchello at 177 won individual crowns in

leading the Wolverines to the team title as the Maize and Blue also put several men into the semi-finals and finals.

The brilliant Barry MacKay swept to the top in tennis singles and, with Dick Potter, retained the doubles honors they'd won the year before, to pace the Michigan bid for the team championship.

There was no disputing the class displayed by Minnesota in winning the Conference baseball title

Minnesota's Big Ten and National Collegiate baseball champions of 1956, front row, from left: Gene Martin, Ron Craven, Jerry Kindall, Woody Erickson, Dean Maas, Doug Gillen, Bob Anderson, Jack McCartan, Jim McNeely, John Clark, manager. Back row, from left: Rod Oistad, Ken Anderson, Shorty Cochran, Bill Horning, Jerry Thomas, Bruce Erickson, Dave Lindblom, Rod Magnuson, John Hoppe, Joe Vancisin, assistant coach; Dick Siebert, head coach; Lloyd Stein, trainer.

JERRY THOMAS

JERRY KINDALL

Leading Minnesota to the Big Ten and national collegiate baseball championships in 1956 were shortstop JERRY KINDALL, and pitcher JERRY THOMAS. Kindall, the league's leading batter (.440), later went on to major league acclaim. Both he and Thomas, Conference mound leader, were All-America.

as the Gophers not only dominated the loop with an 11-2 record but went on to take the national title in the NCAA tourney. Leading the Gophers were Jerry Kindall, the .440 batting championship shortstop who just a few years later would be playing for the Cleveland Indians; and Jerry Thomas, whose 5-0 pitching mark shared the league leadership with Ohio State's Galen Cisco, subsequently a New York Mets hurler.

Proving their all-around excellence, the Gophers won team batting honors with a gaudy .320, as well as fielding laurels with .976. Behind Kindall's .440 were third sacker John McCartan's .436; first baseman Doug Gillen's .345; and outfielded Dave Lindblom's .333. Both Kindall and Thomas were All-America, and McCartan joined them on the Big Ten honor squad. It was a vintage year, all around, for Conference baseball stars; others who became Big Leaguers besides Kindall and Cisco were Frank Howard, Ohio State's towering outfielder-first baseman who went on to star with the Dodgers and Senators; Ron Perranoski, Michigan State hurler who became a Dodger relief star, and Michigan third sacker Steve Boros who later made it with the Tigers.

Illinois added the gymnastics and fencing crowns to its trophy case, somewhat habit-forming in both sports as the Illini gymnasts made it six in a row and the swordsmen six out of seven. Individual titles went to Gavin Blair on side horse (in an unusual tie with Iowa's Sam Bailie); Dan Lirot in tumbling; and all-around to Don Tonry. In fencing, the Illini leaders were Herm Velasco, in foil; and Larry Kauffman, in epee, as Ohio State's Don Little took the sabre championship.

Joe Campbell, a smooth sophomore from Purdue,

won the individual golf crown as he led the Boilermakers to the team title, inaugurating the league's longest streak of individual winners from one school. It would ultimately reach five straight.

In cross-country, Michigan State's machine-like Henry Kennedy repeated as individual titlist and led the Spartans in defense of their team crown, their fifth in the last six years.

It was ho-hum-nothing's-new as Ohio State successfully defended its NCAA swim title, with three individual crowns and balanced point-strength throughout. Al Wiggins took the individual medley in 2:07.5; and Don Harper and Frank Fraunfelter, the latest royalty among Mike Peppe's diving dynasty, won the high and low board crowns respectively. Meanwhile, other Conference schools were taking home a pretty good share of the other individual titles. Northwestern's Al Kuhn captured the 100-freestyle in 49.3; Bill Woolsey, the finest swimmer yet to show up at Indiana (soon, swim

DAN LIROT

Illinois' Big Ten champs successfully defended their NCAA gymnastics team crown in 1956, led by DON TONRY, all-around king, and DAN LIROT, tumbling champ.

DON TONRY

CHARLEY JONES

HENRY KENNEDY

CRAWFORD KENNEDY

The Big Ten's most famous brother act in cross-country were Michigan State's HENRY KENNEDY, and younger brother, CRAWFORD. Henry, two-time individual champ (1955-56) led the Spartans to their fifth team crown in six years in 1956 (and also won the 3000-meters in the NCAA track meet in June). CHARLEY

JONES, Iowa's great distance star, turned the tables on Henry in the 1956 NCAA cross-country meet, however, taking the individual title; the first Big Ten star to do so since 1941. Crawford (Forddy) Kennedy won the NCAA individual crown in 1958 and the Conference championship in 1959.

stars would fall all over Hoosierland), scored a sparkling double with 2:04.7 and 4:31.1 for the 220 and 440 freestyle; and Iowa's sensational Lincoln Hurring pulled off a similar feat in the 100- and 200-yard backstroke, with 58.1 and 2:07.5.

TERRY McCANN, Iowa's Big Ten 115-pound wrestling champ, made it two national titles in a row in 1956 when he repeated as NCAA king.

Although it was an Olympic year, the Conference failed to make a big splash in the NCAA track meet, with only three individual titles going to Big Ten entries and Michigan State took two of them. Henry Kennedy, the cross-country star, won the 3000-meter steeplechase in 9:16.5; and the Spartans' Selwyn Jones took the 10,000-meters in 31:15.3. Indiana's Greg Bell captured the broad jump crown with 25-9¼.

The Conference fared better in cross-country that year, however, as Iowa's Charley Jones won the individual title (the first Big Tenner to do it since Indiana's Fred Wilt, in 1941) and Michigan State took the team crown.

Illinois repeated as national gymnastics king, with the Illini led by Don Tonry, who took the all-around crown, and Dan Lirot who won the tumbling title. Don Harper, of Ohio State, was tops on the trampoline, and keep your eye on him because he's going to show up two years later with one of the unique performances in intercollegiate athletics.

The Illini also picked off the NCCA fencing title under new coach Max Garret , and did it without taking a single individual crown. All around strength in the foil, epee and sabre divisions, however, brought the Orange and Blue a close 90 to 88 bout victory over second place Columbia.

In wrestling, Iowa's aggressive little Terry McCann repeated as NCAA 115-pound champion; Jim

355

College hockey's most successful championship coach was Michigan's VIC HEYLIGER whose Wolverines gave him an all-time high of five NCAA titles in 1951-52-53-55-56.

Sinadinos, of Michigan State, triumphed at 137; Larry Ten Pas, of Illinois, took the 157-pound honors, and Iowa's Ken Leuer won at 191.

Vic Heyliger's Michigan hockey team won a sixth national championship for the youthful Wolverine coach, more than any other team in collegiate hockey, and the Wolves' Neil McDonald led the tourney scorers with five goals.

In boxing, Wisconsin returned to the throne room after evicting Michigan State the defending champions. It was Coach John Walsh's last championship team and his eight team titles were a record high

CHOKEN MAEKAWA, Michigan State's clever little 112-pound Hawaiian, won the Outstanding Boxer Award in the 1956 NCAA tourney.

for one coach and one school. His belters provided Walsh with a fitting valedictory as five of them captured individual crowns, tying the all-time high set by the 1943 Badger team. Dean Plemmons won at 112 pounds; Dick Bartman at 139; Vince Ferguson at 156; Orville Pitts at 178; and Truman Sturdevant took heavyweight honors. The tourney's Outstanding Boxer Award, however, went to Michigan State's marvelous little Hawaiian scrapper, 112-pound Choken Maekawa.

Once again, particularly outstanding athletes proved they possessed brains as well as brawn as the Conference Medal went to, among others, Carl Nystrom, Michigan State's All-America gridder: Al Kuhn, Northwestern's national swim champ; Joe Sexson, Purdue's prolific basketball scorer; and Bob Konovsky, Wisconsin's Big Ten heavyweight wrestling champ.

The 1956 Olympic delegation from the Big Ten broke the record of 1952, with 39 athletes competing for Uncle Sam. (And that doesn't include two young ladies from Michigan State.) To nobody's surprise they harvested their significant share of medals and points.

Indiana's Greg Bell and Milt Campbell took Gold Medals in the broad jump and decathlon respectively, with Campbell's 7939 points setting a new Olympic mark. Ohio State's blazing Glenn Davis posted a new Olympic record of 50.1 in winning the 400-meter hurdles. Illinois' Bob Richards erased his own pole vault figure set four years previously at Helsinki with a new listing of 14-11½, and Minnesota's Fortune Gordien took home a Silver Medal in the discus.

Other Big Ten track and field competitors were Iowa's Charley Jones and Ted Wheeler; and Michigan State's Adolph Weinacker. There were others who competed for their native lands, including the Spartans' David Lean and Kevin Gosper for Australia; and Michigan's Eeles Landstrom and Laird Sloan for Finland and Canada.

In swimming, an Ohio State trio of Bob Clotworthy, Don Harper and Glen Whitten took first, second and fourth against the world in the 3-meter dive. Indiana's Frank McKinney won the Bronze Medal in the 100-meter backstroke; and three Big Ten stars—Ohio State's Ford Konno, Indiana's Bill Woolsey and Michigan's Dick Hanley—swam legs on the second-place 800-meter freestyle relay.

Other Conference swimmers included Indiana's Dick Tanabe, Ohio's Yoshi Oyakawa and Al Wiggins, and divers Don Harper and Nick Silverio, the latter performing for Cuba.

Minnesota provided five hockey players—Jack Petroske, Gene Campbell, Dick Dougherty, Dick Meredith and John Mayasich, and Michigan State added another ice star, Weldon Olson. The Spartans also sent wrestler Dale Thomas; fencer Allan Kwartler; and two feminine stars, Judy Goodrich, a fencer, and Ernestine Russell, who represented Canada in gymnastics. Spartan boxers were Pearce Lane and

Two of the Big Ten's brightest stars kept their lustre in the 1956 Olympics in Melbourne, Australia in 1956. MILT CAMPBELL, Indiana's 215-pound all-around ace, is shown in the 1500-meter event on his way to a smashing victory in the decathlon and a new Olympic mark of 7937 points. Ohio State's GLENN DAVIS, later a world record-holder at 440-yards, is shown hitting the tape in a record 50.1 for his Gold Medal in the 400-meter hurdles. (He repeated at the 1960 Olympics in Rome with a new Olympic mark of 49.3.)

BOB CLOTWORTHY, left, and DON HARPER, both of Ohio State, took the Gold an Silver Medals in the springboard dive in the 1956 Olympics.

Choken Maekawa. Rounding out the U.S. contingent were Indiana's Verle Wright, on the rifle team; Iowa's brilliant duo of Chuck Darling and Carl Cain on the victorious U.S. basketball team; Illinois' Abe Grossfeld in gymnastics; and Ohio State's weight-lifter, Jim George.

On the administrative front in 1956, Ohio State found itself placed on probation for irregularities in its job program and financial assistance rendered by Coach Woody Hayes to football players and the Buckeyes were declared ineligible for Rose Bowl participation for one year.

1957

Woody Hayes, who had made his ground game synonymous with winning football in 1954-55 for straight titles, had misfired slightly in 1956, but not before the Scarlet had racked up 17 straight Conference wins for a modern record. Now, in 1957, there were portents that the Buckeyes could be writing a third chapter in the "Hayes Era" of football—if they could get past Iowa, favored to repeat as champion.

After a stunning 18-14 setback by Texas Christian in the opener, however, there was doubt along High Street and uncertainty around the Conference. Maybe the Buckeyes didn't have much, after all, despite a roster which seemed to proclaim otherwise.

There was a quartet of exceptional ends led by Co-Captain Leo Brown, the remarkable 168-pounder; Jim Houston, a big promising sophomore; and Russ Bowermaster and Chuck Zawacki, talented veterans. Dick Schaffrath, later to be an all-pro selection with the Cleveland Browns; Al Crawford, and another great sophomore, Jim Marshall (who later would run the wrong way for the Minnesota Vikings) were a trio of terrific tackles. Aurelius Thomas, one of the finest in Ohio history; Bill Jobko, and Ernie Spychalskie gave away nothing at guard, and little Danny Fronk, at 185, and Dan James at 250, provided double strength at center.

The backfield was all-a'glitter. Quarterback Frank Kremblas, straight "A" in the classroom, was a fine passer and technician; Don Clark, a streaking halfback; Dick LeBeau, the other half, was a tough man on the reverse and a great defensive player; and at fullback there was Co-Captain Galen Cisco and a rambunctious sophomore named Bob White who was destined to fill in when Cisco got hurt and put on a performance that would become almost legendary. There was other talent, too, including Don Sutherin and Joe Cannavino who logged a lot of time and yardage at halfback.

Once they had shaken off their opening day defeat, the Buckeyes geared up their potential and roared over nine straight opponents, including a 10-7 triumph over Oregon in the Rose Bowl. It was not that easy, however, and there was high drama hanging over Ohio Stadium with more than 82,000 looking on when the Scarlet met Iowa. The Hawkeyes were a team that had been making history, headlines and hot debate all season. Rolling along undefeated at mid-year they came up to a big one in Michigan, who had won 11-straight from the Hawks. It was a real barn-burner, with Iowa coming back with two second half touchdowns to tie the score at 21-21. With three minutes to go and Iowa in possession, Evashevski ordered his crew to stay on the ground. Score, if at all possible, but stay out of the air. Every Big Ten team except Ohio State had lost at least once and if Iowa could get out of the Michigan game with at least a tie they could retain their title by knocking off the Buckeyes in their Conference finale. So, no passing, then, against the Wolverines, and thus no possibility of an interception and a Wolverine victory. The game ended in a tie and Evy was severely criticized.

The following week Iowa set a new Big Ten ground gaining record by ripping off 535 yards—340 rushing and 195 passing—as they swamped Minnesota 44-20. Then the Hawkeyes were in Columbus to face their final hurdle on the way to a second straight title. They had it made, too, with a 13-10 lead going for them late in the fourth quarter. Then, the Bucks got the ball on their own 32 and everybody in the gigantic horseshoe knew it would probably be their last drive. What they didn't know was that fullbacking history was about to be made by 215-pound Bob White, a sophomore who shared the post with Co-Captain Cisco who had been injury-plagued. White had already smashed for 91 yards on a dozen attempts that afternoon, and the Hawkeyes knew he'd be coming at them again as the spearhead of the Scarlet rushing game. They were so right. What happened

AURELIUS THOMAS, Ohio State's bruising All-America guard, and jarring BOB WHITE, fullback, were leaders in the Buckeyes' drive to Big Ten and national championships in 1957. White was the hero of an epic win over Iowa to sew up the title when he carried seven out of eight times for 66 out of 68 yards in the Scarlet's winning touchdown drive. The following year the big redhead was All-America.

was classic in its simplicity, and almost contemptuous in its attitude and execution on consecutive plays.

Quarterback Kremblas pointed his fullback straight ahead and White hammered inside tackle. Then White went up the middle. Next, he cracked over guard. He hit the same spot again. Then he roared over tackle again. The chunks he bit off were big ones and after five straight blasts by White the Bucks were on the Iowa 10-yard line. With the Hawks desperate and unbelieving Kremblas suddenly switched to Dick LeBeau who slashed for two. Then, relentlessly, it was White again and he pounded to the three. In the huddle Kremblas looked at White and the big redhead nodded. He smacked into the line; it bent and surged, and then White was over the goal line, two Hawkeyes draped on his shoulders and back. He had carried seven out of eight times for 66 of the 68 yards which brought the Bucks a title and another trip to Pasadena.

For the season White had carried 88 times for 553 yards (he lost one) for a rampant 6.2 average; but, he scored only one touchdown, the one against Iowa. Even in his All-America days the following season White was never to equal the sustained performance of the '57 Iowa game. There were veteran press box witnesses who said his performance had never been paralleled in Big Ten history.

Don Clark, the sizzling halfback, had been the Bucks' big gainer for the year, however, as he rambled for 655 yards and eight touchdowns. The Buckeyes as a team led the league in rushing with 307 yards per game, making Ohio the only team in Conference history to go over the 300-yard mark twice.

With his club rated number one in the nation, Woody Hayes was the choice of his peers as Coach-of-the-Year, and Aurelius Thomas, the Bucks' magnificent guard, was All-America. Joining Thomas from Big Ten ranks were Alex Karras, the Iowa star repeating at tackle and gaining the Outland Trophy as the country's outstanding interior lineman (the third Big Ten winner in a row); Jim Gibbons, the fast, glue-fingered Hawkeye end; Jim Pace, Michigan's fleet halfback and Conference rushing leader; Walt Kowalczyk, Michigan State's thunderous fullback, and teammate Dan Currie, at guard.

Forrest (Fordy) Anderson, who had left Bradley University in 1954 to take over the Michigan State basketball reins, proved in 1957 that the Spartans were not just a factor in Conference football. It wasn't a very big team he put together, but they could shoot well enough, jump and run—and they did all three in a manner that brought them Michigan State's first cage championship, albeit shared with Indiana, with a 10-4 mark. In fact, in the only head-to-head meeting between the two clubs that year, the Spartans drubbed the Hoosiers 76-61 in the second last game of the season to keep Indiana from an undisputed title.

JIM PACE

ALEX KARRAS

JIM GIBBONS

ALEX KARRAS, Iowa's tremendous tackle, repeated as All-America in 1957 and received the Outland Trophy as the nation's best interior lineman. Other Conference All-America selections were JIM GIBBONS, Iowa's ace pass-grabbing end; and JIM PACE, Michigan's fleet halfback.

The Spartans got there, too, without a prolific scorer, a rarity in big time basketball. Forward Larry Hedden, with a modest 16-point average, was the main threat, but it was a smooth meshing of all the Michigan State gears which brought it off. George Ferguson got the job done at the other forward, with aid from Bob Anderegg. The pivot-man was an amazing 6-5 sophomore, Johnny Green, who was two feet taller off the boards. In the backcourt were Jack Quiggle, a cool, deft play-maker—the best in the Conference—with Anderegg and Pat Wilson helping out.

Co-Champion Indiana had come up with another big man in 6-10 Archie Dees, and Archie the Alp led the league in scoring with a 25.4 average in the Hoosiers' return to the top. Dick Neal was at one forward and Pete Obremsky and Jerry Thompson shared the other. Hallie Bryant and Charley Hodson, quick-moving backcourtmen, filled out the starting team.

It wasn't a big scoring year for Conference individuals, and there was only one other 20-point shooter in the league—Frank Howard, Ohio State's 6'-8" strongman and magnificent rebounder at forward. The All-Big Ten featured Dees (also the Conference MVP) and Howard; George Kline, Minnesota's great forward; Don Ohl, Illinois' heady play-maker and scoring threat at guard; and a

JACK QUIGGLE, play-maker guard, led Michigan State to its first Big Ten title in 1957 (shared with Indiana). Quiggle became the Spartans' second All-America cager, and FRANK HOWARD, the Ohio State forward and base-ball star, joined him on the honor team.

359

brace of Michigan Staters—the smooth Jack Quiggle in backcourt and leaping Johnny Green at center. Quiggle and Howard were the league's All-America contributions.

Having tied with Indiana for the title, Michigan State was given the NCAA bid because the Hoosiers had been there last. The Spartans got off to a rousing start, defeating Notre Dame, 85-83, and Kentucky, 80-68, but couldn't get past North Carolina dropping a 74-70 decision in the Eastern finals, as the Tarheels went on to take the national title.

This was the year, too, that Coach Charley Mc-Cafree made some historical waves with his Michigan State swimmers, who won the first Big Ten team title in Spartan history after years of furnishing individual stars but never putting them together in depth. Now the Spartans had the stars and the all-round strength and McCafree proved he could provide the direction. Although Michigan State took only three individual crowns they scored heavily throughout to turn back perennial powers, Ohio State (after a record eight championships in a row) and Michigan. Paul Reinke took the 100-yard breaststroke in 1:03.8; a foursome of Don Nichols, Reinke, Roger Harmon and Frank Parrish won the 400-yard medley relay in 3:51.4, and a speedy quartet of Don Patterson, Jim Clemens, Gordy Fornell and Parrish flashed to a 3:25 victory in the 400-yard freestyle relay.

Ohio State and Michigan stars, however, provided all the record-breaking at the meet. The Buckeyes' versatile Al Wiggins not only took the 100-yard backstroke in 57.6 but broke the world record in the 100-yard butterfly in 54.3.

An Ohio diving duo, as usual, took both events, with Glen Whitten winning on the low board and Don Harper on the high board. Sensational doubles were also being scored by Michigan's Cy Hopkins and Dick Hanley. Hopkins took the 200-yard butterfly in 2:12.2 and set a new Conference mark of 2:20.5 in the 200-yard breaststroke. Hanley captured the 100-yard freestyle in 49.8 and then smashed the national mark in the 220-freestyle with 2:10.5.

Indiana, which hadn't tasted a team triumph in track since 1941, broke its long drought and took both the indoor and outdoor crowns, with Willie May and Greg Bell leading the way. Indoors, May won the 70-yard high hurdles in 8.6 and took second in the lows, while Bell set a new Conference indoor mark of 25-7 in the broad jump. Braelon Donaldson tied for first in the pole vault at 13'-8" with Ohio's Stan Lyons and Purdue's Jim Johnston. Donaldson also tied for second in the broad jump. Charley Jones, Iowa's great distance man, was another meet star as he posted an iron-man double with mile and two-mile victories in 14:13.8 and 9:23.3.

Outdoors, May flashed to a brilliant hurdle double, with 14.5 and 23.5 in the 120-yard high and 220-

WILLIE MAY, with a double in the low and high hurdles, and GREG BELL, capturing the broad jump, led Indiana to the Conference track title in 1957, the Hoosiers first since 1941. Bell also won the NCAA championship in his specialty. The following year Bell, second only to the legendary Jesse Owens in league broad jump annals, not only retained his Conference crown but leaped 26 feet 7 inches for a new NCAA record.

GREG BELL

TOM HALLER, *Illinois quarterback, played first base for the Illini and led the league in fielding in 1957, but went on to major league stardom as a catcher for the San Francisco Giants.*

Wisconsin's Big Ten champ, NORMAN TYRELL, *was chosen collegiate fencer of the year for all-around performance, sportsmanship, and attitude in the 1957 NCAA tournament.*

yard low, respectively. Bell again triumphed in the broad jump, with 25-3½, and the Hawkeyes' Jones came through with another distance double, with 4:17 and 9:14. Al Urbanckas, of Illinois, set a new league mark of 6-8 and ¾ in the high jump and Northwestern's Wilmer Fowler ripped off a sprint double with 9.8 and 21.5 for the 100 and 220, in other noteworthy performances.

Northwestern took its first baseball title since 1940 as rain trimmed the Conference schedule to its slimmest card in thirty years. Leading the Purple in its 5-2 campaign were Tom Scheuerman, a 4-0 pitcher;

Ed Becker, outfielder-shortstop and the league's leading hitter at .440; and catcher, Chuck Lindstrom, son of the Wildcat coach, Freddy Lindstrom, one-time New York Giant star. Ken Tippery, Michigan second sacker with a .429 average, was an All-America; Tom Haller, Illinois first baseman with the league's best fielding average (.991) was All-Conference but would go on to greater honors as a catcher for the San Francisco Giants.

Wisconsin took its second fencing crown and had to dethrone perennial champ, Illinois, to do it. The Badgers were led by epee champ, Paul Mortensen and his epee teammate Chuck Barnum; Frank Tyrell, who scored in sabre; and Gerry Bedner and Paul Lamba who took points in foil.

Joe Campbell, of Purdue, repeated as individual golf titlist, and Illinois made it eight in a row as gymnastic king. Barry MacKay, one of the all-time Conference tennis greats, repeated as singles champ as the Wolverines took their third straight team crown, and, with Dick Potter, won a third straight doubles championship—the three doubles trick being an all-time league record. In wrestling, Minnesota won its first team title in 16 years, narrowly beating out Michigan, 55-54. Dick Mueller was the Gophers' lone winner, at 123 pounds, but Minnesota got three seconds from Ron Baker, 157; Bill Wright, 177, and Willis Wood, heavyweight.

BARRY McKAY, *of Michigan, an all-time Conference great and later a nationally-ranked star, was singles tennis champion for the second straight year in 1957 and set a league record when he was part of the winning doubles duo with Dick Potter for the third consecutive year. Two weeks later McKay took the NCAA singles crown as the Wolverines became the first Conference school to take the national team championship.*

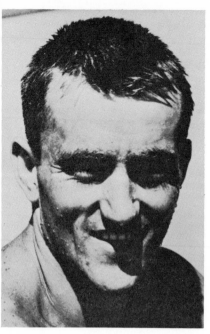

Leading Michigan to the NCAA swim title in 1957 were CY HOPKINS, Big Ten butterfly and breaststroke champ, who took the national collegiate 200-yard breaststroke event; and DICK KIMBALL, the first Wolverine diver to win an NCAA crown in 21 years, cutting into the Ohio State domination with a double on the high and low boards.

In NCAA action for 1957, Conference boxers failed to win a national crown for only the fifth time since the tourney had been held in 1932, but there was no dearth of champions on other fronts.

Although Illinois was dethroned as team titlist in gymnastics, the Illini came up with three individual champions: John Davis, on side horse; Frank Hailand in tumbling, and Abe Grossfeld on horizontal bar. It was the national debut for Grossfeld who would go on to become one of the greatest gymnasts in history.

In the national picture, Michigan made it to the top again in the NCAA swimming meet, resoundingly, with four individual crowns and a relay victory gathered on the way to the team title. Dick Kimball took both the low and high board diving crowns, the first Wolverine to do it in 21 years. Fritz Meyers won the 1500-meter freestyle; Cy Hopkins the 200-yard breaststroke with a new mark of 2:20; and a foursome of Don Adamski, Cy Hopkins, Fred Mowrey and Dick Hanley won the 400-yard medley, a new event on the national program. Meanwhile, Bill Woolsey, the Indiana ace, scored a double of his own for the second straight year, taking the 220 freestyle in a record-breaking 2:02.5 and adding the 440.

Michigan also made tennis news in the NCAA tourney, becoming the first Conference school to take a national team title, led by Barry MacKay's triumph in singles play. The Wolverines came close to the third NCAA crown when they lost the hockey final to Colorado College, 13-6, in the

highest-scoring championship game in tourney history.

Four Conference athletes won individual crowns in NCAA track. Iowa's great Charley Jones took the two-mile; Indiana's Greg Bell leaped to a new NCAA record of 26-7 in the broad jump (the finest effort anywhere, since Jesse Owens' world mark of 28-8¼ more than 20 years previous); Michigan's Dave Owen won the shot-put, and Illinois' Al Urbanckas tied in the high jump with Don Stewart of Southern Methodist.

Simon Roberts and Bob Norman of Illinois, 147-pounder and heavyweight, respectively, took national titles, and in gymnastics the Conference hailed three NCAA titlists from Illinois: John Davis on side horse; Frank Hailand in tumbling, and Abe Grossfeld in all-around.

News was being made on the administrative front in 1957, too. The rules were modified to permit

No one disputes the fact that KARL SCHLADEMAN was one of the most successful cross-country coaches in the history of the Big Ten. Shown here with middle-distance star, WILLIE ATTERBURY, Schlademan, who coached the Michigan State track team from 1941 to 1958, had particularly astounding success with the Spartan hill-and-dalers. As soon as Michigan State was admitted to Big Ten competition in 1951 he led the Spartans to their first cross-country team title, and directed his runners to six out of seven crowns before he retired in 1958. Then, with Schlademan's methods and inspiration to help guide him, Fran Dittrich, whom Schlademan had developed as a distance star in his own right, took over the Spartans and added to an amazing cross-country string that by 1963 had reached 11 out of 14 league crowns. It was the most complete domination by one school the Conference had ever witnessed. The performance by the 1959 Spartans, incidentally, is unmatched by any collegiate conference in the nation. In winning the team title Michigan State runners placed first, second, third, fifth and sixth for a record low-score total of 17 points. (The runners were Crawford Kennedy, Bill Reynolds, Ed Graydon, Gerald Young and Bob Lake.)

granting of basic educational costs for an athlete on a basis of superior scholarship: rank in upper quarter of high school class or upper quarter of college class; and revised recruiting regulations to permit coaches to make off-campus contact with prospects who had signed an acceptance of financial aid tender. (Previousy, coaches were not allowed to visit a prospect under any circumstances until he had matriculated.)

The Conference in July also moved to make Indiana's good standing as a league member conditional upon the suspension for one year of football coach Phil Dickens, who had been found in violation of Conference rules for promising excessive financial aid to perspective students. In September, to strengthen its stand on illegal recruiting practices, the Conference hired an Examiner, John Dewey, to make regular inspections of intercollegiate athletic practices at the member schools and particularly of their administration of financial aid. Then in December, satisfied that all was going well at Indiana, the Faculty Representatives approved the removal of Dickens' suspension.

In the spring of 1957, the Conference Medal for scholarship went to, among others, some athletes who had been singularly distinguished: Bob Hobert, Minnesota's All-America tackle; Terry Barr, Michigan's great halfback; Al Wiggins, Ohio State's national swim champ; and Joe Campbell, Purdue's golf champion.

Quarterback of Iowa's 1958 championship team which rated 1-2 in the nation in various polls was RANDY DUNCAN, a unanimous All-America, second in the balloting for the Heisman Trophy, and Conference MVP. Duncan led the country in pass percentage and yards gained passing; tied for first in TD tosses (12); was second in total offense; and set a Big Ten career mark of 24 touchdown passes.

When the 1958 football season was over there was a whole clutch of politically minded people in Iowa who were convinced that Randy Duncan should seek public office of some kind. The idea was actually broached seriously in many quarters. The only conjecture was the level of office he might seek. Some of the more enthusiastic thought the Iowa quarterback should consider nothing lower than governor, or even Senator. No matter. He'd have the votes merely by declaring himself.

The most talked about Iowa football player in 20 years, Duncan was a sort of latter day Nile Kinnick in the affections of Hawkeye fans—an intellectually gifted, personable, versatile young man who undoubtedly was the big story of the 1958 Big Ten season as the Hawks took the Conference title with their best team in modern history.

Duncan had a marvelous supporting cast but there was no denying the 6-foot 180-pound signal-caller was the star around whom Forest Evashevski mounted his finest production ever. As a sophomore he had been an inspired sub for Kenny Ploen. As a junior he had taken over the post and had a glittering year; but, it was in '58 that he enjoyed the full reach of greatness, and Evy was ready with the corps Duncan would direct.

There were three top ends: Curt Merz, Ray Norton and Bob Prescott. John Burroughs and Mac Lewis were a terrific pair of tackles. Gary Grouwinkel and Don Shipanik gave the Hawks one of the best pair of all-around guards in the country, and Don Suchy was a talented center.

In the backfield, Duncan, when he wasn't flipping the ball, could call on ". . . the greatest and fastest halfback foursome I've ever seen," according to Murray Warmath, Minnesota coach, in describing Willie Fleming, Bob Jauch, Bob Jeter and Kevin Furlong. And in Captain John Nocera and Don Horn, Iowa had two devastating fullbacks.

Evashevski's melding of precision blocking, great passing and brilliant ball-carrying provided Hawkeye fans with an exciting season despite two bumps on the championship road.

After a 17-0 opening win over T.C.U., the Hawkeyes, convinced they were a team of destiny, had their psyche nipped a bit by a hustling Air Force Academy team which played (actually outplayed) Iowa to a 13-13 draw and drew the comment from Evashevski that ". . . if we'd beaten the Air Force we'd never have won the title. We needed that sobering experience to set us right."

After that, things came up roses—except once, when the Hawkeyes found some thorns in what was described by a knowing coach as "the greatest game of offensive football I've ever been in!"

Indiana, Wisconsin, Northwestern and Michigan fell in a row before the swift, slick Hawks, with the glittering halfbacks electrifying the Conference with long runs and Duncan performing feats of wizardry with his passing, ball-handling and rushing. Among the more dramatic moments, Ray Jauch raced 64

JOHN NOCERA

DON SUCHY

BOB JETER

Important cogs in the 1958 Iowa grid machine, called by some observers as "the best ever seen in the Conference," were JOHN NOCERA, hard-hitting fullback; DON SUCHY, a great center; and BOB JETER, flashy halfback.

yards in a scoring dash against the Hoosiers, and Duncan tallied twice on runs as Iowa gained more than 500 yards rushing and passing and equalled the Conference record of 28 first downs. Against Wisconsin the heroics included Ray Norton picking off a mid-air fumble and racing it 21 yards for a score; and Bob Jeter dashing 63 for another. Duncan passed Northwestern into a state of befuddlement with 14 completions in 18 attempts for 174 yards and three TD's. Against Michigan, Willie Fleming flashed 72 yards to score on a punt return for one score and 61 yards for still another; and Bob Jeter contributed a blazing 74-yarder for yet another long distance tally. Willie the Wisp also flashed 46 and 63 yards for TD's against Minnesota.

There was no telling when one of the Hawk speedsters would break open a game or put it out of reach. There was little doubt who would be favored when the Hawkeyes, already having cinched the Big Ten title and a Rose Bowl trip, entertained Ohio State which had a single loss to Northwestern and ties with Wisconsin and Purdue.

It was this game which Woody Hayes described as ". . . the greatest offensive contest I've ever been in." It was 7-7 at the quarter, 21-21 at the half, and 28-28 after three quarters. When the fantastic pyrotechnics were over, Iowa had gained 249 yards passing on 22 completions and 178 yards rushing for a 427-yard total that brought the Hawkeyes four touchdowns—which weren't enough. The Bucks, in pulling it out with a 10-point fourth quarter for a 38-28 victory, had gained 397 yards rushing and completed just a single pass for 65 yards. Don Clark, the Buckeyes' mercurial halfback, picked up 152 yards on only 15 attempts and got two touchdowns,

but it was the bulldozing Bob White, for the second year in a row, who brought most of the devastation to Iowa. White, in carrying 33 times for 209 yards, not only depended on his brute power for short range blasts but on one ferocious charge went 71 yards for the touchdown. It was the big fullback's ability to tear the Iowa line apart in the fourth quarter as thoroughly as he'd done in the first half which was largely responsible for the Buckeye victory.

Despite the loss to Ohio, the Hawks wrote a brilliant end to their regular season by romping over Notre Dame 31-21, with Duncan's sharp passing accounting for two of the touchdowns.

The Hawkeyes' subsequent rout of California in the Rose Bowl was a statistical as well as personal romp for the Hawkeyes as they rolled up 516 yards (429 rushing and 87 passing) in the 38-12 taming of the Golden Bears. Bob Jeter, alone, rolled up a record-breaking 194 yards, featured by a touchdown gallop of 81.

All in all it had been a brilliant year for an Iowa team which, despite a loss and a tie had been called by Ike Armstrong, Minnesota athletic director, "the best team I've ever seen in the Big Ten." The polls ranked the Hawks second in the nation, and, after the bowl games had been played, the Football Writers of America upped the Black and Gold a notch by awarding them the Grantland Rice trophy, symbolic of the best team in the land. As a team, the Hawkeyes led the Big Ten in scoring, rushing, passing, pass-completion average, and set new Conference marks for first downs and total yards gained —the last two for an average of 22 and 416.7 per game.

Randy Duncan was not only Conference MVP but a unanimous All-America, second in the balloting for the Heisman Trophy, and winner of the Camp Trophy as Back-of-the-Year. He ranked first in the nation in pass percentage and yards gained passing;

tied for first with 12 touchdown passes and was second in total offense. His career mark of 24 touchdown tosses was a new league mark. Bob Prescott, the versatile end who the year before had become the highest-scoring lineman in Iowa history with 42 points on three TD'S, a field goal and 21 PAT's, ended his career with a league record 66 PAT's for three years.

Duncan had a lot of Conference company on the All-America lists. Big Curt Merz, his aggressive and versatile teammate, made it at end, as did Sam Williams, Michigan State's devastating flanker, and Jim Houston of Ohio State, the second Houston brother to make it for the Buckeyes. Andy Cvercko, Northwestern's great guard; Gene Selawski, Purdue's top-flight tackle, and Jim Marshall, Ohio State tackle were also named. There was one other Conference back on the All-America squads, and his credentials were awesome: jarring Bob White, the Ohio State fullback, who not only led the Conference

in scoring with 11 touchdowns for 66 points but led in rushing with 713 yards and an unprecedented loss total of exactly zero on his 178 carries.

The 1958 basketball season was pretty much a repeat of the previous season in more ways than one. Not only did Indiana retain the flag it had shared with Michigan State, but for the second year in a row the league failed to produce a team that was truly the class of the Conference. As a result, every night on the schedule was you-take-it-I-dont-want-it. night. Take your eye off the ball and you got cuffed by a tail-ender, and series splits with contenders were the rule rather than exception.

Branch McCracken, a super-scrambler in the coaching ranks, brought his Hoosiers home with a 10-4 mark again, trailed by Purdue and Michigan State with 9-5, and Northwestern and Ohio State with 8-6, in the first division. The situation was so indecisive that Iowa, heading up the second division, was just a notch below at 7-7.

CURT MERZ

GENE SELAWSKI

Among the Big Ten's All-America designees for 1958 were three talented ends: CURT MERZ, of Iowa; JIM HOUSTON, Ohio State; and Michigan State's SAM WILLIAMS; ANDY CVERCKO, Northwestern's great guard; and GENE SELAWSKI, Purdue's tremendous tackle.

SAM WILLIAMS

JIM HOUSTON

ANDY CVERCKO

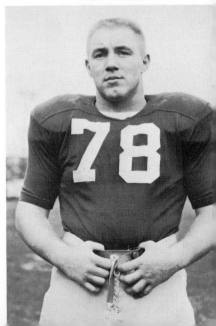

ARCHIE DEES, Indiana's 6-10 center, led the Hoosiers to a second straight Big Ten cage title in 1958 and, for the second year in a row led the league's scorers and was Conference MVP. He was the Big Ten's lone All-America selection for the year.

The Indiana starting five did the best job of holding together, however, winning their last five Conference games in a row to keep in front. Big Archie Dees finished his career by leading the loop's scorers for the second year in a row with a 25.9 average, and the Hoosiers needed every point he got them because their next best shooter Pete Obremsky, at forward, was 23d in the standings with a 15-point average, but he contributed some brilliant floor play. Jerry Thompson at the other forward, and Bob Wilkinson and Sam Gee at guards, rounded out the first five.

Dees not only made All-America but, for the second straight season, was awarded the Conference MVP trophy and was the league's lone All-America designee.

The Hoosiers went to the NCAA tourney but dropped a 94-87 decision to Notre Dame in their opening round.

Dees headed the All-Conference selections, and was joined by Minnesota's high-scoring forward, George Kline, second in the league with a 23-point average; Michigan State's marvelous shooter and rebounder, Johnny Green; Frank Howard, the Ohio State strongman, and Don Ohl, the nifty Illinois backcourt star who was third in Conference scoring with 21.1.

Michigan splashed back into the title picture in swimming after eight years of finishing second to Ohio State and once to Michigan State, and the Wolverines really dominated the meet. Tony Tashnick headed the heroics with three victories in the

Michigan's superb TONY TASHNICK was easily the Conference swimmer of the year in 1958. He took the 100- and 200-yard butterfly and 200-yard individual medley events in the league meet and the 100- and 200-yard butterfly in the national collegiate carnival. DON HARPER, Ohio State's latest diving whiz, scored brilliant doubles off the high and low boards in both the Conference and NCAA meets—and made athletic history when he also won the trampoline championship the same season in the NCAA gymnastics tournament.

GLENN DAVIS of Ohio State was one of the greatest and most versatile trackmen in Big Ten history. He won Conference championships in such varied events as the 60-yard dash; 70-yard high hurdles; the 440 (in which he set a record of 45.8); and was a two-time Olympic winner in the 400-meter hurdles (1956-1960), setting an Olympic record of 49.3 in the 1960 games.

CHARLEY JONES of Iowa was one of the Big Ten's all-time great distance runners. Between 1957 and 1959 in indoor and outdoor competition, he won four league mile crowns, three two-mile championships, an NCAA two-mile crown, an individual Big Ten cross-country title and an NCAA cross-country championship.

FRANK HAILAND, Illinois' Conference gym champ and one of the best in the Illini's long history of the sport, was a two-time National Collegiate tumbling titlist in 1957-58.

100- and 200-yard butterfly and the 200-yard individual medley, and set a new collegiate mark of 2:04.2 in the 200-butterfly. Dick Hanley scored a double in 100- and 200-yard freestyle; and Cy Hopkins got a brilliant duo out of the 100- and 200-yard breaststroke events. A Michigan foursome of Smith, Maten, Pongracz and Hanley added the 400-yard medley relay to the Wolverine harvest. Meanwhile, other brilliant doubles were being posted by Iowa's great Lincoln Hurring in the 100- and 200-yard backstroke; by Don Harper of Ohio State on the high and low diving boards; and by Michigan State's Bill Steuart in the 440- and 1500-meter freestyle.

Illinois pulled off a remarkable reversal of form in track. After finishing a dead last in the indoor meet the previous year the Illini came all the way up to the title, and added the outdoor crown, as well. Indoors the Illini were led by George Kerr's victory in the 440; Dan Imrie's win at 880; Bob Mitchell's record-equalling triumph in the 70-yard low hurdles; and Ernle Haisley's high jump victory. Meanwhile, brilliant doubles were being scored by Ohio State's Glenn Davis in the 60-yard dash and 70-yard high hurdles, and by Iowa's Charley Jones who took the mile and two-mile.

Outdoors, the only Illinois victories were scored by Bob Mitchell in the 220 and by Ernle Haisley in the high jump, but a flock of seconds and thirds wrapped up the title. Of glittering note was Glenn Davis' record-breaking 45.8 for the 440.

For the ninth straight year Illinois won the Conference team title in gymnastics, breaking all league marks for consecutive team championships in any sport. The Illini were led by Abe Grossfeld's victories on the parallel bars and in the all-around, and Frank Hailand's triumph in tumbling.

It was a good year, too, for Illinois swordsmen as the Illini resumed their team leadership in fencing after a brief interruption the previous year. Art Shankin led the Illini with a championship in sabre, with the epee title going to Iowa's Dave Dittmer, and foil going to Wisconsin's Jerrry Bodner.

The league baseball crown was worn by Minnesota as the well-balanced Gophers posted an 11-3 record. Team leaders included all-league selections Jack McCartan, third-sacker, who hit .405; and slick outfielder, Marty Nelson; and John Ericson, a fine second baseman who hit .320. The loop's top hitter was Indiana's Bob Lawrence, with .472; and top pitcher was future Big-Leaguer, Ron Perranoski, of Michigan State, who was 5-0.

Iowa's first and only team championship in tennis was due mostly to the smooth stroking of the Hawkeyes' Art Andrews, singles champ, who paired with Bob Patthast to take the double crown.

It was good news for Iowa again as the Hawkeyes took their first team wrestling honors since 1916. Leading the way with individual titles were Gene Luttrell, 137 pounds, and Simon Roberts, 147 pounds.

SIMON ROBERTS, *with a victory at 147 pounds, was one of Iowa's two individual champions in 1958 as the Hawkeyes won their first league team title in 42 years. (Gene Luttrell at 137 was the other Iowa winner.)*

JACK McCARTEN, *Minnesota's All-America goalie, led the Gophers to the NCAA championship in 1958 and two years later starred for the winning U.S. team in the 1960 Olympic Games.*

ABE GROSSFELD, *one of the greatest gymnasts in collegiate history, led Illinois to the Big Ten title and a tie for the NCAA crown (with Penn State) in 1958. Grossfeld, Big Ten all-around champion for three straight years (1957-58-59) was a triple winner in the 1958 nationals in free exercise, horizontal bar and all-around. Later, he competed in two Olympiads for the U.S.*

Purdue launched a new golf star when John Konsek became the latest Boilermaker in the long string of Purdue individual champions, and led his mates to the team crown.

Michigan State continued its remarkable domination of Conference cross-country under Karl Schlademan, and won its seventh team title in eight years —and the fourth in a row. Iowa's Charley Jones took the individual crown but was pressed by the Spartans' Crawford Kennedy, younger brother of ex-MSU ace Henry Kennedy. Soon, the younger Kennedy would be putting his own title trophies on the family mantel.

In NCAA activity, Michigan retained its national swimming championship on the basis of team balance, as the Wolverines took only two individual titles—both on a sparkling double by Tony Tashnick in the 100- and 200-yard butterfly. Michigan State was the big winner of individual crowns, with five, but couldn't put together enough backup places to nip the Wolves. The Spartans Bill Steuart posted a freestyle double at 440-yards and 1500-meters; Don Patterson streaked to a 100-yard freestyle sprint victory; and Frank Modine triumphed in the 200-yard surface breaststroke. Iowa's Gary Morris was the 50-yard sprint winner; an Ohio State foursome of Bob Connell, Chuck Bechtel, Dick Dewey and Joe Van Horn took the 400-yard freestyle relay in a record 3:23.1; and the Buckeyes' graceful Don Harper pulled off a high and low board double in diving. Illinois' Joe Hunsaker took the 200-yard individual medley to give Conference schools 13 firsts out of the 16 events on the program—an unprecedented haul by any college conference in the history of the nationals.

There was nowhere near that success, however, in track where only a four-way tie for first in the pole vault was accomplished by Purdue's Jim Johnston and Ohio State's Stan Lyons, along with Bob Davis of Missouri and Gene Freudenthal, of Southern California.

Illinois and Michigan State, in an unusual tie for first place, put the Big Ten on top of the gymnastics list again, with the Illini led by Frank Hailand, who repeated as tumbling champ, and Abe Grossfeld, repeating in all-around. Other Conference titlists were Bill Buck of Iowa, on side horse; Tad Muzyczko of Michigan State, on the parallel bar; and Ohio State's trampoline champ, Don Harper, who carved out a unique place in NCAA history for himself, because just a short while previously he had taken the national diving championship and thus became the first man in history to win two NCAA championships in the same season.

Illinois also picked off the NCAA team fencing championship, led by Art Shankin's individual triumph in sabre, and narrowly turned back second-place Columbia, 47 bouts to 43.

Michigan State posted still another national championship for the Conference when Crawford Ken-

In 1933 a Wisconsin boxing team coached by George Downer, the Badgers' athletic publicity director who founded the sport at the school, had a match with St. Thomas College which was coached by one of its student fighters. Downer was so impressed by the student-coach he urged Wisconsin to hire the young man as his replacement the following year.

The young man, JOHN J. WALSH, signed on with the Badgers, practiced law in Madison and simultaneously over the next two and a half decades turned Wisconsin into the most successful collegiate boxing school in the nation.

From 1934 until his retirement in 1958, Walsh tutored Badger belters for 24 seasons, with one year off for military service. During that time his teams won almost 95% of their individual bouts, captured 35 individual crowns at the NCAA tourneys, and won eight team titles —more than twice as many individual and team crowns than his nearest competitor among the more than 30 schools which participated in NCAA boxing. So great was the interest Walsh helped build in national collegiate boxing that when the NCAA tournament was held in Madison in 1948, 50,000 fans attended the three-day tourney. (In 1961, due to pressures opposing the sport, the NCAA discontinued boxing as a national tourney activity.)

nedy, with the individual title, led the Spartans to the cross-country team crown. In boxing, the Spartans got another title from hard-hitting John Horne in the 178-pound division.

In NCAA wrestling, Iowa's Gary Kurdelmeier took 177-pound honors; Ken Maidlow of Michigan State won at 191; and Illinois' Bob Norman repeated as heavyweight champ.

Two items were of paramount significance in administrative matters in 1958. The Conference received announcement from the Pacific Coast Conference that the Westerners wished to discontinue its Rose Bowl agreement with the Big Ten

after the game of January 1, 1960, because of dissolution of their Conference, and the post-season classic, temporarily, was left up in the air as far as the Big Ten was concerned. The Big Ten also approved a 10-game football schedule effective in 1965, and a "round-robin" requirement for Conference games to be effected in progressive stages with the 1969 season. There was some doubt, however, that a true "round-robin" would ever come to pass.

Of a more "passing" nature were some of the recipients of the Conference Medal for scholarship in 1958, including such as Greg Bell, Indiana's broad jump champion; John McCartan, Minnesota's baseball star; and Don Harper, Ohio State's diving and trampoline champion.

The truth of the matter is that the Big Ten didn't come up with a super team of any kind for the 1959 football season but Wisconsin, under Milt Bruhn, took excellent advantage of the talent at hand, put out all the way, and captured the championship with a 5-2 record with a team that wound up seventh in league offensive statistics and seventh in defense. After convincing wins over Stanford and Marquette, the Badgers came unstuck against a Purdue team that had hot-passing Bernie Allen at quarterback, and dropped a 21-0 decision. Four solid wins over Iowa, Ohio State, Michigan and Northwestern preceded a 9-6 setback by Illinois, but the Badgers turned back Minnesota in an important finale, 11-7.

It was a solid and perservering club if not an overpowering one. Henry Derleth and Allan Schoonover were a fine pair of ends. Dan Lanphear, a terrific tackle, paired with Jim Heinke on the other side. Jerry Stalcup, the team's MVP, and Ron Perkins were a tough guard duo, and Bob Nelson an excellent center. Dale Hackbart was a legitimate do-every-

Big Ten champ BOB NORMAN, of Illinois, was two-time NCAA heavyweight wrestling champ in 1957-58.

DAN LANPHEAR DALE HACKBART HENRY DERLETH JERRY STALCUP

Leading Wisconsin to the Big Ten title in 1959 were DAN LANPHEAR, a tremendous tackle who was All-America; and DALE HACKBART, a quarterback who could pass and run, and who was the league's total yardage leader; HENRY DERLETH, a talented end, and JERRY STALCUP, a tremendous guard and the Badgers' MVP.

Three of the Big Ten's six All-America choices for 1959: BILL BURRELL, Illinois' great guard who was also the league MVP; DON NORTON, Iowa's talented pass-grabbing end; and Northwestern's all-purpose center, JIM ANDREOTTI.

BILL BURRELL DON NORTON JIM ANDREOTTI

thing quarterback and was the Conference total yardage leader, rushing 84 times for 319 yards and completing 25 of 52 passes for 367 yards, for a 686-yard total. On defense Hackbart was an alert safetyman and a sure handler of punts. Bill Hobbs and Bob Altmann lent rushing strength at halfback and Ed Hart was a hard-hitting fullback.

Lanphear was an outstanding All-America choice, along with Illinois' tough Bill Burrell at guard, the league's MVP; Don Norton, Iowa's great pass-receiver at end; Dean Look, Michigan State's sparkling rusher-passer at quarterback; Ron Burton, Northwestern's nifty runner and pass-receiver at halfback; and his teammate Jim Andreotti, a bearcat at center. Unfortunately for the Big Ten, Wisconsin ran into a high-scoring Washington club in the Rose Bowl—a Husky eleven that had been upset only once, by Southern California—and took a 44-8 drubbing from the Coast club.

In winning its first undisputed Big Ten basketball title in 1959, Michigan State's speedy Spartans ran away from the pack by the biggest margin in 45 years of Conference cage history. In taking the flag by four full games (with a 12-2 mark) the Spartans had the best season since Wisconsin's all-winning year of 1912, when the Badgers came home by the same margin. The Spartans also accomplished something else never done before or since: they became the first Conference team with two scorers averaging 20 points a game each. Johnny Green, the 6'-4" center, and probably the greatest basketball player in Spartan history; and Bob Anderegg, a 6'-4" forward, both fired for a 20.5 mark as Michigan State handled everybody but Iowa (68-80) and Purdue (81-85) in their surge to the top. Horace Walker, another leaper at forward, and a trio of slick guards—Lance Olson, Dave Fahs, and Tom Rand—rounded out the Spartan starters.

Green, the Big Ten's only All-America as well as Conference MVP, headed an All-Big Ten team that included Ron Johnson, Minnesota's great forward, who tied for second in Conference scoring (21.5); Joe Ruklik, Northwestern's big center who shared the runner-up scoring spot; Willie Merriweather, Purdue's slick, high-scoring backcourtman (21.0); and Dave Gunther, Iowa's ace forward who popped an even 20.0 points per game.

The Spartans, taking high hopes into the NCAA tourney, polished off Marquette, 74-69, in their first effort, but fell before Louisville, 89-81, the next time out.

Michigan turned back Illinois to take the indoor track title, collecting six individual crowns en route. Tom Robinson scored a double with victories in the 60-yard dash, equalling the league mark of 6.1, and setting a new record of 30.3 for the 300-yard run. Tony Seth captured the 880; Pete Stanger won the 70-yard low hurdles; Mamon Gibson the pole vault and Les Bird the broad jump.

Outdoors it was a turnabout affair with Illinois now nipping Michigan. The Illini's Ward Miller took

JOHNNY GREEN

JOHNNY GREEN, only 6-4 but a tremendous leaper at center, and BOB ANDEREGG, a forward, paced Michigan State to its first undisputed Conference basketball title in 1959. Green, probably the greatest cager in Spartan history, was league MVP and the lone Conference All-America selection.

BOB ANDEREGG

a 100 and 220 sprint double, and George Kerr set a new Conference record of 1:50.1 for the 880. Ernle Haisley picked off the high jump and an Illini foursome of John Lattimore, Ted Beastall, Del Coleman and Kerr won the mile relay. Indiana's Willie May was another double star, winning both hurdle events.

A rash of records—most ever in one tourney—were set in the annual Conference swimming meet. Michigan won it with nine new marks posted in 14 events. Leading the Wolverines was the sensational Tony Tashnick with a glittering trio of victories. He took the 100-yard butterfly; set a new American record for the 200 butterfly of 2:02.2; and still another American mark of 2:06.5 for the 200-yard medley. Other Wolverine victories came from Frank Legacki, with a new standard of 49.2 for the 100 freestyle; a new American mark of 2:21.5 by Ron Clark in the 200-yard breaststroke; and a new league record of 3:20.5 by a foursome of McGuire, Woolsey, Dick Hanley and Legacki in the 400-yard freestyle relay.

Other Conference stars were not exactly fading, however. Michigan State's great Bill Steuart took a double in the 440 and 1500-meters; Spartan ace Frank Modine set a new national collegiate record of 1:04.8 for the 100-yard breaststroke; Indiana's Frank McKinney posted a particularly brilliant double with a new collegiate mark of 56.0 for the 100-yard backstroke and a new American record of 2:01.8 for the 200-yard event; a Hoosier quartet of McKinney, Miki, Barton and Nakamura set still another league mark of 3:48 for the 400-yard medley relay; and Ohio State's Sam Hall pulled off a common Buckeye double on the low and high diving boards.

For the first time in its history, Minnesota put together back-to-back baseball championships with a 10-2 mark in league play. Leading the Gophers were All-Conference selections, Ron Causton, league-leading hitter (.475) in the outfield; Wayne Knapp, first baseman who hit .333; and pitcher Fred Bruckbauer (5-1). Also playing strong roles were pitcher Dick Siebert, Jr., (5-0) son of the Gopher coach, and John Ericson, second sacker.

Three Conference stars were destined to go on to Big League status: Bernie Allen, Purdue's brilliant infielder; and Al Luplow, and Dick Radatz, Michigan State outfielder and pitcher. The Conference contribution to All-America in 1959 was Illinois' Bob Klaus, who hit .364 and fielded .979.

Minnesota captured another Conference team title with all-around team balance in wrestling, as the Gophers' Bill Wright was the only individual winner, at 177 pounds. Wisconsin took fencing laurels, led by Ron LeMieux' title in sabre and Dick Green's triumph in foil, with the epee crown going to Illinois' Dave Kennedy. Illinois made it 10 gymnastics team titles in a row to stretch still further its own league mark for consecutive championships in any sport. Don Tonry won at free exercise, and Abe Grossfeld took the still rings and all-around crowns.

Conference baseball stars of 1959 included RON CAUSTON, Minnesota outfielder and league-leading hitter (.475) and BERNIE ALLEN, Purdue's brilliant quarterback and second baseman who later went on to the major leagues.

BOB KLAUS, Illinois' fine fielding shortshop who hit .364 was All-America in 1959.

There was a magnificent performance at the Michigan State cross-country meet when Crawford Kennedy led the Spartans to a new team record of 17 points on a low-point basis. Behind Kennedy came Bill Reynolds in second place; Ed Graydon, in third; Gerald Young, fifth, and Bob Lake, sixth.

Michigan took the tennis title with John Erickson winning the singles and pairing with Gerry Dubie for the doubles crown. Joe Konsek, with his second straight individual title, led Purdue to another golf championship.

On the NCAA lists, no collegiate conference had ever dominated a national tourney as did the Big Ten in swimming. In the 16 swimming events on the program, Big Ten athletes won 12 from the rest of the nation. For the conquering Wolverines, Frank Legacki took the 100 freestyle; Dick Hanley won at 220; Dave Gillanders set a new record of 54.1 in the 100-yard butterfly; a quartet of John McGuire, Carl Woolsey, Dick Hanley and Frank Legacki captured the 400-yard freestyle relay in a record-shattering 3:21.6; and a foursome of John Smith, Ron Clark, Dave Gillanders and Dick Hanley posted a new mark of 3:46.1 for the 400-yard medley.

Meanwhile, Michigan State's Bill Steuart was uncorking a double for the second straight year in the 440 and 1500-meters; Indiana's Frank McKinney scored a double in the 100-yard backstroke and had a record-breaking 2:01.4 for the 200-yard backstroke; Wisconsin's Fred Westphal became the second national titlist in Badger swim history with a victory in the 50-yard sprint; and two Ohio Staters won the usual diving honors collected by the Buckeyes: Sam Hall off the high board, and Ron O'Brien on the low.

BILL STEUART, greatest freestyler who had yet competed for Michigan State and one of the finest on the national scene, captured the major honors in 1959. The year before he had taken the 440-yard and 1500-meters in the Conference meet and a double in the same events in the NCAA; but in 1959 he was even more brilliant, scoring a Big Ten triple at 220, 440 and 1500, and repeating his NCAA triumphs.

Another national crown went to Michigan State as the Spartans took the cross-country team title, and almost got there in still another sport as their hockey team lost to North Dakota in the NCAA final, 4-3. Three league gymnasts won individual titles: Don Tonry of Illinois in free exercise; Michigan State's Stan Tarshis on horizontal bar; and Michigan's Ed Cole on the trampoline. In boxing, Wisconsin's Charley Mohr took 165-pound honors and Michigan State's John Horne repeated as 178-pound champ.

Iowa's Jim Craig was the lone Conference wrestling titlist, at 177 pounds, and it was a lean year for Big Ten national track aspirations, with Illinois' George Kerr taking a lone title, in the 880.

Of significant note in administrative affairs for 1959 was a new recruiting regulation permitting a member school to pay travel expenses for a prospect's campus visit. Also, by a 5-5 vote the Faculty Representatives failed to authorize negotiations for a revival of the Rose Bowl pact with the West Coast but, by the same vote, failed to repeal the standing provision which exempts the Rose Bowl from prohibited post-season contests. The strange stand thus made acceptance of a Bowl bid a matter of individual option—for the time being.

Student-athletes who were awarded the Conference Medal included such luminaries as Abe Grossfeld, Illinois' gymnastics champion; Bob Anderegg, Michigan State's basketball star; and Andy Cvercko, Northwestern's All-America lineman.

FRED WESTPHAL garnered the first Wisconsin NCAA championship in 32 years in 1959 when he won the 50-yard freestyle in the national collegiates.

1960

The 1960's found The Big Ten still the most powerful collegiate athletic conference in the nation, but events of the late Fifties had presaged a tougher fight to remain that way. Admission requirements were being stiffened at all Big Ten schools, and along with raised standards there was a growing trend toward stiffer academic conditions for grants-in-aid; it would not be long before dozens of athletes each year would be denied these aid grants because they could not meet the new qualifications which the Commissioner's office guarded zealously.

The effect would soon be felt in recruiting competition for blue-chip performers. Numerous athletes would be lost to other conferences with lesser standards. It meant, now, that recruiting drives would have to be intensified in a smaller area—the outstanding athletes who could also do a thorough job in the classroom.

The Big Ten schools would meet the challenge and thrive—except in the case of track and field competition—at least in terms of individual NCAA championships. Where the Conference could always count on two or three or more individual crowns and make a strong run for the team title, the 1960's would show a drop off from previous excellence.

On the active scene, championship ties in football had been a rare thing in recent Conference history, but in 1960 Minnesota and Iowa wound up squared off with 5-1 records—with the Gophers getting the Rose Bowl bid because they had tripped the Hawkeyes 27-10 in their head-to-head meeting.

High-scoring Iowa had posted notable victories over Northwestern, Michigan State, Wisconsin and Purdue before bowing to the Vikings. Minnesota, in turn, had scored big wins over Nebraska, Michigan, Illinois and Indiana before being jolted by Purdue, 23-14. Leading the Gopher surge was Sandy Stephens, a daring, running-passing quarterback; and Bill Munsey, a fine halfback, behind a line featuring big, mobile Tom Brown at guard, and the league's MVP; Greg Larson, a center later to star with the New York Giants; Francis Brixius, a tough tackle; Bobby Bell, a growing star at the other tackle; and Bob Deegan, a versatile end. For Iowa, quarterback Wilburn Hollis; swift Larry Ferguson, a breakaway-anytime halfback, and Joe Williams, a just-as-swift fullback, led the Hawkeye offense behind a stout line. Bill Van Buren, a fine all-around center, was flanked by two terrific guards, Mark Manders and Sherwyn Thorson, and Al Hinton was was outstanding at tackle. Good as it was, this Iowa line, and a defensive secondary led by the brilliant Bernie Wyatt, failed to stop Stephens' passing and running in their vital meeting and this one time cost the Hawks dearly. In the Rose Bowl, however, a Washington team that had dropped only a 15-14 decision to Navy, had too much for the Gophers and dumped the Big Ten champs, 17-7.

The Gophers' Brown, however, who won the Outland Trophy as best interior lineman of the year, was an overwhelming All-America choice at guard, and had Conference company on the all-star lists, including Jerry Beabout, Purdue's mighty tackle; Mark Manders, Iowa's great guard; his Hawkeye teammate, Larry Ferguson, at halfback, and Ohio

Big factors in Minnesota's title-sharing team of 1960 were TOM BROWN, the Gophers' magnificent guard who was All-America and the Conference MVP; BILL MUNSEY, a hard-running halfback; and GREG LARSON, a powerful center.

LARRY FERGUSON, a swift All-America halfback; MARK MANDERS, a rousing All-America guard; and tough SHERWYN THORSON, Manders' running mate at guard, were pace-setters for Iowa's 1960 Conference co-champions.

State's bulldozing fullback, Bob Ferguson, the league's leading scorer and rusher with 560 yards on 114 carries for a fraction under 5 yards per carry —without the loss of a single yard all season. For Coach-of-the-Year it was Minnesota's Murray Warmath.

The Cinderella story of the year was Ron Miller of Wisconsin, a fourth-stringer who wasn't even on the initial squad roster for his junior year but came out anyway, and became the league's leading passer with 72 completions on 144 attempts, and was the total offense leader with 966 yards—only 15 of which were by rushing.

In basketball things arrived right on schedule, pre-ordained from the year before when five freshmen reported at Ohio State and promptly gave the varsity fits in every practice scrimmage they held. Not only fits but often a clobbering. The five were Jerry Lucas, John Havlicek, Mel Nowell, Bob Knight and Gary Gearhart. Lucas, Havlicek and Nowell moved right into varsity status with Larry Siegfried, a junior and Joe Roberts, a senior, backed up by still another senior, Dick Furry. A season finale loss to Indiana was their lone Conference blemish, and from then on it would seem an eternity before the Buckeyes would bow to a lodge brother again.

The Bucks went to the NCAA tourney but there was some doubt they might take it all because of

their youth—and waiting in the western bracket if they got to the finals would surely be mighty California. The Bucks disposed of Western Kentucky, Georgia Tech and N.Y.U. in that order, and there they were, pitted against the Golden Bears— whom they promptly demolished 75-55 for the national title. Lucas was the tourney's MVP and a unanimous All-America, and generally hailed as the rising super-star of the era. Other Big Ten representatives on the All-America were Terry Dischinger, another great soph from Purdue headed for three-year stardom; Walt Bellamy, Indiana's 7-foot center; and Minnesota's versatile Ron Johnson, also a center.

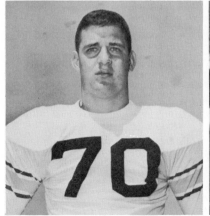

JERRY BEABOUT, a great Purdue tackle, made All-America in 1960 along with Ohio State's pounding full-back, BOB FERGUSON, league rushing leader who gained 560 yards on 114 carries and never lost a yard.

Everybody knew he was something special when he was merely a high school sophomore and led Middletown, Ohio, high school to the 1956 state basketball championship. By the time Jerry Lucas was a 6-8 senior, Middletown had won 76 straight games, and about twice that many college coaches were all but getting on their hands and knees in earnest and legitimate supplication. There was perhaps an equal number who were even more earnest and whose supplication was embroidered with the most lavish athletic fringe benefits ever designed for an American boy of 18.

Middletown is a small city of about 45,000, not too far from Cincinnati. Historically, people talk about Indiana as the real hotbed of schoolboy basketball, but in Middletown a boy who makes the starting five on his fifth grade team in elementary school is SOMEBODY. The boys who make the high school varsity are strictly from Mt. Olympus.

Jerry Lucas was one of the kids who did start out on a fifth grade team, and it would not be until the final game of the season, seven years later, that he would play in a losing contest. By the time he entered junior high school he was 5-7. As a freshman he was 6-4. He shot up to 6-7 as a junior and grew his final inch as a senior. His accomplishments kept growing with him.

Lucas, who probably had more acclaim in the nation's press than any high school athlete in history (because it lasted three years), led Middletown to two straight state titles before going down to defeat in the finals the third year to Columbus North—coached by Frank Truitt, who, just a year later, was to become Jerry's freshman coach at Ohio State.

Along the way, during his three-year varsity career at Middletown, the big 228-pounder with the bushy eyebrows was the first prepster in history to be named as a sophomore to the official SCHOLASTIC COACH MAGAZINE's high school All-America. He turned in yearly point totals of 715, 930 and 805, which was more than 200 points over what Wilt Chamberlain had poured in for Philadelphia's Overbrook High School. Meanwhile, Middletown was also setting a modern national winning streak of 76 games.

This super-nova was also an "A" student, president of his class, and blessed with the instincts of a Boy Scout bucking for Eagle-class merit badges; except, with Big Luke it was all very natural. You add up all those physio-socio virtues and you've got Something Everybody Wants.

The colleges wanted Jerry Lucas like, well, to lose him was perdition; to woo and win him would be the answer to all your problems: artistic, fiscal and alumni. College scouts took all possible paths into Middletown, including a stealthy approach at 5:30 a.m. by (of all people) an Ivy emissary who rapped conspiratorially on his bedroom window. Jerry got up and pulled the blind down in the visitor's face.

You've got to understand why a man should be trying to plead his cause at such an early hour. Nobody was allowed to get to Lucas, personally. Otherwise the competition to gain his ear would have made Middletown a permanent convention city as long as the boy was unhooked, or unpromised.

More than 150 colleges wound up romancing him, or at least getting in touch with him by mail or phone, and their offers were fancy and frantic in many cases,

Middletown High School star, Jerry Lucas, drives for a basket. Lucas later starred for Ohio State during Buckeye's golden basketball years.

including money over and under the table, a new convertible, scholarships for his non-basketball-playing younger brother, and a job for Jerry's father at twice the pay he was currently getting. Finally, Jerry stopped opening the mail and refused to accept long-distance phone calls. A screening committee of his father, his high school coach, Paul Walker, and a local sportswriter evaluated the merit and sincerity of all supplicants. Then Jerry made his decision.

"In the first place," he recalls, "I was pretty disgusted with the easy money prospects. I was just an average kid from an average American family, and the wrong decision could let me in for a peck of problems if not downright trouble.

"So I decided to remain close to home and attend a college which was willing to discuss academics first and then basketball, and which would back it all up with an academic scholarship instead of an athletic grant-in-aid. That way I could quit sports if the grind got too tough and still stay in school."

Lucas' selective philosophy added up to Ohio State. Jerry entered in the fall of 1958, along with four other frosh who combined with Luke (as he came to be called) to give the varsity fits, much to the heady pleasure of Coach Fred Taylor. The other four were Mel Nowell of Columbus; Dave Gearhart of Dixie; Bob Knight of Orrville; and John Havlicek of Bridgeport—all home-grown Buckeyes. (Havlicek had been a great football quarterback and Woody Hayes wanted him desperately for the Bucks' grid team. When Havlicek said he intended to pass up football for basketball, Woody said he respected the boy's decision and immediately helped Freddy Taylor recruit him.)

With the help of this so-called "fabulous five" sent up from the frosh, Taylor started putting together the most successful cage dynasty of modern times. Before it would end, Ohio State would win or share an unprecedented five straight Big Ten basketball championships.

The whole basketball world focused its attention on St. John Arena that first Saturday in December, 1959. Big Luke was going to play his first varsity game against Wake Forest—but already, for the first time in history, an untried sophomore had been unanimously selected as a pre-season All-America. All he had to do now was live up to his advance notices.

Lucas' performance, under the circumstances, according to a dead-pan Fred Taylor was "creditable." Lucas scored fewer than 20 points but he pulled down 28 rebounds. In his second game, again Memphis State, he got eight points in the first 70 seconds and went on to a 34-point total. By the end of the year Taylor was saying: "This kid is the greatest thing since sliced bread!"

He was, indeed, with butter and jam added. Lucas was a unanimous All-America, in support of the earlier predictions, and was chosen Most Valuable Player in the Big Ten (an unprecedented honor for a sophomore, and one he would gain for three straight years). He was also selected MVP in the NCAA tournament when Ohio State scorched California, 75-55 in the finals of the national tourney.

The team which Luke led the following year, including Captain Larry Siegfried, John Havlicek and Mel Nowell, might well have been the greatest club in collegiate history. It won 27 straight games in an undefeated season, picked off number one in national ranking, but, on an off-night, lost in overtime to Cincinnati in the NCAA tournament finale. Both Lucas and Havlicek, for the only time that year, had cold shooting hands, and a Bearcat team that had previously lost three games, proved that on a given night, in a single contest, an acknowledged inferior underdog can commit lese majeste on the high and mighty. It was a stunning defeat, but Lucas, with a wry equanimity which always marked his few defeats, passed it off in typical fashion. "The winners got self-winding watches," he mentioned to a friend. "We got watches, too, but we have to wind ours." This in no way meant that Jerry Lucas didn't mind getting beat. He was too much a competitor for that; but, in coping with reality he had unfailingly good humor. Once, in dropping a direct pass from a teammate he shook his head and offered his excuse. "It caught me in the worst possible place, Coach—the palms of my hands."

Their senior year was virtually a repeat for Luke, Havlicek and Nowell—Perfection. Mechanical and artistic virtuosity. Fred Taylor was the impressario of the most acclaimed basketball show in collegiate history. No team had ever dominated the Big Ten and the national scene in this fashion. When the Buckeyes swept the Los Angeles Christmas Classic (they'd taken the Madison Square Garden Holiday Festival the year before), West Coast fans and coaches shook their heads in disbelief and admiration. "It was a privilege just to see them play," said John Wooden, the UCLA mentor, adding: "West Coast basketball will be better for that gang having appeared out here."

Luke was having more fun, now, in his final season, joyously sweeping both boards and, with defenses ganging up on him, passing off more than ever. (His selflessness was carried to a flaw, according to some critics.) "He looks like a big frog out there," his teammates said, "with his knees bent, his shoulders slumped, and his big eyes peering unblinking beneath his bushy brows. It's enough to make you bust out laughing even as we cut in for a pass from him."

When Lucas wasn't passing off he was demonstrating

Practice makes perfect and Jerry Lucas' long hours on the hardwood paid off handsomely for the Buckeyes.

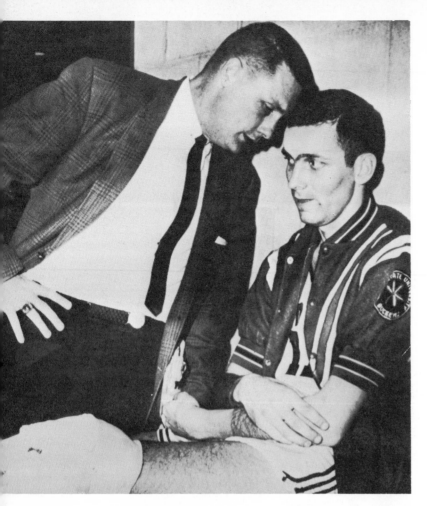

Jerry Lucas' injured knee was big factor in Ohio State's 1962 NCAA title quest.

more uncanny shooting accuracy than any collegiate pivotman ever had exhibited. He hooked gracefully with either hand, took deadly jumpers from any spot on the floor within 25 feet of the basket, had a soft, one-handed push shot when needed and was absolutely unstoppable on tip-ins with either hand if one of his own or a teammate's shot bounced off the board or rim near him. And, of course, Luke was always nearby. His positioning when rebounding the offensive board was fast, slick and instinctive, as though the ball were sending him some remote signal as to which way it would bounce.

Then, one afternoon at Madison, Wisconsin, came the

upset of the year and maybe of all Conference cage history. Wisconsin, with nothing more to look forward to than perhaps a fourth place finish in the league race, shot the eyes out of the basket while Luke and his teammates staggered through a sudden bout of hoopitis myopic, otherwise known as, "Who put the lid on the rim?" It turned out to be a Badger victory, led by Ken Siebel, ending Ohio State's record string of Big Ten victories at 26.

The Bucks went on to close out the season with a third straight Big Ten title and a unique second straight performance in the national polls where they once again were a unanimous Number One selection from the first week of the season through the last. Inexorably, Ohio State and Cincinnati ripped their way through the NCAA preliminaries toward a history-making second straight meeting in the finals. In the semis, however, as the Buckeyes crushed Wake Forest, Lucas went up for a rebound late in the second half, was knocked off balance and tumbled to the floor, falling on one leg.

It just might have been the most costly injury since Achilles took the arrow in his heel. Overnight ministrations did little to relieve the pain and swelling in the knee. At game time the following night Luke gimped onto the floor and gave it all he could against the Bearcats, but a disabled Lucas couldn't cut it. For the second year in a row, opportunistic Cincinnati had beaten the national championship Bucks for the NCAA title.

It was just about all over for Jerry Lucas as a collegian but there was much for him to look back upon. In January of his senior year, Sports Illustrated had named him Sportsman of the Year, the first collegian so honored by the magazine in its annual presentation. He had been a stand-out on the 1960 Olympic team (the first sophomore to make the cage squad) and with Oscar Robertson had led the Yanks to a sensational sweep in the Games. He had won more honors, more awards, more kudos in print than any basketball player since Dr. Henry Naismith pinned up the first peach basket. He had married Treva Gelb, a 5-foot, 9-inch Ohio State coed, and, after sitting out pro ball for a year while mulling over a complex, personal should-I-play-or-shouldn't-I situation, he finally signed for a bundle with the Cincinnati Royals. To nobody's surprise he was pro Rookie-of-the-Year his first season, and a league all-star.

Jerry Lucas, an athlete-scholar, had stopped surprising people back in the fifth grade in Middletown when they said: "This can't be!" But he was.

Michigan did it again in swimming, and there was another power being built in the Big Ten, right behind the Wolverines, as Indiana splashed to second, its highest ranking yet. (Soon, the Hoosiers would found a dynasty of their own.) Leading the Wolverines were Ron Clark, with a double in the 100- and 220-yard breaststroke; and Frank Legacki, with a sparkling double of sprint wins: the 50 in a league record-equalling time of 22.0, and the 100. Fred Wolf added the 200-yard individual medley; Michigan divers interrupted Ohio State's domination of the boards, with Joe Gerlach taking the low and Bob Webster the high; and a Wolverine quartet of Kerr, Morrow, Woolsey and Legacki tied the record of 3:20 for the 400-yard freestyle relay.

There were other scintillating performances by the upcoming Hoosiers. Pete Sintz took a 220 and 440 freestyle double; Mike Troy, soon to be acknowledged as one of the sport's greatest, posted two American record-breaking victories with 53.1 for the 100-yard butterfly and 1:59.4 for the 200-yard butterfly; Frank McKinney, son of the former National Chairman of the Democratic party, added another brilliant double with victories in the 100- and 200-yard backstroke, with a new American record of 55.5 for the shorter distance. Then, a Hoosier

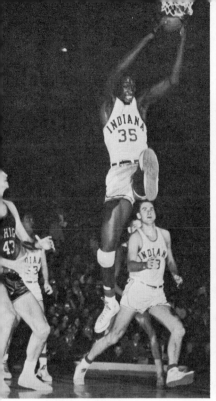

WALT BELLAMY　　　　　　　**HORACE WALKER**　　　　　　　**RON JOHNSON**

Among the bright lights of the 1960 basketball season were Indiana's 7-foot WALT BELLAMY and RON JOHNSON, Minnesota's 6-7 star who tied for fourth place in the Conference scoring race, with both making All-America. Third spot in the league scoring column went to Michigan State's 6-5 center, HORACE WALKER, an All-Conference choice who had the misfortune to do his starring in a year that not only produced Bellamy and Johnson but a couple more centers named Jerry Lucas and Terry Dischinger. Any other season Walker would surely have been All-America, too.

FRANK McKINNEY of Indiana was one of the greatest swimmers ever to come out of the Big Ten and star on the national scene. He won the Conference 100- and 200-yard backstroke events three years in a row (1959-60-61), setting league records in both, and won the NCAA 100-and 200-yard crowns in 1959, also in record time for the latter.

foursome of McKinney, Miki, Troy and Brunnell picked off the 400-yard medley relay in 3:43.4 for still another American mark.

Michigan and Illinois kept playing footsie with each other in track. Indoors—Michigan again, with Illinois second. Outdoors—Illinois first and Michigan second. The same pattern as the year before. The Wolverines' Tom Robinson got another double in the 60-yard dash and 300-yard run; Tom Seth took the 880 again; and Ben McRae, Michigan's halfback ace, equalled the league mark of 7.8 for the 70-yard low hurdles. New records were set by Illinois' Ken Brown in the two-mile (9:04.9) and by an Illini foursome of Ed Houston, Ted Beastall, Jim Hammond, and George Kerr who did 3:16.3 in the mile relay.

GEORGE KERR, Illinois' brilliant middle-distance star, capped a great career in 1960 by taking the indoor 880 and the outdoor 440 and 880 championships. The previous spring he had set a Conference record in the half-mile, and had won the NCAA 880-yard crown.

379

Leading Minnesota to the Big Ten and National Collegiate titles in 1960 were JOHN ERICKSON, slick-fielding second baseman who was the NCAA tourney MVP; and WAYNE KNAPP, hard-hitting first baseman who made All-America along with Ohio State's slugging outfielder and Big Ten batting champ Tom Perdue (.459).

Outdoors, as Illinois reversed things, George Kerr had a 440 and 880 double; Del Coleman won the 220-low hurdles; and Paul Foreman took the broad jump. Michigan's Tom Robinson posted still another double at 100- and 220-yards.

It was getting to be a pleasant habit for Minnesota in baseball as the Gophers' finest era produced a third straight title with a 12-2 mark. Wayne Knapp, first base (.441); Dave Pflepsen, shortstop (.375) and Howie Nathe, a 4-1 pitcher with an ERA of 1.89, were the stars, with strong assists from pitcher Larry Bertelsen (5-0); catcher Neil Junker; third sacker Caldon Rolloff (.383) and second sacker and three year star, John Erickson. At season's end

Knapp and Ohio State outfielder and football star, Tom Perdue, were All-America, with Perdue's .459 leading the Big Ten hitters.

Gerald Young, with the individual crown, led Michigan State to its sixth straight cross-country title (and nine out of the last 10), and Illinois upped its fencing and all-sports consecutive title record with 11 straight in gymnastics. Illini leaders were Ray Hadley with championships in free exercise and all-around; Pat Bird on still rings, and Alvin Barasch in tumbling. The Illini also picked off another league crown, in fencing, led by Abby Silverstone's victory in foil. Iowa's John Youngerman took the epee title and teammate Ralph Sauer triumphed in sabre.

Michigan won the team title in wrestling with four individual crowns: Ambrose Wilbanks, 130 pounds; Fred Kellerman, 137; Jim Blaker, 147, and Dennis Fitzgerald, 167. There was also a team tennis crown for the Wolverines, with the doubles title going to John Wiley and Gerry Dubie, as Northwestern's Denny Konicki stroked his way to the singles championship. Golf was almost a foregone conclusion, with Purdue's brilliant John Konsek's third individual title leading the Boilermakers to their third straight team laurels.

Minnesota headlined the NCAA action as far as the Big Ten was concerned in 1960 when the Gophers battled their way to the national baseball championship, nipping Southern California, 2-1 in a 10-inning finale. A bonus came the Gophers' way when star second sacker John Erickson was chosen as the tournament's MVP for his timely hitting and slick fielding.

Purdue's smooth-swinging JOHN KONSEK was the only man in Big Ten history to win the league individual golf crown three straight years, 1958-59-60.

ART KRAFT, Northwestern's 157-pound Big Ten wrestling champ, added to his 1960 honors by taking the NCAA crown.

Accustomed to seeing either Ohio State or Michigan taking the national swimming title, the Conference took a back seat instead as Southern California came through for its first team title. The Conference, however, recorded plenty of individual triumphs. Indiana's sensational Mike Troy scored a butterfly double, with a record-breaking 53.1 at 100-yards and another mark of 1:57.8 for 200. Michigan's Ron Clark won the 200-yard surface breaststroke; Sam Hall, Ohio State's master of the boards, swept both the high and low dives, and an Indiana quartet of Frank McKinney, Gerald Miki, Mike Troy and Pete Sintz set a mark of 3:40.8 in the 400-yard medley relay.

It was another disappointing year for the Big Ten in track where Illinois' smooth-striding George Kerr, repeating as 880 king, was the lone champ. In wrestling, Northwestern's Art Kraft, at 157 pounds, was the league's lone winner, but Confer-

Two-year Conference champ, STAN TARSHIS, of Michigan State, also won two straight NCAA crowns on the horizontal bars in 1959-60.

BROWN McGHEE · JOHN HORNE

BROWN McGHEE, Wisconsin 132-pounder, won a National Collegiate title in 1960 as the NCAA held its last boxing tourney, in which JOHN HORNE, Michigan State light-heavyweight, repeated as 178-pound champ.

ence boxers did better in the last NCAA tourney that would ever be held. With the 1960 meet, boxing was discontinued as an NCAA event, and it was fitting, perhaps, that Wisconsin, which compiled the finest record in the history of the sport, should help wind it up with two champions—Brown McGhee at 132 pounds, and Jerry Turner, 156. John Horne, Michigan State's fine belter, repeated as 178-pound titlist.

There were honors for Conference gymnasts too, with Illinois' Alvin Barasch and Ray Hadley taking the tumbling and free exercise crowns, respectively; Michigan State's Stan Tarshis repeating on the horizontal bar, and Iowa's Larry Snyder winning on the trampoline.

Champions were well represented in the Conference Medal department, too. Dale Hackbart, Wisconsin's great quarterback of the previous fall; John Konsek, Purdue's golfing great; Art Kraft, Northwestern's wrestling champ; Stan Tarshis, Michigan State's gymnastic ace; and Dick Furry, Ohio State cage captain, were among the recipients.

The 1960 Olympics found 28 athletes, including two young women, contributed by Big Ten schools. As usual, the Conference delegation played an important part in the United States' success at the Games. Glenn Davis, Ohio State's brilliant hurdler, repeated his 1956 triumph with another Olympic record of 49.3 in the 400-meter hurdles, then ran a leg for the Yanks' 1600-meter relay which also set a new mark. Willie May, of Indiana, took a Silver Medal in the 110-meter high hurdles, and Iowa's Charley Jones ran in the 3000-meter steeplechase. It was the smallest Conference track contingent yet to represent the U.S., but the league had the satisfaction of supplying the head coach in Larry Snyder of Ohio State. Two other Big Ten stars competed for their native countries, with Illinois' George Kerr running a leg of the West Indies' third-place 1600-meter relay team, and Michigan's Eeles Landstrom taking third place in the pole vault.

In swimming, Indiana's Mike Troy set a new Olympic mark of 2:12.8 as he won the Gold Medal in the 200-meter butterfly, and swam a leg on the Americans' record-breaking 800-meter relay team. The Hoosiers' Frank McKinney took the Silver Medal in the 100-meter backstroke and swam the first leg for the Yanks' record-breaking 400-meter medley relay. Still another Indianan, Alan Somers, competed in the 1500-meters and 400-meters. Michigan's Bob Webster took the Gold Medal in the platform dive; Ohio State's Sam Hall took a Silver Medal in the 3-meter dive; and Michigan's Dave Gillanders took third place in the 300-meter butterfly.

The Big Ten took particular pride in the basketball proceedings where the Americans swept everything before them. Paced by Ohio State's Jerry Lucas, Purdue's Terry Dischinger and Indiana's Walt Bellamy, plus Cincinnati's Oscar Robertson and West Virginia's Jerry West, this may very well have been the greatest basketball team ever put together, anytime, anywhere.

American success in hockey—for the first time—also took on a decided Big Ten tinge with seven Conference stars on the team. Minnesota sent Bill Christian, Paul Johnson, John Mayasich, John McCartan and Dick Meredith; and Michigan State contributed Gene Grazia and Weldon Olson.

Ohio State's Jim George took a Silver Medal in weightlifting (middleweight) and the Buckeyes' John Pulskamp took fourth place in heavyweight.

Wisconsin's Peter Barrett was on the yachting team and Michigan State's Allan Kwartler was a fencer. The Spartans also sent Judy Goodrich in

1961

TERRY McCANN, Iowa alumnus and ex-Big Ten champ, clamps a leg hold on his opponent on his way to the bantamweight wrestling championship in the 1960 Olympics at Rome.

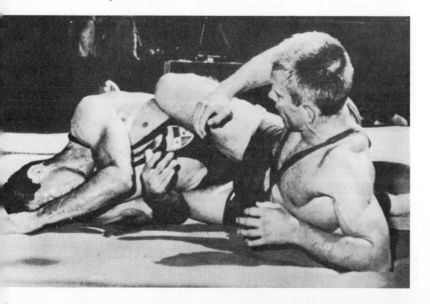

women's fencing, with Illinois furnishing two other pretty stars—Muriel Grossfeld and Carolyn Osborn—for the women's gymnastics' team.

Administratively, the Conference approved a program of financial aid for athletes based on academic achievement without regard for a "need factor," which was in line with what most other collegiate conferences were doing in regard to athletic scholarships. The big news, however, had been the dramatic announcement in July that Commissioner Wilson ruled, on the basis of his investigation, that certain prospective athletes at Indiana had been offered illegal financial assistance, and that the Hoosiers' membership was therefore placed on probation and they could not participate in Conference football television receipts in 1960, and that football games played that year by Indiana wouldn't be counted as Conference games. (Equally stiff penalties by the NCAA would follow, with Hoosier teams being barred from NCAA tournaments for four years. Most affected would be the great Indiana swim teams of that period.)

One of Woody Hayes' finest creations at Ohio State nipped Minnesota for the 1961 football title, but the biggest conflict of all came at the end of the season in the form of a near riot by an enraged Buckeye student body. Before that, however, there was the action on the football field . . .

It was a speedy, solid team which Hayes put together and it posted an undefeated season, following a 7-7 opening tie with Texas Christian which wasn't supposed to happen—certainly not at home.

Hayes, however, had the kind of crew with the power and desire to get right back on course. Up front were a pair of fine ends in Chuck Bryant and Tom Perdue; two tremendous tackles in Bob Vogel and Daryl Sanders; hard-nosed guards Mike Ingram and Gary Moeller, and a smallish but fiery center named Billy Joe Armstrong. Deployed behind them was a backfield featuring John Mummey, a running-passing quarterback; two sensational sophomore halfbacks in Paul Warfield and Matt Snell (later to be rookies-of-the-year in the NFL and AFL) and bulldozing Bob Ferguson at fullback. It was an explosive bunch which averaged 20 first downs and 371 yards gained per game—and had the lowest penalty yardage assessed against them. Ferguson, who repeated as All-America fullback, led the league in scoring and rushing, as the Bucks wound up second in the national polls, just a width of the ball behind Alabama.

Woe lay ahead for this brilliant bunch. The formal Rose Bowl pact between the Coast Conference and Big Ten had not been renewed as such, and although the invite was still being tendered to the Big Ten champion it was left for the school to decide whether to accept. The Ohio State faculty declared itself against the game and the campus erupted. There might have been a full-fledged riot

MIKE INGRAM

MATT SNELL

PAUL WARFIELD

Two sophomores and a senior were among the stars of Ohio State's undefeated 1961 champions who were denied a Rose Bowl trip by faculty edict. Co-Captain MIKE IN-GRAM was a rugged linebacker. PAUL WARFIELD and MATT SNELL were speedy halfbacks. Snell subsequently became one of the most versatile players in recent Buckeye history. As a junior he also played defensive end, and as a senior he was a rampaging fullback. With the New York Jets he became Rookie-of-the-Year in 1964 while Warfield was highly rated for the same honor in the NFL as a flanker for the Cleveland Browns.

Leading a fine Minnesota team to the Rose Bowl fol-lowing the 1961 season, when the Ohio State faculty refused permission for the Buckeyes to go, were SANDY STEPHENS, a do-everything quarterback and BOBBY BELL, one of the greatest tackles in tradition-rich Gopher history. Both Stephens and Bell were named to All-America, with Bell repeating in 1962.

had not Buckeye footballers, themselves, calmed the student body and persuaded the marchers to go home.

Under the circumstances, the Bowl invite then went to Minnesota and the Gophers promptly ac-cepted. The Big Ten didn't have to apologize for its second-place finisher. A derring-do quarterback, Sandy Stephens, directed a unit that had a break-away halfback in Bill Munsey and a jarring full-back in Judge Dickson. Up front, among others, were fine tackles in Carl Eller and Jim Wheeler; two exceptional guards in Julian Hook and Robin Tellor, Dick Enga a bang-up center; and sparkling end Bob Deegan. It might even have been a per-fect season for the Vikings except for the begin-ning and end of the campaign. Missouri startled the Gophers, 6-0 in the opener, and in the finale,

SANDY STEPHENS

BOBBY BELL

a Wisconsin team that had dropped three league games, bushwacked them 23-21 in a barn-burner; but, the Gophers got up, dusted themselves off, and smashed UCLA 21-3 in the Rose Bowl.

Minnesota's Sandy Stephens (the league MVP) and Ohio's Bob Ferguson led the Big Ten's All-America contingent—Ferguson for the second year—and there were three others: Dave Behrman, Michigan State's rousing guard; Pat Richter, Wisconsin's league-leading pass-catcher; and Iowa's fine center, Bill Van Buren.

The 1961 basketball story was pretty much the same as the previous year—only more so—as Fred Taylor's Ohio State five continued to dominate the Conference and the nation. Jerry Lucas, John Havlicek, Larry Siegfried, Mel Nowell and Gang swept to an unbeaten season, in and out of the league, and rated an unquestionable No. 1 in the nation in all the polls. A big honor got away from the Bucks, however, as they suffered a somewhat sub-par night when they met Cincinnati in the finals of the NCAA tourney and were nosed out in overtime.

Lucas, of course, was THE All-America of the season, with Purdue's marvelous Terry Dischinger joining him for a second time, along with Indiana's great Walt Bellamy, another second-timer. Certainly, no Conference, anywhere, ever presented three such All-Americas the same season.

In swimming, it was simply all too apparent. Indiana had arrived! The Hoosiers, under youth-ful Jim Counsilman, put on an absolute swamping act, winning seven individual titles and setting records in six of them. Alan Somers posted a new mark of 4:22.5 for the 440 freestyle and a record of 17:49.9 for the 1500-meters for a tremendous double. Equally sparkling was Frank McKinney's backstroke double with new marks of 54.6 for the 100 and 1:59.8 for the 200. Mike Troy smashed the 200-yard butterfly mark with a clocking of 1:58; John Roethke set a record of 2:04 for the 200-yard individual medley; and Pete Sintz won the 220-yard freestyle. There were other brilliant doubles by other Conference stars, with Minnesota's great Steve Jackman winning the 50- and 100-yard sprints, with a new American collegiate mark of 48.3 for the century.

In track, Michigan made it an indoor-outdoor sweep, with the Wolves making it three straight on the boards, paced by an 880 and mile double by the Lithuanian star, Ergas Leps, and footballer Ben McRae's high and low hurdle victories. Of significant note, too, was Purdue's Dave Mills' record of 47.2 for the 440.

Outdoors, Leps repeated his double, with another twin-win posted by Tom Robinson in the 100 and 220. Records were set by Michigan's Dick Cephas with 23.4 in the 220-low hurdles; Purdue's sparkling George Harvey with a new two-mile mark of 9:02.6; and Indiana's Gene Graham, with 1:19.2 for the 660.

In wrestling, Michigan State came up with its

Not since the Illinois "Whiz Kids" of almost two decades earlier had one team so dominated the All-Conference basketball team as did the Ohio State team of 1961 which had burst upon the league and national scene the year before and ruled the sport for three years. In addition to the incomparable Jerry Lucas, the Buckeyes had backcourtman LARRY SIEGFRIED and JOHN HAVLICEK, the brilliant forward and defensive star.

Backcourt ace MEL NOWELL was on the second team. Siegfried, the Bucks' MVP as a sophomore, was brilliant in the 1960 NCAA championships as a junior and captained the Ohio team in 1961 when they went to the finals again. Havlicek, later a star with the Boston Celtics (as was Siegfried), was All-America in 1962, along with Lucas when the Scarlet made it three straight for the NCAA finals.

JOHN HAVLICEK

LARRY SIEGFRIED

MEL NOWELL

Dashman TOM ROBINSON, of Michigan, was one of the most brilliant stars in the Conference in the early 1960's, winning nine league titles, indoors and outdoors, at distances from 60 yards to 300.

BEN McRAE, Michigan halfback, and ERGAS LEPS, a Canadian from Lithuania, were two of the Big Ten's brightest track stars of the early 1960's. McRae won six hurdling titles over the lows and highs. Leps, a nine-title winner, indoors and outdoors, was the only Conference runner ever to win the outdoor mile crown three years in a row, 1960-61-62.

first league championship, with three Spartans taking individual titles: Okla Johnson at 115 pounds; Fritz Kellerman, 130; and Norm Young, 137. It was Illinois again in fencing—the 17th time the Illini had taken the team title since the tourney began in 1927. Bruce Kwiskey's victory in epee led the Illini, with Michigan State's Don Johnson taking sabre; and Ohio State's Larry Loveland scoring in foils.

Another Illinois dynasty, however, came to an end at long last. After taking the gymnastics championship for 11 straight years—the longest title run in any sport in any major conference—the Illini were dethroned by Michigan. It was a good year for the Wolverines, generally, as they took the baseball title, their first since 1950. Mike Joyce (5-1) and Fritz Fisher (3-1) headed the mound

Highest batting average in Conference history was the .585 posted in 1961 by Michigan's All-America catcher, BILL FREEHAN, who went on to stardom with the Detroit Tigers.

385

Big Ten and NCAA individual golf champ in 1961, Ohio State's husky JACK NICKLAUS served notice that even bigger things lay ahead for the greatest golfer ever to come out of the Western Conference—and one of the greatest the sport has ever known as he went on to win virtually every major golf crown available.

His latest triumph came in 1967 when he won the U. S. Open with record breaking 275, one stroke better than Ben Hogan's 276 of eighteen years ago.

corps, with Bill Freehan, the best college catcher in the nation, their battery-mate. Freehan, who was All-America, posted a batting average of .585 which erased the previous league high of .500 set by Purdue's Bill Skowron.

The Wolverines, headed by Ray Senkowski, who won the singles crown and paired with Wayne Peacock to take the doubles, led Michigan to the team tennis title, but golf was something else as a husky blond from Ohio State won the individual championship and led the Buckeyes to the team honors. His name: Jack Nicklaus.

One other long reign came to an honorable end when Michigan State, winner of six straight cross-country championships and nine of the last 10, was turned back by Iowa, whose Jim Tucker romped home first, with teammates Larry Kramer and Ralph Trimble fourth and fifth respectively.

In NCAA competition something happened which was, perhaps, inevitable but nonetheless a disappointment to the Conference. For the first time in the history of the national collegiate track and field competition the Big Ten failed to win a single individual crown in the annual meet. In swimming, however, the league was still at its triumphant best as Michigan took the team title, headed by four individual victories. Frank Legacki lowered the 50-yard sprint mark to 21.4; Dick Nelson set a new record of 1:02.1 for the 100-yard surface breaststroke; Ron Clark posted a record 2:14.4 for the 200-yard surface breaststroke; and Dave Gillanders won the 200-yard butterfly. Meanwhile, Steve Jackman, the greatest swimmer in Minnesota history, cracked the 100-yard record with 48.5; Ohio State's Lou Vitucci won the high board diving event, and a Buckeye foursome of L.B. Schaefer, Tom Kovacs, Artie Wolfe and John Plain captured the 400-yard medley relay.

In gymnastics, another budding Ohio State diving star, Tom Gompf, won the national trampoline crown. Michigan State's Norm Young took the 137-pound wrestling crown, and in golf the long distance slugger from Ohio State, Jack Nicklaus, offered a portent of things to come when he took the national collegiate title, with Purdue winning the team crown.

Among administrative matters, Indiana got the good news in May of 1961 when the Conference restored the Hoosiers to good standing in the league upon the recommendation of the Commissioner who was satisfied that illegal recruiting practices had been cleaned up.

In July, Kenneth L. (Tug) Wilson, after 16 years of service, and having reached retirement age, stepped down in favor of the new Commissioner, William R. Reed, who had formally been chosen earlier in the Spring. Subsequent important business transacted by the Conference came in December when it enacted new financial aid rules for athletic grants-in-aid, eliminating the "need" principle, and installed an academic requirement of predicted college success based on high school rank

John D. Dewey became Assistant to the Commissioner of the Big Ten in 1961.

John D. Dewey   Kay Fred Schultz

Kay Fred Schultz joined the Conference staff in 1961. He is Director of the Big Ten Service Bureau.

William R. Reed became Commissioner of the Big Ten following Tug Wilson's retirement in 1961.

and aptitude tests. The predicted grade-point-average must not be below 1.7. A new contract with the Coast Conference was authorized to re-establish the closed agreement between the two leagues for the Rose Bowl game.

Three mainstays of Wisconsin's championship team in 1962 were PAT RICHTER, two-time All-America end (1961-62) and one of the great wingmen in Conference

Quite possibly the most exciting thing about the 1962 football season was the last 15 minutes of it. Specifically, the fourth quarter of the Rose Bowl game in which Conference champ, Wisconsin, was squared off with Southern California. A Conference champ which went into that final period dragging a 35-14 thumping behind them with every indication that things would go from bad to abominable. A Conference champ which then proved its real class by getting off the floor and providing

1962

history; ROGER PILLATH, an outstanding tackle; and LOU HOLLAND, a fleet halfback who was the league's leading scorer.

PAT RICHTER   LOU HOLLAND

ROGER PILLATH

what surely must have been the most dramatic turn-about in Rose Bowl history before time ran out with the Badgers obviously needing only one more shot to pull a victory from the 42-37 count remaining against them at the gun.

The Badgers were only a dark horse in the league race that year. Upper second division at best, on the basis of a good tough line that featured the great Pat Richter at one end, and Ron Carlson at the other; rambunctious Roger Pillath and Roger Jacobazzi at tackles; Steve Schenck and Steve Underwood, a fine pair of guards, and tough Ken Bowman at center.

There were a couple of fast, tough halfbacks in Lou Holland and Gary Kronek, and a hard-hitting fullback, Ralph Kurek. At quarterback Coach Milt Bruhn could only come up with a lean, untried third-stringer of the previous two years, Ron Vander-Kelen. Around the league most folks said, "Ron WHO?"

Ron "WHO" turned out to be the most exciting Big Ten quarterback in years, a scrambler who could thread a needle with his passes when he stopped scurrying, and a passer who could change his mind with arm cocked and squirt away for a good gainer on the ground.

The tactics made him the league's total offense leader with 228 yards rushing and 1009 passing, for a new record of 1237 yards. Lou Holland, at halfback, merely turned out to be the Conference scoring champ with 11 touchdowns. All-America Pat Richter repeated as the loop's leading pass receiver with 33 for 440 yards, and, with everything clicking for them, the Badgers turned in such romps as 42-14 over Iowa, 34-12 over Michigan, 35-6 over Illinois, and a 17-8 rouser over Notre Dame. Unfortunately, the Badgers who hadn't beaten Ohio State at Columbus since before The Flood (or at least 1915) got hexed again, 14-7, for their lone defeat of the regular season as they took the Conference title.

VanderKelen's pyrotechnics in the Rose Bowl are, of course, worth noting. The Badger ace left 98,698 spectators limp by completing 33 of 48 passes for a record 419 yards including two touchdowns. He also scored on a 17-yard scrambling run. Such bombing had never been witnessed in the Bowl—and much of it came in that unbelievable fourth quarter when the Badgers got three touchdowns and a safety, with VanderKelen riddling the confused Trojans so mercilessly that it was obvious that all Wisconsin had to do was get hold of the ball once more to score the winning TD. The Badgers, however, had scored with a minute to go and the Trojans desperately ate the ball.

At honors time, the Badgers' Pat Richter repeated as All-America end; Purdue's dynamic Don Brumm made it at tackle; Michigan State's explosive George Saimes was a fullback choice; and Northwestern supplied passing whiz Tom Myers at quarterback, and Jack Cvercko, a larruping guard.

Few Cinderella stories ever matched that of Wisconsin's RON VANDERKELEN who went from obscurity in 1961 to national acclaim in 1962 when his brilliant passing and scrambling led the Badgers to a Big Ten title and an amazing second-half comeback that barely fell short in the Rose Bowl against U.S.C. He was a shoo-in for Conference MVP.

JACK CVERCKO, Northwestern's fine guard, and DON BRUMM, Purdue's mighty tackle, were among a sextet of Big Ten stars who made All-America in 1961.

In brief, there had been just no way to alter things in the 1962 Big Ten basketball race. No way at all. Luke (Lucas), Hondo (Havlicek) and Mel (Nowell) were still at Ohio State as seniors and paced the Buckeyes to an unprecedented modern era record of three straight crowns, and Lucas went on to win the Conference Medal.

There was only one colossal bit of disbelief during their senior season. It came on March 3, 1962 at Madison, the second last game of the Big Ten campaign for both Wisconsin and Ohio State. Coming into the game Ohio had won 47 consecutive regular season games since losing to Indiana, 99-83 on Feburary 29, 1960 at Bloomington. The Bucks had been 74-4 for the three seasons and won 27 straight for Big Ten play (a record) and were 22-0 on the year. Wisconsin was a team with a respectable but not particularly distinguished 16-6 to date.

Coaches had always known there could be a night like this. Fans weren't so easily convinced. The Buckeyes couldn't get the lead out of their pants, couldn't ignite their usual brilliant execution, couldn't find the basket if they'd had an escorted tour of the backboard. Havlicek was 3 for 15 from the field; McDonald was 1 for 6; Doughty 2 for 7; Knight 0 for 10; Gearhart 1 for 5; and even Big Luke was off with 8 for 18. It was the kind of shooting which made Fred Taylor wish Dr. Naismith had never gotten The Idea in the first place. The Badgers, meanwhile, fused like Agena One and got up almost as high, with Ken Seibel's 22 and Don Hearden's 29 points providing the main spark. Certainly it was the most dramatic if not the biggest upset in modern Big Ten cage history. The unbeatables had been had, 86-67. It was somewhat poetic, too. The record 27 straight league wins the Buckeyes had racked up had erased the old mark of 23 set by—naturally—Wisconsin, in the Dr. Walter Meanwell era.

It was Ohio, however, in the NCAA tourney once more—and once again it was Cincinnati fighting its way to the finals in the Bearcats' bracket. In the semi-finals against Wake Forest the night before the big one, Lucas came down from a rebound all in a heap, his knee twisted under him. Overnight ministration fell short of the required medical miracle—and with Lucas obviously sub-par the Bucks, number one in the nation, dropped the NCAA finale.

The All-America lists for the year included, of course, the fabulous Lucas and Buckeye teammate John Havlicek, who for three years had been an explosive scorer and the best defensive forward in the league; and Purdue's tremendous Terry Dischinger. It was the first and only time in the history of college basketball that two men from the same league (Lucas and Dischinger) had made All-America three straight years. For Dischinger, as well, it was the third straight year he'd led the loop in scoring—only the second time it had been done—with his three-year total of 1248 points setting an all-time Conference mark.

Backcourtman KEN SEIBEL was the sparkplug of Wisconsin's victory over Ohio State in 1962 when the Badgers scored one of the most startling upsets in modern Big Ten cage history to hand Jerry Lucas & Co. their lone defeat of the regular season.

Purdue's TERRY DISCHINGER certainly may be labeled one of the greatest players in collegiate basketball annals. The 6-7 center shared the distinction with Jerry Lucas of being the only modern era players to make All-America three straight years (1960-61-62), and his 1248 points in Conference play was a three-year league record (exceeded only by the 1451 scored by Indiana's Don Schlundt who played four seasons under Korean War regulations). A big man who was a smoothie, with all the moves and instincts of a backcourtman, Dischinger's rebounding, passing and play-making were as brilliant as his shooting.

MIKE TROY

ALAN SOMERS

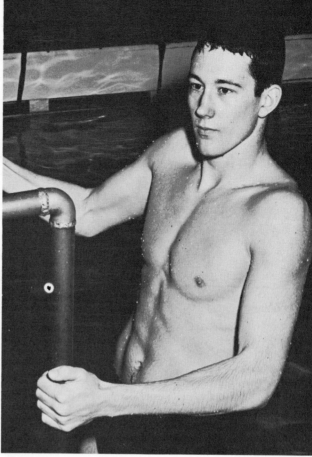

MIKE TROY

ALAN SOMERS

Among the tankful of great Indiana swimmers developed by Coach Jim Counsilman in the 1960's were MIKE TROY, butterfly; ALAN SOMERS, freestyler; CHET JASTREMSKI, breaststroker; and TED STICKELS, individual medley. Troy, Big Ten champ for three straight years, was the only one to win an NCAA title (1960) before the Hoosiers were put on NCAA probation, pre- *venting the others from surely becoming national collegiate champions. Somers was Conference king at 440-yards and 1500-meters; Jastremski, the unbeatable breaststroker, held four world records and shared a fifth in a medley relay; Stickels, a master of all strokes, wore the Big Ten individual medley crown and held two world records for the event.*

TED STICKELS and CHET JASTREMSKI

The kind of waves made by Indiana in repeating as Big Ten swimming champ in 1962 left everybody else awash and quite certain that the Hoosiers were here to stay in the aquatic world. All they did was take eight individual crowns and a relay, which didn't leave too much for the other nine schools. Alan Somers, the Hoosier distance ace, repeated as 440 and 1500-meter king, setting new records in both, 4:20.8 and 17:37.5. Mike Troy captured the 100-yard butterfly event with a new national collegiate mark of 52.9; and repeated as 200-yard butterfly champ in a new American record time of 1:56.9. Records, in fact, were smashed all over the place by Indiana swimmers. Ted Stickels lowered the 200-yard individual medley to 2:00.1; Tom Stack smashed ex-Indianan Frank McKinney's 200-yard backstroke mark with a posting of 1:56.2 for a new American standard; and Chet Jastremski established himself as one of the nation's premier breaststrokers with a brilliant double in the 100 and the 200, setting a new Conference record of 2:13.9 in the 200. Tacked on to all this was a Hoosier victory in the 400-yard medley relay, with a new American mark by a quartet of Tom Stack, Ken Naksone, Larry Schulhof, and Pete Sintz.

There were, of course, some glittering performances by other Conference stars. Minnesota's magnificent Steve Jackman pulled off a sprint double for the second straight year in the 50 and 100, with a new mark of 47.4 in the century. Mike Wood, of Michigan State, set a new record of 2:01.3 for the 220-yard freestyle; Ohio State's L.B. Schaefer posted a record-breaking 54.2 for the 100-yard backstroke; a Michigan State foursome of Jeff Mattson, Doug Rowe, Bill Wood and Mike Wood, set a new record of 3:14.5 for the 400-yard freestyle relay; and there was really pleasant news in the fact that Purdue could boast of its first Conference diving champ, as graceful John Vogel took the high board championship—the first diver the last 30 years and more who did not come from Ohio State or Michigan. Vogel almost brought off a double, but had to take second place behind Ohio's Mexican star, Juan Botella, on the low board.

In track, there was much relief in Madison when Wisconsin ended a lengthy championship dry spell and took its first indoor team title in 30 years. The Badgers were led by Bill Smith's 60-yard dash victory; a record-equalling 70-yard low hurdle flight by Larry Howard; a shotput win by Don Hendrickson and a mile relay victory by Roger Shick, Tom Creagan, Terry Pitts and Elzie Higginbottom. Meanwhile, Michigan's Latvian star, Ergas Leps, loped to a neat double, with a record-breaking 1:52.6 for the 880 and a solid win in the mile.

Michigan repeated as champion outdoors, however. Footballer Ben McRae took the high and low hurdles; Charley Aquino's 1:19.2 tied the 660 mark; Rod Denhart set a new record of 15-¾ for the pole vault and, of course, there was Leps again with a victory in the mile and a second place in the 880 behind a record-tying 1:50.1 by Iowa's Bill Frazier.

Although barred from the NCAA swimming meet in the early 1960's because of football recruiting irregularities, Indiana freestyler PETE SINTZ in 1962 had the satisfaction of turning in a 4:17 for the 440 in Big Ten competition, fastest ever swum by a collegian.

Other traffic of note found Wisconsin's Elmars Ezerins taking the shot-put and discus; Purdue's lithe Nate Adams sped to a sprint double in the 100 and 220; and Ohio State's Paul Warfield, in winning the broad jump, became the second All-America halfback to take a long-jump title that year because Michigan State's Sherman Lewis had won it indoors.

Having ended Illinois' long gymnastic reign the year before, Michigan proved it was no fluke by repeating for the team title. Arno Lascari was the lone Wolverine to take an individual crown (parallel

LARRY HOWARD, with a brilliant double victory in the 70-yard high and low hurdles, led Wisconsin to its first indoor track title in 30 years, in 1962.

ALLEN CARIUS of Illinois was one of the finest cross-country runners in Conference history. He took the league individual crown two straight years, 1962 and 1963.

All-America pitcher, TOM FLETCHER, with a league-leading 5-0 campaign, was a big factor in Illinois' 1962 championship drive.

DOUG MILLS, JR., of Illinois, one of the league's leading pitchers for 1962, had an ERA of 1.03 and hurled a no-hitter against Wisconsin.

bars) but Michigan piled up points in six of the eight events to take the title. Ray Hadley, Minnesota's versatile star, won the all-around crown. Illinois, however, wasn't being budged from its fencing pre-eminence and repeated as titlists (the 9th time in 11 years) with Nick Szluha and Stu Cohn winning titles in sabre and foil. Iowa fought its way to the wrestling championship, with Norm Parker, at 123 pounds, and Tom Huff, 130, leading the Hawkeye point-makers with individual titles. Michigan State regained the cross-country team title after a one-year interruption by Iowa had broken the Spartans' six-year streak, but Illinois' Allen Carius won the individual crown.

Illinois, with tight pitching and league-leading fielding, won the league baseball title as only two Illini hit above .300. All-Conference and All-America pitcher Tom Fletcher, and Doug Mills paced the mound staff with 5-0 marks, with Ron Johnson aiding with 3-1. All-Conference Lloyd Flodin was a fitting battery-mate for them and topped the hitters with .370, with shortstop Tony Eichelberger next with .365. The league's leading hitter was Indiana's second sacker, Eddie LaDuke, with a robust .431.

Michigan made off with its fourth straight team title in tennis but future events were being portented by a senational Northwestern sophomore, Marty Riessen, son of the Wildcat coach, who took the first of three straight singles crowns and teamed up with Jim Erickson for doubles honors.

With Jack Nicklaus out of the way, Indiana took the Conference team title in golf but it was Illinois' Mike Toliuszis who picked off the individual crown.

With Indiana still on NCAA suspension for recruiting violations, Ohio State returned to the throne room in NCAA swimming. L.B. Schaefer and bril-

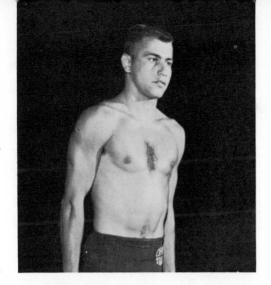

Big Ten champ LOU VITUCCI, latest in a long line of great Ohio State divers, won the low and high board crowns in leading the Buckeyes to the 1962 NCAA championship.

liant diver, Lou Vitucci led the Bucks to their team triumph. Schaefer set a new record of 53.9 for the 100-yard backstroke and also won the 200-yard event. Vitucci repeated as high board titlist and reclaimed his mastery of the low board which he had lost to Florida State's Curt Genders the year before. Artie Wolfe took the 200-yard butterfly for the Buckeyes; Marty Mull picked off the 200-yard individual medley; and a Buckeye quartet of Schaefer Tom Kovacs, Wolfe and John Plain set a new record of 3:37.6 winning the 400-yard medley relay. Other Conference stars were making their presence known, too. Illinois got its first NCAA championship since 1935, from Jim Spreitzer who won the 220 freestyle. Minnesota's Virgil Luken captured the 200-yard breaststroke; Michigan State's foursome of Jeff Mattson, Doug Rowe, and Bill and Mike Wood ripped off a record-shattering 3:15.8 for the 400-yard freestyle relay; and Michigan's Dick Nelson repeated as 100-yard surface breaststroke champ with a new record of 1:01.7.

For the second year in a row, the Big Ten failed to produce a single winner in NCAA track, and it was becoming increasingly apparent that the more stringent admission standards for Conference scholarships were going to have the strongest effect on the cinder sport.

In an unusual situation, both Illinois and Michigan were picked to represent District Four in the NCAA baseball tournament, with the Wolverines eliminating the Illini in a preliminary round and then going on to meet Santa Clara in the finals of the College World Series, in Omaha. There, in a 15-inning title game, the longest ever played in the tourney, the Wolves defeated the Coast entry, 5-4.

Sherwyn Thorson, Iowa's great grid lineman, was the only Big Ten winner in the NCAA wrestling tournament, where he took heavyweight honors in a group which, uniquely, found the Big Ten providing the top four finishers. Behind Thorson were

Roger Pillath, of Wisconsin, John Baum, of Michigan State, and Northwestern's Rory Weber.

Three Conference stars took championships in the national gymnastics meet. Illinois' Mike Aufrecht won on side horse; Michigan State's Dale Cooper took the still rings crown, and the Spartans' Steve Johnson triumphed on the trampoline. There was a close one in tennis, where Northwestern's Marty Riessen lost in the finals to Southern California's Rafael Osuna, of Mexico, later a Davis Cupper.

Two matters of more than transient interest were voted upon by the Conference administrators in 1962. Progression toward a round-robin football schedule was suspended, and in its place the joint group decided upon a seven game league schedule for all members. The Rose Bowl came alive again on a more definite basis when a contract was signed between the Big Ten and Association of Western Universities (Pacific Coast Conference) to provide the bowl adversaries for an indefinite period.

1963

The freshman class which had arrived at Illinois the same year that Pete Elliott took over as head coach from Ray Eliot (1960), grew up a bit late but they did get there, and in 1963, as seniors, they gave the Illini a Big Ten title. It wasn't an overwhelmingly brilliant ball club but it had good depth, fierce desire, just enough individual talent and plenty of muscilage provided by seniors such as Dick Butkus, Archie Sutton, Rich Callaghan and Mike Taliaferro. The Orange and Blue posted a solid 5-1-1 Conference record and went on to knock over a good Washington team in the Rose Bowl, 17-7.

Callaghan and Bill Pasko were excellent ends; Sutton and Bill Minor were thumping tackles; Dick Deller, Wylie Fox and Ed Washington were an unusually fine guard trio, and Butkus, of course, was the all-over, all-purpose center—not only the greatest in Illinois history but one of the all-time greats in the Conference. Behind this line was Mike Taliaferro, a sharp passer and a handy rusher, at quarterback whose running talents were put to use frequently because the Illini offense was geared to just a modicum of passing. In fact, the figures showed a less than average championship overhead game. Taliaferro hit on only 32 passes for 72 yards and his understudy, Fred Custardo was only 14 for 39. The rest of the enemy real estate was picked up by a strong running game featuring Sam Price and Jim Warren, fleet halfbacks, and a big, blasting sophomore fullback, Jim Grabowski, who would obliterate Red Grange's rushing records before he was through.

As a team, Illinois led the league in only one of the 10 departments listed in Conference statistics (such as rushing, passing, first downs, net yards). The one statistic—scoring—was the important one as the Illini led the league with a modest but effective 17.9 points a game.

Two bumps appeared on Illinois' championship road. First came a wild 20-20 tie with Ohio State

| DICK BUTKUS | ARCHIE SUTTON | DON HANSEN | MIKE TALIAFERRO |

Showing the way for Illinois' 1963 championship team were DICK BUTKUS, one of the finest centers and linebackers in the history of collegiate football, the league's MVP and a two-time All-America (1963-64); ARCHIE SUTTON, a booming tackle; DON HANSEN, a fierce linebacker; and MIKE TALIAFERRO, a nimble, pass-pitching quarterback.

and then, later in the season, came a stunning 14-8 setback by a mediocre Michigan team that was to lose four games that season and tie another. In the season finale with Michigan State, with the scent of Roses in the air for both clubs, it was the Illini who "rose" to the challenge and won the invitation with a 13-0 calling card.

Dick Butkus, the 6-3, 250-pound linebacking terror, won the Conference MVP award and All-America honors as well. Other Big Ten All-Americas were Sherman Lewis, the Michigan State speedster halfback; Mike Reilly, Iowa's terrific guard; and Carl Eller, the gigantic and mobile Minnesota tackle.

In basketball, the Conference in 1963 had breathed a sigh of relief. Ohio State had lost Lucas, Havlicek and Nowell. After three years the league could look forward to a new champion; but, a lot of people had overlooked a skinny, burr-topped, 6'-8" center named Gary Bradds who had been Luke's rarely used substitute as a sophomore in Lucas' senior season. Now that Bradds had the job to himself

| MIKE REILLY | SHERMAN LEWIS | CARL ELLER |

Four Big Ten stars were named to the 1963 All-America, including these three: MIKE REILLY, Iowa's stalwart guard; SHERMAN LEWIS, Michigan State's speedy halfback; and CARL ELLER, Minnesota's gigantic and mobile tackle. The fourth designee was Illinois' tremendous center-linebacker, Dick Butkus.

Ohio upset a lot of plans. Bradds led the loop in scoring with a 30-point average, highest yet recorded, and when the firing was over the Buckeyes were still title tinged, for the fourth straight year, although they were sharing the royal purple with Illinois, with identical 11-3 records.

The virtually all new club which Coach Fred Taylor built around Bradds included Jim Doughty and Doug McDonald at forwards, and Dick Reasbeck, a semi-regular the year before, and sophomore Dick Ricketts, at guard. Two early season losses, to Illinois and Iowa all but put the Bucks out of it but they got squared away and went on a winning streak that almost took the all the marbles. In the season finale at Bloomington, against Indiana, the Buckeyes and Hoosiers engaged in a barn-burner which almost had repercussions on an administrative level as Hoosier fans left their seats in the last minute of play and ringed the playing floor when Indiana started to cut an apparently safe Ohio lead in the last two minutes of play. Things almost got out of hand, and then Gary Bradds went out on personals just before the end with everything all tied up. The Hoosiers took it 87-85 in overtime and it cost the Buckeyes the undisputed title.

Meanwhile, it had been a beautifully co-ordinated Illinois team which carved out—and deserved—a share of the league championship honors. Dave Downey, a 20-point a game scorer, led the Illini at forward, with swift Bob Starnes his running mate. Bill Burwell, a New York City import, gave Illinois strength at center, and Bill Small and Tal Brody were two smooth, play-making backcourtmen.

Strangely enough, it was also an encounter with Indiana which cost the Illini a possible undisputed title. In an early season game Illinois had turned back the Hoosiers 104-101, but then came a totally unexpected 84-77 defeat by Wisconsin which made

Slender JIMMY RAYL, Indiana backcourtman and 1963 All-America, set a Conference single game scoring record of 56 points against Michigan State. (He had also hit for 56 the previous year against Minnesota in overtime.) His average for the year was 27 per game.

the Illini become somewhat unstuck for its next contest which was a return with the Hoosiers. In an almost identical turnabout of the score, Indiana nipped the Illini 103-100. The third Illinois loss was an 84-81 affair with Michigan, with only three games to go. The Illini pulled out their finale with Iowa, 73-69, and when the Buckeyes ran afoul of Indiana it was an Illinois-Ohio tie.

Ohio had been to the NCAA three years in a row, therefore Illinois became the Conference representative; but, after an opening victory over Bowling Green, the Illini were knocked out of the tourney by Loyola of Chicago, the eventual champion.

Bradds, the Conference MVP as well as scoring leader, led the All-Conference selections, and had distinguished company in Downey, the Illinois star forward; Bill Buntin, Michigan's great sophomore center; Jimmy Rayl, Indiana's splended splinter and shooting whiz in the backcourt; his Hoosier teammate Tom Bolyard, a fine forward; and Purdue's hot scorer, Mel Garland, a guard. Bradds was Conference MVP and he and Rayl made All-America.

Indiana made it three straight in the Conference swimming meet, and people were wondering whether there was any reason why the Hoosiers might not make it 23, the way Jim Counsilman was attracting youthful aquatic stars to Bloomington and shaping them into champions. His 1963 edition tied Ohio State's record of nine individual titles to make another runaway of the team crown. Double winners accounted for six of them. Gary Verhoeven set a national collegiate mark of 1:48.2 for the 200-yard freestyle and a Big Ten record of 4:59 for 500-yards. Chet Jastremski repeated as 100- and 200-yard breaststroke champ, and posted a new national collegiate mark of 2:13.2 for the latter. Ted Stickels, the jack-of-all-strokes, took a brilliant pair of vic-

DAVE DOWNEY, a virtually unanimous choice at forward on the All-Conference team, led Illinois to a share of the championship in 1963.

tories in the 200- and 400-yard individual medleys, tying the meet mark and setting a new American collegiate record of 2:00.1 over the shorter route, and posting still another American mark of 4:17.6 for the 400. Meanwhile, the Hoosier point total soared with Alan Somers' American record of 17:36.0 for the 1650-yard freestyle, Tom Stock's national collegiate mark of 1:56.9 for the 200-yard backstroke; and Rick Gilbert's diving victory off the low board.

It was almost a two-school tourney as far as firsts were concerned, with Minnesota picking up six, it's most ever. The Gophers' sensational Steve Jackman repeated as 50- and 100-yard sprint champ, with an American record of 21.0 and a Big Ten mark of 47.3, respectively. Walt Richardson posted and American mark of 50.6 for the 100-yard butterfly and another of 1:53.7 for the 200-yard event for a sparkling double; and two Gopher relay teams splashed to victory; Al Erickson, Virg Luken, Walt Richardson and Steve Jackman set a new national collegiate mark of 3:34.8 for the 400-yard medley, and Mike Stauffer, Richardson, Ralph Allen and Jackman took the 400-yard freestyle event in a new collegiate time of 3:13.4. The only non-Indiana or Minnesota victories were taken by Michigan State's Jeff Mattson in the 100-yard backstroke and by Ohio's Lou Vitucci off the high board.

Track news in 1963 was made by Iowa when the Hawkeyes took their first indoor crown since 1929 and their first outdoor title, ever. The outdoor title was a special kind of record. No Conference school had ever gone that long (since 1899) without winning a championship in any major, popular sport. Good balance did it for Coach Francis Cretzmeyer's bunch. Indoors, Gary Hollingsworth took the 440; Roger Kerr set a new league mark of 1:10 for the

Middle distance aces BILL FRAZIER in the half mile and ROGER KERR in the 660 both won their specialties indoors and outdoors in 1963 as Iowa took its first title in almost 35 years on the boards and their first ever outdoors.

DICK SCHLOEMER

Michigan State's DICK SCHLOEMER won the foils title and LOU SALAMONE the sabre crown as the Spartans took their first league fencing championship in 1963.

LOU SALAMONE

660; Bill Frazier took the 880 in a record-breaking 1:51.8; Gary Fischer won the mile, and a foursome of Gary Richards, Scott Rocker, Hollingsworth and Kerr set a mile relay mark of 3:14.7. Other league marks were posted by Wisconsin high-jumper Bill Holden, with 6'-10", and Michigan's Chuck Aquino with 2:09.9 for the 1000-yards.

Outdoors, the Hawks just got by Wisconsin, 48-47, with pretty much the same cast. Roger Kerr took the 660 in a record-setting 1:17.4; Bill Frazier again took the half-mile; a Hawk mile relay team of Richards, Hollingsworth, Frazier and Kerr set a new league mark of 3:11.2; and Don Gardner captured a new event on the program, the 330-yard intermediate hurdles.

Michigan took the league wrestling championship, led by individual victories by Rick Bay, at 157 pounds, and Jack Barden, heavyweight. The Wolverines also repeated as gymnastics champs—their third in a row—with Gil Larose scoring victories in free exercise, long horse and all-around; and Arno Lascari winning the high bar, parallel bars and side horse. Fred Sanders on trampoline was another Wolverine individual king.

Michigan State won its first Conference fencing title, led by Dick Schloemer, foil champ, and Lou Salamone, sabre victor. Foil was taken by Ohio State's Gary Price.

In Spring sports, Illinois repeated as baseball champ with a 10-5 record, led by Jerry Weygandt, league-leading pitcher who was 5-0 and had an ERA of 1.71. Lloyd Flodin, his capable batterymate, Jerry Renner, a .381-hitting first baseman, and Tony Provenzano, all-league centerfielder (.318), were other Illinois stars. Top hitter in the loop was a powerful Wisconsin halfback named Fred (Rick) Reichardt, who posted .429 and who would be heard from even more dramatically in another year.

Northwestern's brilliant Marty Riessen repeated as Conference tennis singles champ and paired with Clark Graebner, Jr., to take the doubles and lead the Wildcats to the team title. Both, of course, would subsequently be international stars of note and American Davis Cuppers. Roger Eberhardt became Wisconsin's third individual golf titlist but Minnesota took the team crown.

The Big Ten took only one team championship in NCAA competition in 1963 but for Michigan it was a welcome first. Under Newt Loken, the ex-Minnesota star, the Wolverines had made rapid progress in gymnastics competition in recent years, and now Luken put together one of the strongest teams that the league—and the nation—had ever seen. Gil Larose, possibly the finest gymnast in Michigan history, led the team triumph in the nationals with three brilliant victories: long horse, horizontal bar and all-around. Arno Lascari added the parallel bar title, Gary Erwin took top honors on trampoline, and Mike Henderson tied for first in free exercise. The six Wolverine titles equalled the record set by Penn State in 1954 and again in 1959.

Eight swim crowns went to Conference athletes, but the team title got away to Southern California for the second time. Minnesota's great Steve Jackman repeated as 50-yard sprint champ; Ohio State's Marty Mull took his second straight 200-yard individual medley crown in a record-breaking 2:01.6; the Buckeyes' diving ace, Lou Vitucci, repeated his double on the high and low boards; and Michigan's Dick Nelson held onto his 100-yard surface breaststroke championship but had to share it with Princeton's Gardiner Green who touched out with him. First time winners were Michigan's Ed Bartsch in the 200-yard backstroke and Minnesota's new rising star, Walt Richardson, in the 100-yard butterfly. A Minnesota foursome of Al Ericksen, Virgil Luken, Richardson and Jackman captured the 400-yard medley relay in record time of 3:35.2.

For the third time in history, the Conference

STEVE JACKMAN

Never noted for swimming supremacy, Minnesota in recent years, nevertheless, produced two of the finest tankmen of modern times. STEVE JACKMAN was easily the greatest sprinter in Conference annals, becoming the only man ever to score 50- and 100-yard doubles for three years in a row (1961-62-63). He also added the NCAA 100-yard crown in 1961; both the 50 and 100 NCAA titles in 1962 and the 50-yard championship in 1963. WALT RICHARDSON, master of the butterfly stroke, took Conference crowns at 100- and 200-yards and the NCAA 100-yard title in 1963; and in 1964 won the Conference 100-yard title again and added two more NCAA championships at 100- and 200-yards.

WALT RICHARDSON

failed to take even a single individual title in track, and there was only one collected in wrestling as Michigan's Jack Barden took the 191-pound crown.

On the administrative front, the Conference approved of participation in the "Inter-Conference Letter of Intent," which meant that collegiate leagues who were part of the agreement would not be able to recruit a prospective athlete once he had signed a letter of intent to any of the participating Conference schools. The Big Ten athletic directors also voted to limit football scouting of league opponents to no more than one game but with unlimited film exchange for scouting purposes. The Joint Group also amended league policies to allow one personal visit by a Conference coach to the home of a prospect between December 1 and the first date for the issuance of tenders.

Never, perhaps, had a year produced so many scholars among the league's outstanding athletes. Winners of the Conference Medal in the spring of 1963 were Pat Richter, Wisconsin's All-America end; Dave Downey, Illinois' All-Conference forward; Paul Flatley, Northwestern's great end; Chet Jastremski, Indiana's record-smashing swimmer; Chuck Aquino, Michigan's Big Ten track champion; Dick Schloemer, Michigan State fencing titlist; and the greatest name in Big Ten basketball history, Ohio's Jerry Lucas.

1964

On a piercingly cold late November afternoon, with the temperature in Ohio Stadium hovering around 20 degrees, a booming Michigan punt with less than a minute to go in the first half carried from the Wolverines' 20-yard line to the waiting Buckeye safetyman on about his own 30—and nobody among the 83,000 in the huge horseshoe had an idea that the story of the Big Ten season and a Rose Bowl invitation were carrying with that punt.

Going into the game the Bucks were 5-0 in the Conference and 7-1 for the season, with only an

Stars galore paced Michigan to its 1964 Big Ten championship, including triple-threat BOB TIMBER-LAKE, All-America quarterback and Conference MVP; MEL ANTHONY, hard-hitting fullback; and JOHN HENDERSON, a talented end.

upset by Penn State blotching their record. Michigan had wins over the Air Force Academy and Navy, but were 5-1 in the league, having taken a 21-20 nip by Purdue, fummixed mostly by the brilliant Boilermaker sophomore quarterback whiz, Bob Griese, and slick Bob Hadrick, his pass-grabbing end.

The Wolverines were big, deep and good. John Henderson and Jim Conley sparkled at end while Bill Yearby and Tom Mack were huge, mobile tackles. Dave Butler, John Marcum and Bill Keating were top guards and Brian Patchen a steady center. Triple-threat Bob Timberlake was a strong-armed, hard-running quarterback, directing swift halfbacks Carl Ward and Jim Detwiler, and a tough fullback, Mel Anthony. Tom Cecchini was an ace linebacker and Dick Rindfuss and Rick Volk were brilliant defensive halfbacks.

The Buckeye line was bulwarked by Bill Spahr, a crack end; Bill Davidson, a tremendous tackle and Dan Poretta, a great guard. Ike Kelley and Tom Bugel were the best pair of linebackers in the league. Arnie Chonko was the loop's best safety man. Quarterback Don Unverfurth directed a strong running attack built around Willard Sander, a pulverizing fullback, and hard-nosed Bo Rein, a terrific sophomore halfback.

It was Rein who waited to field that Michigan punt in the waning seconds of a scoreless first half. As Woody Hayes said afterwards: "He's a tremendous punt-handler. He's fielded a hundred of them in his day." On this day, however, the sun produced a brilliant glare, the frigid wind made fingers icy and every punt situation was a second act curtain in this drama for all the marbles.

The wind shifted violently as the ball tumbled down toward Rein. He clutched for it but the ball slid off his fingers, bounded toward the Ohio goal and was smothered by a white Michigan jersey on

BOB TIMBERLAKE

MEL ANTHONY

JOHN HENDERSON

GARY SNOOK, *Iowa's pin-point passing quarterback, set an all-time Conference aerial mark in 1964 when he fired for 1544 yards on 110 completions (out of 234 attempts). His chief target was All-America flanker, Karl Noonan, who set a new league mark of 40 catches. Snook's total of 1560 yards (with 16 rushing) also made him the league's new total offense champion.*

about the 20. Two plays later Bob Timberlake drilled a pass to Jim Detwiler who took it on the four and twisted between two Buckeye defenders for the TD, with only seconds remaining in the half.

Up until then the two teams might have played all day without scoring, and, except for a Timberlake field goal in the third quarter, nobody got too close to a goal line. So, the Wolverines had a 10-0 victory, the Big Ten title and a Rose Bowl date with Oregon State—whom they creamed 34-7.

The Conference contributed a record (for any league) 11 players to the All-America lists. Conference MVP Bob Timberlake and mighty tackle, Bill Yearby, came from Michigan. Illinois' Jim Grabowski and Indiana's jarring Tom Nowatzke shared fullback honors. Two other Illini—the tremendous center and linebacker, Dick Butkus, and safety-man George Donnelly, were choices, along with Indiana's fierce guard, Don Croftchek; Iowa's brilliant pass-catching flanker, Karl Noonan; Purue's hard-hitting end, Harold Wells; and two superb Ohio State defensive stars, Arnie Chonko, at safety, and Dwight (Ike) Kelley, the linebacker.

Not since 1948 had Michigan won a league basketball championship, and 16 years was a long time to go without a major sport title for a school with the Wolverines' proud and accomplished athletic background. The 1964 season was the one Michigan fans had been waiting for—the varsity debut of the greatest basketball player ever to

TOM NOWATZKE, *Indiana fullback, proved himself one of the more remarkable competitors of the modern Big Ten era even though he played for a ninth place team as a sophomore and a last place club as a junior and senior. The 220-pounder made All-America in 1964 playing both ways, although he may even have had a better season as a junior and a one-man gang for the Hoosiers. In his junior year he led the league in rushing with 486 yards on 98 carries for a 5-yard average in seven Conference games; set an Indiana season rushing mark of 756 yards for all games; a school scoring record of 58 points; a field goal mark of five; led in interceptions with four; fumble recoveries with five; and was an outstanding linebacker.*

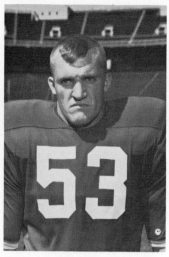

KARL NOONAN　　　　GEORGE DONNELLY　　　　IKE KELLEY　　　　HAROLD WELLS

The Big Ten contributed eleven players to the All-America squad in 1964, the most ever picked from a single Conference. They included Illinois' alert safety-man, GEORGE DONNELLY; Purdue's brilliant end, HAROLD WELLS; Ohio State's demon linebacker, IKE KELLEY; and Iowa's record-setting, pass-snatching end, KARL NOONAN.

enroll at Ann Arbor. None other, of course, than Cazzie Russell, the 6-5 sophomore out of Chicago who, it was reported, could do everything that needed to be done with a basketball. Maybe it was true; but, there was nothing to worry about. Cazzie and a basketball went together like Brigitte Bardot and her towel, and just as effectively. He averaged 26.1 per game from his backcourt position and, with Bill Buntin, the Wolves' star junior center, averaging 24.6, they formed the highest scoring tandem in Big Ten court history. They had to. Oliver Darden, the next high Wolverine pointmaker, hit for only 10.6 (but was a demon on the boards). With Larry Tregoning at forward, and Bob Cantrell at the other guard spot, they put together an 11-3 season, and if it hadn't been for a couple of in-and-out-again field goal attempts the Wolverines could have had quite a year. A late roll-around-the-rim cost them an 86-85 defeat by Ohio State, and a final shot by Purdue got there just right to give the Boilermakers an 81-79 decision in the season finale. In between came the Wolverines' lone real larruping of the year, 89-75 by Minnesota.

So Michigan had to accept an 11-3 title-tie with no stranger to such emminence—Ohio State—and for the Buckeyes it made it an all-time league record of five straight championships as Gary Bradds had a phenomenal season that found him hitting for 40 or more points in six straight games, a loop mark a way off by itself, and posting still another Conference scoring high of 33.9 points per game. Dick Ricketts, a smooth-geared guard, was Bradds' chief aider-and-abetter in the Bucks' pennant drive.

Bradds, the Conference MVP for the second year in a row, led the league's All-America choices, which also included Michigan's Bill Buntin and Rus-

sell. Meanwhile, a new star was rising in the Conference in a 6-4 Purdue forward named Dave Schelhase, whose second-place finish to Bradds in the loop scoring race gave notice that for two more years he'd be The Man With The Gun . . . as indeed it would turn out.

In swimming it was again no contest as Indiana made it four team crowns in a row, with the Hoosiers winning seven individual titles and a relay. Ted Stickels repeated his double championship in the 200- and 400-yard individual medley; graceful Rick Gilbert was a double winner off the high and low diving boards; Pete Hammer took two backstroke wins at 100- and 200-yards; Fred Schmidt

DICK and TOM VAN ARSDALE, Indiana's twin forwards, were unique in Big Ten basketball history. Stars for three years (1962-63-64), the hot-shooting, all-around virtuosos were as close in their cage efforts as they were fraternally. In their senior year Dick, who was fifth in the league scoring race, made the All-Big Ten first team; Tom, seventh in the loop scoring column, made the second all-star team, and both of them shared the Hoosiers' MVP award.

400

Ohio State's 6'-8" GARY BRADDS who rode the bench for Jerry Lucas as a sophomore became a star in his own right as a junior in 1963 when he averaged 30 points a game. He was chosen College Player of the Year in 1964 when he was unanimous All-America after his prodigious scoring feats astounded the league and the nation. On the way to his 33.9-point average, a Big Ten record, Bradds, in one stretch, hit for 40 or more points in six Conference games for a major collegiate record: 47 against Purdue; 48 against Michigan State; 42 against Michigan; 40 against Indiana; 49 against Illinois, and 40 against Wisconsin. For two straight seasons, 1963-64, he was the Conference MVP. His junior year pace brought the Buckeyes a co-championship with Illinois, and his senior season heroics led the Scarlet to a title share with Michigan, for an unprecedented five straight championships.

Big, powerful BILL BUNTIN led Michigan to a share of the 1964 basketball title. His 24.6 average, third best in the loop, and strong rebounding brought him All-America honors.

won the 200-yard butterfly event; and a Hoosier foursome of Tom Stock, Tom Tretheway, Larry Schulhof, and Chuck Ogilby posted a new record of 3:34.7 for the 400-yard medley relay. Michigan, meanwhile, came up with two double winners who paced the Wolverines to second place. Dick Walls won the 100- and 200-yard freestyle, with a new league mark of 1:47.3 in the latter; and Bill Farley captured the 500-yard freestyle in a record 4:57.6, and tied the mark of the 1650 freestyle in 17:36.

In wrestling, however, Michigan climbed a notch to championship status, repeating the honors won a year before. Leading the Wolves were Ralph Bahna's triumph at 123 pounds, and Lee Detrick's win at 147.

The Wolverines also took the indoor track crown, but were turned back by Wisconsin outdoors. Five individual titles went to Michigan on the boards. Kent Bernard took the 600; Ted Kelly won the 880; Des Ryan captured the mile; Al Ammermann won the high jump crown and Roger Schmitt took the shot-put. Michigan State's Bob Moreland retained his 60-yard dash crown with a record-tying 6.1; Wisconsin's Billy Smith equalled the record of 7.8 for the 70-yard low hurdles; and Ohio State's Bob Neutzling set a mark of 15-8¼ in the pole vault.

On the cinders, the first Wisconsin championship since 1931 was also marked by five individual victories. Mike Manley took the mile; Gene Dix the 120-yard high hurdles; Barry Ackerman the broad jump; Brian Bergemann the pole vault; and Don Hendrickson repeated as discus champ. The only record that went into the books was a brilliant 3:10.2 mile relay by a Michigan quartet of Romain, Hughes, Wade and Bernard.

Minnesota came back to the baseball heights in 1964 when the Gophers took the league championship with an 11-3 mark and then went on to win its third NCAA title, defeating Missouri for the national crown. It wasn't an overpowering club which canny Dick Siebert put together, placing second in team fielding but only seventh in batting. There was, however, a strong mound staff led by all-league Joe Pollack (4-1 and ERA of 1.50) and Frank Brosseau (4-1 and an ERA of 1.56). All-Conference Ron Wojciak was a brilliant battery-mate behind the plate. Bill Davis, slick first sacker, hit .377; second baseman Duane Marcus swung for a robust .333 and, although they were light hitters, outfielders Dave Huffman and Al Druskin were among the best in the league. And for the second straight year, the loop batting crown went to future Big League star, Rick Reichardt (.472) of Wisconsin.

Michigan, a rising power in the sport, took its fourth straight gymnastics crown, led by Gary Erwin's victory on trampoline; Arno Lascari's triumph on the parallel bars; and Jim Henderson's individual crown in tumbling. It was Michigan State's versatile Jim Curzi, however, who took the all-around championship. Illinois was back on top

RICK REICHARDT, *Wisconsin's star halfback, earned even bigger honors in baseball, leading the league in batting for two straight years (1963-64), being named All-America outfielder in 1964, and then signing with the Los Angeles Angels for what was reputed to be the biggest ($200,000) bonus offer ever paid.*

BYRON COMSTOCK, *of Indiana, became the first and only Hoosier golfer to win the Conference individual crown, taking the honors in 1964.*

once again, Riessen teamed with Clark Graebner, Jr., to take the doubles crown. There was also an historic first for Northwestern as Lee Assenheimer became the first Purple harrier to win the Conference individual cross-country crown—and a first for Minnesota as the Gophers took their initial team title, led by Norris Peterson, who came in second, and Tom Heinonen, who took fourth.

Two national team titles were won by Conference schools in NCAA competition for 1964. Minnesota's league baseball champs disposed of Kent State, Texas A. & M., Maine and Southern California in preliminary rounds, dropped the semi-final to Missouri, 4-0, and then, under the tourney setup of two-defeats-and-out, the Gophers took a 5-1 finals from Missouri (who had lost one to U.S.C.) to win their third national crown, the first Conference school to do so.

MARTY RIESSEN

Possibly the finest player in Conference tennis history and one of the great all-time collegians was Northwestern's MARTY RIESSEN, *only man ever to win three straight singles and three straight doubles titles (1962-63-64). His doubles partner in 63-64 was* CLARK GRAEBNER, JR., *and both later became national and international stars.*

of the fencing lists, headed by Jim Tibbetts' epee title and Bob Frase's sabre championship. Individual foil honors went to Iowa's Mike Kinsinger.

Byron Comstock became Indiana's first Conference individual golf titlist and Northwestern's brilliant Marty Riessen became the first man in 36 years to became a three-time tennis singles champion as the Wildcats also made it three straight as team champs.

In hockey, new coach Al Renfrew took a well-drilled Michigan sextet into the national tourney and beat Denver in the final, 6-3. The Wolverines were led by Tom Polonik and Gordon Wilkie, who tied for the tournament scoring championship with five goals each, but it was the Wolves' steady Bob Gray who won tournament MVP honors.

Two other league teams came close to winning national titles. Michigan State, coming on fast in soccer, went all the way to the finals before losing to Navy, 1-0, and Indiana, restored to good grace in NCAA competition, was nosed out for the swim crown by Southern California, 96-91. Balanced strength took the Hoosiers up there, as they won only two individual titles. Fred Schmidt set a new mark of 1:53.5 for the 200-yard butterfly event and Rick Gilbert won the low board diving championship. Other league winners were Minnesota's stellar Walt Richardson, repeating as 100-yard butterfly champ in a record time of 50.2; and Ohio State's latest springboard star, Randy Larson who captured high board honors.

Michigan had represented the Conference in basketball but, after getting past Loyola of Chicago and Ohio University, the Wolverines lost to Duke, 90-81 for the Eastern title.

Illinois' Craig Bell, who had taken second place in sabre in the Big Ten tourney, rose to the occasion in the nationals and won the championship while Michigan's Gary Erwin repeated as trampoline champion in gymnastics. A new tourney showed for the first time on the NCAA calendar with the appearance of the national collegiate indoor track carnival, but only one event went to a Conference school—the 60-yard high hurdles—taken by Michigan

Michigan's BOB WEBSTER, winner of the platform dive in the 1960 Olympics, received still another Gold Medal in 1964 when he successfully defended his crown. Ohio State's TOM GOMPF, winner of the Bronze Medal, stands alongside.

State grid star, Gene Washington. In the invitational mile, however, an open event, Illinois graduate, Al Carrius, former Conference distance champ and cross-country star won the event's first running. Outdoors, the Conference had an equally frustrating time of it, with only Illinois taking a title—the new 440-yard relay event—with a trio of Gilwyn Williams, Mel Blanheim, and Trent Jackson streaking home in 40.1.

Among the winners of the Conference Scholarship Medal in the Spring of 1964 were Mel Garland, Purdue's All-Conference basketball star, and Marty Riessen, Northwestern's all-time great tennis ace.

Although only two track and field athletes—a record low number—represented the Big Ten in the 1964 Olympics, there was a solid contingent of 20 Conference stars on the various Olympic squads. Seven of them were medal winners.

Michigan's Bob Webster retained the platform diving crown he'd won in 1956 and Indiana's Ken Sitzberger took the Gold Medal in the 3-meter springboard dive. Michigan's Carl Robie won the Silver Medal in the 200-meter butterfly, and Michigan State's Gary Dilley captured the Silver Medal in the 200-meter backstroke. Bronze Medals went to Ohio State's Tom Gompf in the platform dive; Indiana's Chet Jastremski in the 200-meter breaststroke; and Indiana's Fred Schmidt in the 200-meter butterfly. Schmidt also swam a leg on the Americans' record-setting 400-meter medley relay team.

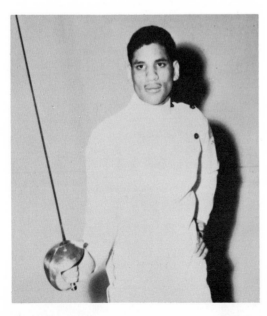

Although he only took second spot in the Big Ten fencing tournament in 1964, Illinois' CRAIG BELL reached much more stature in the NCAA meet that same year, not only winning the national collegiate sabre crown but the "Outstanding Fencer Award" as well.

1965

In track competition, Minnesota's Leonard (Buddy) Edelen ran in the marathon; Illinois' Trent Jackson was a sprinter, and the Illini's George Kerr once again raced the 800-meters for his native West Indies. Also on the swimming and diving teams —which were coached, incidentally, by Indiana's brilliant Jim Counsilman and Michigan's Dick Kimball—were Ohio State diver Lou Vitucci, Minnesota swimmers Virgil Luken and Walt Richardson, Indiana's Mike Wall, and Michigan's Bill Farley.

Michigan's Jim Kerr competed in the modern Pentathlon; Michigan State's Bill Smoke was a canoeist; Gary Cleveland, of Minnesota, a weightlifter; Wisconsin's Pete Barret was on the yachting team; Wisconsin's Bob Pickens was a wrestler; Michigan State coed, Patti Bright, was on the women's volleyball team; and Minnesota, making it a habit, contributed three hockey players to the Yanks' team: Dick Meredith, John Mayasich and Jack McCartan.

Two matters of some significance were resolved by Conference administrators. The Joint Group re-affirmed Regulation III which prohibits use of Conference athletic facilities for admission-paid exhibitions or contests by professional sports teams; and the school year of 1964 became the first in which a yearly limit of 70 tenders of grant-in-aid were placed on each member institution for any given year, with no more than 30 going to football and six to basketball, and 34 for sports other than football, basketball, hockey, soccer, lacrosse and crew. In effect, this would mean the Big Ten would be recruiting fewer athletes each year than any other major college conference.

Leading Michigan State to the Big Ten and national titles in 1965 were a whole constellation of stars including a sophomore fullback from Samoa (via Hawaii), BOB APISA; quarterback STEVE JUDAY; and guard HAROLD LUCAS, who bulwarked a ferocious Spartan defense that held three major foes (Michigan, Ohio State and Notre Dame) to minus-yardage.

The Big Ten Sky-Writers are a group of midwestern newspapermen who charter a plane each year and make the rounds of the Conference schools during pre-season football practice. Then they sagely predict how the league race will go. The Sky-Writers are quick to admit they're not always correct. In September, 1965, their consensus was that Michigan State was a young, inexperienced team and Duffy Daugherty would be fortunate to nail down a fifth place finish.

Everyone believed it but Michigan State. The Spartan non-believers simply went out and shot down the Sky-Writers with the kind of ammunition such as hadn't been brought up in the Big Ten in years.

The "young and inexperienced" Spartans under Daugherty's direction crushed 10 straight foes for an undefeated regular season and became the "most decorated" team in Conference history, if not all-time modern collegiate annals.

The backfield of senior Steve Juday, quarterback; Clint Jones, a junior; Dwight Lee, a sophomore; and Bob Apisa, the sophomore from Samoa by way of Hawaii, had perfect balance; Juday's passing and ability to roll out; slashing, breakaway speed by Jones and Lee; and blasting power by Apisa. Big Ten hurdle champ, Gene Washington, a great receiver, and Bob Viney, were talented ends; Jerry West, Don Bierowicz and Buddy Owens headed a strong tackle corps; John Karpinsky, Buddy Owens and Dave Techlin were ferocious guards; and Boris Dimitroff was a stellar center. On defense the Spartans were something special, with 280-pound Bubba Smith at end; 265-pound Harold Lucas, middle guard; Ron Goovert and Charley Thornhill, leather-sniffing linebackers, and Don Jappinga and George Webster, deadly defenders at cornerback.

Sweeping to a 7-0 Big Ten championship season on its way to 10 straight for the year, the Spartans led the Conference in offense and defense, and led

BOB APISA

HAROLD LUCAS

STEVE JUDAY

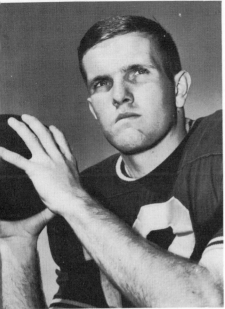

BOB GRIESE

KARL SINGER

CLINT JONES

Fifteen Big Ten stars made the various All-America teams in 1965, a new record high number for any collegiate conference. Included were BOB GRIESE, Purdue's tremendously-talented do-everything quarterback; KARL

SINGER, his teammate at tackle; and CLINT JONES, Michigan State's swift halfback and rushing star, who was just one of an incredible seven selections from the mighty Spartans.

the nation defensively, limiting its opponents to rushing yardage of 45.6 per game. Against three mighty foes—Michigan, Ohio State and Notre Dame—the Spartans held the opposition to minus-51, minus-22 and minus-12 yards respectively. Quarterback Juday ended up with 12 school passing marks, and Clint Jones and Bob Apisa rushed for 538 yards and 486 yards respectively in leading the spectacular Spartan ground attack.

At season's end the team was showered with honors: National Champion in the UPI poll; The Robert Zuppke Award from the Columbus Touchdown Club for "The Best Team with the Most Demanding Schedule;" The MacArthur Bowl presented by the National Football Foundation and Hall of Fame, as national champion, and a roomful of other trophies and awards, including an observance by Bud Wilkinson in his nationally syndicated column that in his judgment ". . . the Spartans have . . . perhaps the finest team in the history of intercollegiate football."

As if all these team honors weren't enough, Michigan State also contributed more players to the various All-America teams than any squad in the annals of modern collegiate history. There were seven Spartans honored: Steve Juday, quarterback, who erased Earl Morrall's career marks at Michigan State; Clint Jones, halfback; Gene Washington, end; Harold Lucas, middle guard; Bubba Smith, defensive end; George Webster, defensive halfback; Ron Goovert, linebacker.

On the All-Conference teams, the Spartans dominated the selection with 11 men on the first and second teams, offensively and defensively.

Michigan State's All-America contributions also helped considerably in giving the Conference 14 designees to the honor teams, the most ever by any

JIM GRABOWSKI, Illinois fullback, on his way to his second year of All-America selection in 1965, broke Red Grange's career rushing record of 2071 yards by smashing for more than 2500 during his three-year stint with the Illini. Grabowski, in 1965, also set a new single season rushing mark for the Big Ten with 996 yards and another mark of 201 carries for the year as he won the Conference MVP award.

Conference in the nation. Included were Illinois' line-smashing Jim Grabowski repeating at fullback; Michigan's Bill Yearby, repeating at tackle; Minnesota's rousing Aaron Brown, at end; Ohio State's Doug Van Horn, at tackle and Ike Kelley, repeating as linebacker; Purdue's Karl Singer, tackle, and the tremendously versatile Bob Griese, the most complete quarterback the league had seen in decades.

For Michigan State in 1965 there was only one blemish—although a major one—on an otherwise fantastic season. Coach-of-the-Year Duffy Daugherty took his titans West to Pasadena for a Rose Bowl date with so-so UCLA and for 60 minutes on New Year's Day there was evidence, once again, that "a football bounces funny," and the Spartans went home

CAZZIE RUSSELL, the greatest basketball player in Michigan history and certainly one of the finest all-time collegians, was a two-year All-America for the Wolverines in their championship years of 1964 and 1965 after serving an all-star apprenticeship as All-Big Ten in his sophomore season. A 6-5 backcourtman with a sensational shooting touch, Russell was more than a scoring threat, however; he was a rallying force for the Wolverines and everyone on the floor knew that when Michigan was in trouble Cazzie would bail them out. So well did he do it that at least six times Russell won games for Michigan with winning goals in the last 10 seconds. His all-everything virtues and his 33.2 scoring average in his senior season brought him national Player-of-the-Year honors as well as Conference MVP, the latter award having been shared with Bill Buntin, his teammate, the year before.

with a 14-12 defeat as a last-minute two-point conversion attempt by Bob Apisa was throttled on the one-yard line.

In basketball, Michigan burned up the boards and for the second straight season won the league crown —the first undisputed title for them in 17 years. On the way to a 13-1 Conference mark and 20-4 overall, Coach Dave Strack's big and bounding Wolverines got off to a shaky start by dropping early season games, 74-73 and 75-74 to Nebraska and St. Johns, but then Michigan took off and roared to 12 straight within the league before the lid shut down on the basket for them in their Conference finale as they lost to Ohio State 93-85.

Yet it was clearly the finest team in Michigan history and one of the best ever to come out of the Conference which Strack took into the NCAA tournament. Oliver Darden and Larry Tregoning at forwards, Bill Buntin at center and the amazing Cazzie Russell and George Pomey at guards, gave the Wolverines the highest scoring team in Conference annals as they set a new league mark of 1300 points for the 14-game Big Ten campaign. Every Wolverine starter averaged double figures for the only time in Michigan history and for only the second time in Conference play (Ohio State had been the first in the Lucas days of 1960).

The figures were 26.2 for Russell; 21.3 for Buntin; 14.5 for Darden; 13.1 for Tregoning and 10.1 for Pomey. Russell and Buntin with 47.5 together were a new league record tandem, as both made All-America, along with Purdue's net-burning Dave Schelhase who led the loop scorers with a 27.9 average. These three, of course, were All-Conference choices along with Lou Hudson, who posted the highest scoring average (24.8) in Minnesota history; and Skip Thoren and Tal Brody of Illinois who tied for the fifth position. It was the first time Illinois ever had two 20-plus scorers the same year (22.3 and 21.4 respectively).

The Wolverines went into the NCAA tourney with high hopes and disposed of Dayton, Vanderbilt and Princeton to gain the final with UCLA, but the speedy Westerners, the quickest team that ever played in the national tournament, raced and shot the bigger Wolverines into a 91-80 defeat.

In swimming, it began to look like the only way to stop Indiana was to pull the plug and drain the pool. The Hoosiers won their fifth straight team crown in 1965 as Jim Councilman developed balanced strength throughout. There were, however, three brilliant individual wins for the Hoosiers. Fred Schmidt took a butterfly double at 100- and 200-yards, successfully defending his league championship in the longer event with a new record of 1:51.9. An Indiana foursome of Pete Hammer, Tom Tretheway, Schmidt and Bob Williamson then set a new Conference and American mark of 3:31.55 for the 400-yard freestyle relay.

Records, in fact, were splashed up on all sides. Bill Farley, Michigan's superb freestyler, set new

A two-year All-America (1965 and 1966), Purdue's DAVE SCHELHASE was a member of that rare breed in the Big Ten who were their team's MVP three straight years. Schelhase, second in league scoring as a sophomore with a 27.1 average per game, captured point-making honors in his junior season with 27.9 and was barely beaten out by Michigan's Cazzie Russell in 1966, 33.2 to 32.2, with Russell nipping him for Conference MVP honors in his last two years.

LOU HUDSON, considered by most critics to be the outstanding basketball player in Minnesota history, was All-America for the Gophers in 1965, and posted a 24.8 scoring average for the league season.

standards in his 200-yard and 500-yard double, of 1:45.68 and 4:46.14. Teammate Carl Robie posted a two-ply spectacular with a new record of 16:54.06 for the 1650-yard event; and 4:17.54, a new mark for the 400-yard individual medley. It was a rare finish in the 1650, incidentally, with Robie being judged the winner over Farley who posted the same time but lost by a finger-length in his bid for three titles. Wolverine Paul Scheerer added two more records with a breaststroke double: 1:00.39 for 100-yards and a new American listing of 2:13.09 in the 200-yard preliminary before taking the final. Then a Michigan quartet of Hoag, Williams, Farley and Robie ripped home in 7:06.91 for a new league and American mark in the 800-yard freestyle relay.

Michigan State got into the record-busting business when Gary Dilley backstroked to the 100- and 200-yard crowns, with a new mark of 53.15 for the century; and a Spartan foursome of Darryle Kifer, Dick Gretzinger, Dilley and Jim MacMillan tore off the 400-yard freestyle in 3:11.54. One other record fell to Ohio State's versatile Bob Hopper who won the 200-yard individual medley in 1:59.91.

Illinois continued its domination of fencing by winning its 20th team crown, more than all other Conference school titles combined, as the Illini pulled off the rare feat of taking all three individual titles in addition to piling up team points. Steve Stoll won at foil; Mark Gates at epee; and Craig Bell in sabre.

Michigan almost made it a one-team show in the wrestling tournament, with five of the eight individual crowns falling to the Wolverines as they took the team title. Bob Fehrs won at 123 pounds; Bill Johannensen at 137; Jim Kamman at 147; Rick Bay at 167 and Chris Stowell at 177.

Wisconsin barely nipped Michigan State for the indoor track crown, 46 points to 45½, with four

KENT BERNARD, Michigan's great middle-distance ace, scored outstanding doubles in 1964 and 1965 when he won the 600 indoors and 440 outdoors two straight years.

Badgers taking individual crowns. Ken Latigolal took the 880; Barney Peterson won the 1000 in record time of 2:09.2; Gerry Beatty picked off the 70-yard high hurdles and Bill Holden the high jump. There were other noteworthy record performances by Michigan State's fleet football end, Gene Washington, who won the 70-yard low hurdles in 7.7; and Minnesota's Norris Peterson's repeat as two-mile champ in 9:01.8; and Michigan's Kent Bernard's repeat as 600-yard king in 1:09.9.

Michigan State came back, however, to hoist its first league track flag, with a solid team performance in the outdoor meet. Five individual crowns went to the Spartans, led by Jim Garrett's double in the 220-yard dash and broad jump. Keith Coats set a new Conference mile mark of 4:08.2; Gene Washington took the 120-yard high hurdles and Mike Bowers triumphed in the high jump. Minnesota's Norris Peterson in a remarkable replay of his indoor victory, set a new two-mile mark of 9:01.5, bettering his indoor listing by three-tenths. Iowa's Jon Reimer set a new league mark and tied the National Collegiate listing of 36.1 for the 300-yard intermediate hurdles; Michigan's George Canamare pole vaulted to a new record height of 15-9¼; and the Wolverines' Kent Bernard repeated as quarter-mile king.

A glittering 11-2 league season brought Ohio State the Conference baseball crown and took the Buckeyes into the NCAA World Series. Led by a superlative battery of Steve Arlin, ace pitcher, and Chuck Brinkman, a smart receiver; Arnie Chonko, the football All-America at first base; and Bo Rein, the star football halfback, a shortstop, the Bucks went to the NCAA tournament finals in the two-losses-and-out system which governs the college World Series. Coach Marty Karow led his club past Florida State and Washington State, then lost to Arizona State. The Bucks came back to win over Washington State in 15 innings, then tripped Arizona State 7-3, the second time around. This left only the Buckeyes and Arizona State in the finale which went to the Southwesterners in a 2-1 squeaker. Ohio State's Arnie Chonko and Steve Arlin, both of whom had made All-Conference, were picked for the All-America team. Michigan outfielder, Carl Cmejrek, meanwhile, had taken the Big Ten batting crown with .453.

Clark Graebner succeeded his former Northwestern teammate, Marty Riessen, as Conference tennis singles champion; and Indiana's brilliant duo of Dave Power and Rod McNerney took the doubles crown. Michigan, under a new scoring system of a combination of season dual meet match points and individual points earned in the Conference tournament, took the team crown.

The Wolverines' Bill Newton brought the individual golf title to Michigan for the first time in more than 20 years, but Purdue captured the team crown.

In NCAA activity, Indiana was nipped for the national swimming championship by Southern California, 285 to 278½ but Big Ten stars were very much aglow. Indiana's Sitzberger became the first Hoosier diver to score an NCAA double by taking the low and high board events; teammate Fred Schmidt, one of the greatest of modern Indiana swimmers, scored a sensational double in the 100- and 200-yard butterfly, with new records in both, 51.0 and 1:51.4; still another Hoosier, Tom Tretheway posted a new collegiate mark of 2:10.4 for the 200-yard surface breaststroke; and an Indiana foursome of Glen Hammer, Tretheway, Schmidt and Bob Williamson splashed to a new record of 3:30.7 in the 400-yard medley relay.

Meanwhile, Michigan State's sensational Gary Dilley was making waves, too. He set a new record of 52.6 for the 100-yard backstroke and tied the mark of 1:56.2 for the 200. Michigan's brilliant Carl Robie smashed the 400-yard individual medley mark with 4:16.6; and Ohio State's versatile Bob Hopper posted a new collegiate record of 1:51.8 for the 200-yard individual medley.

The Conference was shut out in 1965 as far as track and wrestling were concerned, but gymnastics produced three individual titles for Big Ten performers. Michigan State's Jim Curzi won on parallel bars and tied for first on the horizontal bar. Iowa's Glenn Gailis triumphed on still rings.

When the Conference Scholarship Medals were given out in the Spring of 1965 the recipients included the biggest batch of All-Americas and national champions, ever: Michigan's Bob Timberlake; Ohio State's Arnie Chonko; and Northwestern's Tom Myers, all of whom had been football All-Americas the previous autumn; Walt Richardson, Minnesota's swimming champion, and Glenn Gailis, Iowa's gymnastics champ.

It was a busy year on the administrative level, too. The Directors, among other matters, established a "Catastrophic Self-Insurance Plan," to provide reimbursement to a member institution for loss of income by a catastrophy resulting in the cancellation of a football game or series of games. The plan funded through television receipts, would reach a maximum of $250,000. The Joint Group also authorized two intercollegiate freshman football games

GLENN GAILIS was Iowa's first Big Ten all-around gymnastics champion in 30 years. He won the crown in 1965.

BUBBA SMITH   GENE WASHINGTON   GEORGE WEBSTER

each season. Heretofore, the Big Ten was the only major conference in the nation which didn't allow freshmen to play interschool games.

Winning back-to-back football championships in the Big Ten is one of the rarities in collegiate sports. Michigan State pulled it off in 1965-66—the first time it had been done since Ohio State's big double of 1954-55—and for good measure the Spartans survived the jinx that says champions picked to repeat just DON'T in the Western Conference. Of course, Duffy Daugherty's holdovers in 1966 could no more fail their destiny than Thursday fail to follow Wednesday. Stars in their courses, and all that . . .

What Duffy had to begin with was an awesome veteran backfield threesome of Clint Jones and Dwight Lee at halfbacks and the explosive Bob Apisa at fullback. The question was whether little, skittery Jimmy Raye could pass well enough and call the plays smart enough to make it at quarterback. From Day One in pre-season practice until the season finale, Jimmy Raye was a star.

Up front, a veteran line was led by the remarkable pass-catching end, Gene Washington, and Jerry West, a ferocious tackle. On defense the Spartans were as shatterproof as in '65, with 6-7, 285-pound Bubba Smith at end; Pat Gallinagh at tackle; and George Webster and Charley Thornhill, possibly the best brace of backer-uppers the league had ever seen. So talented were the Spartan holdovers that only two sophomores—Al Brenner, offensive end; and Charley Bailey, defensive tackle—were able to crack the starting line-up (until Apisa got hurt and sophomore Regis Cavender got the call at fullback).

For the Spartans it was a delicious romp with only two occasions forcing them to prove their consummate class. In the rain against Ohio State they trailed the fired-up Bucks 2-0 until late in the third quarter when Jimmy Raye led them on a now-or-never 85-yard touchdown drive (with two key passes paving the way) to pull it out 8-2.

This trio of All-America stars led Michigan State to its second straight league championship in 1966 and second ranking to Notre Dame in a disputed battle for top national honors. BUBBA SMITH, 6'-8", 280-pounder, was an immovable defensive end and middle guard; GENE WASHINGTON was a tremendous pass-catching end; and GEORGE WEBSTER was considered the finest corner linebacker in the nation. Other Conference All-America designees were Michigan State halfback Clint Jones and tackle Jerry West; Michigan's record setting end Jack Clancy who broke the Big Ten pass reception mark; Ohio State center Ray Prior; and Purdue's versatile quarterback Bob Griese.

1966

Then with all the national championship chips pushed to the center of the table against Notre Dame a few weeks later, observers saw the collegiate football titans battle to a 10-10 tie.

When Michigan State wound up the season with a shellacking of Indiana for its second straight undefeated regular season and another league crown, the Spartans and Irish owned a Number One Poll apiece. Then Notre Dame, with one game remaining, clobbered Southern California a week later and the Irish edged ahead for the top spot. Great claims are still being made for the 1966 Spartans, who were co-winners (with Notre Dame) of the MacArthur Bowl by the National Football Foundation as the nation's top team.

With Michigan State ineligible to return to the Rose Bowl a second straight time, second-place Purdue went to Pasadena as the Conference representative and edged out Southern California, 14-13. The Boilermakers were a sound, versatile club and it took the two best teams in the nation to beat them, with their two losses being inflicted by Notre Dame and Michigan State. The brilliant Bob Griese at quarterback was the Boilermaker energizer all year, as he was the year before, with plenty of fizz added by halfbacks Bob Baltzell, Jim Finley and Bob Hurst, and a fine sophomore fullback, Perry Williams.

Up front, Jim Beirne was one of the nation's finest pass-catching ends; Pat Labus was a hard-hit-

ting center; Jack Calcaterra, Clanton King and Lance Olssen were rousing tackles; Chuck Kyle was a sophomore find at middle guard; and George Olion was a crack defensive end. In addition, two of the the greatest defensive backs in the league were George Catavolos and John Charles, with the latter voted the outstanding player in the Rose Bowl.

In basketball, the 1966 season had marked the end of "The Cazzie Russell Era" at Michigan, and the Wolverines, in repeating as Conference champs, became only the third Big Ten team in history to win three straight titles. Russell, the Wolves' All-America backcourtman, and a two-time choice for league MVP, led the Maize and Blue to an 11-3 Conference record and a fine 23-5 overall. As league representative in the NCAA tourney the Wolverines were eliminated by Kentucky, 84-77.

Michigan State scored its first track sweep in 1966, taking both the indoor and outdoor crowns. Gene Washington, the Spartans' great football end, won both the 70-yard high and low hurdles to pace the Green and White, setting a new league mark in the highs. Another record fell to Spartan Dick Sharkey who posted 9:01.4 for two-miles. A fourth individual crown went to Michigan State's

BOB GRIESE, Purdue's two-time All-America quarterback, set an all-time Conference record for total yardage gained in three years of play with 4829 yards passing and running. His 288 yards, passing, against Illinois in 1966 was another league mark for a single game as he won Big Ten MVP honors and was runner-up in the balloting for the Heisman Trophy. The versatile Boilermaker also handled Purdue's punting, point-after and field goal attempts, and kick-offs.

Four generations of Indiana athletic greats in a recent get-together on the Hoosier campus: LOU WATSON, current Indiana basketball coach, who starred in the early '50s under Coach BRANCH McCRACKEN, second from left, who starred in mid '20s under Coach EVERETT DEAN, second from right, who starred in early '20s when ZORA CLEVENGER, right, was highly-respected Director of Athletics (and who coached early Hoosier team shortly after turn of the century).

JIM COUNSILMAN, BILLY BARTON, & FRANK McKINNEY

Indisputably, there is a new coaching genius in the making at Indiana where dynamic JIM COUNSILMAN, the Hoosiers' swim coach, some day will be ranked with Michigan's Matt Mann, Ohio State's Mike Peppe, and Yale's Bob Kiputh. A scholarly Ph. D., Counsilman, with his drive and dedicated study of the mechanics of the sport, in a few short years has taken Indiana from virtual aquatic obscurity to the pinnacle of success.

A collegiate star, himself, under Peppe at Ohio State,

Counsilman, since coming to Bloomington in 1958, has seen his Hoosiers win 55 individual Conference titles, 6 league team crowns and 17 individual national collegiate championships. His NCAA bag would have been considerably fatter (and surely would have included a few team titles, as well) had not the Hoosiers been beached for three years in the early 1960's as a result of an NCAA ban for football recruiting excesses. Ten of his stars have represented the United States at the Olympics.

Jim Garrett in the broad jump. Outdoors, Washington again took the 120-yard high hurdles in a wind-aided mark of 13.8, with an official league mark going to Indiana's Bob White who posted 13.9 in the semi-finals. The Spartans' John Spain set a new Conference record of 1:48 in the 880 to further help the cause, along with a record-breaking 50.7 for the 440-yard intermediate hurdles by Bob Steele, and a mile-relay triumph by a quartet consisting of Mike Martens, Rick Dunn, Daswell Campbell and John Spain.

The Spartans also came up with the league wrestling crown led by individual victories scored by Dale Anderson at 137 pounds and Mike Bradley at 177.

Indiana in 1966 was edging up on Ohio State's mark of eight straight swimming championships by posting its sixth in a row, with seven titles

picked up en route. Bill Utley's 1:43.9 was a new record for the 200-yard freestyle; Bob Windle's 16:50.4 was a new mark for the 1650-yard freestyle; Ken Webb took the 400-yard individual medley in a record-breaking 4:17.3; Kevin Berry won the 200-yard butterfly; a Hoosier foursome of Utley, Cordin, Webb, and Windle posted a new league and American mark of 7:02.6 for the 800-yard relay; and the brilliant Ken Sitzberger ruled the diving boards with victories on the high and low.

Michigan, which in 1961 had ended Illinois' phenomenal streak of 11 straight gymnastics championships, was adding to its own skein with its sixth straight team title in 1966, although it was strictly team balance that did it, with the Spartans scoring only one individual victory—by Wayne Miller, on trampoline. To prove what balance means, Michigan State took six of the eight individual titles

KEN SITZBERGER

RICK GILBERT

*Divers as well as swimmers sparkled for all-winning
Indiana in the 1960's, with RICK GILBERT and KEN
SITZBERGER competing against each other as well as
the nation. Gilbert won the Big Ten low board crown in
1963, was double champ on low and high boards in 1964,
as well as NCAA low board titlist; and repeated as Conference king on both boards in 1965. Sitzberger burst
on the scene as Olympic champion in 1964; took the
NCAA crowns, high and low in 1965, and added the
Big Ten titles in 1966 and the low board NCAA crown.*

and came in second. The Spartans' Dave Thor, incidentally, was a three-ply winner in floor exercises,
side horse, and all-around.

In fencing, Illinois took the team crown, led by
John Tocks' victory in foils; Wisconsin's Todd Ballinger won the Conference singles tennis crown; and
Northwestern's John Seehausen was the league golf
king.

Ohio State repeated as Conference baseball champions with what was possibly the best club in
Buckeye history, led by Steve Arlin, one of the
nation's finest collegiate pitchers (he signed at
season's end for more than $100,000 with the Phil-
lies), his batterymate Chuck Brinkman, a fine receiver; and Bob Baker and footballer Bob Rein,
two hard-hitting outfielders. It was a team that
went into the NCAA tourney determined to go one
step beyond its second-place finish of the year
before and did just that—knocking over Arizona in
the finals for the national collegiate championship.
Arlin was named to the All-America team, and
subsequently, Marty Karow, the Buckeyes' veteran
tutor, was named Coach-of-the-Year by the American College Baseball Coaches Association.

In other NCAA action, Michigan State's Bob
Steele, in the 440-yard hurdles, was the league's

1967

lone track champion, but nine titles went to Conference schools in swimming, with Indiana just
barely being nipped for the team crown by Southern California. Meanwhile, Michigan State's Gary
Dilley for the second straight year scored a brilliant double in the 100- and 200-yard backstroke;
Michigan's Paul Scheerer took the 100-yard breaststroke; the Wolverines' Carl Robie captured the
200-yard butterfly; Indiana's Ken Webb took the
400-yard individual medley; the Hoosiers' Bill Utley
won the 200-yard medley; Ken Sitzberger successfully defended his low board diving crown; a
Hoosier foursome of Ken Webb, Scott Cordin, Bill
Utley and Bob Windle took the 800-yard relay;
and Michigan's Rees Orland, Paul Scheerer, Carl
Robie, and Bill Groft won the 400-yard medley
relay.

In fencing, Iowa's Bernhardt Hermann, in epee,
gave the Hawkeyes their first national collegiate
champion, and in wrestling the Conference won
three individual crowns: Dick Cook, of Michigan
State, at 152 pounds; Dave Reinbolt, of Ohio State,
at 167; and Dave Porter, of Michigan, heavyweight.

The Conference also hailed two firsts for Michigan State and Wisconsin as the Spartans captured
the NCAA hockey championship and the Badger
eight-oared crew, after more than a half century
of trying, won the Intercollegiate Rowing Association crown.

The Big Ten Medal for Scholarship went to some
particularly outstanding athletes in 1966, with the
prestigious award going to Jim Grabowski, Illinois'
All-America fullback; Dave Schelhase, Purdue's All-
America basketball star; Steve Juday, Michigan
State's All-America quarterback; Dick Abrahams,
Northwestern's Big Ten swimming sprint champion;
and Don Unverfurth, Ohio State's fine quarterback.

The winter of 1967 brought its customary bag of
championships to Big Ten schools, but even before

*GARY DILLEY, Michigan State's tremendous backstroker,
splashed to fame even before his varsity career had
started when he won the Silver Medal in the 200-meter
backstroke in the 1964 Olympics. Then, as a varsity star,
he swept the Big Ten and NCAA 100-yard and 200-yard
events in 1965 and 1966.*

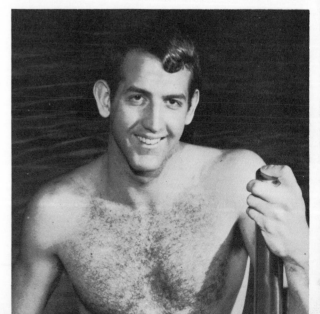

BERNHARDT HERMANN, Iowa's Big Ten epee champion in 1966, brought the Hawkeyes their first national fencing championship when he won the NCAA epee crown.

all the trophies were shined and displayed there was a bit of tarnish that lay over one of the lodge members. . .

Indiana and Michigan State went down to the wire for the basketball title with identical 10-4 reccords, the most undistinguished winning margin in

almost a decade. Harry Joyner, a 20.3 scorer for the league season; Irv Ininger and Vernon Payne, both 15-plus, led the Hoosiers. Matt Aitch (16.3) and Lee Lafayette, a hot soph (15.1), paced the Spartans. Neither team could be considered a strong champ by previous standards and Indiana got the NCAA bid because Michigan State had been there most recently, and the Hoosiers were eliminated by Virginia Tech. The league's leading scorer, meanwhile, had been Minnesota's Tom Kondla, a slick junior, with 28.3.

Although they had faltered in basketball, the Hoosiers didn't slip up in their by-now annual domination of Big Ten swimming. They won their seventh straight team crown, led by Ken Sitzberger's repeat double in the low and high board diving events and a record-shattering (league and American) 800-yard freestyle relay, swum by Bill Utley, Scott Cordin, Ken Webb and Bob Windle.

The star of the meet, however, was Michigan's versatile Carl Robie one of the few men in league history to score a triple when he won the 500-yard freestyle; the 1650-yard freestyle; and the 200-yard butterfly, setting new records for the 500 and the 1650.

Wisconsin took two winter sports crowns, dethroning virtually perennial champ, Illinois, in fencing, and winning its third indoor track title in six years. Pat Laper, in epee, and Bruce Taubman, in foil, were Badger individual champs. On the boards,

It was a big "first" for the Wisconsin crew in 1966 when the Badger eight scored the first Wisconsin triumph in the Intercollegiate Rowing Regatta (formerly Poughkeepsie Regatta) emblematic of the national rowing championship. Coach Norm Sonju's varsity, from left to right: Dave Quam, Neil Halleen, Greg Farnham, Tom Mitchell, John Norsetter, Roger Seeman, Bill Clapp, and Steve Bergum. Kneeling is Coxswain Bill Witte.

sophmore Mike Butler with two new marks in the 70-yard low and high hurdles, defeated Michigan State's defending champ, All-America gridder, Gene Washington.

Iowa broke an 18-year monopoly by Illinois and Michigan in gymnastics, when the Hawkeyes took their first team title in 30 years. Michigan had held the crown for six straight years and Illinois for 11 straight before that.

Michigan State took the league wrestling title as the Spartans and runner-up Michigan won all the individual championships, the first time two teams had ever done the trick. Then Michigan State went on to win the NCAA team crown, a first for the Spartans, paced by individual wins by Big Ten champs Dale Anderson, at 137 pounds, and George Radman, 167.

Six national collegiate swim titles went to Conference stars in the NCAA meet, as Stanford and Southern California slipped in ahead of Indiana for team honors. Two Hoosiers scored brilliant doubles—Ken Sitzberger in both diving events, and Charles Hickcox in the 100- and 200-yard backstroke. Michigan's great Carl Robie repeated as 200-yard butterfly champ and Ken Walsh of Michigan State set a new NCAA mark of 45:6.7 for the 100-yard free-style.

The big news out of the Big Ten in the winter and spring of 1967 stunned the entire league. In the late fall, Doug Mills had resigned as Illinois Athletic Director. A few weeks later, Mel Brewer, an assistant who had been passed over for promotion to the top job, walked into the office of the university president, Dr. David D. Henry, and revealed the existence of a slush fund for athletes in violation of Conference rules. Sums of money, reportedly up to $50 a month beyond the legitimate athletic scholarship of tuition, books, room and board had been given to several athletes, many of them still in school. One halfback had also received several hundred dollars in transportation money between his Florida home and campus—also illegal. Money in the slush fund had been contributed by alumni and businessmen.

Unfalteringly, Dr. Henry on December 12 immediately reported the situation to Big Ten Commissioner William R. Reed. A week later a dozen athletes were suspended from further competition; subsequently seven suffered loss of eligibility, five of them permanently.

When it was revealed that Illinois coaches had been aware of the slush fund, the Conference imposed an even stronger penalty on Illinois. The varsity football coach, Pete Elliott; varsity basketball coach Harry Combes, and assistant cage coach Howard Braun had to be fired or Illinois would have to "show cause why it should not be suspended from membership in the Big Ten." The furor among Illini alumni, and in the press and even the state legislature, was intense. Many wanted the university to stand by its coaches and go its own way. The university seemed torn between loyalty to its coaches and withdrawal from the Conference. Just before the deadline handed down by the league, Elliott, Combes, and Braun resigned ". . . rather than force the University of Illinois to act in an impossible situation."

The Big Ten had weathered its most critical storm of modern times. The University of Illinois had preserved its integrity in reporting violtations it had, itself, uncovered. The Conference had backed up its most important regulation despite the possible loss of one of its most honored members. The wounds, in healing, would find the Big Ten morally stronger than ever before.

OFFICIAL ALL-TIME BIG TEN RECORDS, STATISTICS AND AWARDS

ALL-SPORTS—TEAM CHAMPIONS—ALL TIME

Season	Football	Basketball	Baseball	Outdoor Track	Indoor Track	Swimming
1896	Wisconsin		Chicago			
1897	Wisconsin		Chicago			
1898	Michigan		Chicago			
1899	Chicago		Michigan			
1900	Minn., Iowa		Illinois			
1901	Mich., Wis.		Michigan	Mich.		
1902	Michigan		Wisconsin	Mich.		
1903	Mich., Minn., NU		Illinois	Mich.		
1904	Mich., Minn.		Illinois	Mich.		
1905	Chicago		Michigan	Chicago		
1906	Mich., Minn., Wis.	Minnesota	Illinois	Mich.		
1907	Chicago	Chi., Minn., Wis.	Illinois	Illinois		
1908	Chicago	Chicago	Illinois	Chicago		
1909	Minnesota	Chicago	Purdue	Illinois		
1910	Ill., Minn.	Chicago	Illinois	N Dame		
1911	Minnesota	Purdue	Illinois	Missouri	Chicago	Illinois
1912	Wisconsin	Purdue, Wis.	Wisconsin	Calif.	Illinois	Illinois
1913	Chicago	Wisconsin	Chicago	Illinois	Illinois	Illinois
1914	Illinois	Wisconsin	Illinois	Illinois	Chicago	NU
1915	Ill., Minn.	Illinois	Illinois	Wis.	Illinois	NU
1916	Ohio State	Wisconsin	Illinois	Wis.	Illinois	Chi., NU
1917	Ohio State	Ill., Minn.	Ohio	Chicago	Chicago	NU
1918	Ill., Mich., Pur.	Wisconsin	Michigan	Mich.	Mich.	NU
1919	Illinois	Minnesota	Michigan	Illinois	Mich.	Chicago
1920	Ohio State	Chicago	Michigan	Illinois	Illinois	NU
1921	Ia., Mich.	Mich., Pur., Wis.	Illinois	Illinois	Illinois	Chicago
1922	Ill., Mich.	Purdue	Illinois	Illinois	Illinois	Minn.
1923	Ill., Mich.	Iowa, Wis.	Michigan	Mich.	Mich.	NU
1924	Chicago	Chi., Ill., Wis.	Mich., Ohio	Illinois	Illinois	NU
1925	Ohio State	Ohio State	Indiana	Mich.	Mich.	NU
1926	Mich., N.U.	Ind., Mich.	Michigan	Mich.	Iowa	Minn.
1927	Illinois	Pur., Iowa	Ill., Iowa	Illinois	Wis.	Mich.
1928	Illinois	Michigan	Michigan	Illinois	Illinois	Mich.
1929	Purdue	Ind., Pur.	Michigan	Illinois	Iowa	Mich.
1930	Mich., NU	Purdue	Wisconsin	Mich.	Wis.	NU
1931	Mich., NU, Pur.	Northwestern	Indiana	Wis	Mich.	Mich.
1932	Michigan	Purdue	Minnesota	Mich.	Indiana	Mich.
1933	Michigan	Purdue	Illinois	Illinois	Mich.	Mich.
1934	Minn., Ohio	Ill., Pur., Wis.	Minnesota	Mich.	Mich.	Mich.
1935	Minnesota	Ind., Purdue	Michigan	Mich.	Mich.	Mich.
1936	Northwestern	Purdue	Minnesota	Indiana	Mich.	Iowa
1937	Minnesota	Ohio State	Ind., Iowa	Mich.	Mich.	Mich.
1938	Minnesota	Purdue	Iowa	Mich.	Mich.	Ohio
1939	Ohio State	Wisconsin	Ill., NU	Mich.	Mich.	Mich.
1940	Minnesota	Illinois	Michigan	Mich.	Mich.	Mich.
1941	Minnesota	Illinois	Ia., Mich.	Indiana	Indiana	Mich.
1942	Ohio State	Iowa	Ohio	Ohio	Ohio	Ohio
1943	Mich., Pur.	Ohio State	Michigan	Mich.	Mich.	Mich.
1944	Ohio State	Wisconsin	Michigan	Mich.	Mich.	Mich.
1945	Indiana	Michigan	Wisconsin	Illinois	Illinois	Mich.
1946	Illinois	Illinois	Illinois	Illinois	Illinois	Ohio
1947	Michigan	Ohio State	Ill., Mich.	Illinois	Illinois	Ohio
1948	Michigan	Illinois	Ind., Iowa, Mich.	Ohio	Ohio	Mich
1949	Ohio, Mich.	Illinois	Mich., Wis.	Minnesota	Michigan	Ohio
1950	Michigan	Ohio State	Ohio	Indiana	Ohio	Ohio
1951	Illinois	Indiana	Ill., Mich.	Illinois	Illinois	Ohio
1952	Pur., Wis.	Indiana	Mich., Ill.	Illinois	Illinois	Ohio
1953	Ill., MSC	Iowa	Mich. State	Illinois	Illinois	Ohio
1954	Ohio State	Ind., MSU	Ohio	Michigan	Michigan	Ohio
1955	Ohio State	Indiana	Minnesota	Michigan	Michigan	Ohio
1956	Iowa	MSU	NU	Michigan	Michigan	Ohio
1957	Ohio State	Ohio State	Minnesota	Indiana	Indiana	MSU
1958	Illinois	Ohio State	Minnesota	Illinois	Illinois	Mich.
1959	Wisconsin	Ohio State	Minnesota	Illinois	Michigan	Mich.
1960	Minn., Iowa	Illinois	Michigan	Michigan	Michigan	Mich.
1961	Ohio State	Indiana	Michigan	Michigan	Michigan	Indiana
1962	Wisconsin	Indiana	Illinois	Michigan	Wisconsin	Indiana
1963	Illinois	Iowa	Illinois	Iowa	Iowa, Mich.	Iowa, Mich.
1964	Michigan	Michigan	Minnesota	Wisconsin	Wisconsin	Indiana
1965	MSU	Michigan	Ohio State	MSU	MSU	Indiana
1966	MSU	Michigan	Ohio State	MSU	MSU	Indiana

ALL-TIME CHAMPIONSHIP COMPETITION
(as of September, 1966)

	Chi.	Ill.	Ind.	Iowa	Mich.	MSU	Minn.	NU	OSU	Pur.	Wis.
FOOTBALL Championship	6	7	1	3	9	1	7	1	10	1	5
FOOTBALL Co-Champ.	—	5	—	3	12	1	8	4	2	4	3
BASKETBALL Championship	4	6	3	3	4	1	2	1	8	7	6
BASKETBALL Co-Champ.	2	5	4	2	4	1	3	1	3	6	7
BASEBALL Championship	4	19	2	1	15	1	7	1	6	1	4
BASEBALL Co-Champ.	—	5	2	4	7	—	—	1	1	—	1
OUT. TRACK Championship	3	22	4	1	24	2	1	0	2	0	4
IN. TRACK Championship	3	16	4	2	21	1	0	0	3	0	4
IN. TRACK Co-Champ.	—	—	—	1	1	—	—	—	1	—	1
SWIMMING Championship	2	3	6	1	19	1	2	9	12	0	0
SWIMMING Co-Champ.	1	—	—	—	—	—	—	1	—	—	—
C. COUNTRY Championship	0	2	8	1	2	11	3	1	1	3	14
C. COUNTRY Co-Champ.	—	—	1	—	—	—	—	—	—	—	1
WRESTLING Championship	0	12	9	3	10	2	3	0	0	6	0
WRESTLING Co-Champ.	—	4	3	0	0	0	1	0	1	0	0
GOLF Championship	3	6	1	0	12	0	3	4	6	9	1
GYMNASTICS Championship	15	18	0	1	6	0	10	0	0	0	8
FENCING Championship	8	21			0	1	0	2	3	0	3
TENNIS Championship.*	10	4	4	1	13	1	2	8	1	0	0
TENNIS Co-Champ.*	10	5	1	—	3	0	4	—	1	—	—
HOCKEY Championship					3	1	4				
CHAMPIONSHIP	58	136	42	17	138	23	44	27	53	27	49
CO-CHAMP.	13	24	11	10	27	2	16	7	9	10	13

*—From 1910 through 1933, only singles and doubles champions were named in tennis. Starting in 1934, team champions were named on the basis of matches won in both singles and doubles competition. In the above, "Championship" denotes the number of team titles since 1933 and clean sweeps of both singles and doubles prior to that date. "Co-Champ" denotes either singles or doubles victory prior to 1934. Starting in 1965 a combination of round-robin dual-meet and championship results determined team champion.

FOOTBALL SECTION

ALL-TIME CONFERENCE FOOTBALL RECORDS

(Includes marks during the Pre-Modern Era, 1896-1938)

Team Scoring, One Game
146, Minnesota vs. Grinell (0), 10-22-04
119, Michigan vs. Michigan State (0), 10-8-02
*107, Michigan vs. Iowa (0), 11-8-02

Two Teams' Scoring, One Game
104, Ohio State (83), Iowa (21), 10-28-50

Team Scoring, Season
644, Michigan (11 games), 1902
*218, Ohio State (7 games), 1950

Highest Losing Score
34, Wisconsin vs. Ohio State (46), 11-8-41

Most Points, Individual
30, Harold (Red) Grange (Illinois) vs. Michigan, 10-18-24

Most Field Goals
5, Walter Eckersall (Chicago) vs. Illinois, 11-18-05

Run From Scrimmage
100 Yds., Mickey Erehart (Indiana) vs. Iowa, 11-9-12.
96 Yds., HB Eddie Vincent (Iowa) vs. Purdue, 11-6-54

Kickoff Return
106 yds., Walter Eckersall (Chicago) vs. Wisconsin, 11-26-04
100 yds., Eddie Cochems (Wisconsin) vs. Chicago, 11-28-01
100 yds., Walter Steffan (Chicago) vs. Wisconsin, 11-14-08
100 yds., Jack Brown (Purdue) vs. Indiana, 11-19-38
100 yds., George Rice (Iowa) vs. Purdue, 10-6-51
100 yds., William Wentz (Ohio State) vs. Illinois 10-8-60

Punt Return
110 yds., Al Barlow (Michigan) vs. Ohio State, 11-11-05**
92 yds., Phil Mateja (Purdue) vs. Iowa, 10-6-51
92 yds., Dean Look (MSU) vs. Michigan, 10-4-58
92 yds., Earl Faison (Indiana) vs. MSU, 11-8-58**
91 yds., Fred Hovde, (Minnesota) vs. Iowa, 10-27-28

Run With Recovered Fumble
105 yds., H. M. Coleman (Wisconsin) vs. Minnesota, 10-24-91
105 yds., Chuck Palmer (N.U.) vs. Minnesota, 10-21-22

Run With Intercepted Pass
105 yds., Coots Cunningham (Wisconsin) vs. Purdue, 11-16-07
105 yds., Clark Sauer (Chicago) vs. N.U., 10-22-10
105 yds., Clark Sauer (Chicago) vs. Ind., 10-7-11
103 yds., B. E. Hutchinson (Chicago) vs. Northwestern, 10-25-19
100 yds., Coots Cunningham (Wisconsin) vs. Illinois, 11-22-07
100 yds., Edgar Williams (N.U.) vs. Purdue, 11-18-16
100 yds., Buell Hutchinson (Chicago) vs. N.U., 10-25-19

Run With Blocked Kick
92 yds., Earl Faison (Ind.) vs. MSU, 11-8-58 (FG att.)
40 yds., August Hook (Purdue) vs. N.U., 11-5-27

Completed Forward Pass Play
95 yds., Len Dawson to Erich Barnes (Purdue) vs. N.U., 11-12-55

Longest Punt
110 Yds., Pat O'Dea (Wisconsin) vs. Minn., 10-30-97. Field was 110 yds. long
(With Roll) 96 yds., George O'Brien (Wisconsin) vs. Iowa, 10-18-52
(Without Roll) 78 yds., Howard Wedebrook (Ohio State) vs. Michigan, 11-21-36

Longest Field Goal
65 yds., (Drop Kick), Pat O'Dea (Wisconsin) vs. N.U. 11-24-98
57 yds., (Place Kick), Pat O'Dea (Wisconsin) vs. Ill., 11-11-99

*—Record For Conference Games Only   **—Return of Field Goal Attempt

Season	Cross Country	Wrestling	Golf	Gymnastics	Fencing	Tennis
1902				Wisconsin		
1903				Minnesota		
1904				Wisconsin		
1905				Wisconsin		
1906				No Record		
1907	Nebr.			Minnesota		Chi.-Minn.
1908	Minn.			Wisconsin		Minn.
1909	Wis.	No record		Wisconsin		
1910	Wis.	Illinois, Minn.		Chicago		Minn.
1911	Ia. State	Indiana		Minnesota		Chicago
1912	Wis.	Nebraska		Illinois		Chi.-Ill.
1913	Wis	Iowa		Wisconsin		Ohio-Chi.
1914	Minn.		Minn.	Chicago		Chicago
1915	Wis.		Illinois	Wisconsin		Chicago
1916	Purdue		Illinois	Wisconsin		
1917	No Meet	Illinois		Chicago		Illinois
1918	No Meet	No meet		No Meet		Chi.-Minn
1919	Ia. State	No meet		No Meet		Mich.
1920	Ia. State	Illinois	Drake	Chicago		Mich.-Chi.
1921	Illinois	Indiana	Drake	Chicago		Ind.-Chi.
1922	Mich.	Illinois	Chicago	Chicago		Ill.-Chi.
1923	Ohio	Ohio, Iowa State	Illinois	Wisconsin		Mich.-Chi.
1924	Wis.	Ill., Ind	Chicago	Minnesota		Chi.-Ill.
1925	Wis.	Ill., Ind	NU	Chicago		Butler
1926	Wis.	Illinois	Chicago	Chicago	Ohio	Illinois
1927	Wis.	Illinois	Illinois	Chicago	Ohio	Ill.-Mich.
1928	Indiana	Illinois	Ohio	Chicago	Chicago	Illinois
1929	Indiana	Michigan	Minn.	Illinois	Illinois	Chicago
1930	Indiana	Indiana	Illinois	Chicago	Illinois	Chicago
1931	Indiana	Indiana	Illinois	Chicago	Illinois	Chicago
1932	Indiana	Ind., Ill.	Mich.	Chicago	Illinois	Ill.-Minn.
1933	No Meet	Indiana	Mich.	Illinois	Illinois	Minn.-Chi.
1934	Indiana	Indiana	Mich.	Chicago	Chicago	Chicago
1935	No Meet	Illinois	Mich.	Chicago	Illinois	Chicago
1936	No Meet	Indiana	Mich.	Minn.	Chicago	NU
1937	No Meet	Illinois	NU	Iowa	Chicago	Chicago
1938	Indiana	Mich.	Minn.	Minn.	Chicago	Chicago
1939	Indiana	Indiana	NU	Illinois	Chicago	Chicago
1940	Indiana	Indiana	Illinois	Minn.	Chicago	NU
1941	Purdue	Minn.	Illinois	Illinois	Chicago	Michigan
1942	Indiana	Purdue	Mich.	Illinois	Illinois	NU
1943	Purdue	Indiana	Mich.	No Meet	Illinois	Ohio
1944	Wis.	Mich.	Ohio	No Meet	No Meet	Michigan
1945	Wis.	Purdue	Ohio	No Meet	No Meet	Michigan
1946	Ind.-Wis.	Illinois	Mich.	No Meet	No Meet	Illinois
1947	Illinois	Illinois	Mich.	Illinois	NU	NU
1948	Wis.	Purdue	NU	Minn.	NU	NU
1949	Wis.	Purdue	Mich.	Minn.	Ohio	NU
1950	Wis.	Purdue	Purdue	Illinois	Illinois	NU
1951	MSC	Ohio	Ohio	Illinois	Illinois	MSC
1952	MSC	Illinois	Mich.	Illinois	Indiana	Indiana
1953	MSC	Michigan	Purdue	Illinois	Indiana	Indiana
1954	Michigan	Purdue	Ohio	Illinois	Indiana	Indiana
1955	MSU	Michigan	Purdue	Wisconsin	Wisconsin	Michigan
1956	MSU	Michigan	Purdue	Illinois	Illinois	Michigan
1957	MSU	Minnesota	Wisconsin	Illinois	Wisconsin	Michigan
1958	MSU	Iowa	Purdue	Illinois	Illinois	Iowa
1959	MSU	Minnesota	Purdue	Illinois	Wisconsin	Michigan
1960	MSU	Michigan	Purdue	Illinois	Illinois	Michigan
1961	Iowa	MSU	Ohio State	Michigan	Illinois	Michigan
1962	MSU	Iowa	Indiana	Michigan	Illinois	Michigan
1963	MSU	Michigan	Minnesota	Michigan	MSU	Northwestern
1964	Minnesota	Michigan	Purdue	Michigan	Illinois	Indiana
1965	NU	Michigan	Purdue	Michigan	Illinois	Michigan
1966		MSU	Ohio State	Michigan	Michigan	Michigan

Hockey: 1959, Michigan State   1962, Michigan   1965, Minnesota
1960, Minnesota   1963, Michigan   1966, Minnesota
1961, Michigan   1964, Michigan

NOTE: Wrestling championships determined on basis of dual meet records, 1922-1933. In earlier years, some of the competitions were held as open meets explaining the fact that non-Conference schools sometimes are listed as Conference champions.

MODERN ERA (Since 1939) RECORDS
(Based on Conference Games Only)

INDIVIDUAL SINGLE GAME RECORDS
(Home Team in Caps)

SCORING
Most Points: 27, HB Tom Harmon (4 TD, 3 PAT) MICH. vs. Iowa 10-14-39
Most Touchdowns: 4, HB Tom Harmon, MICH. vs. Iowa 10-14-39; HB George Franck, MINN. vs. Iowa 10-26-40; FB Tony Butkovich, PURDUE vs. Ill. 10-2-43; HB Otto Graham, N'western vs. WIS. 11-6-43; HB Red Williams, MINN. vs. Iowa 11-13-43; Jerry Witt, Wis. vs. NU, 10-27-51; Mickey Bates, Ill., vs. OHIO 10-10-53; Boris Dimancheff, Pur., vs. WIS. 11-4-44; Don Clark, OHIO, vs. N'western, 11-2-57; Bob White, OHIO, 11-16-58; Bob Ferguson, OHIO vs. Ill., 10-14-61, and vs. MICH. 11-25-61; Louis Holland, Wis. vs. ILL., 11-17-62; Clinton Jones, MSU vs. IOWA, 11-6-65
Most PAT Attempts: 11, HB Vic Janowicz (10 made), OHIO vs. Iowa 10-28-50
Most PAT Made: 10, HB Vic Janowicz (11 att.), OHIO vs. Iowa 10-28-50
Most Field Goals: 2, Omer Ohl, PURDUE, vs. Ill, 11-1-58; and vs. MINNESOTA, 11-17-62; Jim Bakken, Wisconsin, vs. Ind., 10-7-61; Luke George, Indiana, vs. PURDUE, 11-24-62; Dick Van Raaphorst, Ohio, vs. INDIANA, 10-5-63 and vs. Illinois, 10-12-63; Bob Funk, Ohio, vs. ILLINOIS, 10-10-64; Dick Kenney, MSU vs. IOWA, 11-6-65; Bob Anderson, Iowa vs. WIS., 10-2-65

LONGEST SCORING PLAYS
Run from Scrimmage: 96 yds., HB Eddie Vincent, IOWA vs. Pur., 11-6-54
Pass: 95 yds., QB Len Dawson to HB Erich Barnes, PUR., vs. N.U., 11-12-55
Field goal: 50 yds., FB Tom Nowatzke, Indiana vs. OHIO, 10-3-64
Pass Interception: 98 yds., HB Julie Rykovich, ILL. vs. Ohio, 11-16-46; Billy Lowe, WIS., vs. Pur., 10-16-54
K.O. Return: 100 yds. HB George Rice, Iowa vs. PUR., 10-6-51; 100 yds., HB Bill Wentz, Ohio vs. ILL., 10-8-60
Punt Return: 92 yds., HB Philip Mateja, PUR. vs. Iowa, 10-6-51; Dean Look, MSU, vs. Mich., 10-4-58
Recovered Fumble: 90 yds., E Norm Maloney, PUR. vs. Ind. 11-23-46
Blocked Kick Return: 92 yds., Earl Faison, Ind., vs. MSU, 11-8-58 (FG att.)

RUSHING
Most Rushes: 38, HB Ernie Parks (158 yds.) OHIO vs. Illinois 11-14-43 and FB Jim Grabowski (196 yds.) Illinois vs. WISCONSIN, 11-13-65
Most Yds. Gained: 239, FB Jim Grabowski (33 rushes) ILLINOIS vs. Wisconsin, 11-14-64

PASSING
Most Attempts: 49, QB Gary Snook (26 compl., 310 yds.) IOWA vs. Purdue, 10-24-64
Most Completed: 26, QB Olen Treadway (41 att., 304 yds.), Iowa, vs. WIS., 10-17-59 and QB Gary Snook (49 att., 310 yds.) IOWA vs. Purdue, 10-24-64
Most Yds. Gained: 310, QB Gary Snook, (49 att., 26 compl.) IOWA vs. Purdue, 10-24-64
Best Compl. Percentage: .857 QB Dale Samuels, Purdue vs. ILLINOIS (12 of 14), 10-25-52
Most Had Interc.: 6, Tom O'Connell (34 att., 22 compl.), Illinois vs. IOWA, 11-8-52; Don Swanson (17 att., 6 compl.), Minn. vs. WIS., 11-20-54
Most TD Passes: 5, QB Fred Riddle (16 att., 10 compl., 155 yds.), IOWA, vs. Indiana, 10-12-63 (TD Passes of 5, 5, 3, 76 and 4 yds.)

TOTAL OFFENSE
Most Plays: 53, HB Paul Giel (35 rush, 18 pass), MINN. vs. Mich., 10-24-53 and 52, QB Gary Snook (3 rush, 49 pass) IOWA vs. Purdue, 10-24-64
Most Yds. Gained: 309, Ron Miller (7 rush, 12 yds.; 37-19-297 yds., pass) Wis. vs. MINN., 11-25-61, 308, QB Tony Curcillo (9 rush, 14-10-292 yds., pass), OHIO, vs. Iowa, 10-27-51; 307, HB Bob Chappuis (17 rush, 90 yds.; 26-12-217 yds. pass) MICH. vs. Ohio 11-22-47
Yds. Per Play: 14.25, QB Len Dawson (6 rush, 14 pass) Pur. vs. MSC, 10-23-54

RECEIVING
Most Caught: 13, E Don Stonesifer (140 yds., 2 TD) N.U. vs. Minn. 10-14-50
Most Yds. Gained: 190, Rex Smith (11 catches) Illinois vs. IOWA, 11-8-52
Most Passes Interc.: 4, Clarence Bratt, WIS. vs. Minn., 11-20-54
Most Yds. Interc. Ret.: 116, HB Tom Worthington (3 interc.) N.U. vs. Ind. 10-25-47
Most TD Passes: 3, Erwin Prasse, IOWA vs. Ind. 10-7-39; Emlen Tunnell, IOWA vs. Ind., 10-11-47; Bernie Flowers, Purdue, vs. ILL. 10-25-52; Dave Howard, WIS., vs. Iowa, 10-1-55; Pat Richter, WIS., vs. Ill., 11-18-61; Gene Washington, MSU vs. Ind., 11-13-65

PUNTING
Most Kicked: 24, HB Chuck Ortmann (723 yds.) Mich. vs. OHIO 11-25-50
Most Yds. Kicked: 723 yds., HB Chuck Ortmann (24 punts) Mich. vs. OHIO, 11-25-50
685 yds., FB Vic Janowitz (21 punts) OHIO vs. Wis. 10-22-49
Best Average: 57.3, FB Fred Morrison (4 punts, 229 yds.) IOWA vs. PURDUE 11-4-39
Longest Punt: 96 yds., G Geo. O'Brien, Wis. vs. IOWA, 10-18-52
Most Punts Returned: 10, William Lane (83 yds.), WIS. vs. Ind., 11-3-51
Most Yards Returned: 201, Nile Kinnick, Iowa vs. Ind., 10-7-39
Most Blocked: 2, T Mike Ennich, Iowa vs. PURDUE 11-4-39

KICKOFFS
Most Returned: 7, Ron Engel (203 yds.), Minn. vs. MICH., 10-27-51
Most Yds. Returned: 203, Ron Engel (7 ret.), Minn. vs. MICH., 10-27-51

INDIVIDUAL SEASON RECORDS
(Figures in parentheses denote number of Conference games played in season.)

SCORING
Most Points: 78, FB Tony Butkovich, Purdue (4), 1943 (13 TD)
Most Touchdowns: 13, FB Tony Butkovich, Purdue (4), 1943
Most PAT: 22, C Jim Brieske, Michigan (7), 1946 (23 att.)
22, C Jim Brieske, Michigan (6), 1947 (24 att.)
22, E Harry Allis, Michigan (6), 1948 (28 att.)
Most Field Goals: 6, PK Dick Van Raaphorst, Ohio State (6), 1963
6, PK Dick Kenney, Michigan State (7) 1965
6, PK Bob Funk, Ohio State (7), 1965

RUSHING
Most Rushes: 201, FB Jim Grabowski, Illinois (7), 1965
Highest Ave. Rushes Per Game: 28.71, FB Jim Grabowski, Illinois (7), 1965
Most Yards Gained (Net): 996, FB Jim Grabowski, Illinois (7), 1965
Highest Ave. Per Game: 167.3, FB Bill Daley, Michigan (3), 1943
Highest Ave. Gain Per Rush:
20 to 40 Attempts: 11.85, HB Tom James, Ohio State, 1942 (20 Att.)
40 to 50 Attempts: 8.8, HB Willie Fleming, Iowa, 1958 (41 Att.)
50 to 75 Attempts: 8.8, HB Bob Mitchell, Illinois, 1955 (53 Att.)

PASSING
Most Attempted: 234, Gary Snook, Iowa (6), 1964
Most Passes Completed: 110, Gary Snook, Iowa (6), 1964
Best Completion Percentage: .642, QB John Coatta, Wis. (7), 1950 (52 comp., 81 atts.)
Most Yards Gained: 1,544, Gary Snook, Iowa (6), 1964
Most TD Passes: 10, Ron Vander Kelen, Wisconsin (7), 1962

TOTAL OFFENSE
Most Plays: 276, Gary Snook, Iowa (42 rushes, 234 passes) (6), 1964
Most Yards Gained Rushing and Passing: 1560, QB Gary Snook, Iowa (16 rush, 1544 pass) (6), 1964

PASS RECEIVING
Most Caught: 40, FL Karl Noonan, Iowa (6), 1964
Most Yards Gained: 656, E Pat Richter, Wisconsin (7), 1961 (36 catches); 652, FL Karl Noonan, Iowa (6), 1964 (40 catches)
TD Passes Caught: 7, E Joe Collier, Northwestern (7), 1952; and E Pat Richter, Wisconsin (7), 1961

PASS INTERCEPTIONS
Most: 7, HB Chuck Lentz, Michigan (6), 1949 (79 yds. ret.); Al Brosky, Ill. (6) 1951 (130 yds. ret.),
Most Yds. Returned: 167, HB Tom Worthington, N.U. (6), 1947 (6 intrc.)

PUNTING
Most Kicked: 56, G Don Roedel, Minnesota (6), 1950 (37.1 ave.)
Best Ave.: 44.2, FB Kevin Kleber, Minnesota (7), 1955 (25 punts, 1106 yds.)
43.3, HB Dwight Eddelman, Illinois (7), 1948 (52 punts, 2252 yds.)

PUNT RETURNS
Most: 18, HB Bob Thompson, Minnesota (6), 1950 (217 yds.); HB William Lane, Wis. (7) 1951 (119 yds.)
Best Ave.: 32.5 yds., HB Dean Look MSU (6), 1958 (6 ret.)

KICKOFF RETURNS
Most: 14, HB Howard Cassady, Ohio State (7), 1953 (328 yds.) and HB Trent Walters, Indiana (7), 1965 (357 yds.)
Best Ave.: 37.2, HB Chuck Ortmann, Michigan (6) 1949 (4 ret. 149 yds.)

TEAM SINGLE GAME RECORDS
(Home Team in Caps)

SCORING
Most Points: 85, Mich. vs. CHICAGO 10-21-39
83, OHIO vs. Iowa 10-28-50
Most Touchdowns: 12, Mich. vs. CHICAGO 10-21-39
12, OHIO vs. Iowa 10-28-50

TEAM SEASON RECORDS

(Because of the varying number of Conference games played from year to year, the statistical marks are per game averages rather than totals. Figures in parenthesis denote number of Conference games played in season.)

SCORING
Most Points: 34.5, Michigan (6), 1943
Fewest Points: 0, Chicago (3), 1939
2.6, Illinois (5), 1941
Most Points by Opponents: 64, Chicago (3), 1939
38, Iowa (6), 1945
Fewest Points by Opponents: 3.8, Illinois (6), 1951

RUSHING
Most Rushes: 61.6, Ohio State (6), 1944
Fewest Rushes: 26.7, Iowa (6), 1964
Most Yards Gained: 320, Michigan (6), 1943
Fewest Yards Gained: 59.0, Indiana (6), 1948
Most Yards Gained by Opponents: 363.3, Chicago (3), 1939
Fewest Yards Gained by Opponents: 34.6, Michigan State (7), 1965

PASSING
Most Attempted: 39.8, Iowa (6), 1964
Most Completed: 18.7, Iowa (6), 1964
Fewest Attempted: 4, Minnesota (5), 1943
Fewest Completed: 1, Minnesota (5), 1943
1, Minnesota (5), 1943
Most Yards Gained: 266.8, Iowa (6), 1964
Fewest Yards Gained: 12.8, Ohio State (6), 1955
Most Yards Gained by Opponents: 175.4, Iowa (6), 1952
Fewest Yards Gained by Opponents: 26, Michigan (6), 1943
Highest Average Completed: .575, Wisconsin (6), 1952
Lowest Average Completed: .193, Minnesota (6), 1940
Highest Average Opponents' Passes Completed: .587, Iowa (6), 1951
Lowest Average Opponents' Passes Completed: .237, Illinois (6), 1945

TOTAL OFFENSE
Most Yards Gained: 416.7, Iowa (6), 1958
Fewest Yards Gained: 118.6, Purdue (5), 1942
Most Yards Gained by Opponents: 450, Chicago (3), 1939
Fewest Yards Gained by Opponents: 131, Michigan (6), 1943

PUNTING
Most Punts: 10.8, Northwestern (6), 1939
Fewest Punts: 2.7, Ohio State (6), 1961
Highest Average: 43.2, Illinois (7), 1948
Lowest Average: 27.8, Minnesota (7), 1953

FIRST DOWNS
Most: 22.0, Iowa (6), 1958
Fewest: 6.5, Iowa (6), 1944
Most Opponents' First Downs: 21.6, Indiana (7), 1965
Fewest Opponents' First Downs: 6, Michigan (4), 1940

FUMBLES
Most: 5.5, Indiana (6), 1946 and Michigan State (6), 1962
Fewest: 1.3, Minnesota (7), 1961; Ohio State (6), 1963 and Purdue (7), 1965
Most Fumbles Lost: 3.7, Michigan State (6), 1962
Fewest Fumbles Lost: .4, Minnesota (7), 1961
Most Opponents' Fumbles Recovered: 3, Purdue (6), 1943; Illinois (6), 1943; Minn. (6), 1952
Fewest Opponents' Fumbles Recovered: .25, Indiana (4), 1942

PENALTIES
Most: 8.5, Michigan State (6), 1964
Fewest: 2.0, Indiana (6), 1946; Northwestern (6), 1960
Most Yards Penalized: 82.8, MSU (6), 1956
Fewest Yards Penalized: 15.2, Wisconsin (6), 1948

Safeties: 2, Iowa vs. PUR. 11-4-39; Pur. vs. IND., 11-19-55; Wis. vs. PUR. 10-20-51
Most PAT made: 11, OHIO vs. Iowa (12 att.) 10-28-50
Most Field Goals: 2, PURDUE vs. CHICAGO (12 att.) 10-21-39
10, Mich. vs. ILL., 11-1-58 and vs. MINN., 11-17-62; Wisconsin vs. INDIANA, 10-5-63, vs. Illinois, 10-12-63 and vs. ILLINOIS, 10-10-64; MSU vs. MICH., 10-9-65 and vs. Ind., 11-13-65; Iowa vs. WIS., 10-2-65

RUSHING
Most Rushes: 86, OHIO vs. Ill. (377 yds.) 11-13-43
Fewest Rushes: 21, Ind. vs. PUR. (47 yds.) 11-20-48
Most Yards Gained: 517, Ohio vs. ILL. (56 rushes), 10-13-62
465, OHIO vs. Ind., 11-10-56
Fewest Yards Gained: (-87), Iowa vs. WIS. (29 rushes) 10-18-41
Best Ave. Per Rush: 10.33 yds., PUR. vs. Ill. (39 rushes, 403 yds.) 10-2-43

PASSING
Most Attempts: 50, IOWA, vs. Purdue (26 compl., 310 yds.), 10-24-64
Fewest Attempts: 0, Minn. vs. OHIO 10-19-40
Most Completed: 26, Iowa, vs. WIS. (41 att.), 10-17-59 and vs. Purdue (50 att.), 10-24-64
Fewest Yards Gained: 0, by numerous teams
Most Yards Gained: 322, Illinois vs. IOWA (37 att., 23 comp.), 11-8-52
Best Completion Ave.: 1,000 WIS. vs. Ind. (5-5-126 yds.) 10-25-41
(More than 5 attempts): .889, MICH. vs. Minn. (9-8-203 yds.), 10-27-51
.883, Ohio State vs. IND. (10-12-204 yds.), 10-13-56
Most TD passes: 5, OHIO vs. Iowa 10-28-50 and IOWA vs. Indiana, 10-12-63
Most Had Interc.: 7, Minn. vs. WIS. 11-20-54

TOTAL OFFENSE
Most Plays: 96, PUR. vs. Ind. (85 rush, 11 pass) 11-20-48; (79 rush, 17 pass) 11-19-60; and vs. IOWA (61 rush, 35 pass), 10-9-65
93, Wis. vs. NORTHWN. (67 rush, 26 pass), 10-27-51
93, MICH. vs. Wis. (78 rush, 15 pass), 10-30-65
92, NORTHWESTERN vs. Illinois (63 rush, 29 pass), 10-6-62
Fewest Plays: 34, Iowa vs. IND. (31 rush, 3 pass) 10-28-44
35, ILL. vs. Ohio (28 rush, 7 pass) 11-16-46
Most Yards Gained: 572, Wis. vs. NORTHWN. (67 rush, 26 pass., 201 yds.), 10-27-51
Fewest Yards Gained: 19, IOWA vs. Minn. (39 plays) 11-18-44

PUNTING
Most Punts: 24, Mich. vs. OHIO (723 yds.) 11-25-50
Fewest Punts: 0, ILL. vs. Pur. 10-7-44
0, Ind. vs. MINN. 10-5-46
0, NORTHWESTERN, vs. Illinois, 10-6-62
0, MSU, vs. Michigan, 10-13-62
0, WISCONSIN, vs. Iowa, 10-17-64
0, MINNESOTA, vs. Indiana, 10-9-65
Most Yards Kicked: 723 yds., Mich. vs. OHIO (24 punts) 11-25-50
685 yds., Mich. vs. OHIO (21 punts) 11-25-50
531, ILL. vs. N'western (14 punts) 10-28-39
Best Average: 52.5 yds., ILL. vs. OHIO (6-315 yds.) 11-13-48
52.4 yds., Ohio vs. IND. (5-262 yds.) 10-14-50

FIRST DOWNS
Most by Rushing: 25, PURDUE vs. Indiana, 11-20-48
Fewest by Rushing: 0, Ind. vs. MICH. 11-12-49
0, Mich. vs. OHIO 11-25-50
0, Ind. vs. MSU, 10-16-65
Most by Passing: 18, Ill. vs. IOWA, 11-8-52
Fewest by Passing: 0, by numerous teams
Most Total First Downs: 32, MSU, vs. Ind., 9-28-57
Fewest Total First Downs: 0, Mich. vs. OHIO 11-25-50
1, Pur. vs. OHIO (1 rush) 10-17-42

FUMBLES
Most: 12, Wis. vs. MICH. (5 lost) 11-8-44
11, Ill. vs. WIS. (8 lost) 10-20-45
Fewest: 0, by numerous teams
Most Lost: 8, Ill. vs. WIS (11 fumbles) 10-20-48

PENALTIES
Most: 17, MSU, vs. Ind. 9-28-57
Most Yards: 155, MSU, vs. Ind. 9-28-57
Fewest Penalties: 0, ILL. vs. Mich. 9-28-57
0, ILL. vs. Mich. 10-30-43
0, MICH. vs. Ind. 9-30-44
0, PUR. vs. Mich. 10-9-48
0, Wis. vs. OHIO, 11-11-50
0, IOWA vs. Wisconsin, 10-18-52
0, MICH. vs. N.U. 10-17-53
0, WIS., vs. MSU, 10-3-56
0, N.U. vs. Ohio, 10-21-61
0, Iowa, vs. MINN., 11-10-62
0, MINN., vs. Mich., 11-24-62
0, Wis. vs. Mich., 10-26-63
0, OHIO, vs. NU, 11-16-63

419

INDIVIDUAL DEPARTMENTAL CHAMPIONS
(No. of Conference games in parenthesis)

SCORING

	TD	PAT	FG	TOTAL
1939—HB Tom Harmon, Michigan (5)	8	10	1	61
1940—HB Tom Harmon, Michigan (4)	5	7	1	40
1941—FB Pat Harder, Wisconsin (6)	5	7	1	40
1942—HB Gene Fekete, Ohio State (6)	6	13	0	58
1943—FB Tony Butkovich, Purdue (4)	*13	0	0	52
1944—FB Boris Dimancheff, Purdue (6)	9	0	0	*78
1945—FB Ollie Cline, Ohio State (7)	9	0	0	54
1946—HB Bill Canfield, Purdue (6)	6	0	0	54
1947—HB Don Kindt, Wisconsin (6)	6	0	0	36
1946—HB Vic Schwall, Northwestern (6)	6	5	0	36
1947—HB Chalmers Elliott, Michigan (6)	6	0	0	36
1948—E Harry Allis, Michigan (6)	3	22	0	36
1949—HB Fred Morrison, Ohio State (6)	6	0	0	36
1950—HB Vic Janowicz, Ohio State (6)	4	21	1	48
1951—HB Jerry Witt, Wisconsin (5)	8	0	0	48
1952—FB Chuck Hren, Northwestern (7)	8	0	0	48
1953—HB Mickey Bates, Illinois (6)	9	0	0	54
1954—FB Earl Smith, Iowa (7)	11	0	0	66
1955—HB Howard Cassady, Ohio State (6)	6	3	0	39
1956—QB Frank Ellwood, Ohio State (6)	11	0	0	54
1957—HB Jim Pace, Michigan (7)	11	0	2	66
1958—FB Bob White, Ohio State (7)	3	9	0	33
1959—HB Mike Stock, Northwestern (7)	8	0	0	48
1960—FB Bob Ferguson, Ohio State (6)	9	0	0	54
QB Wilburn Hollis, Iowa (6)	9	0	0	54
1961—FB Bob Ferguson, Ohio State (6)	5	0	0	30
1962—HB Louis Holland, Wisconsin (7)	5	0	0	30
1963—HB Louis Holland, Wisconsin (7)	7	16	3	67
1964—QB Bob Timberlake, Michigan (7)	11	2	0	68
1965—HB Clinton Jones, Michigan State (7)				

RUSHING

	NO.	NET. YDS.	AVE.
1939—HB Harold Van Every, Minnesota (6)	106	452	4.3
1940—HB Tom Harmon, Michigan (5)	76	444	5.8
1940—FB Bob Westfall, Michigan (4)	109	443	4.1
1941—FB Pat Harder, Wisconsin (6)	106	590	5.6
1942—HB Gene Fekete, Ohio State (6)	134	550	3.4
1943—FB Tony Butkovich, Purdue (4)	95	626	6.6
1944—FB Les Horvath, Ohio State (6)	126	606	4.8
1945—FB Ollie Cline, Ohio State (7)	84	443	5.3
1946—HB Bob Chappuis, Michigan (7)	82	503	6.1
1947—FB Jack Weisenburger, Michigan (6)	88	503	5.8
1948—HB Harry Szulborski, Purdue (6)	125	631	5.0
1949—HB Harry Szulborski, Purdue (7)	109	732	6.7
1950—HB John Karras, Illinois (6)	92	431	4.6
1951—FB Dick Raklovits, Illinois (7)	147	774	5.3
1952—FB Alan Ameche, Wisconsin (7)	146	721	4.9
1953—FB Alan Ameche, Wisconsin (6)	141	919	6.5
1954—HB J. C. Caroline, Illinois (6)	81	566	6.9
1955—HB Eddie Vincent, Iowa (7)	118	711	6.0
1956—FB Howard Cassady, Ohio State (6)	144	634	4.4
1957—FB Mel Dillard, Purdue (7)	100	584	5.8
1958—FB Jim Pace, Michigan (7)	178	713	4.0
1959—HB Bob White, Ohio State (7)	71	443	6.2
1960—FB Bob Ferguson, Ohio State (6)	114	560	4.9
1961—FB Bob Ferguson, Ohio State (6)	129	671	5.2
1962—FB Dave Francis, Ohio State (6)	75	418	5.6
1963—FB Tom Nowatzke, Indiana (6)	98	486	5.0
1964—HB Jim Grabowski, Illinois (7)	139	723	5.2
1965—HB Jim Grabowski, Illinois (7)	*201	*996	5.0

PASSING

	ATT.	COMP.	YDS.	PCT.	INTRC.	T.D.
1939—HB Harold Hursh, Indiana (5)	56	27	592	.482	—	—
1940—HB Harold Hursh, Indiana (5)	65	32	465	.492	3	7
1941—HB Len Seelinger, Wisconsin (6)	48	26	419	.542	3	7
1942—HB Otto Graham, Northwestern (6)	104	53	714	.514	12	6
1943—HB Bob Hoernschemeyer, Indiana (7)	97	44	523	.509	4	
1944—QB Ben Raimondi, Indiana (6)	82	37	541	.451		
1945—QB Ben Raimondi, Indiana (6)	62	31	470	.500		
1946—HB Bob Chappuis, Michigan (6)	89	48	598	.539	5	
1947—HB Chuck Ortmann, Michigan (6)	71	39	655	.549	2	
1948—HB Chuck Ortmann, Michigan (6)	59	29	547	.492	2	
1949—QB Don Burson, Northwestern (7)	95	44	664	.463	2	
1950—QB John Coatta, Wisconsin (7)	81	52	610	*.642		

PASSING (continued)

	ATT.	COMP.	YDS.	PCT.	INTRC.	T.D.
1951—QB John Coatta, Wisconsin (7)	146	76	1030	.521	12	8
1952—QB John Borton, Ohio (6)	135	75	961	.526	5	8
1953—Qb Jim Miller, Wisconsin (6)	68	36	683	.529	6	6
1954—QB Len Dawson, Purdue (6)	122	63	1019	.516	13	7
1955—QB Len Dawson, Purdue (7)	134	76	901	.567	9	7
1956—QB Len Dawson, Purdue (7)	99	55	691	.556	2	7
1957—QB Jim Van Pelt, Michigan (7)	64	30	465	.469	3	7
1958—QB Randy Duncan, Iowa (6)	111	66	898	.595	1	4
1959—QB Olen Treadway, Iowa (6)	111	63	663	.568		4
1960—QB Ron Miller, Wisconsin (7)	144	72	966	.500	14	4
1961—QB Ron Miller, Wisconsin (7)	153	80	1168	.523	8	9
1962—QB Ron Vander Kelen, Wisconsin (7)	146	77	1009	.527	4	*10
1963—QB Ron DiGravio, Purdue (7)	134	74	941	.552	13	7
1964—QB Gary Snook, Iowa (6)	*234	*110	*1544	.470	4	9
1965—QB Bob Griese, Purdue (7)	178	96	1097	.539	6	4

TOTAL OFFENSE

	RUSHING	PASSING	TOTAL
1939—HB Tom Harmon, Michigan (5)	76-444	57-27-394	133-838
1940—HB Tom Harmon, Michigan (4)	73-330	48-25-306	121-636
1941—HB Tom Kuzma, Michigan (5)	91-398	45-20-267	136-592
1942—HB Otto Graham, Northwestern (6)	82-148	104-53-714	186-862
1943—HB Bob Hoernschemeyer, Indiana (6)	123-277	97-44-596	220-873
1944—HB Les Horvath, Ohio State (6)	126-669	24-12-284	150-953
1945—FB Ollie Cline, Ohio State (7)	126-606	0- 0- 0	126-606
1946—HB Bob Chappuis, Michigan (7)	84-443	64-36-596	148-1039
1947—HB Bob Chappuis, Michigan (6)	88-365	71-39-655	159-1019
1948—HB Chuck Ortmann, Michigan (6)	58-165	59-29-547	117-712
1949—HB Chuck Ortmann, Michigan (6)	78-268	100-36-500	178-768
1950—HB Vic Janowicz, Ohio State (7)	104-293	67-26-410	171-703
1951—HB Paul Giel, Minnesota (6)	123-651	78-35-428	201-1079
1952—QB Tom O'Connell, Illinois (7)	32-(14)	191-108-1308	223-1294
1953—HB Paul Giel, Minnesota (7)	163-580	69-38-457	232-1037
1954—QB Len Dawson, Purdue (6)	31-(95)	122-63-1019	153-924
1955—QB Len Dawson, Purdue (7)	29-(14)	134-76-901	163-887
1956—QB Len Dawson, Purdue (7)	26-52	99-55-691	128-669
1957—QB Randy Duncan, Iowa (6)	29-(22)	90-50-695	116-747
1958—QB Dick Thornton, Northwestern (7)	82-206	108-48-751	190-957
1959—QB Dale Hackbart, Wisconsin (7)	84-319	56-25-367	140-686
1960—QB Ron Miller, Wisconsin (7)	43-15	144-72-966	187-981
1961—QB Sandy Stephens, Minnesota (7)	79-394	123-44-757	202-1151
1962—QB Ron Vander Kelen, Wisconsin (7)	52-228	146-77-1009	198-1237
1963—HB Ron DiGravio, Purdue (7)	68-(14)	134-74-941	202-927
1964—QB Gary Snook, Iowa (7)	42-16	234-110-1544	276-*1560
1965—QB Bob Griese, Purdue (7)	82-(4)	178-96-1097	260-1093

PASS RECEIVING

	NO.	YDS.	T.D.
1940—HB Laverne L. Astroth, Illinois (5)	12	162	—
1941—E Dave Schreiner, Wisconsin (6)	12	249	4
1942—E Bob Motl, Northwestern (6)	16	219	1
1943—E Pete Pihos, Indiana (6)	11	105	2
1944—HB Abe Addams, Indiana (6)	13	207	1
1945—HB Bill Canfield, Purdue (6)	18	245	0
1946—E Lou Mihajlovich, Indiana (6)	16	188	2
1947—HB Chalmers Elliott, Michigan (6)	14	303	0
1948—E Dick Rifenburg, Michigan (6)	17	313	4
1949—E Clifton Anderson, Indiana (6)	21	329	2
1950—E Don Stonesifer, Northwestern (6)	28	394	2
1951—HB Jerry Witt, Wisconsin (5)	16	372	3
1952—E Rex Smith, Illinois (7)	36	515	4
1953—E Bob Topp, Michigan (5)	16	226	1
1054—E John Kerr, Purdue (6)	15	261	0
1955—E Bob Khoenle, Purdue (7)	25	320	1
1956—E Brad Bomba, Indiana (6)	26	376	3
1957—E Jim Gibbons, Iowa (6)	29	548	5
1958—E Rich Kreitling, Illinois (6)	19	283	3
1959—E Don Norton, Iowa (6)	23	321	2
1960—E El Kimbrough, Northwestern (6)	21		
1961—E Hugh (Pat) Richter, Wisconsin (7)	36	*656	*7
1962—E Hugh (Pat) Richter, Wisconsin (7)	33	440	2
1963—E Fred Reichardt, Wisconsin (7)	*40	383	1
1964—FL Karl Noonan, Iowa (6)	26	652	3
1965—E John Wright, Illinois (7)	38	561	2

PUNTING

	NO.	YDS.	AVE.
1940—HB Don Scott, Ohio State (6)	35	1490	42.6
1941—HB Walter Correll, Illinois (5)	17	688	40.5
1942—HB Earl Dolaway, Wisconsin (4)	13	534	41.0
1943—HB Ray Dooney, Wisconsin (7)	19	759	39.9
1944—HB Bob Wiese, Michigan (4)	15	643	42.9
1945—T Rex John, Wisconsin (6)	27	1101	40.8

*—Conference Record

NET YARDS GAINED PASSING

Year	Team	Yards
1939	Indiana (5)	132.6
1940	Illinois (5)	104.0
1941	Wisconsin (6)	99.6
1942	Northwestern (6)	135.0
1943	Indiana (6)	98.0
1944	Indiana (7)	88.0
1945	Indiana (6)	108.0
1946	Michigan (7)	145.5
1947	Michigan (6)	136.8
1948	Michigan (6)	151.0
1949	Ohio State (6)	150.0
1950	Northwestern (6)	141.3
1951	Wisconsin (6)	155.4
1952	Wisconsin (6)	192.1
1953	Indiana (6)	140.8
1954	Purdue (7)	184.3
1955	Purdue (7)	146.8
1956	Indiana (6)	128.7
1957	Iowa (6)	125.7
1958	Iowa (6)	166.5
1959	Iowa (6)	125.0
1960	Wisconsin (7)	157.1
1961	Wisconsin (7)	196.7
1962	Northwestern (6)	199.5
1963	Wisconsin (7)	170.0
1964	Iowa (6)	*266.8
1965	Purdue (7)	161.1

PASSING COMPLETION PERCENTAGE

Year	Team	Pct.
1939	Indiana (5)	.493
1940	Michigan (4)	.500
1941	Wisconsin (6)	.500
1942	Northwestern (6)	.481
1943	Michigan (6)	.500
1944	Minnesota (6)	.461
1945	Indiana (6)	.489
1946	Indiana (6)	.500
1947	Illinois (6)	.509
1948	Michigan (6)	.462
1949	Northwestern (7)	.468
1950	Wisconsin (6)	.545
1951	Wisconsin (7)	.516
1952	Wisconsin (6)	*.575
1953	Wisconsin (6)	.514
1954	Illinois (6)	.550
1955	Purdue (7)	.557
1956	Purdue (7)	.507
1957	Michigan State (6)	.535
1958	Iowa (6)	.552
1959	Iowa (6)	.535
1960	Iowa (6)	.536
1961	Iowa (6)	.556
1962	Northwestern (6)	.554
1963	Indiana (6)	.549
1964	Michigan State (6)	.534
1965	Purdue (7)	.530

TOTAL NET YARDS GAINED

Year	Team	Yards
1939	Ohio State (6)	291.7
1940	Michigan (4)	272.0
1941	Minnesota (5)	343.0
1942	Ohio State (6)	351.6
1943	Michigan (6)	376.0
1944	Ohio State (6)	351.1
1945	Indiana (6)	310.0
1946	Michigan (7)	340.9
1947	Michigan (6)	379.3
1948	Minnesota (7)	332.0
1949	Illinois (7)	338.1
1950	Northwestern (6)	331.2
1951	Wisconsin (7)	391.3
1952	Wisconsin (6)	415.5
1953	Illinois (6)	359.3
1954	Purdue (6)	318.0
1955	Ohio State (6)	322.5
1956	Michigan State (6)	325.5
1957	Michigan State (6)	372.2
1958	Iowa (6)	*416.7
1959	Iowa (6)	351.5
1960	Ohio State (6)	307.7
1961	Ohio State (6)	371.5
1962	Ohio State (7)	337.0
1963	Wisconsin (7)	305.4
1964	Iowa (6)	346.0
1965	Michigan State (7)	377.1

PUNTING AVERAGE

Year	Team	Yards
1939	Ohio State (6)	42.2
1940	Michigan (4)	41.5
1941	Illinois (5)	38.0
1942	Indiana (4)	37.6
1943	Michigan (6)	40.0
1944	Indiana (6)	39.0
1945	Wisconsin (6)	37.1
1946	Wisconsin (6)	39.3
1947	Northwestern (6)	39.4
1948	Illinois (7)	*43.2
1949	Iowa (6)	39.4
1950	Indiana (6)	40.8
1951	Indiana (6)	37.9
1952	Northwestern (7)	42.4
1953	Iowa (6)	41.2
1954	Michigan State (6)	39.9
1955	Michigan State (6)	41.3
1956	Northwestern (7)	37.6
1957	Wisconsin (7)	38.5
1958	Michigan (7)	38.6
1959	Michigan (7)	38.3
1960	Northwestern (6)	37.0
1961	Wisconsin (7)	41.2
1962	Wisconsin (7)	39.5
1963	Michigan State (6)	41.1
1964	Michigan State (7)	42.0
1965	Northwestern (7)	38.7

BALL LOST ON FUMBLES FEWEST TIMES

Year	Team	No.
1939	Illinois (6)	.3
1940	Northwestern (6)	.6
	Illinois (5)	.6
1941	Northwestern (6)	.6
1942	Purdue (5)	
1943	Michigan (6)	.6
1944	Ohio State (6)	1.0
1945	Minnesota (6)	.6
1946	Minnesota (6)	.7
1947	Minnesota (6)	.8
1948	Ohio State (6)	.8
1949	Wisconsin (6)	.8
1950	Ohio State (6)	.7
1951	Northwestern (7)	1.2
1952	Northwestern (7)	1.1
1953	Wisconsin (6)	.8
1954	Purdue (6)	.8
1955	Ohio State (6)	.8
1956	Iowa (6)	1.2
1957	Ohio State (6)	1.1
1958	Illinois (7), Wisconsin (7), Ohio State (7)	1.3
1959	Indiana (7), Ohio State (7)	1.1
1960	Ohio State (6)	1.1
1961	Minnesota (7)	*.7
1962	Indiana (6)	.8
1963	Ohio State (6)	.7
1964	Indiana (6)	.8
1965	Illinois (7)	.9

*—Conference Record

PUNTING (Continued)

Year	Player	NO.	YDS.	AVE.
1946	QB John Galvin, Purdue (6)	34	1322	*38.9
1947	FB T. A. Cox, Wisconsin (6)	16	688	43.0
	QB Pete Perini, Ohio State (5)	46	1821	39.8
1948	HB Earl Girard, Wisconsin (6)	18	700	38.9
1949	HB Dwight Eddelman, Illinois (7)	52	2252	43.3
1950	HB Bob Robertson, Indiana (6)	32	1306	*40.8
1951	HB Jim Hammond, Wisconsin (7)	22	926	42.0
1952	HB Bob Robertson, Indiana (3)	25	973	*38.8
1953	HB Ken Miller, Illinois (6)	28	1126	40.2
1954	E Ron Kramer, Michigan (7)	22	908	41.2
1955	FB George Broeder, Iowa (6)	18	746	41.4
1956	FB Kevin Kleber, Minnesota (3)	25	1106	44.2
1957	HB Clarence Peaks, Mich. State (3)	13	532	40.9
1958	HB Kenny Mikes, Purdue (7)	26	1007	38.8
1959	FB Brad Myers, Michigan (7)	20	856	42.8
1960	FB Tom Robbins, Minnesota (7)	42	1630	38.8
1961	QB Jim Bakken, Wisconsin (7)	28	1163	41.5
1962	QB Jim Bakken, Wisconsin (7)	31	1277	41.2
1963	HB Russ Pfahler, Purdue (6)	21	855	40.7
1964	FB Lou Bobich, Michigan State (6)	27	1110	41.1
1965	FB Lou Bobich, Michigan State (6)	21	882	42.0
	HB Ron Rector, Northwestern (7)	27	1080	40.0

*—one kick blocked.

TEAM DEPARTMENTAL CHAMPIONS

(all figures are per game averages)

SCORING

Year	Team	Ave.
1939	Michigan (5)	29.4
1940	Michigan (4)	23.5
1941	Minnesota (5)	24.8
1942	Ohio State (6)	25.0
1943	Michigan (6)	*34.5
1944	Ohio State (6)	25.5
1945	Indiana (6)	25.5
1946	Michigan (7)	23.6
1947	Michigan (6)	28.7
1948	Michigan (6)	31.7
1949	Minnesota (6)	21.8
1950	Ohio State (7)	31.1
1951	Purdue (5)	23.2
1952	Wisconsin (6)	26.3
1953	Illinois (6)	25.7
1954	Wisconsin (6)	19.3
1955	Ohio State (6)	26.5
1956	Michigan State (6)	22.0
1957	Michigan State (6)	30.7
1958	Iowa (6)	28.8
1959	Iowa (6)	19.8
1960	Iowa (6)	27.2
1961	Ohio State (6)	29.8
1962	Wisconsin (7)	28.4
1963	Illinois (7)	17.9
1964	Michigan (7)	22.3
1965	Michigan State (7)	29.0

FIRST DOWNS

Year	Team	Ave.
1939	Ohio State (6)	12.7
1940	Michigan (4)	15.7
1941	Ohio State (5)	13.6
1942	Michigan (6)	16.0
1943	Michigan (6)	15.0
1944	Ohio State (6)	15.0
1945	Indiana (6)	15.6
1946	Iowa (6)	15.5
1947	Michigan (6)	15.5
1948	Michigan (6)	17.5
1949	Minnesota (7)	15.1
1950	Wisconsin (6)	15.7
1951	Northwestern (7)	17.3
1952	Wisconsin (6)	19.3
1953	Wisconsin (6)	19.2
1954	Illinois (6)	16.6
1955	Purdue (6)	17.2
1956	Wisconsin (6)	17.7
1957	Michigan State (6)	18.3
1958	Iowa (6)	19.7
1959	Iowa (6)	*22.0
1960	Iowa (6)	18.0
1961	Illinois (6)	17.7
1962	Ohio State (6)	19.8
1963	Wisconsin (7)	20.3
1964	Michigan (7)	17.4
1965	Michigan State (7)	19.3
	Northwestern (7)	21.1

NET YARDS GAINED RUSHING

Year	Team	Yards
1939	Minnesota (6)	241.2
1940	Minnesota (6)	221.0
1941	Minnesota (5)	277.8
1942	Ohio State (6)	270.1
1943	Michigan (6)	*320.0
1944	Ohio State (6)	274.3
1945	Indiana (6)	214.0
	Ohio State (7)	214.0
1946	Northwestern (6)	205.5
1947	Michigan (6)	242.5
1948	Ohio State (6)	212.3
1949	Illinois (6)	283.9
1950	Northwestern (6)	198.0
1951	Wisconsin (6)	235.9
1952	Wisconsin (6)	256.3
1953	Illinois (6)	284.5
1954	Ohio State (7)	239.1
1955	Ohio State (6)	309.7
1956	Ohio State (6)	260.3
1957	Ohio State (6)	307.0
1958	Iowa (6)	250.2
1959	Iowa (6)	226.5
1960	Iowa (6)	243.7
1961	Ohio State (6)	279.3
1962	Ohio State (6)	275.2
1963	Michigan State (6)	187.2
1964	Michigan (7)	222.6
1965	Michigan State (7)	249.4

*—Conference Record

HONOR TEAMS
ALL-CONFERENCE ACADEMIC

(Sponsored by Conference Sports Information Directors)

A player qualifies for nomination by having a B or better scholastic average.

Pos.	1953	1954	1955
E	Carl Diener, MSU	Brad Bomba, Ind.	Brad Bomba, Ind.#
E	Bill Fenton, Iowa#	Don Kauth, MSU	Fred Kriss, OSU
T	Don Ernst, Ill.	Sandy Sacks, NU#	Bob Hobert, Minn.#
T	Bob Lezinski, Ill.#	Dick Hilinski, OSU#	Jim Orwig, Mich.
G	Tom Dailey, Ind.	Clarence Stensby, Wis.#	Dick Dessy, Iowa
G	John Dixon, Wis.#	Jack Chamblin, Ill.#	Carl Nystrom, MSU#
C	Jerry Hilgenberg, Ia.*	Warren Lawson, Ia.#	Jim Minor, Ill.
B	John Borton, OSU#	John Borton, Ia.#	Frank Ellwood, OSU
B	Froncie Gutman, Pur.	Froncie Gutman, Pur.	Jim Whitmer, Pur.
B	Dick Balzhiser, Mich.#	Pat Levenhagen, Wis.	Pat Levenhagen, Wis.#
B	Paul Giel, Minn.*	John Baumgartner, Minn.#	Dick Borstad, Minn.#

Pos.	1956	1957	1958
E	Brad Bomba, Ind.#	Perry Gehring, Minn.	Perry Gehring, Minn.
E	Perry Gehring, Minn.	Bob Jewitt, MSU	Dick Barker, MSU
T	Bob Hobert, Minn.*	Jim Orwig, Mich.#	Andy Cvercko, NU*
T	John Smith, Minn.#	Andy Cvercko, NU#	Gene Selawski, Pur.*
G	Frank Bloomquist, Ia.#	Bob Allen, Ill.	Ellison Kelly, MSU#
G	Jim Orwig, Mich.#	John Heineke, Wis.#	Jerry Stalcup, Wis.#
C	Jim Minor, Ill.	Mike Svendsen, Minn.#	Mike Svendsen, Minn.#
B	Len Dawson, Pur.#	Frank Kremblas, OSU#	Tommy Kendrick, Ind.
B	Frank Ellwood, OSU#	Dale Smith, Ill.#	Bob Zeman, Wis.
B	Pat Levenhagen, Wis.#	Blanche Martin, MSU#	Jon Hobbs, Wis.#
B	Dick Borstad, Minn.#	Bob White, OSU#	Bob White, OSU#

Pos.	1959	1960	1961
E	Henry Derleth, Wis.#	Bill Freehan, Mich.	Jack Elwell, Pur.#
E	Leonard Jardine, Pur.	Henry Derleth, Wis.#	Tom Perdue, OSU#
T	Gene Gossage, NU#	Frank Brixius, Minn.#	Jon Schopf, Mich.#
T	Michael Wright, Minn.#	Jerry Beabout, Pur.*	Jim Wheeler, Minn.#
G	Donald Noone, Ind.	Darrel DeDecker, Ind.	Boyd Melvin, Mich.
G	Jerome Shetler, Minn.	Alex Trombetta, Ind.	Brian Moore, Wis.
C	Dave Ash, Ill.	Jerry Smith, Mich.#	Larry Onesti, NU*
B	Dale Hackbart, Wis.#	Bob Eickhoff, NU	Bob Eickhoff, NU
B	Darrell Harper, Mich.	Bill Wentz, OSU	Bennie McRae, Mich.#
B	Blanche, Martin, MSU	Ed Ryan, MSU	Judge Dickson, Minn.#
B	Bob White, OSU	Mike Stock, NU#	Bill Tunnicliff, Mich.#

Pos.	1962	1963	1964
E	Ron Carlson, Wis.#	George Burman, NU	Gene Washington, MSU
E	Pat Richter, Wis.*	Dave Ellison, Pur.	Dave Cyranoski, NU
T	Dick Deller, Ill.	Milt Sunde, Minn.#	Mike Schwager, NU
T	Joe O'Donnell, Mich.#	Joe Szczecko, NU	Joe Szczecko, NU
G	Ken Ellis, Ind.	Dick O'Donnell, Mich.#	Bill Keating, Mich.
G	Kent Pike, NU	Dick Deller, Ill.#	John Marcum, Mich.#
C	Jerry Goshgarian, NU	Ken Bowman, Wis.#	Bruce Capel, Ill.
QB	Ron Meyer, Pur.	Mike Taliaferro, Ill.#	Bob Timberlake, Mich.*
HB	Harvey Chapman, Mich.	Bob Timberlake, Mich.#	Dick Gordon, MSU#
HB	Paul Flatley, NU#	Billy Smith, Wis.	Arnie Chonko, OSU*
FB	Dave Katterhenrich, OSU	Mike Dundy, Ill.#	Jim Grabowski, Ill.*

Pos.	1965
E	John Wright, Ill.#
E	Jim Proebstle, MSU#
T	Don Bierowicz, MSU#
G	Ken Ramsey, NU#
G	Bill Ridder, OSU#
C	Mike Beinor, NU#
QB	Ray Pryor, OSU#
HB	Steve Juday, MSU*
HB	Gordon Teter, Pur.
FB	Don Japinga, MSU#
FB	Jim Grabowski, Ill.*

*—All-America 1st team selection   #—All-Big Ten selection or mention

*—All-Big Ten selection

BALL LOST ON FUMBLES — MOST TIMES

Year	Team	Avg.
1939	Ohio State (6)	2.0
1940	Indiana (5)	2.4
1941	Illinois (5)	2.6
1942	Ohio State (6)	2.0
1943	Purdue (6)	3.0
	Illinois (6)	3.0
1944	Iowa (6)	2.3
1945	Ohio State (7)	2.5
1946	Indiana (6)	3.3
1947	Purdue (6)	2.3
1948	Northwestern (6)	2.2
1949	Purdue (6)	2.5
1950	Iowa (6)	2.8
1951	Ohio State (6)	3.0
1952	Purdue (6)	2.0
1953	Minnesota (7)	2.0
	Purdue (6)	2.0
1954	Northwestern (6)	3.0
1955	Michigan State (6)	1.8
	Purdue (7)	1.8
1956	Purdue (7)	2.6
1957	Illinois (7)	2.7
	Michigan State (6)	2.7
1958	Iowa (6)	2.5
1959	Iowa (6)	2.5
1960	Michigan (6)	2.0
1961	Northwestern (6)	2.0
1962	Michigan State (6)	*3.7
1963	Minnesota (7)	2.6
	Wisconsin (7)	2.6
1964	Iowa (6)	2.5
1965	Wisconsin (7)	2.1

FEWEST YARDS PENALIZED

Year	Team	Avg.
1939	Purdue (5)	20.0
1940	Purdue (5)	20.6
1941	Purdue (5)	18.2
1942	Purdue (5)	21.6
1943	Ohio State (5)	24.0
	Iowa (5)	24.3
1944	Northwestern (6)	18.8
1945	Northwestern (7)	17.7
1946	Minnesota (6)	25.8
1947	Michigan (6)	*15.2
1948	Michigan (6)	34.2
1949	Wisconsin (6)	34.2
1950	Wisconsin (7)	22.3
1951	Minnesota (6)	39.2
1952	Minnesota (6)	37.8
1954	Northwestern (6)	33.8
1955	Illinois (6)	29.5
1956	Wisconsin (7)	18.7
1957	Michigan (7)	24.4
1958	Ohio State (7)	21.3
1959	Ohio State (6)	16.2
1960	Northwestern (6)	26.0
1961	Ohio State (6)	22.3
1962	Ohio State (6)	28.5
1963	Ohio State (6)	34.4
1964	Wisconsin (6)	26.7
1965	Ohio State (7)	

*—Conference Record

Harry Hawkins, g, 1925
Bob Brown, c, 1925
Otto Pommerening, t, 1928
Maynard Morrison, c, 1931
Ted Petoskey, e, 1932-33
Charles Bernard, c, 1932-33
Harry Newman, qb, 1932
Francis Wistert, t, 1933
Ralph Heikkinen, g, 1938
*Tom Harmon, hb, 1939-40
Ed Frutig, e, 1940
Bob Westfall, fb, 1941
Albert Wistert, t, 1942
Julius Franks, g, 1942
Mervin Pregulman, t, 1943
Bill Daley, fb, 1943
Elmer Madar, e, 1946
Bob Chappuis, hb, 1947
Chalmers (Bump) Elliott, hb, 1947
Richard Rifenburg, e, 1948
Alvin Wistert, t, 1948-49
Pete Elliott, qb 1948
Allen Wahl, t, 1949-50
Lowell Perry, e, 1951
Art Walker, t, 1954
Ron Kramer, e, 1955-56
Jim Pace, hb, 1957
Bob Timberlake, qb, 1964
Bill Yearby, t, 1964-65

MICHIGAN STATE
Neno J. DaPrato, hb, 1915
Sidney Wagner, g, 1935
John Pingel, hb, 1938
Ed Bagdon, g, 1949
Lynn Chandnois, hb, 1949
Everett Grandelius, hb, 1950
Don Coleman, t, 1951
Bob Carey, e, 1951
Al Dorow, qb, 1951
Frank Kush, g, 1952
Dick Tamburo, c-lb, 1952
Don McAuliffe, hb, 1952
Don Dohoney, e, 1953
Earl Morrall, b, 1955
Norman Masters, t, 1955
Dan Currie, c, 1957
Walt Kowalczyk, b, 1957
Sam Williams, e, 1957
Dean Look, b, 1959
Dave Behrman, g, 1961
George Saimes, fb, 1962
Sherman Lewis, hb, 1963
Harold Lucas, mg, 1965
Steve Juday, qb, 1965
Charles (Bubba) Smith, e, 1965
George Webster, dhb, 1965
Gene Washington, e, 1965
Clinton Jones, hb, 1965

*Clarence Munn, g, 1931
Frank (Butch) Larson, e, 1933-34
*Francis (Pug) Lund, hb, 1933-34
Bill Bevan, g, 1934
Sheldon Beise, b, 1935
Charles (Bud) Wilkinson, g, 1935
Dick Smith, t, 1935
*Ed Widseth, t, 1934-35-36
Andrew Uram, b, 1936
Ray King, e, 1937
Francis Twedell, g, 1938
George Franck, hb, 1940
Urban Odson, t, 1940
Helge Pukema, g, 1940
Bruce Smith, hb, 1941
Dick Wildung, t, 1941-42
Leo Nomellini, g, 1948-49
Clayton Tonnemaker, c, 1949
Paul Giel, hb, 1952, 1953
Bob McNamara, b, 1954
Tom Brown, g, 1960
Sandy Stephens, qb, 1961
Bobby Bell, t, 1961-1962
Carl Eller, t, 1963
*Aaron Brown, e, 1965

NORTHWESTERN
Alton Johnson, hb, 1901
Tim Lowry, c, 1925
Robert Johnson, t, 1926
Ralph (Moon) Baker, hb, 1926
Henry Anderson, g, 1929
Frank Baker, hb, 1930
Wade Woodworth, g, 1930
Fayette (Reb) Russell, fb, 1930
Jack Riley, t, 1931
Dal Marvil, t, 1931
Ernest (Pug) Rentner, hb, 1931
Edgar Manske, e, 1933
Paul Tangora, g, 1935
Steve Reid, g, 1936
Bob Voigts, t, 1938
John Haman, c, 1939
Alf Bauman, t, 1940-41
Herb Hein, e, 1943
Otto Graham, hb, 1943
Max Morris, e, 1945
Alex Sarkisian, c, 1948
Art Murakowski, hb, 1948
Don Stonesifer, e, 1950
Joe Collier, e, 1952, 1953
Andy Cvercko, t, 1958
Ron Burton, b, 1959
Jim Andreotti, c, 1959
Larry Onesti, c, 1961
Jack Cvercko, g, 1962
Tom Myers, qb, 1962

OHIO STATE
Robert Karch, t, 1916
*Charles Harley, fb, 1916-17-19
*Charles Bolen, e, 1917
Gaylord Stinchcomb, hb, 1920
Iolas Huffman, g-t, 1920-21
Edwin Hess, g, 1925-26
Marty Karow, hb, 1926
Leo Raskowski, t, 1927
*Wes Fesler, e, 1928-29-30
Joseph Gailus, g, 1932
Regis Monahan, g, 1934-35
George Gibson, g, 1928
Kenneth Haycraft, e, 1928
Robert Tanner, e, 1929
*Bronko Nagurski, t, 1929

Merle Wendt, e, 1934-35
Inwood Smith, g, 1935
Gomer Jones, c, 1935
Gust Zarnas, g, 1937

Esco Sarkkinen, e, 1939
Don Scott, hb, 1939
Bob Shaw, e, 1942
Charles Csuri, t, 1942
Lindell Houston, g, 1942
Jack Dugger, e, 1944
Bill Willis, t, 1944
Bill Hackett, g, 1944
Les Horvath, hb, 1944
Warren Amling, g-t, 1945-46
Vic Janowicz, hb, 1950
Robert Momsen, g, 1950
Robert McCullough, c, 1950
Mike Takacs, g, 1952
Howard Cassady, hb, 1954, 1955
Dean Dugger, e, 1954
Jim Parker, g, 1955, 1956
Aurelius Thomas, g, 1957
James Houston, e, 1958-59
Robert White, fb, 1958
Jim Marshall, t, 1958
Bob Ferguson, fb, 1960-61
Jim Davidson, t, 1964
Arnie Chonko, saf, 1964
Dwight Kelley, lb, 1964-65
Doug Van Horn, g, 1965

PURDUE
*Elmer Oliphant, hb, 1916##
Ralph Welch, hb, 1929
Elmer Sleight, t, 1929
Paul Moss, e, 1931-32
Charles Miller c, 1931
Roy Horstmann, fb, 1932
Duane Purvis, hb, 1933-34
Dave Rankin, e, 1939-40
Tony Butkovich, fb, 1943
Alex Agase, t, (1942#)-43-(46#)
Boris Dimancheff, hb, 1944
Tom Hughes, t, 1945
Leo Sugar, g, 1951
Bernie Flowers, e, 1952
Tom Bettis, g, 1954
Gene Selawski, t, 1958
Jerry Beabout, g, 1960
Don Brumm, t, 1962
Harold Wells, e, 1964
Jerry Shay, t, 1965
Karl Singer, t, 1965
Bob Griese, qb, 1965

WISCONSIN
*Pat O'Dea, fb, 1899
Robert (Butts) Butler, t, 1912
Ray (Tubby) Keeler, g, 1913
Arlie Mucks, g, 1914
Howard (Cub) Buck, t, 1915
Charles Carpenter, c, 1919
Frank Weston, e, 1920
Ralph Scott, t, 1920
Martin Below, t, 1923
Milo Lubratovich, t, 1930
Howard Weiss, fb, 1938
Dave Schreiner, e, 1941-42
Pat Harder, fb, 1942
Earl (Jug) Girard, fb, 1944
Ed Withers, hb, 1950
Pat O'Donahue, e, 1951
Hal Faverty, e, 1951
Don Voss, e, 1952
David Suminski, t, 1952
Alan Ameche, fb, 1953-54
Dan Lanphear, t, 1959
Pat Richter, e, 1961-1962

#at Illinois
##at Army

*Hall of Fame (Player)   **Hall of Fame (Coach)

ALL-AMERICAN

(Consensus of Major Team Selections, Compiled by National Collegiate Athletic Bureau)

1965 Consensus Team

OFFENSE
E—Howard Twilley, Tulsa
E—Freeman White, Nebraska
T—Sam Ball, Kentucky
T—Glen Ray Hines, Arkansas
G—Dick Arrington, Notre Dame
G—Stas Maliszewski, Princeton
C—Paul Crane, Alabama
QB—BOB GRIESE, PURDUE

HB—Donny Anderson, Texas Tech
HB—Mike Garrett, Southern California
FB—JIM GRABOWSKI, ILLINOIS

DEFENSE
E—AARON BROWN, MINNESOTA
E—CHARLES (BUBBA) SMITH, MICHIGAN STATE
T—Walt Barnes, Nebraska
T—Lloyd Phillips, Arkansas
T—BILL YEARBY, MICHIGAN
LB—Carl McAdams, Oklahoma
LB—Frank Emanuel, Tennessee
HB—Tommy Nobis, Texas
HB—GEORGE WEBSTER, MICH. STATE
HB—Johnny Roland, Missouri
HB—Nick Rassas, Notre Dame

OTHER FIRST TEAM SELECTIONS

ENDS—GENE WASHINGTON, MICHIGAN STATE; Chuck Casey, Florida; Bobby Crockett, Arkansas; Tony Jeter, Nebraska; Ed Weisacosky, Miami (Fla.); Lynn Matthews, Florida.
TACKLES—KARL SINGER, PURDUE; HAROLD LUCAS, MICHIGAN STATE; Jack Thornton, Auburn; Wayne Foster, Washington State; George Patton, Georgia.
GUARDS—RON GOOVERT, MICHIGAN STATE; DOUG VAN HORN, OHIO STATE; JERRY SHAY, PURDUE.
CENTER—DWIGHT KELLEY, OHIO STATE.
BACKS—CLINTON JONES, MICHIGAN STATE; STEVE JUDAY, MICHIGAN STATE; Floyd Little, Syracuse; Steve Spurrier, Florida; Bruce Bennett, Florida.

BIG TEN CONFERENCE FOOTBALL ALL-AMERICANS

CHICAGO
*Andrew R. E. Wyant, c, 1894
Clarence Herschberger, fb, 1898
Frederick A. Speik, e, 1904, '05, '06
*Walter Eckersall, qb, 1904, '05, '06
Mark S. Catlin, e, 1905
Walter Steffen, qb, 1908
*Paul Des Jardien, c, 1913
Charles E. Higgins, g, 1917, 1920, '21
John W. Thomas, fb, 1922
Franklin K. Gowdy, g, 1924
Joseph Pondelik, g, 1924
Elmore Patterson, c, 1934

ILLINOIS
Ralph Chapman, g, 1914
Perry Graves, e, 1914
Bart Macomber, hb, 1915
John Depler, c, 1918
*Charles Carney, e, 1920
James McMillen, g, 1923
*Harold Grange, hb, 1923-24-25
Bernie Shively, g, 1926
Russ Crane, g, 1927
Robert Reitsch, c, 1927
Leroy Wietz, g, 1928
Albert (Butch) Nowack, t, 1928
Lou Gordon, t, 1929
Jim Reeder, t, 1939
*Alex Agase, g, 1942-(43#)-46
Claude (Buddy) Young, hb, 1944
Ralph Serpico, g, 1944

INDIANA
Chuck Bennett, hb, 1928
Corby Davis, fb, 1937
Billy Hillenbrand, hb, 1942
*Pete Pihos, e, 1943
John Tavener, c, 1944
Bob Ravensburg, e, 1945
George Taliaferro, hb, 1948
Tom Nowatzke, fb, 1964
Don Croftcheck, g, 1964

IOWA
Fred Becker, t, 1916
Lester Belding, e, 1919
*Fred (Duke) Slater, t, 1921
Aubrey Devine, qb, 1921
Gordon Locke, qb, 1921-22
Richard Romey, e, 1925
Emerson Nelson, t, 1925
Willis Glassgow, hb, 1929
Francis Schammel, g, 1933
Ozzie Simmons, hb, 1935
*Nile Kinnick, hb, 1939

MICHIGAN
William Cunningham, c, 1898
*Neil Snow, e, 1901
*William Heston, hb, 1903-04
*Adolph (Germany) Schultz, c, 1907
Albert Benbrook, g, 1909-10
Stanfield Wells, e, 1910
Miller H. Pontius, t, 1913
James Craig, hb, 1913
John Maulbetsch, hb, 1914
Frank Culver, c, 1917
Cedric Smith, fb, 1917
Ernest Allmendinger, g, 1917
Ernest Steketee, fb, 1918
Henry Vick, c, 1921
Paul Goebel, e, 1922
*Harry Kipke, hb, 1922
Jack Blott, c, 1923
Edliff R. Slaughter, g, 1924
*Bennie Friedman, qb, 1925-26
*Bennie Oosterbaan, e, 1925-26-27

*Hall of Fame (Player)

School	1939	1940	1941
Chicago	Robert Wasem, hb	George Bernhardt, fb	Nate Johnson, t
Illinois	Bill Lenich, c	Dwight Gahm, c	
Indiana			Bill Hillenbrand, hb
Iowa	Nile Kinnick, hb*	Mike Enich, t	Bill Diehl, c
Michigan	Tom Harmon, hb	Tom Harmon, hb*	Reuben Kelto, t
Michigan State	Lyle Rockenbach, hb	Jack Amon, fb	Anthony Arena, c
Minnesota	Harold Van Every, hb	Bob Paffrath, qb	Bob Sweiger, b
Northwestern	John Haman, c	Paul Hiemenz, c	Alf Bauman, t
Ohio State	Stephen Andrako, c	Claude White, c	Jack Graf, fb*
Purdue	Fred Bykowski, g	Dave Rankin, e	Bill Combs, e
Wisconsin	George Paskvan, fb	George Paskvan, fb	Marlin (Pat) Harder, fb

School	1942	1943	1944
Illinois	Elmer Engel, e	Eddie Bray, b	Buddy Young, b
Indiana	Lou Saban, b	John Tavener, c	John Tavener, c
Iowa	Tom Farmer, b	Bob Liddy, b	Robert Snyder, t
Michigan	Al Wistert, t	Bob Wiese, b	Don Lund, b
Michigan State	Richard Kieppe, hb	No Award	Jack Breslin, fb
Minnesota	Ed Hirsch, b	Paul Mitchell, t	John Lundquist, b
Northwestern		Otto Graham, hb*	Max Morris, b*
Ohio State	Charles Csuni, t	Gordon Appleby, c	Les Horvath, b*
Purdue	Bill Buffington, b	Dick Barwegen, g	Boris Dimancheff, b
Wisconsin	Dave Schreiner, e*	Joe Keenan, c	Clarence Esser, t

School	1945	1946	1947
Illinois	Mac Wenskunas, c	Alex Agase, g*	Ike Owens, e
Indiana	Howard Brown, g	Pete Pihos, fb	Howard Brown, g
Iowa	Arthur Johnson, hb	Bill Kay, t	
Michigan	Harold Watts, c	Bob Chappius, hb	Chalmers Elliott, hb*
Michigan State	Stephen Contos, hb	George Guerre, hb	Warren Huey, e
Minnesota	Bob Fitch, t	Bill Bye, hb	Larry Olsonowski, b
Northwestern		Ed Hirsch, g	Art Murakowski, b
Ohio State	Ollie Cline, fb*	Cecil Seuders, e	
Purdue	Norman Maloney, e		Phil O'Reilly, t
Wisconsin	Clarence Esser, e*	Fred Negus, c	Bob Wilson, c

School	1948	1949	1950
Illinois	James Valek, e	John Karras, hb	Tony Klimek, e
Indiana	George Taliaferro, b	Nick Sebek, b	Bob Robertson, hb
Iowa	Alfonso DiMarco, b	Jack Dittmer, e	
Michigan	Dominic Tomasi, g	Dick Kempthorn, b	Don Dufek, fb
Michigan State	Lynn Chandnois, hb	Eugene Glick, qb	Everett Grandelius, hb
Minnesota	Everette Faunce, b	Bud Grant, e	Wayne Robinson, c
Northwestern	Art Murakowski, b*	Don Stonesifer, e	
Ohio State			
Purdue			Chuck Hagmann, e
Wisconsin		Gaspar Perricone, fb	

School	1951	1952	1953
Illinois	Charles Boerio, lb	Al Brosky, b	Don Ernst, t
Indiana	Gene Gedman, fb	Eugene Gedman, fb	Harry Jagielski, t
Iowa	Bill Reichardt, fb*	Bill Fenton, e	Bill Fenton, t
Michigan	Don Peterson, fb	Ted Topor, qb	Tony Branoff, hb
Michigan State	Donald Coleman, t	Richard Tamburo, c	LeRoy Bolden, hb
Minnesota	Ron Engel, fb	Paul Giel, hb*	Paul Giel, hb*
Northwestern	John Steeb, g	Charles Hren, fb	Bob Lauer, t
Ohio State	Vic Janowicz, hb	Fred Bruney, hb	George Jacoby, t
Purdue	Darrell Brewster, e	Earl Heninger, hb	Tom Bettis, g
Wisconsin	Harold Faverty, e	Dave Suminski, t	Alan Ameche, fb

School	1954	1955	1956
Illinois	Jack Chamblin, c	Em Lindbeck, qb	Dave Walker, g
Indiana	Florian Helinski, qb	Bob Skoronski, t	Bob Fee, fb
Iowa	Warren Lawson, c	Jerry Reichow, qb	Kenny Ploen, qb*
Michigan	Fred Baer, fb	Terry Barr, hb	Dick Hill, g
Michigan State	John Matsock, hb	Carl Nystrom, g	Jim Hinesly, e
Minnesota	Bob McNamara, fb	Don Swanson, qb	Bobby Cox, qb
Northwestern	Ziggie Niepokoj, e	Kurt Krueger, e	Al Viola, g
Ohio State	Howard Cassady, hb	Howard Cassady, hb*	Jim Parker, g
Purdue	Tom Bettis, g	Joe Krupa, t	Lamar Lundy, e
Wisconsin	Alan Ameche, fb*	Wells Gray, g	Dave Howard, t

*—Received Chicago Tribune Trophy as Most Valuable in Conference. (Tribune Trophy winners prior to 1930 were Red Grange, Illinois, 1924; Tim Lowry, Northwestern, 1925; Benny Friedman, Michigan, 1926; Ken Rouse, Chicago, 1927; Chuck Bennett, Indiana, 1928; Bill Glassgow, Iowa, 1929.)

HALL OF FAME—COACHES

The following are current or former Big Ten officials and coaches who are members of the National Football Foundation Hall of Fame as coaches:

Ike Armstrong—Utah (MINNESOTA Athletic Director, 1950-1963).

Bernard W. Bierman—Mississippi A & M, Tulane and MINNESOTA (1932-1941 & 1945-1950).

Herbert O. (Fritz) Crisler—MINNESOTA (1930-1931), Princeton and MICHIGAN (1938-1947).

Edward K. Hall—ILLINOIS (1892-1893).

Howard H. Jones—Syracuse, Yale, OHIO STATE (1910), IOWA (1916-1923), Duke and Southern California.

George E. Little—Miami (Ohio), MICHIGAN (1924), WISCONSIN (1925-1926) and Cincinnati.

Clarence (Biggie) Munn—Albright, Syracuse and MICHIGAN STATE (1947-1953).

Andrew L. Smith—Pennsylvania, PURDUE (1913-1915) and California.

Amos Alonzo Stagg—Springfield, CHICAGO (1892-1932) and College of Pacific.

Lynn (Pappy) Waldorf—Oklahoma State, Kansas State, NORTHWESTERN (1935-1945) and California.

E. E. (Tad) Wieman—MICHIGAN (1927-1928) and Princeton.

Dr. John W. Wilce—OHIO STATE (1913-1928).

Dr. Henry L. Williams—MINNESOTA (1900-1921).

Fielding H. Yost—MICHIGAN (1901-1923 & 1925-1926).

Robert C. Zuppke—ILLINOIS (1913-1941).

MOST VALUABLE FOOTBALL PLAYERS

School	1930	1931	1932
Chicago	Wally Knudson, fb	Sam Horwitz, g	William B. Cassels, t
Illinois	Stan Bodman, g	Fred Frink, e	Gil Berry, hb
Indiana	Joe Zeller, g	Joe Zeller, g	John Keckich, g
Iowa	Oliver Sansen, hb	Oliver Sansen, b	Joe Laws, g
Michigan	Jack Wheeler, hb	William Hewitt, b	Harry Newman, qb*
Michigan State		Abe Eliowitz, fb	Robert Monnett, hb
Minnesota	Clarence Munn, g	Clarence Munn, g*	Roy Oen, c
Northwestern	Robert Clark, c	Paul Engebretsen, g	Ernest Rentner, hb
Ohio State	Wesley Fesler, e*	Robert Haubrich, t	Lewis Hinchman, fb
Purdue	George Stears, g	Jim Purvis, b	Roy Horstmann, fb
Wisconsin	William Lusby, fb	Harold Smith, t	Mickey McGuire, hb

School	1933	1934	1935
Chicago	Jay Berwanger, b	Ell Patterson, c	Jay Berwanger, b*
Illinois	Dave Cook, t	Les Lindberg, b	Ed Gryboski, g
Indiana	Robert Jones, fb	Don Veller, b	Wendell Walker, b
Iowa	Joe Laws, b*	Dick Crayne, b	Dick Crayne, b
Michigan	Herman Everhardus, b	Gerald Ford, c	Bill Renner, b
Michigan State	Arthur Buss, t	Edward Klewicki, e	Sidney Wagner, g
Minnesota	Michael Vuchinich, c	Pug Lund, b*	Vernal LeVoir, b
Northwestern	Edgar Manske, e	Edward Whalen, g	Walter Cruice, b
Ohio State	Fred Hecker, b	Gomer Jones, c	Frank Loebs, e
Purdue	Robert Schiller, b	Duane Purvis, b	
Wisconsin		Milt Kummer, g	Eddie Jankowski, b

School	1936	1937	1938
Chicago	Sam Whiteside, c	Kendall Petersen	Lew Hamity
Illinois	Cliff Kuhn, g	Jack Berner, qb	James Hodges, g
Indiana	Vernon Huffman, b*	Corbett Davis, fb*	Bob Haak, t
Iowa	Homer Harris, e	Bob Lannon	Erwin Prasse, e
Michigan	Matt Patanelli, e	Ralph Heikkinen, t	Ralph Heikkinen, g
Michigan State	Sam Ketcham, c	Harry Speelman, t	John Pingel, hb
Minnesota	Ed Widseth, t	Rudy Gmitro, hb	Larry Buhler
Northwestern	Steve Reid, t	Don Heap, fb	Robert Voigts, t
Ohio State	Ralph Wolfe, c	Ralph Wolfe	James Langhurst, hb
Purdue	John Drake, b	Cecil Isbell, hb	Joe Mihal
Wisconsin	Eddie Jankowski, b	Howard Weiss, fb	Howard Weiss, fb*

*—Received Chicago Tribune Trophy as Most Valuable in Conference. (Tribune Trophy winners prior to 1930 were Red Grange, Illinois, 1924; Tim Lowry, Northwestern, 1925; Benny Friedman, Michigan, 1926; Ken Rouse, Chicago, 1927; Chuck Bennett, Indiana, 1928; Bill Glassgow, Iowa, 1929.)

National Rankings (continued)

1944
1. Army
2. OHIO STATE
3. Randolph Field
4. Navy
5. Bainbridge Navy
6. Iowa Seahawks
7. S. California
8. MICHIGAN
9. Notre Dame
10. Fourth Air Force

1945
1. Army
2. Alabama
3. Navy
4. INDIANA
5. Okla. A. & M.
6. MICHIGAN
7. St. Mary's
8. Pennsylvania
9. Notre Dame
10. Texas

1946
1. Notre Dame
2. Army
3. Georgia
4. U.C.L.A.
5. ILLINOIS
6. MICHIGAN
7. Tennessee
8. Louisiana State
9. N. Carolina
10. Rice

1947
*1. Notre Dame
2. MICHIGAN
3. S. Methodist
4. Penn State
5. Univ. of Texas
6. Univ. of Penn.
7. S. California
8. North Carolina
9. Georgia Tech
10. Georgia

1948
1. MICHIGAN
2. Notre Dame
3. North Carolina
4. California
5. Oklahoma
6. Army
7. N'WESTERN
8. Georgia
9. Oregon
10. S. Methodist

1949
1. Notre Dame
2. Oklahoma
3. California
4. Army
5. Rice
6. OHIO STATE
7. MICHIGAN
8. MINNESOTA
9. Louisiana State
10. College of Pacific

1950
1. Oklahoma
2. Army
3. Texas
4. Tennessee
5. California
6. Princeton
7. Kentucky
8. MICH. STATE
9. MICHIGAN
10. Clemson

1951
1. Tennessee
2. MICH. STATE
3. Maryland
4. ILLINOIS
5. Georgia Tech.
6. Princeton
7. Stanford
8. WISCONSIN
9. Baylor
10. Oklahoma

1952
1. MICH. STATE
2. Georgia Tech
3. Notre Dame
4. Oklahoma
5. So. California
6. UCLA
7. Mississippi
8. Tennessee
9. Alabama
10. Texas

1953
1. Maryland
2. Notre Dame
3. MICH. STATE
4. Oklahoma
5. UCLA
6. Rice
7. ILLINOIS
8. Georgia Tech
9. IOWA
10. West Virginia

1954
1. OHIO STATE
2. UCLA
3. Oklahoma
4. Notre Dame
5. Navy
6. Mississippi
7. Army
8. Maryland
9. WISCONSIN
10. Arkansas

1955
1. Oklahoma
2. MICH. STATE
3. Maryland
4. UCLA
5. OHIO STATE
6. Texas Christian
7. Georgia Tech
8. Auburn
9. Notre Dame
10. Mississippi

1956
1. Oklahoma
2. Tennessee
3. IOWA
4. Georgia Tech
5. Texas A&M
6. Miami
7. MICHIGAN
8. Syracuse
9. MICH. STATE
10. Oregon State

1957#
1. Auburn
2. OHIO STATE**
3. MICH. STATE
4. Oklahoma
5. Navy
6. IOWA***
7. Mississippi
8. Rice
9. Texas A&M
10. Notre Dame

1958#
1. Louisiana State
2. IOWA
3. Army
4. Auburn
5. Oklahoma
6. Air Force
7. WISCONSIN
8. OHIO STATE
9. Syracuse
10. Texas Christian

1959
1. Syracuse
2. Mississippi
3. Louisiana State
4. Texas
5. Georgia
6. WISCONSIN
7. Texas Christian
8. Washington
9. Arkansas
10. Alabama

1960
1. MINNESOTA
2. Mississippi
3. IOWA****
4. Navy
5. Missouri
6. Washington
7. Arkansas
8. OHIO STATE
9. Alabama
10. Duke

1961
1. Alabama
2. OHIO STATE
3. Texas
4. Louisiana State
5. Mississippi
6. MINNESOTA
7. Colorado
8. MICH. ST.*****
9. Arkansas
10. Utah State

1962
1. So. California
2. WISCONSIN
3. Mississippi
4. Texas
5. Alabama
6. Arkansas
7. Louisiana State
8. Oklahoma
9. Penn State
10. MINNESOTA

1963
1. Texas
2. Navy
3. ILLINOIS******
4. Pittsburgh
5. Auburn
6. Nebraska
7. Mississippi
8. Oklahoma
9. Alabama
10. MICHIGAN ST.

1964
1. Alabama
2. Arkansas
3. Notre Dame
4. MICHIGAN
5. Texas
6. Nebraska
7. Louisiana State
8. Oregon State
9. OHIO STATE
10. Southern Calif.

1965%
1. Alabama
2. MICH. ST.*******
3. Arkansas
4. UCLA
5. Nebraska
6. Missouri
7. Tennessee
8. Louisiana State
9. Notre Dame
10. Southern Calif.

*—Supplementary AP poll later voted Michigan nation's No. 1 team.
**—Ranked first by United Press coaches' poll.
***—Ranked fifth by United Press.
****—Ranked second by United Press.
*****—Ranked ninth by United Press.
******—Ranked fourth by United Press.
*******—Ohio State and Iowa ranked first by United Press.
#—Michigan State named co-national champion with Alabama by Football Writers Association in 1957 and 1958 respectively.

Most Valuable Football Players (Continued)

1957
Illinois — Rod Hanson, e
Indiana — Tony Aloisio, g
Iowa — Bob Commings, g
Michigan — Jim Pace, hb*
Michigan State — Dan Currie, c
Minnesota — Dick Larson, qb
Northwestern — Willmer Fowler, hb
Ohio State — Bill Jobko, g
Purdue — Neil Habig, c
Wisconsin — Danny Lewis, hb

1958
Illinois — Gene Cherney, c
Indiana — Mike Rabold, g
Iowa — Randy Duncan, qb*
Michigan — Bob Ptacek, hb
Michigan State — Sam Williams, e
Minnesota — Everett Gurths, g
Northwestern — Ron Burton, hb
Ohio State — James Houston, e
Purdue — {Tom Franckhauser, e
Wisconsin — {Dick Teteak, g

1959
Illinois — Bill Burrell, g*
Indiana — Ted Aucerman, e
Iowa — Don Norton, e
Michigan — Tom Moe, e
Northwestern — Jim Andreotti, c
Ohio State — Jim Houston, e
Purdue — Leonard Jardine, e
Wisconsin — Jerry Stalcup, g

1960
Illinois — Joe Rutgens, t
Indiana — Earl Faison, e
Michigan — Dennis Fitzgerald, b
Michigan State — Tom Brown, g*
Northwestern — Mike Stock, b
Ohio State — Tom Matte, b
Purdue — Bernie Allen, b
Wisconsin — Tom Wiesner, b

1961
Illinois — Tony Parrilli, g
Indiana — Byron Broome, qb
Iowa — Alfred Hinton, t
Michigan — John Walker, c
Michigan State — George Saimes, fb
Minnesota — Boyd Melvin, t
Ohio State — Bob Ferguson, fb
Purdue — Jack Elwell, e
Wisconsin — Ron Miller, qb

1962
Illinois — Ken Zimmerman, hb
Indiana — Woody Moore, qb
Iowa — Larry Ferguson, hb
Michigan — Dave Raimey, hb
Michigan State — George Saimes, fb*
Minnesota — George Thomas, t
Northwestern — Bill Armstrong, c
Purdue — Roy Walker, fb
Wisconsin — Ron VanderKelen, qb*

1963
Illinois — Dick Butkus, c*
Indiana — Tom Nowatzke, fb
Iowa — Mike Reilly, g
Michigan — Tom Keating, t
Michigan State — Sherman Lewis, hb
Minnesota — Carl Eller, t
Northwestern — Bill Swingle, fb
Ohio State — Matt Snell, fb
Purdue — Ron DiGravio, qb
Wisconsin — Jim Purnell, lb

1964
Illinois — Dick Butkus, lb
Indiana — Rich Badar, qb
Iowa — Karl Noonan, fl
Michigan — Bob Timberlake, qb*
Michigan State — Dick Gordon, hb
Minnesota — Joe Pung, c
Northwestern — Pat Riley, c
Ohio State — Ed Orazen, t
Purdue — Bob Hadrick, hb
Wisconsin — Carl Silvestri, hb

1965
Illinois — Jim Grabowski, fb*
Indiana — Bill Malinchak, e
Iowa — Dave Long, t
Michigan — Bill Yearby, t
Michigan State — Steve Juday, qb
Minnesota — John Hankinson, qb
Northwestern — Jim Burns, t
Ohio State — Doug Van Horn, g
Purdue — Bob Griese, qb
Wisconsin — Tom Brigham, hb

*—Received Chicago Tribune Trophy as Most Valuable in Conference.

National Football Rankings

(Selected by the nation's sports writers as polled by the Associated Press, with associated notations for Big Ten teams when ranked differently by United Press International's coach's poll.) Prior to the AP poll in 1936, the Rissman and Knute Rockne trophies, symbolic of the national title, were awarded as follows: Illinois, 1927; Michigan, 1932-33; Minnesota, 1934; Notre Dame, 1924-30; So. California, 1928-31; So. Methodist, 1935; Stanford, 1926; Dartmouth, 1925.

1936
1. MINNESOTA
2. Louisiana State
3. Pittsburgh
4. Alabama
5. Washington
6. Santa Clara
7. N'WESTERN
8. Notre Dame
9. Nebraska
10. Pennsylvania

1937
1. Pittsburgh
2. California
3. Fordham
4. Alabama
5. MINNESOTA
6. Villanova
7. Dartmouth
8. Louisiana State
9. Notre Dame
10. Santa Clara

1938
1. Texas Christian
2. Tennessee
3. Duke
4. Oklahoma
5. Notre Dame
6. Carnegie Tech
7. S. California
8. Pittsburgh
9. Holy Cross
10. MINNESOTA

1939
1. Texas A. & M.
2. Tennessee
3. S. California
4. Cornell
5. Tulane
6. U.C.L.A.
7. Duke
8. IOWA
9. Duquesne
10. Duquesne

1940
1. MINNESOTA
2. Stanford
3. MICHIGAN
4. Tennessee
5. Boston College
6. Texas A. & M.
7. N'WESTERN
8. Nebraska
9. Mississippi State
10. Washington

1941
1. MINNESOTA
2. Duke
3. Notre Dame
4. Texas
5. MICHIGAN
6. Fordham
7. Missouri
8. Duquesne
9. Texas A. & M.
10. Navy

1942
1. OHIO STATE
2. Georgia
3. WISCONSIN
4. Tulsa
5. Georgia Tech
6. Notre Dame
7. Tennessee
8. Boston College
9. MICHIGAN
10. Alabama

1943
1. Notre Dame
2. Iowa Seahawks
3. MICHIGAN
4. Navy
5. PURDUE
6. Great Lakes
7. Duke
8. Del Monte Pre-Fl.
9. N'WESTERN
10. March Field

CROSS COUNTRY

CONFERENCE MEETS

Year	Site	Individual Winner	Time	Team Champion	Points
1908	Chicago	Walter P. Comstock, Chicago	28:12	Nebraska	41
1909	Chicago	H. B. Wasson, Purdue	27:08	Minnesota	40
1910	Madison	E. J. Dohmen, Wisconsin	26:21	Wisconsin	33
1911	Iowa City	C. R. Cleveland, Wisconsin	29:43.2	Iowa State	32
1912	Evanston	Irving White, Wisconsin	27:29	Wisconsin	61
1913	Columbus	F. O. Watson, Wisconsin	26:44.5	Wisconsin	72
1914	Madison	F. O. Watson, Minnesota		Minnesota	45
1915	Lafayette	F. O. Watson, Minnesota	26:14	Minnesota	38
1916	Lafayette	Glenn I. Tenney, Chicago	26:25	Purdue	56
1917-1918	No Meet Held				
1919	Columbus	G. L. Otis, Chicago	26:30.6	Iowa State	38
1920	Champaign	C. C. Furnas, Purdue	29:12	Iowa State	32
1921	Bloomington	G. H. Finkle, Michigan	26:33.2	Illinois	46
1922	Lafayette	E. R. Isbell, Michigan	26:16	Michigan	41
1923	Columbus	H. R. Phelps, Iowa	25:59.7	Ohio State	55
1924	Ann Arbor	H. R. Phelps, Iowa	26:12	Wisconsin	52
1925	Ann Arbor	Vic Chapman, Wisconsin	26:27.8	Wisconsin	39
1926	Minneapolis	Jock Hunn, Iowa	24:57	Wisconsin	34
1927	Ann Arbor	John Zola, Wisconsin	26:26	Wisconsin	51
1928	Madison	David Abbott, Illinois	26:27.7	Indiana	72
1929	Columbus	Orville Martin, Purdue	21:59.7	Indiana	36
1930	Champaign	Leas, Indiana	21:00.3	Indiana	51
1931	Iowa City	Henry Brocksmith, Indiana		Indiana	38
1932	Lafayette	Dean Woolsey, Illinois		Indiana	42
1933-1937	No Meet Held				
1938	Lafayette	Mel Trutt, Indiana	20:11.8	Indiana	30
1939	Chicago	Walter Mehl, Wisconsin	20:34.7	Indiana	28
1940	Chicago	Wayne Tolliver, Indiana	22:25.2	Indiana	31
1941	Lafayette	Fred Wilt, Indiana	20:01.5	Purdue	33
1942	Chicago	Earl Mitchell, Indiana	21:09.2	Indiana	34
1943	Chicago	Ericsson, Purdue	21:53.6	Purdue	26
1944	Chicago	Wm. Lawson, Wisconsin	21:16	Wisconsin	38
1945	Chicago	Victor Twomey, Illinois	21:28.9	Wisconsin	43
1946	Chicago	Earl Mitchell, Indiana	21:10.8	Indiana } Illinois	48
1947	Chicago	Don Gehrmann, Wisconsin	20:26.4	Illinois	48
1948	Chicago	Don Gehrmann, Wisconsin	20:31.4	Wisconsin	44
1949	Chicago	Don McEwen, Michigan	19:44.5	Wisconsin	49
1950	Chicago	Don McEwen, Michigan	19:34.1	Wisconsin	56
1951	Chicago	Walter E. Deike, Wisconsin	21:12.3	Michigan State	49
1952	Chicago	Rich Ferguson, Iowa	19:40.5	Michigan State	28
1953	Chicago	Rich Ferguson, Iowa	19:43.2	Michigan State	39
1954	Chicago	James Lambert, Indiana	19:59.6	Michigan	55
1955	Chicago	Henry Kennedy, MSU	19:06.0	Michigan State	36
1956	Chicago	Leonard Edelen, Minn.	20:25.3	Michigan State	21
1957	Chicago	Charles Jones, Iowa	21:09.4	Michigan State	43
1958	Chicago	Crawford Kennedy, MSU	20:18.0	Michigan State	43
1959	Chicago	Gerald Young, MSU	20:12.3	Michigan State	17
1960	Chicago	James Tucker, Iowa	19:35.3	Michigan State	30
1961	Iowa City	Allen Carius, Illinois	19:50.4	Iowa	45
1962	Illinois	Allen Carius, Illinois	19:45.2	Michigan State	39
1963	Illinois	Lee Assenheimer, Northwestern	19:39.4	Michigan State	46
1964	Minnesota	Lee Assenheimer, Northwestern	20:11	Minnesota	27
1965			20:05.2	Northwestern	40

RECORDS

Team Record
17, by Michigan State, 1959, Crawford Kennedy, 1st; William Reynolds, 2nd; Edward Graydon, 3rd; Gerald Young, 5th; Robert Lake, 6th

Individual Records
21:01.5, for standard four-mile course set by Fred Wilt of Indiana at West Lafayette, Ind., 1941.
19:44.5, for four-mile course at Washington Park, Chicago, set by Gerald Young, MSU, 1960.
19:35.3, for double-loop four-mile course at Washington Park, Chicago, set by Don McEwen, Michigan, 1949.
19:34.1, for four-mile emergency course at Washington Park, Chicago, set by Don McEwen, Michigan, 1950.
19:06.0, for unsurveyed four-mile course at Washington Park, Chicago, set by Henry Kennedy, MSU, 1955.
Three Individual Titles—F. O. Watson, Minnesota, 1913-14-15.

MISCELLANEOUS RECORDS

ATTENDANCE

CONFERENCE
*1965 Conference Games Only (35) 2,140,891; 61,168 Ave.—2.9% Increase
**1965 Home Games (54) 3,054,643; 56,567 Ave.—3.9% Decrease
1965 Season (64) 3,523,892; 55,061 Ave.—3.6% Decrease
*—Represents 89.3% of stadium capacities.
**—Represents 83.5% of stadium capacities.

Record Seasons:
1965 Conference Games Only (35)—Average: 61,168
1965 Conference Games Only (35)—Total: 2,140,891
1964 Home Games (49)—Average: 58,889
1965 Home Games (54)—Total: 3,054,643
1956 Full Season—57 Games—Average: 58,144
1965 Full Season—64 games—Total: 3,523,892

Record Days:
4 Home Games	263,221; 65,805 Ave.	Nov. 19, 1949
5 Home Games	351,940; 70,388 Ave.	Oct. 12, 1963
6 Home Games	378,584; 63,097 Ave.	Oct. 3, 1959

TEAM
One Game: 103,234, Michigan vs. Michigan State, 10-3-59
Home Games, One Season: 566,096, Michigan, 1956 (7 games)
All Games, One Season: 772,482, Michigan, 1965 (9 games)

Home Records of Member Schools:
Illinois: 75,119, Notre Dame 9-28-46
Indiana: 50,046, Purdue, 11-20-65
Iowa: 60,150, Wisconsin, 10-21-61
Michigan: 103,234, Michigan State 10-3-59
Michigan State: 78,234, Michigan, 10-10-64

Minnesota: 67,081, Purdue, 11-18-61
Northwestern: 55,752, Notre Dame, 10-27-62
Ohio State: 84,712, Illinois, 10-12-63
Purdue: 62,113, Michigan State, 10-23-65
Wisconsin: 65,728, Michigan State, 10-31-64

LONGEST WINNING STREAKS

CONFERENCE GAMES ONLY
17 straight games were won by Ohio State, 1954-1956
15 straight games were won by Michigan, 1946-48
14 straight games were won by Iowa, 1920-23
13 straight games were won by Minnesota, 1933-1936.

CONFERENCE AND NON-CONFERENCE GAMES
28 straight games were won by MSC, 1950-1953 (including 3 as a Conference member, 1953)
25 straight games were won by Michigan, 1946-49
21 straight games were won by Iowa, 1920-23
21 straight games were won by Minnesota, 1933-1936

Tied but Undefeated
Michigan was tied but undefeated in 22 straight Conference games, 1901-1905
Michigan was tied but undefeated in 56 straight games, Conference and non-Conference, 1900-1905.

All-Time Conference Standings (1896-1965)

	Won	Lost	Tied	Pct.#	Years
Ohio State (1913)	186	89	19	.665	53
Michigan (1896)	194	103	13	.647	60*
Michigan State (1953)	49	28	2	.633	13
Minnesota (1896)	188	136	23	.575	70
Chicago (1896)	120	99	14	.545	44**
Wisconsin (1896)	169	165	32	.505	70
Illinois (1896)	180	179	22	.501	70
Purdue (1896)	141	170	26	.457	70
Iowa (1900)	115	174	17	.404	66
Northwestern (1896)	137	208	18	.402	68***
Indiana (1900)	80	208	20	.292	64****

#—Ties count half game won, half game lost.
*—Out of Conference from 1907 through 1916.
**—Dropped out of Conference in 1939.
***—Out of Conference in 1906 and 1907.
****—Out of Conference in 1918 and 1960.

OUTSIDE THE FAMILY

(Record of Big Ten Teams Against Non-Conference Opponents Since 1945)

	AAWU	Big Eight	South-West	Notre Dame	Midwest	South & SE	Eastern	Other	Grand Total
Won	100	51	13	33	54	21	70	17	359
Lost	58	15	8	39	7	18	26	0	171
Tied	6	6	2	3	1	2	3	1	24

.670 pct.

BASKETBALL SECTION

(These are all-time records, based on Conference games only.)
Compiled in cooperation with Vic Rensberger, Indianapolis News

INDIVIDUAL RECORDS

Most Points, One Game

57, Dave Schellhase (Purdue) vs. Mich., 2-19-66 (23 FG, 11 FT)
56, Jimmy Rayl (Indiana) vs. MSU, 2-23-63 (23FG, 10 FT)
56, Jimmy Rayl (Indiana) vs. Minn., 1-27-62 (23FG, 16FT)
53, Dave Downey (Illinois) vs. Ind., 2-16-63 (Overtime) (20FG, 16FT)
52, Terry Dischinger (Purdue) vs. MSU 2-25-61 (19FG, 14 FT)
50, Terry Dischinger (Purdue) vs. Wis., 1-27-62 (17FG, 16 FT)
49, Gary Bradds (OSU) vs. Ill., 2-10-64
49, Rich Falk (NU) vs. Iowa, 2-24-64
48, Jerry Lucas (OSU) vs. MSU 2-11-61
48, Gary Bradds (OSU) vs. NU, 1-27-64
48, Don Schlundt (Indiana) vs. OSU 1-18-54 and 3-5-55
47, Terry Dischinger (Purdue) vs. Ind., 2-10-62
47, Gary Bradds (OSU) vs. Pur., 1-25-64
46, Robin Freeman (Purdue) vs. MSU, 1-28-56
46, Terry Dischinger (Purdue) vs. Minn., 2-24-62
45, Terry Dischinger (Purdue) vs. Ill., 1-8-62 and 2-17-62
44, Jimmy Rayl (Indiana) vs. Wis., 2-12-62 and vs. MSU, 1-5-63
43, Dick Ives (Iowa) vs. Chicago, 2-5-44
43, Robin Freeman (OSU) vs. Ill., 2-25-56, and vs. MSU, 3-3-56
43, Terry Dischinger (Purdue) vs. Ill., 1-11-60
43, John Tidwell (Mich.) vs. Minn., 3-4-61
42, Walt Bellamy (Indiana) vs. Ill. 2-15-60
42, Eric Magdanz (Minn.) vs. Mich., 3-5-62
42, Gary Bradds (OSU) vs. Mich., 2-3-64
42, Ken Barnes (Wis.) vs. Ind., 2-4-56
41, Robin Freeman (OSU) vs. Ind., 2-6-56
41, Julius McCoy (MSU) vs. Mich., 2-27-60
41, John Tidwell (Mich.), vs. MSU, 2-27-61
41, Terry Dischinger (Purdue) vs. NU, 1-7-61
41, Dave Schellhase (Pur.) vs. Ill., 2-6-65
40, Andy Phillip (Ill.) vs. Chicago, 3-1-43
40, Paul Ebert (Ohio) vs. Mich., 2-23-52
40, Julius McCoy (MSU) vs. OSU, 2-28-56
40, George Kline (Minn.) vs. Iowa, 2-25-57
40, Joe Ruklick (NU) vs. Ill., 3-8-58
40, Gary Bradds (OSU) vs. Iowa, 2-23-64; vs. Indiana (Overtime), 2-8-64; vs. Wisconsin, 2-15-64
40, Rich Lopossa (NU) vs. Ill., 2-1-64
40, Cazzie Russell (Mich.) vs. MSU, 1-22-66

Most Points a Game, One Season

33.9, Gary Bradds (Ohio State), 1964 (474 in 14)
33.2, Cazzie Russell (Michigan), 1966 (465 in 14)
32.8, Terry Dischinger (Purdue), 1962 (459 in 14)
32.5, Robin Freeman (Ohio), 1956 (455 in 14)
32.4, Jimmy Rayl (Indiana), 1962 (454 in 14)
32.2, Dave Schellhase (Purdue), 1966 (451 in 14)
30.9, Gary Bradds (OSU), 1963 (433 in 14)
28.9, Terry Dischinger (Purdue), 1961
27.9, Dave Schellhase (Purdue), 1965
27.5, Don Freeman (Illinois), 1966
27.4, Terry Dischinger (Purdue), 1960
27.3, Julius McCoy (MSU) 1956
27.1, Don Schlundt (Ind.) 1954
27.1, Dave Schellhase (Purdue), 1964
27.0, Jimmy Rayl (Indiana) 1963

Consecutive 40-Point Games

6, Gary Bradds (OSU), Jan. 25 to Feb. 15, 1964 (47, 48, 42, 40-OT, 49, 40)
2, Terry Dischinger (Purdue), Feb. 17 & Feb. 24, 1962 (45 & 46)

Most Field Goals, One Game

23, Jimmy Rayl (Indiana) vs. MSU, 2-23-63
23, Dave Schellhase (Purdue) vs. Mich., 2-19-66
22, Dave Downey (Illinois) vs. Ind., 2-16-63 (overtime)
20, John Tidwell (Mich.), vs. Minn., 3-4-61
20, Jimmy Rayl (Indiana) vs. Minn., 1-27-62
20, Terry Dischinger (Purdue) vs. NU, 1-7-61
20, Gary Bradds (OSU) vs. Pur., 1-25-64
19, Dick Ives (Iowa), vs. Chicago, 2-5-44
19, Cazzie Russell (Michigan) vs. MSU, 2-1-66
19, Jerry Lucas (OSU) vs. MSU, 2-11-61
19, Terry Dischinger (Purdue), vs. MSU 2-25-61
19, Rich Falk (NU) vs. Iowa, 2-24-64

Most Field Goals a Game, One Season

13.0, Cazzie Russell (Michigan), 1966 (182 in 14)
12.4, Gary Bradds (OSU), 1964 (174 in 14)
11.6, Robin Freeman (OSU), 1956 (163 in 14)
11.4, Dave Schellhase (Purdue), 1966 (160 in 14)
11.0, Gary Bradds (OSU), 1963 (154 in 14)
11.0, Don Freeman (Illinois), 1966 (154 in 14)
10.9, Jimmy Rayl (Indiana), 1962 (152 in 14)
10.4, Cazzie Russell (Michigan), 1965 (135 in 13)
10.2, Jerry Lucas (Ohio State), 1960 (143 in 14)
10.14, Dave Schellhase (Purdue), 1964 (142 in 14)
10.07, Jimmy Rayl (Indiana), 1962 (141 in 14)
10.0, Terry Dischinger (Purdue), 1962 (140 in 14)

Most Free Throws, One Game

25, Don Schlundt (Ind.) vs. Ohio, 3-5-55
21, Al Ferrari (MSU), vs. Indiana, 2-28-55
21, Terry Dischinger (Purdue) vs. Iowa, 2-27-61
21, Don Nelson (Iowa) vs. Ind., 2-17-62
18, Terry Dischinger (Purdue), vs. Minn., 2-24-62
18, Jimmy Rayl (Indiana) vs. MSU, 1-27-64
18, Dave Schellhase (Purdue) vs. Iowa, 2-27-65
17, Don Schlundt (Ind.) vs. Mich., 3-5-61
17, Terry Dischinger (Purdue) vs. Michigan, 1-3-61; vs. MSU, 2-3-62; and vs. Ind., 2-10-62.
17, Tom Cole (Mich.) vs. Ind., 2-26-62
17, Dick Van Arsdale (Ind.) vs. OSU, (Overtime), 2-8-64

Most Free Throws a Game, One Season

12.8, Terry Dischinger (Purdue), 1962 (179 in 14)
11.2, Don Schlundt (Ind.), 1955 (157 in 14)
10.9, Don Schlundt (Ind.), 1954 (153 in 14)
10.7, Jimmy Rayl (Indiana), 1962 (150 in 14)
10.2, Terry Dischinger (Purdue), 1961 (143 in 14)

Best Field Goal Shooting Averages: One Game (10 or more attempts)

.933, Jerry Lucas (OSU) vs. Minn. (14 of 15), 2-10-62
.933, Terry Kunze (Minnesota) vs. Mich. (14 of 15), 1-14-63
.917, Willie Merriweather (Purdue) vs. Illinois (11 of 12), 1-31-59
.909, Jim McConnell (Iowa) vs. Minnesota (10 of 11), 1-12-57
.909, Tom McGrann (Minnesota) vs. OSU (10 of 11), 1-5-63
.900, Jerry Lucas (OSU) vs. NU (9 of 10), 2-3-62
.900, George Peeples (Iowa) vs. OSU (9 of 10), 1-24-66
.857, Mel Nowell (OSU) vs. NU (12 of 14), 2-13-61
.857, John Havlicek (OSU) vs. MSU (12 of 14), 3-4-61

One Season (100 or more attempts)

.678, Jerry Lucas, OSU (122 of 180), 1962
.656, Jerry Lucas, OSU (143 of 218), 1960
.612, Jerry Lucas, OSU (137 of 224), 1961
.5752, Don Nelson, Iowa (127 of 220), 1962
.5746, Skip Thoren, Ill. (130 of 226), 1965
.5746, Terry Dischinger (Purdue) (131 of 228), 1961
.566, Ron Johnson, Minn. (121 of 219), 1960
.563, John Havlicek, OSU (89 of 158), 1961

Best Free Throw Shooting Averages: One Game (14 or more attempts)

1.000, Larry Siegfried (OSU), vs. Purdue (16 of 16), 3-7-59
1.000, Jimmy Rayl (Indiana) vs. Mich. (15 of 15), 2-26-62
1.000, Don Schlundt (Ind.), vs. Minn. (14 of 14), 2-8-54
1.000, Robin Freeman (Ohio), vs. MSU (14 of 14), 1-28-56
1.000, Larry Huston (Ohio State), vs. Illinois (14 of 14), 1-3-59
1.000, Lance Olson (MSU) vs. Minnesota (14 of 14), 2-1-60

One Season (30 or more attempts)

.923, Jon McGlocklin (Ind.), (36 of 39), 1965
.922, Henry Ebershoff (Pur.), (59 of 64), 1966
.920, Sam Gee (Ind.) (46 of 50), 1958
.918, Larry Siegfried (OSU), (56 of 61), 1961
.8857, Meyer Skoog (Minn.), (31 of 35), 1951
.8857, Bob Griggas (Minn.), (31 of 35), 1961
.8852, Jimmy Rayl (Ind.), (108 of 122), 1963
.884, Bill Cacciatore, NU (38 of 43), 1962
.882, Hallie Bryant (Ind.), (45 of 51), 1956

Most Consecutive Free Throws

32, Jimmy Rayl (Indiana), 1962
31, Gary Bradds (OSU), 1963
29, Dick Miller (Wis.), 1955-56 (25 in 1956)
28, Bill Tosheff (Wis.), 1951
27, Jerry Lucas (OSU), 1961
27, Terry Dischinger (Purdue), 1962
24, Ken Buckles (Iowa), 1953
23, Wally Choice (Ind.), 1956
22, Mike O'Melia (Wis.), 1962
21, Terry Dischinger (Pur.) 1961
21, Dick Van Arsdale (Indiana), 1964-65 (15 in 1965)
20, Don Sunderlage (Ill.), 1950
20, Bill Burwell (Ill.), 1962

Most Free Throws Missed, One Game

15, Jack Runyan (Purdue) vs. Mich., 3-2-53
11, Paul Ebert (Ohio) vs. Indiana, 1-18-54
11, Tom McGrann (Minn.) vs. Ill., 2-27-61
10, Max Morris (N.U.) vs. Minn., 1946
10, Wally Osterkorn (Illinois) vs. Ohio. 1950
10, Jack Runyan (Purdue) vs. N.U., 1953
10, Jim Barron (Mich.) vs. Pur., 1954
10, Jim Pitts (NU) vs. Ind., 1965

Most Free Throws Missed a Game, One Season

6.3, Jack Runyan (Purdue), 1953 (114 in 18)
*4.7, Andy Butchko (Purdue), 1950 (56 in 12)

Most Free-Throw Attempts, One Game

30, Don Schlundt (Ind.), vs. Ohio, 3-5-55
29, Jack Runyan (Purdue) vs. Mich., 3-2-53
26, Al Ferrari (MSU) vs. Ind., 2-28-55
25, Don Nelson (Iowa) vs. Ind., 2-17-62
24, Terry Dischinger (Purdue) vs. Iowa, 2-27-61
23, Paul Morrow (Wis.) vs. Mich., 2-21-53
23, Terry Dischinger (Purdue) vs. Minn., 2-24-62
23, Dave Schellhase (Purdue) vs. Iowa, 2-27-65
*21, Charles Darling (Iowa) vs. Minn., 1952
*20, Tony Jaros (Minn.) vs. Wis., 1946

Most Free-Throw Attempts a Game, One Season

15.4, Terry Dischinger (Pur.), 1962 (215 in 14)
13.8, Don Schlundt (Ind.), 1954 (193 in 14)
13.6, Don Schlundt (Ind.), 1955 (190 in 14)
13.1, Dick Garmaker (Minn.), 1954 (183 in 14)
12.5, Jimmy Rayl (Ind.), 1962 (175 in 14)
12.43, Don Nelson (Iowa), 1962 (174 in 14)
12.39, Jack Runyan (Purdue), 1953 (223 in 18)
12.3, Terry Dischinger (Pur.), 1960 (172 in 14)

Most Field-Goal Attempts, One Game

48, Jimmy Rayl (Indiana) vs. MSU, 2-23-63
42, Dave Schellhase (Purdue) vs. Mich., 2-19-66
39, Jimmy Rayl (Indiana) vs. Minn., 1-27-62 (overtime)

*Before one-and-one rule

(Note: 12 games for years prior to 1951 and thereafter, except 18 in 1953.)

Most Points, One Game, Two Teams

222, Michigan (120) vs. Wisconsin (102), Feb. 12, 1966
222, Michigan (128) vs. Purdue (94), Feb. 19, 1966
214, Indiana (122) vs. Ohio State (92), Feb. 2, 1959
214, Illinois (121) vs. Purdue (93), Feb. 6, 1965
210, Michigan State (107) vs. Indiana (103), Jan. 11, 1964
210, Illinois (121) vs. Michigan State (89), Mar. 9, 1965
209, Indiana (105) vs. Minnesota (104), Jan. 27, 1962 (Overtime)
208, Northwestern (111) vs. Purdue (97), Jan. 8, 1966
207, Indiana (113) vs. Michigan State (94), Feb. 23, 1963
207, Illinois (113) vs. Michigan State (94), Feb. 20, 1965
206, Indiana (112) vs. Michigan State (94), Feb. 8, 1965
205, Illinois (104) vs. Indiana (101), Feb. 4, 1963
204, Indiana (109) vs. Purdue (95) March 1, 1958
204, Minnesota (104) vs. Indiana (100), Jan. 8, 1962
204, Wisconsin (103) vs. Illinois (101), Feb. 19, 1962
204, Michigan State (107) vs. Northwestern (97), Feb. 29, 1964
203, Illinois (112) vs. Indiana (91), Jan. 14, 1957
203, Indiana (103) vs. Illinois (100), Feb. 16, 1963
203, Minnesota (111) vs. Wisconsin (92), Feb. 1, 1964
202, Ohio State (110) vs. Illinois (92), Feb. 10, 1964
202, Michigan State (110) vs. Purdue (92), Mar. 1, 1965
201, Illinois (104) vs. Northwestern (97), Feb. 11, 1957
201, Michigan State (102) vs. Ohio State (99), Jan. 27, 1964
201, Minnesota (105) vs. Wisconsin (96), Mar. 2, 1964
201, Michigan (103) vs. Michigan State (98), Jan. 26, 1965 (Overtime)
200, Illinois (102) vs. Northwestern (98), Feb. 1, 1958 (overtime)
200, Illinois (103) vs. Iowa (97), Jan. 12, 1959
200, Indiana (104) vs. Michigan (96), Mar. 4, 1963
200, Indiana (104) vs. Illinois (96), Feb. 3, 1964
200, Indiana (110) vs. Ohio State (90), Mar. 1, 1965
200, Ohio State (102) vs. Minnesota (98), Feb. 21, 1966

Most Points a Game, One Season

95.4, Michigan, 1966 (1336 in 14)
92.9, Michigan, 1965 (1300 in 14)
92.4, Illinois, 1965 (1293 in 14)
92.1, Michigan State, 1964 (1290 in 14)
91.2, Illinois, 1956 (1,277 in 14)
90.4, Indiana, 1965 (1266 in 14)
89.1, Indiana, 1963 (1247 in 14)
88.8, Ohio State, 1964 (1243 in 14)
87.4, Illinois, 1966 (1221 in 14)
87.2, Illinois, 1963 (1221 in 14)
86.7, Indiana, 1962 (1214 in 14)
86.6, Minnesota, 1965 (1213 in 14)
86.4, Ohio State, 1962 (1209 in 14)
86.2, Ohio State, 1961 (1207 in 14)

Most Field Goals, One Game

52, Michigan vs. Purdue, Feb. 19, 1966
50, Indiana, vs. Ohio State, Feb. 2, 1959
50, Illinois, vs. Michigan State, Feb. 20, 1965 & Mar. 9, 1965
49, Ohio State, vs. Michigan State, Jan. 30, 1960
49, Michigan, vs. Wisconsin, Feb. 12, 1966
49, Indiana, vs. Michigan State, Feb. 23, 1963
48, Indiana vs. Michigan State, Feb. 8, 1965
47, Illinois, vs. Indiana, Jan. 14, 1957 & vs. Purdue, Feb. 6, 1965
47, Michigan vs. Northwestern, Mar. 5, 1966
46, Ohio State, vs. Michigan, Feb. 28, 1959; and vs. Illinois, Feb. 24, 1962
46, Iowa vs. Chicago, Feb. 5, 1944
45, Ohio State vs. Wis., 2-8-60; vs. Ill., 2-15-60; and vs. Wis., 1-4-64
45, Michigan, vs. Wisconsin, Feb. 1, 1964
45, Indiana, vs. Ohio State, Mar. 1, 1965

Most Field Goals, One Game, Two Teams

89, Indiana (49) vs. Michigan State (40), Feb. 8, 1965
89, Illinois (50) vs. Michigan State (39), Feb. 20, 1965
87, Michigan (49) vs. Wisconsin (38), Feb. 12, 1966
87, Michigan (52) vs. Purdue (35), Feb. 19, 1966
85, Wisconsin (43) vs. Illinois (42), Feb. 19, 1962
84, Indiana (50) vs. Ohio State (34), Feb. 2, 1959
84, Michigan State (43) vs. Northwestern (41), Feb. 29, 1964
83, Illinois (47) vs. Indiana (36), Jan. 14, 1957
83, Illinois (42) vs. Indiana (41), Feb. 21, 1959
83, Minnesota (45) vs. Wisconsin (38), Feb. 1, 1964
83, Illinois (50) vs. Michigan State (33), Mar. 9, 1965
83, Indiana (47) vs. Northwestern (36), Mar. 5, 1966

Most Field Goals a Game, One Season

38.2, Illinois, 1965 (534 in 14)
37.7, Michigan, 1966 (528 in 14)
37.4, Ohio State, 1960 (523 in 14)
36.9, Michigan State, 1964 (516 in 14)
36.7, Michigan, 1965 (514 in 14)
35.3, Ohio State, 1962 (494 in 14)
34.9, Illinois, 1959 (488 in 14)
34.9, Illinois, 1966 (488 in 14)
34.9, Ohio State, 1964 (484 in 14)
34.43, Illinois, 1963 (482 in 14)
34.4, Ohio State, 1961 (481 in 14)
34.4, Minnesota, 1964 (481 in 14)
34.1, Michigan, 1964 (477 in 14)

Most Free Throws, One Game

43, Indiana, vs. Michigan, Jan. 3, 1955
42, Indiana, vs. Purdue, Jan. 19, 1953
41, Wisconsin vs. Illinois, Jan. 1, 1955
*38, Indiana, vs. Northwestern, Feb. 16, 1952
*31, Illinois, vs. Indiana, 1949
*31, Wisconsin vs. Michigan, 1952
*Before One & One

38, Rick Falk (NU vs. Iowa, 2-24-64
35, Bob Leonard (Indiana) vs. Iowa, 1953
34, John Tidwell (Michigan) vs. Minn., 3-4-61
34, George Kline (Minnesota) vs. Wis., 2-24-58
34, Dave Downey (Illinois) vs. Ind., 2-16-63
33, Ron Johnson (Minnesota) vs. OSU, 1-31-59
33, Gary Bradds (OSU) vs. Ill., 1-7-63
33, Jimmy Rayl (Indiana) vs. Ill., 2-4-63

Most Field-Goal Attempts a Game, One Season

25.9, Don Freeman (Ill.), 1966 (362 in 14)
25.8, Murray Wier (Iowa), 1948 (309 in 12)
25.7, Dave Schellhase (Pur.), 1966 (360 in 14)
25.6, Robin Freeman (Ohio), 1956 (359 in 14)
24.9, Julius McCoy (MSU), 1956 (348 in 14)
24.7, Jimmy Rayl (Ind.), 1962 (346 in 14)
24.2, John Kerr (Ill.), 1954 (339 in 14)
24.0, Cazzie Russell (Mich) 1966 (336 in 14)

Most Personal Fouls a Game, One Season

4.57, Jim Clinton (Wis.), 1951 (64 in 14)
4.39, Paul Morrow (Wis.), 1953 (79 in 18)
4.36, Bob Carey (MSC) 1952 (61 in 14)
4.36, Harry Joyner (Ind.), 1966 (61 in 14)

Most Rebounds, One Season

256, Horace Walker (MSU) 1960
253, Jerry Lucas (OSU), 1962
247, Walt Bellamy (Indiana) 1961

Most Points, College Career

1451, Don Schlundt (Indiana) 1952-244; 1953-459; 1954-379; 1955-369

4 Seasons

1248, Terry Dischinger (Purdue) 1960-384; 1961-405; 1962-459

3 Seasons

1221, Dave Schellhase (Purdue) 1964-379; 1965-391; 1966-451
1207, Don Schlundt (Indiana) 1953-459; 1954-379; 1955-369
1171, Cazzie Russell (Michigan) 1964-366; 1965-340; 1966-465
1027, Paul Ebert (OSU) 1952-300; 1953-406; 1954-321
1019, Jerry Lucas (OSU) 1960-362; 1961-345; 1962-312

2 Seasons

907, Gary Bradds (OSU) 1963-433; 1964-474
864, Terry Dischinger (Purdue) 1961-405; 1962-459
842, Dave Schellhase (Purdue) 1965-391; 451-1966
838, Don Schlundt (Indiana) 1953-459; 1954-379
832, Jimmy Rayl (Indiana) 1962-454; 1963-378
805, Cazzie Russell (Michigan) 1965-340; 1966-465
727, Paul Ebert (OSU) 1953-406; 1954-321
718, Archie Dees (Indiana) 1957-356; 1958-362
707, Jerry Lucas (OSU) 1960-362; 1961-345

Most Points a Game, College Career

29.72, Terry Dischinger, Purdue (1248 in 42) 1960-61-62
29.07, Dave Schellhase, Purdue (1221 in 42) 1964-65-66
28.56, Cazzie Russell, Michigan (1171 in 41) 1964-65-66
27.03, Robin Freeman, OSU (919 in 34) 1954-55-56
24.75, Dick Garmaker, Minnesota (693 in 28) 1954-55
24.26, Jerry Lucas, OSU (1019 in 42) 1960-61-62
24.18, Don Schlundt, Indiana (1451 in 60) 1952-53-54-55
23.46, Gary Bradds, OSU (962 in 41), 1962-63-64
23.12, Bill Buntin, Michigan (971 in 42) 1963-64-65
22.93, Archie Dees, Indiana (963 in 42) 1956-57-58
22.33, Paul Ebert, OSU (1027 in 46) 1952-53-54
21.86, Julius McCoy, MSU (918 in 42) 1954-55-56
21.85, Jimmy Rayl, Indiana (874 in 40) 1961-62-63

TEAM RECORDS

Most Points, One Game

128, Michigan vs. Purdue, Feb. 19, 1966
122, Indiana vs. Ohio State, Feb. 2, 1959
121, Illinois vs. Purdue, Feb. 6, 1965, & vs. Michigan State, Mar. 9, 1965
120, Michigan vs. Wisconsin, Feb. 12, 1966
113, Indiana vs. Purdue, Feb. 23, 1953 & vs. Michigan State, Feb. 23, 1963
113, Illinois vs. Michigan State, Feb. 20, 1965
112, Illinois vs. Indiana, Jan. 14, 1957
111, Indiana vs. Michigan State, Feb. 8, 1965
111, Illinois vs. Michigan State, Jan. 30, 1960
111, Minnesota, vs. Wisconsin, Feb. 1, 1964
111, Iowa vs. Michigan State, Jan. 16, 1965
111, Northwestern vs. Purdue, Jan. 8, 1966
110, Michigan vs. Indiana, Feb. 26, 1962
110, Ohio State, vs. Illinois, Feb. 10, 1964
110, Indiana vs. Illinois, Mar. 1, 1965
110, Michigan State vs. Purdue, Mar. 1, 1965

Most Points, One Game, Losing Team

104, Minnesota, vs. Indiana, Jan. 27, 1962. (Overtime)
103, Indiana, vs. Michigan State, Jan. 11, 1964
102, Wisconsin vs. Michigan, Feb. 12, 1966
101, Illinois, vs. Wisconsin, Feb. 19, 1962
101, Indiana, vs. Illinois, Feb. 4, 1963
100, Indiana, vs. Minnesota, Jan. 8, 1962
100, Illinois vs. Indiana, Feb. 16, 1963
99, Ohio State, vs. Michigan State, Jan. 27, 1964
98, Wisconsin, vs. Ohio, Jan. 14, 1956 (Double overtime)
98, Northwestern vs. Illinois, Feb. 1, 1958 (Overtime)
98, Indiana, vs. Illinois, Feb. 21, 1959
98, Michigan State, vs. Purdue, Feb. 3, 1964
98, Michigan State vs. Michigan, Jan. 26, 1965 (Overtime)
98, Minnesota vs. Ohio State, Feb. 21, 1966

Most Personal Fouls, One Game

41, Michigan State vs. Northwestern, Feb. 2, 1952
40, Purdue vs. Illinois, Mar. 1, 1952

Most Personal Fouls, One Game, Two Teams

73, Purdue (40) vs. Illinois (33), Mar. 1, 1952
72, Indiana (38) vs. Northwestern (34), Feb. 16, 1952

Most Personal Fouls a Game, One Season

28.8, Indiana, 1952 (403 in 14)
27.7, Purdue, 1952 (388 in 14)

Most Consecutive Victories Conference Games

27, Ohio State, 1960-62
23, Wisconsin, 1912-1913
20, Indiana, 1952-1953
17, Illinois, 1914-1916

All Games

32, Ohio State, 1960-1961
29, Minnesota, 1901-1904
29, Wisconsin, 1912-1913
25, Illinois, 1914-1916

Most Overtimes

6, Minnesota (59) vs. Purdue (56), Jan. 29, 1955

Most Field-Goal Attempts a Game, One Season

87.9, Michigan State, 1964 (1,230 in 14)
86.6, Minnesota, 1956 (1,212 in 14)
85.9, Northwestern, 1952 (1,203 in 14)
85.7, Indiana, 1950 (1,028 in 12)
85.4, Michigan, 1959 (1196 in 14)

Most Free-Throw Attempts, One Game

65, Purdue vs. Michigan, Mar. 2, 1953
60, Indiana vs. Michigan, Jan. 3, 1955
56, Indiana vs. Ohio State, Mar. 5, 1955
55, Iowa vs. Michigan, Jan. 11, 1954
55, Illinois vs. Purdue, Dec. 22, 1952
54, Indiana vs. Purdue, Jan. 19, 1953
54, Iowa vs. Minnesota, Mar. 2, 1953
54, Wisconsin vs. Illinois, Jan. 1, 1955

Most Free-Throw Attempts, One Game, Two Teams

106, Purdue (65) vs. Michigan (41), Mar. 2, 1953
99, Purdue (51) vs. Michigan (48), Dec. 22, 1952
99, Indiana (55) vs. Purdue (44), Jan. 19, 1953

Most-Free-Throw Attempts a Game, One Season

39.2, Minnesota, 1954 (549 in 14)
38.6, Indiana, 1954 (541 in 14)
38.2, Purdue, 1953 (688 in 18)
36.9, Iowa, 1954 (517 in 14)
36.0, Iowa, 1953 (648 in 18)

SCHOOL RECORDS

(Conference Games Only)

Single Game Scoring, Individual

Illinois	53, Dave Downey vs. Chicago, 1944
Indiana	56, Jimmy Rayl vs. Minnesota, 1962 (overtime)—and vs. MSU, 1963
Iowa	43, Dick Ives vs. Chicago, 1944
Michigan	48, Cazzie Russell vs. Northwestern, 1966
Michigan State	41, Julius McCoy, vs. Michigan, 1956
Minnesota	42, Eric Magdanz, vs. Michigan, 1962
Northwestern	49, Rich Falk, vs. Iowa, 1964
Ohio State	49, Gary Bradds, vs. Ill., 1964
Purdue	*57, Dave Schellhase vs. Michigan, 1966
Wisconsin	42, Ken Barnes vs. Indiana, 1965

Single Game Scoring, Team

Illinois	121, vs. Purdue (93), and vs. Michigan State (89), both 1965
Indiana	122, vs. Ohio State (92), 1959
Iowa	111, vs. Michigan State (68), 1965
Michigan	*128, vs. Purdue (94), 1966
Michigan State	110, vs. Purdue (92), 1965
Minnesota	111, vs. Wisconsin (92), 1964
Northwestern	111, vs. Purdue (97), 1966
Ohio State	111, vs. Michigan State (79), 1960
Purdue	105, vs. Indiana (93), 1962
Wisconsin	105, vs. Michigan (93),
	105, vs. Indiana (94), 1962

*Conference Record

Most Free Throws, One Game, Two Teams

73, Indiana (42) vs. Purdue (31), Jan. 19, 1953
69, Illinois (36) vs. Northwestern (33), Feb. 5, 1955
68, Indiana (36) vs. Northwestern (32), 2-2-53 (Overtime)
*65, Indiana (38) vs. Northwestern (27) 1952
*54, Illinois (28) vs. Indiana (26), 1950

Most Free Throws a Game, One Season

26.9, Ohio State, 1956 (376 in 14)
25.9, Indiana, 1954 (363 in 14)
25.4, Indiana, 1955 (356 in 14)
25.0, Minnesota, 1954 (350 in 14)
*20.1, Indiana, 1952 (281 in 14)
*18.9, Iowa, 1952 (264 in 14)

Best Field Goal Shooting Averages, One Game

.723, Minnesota, vs. Iowa (34 of 47), Jan. 25, 1960
.645, Purdue, vs. Ohio State (40 of 62), Feb. 2, 1963
.636, Michigan vs. Iowa (42 of 66), Feb. 28, 1966
.633, Indiana, vs. Ohio State (50 of 79), Feb. 2, 1959
.625, Minnesota vs. Indiana (40 of 64) Feb. 28, 1966
.613, Iowa, vs. N.U. (38 of 62), Feb. 28, 1953
.600, Purdue, vs. MSU (33 of 55), Feb. 3, 1962
.600, Michigan vs. Purdue (42 of 70), Feb. 26, 1966
.592, Ohio State, vs. Illinois (45 of 76), Feb. 15, 1960
.592, Ohio State, vs. Ind. (42 of 71), 2-6-61

Best Field Goal Shooting Average, One Season

.497, Ohio State (523 of 1053), 1960
.495, Ohio State (481 of 972), 1961
.490, Ohio State (494 of 1009), 1962
.489, Michigan (528 of 1080), 1966
.482, Illinois (534 of 1108), 1965
.479, Ohio State (484 of 1010), 1964
.466, Purdue (395 of 828), 1959
.465, Purdue (477 of 1026), 1964
.458, Indiana (472 of 1030), 1960
.456, Purdue (466 of 1021), 1964
.4534, Illinois (482 of 1063), 1963
.4532, Minnesota (474 of 1046), 1965
.451, Michigan (514 of 1140), 1965

Best Free Throw Shooting Averages, One Game

.952, Indiana, vs. Wisconsin (20 of 21), Feb. 24, 1964
.952, Indiana, vs. Northwestern (20 of 21), Jan. 9, 1965
.950, Illinois, vs. Wisconsin (19 of 20) Feb. 23, 1963
.950, Wisconsin, vs. Michigan State (19 of 20), Feb. 27, 1965
.947, Wisconsin vs. Michigan State (18 of 19), Feb. 19, 1966
.944, Ohio State, vs. Northwestern (17 of 18), Jan. 16, 1960
.941, Ohio State, vs. Northwestern (16 of 17), Jan. 28, 1963
.935, Wisconsin, vs. MSC (29 of 31), Mar. 1, 1954
.933, Indiana, vs. NU (14 of 15), 2-27-61
.929, Ohio State, vs. NU (13 of 14), 1-14-61

Best Free Throw Shooting Averages, One Season

.781, Indiana (271 of 347), 1965
.768, Purdue (285 of 371), 1966
.765, Indiana (328 of 429), 1963
.758, Indiana (257 of 339), 1964
.758, Indiana (235 of 310), 1966
.749, Illinois (257 of 343), 1963
.745, Michigan (280 of 376), 1966
.7441, Ohio State (221 of 297), 1962
.7439, Illinois (337 of 453), 1956
.7425, Michigan (248 of 334) 1964
.7424, Ohio State (245 of 330), 1961
.7417, Indiana (356 of 480), 1955
.7406, Purdue (297 of 401), 1962

Most Free Throws Missed, One Game

30, Purdue vs. Michigan, Mar. 2, 1953
25, Ohio State vs. Indiana, Jan. 18, 1954
*24, Illinois vs. Indiana, Jan. 8, 1949
*24, Iowa vs. Indiana, Dec. 22, 1952

Most Free Throws Missed, One Game, Two Teams

46, Purdue (30) vs. Michigan (16), Mar. 2, 1953
40, Ohio State (25) vs. Indiana (15), Jan. 8, 1954

Most Free Throws Missed a Game, One Season

15.9, Purdue, 1953 (286 in 18)
14.2, Minnesota, 1954 (199 in 14)
13.6, Iowa, 1954 (191 in 14)

Most Field-Goal Attempts, One Game

114, Indiana, vs. Purdue, 2-23-53
113, Wisconsin, vs. Michigan State, 1-6-64
110, Indiana, vs. Iowa, 2-25-50
110, Indiana, vs. Michigan State, 1-11-64
109, Michigan, vs. Purdue, 1-23-65
108, Illinois, vs. Indiana, 2-22-60
104, Illinois, vs. Purdue, 2-7-59
104, Illinois, vs. Purdue, 2-13-60
101, Illinois, vs. Indiana, 3-3-58
101, Michigan State, vs. Indiana, 3-5-60

Most Field-Goal Attempts, One Game, Two Teams

207, Wisconsin (113) vs. Michigan State (94), 1-6-64
206, Indiana (110) vs. Michigan State (96), 1-11-64
196, Michigan (104) vs. Indiana (92), 2-7-59
194, Northwestern (98) vs. Iowa (96), 1-24-59
193, Ohio State (100) vs. Michigan (93), 1-10-59
191, Illinois (108) vs. Indiana (83), 2-22-60
190, Illinois (101) vs. Indiana (89), 3-3-58

*Before one-and-one rule

MOST FREE THROWS

1939—F Louis Debner, Illinois, 43
1940—C Joe Stampf, Chicago, 49
1941—C Joe Stampf, Chicago, 82
*1942—F Otto Graham, N'western, 58
1943—F Otto Graham, N'western, 41
   F Ralph Hamilton, Indiana, 41
1944—G Walt Kirk, Illinois, 39
1945—F Max Morris, N'western, 53
1946—F Tony Jaros, Minnesota, 79
1947—C Jim McIntyre, Minnesota, 69
1948—C Jim McIntyre, Minnesota, 73
1949—G Andy Butchko, Purdue, 67
1950—F Dick Schnittker, Ohio State, 91
*1951—C Ray Ragelis, N'western, 99
*1952—C Charles Darling, Iowa, 100

*1953—C Don Schlundt, Indiana 175
*1954—C Don Schlundt, Indiana 153
*1955—C Don Schlundt, Indiana, 157
*1956—G Robin Freeman, Ohio State, 129
*1957—C Archie Dees, Indiana, 106
1958—C Archie Dees, Indiana, 84
*1959—G Larry Seigfried, Ohio State, 106
*1960—C Terry Dischinger, Purdue, 130
*1961—C Terry Dischinger, Purdue, 143
*1962—C Terry Dischinger, Purdue, 179
*1963—C Gary Bradds, Ohio State, 125
*1964—C Gary Bradds, Ohio State, 126
*1965—F Dave Schellhase, Purdue, 117
*1966—F Dave Schellhase, Purdue, 131

BEST FIELD GOAL SHOOTING AVERAGE

	FG	FGA	FG Pct.
1947—F Ralph Hamilton, Indiana	73	195	.374
1948—F Dick Schnittker, Ohio	70	190	.368
1949—C Jim McIntyre, Minnesota	68	181	.376
1950—F Bob Donham, Ohio State	49	114	.430
*1951—G Ralph Gelle, Minnesota	43	98	.439
*1952—C Don Schlundt, Indiana	84	194	.433
*1953—F Dick Farley, Indiana	69	151	.457
*1954—C Don Schlundt, Indiana	113	224	.504
*1955—F John Miller, Ohio State	93	193	.482
*1956—F Wally Choice, Indiana	93	185	.503
*1957—C Dick Neal, Indiana	84	164	.512
*1958—C John Green, MSU	107	199	.538
*1959—C Walt Bellamy, Indiana	95	181	.525
*1960—C Jerry Lucas, Ohio State	143	218	.656
*1961—C Jerry Lucas, Ohio State	137	224	.612
*1962—C Jerry Lucas, Ohio State	122	180	.678
*1963—C Gary Bradds, Ohio State	154	293	.526
*1964—C Gary Bradds, Ohio State	174	325	.535
*1965—C Skip Thoren, Illinois	130	226	.575
*1966—C Cazzie Russell, Michigan	182	336	.542

*Conference teams played 12-game conference schedules from 1939 through 1950 (except 1942, 14 games) and 14-game schedules beginning 1951 (except 1953, 18 games).

BEST FREE THROW SHOOTING AVERAGE

	FT	FTA	FT Pcts.
1947—F Bob Cook, Wisconsin	47	63	.746
1948—F Ward Williams, Indiana	27	34	.794
1949—G Howie Williams, Purdue	30	35	.857
1950—F Don Page, Wisconsin	28	32	.875
*1951—G Myer Skogg, Minnesota	31	35	.886
*1952—F Clive Follmer, Illinois	40	51	.784
F Gordon Stauffer, MSC	40	51	.784
*1953—G Don Schlundt, Indiana	175	213	.822
*1954—G Walter Stoeppelwerth, NU	26	32	.813
*1955—F Robin Freeman, OSU	45	53	.849
*1956—C Hallie Bryant, Indiana	45	51	.882
*1957—C Archie Dees, Indiana	106	125	.848
*1958—G Sam Gee, Indiana	46	50	.920
*1959—G Roger Taylor, Illinois	48	55	.873
*1960—F Govoner Vaughn, Illinois	42	48	.875
*1961—F Larry Siegfried, OSU	56	61	.918
*1962—G Bill Cacciatore, NU	38	43	.884
*1963—G Jimmy Rayl, Purdue	108	122	.885
*1964—G Mel Garland, Purdue	59	69	.885
*1965—G-C Jimmy Rodgers, Iowa	59	69	.855
G-C Jon McGlocklin, Indiana	36	39	.923
*1966—G Henry Ebershoff, Purdue	59	64	.922

TEAM DEPARTMENTAL CHAMPIONS

SCORING

1939—Indiana	508	1949—Illinois	783	*1959—Illinois	1202
1940—Wisconsin	519	1950—Illinois	798	*1960—Ohio State	1271
1941—Ohio State	536	*1951—Illinois	989	*1961—Ohio State	1207
*1942—Iowa	721	*1952—Indiana	1035	*1962—Indiana	1214
1943—Illinois	755	*1953—Indiana	1452	*1963—Indiana	1266
1944—Ohio State	702	*1954—Ohio State	1087	*1964—Mich. State	1290
1945—Ohio State	632	*1955—Illinois	1174	*1965—Michigan	1300
1946—Indiana	661	*1956—Illinois	1277	*1966—Michigan	1336
1947—Wisconsin	677	*1957—Illinois	1180		
1948—Illinois	692	*1958—Indiana	1170		

Highest Opponents' Score

Illinois 110, by Ohio State 1964
Indiana 112, by Illinois, 1957
Iowa 107, by Michigan State, 1964 (twice)
Michigan 106, by Ohio State, 1959
Michigan State 121, by Illinois, 1965
Minnesota 105, by Indiana, 1962 (overtime)
Northwestern 107, by Michigan State, 1964
Ohio State 122, by Indiana, 1959
Purdue *128, by Michigan, 1966
Wisconsin 120, by Michigan, 1966

Highest Losing Score

Illinois 101, vs. Wisconsin (103), 1962
Indiana 103, vs. Michigan State (107), 1964
Iowa 97, vs. Illinois (103), 1959
Michigan 97, vs. Indiana (104), 1963
Michigan State 98, vs. Purdue (101), 1964 and vs. Michigan (103), 1965
Minnesota *104, vs. Indiana (105) 1962 (Overtime)
Northwestern 58, vs. Illinois (102), 1958 (overtime)
Ohio State 99, vs. Michigan State (102), 1964
Purdue 97, vs. Northwestern (111), 1966
Wisconsin 102, vs. Michigan (120), 1966

Individual Scoring, Big Ten Career

Illinois 880, John Kerr, 1952-1953-1954
Indiana #1451, Don Schlundt, 1952-1953-1954-1955 (1207 in 1953-54-55)
Iowa 903, Don Nelson, 1960-61-62
Michigan 1171, Cazzie Russell, 1964-65-66
Michigan State 918, Julius McCoy, 1954-55-56
Minnesota 958, Chuck Mencel, 1952-1953-1954-1955 (766 in 1953-54-55)
   858, Lou Hudson, 1964-65-66
Northwestern 816, Joe Ruklick, 1957-1958-1959
Ohio State 1027, Paul Ebert, 1952-1953-1954
Purdue ##1248, Terry Dischinger, 1960-61-62
Wisconsin 810, Dick Cable, 1952-1953-1954-1955 (697 in 1953-54-55)
   738, Ken Siebel, 1961-1962-1963

*Conference Record #4 Year Conference Record ##3 Year Conference Record

INDIVIDUAL DEPARTMENTAL CHAMPIONS

SCORING

	POINTS
1939—F Jimmy Hull, Ohio State	169
1940—F Bill Hapac, Illinois	164
1941—C Joe Stampf, Chicago	166
*1942—F Dick Ives, Iowa	242
1943—F Andy Philip, Illinois	255
1944—F Dick Ives, Iowa	208
1945—F Max Morris, N'western	189
1946—F Max Morris, N'western	198
1947—F Murray Wier, Iowa	272
1948—C Bob Cook, Wisconsin	229
1949—C Don Rehfeldt, Wisconsin	265
1950—C Don Rehfeldt, Wisconsin	277
*1951—C Ray Ragelis, N'western	277
*1952—C Charles Darling, Iowa	364

	POINTS
*1953—C Don Schlundt, Indiana	459
*1954—C Don Schlundt, Indiana	379
*1955—G Don Schlundt, Indiana	369
*1956—G Robin Freeman, Ohio State	455
*1957—C Archie Dees, Indiana	356
1958—F Archie Dees, Indiana	362
*1959—F M. C. Burton, Michigan	316
*1960—C Terry Dischinger, Purdue	384
*1961—C Terry Dischinger, Purdue	405
*1962—C Terry Dischinger, Purdue	459
*1963—C Gary Bradds, Ohio State	459
*1964—C Gary Bradds, Ohio State	474
*1965—F Dave Schellhase, Purdue	391
*1966—G Cazzie Russell, Michigan	465

MOST FIELD GOALS

1939—F Jimmy Hull, Ohio State, 66
1940—F Bill Hapac, Illinois, 60
*1942—F Dick Fisher, Ohio State, 62
*1943—C John Kotz, Wisconsin, 95
1944—F Andy Philip, Illinois, 111
1945—F Dick Ives, Iowa, 89
1945—F Max Morris, N'western, 68
1946—F Max Morris, N'western, 77
1947—F Ralph Hamilton, Indiana, 73
1948—F Murray Wier, Iowa, 107
1949—C Don Rehfeldt, Wisconsin, 85
1950—C Don Rehfeldt, Wisconsin, 101
*1951—F Carl McNulty, Purdue, 97
*1952—C Charles Darling, Iowa, 132

*1953—C Paul Ebert, Ohio, 145
*1954—F John Kerr, Illinois, 133
*1955—G Frank Ehmann, Northwestern, 163
*1956—G Robin Freeman, Ohio State, 123
*1957—C Archie Dees, Indiana, 125
1958—C Archie Dees, Indiana, 139
*1959—G Willie Merriweather, Purdue, 125
*1960—C Jerry Lucas, Ohio State, 143
*1961—C Jerry Lucas, Ohio State, 137
*1962—C Jimmy Rayl, Indiana, 152
*1963—C Gary Bradds, Ohio State, 154
*1964—C Gary Bradds, Ohio State, 174
*1965—F Lou Hudson, Minnesota, 139
*1966—G Cazzie Russell, Michigan, 182

HONOR TEAMS

BIG TEN CONFERENCE ALL-AMERICANS

ILLINOIS
Chuck Carney, f, 1922
Louis (Pick) Dehner, c, 1938-39
Bill Hapac, f, 1940
Andy Phillip, f, 1943
Walton (Junior) Kirk, g, 1945
Bill Erickson, g, 1949
Don Sunderlage, g, 1951
Rod Fletcher, g, 1952

INDIANA
Everett Dean, c, 1921
Branch McCracken, f, 1930
Vern Huffman, g, 1936
Ernie Andres, g, 1938
Marvin Huffman, f, 1940
Ralph Hamilton, f, 1947
Bill Garrett, c, 1951
Don Schlundt, c, 1953-54-55
Bob Leonard, g, 1953-54
Archie Dees, c, 1958
Walt Bellamy, c, 1960-61
Jimmy Rayl, g, 1963

IOWA
Dick Ives, f, 1945
Herb Wilkinson, g, 1946-47
Murray Wier, f, 1948
Chuck Darling, c, 1952
Carl Cain, f, 1956

MICHIGAN
Bennie Oosterbaan, f, 1928
John Townsend, f, 1938
Bill Buntin, c, 1964-65
Cazzie Russell, g, 1964-65-66

MICHIGAN STATE
Chet Aubuchon, g, 1940
Jack Quiggle, g, 1957
Johnny Green, c, 1959

MINNESOTA
Martin Rolek, g, 1938
Meyer (Whitey) Skoog, g, 1951
Dick Garmaker, g, 1955
Chuck Mencel, g, 1955
Ron Johnson, c, 1960
Lou Hudson, f, 1965

NORTHWESTERN
Joe Reiff, c, 1931
Otto Graham, f, 1944
Max Morris, f, 1946
Ray Ragelis, c, 1951
Frank Ehmann, f, 1955

OHIO STATE
Johnny Miner, f, 1925
Jimmy Hull, f, 1939
Dick Schnittker, f, 1950
Paul Ebert, f, 1954
Robin Freeman, g, 1955-56
Frank Howard, f, 1957
Jerry Lucas, c, 1960-61-62
Larry Siegfried, g, 1961
John Havlicek, f, 1962
Gary Bradds, c, 1963-64

PURDUE
Donald White, g, 1921
Ray Miller, g, 1922
George Spaulding, f, 1926
Charles Murphy, c, 1928-29-30
John Wooden, g, 1930-31-32
Emmett Lowery, g, 1934
Norman Cottom, f, 1934
Robert Kessler, f, 1936
Jewell Young, f, 1937-38
Fred Beretta, g, 1940
Terry Dischinger, c, 1960-61-62
Dave Schellhase, f, 1965-66

WISCONSIN
Chris Steinmetz, 1905
Harold (Bud) Foster, g, 1930
Gene Englund, f, 1941
John Korz, f, 1942
Don Rehfeldt, c, 1950

MOST FIELD GOALS

1940—Indiana, 216
1941—Indiana, 210
*1942—Indiana, 288
1043—Illinois, 325
1944—Ohio State, 294
1945—Ohio State, 257
1946—Michigan, 267
1947—Wisconsin, 248
1948—Illinois, 274

1949—Illinois, 297
1950—Illinois, 291
*1951—Northwestern, 368
*1952—Illinois, 380
1953—Illinois, 531
*1954—Ohio State, 381
*1955—Illinois, 442
*1956—Illinois, 470
*1957—Illinois, 461

*1958—Northwestern, 453
*1959—Illinois, 488
*1960—Ohio State, 523
*1961—Ohio State, 481
*1962—Ohio State, 494
*1963—Illinois, 516
*1964—Mich. State, 516
*1965—Illinois, 534
*1966—Michigan, 528

MOST FREE THROWS

1940—Purdue, 130
1941—Wisconsin, 146
*1942—Northwestern, 161
1943—Indiana, 139
1944—Purdue, 118
1945—Iowa, 146
1946—Minnesota, 172
1947—Wisconsin, 181
1948—Iowa, 169

1949—Purdue, 209
1950—Ohio State, 221
*1951—Illinois, 255
*1952—Indiana, 281
*1953—Indiana, 442
*1954—Indiana, 363
*1955—Indiana, 356
*1956—Ohio State, 376
*1957—Indiana, 284

*1958—Purdue, 276
*1959—Ohio State, 278
*1960—Minnesota, 254
*1961—Purdue, 288
*1962—Minnesota, 312
*1963—Indiana, 328
*1964—Ohio State, 275
*1965—Iowa, 303
*1966—Purdue, 285

BEST FIELD GOAL SHOOTING AVERAGE

	FG	FGA	FG Pct.
1947—Wisconsin	248	833	.298
1948—Minnesota	226	778	.290
1949—Minnesota	228	713	.320
1950—Ohio State	283	812	.349
*1951—Northwestern	368	1001	.368
*1952—Indiana	377	1079	.349
*1953—Ohio State	505	1410	.358
*1954—Ohio State	381	1010	.377
1955—Iowa	418	1011	.413
*1956—Iowa	415	1024	.405
*1957—Ohio State	418	969	.431
*1958—Northwestern	453	1115	.4062
*1959—Purdue	458	1066	.430
*1960—Ohio State	523	1053	.497
*1961—Ohio State	481	972	.495
*1962—Ohio State	494	1009	.490
*1963—Illinois	482	1063	.453
*1964—Ohio State	484	1010	.479
*1965—Illinois	534	1108	.482
*1966—Michigan	528	1080	.489

*—Conference teams played 12-game conference schedules from 1939 through 1950 (except 1942, 14 games) and 14-game schedules beginning 1951 (except 1953, 18 games).

BEST FREE THROW SHOOTING AVERAGE

	FT	FTA	FT Pct.
1947—Indiana	171	258	.663
1948—Wisconsin	168	253	.664
1949—Purdue	209	308	.641
1950—Wisconsin	179	265	.675
*1951—Minnesota	172	234	.735
*1952—Iowa	264	390	.677
*1953—Minnesota	385	558	.690
*1954—Wisconsin	324	457	.707
1955—Indiana	356	480	.742
*1955—Indiana	337	453	.7439
*1957—Indiana	251	342	.734
*1958—Michigan	387	490	.734
*1959—Ohio State	278	390	.713
*1960—Michigan State	231	318	.726
*1961—Ohio State	245	330	.742
*1962—Ohio State	221	297	.7441
*1963—Indiana	328	429	.765
*1964—Indiana	257	339	.758
*1965—Indiana	271	347	.781
*1966—Purdue	285	371	.768

*—Conference teams played 12-game conference schedules from 1939 through 1950 (except 1942, 14 games) and 14-game schedules beginning 1951 (except 1953, 18 games).

MOST VALUABLE BASKETBALL PLAYERS

	1946	1947	1948
Chicago	George Raby, c		
Illinois	Bob Doster, f	Jack Smiley, g	Jack Burmaster, g
Indiana	John Wallace, f	Ralph Hamilton, f	Ward Williams, f
Iowa	Herb Wilkinson, g	Murray Wier, f	Murray Wier, f*
Michigan	Dave Strack, f-g	Mack Suprunowicz, f	Pete Elliott, g
Minnesota	Tony Jaros, f	Jim McIntyre, c	Harry (Bud) Grant, f
Northwestern	Max Morris, f*	Bernard Schadler, g	Charles Tourek, f
Ohio State	Paul Huston, g	Jack Underman, c	Dick Schnittker, f
Purdue	Rudy Lawson, g	Paul Hoffman, g	Bill Berberian, g
Wisconsin	Bob Cook, f	Glen Selbo, g*	Bob Cook, f

	1949	1950	1951
Illinois	Dwight Eddleman, f*	Wally Osterkorn, c	Don Sunderlage, g*
Indiana	Lou Watson, g	Lou Watson, g	Bill Garrett, c
Iowa	Charlie Mason, f	Franklin Calsbeek, f	Franklin Calsbeek, f
Michigan	Bob Harrison, g	Mack Suprunowicz, f	Leo VanderKuy, f
Michigan State			Jim Snodgrass
Minnesota	Harold Olson, g	Meyer (Whitey) Skoog, g	Meyer (Whitey) Skoog, g
Northwestern	Bill Stricklen, f	Ray Ragelis, g	Ray Ragelis, g
Ohio State	Dick Schnittker, f	Bob Donham, f	Jim Remington, f
Purdue	Howie Williams, f	Howie Williams, f	Carl McNulty, c
Wisconsin	Don Rehfeldt, c	Don Rehfeldt, c*	Ab Nicholas, g

	1952	1953	1954
Illinois	Rod Fletcher, g	Irv Bemoras, g	John (Red) Kerr, c*
Indiana	Bob Leonard, f	Don Schlundt, c*	Don Schlundt, c
Iowa	Jim Skala, f	Herb Thompson, f	Carl Cain, f
Michigan	Bill Bower, f	Paul Groffsky, c	Jim Barron, g
Michigan State	Dick Means, f	Al Ferrari, c	Al Ferrari, c
Minnesota	Frank Petrancek, c	Bob Gelle, f	Ed Kalafat, c
Northwestern		John Biever, g	Frank Ehmann, f
Ohio State	Paul Ebert, c	Paul Ebert, c	Paul Ebert, c
Purdue	Carl McNulty, c	Jack Runyan, g	Dennis Blind, g
Wisconsin	Ab Nicholas, g	Chuck Siefert, g	Paul Morrow, c

	1955	1956	1957
Illinois	Paul Judson, g	Bruce Brothers, f	Harv Schmidt, f
Indiana	Don Schlundt, c	Wally Choice, f	Archie Dees, c*
Iowa	Bill Seaburg, g	Carl Cain, f	Dave Gunther, f
Michigan	Ron Kramer, c	Ron Kramer, c	Ron Kramer, c
Michigan State	Al Ferrari, f	Julius McCoy, f	George Ferguson, f
Minnesota	Chuck Mencel, g*	Dave Tucker, f	Jed Dommeyer, c
Northwestern	Frank Ehmann, f	Dick Mast, g	Joe Ruklick, c
Ohio State	John Miller, f	Robin Freeman, g*	Gene Millard, c
Purdue	Don Beck, f	Joe Sexson, f	Lamar Lundy, c
Wisconsin	Dick Cable, f	Dick Miller, g	Bob Litzow, g

	1958	1959	1960
Illinois	Don Ohl, g	Roger Taylor, g	Govoner Vaughn, f
Indiana	Archie Dees, c*	Walt Bellamy, c	Walt Bellamy, c
Iowa	Dave Gunther, f	Dave Gunther, f	Don Nelson, c
Michigan	Pete Tillotson, c-f	M. C. Burton, f	Lovell Farris, f-c
Michigan State	John Green, c	John Green, c*	Horace Walker, f
Minnesota	George Kline, f	Roger Johnson, g	Willie Johnson, c
Northwestern	Joe Ruklick, c	Willie Jones, f	Willie Jones, f
Ohio State	Ken Sidle, f	Larry Siegfried, g	Jerry Lucas, c*
Purdue	Wilson Eison, c	Willie Merriweather, g	Terry Dischinger, c
Wisconsin	Walter Holt, f	Bob Barneson, c	Fred Clow, f

	1961	1962	1963
Illinois	Dave Downey, f	Dave Downey, f	Dave Downey, f
Indiana	Walt Bellamy, c	Jimmy Rayl, g	Tom Bolyard, f
Iowa	Don Nelson, c-f	Don Nelson, f	Jerry Messick, c
Michigan	John Tidwell, g	John Harris, c	Bill Buntin, c
Michigan State	Art Schwarm, g	Pete Gent, f	Ted Williams, c
Minnesota	Dick Erickson, g	Ray Cronk, f	Eric Magdanz, f
Northwestern	Ralph Wells, g, & Brad Snyder, f	Ralph Wells, g	Rich Falk, g
Ohio State	Jerry Lucas, c*	Jerry Lucas, c*	Gary Bradds, c*
Purdue	Terry Dischinger, c	Terry Dischinger, c	Mel Garland, g
Wisconsin	Ken Siebel, f	Ken Siebel, f	Ken Siebel, f

*—Received Chicago Tribune Trophy as Most Valuable in Conference. (Earlier Most Valuable designations went to Gene Englund, Wisconsin, 1941; John Kotz, Wisconsin, 1942; and Andy Phillip, Illinois, 1943.)

MOST VALUABLE BASKETBALL PLAYERS (Cont.)

	1964	1965	1966
Illinois	Skip Thoren, f	Skip Thoren, f	Don Freeman, f
Indiana	Tom and Dick Van Arsdale, f	Dick and Tom Van Arsdale, f	Max Walker, g
Iowa	Jimmy Rodgers, g	Jimmy Rodgers, g	Denny Pauling, g
Michigan	Cazzie Russell, g	Bill Buntin, c, and Cazzie Russell, g*	Cazzie Russell, g*
Michigan State	Fred Thomann, c	Stan Washington, g	Stan Washington, f
Minnesota	Bill Davis, f	Lou Hudson, f	Archie Clark, g
Northwestern	Rich Falk, g, & Rick Lopossa, f	Jim Pitts, c	Jim Pitts, c
Ohio State	Gary Bradds, c*	Dick Ricketts, g	Bob Dove, c
Purdue	Dave Schellhase, f	Dave Schellhase, f	Dave Schellhase, f
Wisconsin	Ken Gustafson, f	Jim Bohen, g	Paul Morenz, g

*—Received Chicago Tribune Trophy as Most Valuable in Conference. (Earlier Most Valuable designations went to Gene Englund, Wisconsin, 1941; John Kotz, Wisconsin, 1942; and Andy Phillip, Illinois, 1943.)

BIG TEN IN NCAA TOURNAMENT

	W	L	Pct.	Pts.	O. Pts.
Indiana (1940-53-54-58)	9	2	.818	770	688
Wisconsin (1941-47)	4	1	.800	232	233
Ohio State (1939-44-45-46-50-60-61-62)	17	7	.708	1611	1400
Michigan (1948-64-65-66)	8	4	.667	959	916
Iowa (1955-56)	5	3	.625	634	604
Illinois (1942-49-51-52-63)	9	6	.600	965	946
Michigan State (1957-59)	3	3	.500	440	449
Totals	55	26	.679	5611 (69.3)	5236 (64.6)

Big Ten Teams in NCAA Finals

	FINISH	SCORE
1939—Ohio State	2nd	Oregon 46—OHIO STATE 33
*1940—Indiana	1st	INDIANA 60—Kansas 42
*1941—Wisconsin	1st	WISCONSIN 39—Washington State 34
1946—Ohio State	3rd	OHIO STATE 63—California 45
1949—Illinois	3rd	ILLINOIS 57—Oregon State 53
1951—Illinois	3rd	ILLINOIS 61—Oklahoma A&M 46
1952—Illinois	3rd	ILLINOIS 67—Santa Clara 64
*1953—Indiana	1st	INDIANA 69—Kansas 68
1955—Iowa	4th	Colorado 75—IOWA 54
1956—Iowa	2nd	San Francisco 83—IOWA 71
1957—Michigan State	4th	San Francisco 67—MICHIGAN STATE 60
*1960—Ohio State	1st	OHIO STATE 75—California 55
1961—Ohio State	2nd	Cincinnati 70—OHIO STATE 65—OT
1962—Ohio State	2nd	Cincinnati 71—OHIO STATE 59
1964—Michigan	3rd	MICHIGAN 100—Kansas State 90
1965—Michigan	2nd	U.C.L.A. 91—MICHIGAN 80

*—National Championship

NATIONAL BASKETBALL RANKINGS

(Selected by the nation's sports writers as polled by the Associated Press, with associated notations for Big Ten teams when ranked differently by United Press International's coach's poll.)

1949
1. Kentucky
2. Oklahoma A & M
3. St. Louis
4. ILLINOIS
5. Western Kentucky
6. MINNESOTA
7. Bradley
8. San Francisco
9. Tulane
10. Bowling Green

1950
1. Bradley
2. OHIO STATE
3. Kentucky
4. Holy Cross
5. North Carolina State
6. Duquesne
7. U.C.L.A.
8. Western Kentucky
9. St. John's (N.Y.)
10. LaSalle

1951#
1. Kentucky
2. Oklahoma A & M
3. Columbia
4. Kansas State
5. ILLINOIS-a
6. Bradley
7. INDIANA-b
8. North Carolina State
9. St. John's (N.Y.)
10. St. Louis

1952
1. Kentucky
2. ILLINOIS
3. Kansas State
4. Duquesne
5. St. Louis
6. Washington
7. IOWA-c
8. Kansas
9. West Virginia
10. St. John's (N.Y.)

1953
1. INDIANA
2. Seton Hall
3. Kansas
4. Washington
5. Louisiana State
6. LaSalle
7. St. John's (N.Y.)
8. Oklahoma A & M
9. Duquesne
*10. Notre Dame

1954
1. Kentucky
2. LaSalle
3. Holy Cross
4. INDIANA-d
5. Duquesne
6. Notre Dame
7. Bradley
8. Western Kentucky
9. Penn State
**10. Oklahoma A & M

1955
1. San Francisco
2. Kentucky
3. LaSalle
4. North Carolina State
5. IOWA
6. Duquesne
7. Utah
8. Marquette
9. Dayton
10. Oregon State

1956
1. San Francisco
2. North Carolina State
3. Dayton
4. IOWA
5. Alabama
6. Louisville
7. Southern Methodist
8. U.C.L.A.
9. Kentucky
10. ILLINOIS-e

1957
1. North Carolina
2. Kansas
3. Kentucky
4. Southern Methodist
5. Seattle
6. Louisville
7. West Virginia
8. Vanderbilt
9. Oklahoma City
***10. St. Louis

1958
1. West Virginia
2. Cincinnati
3. Kansas State
4. San Francisco
5. Temple
6. Maryland
7. Kansas
8. Notre Dame
9. Kentucky
****10. Duke

1959
1. Kansas State
2. Kentucky
3. Mississippi State
4. Bradley
5. Cincinnati
6. North Carolina State
7. MICHIGAN STATE-f
8. Auburn
9. North Carolina
10. West Virginia

1960
1. Cincinnati
2. California
3. OHIO STATE
4. Bradley
5. West Virginia
6. Utah
7. INDIANA-g
8. Utah State
9. St. Bonaventure
10. Miami (Fla.)

1961
1. OHIO STATE
2. Cincinnati
3. St. Bonaventure
4. Kansas State
5. North Carolina
6. Bradley
7. Southern California
8. IOWA-h
9. West Virginia
10. Duke

1962
1. OHIO STATE
2. Cincinnati
3. Kentucky
4. Mississippi State
5. Bradley
6. Kansas State
7. Utah
8. Bowling Green
9. Colorado
10. Duke

1963
1. Cincinnati
2. Duke
3. Loyola (Chicago)
4. Arizona State
5. Wichita
6. Mississippi State
7. OHIO STATE-i
8. ILLINOIS-j
9. N.Y.U.
10. Colorado

1964
1. U.C.L.A.
2. MICHIGAN
3. Duke
4. Kentucky
5. Wichita
6. Oregon State
7. Villanova
8. Loyola (Chicago)
9. DePaul
10. Davidson

1965
1. MICHIGAN
2. U.C.L.A.
3. St. Joseph's (Pa.)
4. Providence
5. Vanderbilt
6. Davidson
7. MINNESOTA-k
8. Villanova
9. Brigham Young
10. Duke

1966
1. Kentucky
2. Duke
3. Texas Western
4. Kansas
5. St. Joseph's (Pa.)
6. Loyola (Chicago)
7. Cincinnati
8. Vanderbilt
9. MICHIGAN-l
10. Western Kentucky

#—UPI's initial Coach's poll.
a—Ranked 4th by UPI.
b—Ranked 8th by UPI.
c—Ranked 8th by UPI.
d—Ranked 1st by UPI.
e—Ranked 5th by UPI.
f—Ranked 3rd by UPI.
g—Ranked 10th-tie by UPI.
h—Ranked 10th by UPI.
i—Ranked 10th by UPI.
j—Ranked 5th by UPI.
k—Ranked 7th by UPI.
l—Ranked 10th by UPI.

*—ILLINOIS ranked 10th by UPI. ***—MICHIGAN STATE ranked 7th by UPI.
—IOWA ranked 10th by UPI. **—INDIANA ranked 10th by UPI.

TEAM CHAMPIONS: Chicago—1909, '14, '17, '20, '21, '22, '24, '26, '27, '28, '30, '31, '32, '33, '34.
Illinois—1911, '12, '29, '35, '39, '41, '42, '50, '51, '52, '53, '54, '55, '56, '57, '58, '59, '60.
Iowa—1957.
Michigan—1961, '62, '63, '64, '65, '66.
Minnesota—1903, '07, '10, '25, '36, '38, '40, '47, '48, '49.
Wisconsin—1902, '04, '05, '08, '13, '15, '16, '23.

SWIMMING SECTION

CONFERENCE SHORT COURSE (75 FT.) RECORDS
(Annual Championship Meet)

Event	Individual	School	Record	Year	Place
50-Yd. Free Style	Steve Jackman	Minnesota	:21.0	1963	Purdue
100-Yd. Free Style	Steve Jackman	Minnesota	:47.3	1963	Purdue
200-Yd. Free Style	Bill Utley	Indiana	1:43.9	1966	Iowa
220-Yd. Free Style	Mike Wood	Mich. State	2:01.3	1962	Indiana
440-Yd. Free Style	Alan Somers	Indiana	4:20.8	1962	Indiana
500-Yd. Free Style	Bill Farley	Michigan	4:46.14	1965	Wisconsin
1500-Meter Free Style	Alan Somers	Indiana	17:37.5	1962	Indiana
1650-Yd. Free Style	Robert Windle	Indiana	16:50.4	1966	Wisconsin
100-Yd. Back Stroke	Gary Dilley	MSU	:53.15	1965	NU
150-Yd. Back Stroke	Harry Holiday	Michigan	1:31.7	1943	Indiana
200-Yd. Back Stroke	Tom Stock	Indiana	1:56.20	1962	Purdue
100-Yd. Butterfly Stroke	Walt Richardson	Minnesota	:50.6	1963	Wisconsin
200-Yd. Butterfly Stroke	Fred Schmidt	Indiana	1:51.90	1965	Wisconsin
100-Yd. Breast Stroke	Paul Scheerer	Michigan	1:00.39	1965	Wisconsin
200-Yd. Breast Stroke	Paul Scheerer	Michigan	2:12.81	1965#	Iowa
200-Yd. Indiv. Medley	Bob Hopper	Ohio State	1:59.9	1966	Iowa
400-Yd. Indiv. Medley	Ken Webb	Indiana	4:17.3	1966	Wisconsin
400-Yd. Medley Relay	Pete Hammer / Tom Tretheway / Fred Schmidt / Bob Williamson	Indiana	3:31.55	1965	Wisconsin
400-Yd. Free Style Relay	John Salassa / Rich Walls / Ken Wiebeck / Bill Groft	Michigan	3:09.2	1966	Iowa
800-Yd. Free Style Relay	Bill Utley / Scott Cordin / Ken Webb / Robert Windle	Indiana	7:02.6	1966	Iowa

#—Mark set in preliminaries.

CONFERENCE LONG COURSE (150 FT.) RECORDS
(Annual Championship Meet)

Event	Individual	School	Record	Year	Place
50-Yd. Free Style	Keith Carter	Purdue	:23.3	1948	Iowa
100-Yd. Free Style	Wally Ris	Iowa	:51.5	1948	Iowa
220-Yd. Free Style	Wally Ris	Iowa	2:15.3	1948	Iowa
440-Yd. Free Style	Bill Heusner	NU	4:56.7	1948	Iowa
150-Yd. Back Stroke	Harry Holiday	Michigan	1:37.9	1948	Iowa
200-Yd. Breast Stroke	Keith Carter	Purdue	2:24	1948	Iowa
300-Yd. Medley Relay	Holiday, Sohl and Kogen	Michigan	2:58:5	1948	Iowa
400-Yd. Free Style Relay	Marsh, Draves Straub, Ris	Iowa	3:33.4	1948	Iowa
1500-Meter Free Style	Matt Mann III	Michigan	20:17.5	1948	Iowa

TEAM CHAMPIONS:
Chicago—1916 (co), '19, '21.
Illinois—1911, '12, '13.
Indiana—1961, '62, '63, '64, '65, '66.
Iowa—1936.
Michigan—1927, '28, '29, '31, '32, '33, '34, '35, '37, '39, '40, '41, '42, '44, '45, '48, '58, '59, '60.
Michigan State—1957.
Minnesota—1922, '26.
Northwestern—1914, '15, '16 (co), '17, '18, '20, '23, '24, '25, '30.
Ohio State—1938, '43, '46, '47, '49, '50, '51, '52, '53, '54, '55, '56.

FENCING TEAM CHAMPIONS:
Chicago—1928, '34, '36, '37, '38, '39, '40, '41.
Illinois—1929, '30, '31, '32, '33, '35, '42, '43, '50, '51, '52, '53, '54, '56, '58, '60.
Michigan State—1963.
Northwestern—1947, '48.
Ohio State—1926, '27, '49.
Wisconsin—1955, '57, '59.

GYMNASTICS

CONFERENCE MEETS

Year	Site	All-Around Winner	Points	Team Champion	Points
1902	Wis.	J. W. Dye, Minn.	98.16	Wisconsin	No Record
1903	Minn.	Walleser, Grinnell		Minnesota	37.00
1904	Wis.	Johnson, Nebr.		Wisconsin	31.00
1905	Chi.			Wisconsin	40.00
1906	No Meet				
1907	Chi.	Felix Zeidelhock, Wis.	515.25	Minnesota	25.00
1908	Wis.	Felix Zeidelhock, Wis.		Wisconsin	31.50
1909	Nebr.	D. C. Mitchell, Nebr.	385.20	Chicago	1263.40
1910	Minn.	E. B. Styles, Ill.		Minnesota	1156.65
1911	Chi.	E. B. Styles, Ill.	359.00	Illinois	1103.75
1912	Ill.	E. B. Styles, Ill.	370.00	Illinois	1174.75
1913	Wis.	Parkinson, Chicago	353.44	Wisconsin	1161.47
1914	Chi.	Replinger, Wis.	370.50	Chicago	1103.00
1915	Nebr.	J. C. West, Minn.	377.00	Wisconsin	1257.00
1916	Minn.	Ernest Carlson, Minn.	357.63	Wisconsin	1265.00
1917	Iowa	Drewing, Nebr.	364.50	Chicago	1267.75
1918	No Meet				
1919	No Meet				
1920	Ill.	Ziegler, Ill.	327.50	Chicago	1102.50
1921	Ind.	Ernest Carlson, Minn.	332.70	Chicago	1114.90
1922	Wis.	Schneidenbach, Chi.	355.30	Wisconsin	1117.25
1923	Ohio	Thomkins, Ia.	303.00	Chicago	1114.00
1924	Chi.	Schmidt, Wis.	345.50	Minnesota	1189.50
1925	Minn.	Schmidt, Wis.	374.00	Chicago	1224.50
1926	Pur.	McDonald, Illinois	340.00	Chicago	1234.80
1927	Chi.	Floyd H. Davidson, Chicago	386.75	Chicago	1235.75
1928	Chi.	Floyd H. Davidson, Chicago	395.90	Chicago	1249.20
1929	Ill.	John E. Menzies, Chicago	370.75	Illinois	1143.85
1930	Chi.	John E. Menzies, Chicago	403.60	Chicago	1212.05
1931	Ill.	Everett C. Olson, Chicago	377.15	Chicago	1121.95
1932	Chi.	Everett C. Olson, Chicago	393.1	Chicago	1133.0
1933	Chi.	George H. Wrighte, Chicago	360.15	Chicago	1053.45
1934	Chi.	George H. Wrighte, Chicago	316.95	Chicago	1065.20
1935	Ill.	Eugene Wettstein, Iowa	320.80	Illinois	1001.05
1936	Ill.	George Matison, Minnesota	370.75	Minnesota	97.5
1937	Iowa	Eugene Wettstein, Iowa	362.50	Iowa	1051.00
1938	Minn.	Joseph Giallombardo, Illinois	166.15	Minnesota	112.0
1939	Ill.	Joseph Giallombardo, Illinois	187.75	Minnesota	111.5
1940	Chi.	Delver Daly, Minnesota	178.00	Minnesota	105.5
1941	Iowa	Newt Loken, Minnesota	182.00	Illinois	105.5
1942	Minn.	Newt Loken, Minnesota	229.9	Illinois	111.0
1943-1946—No Meet Held.					
1947	Chi.	James Peterson, Minn.	211.00	Minnesota	92.00
1948	Ill.-X	James Peterson, Minnesota	1475.	Minnesota	71.0
1949	Mich.	James Peterson, Minnesota	1053.	Minnesota	52.0
1950	Iowa	Frank Dolan, Illinois	1032.	Illinois	66.0
1951	Wis.	Mel Stout, Michigan State	1494½	Illinois	62.0
1952	Ind.	Bob Sullivan, Illinois	1499.00	Illinois	94.50
1953	MSC	Kenneth Bartlett, Minnesota State	1287.	Illinois	133.
1954	Ohio	Carlton Rintz, Michigan State	1517.	Illinois	125.5
1955	Minn.	Carlton Rintz, Michigan State	1560.	Illinois	139.5
1956	Ill.	Don Tonry, Ill.	1516.	Illinois	162.5
1957	Mich.	Edward Gagnier, Mich.	1068.	Illinois	143.5
1958	Iowa	Abraham Grossfeld, Ill.	1061.	Illinois	149.5
1959	Ind.	Abraham Grossfeld, Ill.	536.5	Illinois	143.0
1960	Minn.	Ray Hadley, Ill.	535.75	Illinois	114.5
1961	Mich.	Rich Montpetit, Mich.	551.	Michigan	147.0
1962	Ohio	Ray Hadley, Ill.	538.75	Michigan	163.0
1963	MSU	Gil LaRose, Mich.	548.5	Michigan	210.5
1964	Wis.	Jim Curzi, MSU	516.75	Michigan	131
1965	Ill.	Glenn Gailis, Iowa	53.75	Michigan	Dual Record
1966	Ind.	Dave Thor, MSU	55.00	Michigan	#

X—1948 meet at Navy Pier, Chicago
#—Team title based on combination of dual & championship meet points.

Illinois—1913 (tie), '17, '20, '22, '24 (tie), '25 (tie), '26, '27, '28, '30, '32 (tie), '35, '37, '46, '47, '52
Indiana—1914, '21, '24 (tie), '25 (tie), '31, '32 (tie), '33, '34, '36, '39, '40, '43.
Iowa—1916, '58, '62.
Michigan—1929, '38, '44, '53, '55, '56, '60, 63,
Michigan State—1961, '66
Minnesota—1913 (tie), '41, '57, '59
Ohio State—1923 (tie), 1951
Purdue—1942, '45, '48, '49, '50, '54

From 1912 through 1921 team champions were determined in the "Western Intercollegiate Wrestling, Gymnastics and Fencing Association," which was an open meet. From 1922 through 1933 team championships were based on dual meet records. In 1926 the Conference sponsored its own meet, but individual champions only were named until 1934, when a point system was adopted to name a team champion in that meet.

BASEBALL SECTION

(These Modern-era Records, since 1939, are based on Conference Games Only.)

INDIVIDUAL SINGLE GAME RECORDS

MOST TIMES AT BAT
7. equaled by numerous players

MOST HITS
6, SS Don Burson, N.U. vs. Wis., 5-22-48
6, 3B Bill Gorman, PUR. vs. Iowa, 5-4-57

MOST RUNS
6, CF Bill Hess, OHIO vs. NU, 4-21-62
5, C Jack Gannon, Ohio vs. WIS, 5-10-52
5, 3B Bill Gorman, PUR. vs. Iowa, 5-4-57
5, 2B Ken Peters, OHIO vs. NU, 4-21-62
5, RF Pat Richter, Wis., vs. IND., 4-21-62

MOST TOTAL BASES
13, P Jerry Thomas, Minn., vs. Ill., 5-4-57
12, 3B John McCartan, MINN, vs. Iowa 5-12-56
12, P Ernie Kumerow, ILL. vs. Minn., 5-13-61
11, 2B Bill Hapac, ILL. vs. Purdue, 5-10-40
11, 2B Jack Dittmer, IOWA vs. Ill., 4-23-49
11, SS Jerry Kindall, MINN, vs. Iowa 5-12-56
11, OF Ethan Blackaby, Ill., vs. MSU, 4-23-60
11, C Jerry Cawley, Minn. vs. NU, 5-21-65

MOST DOUBLES
3, 3B Bob Belsole, ILL., vs. OSU, 5-9-64

MOST TRIPLES
2, equaled by numerous players

MOST HOME RUNS
3, 3B John McCartan, MINN, vs. Iowa, 5-12-56
3, P Jerry Thomas, Minn. vs. Ill., 5-4-57
3, P Ernie Kumerow, ILL., vs. Minn., 5-13-61

MOST RUNS BATTED IN
8, LF Elbert Gutzwiller, OHIO vs. Purdue, 5-5-51
8, LF Jack Tosh, NU, vs. MSC, 5-23-55

MOST STOLEN BASES
4, CF Robert Wahl, ILL. vs. Ohio State, 5-16-41
4, 3B John Machado, OSU, vs. ILL, 5-9-64
4, 2B Duane Markus, MINN, vs. NU, 5-22-64
4, 2B Ron Roalstad, Minn. vs. PUR., 4-30-66
4, LF Reggie Woods, Ind. vs. NU, 5-6-66

MOST SACRIFICES
3, 2b Frank Marik, Wis. vs. Ohio, 5-15-59

MOST PUTOUTS
21, 1B Arnie Chonko, OSU vs. Mich., 5-21-65
20, 1B Harold Morrill, MICH. vs. Minn., 4-22-50
19, 1B Art Davis, MINN. vs. Iowa, 5-26-62
18, 1B Chet Ziemba, ILL. vs. Ohio State, 4-29-39
18, 1B Ed Parker, ILL. vs. Mich., 4-16-42
18, C John Gugala, Ill. vs. PURDUE, 4-30-48
18, 1B Roscoe Davis, MSU, vs. WIS., 5-4-56
18, 1B Wayne Knapp, MINN. vs. Iowa, 5-20-61
18, 1B Max Bailey, IND. vs. Iowa, 5-4-62
18, C Al Silverman, OHIO vs. Purdue, 5-4-63

MOST ASSISTS
10, SS Bob Klaus, Ill. vs. Purdue 5-1-59
10, SS Tony Eichelberger, Ill. vs. NU, 5-5-62
9, 3B Don Peden, Iowa vs. Ill., 5-9-58
9, P Steve Arlin, OSU vs. Mich., 5-21-65

MOST DOUBLEPLAYS
5, 1B Ronald Barbian, Wis. vs. MINN., 4-27-51
5, 2B Sheldon Fink, Wis. vs. MINN., 4-27-51

MOST ERRORS
5, 3B Earl Morrall, MSC, vs. Iowa, 5-7-55

MOST INNINGS PITCHED
16, Steve Arlin, OSU (4) vs. Mich. (3) 5-21-65
15, Howie Judson, Ill. (6) vs. IND. (6), 4-28-45

BEST PERFORMANCES BY BIG TEN SWIMMERS AS UNDER-GRADUATES

Compiled in cooperation with Robert Ries of Ohio State University
All marks are for a 25-yard pool.

50-Yd. Free Style
1. Steve Jackman, Minnesota, 1963, :21.0
2. Bill Groft, Michigan, 1965 } :21.3
3. Dick Abrahams, N.U., 1965 }
4. Frank Legacki, Michigan, 1961, :21.4
5. Gary Dilley, MSU, 1965, :21.68

100-Yd. Free Style
1. Steve Jackman, Minnesota, 1963, :46.5
2. Ken Walsh, MSU, 1965, :46.7
3. Bill Utley, Indiana, 1966, :46.9
4. Jim MacMillan, MSU, 1965, :47.3
5. Bill Groft, Michigan, 1965, :47.4

200-Yd. Free Style
1. Bill Utley, Indiana, 1966, 1:43.9
2. Bob Windle, Michigan, 1966, 1:44.5
3. Bob Hoag, Michigan, 1965, 1:44.8
4. Jim MacMillan, MSU, 1965, 1:45.2
5. Bill Farley, Michigan, 1965, 1:45.4

220-Yd. Free Style
1. Jim Spreitzer, Illinois, 1962 } 2:00.9
2. Mike Troy, Indiana, 1962 }
3. Mike Wood, MSU, 1962 } 2:01.3
   Steve Jackman, Minnesota, 1962 }
5. Dick Hanley, Michigan, 1957 } 2:01.5
   Bill Darnton, Michigan, 1961 }
   Tom Verth, Indiana, 1962 }

440-Yd. Free Style
1. Pete Sintz, Indiana, 1962, 4:17.0
2. Alan Somers, Indiana, 1962, 4:20.8
3. Mike Troy, Indiana, 1962, 4:21.9
4. Bill Darnton, Michigan, 1961, 4:22.2
5. Claude Thompson, Indiana, 1962, 4:25.7

500-Yd. Free Style
1. Carl Robie, Michigan, 1965, 4:44.1
2. Bill Farley, Indiana, 1966, 4:44.3
3. Bob Windle, Indiana, 1966, 4:49.9
4. Gary Verhoeven, Indiana, 1965, 4:50.0
5. Ken Walsh, MSU, 1965, 4:51.2

1500-Meter Free Style
1. Alan Somers, Indiana, 1962, 17:37.5
2. Claude Thompson, Indiana, 1962, 17:40.0
3. Roy Burry, Michigan, 1963, 17:43.5
4. Gary Verhoeven, Indiana, 1962, 17:45.4
5. Win Pendleton, Michigan, 1961, 17:46.5

1000-Yd. Free Style
1. Bill Farley, Michigan, 1966, 10:12.9
2. Carl Robie, Michigan, 1966, 10:17.2
3. Bob Windle, Indiana, 1966, 10:20.9
4. Ed Glick, MSU, 1966, 10:22.9
5. Ken Webb, Indiana, 1966, 10:24.7

1650-Yd. Free Style
1. Carl Robie, Michigan, 1965, 16:49.7
2. Bob Windle, Indiana, 1966, 16:54.0
3. Bill Farley, Michigan, 1965 16:54.1
4. Ed Glick, MSU, 1966, 16:59.0
5. Gary Verhoeven, Indiana, 1965, 17:11.18

100-Yd. Back Stroke
1. Gary Dilley, MSU, 1966, :52.39x*
2. Pete Hammer, Indiana, 1965, :53.1
3. Ed Bartsch, Michigan, 1963, :53.5
4. L. B. Schaefer, Ohio State, 1962, :53.9
5. Jeff Mattson, MSU, 1963, :54.0
   Charles Hickcox, Indiana, 1966, :54.0

200-Yd. Back Stroke
1. Tom Stock, Indiana, 1963, 1:55.9
2. Gary Dilley, MSU, 1965, 1:56.2
3. Ed Bartsch, Michigan, 1963, 1:56.5
4. Pete Hammer, Indiana, 1965, 1:56.84
5. Russ Kingery, Michigan, 1965, 1:57.5

100-Yd. Butterfly
1. Walt Richardson, Minnesota, 1964, :50.2x*
2. Fred Schmidt, Indiana, 1965, :50.9
3. Lary Schulhof, Michigan, 1966, :51.6
4. Tom O'Malley, Michigan, 1966, :51.73
5. Frank Legacki, MSU, 1965, :51.9

200-Yd. Butterfly
1. Fred Schmidt, Indiana, 1965, 1:51.4x*
2. Carl Robie, Michigan, 1965, 1:52.1
3. Walt Richardson, Minnesota, 1963, 1:53.7
4. Kevin Berry, Indiana, 1966, 1:54.46
5. Lary Schulhof, Indiana, 1965, 1:55.8

100-Yd. Breast Stroke
1. Chet Jastremski, Indiana, 1963, :58.5x
2. Tom Trethewey, Indiana, 1965, 1:00.0
3. Paul Scheerer, Michigan, 1965, 1:00.3
4. Bob Blanchard, Wisconsin, 1965, 1:00.6
5. Ken Frost, Indiana, 1964 }
   Dick Schaible, Indiana, 1964 } 1:01.1

200-Yd. Breast Stroke
1. Chet Jastremski, Indiana, 1963, 2:09.0x
2. Tom Trethewey, Indiana, 1965, 2:10.4*
3. Paul Scheerer, Michigan, 1965, 2:12.8
4. Ken Frost, Indiana, 1964, 2:13.0
5. Ron Clark, Michigan, 1961, 2:13.4

200-Yd. Individual Medley
1. Bill Utley, Indiana, 1966, 1:57.8
2. Bob Hopper, Ohio State, 1965, 1:58.1
3. Chet Jastremski, Indiana, 1963, 1:58.5
4. Ted Stickles, Indiana, 1962, 1:59.5
5. Chuck Richards, Indiana, 1966, 1:59.8

400-Yd. Individual Medley
1. Ted Stickles, Indiana, 1964, 4:16.3
2. Ken Webb, Indiana, 1966, 4:17.3
3. Bob Hopper, Ohio State, 1966, 4:18.8

400-Yd. Free Style Relay
1. MSU (Kifer, MacMillan, Walsh, Dilley), 1965, 3:07.7
2. Michigan (Hoag, Walls, Groft, Wiebeck), 1966, 3:08.0
3. MSU (Walsh, Glick, Dilley, MacMillan), 1966, 3:08.6
4. Michigan (Salassa, Walls, Wiebeck, Groft), 1966, 3:09.2

800-Yd. Free Style Relay
1. Indiana (Utley, Cordin, Webb, Windle), 1966, 7:02.6x*
2. Michigan (Hoag, Walls, Farley, Robie), 1966, 7:03.7
3. MSU (Glick, Hill, Walsh, MacMillan), 1966, 7:21.1
4. Indiana (Webb, Newman, Utley, Windle), 1966, 7:21.2

400-Yd. Medley Relay
1. Indiana (Hammer, Trethewey, Schmidt, Williamson), 1965, 3:30.7x*
2. Michigan (Bartsch Robie, Scheerer Groft, 1965, 3:32.3
3. Indiana (Stock, Jastremski, Schulhof, Hayden), 1963, 3:33.2
4. Michigan (Orland, Robie, Scheerer, Groft), 1966, 3:33.3 Indiana (Hammer, Berry, Trethewey, Williamson), 1966, 3:33.3

xAmerican Record
*Intercollegiate Record

Individuals or relay teams qualifying by their times for repeat listings are not so listed; their best times only are given.

MOST STRIKEOUTS
18, Marv Rotblatt, Ill. (9) vs. PURDUE (2), 4-30-48
16, R. E. Bailey, Pur. vs. OSU, 5-12-39

NO-HIT GAMES (Complete Game)
Chuck Schiller, ILL. (6) vs. Chicago (0), 4-25-42
Don Zitek, N'western (2) vs. IOWA (0), 5-22-54 (7 innings)
Albin Hayes, Ind. (1) vs. Ohio (2), 5-4-57 (7 innings)
Doug Mills, ILL. (4) vs. Wis. (0), 4-29-61 (7 innings)
Joe Sparma, OHIO (3) vs. Michigan (0), (7 innings) 5-18-63

INDIVIDUAL SEASON HITTING RECORDS

BEST BATTING AVERAGE (30 or more A.B.)
.585, C Bill Freehan, Michigan, 1961 (41 AB, 24 Hits)
.500, SS Bill Skowron, Purdue, 1950 (40 AB, 20 Hits)
.485, 2B George Smith, MSC, 1955 (33 AB, 16 Hits)
.484, C Lee Eilbracht, Illinois, 1946 (31 AB, 15 Hits)

MOST HITS
28, SS Harvey Kuenn, Wisconsin, 1952 (63 AB)
26, SS Bob Klein, OSU 1962, (61 AB)
25, 1B Don Ritter, Indiana, 1949, (57 AB)
25, 1B Bob Lawrence, Ind., 1958 (53 AB)
25, CF Don Foreman, Ind., 1958 (59 AB)
25, CF Fred Reichardt, Wisconsin, 1964 (53 AB)

MOST TOTAL BASES
47, SS Harvey Kuenn, Wisconsin, 1952 (63 AB 28 Hits)
44, 1B Bob Lawrence, Ind., 1958 (53 AB, 23 Hits)
43, SS Jerry Kindall, Minnesota, 1956 (50 AB, 22 Hits)
42, RF Dick Wakefield, Michigan, 1941 (55 AB, 21 Hits)

MOST RUNS
21, Dave Pflepsen, Minnesota, 1960
29, Dave Nelson, Michigan, 1942
18, CF Walt Evers, Illinois, 1940
18, SS Jerry Kindall, Minnesota, 1956
18, OF John Jurasevich, Illinois, 1958
18, 2B Joe Jones, Michigan, 1962

MOST DOUBLES
8, 1B Russ Steger, Illinois, 1949 (51AB, 19 Hits)
8, C Chuck Lindstrom, NU, 1956 (41 AB, 17 Hits)
8, 1B Arnie Chonko, OSU, 1964 (53 AB, 24 Hits)
8, CF Dick Schryer, Michigan, 1965 (63 AB, 23 Hits)
7, 1B Don Ritter, Indiana, 1949 (57 AB, 25 Hits)
7, OF John DeMerit, Wisconsin, 1956 (48 AB, 17 Hits)
7, OF Dean Look, MSU, 1958 (51 AB, 21 Hits)

MOST TRIPLES
5, CF, Walt Evers, Illinois, 1940 (51 AB, 18 Hits)
5, OF-P Don Blanken, Purdue, 1941
5, 1B Norm Banas, Purdue, 1951 (31 AB, 9 Hits)
5, SS Harvey Kuenn, Wisconsin, 1952 (63 AB, 28 Hits)
5, OF Don Dilly, Indiana, 1964 (61 AB, 16 Hits)

MOST HOME RUNS
7, 1B Doug Gillen, Minnesota, 1956
6, SS Jerry Kindall, Minnesota, 1956
6, 3B John McCartan, Minnesota, 1956
6, 1B, Vic Petreshne, Illinois, 1955 (36AB, 12 Hits)
6, 1B Wayne Knapp, Minnesota, 1960

MOST RUNS BATTED IN
25, RF Dick Wakefield, Michigan, 1941 (55 AB, 21 Hits)
25, 3B Francis Chamberlain, Michigan, 1942 (49 AB, 19 Hits)

FEWEST STRIKEOUTS (50AB)
0, 1B Bill Roman, Michigan, 1960 (53 AB)
0, SS Ron Henderson, MSU 1961 (50 AB)
1, SS Harvey Kuenn, Wisconsin, 1952 (63 AB)
1, 2B John Erickson, Minnesota, 1958 (50 AB)
1, OF Jim Howe, Indiana, 1959 (53 AB)
1, 1B Arnie Chonko, OSU, 1964 (53 AB)

INDIVIDUAL SEASON PITCHING RECORDS

MOST STRIKEOUTS
68, Steve Arlin, Ohio State, 1965 (W6, L0, 57⅓ IP)
66, Jack Bruner, Iowa, 1949 (W5, L1, 62 IP)
62, Marv Rotblatt, Illinois, 1948 (W5, L1, 53⅓ IP)

FEWEST HITS PERMITTED (40 or more innings)
17, Joe Pollack, Minnesota, 1964 (W4, L1, 42IP)
18, Marv Rotblatt, Illinois, 1947 (W6, L0, 54 IP)

MOST INNINGS PITCHED
62, Pete Perini, Ohio State, 1948; Jack Bruner, Iowa, 1949

FEWEST BASES ON BALLS (40 or more innings)
3, Bill Robichaud, Wis., 1954 (W4, L0, 43 IP)
6, Melvin [illegible], Purdue, 1949 (W3, L3, 42 IP)

6, George Schmid, Wis., 1958 (W4, L1, 44 IP)
6, Jack Wiland, Iowa, 1963 (W3, L2, 41 IP)

LOWEST BATTING AVERAGE AGAINST (40 or more innings)
.122, Joe Pollack, Minnesota, 1964 (139 AB, 17 Hits, 42 IP)

MOST VICTORIES
6, Gene Jaroch, Wisconsin, 1946; Marv Rotblatt, Illinois, 1947;
Peter Perini, Ohio State, 1948, Steve Arlin, Ohio State, 1965; Bob Reed, Michigan, 1966

EARNED RUN AVERAGE
0.28, Bob Schauenberg, Iowa, 1965 (32⅓ IP)
0.40 Tom Fletcher, Illinois, 1962 (45 IP)
0.42 Paul Giel, Minnesota, 1952 (43 IP)
0.53 Mike McNair, Minnesota, 1966 (34 IP)

LEADING HITTERS YEAR-BY-YEAR

Year	Name	Pos.	School	AB	R	H	TB	AVE.
1939	James George	RF	Iowa	42	—	19	25	.452
1940	R. Smith	3B	Wisconsin	34	—	15	—	.441
1941	Clarence Dunagan	SS	Iowa	38	6	15	16	.395
1942	John Kasper	LF	Wisconsin	44	9	19	25	.431
1943	Boyd Bartley	SS	Illinois	30	—	12	—	.400
1944	Merlin Brinker	RF	Wisconsin	33	6	15	—	.455
1945	Jim Ackeret	SS	Wisconsin	49	5	21	—	.429
1946	Lee Eilbracht	C	Illinois	31	6	15	23	.484
1947	Bob Wilson	CF	Northwestern	42	4	18	18	.429
1948	Herbert Plews	2B	Illinois	52	11	21	25	.404
1949	Don Ritter	1B	Indiana	57	13	25	41	.439
1950	Bill Skowron	SS	Purdue	40	7	20	35	.500
1951	Bob Montebello	3B	Ohio State	45	9	21	24	.467
1952	Harold Hanes	OF	Purdue	40	8	18	20	.450
1953	Gene Steiger	C	Minnesota	39	8	18	23	.462
1954	Bob Robertson	OF	Indiana	48	2	21	28	.438
1955	George Smith	2B	Michigan State	33	10	16	24	.485
1956	Jerry Kindall	SS	Minnesota	50	18	22	43	.440
1957	Ed Broeker	SS-OF	Northwestern	25	7	11	14	.440
1958	Bob Lawrence	1B	Indiana	53	13	25	44	.472
1959	Ron Causton	OF	Minnesota	40	8	19	22	.475
1960	Tom Perdue	OF	Ohio State	37	8	17	26	.459
1961	Bill Freehan	C	Michigan	41	14	24	39	.585
1962	Eddie LaDuke	2B	Indiana	51	10	22	28	.431
1963	Fred Reichart	OF	Wisconsin	49	13	21	37	.429
1964	Fred Reichart	CF	Wisconsin	53	12	25	38	.472
1965	Carl Cmejrek	RF	Michigan	53	6	24	34	.453
1966	Jack Campbell	1B	Indiana	42	7	16	20	.381

LEADING PITCHERS YEAR-BY-YEAR

Year	Name	School	G	IP	H	SO	BB	W	L	PCT.
1939	Harold Haub	Iowa	6	48	30	35	14	4	0	1.000
1940	John Pacotti	Illinois	6	32	32	38	28	5	1	.833
	Fred Rosch	N'western	7	54	53	19	14	5	1	.833
1941	Don Dunker	Indiana	10	59⅔	48	44	10	5	1	.833
	Alan Grant	Illinois	6	53	30	20	21	5	1	.833
	Clifford Wise	Michigan	6	51⅔	44	39	11	5	1	.833
1942	Richard Hein	Iowa	6	36⅔	25	20	13	5	0	1.000
1943	Al Scharf	Illinois	3	20	10	15	1	3	0	1.000
1944	Bliss Bowman	Michigan	5	42	26	32	12	4	0	1.000
1945	Bliss Bowman	Michigan	4	33⅔	25	28	11	4	0	1.000
	Ray Louthen	Michigan	4	38½	21	38	13	4	0	1.000
1946	Gene Jaroch	Wisconsin	6	46½	29	52	16	6	0	1.000
1947	Marv Rotblatt	Illinois	6	54	18	49	14	6	0	1.000
1948	Pete Perini	Ohio State	7	62	35	36	21	6	1	.875
1949	Jack Bruner	Iowa	7	62	32	66	32	5	1	.833
1950	Thornton Kipper	Wisconsin	6	50	50	25	23	5	0	1.000
1951	Ed Bohnslay	Ohio State	4	25	13	18	14	3	0	1.000
	George Maier	Illinois	6	53	34	56	23	5	1	.833
1952	Paul Giel	Minnesota	5	43	30	43	8	5	0	1.000
	Gerry Smith	Illinois	5	45	38	24	14	5	0	1.000
	Paul Ebert	Ohio	5	42	25	35	35	5	0	1.000
1953	Merle Jensen	Iowa	5	36	36	14	8	4	0	1.000
1954	Bud Erickson	MSC	6	40	37	28	9	5	0	1.000
1955	Dick Idzkowski	MSC	5	28	20	18	15	4	0	1.000
1956	Jerry Thomas	Minnesota	8	42	26	33	13	5	0	1.000
	Galen Cisco	Ohio	6	43	33	40	24	5	0	1.000
1957	Tom Scheuerman	Northwestern	4	34	20	24	10	4	0	1.000
	Glenn Girardin	Michigan	6	24	23	13	9	4	0	1.000
1958	Ron Perranoski	MSU	5	45	33	37	4	5	0	1.000
	Dick Radatz	MSU	5	43	37	40	12	5	0	1.000
1959	Terry Gellinger	Illinois	6	50	33	32	17	5	0	1.000
1960	Larry Bertelsen	Minnesota	5	38	34	21	7	5	0	1.000
1961	Douglas Mills	Illinois	5	35	14	26	21	4	0	1.000
	Ron Johnson	Illinois	4	29	19	25	15	4	0	1.000
	Paul Deem	Indiana	5	35	26	25	13	4	0	1.000
1962	Tom Fletcher	Illinois	5	45	32	42	31	5	0	1.000
	Douglas Mills	Illinois	5	45	32	24	12	5	0	1.000
1963	Jerry Weygandt	Illinois	5	42	29	28	13	5	0	1.000
1964	Joe Pollack	Minnesota	5	42	17	22	17	4	1	.800
1965	Steve Arlin	Ohio State	6	57⅓	35	68	20	6	0	1.000
1966	Bob Reed	Michigan	10	53	46	47	15	6	3	.667

HONOR TEAMS

BIG TEN CONFERENCE BASEBALL ALL-AMERICANS
(Since 1949)

ILLINOIS
Dick Raklovits, 3b, 1951
Bob Klaus, ss, 1959
Tom Fletcher, p, 1962

INDIANA
Don Ritter, of, 1949

IOWA
Jack Bruner, p, 1949

MICHIGAN
Bruce Haynam, ss, 1953
Don Eaddy, ss, 1955

OHIO STATE
Fred Taylor, 1b, 1950
Stewart Hein, of, 1951
Paul Ebert, p, 1954
Tom Perdue, of, 1960
Steve Arlin, p, 1965-66

MICHIGAN STATE
Tom Yewcic, c, 1954

MINNESOTA
Paul Giel, p, 1953
Jerry Kindall, ss, 1956
Jerry Thomas, p, 1956
Wayne Knapp, 1b, 1960
Jon Andresen, 2b, 1963

WISCONSIN
Harvey Kuenn, ss, 1952
Ron Nieman, of, 1958
Rick Reichardt, cf, 1964

GOLF
CONFERENCE TOURNAMENTS

Year	Site	Individual Champion	Score	Team Champion	Score
1920	Olympia Fields	Robert McKee, Drake	1 up	Drake	28 down
1921	Indian Hills	B. E. Ford, Chicago	1 up	Drake	684
1922	Midlothian C.C.	Rudolph E. Knepper, Chicago	303	Chicago	639
1923	Evanston G.C.	R. E. Rolfe, Illinois	5 & 3	Illinois	643
1924	Briergate G.C.	M. J. Holdsworth, Michigan	3 & 1	Chicago	663
1925	Sunset Ridge	K. E. Hisert, Chicago	3 & 2	Chicago	669
1926	Knollwood G.C.	K. E. Hisert, Chicago	316	N'western	659
1927	Tam O'Shanter	Les Bolstad, Minnesota	313	Chicago	1305
1928	Scioto, Columbus, O.	John Lehman, Purdue	314	Minnesota	1323
1929	Interlochen C.C.	Les Bolstad, Minnesota	313	Ohio State	1331
1930	Westmoreland C.C.	Richard Martin, Illinois	305	Illinois	1247
1931	Univ. of Michigan	Richard Martin, Illinois	311	Illinois	1293
1932	Univ. of Minnesota	John Fischer, Michigan	303	Illinois	1248
1933	Kildeer C.C.	John Fischer, Michigan	301	Michigan	1291
1934	Kildeer C.C.	Charles Kocsis, Michigan	283	Michigan	1228
1935	Kildeer C.C.	John Fischer Michigan	281	Michigan	1163
1936	Kildeer C.C.	Charles Kocsis, Michigan	286	Michigan	1190
1937	Kildeer C.C.	Sid Richardson, N'western	301	Michigan	1244
1938	Univ. of Minnesota	Sid Richardson, N'western	305	N'western	1255
1939	Kildeer C.C.	Chase Fannon, N'western	295	Minnesota	1197
1940	Mill Road Farm G.C.	William Gilbert, Ohio	298	Illinois	1245
1941	Univ. Michigan	Alex Welsh, Illinois	297	Illinois	1228
1942	Westmoreland C.C.	James McCarthy, Illinois	301	Michigan	1255
1943		Ben Smith, Michigan / James Teale, Minnesota	311	Michigan	1289
1944	Medinah C.C.	John Jenswold, Michigan / Howard Baker, Ohio State	153	Michigan	623
1945	Northwestern Univ.	John Lorms, Ohio State	148	Ohio State	603
1946	Univ. of Minnesota	John Jacobs, Iowa	294	Michigan	1220
1947	Purdue University	Ed Schalon, Michigan	297	Michigan	1237
1948	Northwestern Univ.	Howard B. Saunders, Ohio	296	N'western	1531
1949	Univ. of Michigan	Fred Wampler, Purdue / Ed Schalon, Michigan	297	Michigan	1499
1950	Ohio State Univ.	Fred Wampler, Purdue	284	Purdue	1464
1951	Northwestern	Gene Coulter, Purdue	290	Ohio State	1528
1952	Univ. of Illinois	Doug Koepcke, Wisconsin	306	Michigan	1559
1953	Univ. of Wisconsin	Don Albert, Purdue	290	Purdue	1514
1954	Univ. of Minnesota	Bob Benning, Purdue	298	Ohio State	1527
1955	Purdue University	Roger Rubendall, Wisconsin	216	Purdue	1141
1956	Northwestern	Joe Campbell, Purdue	281	Wisconsin	1501
1957	University of Iowa	Joe Campbell, Purdue	290	Purdue	1512
1958	Ohio State Univ.	John Konsek, Purdue	293	Purdue	1522
1959	Univ. of Michigan	John Konsek, Purdue	301	Purdue	1555
1960	Michigan State	John Konsek, Purdue	282	Purdue	1520
1961	Indiana	Jack Nicklaus, OSU	283	Ohio State	1527
1962	Wisconsin	Mike Toluszis, Illinois	288	Indiana	1523
1963	Minnesota	Roger Eberhardt, Wisconsin	292	Minnesota	1509
1964	Purdue	Byron Comstock, Indiana	290	Purdue	1487
1965	Purdue	Bill Newton, Michigan	287	Purdue	1472
1966	Iowa	John Seehausen, Northwestern	286	Ohio State	1480

TEAM CHAMPIONS: Chicago—1922, '24, '26
Illinois—1923, '27, '30, '31, '40, '41
Indiana—1962

Michigan—1932, '33, '34, '35, '36, '42, '43, '44, '46, '47, '49, '52
Minnesota—1929, '38, '63
Northwestern—1925, '37, '39, '48
Purdue—1950, '53, '55, '56, '58, '59, '60, '64, '65
Wisconsin—1957

TENNIS
CONFERENCE TOURNAMENTS

Year	Site	Singles Winner	School	Doubles Winner	School
1910	Chi.	Paul E. Gardner	Chicago	Adams & Sischo	Minnesota
1911	Chi.	J. J. Armstrong	Minnesota	Adams & Armstrong	Minnesota
1912	Chi.	J. J. Armstrong	Minnesota	Armstrong & Stellwagen	Minnesota
1913	Chi.	A. L. Green	Chicago	Green & Squair	Chicago
1914	Wis.	A. M. Squair	Chicago	Moses & Buhai	Chicago
1915	Chi.	Charles Carran	Ohio	MacNeal & Gross	Illinois
1916	Chi.	Albert J. Lindauer	Chicago	Lindauer & Clark	Chicago
1917	Chi.	Walter Becker	Illinois	Becker & McKay	Chicago
1918	Chi.	Ruthven W. Pike	Chicago	Widen & Adams	Illinois
1919	Chi.	Walter K. Westbrook	Michigan	Westbrook & Bartz	Minnesota
1920	Chi.	Walter K. Westbrook	Michigan	Vories & Segal	Chicago
1921	Chi.	Frederick E. Bastian	Indiana	Vories & Segal	Chicago
1922	Chi.	Frank Myers	Illinois	Frankenstein-Stagg	Chicago
1923	Chi.	Charles Merkel	Michigan	Wilson-Frankenstein	Chicago
1924	Chi.	Edward Wilson	Chicago	Goodwillie & Dubach	Illinois
1925	Chi.	Kurzrok	Butler	Sagalowsky-Kurzrok	Butler
1926	Chi.	Thomas O'Connell	Illinois	O'Connell & Shoaff	Illinois
1927	Chi.	Thomas O'Connell	Illinois	Barton & Moore	Illinois
1928	Pur.	Thomas O'Connell	Illinois	O'Connell & Brandt	Illinois
1929	Ohio	George Lott	Chicago	Lott-Calohan	Chicago
1930	Chi.	Scott Rexinger	Chicago	Rexinger-Calohan	Chicago
1931	Ohio	Scott Rexinger	Chicago	Rexinger-Heyman	Chicago
1932	N.U.	Edward Lejeck	Illinois	Britzius-Scherer	Minnesota
1933	Ill.	Charles Britzius	Minnesota	Davidson & Weiss	Chicago
1934	Chi.	Max Davidson	Chicago	Davidson & Weiss	Chicago
1935	N.U.	William Schommer	Chicago	Schommer & Huber	Minnesota
1936	Chi.	Norman F. Bickel	Michigan	Bickel & Burgess	Chicago
1937	Mich.	Robert Nihousen	N.U.	Bickel & Burgess	Chicago
1938	N.U.	John Shostrom	Chicago	Chester & Wm. Murphy	Chicago
1939	Chi.	Chester Murphy	Chicago	Chester & Wm. Murphy	Chicago
1940	N.U.	Seymour Greenberg	N'western	Greenberg & Clifford	Chicago
1941	Chi.	Seymour Greenberg	N'western	Greenberg & Richards	N'western
1942	Ohio	Calvin P. Sawyier	Chicago	Greenberg & Jake	N'western
1943	N.U.	Roger Downs	N'western	Wasserman & Samson	N'western
1944	N.U.	Ted Park	Wisconsin	Aris Franklin & Mitchell	Ohio
1945	N.U.	Aris Franklin	Ohio	Aris & Alex Franklin	Ohio
1946	N.U.	Robert Jake	N'western	Jake & Daly	Ohio
1947	N.U.	Ted Petersen	N'western	Downs & Migdow	N'western
1948	N.U.	Andy Paton	Michigan	Paton & Mikulich	Illinois
1949	N.U.	Ted Peterson	N'western	Paton & Mikulich	Michigan
1950	N.U.	Grant Golden	Mich. State	Golden & Landin	Michigan
1951	N.U.	Leonard Brose	Iowa	Brose & Sahratian	N'western
1952	N.U.	Norman Barnes	Mich. State	Drobac & Belton	Mich. State
1953	N.U.	Stan Drobac	Mich. State	Drobac & Belton	Mich. State
1954	Ill.	Al Kuhn	Ill.	Hironimus & Martin	Indiana
1955	Minn.	Warren Mueller	Wisconsin	MacKay & Potter	Michigan
1956	N.U.	Barry MacKay	Michigan	MacKay & Potter	Michigan
1957	N.U.	Barry MacKay	Michigan	MacKay & Potter	Michigan
1958	N.U.	Art Andrews	Michigan	Andrews & Porthast	Iowa
1959	MSU	Jon Erickson	Iowa	Erickson & Dubie	Michigan
1960	N.U.	Denny Konicki	Michigan	Wiley & Dubie	Michigan
1961	MSU	Raymond Senkowski	Michigan	Senkowski & Peacock	Michigan
1962	Minn.	Marty Riessen	N'western	Riessen & Erickson	N'western
1963	N.U.	Marty Riessen	N'western	Riessen & Graebner	N'western
1964	Ill.	Clark Graebner	N'western	Power & McNerney	Indiana
1965	Ind.	Todd Ballinger	Wisconsin	Hedrick & Stewart	Michigan

*TEAM CHAMPIONS:

Chicago—1934, '35, '37, '38, '39.   Mich.—1941, '44, '45, '55, '56, '57, '59, '60, '61, '62, '65, '66.
Illinois—1946.   Michigan State—1951.
Indiana—1952, '53, '54, '64.   N'western—1936, '40, '42, '47, '48, '49, '50, '63.
Iowa—1958.   Ohio State—1943.

*Team championship officially decided starting in 1934.

TRACK SECTION

CONFERENCE INDOOR MEET RECORDS

Event	Individual	School	Record	Date
60-Yard Dash	Jesse Owens Sam Stoller Tom Robinson Bob Moreland	Ohio State Michigan Michigan MSU	6.1 sec. 6.1 sec. 6.1 secs. 6.1 sec.	1935 1936 1960 1963 & 1964
300-Yard Dash	Tom. Robinson	Michigan	30.3 secs.	1959
440-Yard Dash	Dave Mills	Purdue	47.2 secs.	1961
600-Yard Run	Kent Bernard	Michigan	1:09.9	1965
880-Yard Run	Bill Frazier	Iowa	1:51.8	1963
1000-Yard Run	Barney Peterson	Wisconsin	2:09.2	1965
One Mile Run	John Ross	Michigan	4:09.4	1952
Two Mile Run	Dick Sharkey	MSU	9:01.4	1966
70-Yard High Hurdles	Gene Washington	MSU	8.3 sec.	1966
70-Yard Low Hurdles	Gene Washington	MSU	7.7 sec.	1965
One Mile Relay	Richards, Rocker, Hollingsworth, Kerr	Iowa	3:14.7	1963
Shot Put	Jack Harvey	Michigan	58′ 3¼″	1966
High Jump	Bill Holden	Wisconsin	6′ 10″	1963
Broad Jump	Greg Bell	Indiana	25′ 7″	1957
Pole Vault	Bob Neutzling	Ohio State	15′ 8¼″	1964

CONFERENCE OUTDOOR MEET RECORDS

Event	Individual	School	Record	Date
100-Yard Dash	Jesse Owens	Ohio State	9.4 sec.	1935
220-Yard Dash (Straightaway) (Around Curve)	 Jesse Owens Nate Adams	 Ohio State Purdue	 20.3 sec. 20.8 sec.	 1935 1963
440-Yard Dash (Two Turns)	Glenn Davis	Ohio State	45.8 sec.	1958
660-Yard Run	Roger Kerr	Iowa	1:17.4	1963
880-Yard Run	John Spain	MSU	1:48.0	1966
One Mile Run	Keith Coates	MSU	4:08.2	1965
Two Mile Run	Norris Peterson	Minnesota	9:01.5	1965
120-Yd. H. Hurdles	Bob White	Indiana	13.9 sec.*	1966
220-Yd. L. Hurdles (Straightaway) (One Turn)	 Jesse Owens Dick Cephas	 Ohio State Michigan	 22.6 sec. 23.4 sec.	 1935 1961
330-Yd. Interm. Hurdles	Jon Reimer	Iowa	36.1 sec.	1965
440-Yd. Interm. Hurdles	Bob Steele	MSU	50.7 sec.	1966
One Mile Relay	Romain, Hughes, Wade, Bernard	Michigan	3:10.2 sec.	1964
Shot Put	Jack Harvey	Michigan	57′ 2¾″	1966
Discus Throw	Fortune Gordien	Minnesota	178′ 11½″	1948
High Jump	Al Urbanckas	Illinois	6′ 8¾″	1957
Broad Jump	Jesse Owens	Ohio State	26′ 8¼″	1935
Pole Vault	George Canamare	Michigan	15 9¼″	1965

*—Set in semi-finals

BEST PERFORMANCES OF BIG TEN TRACK ATHLETES AS UNDERGRADUATES

INDOORS

Event	Individual	School	Record	Date
60-Yard Dash	Jim Golliday	N.U.	:06.0	at Wis., 2-25-56
300-Yard Dash	Herb McKenley Tom Robinson	Illinois Michigan	:30.3 :30.3	*Central AAU, 3-14-47 Big Ten 3-7-59
440-Yard Dash	Dave Mills	Purdue	:47.2	Big Ten, 3-4-61
600-Yard Run	Al Montalbano	Wisconsin	1:09.8	vs. Ind. & MSU, 2-22-64
880-Yard Run	John Spain Don Gehrmann	MSU Wisconsin	1:51.4 1:51.5	Frosh Exhib., 2-20-66 vs. Marquette, 2-26-49
1000-Yard Run	Ray Arrington	Wis. Frosh	2:08.5	Varsity-Fresh., 12-16-65
Mile Run	Craig Boydston Earl Mitchell	Northwestern Indiana	4:07.6 4:08.6†	Ill., Fed. 2-26-66 *Millrose Games, 2-6-43
2-Mile Run	Don Lash Tom Heinonen Dick Sharkey	Indiana Minnesota MSU	8:58.0† 8:55.3-N† 9:01.4	*Boston AA Games, 2-13-37 NCAA 3-12-66 Big Ten, 3-5-66
70-Yard H. Hurdles	Gene Washington	MSU	:08.3	Big Ten, 3-5-66
70-Yard L. Hurdles	Jesse Owens	Ohio	:07.6	at Indiana, 2-8-35
High Jump	Bill Holden	Wisconsin	6′ 10¼″	vs. Iowa State, 2-6-65
Pole Vault	Bob Neutzling	Ohio State	15′ 8¼″	Big Ten, 3-7-64
Broad Jump	Jesse Owens Greg Bell	Ohio Indiana	25′ 9″† 25′ 7″	*National AAU, 2-23-35 Big Ten, 3-7-57
Shot Put	Dave Owen	Mivchigan	59′ 0″	Michigan AAU, 2-8-57
880-Yard Relay	Konrad, Dan Hickman, LaRue & Carroll	Michigan	1:30.2	Mich. AAU, 2-2-52
Mile Relay	Sneed, Cochran, Washington, Adams	Purdue	3:13.8	vs. Ill., Iowa & NU, 2-22-64
2-Mile Relay	Christiansen, Moule, Ross, Gray	Michigan	7:35.0†	Chi Relays, 3-27-54
4-Mile Relay	Kendall, Broertjes, Wilt, Tolliver	Indiana	17:34.6	Ill. Relays, 2-15-41
Sprint Med. Relay	Scruggs, Floqin, Rudesill, Wallingford	Michigan	3:26.5	MSU Relays, 2-11-56
Dist. Med. Relay	Jacobi, Carroll, McEwen & Ross	Michigan	10:04.5	MSU Relays, 2-16-52

†On Boards
*—Non-Collegiate Competition

OUTDOORS

1961 (at Iowa)

	Points
Michigan	55-1/5
Indiana	36
Illinois	27-1/5
Iowa	24-2/5
Northwestern	24-1/5
Mich. State	16
Minnesota	15
Ohio State	14-1/5
Purdue	13-1/5
Wisconsin	5-1/5

1962 (at Purdue)

	Points
Michigan	48¾
Wisconsin	41
Michigan State	34-2/5
Iowa	30
Purdue	21-9/20
Indiana	19
Illinois	14½
Ohio State	14-9/20
Minnesota	7-9/20
Northwestern	0

1963 (at Minnesota)

Iowa	48
Wisconsin	47
Michigan	37
Michigan State	31
Illinois	29
Purdue	14
Minnesota	11
Ohio State	8
Indiana	5
Northwestern	1

1964 (at Northwestern)

Wisconsin	64
Michigan	52
Illinois	33
Michigan State	22
Northwestern	16
Iowa	12
Indiana	11
Minnesota	9
Ohio State	9
Purdue	2

1965 (at Iowa)

Michigan State	56
Michigan	43
Iowa	37
Wisconsin	28
Northwestern	13
Illinois	9
Indiana	6
Purdue	6
Minnesota	5

1966 (at Indiana)

Michigan State	52½
Iowa	43
Michigan	33
Minnesota	33
Wisconsin	31
Northwestern	15
Illinois	11½
Indiana	5
Ohio State	4
Purdue	3

1955 (at Ohio State)

	Points
Michigan	62-1/6
Illinois	31-13/18
Iowa	25-2/9
Minnesota	24-1/9
Michigan State	19-4/9
Ohio State	16-2/9
Indiana	12-1/9
Wisconsin	12
Purdue	10
Northwestern	3

1956 (at Minnesota)

Michigan	41
Iowa	37½
Indiana	34½
Michigan State	28½
Minnesota	21½
Ohio State	19½
Illinois	15
Northwestern	13
Wisconsin	4½
Purdue	1

1957 (at Northwestern)

Indiana	54
Ohio State	32
Michigan	25
Illinois	19
Purdue	16
Michigan State	16
Northwestern	15
Iowa	15
Minnesota	15
Wisconsin	9

1958 (at Purdue)

Illinois	46½
Indiana	41
Ohio State	35
Michigan State	23½
Minnesota	16
Iowa	15
Purdue	15
Michigan	11½
Wisconsin	8
Northwestern	6½

1959 (at Michigan)

Illinois	65½
Michigan	45
Indiana	19
Iowa	17
Ohio State	16½
Northwestern	13-5/6
Minnesota	12-1/3
Mich. State	11
Wisconsin	9
Purdue	7-5/6

1960 (at Michigan State)

Illinois	61½
Michigan	45
Minnesota	25½
Michigan State	22
Ohio State	17½
Iowa	16
Indiana	14½
Purdue	12½
Northwestern	1½
Wisconsin	0

1949 (at Northwestern)

	Points
Minnesota	49
Ohio State	37¾
Wisconsin	36
Illinois	35
Indiana	34
Michigan	15
Purdue	10¾
Northwestern	6¾
Iowa	¾

1950 (at Northwestern)

Indiana	37
Minnesota	36
Illinois	36
Wisconsin	31
Ohio State	25½
Michigan	23
Iowa	14½
Purdue	12
Northwestern	10

1951 (at Northwestern)

Illinois	55½
Michigan State	49
Indiana	32
Michigan	27
Iowa	20
Purdue	17
Minnesota	9
Wisconsin	8
Ohio State	7½
Northwestern	0

1952 (at Michigan)

Illinois	67-3/5
Michigan	65-1/10
Iowa	28
Northwestern	12½
Michigan State	10-17/20
Ohio State	10½
Indiana	10¼
Purdue	7
Wisconsin	7-3/5
Minnesota	5-3/5

1953 (at Illinois)

Illinois	69½
Michigan	43½
Michigan State	25
Iowa	17½
Indiana	14½
Minnesota	12
Ohio State	10½
Northwestern	5
Wisconsin	4½

1954 (at Purdue)

Illinois	57
Michigan	40-1/7
Michigan State	37-9/14
Indiana	28-1/7
Iowa	12-9/14
Purdue	12
Northwestern	10-1/7
Ohio State	5-1/7
Wisconsin	2-1/7

Event	Individual	School	Record	Date
100-Yard Dash	Jim Golliday	Northwestern	:09.3	Big Ten Relays, 5-14-55
220-Yard Dash (Straightaway)	Jesse Owens	Ohio	:20.3	Big Ten, 5-25-35
(One Turn)	Nate Adams	Purdue	:20.7	vs. Michigan, 5-4-63
440-Yard Dash (Two Turns)	Glenn Davis	Ohio	:45.7	NCAA, 6-14-58
660-Yard Run	Roger Kerr	Iowa	1:17.4	Big Ten, 5-18-63
880-Yard Run	George Kerr	Illinois	1:47.8	NCAA, 6-13-59
Mile Run	Craig Boydston	Northwestern	4:04.1-N	USTFF, 6-11-66
	Larry Wieczorek	Iowa	4:06.9	vs. C.T.C. & Drake, 5-7-66
	Dave Martin	Michigan	4:06.9	vs. Western Michigan, 5-13-61
2-Mile Run	Charles Jones	Iowa	8:57.6	NCAA, 6-15-57
3-Mile Run	Tom Heinonen	Minnesota	13:58-3-N	Texas Relays, 4-3-66
120-Yard H. Hurdles	Willard Thomson	Illinois	:13.7	Big Ten Relays, 5-14-55
220-Yard L. Hurdles (Straightaway)	Jesse Owens	Ohio	:22.6	Big Ten, 5-25-35
	George Walker	Illinois	:22.6	vs. MSC, 5-22-48
(One Turn)	Joe Corley	Illinois	:22.6	NCAA, 6-12-54
330-Yard Hurdles	Jon Reimer	Iowa	:36.1	Big Ten, 5-22-65
440-Yard Hurdles	Glenn Davis	Ohio	:49.9	*AAU, 6-20-58
	Bob Steele	MSU	:50.1	NCAA Semis, 6-17-66
3000-Meter Steeplechase	Charles Jones	Iowa	8:57.3	*AAU, 6-21-58
High Jump	Mel Walker	Ohio	6' 10¼"	*Malmoe, Sweden, 8-12-37
	Al Ammerman	Michigan	6' 10"	vs. Penn State, 5-2-64
	Mike Bowers	MSU	6 10"-N	NCAA, 6-19-65
Pole Vault	Bob Neutzling	Ohio State	16' ¼"	vs. Mich State, 5-2-64
Broad Jump	Jesse Owens	Ohio	26' 8¼"	Big Ten, 5-25-35
Triple Jump	Koutonen Erkki	Ohio	48' 8¼"	1949
Shot Put	Dave Owen	Michigan	59' 5¾"	NCAA, 6-15-57
Discus Throw	Ernst Soudek	Michigan	185' 5"	vs. Penn State, 5-2-64
440-Yard Relay	Williams, Blanheim, Yavorski, Jackson	Illinois	:40.1	NCAA, 6-20-64
880-Yard Relay	Owens, Briggs, Dooley, Nelson	Iowa	1:25.2 (chute)	K.U. Relays, 4-20-35
	Parker, Beverly Lewis, Moreland	MSU	1:25.1	Penn Relays, 4-27-63
	Goldston, Kohl, Richards, Hollingsworth	Iowa	1:25.0-N	Drake Relays, 4-25-64
Mile Relay	Goldston, Ferree, Randolph, Reimer	Iowa	3:08.7	USTFF, 6-12-65
2-Mile Relay	Castle, Lake, Lean, Atterbery	MSU	7:24.8	Kan. Relays, 4-19-58
4-Mile Relay	Moule, Bill Hickman, Ross & McEwen	Michigan	17:08.6	vs. MSC-MSNC at MSNC, 5-2-52
	Humbarger, Kaines, Bowen, Castle	MSU	16:59.4-N	Penn Relays, 4-27-63
Sprint Med. Relay	Coleman Lattimore, Miller, Kerr	Illinois	3:17.8	Drake Relays, 4-24-59
Dist. Med. Relay	Brubacher, Mondane, Griffith, Wieczorek	Iowa	9:53.6-N	Drake Relays, 4-30-66
	Carroll, Gordon, Ross & McEwen	Michigan	9:56.3	Ohio Relays, 4-19-52
480-Yard Shuttle Relay	Walker (Ill.), Mitchell (Ind.), Maxwell (Ohio), Porter (N.U.)		:56.8	Big Ten-PCC, 6-22-48
	Jones, Steele, McKoy, Washington	MSU	:57.4	Drake Relays, 4-30-66

*—Non-collegiate competition.   N—Non-winning.

PERSONNEL HISTORY SECTION

OFFICE OF COMMISSIONER OF ATHLETICS

Commissioner
1922-1944 Major John L. Griffith
1945-1961 Kenneth L. (Tug) Wilson
1961- William R. Reed

Assistant Commissioner
1951-1961 William R. Reed

Examiner
1957-1961 John D. Dewey

Assistant to Commissioner (also Examiner)
1961- John D. Dewey

Service Bureau Director
1939-1942 William R. Reed
1942-1943 James R. Maher
1946-1947 William R. Reed
1947-1951 Walter Byers
1951-1961 William R. Reed
1961- Kay Fred Schultz

Supervisor of Officials
1945-1948 James C. Masker
1950- William Haarlow (Basketball)
1952-1953 William A. Blake (Football)
1953-1954 William A. Blake (Tech. Adv. Ftbl.)
1953-1960 E. C. (Irish) Krieger (Tech. Adv. Ftbl.)
1961- Carlisle O. Dollings (Tech. Adv. Ftbl.)
1963- Ike J. Armstrong (Football)

1935 Gerald Huff
1936-1937 Caspar H. Nannes
1938-1942 Howard J. Braun
1943-1946 Ralph Johnson
1946-1964 Howard J. Braun
1965 Bob Lansford (Acting)
1966- Dan Olson

Track Coaches
1895 Harvey Cornish
1896-1898 H. H. Everett
1899-1900 Jacob K. Shell
1901-1903 William R. Reed
1904-1929 Harry L. Gill
1930 C. D. Werner
1930 Harry L. Gill
1931-1933 Don Cash Seaton
1934-1937 Leo T. Johnson
1965- Robert C. Wright

Wrestling Coaches
1911 R. N. Fargo
1912-1913 Alexander Elston
1914 Theodore Paulsen
1915-1917 Walter Evans
1921-1928 Paul Prehn
1929-1943 H. E. Kenney
1944-1946 Glenn C. Law
1946-1947 H. E. Kenney
1948-1950 Glenn C. Law
1950- B. R. Patterson

1926-1929 R. C. Heidloff
1930-1942 H. D. Price
1943-1946 Discontinued
1947-1948 H. D. Price
1949-1961 Charles Pond
1961-1962 Pat Bird (Acting)
1962- Charles Pond

Hockey Coaches
1938-1939 Ray Eliot
1940-1943 Victor Heyliger
1944- No Team

Swimming Coaches
1906-1909 W. H. Hockmeister
1910-1911 George B. Norris
1912-1917 E. J. Manley
1918-1919 No Team
1920-1952 E. J. Manley
1953- Allen B. Klingel

Tennis Coaches
1908-1913 P. B. Hawk
1914 W. A. Oldfather
1920-1924 E. E. Bearg
1925 B. P. Hoover
1926-1929 A. R. Cohn
1930 E. A. Shoaff
1931-1934 C. W. Gelwick

UNIVERSITY OF ILLINOIS

Faculty Representatives
1896-1898 Henry H. Everett
1898-1899 Jacob K. Shell
1899-1906 Herbert A. Barton
1906-1929 George A. Goodenough
1929-1936 Alfred C. Callen
1936-1949 Frank E. Richart
1950-1959 Robert B. Browne
1959- Leslie A. Bryan

Athletic Directors
1896-1935 George A. Huff
1936-1941 Wendell S. Wilson
1941- Douglas R. Mills

Athletic Publicity Directors
1922-1943 L. M. (Mike) Tobin
1943-1956 Charles E. Flynn
1956 Charles M. Bellatti

Baseball Coaches
1896-1919 George A. Huff
1920 George Clark
1921-1934 Carl Lundgren
1935-1951 Walter Roettger
1952- Lee Eilbracht

Basketball Coaches
1906 Elwood Brown
1907 F. L. Pinckney
1908 Fletcher Lane
1909-1910 H. V. Juul
1911-1912 T. E. Thompson
1913-1920 Ralph R. Jones
1921-1922 Frank J. Winters
1923-1936 J. Craig Ruby
1937-1947 Douglas R. Mills
1948- Harry Combes

Cross Country Coaches
1938-1960 Leo T. Johnson
1961 Edward Bernauer
1962-1963 Phillip Coleman
1965- Robert C. Wright

Fencing Coaches
1911 R. N. Fargo
1912 K. J. Beebe
1913-1916 H. E. Pengilly
1917-1921 A. J. Schuettner
1922 R. G. Tolman
1924-1928 Waldo Shumway
1929-1938 Herbert W. Craig
1939-1940 James L. Jackson
1941 Maxwell R. Garret

Football Coaches
1895-1899 George A. Huff
1900 F. L. Smith
1901-1902 E. G. Holt
1903 George Woodruff
1904-1905 George A. Huff
1906 J. M. Lindgren
1907-1911 A. R. Hall
1912 J. M. Lindgren, R. R. Hall, Fred Lowenthal, E. A. White
1913-1941 R. C. Zuppke
1942-1959 Ray Eliot
1960- Pete Elliott

Golf Coaches
1922-1923 George Davis
1924 Ernest E. Bearg
1925-1928 D. L. Swank
1929-1932 J. H. Utley
1933 Robert Martin
1934 F. H. Renwick
1935-1938 J. H. Utley
1939-1943 W. W. Brown
1944- Ralph Fletcher

Gymnastics Coaches
1898 Adolph Kreikenbaum
1902 Adolph Kreikenbaum
1905 Leo G. Hana
1910-1913 Leo G. Hana
1914-1917 R. N. Fargo
1921 A. J. Schuettner
1922 S. C. Staley
1924-1925 J. C. Wagner

INDIANA UNIVERSITY

Faculty Representatives
1900-1906 M. W. Sampson
1906-1907 U. G. Weatherly
1907-1908 E. O. Holland
1908-1912 H. W. Johnston
1912-1919 Charles W. Sembower
1919-1941 William J. Moenkhaus
1941-1942 Bernard C. Gavit
1942-1943 Lee Norvelle
1943-1951 William R. Breneman
1951-1962 John F. Mee
1962- Edwin H. Cady

Athletic Directors
1894-1896 Edgar Syrett
1897-1898 Madison G. Gonterman
1899-1905 James H. Horne
1906 Zora G. Clevenger
1907-1910 James M. Sheldon
1911-1913 Dr. C. P. Hutchins
1914-1915 Clarence C. Childs
1916-1922 E. O. Stiehm
1923-1946 Zora G. Clevenger
1946-1947 A. N. McMillin
1948-1954 Paul J. Harrell
1954-1955 W. W. Patty (acting)
1955-1961 Frank E. Allen
1961- J. W. (Bill) Orwig

Athletic Publicity Directors
1935-1939 George Gardner
1939-1944 Bob Cook
1944-1946 Jack Overmeyer (Acting)
1946-1953 Bob Cook
1953- Tom Miller

Baseball Coaches
1898-1900 James H. Horne
1901 Robert K. Wicker
1902 George W. Moore
1903-1904 Philip O'Neil
1905-1906 Zora G. Clevenger
1907 Jake Stahl
1908 Robert K. Wicker
1909-1911 Ralph C. Roach
1912 John Corbett
1913-1915 Arthur H. Berndt
1916 Frederick L. Beebe
1917 Roy M. Whisman
1918 Guy L. Rathbun
1919-1920 Harry Scholler
1921-1922 George W. Levis
1923-1924 Roscoe Minton
1925-1938 Everett S. Dean
1948 Paul J. Harrell
Donald Danielson
1949- Ernest Andres

Basketball Coaches
1901 James H. Horne
1902 Phelps Darby
1903-1904 Willis N. Coval
1905 Zora G. Clevenger
1906-1907 James M. Sheldon
1908 Edward Cook
1909 Robert Harris
1910 John Georgen
1911 Oscar Rackle
1912 James Kase
1914-1915 Arthur I. Powell
1916 Arthur H. Berndt
1917 Allan Williford
1918-1919 Guy S. Lowman
1920-1921 Dana M. Evans
1922-1923 Ewald O. Stiehm
1924 George C. Levis
1925-1937 Leslie Mann
1938-1942 Everett S. Dean
1943-1945 Harry C. Good
1946-1965 Branch McCracken
1965- Lou Watson

Gymnastics Coaches

1913-1914	E. G. Schroeder
1915-1919	Frank Wheeler
1920	Joe Sharp
1921	Frank Wheeler
1922-1923	Harold Briceland
1924-1942	Albert Baumgartner
1943-1947	No Team
1948-1966	N. R. Holzaepfel
1967-	Sam Bailie

Swimming Coaches

1917-1958	David Armbruster
1959	Robert Allen

Tennis Coaches

1922-1937	E. G. Schroeder
1938-1947	Arthur Wendler
1948-	Donald Klotz

Track Coaches

1898	Dad Moulton
1899-1902	A. A. Knipe
1903-1904	No Coach
1905	Jerry Delaney
1906-1908	Mark Catlin
1909-1910	Jerry Delaney
1911-1913	Nelson Kellogg
1914-1920	Jack Watson
1921-1948	George Bresnahan
1949-	Francis Cretzmeyer

Wrestling Coaches

1911-1915	E. G. Schroeder
1916-1920	Pat Wright
1921	E. G. Schroeder
1922-1952	Harold Howard
1953-	David McCuskey

Fencing Coaches

1950-1954	Lucien Morris
1955	Harry Hollien
1956	Joseph Mastropaolo
1957	Frank Craig
1958	C. David Hartmann
1959-1960	Charles Simonian
1961	David Dittmer
1962	Achilles Nickles
1963-1964	James White
1965-	Richard Marks

Football Coaches

1896	A. E. Ball
1897	T. Wagonhurst
1898-1901	A. A. Knipe
1902	S. W. Hobbs
1903-1905	J. G. Chalmers
1906-1908	Mark Catlin
1909	J. G. Griffith
1910-1915	Jesse Hawley
1916-1923	Howard Jones
1924-1931	Burt Ingwersen
1932-1936	Ossie Solem
1937-1938	Irl Tubbs
1939-1942	Eddie Anderson
1943-1944	Slip Madigan
1945	Clem Crowe
1946-1949	Eddie Anderson
1950-1951	Leonard Raffensperger
1952-1960	Forest Evashevski
1961-1965	Jerry Burns
1966	Ray Nagel

Golf Coaches

1921-1922	E. G. Schroeder
1923-1948	Charles Kennett
1948-1956	Frank O'Connor
1957	Glenn Devine
1958	Charles Zwiener

UNIVERSITY OF MICHIGAN

Baseball Coaches

1904	Jerome Utley
1905-1906	L. W. McAllister
1907	R. L. Lowe
1908-1909	L. W. McAllister
1910-1913	Branch Rickey
1914-1920	Carl Lundgren
1921-1958	Ray Fisher
1959-1962	Don Lund
1963-	Milbry E. Benedict

Faculty Representatives

1896	Dr. Joseph Nancrede
1896-1897	J. C. Knowlton
1898-1905	A. H. Pattengill
1906-1907	V. H. Lane
1907	H. M. Bates
1908	G. W. Patterson
1917-1955	Ralph W. Aigler
1955-	Marcus Plant

Athletic Directors

1898-1908	Charles Baird
1908-1921	Philip Bartelme
1921-1940	Fielding H. Yost
1941-	H. O. Crisler

Athletic Publicity Directors

1925-1938	Phil Pack
1938-1940	William R. Reed
1940-1944	Fred DeLano
1944-	Les Etter

Basketball Coaches

1909	G. D. Corneal
1917-1918	Elmer Mitchell
1919-1928	E. J. Mather
1929-1930	George Veenker
1931-1937	Franklin Cappon
1938-1946	Bennie Oosterban
1946-1948	Osborne Cowles
1948-1952	Ernest B. McCoy
1953-1960	William Perigo
1960-	David Strack

Fencing Coaches

1928-1933	John Johnstone

Football Coaches

1891	Mike Murphy
1892-1893	F. E. Barbour
1894-1896	W. U. McCauley
1897-1899	G. H. Ferbert
1900	Biff Lea
1901-1923	Fielding Yost

Football Coaches

1891	Billy Herod
1894	Ferbert and Huddleson
1895	Osgood and Wren
1896-1897	Madison G. Gonterman
1898-1904	James H. Horne
1905-1913	James M. Sheldon
1914-1915	Clarence C. Childs
1916-1921	Ewald O. Stiehm
1922	James P. Herron
1923-1925	William A. Ingram
1926-1930	Harlan O. "Pat" Page
1931-1933	Earle C. "Billy" Hayes
1934-1947	Alvin N. "Bo" McMillin
1948-1951	Clyde B. Smith
1952-1956	Bernie Crimmins
1957	Bob Hicks (Acting)
1958-1964	Phil Dickens
1965-	John Pont

Golf Coaches

1929	Harper Miller
1930	Gerald Redding
1931	Joe Greenwood
1932	Phil Talbot
1933	No Coach
1934-1941	Hugh E. Willis
1942-1947	James Soutar
1948-1957	Owen L. Cochrane
1958-	Robert Fitch

Gymnastics Coaches

1947-	Otto Ryser

Swimming Coaches

1919-1920	Guy L. Rathbun
1921	Robert Shafer
1922	Lester Null
1923-1924	William S. Merriam
1925	Oscar Tharp
1926	William S. Merriam
1927-1930	Paul Thompson
1931	No Coach
1932-1944	Robert Royer
1945-1946	Robert Stumper
1946-1957	Robert Royer
1958-	James Counsilman

Tennis Coaches

1930	Harlan Logan
1931-1933	Ralph Esarey
1934-1940	Ralph Graham
1941-1943	Ralph Collins
1944	Emory Clark
1945-1946	Ralph Collins
1947	William Johnson
1948	Don Veller
1949-1957	Dale Lewis
1958-	William Landin

Track Coaches

1915-1916	Clarence C. Childs
1917	Harvey Cohn
1918-1819	Dana M. Evans
1920	Guy L. Rathbun
1921	John Millen
1922	Lester Null
1923-1924	Jesse Ferguson
1925-1943	Earle C. "Billy" Hayes
1944	Clifford Watson
1945-1962	Gordon R. Fisher
1962-	James Lavery

Wrestling Coaches

1910-1914	Prof. Elmer E. Jones
1915-1916	Edgar Davis
1917-1921	James A. Kase
1922	Guy L. Rathbun
1923-1927	Jack Reynolds
1927-1945	W. H. Thom
1946-	Charles McDaniel

UNIVERSITY OF IOWA

Faculty Representatives

1900-1914	Arthur G. Smith
1914-1916	W. J. Teeters
1916-1917	B. J. Lambert
1917-1920	H. J. Prentiss
1920-1923	B. J. Lambert
1923-1929	Louis Pelzer
1929-1932	Clement C. Williams
1932-1938	Clarence M. Updegraff
1938-1947	Karl E. Leib
1947-1956	Paul J. Blommers
1956-	Robert Ray

Athletic Directors

1910-1917	Nelson Kellogg
1918-1923	Howard Jones
1924-1928	Paul Belting
1929-1934	Edward Lauer
1934-1936	Ossie Solem
1936-1947	Ernest G. Schroeder
1947-1960	Paul W. Brechler
1960-	Forest Evashevski

Athletic Publicity Directors

1923-	Eric C. Wilson

Baseball Coaches

1902-1903	S. C. Williams
1904-1905	J. G. Chalmers
1906	John G. Griffith
1907	L. J. Storey
1908	Maury Kent
1909	Charles Kirk
1910	Ted Green
1911-1912	Walter Stewart
1913-1918	Lindemann
1919	Howard Jones
1920-1922	James Ashmore
1923-1924	Sam Barry
1925-1942	Otto Vogel
1943-1945	J. E. Davis
1946-1966	Otto Vogel
1967-	Richard Schultz

Basketball Coaches

1902	Ed Rule
1903	Fred Bailey
1904	J. G. Chalmers
1905-1906	Ed Rule
1907	John G. Griffith
1908	Ed Rule
1909-1910	John G. Griffith
1911	Walter Stewart
1912	No Coach
1913	Floyd Thomas
1914-1918	Maury Kent
1919	Ed Bannick
1920-1922	James Ashmore
1923-1929	Sam Barry
1930-1942	Rollie Williams
1943-1949	Lawrence Harrison
1950-1951	Rollie Williams
1952-1958	Frank O'Connor
1958-1964	Milton Scheuerman
1964-	Ralph Miller

University of Michigan (continued)

Football Coaches
1924	George Little
1925-1926	Fielding Yost
1927-1928	Elton Wieman
1929-1937	Harry Kipke
1938-1947	H. O. Crisler
1948-1958	Bennie G. Oosterbaan
1959-	Chalmers W. Elliott

Tennis Coaches
1913-1915	A. O. Lee
1916-1917	No Coach
1918	Chris Mack
1919-1920	No Coach
1921	Walter Wesbrook
1922	Thomas Trueblood
1923	Paul Leidy
1924	Robert Angell
1925	Henry Hutchins
1926-1928	No Coach
1929-1936	John Johnstone
1937-1947	LeRoy Weir
1948	W. Robert Dixon
1949-	William Murphy

Golf Coaches
1921-1935	Thomas Trueblood
1936-1944	Ray Courtright
1945-1947	William Barclay
1947-	Bert Katzenmeyer

Gymnastics Coaches
1930-1932	Wilbur West
1933-1946	No coach
1947-	Newton C. Loken

Hockey Coaches
1922-1927	Richard Barss
1928-1944	Eddie Lowrey
1945-1957	Vic Heyliger
1957-	Allen Renfrew

Track Coaches
1911-1912	Dr. A. C. Kraenzlein
1913-1929	Stephen J. Farrell
1930-1939	Charles B. Hoyt
1940-1948	J. Kenneth Doherty
1948-	Donald B. Canham

Swimming Coaches
1922	J. Jerome
1923-1924	W. S. Brown
1925	Gerald Barnes
1926-1954	Matt Mann
1954-	August P. Stager, Jr.

Wrestling Coaches
1922	Thorn
1923-1924	Richard Barker
1925-	Clifford Keen

MICHIGAN STATE UNIVERSITY

Faculty Representatives
1949-1953	Lloyd C. Emmons
1953-1955	Edgar L. Harden
1955-1956	Leslie W. Scott
1956-1959	Harold B. Tukey
1959-	John A. Fuzak

Athletic Directors
1899-1900	Charles O. Bemies
1901-1902	George E. Denham
1903-1910	Chester L. Brewer
1911-1915	John F. Macklin
1916	Chester L. Brewer
1917	George E. Gauthier (acting)
1918	Chester L. Brewer
1919-1921	George E. Gauthier (acting)
1922	Albert M. Barron
1923-1954	Ralph H. Young
1954-	Clarence L. (Biggie) Munn

Athletic Publicity Directors
1917-1924	Jim Hasselman
1924-1930	Student Directors, incl.: Keith Himebaugh, Ted Smits, Dale Stafford, Will Muller
1930-1944	George Alderton
1944-1948	Nick Kerbawy
1948-	Fred Stabley

Baseball Coaches
1883-1886	No established coach
1887-1888	Professor Carpenter
1889-1895	No established coach
1896-1898	Robert T. Gale
1899	Ferguson
1900-1901	Charles O. Bemies
1902-1903	George E. Denham
1911-1915	John F. Macklin
1916-1917	John Morrissey
1918-1920	Chester L. Brewer
1921	George "Potsy" Clark
1922	John Morrissey
1923-1924	Fred M. Walker
1925-1963	John H. Kobs
1964-	Dan Litwhiler

Basketball Coaches
1899	No established coach
1900-1901	Charles O. Bemies
1902-1903	George E. Denham
1904-1910	Chester L. Brewer
1911-1916	John F. Macklin
1917-1920	Lyman L. Frimodig
1921-1922	George E. Gauthier
1923-1924	Fred M. Walker
1925-1926	John H. Kobs
1927-1949	Benjamin F. Van Alstyne
1950-1951	Alton S. Kircher
1951-1954	Peter F. Newell
1954-1965	Forrest Anderson
1965-	John Benington

Boxing Coaches
1935-1941	Leon D. Burhans
1942-1943	Albert P. Kawal
1944-1945	No team
1946-1947	Louis F. Zarza
1948-1955	George Makris
1956-1958	John Brotzmann

Cross Country Coaches
1922	Albert M. Barron
1923	Jack Heppinstall
1924	Ralph H. Young
1925-1930	Morton F. Mason
1931-1946	Lauren P. Brown
1947-1957	Karl A. Schlademan
1958-	Fran Dittrich

Soccer Coaches
1957-	Willard Kenney

Swimming Coaches
1922	S. S. Flynn
1923	Richard H. Rauch
1924-1925	W. B. Jones
1926	R. D. Keifaber
1927-1928	W. Sterry Brown
1929	F. R. Hoercher
1930-1941	Russell B. Daubert
1942	Charles McCaffree, Jr.

Fencing Coaches
1926-1929	Joseph Waffa
1930-1937	George T. Bauer
1938	Thomas L. Caniff
1939-	Charles R. Schmitter

Football Coaches
1897-1898	Henry Keep
1899-1900	Charles O. Bemies
1901-1902	George Denman
1903-1910	Chester L. Brewer
1911-1915	John F. Macklin
1916	Frank Sommers
1917	Chester L. Brewer
1918	George E. Gauthier
1919	Chester L. Brewer
1920	George "Potsy" Clark
1921-1922	Albert M. Barron
1923-1927	Ralph H. Young
1928	Harry G. Kipke
1929-1932	James H. Crowley
1933-1946	Charles W. Bachman
1947-1953	Clarence L. (Biggie) Munn
1954-	Hugh Duffy Daugherty

Tennis Coaches
1921-1922	H. C. Young
1923-1946	Charles D. Ball, Jr.
1947	Gordon A. Dahlgren
1948-1951	Harris F. Beeman
1952	John Friedrich
1953-1958	Harris F. Beeman
1959-	Stan Drobac

Golf Coaches
1929	Harry G. Kipke
1930-1931	James H. Crowley
1932-1961	Benjamin F. VanAlstyne
1962-1965	John Brotzmann
1966-	Bruce Fossum

Track Coaches
1897-1898	Henry Keep
1899	Max Beutner
1900-1901	Charles O. Bemies
1902-1903	George E. Denham
1904-1910	Chester L. Brewer
1911-1913	John F. Macklin
1914	Ion J. Cartright
1915-1916	George E. Gauthier
1917	Howard E. Beatty
1918-1919	George E. Gauthier
1920-1921	Arthur Smith
1922-1923	Albert M. Barron
1924-1940	Ralph H. Young
1941-1958	Karl A. Schlademan
1959-	Fran Dittrich

Gymnastics Coaches
1948-	George Szypula

Wrestling Coaches
1922-1923	James H. Devers
1924-1926	Leon D. Burhans
1927-1928	Ralph G. Leonard
1929	Glenn L. Rickes
1930-1962	Fendley A. Collins
1963-	Grady J. Peninger

Hockey Coaches
1922-1924	No established coach
1925-1930	John H. Kobs
1931-1949	No team
1950-1951	Harold Paulsen
1952-	Amo Bessone

UNIVERSITY OF MINNESOTA

Faculty Representatives
1896	Conway McMillan
1896	F. W. Denton
1897	Prof. Woodbridge
1897-1906	F. S. Jones
1906-1934	James Paige
1934-1957	Henry Rottschaefer
1957-1962	Stanley V. Kinyon
1962-	Max O. Schultze

Athletic Publicity Directors
1930-1935	Les Etter
1935-1944	Various persons in News Service
1944-	Otis J. Dypwick

Athletic Directors
1922-1930	Fred Leuhring
1930-1932	H. O. Crisler
1932-1941	Frank G. McCormick
1941-1946	Lou Keller (Acting)
1946-1950	Frank G. McCormick
1950-1963	Ike J. Armstrong
1963-	Marshall W. Ryman

Baseball Coaches
1923-1926	Lee R. Wattrous, Jr.
1927	Geo. "Potsy" Clark
1928-1930	A. J. Bergman
1931-1941	Frank G. McCormick
1942-1947	Dave MacMillan
1948-	Dick Siebert

Basketball Coaches
1923	L. J. Cooke
1924-1927	Harold Taylor
1928-1930	Dave MacMillan
1943-1944	Carl L. Nordly
1945	Weston Mitchell
1946-1948	Dave MacMillan
1948-1959	Osbone B. Cowles
1959-	John Kundla

Boxing Coaches
1946-1952	Ray Chisholm
1953	Frank Wolynski

Swimming Coaches
1933-1945 Ted Payseur
1946- Sid Richardson

Swimming Coaches
1910-1943 Tom Robinson
1944- William Peterson

Tennis Coaches
1921-1922 Henry Raeder
1923-1930 Arthur Nethercot
1931-1958 Paul Bennett
1959- Clare Riessen

Track Coaches
1895-1896 Otto Miller
1897-1901 W. J. Bryan
1902 Walter Hempel
1903 Horace Butterworth
1904 J. D. Delaney
1905 Tom Holland
1906 Louis Gillesby
1907-1910 R. W. Albertson
1911-1917 Louis Omer
1918 Percy Bradley
1919 Charles Bachman
1920 Ray Edler
1921-1952 Frank Hill
1953-1960 Rur Walter
1960- Robert Ehrhart

Wrestling Coaches
1917 Elmer Jones
1918-1919 Tom Robinson
1920-1921 Jack Sawtelle
1922-1923 Henry Szymanski
1924-1925 Eugene Maynor
1926 Bryan Hines
1927-1936 Orion Stuteville
1937-1942 Wesley Brown
1943-1945 Roy Greening
1946-1947 Wesley Brown
1948-1957 Jack Riley
1958- Kenneth Kraft

1919 Tom Robinson
1920 Norman Elliott
1921 Ray Edler
1922 Dana Evans
1923-1927 Maury Kent
1928-1950 Arthur Lonborg
1950-1952 Harold G. Olsen
1953-1957 Waldo Fisher
1957-1963 William Rohr
1963 Larry Glass

Fencing Coaches
1927-1929 Leon Kranz
1930-1931 Henry Zettleman
1932-1934 Otto Haier
1935-1943 Henry Zettleman
1944-1945 No Teams
1946-1956 Tully Friedman

Football Coaches
1893 Paul Noyes
1894 A. A. Ewing
1895-1896 Alvin H. Culver
1897 Jesse Van Doozer
1898 W. H. Bannard
1899-1902 Dr. C. M. Hollister
1903-1905 Walter McCornac
1906-1907 No Intercollegiate Teams
1908 Alton Johnson
1909 William Horr
1910-1912 C. E. Hammett
1913 Dennis Grady
1914-1918 Fred Murphy
1919 Charles Bachman
1920-1921 Elmer McDevitt
1922-1926 Glenn Thistlethwaite
1927-1934 Dick Hanley
1935-1946 Lynn Waldorf
1947-1954 Bob Voigts
1955 Lou Saban
1956-1963 Ara Parseghian
1964- Alex Agase

Golf Coaches
1920 Arthur Sweet
1923-1932 Leon Kranz

OHIO STATE UNIVERSITY

Faculty Representatives
1912-1944 Thomas E. French
1944-1946 James E. Pollard
1947-1961 Wendell Postle
1961- James R. McCoy

Athletic Directors
1912-1947 L. W. St. John
1947- R. C. Larkins

Athletic Publicity Directors
1923-1933 William Griffith
1934-1935 James B. Reston
1936-1943 James L. Renick
1944- Wilbur E. Snypp

Basketball Coaches
1902-1903 D. C. Huddleson
1909-1910 Thomas Kibler
1912-1919 L. W. St. John
1920-1921 George M. Trautman
1922-1946 Harold G. Olsen
1946-1950 W. H. H. Dye
1950-1958 Floyd S. Stahl
1958- Fred Taylor

Cross Country Coaches
1955-1964 Charles Beetham
1965- Robert Epskamp

Fencing Coaches
1922-1924 L. A. Kunzig
1925-1926 F. A. Riebel

Baseball Coaches
1901-1902 Jack Reed
1903 C. W. Dickerson
1913-1928 L. W. St. John
1929-1932 Wayne Wright
1933-1938 Floyd Stahl
1939-1944 Fred Mackey
1945-1946 Lowell Wrigley
1947-1950 Floyd Stahl
1950- Martin G. Karow

Football Coaches
1883 Thomas Peebles
1886-1889 Fred S. Jones
1890 Tom Eck
1891 Edward Moulton
1892 No Coach
1893 Wallie Winter
1894 Thomas Cochrane, Jr.
1895 W. W. Heffelfinger
1896-1897 Alexander N. Jerrems
1898 Jack Minds
1899 Wm. C. Leary, John Harrison
1900-1921 Dr. Henry L. Williams
1922-1924 William Spaulding
1925-1929 Dr. C. W. Spears
1930-1931 H. O. Crisler
1932-1941 Bernie Bierman
1942-1944 Dr. George W. Hauser
1945-1950 Bernie Bierman
1951-1953 Wesley E. Fesler
1954- Murray Warmath

Golf Coaches
1930-1945 W. R. Smith
1946- Les Bolstad

Gymnastics Coaches
1902-1906 Dr. L. J. Cooke
1907-1929 Dr. W. K. Foster
1930-1962 Dr. Ralph A. Piper
1962-63 Pat Bird (Acting)
1963-1965 Pat Bird (Acting)
1965-66 Dr. Ralph A. Piper
1966- Dr. Ralph A. Piper

Hockey Coaches
1922-1930 Emil W. Iverson
1931-1935 Frank Pond
1936-1946 Larry S. Armstrong
1947-1952 Elwin Romnes
1953-1966 John Mariucci
1966- Glen Sonmor

Swimming Coaches
1920-1957 Niels Thorpe
1958-1962 William Heusner
1962- G. Robert Mowerson

Tennis Coaches
1928-1956 Phil Brain
1957-1959 Chet Murphy
1960-1965 Donald R. Lewis
1966- Joseph A. Walsh

Track Coaches
1922-1923 T. Nelson Metcalf
1924- Leo Frank
1925-1933 Sherman Finger
1934-1935 Clarence Munn
1936 George Otterness
1937-1963 James Kelly
1963- Roy Griak

Wrestling Coaches
1932-1935 Blain McKusick
1936-1942 Dave Bartelma
1943-1944 Stanley Hanson
1945 Clarence R. Osell
1947 Dave Bartelma
1948-1952 Stanley Hanson
1953- Wallace Johnson

NORTHWESTERN UNIVERSITY

Baseball Coaches
1894-1897 John Kedzie
1898-1902 W. J. Bryan
1903 Horace Butterworth
1904 Harry Fleager
1905 Harley Parker
1906 Charles Hollister
1907-1908 A. B. Cunningham
1909-1911 A. G. Rundle
1912 L. C. Holsinger
1913 Dennis Grady
1914-1916 Fred Murphy
1917-1920 William McGill
1921 Jack Sawtelle
1922 Henry Szymanski
1923-1928 Maury Kent
1929-1935 Paul Stewart
1936-1939 Burt Ingwersen
1940-1941 Stanley Klores
1942-1943 Maury Kent
1944-1946 Wesley Fry
1947-1948 Don Heap
1948-1961 Freddie Lindstrom
1961- George McKinnon

Basketball Coaches
1905-1906 Tom Holland
1907-1910 Louis Gillesby
1911 Stuart Templeton
1912 Charles Hammett
1913-1914 Dennis Grady
1915-1917 Fred Murphy
1918 Norman Elliott

Faculty Representatives
1896-1898 J. Scott Clark
1898-1900 H. S. White
1900-1901 W. A. Locy
1901-1906 O. F. Long
1906-1914 R. E. Wilson
1914-1918 G. V. Pooley
1918-1919 R. E. Wilson
1919-1940 O. F. Long
1940-1943 Walter K. Smart
1943-1945 Ward V. Evans
1945-1948 G. R. Lundquist
1949-1956 F. George Seulberger
1956- T. Leroy Martin

Athletic Directors
1895-1896 Otto Miller
1897-1898 W. J. Bryan
1898-1902 Dr. C. M. Hollister
1903-1904 Horace Butterworth
1905-1906 F. O. Smith
1906-1910 Louis Gillesby
1910-1913 Charles Hammett
1913-1918 Fred Murphy
1919-1920 Charles W. Bachman
1921-1924 Dana Evans
1925-1945 Kenneth L. Wilson
1945-1956 Theodore B. Payseur
1956- Stuart K. Holcomb

Athletic Publicity Directors
1926- Walt Paulison

443

Gymnastics Coaches

1945	Sam Voinoff
1946-1950	Loomis Heston
1951-	Sam Voinoff
1921-1930	M. L. Clevett

Swimming Coaches

1920-1921	M. L. Clevett
1922	Barr
1923	C. J. Merriam
1924	G. H. Aylesworth
1925-1938	L. W. LaBree
1939-	R. O. Papenguth

Tennis Coaches

1915-1916	C. M. James
1920-1923	E. R. Sidwell
1924	G. H. Aylesworth
1925-1964	L. W. LeBree
1965-	Edward C. Eicholtz

Track Coaches

1900	Curtiss
1901	W. J. Hyland
1902-1903	C. I. Freeman
1904	E. L. Wheeler
1905	J. J. Nufer
1906-1907	C. B. Jamison
1908-1909	H. E. Wilson
1910-1912	R. R. Jones
1913	Arbor W. Clow
1914	J. Mahan
1915-1916	J. Temple
1917-1929	E. J. O'Connor
1930-1931	Earl T. Martineau
1932-1936	H. E. Phillips
1937-1943	O. J. Martin
1944	H. E. Phillips, Homer Allen
1945-1946	Homer Allen
1947-	David Rankin

Wrestling Coaches

1914	N. Embleton
1915-1922	Frederick Paulsen
1923-1924	W. S. Von Bermuth
1925-1929	H. A. Miller
1930-1932	L. B. Beers
1933-1936	G. J. Mackey
1937-	C. C. Reeck

Basketball Coaches

1901-1902	W. C. Curd
1903	C. I. Freeman
1905	J. J. Nufer
1906-1908	C. B. Jamison
1909	E. J. Stewart
1910-1912	R. R. Jones
1913-1916	R. E. Vaughan
1917	Ward L. Lambert
1918	J. J. Molony
1919-1946	Ward L. Lambert
1946-1950	Mel Taube
1950-1965	Ray Eddy
1965-	George King

Fencing Coaches

1922-1925	A. C. Staley
1926	W. E. Phillips
1927-1928	L. L. Huxtable
1930-1931	R. P. Hollis
1932-1933	M. L. Clevett
1934-1938	R. V. Finney

Football Coaches

1895	D. M. Balliet
1896	S. M. Hammond
1897	W. S. Church
1898-1899	A. P. Jamison
1900-1901	D. M. Balliet, A. P. Jamison
1902	C. M. Best
1903-1904	O. F. Cutts
1905	A. E. Herrnstein
1906	M. E. Witham
1907	L. C. Turner
1908-1909	Frederick Speik
1910-1911	M. H. Horr
1912	M. H. Horr, J. E. Moll
1913-1915	H. L. Smith
1916-1917	A. S. Scanlon
1918-1920	C. O. O'Donnell
1921	W. H. Dietz
1922-1929	James Phelan
1930-1936	Noble Kizer
1937-1941	A. H. Elward
1942-1943	Elmer H. Burnham
1944-1946	Cecil Isbell
1947-1955	Stu Holcomb
1956-	Jack Mollenkopf

Golf Coaches

1922	G. A. Young
1923-1927	B. S. Swezey
1929-1937	J. E. Bixler
1938-1944	Harry Allspaw

UNIVERSITY OF WISCONSIN

Athletic Directors

1920-1924	Tom E. Jones (acting)
1925-1932	George Little
1933-1935	Walter Meanwell
1936-1950	Harry Stuhldreher
1950-1955	Guy Sundt
1955-	Ivan Williamson

Athletic Publicity Directors

1923-1929	Les Gage
1929-1941	George Downer
1941-1946	Bob Foss

Faculty Representatives

1896	C. R. Barnes
1896-1899	E. A. Birge
1899-1905	C. S. Slichter
1905-1906	T. S. Adams
1906-1909	W. L. Lambert
1910-1912	G. W. Ehler
1912-1931	J. F. A. Pyre
1932-1935	A. T. Weaver
1936-1947	William F. Lorenz
1947-1951	Kenneth Little
1951-1954	Kurt F. Wendt
1954-1959	George Young
1959-	Frank Remington

Fencing Coaches

1927	Ted Lorber
1928-1943	F. A. Riebel
1944-1945	Ben Burtt
1946-1947	Joseph Craig
1947	A. R. Deladrier
1948-1963	Robert Kaplan
1964-	Charles Simonian

Football Coaches

1886-1890	Jack Ryder
1891	Alexander S. Lilley
1892-1898	Jack Ryder
1899-1902	Dr. J. B. C. Eckstorm
1903	Perry Hale
1904-1905	E. R. Sweetland
1906-1909	A. E. Herrnstein
1910	Howard Jones
1911	Harry Vaughn
1912	John R. Richards
1913-1928	Dr. J. W. Wilce
1929-1933	Sam S. Willaman
1934-1940	Francis A. Schmidt
1941-1943	Paul E. Brown
1944-1945	Carroll C. Widdoes
1946-	Paul O. Bixler
1947-1950	Wesley E. Fesler
1951-	W. W. Hayes

Golf Coaches

1921-1923	Mike Godman
1924-1925	George Eckelberry
1926-1931	George Sargent
1932	Francis Marzolf
1933-1937	Harold G. Olsen
1938-1965	Robert Kepler
1966	Floyd S. Stahl
1967-	Rodney W. Myers

Gymnastics Coaches

1923	Glenn Alexander
1924-1932	Leo G. Staley
1947-1966	Joseph M. Hewlett
1967-	James Sweeney

Hockey Coaches

1963-1965	Thomas Bedecki
1965-1966	Glen Sonmor

Lacrosse Coaches

1953	Jack Corkery
1954	Ed Baker
1955-1959	Howard Knuttgen
1960-	Paul Hartman

Soccer Coaches

1953	Bruce Bennett
1954-1957	Howard Knuttgen
1958-	Walter Ersing

Swimming Coaches

1930-1963	Michael Peppe
1963-	Robert Bartels

Tennis Coaches

1921	T. H. Connell
1922-1924	R. L. Grismer
1926-1957	Herman Wirthwein
1958-	John W. Hendrix

Track Coaches

1902-1903	D. C. Huddleson
1908	W. T. McCarty
1910-1912	Steve Farrell
1913-1931	Frank R. Castleman
1932-1942	Larry Snyder
1943-1945	George Haney
1946-1965	Larry Snyder
1965-	Robert Eipskamp

Wrestling Coaches

1921-1925	Al Haft
1926-1942	Bernard Mooney
1943-1944	Lawrence Hicks
1945-1947	Bernard Mooney
1948-	Casey Fredericks

PURDUE UNIVERSITY

Athletic Publicity Directors

1925-1928	Robert A. McMahon
1928-1964	Robert C. Woodworth
1964-	Karl W. Klages

Baseball Coaches

1892-1893	W. M. Phillips
1901	W. H. Fox
1902	Friel
1903-1904	J. C. Kelsey
1905	P. O'Neil
1906-1914	H. Nicol
1915-1916	B. P. Pattison
1917	W. L. Lambert
1918	J. Pierce
1919-1935	W. L. Lambert
1936-1942	W. P. Fehring
1943	W. P. Fehring, C. S. Doan
1944	C. S. Doan
1945-1946	W. L. Lambert
1947-1950	Mel Taube
1950-1955	Henry Stram
1956-1959	Paul Hoffman
1960-	Joe Sexson

Faculty Representatives

1896-1897	W. E. Stone
1897-1900	C. A. Waldo
1900-1901	H. A. Huston
1901-1928	Thomas F. Moran
1928-1939	William Marshall
1939-1941	G. A. Young
1941-1945	J. A. Estey
1946-	V. C. Freeman

Athletic Directors

1904-1905	O. F. Cutts
1906-1914	Hugh Nichols
1915-1918	O. F. Cutts
1919-1930	N. A. Kellogg
1931-1936	Noble E. Kizer
1937	R. C. Woodworth (Acting)
1938-1939	Noble E. Kizer
1940	E. C. Elliott (Acting)
1941	A. H. Elward
1942-	Guy J. Mackey

Wrestling Coaches

1914-1916 Fred Schlatter
1917-1918 Arthur Knott
1919-1920 Joe Steinauer
1921-1933 George Hitchcock
1934-1935 Paul Gerlin
1936-1942 George Martin
1943 John Roberts
1944 Jim Dailey, Frank Jordan
1945 Frank Jordan
1946- George Martin

Tennis Coaches

1919-1922 George E. Linden
1923-1925 Arpad Masley
1926-1930 William Winterble
1931 Loren Cockrell
1932-1935 Arpad Masley
1936-1937 William Kaeser
1938-1939 Roy Black
1941-1943 Carl Sanger
1944-1945 Harold A. Taylor
1946-1947 Carl Sanger
1947-1951 Al Hildebrandt
1952-1962 Carl Sanger
1963 David G. Clark
1964- John Powless

Track Coaches

1899 John T. Moakley
1900-1904 C. H. Kilpatrick
1905 James Temple

Fencing Coaches

1911 Walter Meanwell
1912-1914 H. D. MacChesney
1915 George Breen
1916-1917 H. D. MacChesney
1918-1919 No Teams
1920-1926 Fred Schlatter
1927-1952 A. L. Masley
1953- Archie Simonson

Football Coaches

1890 Ted Mestre
1891 Herb Alward
1892 Crawford
1893 Parke Davis
1894-1895 H. O. Stickney
1896-1902 Phil King
1903-1904 Art Curtis
1905 Ed Cochems
1906-1907 Phil King
1908-1910 C. P. Hutchins
1911 J. A. Barry
1912-1915 J. R. Richards
1916 W. J. Juneau
1917 P. Withington
1918 J. R. Richards
1919-1922 Guy Lowman
1923-1924 J. R. Richards
1925-1926 Jack Ryan
1927-1931 George Little
1932-1935 Glenn Thistlethwaite
1936-1948 Dr. C. W. Spears
1949-1955 Harry Stuhldreher
1956- Ivan B. Williamson
Milt Bruhn

Golf Coaches

1926 Joe Steinhauer
1927-1931 George Levis
1932-1951 Joe Steinhauer
1952- John Jamieson

Gymnastics Coaches

1902-1905 J. C. Elsom
1906-1907 Emett Angell
1908-1909 J. C. Elsom
1910 Felix Zeidelbach
1911-1917 H. D. MacChesney
1918 Joe Steinauer
1919-1922 Fred Schlatter
1923 Frank Leitz
1924-1926 Fred Schlatter
1927-1935 A. L. Masley
1936-1947 Dean Mory
1948-1959 George Bauer and Gordon Johnson
1960-1961 George Johnson
1962- George Bauer

Hockey Coaches

1916-1919 Joe Steinauer
1921-1925 Dr. A. C. Viner
1926-1935 Kay Iverson
1935-1963 No teams
1963-1964 Art Thomsen and John Riley
1964-1966 John Riley
1966- Robert Johnson

Swimming Coaches

1912-1913 Chauncey Hyatt
1914-1919 Harry H. Hindman
1920-1951 Joe Steinhauer
1951- John Hickman

Baseball Coaches

1900-1901 Phil King
1902-1903 Oscar Bandelin
1904-1905 Bemis Pierce
1906 No Team
1907 C. P. Hutchins
1908-1911 Tom Barry
1912 Gordon (Slim) Lewis
1913 William Juneau
1914-1917 Gordon (Slim) Lewis
1918 Guy Lowman
1919-1920 Maurice A. Kent
1921-1932 Guy Lowman
1933-1934 Irvin Uteritz
1935-1936 Robert Poser
1937-1939 Lowell Douglas
1940- Arthur Mansfield

Basketball Coaches

1905-1908 E. D. Angell
1909-1910 Haskell Noyes
1911 George Kirchgasser
1912-1917 Dr. Walter Meanwell
1918-1920 Guy Lowman
1921-1934 Dr. Walter Meanwell
1935-1959 Harold Foster
1960- John E. Erickson

Boxing Coaches

1923 Eddie Borg
1924-1926 Ray Moore
1927 W. G. Storch
1928-1930 Leonard "Stub" Allison
1934-1944 John Walsh
1945 Tom Kenneally
1946 John Walsh, DeWitt Portal
1947-1958 John Walsh
1959-1960 Vern Woodward

Crew Coaches

1894 Amos W. Marston
1895-1898 Andrew O'Dea
1899 C. C. McConville
1900-1906 Andrew O'Dea
1907-1910 Edward Ten Eyck
1911-1928 "Dad" Vail
1929-1933 Mike Murphy
1934-1939 Ralph Hunn
1934-1942 Allen Walz
1943 George Rea
1944 Curt Drewes
1945 Ray Rom
1946 Allen Walz
1947- Norm Sonju

Cross Country Coaches

1910-1911 Charles Wilson
1912 Clarence Cleveland
1913 Thomas E. Jones
1914 George T. Bresnahan
1915 Fred G. Lee
1916 Irvin A. White
1917 George Benish
1918-1920 George T. Bresnahan
1921-1925 Meade Burke
1926-1948 Thomas E. Jones
1948-1950 Guy Sundt
1950-1959 J. Riley Best
1960- Tom Bennett

CHRONOLOGY SECTION

Pres. James H. Smart
Purdue University

Jan. 11, 1895—President James H. Smart of Purdue University called meeting of the presidents of seven midwestern universities at Chicago for purpose of considering regulation and control of intercollegiate athletics. At meeting, organization for control of athletics was blueprinted, consisting of an appointed faculty representative from each institution.

Jan. 11, 1895—Voted to restrict eligibility for athletics to bona-fide, full-time students who were not delinquent in their studies.

Feb. 8, 1896—One faculty representative from each of seven institutions met at Palmer House, Chicago, Ill., to establish standards and machinery for regulation and administration of intercollegiate athletics. They designated themselves as "Intercollegiate Conference of Faculty Representatives." The organization eventually was labeled popularly the "Big Ten" or "Western Conference," although the original title still is the official name. Original use of the word "Conference" has since been applied to any group of institutions for similar purposes. The seven original members of the Conference were:

UNIVERSITY OF CHICAGO
UNIVERSITY OF ILLINOIS
UNIVERSITY OF MICHIGAN
UNIVERSITY OF MINNESOTA
NORTHWESTERN UNIVERSITY
PURDUE UNIVERSITY
UNIVERSITY OF WISCONSIN

Note: Lake Forest College was at the 1895 meeting but was replaced by Michigan in the 1896 sessions.

Nov. 26, 1897—Voted to require a year's residence after changing institutions.

Nov. 26, 1897—Prof. J. Scott Clark of Northwestern submitted the following figures regarding men available for athletics:

Chicago	1,345	Northwestern	317
Illinois	746	Purdue	569
Michigan	2,081	Wisconsin	1,229
Minnesota	1,813		

Nov. 25, 1898—Committee devised and printed set of football rules for Conference teams in contrast to rules used by Eastern institutions. (Later it was decided to use the Eastern rules.)

Dec. 1, 1899—There were admitted to membership:
INDIANA UNIVERSITY
STATE UNIVERSITY OF IOWA

Nov. 30, 1900—H. S. White of Northwestern presented legislation providing that any university may object to new legislation if objection made within 30 days after legislation was passed, otherwise the Conference action would be binding on all members. (The following year this time limit was raised to 60 days and final action on the subject specified that these days must be during school session.) This legislative procedure has since been known as the *White Resolution.*

June 1, 1901—First Conference Outdoor Track meet held at University of Chicago.

Nov. 29, 1901—Voted "to limit preliminary football practice to two weeks immediately preceding the opening of college."

Nov. 29, 1901—Voted to drop the bicycle event from the Conference track meet.

Nov. 27, 1903—Proposed that if rules of Eastern Football Rules Committee were to be followed the West should have representation on the Rules Committee.

Nov. 25, 1904—Conference pioneered residence rule requiring that a student to be eligible to participate in intercollegiate sports must first complete a full semester's work in residence. No such rule had been enacted before; it was termed a radical departure in college athletics.

May 13, 1905—The Intercollegiate Conference Athletic Association (ICAA) was incorporated under the laws of Illinois "to promote public interest in track and field athletics and other forms of amateur sports, to maintain a high standard of amateurism in athletics and to conduct and manage athletic contests, exhibitions and meets in furtherance of the purpose above named." Members of the corporation are the institutions making up the Conference. Meets in indoor and outdoor track and field, gymnastics, swimming and wrestling, a cross country run and tournaments in fencing, golf and tennis held under the auspices of the Conference are conducted by this corporation. Operating the corporation were graduate directors representing each member institution.

March 9, 1906—Meeting held this date commonly called "Angell Conference," since it was called by President A. A. Angell of Michigan. Following far-sighted regulations for participation in and control of intercollegiate athletics were agreed upon and adopted following day:

1. One year of residence necessary for eligibility. This rule also required the meeting of all entrance requirements and completion of a full year's work.
2. Only three years of competition allowed and no graduate student to be eligible.
3. Football season limited to five games.
4. No training table or training quarters permitted.
5. Student and faculty tickets not to cost over fifty cents.

Nov. 30, 1907—Raised limit on football games per season from five to seven.

Jan. 14, 1908—University of Michigan withdrew from Conference in protest against "retroactive provisions" of certain Conference enactments.

Nov. 15, 1908—First Conference cross country meet held over five mile course at Chicago.

Jan. 2, 1909—Conference institutions took an active part in National Collegiate Athletic Association as evidenced by early membership of Chicago and Minnesota.

May 19-21, 1910—First Conference Tennis meet held at University of Chicago.

March 25, 1911—First Conference Indoor Track and Swimming meet held at Northwestern University.

April 6, 1912—There was admitted to membership:
OHIO STATE UNIVERSITY

April 6, 1912—Voted that "the Faculty Representative of each University in the Conference must be a person who receives no pay for any services connected with Athletics or the Department of Physical Culture."

April 16, 1912—Voted down recommendation of University Presidents for dual representation, one of the two men from each institution to be a member of the athletic staff.

Nov. 29, 1912—Voted to permit Conference basketball teams to play 12 Conference games and five non-Conference contests.

Dec. 6, 1913—Post-season basketball games were prohibited.

Dec. 5, 1914—The Board of Directors of the ICAA set aside the sum of $2,000 (increased by the Directors in 1926 to $3,000) for the endowment of the ICAA Medal (Medal of Honor), which is annually awarded by each Conference institution to the student of the graduating class who has attained the greatest proficiency in scholarship and athletics.

June 5, 1915—Enacted regulation permitting two secret practices per week only.

Dec. 4, 1916—Javelin throw was added to outdoor track meet.

Dec. 9, 1916—Date of the opening of fall football practice was moved up to Sept. 15.

Nov. 20, 1917—University of Michigan resumed membership in the Conference.

Sept. 26, 1918—Conference suspended "its activities as a controlling body" at the same time tendering to War Department "its services in carrying on athletic activities, both intramural and intercollegiate, in and among its members."

Dec. 7, 1918—Conference declared former authority in effect.

June 2, 1921—Official action against post-season football games was taken. Following fall, a Tournament of Roses invitation received by University of Iowa was ruled out on the grounds that it constituted a post-season game.

June 2, 1922—Established the office of "Commissioner of Athletics" with the Commissioner to serve as a general secretary, promote educational campaigns on amateurism and carry on investigations regarding intercollegiate athletic problems. Major John L. Griffith was elected to the post.

Sept. 13, 1922—Meeting held with basketball officials to work out procedure for improvement of crowd behavior at basketball games.

June 1, 1923—Voted that student who previously left college while failing work or on probation must be in residence for two years after entering a Conference institution before becoming eligible. Any student leaving school twice while under probation not eligible.

June 1, 1923—Raised limit on football games per season from seven to eight games.

March 12-13, 1926—First Conference meets in fencing, gymnastics and wrestling held at Purdue University.

March 13, 1926—Conference Athletic Directors were elected directors of the ICAA in a corporate reorganization. The directors assumed control over ICAA activities as the agent running Conference meets and tournaments. Amos Alonzo Stagg, Chicago Athletic Director, was elected the first ICAA president under the reorganization.

May 27, 1927—Ruled that athletes should not engage in athletic writing or use their names for commercial advertising.

Major John L. Griffith
First Commissioner

May 27, 1927—Voted that Conference members should not employ coaches from other Conference institutions without first obtaining permission to negotiate from employers of such coaches.

Dec. 7, 1928—Approved athletic standards of North Central Association of Colleges and Secondary schools as paralleling regulations long enforced by the Conference. Agree not to play a college in the Conference territory dropped from the accredited list by the N.C.A. for athletic irregularities.

May 25, 1929—University of Iowa was suspended from Conference membership due to infractions of an athletic nature.

Feb. 1, 1930—University of Iowa resumed membership in the Conference.

May 25, 1935—Regulations governing broadcasting rights to home Conference games adopted.

May 22, 1936—Voted to accept resolution by University of Wisconsin that its Faculty considers itself in control of athletic affairs. The University had been threatened with suspension from the Conference on February 29, 1936.

Dec. 4, 1937—Amended Regulations to permit Conference teams to compete against U. S. Military Academy.

May 21, 1938—Voted to re-establish training table for football players.

Dec. 3, 1938—Reaffirmed ruling that football season shall end the last Thursday before Thanksgiving day.

Aug. 15, 1939—William R. Reed was hired to establish Big Ten Service Bureau.

September, 1939—The beginning of "Modern Era" of Big Ten Athletic competition.

May 24, 1940—Voted to permit nine football games per season, six Conference games to be required and at least two at each home institution. (For seasons of 1943 and 1944.)

Sept. 13, 1941—Conference permitted certain Service teams to schedule a limited number of football and basketball games with Conference teams.

Dec. 6, 1941—Javelin throw was dropped from outdoor track meet.

March 7, 1942—Certain rules were waived because of the war-time conditions, permitting a 10-game football schedule for 1942, permitting inter-freshman team competition, and permitting games with teams that do not observe Conference rules.

Feb. 21, 1943—Certain Eligibility Rules waived for the duration of the war to permit use of freshmen on varsity teams. All eligibility rules waived for students in armed forces, receiving major instruction at a member institution.

May 15, 1943—Summer football practice permitted.

June 23, 1943—In order to maintain athletic programs the Conference voted to waive its Eligibility Rules, with two exceptions (a) regular enrollment as a student and (b) non-receipt of compensation for athletic participation.

May 26, 1944—The University of Chicago announced its withdrawal from scheduling athletic meets for 1944-45.

Dec. 7, 1944—Major John L. Griffith, Commissioner (1922-1944), died.

Dec. 11, 1949—Approved Conference football schedules for the season of 1953 and 1954, with Michigan State College as a football-playing member of the Conference.

Dec. 11, 1949—Voted to limit the opening of freshman football practice to the opening day of the school year.

March 11, 1950—Approved a 14-game Conference basketball schedule for member schools, but maintained the limit of 22 games in all.

March 11, 1950—Increased the football traveling squad limit from 36 to 40 players.

March 11, 1950—Adopted an eligibility rule requiring that a student, to be eligible for intercollegiate athletic competition, must maintain each year normal progress toward his degree.

May 25, 1950—Voted to prohibit for the 1950 football season simultaneous general television broadcast of games played on the home grounds of Conference institutions; and at the same time sanctioned "deferred" television of Conference football games whereby the complete films of games played at Conference institutions shall be made available for post-game general television broadcast.

July 31, 1950—Approved as a one-year experiment simultaneous theatre-television of Conference football games for the 1950 season, subject to the individual approval of all details by each participating institution.

December 7, 1950—Disapproved a proposal for establishment of a Mid-West Intercollegiate Ice Hockey League to be composed of three Conference institutions and four non-conference institutions.

December 8, 1950—Voted that five-man officiating crews shall be assigned to all football games played on the home grounds of Big Ten institutions in 1951.

February 23, 1951—Voted to prohibit the simultaneous general television broadcast of football games played on the home grounds of Conference institutions during the 1951 season, but authorized Conference institutions to co-operate with the NCAA in the conduct of any controlled experiments with simultaneous or delayed television which the NCAA might consider to be worthwhile for experimental purposes; and further voted that Conference institutions could make available for general simultaneous television broadcast any other intercollegiate contest under their control.

March 19, 1951—Voted that for the academic year 1951-52, the one-year residence rule be suspended for new freshmen entering in the summer or fall of 1951, students who entered Conference institutions during 1950-51 but had not completed one year of residence by the time the 1951 fall term opened, and for transfer graduates of junior colleges.

May 25, 1951—Renewed the contract of Commissioner Kenneth L. Wilson for a period of five years.

May 25, 1951—Voted that freshmen candidates for 1951 Conference football teams report for 1951 fall practice on September 1.

May 25, 1951—Voted to renew the Rose Bowl agreement with the Pacific Coast Conference for a three-year period with the understanding that no Big Ten institution be permitted to compete in the game more often than once in a two-year period.

Kenneth L. (Tug) Wilson
Second Commissioner

March 10, 1945—Faculty approved the appointment of Kenneth L. (Tug) Wilson, Athletic Director of Northwestern University, as new Commissioner.

May 1, 1945—Kenneth L. (Tug) Wilson took office as Major Griffith's successor.

Dec. 7, 1945—"Duration of the war," as referred to on Feb. 21, 1943, was considered concluded insofar as Conference administration is concerned.

Dec. 7, 1945—Voted nine-game football schedule as permanent legislation, the first game of the season not to be played before the last Saturday in September and the last game not to be played after the last Saturday before the last Thursday in Nov.

March 8, 1946—University of Chicago formally withdrew from the Conference due to inability "to provide reasonable equality of competition."

Sept. 1, 1946—Voted to enter into a five-year agreement with the Pacific Coast Intercollegiate Conference permitting a Conference representative to play a PCC representative in the Jan. 1 Rose Bowl football game. This marked a singular exception to the Conference's stand against post-season games.

March 30, 1947—Conference took official notice of unusual circumstance "whereas, the year just ending has been marked by the retirement or withdrawal from its active ranks of four men who for a combined total of nearly eighty years have played major roles in the affairs of the Conference":

L. W. St. John, Ohio State University, 1913-1947
Z. G. Clevenger, Indiana University, 1923-1946
Dr. Wm. F. Lorenz, Univ. of Wisconsin, 1936-1947
E. G. Schroeder, Univ. of Iowa, 1936-1947

May 31, 1947—Removal of grade of failure by special examination prohibited.

Oct. 1, 1947—Four institutions, Illinois, Michigan, Ohio State and Wisconsin, began 150-pound, intercollegiate football competiton.

May 27, 1948—Reaffirmed traditional rule requiring Junior College transfers to spend one year in residence prior to becoming eligible for intercollegiate athletic competition.

June 5, 1948—Ruled 11 athletes ineligible for a period of one year due to infractions of the Conference rule dealing with aid to athletes.

Sept. 12, 1948—Adopted new Eligibility Rule 6, providing that the award of scholarships to athletes must conform to academic standards set by the Conference.

Dec. 12, 1948—Voted that Michigan State College, East Lansing, be admitted to membership in the Conference, the admission to take effect at such time as a Committee of the Faculty Representatives shall have certified to the Conference that rules and regulations and other requirements of the Conference are completely in force at that institution.

May 20, 1949—There was admitted to membership:
MICHIGAN STATE COLLEGE

It was voted that Conference competition by Michigan State College would begin with the academic year of 1950-51 and in the case of football at the expiration of schedules heretofore drawn. (At the December, 1948, meeting, Conference football schedules had been drawn through the 1952 season.)

Feb. 22, 1953—The Faculty Representatives confirmed disciplinary action of the Commissioner in placing Michigan State College on probation for its delinquencies in permitting to exist an organization, known as the Spartan Foundation of Lansing, which had solicited funds for the assistance of Michigan State College athletes, which funds were not administered by the College in accordance with Rule 7.

March 6, 1953—Football traveling squads reduced to 38 and 14-game Conference basketball schedules voted for 1954 and 1955.

April 27, 1953—Council of Ten, meeting with presidential representatives from five other Conferences, requested North Central Association to review and modify its athletic policy with regard to financial aids for athletes.

May 28, 1953—Faculty representatives voted to renew Rose Bowl agreement for three years, an invitation to that effect having been received from the Pacific Coast Conference Jan. 19, 1953 and referred at that time to the member institutions as under the White Resolution.

May 28, 1953—Voted to abandon pro-rata assessments based on football receipts to support Commissioner's office, in favor of equal shares. Special assessments for supervision and training of officials also abandoned; funds for purpose to come from Commissioner's regular budget.

Dec. 10, 1953—On recommendation of the Commissioner the Faculty Representatives removed Michigan State College from the state of probation imposed Feb. 22, 1953.

Dec. 10, 1953—Conference approved an operating principle for regional televising of football games, but released a critical statement on NCAA television plans.

Dec. 11, 1953—Directors approved addition of the 300, 600- and 1000-yard run events for the Conference Indoor Track Meet.

Dec. 12, 1953—Prof. Ralph W. Aigler of Michigan retired as chairman of the Eligibility Committee after more than 25 years service on that Committee.

March 4, 1954—Directors released details of a Conference approved plan for regional televising of football games.

April 25, 1954—Joint Group received the report of a third Committee on Rules Revision, which set up procedures for administering all aid to athletes on a basis of need, need to be calculated by formula.

April 26, 1954—Joint Group met with Council of Ten to discuss television policies and the report of Rules Revision Committee #3.

May 25, 1954—Directors, Football Coaches and Publicity Directors met for a discussion of public relations problems and programs.

May 28, 1954—Directors adopted procedure for selection of Rose Bowl representative.

May 28-29, 1954—Joint Group adopted benefit plans for employees in Commissioner's office; created a standing Finance Committee; modified rule on competition with non-Conference institutions.

Sept. 8-9-1954—Joint Group liberalized rule on TV and radio appearances of athletes; tabled Rules Revision Report #3; Directors raised basketball officials fees to $75.

March 5, 1955—Faculty voted to count certain pre-matriculation competition of alien students the equivalent of inter-college competition; R. C. Larkins succeeded Ted Payseur as Chairman of the Television Committee.

May 25, 1951—Voted approval of a re-organization of the Conference rules and regulations which more clearly defined the jurisdiction of the Faculty Representatives and Athletic Directors in matters of Conference legislation, and which established the Commissioner as the primary enforcement agency of all legislation.

November 1, 1951—William R. Reed became Assistant Commissioner.

December 8, 1951—Rejected a proposed work-aid program for athletes described as "an equality of offer" basis for aids, indicating a desire to tighten rather than relax standards for assistance to athletes.

December 8, 1951—Athletic Directors, instead of Faculty Representatives, designated to cast ballots for selection of a "representative team" to play in Rose Bowl.

February 3, 1952—Special Meeting called to consider Report on Athletic Policy of a Committee of the American Council on Education. A brief comparing Conference regulations with the report, together with certain recommendations, was authorized for presentation to the ACE.

February 3, 1952—Approved, with definitions, the NCAA limitation upon out-of-season practice in football (20 sessions in 30 days) and basketball (20 sessions in 24 days).

March 16, 1952—Met jointly with the Conference Presidents to consider recommendations of the Special Committee on Athletic Policy of the American Council on Education. The Presidents issued a statement that they were "impressed with the substantial area of agreement between the ACE Report and regulations of the Conference," noting "with gratification certain Conference standards that are higher than those proposed by the ACE," and called for further action along four major lines as follows: (1) The elimination of the subsidization of athletes; (2) The elimination of recruiting methods that are contrary to Conference regulations; (3) The granting of special academic favor to athletes; (4) the over-emphasis is on competition in athletics, especially on a national basis.

March 16, 1952—Adopted an 18-game round-robin Conference basketball schedule, within the previous limit of 22 games in a season.

May 30, 1952—Provided that the Conference Commissioner shall be employed by the ten Conference Presidents, and that he shall report to them semi-annually on the enforcement of Conference rules and regulations.

May 31, 1952—Finalized action (taken, in part, at meetings earlier in the year) which (1) Limits any institutional aid to athletes on basis of superior scholarship to a renewable one-year term and an amount not exceeding "normal expenses of attending the institution"; (2) Re-defines "superior" scholarship" as a position in the upper one-third of a high school graduating class or, in college, a cumulative scholastic average no lower than mid-way between B and C; (3) Requires any athlete receiving unearned aid from an institution to be notified in writing of the terms and basis of the award; (4) Establishes a "qualitative progress" rule of eligibility paralleling the "rule of normal quantitative progress" toward a degree adopted March 11, 1950; and (5) Limits any athlete's eligibility to a residence period of ten semesters or 15 quarters.

Dec. 5, 1952—Conference voted to sponsor amendment to NCAA limitation on out-of-season practices which would permit 30 practice sessions for spring football and basketball. (The proposal was defeated at NCAA Convention Jan. 9, 1953.)

Dec. 6, 1952—Provided that all penalties imposed by Commissioner and the Conference be announced publicly.

449

March 14, 1955—Special Joint Group meeting approved pending NCAA TV plan and voted to pool all football television rights of members and to share television proceeds equally.

July 1, 1955—By action of the State Legislature Michigan State College became known as Michigan State University.

Dec. 9, 1955—Opening date of football practice moved to Sept. 1 to conform to NCAA regulation.

March 3, 1956—Joint Group approved continuation of Rose Bowl agreement with Pacific Coast Conference on an indefinite term basis.

April 26, 1956—Ohio State placed on probation by Commissioner and made ineligible for Rose Bowl participation for one year because of irregularities in job program for football players and for irregular financial assistance to football players by the coach.

April 30, 1956—K. L. Wilson's contract as Commissioner extended for five-year term by Council of Ten.

Aug. 4, 1956—A special Joint Group meeting received a report from the Special Committee appointed the previous December, which was described as a "critical self-appraisal" of Conference policies and practices. The Joint Group endorsed a principle of administering financial aids to athletes on a basis of proven need, and directed the Special Committee to prepare and submit legislation giving effect to that principle.

Dec. 8, 1956—Conference approved a new Rule 7, governing financial assistance on a basis of demonstrated need.

Feb. 22, 1957—Confirmed enactment of new financial assistance rule; created a new Financial Aids Service to make determinations of financial need.

May 25, 1957—Modified Rule 7 to permit award of basic educational costs on a basis of superior scholarship—rank in upper quarter of high school class or in upper quarter of college class; revised recruiting regulation to permit coaches off-campus contact with prospective students who had signed acceptances of financial aid tenders.

July 28, 1957—Faculty Representatives moved to make Indiana University's good standing as a Conference member conditional upon the suspension for one year of football coach Phil Dickens, who had been found in violation of Conference rules by promising excessive financial aid to prospective students.

Sept. 1, 1957—Pursuant to action of Faculty Representatives in May, the Conference employed an Examiner, John Dewey, whose duties are to make regular inspections of intercollegiate athletic practices at the member schools and particularly of the administration of financial aid, for the information of the Commissioner and the Faculty Representatives.

Dec. 14, 1957—Faculty Representatives approved removal of the suspension of Indiana football coach Phil Dickens.

March 7, 1958—Faculty Representatives adopted a rule limiting eligibility (except in hardship cases) to a period of four years following initial college enrollment.

Dec. 12, 1958—Received announcement of Pacific Coast Conference regarding its dissolution, and termination of Rose Bowl participation agreement after January 1, 1960. Joint Group affirmed its approval of a 10-game football schedule effective in 1965 and a "round-robin" requirement for Conference games to be effective in progressive stages with the 1969 season.

May 22, 1959—Joint Group affirmed adoption of a new recruiting regulation, permitting a university to pay travel expenses for a prospect's campus visit. By a 5-5 vote the Faculty Representatives failed to authorize negotiations for a revival of the Inter-Conference agreement on Rose Bowl participation, but by the same division failed to repeal the standing provision which exempts the Rose Bowl from the prohibition on post-season contests, thus making acceptance of a bid for participation in that event a matter of individual option.

Dec. 10-11, 1959—Basketball officials' fees raised to $100; summer competition rule revised to permit limited basketball play.

March 3-5, 1960—Junior college graduates made immediately eligible upon enrollment in a Conference University; rejected a proposal that the Conference contract with the Athletic Association of Western Universities for participation in the Rose Bowl.

May 19-21, 1960—Voted, in principle, to approve a program of financial aid based on academic achievement without regard to a need factor; reaffirmed privilege of members on an individual option basis to accept an invitation to play in the Rose Bowl; rejected a proposal that all post-season competition following Conference meets be prohibited.

July 30, 1960—Commissioner Wilson ruled, on the basis of findings that certain prospective athletes at Indiana University had been offered or had received illegal financial assistance, that Indiana University's membership should be placed on probation, that the University should not participate in the Conference division of football television receipts in 1960, and that football games played by Indiana in 1960 should not be counted as Conference games.

Dec. 8-10, 1960—Duties and responsibilities of the Commissioner re-defined by the Joint Group and enforcement procedures revised to give the Athletic Directors new responsibilities, with the Commissioner, for the determination of violations and the imposition of penalties.

May 18-20, 1961—Indiana University was restored to good standing in the Conference, by vote of the Faculty Representatives upon recommendation of the Commissioner.

July 1, 1961—Kenneth L. (Tug) Wilson retired as Commissioner after 16 years of service (1945-1961) and, pursuant to his election by the Council of Ten on April 24, 1961, William R. Reed became the third Conference Commissioner; John Dewey, named Assistant to the Commissioner and Kay Fred Schultz became Service Bureau Director.

Dec. 7-8, 1961—The Faculty Representatives enacted new financial aid rules, eliminating the "need principle" and installing a requirement of predicted college success on the basis of high school rank and aptitude tests, and strengthened the "normal progress" requirements of the eligibility rules. The Joint Group authorized a contract for Rose Bowl participation with the Athletic Association of Western Universities (AAWU).

May 17-18, 1962—The Joint Group voted to suspend progression toward "round robin" football schedules with a requirement of seven Conference games, and endorsed the new Sports Federations.

July 1, 1962—The Conference offices were moved to the Sheraton-Chicago Hotel.

Aug. 1, 1962—A contract was signed between the Big Ten and the AAWU to provide opponents in the Jan. 1, Rose Bowl game for an indefinite period.

March 8, 1963—Conference participation in the "Inter-Conference Letter of Intent Plan" was approved.

Amos Alonzo Stagg
University of Chicago

March 17, 1965—Amos Alonzo Stagg died at age of 102. He served as the first athletic director and football coach at the University of Chicago from 1892 to 1932, when after 41 seasons he reached the compulsory retirement age of 70. His Maroon teams won 255 games and six Big Ten championships.

April 26, 1965—William R. Reed's contract as Commissioner extended to June 30, 1970, by the Council of Ten.

May 19, 1965—Athletic Directors established television production guidelines for coverage of Conference football and basketball based on principles of non-interference with the conduct of the game.

May 21, 1965—Joint Group established a "Catastrophic Self-Insurance Plan" to provide reimbursement to member institutions for the loss of income brought about by catastrophy resulting in the cancellation of a football game or series of games. Plan to be funded through television receipts, reaching maximum of $250,000.

Dec. 9, 1965—Joint Group authorized two intercollegiate freshman football games to be played in the final four weeks of season.

March 2, 1966—Athletic Directors raised limit of football traveling squads from 38 to 40. Changed the 330-yard intermediate hurdles to 440-yards for 1966 outdoor track championship program; changed two mile run to three miles and added 3000 meter steeplechase, 440-yard relay and triple jump to 1967 outdoor track program.

May 17, 1963—Athletic Directors voted to limit football scouting of Conference opponents to no more than one game with unlimited film exchange for scouting purposes. The Joint Group amended Conference recruiting policies to allow one personal visit on behalf of the member institution in the home of a prospective student-athlete between Dec. 1 and the first date for the issuance of tenders. Approved the appointment of Ike J. Armstrong, retiring University of Minnesota Athletic Director, as Supervisor of Conference Football Officials and as the Commissioner's special representative in Rose Bowl liaison.

Dec. 5, 1963—Under the White Resolution, Joint Group limited initial accepted tenders of athletic grants-in-aid to 70 per Conference institution each year; with further limitation of 30 for football, six for basketball and 34 for sports other than football, basketball, hockey, soccer, lacrosse and crew.

Mar. 13, 1964—Joint Group reaffirmed Regulation III, which states the Conference athletic facilities are not available for the conduct of admissions-paid exhibitions or contests by professional sports team or professional sports organization.

May 21, 1964—Athletic Directors added the 800-yard free style relay to the Conference championship swimming meet program.

May 22, 1964—Joint Group established a committee to study interpretations of Regulation III. Approved a "Declaration of Policy" implementing Conference support of the several sports Federations.

Dec. 8, 1964—Big Ten Sports Information Directors established the "Robert C. Woodworth Award" to honor long-time Purdue publicist, who died April 4, 1964. Recipients are members of press, radio and/or television who have made meritorious contributions in the interest of Big Ten and intercollegiate athletics. Awards made at such time the individual left active coverage.

Dec. 11, 1964—Under the White Resolution, Joint Group Approved: a "Declaration of Policy" implementing Conference support of the several Federations.

Dec. 11, 1964—Faculty Representatives established procedures to expedite eligibility rulings by empowering Commissioner to make authoritative rulings. Joint Group amended and interpreted Regulation III (Facilities) to restore authority for discrimination in the control of athletic facilities to the respective institutions. Excepted were contests by professional sports teams or organizations which engage in championship competition and professional boxing and wrestling. Under amended Regulation, institutions authorized to permit use of their facilities for events such as golf and tennis exhibitions.

Jan. 12, 1965—Faculty Representatives changed date for issuance of tenders of financial assistance for sports other than football to May 1. Football remained at April 1.

March 3, 1965—Athletic Directors voted to provide, for the first time in history, team championship trophies in football, basketball, baseball and hockey. Approved guidelines for relations with professional football. Under White Resolution procedure, Faculty Representatives adopted legislation which accepts sanctioning authority for open competition of Federations in baseball, basketball, gymnastics and track and field. Student-athletes limited to competition which is exclusively intercollegiate or events sanctioned by respective Federation.

March 4, 1965—Athletic Directors raised fees for football officials to $150 per game and basketball officials to $110 per game.

451

CONFERENCE MEDAL WINNERS

In 1914 the Conference endowed a Medal of Honor, to be awarded annually at each institution to the student demonstrating the greatest proficiency in scholarship and athletics. Winners in 1964 were 50th Anniversary Winners of the Medal of Honor.

Following is a list of past winners of the Conference Medal of Honor:

CHICAGO

Year	Winner	Year	Winner	Year	Winner
1915	F. T. Ward	1925	Harry G. Frieda	1935	E. C. Patterson, Jr.
1916	Paul S. Russell	1926	Graham A. Kernwein	1936	Gordon C. Peterson
1917	Daniel J. Fisher	1927	Anton B. Burg	1937	Floyd R. Stauffer
1918	Walter C. Earle	1928	Kenneth A. Rouse	1938	George C. Halcrow
1919	William C. Gorgas	1929	Rudolph P. Leyers	1939	Robert E. Cassels
1920	Charles G. Higgins	1930	Harold E. Haydon	1940	Martin Levit
1921	Harold L. Hanisch	1931	Dale Allen Letts	1941	James Lloyd Ray
1922	Herbert O. Crisler	1932	Everett C. Olson	1942	Calvin C. Sawyier
1923	Harold A. Fletcher	1933	Keith I. Parsons	1943	Raymond Siever
1924	Campbell Dickson	1934	George H. Wrighte	1944	Edward A. Cooperrider

ILLINOIS

Year	Winner	Year	Winner	Year	Winner
1915	Edward A. Williford	1933	R. Dean Woolsey	1951	Don Laz
1916	Elmo Paul Hohman	1934	Ralph J. Eipstein	1952	Richard Calisch
1917	Clyde Gobel Alwood	1935	Irving Seely	1953	Clive Follmer
1918	John Leo Klein	1936	Arthur Fisher	1954	Robert Lenzini
1919	G. C. Bucheit	1937	Harry Combes	1955	Edwin G. Jackson, Jr.
1920	John B. Felmley	1938	Allen Sapora	1956	Daniel E. Dudas
1921	John S. Prescott	1939	Archie Deuschman	1957	Robert Dintelmann
1922	Clarence Crossley	1940	Frank E. Richart, Jr.	1958	Lee Sentman
1923	Otto H. Vogel	1941	Park Brown	1959	Abraham Grossfeld
1924	Walter Roetger	1942	William Hocking	1960	Robert J. Madix
1925	Gilbert J. Roberts	1943	Edwin S. Parker	1961	Charles Campbell
1926	John W. Mauer	1944	Warren F. Goodell	1962	Stuart R. Cohn
1927	Doran T. Rue	1945	Donald Delaney	1963	David J. Downey
1928	Richard G. Finn	1946	Robert Phelps	1964	Richard W. Deller
1929	Robert B. Orlovich	1947	Robert Richards	1965	G. Bogie Redmon
1930	Richard C. Oeler	1948	George Fischer	1966	James S. Grabowski
1931	Lee Sentman	1949	T. Dwight Eddleman		
1932	Edward F. Gbur	1950	Russell W. Steger		

INDIANA

Year	Winner	Year	Winner	Year	Winner
1915	Matthew Winters	1933	Noble L. Biddinger	1951	John H. Phillips
1916	George J. Shively	1934	Raymond F. Dauer	1952	Robert Watson Masters
1917	DeWitt T. Mullett	1935	Don A. Veller	1953	George E. Branam
1918	Wilbur J. Dalzell	1936	Reed H. Kelso	1954	E. Duane Gomer
1919	William M. Zeller	1937	Vernon R. Huffman	1955	Arthur Michael Cusick
1920	Willard Rauschenback	1938	Charles E. McDaniel	1956	Sam Reed
1921	Everitt S. Dean	1939	Christopher Traicoff	1957	Harold Richard Neal
1922	William G. McCaw	1940	Robert I. Hoke	1958	Gregory Bell
1923	Omar Held	1941	Harold L. Zimmer	1959	Ronald Walden
1924	John Milton Nay	1942	Hugh B. McAdams	1960	Donald G. Noone
1925	Harlan Logan	1943	Fred Huff	1961	Gary V. Long
1926	Daniel G. Bernoske	1944	No award	1962	William D. Elyea
1927	Charles F. Beckner	1945	No award	1963	Chester A. Jastremski
1928	Arthur J. Beckner	1946	Ralph Hamilton	1964	James L. Binkley
1929	Wilmer T. Rinehart	1947	LeRoy Thomas Deal	1965	Douglas A. Spicer
1930	W. E. Clapham	1948	Joseph Lawecki	1966	Wayne L. Witmer
1931	J. E. Hatfield	1949	Walter C. Bartkiewicz		
1932	Henry A. Brocksmith	1950			

IOWA

Year	Winner	Year	Winner	Year	Winner
1915	Herman L. Von Lackun	1933	William A. McCloy	1951	Ralph W. Thomas
1916	Forrest W. Deardorff	1934	Tom W. Moore	1952	Charles F. Darling
1917	Wayne J. Foster	1935	James P. McClintock	1953	J. Burton Britzmann
1918	John K. VonLackum	1936	Francis X. Cretzmeyer	1954	William Fenton
1919	Homer W. Scott	1937	Cornelius J. Walker	1955	LeRoy Anton Ebert
1920	Charles Mockmore	1938	Robert G. Lannon	1956	Andrew Marc Houg
1921	Robert J. Kaufman	1939	Wilbur V. Nead	1957	Frank Otis Sebolt
1922	Aubrey Devine	1940	Andrew J. Kantor	1958	Gary E. Meyer
1923	Gordon C. Locke	1941	James R. Murphy, Jr.	1959	James Van Young
1924	Wayland Hicks	1942	Richard E. Hein	1960	William Lloyd Voxman
1925	John Hancock	1943	Thomas Farmer	1961	William Davis Buck
1926	D. M. Graham	1944	No award	1962	Joel D. Novak
1927	Carl D. Voltmer	1945	No award	1963	Ralph W. Trimble
1928	Lawrence Harrison	1946	Arthur Harold Johnson	1964	Andrew J. Hankins, Jr.
1929	Forest Twogood	1947	John Kenneth Hunter	1965	Glenn Gailis
1930	Willis A. Glassgow	1948	Herbert W. Wilkinson	1966	James M. Moses
1931	No award	1949	Evan LeRoy Hultman		
1932	Stuart W. Skowbo	1950	Donald C. Hays		

MICHIGAN

Year	Winner	Year	Winner
1918	Alan W. Boyd	1935	Harvey Smith
1919	No award	1936	Harvey W. Patton
1920	Carl E. Johnson	1937	John A. Gee
1921	Elton E. Wieman	1938	John Townsend
1922	Robert J. Dunne	1939	Leo C. Beebe
1923	Paul C. Goebel	1940	James R. Rae
1924	Franklin C. Cappon	1941	Forest Evashevski
1925	William E. Giles	1942	David M. Nelson
1926	Harold Freyberg	1943	George F. Ceithaml
1927	Paul C. Samson	1944	Paul Grover White
1928	Norman Gabel	1945	Robert L. Wiese
1929	Edwin B. Poorman	1946	Bliss Bowman, Jr.
1930	J. Perry Austin	1947	Paul G. White
1931	Edwin F. Russell	1948	John E. Weisenburger
1932	Ivan B. Williamson	1949	Peter R. Elliott
1933	James C. Cristy, Jr.	1950	Thomas R. Peterson
		1951	Loe R. Koceski

MICHIGAN STATE

Year	Winner	Year	Winner	Year	Winner
1951	Everett Grandelius	1957	Selwyn Jones	1963	Richard Schloemer
1952	Orris H. Bender	1958	Robert W. Jasson	1964	George (Pete) Gent
1953	John D. Wilson	1959	Robert Anderegg	1965	David Price
1954	Bob Hoke	1960	Stanley Tarshis	1966	Stephen A. Juday
1955	R. Kevan Gosper	1961	William Reynolds		
1956	Carl Nystrom	1962	Edward J. Ryan		

MINNESOTA

Year	Winner	Year	Winner	Year	Winner
1915	Boles A. Rosenthal	1933	Kenneth Gay	1951	Myer U. Skoog
1916	Bernard W. Bierman	1934	Marshall Wells	1952	Richard K. Means
1917	Joseph M. Spafka	1935	Robert Tenner	1953	Robert D. Gelle
1918	George W. Hauser	1936	Glenn Seidel	1954	Paul R. Giel
1919	Erling S. Platou	1937	Charles B. Wilkinson	1955	Charles J. Mencel
1920	Norman W. Kingsley	1938	Dominic Krezowski	1956	Darrell R. Cochran
1921	Neal A. Arntson	1939	John A. Kundla	1957	Robert D. Hobert
1922	Arnold Oss	1940	Harold Van Every	1958	John W. McCartan
1923	Rudolph Hultkrans	1941	George Franck	1959	Leroy J. Gehring
1924	Earl Martineau	1942	Eugene Flick	1960	Orville Peterson
1925	Louis Gross	1943	Christie Geankoplis	1961	Robert J. Schwarzkopf
1926	Raymond F. Rasey	1944	Stuart A. Olson	1962	James A. Fischer
1927	Roger Wheeler	1945	Arnold Lehman	1963	Robert J. Bateman
1928	Malvin J. Nydahl	1946	John Adams	1964	Arthur (Bill) Davis
1929	George E. MacKinnon	1947	Robert Sandberg	1965	Walter P. Richardson
1930	Robert Tanner	1948	Steve Silianoff	1966	Paul T. Faust
1931	Lowell Marsh	1949	James B. Peterson		
1932	Earl W. Loose	1950	Richard S. Kilty		

1902

(Game not divided into quarters until 1910)

Michigan	17	32	49
Stanford	0	0	0

Michigan—Touchdowns: Snow 5 (5, 2, 6, 15, 3, center rushes), Redden 2 (25, punt return; 25, run with recovered fumble), Herrnstein (22, right tackle). Field goal: Sweeley (20, placekick). Points after touchdown: Shorts 4.

Michigan		Stanford
Redden	LE	Clark
White (c)	LT	Traeger
McGugin	LG	Roosevelt
Gregory	C	Lee
Wilson	RG	Thompson
Shorts	RT	McFadden
Sweeley	RE	Cooper
Weeks	QB	Tarpay
Heston	LH	Slaker
Herrnstein	RH	Fisher (c)
Snow	FB	McGilvray

STATISTICS

Michigan		Stanford
27	First downs	5
503	Net yards rushing	67
21	Number of punts	16
38.9	Punting average	31
1	Fumbles lost	8
10	Yards penalized	15

Substitutions—Michigan: none. Stanford: Preston, Sefton, ends; Hauverman, tackle; Van Sickle, guard; Allen, halfback.

1921

California	7	14	0	7	28
Ohio State	0	0	0	0	0

California—Touchdowns: Sprott 2 (1, center plunge; 5, left end), Stephens (37, pass from Muller), Deeds (1, right tackle). Points after touchdown: Toomey 3, Erb.

California		Ohio State
Stephens	LE	Myers
Dean	LT	Huffman
Majors (c)	LG	J. Taylor
Latham	C	Nemecek
Cranmer	RG	Wieche
McMillan	RT	Trott
Muller	RE	N. Workman
Erb	QB	H. Workman
Sprott	LH	Stinchcomb
Toomey	RH	Blair
Nisbet	FB	C. Taylor

STATISTICS

California		Ohio State
17	First downs	11
234	Net yards rushing	85
12	Passes attempted	27
8	Passes completed	10
1	Passes had intercepted	4
134	Net yards passing	121
368	Total net yards	206
10	Number of punts	7
38.3	Punting average	41.2

STATISTICS

California		Ohio State
0	Fumbles lost	3
45	Yards penalized	0

Substitutes—California: Hall, end; Barnes, tackle; Clark, guard; Deeds, Eells, halfbacks; Morrison, fullback. Ohio State: Slyker, end; Spiers, guard; Bliss, Cott, Wiper, Isabel, Henderson, Wilder, halfbacks; Willaman, fullback.

1947

Illinois	6	19	0	20	45
UCLA	7	7	0	0	14

Illinois—Touchdowns: Rykovich (1, left guard), Young 2 (2, right tackle; 1, left tackle), Patterson (4, left end), Moss (1, sneak), Steger (64, intercepted pass by Case), Green (20, intercepted pass by Case). Points after touchdown: Maechtle 3.

UCLA—Touchdowns: Case (1, sneak), Hoisch (103, kickoff return). Points after touchdown: Case 2.

Illinois		UCLA
Zatkoff	LE	Baldwin (c-c)
L. Agase	LT	Malmberg
Wrenn	LG	Dimitro
Wenskunas (c)	C	Paul
A. Agase	RG	Clements
Genis	RT	Chambers
Huber	RE	Fears
Moss	QB	Case (c-c)
Rykovich	LH	Rowland
Young	RH	Rossi
Steger	FB	Myers

STATISTICS

Illinois		UCLA
23	First downs	12
320	Net yards rushing	72
15	Passes attempted	29
4	Passes completed	14
2	Passes had intercepted	4
76	Net yards passing	176
396	Total net yards	248
5	Number of punts	8
33.8	Punting average	32
0	Fumbles lost	0
55	Yards penalized	45

Substitutes—Illinois: Owens, Maechtle, Valek, Heiss, Buscemi, Ciszek, ends; Green, Kasap, Bingaman, Franks, tackles; Prymuski, Serpico, Gottfried, Siegert, Martignago, guards; Seliger, Mastrangeli, Cahill, centers; Gallagher, Stewart, quarterbacks; Patterson, Eddleman, Dufelmeier, Kwasniewski, Maggioli, Zaborac, halfbacks; Grierson, Piggott, Dimit, fullbacks. UCLA: Kurrasch, Tinsley, Hoyt, Dobrow, Breeding, Kiefer, ends; Asher, Mathews, Griswold, Mike, Boom, Versen, Pastre, tackles; Nikcevich, Steiner, Russell, Watts, guards; McLaughlin, center; Reiges, quarterback; Hoisch, Shipkey, E. Johnson, Roesch, Brown, Schneider, halfbacks; Steffen, J. Johnson, Hunt, fullbacks.

1948

Michigan	7	14	7	21	49
Southern California	0	0	0	0	0

Michigan—Touchdowns: Weisenburger 3 (1, center plunge; 1, plunge; 1, plunge), C. Elliott (11, pass from Chappuis, run of 11), Yerges (18, pass from Chappuis of 13, run of 5), Derricotte (45, pass, pass from Fonde of 24, run of 21), Rifenburg (28, pass from Yerges). Points after touchdown: Brieske 7.

Michigan		Southern California
Mann	LE	Tolman
Hilkene (c)	LT	Ferraro
Tomasi	LG	Clark (c)
White	C	McCormick
Wilkins	RG	McCall
Pritula	RT	Bird
Rifenburg	RE	Cleary
Yerges	QB	Murphy
Chappuis	LH	McCardle
C. Elliott	RH	Doll
Weisenburger	FB	Lillywhite

STATISTICS

Michigan		Southern California
21	First downs	10
219	Net yards rushing	91
27	Passes attempted	11
17	Passes completed	6
1	Passes had intercepted	1
272	Net yards passing	42
491	Total net yards	133
4	Number of punts	8
38.2	Punting average	43.7
1	Fumbles lost	2
40	Yards penalized	10

Substitutes—Michigan: McNeill, Ford, Wisniewski, Hershberger, Andersen, ends; Wistert, Kohl, Johnson, Dendrinos, tackles; Soboleski, Sickels, Kampe, Heneveld, guards; Dworsky, Brieske, centers; P: Elliott, Kiesel, quarterbacks; Derricotte, Teninga, Fonde, Kuick, halfbacks; Kempthorn, Peterson, fullbacks. Southern California: Linehan, Stillwell, Cramer, Salata, Lloyd, Willumson, ends; Schutte, Swope, Perrin, tackles; Bastian, Rea, Colley, Lowell, Monson, guards; Davis, Busch, centers; Powers, Dill, Robertson, quarterbacks; Tannehill, Garlin, Gray, Curry, Kirby, Roundy, Cantor, Craig, Futrell, halfbacks; Betz, Oestreich, Rossetto, Burke, fullbacks.

1949

Northwestern	7	6	0	7	20
California	7	0	7	0	14

Northwestern—Touchdowns: Aschenbrenner (73, right tackle), Murakowski (2, right tackle), Tunnicliff (43, right end). Points after touchdown: Farrar 2.
California—Touchdowns: Jensen (67, left end), Swaner (4, left tackle). Points after touchdown: Cullom 2.

Northwestern		California
Zuravleff	LE	Van Deren
Sawle	LT	Cullom
Nemeth	LG	Baker
Sarkisian (c)	C	Duncan
Fatso Day	RG	Franz
Cernoch	RT	Frassetto (c)
Hagmann	RE	Cunningham
Burson	QB	Erickson
Aschenbrenner	LH	Main
Tunnicliff	RH	Swaner
Murakowski	FB	Jensen

STATISTICS

Northwestern		California
6	First downs	12
273	Net yards rushing	173
4	Passes attempted	16
1	Passes completed	6

STATISTICS

Northwestern		California
0	Passes had intercepted	4
17	Net yards passing	83
290	Total net yards	256
7	Number of punts	4
43	Punting average	33
2	Fumbles lost	1
15	Yards penalized	6

Substitutions—Northwestern: Stonesifer (l), Keddie (r), ends; Maddock (l), Forman (r), tackles; Anderson (r), guard; Wietecha, Petter, Price, centers; Farrar, Flowers, J. Miller, quarterbacks; PeeWee Day (l), Worthington (r), G. Miller (r), halfbacks; Sundheim, Perricone, Rossi, fullbacks. California: Souza (l), Pressley (r), ends; Turner (l), Schmalenberger (l), Borghi (r), Najarian (r), tackles; DeJong (l), Poddig (r), guards; Hileman, Papais, centers; Celeri, Minahen, Erb, quarterbacks; Keckley (l), Sarver (l), Dal Porto (l), Montagne (r), Webster (r), halfbacks;; Lotter, Brunk, Navarro, fullbacks.

1950

Ohio State	0	0	14	3	17
California	0	7	7	0	14

Ohio State—Touchdowns: Morrison (1, center dive), Krall (2, right tackle). Field goal: Hague (28, placekick). Points after touchdown: Hague 2.
California—Touchdowns: Monachino 2 (7, left tackle; 44, left end). Points after touchdown: Cullom 2.

Ohio State		California
Schnittker	LE	Begovich
O'Hanlon	LT	Cullom
Toneff	LG	DeJong
Lininger	C	Richter
Biltz	RG	Franz (c-c)
Wilson (c)	RT	Turner (c-c)
Hague	RE	Pressley
Savic	QB	Celeri
Krall	LH	Brunk
Hamilton	RH	Monachino
Morrison	FB	Schabarum

STATISTICS

Ohio State		California
19	First downs	12
221	Net yards rushing	133
14	Passes attempted	13
5	Passes completed	3
1	Passes had intercepted	4
34	Net yards passing	106
255	Total net yards	239
4	Number of punts	6
28.5	Punting average	22.5
1	Fumbles lost	0
50	Yards penalized	45

Substitutions—Ohio State: Armstrong (l), Gilbert (l), Watson (r), ends; Jennings (l), Miller (l), Wittman (l), Trautwein (r), Edwards (r), tackles; Mattey (l), Manz (l), Thomas (r) Wittman (r), guards; McCullough, Heid, centers; Widdoes, Wertz, quarterbacks; Swinehart (l), Newell (l), Klevay (r), Sturtz (r), halfbacks; Janowicz, Perini, Gandee, fullbacks. California: Minahen (l), Bartlett (l), Souza (l), LemMon (l), Cummings (r), ends; Muehlberger (l), Nelson (l), Jones (r), Schmalenberger (r), tackles; Klein (l), Harris (l), Solari (l), Dodds (r), Fox (r), guards; Humpert, Stathakis, Harris, centers; Erb, Van Heuit, quarterbacks; Baldwin (l), Montagne (r), halfbacks; Robison, Groger, fullbacks.

1951

| Michigan | 0 | 0 | 0 | 14 | 14 |
| California | 0 | 6 | 0 | 0 | 6 |

Michigan—Touchdowns: Dufek 2 (1, right guard; 7, right end). Points after touchdown: Allis 2.

California—Touchdown: Cummings (39, pass from Marinos of 32, run of 7).

Michigan		California
Perry	LE	Fitzgerald
Johnson	LT	Karpe
Kinyon	LG	Laster
Kreager	C	Harris
Wolter	RG	Bagley
Wahl (c)	RT	Krueger
Allis	RE	Cummings
Putich	QB	Marinos
Ortmann	LH	Monachino
Koceski	RH	Schabarum
Dufek	FB	Olszewski

STATISTICS

Michigan		California
17	First downs	12
145	Net yards rushing	175
21	Passes attempted	8
15	Passes completed	4
2	Passes had intercepted	0
146	Net yards passing	69
291	Total net yards	244
2	Number of punts	4
32.5	Punting average	33.7
2	Fumbles lost	2
20	Yards penalized	50

Substitutions—Michigan: Clark (l), Pickard (l), Green (r), Popp (r), ends; Zatkoff (l), Ohlenroth (r), Stribe (r), tackles; McWilliams (l), Strozewski (l), Kelsey (r), Timm (r), Jackson (r), guards; Momsen, Padjen, centers; Palmer, Topor, quarterbacks; Osterman (l), Bradford (r), Peterson (r), halfbacks; Straffon, fullback. California: Minahen (l), Ward (l), Bartlett (l), Beal (r), Parker (r), ends; Gulvin (l), Curran (r), tackles; Solari (l), Mering (l), Richter (r), Wardlaw (r), Ely (r), guards; Groger, Cadenasso, centers; Ogden, Van Heuit, quarterbacks; Pappa (l), Robison (l), West (r), LemMon (r), halfbacks; Braham, Richter, fullbacks.

1952

| Illinois | 6 | 0 | 7 | 27 | 40 |
| Stanford | 7 | 0 | 0 | 0 | 7 |

Illinois—Touchdowns: Bachouros (6, right tackle), W. Tate 2 (5, right end; 8, right end), Karras (7, left end), D. Stevens (7, right tackle), Ryan (6, pass from Engels). Points after touchdown: Rebecca 4.

Stanford—Touchdown: Hugasian (1, right guard). Point after touchdown: Kerkorian.

Illinois		Stanford
Vernasco	LE	Storum
Ulrich	LT	Vick
Studley (c)	LG	Manoogian
Sabino	C	Garner
Gnidovic	RG	Bonetti
Jenkins	RT	Pyle
Smith	RE	McColl
O'Connell	QB	Kerkorian
Bachouros	LH	Hugasian
Karras	RH	Cook
W. Tate	FB	Meyers

STATISTICS

Illinois		Stanford
19	First downs	16
361	Net yards rushing	53
15	Passes attempted	29
7	Passes completed	14
1	Passes had intercepted	3
73	Net yards passing	180
434	Total net yards	233
2	Number of punts	6
50.5	Punting average	30.3
0	Fumbles lost	0
43	Yards penalized	50

Substitutions—Illinois: Wodziak (l), Nosek (l), Waldbeser (r), L. Stevens (r), Ryan (r), ends; Berschet (l), Baughman (l), Kasap (l), Weddell (r), D. Tate (r), Peterson (r), tackles; Lenzini (l), Valentino (l), Boerio (r), Ernst (r), Murphy (r), Bauer (r), guards; Popa, Cole, Borman, Luhrsen, centers; Engels, Henss, Rebecca, quarterbacks; D. Stevens (l), Neathery (l), Dusenbury (l), Taliaferro (l), Wallace (r), Miller (r), De Moss (r), halfbacks; Brosky, Duke, fullbacks. Stanford: Rye (l), Morley (l), Hoegh (l), Tennefoss (l), Eadie (r), Steinberg (r), ends; Latham (l), Hokanson (l), Calfee (l), Kirkland (r), Broderick (r), tackles; King (l), Griffin (l), Powell (l), Cone (r), Essegian (r), Powell (r), guards; Tobin, Worley, Tanner, centers; Garrett, Horn, quarterbacks; McKay (l), Thompson (l), Laubscher (r), St. Geme (r), halfbacks; Mathias, Crist, Sanders, fullbacks.

1953

| Southern California | 0 | 0 | 7 | 0 | 7 |
| Wisconsin | 0 | 0 | 0 | 0 | 0 |

Southern California—Touchdown: Carmichael (22, pass from Bukich). Point after touchdown: Tsagalakis.

Southern California		Wisconsin
Miller	LE	Peters
Thompson	LT	Prchlik
Willhoite	LG	Steinmetz
Welsh (c-c)	C	Simkowski
Cox	RG	Stensby
Weeks	RT	Suminski
Nickoloff	RE	Andrykowski
Bozanic	QB	Haluska
Sears	LH	Hutchinson
Carmichael	RH	Witt
Sellers	FB	Ameche

STATISTICS

Southern California		Wisconsin
16	First downs	19
48	Net yards rushing	211
27	Passes attempted	26
18	Passes completed	11
2	Passes had intercepted	2
185	Net yards passing	142
233	Total net yards	353
8	Number of punts	5
52	Punting average	39.2
0	Fumbles lost	1
62	Yards penalized	20

Substitutions—Southern California: Hattig (l), Stillwell (l), Hooks (r), Petty (r), ends; Ane (l), Ashcraft (l), Fouch (l), Van Doren (c-c), (r), Da Re (r), tackles; Pucci (l), Peviani (r), Pavich (r), guards; Timberlake, center; Goux, Riddle, quarterbacks; Bukich (l), Welch (l), Dandoy (l), Crow (r), Kirkland (r), Exley (r), halfbacks; Han, Koch, Tsagalakis, fullbacks. Wisconsin: Wuhrman (l), Esser (l), Lundin (l), Voss (r), Locklin (r), ends; Hoegh (l), Ursin (l), Berndt (r), Martin (r), Gulseth (r), tackles; Kennedy (l), Brandt (l), O'Brien (r), Amundsen (r), guards; Durkin, Messner, centers; Hable, quarterback; Canny (l), Carl (l), Shwaiko (l), Gingrass (l), Dornburg (r), Burks (r), halfbacks; Lamphere, Dixon, fullbacks.

1954

Michigan State	0	7	14	7	28
UCLA	7	7	0	6	20

Michigan State—Touchdowns: Duckett (blocked Cameron's punt from UCLA 25, recovered on 6 and carried over), Bolden (1, left guard), Wells 2 (2, left tackle; 62, punt return). Points after touchdown: Slonac 4.

UCLA—Touchdowns: Stits (13, pass from Cameron), Cameron (2, left tackle), Loudd (28, pass from Cameron). Points after touchdown: Herman 2.

Michigan State		*UCLA*
Duckett	LE	Heydenfeldt
Jebb	LT	Ellena
Hallmark	LG	Boghosian
Neal	C	Pauly
Bullough	RG	Feldman
Fowler	RT	Doud
Dohoney	RE	Berliner
Yewcic	QB	Foster
Bolden	LH	Cameron
Wells	RH	Stits
Slonac	FB	Dailey

STATISTICS

Michigan State		*UCLA*
14	First downs	16
195	Net yards rushing	90
10	Passes attempted	24
2	Passes completed	9
1	Passes had intercepted	2
11	Net yards passing	152
206	Total net yards	242
5	Number of punts	6
35.4	Punting average	38.6
4	Fumbles lost	3
15	Yards penalized	30

Substitutions—Michigan State: Quinlan (l), Lewis (l), Knight (l), Kauth (r), Diener (r), W. Postula (r), ends; Nystrom (l), Frank (l), Robinson (l), Murphy (r), Dotsch (r), tackles; Hollern (l), Ross (l), guards; Badaczewski, Rody, centers; Morall, Matsock, quarterbacks; Ellis (l), Zagers (l), halfbacks; Planutis, V. Postula, fullbacks. UCLA: Smith (l), Loudd (l), Long (l), Smith (l), ends; Benjamin (l), Britten (l), Andrews (l), Ray (r), Moreno (r), tackles; Cureton (l), Levy (l), Salsbury (r), guards; Peterson, center; Debay, Okuneff, quarterbacks; Villanueva (l), Brown (l), Davis (l), Stalwick (r), Hermann (r), halfbacks; Davenport, fullback.

1955

Ohio State	0	14	0	6	20
Southern California	0	7	0	0	7

Ohio State—Touchdowns: Leggett (3, left guard), Watkins (21, pass from Leggett of 12, run of 9), Harkrader (9, left end). Points after touchdown: Weed, Watkins.

Southern California—Touchdown: Dandoy (86, punt return). Point after touchdown: Tsagalakis.

Ohio State		*Southern California*
Dugger	LE	Clarke
Hilinski	LT	Da Re
D. Williams	LG	Galli
Thornton	C	Goux
Reichenbach	RG	Ferrante
Machinsky	RT	Fouch
Brubabaker	RE	Greenwood
Leggett	QB	Contratto
Cassady	LH	Dandoy
Watkins	RH	Crow
Bobo	FB	Duvall

STATISTICS

Ohio State		*Southern California*
22	First downs	6
305	Net yards rushing	177
11	Passes attempted	8
6	Passes completed	3
1	Passes had intercepted	0
65	Net yards passing	29
370	Total net yards	206
4	Number of punts	5
38.3	Punting average	46.6
0	Fumbles lost	3
40	Yards penalized	60

Substitutions—Ohio State: Michael (l), Spears (l), Ellwood (l), Ludwig (r), Kriss (r), Collmar (r), ends; Swartz (l), Stoeckel (l), Krisher (r), Guy (r), Cummings (r), tackles; Parker (l), Jobko (l), Howley (l), Weaver (r), Blazeff (r), Ramser (r), guards; Vargo, Bond, Dillman, centers; Booth, Weed, quarterbacks; Howell (l), Archer (l), Roseboro (r), Young (r), Harkrader (r), Thompson (r), halfbacks; Gibbs, Vicic, L. Williams, fullbacks. Southern California: Leimbach (l), McFarland (l), Perpich (l), Bordier (r), Griffith (r), Hilario (r), ends; Belotti (l), Fletcher (l), Westphal (l), Pavich (r), Adams (r), Smith (r), tackles; Miller (l), Isaacson (l), Torena (l), Spector (r), Enright (r), Willott (r), guards; Sampson, Eldredge, centers; Hall, Kissinger, quarterbacks; Arnett (l), Clayton (l), Pierce (l), Calabria (r), Merk (r), halfbacks; Brown, Tisdale, Kurlak, Tsagalakis, fullbacks.

1956

Michigan State	0	7	0	10	17
UCLA	7	0	0	7	14

Michigan State—Touchdowns: Peaks (13, pass from Morrall of 12, run of 1), Lewis (67, pass from Peaks of 30, run of 37). Field goal: Kaiser (41, place kick). Points after touchdown: Planutis 2.

UCLA—Touchdowns: Davenport (2, left guard), Peters (1, dive). Points after touchdown: Decker 2.

Michigan State		*UCLA*
Lewis	LE	Hermann
Masters	LT	White
Currie	LG	Cureton
Badaczewski	C	Palmer
Nystrom (c)	RG	Moreno
Haidys	RT	J. Brown
Kaiser	RE	Loudd
Morrall	QB	Ballard
Peaks	LH	S. Brown
Kowalczyk	RH	Decker
Planutis	FB	Davenport

Michigan State		UCLA
18	First downs	13
251	Net yards rushing	136
18	Passes attempted	10
6	Passes completed	2
2	Passes had intercepted	1
130	Net yards passing	61
381	Total net yards	197
2	Number of punts	7
40	Punting average	39.6
1	Fumbles lost	0
98	Yards penalized	60

Substitutions—Michichan State: Kolodziej (l), Jones (l), Jewett (l), Hinesly (r), ends; Rutledge (l), Burke (r), tackles; Matsos (l), Hollern (r), guards; Matsko, center; Wilson, quarterback; Mendyk (l), Wulff (r), Zysk (r), Gaddini (r), halfbacks; Lowe, fullback. UCLA: J. Smith (l), O'Garro (l), Adams (r), H. Smith (r), ends; Shinnick (l), Hampton (l), Penner (r), tackles; Birren (l), Harris (r), guards; Matheny, center; Bergdahl, quarterback; Bradley (l), Knox (l), Hollaway (r), halfbacks; Peters, fullback.

1957

Iowa	17	7	7	7	35
Oregon State	0	6	6	7	19

Iowa—Touchdowns: Ploen (49, right end), Hagler 2 (9, left tackle; 66, left guard), Happel (5, left end), Gibbons (16, pass from Ploen). Points after touchdown: Prescott 5.

Oregon State—Touchdowns: Berry (3, left guard), Beamer (1, center plunge), Hammack (35, pass from Francis of 33, run of 2). Points after touchdown: Beamer (plunge).

Iowa		Oregon State
Gibbons	LE	Thiel
A. Karras	LT	Witte
Bloomquist	LG	Sniffen
Suchy (c-c)	C	Corrick (c-c)
Commings	RG	Brackins
Klein	RT	Jesmer
Gilliam	RE	DeGrant
Ploen	QB	Laird (c-c)
Dobrino	LH	Francis
Hagler	RH	Durden
Nocera	FB	Berry

STATISTICS

Iowa		Oregon State
16	First downs	16
301	Net yards rushing	166
15	Passes attempted	14
11	Passes completed	10
1	Passes had intercepted	0
107	Net yards passing	130
408	Total net yards	296
2	Number of punts	3
36	Punting average	35
3	Fumbles lost	3
50	Yards penalized	60

Substitutions—Iowa: Ahlgren (l), Haussman (l), Jenkinson (l), Prescott (r), Hatch (r), ends; Burroughs (l), Kress (l), Scott (l), Deasy (c-c) (r), Rigney (r), tackles; Theer (l), Grouwinkel (l), Drake (r), P. Karras (r), guards; Pierce, Lewis, centers; Duncan, Veit, Coppotelli, quarterbacks; Gravel (l), Kloewer (l), Knotts (l), Happel (r), Furlong (r), halfbacks; Harris, Walker, Janda,

Stifter, fullbacks. Oregon State: Fournier (l), Negri (r), Clarke (r), ends; Zwahlen (l), Bates (r), Rogers (r), tackles; McKittrick (l), Ellison (r), guards; Randall, Anagnos, centers; Searle, Lukehart, quarterbacks; Lowe (l), Arana (l), Hammack (r), Marsh (r), Owings (r), halfbacks; Beamer, Milum, fullbacks.

1958

Ohio State	7	0	0	3	10
Oregon	0	7	0	0	7

Ohio State—Touchdown: Kremblas (1, sneak). Point after touchdown: Kremblas. Field goal: Sutherin (34, placekick).

Oregon—Touchdown: Shanley (5, left end). Point after touchdown: Morris.

Ohio State		Oregon
Houston	LE	Wheeler
Schafrath	LT	Kershner
Jobko	LG	Mondale (c-c)
Fronk	C	Peterson
Thomas	RG	Grottkau
Marshall	RT	Linden
Bowermaster	RE	Stover
Kremblas	QB	Crabtree
LeBeau	LH	Tourville
Cannavino	RH	Shanley (c-c)
White	FB	Morris (c-c)

STATISTICS

Ohio State		Oregon
19	First downs	21
245	Net yards rushing	160
6	Passes attempted	21
2	Passes completed	14
0	Passes had intercepted	2
59	Net yards passing	191
304	Total net yards	351
2	Number of punts	0
19	Punting average	0
0	Fumbles lost	2
15	Yards penalized	25

Substitutions—Ohio State: Morgan (r), Brown (c-c) (r), ends; Crawford (l), Arnold (r), tackles; Baldacci (l), Spychalski (r), guards; White, James, centers; Okulovich, quarterback; Clark (l), Sutherin (l), Trivisonno (r), Sutherin (r), halfbacks; Cisco (c-c), fullback. Oregon: Kimbrough (l), Brenn (l), Altenhofen (r), Robinson (r), ends; Aschbacher (l), Willener (l), Keele (r), White (r), Frost (r), tackles; Schaffeld (l), Heard (l), Newsom (l), Reeve (r), Todd (r), guards; Fish, Powell, centers; Fraser, Grover, quarterbacks; West (l), Phelps (l), Read (r), Laudenslager (r), halfbacks; Osborne, Holland, fullbacks.

1959

Iowa	7	13	12	6	38
California	0	0	6	6	12

Iowa—Touchdowns: Fleming 2 (37, left tackle; 7, left tackle), Duncan (1, right guard), Langston (7, pass from Duncan), Horn (4, center), Jeter (81, right tackle). Points after touchdown: Prescott 2.

California—Touchdowns: Hart 2 (1, right guard; 17, pass from Kapp).

Iowa		California
Langston	LE	Lundgren
Burroughs	LT	Newell
Grouwinkel	LG	Domoto

Iowa		California
Lapham	C	Jones
Drake	RG	Piestrup
Lewis	RT	Sally
Norton	RE	T. Bates
Duncan	QB	Kapp (c-c)
Jeter	LH	Olguin
Fleming	RH	Hart (c-c)
Nocera (c)	FB	Patton

STATISTICS

Iowa		California
24	First downs	20
429	Net yards rushing	214
14	Passes attempted	20
9	Passes completed	9
0	Passes had intercepted	2
87	Net yards passing	130
516	Total net yards	344
3	Number of punts	5
40.7	Punting average	37
1	Fumbles lost	2
55	Yards penalized	35

Substitutions—Iowa: Miller (l), Merz (l), Prescott (r), Spaan (r), Clauson (r), ends; Lee (l), Scott (l), Sawin (r),, Hain (r), tackles; Novack (l), Ringer (l), Mielke (l), Clark (l), Shipanik (r), Manders (r), Dunn (r), Sonnenberg (r), guards; Humphreys, Turner, Leshyn, centers; Ogiego, Treadway, Moore, quarterbacks; Furlong (l), Gravel (l), McMeekins (l), Jauch (r), Mauren (r), Gajda (r), halfbacks; Horn, Brown, Long, Mosley, fullbacks. California: Holston (l), George (l), Fraser (l), Huber (r), Cooper (r), ends; Streshly (l), Dinkler (l), Michael (r), Thomas (r), tackles; Green (l), Gonzales (l), Lasher (r), Snow (r), Johnson (r), Byrd (r), guards; Segale, Doretti, centers; Parque, quarterback; S. Bates (l), Garvin (r), Crow (r), halfbacks; Arnold, Yerman, Perrin, fullbacks.

1960

Washington	17	7	7	13	44
Wisconsin	0	8	0	0	8

Washington—Touchdowns: McKeta (6, right end), Fleming (53, punt return), Folkins (23, pass from Schloredt), Jackson (2, right tackle), Schloredt (3, left tackle), Millich (1, pass from Hivner). Points after touchdown: Fleming 5. Field goal: Fleming (36, placekick).

Wisconsin—Touchdown: Wiesner (4, left tackle). Points after touchdown: Schoonover (pass from Hackbart).

Washington		Wisconsin
Folkins	LE	Schoonover
Gegner	LT	Lanphear
Allen	LG	Perkins
McKasson	C	Nelson
Kinnune	RG	Stalcup (c-c)
B. Bullard	RT	Heineke
Meyers	RE	Derleth
Schloredt	QB	Hackbart
Fleming	LH	Hobbs
McKeta	RH	Zeman (c-c)
Jackson	FB	Hart

STATISTICS

Washington		Wisconsin
16	First downs	13
215	Net yards rushing	123
13	Passes attempted	32

STATISTICS

Washington		Wisconsin
7	Passes completed	14
0	Passes had intercepted	0
137	Net yards passing	153
352	Total net yards	276
6	Number of punts	6
36	Punting average	36
0	Fumbles lost	4
85	Yards penalized	18

Substitutions—Washington: Claridge (l), Peasley (l), Quessenberry (r), Chapple (r), ends; White (l), Cordes (l), Echols (r), Davidson (r), Enslow (r), tackles; Walters (l), Clanton (l), Skaggs (r), Crawford (r), guards; Pitt, F. Bullard, Dunn, Nelson, centers; Hivner, Everett, quarterbacks; Millich (l), Gayton (l), Wooten (r), halfbacks; Jones, Hurworth, Wheatley, fullbacks. Wisconsin: Holmes (l), Rogers (r), ends; Holzwarth (l), Huxhold (l), Jenkins (r), Moore (r), Zouvas (r), tackles; Schade (l), Kulcinski (r), guards; Gotta, center; Bakken, quarterback; Clark (l), Kunesh (r), halfbacks; Wiesner, Neumann, fullbacks.

1961

Washington	3	14	0	0	17
Minnesota	0	0	7	0	7

Washington—Touchdowns: Wooten (4, pass from Schloredt of 1, run of 3), Schloredt (1, left tackle sneak). Points after touchdown: Fleming 2. Field goal: Fleming (44, placekick).

Minnesota—Touchdown: Munsey (18, left end). Point after touchdown: Rogers.

Washington		Minnesota
Claridge	LE	R. Larson
Gegner	LT	Bell
Allen	LG	Mulvena
McKasson	C	G. Larson (c)
Kinnune	RG	Brown
Enslow	RT	Brixius
Chapple	RE	Deegan
Hivner	QB	Stephens
Fleming	LH	Dickson
McKeta	RH	Munsey
Jackson	FB	Hagberg

STATISTICS

Washington		Minnesota
11	First downs	14
177	Net yards rushing	202
5	Passes attempted	18
2	Passes completed	5
0	Passes had intercepted	3
16	Net yards passing	51
193	Total net yards	253
8	Number of punts	6
41.3	Punting average	43.3
2	Fumbles lost	0
50	Yards penalized	35

Substitutions—Washington: Folkins (l), Meyers (r), Davidson (r), ends; Mansfield (l), B. Bullard (l), tackles; Hurworth (l), Skaggs (r), Scheyer (r), T. Bullard (r), Locknane (r), guards; Nelson, center; Schloredt, Jorgensen, quarterbacks; Mitchell (l), Wooten (r), halfbacks. Minnesota: Prawdzik (l), Hall (r), ends; Frisbee (l), Miller (r), Wheeler (r), tackles; Hook (l), Tellor (l), Odegard (r), Perkovich (r), guards; Annis, center; Johnson, Salem, quarterbacks; Mulholland (l), Kauth (r), King (r), halfbacks; Enga, Rogers, fullbacks.

1962

Minnesota	7	7	0	7	21
UCLA	3	0	0	3	3

Minnesota—Touchdowns: Stephens 2 (1, left guard; 2, left tackle). Munsey (3, left guard). Points after touchdown: Loechler 3.

UCLA—Field goal: B. Smith (28, placekick).

Minnesota		UCLA
Hall	LE	Vena
Eller	LT	Andersen
Hook	LG	Macari
Frisbee	C	Hull
Tellor	RG	Paton
Bell	RT	Shirk
Deegan	RE	Gutman
Stephens	QB	Stevens
Mulholland	LH	B. Smith
Munsey	RH	Alexander
Dickson	FB	Thompson

STATISTICS

Minnesota		UCLA
21	First downs	8
222	Net yards rushing	55
11	Passes attempted	8
7	Passes completed	5
0	Passes had intercepted	0
75	Net yards passing	52
297	Total net yards	107
3	Number of punts	5
40	Punting average	37
2	Fumbles lost	2
70	Yards penalized	5

Substitutions—Minnesota: Park (l), Prawdzik (l), Rognlie (l), Campbell (r), Rude (r), Lothner (r), ends; Wheeler (l), Tyskiewicz (l), Maus (l), Loechler (r), Sunde (r), Schwantz (r), tackles; Mulvena (l), McNeil (l), Hartse (l), Perkovich (r), Mudd (r), guards; Enga, center; Teigen, Pelletier, Blaska, quarterbacks; King (l), Fischer (l), Cashman (l), Cairns (r), Smith (r), halfbacks; Jones, Benson, fullbacks. UCLA: Profit (l), Geverink (l), Hicks (r), Gibbs (r), ends; Fiorentino (l), S. Bauwens (l), Jones (l), Oram (r), Weeden (r), tackles; J. Bauwens (l), Allen (l), Stout (r), Dathe (r), guards; Von Sonn, Truesdell, centers; Walker, LoCurto, quarterbacks; Singleton (l), Haffner (l), Jenson (l), R. Smith (r), DiPoalo (r), Rosenkrans (r), halfbacks; Dimkich, Zeno, Rojas, fullbacks.

1963

Southern California	7	14	14	7	42
Wisconsin	7	0	7	23	37

Southern California—Touchdowns: Bedsole 2 (57, pass from Beathard of 5, run of 52; 23, pass from Beathard), Butcher (13, pass from Beathard of 9, run of 4), Wilson (1, left tackle), Heller (25, right end), F. Hill (13, pass from Beathard). Points after touchdown: Lupo 6.

Wisconsin—Touchdowns: Kurek (1, left tackle), VanderKelen (17, right end), Holland (13, right end), Kroner (4, pass from VanderKelen), Richter (19, pass from VanderKelen of 16, run of 3). Points after touchdown: Kroner 5. Safety: Lubisich's center snap to E. Jones from Southern California 25 went over punter's head who downed it in the end zone.

Southern California		Wisconsin
Bedsole	LE	Leafblad
Kirner	LT	Pillath

Southern California		Wisconsin
Fisk	LG	Gross
Sagouspe	C	Bowan
Lubisich	RG	Underwood
Marinovich	RT	Wojdula
Pye	RE	Richter
Beathard	QB	Norvell
Brown	LH	Holland
Del Conte	RH	Kroner
Byrd	FB	Kurek

STATISTICS

Southern California		Wisconsin
15	First downs	32
114	Net yards rushing	67
20	Passes attempted	49
10	Passes completed	34
0	Passes had intercepted	3
253	Net yards passing	419
367	Total net yards	486
5	Number of punts	4
40.4	Punting average	40.3
1	Fumbles lost	0
93	Yards penalized	77

Substitutions—Southern California: Hoover (l), E. Jones (l), Thurlow (l), Brownwood (r), F. Hill (r), Potter (r), Austin (r), ends; Byrd (l), Butcher (l), Eaton (r), R. Jones (r), Gonta (r), tackles; Johnson (l), Svihus (l), Ratliff (l), Smedley (r), Gonta (r), guards; Schmidt, Sanchez, centers; Lupo, Nelsen, quarterbacks; Clark (l), G. Hill (l), Heller (r), Hunt (r), halfbacks; Bame, Wilson, McMahon, E. Jones, Pye, fullbacks. Wisconsin: Carlson (l), Ezerins (l), Howard (r), ends; Bernet (l), Jacobazzi (r), tackles; Paar (l), Monk (l), Schenk (r), guards; Heckl, Bruhn, centers; VanderKelen, Frain, Reichardt, quarterbacks; Nettles (l), Silvestri (l), W. Smith (r), R. Smith (r), halfbacks; Purnell, Norvell, fullbacks.

1964

Illinois	0	3	7	7	17
Washington	0	7	0	0	7

Illinois—Field goal: Plankenhorn, 32. Touchdowns: Warren (1, run) Grabowski (1, run). Points after touchdown: Plankenhorn, 2.

Washington: Touchdown: Kopay (7, run). Point after touchdown: Medved.

STATISTICS

Illinois		Washington
22	First downs	12
291	Rushing yards	114
59	Passing yards	69
6-15	Passes	8-19
3	Interceptions by	0
4 for 39	Punts	3 for 43
3	Fumbles lost	3
64	Yards penalized	25

Substitutions—Illinois: Schumacher, Callaghan, Mueller, Summers, Rutherford, Russell, ends; Sutton, Minor, Easter, Fitzgerald, Greco, Eickman, Hochleutner, tackles; Fox, Deller, Powless, Washington, Stewart, Saunders, Wainwright, guards; Plankenhorn, Butkus, Capel, centers; Taliaferro, Custardo, Donnelly, Acks, Dorr, quarterbacks; Dundy, Price, Paulson, McCaskill, D. Anderson, Warren, Fearn, Lee, Jackson, halfbacks; Grabowski, Wheatland, Hansen, Parola, N. Anderson, fullbacks. Washington: Libke, Hainz, Winters, Mancuso, Greenlee, ends; Kupa,

J. Knoll, Briggs, Norton, tackles; Redman, Otis, O'Brien, Hagen, Sartin, guards; Forsberg, center; Douglas, Siler, Sampson, Hullin, quarterbacks; Medved, Stroud, Kopay, Bramwell, halfbacks; Browning, Kukenski, Coffey, fullbacks.

1965

| Michigan | 0 | 12 | 15 | 7 | 34 |
| Oregon State | 0 | 7 | 0 | 0 | 7 |

Oregon State—McDougal, 5, pass from Brothers (Clark, kick).
Michigan—Anthony, 84, run (kick failed); Ward, 43, run (pass failed); Anthony, 1, run (Timberlake, run); Anthony, 7, run, (Timberlake, kick); Timberlake, 24, run (Sygar, kick).

STATISTICS

Michigan		Oregon State
18	First downs	14
332	Rushing yards	64
132	Passing yards	175
8-15	Passing	19-33
0	Interceptions by	0
5 for 33.6	Punts	9 for 44
1	Fumbles lost	1
55	Yards penalized	57

Substitutions—Michigan: Farabee, Conley, S. Smith, Wilhite, Henderson, Laskey, Hoyne, Kirby, ends; Kines, Mader, Bailey, Ruzicka, Yearby, Mack, Haverstock, tackles; Butler, Simkus, Hahn, Flanagan, Marcum Mielke, guards; Patchen, Cecchini, Muir, centers; Timberlake, Sygar, Evaskshevski, Gabler, quarterbacks; Detwiler, Volk, Lee, Parkhill, Ward, Rindfuss, Wells, Bass, halfbacks; Anthony, Nunley, Fisher, Dehlin, Schick, fullbacks. Oregon State: Grim, Hartman, Bell, Miller, McDougald, East, Freketich, Sullivan, Coccione, ends; Stellmacher, Rozario, Bruaren, Aarts, Koeper, Carr, Wilkin, tackles; Cole, Winton, Heacock, Gould, Funston, John, Neil, guards; Keeney, O'Billovich, Freitas, Sucklin, Graham, centers; Brothers, Espalin, Queen, quarterbacks; Watkins, Shaw, Crowston, Moreland, J. Smith, Osmer, halfbacks; Washington, Ruhl, fullbacks.

1966

| U.C.L.A. | 0 | 14 | 0 | 0 | 14 |
| Michigan State | 0 | 0 | 0 | 12 | 12 |

UCLA: Beban, 1, run (Zimmerman, kick). Beban, 1, run Zimmerman, kick).

MSU: Apisa, 38, run (pass failed); Juday, 1, run (run failed).

STATISTICS

UCLA		*Michigan State*
10	First downs	13
65	Rushing yards	204
147	Passing	110
8-20	Passing yards	8-22
3	Interceptions by	0
11-40	Punts	5-42
2	Fumbles lost	2
86	Yards penalized	14

Substitutions—Michigan State: Proebstle, Washington, Viney, Richardson, Chatlos, Smith, Hoag, ends; Bierowicz, West, Przybycki, Owens, tackles; Jenkins, Karpinsky, Gallinagh, Lucas, Techlin, guards; Dimitroff, center; Juday, quarterback; C. Jones Lee, Garrett, Japinga, Phillips, J. Jones, Thornhill, Webster, Summers, Goovert, halfbacks; Cotton, Apisa, Kenney, fullbacks.
UCLA (Starting Line-up): Attenberg, Nelson, ends; Banducci, Slagle, tackles; Deakers, Leventhal, guards; Freedman, center; Beban, quarterback; Farr, Witcher, halfbacks; Horgan, fullback.

1967

| Purdue | 0 | 7 | 7 | 0 | 14 |
| Sthn. California | 0 | 7 | 0 | 6 | 13 |

Purdue—Williams, 1, run (Griese, kick). Williams, 2, run (Griese, kick).
U.S.C.—McCall, 1, run (Roosovich, kick). Sherman, 19, pass from Winslow (pass failed).

Purdue (14): Beirne, Griffin, Olson, Homes, ends; Barnes, Burke, Calcaterra, Rafa, Olssen, tackles; Erlenbaugh, Sebeck, Kyle, Piper, guards; Labus, center; King, Burke, Marvel, linebackers; Griese, Connors, Emch, quarterbacks; Baltzell, Finley, Hurst, Charles, Catavolos, Frame, Keyes, halfbacks; P. Williams, Cirbes, fullbacks.
U.S.C. (13): Rossovich, Almon, Cahill, Klein, Mayes, Miller, B. Hayhoe, ends; Yary, Magner, Moore, J. Hayhoe, Wells, Crane, tackles; Oliver, Petrill, Homan, Blanche, Scarpace, guards; Baccitich, center; Young, Snow, King, linebackers; Winslow, quarterback; McCall, Sherman, Lawrence, Cashman, Shaw, Jaronyck, Salness, Nyquist, halfbacks; H. Williams, Hull, fullbacks.

UNIVERSITY OF ILLINOIS

Founded: *1867*
Location: *CHAMPAIGN-URBANA*
Colors: *ORANGE AND BLUE*
Nickname: *FIGHTING ILLINI*
Total Enrollment: 27,020
Undergraduate: 20,640
Undergraduate Men: 13,743

INDIANA UNIVERSITY

Founded: *1820*
Location: *BLOOMINGTON*
Colors: *CREAM AND CRIMSON*
Nickname: *FIGHTIN' HOOSIERS*
Total Enrollment: 26,199
Undergraduate: 20,953
Undergraduate Men: 12,240

STATE UNIVERSITY OF IOWA

Founded: *1847*
Location: *IOWA CITY*
Colors: *OLD GOLD & BLACK*
Nickname: *HAWKEYES*
Total Enrollment: 14,480
Undergraduate: 10,222
Undergraduate Men: 5,250

UNIVERSITY OF MICHIGAN

Founded: *1837*
Location: *ANN ARBOR*
Colors: *MAIZE AND BLUE*
Nickname: *WOLVERINES*
Total Enrollment: 27,659
Undergraduate: 16,665
Undergraduate Men: 9,390

MICHIGAN STATE UNIVERSITY

Founded: *1855*
Location: *EAST LANSING*
Colors: *GREEN AND WHITE*
Nickname: *SPARTANS*
Total Enrollment: 31,268
Undergraduate: 25,603
Undergraduate Men: 14,632

UNIVERSITY OF MINNESOTA

Founded: *1851*
Location: *MINNEAPOLIS*
Colors: *MAROON AND GOLD*
Nickname: *GOPHERS*
Total Enrollment: 38,403
Undergraduate: 32,100
Undergraduate Men: 20,603

NORTHWESTERN UNIVERSITY

Founded: *1851*
Location: *EVANSTON, ILLINOIS*
Colors: *PURPLE AND WHITE*
Nickname: *WILDCATS*
Total Enrollment: 9,505
Undergraduate: 6,127
Undergraduate Men: 3,417

OHIO STATE UNIVERSITY

Founded: *1873*
Location: *COLUMBUS*
Colors: *SCARLET AND GRAY*
Nickname: *BUCKEYES*
Total Enrollment: 36,775
Undergraduate: 33,100
Undergraduate Men: 24,182

PURDUE UNIVERSITY

Founded: *1869*
Location: *LAFAYETTE, INDIANA*
Colors: *OLD GOLD AND BLACK*
Nickname: *BOILERMAKERS*
Total Enrollment: 19,700
Undergraduate: 15,400
Undergraduate Men: 11,348

UNIVERSITY OF WISCONSIN

Founded: *1849*
Location: *MADISON*
Colors: *CARDINAL AND WHITE*
Nickname: *BADGERS*
Campus Enrollment: 26,293
Undergraduate: 18,711
Undergraduate Men: 10,788

The famous Michigan-Minnesota Little Brown Jug, the first intercollegiate athletic trophy.

TRADITIONAL TROPHIES

TRADITIONAL BIG TEN TROPHIES

It was perhaps fitting that one of the most dramatic football games in Big Ten history should have produced the first—and now the most famous—of all intercollegiate athletic trophies—the famed Little Brown Jug that goes to the winner of the Michigan-Minnesota game each year.

From the time the awesome Michigan "point-a-minute" squads started dominating Conference football in 1901 until the streak ended in 1905, there was only one roadblock thrown up before the Maize and Blue steam-roller. In 1903 Michigan traveled to Minneapolis to meet high-scoring Minnesota, and the Gophers battled the visitors on even terms all the way. If there can be such a thing as a perfect stalemate, the 6-6 tie was it.

But, back to the Little Brown Jug . . .

These were the days when the visiting team not only thought that a sudden switch to the local drinking water could be harmful but it was not uncommon for a local sport to doctor the water if the visitors were dumb enough to fill up their jugs from local sources.

So, visiting teams brought along their own water in large stone jugs. In the excitement following the 6-6 tie, the Michigan trainer forgot to pick up the biggest Wolverine jug and it was confiscated by Oscar Munson, the Minnesota trainer. When the Wolverines returned to Ann Arbor, Fielding Yost, the Michigan coach, discovering the jug was missing, wrote Minnesota authorities to ship it home.

The reply he got, in essence, was "if you want it, come and get it!"

Nobody could mistake the clear challenge, although it wasn't until 1909 that the issue could be met again. Michigan returned to Minneapolis that year and somebody ostentatiously placed the big jug on the sidelines.

When the Wolverines whipped Minnesota 15-6 the Wolverine trainer dashed over to pick up the jug and take it back to Ann Arbor. There it was decorated in both Michigan and Minnesota

colors and inscribed with a suitable legend, along with the score of the game. From then on the jug was placed in an honored spot on the sidelines, to be claimed by the winner.

In 1925, the men's junior class honorary societies at Ohio State and Illinois came up with the second oldest Big Ten trophy for the winner of the annual Illini-Buckeye game. A live turtle—dubbed "Illibuck" to combine both school names—was envisioned as a durable symbol, with scores of 50 and more games carved on his back. The turtle disproved the antiquarian theory of its kind, however, and died about 10 years later. A wooden replica now serves the purpose.

Just about the same time that Illibuck crawled slowly toward immortality, Chicago alumni of Purdue and Indiana got hold of an old oaken bucket, found in a well in Indiana, and estimated to be more than 100 years old. Legend had it that Morgan's Raiders had used it to quench their thirst during an invasion of Yankee territory. The bucket was considered typically Hoosier memorabilia and the alumni gussied it up and offered it as a trophy for the annual bitter-ender between Purdue and Indiana. A chain made of bronze block "I" and "P" letters was planned for it. With each game the winner was to add a link of the school's initial. In case of ties a joint "IP" link was added.

The bucket has led a precarious existence because of student pranks. Once, at the beginning of the season it disappeared from the display case in the Purdue Field House and was gone for two months. At noon of the day of the game, late in November, a contingent from an Indiana fraternity marched into the living room of its brother chapter at Purdue and grinningly set the bucket on a table.

Another time, the bucket disappeared for months before an anonymous tip led a search party to a spot where it was buried in the basement of the Indiana University Library.

Once, after Indiana had upset Purdue, the bucket was shipped to Indianapolis where it was to be turned over to I.U. representatives. There, a railroad station agent turned it over to a group of students wearing Indiana sweaters who said they were an honor guard to escort the bucket to Bloomington. It never arrived. Again, it was a long time before *that* caper ended happily.

"Illibuck" commemorates the annual clash between Illinois and Ohio State.

The Old Oaken Bucket records the rivalry between Indiana and Purdue.

In 1935 Governor Clyde Herring of Iowa and Governor Floyd Olson of Minnesota agreed to bet a prize pig on the outcome of the Gopher-Hawkeye game. There had been bad blood and a lot of student tension because of incidents at the previous year's game and the wager was considered to be a bit of gubernatorial diplomacy aimed at patching things up. When Minnesota's national champions clobbered Iowa, the Iowa governor paid off with a full-blooded champion named

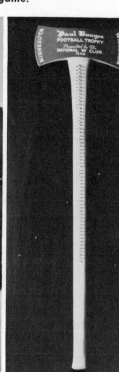

The Sweet Sue Tomahawk (left) goes each year to the winner of the Northwestern-Illinois game.

The Paul Bunyan Axe (right) is claimed annually by the victor of the Minnesota-Wisconsin game.

Floyd of Rosedale. At Minnesota the blue-blooded porker was the model for a bronzed statue 21 inches long, with a sash around the middle for game scores.

Other trophies, more recently established, include the Sweet Sioux Tomahawk, going to the winner of the Northwestern-Illinois game, the Paul Bunyan Axe for the victor of the Minnesota-Wisconsin game, and the Old Brass Spittoon to the winner of the Michigan State-Indiana game. The Indian skull-cracker originally started out as a substitute for the original series trophy—a life-sized wooden cigar store Indian. The chief, however, posed too much of a transportation problem and the handier tomahawk, a genuine article that may or may not have laid open an old-time settler's skull or two, was sanctified.

Spartan and Hoosier die-hards estimated the venerable brass spittoon, found at an old Michigan trading post, had been around when both universities were founded.

The Boilermakers and Illini battle yearly for possession of the Purdue-Illinois Cannon.

WHERE

ARE THEY NOW?

JACK NICKLAUS, Ohio State golf star of late-1950s; now leading pro; U.S. Open, Masters, British Open and P.G.A. titlist.

JACK DREES, Iowa basketball star of late-1930's; nationally-known CBS TV-Radio sportscaster.

NILS A. BOE, Wisconsin track star of mid-1930's; now Governor of South Dakota.

EARL B. HATHAWAY, Northwestern basketball ace in mid-1920's; now President, The Firestone Tire & Rubber Co., Akron, O.

WILLIAM H. ABBOTT, Chicago football and basketball star, mid-1920's; Vice-President, legal affairs, Minnesota Mining & Manufacturing Co., Minneapolis.

HOWARD MITHUN, Minnesota track ace, early-1930's; now Vice-President, Secretary & General Counsel, Minneapolis Star and Tribune Company.

ROBERT L. KESSLER, Purdue All-America cager of late 1930's; now General Manager, Buick Motor Division of General Motors, Flint, Mich.

GERALD R. FORD, Michigan grid star of early-1930's; now U.S. Congressman from Michigan, and House Minority Leader.

466 **PAUL G. JASPER,** Indiana football and cage star of late-1920's; now General Counsel, Public Service Company of Indiana.

MARTIN F. RUMMEL, Michigan State football star of mid-1920's; now Director of Purchasing & Production Control, Pontiac Motor Division of General Motors Corp., Detroit.

JAMES B. RESTON, Illinois golf ace of early-1930's; now emminent columnist and Associate Editor, The New York Times.

ALBERT O. NICHOLAS, Wisconsin basketball star of early-1950's; now assistant vice-president, Marshall & Isley Bank, Milwaukee.

JOHN E. ROBERTS, Wisconsin football and wrestling star of early 1940's; now Executive Director of Wisconsin Interscholastic Athletic Assn.

STUART W. SKOWBO, Iowa track star of early-1940's; vice-president, U.S. Plywood and Champion Paper Co., Hamilton, O.

LEONARD L. LOVSHIN, M.D.; Wisconsin grid star of mid-1930's; now eminent physician on staff of famed Cleveland Clinic.

WALTER MEHL, distance ace on Wisconsin track teams of late 1930's; now Minister of First Presbyterian Church, Edwardsville, Ill.

467

ELROY HIRSCH, great Wisconsin halfback of early 1940's; now Assistant to the President, The Los Angeles Rams.

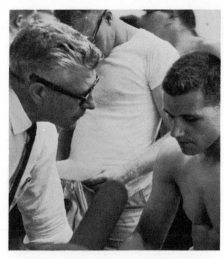

JAMES W. NELLEN, M.D., Wisconsin grid star of mid-1930's; now team physician for Green Bay Packers.

JAMES HULL, D.D.S., Ohio State All-America cager, 1939; now prominent Columbus orthodontist.

LEO HOEGH, Iowa swimming star of late-1920's; ex-Governor of Iowa; now prominent Denver attorney.

TIM LOWRY, Northwestern All-America football center, 1925; now outstanding Chicago attorney.

SAUL WEISLOW, Chicago grid star of the late 1920's; now vice-president, legal and business affairs, Bing Crosby Productions, Inc., Beverly Hills, Calif.

PRESCOTT JORDAN, M.D., Chicago football star of mid-1930's; prominent Detroit cardio-vascular surgeon.

MERRILL (BABE) MEIGS, great Chicago football lineman of early Stagg era; ex-publisher of Chicago Herald & Examiner and Chicago American; now business consultant.

A. WILLIAM HAARLOW, Chicago All-America cager of mid-1930's; General Traffic Manager, Illinois Bell Telephone Co., Chicago.

ROBERT E. MERRIAM, Chicago track star of late-1930's; President, University Patents, Inc., patent management and marketing, Chicago.

GEORGE NISSEN, Iowa gymnastics ace of mid-1940's; President, Nissen Trampoline and Gymnastics Equipment Co.

NOLDEN GENTRY, Iowa basketball ace of 1950's; now a leading attorney in Des Moines.

469

WILLIAM A. McCULLOUGH, Iowa swim star of 1920's; attorney, retired judge of Clinton Municipal and Juvenile Courts.

JUSTIN DART, Northwestern star football lineman and track ace of late 1920's; President, Rexall Drug and Chemical Co.

SID GILLMAN, star Ohio State end of early 1930's; now Coach and General Manager, San Diego Chargers, A.F.L.

SAMUEL L. DEVINE, Ohio State track star of mid-1930's; U.S. Congressman from Ohio.

KEO NAKAMA, Ohio State national swimming champ of 1940's; member, Hawaiian State Legislature.

PAUL A. EBERT, M.D.; Ohio State All-America basketball and baseball in mid-1950's; faculty member, Duke University Medical School.

LYLE H. FISHER, Northwestern basketball star of mid-1930's; Vice President, Minnesota Mining & Manufacturing Co., Minneapolis.

ARTHUR T. McINTOSH, JR., Northwestern track ace of early-1930's; now President, Arthur T. McIntosh Real Estate Co., Chicago.

EDWIN M. MARTIN, Northwestern tennis star of late-1920's; now United States Ambassador to Argentina.

ROBERT H. WIENECKE, Northwestern grid star of early-1920's; Chief-of-Staff, 82d Airborne in Italy and Normandy, World War II; Maj. Gen. U.S. Army, Ret.

BURTON M. JOSEPH, Minnesota hockey star of early 1940's; now President, I.S. Joseph Co., Grain Merchants, Minneapolis.

CHARLES DARLING, Iowa All-America basketball star of early-1950's; Senior exploration geologist, Phillips Petroleum Co., Shreveport, La.

EMLEN TUNNELL, Iowa grid star of early-1950's; assistant coach, New York Football Giants.

PAUL E. HUMPHREY, M.D., Purdue football star of late-1930's; now prominent urologist and surgeon, Terre Haute, Ind.

HARRY G. KEMMER, Purdue basketball and baseball star of late-1920's; now President, Kemmer Construction Co., Lafayette, Ind.

RICHARD C. POTTER, Purdue grid star of the late-1930's; now President, Northrop Institute of Technology, Inglewood, Calif.

472 HENRY (HANK) STRAM, Purdue football and baseball star in early-1940's; now head coach, Kansas City Chiefs of American Football League.

HARVEY S. OLSON, Purdue grid star of late-1920's; now President, Olson Travel Organization, Chicago.

RICHARD BATEMAN, Purdue football star, early-1930's; now President, Tri-State College, Angola, Ind.

CHARLES H. FENSKE, Wisconsin track great of late-1930's; now Vice-President, Oscar Meyer Meat Packing Co., Madison, Wisc.

R. CONRAD COOPER, Minnesota grid star of mid-1920's; now executive Vice-President for Personnel Services, United States Steel Corp.

HORACE D. BELL, M.D., outstanding Minnesota football lineman of late 1930's; now physician in South Bend, Ind.

MALVIN J. NYDAHL, Minnesota football, basketball and baseball star of mid-1920's; now orthopedic surgeon in Minneapolis.

GLENN E. SEIDEL, Minnesota brilliant quarterback of mid-1930's; now President, Marquette Corporation, Minneapolis.

CYRIL P. PESEK, Minnesota cage ace of mid-1920's; now Vice-President Minnesota Mining and Manufacturing Co., Minneapolis.

MARCUS W. K. HEFFELFINGER, Minnesota football and swimming ace of late 1940's; now Executive Vice-President, Peavey Company, Flour Mills, Minneapolis.

FRANK E. McNALLY, Minnesota track ace of early-1920's; now Chairman of the Board, B. F. Nelson Mfg. Co., Minneapolis.

MICHAEL N. (MICKEY) VUCHNICH, Ohio State star football center of early-1930's; President, Lincoln Electric Co. of Canada, Ltd.

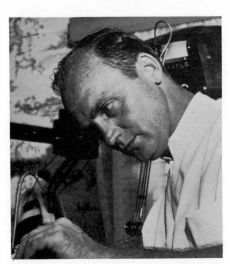

474   LESLIE HORVATH, D.D.S., Ohio State All-America and Heisman Trophy-winning halfback, 1944; prominent Los Angeles dentist.

JACK KELLER, Ohio State national hurdles champion in early-1930's; now managing editor, The Columbus Citizen-Journal.

WILLIAM F. PORTER, II, Northwestern Olympic hurdles champion of 1948; President, American Hospital Supply, Division of American Hospital Supply Corp.

C. DON CLAWSON, Northwestern grid and cage star of late 1930's; Chicago Manager, Mutual Life Insurance Co. of New York.

STEPHEN E. REID, M.D., Northwestern All-America football guard, 1936; prominent orthodpedist, Evanston, Ill.

CHARLES (CHIC) EVANS, Northwestern golf ace prior to World War I, and subsequent national star; founder of famed Chic Evans National Caddy Scholarship Program.

CHARLES CSURI, Ohio State All-America tackle, 1942; artist and Professor of Fine Arts, Ohio State University.

RICHARD T. BAKER, Ohio State basketball star, late-1930's; Managing Partner (President) Ernst & Ernst, Accounting, Cleveland.

DAVID D. ALBRITTON, Ohio State national high jump champion in mid-1930's; Member, Ohio State Legislature.

TOM HARMON, Michigan All-America halfback, 1939-40 and Heisman Trophy winner in '40; now nationally-famed ABC Television-Radio sportscaster, Los Angeles, Calif.

HARRY G. KIPKE, Michigan All-America halfback, 1922, and basketball and baseball star; Vice-President (ret.) and consultant to Coca Cola Export Co.

RICHARD K. DEGENER, Michigan diving champion of mid-1930's; now General Manager, Lear-Siegler Corp., Detroit.

476 ALLAN SEAGER, Michigan swim star, late-1920's; now outstanding author; professor of English, University of Michigan.

BRUCE L. HILKENE, Michigan grid star of mid-1930's; now Director of Salaried Personnel, Chevrolet Motor Division, General Motors Corp., Detroit.

ERNEST B. McCOY, Michigan basketball and baseball star of late-1920's; now Director of Athletics, Pennsylvania State University.

FRANCIS WISTERT, Michigan All-America lineman, 1933; now Vice-President, Autolite Co. (Eltra Corp.) Toledo, O.

DOUGLAS F. ROBY, Michigan football and baseball star of early-1920's; now President, American Metal Product, Detroit, and President of U.S. Olympic Committee.

LOUIS R. KING, JR., Iowa grid star, early-1950's; vice-president, sales, Amana Refrigeration, Inc., Amana, Iowa.

LOU SABAN, Indiana grid and track ace of early-1940's; now Head Coach and General Manager, Denver Broncos of American Football League.

EVAN HULTMAN, Iowa track star, early-1950's; Waterloo, Iowa attorney; ex-Attorney General of Iowa.

477

ROBERT L. DELLINGER, distance star on Indiana track squad, early-1950's; now Vice-President, Petersen Publishing Co., Los Angeles.

ROBERT H. MENKE, Indiana cage star of early-1940's; now President, Menke Furniture Manufacturing Co., Huntingburg, Ind.

TED KLUZEWSKI, Indiana grid ace of mid-1940's; ex-Cincinnati Reds star and now well-known restauranteur in Cincinnati.

JOHN S. PINGEL, Michigan State All-America halfback of 1938; now President, Ross Roy, Inc., Advertising, Detroit, Mich.

FRANK G. McINNIS, Michigan State baseball star of mid-1920's; now Director, Zoological Park Commission, City of Detroit.

FRANK GAINES, Jr., Michigan State grid star of mid-1930's; now Assistant Coordinator, Executive Development and Compensation Division, Standard Oil Company of New Jersey.

JACWEIR BRESLIN, Michigan State football, basketball and baseball star of mid-1940's; now Secretary of Michigan State University and Board of Trustees.

JOHN WOODEN, Purdue All-America cager, 1932; now head basketball coach at U.C.L.A. and three-time NCAA championship winner.

CAMPBELL KANE, Indiana track star of early-1940's; now an architect in Valparaiso, Ind.

GREGORY BELL, D.D.S., Indiana track star of late-1940's; now a dentist in Terre Haute, Ind.

ORVILLE FREEMAN, Minnesota grid star of late-1930's; now U.S. Secretary of Agriculture, Washington, D.C.

EARL R. LARSEN, Minnesota golf ace of early-1930's; now a Federal Judge, Minneapolis, Minn.

ARTHUR F. BRANDSTATTER, Michigan State grid star of mid-1930's; now Director of Michigan State University School of Police Administration.

ELLMORE C. PATTERSON, Chicago All-America football guard, 1934; Vice-Chairman, Morgan Guarantee Trust Co., New York City.

WALTER A. ARRINGTON, Michigan State track ace of late-1940's; Lt. Colonel and Chief of War Plans, Logistics, U.S. Air Force (ret.). now Depot Manager, General Services Admn., Washington, D.C.

SIDNEY P. WAGNER, Michigan State All-America guard, 1935; now Vice-President, Edward E. Gillen Construction Co., Milwaukee, Wisc.

ROBERT B. McCURRY, Michigan State grid star in late-1940's; now Vice-President and General Manager, Dodge Division of Chrysler Motors Corp., Detroit.

JAY BERWANGER, Chicago All-America halfback, 1934-35 and first Heisman Trophy winner; now prominent manufacturer's representative, Chicago.

RICHARD L. M. LORD, Michigan State All-America hockey, 1953; now consulting engineer, Montreal, Que.; Vice-President of Liberal Party of Quebec.

STEVE SEBO, Michigan State football and baseball star of mid-1930's; now Director of Athletics at University of Virginia.

HUGH J. WADE, Iowa football star of early-1930's; now Secretary of State, State of Alaska.

WILL LANG, outstanding Chicago basketballer of mid-1930's; now Director, News Bureaus, LIFE Magazine, New York City.

GEORGE HALAS, Illinois football, basketball and baseball star shortly before the 1920's; now Chairman and Head Coach, Chicago Bears, N.F.L.

DWIGHT (DIKE) EDDLEMAN, Illinois football, basketball and track ace of late-1940's; now Personnel Manager, Central Soya Co., Gibson City, Ill.

CHARLES H. PERCY, Chicago swimming and water polo star of late-1930's; now U.S. Senator from Illinois.

BERNIE A. SHIVELY, Illinois All-America football lineman, 1926; now Director of Athletics, University of Kentucky.

MARTIN BELOW, Wisconsin All-America end in 1923; Vice-President and General Sales Manager, Kieffer-Nolde Engraving Co., Milwaukee.

DONALD R. LAZ, Illinois' pole vault champion of early-1950's; now architect, Champaign-Urbana, Ill.

CHARLES S. GALBREATH, Illinois football star of mid-1930's; now Resident Vice-President, Merrill Lynch, Pierce, Fenner & Smith, Inc., Indianapolis.

BARTON A. CUMMINGS, Illinois basketball and track star, mid-1930's; now Chairman of the Board, Compton Advertising, Inc., New York.

FREDERICK S. GREEN, Illinois basketball luminary, late-1940's; now Circuit Court Judge, Champaign County, Ill.

CHARLES R. CARNEY, Illinois All-America football and basketball star, early-1920's; Investment Executive, Dominick & Dominick, Boston, Mass.

FRED HOVDE, Minnesota grid star of late-1920's and Rhodes Scholar; now President, Purdue University.

ALBERT H. VONDENBUSCH, Illinois wrestling star, mid-1920's; now Vice-President, Harris Trust and Savings Bank, Chicago.

FRED L. WHAM, Illinois football star prior to World War I; now U.S. District Judge, Centralia, Ill.

LELAND J. HAWORTH, Indiana baseball star of mid-1920's; now Director, National Science Foundation, Washington, D.C.

ELMER N. SLEIGHT, Purdue All-America tackle, 1929; now Vice-President, Gustin-Bacon Manufacturing Co., Chicago.

CLIFFORD C. FURNAS, Purdue track ace of early-1920's; President Emeritus, State University of New York at Buffalo, and President, Western New York Nuclear Research Center, Buffalo.

NOBLE L. BIDDINGER, Indiana track ace of mid-1930's; now President, City Securities Corp., Indianapolis, Ind.

PATRICK H. DEVINE, Indiana wrestling star of early-1930's; now Brigadier General, U.S. Army.

PAUL E. TOBIN, Indiana football and baseball star of mid-1920's; now Vice-President, White Trucks Division, the White Motor Co., Cleveland.

DON LASH, famed Indiana trackman of mid-1930's; now Regional Secretary Fellowship of Christian Athletes, Indianapolis, Ind.

BRAD BOMBA, M.D., Indiana football star of mid-1950's; now Bloomington, Ind., physician and Indiana University team physician.

SAMUEL DEVINE, Ohio State track star of mid-1930's; U.S. Congressman from Ohio.

OTTO GRAHAM, Northwestern All-America halfback of 1943, coach of Washington REDSKINS

SAMUEL H. MILLER, Indiana track luminary of late-1930's; formerly Chief Pilot for Pan-American Airways; now Manager, Flight Operations, New York.

AVERY BRUNDAGE, Illinois track ace shortly before World War I; now leading philanthropist, real estate magnate and President of the International Olympic Committee.

WALTER HASS, Minnesota grid star of early-1930's; now Director of Athletics, University of Chicago.

A

Abbott, Dave, 115, 151, 152, 158
Abrahams, Dick, 412
Adams, Norb, 309
Adkins, John, 245
Agase, Alex, 248-249, 253, 255, 270-271
Ahrens, Carl, 329
Aigler, Ralph W., 106
Aihara, Henry, 270
Aitch, Matt, 413
Albershardt, Dick, 350
Albritton, Dave, 211
Alderman, Fred, 147, 151
Alfonse, Julie, 178, 180, 182
Allen, Bernie, 372
Allen, Harry, 59
Allis, Harry, 283, 284, 293
Allmendinger, Ernie, 100, 163
Allwardt, Bob, 290
Alwood, Chuck, 101
Ameche, Alan (The Horse), 310, 317, 335-336
Amling, Warren, 267, 268, 271, 283
Amundsen, Bob, 253
Anderegg, Bob, 371, 373
Anderson, Bob, 353
Anderson, Cliff, 306
Anderson, Dale, 414
Anderson, Eddie, 111, 222
Anderson, Forrest (Fordy), 358
Anderson, Henry, 154
Anderson, Karl, 130
Anderson, Ken, 353
Anderson, Miller, 272, 281, 288, 291, 324
Andreotti, Jim, 370, 371
Andres, Ernie, 228
Angell, J.B., 68, 74
Angier, Milt, 110
Anthony, Mel, 398
Apisa, Bob, 404, 406, 409
Appleby, Gordon, 260
Aquino, Chuck, 391, 398
Arlin, Steve, 408, 412
Armbruster, Dave, 106
Arms, Dick, 55
Armstrong, Billy Joe, 382
Armstrong, Ike, 148
Armstrong, Ralph, 293
Aschenbrenner, Frank, 285, 286
Assenheimer, Lee, 402
Atkin, Leonard, 313
Atterbury, Willie, 362
Aubuchon, Chet, 233

B

Bachman, Charley, 207
Bagdon, Ed, 294-295
Bailey, Charley, 409
Baird, Charles, 59, 151, 152
Baker, Bob, 412
Baker, Frank, 160-161, 163
Baker, Howard, 268
Baker, Ralph (Moon), 131, 139, 140, 144, 165
Ballinger, Todd, 412
Balmores, Jose, 307, 313
Baltzell, Bob, 409
Barclay, Dave, 283
Bare, Frank, 323, 339
Barker, Charley, 245
Barnes, Harrison, 126-127
Barnes, Norman, 322
Barr, Ron, 330

Barr, Terry, 363
Bartelma, Dave, 245
Barten, Herb, 292
Barton, Bill, 308
Barwegan, Dick, 254-255
Baston, Bert, 93-94, 99
Bates, Mickey, 326
Batterman, Charley, 264
Bauman, Alf, 243
Baxter, Virginia, 324
Bay, Rick, 407
Beabout, Jerry, 374, 375
Beatty, Gerry, 408
Becker, Fred, 99
Beckner, Art, 144, 151
Bedard, Irv, 308
Beecher, Bryce, 172
Beers, Leslie, 151, 152
Beetham, Charley, 202
Behrman, Dave, 384
Beirne, Jim, 409
Beise, Sheldon, 178, 180
Beitner, Bill, 176
Belding, Lester, 108, 111, 114
Bell, Bobby, 374, 383
Bell, Craig, 403
Bell, Craig, 407
Bell, Greg, 355, 356, 360, 362, 369
Bellamy, Walt, 375 382 384
Bellows George, 64
Below, Martin, 123
Belshaw, Ed, 173
Bemoras, Irv, 312, 328
Benbrook, Albert, 78, 134
Benner, Tom, 339, 341
Benners, Fred, 300
Bennett, Basil, 110
Bennett, Chuck, 148, 149
Bennett, Paul, 175
Beretta, Fred, 105, 233
Bergum, Steve, 413
Bernard, Chuck, 169-170, 174
Bernard, Kent, 407, 408
Berry, Kevin, 411
Berry, Sam, 170
Bertelli, Angelo, 255
Berwanger, Jay, 175, 192-194
Bettis, Tom, 318, 336
Bevan, Bill, 175, 178, 180, 182, 183
Beyer, Ralph, 130
Beynon, Jack, 183
Bezdek, Hugo, 65, 70
Bickell, Norm, 203
Bierman, Bernie, 93, 112, 174, 178, 179-182
Billingsley, Hobie, 268-269
Billman, John, 241
Biltz, John, 300
Bjorkman, Rube, 292
Black, Gerald, 316
Blott, Jack, 123, 134
Bobo, Doug, 316
Bobo, Hubert, 334
Boerio, Charley, 310
Boesel, Dick, 100
Bohnslay, Ed, 313
Bolden, Leroy, 310, 325, 327
Bolen, Charles, 100
Bollas, George, 273
Bolstad, Les, 147
Booth, Albie, 71
Booth, Mark, 352
Borland, G.H., 245
Boros, Steve, 354

Borton, John, 333
Boudreau, Lou, 210, 304
Bouschor, Royal, 138
Bowman, Bliss, 268, 273
Bradds, Garry, 394-395, 400, 401
Brandt, Gordon, 145
Brass, Fred, 289
Braun, Howard, 325, 330, 414
Breen, Bill, 269
Brenner, Al, 409
Brenniff, Bob, 316
Brewer, Don, 176
Brewer, Mel, 414
Breyer, Larry, 138
Breyer, Ralph, 128, 129, 138
Bricker, John W., 88, 94
Brieske, Jim, 271, 284
Brill, Marty, 162
Brindley, Audley, 262
Brinkman, Chuck, 408, 412
Britton, Earl, 120, 123, 132
Brixius, Francis, 374
Brocksmith, Henry, 169, 201
Brooker, Jim, 130
Brookins, Charles, 118, 124, 125, 130
Brooks, John, 176
Brose, Leonard, 314
Brosky, Al, 310
Brousseau, Frank, 401
Brown, Aaron, 406
Brown, Bob, 305
Brown, Chuck, 300
Brown, Howard, 264, 266, 267
Brown, Paul, 170, 245, 246, 258-259
Brown, Tom, 374
Browning, Dick, 341
Browning, Skippy, 315
Brubaker, Dick, 333, 335
Bruder, Hank (Hard-Luck), 160, 161-162
Brugge, Bob, 259, 261
Bruhn, Milt, 178, 369
Brumm, Don, 388
Brundage, Avery, 84, 114, 340, 344
Bruner, Jack, 296
Bruney, Bob, 300
Bryant, Chuck, 382
Bullough, Hank, 317, 325
Bunker, Ray, 138
Buntin, Bill, 400, 401, 406
Burford, Gil, 299, 316
Burkholder, Bob, 305
Burks, Archie, 317
Burrell, Bill, 370, 371
Burson, Don, 285, 309
Burton, Bill, 253
Burtt, Ben, 252-253
Butkovich, Tony, 254-255
Butkus, Dick, 393, 394, 399
Butler, Robert (Butts), 82, 84
Butterworth, Horace, 54
Buxton, Ed, 95
Bye, Billy, 293

C

Cain, Carl, 337, 346, 351, 352, 357
Calcaterra, Jack, 410
Calderwood, Bill, 150
Calhoun, Jack, 324
Callaghan, Rich, 393
Cameron, John, 329
Camp, Walter, 53-54, 86, 99, 265

Campanella, Joe, 300
Campbell, Daswell, 411
Campbell, Holley, 164
Campbell, Joe, 350, 363
Campbell, Milt, 323-324, 356, 357
Cannady, John, 267
Capron, George, 74
Carey, Bill, 310
Carey, Bob, 310
Carius, Allen, 392
Carl, Harland, 317
Carle, Jerry, 254
Carlson, Ron, 388
Carney, Chuck, 110, 117, 135, 137
Caroline, J.C., 326, 327
Carpenter, Charles, 108
Carran, Charles, 94
Carter, Keith, 288, 297, 299
Cassady, Howard (Hopalong), 299, 319, 334-336, 343, 344, 345, 349
Catavolos George, 410
Catlin, Maurice, 62
Causton, Ron, 372
Cavender, Regis, 409
Ceithaml, George, 258
Cephas, Dick, 384
Cernoch, Rudy, 284
Chamberlain, Clark, 168, 169
Chandler, Bill, 83, 100-101
Chandnois, Lynn, 294-295
Chapman, Ralph (Slooie), 89
Chappuis, Bob, 273, 276, 278, 279, 284
Charboneau, Ernie, 290
Charles, John, 410
Chin, George, 330
Chinielewski, Ed, 151
Chonko, Arnie, 399, 408
Christmann, Bill, 131
Church, Mert, 257, 263, 269
Cisco, Galen, 344, 354, 357-358
Clapp, Bill, 413
Clark, Bob, 162
Clark, Denny, 62
Clark, Don, 357-358
Clark, Earl, 245, 257, 258
Clark, Ellery, 115
Clark, George (Potsy), 89
Clark, Jimmy, 293
Clark, John, 353
Clark, Meyers, 140
Clark, Ron, 372, 378, 381, 386
Clarkson, Art, 178
Cleveland, Dick, 321-322, 324, 330, 338, 341
Cleveland, Dick, 341
Clevenger, Zora G., 66, 154, 174, 196, 410
Clifford, Bill, 282, 287, 288
Cline, Ollie, 259, 261, 268
Clotworthy, Bob, 313, 321, 324, 329, 330, 331, 356, 357
Cmejrek, Carl, 408
Coats, Keith, 408
Coatta, John, 304, 310-311
Cobb, Caton, 244, 245, 252
Cochran, Shorty, 353
Cochrane, Roy, 291
Cogswell, Harry, 287, 288, 306
Colbath, Wally, 146, 147, 150, 152, 158
Colburn, Bobby, 176
Cole, Gene, 306, 323
Coleman, Dick, 321, 323
Coleman, Don, 310, 311
Collier, Blanton, 170

Collier, Joe, 319, 327
Combes, Harry, 325, 330, 414
Comer, Bob, 289
Comstock, Byron, 402
Cook, Bob, 279-280, 287
Cook, Dick, 412
Cook, John, 330
Cooke, Clement, 84
Corbett, Jack, 321, 329
Cordin, Scott, 412, 413
Corless, Rex, 317
Corley, Joe, 341
Correll, Bob, 150
Cory, Ace, 257
Cottom, Norm, 105, 184
Coulter, Chan, 130
Coulter, Gene, 313
Counsilman, James, 272, 384, 411
Courtwright, Bill, 273
Cox, Rod, 176
Crafts, H.K., 59
Craig, Herb, 159, 257
Craig, James, 134
Craig, Ralph, 84, 86
Crain, Russ, 145
Crangle, Jack, 131-132
Craven, Ron, 353
Crisler, Herbert Orrin (Fritz), 70, 72, 118, 273, 274-277,
    279, 283, 301
Cristy, Jim, 174
Crocker, Ray, 229
Croftchek, Don, 399
Cromwell, Dean, 282
Crosbie, Ernie, 174, 292
Crowley, Sleepy Jim, 162-163
Cryder, Hank, 320
Csuri, Chuck, 246, 247
Cudzik, Walt, 318
Cuhel, Frank, 151, 152
Cuhel, Joe, 164
Culver, Nelson, 176
Cunningham, Harold (Cookie), 132, 137
Cunningham, William, 54
Curcillo, Tony, 300, 302, 311
Currier, Ken, 246
Curzi, Jim, 401, 408
Cusick, Mike, 338
Cvercko, Andy, 365, 373
Cvercko, Jack, 388

D

Daley, Bill, 249, 253, 255
Daly, Del, 245
Daly, Larry, 272
Daniels, Harry, 152
Danner, Dave, 262
Darden, Oliver, 400, 406
Darling, Chuck, 320, 337, 357
Darnall, Carl, 147, 150-151
Dart, Justin, 140, 165
Daugherty, Hugh (Duffy), 316, 334, 345-346, 406
Davenport, Ira, 84
Davey, Chuck, 257, 282, 290, 292, 297, 298
Davidson, Floyd, 147
Davies, John, 291, 322, 324
Davis, Corby, 208
Davis, Glenn, 357, 367, 381
Davis, John, 321
Davis, W.S., 170
Dawson, Len, 345-346
Day, Loran (Pee Wee), 284, 285

Dean, Everett, 113, 410
Dean, Russ, 267
Dearden, Don, 389
Deckard, Tom, 201
Deegan, Bob, 383
Dees, Archie, 359-360, 366
DeField, Jack, 257
Degener, Dick, 174, 176, 186
deGroot, Bob, 296-297
Dehner, Lew (Pick), 218
Dekker, Paul, 316
Delaney, John, 349
Demmel, Bob, 300
Dempsey, Frank, 253
DePrato, Neno (Jerry), 93-94
Deranek, Dick, 267
Derleth, Henry, 370
Derricotte, Gene, 278, 284
Des Jardiens, Paul, 70, 86
Desmond, Binga, 101
Detwiler, Jom, 398
Devine, Aubrey, 111, 112-115, 118
Devine, Glenn, 111, 114
Devine, Pat, 176
Dewey, John, 305, 312, 323, 363
Dibble, Dorne, 304
Dick, Leo, 86
Dickens, Phil, 299, 301, 305, 363
Dickenson, Dick, 290
Dickenson, Don, 290
Dickson, Judge, 383
Diebold, Marshall, 126
Dilley, Gary, 403, 407, 408, 412
Dimancheff, Boris, 254, 255, 262
Dischinger Terry, 375, 382, 384, 389
Dobie, Gil, 79
Doheny, Don, 316, 325, 327
Dolan, Frank, 308, 313
Domney, Dick, 136
Donham, Bob, 305
Donnelly, George, 399, 400
Dooley, Frank, 307, 321, 324
Dorais, Gus, 93
Dorr, Gerry, 306
Dorrow, Al, 310
Dougovito, Carl, 173, 174
Downey, Dave, 395, 398
Doyle, Dick, 144
Draves, Duane, 297
Dreutzler, Warren, 315, 324
Driscoll, John Leo (Paddy), 93, 95
Drobac, Stan, 330
Droegemueller, Bill, 147, 151, 152
Drysdale, Taylor, 172, 185
Duckett, Ellis, 325
Dudeck, John, 339
Dufek, Don, 293, 301
Duff, Lloyd, 287
Dugger, Dean, 333, 334
Dugger, Jack, 259, 261, 270
Duke, Jim, 290
Duncan, Randy, 363-365
Dunn, Rick, 411
Dworsky, Dan, 278, 283, 284
Dye, J.W., 61
Dye, William Henry Harrison (Tippy), 209

E

Eaddy, Don, 321, 329, 349
Ebert, Paul, 320-321, 328, 337-338, 339-340, 342
Eckersall, Walter, 62, 64-65, 67, 70, 82, 123-124

Eddleman, Dwight (Dike), 287, 289, 292, 295, 299, 304
Egan, Eddie, 143
Ehmann, Frank, 347
Einbender, Irv, 257
Eller, Carl, 383, 394
Elliott, Bruce, 306
Elliott, Chalmers (Bump), 106, 273, 276, 278, 279, 284
Elliott, Norman, 106
Elliott, Pete, 106, 276, 278, 284, 287, 299, 324-325, 330, 414
Elliott, Ray, 270
Ellis, Jim, 310, 317
Elwood, Frank, 343
Emery, Bob, 110
Enga, Dick, 383
Englund, Gene, 243
Engregretsen, Paul, 166
Enich, Mike, 232
Erben, Bob, 283
Erickson, Bill, 295, 296
Erickson, Bruce, 353
Erickson, Bud, 339
Erickson, John, 380
Erickson, Woody, 353
Ernst, Don, 327
Eubank, Weeb, 170
Evans, Dana, 154
Evashevski, Forest, 221, 245, 276, 350-351
Everhardus, Herman, 165, 169, 174
Ewing, Bill, 289
Ewry, Ray, 58-59, 76, 77
Ezerins, Elmars, 391

F

Fadner, Bob, 203
Farina, Charles, 307
Faricy, John, 138
Farley, Bill, 404, 406-407
Farley, Dick, 328, 336
Farnham, Greg, 413
Farrell, Steve, 85-86
Faverty, Hal, 310
Feathers, Beattie, 157
Fekete, Gene, 246
Fencl, Dick, 161
Fenske, Chuck, 95, 211
Ferguson, Bob, 375, 382, 384
Ferguson, Larry, 374, 375
Ferguson, Richard, 330
Fesler, Wesley, 148, 149, 160, 163, 293, 299-300, 301, 303
Fessenden, Ralph, 338
Fetterman Dick, 272
Fina, Lou, 245
Finley, Jim, 409
Fischer, Gary, 396
Fischer, Johnny, 172, 176
Fisher, Fritz, 385
Fisher, Waldo, 131, 139, 163
Fitch, Horatio M., 114
Fitzpatrick, Keene, 59
Flachman, Charley, 185
Flannagan, Christy, 140
Flannagan, Dick, 259, 261
Flatley, Paul, 398
Fleming, Willie, 363-364
Fletcher, Bobby, 108, 137
Fletcher, Ray, 312
Fletcher, Rod, 320
Fletcher, Tom, 392
Flowers, Bernie, 318-319
Floyd, Tom, 312-313, 329

Fonville, Charles, 282, 288, 289
Ford, Alan, 263
Ford, B. E., 114
Ford, Gerald, 183-184
Ford, Len, 276, 278
Foster, Harold (Bud), 154, 163, 164
Fowler, Larry, 316, 325, 327
Fowler, Wilmer, 361
Franck, Sonny, 232, 245
Frank, Leonard, 78
Franklin, Alex, 269
Franklin, Aris, 268, 269
Franks, Julius, 248
Frazier, Bill, 396
Frazier, Bruce, 321
Fredericks, Casey, 250
Freehan, Bill, 306, 385, 386
Freeman, Robin, 346, 352
French, Ed, 55
Frickey, Herm, 254
Frieda, Harry, 125, 138
Friedman, Benny, 131-132, 135, 140, 144, 163
Friedman, Tully, 281
Fries, Charley, 263
Frimodig, Lyman, 106
Froschauer, Frank, 195
Frues, Charley, 269
Fuqua, Ivan, 174, 201
Furry, Dick, 375, 381
Furseth, Paul, 306

G

Gacek, Wally, 290-291
Gagne, Vern, 291, 292, 298-299
Gailis, Glenn, 408
Gailus, Joe, 165, 170
Gallinagh, Pat, 409
Gandee, Chuck, 300
Garbe, Lyle, 330
Garland, Mel, 403
Garmaker, Dick, 346, 347
Garnass, Bill, 241
Garret, Max, 159, 257, 355
Garrett, Bill, 312
Garrett, Jim, 408, 411
Garst, Ed, 308
Gates, Mark, 407
Gearhart, Gary, 375
Gee, Johnny, 105
Gehrmann, Don, 95, 281, 289, 290, 292, 297, 299, 306, 308
Gelein, Max, 82
Genske, Gene, 290
George, Ed Don, 151
George, Jim, 382
George, Ray, 316
Giallombardo, Joe, 220
Gibbons, Jim, 350-351, 358, 359
Gibson, Gene, 316
Gibson, George, 145, 157
Giel, Paul, 318, 321, 327, 329, 342
Gilbert, Abel, 290
Gilbert, Rick, 400, 403, 412
Gilders, Fletcher, 349
Gill, Harry, 64, 114-115, 127, 140
Gillanders, Dave, 382, 386
Gillen, Doug, 353
Gillen, Harold, 100-101
Gillette, Eddie, 82
Gilliam, Frank, 350-351
Gilman, Sid, 165
Girard, Earl (Jug), 254, 261-262

Glassgow, Willis, 148, 153, 154, 159
Gnidovic, Don, 310
Goebel, Paul, 116, 134
Gola, Tom, 346
Goldin, Grant, 308
Goldsberry, John, 266-267
Golliday, Jim, 323, 346-347
Gompf, Tom, 386, 403
Gonzales, Joe, 312, 313
Good, Roy, 289
Goodrich, Judy, 356, 382
Googerhyde, George, 291
Gora, Ron, 339, 341, 349
Gordien, Fortune, 282, 288, 289, 324, 356
Gordon, Ed, 151, 158, 164, 168, 173-174
Gordon, Lou, 154
Gowdy, Frankiln, 126
Graber, Bill, 158, 168
Grabowski, Jim, 393, 399, 405, 412
Graebner, Clark, Jr., 397, 402, 408
Graf, Jack, 242
Graham, Gene, 384
Graham, Otto, 239-240, 249, 255-256, 262
Grandelius, Everett (Sonny), 304, 316
Grange, Harold (Red), 91-92, 118, 119-123, 125-126, 132, 135, 304
Grant, Bud, 293
Grate, Don, 262
Graver, Herb, 59
Green, Fred, 251
Green, Johnny, 359-360, 371
Greenberg, Seymour, 244, 252
Gregory, Dick, 293
Gregory, George, 59
Gremban, Steve, 290
Gretzinger, Dick, 407
Griese, Bob, 405-406, 409, 410
Griffith, Major John L., 118, 145, 154, 160, 174, 196, 322
Groft, Bill, 412
Groh, Gordon, 281
Groomes, George, 266
Grossfeld, Abe, 357, 362, 367-368, 373
Grossfeld, Muriel, 382
Guarasci, Ralph, 302
Gustafson, Vic, 166
Guthrie, George (Phin), 130, 144
Gutzweiler, Elbert, 313

H

Haarlow, Bill, 196
Hackbart, Dale, 370, 381
Hackett, Bill, 259, 261
Haff, Carol, 84
Hagmann, Chuck, 284
Hague, Jimmy, 292-293, 294
Hahn, Archie, 63, 64
Hahn, Bernard, 176
Hailand, Frank, 367, 368
Halas, George, 107, 118, 157, 304
Hall, Sam, 382
Halleen, Neil, 413
Haller, Tom, 361
Hallmark, Ferris, 316, 325
Haluska, Jim, 318
Haman, John, 227
Hamilton, Brutus, 143
Hamilton, Ralph, 279-280
Hammil, Ralph, 70
Hamrick, Charlie, 183
Hanes, Harold, 321
Hanley, Dan, 162

Hanley, Dick, 160, 169, 172-173, 356-360, 362, 367, 372
Hanley, Lee, 161-162
Hanner, Glen, 408
Hansen, Don, 394
Hanson, Dale, 229
Hapac, Bill, 233
Harder, Pat, 246, 248
Harkrader, Jerry, 344
Harlan, Bruce, 290, 291, 296-297, 299, 307, 308-309
Harley, Charles W. (Chic), 95, 96-100, 108, 109, 135, 319
Harmeson, Glenn, 153
Harmeson, Harold, 153
Harmon, Tom, 213-217, 276
Harper, Carl, 86, 89
Harper, Don, 352, 354, 355, 356, 357, 360, 366, 367, 368
Harper, Jesse, 65
Harper, William Rainey, 51
Harris, Archie, 237, 245
Harris, Fred, 350-351
Harris, Sig, 79
Harrison, Bob, 287, 294
Harrison, Gerry, 330, 331, 348, 349
Harvey, George, 384
Hass, Mell, 89
Hauser, George, 99
Havlicek, John, 375, 384, 389
Hawkins, Harry, 135-136, 144
Hawley, Jesse, 86
Haycraft, Ken, 145, 148
Hayes, Billy, 201
Hayes, Wayne Woodrow (Woody), 319, 331-333, 351-352, 357
Haynam, Bruce, 329
Heekin, Dick, 183
Hefflefinger, Pudge, 63, 78
Hein, Herb, 255
Hein, Herm, 254
Hein, Stew, 313-314, 325
Heldt, John, 111, 114
Henderson, John, 398
Heneveld, Lloyd, 293
Hermann, Bernhardt, 412, 413
Herrnstein, Albert, 59, 62
Herschberger, Clarence, 54, 70
Hess, Ed, 135, 137, 144
Hester, George, 151
Heston, Willie, 59, 61-63, 64
Heusner, Bill, 290, 297, 298, 299
Hewitt, Bobby, 151
Heydt, Francis, 245
Heyliger, Vic, 323, 356
Higgins, Charley, 100
Highland, Art, 172, 176
Hilgenberg, Jerry, 327
Hill, Don, 331, 338-339, 341
Hill, Frank, 175, 323
Hill, Jim, 144, 145, 147
Hill, Sam, 147
Hillenbrand, Billy, 248, 266
Himes, Bryan, 130
Hinch, Dick, 158, 163
Hinchman, Lew, 165, 176
Hirose, Halo, 282
Hirsbrunner, Paul, 246
Hirsch, Elroy (Crazy Legs), 246, 253, 255
Hisert, K. E., 145
Hobert, Bob, 351, 363
Hobert, Ted, 282
Hoeffel, Ed, 82
Hoernschemeyer, Bob (Hunchy), 253, 254, 266

Hofacre, Lee, 289
Hoffman, Dave, 315
Hoffman, Frank, 162
Hoffman, Howard, 118
Hoffman, Paul, 262, 272
Hoke, Bob, 342
Holan, Gerry, 315, 321, 324, 329-330
Holcomb, Stu, 165, 318
Holden, Bill, 408
Holiday, Harry, 257, 258, 282, 288, 290
Holland, Lou, 387, 388
Hollis, Wilburn, 374
Holmer, Walt, 140
Hoogerhyde, George, 281, 282, 290, 315
Hook, Julian, 383
Hopkins, Cy, 360, 362, 367
Hoppe, John, 353
Hopper, Bob, 407, 408
Horn, Donald, 176
Hornbostel, Charles, 174, 176, 201
Horne, John, 369, 381
Horning, Bill, 353
Horstman, Roy, 165, 170, 176
Horvath, Leslie, 246, 259, 260, 261
Hosket Bill, 175-176
Hosket, Bill, Jr., 175
Houston, Jack, 318
Houston, Jim, 365
Houston, Lindell, 246, 247
Hovde, Fred, 150, 156-157
Howard, Frank, 353, 359, 360
Howard, Larry, 391
Howell, Dick, 128, 129, 130, 138
Howlett, Bob, 163
Hubbard, Cal, 266
Hubbard, William DeHart, 125, 130, 137
Hubbell, George, 151
Hudson, Lou, 406, 407
Huff, George, 58, 59, 108, 109, 118, 137, 154, 158, 174, 196
Huff, Tom, 392
Huffman, Iolas, 112, 113, 118
Huffman, Marv, 234
Huffman, Vern, 201
Hughes, Tom, 267, 268
Hull, Jimmy, 228
Hume, Robert, 263
Hume, Ross, 263, 269
Hunter, Joe, 59
Hurring, Lincoln, 353, 367
Hurst, Bob, 409
Huston, Paul, 272
Huszagh, Ken, 84
Hutchinson, Bill, 317

I

Ingram, Mike, 382, 383
Ingwersen, Burt, 150
Ives, Dick, 262, 268

J

Jackman, Steve, 384, 386, 396, 397
Jacobazzi, Roger, 388
Jacobs, John, 272
Jacobs, Walter, 203
Jake, Bob, 252, 272
Jake, Bob, 272
James, Jack, 170
James, Tom, 246, 249
Janowicz, Vic, 293, 300-303
Jaroch, Gene, 272

Jastremski, Chet, 390, 396, 398, 403
Jennings, Burl, 244, 245, 252
Jennings Merle, 244, 245, 252
Jensen, Jackie, 286
Jensen, Merle, 329
Jenswold, John, 263
Jeter, Bob, 363-364
Joesting, Herb, 144, 145-146
John, Verdayne, 257
Johannensen, Bill, 407
Johnson, Allan, 86
Johnson, Alton, 59-60
Johnson, Bob, 131, 139-140
Johnson, Carl, 110
Johnson, Elmer, 176
Johnson, Fred, 299
Johnson, Howie, 128
Johnson, Leo, 272, 338
Johnson, Lyndon B., 337
Johnson, Okla, 385
Johnson, Ron, 375
Johnson, Walter, 87
Johnsos, Luke, 140, 165
Jollymore, Warren, 252
Jones, Burwell, 329, 331, 339, 340, 341, 348
Jones Calvin, 336, 345
Jones, Charley, 355, 362, 367, 381
Jones, Clint, 405, 409
Jones, Gomer, 175, 191
Jones, Howard Harding, 100, 111-112, 114, 154, 170-172
Jones, Selwyn, 355
Jones, Tad, 100, 116
Jones, Tom, 87, 95, 110, 154
Joyce, Mike, 385
Joyner, Harry, 413
Juday, Steve, 404-405, 412
Juneau, Bill, 56, 82

K

Kadesky, Max, 114
Kallenberg, H. F., 54
Kamman, Kim, 407
Kane, Campbell, 244, 245
Karow, Marty, 144, 412
Karras, Alex, 350-351, 358, 359
Karras, Johnny, 300, 309, 310, 311
Kauffman, George B., 58
Kawachika, Ed, 338, 349, 352
Keeler, Ray, 82, 86
Keller, Jack, 168, 172, 173, 174, 176
Kelley, Bob, 263
Kelley, Don 349
Kelley, Dwight (Ike), 399, 400, 406
Kelley, Otto, 164
Kellogg, N. A., 196
Kellogg, Ned, 154
Kelly, Jim, 289
Kempthorn, Dick, 278, 284, 293
Kennedy, Bob, 318
Kennedy, Crawford (Forddy), 355, 368-369, 373
Kennedy, Henry, 354-355
Kennen, Lloyd, 150
Keough, Bryce, 313
Kerr, Bob, 320, 337-338
Kerr, George, 372, 373, 379, 381, 382, 404
Kerr, Jim, 404
Kerr, John, 328
Kerr, Roger, 396
Kessler, Bob, 102, 105
Ketz, Wilford, 151
Kifer, Darryle, 407

Kilty, Dick, 289
Kimball, Dick, 362
Kindall, Jerry, 353-354
King, Clanton, 410
King, Phil, 56-57
King, Ray, 208
Kingsley, N. Y., 109
Kinnick, Nile, 223-227
Kinsey, Dan, 114
Kipke, Harry, 116, 126, 134, 162, 169-170
Kipper, Thornton, 306
Kirk, Walton, 268
Kivi, Lou, 253
Kizer, Noble, 169, 170, 171, 174
Klaus, Bob, 372
Klevay, Walt, 293, 299
Klimek, Tony, 300
Kline, George, 366
Klusewski, Ted, 264, 266-267
Knapp, Wayne, 372, 380
Knight, Bob, 375
Knight, Dave, 257
Kobayashi, Herb, 315, 321
Kobs, John, 128, 129
Koepcke, Doug, 322
Kogen, Bill, 263, 288
Kohl, Ralph, 278, 283
Kondla, Tom, 413
Konno, Ford, 321-322, 324, 329, 338, 340, 341, 347-348,
    349, 356
Konovsky, Bob, 356
Konsek, John, 368, 380, 381
Kostka, Stan, 178, 182
Kotz, John, 243, 249, 256
Koutenen, Erkki, 292
Kowalczyk, Walt, 358
Kozlowski, Henry, 258
Kraak, Charley, 328, 336
Kraft, Art, 381
Krall, Jerry, 293
Kramer, Larry, 386
Kramer, Ron, 345, 350-351, 352
Kratz, Winston, 147
Kremblas, Frank, 357-358
Kreuger, Julius, 144
Kuenn, Harvey, 321
Kuh, Dick, 310
Kuhn, Al, 356
Kunz, Howie, 306
Kurth, Joe, 162
Kush, Frank, 310, 317, 318
Kutch, Nicholas, 136
Kuzma, Frank, 293
Kuzma, Tom, 276
Kwiskey, Bruce, 385
Kyle, Chuck, 410

L

La Beach, Lloyd, 95
Labus, Pat, 409
Lad, Bob, 172
Lafayette, Lee, 413
Lambert, Jim, 341
Lambert, Ward (Piggy), 101, 102-105, 108, 110, 117, 163
La Mois, Lloyd, 289
Landin Bill, 308
Landowski, John, 118
Lange, Ernie, 89
Lanphear, Dan, 370
Laper, Pat, 413
Lardner, Ring, 62
Larkins, Richard C., 163, 169, 301

Larose, Gil, 397
Larson, Frank (Butch), 174, 178, 183
Larson, Greg, 374
Lascari, Arno, 397, 401
Lash, Don, 201
Latigolal, Ken, 408
Lattner, John, 327
Lauer, E. H., 196
Lauer, Edward, 174
Laws, Joe, 174-175
Lawson, Bill, 263
Layden, Elmer, 126, 140
Laz, Don, 306, 313, 315, 316
Leach, Felix (Lefty), 161
LeBeau, Dick, 357-358
Legacki, Frank, 372, 373, 378, 386
Leggett, Dave, 333-335
Lekenta, Gene, 317
Lemak, Lou, 172
Lenski, John, 282
Lentz, Chuck, 293, 344
Lenzini, Bob, 326, 342
Leonard, Bob, 320, 328, 336, 337
Leonhart, Dave, 313
Lepley, Paul, 329
Leps, Ergas, 384, 385, 391
Letts, Dale, 168-169
Leuhring, Fred, 154
Levis, George, 100
Levinson, Yatz, 165
LeVoir, Babe, 178
Lewis, Leland (Tiny), 131, 139, 147, 163
Lewis, Sherman, 394
Licht, Virgil, 172
Lick, Lou, 263-264
Lidberg, Carl, 126
Lindberg, Les, 183
Lindbloom, Dave, 353
Lindekugel, Charles, 289
Lininger, Jack, 293
Lirot, Dan, 354-355
Little, George, 196
Loceski, Leo, 284, 306
Locke, Gordon, 110-111, 112, 114-115, 116, 255
Logan, Bill, 337, 346, 351, 352
Logan, Dick, 300
Loken, Newt, 245, 252
Lonborg, Arthur (Dutch), 168, 175, 250
Lorms, John, 268, 269
Lott, George, 159
Lowery, Emmett, 105, 184
Lowry, Tim, 131-132, 137, 163
Lubratovich, Milo, 160, 163
Lucas, Harold, 404
Lucas, Jerry, 375, 376-378, 382, 384, 389, 398
Luehring, Fred W., 196
Luke, Ed, 316
Lund, Don, 260
Lund, Francis (Pug), 174, 178, 180, 182, 183
Lundgren, Carl, 114
Lupton, Ralph, 151
Lutz, Cliff, 252, 257, 282-283
Lynn, George, 246

M

Maas, Dean, 353
McAuliffe, Don, 310, 316, 318
McCafree, Charley, 360
McCann, Terry, 350, 355, 382
McCarnes, Bob, 168
McCartan, John, 369
McCarten, Jack, 353, 368

McCarty, Austin (Five-Yards), 70, 120, 125, 126
McClain, Mayes, 148
McConnell, Charley, 144
McCormick, Frank, 174
McCoy, Ernie, 154, 159
McCoy, Julius, 352
McCracken, Branch, 113, 163-164, 234-236, 328, 336, 410
McCullough, Bob, 300, 304
McDaniel, Charley, 197
McDermott, Verne, 115, 168
McDonald, Pat, 142
McEwan, Don, 297, 308, 313, 315, 327
McGhee, Brown, 381
McGinnis, Chuck, 151
McGovern, John, 76-77
McGugin, Dan, 59, 62, 116
McGuire, Charles, 70, 112, 113
McIntyre, Jim, 280, 287, 295
MacKay, Barry, 353, 361, 362
McKee, Robert, 110
McKenley, Herb, 273, 280-281, 282, 323
McKinney, Frank, 356, 378, 381, 382, 384
Macklin, John F., 81-82
MacMillan, Jim, 407
McMillen, Jim, 123
McMillin, Alvin Nugent (Bo), 178, 265-268
McNamara, Bob, 336
McNamara, Ed, 245
McNeely, Jim, 353
McNeil, Ed, 278, 283
McNerney, Rod, 408
McNulty, Carl, 320
McNulty, Joel, 320, 328-329
McNulty, Paul, 312
Macomber, Bart, 89, 94
McRae, Ben, 384, 385, 391
McSween, Cirilo, 312-313, 321
Madar, Elmer, 271
Maekawa, Choken, 356, 357
Magnuson, Rod, 353
Major, Fred, 300
Makris, George, 252, 257, 316
Maldegan, Bob, 292
Mallory, Bill, 114
Maloney, Norm, 271
Manders, Mark, 374, 375
Mann, Matt, III, 138, 146, 245, 288, 290, 348
Manske, Edgar (Eggs), 174, 176
March, Lowell, 168
Marek, Elmer, 140
Marshall, Bobby, 74
Marshall, Frank, 168
Marston, Amos, 55
Martens, Mike, 411
Marter, Perry, 126, 128, 130
Martin, Alvo, 144
Martin, Gene, 353
Martin, Orval, 164
Martin, Richard, 169
Martineau, Earl, 123
Marvin, Dallas, 161, 166-167
Mason, Don, 294-295
Mason, Tom, 289
Masters, Norm, 345
Mathis, Bill, 273
Mathisen, Art, 249, 250-251, 256
Matthews, Charley, 339
Mattison, Howie, 176
Maulbetsch, John, 89, 134
Maxwell, Tiny, 70
May, Willie, 360, 381

Mayasich, John, 342
Maynard, Gene, 338
Mead, Milt, 321
Mean, Chet, 114
Meanwell, Dr. Walter, 82-83, 86, 89, 174
Meath, Dob, 341
Mehl, Walter, 95, 211, 290
Meigs, Babe, 65-66, 70, 75
Mencel, Chuck, 320, 328, 346, 347
Menke Ken, 249, 250-251, 256
Menzies, John, 147
Merrill, Leland, 292
Merz, Curt, 363, 365
Metcalfe, Nelson, 174
Metzger, Bert, 162
Meyers, Bob, 265
Meyers, Paul, 101
Miki, Gerald, 379, 381
Mikles, Gail, 282
Miller, Bill, 313
Miller, Chuck, 165, 166, 257
Miller, Myron, 257
Miller, Ray, 104
Miller, Ron, 375
Miller, Wayne, 411
Mills, Allen, 313
Mills, Dave, 384
Mills, Doug, 164, 249, 250-251, 414
Mills, Doug, Jr., 392
Millstead, Century, 114
Miner, Johnny, 137
Miner, Moe, 164
Minick, Paul, 111, 114
Minot, George, 159
Mitchell, Charles, 57
Mitchell, Earl, 252
Mitchell, Ron, 321, 338
Mitchell, Tom, 413
Modine, Frank, 372
Moeller, Gary, 382
Momsen, Bob, 293, 300, 303, 304
Momsen, Tony, 301
Monahan, Regis, 183
Montebello, Bob, 313-314
Moore, Bill, 273, 282
Moore, Bob, 321, 329
Moran, Charley, 265
Moreno, Charles, 307
Morgan, Jack, 316
Morgan, Bob, 323
Morrall, Earl, 345
Morris, Max, 267, 268, 271, 272
Morrison, Albi, 152
Morrison, Fred, 293-294
Morrison, Maynard, 165-167
Moss, Paul, 165-166, 170
Moss, Perry, 270-271
Mountbatten, Lord Phillip, 253
Muchanan, Edwel, 316
Mueller, Brick, 109
Mueller, Dick, 331, 361
Mueller, Warren, 348
Mull, Marty, 397
Mummey, John, 382
Munn, Clarence (Biggie), 167-168, 310, 316, 319, 325, 334
Munsey, Bill, 374, 383
Murakowki, Art, 285, 286
Murphy, Bill, 220
Murphy, Dick, 316
Murphy, Charles (Stretch), 102, 105, 150, 163-164, 168
Murphy, Chet, 220

Mydahl, Mal, 151
Myers, Tom, 388, 408

N

Nagusrki, Bronko, 145, 154, 155-157
Naismith, Dr. James, 54
Nakama, Keo, 257, 258, 263-264
Nalon, Norvard (Snip), 329, 331, 342
Neal, Jim, 316, 325
Neff, Paul, 289
Negus, Fred, 246
Nelson, Dave, 238, 253
Nelson, Dick, 386, 393, 397
Nelson, Emerson, 144
Nelson, Irv, 150
Nemeth, Eddie, 284, 293
Newman, Harry, 165, 169-170
Newton, Bill, 408
Nicholas, Ab, 312, 320
Nichols, Dave, 263
Nicklaus, Jack, 386
Nielsen, Jim, 289
Niemic, John, 140
Nieport, Gene, 315
Nocera, John, 363-364
Nomellini, Leo, 287, 292, 293, 294
Noonan, Karl, 399, 400
Norgren, Nels, 70, 86, 87
Norman, Bob, 369
Norsetter, John, 413
Northrop, Phil, 144
Norton, Don, 370
Norton, Ray, 363-365
Nowack, Al, 145, 148
Nowatzke, Tom, 399
Nowell, Mel, 375, 384
Nystrom, Carl, 345, 356

O

O'Brien, George, 318, 319
O'Brien, Willis (Fat), 81
O'Connell, Thomas F., 145
O'Connell, Tommy, 309, 319
O'Connor, Frank, 351
O'Dea, Andrew, 55-56
O'Dea, Pat, 56-57
Odom, Herb, 350
O'Donahue, Pat, 310
Oech, Vern, 178
Oftshun, Neil, 316, 323
Ofstie, Hod, 82
O'Hanlon, Dick, 293
Oistad, Rod, 353
Olander, Bon, 308
Olion, George, 410
Oliphant, Elmer, 81
Olsen, Harold, 83, 100-101
Olson, Oliver, 170
Olssen, Lance, 410
Oosterbaan, Bennie, 132, 135, 136, 140, 141-143, 144,
     146, 150, 163, 283, 284, 301
Opsahl, Allan, 292
Orland, Rees, 412
Ortmann, Chuck, 284, 293, 301-302
Osborn, Carolyn, 382
Osborne, Harold, 114, 118, 130
O'Shaughnessy, Dick, 329
Oss, Arnie, 108, 109, 113
Ottey, Tom, 174
Owen, Dave, 352
Owen, Russ, 287

Owens, Jesse, 204-206, 362
Oyakawa, Yoshi, 322, 324, 330, 338, 340, 341, 347,
     349, 356

P

Pace, Jim, 358-359
Pacetti, Nello, 164
Padway, Milt, 95
Page, Harlan O. (Pat), 70, 74, 75, 76
Paine, Norman, 78
Palmer, Chuck, 116
Palmer, Dick, 308
Palmer, Pete, 306
Panfil, Ken, 318
Panin, Dick, 310
Pape, Oran, 148, 150, 153, 154, 159
Parisi, Vito, 290
Parisien, Art, 140
Park, Ted, 263
Parker, Jim, 345, 351
Parkin, Lee, 114
Patascil, Joe, 288, 306, 308-309
Patnik, Al, 186, 245
Paton, Andy, 288
Patten, James, 79, 80
Patten, John, 253, 257
Patterson, Ellmore, 183, 184
Patterson, Howard, 291
Payne, Russ, 130
Payne, Vernon, 413
Payseur, Ted, 175
Peacock, Wayne, 386
Peakes, Clarence, 345
Peppe, Mike, 296, 313, 341, 348
Perranoski, Ron, 354
Perry, Lowell, 301, 310
Peters, Charley, 306
Peterson, Barney, 408
Peterson, Don, 158, 284, 293
Peterson, Jim, 289, 297
Peterson, Norris, 408
Peterson Ted, 281, 297
Peterson, Tom, 309
Petoskey, Ted, 165, 169, 170, 174
Phelan, Jimmy, 152, 170
Phelps, Bob, 263, 273
Phelps, H. R., 128
Phelps, Harold, 129, 130
Phillip, Andy, 249, 250-251, 256
Philpott, Doug, 330
Pihos, Pete, 255, 266, 267
Pillath, Roger, 387, 388
Pincura, Stan, 183
Pingel, John, 212
Piper, Ralph, 281
Pisano, Vince, 310
Planutis, Gerry, 345
Platou, Erling, 109
Plaza, Arnold, 288, 290, 297, 298, 306, 307
Plews, Herb, 288
Ploen, Kenny, 350-351
Pogue, Harold, 89
Pollack, Joe, 401
Pommerening, Otto, 148
Pondelik, Joe, 70, 126
Poney, George, 406
Pontius, Miller, 86
Porter, Bill, 291
Porter, Dave, 412
Porter, Ed, 288
Poser, Rolf, 195
Potter, Al, 53

Potter, Dick, 353, 361
Potter, George, 170
Power, Dave, 408
Pregulman, Merv, 255
Price, Hartley, 252, 308
Puerta, Joe, 173
Pulford, Gurdon, 263, 269
Purdy, Charles, 147
Purma, Frank, 115
Purvis, Duane, 174, 175, 176, 183
Purvis, Jim, 165

Q

Quam, Dave, 413
Quiggle, Jack, 359-360
Quigley, Jim, 315
Quiros, Jorge, 313

R

Racklovits, Dick, 309
Radman, George, 414
Ragelis, Ray, 312
Raimondi, Ben, 264, 266-268
Raklovits, Dick, 300, 313
Ranck, Bob, 316, 323
Rankin, Dave, 232
Rankin, Gene, 245, 252
Raskowski, Leo, 146
Rasmus, Pete, 158
Ravensburg, Bob, 266-268
Raye, Jimmy, 409
Rayl, Jimmy, 395
Redden, Curtis, 59
Redner, Arthur, 59
Reeck, C. C., 306
Reed, William R., 316, 322, 323, 344, 386, 414
Rehberg, Bob, 273
Rehfeldt, Don, 295, 304-305
Reichardt, Bill, 310-311
Reichardt, Rick, 401, 402
Reichenbach, Jim, 333
Reid, Steve, 200
Reilly, Mike, 394
Reimer, Jon, 408
Rein, Bob, 408, 412
Reinbolt, Dave, 412
Reinke, Paul, 360
Rennebohm, Dale, 178, 180
Rentner, Ernest (Pug), 161-162, 165, 166-167, 170
Rexinger, Scott, 169
Rice, Clark, 289
Richards, John, 112
Richards, John R., 85
Richards, Bob, 282, 283, 292, 304, 323, 356
Richardson Sid, 211
Richardson, Walt, 396, 397, 408
Richter, Pat, 384, 387, 388, 398
Rickey, Branch, 87
Riddle, Fred, 300
Rieff, Joe, 168, 169, 172, 176
Riel, Bert, 168
Riessen, Marty, 392, 397, 402, 403, 408
Rifenburg, Dick, 276, 278 283, 284, 286
Riis, Wally, 290
Riley, Jack, 161, 166-167, 169, 173-174
Rintz, Carlton, 331, 339, 349-350
Ris, Walter, 291, 297, 298
Risch, Jack, 339
Risen, Arnie, 262
Ritter, Don, 296
Roberts, Joe, 375

Roberts, Robin, 280, 281
Roberts, Simon, 368
Robertson, Oscar, 382
Robie, Carl, 403, 407, 408, 412, 413, 414
Robinson, Tom, 86, 128, 138, 145, 175, 256, 371, 379, 380, 384, 385
Roby, Douglas F., 342, 344
Rockaway, Dick, 158
Rockne, Knute, 93
Rockwell, Tod, 123-124
Roedel, Don, 304
Roethke, John, 384
Rolek, Marty, 218
Romig, John, 178
Roper, Bill, 72
Rose, Ralph, 64, 76
Roseboro, Jim, 344
Ross, John, 321
Rotblatt, Marv, 280-281
Rote, Kyle, 300
Rouse, Ken, 70, 146, 151
Russell, Cazzie, 400, 406, 410
Russell, Ernestine, 356
Russell, Justin, 138
Russell, Fayette (Reb), 160, 161-163
Ryan, Pat, 142
Rykovich, Julie, 270-271, 336

S

Sahratian, John, 314
Saimes, George, 388
St. John, Lynn W., 85, 137, 154, 174, 196
Salamone, Lou, 396
Saling, George, 172, 173, 174
Saltau, Gordy, 293
Samp, Ed, 82
Samse, Leroy, 64
Samson, Paul, 147, 151, 152
Samuels, Dale, 318
Sanders, Daryl, 382
Sands, Al, 89
Sapora, Joe, 159, 163
Sarkisian, Alex, 284, 286
Sarkkinen, Esco, 227
Sarringhaus, Paul, 246
Saver, Russ, 151
Savic, Pandel, 293
Sawle, Steve, 284
Sawyier, Cal, 249, 253
Scarpello, Joe, 282, 292, 308
Schaefer, L.B., 391, 392-393
Schalon, Ed, 297
Schammel, Francis, 174
Scheerer, Paul, 407, 412
Schelhase, Dave, 400, 406, 407, 412
Scheuerman, Milt (Sharm), 346, 351
Schlademan, Karl, 297, 314, 362
Schlanger, Seymore, 268
Schloemer, Dick, 396, 398
Schlundt, Don, 299, 320, 328, 331, 336, 337-338, 346
Schmaling, Max, 318
Schmidt, Francis, 182, 188, 246
Schmidt, Fred, 403, 406, 408
Schmidt, John, 263
Schmieler, John, 168, 172
Schnittker, Dick, 295, 304, 305, 306
Schobinger, Gene, 89
Scholes, Clark, 308, 313-315, 324
Schommer, John, 70, 75-77
Schrecengost, Randy, 325
Schreiner, Dave, 243, 246, 248

Schulhof, Larry, 391
Schulz, Adolph (Germany), 62, 74, 75
Schutte, Clarence, 126
Schwartz, Al, 158, 163, 185
Schwartz, Marchy, 162
Scott, Burke, 328, 336
Scott, Don, 227
Scott, Ralph, 110
Scott, Walter Dill, 116, 117, 158
Scoville, Wallie, 84
Seaburg, Bill, 351
Seager, Allan, 147, 151
Seehausen, John, 412
Seeman, Roger, 413
Seibel, Ken, 389
Seidel, Glenn, 178, 180, 182
Seiler, Otto, 80
Selawski, Gene, 365
Senkowski, Ray, 386
Senol, Ahmet, 339
Sensanbaugher, Dean, 254
Sentman, Lee, 115, 164, 169
Serpico, Ralph, 262
Serr, Gordon, 316
Sexson, Joe, 352, 356
Shanken, Courtney, 244, 245
Shanken, Earl, 244, 245, 252
Shapiro, Morley, 321, 338, 341
Sharemet, John, 253
Sharkey, Dick, 410
Shaughnessy, Clark, 86
Shaver, Ed, 195
Shaw, Bob, 246, 247
Sheridan, Matt, 77
Shick, Roger, 391
Shively, Bernie, 144
Shoaff, Ed, 145
Shorts, Bruce, 59
Shuttleworth, Craven, 111, 114
Siders, Stacey, 321, 328-329
Siebert, Dick, 353, 401
Siegfried, Larry, 384
Sigrist, John L., 60
Silverio, Nick, 321, 329, 356
Simmons, Ozzie, 175, 192
Simpson, George, 158, 164, 173-174
Singer, Karl, 405, 406
Sintz, Pete, 384, 391
Sisler, George, 87-88
Sittig, John, 115, 147
Sitzberger, Ken, 403, 411, 412, 413, 414
Skinner, Jim, 245
Skinner, John, 253
Skoog, Meyer (Whitey), 295, 306, 312, 316
Skowron, Bill (Moose), 288, 306
Slater, Duke, 111, 112, 113, 114, 115
Slaughter, Ed, 126
Sleight, Elmer (Red), 153, 154
Slonak, Evan, 316
Smart, Floyd, 107
Smart, James H., 50
Smiley, Ed, 249, 250-251, 256
Smith, Andy, 109
Smith, Bill, 257, 281-282, 290, 291, 296-297, 298, 349
Smith, Bruce, 241, 243
Smith, Bubba, 404-405, 409
Smith, Cedric, 100
Smith, Dick, 178
Smith, Ed, 95
Smith, Gerry, 321
Smith, Gideon E., 94
Smith, Jack, 183

Smith, Rex, 309, 319
Snell, Matt, 382, 383
Snook, Gary, 399
Snow, Neil, 59-60, 62
Snyder, Lawrence M., 138
Snyder, Tom, 260
Soboleski, Joe, 283
Sohl, Bob, 282, 288, 290, 291
Somers, Alan, 382, 384, 396
Somers, Mike, 390
Sommer, Bill, 307, 308
Sommerfield, Art, 164
Souders, Cecil, 260
Sowenski, Joe, 267
Spain, John, 411
Spears, Dr. Clarence, 140, 155-156
Speik, Fred, 64
Speiser, Chuck, 292, 315, 316, 323, 324
Spellerberg, Tom, 288
Spradling, George, 105, 126, 127, 144
Sprowl, Forrest, 249
Stack, Tom, 391
Stadsvold, Fred, 100-101
Stagg, Amos Alonzo, 53, 54, 62, 69-73, 74, 78, 81, 82, 125, 137, 144, 154, 165-166, 172, 196, 203
Stagg, Amos Alonzo, Jr., 71, 72
Stalcup, Jerry, 370
Stangel, Otto, 84
Stassforth, Bowen, 324
Steel, Harry, 130
Steele, Bob, 412
Steffen, Walter (Wally), 70, 76
Steiger, Gene, 329
Stein, Lloyd, 353
Steinauer, Joe, 110, 149-150
Steinmetz, Chris, 65
Steinmetz, George, 318
Steketee, Frank, 106
Stensby, Clarence, 318
Stephens, Sandy, 374, 383-384
Steuart, Bill, 368, 373
Stevens, Don, 300
Stickels, Ted, 390, 391, 395
Stilwell, Leland, 126, 127
Stinchcomb, Gaylord (Pete), 100, 107, 109-110, 114
Stock, Tom, 401
Stoefer, Lester, 159
Stoll, Steve, 407
Stonesifer, Don, 286, 303, 304
Stout, Mel, 313, 315
Stowell, Chris, 407
Strange, Ernie, 60
Strassforth, Bowen, 297
Straug, Erv, 297
Studley, Chuck, 309-310
Stuhldreher, Harry, 246
Stungis, John, 256
Sturtz, Karl, 300
Styles, E. B., 79
Suchy, Don, 364
Sugar, Leo, 310, 311
Sullivan, Bob, 313, 316, 322, 323, 331
Sullivan, Humphrey, 288
Suminski, Dave, 318, 319
Sunderlage, Don, 312
Supronowicz, Mack, 287, 294
Sutherland, Jock, 182
Sutton, Archie, 394
Svendsen, Earl, 178
Sweeley, Everett, 59

T

Takacs, Mike, 319
Taliaferro, George, 266, 267
Taliaferro, Mike, 393, 394
Tamburo, Dick, 310, 317, 318-319
Tanberg, Al, 82
Tarshis, Stan, 381
Tashnick, Tony, 366, 369, 372
Tate, Al, 300, 303, 304
Taube, Mel, 153
Tavener, John, 261-262
Taylor, Fred, 305, 306, 307
Taylor, Jack, 308, 313, 314, 315, 321, 322, 324
Tellor, Robin, 383
Temlin, Ed (Killer), 126, 128
Teninga, Wally, 284, 293
Tenner, Bob, 178, 180
Thistlethwaite, Glen, 139, 160, 166-167
Thomas, Aurelius, 357-358
Thomas, Dale, 324
Thomas, Jerry, 353-354
Thomas, John, 70, 116, 117
Thomas, Russ, 260
Thompson, Jay, 151
Thompson, William Oxley, 58, 66
Thomson, Willard, 329, 338, 341, 346-347
Thor, Dave, 412
Thornhill, Charley, 409
Thornton, Bob, 333
Thorson, Sherwyn, 375, 393
Timberlake, Bob, 398-399, 408
Timm, Jud, 145, 148
Timmerman, Ed, 317
Tinker, Joe, 113
Title, Dave, 290
Tocks, John, 412
Tolan, Eddie, 168, 173
Tomasi, Bon, 283
Toneff, George, 293
Tonnemaker, Clayton, 292, 293, 294
Tonry, Don, 354-355, 372, 373
Townsend, John, 105, 218
Trautman, George (Red), 94
Trautwein, Bill, 293, 300
Tregoning, Larry, 406
Tretheway, Tom, 406, 408
Trosko, Freddy, 277
Troup, Paul, 172
Troy, Mike, 378, 379, 381, 382, 384, 390, 391
Trutt, Mel, 219
Tucker, Jim, 386
Tunnicliff, Ed, 285, 286
Turner, Herman, 306
Turner, Ned, 174
Twomey, Vic, 268
Tykodi, Ralph, 288
Tyler, Ralph, 263
Tyrell, Norman, 361

U

Underman, Jack, 272
Unverfurth, Don, 412
Utley, Bill, 411, 412, 413

V

Vahaska, Bill, 300
Vail, Harry (Dad), 93
Van Arsdale, Dick, 400
Van Arsdale, Tom, 400
Van Bibber, George, 169

Van Buren, Bill, 374, 384
Vance, Gene, 249, 250-251, 256
Vancisin, Joe, 353
Van Cott, Wald, 288, 307
VanderKelen, Ron, 388
Van Doozer, Jesse, 53
Van Gent, Gene, 86, 89
Van Heyde, Bob, 338, 341
Van Hise, Charles, 61
Van Horn, Doug, 406
Van Riper, John, 82, 86
Vargo, Ken, 333
Vega, Al, 339
Verhoeven, Gary, 395
Vernon, Cal, 290
Vicic, Don, 344
Vick, Ernie, 112, 113
Vick, Harry, 134
Vickroy, Bill, 258
Vitucci, Lou, 386, 393, 396, 397, 404
Vogds, Evan, 246
Vogel, Bob, 382
Vogel, John, 391
Vohaska, Bob, 304
Voigts, Bob, 212, 289
Voliva, Dick, 185
Voss, Don, 318, 319
Vuchinich, Mickey, 165

W

Wagner, Sid, 191
Wahl, Allen, 293, 301, 304
Walaitis, Frank, 151
Waldorf, Lynn (Pappy), 176-177, 199, 285
Walker, Art, 336
Walker, Bob, 150-151
Walker, George, 269, 270
Walsh, Ed, 113
Walsh, John J., 356, 369
Walsh, Ken, 414
Walter, Russell (Rut), 158
Wampler, Fred, 289, 297, 308
Ward, Arch, 173
Ward, Charley, 55, 61
Ward, Don, 352
Wardrop, Jack, 349
Warfield, Paul, 382, 383, 391
Warmath, Murray, 306, 375
Warne, Tom, 158, 164, 168
Washington, Gene, 404, 408, 409-411, 414
Watkins, Bobby, 334
Watson, Al, 151
Watson, F. O., 94
Watson, Lou, 306, 410
Watson, Tom, 147, 300
Weaver, Dave, 333
Weaver, Red, 265
Webb, Ken, 411, 412, 413
Webster, Bob, 382, 403
Webster, George, 404-405, 409
Weeks, Boss, 62
Weeks, Harrison, 59
Weick, Bob, 339
Weinacker, Adolph, 292
Weinberg, Dick, 282, 297
Weir, Murray, 268, 287,
Weisenburger, Jack, 273, 278, 284
Weiss, Howie, 212
Welbourn, Jerry, 321
Welch, Ralph (Pest), 153-154
Wells, Billy, 316, 325

Wells, Elmo, 150
Wells, Harold, 399, 400
Wells, Stanfield, 134
Welsh, Alex, 245
Welsh, Jim, 245
Wendt, Merle, 183
West, Jerry, 382, 409
Westbrook, Walter K., 109
Westfall, Bob, 243, 276
Westphal, Fred, 373
Weston, Frank, 110
Wettstone, Gene, 211
Wetzel, Buzz, 183
Wham, Dick, 329
Wheeler, Jim, 383
Whitaker, Mark, 287-288
White, Bob, 358, 364-365, 411
White, Don, 105, 113
White, Hugh, 59
White, Irving, 84
White, Paul, 283
Whiteleather, Tom, 341
Whitfield, Mal, 288, 289, 291, 299, 323
Whitney, Casper, 54, 60
Whitten, Glen, 356, 360
Whittle, Glenn, 89
Widdoes, Carroll, 259-260
Widdoes, Dick, 300
Widseth, Ed, 178, 200
Wiese, Bob, 260, 270
Wiggins, Al, 349, 352, 353, 354, 356, 360, 363
Wikoff, Garnett, 84
Wilce, Dr. John W., 86, 96, 135, 163
Wilcox, Mert, 172
Wilder, Lloyd, 114
Wildung, Dick, 241, 248
Wilford, Ernie, 94
Wilkins, Stu, 283
Wilkinson, Charles (Bud), 175, 178, 191, 198
Wilkinson, Herb, 262, 268, 271, 272
Willaman, Sam, 174, 182
Williams, Dr. Henry, 59, 63, 64, 74, 77, 78-79, 93, 99
Williams, Joe, 374
Williams, Perry, 409
Williams, Red, 271
Williams, Sam, 365
Williams, Willie, 320, 321, 328-329, 330, 338, 341
Williamson, Bob, 408
Williamson Ivan, 169, 170, 176, 317, 335
Willis, Bill, 259, 261
Wilson, Bob, 294, 306, 309
Wilson, Ebin, 59
Wilson, Eric, 114, 124, 125, 130
Wilson, John, 317
Wilson, Kenneth L. (Tug), 136, 139, 159, 169, 174, 196, 203, 208, 253, 304, 337, 341-342, 386

Wilson, Volney, 163, 172
Wilt, Fred, 244-245, 292, 324
Windle, Bob, 411, 412, 413
Wing, Jack, 246
Wink, Jack, 253
Wistert, Albert, 294
Wistert, Alvin, 276, 278, 283, 286, 293, 294
Wistert, Francis, 165, 169, 174, 294
Withers, Ed, 304
Witsiepie, Bill, 308
Witt, Gerry, 317
Witte, Bill, 413
Wojciak, Ron, 401
Wolmer, Walt, 150
Wood, Mike, 391
Wooden, Johnny, 105, 163-164, 168-169, 172
Woods, Ralph, 101
Woods, Raymond, 101
Woodson, Abe, 338
Woodworth, Wade (Red), 160, 161, 163
Woolsey, Bill, 324, 352, 353, 354, 356, 362
Woolsey, Dean, 173
Worthington, Tom, 285
Wright, Bill, 372
Wright, Bob, 244, 245
Wright, Jim, 329
Wrighte, George H., 184
Wyant, Andrew R. E. (Andy), 61, 70
Wyatt, Bernie, 374
Wyman, Arnold (Pudge), 93, 99

Y

Yarr, Tommy, 162
Yearby, Bill, 399, 406
Yerges, Howard, 100, 273, 278-279, 284
Yewcic, Tom, 310, 316, 325, 339, 342
Yirkoski, Dick, 321
Yost, Fielding (Hurry-Up), 59, 62, 116, 132, 133-135, 137, 140, 154, 163, 174, 196
Young, Claude (Buddy), 261, 262, 263, 270
Young, Gerald, 380
Young, Kewell, 105
Young, Ralph, 339

Z

Zale, Ray, 331
Zarnas, Gus, 208
Zemer, Bill, 282
Zimmer, Andy, 249
Zola, John, 147
Zuppke, Robert, 60, 65, 73, 78-79, 86, 88-89, 99, 112, 118-120, 145, 148
Zurakowski, Bill, 257
Zuravlef, Joe, 284-285